# The Sociology of Organizations
## BASIC STUDIES

# The Sociology of Organizations

## BASIC STUDIES

---

edited by

**OSCAR GRUSKY and**

**GEORGE A. MILLER**

---

**THE FREE PRESS**
A Division of Macmillan Publishing Co., Inc.
*New York*

Collier Macmillan Publishers
*London*

THE FREE PRESS
*A Division of Macmillan Publishing Co., Inc.*
866 Third Avenue, New York. N.Y. 10022

Collier Macmillan Canada, Ltd.

Library of Congress Catalog Card Number: 69-20286

Printed in the United States of America

printing number
9 10

# Contents

# Preface

In 1952 the Free Press published the *Reader in Bureaucracy* edited by Robert K. Merton, Ailsa P. Gray, Barbara Hockey and Hanan C. Selvin. This important book directed interest to the problems of organizations for over two decades and remains a major contribution to this day. Since the present volume is by the same publisher some comparisons of the non-invidious kind are in order.

First, unlike its predecessor, we sought deliberately to present a uniquely sociological orientation. That is not to say that non-sociologists were excluded from the "club", but rather that the aim was to present the student, insofar as possible, with the conceptual elements of a sociology of organizations. This field emerged from what was earlier called industrial sociology and the sociology of occupations, on the one hand, and the more general area, social organization, on the other. The object of study—the organization—has been labelled the complex, the formal, the bureaucratic, and the large-scale organization. The study of organizations has now reached a stage of development where the outlines of a sociological perspective can be identified. We do not consider it anti-interdisciplinary to believe such a condition both desirable and deserving of encouragement.

Second, we decided against dividing up the work of major theorists by selected substantive areas in favor of reprinting large, unified sections of their work in one place. The main advantage of this procedure is that it enables the reader to grasp the whole perspective. Obviously, however, reading the entire work of the author is superior to either approach. This technique sought to encourage direct theoretical comparisons among the classical theorists as well as between classical and current theoretical perspectives. We called upon the work of Talcott Parsons to serve as a bridge between the classical and current theorists.

The current theorists were also presented in one unit with the aim of emphasizing the broad inter-relationships between the specialized field of organizations and the general study of social systems. In this respect as well, Parsons is a leader. We hope the instructor will encourage students to re-examine empirical studies presented later in the book in terms of contrasting theories. For this purpose, the theoretical material is lengthy and detailed and the empirical studies, whenever possible, are presented in full.

Third, a broadly-based selection of research techniques is provided in the early part of the book so as to emphasize the obviously close relationship between methods and theory. A comparison with the *Reader in Bureaucracy*, which dealt exclusively with field methods, is evidence of the degree of progress, increased sophistication, and self-awareness, that has characterized the field since the 1950's.

Fourth, the selections on substantive problems differentiated the two collections most of all and in the case of the present volume, presented the most difficult problems. Like its predecessor, we sought to focus on universal organizational problems. Yet, not only are the problems different, but the way of approaching them, and especially the more rigorous theoretical and methodological equipment used, distinguish the studies included in this book. Moreover, a somewhat broader range of organizational types may be found including religious organizations, prisons, the military, industry, ships, unions, and so on. Sociologists may very well fault us for failing to stress such important problem-areas as inter-organizational relationships, organization-client relations, de-bureaucratization, and others. Some may also feel that too much attention is given to problems stemming from professionalization. This emphasis reflects both the great commitment of contemporary researchers to this topic and the realities of living and working in a post-industrial society.

The decisions to include and exclude studies were very difficult ones. Almost every selection has been used at some time during our combined total of twelve years of teaching an advanced undergraduate course on formal organizations at UCLA. We apologize to the many talented scholars whose work we were compelled by space limitations to omit and thank the authors and publishers who graciously permitted the use of their material. We are deeply grateful to Peter Blau for advice and suggestions, to Carl Beers of The Free Press for his interest and assistance, and to Keiko Shimabukuro for secretarial help.

O.G.
G.A.M.

# Part One

# Classical Theoretical Perspectives

Social scientists are not notorious for their agreement on what constitutes the basic issues or most fruitful approaches to their fields, or even as to who in the past have been the major contributors to their discipline. However, when the position of Max Weber is evaluated, organizational sociologists, almost to a man, are in agreement on his pre-eminence. It is therefore altogether fitting—one could say that there was almost no other alternative—for the present collection to begin with the work of this man.

The excerpts selected cover three main areas: Weber's three pure types of authority, a detailed description and analysis of the characteristics and development of bureaucracy, and the process of routinization of charismatic authority. The concept of legitimacy is fundamental to Weber's treatment of organizations. By legitimacy he referred to the acceptance of influence because of its perceived justifiability. The three ideal types of authority are based on the types of legitimation applied. In the rational-legal or bureaucratic kind, members accepted a ruling as proper because it was based on abstract rules which they accepted as just. Under traditional authority legitimacy was based on the simple fact that things had normally been accomplished in that fashion in the past. Acceptance of charismatic authority was based on the member's emotional commitment to the leader or to his mission.

The longest selection describes both the fundamental features of bureaucratic organizations and their historical development. The ponderousness of the system, its emphasis on efficiency, and the political characteristics of bureaucracies, with illustrations from Greece, Rome, Weber's native Germany, and even the United States, are analyzed. Weber sought to account for organizational changes in part by an extensive analysis of the succession process. The last brief selection examines the mechanisms involved when an established system seeks to maintain itself beyond the first generation of leadership. This description of the process by which charismatic authority is transformed to other directions may also be considered with the readings in Part IV, where the central problem is succession and mobility.

Michels is most famous for his study of the process of goal displacement, whereby organizations subvert their original objectives and replace them with other goals, sometimes even with objectives that are alien to their original purposes. *Political Parties* is a detailed study of pre-World War I European labor unions and Socialist parties. The excerpts from this book illustrate some of the major components of Michels' theory of organizational leadership. The organizations studied, although originally seeking a Socialist revolution, soon abandoned this goal in part because of the leaders' desires to maintain their relatively high status position. Organizations become conservative because once in power leaders refuse to engage in activities that will endanger loss of their position. Moreover, the leaders are able to ensconce themselves in office because of the built-in advantages of their position. These advantages include control over communication to the ordinary members and superior political skills and experience. This does not mean that every organization, even those with avowedly democratic objectives, *must* become oligarchical, but instead that voluntary, political organizations and perhaps other types as well contain certain elements that can interfere with rank-and-file control. The problem is to specify carefully the conditions and circumstances, no doubt varying for particular types of organizations, that encourage or interfere with the democratic process. Readers will be especially interested in Lipset, Coleman, and Trow's *Union Democracy* which explicates and qualifies several propositions from Michels by means of a detailed study of the history and political structure of the International Typographers Union. (See the section on substantive problems for a summary of this study.)

The selection from Taylor's *Scientific Management* presents the basic assumptions of this classic approach to the study of organizations. A major feature of this orientation rests in the notion that careful definition of the requirements of each worker's job can assure effectiveness, as defined by the management. Hence, in Taylor's system: "The work of every workman is fully planned out by the management . . . and each man receives in most cases written instructions, describing in detail the task he is to accomplish, as well as the means to be used in doing the work." (p. 39) In addition to rigorous planning of work tasks, scientific management encouraged close supervisory control of the worker and the application of narrow economic incentives. The administrative theory of Gulick and Urwick (editors), *Papers on the Science of Administration* (New York: Institute of Public Administration, Columbia University, 1937) which is not represented in this volume, is closely related to the scientific-management approach. This orientation also emphasized the importance of breaking complex tasks down into simpler components and thereby specifying carefully the task expectations associated with each position.

The case of Schmidt, a pig-iron handler, which is presented in the excerpt, illustrates the principles of task specification, close control, and economic incentives. The derogation of the worker and his assumed inferiority, that is, the moral components of the approach, are also apparent in the account.

The human relations approach sought to counter scientific managements' focus on formal requirements and simple economic rewards as crucial motivational elements. The point of view was that *non*economic, social rewards were more important in inducing workers to behave in line with or in opposition to managerial goals. The famous studies of the Relay Assembly Test Room, the Mica Splitting Test Room, and the Bank-Wiring Observation Room served as the empirical basis for the authors' conclusions that informal group behavior was fundamental to the operation of industrial and other organizations. However, other elements in the social structure of the plant, such as technology and formal structure, were not totally overlooked. Nevertheless, as shown in the selection from *Management and the Worker*, which summarizes the author's main theoretical perspective, these features are not emphasized. While only one half page is devoted to the formal organization of the plant, seven times as much space is devoted to the plants' informal organization. The human-relations approach stressed—some would say "discovered"—the key role of informal group behavior for the functioning of complex organizations. The reader may be especially interested in two other studies that are noteworthy contributions to the human relations approach: Elton Mayo, *The Human Problems of an Industrial Civilization*, 1933, and Burleigh Gardner, *Human Relations in Industry*. In addition, the reader will find it useful to examine criticisms of this perspective by Henry Landsberger (*Hawthorne Revisited*, Ithaca, N.Y.: Cornell University Press, 1958), Morris S. Viteles (*Motivation and Morale in Industry*, London: Staples, 1954), and Alex Carey ("The Hawthorne Studies: A Radical Criticism," *American Sociological Review*, 32 [June, 1967], 403–16).

The next classical theoretical perspective is that of Chester I. Barnard, former president of New Jersey Bell Telephone Company and a man of varied experiences in business, academic, and government organizations. Barnard's theory of cooperation stresses the joint importance of factors emanating from the system as a whole and from the individual member. This distinction underlies the use of the concepts of effectiveness and efficiency, as well as the analysis of the three requirements for organization: willingness to cooperate, common purpose, and communication. There tends to be a much stronger focus on motivational elements than on structural features in Barnard's orientation. Hence, the brief excerpt from Barnard's theory of authority stresses personal predilection and perception as elements in the acceptance or rejection of authority. The interest in incentives as a means of inducing members of an organization to cooperate in achieving the organization's objectives served as the cornerstone of his theory and was a direct intellectual predecessor to the March and Simon theory described in the following section.

The last selection is from the foremost sociological theorist of recent times, Talcott Parsons. Like Weber before him, Parsons has sought as his point of departure the exploration of the general relation of economics and sociology. Parsons has sought in his essay to isolate the fundamental defining features of organizations. Four main categories derived from his well-known general classification system are applied: the value system of the organization, the mechanisms of procuring resources, the means of policy-making, allocating, and integrating the units of the system, and lastly, its institutional connections to the larger society. The focus on goal-attainment is seen as the basic characteristic of the organization. Parsons' concern with the organization's value pattern and the relationship of this value pattern to the more generalized values of the society is a forerunner of open-systems theory and a key feature of his orientation. Parsons' approach also resembles Max Weber's in its concern with the problem of power, "the generalized capacity to mobilize resources in the interest of attainment of the system goal." The concluding substantive section presents the author's typology of organizations: economic, political, integrative, and pattern-maintenance systems.

The reader should seek to evaluate the utility of each of the theoretical perspectives presented in enhancing his understanding of the substantive problems raised in later sections. He also will find it valuable to contrast the orientations of the classical theorists with those presented in the following section.

MAX WEBER

# Bureaucracy

## The three pure types of legitimate authority

There are three pure types of legitimate authority. The validity of their claims to legitimacy may be based on:

1. Rational grounds—resting on a belief in the "legality" of patterns of normative rules and the right of those elevated to authority under such rules to issue commands (legal authority).
2. Traditional grounds—resting on an established belief in the sanctity of immemorial traditions and the legitimacy of the status of those exercising authority under them (traditional authority); or finally,
3. Charismatic grounds—resting on devotion to the specific and exceptional sanctity, heroism or exemplary character of an individual person, and of the normative patterns or order revealed or ordained by him (charismatic authority).

In the case of legal authority, obedience is owed to the legally established impersonal order. It extends to the persons exercising the authority of office under it only by virtue of the formal legality of their commands and only within the scope of authority of the office. In the case of traditional authority, obedience is owed to the *person* of the chief who occupies the traditionally sanctioned position of authority and who is (within its sphere) bound by tradition. But here the obligation of obedience is not based on the impersonal order, but is a matter of personal loyalty within the area of accustomed obligations. In the case of charismatic authority, it is the charismatically qualified leader as such who is obeyed by virtue of personal trust in him and his revelation, his heroism or his exemplary qualities so far as they fall within the scope of the individual's belief in his charisma.

1. The usefulness of the above classification can only be judged by its results in promoting systematic analysis. The concept of 'charisma' ('the gift of grace') is taken from the vocabulary of early Christianity. For the Christian religious organization Rudolf Sohm, in his *Kirchenrecht*, was the first to clarify the substance of the concept, even though he did not use the same terminology. Others (for instance, Hollin, *Enthusiasmus und Bussgewalt*) have clarified certain important consequences of it. It is thus nothing new.

Reprinted from *The Theory of Social and Economic Organization*, translated by A. M. Henderson and Talcott Parsons, edited by Talcott Parsons (New York: Free Press, 1957), p. 328.

* * * * * *

## Characteristics of bureaucracy

Modern officialdom functions in the following specific manner:

I. There is the principle of fixed and official jurisdictional areas, which are generally ordered by rules, that, is, by laws or administrative regulations.

Reprinted from *From Max Weber: Essays in Sociology*, edited and translated by Hans H. Gerth and C. Wright Mills, pp. 196–204, 209–16, 221–26, 228–30, by permission of the publisher. (Copyright 1946 by Oxford University Press, Inc.)

1. The regular activities required for the purposes of the bureaucratically governed structure are distributed in a fixed way as official duties.

2. The authority to give the commands required for the discharge of these duties is distributed in a stable way and is strictly delimited by rules concerning the coercive means, physical, sacerdotal, or otherwise, which may be placed at the disposal of officials.

3. Methodical provision is made for the regular and continuous fulfilment of these duties and for the execution of the corresponding rights; only persons who have the generally regulated qualifications to serve are employed.

In public and lawful government these three elements constitute "bureaucratic authority." In private economic domination, they constitute bureaucratic "management." Bureaucracy, thus understood, is fully developed in political and ecclesiastical communities only in the modern state, and, in the private economy, only in the most advanced institutions of capitalism. Permanent and public office authority, with fixed jurisdiction, is not the historical rule but rather the exception. This is so even in large political structures such as those of the ancient Orient, the Germanic and Mongolian empires of conquest, or of many feudal structures of state. In all these cases, the ruler executes the most important measures through personal trustees, table-companions, or court-servants. Their commissions and authority are not precisely delimited and are temporarily called into being for each case.

II. The principles of office hierarchy and of levels of graded authority mean a firmly ordered system of super- and subordination in which there is a supervision of the lower offices by the higher ones. Such a system offers the governed the possibility of appealing the decision of a lower office to its higher authority, in a definitely regulated manner. With the full development of the bureaucratic type, the office hierarchy is monocratically organized. The principle of hierarchical office authority is found in all bureaucratic structures: in state and ecclesiastical structures as well as in large party organizations and private enterprises. It does not matter for the character of bureaucracy whether its authority is called "private" or "public."

When the principle of jurisdictional "competency" is fully carried through, hierarchical subordination—at least in public office—does not mean that the "higher" authority is simply authorized to take over the business of the "lower." Indeed, the opposite is the rule. Once established and having fulfilled its task, an office tends to continue in existence and be held by another incumbent.

III. The management of the modern office is based upon written documents ("the files"), which are preserved in their original or draught form. There is, therefore, a staff of subaltern officials and scribes of all sorts. The body of officials actively engaged in a "public" office, along with the respective apparatus of material implements and the files, make up a "bureau." In private enterprise, "the bureau" is often called "the office."

In principle, the modern organization of the civil service separates the bureau from the private domicile of the official, and, in general, bureaucracy segregates official activity as something distinct from the sphere of private life. Public monies and equipment are divorced from the private property of the official. This condition is everywhere the product of a long development. Nowadays, it is found in public as well as in private enterprises; in the latter, the principle extends even to the leading entrepreneur. In principle, the executive office is separated from the household, business from private correspondence, and business assets from private fortunes. The more consistently the modern type of business management has been carried through the more are these separations the case. The beginnings of this process are to be found as early as the Middle Ages.

It is the peculiarity of the modern entrepreneur that he conducts himself as the "first official" of his enterprise, in the very same way in which the ruler of a specifically modern bureaucratic state spoke of himself as "the first servant" of the state. The idea that the bureau activities of the state are intrinsically different in character from the management of private economic offices is a continental European notion and, by way of contrast, is totally foreign to the American way.

IV. Office management, at least all specialized office management—and such management is distinctly modern—usually presupposes thorough and expert training. This increasingly holds for the modern executive and employee of private enterprises, in the same manner as it holds for the state official.

V. When the office is fully developed, official activity demands the full working capacity of the official, irrespective of the fact that his obligatory time in the bureau may be firmly delimited. In the normal case, this is only the product of a long development, in the public as well as in the private office. Formerly, in all cases, the normal state of affairs was reversed: official business was discharged as a secondary activity.

VI. The management of the office follows general rules, which are more or less stable, more or less exhaustive, and which can be learned. Knowledge of these rules represents a special technical learning which the officials possess. It involves jurisprudence, or administrative or business management.

The reduction of modern office management to rules is deeply embedded in its very nature. The theory of modern public administration, for instance, assumes that the authority to order certain matters by decree—which has been legally granted to public authorities—does not entitle the bureau to regulate the matter by commands given for each case, but only to regulate the matter abstractly. This stands in extreme contrast to the regulation of all relationships through individual privileges and bestowals of favor, which is absolutely dominant in patrimonialism, at least in so far as such relationships are not fixed by sacred tradition.

### THE POSITION OF THE OFFICIAL

All this results in the following for the internal and external position of the official:

I. Office holding is a "vocation." This is shown, first, in the requirement of a firmly prescribed course of training, which demands the entire capacity for work for a long period of time, and in the generally prescribed and special examinations which are prerequisites of employment. Furthermore, the position of the official is in the nature of a duty. This determines the internal structure of his relations, in the following manner: Legally and actually, office holding is not considered a source to be exploited for rents or emoluments, as was normally the case during the Middle Ages and frequently up to the threshold of recent times. Nor is office holding considered a usual exchange of services for equivalents, as is the case with free labor contracts. Entrance into an office, including one in the private economy, is considered an acceptance of a specific obligation of faithful management in return for a secure existence. It is decisive for the specific nature of modern loyalty to an office that, in the pure type, it does not establish a relationship to a *person*, like the vassal's or disciple's faith in feudal or in patrimonial relations of authority. Modern loyalty is devoted to impersonal and functional purposes. Behind the functional purposes, of course, "ideas of culture-values" usually stand. These are *ersatz* for the earthly or supramundane personal master: ideas such as "state," "church," "community," "party," or "enterprise" are thought of as being realized in a community; they provide an ideological halo for the master.

The political official—at least in the fully developed modern state—is not considered the personal servant of a ruler. Today, the bishop, the priest, and the preacher are in fact no longer, as in early Christian times, holders of purely personal charisma. The supramundane and sacred values which they offer are given to everybody who seems to be worthy of them and who asks for them. In former times, such leaders acted upon the personal command of their master; in principle, they were responsible only to him. Nowadays, in spite of the partial survival of the old theory, such religious leaders are officials in the service of a functional purpose, which in the present-day "church" has become routinized and, in turn, ideologically hallowed.

II. The personal position of the official is patterned in the following way:

1. Whether he is in a private office or a public bureau, the modern official always strives and usually enjoys a distinct *social esteem* as compared with the governed. His social position is guaranteed by the prescriptive rules of rank order and, for the political official, by special definitions of the criminal code against "insults of officials" and "contempt" of state and church authorities.

The actual social position of the official is normally highest where, as in old civilized countries, the following conditions prevail: a strong demand for administration by trained experts; a strong and stable social differentiation, where the official predominantly derives from socially and economically privileged strata because of the social distribution of power; or where the costliness of the required training and status conventions are binding upon him. The possession of educational certificates—to be discussed elsewhere—are usually linked with qualification for office. Naturally, such certificates or patents enhance the "status element" in the social position of the official. For the rest this status factor in individual cases is explicitly and impassively acknowledged; for example, in the prescription that the acceptance or rejection of an aspirant to an official career depends upon the consent ("election") of the members of the official body. This is the case in the German army with the officer corps. Similar phenomena, which promote this guildlike closure of officialdom, are typically found in patrimonial and, particularly, in prebendal officialdoms of the past. The desire to resurrect such phenomena in changed forms is by no means infrequent among modern bureaucrats. For instance, they have played a role among the demands of the quite proletarian and expert officials (the *tretyj* element) during the Russian revolution.

Usually the social esteem of the officials as such is especially low where the demand for expert administration and the dominance of status conventions are weak. This is especially the case in the United States; it is often the case in new settlements by virtue of their wide fields for profit-making and the great instability of their social stratification.

2. The pure type of bureaucratic official is *appointed* by a superior authority. An official elected by the governed is not a purely bureaucratic figure. Of course, the formal existence of an election does not by itself mean that no appointment hides behind the election—in the state, especially, appointment by party chiefs. Whether or not this is the case does not depend upon legal statutes but upon the way in which the party mechanism functions. Once firmly organized, the parties can turn a formally free election into the mere acclamation of a candidate designated by the party chief. As a rule, however, a formally free election is turned into a fight, conducted according to definite rules, for votes in favor of one or two designated candidates.

In all circumstances, the designation of officials by means of an election among the governed modifies the strictness of hierarchical subordination. In principle, an official who is so elected has an autonomous position opposite the superordinate official. The elected official does not derive his position "from above" but "from below," or at least not from a superior authority of the official hierarchy but from powerful party men ("bosses"), who also determine his further career. The career of the elected official is not, or at least not primarily, dependent upon his chief in the administration. The official who is not elected but appointed by a chief normally functions more exactly, from a technical point of view, because, all other circumstances being equal, it is more likely that purely functional points of consideration and qualities will determine his selection and career. As laymen, the governed can become acquainted with the extent to which a candidate is expertly qualified for office only in terms of experience, and hence only after his service. Moreover, in every sort of selection of officials by election, parties quite naturally give decisive weight not to expert considerations but to the services a follower renders to the party boss. This holds for all kinds of procurement for officials by elections, for the designation of formally free, elected officials by party bosses when they determine the slate of candidates, or the free appointment by a chief who has himself been elected. The contrast, however, is relative: substantially similar conditions hold where legitimate monarchs and their subordinates appoint officials, except that the influence of the followings are then less controllable.

Where the demand for administration by trained experts is considerable, and the party followings have to recognize an intellectually developed, educated, and freely moving "public opinion," the use of unqualified officials falls back upon the party in power at the next election. Naturally, this is more likely to happen when the officials are appointed by the chief. The demand for a trained administration now exists in the United States, but in the large cities, where immigrant votes are "corralled," there is, of course, no educated public opinion. Therefore, popular elections of the administrative chief and also of his subordinate officials usually endanger the expert qualification of the official as well as the precise functioning of the bureaucratic mechanism. It also weakens the dependence of the officials upon the hierarchy. This holds at least for the large administrative bodies that are difficult to supervise. The superior qualification and integrity of federal judges, appointed by the President, as over against elected judges in the United States is well known, although both types of officials have been selected primarily in terms of party considerations. The great changes in American metropolitan administrations demanded by reformers have proceeded essentially from elected mayors working with an apparatus of officials who were appointed by them. These reforms have thus come about in a "Caesarist" fashion. Viewed technically, as an organized form of authority, the efficiency of "Caesarism," which often grows out of democracy, rests in general upon the position of the "Caesar" as a free trustee of the masses (of the army or of the citizenry), who is unfettered by tradition. The "Caesar" is thus the unrestrained master of a body of highly qualified military officers and officials whom he selects freely and personally without regard to tradition or to any other considerations. This "rule of the personal genius," however, stands in contradiction to the formally "democratic" principle of a universally elected officialdom.

3. Normally, the position of the official is held for life, at least in public bureaucracies; and this is increasingly the case for all similar structures. As a factual rule, *tenure for life* is presupposed, even where the giving of notice or periodic reappointment occurs. In contrast to the worker in a private enterprise, the official normally holds tenure. Legal or actual life-tenure, however, is not recognized as the official's right to the possession of office, as was the case with many structures of authority in the past. Where legal guarantees against arbitrary dismissal or transfer are developed, they merely serve to guarantee a strictly objective discharge of specific office duties free from all personal considerations. In Germany, this is the case for all juridical and, increasingly, for all administrative officials.

Within the bureaucracy, therefore, the measure of "independence," legally guaranteed by tenure, is not always a source of increased status for the official whose position is thus secured. Indeed, often the reverse holds, especially in old cultures and communities that are highly differentiated. In such communities, the stricter the subordination under the arbitrary rule of the master, the more it guarantees the maintenance of the conventional seigneurial style of living for the official. Because of the very absence of these legal guarantees of tenure, the conventional esteem for the official may rise in the same way as, during the Middle Ages, the esteem of the nobility of office rose at the expense of esteem for the freemen, and as the king's judge surpassed that of the people's judge. In Germany, the military officer or the administrative official can be removed from office at any time, or at least far more readily than the "independent judge," who never pays with loss of his office for even the grossest offense against the "code of honor" or against social conventions of the salon. For this very reason, if other things are equal, in the eyes of the master stratum the judge is considered less qualified for social intercourse than are officers and administrative officials, whose greater dependence on the master is a greater guarantee of their conformity with status conventions. Of course, the average official strives for a civil-service law, which would materially secure his old age and provide increased guarantees against his arbitrary removal from office. This striving, however, has its limits. A very strong development of the "right to the office" naturally makes it more difficult to staff them with regard to technical efficiency, for such a development decreases the career opportunities of ambitious candidates for office. This makes for the fact that officials, on the whole, do not feel their dependency upon those at the top. This lack of a feeling of dependency, however, rests primarily upon the inclination to depend upon one's equals rather than upon the socially inferior and governed strata. The present conservative movement among the Badenia clergy, occasioned by the anxiety of a presumably threatening separation of church and state, has been expressly determined by the desire not to be turned "from a master into a servant of the parish."

4. The official receives the regular *pecuniary* compensation of a normally fixed *salary* and the old age security provided by a pension. The salary is not measured like a wage in terms of work done, but according to "status," that is, according to the kind of function (the "rank") and, in addition, possibly, according to the length of service. The relatively great security of the official's income, as well as the rewards of social esteem, make the office a sought-after position, especially in countries which no longer provide opportunities for colonial profits. In such countries, this situation permits relatively low salaries for officials.

5. The official is set for a "*career*" within the hierarchical order of the public service. He moves from the lower, less important, and lower paid to the

higher positions. The average official naturally desires a mechanical fixing of the conditions of promotion: if not of the offices, at least of the salary levels. He wants these conditions fixed in terms of "seniority," or possibly according to grades achieved in a developed system of expert examinations. Here and there, such examinations actually form a character *indelebilis* of the official and have lifelong effects on his career. To this is joined the desire to qualify the right to office and the increasing tendency toward status group closure and economic security. All of this makes for a tendency to consider the offices as "prebends" of those who are qualified by educational certificates. The necessity of taking general personal and intellectual qualifications into consideration, irrespective of the often subaltern character of the educational certificate, has led to a condition in which the highest political offices, especially the positions of "ministers," are principally filled without reference to such certificates.

* * * * * *

### THE QUANTITATIVE DEVELOPMENT OF ADMINISTRATIVE TASKS

The proper soil for the bureaucratization of an administration has always been the specific developments of administrative tasks. We shall first discuss the quantitative extension of such tasks. In the field of politics, the great state and the mass party are the classic soil for bureaucratization.

This does not mean that every historically known and genuine formation of great states has brought about a bureaucratic administration. The permanence of a once-existing great state, or the homogeneity of a culture borne by such a state, has not always been attached to a bureaucratic structure of state. However, both of these features have held to a great extent, for instance, in the Chinese empire. The numerous great Negro empires, and similar formations, have had only an ephemerical existence primarily because they have lacked an apparatus of officials. And the unity of the Carolingian empire disintegrated when its organization of officials disintegrated. This organization, however, was predominantly patrimonial rather than bureaucratic in nature. From a purely temporal view, however, the empire of the Caliphs and its predecessors on Asiatic soil have lasted for considerable periods of time, and their organization of office was essentially patrimonial and prebendal. Also, the Holy Roman Empire lasted for a long time in spite of the almost complete absence of bureaucracy. All these realms have represented a cultural unity of at least approximately the same strength as is usually created by bureaucratic polities.

The ancient Roman Empire disintegrated internally in spite of increasing bureaucratization and even during its very execution. This was because of the way the tax burdens were distributed by the bureaucratic state, which favored the subsistence economy. Viewed with regard to the intensity of their purely *political* unities, the temporal existences of the empires of the Caliphs, Carolingian and other medieval emperors were essentially unstable, nominal, and cohesive conglomerates. On the whole, the capacity for political action steadily diminished, and the relatively great unity of *culture* flowed from ecclesiastic structures that were in part strictly unified and, in the Occidental Middle Ages, increasingly bureaucratic in character. The unity of their cultures resulted partly from the far-going homogeneity of their social structures, which in turn was the aftermath and transformation of their former political unity. Both are phenomena of the traditional stereotyping of culture, which favors an unstable equilibrium. Both of these factors proved so strong a foundation that even grandiose attempts at expansion, such as the Crusades, could be undertaken in spite of the lack of intensive political unity; they were, one might say, performed as "private undertakings." The failure of the Crusades and their often irrational political course, however, is associated with the absence of a unified and intensive state power to back them up. And there is no doubt that the nuclei of intensive "modern" states in the Middle Ages developed concomitantly with bureaucratic structures. Furthermore, in the end these quite bureaucratic political structures undoubtedly shattered the social conglomerates, which rested essentially upon unstable equilibriums.

The disintegration of the Roman Empire was partly conditioned by the very bureaucratization of its army and official apparatus. This bureaucratization could only be realized by carrying through at the same time a method of taxation which by its distribution of burdens was bound to lead to relative increase in the importance of a subsistence economy.

Individual factors of this sort always enter the picture. Also the "intensity" of the external and the internal state activities play their part. Quite apart from the relation between the state influence upon culture and the degree of bureaucratization, it may be said that "normally"—though not without exception—the vigor to expand is directly related to the degree of bureaucratization. For two of the most expansive polities, the Roman Empire and the British world empire, during their most expansive periods, rested upon bureaucratic foundations only to a small extent. The Norman state in England carried through a strict organization on the basis of a feudal hierarchy. To a large extent, it received its unity and its push through the bureaucratization of the royal exchequer, which, in comparison to other political structures of the feudal period, was extremely strict. Later on, the English state did not share in the continental development towards bureaucratization, but remained an administration of notables. Just as in the republican administration of Rome, this English rule by notables was a result of the relative absence of a continental character, as well as of absolutely unique preconditions, which at the present time are disappearing. The dispensability of the large standing armies, which a continental state with equally expansive tendencies requires for its land frontiers, is among these special preconditions. In Rome, bureaucratization advanced with the transition from a coastal to a continental ring of frontiers. For the rest, in the domination structure of Rome, the strictly military character of the magistrate authorities—in the Roman manner unknown to any other people—made up for the lack of a bureaucratic apparatus with its technical efficiency, its precision and unity of administrative functions, especially outside the city limits. The continuity of administration was safeguarded by the unique position of the Senate. In Rome, as in England, one presupposition for this dispensability of bureaucracy which should not be forgotten was that the state authorities increasingly "minimized" the scope of their functions at home. They restricted their functions to what was absolutely demanded for direct "reasons of state."

At the beginning of the modern period, all the prerogatives of the continental states accumulated in the hands of those princes who most relentlessly took the course of administrative bureaucratization. It is obvious that technically the great modern state is absolutely dependent upon a bureaucratic basis. The larger the state, and the more it is or the more it becomes a greater power state, the more unconditionally is this the case.

The United States still bears the character of a polity which, at least in the technical sense, is not fully bureaucratized. But the greater the zones of friction with the outside and the more urgent the needs for administrative unity at home become, the more this character is inevitably and gradually giving way formally to the bureaucratic structure. Moreover, the partly unbureaucratic form of the state structure of the United States is materially balanced by the more strictly bureaucratic structures of those formations which, in truth, dominate politically, namely, the parties under the leadership of professionals or experts in organization and election tactics. The increasingly bureaucratic organization of all genuine mass parties offers the most striking example of the role of sheer quantity as a leverage for the bureaucratization of a social structure. In Germany, above all, the Social Democratic party, and abroad both of the "historical" American parties are bureaucratic in the greatest possible degree.

### QUALITATIVE CHANGES OF ADMINISTRATIVE TASKS

Bureaucratization is occasioned more by intensive and qualitative enlargement and internal deployment of the scope of administrative tasks than by their extensive and quantitative increase. But the direction bureaucratization takes and the reasons that occasion it vary widely.

In Egypt, the oldest country of bureaucratic state administration, the public and collective regulation of waterways for the whole country and from the top could not be avoided because of technical economic factors. This regulation created the mechanism of scribes and officials. Once established, this mechanism, even in early times, found its second realm of business in the extraordinary construction activities which were organized militarily. As mentioned before, the bureaucratic tendency has chiefly been influenced by needs arising from the creation of standing armies as determined by power politics and by the development of public finance connected with the military establishment. In the modern state, the increasing demands for administration rest on the increasing complexity of civilization and push towards bureaucratization.

Very considerable expansions, especially overseas, have, of course, been managed by states ruled by notables (Rome, England, Venice), as will become evident in the appropriate context. Yet the "intensity" of the administration, that is, the transfer of as many tasks as possible to the organization of the state proper for continuous management and discharge, has been only slightly developed among the great states ruled by notables, especially Rome and England, if we compare them with bureaucratic polities.

Both in notable and bureaucratic administrations the *structure* of state power has influenced culture very strongly. But it has done so relatively slightly in the form of management and control by the state. This holds from justice down to education. The growing demands on culture, in turn, are determined, though to a varying extent, by the growing wealth of the most influential strata in the state. To this extent increasing bureaucratization is a function of the increasing possession of goods used for consumption, and of an increasingly sophisticated technique of fashioning external life—a technique which corresponds to the opportunities provided by such wealth. This reacts upon the standard of living and makes for an increasing subjective indispensability of organized, collective, interlocal, and thus bureaucratic, provision for the most varied wants, which previously were either unknown, or were satisfied locally or by a private economy.

Among purely political factors, the increasing demand of a society, accustomed to absolute pacification, for order and protection ("police") in all fields exerts an especially persevering influence in the direction of bureaucratization. A steady road leads from modifications of the blood feud, sacerdotally, or by means of arbitration, to the present position of the policeman as the "representative of God on earth." The former means placed the guarantees for the individual's rights and security squarely upon the members of his sib, who are obligated to assist him with oath and vengeance. Among other factors, primarily the manifold tasks of the so-called "policy of social welfare" operate in the direction of bureaucratization, for these tasks are, in part, saddled upon the state by interest groups and, in part, the state usurps them, either for reasons of power policy or for ideological motives. Of course, these tasks are to a large extent economically determined.

Among essentially technical factors, the specifically modern means of communication enter the picture as pacemakers of bureaucratization. Public land and water-ways, railroads, the telegraph, et cetera—they must, in part, necessarily be administered in a public and collective way; in part, such administration is technically expedient. In this respect, the contemporary means of communication frequently play a role similar to that of the canals of Mesopotamia and the regulation of the Nile in the ancient Orient. The degree to which the means of communication have been developed is a condition of decisive importance for the possibility of bureaucratic administration, although it is not the only decisive condition. Certainly in Egypt, bureaucratic centralization, on the basis of an almost pure subsistence economy, could never have reached the actual degree which it did without the natural trade route of the Nile. In order to promote bureaucratic centralization in modern Persia, the telegraph officials were officially commissioned with reporting all occurrences in the provinces to the Shah, over the heads of the local authorities. In addition, everyone received the right to remonstrate directly by telegraph. The modern Occidental state can be administered the way it actually is only because the state controls the telegraph network and has the mails and railroads at its disposal.

Railroads, in turn, are intimately connected with the development of an interlocal traffic of mass goods. This traffic is among the causal factors in the formation of the modern state. As we have already seen, this does not hold unconditionally for the past.

### TECHNICAL ADVANTAGES OF BUREAUCRATIC ORGANIZATION

The decisive reason for the advance of bureaucratic organization has always been its purely technical superiority over any other form of organization. The fully developed bureaucratic mechanism compares with other organizations exactly as does the machine with the non-mechanical modes of production.

Precision, speed, unambiguity, knowledge of the files, continuity, discretion, unity, strict subordination, reduction of friction and of material and personal costs—these are raised to the optimum point in the strictly bureaucratic administration, and especially in its monocratic form. As compared with all collegiate, honorific, and avocational forms of administration, trained bureaucracy is superior on all these points. And as far as complicated tasks are concerned, paid bureaucratic work is not only more precise but, in the last analysis, it is often cheaper than even formally unremunerated honorific service.

Honorific arrangements make administrative work an avocation and, for this reason alone, honorific service normally functions more slowly; being less bound to schemata and being more formless. Hence it is less precise and less unified than bureaucratic work because it is less dependent upon superiors and because the establishment and exploitation of the apparatus of subordinate officials and filing services are almost unavoidably less economical. Honorific service is less continuous than bureaucratic and frequently quite expensive. This is especially the case if one thinks not only of the money costs to the public treasury—costs which bureaucratic administration, in comparison with administration by notables, usually substantially increases—but also of the frequent economic losses of the governed caused by delays and lack of precision. The possibility of administration by notables normally and permanently exists only where official management can be satisfactorily discharged as an avocation. With the qualitative increase of tasks the administration has to face, administration by notables reaches its limits—today, even in England. Work organized by collegiate bodies causes friction and delay and requires compromises between colliding interests and views. The administration, therefore, runs less precisely and is more independent of superiors; hence, it is less unified and slower. All advances of the Prussian administrative organization have been and will in the future be advances of the bureaucratic, and especially of the monocratic, principle.

Today, it is primarily the capitalist market economy which demands that the official business of the administration be discharged precisely, unambiguously, continuously, and with as much speed as possible. Normally, the very large, modern capitalist enterprises are themselves unequalled models of strict bureaucratic organization. Business management throughout rests on increasing precision, steadiness, and, above all, the speed of operations. This, in turn, is determined by the peculiar nature of the modern means of communication, including, among other things, the news service of the press. The extraordinary increase in the speed by which public announcements, as well as economic and political facts, are transmitted exerts a steady and sharp pressure in the direction of speeding up the tempo of administrative reaction towards various situations. The optimum of such reaction time is normally attained only by a strictly bureaucratic organization.*

Bureaucratization offers above all the optimum possibility for carrying through the principle of specializing administrative functions according to purely objective considerations. Individual performances are allocated to functionaries who have specialized training and who by constant practice learn more and more. The "objective" discharge of business primarily means a discharge of business according to *calculable rules* and "without regard for persons."

"Without regard for persons" is also the watchword of the "market" and, in general, of all pursuits of naked economic interests. A consistent execution of bureaucratic domination means the leveling of status "honor." Hence, if the principle of the free-market is not at the same time restricted, it means the universal domination of the "class situation." That this consequence of bureaucratic domination has not set in everywhere, parallel to the extent of bureaucratization, is due to the differences among possible principles by which polities may meet their demands.

The second element mentioned, "calculable rules," also is of paramount importance for modern bureaucracy. The peculiarity of modern culture, and specifically of its technical and economic basis, demands this very "calculability" of results. When fully developed, bureaucracy also stands, in a specific sense, under the principle of *sine ira ac studio*. Its specific nature, which is welcomed by capitalism, develops the more perfectly the more the bureaucracy is "dehumanized," the more completely it

* Here we cannot discuss in detail how the bureaucratic apparatus may, and actually does, produce definite obstacles to the discharge of business in a manner suitable for the single case.

succeeds in eliminating from official business love, hatred, and all purely personal, irrational, and emotional elements which escape calculation. This is the specific nature of bureaucracy and it is appraised as its special virtue.

The more complicated and specialized modern culture becomes, the more its external supporting apparatus demands the personally detached and strictly "objective" *expert*, in lieu of the master of older social structures, who was moved by personal sympathy and favor, by grace and gratitude. Bureaucracy offers the attitudes demanded by the external apparatus of modern culture in the most favorable combination. As a rule, only bureaucracy has established the foundation for the administration of a rational law conceptually systematized on the basis of such enactments as the latter Roman imperial period first created with a high degree of technical perfection. During the Middle Ages, this law was received along with the bureaucratization of legal administration, that is to say, with the displacement of the old trial procedure which was bound to tradition or to irrational presuppositions, by the rationally trained and specialized expert.

* * * * * *

### THE CONCENTRATION OF THE MEANS OF ADMINISTRATION

The bureaucratic structure goes hand in hand with the concentration of the material means of management in the hands of the master. This concentration occurs, for instance, in a well-known and typical fashion, in the development of big capitalist enterprises, which find their essential characteristics in this process. A corresponding process occurs in public organizations.

The bureaucratically led army of the Pharaohs, the army during the later period of the Roman republic and the principate, and, above all, the army of the modern military state are characterized by the fact that their equipment and provisions are supplied from the magazines of the war lord. This is in contrast to the folk armies of agricultural tribes, the armed citizenry of ancient cities, the militias of early medieval cities, and all feudal armies; for these, the self-equipment and the self-provisioning of those obliged to fight was normal.

War in our time is a war of machines. And this makes magazines technically necessary, just as the dominance of the machine in industry promotes the concentration of the means of production and management. In the main, however, the bureaucratic armies of the past, equipped and provisioned by the lord, have risen when social and economic development has absolutely or relatively diminished the stratum of citizens who were economically able to equip themselves, so that their number was no longer sufficient for putting the required armies in the field. They were reduced at least relatively, that is, in relation to the range of power claimed for the polity. Only the bureaucratic army structure allowed for the development of the professional standing armies which are necessary for the constant pacification of large states of the plains, as well as for warfare against far-distant enemies, especially enemies overseas. Specifically, military discipline and technical training can be normally and fully developed, at least to its modern high level, only in the bureaucratic army.

Historically, the bureaucratization of the army has everywhere been realized along with the transfer of army service from the propertied to the propertyless. Until this transfer occurs, military service is an honorific privilege of propertied men. Such a transfer was made to the native-born unpropertied, for instance, in the armies of the generals of the late Roman republic and the empire, as well as in modern armies up to the nineteenth century. The burden of service has also been transferred to strangers, as in the mercenary armies of all ages. This process typically goes hand in hand with the general increase in material and intellectual culture. The following reason has also played its part everywhere: the increasing density of population, and therewith the intensity and strain of economic work, makes for an increasing "indispensability" of the acquisitive strata for purposes of war. Leaving aside periods of strong ideological fervor, the propertied strata of sophisticated and especially of urban culture as a rule are little fitted and also little inclined to do the coarse war work of the common soldier. Other circumstances being equal, the propertied strata of the open country are at least usually better qualified and more strongly inclined to become professional officers. This difference between the urban and the rural propertied is balanced only where the increasing possibility of mechanized warfare requires the leaders to qualify as "technicians."

The bureaucratization of organized warfare may be carried through in the form of private capitalist enterprise, just like any other business. Indeed, the procurement of armies and their administration by private capitalists has been the rule in mercenary armies, especially those of the Occident up to the turn of the eighteenth century. During the Thirty Years' War, in Brandenburg the soldier was still the predominant owner of the material implements of his business. He owned his weapons, horses, and dress, although the state, in the role, as it were, of the merchant of the "putting-out system," did supply him to some extent. Later on, in the standing army of Prussia, the chief of the company owned the material means of warfare, and only since the peace of Tilsit has the concentration of the means of warfare in the hands of the state definitely come about. Only with this concentration was the introduction of uniforms generally carried through. Before then, the introduction of uniforms had been left to a great extent to the arbitrary discretion of the regimental officer, with the exception of individual categories of troops to whom the king had "bestowed" certain uniforms, first, in 1620, to the royal bodyguard, then, under Frederick II, repeatedly.

Such terms as "regiment" and "battalion" usually had quite different meanings in the eighteenth century from the meanings they have today. Only the battalion was a tactical unit (today both are); the "regiment" was then a managerial unit of an economic organization established by the colonel's position as an "entrepreneur." "Official" maritime ventures (like the Genoese *maonae*) and army procurement belong to private capitalism's first giant enterprises of far-going bureaucratic character. In this respect, the "nationalization" of these enterprises by the state has its modern parallel in the nationalization of the railroads, which have been controlled by the state from their beginnings.

In the same way as with army organizations, the bureaucratization of administration goes hand in hand with the concentration of the means of organization in other spheres. The old administration by satraps and regents, as well as administration by farmers of office, purchasers of office, and, most of all, administration by feudal vassals, decentralize the material means of administration. The local demand of the province and the cost of the army and of subaltern officials are regularly paid for in advance from local income, and only the surplus reaches the central treasure. The enfeoffed official administers entirely by payment out of his own pocket. The bureaucratic state, however, puts its whole administrative expense on the budget and equips the lower authorities with the current means of expenditure, the use of which the state regulates and controls. This has the same meaning for the "economics" of the administration as for the large centralized capitalist enterprise.

In the field of scientific research and instruction, the bureaucratization of the always existing research institutes of the universities is a function of the increasing demand for material means of management. Liebig's laboratory at Giessen University was the first example of big enterprise in this field. Through the concentration of such means in the hands of the privileged head of the institute, the mass of researchers and docents are separated from their "means of production," in the same way as capitalist enterprise has separated the workers from theirs.

In spite of its indubitable technical superiority, bureaucracy has everywhere been a relatively late development. A number of obstacles have contributed to this, and only under certain social and political conditions have they definitely receded into the background.

### THE LEVELING OF SOCIAL DIFFERENCES

Bureaucratic organization has usually come into power on the basis of a leveling of economic and social differences. This leveling has been at least relative, and has concerned the significance of social and economic differences for the assumption of administrative functions.

Bureaucracy inevitably accompanies modern *mass democracy* in contrast to the democratic self-government of small homogeneous units. This results from the characteristic principle of bureaucracy: the abstract regularity of the execution of authority, which is a result of the demand for "equality before the law" in the personal and functional sense—hence, of the horror of "privilege," and the principled rejection of doing business "from case to case." Such regularity also follows from the social preconditions of the origin of bureaucracies. The nonbureaucratic administration of any large social structure rests in some way upon the fact that existing social, material, or honorific preferences and ranks are connected with administrative functions and duties. This usually means that a direct or indirect economic exploitation or a "social" exploitation of position, which every sort of administrative activity gives to its bearers, is equivalent to the assumption of administrative functions.

Bureaucratization and democratization within the administration of the state therefore signify and increase the cash expenditures of the public treasury. And this is the case in spite of the fact that bureaucratic administration is usually more "economical" in character than other forms of administration. Until recent times—at least from the point of view of the treasury—the cheapest way of satisfying the need for administration was to leave almost the entire local administration and lower judicature to the landlords of Eastern Prussia. The same fact applies to the administration of sheriffs in England. Mass democracy makes a clean sweep of the feudal, patrimonial, and—at least in intent—the plutocratic privileges in administration. Unavoidably it puts paid professional labor in place of the historically inherited avocational administration by notables.

This not only applies to structures of the state. For it is no accident that in their own organizations, the democratic mass parties have completely broken with traditional notable rule based upon personal relationships and personal esteem. Yet such personal structures frequently continue among the old conservative as well as the old liberal parties. Democratic mass parties are bureaucratically organized under the leadership of party officials, professional party and trade union secretaries, et cetera. In Germany, for instance, this has happened in the Social Democratic party and in the agrarian mass movement; and in England, for the first time, in the caucus democracy of Gladstone-Chamberlain, which was originally organized in Birmingham and since the 1870's has spread. In the United States, both parties since Jackson's administration have developed bureaucratically. In France, however, attempts to organize disciplined political parties on the basis of an election system that would compel bureaucratic organization have repeatedly failed. The resistance of local circles of notables against the ultimately unavoidable bureaucratization of the parties, which would encompass the entire country and break their influence, could not be overcome. Every advance of the simple election techniques, for instance the system of proportional elections, which calculates with figures, means a strict and interlocal bureaucratic organization of the parties and therewith an increasing domination of party bureaucracy and discipline, as well as the elimination of the local circles of notables—at least this holds for great states.

The progress of bureaucratization in the state administration itself is a parallel phenomenon of democracy, as is quite obvious in France, North America, and now in England. Of course one must always remember that the term "democratization" can be misleading. The *demos* itself, in the sense of an inarticulate mass, never "governs" larger associations; rather, it is governed, and its existence only changes the way in which the executive leaders are selected and the measure of influence which the *demos*, or better, which social circles from its midst are able to exert upon the content and the direction of administrative activities by supplementing what is called "public opinion." "Democratization," in the sense here intended, does not necessarily mean an increasingly active share of the governed in the authority of the social structure. This may be a result of democratization, but it is not necessarily the case.

We must expressly recall at this point that the political concept of democracy, deduced from the "equal rights" of the governed, includes these postulates: (1) prevention of the development of a closed status group of officials in the interest of a universal accessibility of office, and (2) minimization of the authority of officialdom in the interest of expanding the sphere of influence of "public opinion" as far as practicable. Hence, wherever possible, political democracy strives to shorten the term of office by election and recall and by not binding the candidates to a special expertness. Thereby democracy inevitably comes into conflict with the bureaucratic tendencies which, by its fight against notable rule, democracy has produced. The generally loose term "democratization" cannot be used here, in so far as it is understood to mean the minimization of the civil servants' ruling power in favor of the greatest possible "direct" rule of the *demos*, which in practice means the respective party leaders of the *demos*. The most decisive thing here—indeed it is rather exclusively so—is the *leveling of the governed* in opposition to the ruling and bureaucratically articulated group, which in its turn may occupy a quite autocratic position, both in fact and in form.

* * * * * *

### THE PERMANENT CHARACTER OF THE BUREAUCRATIC MACHINE

Once it is fully established, bureaucracy is among those social structures which are the hardest to destroy. Bureaucracy is *the* means of carrying "community action" over into rationally ordered "societal action." Therefore, as an instrument for "societalizing" relations of power, bureaucracy has been and is a power instrument of the first order—for the one who controls the bureaucratic apparatus.

Under otherwise equal conditions, a "societal action," which is methodically ordered and led, is superior to every resistance of "mass" or even of "communal action." And where the bureaucratization of administration has been completely carried through, a form of power relation is established that is practically unshatterable.

The individual bureaucrat cannot squirm out of the apparatus in which he is harnessed. In contrast to the honorific or avocational "notable," the professional bureaucrat is chained to his activity by his entire material and ideal existence. In the great majority of cases, he is only a single cog in an ever-moving mechanism which prescribes to him an essentially fixed route of march. The official is entrusted with specialized tasks and normally the mechanism cannot be put into motion or arrested by him, but only from the very top. The individual bureaucrat is thus forged to the community of all the functionaries who are integrated into the mechanism. They have a common interest in seeing that the mechanism continues its functions and that the societally exercised authority carries on.

The ruled, for their part, cannot dispense with or replace the bureaucratic apparatus of authority once it exists. For this bureaucracy rests upon expert training, a functional specialization of work, and an attitude set for habitual and virtuoso-like mastery of single yet methodically integrated functions. If the official stops working, or if his work is forcefully interrupted, chaos results, and it is difficult to improvise replacements from among the governed who are fit to master such chaos. This holds for public administration as well as for private economic management. More and more the material fate of the masses depends upon the steady and correct functioning of the increasingly bureaucratic organizations of private capitalism. The idea of eliminating these organizations becomes more and more utopian.

The discipline of officialdom refers to the attitude-set of the official for precise obedience within his *habitual* activity, in public as well as in private organizations. This discipline increasingly becomes the basis of all order, however great the practical importance of administration on the basis of the filed documents may be. The naïve idea of Bakuninism of destroying the basis of "acquired rights" and "domination" by destroying public documents overlooks the settled orientation of *man* for keeping to the habitual rules and regulations that continue to exist independently of the documents. Every reorganization of beaten or dissolved troops, as well as the restoration of administrative orders destroyed by revolt, panic, or other catastrophes, is realized by appealing to the trained orientation of obedient compliance to such orders. Such compliance has been conditioned into the officials, on the one hand, and, on the other hand, into the governed. If such an appeal is successful it brings, as it were, the disturbed mechanism into gear again.

The objective indispensability of the once-existing apparatus, with its peculiar, "impersonal" character, means that the mechanism—in contrast to feudal orders based upon personal piety—is easily made to work for anybody who knows how to gain control over it. A rationally ordered system of officials continues to function smoothly after the enemy has occupied the area; he merely needs to change the top officials. This body of officials continues to operate because it is to the vital interest of everyone concerned, including above all the enemy.

During the course of his long years in power, Bismarck brought his ministerial colleagues into unconditional bureaucratic dependence by eliminating all independent statesmen. Upon his retirement, he saw to his surprise that they continued to manage their offices unconcerned and undismayed, as if he had not been the master mind and creator of these creatures, but rather as if some single figure had been exchanged for some other figure in the bureaucratic machine. With all the changes of masters in France since the time of the First Empire, the power machine has remained essentially the same. Such a machine makes "revolution," in the sense of the forceful creation of entirely new formations of authority, technically more and more impossible, especially when the apparatus controls the modern means of communication (telegraph, et cetera) and also by virtue of its internal rationalized structure. In classic fashion, France has demonstrated how this process has substituted *coups d'état* for "revolutions": all successful transformations in France have amounted to *coups d'état*.

## The routinization of charisma

In its pure form charismatic authority has a character specifically foreign to everyday routine structures. The social relationships directly involved are strictly personal, based on the validity and practice of charismatic personal qualities. If this is not to remain a purely transitory phenomenon, but to take on the character of a permanent relationship forming a stable community of disciples or a band of followers or a party organization or any sort of political or hierocratic organization, it is necessary for the character of charismatic authority to become radically changed. Indeed, in its pure form charismatic authority may be said to exist only in the process of originating. It cannot remain stable, but becomes either traditionalized or rationalized, or a combination of both.

The following are the principal motives underlying this transformation: (*a*) The ideal and also the material interests of the followers in the continuation and the continual reactivation of the community, (*b*) the still stronger ideal and also stronger material interests of the members of the administrative staff, the disciples or other followers of the charismatic leader in continuing their relationship. Not only this, but they have an interest in continuing it in such a way that both from an ideal and a material point of view, their own status is put on a stable everyday basis. This means, above all, making it possible to participate in normal family relationships or at least to enjoy a secure social position in place of the kind of discipleship which is cut off from ordinary worldly connections, notably in the family and in economic relationships.

These interests generally become conspicuously evident with the disappearance of the personal charismatic leader and with the problem of succession, which inevitably arises. The way in which this problem is met—if it is met at all and the charismatic group continues to exist—is of crucial importance for the character of the subsequent social relationships. The following are the principal possible types of solution:—

(*a*) The search for a new charismatic leader on the basis of criteria of the qualities which will fit him for the position of authority. This is to be found in a relatively pure type in the process of choice of a new Dalai Lama. It consists in the search for a child with characteristics which are interpreted to mean that he is a reincarnation of the Buddha. This is very similar to the choice of the new Bull of Apis.

In this case the legitimacy of the new charismatic leader is bound to certain distinguishing characteristics; thus, to rules with respect to which a tradition arises. The result is a process of traditionalization in favour of which the purely personal character of leadership is eliminated.

(*b*) By revelation manifested in oracles, lots, divine judgments, or other techniques of selection. In this case the legitimacy of the new leader is dependent on the legitimacy of the technique of his selection. This involves a form of legalization. It is said that at times the *Schofetim* of Israel had this character. Saul is said to have been chosen by the old war oracle.

(*c*) By the designation on the part of the original charismatic leader of his own successor and his recognition on the part of the followers. This is a very common form. Originally, the Roman magistracies were filled entirely in this way. The system survived most clearly into later times in the appointment of "dictators" and in the institution of the "interrex." In this case legitimacy is acquired through the act of designation.

(*d*) Designation of a successor by the charismatically qualified administrative staff and his recognition by the community. In its typical form this process

Reprinted from *The Theory of Social and Economic Organization* (trans. A. M. Henderson and Talcott Parsons, ed. Talcott Parsons), pp. 363–73, by permission of the publisher. 

should quite definitely not be interpreted as "election" or "nomination" or anything of the sort. It is not a matter of free selection, but of one which is strictly bound to objective duty. It is not to be determined merely by majority vote, but is a question of arriving at the correction designation, the designation of the right person who is truly endowed with charisma. It is quite possible that the minority and not the majority should be right in such a case. Unanimity is often required. It is obligatory to acknowledge a mistake and persistence in error is a serious offence. Making a wrong choice is a genuine wrong requiring expiation. Originally it was a magical offence.

Nevertheless, in such a case it is easy for legitimacy to take on the character of an acquired right which is justified by standards of the correctness of the process by which the position was acquired, for the most part, by its having been acquired in accordance with certain formalities, such as coronation. This was the original meaning of the coronation of bishops and kings in the Western World by the clergy or the nobility with the "consent" of the community. There are numerous analogous phenomena all over the world. The fact that this is the origin of the modern conception of "election" raises problems which will have to be gone into later.

(*e*) By the conception that charisma is a quality transmitted by heredity; thus that it is participated in by the kinsmen of its bearer, particularly by his closest relatives. This is the case of hereditary charisma. The order of hereditary succession in such a case need not be the same as that which is in force for appropriated rights, but may differ from it. It is also sometimes necessary to select the proper heir within the kinship group by some of the methods just spoken of; thus in certain Negro states brothers have had to fight for the succession. In China, succession had to take place in such a way that the relation of the living group to the ancestral spirits was not disturbed. The rule either of seniority or of designation by the followers has been very common in the Orient. Hence, in the house of Osman, it has been obligatory to eliminate all other possible candidates.

Only in Medieval Europe and in Japan universally, elsewhere only sporadically, has the principle of primogeniture, as governing the inheritance of authority, become clearly established. This has greatly facilitated the consolidation of political groups in that it has eliminated struggle between a plurality of candidates from the same charismatic family.

In the case of hereditary charisma, recognition is no longer paid to the charismatic qualities of the individual, but to the legitimacy of the position he has acquired by hereditary succession. This may lead in the direction either of traditionalization or of legalization. The concept of "divine right" is fundamentally altered and now comes to mean authority by virtue of a personal right which is not dependent on the recognition of those subject to authority. Personal charisma may be totally absent. Hereditary monarchy is a conspicuous illustration. In Asia there have been very numerous hereditary priesthoods; also, frequently, the hereditary charisma of kinship groups has been treated as a criterion of social rank and of eligibility for fiefs and benefices.

(*f*) The concept that charisma may be transmitted by ritual means from one bearer to another or may be created in a new person. The concept was originally magical. It involves a dissociation of charisma from a particular individual, making it an objective, transferrable entity. In particular, it may become the charisma of office. In this case the belief in legitimacy is no longer directed to the individual, but to the acquired qualities and to the effectiveness of the ritual acts. The most important example is the transmission of priestly charisma by anointing, consecration, or the laying on of hands; and of royal authority, by anointing and by coronation. The *caracter indelibilis* thus acquired means that the charismatic qualities and powers of the office are emancipated from the personal qualities of the priest. For precisely this reason, this has, from the Donatist and the Montanist heresies down to the Puritan revolution, been the subject of continual conflicts. The "hireling" of the Quakers is the preacher endowed with the charisma of office.

Concomitant with the routinization of charisma with a view to insuring adequate succession, go the interests in its routinization on the part of the administrative staff. It is only in the initial stages and so long as the charismatic leader acts in a way which is completely outside everyday social organization, that it is possible for his followers to live communistically in a community of faith and enthusiasm, on gifts, "booty," or sporadic acquisition.

Only the members of the small group of enthusiastic disciples and followers are prepared to devote their lives purely idealistically to their call. The great majority of disciples and followers will in the long run "make their living" out of their "calling" in a material sense as well. Indeed, this must be the case if the movement is not to disintegrate.

Hence, the routinization of charisma also takes the form of the appropriation of powers of control and of economic advantages by the followers or disciples, and of regulation of the recruitment of these groups. This process of traditionalization or of legalization, according to whether rational legislation is involved or not, may take any one of a number of typical forms.

1. The original basis of recruitment is personal charisma. With routinization, the followers or disciples may set up norms for recruitment, in particular involving training or tests of eligibility. Charisma can only be "awakened" and "tested"; it cannot be "learned" or "taught." All types of magical asceticism, as practiced by magicians and heroes, and all novitiates, belong in this category. These are means of closing the group which constitutes the administrative staff.

Only the proved novice is allowed to exercise authority. A genuine charismatic leader is in a position to oppose this type of prerequisite for membership. His successor is not, at least if he is chosen by the administrative staff. This type is illustrated by the magical and warrior asceticism of the "men's house" with initiation ceremonies and age groups. An individual who has not successfully gone through the initiation, remains a "woman"; that is, is excluded from the charismatic group.

2. It is easy for charismatic norms to be transformed into those defining a traditional social status on a hereditary charismatic basis. If the leader is chosen on a hereditary basis, it is very easy for hereditary charisma to govern the selection of the administrative staff and even, perhaps, those followers without any position of authority. The term "familistic state" will be applied when a political body is organized strictly and completely in terms of this principle of hereditary charisma. In such a case, all appropriation of governing powers, of fiefs, benefices, and all sorts of economic advantages follow the same pattern. The result is that all powers and advantages of all sorts become traditionalized. The heads of families, who are traditional gerontocrats or patriarchs without personal charismatic legitimacy, regulate the exercise of these powers which cannot be taken away from their family. It is not the type of position he occupies which determines the rank of a man or of his family, but rather the hereditary charismatic rank of his family determines the position he will occupy. Japan, before the development of bureaucracy, was organized in this way. The same was undoubtedly true of China as well where, before the rationalization which took place in the territorial states, authority was in the hands of the "old families." Other types of examples are furnished by the caste system in India, and by Russia before the *Mjestnitschestvo* was introduced. Indeed, all hereditary social classes with established privileges belong in the same category.

3. The administrative staff may seek and achieve the creation and appropriation of individual positions and the corresponding economic advantages for its members. In that case, according to whether the tendency is to traditionalization or legalization, there will develop (*a*) benefices, (*b*) offices, or (*c*) fiefs. In the first case a prebendal organization will result; in the second, patrimonialism or bureaucracy; in the third, feudalism. These become appropriated in the place of the type of provision from gifts or booty without settled relation to the everyday economic structure.

Case (*a*), benefices, may consist in rights to the proceeds of begging, to payments in kind, or to the proceeds of money taxes, or finally, to the proceeds of fees. Any one of these may result from the regulation of provision by free gifts or by "booty" in terms of a rational organization of finance. Regularized begging is found in Buddhism; benefices in kind, in the Chinese and Japanese "rice rents"; support by money taxation has been the rule in all the rationalized conquering states. The last case is common everywhere, especially on the part of priests and judges and, in India, even the military authorities.

Case (*b*), the transformation of the charismatic mission into an office, may have more of a patrimonial or more of a bureaucratic character. The former is much the more common; the latter is found principally in Mediterranean Antiquity and in the modern Western World. Elsewhere it is exceptional.

In case (*c*), only land may be appropriated as a fief, whereas the position as such retains its originally charismatic character. On the other hand, powers and authority may be fully appropriated as fiefs. It is difficult to distinguish the two cases. It is, however, rare that orientation to the charismatic character of the position disappears entirely; it did not do so in the Middle Ages.

For charisma to be transformed into a permanent routine structure, it is necessary that its anti-economic character should be altered. It must be adapted to some form of fiscal organization to provide for the needs of the group and hence to the economic conditions necessary for raising taxes and contributions. When a charismatic movement develops in the direction of prebendal provision, the "laity" become differentiated from the "clergy"; that is, the participating members of the charismatic administrative staff which has now become routinized. These are the priests of the developing "church." Correspondingly, in a developing political body the vassals, the holders of benefices, or officials are differentiated from the "taxpayers." The former, instead of being the "followers" of the leader, become state officials or appointed party officials. This process is very conspicuous in Buddhism and in the Hindu sects. The same is true in all the states resulting from conquest which have become rationalized to form permanent structures; also of parties and other movements which have originally had a purely charismatic character. With the process of routinization the charismatic group tends to develop into one of the forms of everyday authority, particularly the patrimonial form in its decentralized variant or the bureaucratic. Its original peculiarities are apt to be retained in the charismatic standards of honor attendant on the social status acquired by heredity or the holding of office. This applies to all who participate in the process of appropriation, the chief himself, and the members of his staff. It is thus a matter of the type of prestige enjoyed by ruling groups. A hereditary monarch by "divine right" is not a simple patrimonial chief, patriarch, or sheik; a vassal is not a mere household retainer or official. Further details must be deferred to the analysis of social stratification.

As a rule the process of routinization is not free of conflict. In the early stages personal claims on the charisma of the chief are not easily forgotten and the conflict between the charisma of office or of hereditary status with personal charisma is a typical process in many historical situations.

1. The power of absolution—that is, the power to absolve from mortal sins—was held originally only by personal charismatic martyrs or ascetics, but became transformed into a power of the office of bishop or priest. This process was much slower in the Orient than in the Occident because in the latter case it was influenced by the Roman conception of office. Revolutions under a charismatic leader, directed against hereditary charismatic powers or the powers of office, are to be found in all types of corporate groups, from states to trade unions. The more highly developed the interdependence of different economic units in a monetary economy, the greater the pressure of the everyday needs of the followers of the charismatic movement becomes. The effect of this is to strengthen the tendency to routinization, which is everywhere operative, and as a rule has rapidly won out. Charisma is a phenomenon typical of prophetic religious movements or of expansive political movements in their early stages. But as soon as the position of authority is well established, and above all as soon as control over large masses of people exists, it gives way to the forces of everyday routine.

2. One of the decisive motives underlying all cases of the routinization of charisma is naturally the striving for security. This means legitimization, on the one hand, of positions of authority and social prestige, on the other hand, of the economic advantages enjoyed by the followers and sympathizers of the leader. Another important motive, however, lies in the objective necessity of adaptation of the patterns of order and of the organization of the administrative staff to the normal, everyday needs and conditions of carrying on administration. In this connection, in particular, there are always points at which traditions of administrative practice and of judicial decision can take hold; since these are needed both by the normal administrative staff and by those subject to its authority. It is further necessary that there should be some definite order introduced into the organization of the administrative staff itself. Finally, as will be discussed in detail below, it is necessary for the administrative staff and

all its administrative practices to be adapted to everyday economic conditions. It is not possible for the costs of permanent, routine administration to be met by "booty," contributions, gifts, and hospitality, as is typical of the pure type of military and prophetic charisma.

3. The process of routinization is thus not by any means confined to the problem of succession and does not stop when this has been solved. On the contrary, the most fundamental problem is that of making a transition from a charismatic administrative staff, and the corresponding principles of administration, to one which is adapted to everyday conditions. The problem of succession, however, is crucial because through it occurs the routinization of the charismatic focus of the structure. In it, the character of the leader himself and of his claim to legitimacy is altered. This process involves peculiar and characteristic conceptions which are understandable only in this context and do not apply to the problem of transition to traditional or legal patterns of order and types of administrative organization. The most important of the modes of meeting the problem of succession are the charismatic designation of a successor and hereditary charisma.

4. As has already been noted, the most important historical example of designation by the charismatic leader of his own successor is Rome. For the *rex*, this arrangement is attested by tradition; while for the appointment of the "dictator" and of the co-emperor and successor in the principate, it has existed in historical times. The way in which all the higher magistrates were invested with the *imperium* shows clearly that they also were designated as successors by the military commander, subject to recognition by the citizen army. The fact that candidates were examined by the magistrate in office and that originally they could be excluded on what were obviously arbitrary grounds shows clearly what was the nature of the development.

5. The most important examples of designation of a successor by the charismatic followers of the leader are to be found in the election of bishops, and particularly of the Pope, by the original system of designation by the clergy and recognition by the lay community. The investigations of U. Stutz have made it probable that, though it was later altered, the election of the German emperor was modeled on that of the bishops. He was designated by a group of qualified princes and recognized by the "people," that is, those bearing arms. Similar arrangements are very common.

6. The classical case of the development of hereditary charisma is that of caste in India. All occupational qualifications, and in particular all the qualifications for positions of authority and power, have there come to be regarded as strictly bound to the inheritance of charisma. Eligibility for fiefs, involving governing powers, was limited to members of the royal kinship group, the fiefs being granted by the eldest of the group. All types of religious office, including the extraordinarily important and influential position of *guru*, the *directeur de l'âme*, were treated as bound to hereditary charismatic qualities. The same is true of all sorts of relations to traditional customers and of all positions in the village organization, such as priest, barber, laundryman, watchman, etc. The foundation of a sect always meant the development of a hereditary hierarchy, as was true also of Taoism in China. Also in the Japanese "feudal" state, before the introduction of a patrimonial officialdom on the Chinese model, which then led to prebends and a new feudalization, social organization was based purely on hereditary charisma.

This kind of hereditary charismatic right to positions of authority has been developed in similar ways all over the world. Qualification by virtue of individual achievement has been replaced by qualification by birth. This is everywhere the basis of the development of hereditary aristocracies, in the Roman nobility, in the concept of the *stirps regia*, which Tacitus describes among the Germans, in the rules of eligibility to tournaments and monasteries in the late Middle Ages, and even in the genealogical research carried on on behalf of the parvenu aristocracy of the United States. Indeed, this is to be found everywhere where a differentiation of hereditary social classes has become established.

The following is the principal relation to economic conditions: The process of routinization of charisma is in very important respects identical with adaptation to the conditions of economic life, since this is one of the principal continually operating forces in everyday life. Economic conditions in this connection play a leading role and do not constitute merely a dependent variable. To a very large extent the transition to hereditary charisma or the charisma of office serves in this connection as a means of legitimizing existing or recently acquired powers of control over economic goods. Along with the ideology of loyalty, which is certainly by no means unimportant, allegiance to hereditary monarchy in particular is very strongly influenced by the consideration that all inherited property and all that which is legitimately acquired would be endangered if subjective recognition of the sanctity of succession to the throne were eliminated. It is hence by no means fortuitous that hereditary monarchy is more acceptable to the propertied classes than, for instance, to the proletariat.

Beyond this, it is not possible to say anything in general terms, which would at the same time be substantial and valuable, on the relations of the various possible modes of adaptation to the economic order. This must be reserved to a special investigation. The development of a prebendal structure, of feudalism and the appropriation of all sorts of advantages on a hereditary charismatic basis, may in all cases have the same stereotyping effect on the economic order if they develop from charismatic starting points as if they developed from patrimonial or bureaucratic origins. The immediate effect of charisma in economic as in other connections is usually strongly revolutionary; indeed, often destructive, because it means new modes of orientation. But in case the process of routinization leads in the direction of traditionalism, its ultimate effect may be exactly the reverse.

ROBERT MICHELS

# Oligarchy

## Introductory—the need for organization

Democracy is inconceivable without organization. A few words will suffice to demonstrate this proposition.

A class which unfurls in the face of society the banner of certain definite claims, and which aspires to the realization of a complex of ideal aims deriving from the economic functions which that class fulfils, needs an organization. Be the claims economic or be they political, organization appears the only means for the creation of a collective will. Organization, based as it is upon the principle of least effort, that is to say, upon the greatest possible economy of energy, is the weapon of the weak in their struggle with the strong.

The chances of success in any struggle will depend upon the degree to which this struggle is carried out upon a basis of solidarity between individuals whose interests are identical. In objecting, therefore, to the theories of the individualist anarchists that nothing could please the employers better than the dispersion and disaggregation of the forces of the workers, the socialists, the most fanatical of all the partisans of the idea of organization, enunciate an argument which harmonizes well with the results of scientific study of the nature of parties.

We live in a time in which the idea of cooperation has become so firmly established that even millionaires perceive the necessity of common action. It is easy to understand, then, that organization has become a vital principle of the working class, for in default of it their success is *a priori* impossible. The refusal of the worker to participate in the collective life of his class cannot fail to entail disastrous consequences. In respect of culture and of economic, physical, and physiological conditions, the proletarian is the weakest element of our society. In fact, the isolated member of the working classes is defenseless in the hands of those who are economically stronger. It is only by combination to form a structural aggregate that the proletarians can acquire the faculty of political resistance and attain to a social dignity. The importance and the influence of the working class are directly proportional to its numerical strength. But for the representation of that numerical strength organization and coordination are indispensable. The principle of organization is an absolutely essential condition for the political struggle of the masses.

Yet this politically necessary principle of organization, while it overcomes that disorganization of forces which would be favorable to the adversary, brings other dangers in its train. We escape Scylla only to dash ourselves on Charybdis. Organization is, in fact, the source from which the conservative currents flow over the plain of democracy, occasioning there disastrous floods and rendering the plain unrecognizable.

* * * * * *

Reprinted from *Political Parties* (New York: Free Press Paperback, 1966), pp. 61–62, 65–73, 81–84, 87–89, 99–100, 103–4, 109–11, 167–68, 170–71, 172–73, 177–80, 364–71, by permission of The Macmillan Company. First published in the United States by The Free Press of Glencoe, Inc. 1958.

## Government by the masses

It is obvious that such a gigantic number of persons belonging to a unitary organization cannot do any practical work upon a system of direct discussion. The regular holding of deliberative assemblies of a thousand members encounters the gravest difficulties in respect of room and distance; while from the topographical point of view such an assembly would become altogether impossible if the members numbered ten thousand. Even if we imagined the means of communication to become much better than those which now exist, how would it be possible to assemble such a multitude in a given place, at a stated time, and with the frequency demanded by the exigencies of party life? In addition must be considered the physiological impossibility even for the most powerful orator of making himself heard by a crowd of ten thousand persons. There are, however, other persons of a technical and administrative character which render impossible the direct self-government of large groups. If Peter wrongs Paul, it is out of the question that all the other citizens should hasten to the spot to undertake a personal examination of the matter in dispute, and to take the part of Paul against Peter. By parity of reasoning, in the modern democratic party, it is impossible for the collectivity to undertake the direct settlement of all the controversies that may arise.

Hence the need for delegation, for the system in which delegates represent the mass and carry out its will. Even in groups sincerely animated with the democratic spirit, current business, the preparation and the carrying out of the most important actions, is necessarily left in the hands of individuals. It is well known that the impossibility for the people to exercise a legislative power directly in popular assemblies led the democratic idealists of Spain to demand, as the least of evils, a system of popular representation and a parliamentary state.[1]

Originally the chief is merely the servant of the mass. The organization is based upon the absolute equality of all its members. Equality is here understood in its most general sense, as an equality of like men. In many countries, as in idealist Italy (and in certain regions in Germany where the socialist movement is still in its infancy), this equality is manifested, among other ways, by the mutual use of the familiar "thou," which is employed by the most poorly paid wage-laborer in addressing the most distinguished intellectual. This generic conception of equality is, however, gradually replaced by the idea of equality among comrades belonging to the same organization, all of whose members enjoy the same rights. The democratic principle aims at guaranteeing to all an equal influence and an equal participation in the regulation of the common interests. All are electors, and all are eligible for office. The fundamental postulate of the *Déclaration des Droits de l'Homme* finds here its theoretical application. All the offices are filled by election. The officials, executive organs of the general will, play a merely subordinate part, are always dependent upon the collectivity, and can be deprived of their office at any moment. The mass of the party is omnipotent.

At the outset, the attempt is made to depart as little as possible from pure democracy by subordinating the delegates altogether to the will of the mass, by tieing them hand and foot. In the early days of the movement of the Italian agricultural workers, the chief of the league required a majority of four-fifths of the votes to secure election. When disputes arose with the employers about wages, the representative of the organization, before undertaking any negotiations, had to be furnished with a written authority, authorized by the signature of every member of the corporation. All the accounts of the body were open to the examination of the members, at any time. There were two reasons for this. First of all, the desire was to avoid the spread of mistrust through the mass, "this poison which gradually destroys even the strongest organism." In the second place, this usage allowed each one of the members to learn bookkeeping, and to acquire such a general knowledge of the working of the corporation as to enable him at any time to take over its leadership.[2] It is obvious that democracy in this sense is applicable only on a very small scale. In the infancy of the English labor movement, in many of the trade unions, the delegates were either

1. Cf. the letter of Antonio Quiroga to King Ferdinand VII, dated January 7, 1820 (Don Juan van Halen, *Mémoires*, Renouard, Paris, 1827, Part II, p. 382).

2. Egidio Bernaroli, *Manuale per la constituzione e il funzionamento delle leghe dei contadini*, Libreria Soc. Ital., Rome, 1902, pp. 20, 26, 27, 52.

appointed in rotation from among all the members, or were chosen by lot.[3] Gradually, however, the delegates' duties became more complicated; some individual ability becomes essential, a certain oratorical gift, and a considerable amount of objective knowledge. It thus becomes impossible to trust to blind chance, to the fortune of alphabetic succession, or to the order of priority, in the choice of a delegation whose members must possess certain peculiar personal aptitudes if they are to discharge their mission to the general advantage.

Such were the methods which prevailed in the early days of the labor movement to enable the masses to participate in party and trade-union administration. Today they are falling into disuse, and in the development of the modern political aggregate there is a tendency to shorten and stereotype the process which transforms the led into a leader—a process which has hitherto developed by the natural course of events. Here and there voices make themselves heard demanding a sort of official consecration for the leaders, insisting that it is necessary to constitute a class of professional politicians, of approved and registered experts in political life. Ferdinand Tönnies advocates that the party should institute regular examinations for the nomination of socialist parliamentary candidates, and for the appointment of party secretaries.[4] Heinrich Herkner goes even farther. He contends that the great trade unions cannot long maintain their existence if they persist in entrusting the management of their affairs to persons drawn from the rank and file, who have risen to command stage by stage solely in consequence of practical aptitudes acquired in the service of the organization. He refers, in this connection, to the unions that are controlled by the employers, whose officials are for the most part university men. He foresees that in the near future all the labor organizations will be forced to abandon proletarian exclusiveness, and in the choice of their officials to give the preference to persons of an education that is superior alike in economic, legal, technical, and commercial respects.[5]

3. Sidney and Beatrice Webb, *Industrial Democracy* (German edition), Stuttgart, 1898, vol. i, p. 6.

4. Ferdinant Tönnies, *Politik und Moral*, Neuer Frankf. Verl., Frankfort, 1901, p. 46.

5. Heinrich Herkner, *Die Arbeiterfrage*, Guttentag, Berlin, 1908, 5th ed., pp. 116, 117.

Even today, the candidates for the secretaryship of a trade union are subject to examination as to their knowledge of legal matters and their capacity as letter-writers. The socialist organizations engaged in political action also directly undertake the training of their own officials. Everywhere there are coming into existence "nurseries" for the rapid supply of officials possessing a certain amount of "scientific culture." Since 1906 there has existed in Berlin a Party-School in which courses of instruction are given for the training of those who wish to take office in the socialist party or in trade unions. The instructors are paid out of the funds of the socialist party, which was directly responsible for the foundation of the school. The other expenses of the undertaking, including the maintenance of the pupils, are furnished from a common fund supplied by the party and the various trade unions interested. In addition, the families of the pupils, in so far as the attendance of these at the school deprives the families of their breadwinners, receive an allowance from the provincial branch of the party or from the local branch of the union to which each pupil belongs. The third course of this school, from October 1, 1908, to April 3, 1909, was attended by twenty-six pupils, while the first year there had been thirty-one and the second year thirty-three. As pupils, preference is given to comrades who already hold office in the party or in one of the labor unions.[6] Those who do not already belong to the labor bureaucracy make it their aim to enter that body, and cherish the secret hope that attendance at the school will smooth their path. Those who fail to attain this end are apt to exhibit a certain discontent with the party which, after having encouraged their studies, has sent them back to manual labor. Among the 141 students of the year 1910–11, three classes were to be distinguished: one of these consisted of old and tried employees in the different branches of the labor movement (fifty-two persons); a second consisted of those who obtained employment in the party or the trade unions directly the course was finished (forty-nine persons); the third consisted of those who had to return to manual labor (forty persons).[7]

6. *Protokoll des Parteitags zu Leipzig*, 1909, "Vorwärts," Berlin, 1909, p. 48.

7. Heinrich Schulz, *Fünf Jahre Parteischule*, "Neue Zeit," anno xxix, vol. ii, fasc. 49, p. 807.

In Italy, *L'Umanitaria*, a philanthropic organization run by the socialists, founded at Milan in 1905 a "Practical School of Social Legislation," whose aim it is to give to a certain number of workers an education which will fit them for becoming factory inspectors, or for taking official positions in the various labor organizations, in the friendly societies, or in the labor exchanges.[8] The course of instruction lasts for two years, and at its close the pupils receive, after examination, a diploma which entitles them to the title of "Labor Expert." In 1908 there were two hundred and two pupils, thirty-seven of whom were employees of trade unions or of cooperative societies, four were secretaries of labor exchanges, forty-five employees in or members of the liberal professions, and a hundred and twelve working men.[9] At the outset most of the pupils came to the school as a matter of personal taste, or with the aim of obtaining the diploma in order to secure some comparatively lucrative private employment. But quite recently the governing body has determined to suppress the diploma, and to institute a supplementary course open to those only who are already employed by some labor organization or who definitely intend to enter such employment. For those engaged upon this special course of study there will be provided scholarships of £2 a week, the funds for this purpose being supplied in part by *L'Umanitaria* and in part by the labor organizations which wish to send their employees to the school.[10] In the year 1909, under the auspices of the *Bourse du Travail*, there was founded at Turin a similar school (*Scuola Pratica di Cultura e Legislazione Sociale*), which, however, soon succumbed.

In England the trade unions and cooperative societies make use of Ruskin College, Oxford, sending thither those of their members who aspire to office in the labor organizations, and who have displayed special aptitudes for this career. In Austria it is proposed to found a party school upon the German model.

It is undeniable that all these educational institutions for the officials of the party and of the labor organizations tend, above all, towards the artificial creation of an *élite* of the working class, of a caste of cadets composed of persons who aspire to the command of the proletarian rank and file. Without wishing it, there is thus effected a continuous enlargement of the gulf which divides the leaders from the masses.

The technical specialization that inevitably results from all extensive organization renders necessary what is called expert leadership. Consequently the power of determination comes to be considered one of the specific attributes of leadership, and is gradually withdrawn from the masses to be concentrated in the hands of the leaders alone. Thus the leaders, who were at first no more than the executive organs of the collective will, soon emancipate themselves from the mass and become independent of its control.

Organization implies the tendency to oligarchy. In every organization, whether it be a political party, a professional union, or any other association of the kind, the aristocratic tendency manifests itself very clearly. The mechanism of the organization, while conferring a solidity of structure, induces serious changes in the organized mass, completely inverting the respective position of the leaders and the led. As a result of organization, every party or professional union becomes divided into a minority of directors and a majority of directed.

It has been remarked that in the lower stages of civilization tyranny is dominant. Democracy cannot come into existence until there is attained a subsequent and more highly developed stage of social life. Freedoms and privileges, and among these latter the privilege of taking part in the direction of public affairs, are at first restricted to the few. Recent times have been characterized by the gradual extension of these privileges to a widening circle. This is what we know as the era of democracy. But if we pass from the sphere of the state to the sphere of party, we may observe that as democracy continues to develop, a backwash sets in. With the advance of organization, democracy tends to decline. Democratic evolution has a parabolic course. At the present time, at any rate as far as party life is concerned, democracy is in the descending phase. It may be enunciated as a general rule that the increase in the power of the leaders is directly proportional with the extension of the organization. In the various parties and labor organizations of different countries the influence of the leaders is

8. *Scuola Prat. di Legislaz. Sociale* (Programma e Norme), anno iii, Soc. Umanitaria, Milan, 1908.

9. *Ibid.*, anno iv, Milan, 1909, p. 5.

10. Rinaldo Rigola, *I funzionari delle organizzazioni* "Avanti," anno xiv, No. 341.

mainly determined (apart from racial and individual grounds) by the varying development of organization. Where organization is stronger, we find that there is a lesser degree of applied democracy.

Every solidly constructed organization, whether it be a democratic state, a political party, or a league of proletarians for the resistance of economic oppression, presents a soil eminently favorable for the differentiation of organs and of functions. The more extended and the more ramified the official apparatus of the organization, the greater the number of its members, the fuller its treasury, and the more widely circulated its press, the less efficient becomes the direct control exercised by the rank and file, and the more is this control replaced by the increasing power of committees. Into all parties there insinuates itself that indirect electoral system which in public life the democratic parties fight against with all possible vigor. Yet in party life the influence of this system must be more disastrous than in the far more extensive life of the state. Even in the party congresses, which represent the party-life seven times sifted, we find that it becomes more and more general to refer all important questions to committees which debate *in camera*.

As organization develops, not only do the tasks of the administration become more difficult and more complicated, but, further, its duties become enlarged and specialized to such a degree that it is no longer possible to take them all in at a single glance. In a rapidly progressive movement, it is not only the growth in the number of duties, but also the higher quality of these, which imposes a more extensive differentiation of function. Nominally, and according to the letter of the rules, all the acts of the leaders are subject to the ever vigilant criticism of the rank and file. In theory the leader is merely an employee bound by the instruction he receives. He has to carry out the orders of the mass, of which he is no more than the executive organ. But in actual fact, as the organization increases in size, this control becomes purely fictitious. The members have to give up the idea of themselves conducting or even supervising the whole administration, and are compelled to hand these tasks over to trustworthy persons specially nominated for the purpose, to salaried officials. The rank and file must content themselves with summary reports, and with the appointment of occasional special committees of inquiry. Yet this does not derive from any special change in the rules of the organization. It is by very necessity that a simple employee gradually becomes a "leader," acquiring a freedom of action which he ought not to possess. The chief then becomes accustomed to dispatch important business on his own responsibility, and to decide various questions relating to the life of the party without any attempt to consult the rank and file. It is obvious that democratic control thus undergoes a progressive diminution, and is ultimately reduced to an infinitesimal minimum. In all the socialist parties there is a continual increase in the number of functions withdrawn from the electoral assemblies and transferred to the executive committees. In this way there is constructed a powerful and complicated edifice. The principle of division of labor coming more and more into operation, executive authority undergoes division and subdivision. There is thus constituted a rigorously defined and hierarchical bureaucracy. In the catechism of party duties, the strict observance of hierarchical rules becomes the first article. The hierarchy comes into existence as the outcome of technical conditions, and its constitution is an essential postulate of the regular functioning of the party machine.

It is indisputable that the oligarchical and bureaucratic tendency of party organization is a matter of technical and practical necessity. It is the inevitable product of the very principle of organization. Not even the most radical wing of the various socialist parties raises any objection to this retrogressive evolution, the contention being that democracy is only a form of organization and that where it ceases to be possible to harmonize democracy with organization, it is better to abandon the former than the latter. Organization, since it is the only means of attaining the ends of socialism, is considered to comprise within itself the revolutionary content of the party, and this essential content must never be sacrificed for the sake of form.

In all times, in all phases of development, in all branches of human activity, there have been leaders. It is true that certain socialists, above all the orthodox Marxists of Germany, seek to convince us that socialism knows nothing of "leaders," that the party has "employees" merely, being a democratic party, and the existence of leaders being incompatible with democracy. But a false assertion such as this cannot override a sociological law. Its only result is, in fact, to strengthen the rule of the leaders, for it serves to conceal from the mass a danger which really threatens democracy.

For technical and administrative reasons, no less than for tactical reasons, a strong organization needs an equally strong leadership. As long as an organization is loosely constructed and vague in its outlines, no professional leadership can arise. The anarchists, who have a horror of all fixed organization, have no regular leaders. In the early days of German socialism, the *Vertrauensmann* (homme de confiance) continued to exercise his ordinary occupation. If he received any pay for his work for the party, the remuneration was on an extremely modest scale, and was no more than a temporary grant. His function could never be regarded by him as a regular source of income. The employee of the organization was still a simple workmate, sharing the mode of life and the social condition of his fellows. Today he has been replaced for the most part by the professional politician, *Bezirksleiter* (U.S. ward boss), etc. The more solid the structure of an organization becomes in the course of the evolution of the modern political party, the more marked becomes the tendency to replace the emergency leader by the professional leader. Every party organization which has attained to a considerable degree of complication demands that there should be a certain number of persons who devote all their activities to the work of the party. The mass provides these by delegations, and the delegates, regularly appointed, become permanent representatives of the mass for the direction of its affairs.

For democracy, however, the first appearance of professional leadership marks the beginning of the end, and this, above all, on account of the logical impossibility of the "representative" system, whether in parliamentary life or in party delegation.

* * * * * *

## The establishment of a customary right to the office of delegate

One who holds the office of delegate acquires a moral right to that office, and delegates remain in office unless removed by extraordinary circumstances or in obedience to rules observed with exceptional strictness. An election made for a definite purpose becomes a life incumbency. Custom becomes a right. One who has for a certain time held the office of delegate ends by regarding that office as his own property. If refused reinstatement, he threatens reprisals (the threat of resignation being the least serious among these) which will tend to sow confusion among his comrades, and this confusion will continue until he is victorious.

Resignation of office, in so far as it is not a mere expression of discouragement or protest (such as disinclination to accept a candidature in an unpromising constituency), is in most cases a means for the retention and fortification of leadership. Even in political organizations greater than party, the leaders often employ this stratagem, thus disarming their adversaries by a deference which does not lack a specious democratic color. The opponent is forced to exhibit in return an even greater deference, and this above all when the leader who makes use of the method is really indispensable, or is considered indispensable by the mass. The recent history of Germany affords numerous examples showing the infallibility of this machiavellian device for the maintenance of leadership. During the troubled period of transition from absolute to constitutional monarchy, during the ministry of Ludolf Camphausen, King Frederick William IV of Prussia threatened to abdicate whenever liberal ideas were tending in Prussian politics to gain the upper hand over the romanticist conservatism which was dear to his heart. By this threat the liberals were placed in a dilemma. Either they must accept the king's abdication, which would involve the accession to the throne of Prince William of Prussia, a man of ultrareactionary tendencies, whose reign was likely to be initiated by an uprising among the lower classes; or else they must abandon their liberal schemes, and maintain in power the king now become indispensable. Thus Frederick William always succeeded in getting his own way, and in defeating the schemes of his political opponents. Thirty-five years later Prince Bismarck, establishing his strength with the weapon of his indispensability, consolidated his omnipotence over the German empire which he had recently created, by again and again handing in his resignation to the Emperor William I. His aim was to reduce the old monarch to obedience, whenever the latter showed any signs of exercising an independent will, by suggesting the chaos in internal and external policy which would necessarily result from the retirement of the "founder of the empire," since the aged emperor was not competent to undertake the personal direction of affairs.[11] The present president of the Brazilian republic, Hermes da Fonseca, owes his position chiefly to a timely threat of resignation. Having been appointed Minister of War in 1907, Fonseca undertook the reorganization of the Brazilian army. He brought forward a bill for the introduction of universal compulsory military service, which was fiercely resisted in both houses of parliament. Through his energetic personal advocacy, sustained by a threat of resignation, the measure was ultimately carried, and secured for its promoter such renown, that not only did he remain in office, but in the year 1910 was elected President of the Republic by 102,000 votes against 52,000.

It is the same in all political parties. Whenever an obstacle is encountered, the leaders are apt to offer to resign, professing that they are weary of office, but really aiming to show to the dissentients the indispensability of their own leadership. In 1864, when Vahlteich proposed a change in the rules of the General Association of German Workers, Lassalle, the president, was very angry, and, conscious of his own value to the movement, propounded the following alternative: Either you protect me from the recurrence of such friction as this, or I throw up my office. The immediate result was the expulsion of the importunate critic. In Holland today, Troelstra, the Dutch Lassalle, likewise succeeds in disarming his opponents within the party by pathetically threatening to retire into private life, saying that if they go on subjecting his actions to an inopportune criticism, his injured idealism will force him to withdraw from the daily struggles of party life. The same thing has occurred more than once in the history of the Italian socialist party. It often happens that the socialist members of parliament find themselves in disagreement with the majority of the party upon some question of importance, such as that of the opportuneness of a general strike; or in the party congresses they may wish to record their votes in opposition to the views of their respective branches. It is easy for them to get their own way and to silence their opponents by threatening to resign. If necessary, they go still further, and actually resign their seats, appealing to the electors as the only authority competent to decide the question in dispute. In such cases they are nearly always re-elected, and thus attain to an incontestable position of power. At the socialist congress held at Bologna in 1904, some of the deputies voted in favor of the reformist resolution, in opposition to the wishes of the majority of the comrades whose views they were supposed to represent. When called to account, they offered to resign their seats, and the party electors, wishing to avoid the expense and trouble of a new election, and afraid of the loss of party seats, hastened to condone the deputies' action. In May, 1906, twenty-four out of the twenty-seven members of the socialist group in the Chamber resigned their seats, in consequence of the difference of views between themselves and the rank and file on the subject of the general strike, which the deputies had repudiated. All but three were re-elected.

Such actions have a fine democratic air, and yet hardly serve to conceal the dictatorial spirit of those who perform them. The leader who asks for a vote of confidence is in appearance submitting to the judgment of his followers, but in reality he throws into the scale the entire weight of his own indispensability, real or supposed, and thus commonly forces submission to his will. The leaders are extremely careful never to admit that the true aim of their threat to resign is the reinforcement of their power over the rank and file. They declare, on the contrary, that their conduct is determined by the purest democratic spirit, that it is a striking proof of their fineness of feeling, of their sense of personal dignity, and of their deference for the mass. Yet if we really look into the matter we cannot fail to see that, whether they desire it or not, their action is an oligarchical demonstration, the manifestation of a tendency to enfranchise themselves from the control of the rank and file. Such resignations, even if not dictated by a self-seeking policy, but offered solely in order to prevent differences of opinion between the leaders and the mass, and in order to maintain the necessary harmony of views, always

11. *Denkwürdigkeiten des Fürsten Chlodwig zu Hohenlohe-Schillingsfürst*, ed. by Friedrich Curtius, Deutsche Verlags-anstalt, Stuttgart and Leipzig, 1907, vol. ii.

have as their practical outcome the subjection of the mass to the authority of the leader.

* * * * * *

## The need for leadership felt by the mass

. . . The same thing happens in party life as happens in the state. In both, the demand for monetary supplies is upon a coercive foundation, but the electoral system has no established sanction. An electoral right exists, but no electoral duty. Until this duty is superimposed upon the right, it appears probable that a small minority only will continue to avail itself of the right which the majority voluntarily renounces, and that the minority will always dictate laws for the indifferent and apathetic mass. The consequence is that, in the political groupings of democracy, the participation in party life has an echeloned aspect. The extensive base consists of the great mass of electors; upon this is superposed the enormously smaller mass of enrolled members of the local branch of the party, numbering perhaps one tenth or even as few as one thirtieth of the electors; above this, again, comes the much smaller number of the members who regularly attend meetings; next comes the group of officials of the party; and highest of all, consisting in part of the same individuals as the last group, come the half-dozen or so members of the executive committee. Effective power is here in inverse ratio to the number of those who exercise it. Thus practical democracy is represented by the following diagram:[12]

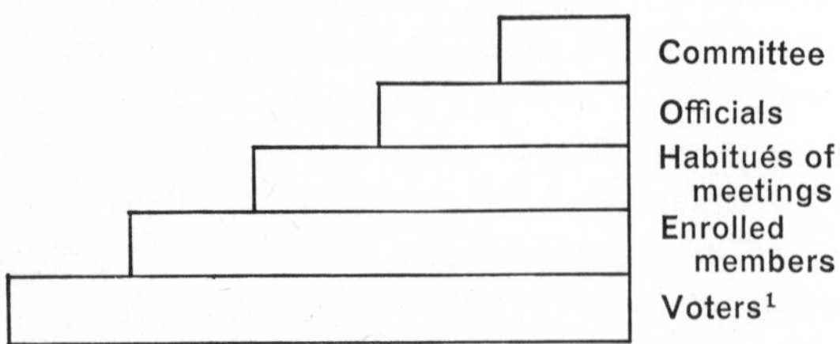


Though it grumbles occasionally, the majority is really delighted to find persons who will take the trouble to look after its affairs. In the mass, and even in the organized mass of the labor parties, there is an immense need for direction and guidance. This need is accompanied by a genuine cult for the leaders, who are regarded as heroes. Misoneism, the rock upon which so many serious reforms have at all times been wrecked, is at present rather increasing than diminishing. This increase is explicable owing to the more extensive division of labor in modern civilized society, which renders it more and more impossible to embrace in a single glance the totality of the political organization of the state and its ever more complicated mechanism. To this misoneism are superadded, and more particularly in the popular parties, profound differences of culture and education among the members. These differences give to the need for leadership felt by the masses a continually increasing dynamic tendency.

This tendency is manifest in the political parties of all countries. It is true that its intensity varies as between one nation and another, in accordance with contingencies of a historical character or with the influences of racial psychology. The German people in especial exhibits to an extreme degree the need for someone to point out the way and to issue orders. This peculiarity, common to all classes not excepting the proletariat, furnishes a psychological soil upon which a powerful directive hegemony can flourish luxuriantly. There exist among the Germans all the preconditions necessary for such a development: a psychical predisposition to subordination, a profound instinct for discipline, in a word, the whole still-persistent inheritance of the influence of the Prussian drill-sergeant, with all its advantages and all its disadvantages; in addition, a trust in authority which verges on the complete absence of a critical faculty. It is only the Rhinelanders, possessed of a somewhat more conspicuous individuality, who constitute, to a certain extent, an exception to this generalization. The risks to the democratic spirit that are involved by this peculiarity of the German character were well known to Karl Marx. Although himself a party leader in the fullest sense of the term, and although endowed to the highest degree with the qualities necessary for leadership, he thought it necessary to warn the German workers against entertaining too rigid a conception of organization. In a letter from Marx to Schweitzer we are told that in Germany, where the workers are bureaucratically controlled from birth upwards, and for this reason have a blind

12. This figure must not be regarded as intended to represent such relationships according to scale, for this would require an entire page. It is purely diagrammatic.

faith in constituted authority, it is above all necessary to teach them to walk by themselves.[13]

* * * * * *

## Accessory qualities requisite to leadership

... Those who aspire to leadership in the labor organizations fully recognize the importance of the oratorical art. In March 1909 the socialist students of Ruskin College, Oxford, expressed discontent with their professors because these gave to sociology and to pure logic a more important place in the curriculum than to oratorical exercises. Embryo politicians, the students fully recognized the profit they would derive from oratory in their chosen career. Resolving to back up their complaint by energetic action, they went on strike until they had got their own way.

The prestige acquired by the orator in the minds of the crowd is almost unlimited. What the masses appreciate above all are oratorical gifts as such, beauty and strength of voice, suppleness of mind, badinage; whilst the content of the speech is of quite secondary importance. A spouter who, as if bitten by a tarantula, rushes hither and thither to speak to the people, is apt to be regarded as a zealous and active comrade, whereas one who, speaking little but working much, does valuable service for the party, is regarded with disdain, and considered but an incomplete socialist.

Unquestionably, the fascination exercised by the beauty of a sonorous eloquence is often, for the masses, no more than the prelude to a long series of disillusionments, either because the speaker's practical activities bear no proportion to his oratorical abilities, or simply because he is a person of altogether common character. In most cases however, the masses, intoxicated by the speaker's powers, are hypnotized to such a degree that for long periods to come they see in him a magnified image of their own ego. Their admiration and enthusiasm for the orator are, in ultimate analysis, no more than admiration and enthusiasm for their own personalities, and these sentiments are fostered by the orator in that he undertakes to speak and to act in the name of the mass, in the name, that is, of every individual. In responding to the appeal of the great orator, the mass is unconsciously influenced by its own egoism.

Numerous and varied are the personal qualities thanks to which certain individuals succeed in ruling the masses. These qualities, which may be considered as specific qualities of leadership, are not necessarily all assembled in every leader. Among them, the chief is the force of will which reduces to obedience less powerful wills. Next in importance come the following: a wider extent of knowledge which impresses the members of the leader's environment; a catonian strength of conviction, a force of ideas often verging on fanaticism, and which arouses the respect of the masses by its very intensity; self-sufficiency, even if accompanied by arrogant pride, so long as the leader knows how to make the crowd share his own pride in himself; in exceptional cases, finally, goodness of heart and disinterestedness, qualities which recall in the minds of the crowd the figure of Christ, and reawaken religious sentiments which are decayed but not extinct.

* * * * * *

Thus the dominion dependent upon distinction acquired outside the party is comparatively ephemeral. But age in itself is no barrier whatever to the power of the leaders. The ancient Greeks said that white hairs were the first crown which must decorate the leaders' foreheads. Today, however, we live in an epoch in which there is less need for accumulated personal experience of life, for science puts at every one's disposal efficient means of instruction that even the youngest may speedily become thoroughly well instructed. Today everything is quickly acquired, even that experience in which formerly consisted the sole and genuine superiority of the old over the young. Thus, not in consequence of democracy, but simply owing to the technical type of modern civilization, age has lost much of its value, and therefore has lost, in addition, the respect which it inspired and the influence

13. Letter from Karl Marx to J. B. von Schweitzer dated London, October 13, 1868, published, with comments by Ed. Bernstein, "Neue Zeit," xv, 1897, p. 9. Bernstein himself appears to share the views of Marx. (Cf. Ed. Bernstein, *Gewerkschaftsdemokratie*, "Sozial. Monatshefte," 1909, p. 83.)

which it exercised. It might rather be said that age is a hindrance to progress within the party, just as in any other career which it is better to enter in youth because there are so many steps to mount. This is true at least in the case of well organized parties, and where there is a great influx of new members. It is certainly different as far as concerns leaders who have grown old in the service of the party. Age here constitutes an element of superiority. Apart from the gratitude which the masses feel towards the old fighter on account of the services he has rendered to the cause, he also possesses this great advantage over the novice that he has a better knowledge of his trade. David Hume tells us that in practical agriculture the superiority of the old farmer over the young arises in consequence of a certain uniformity in the effects of the sun, the rain, and, the soil upon the growth of plants, and because practical experience teaches the rules that determine and guide these influences.[14] In party life, the old hand has a similar advantage. He possesses a profounder understanding of the relationships between cause and effect which form the framework of popular political life and the substance of popular psychology. The result is that his conduct is guided by a fineness of perception to which the young have not yet attained.

* * * * * *

## Superiority of leaders

. . . All parties today have a parliamentary aim. (There is only one exception, that of the anarchists, who are almost without political influence, and who, moreover, since they are the declared enemies of all organization, and who, when they form organizations, do so in defiance of their own principles, cannot be considered to constitute a political party in the proper sense of the term.) They pursue legal methods, appealing to the electors, making it their first aim to acquire parliamentary influence, and having for their ultimate goal "the conquest of political power." It is for this reason that even the representatives of the revolutionary parties enter the legislature. Their parliamentary labors, undertaken at first with reluctance, but subsequently with increasing satisfaction and increasing professional zeal, remove them further and further from their electors. The questions which they have to decide, and whose effective decision demand on their part a serious work of preparation, involve an increase in their own technical competence, and a consequent increase in the distance between themselves and their comrades of the rank and file. Thus the leaders, if they were not "cultured" already, soon become so. But culture exercises a suggestive influence over the masses.

In proportion as they become initiated into the details of political life, as they become familiarized with the different aspects of the fiscal problem and with questions of foreign policy, the leaders gain an importance which renders them indispensable so long as their party continues to practice a parliamentary tactic, and which will perhaps render them important even should this tactic be abandoned. This is perfectly natural, for the leaders cannot be replaced at a moment's notice, since all the other members of the party are absorbed in their everyday occupations and are strangers to the bureaucratic mechanism. This special competence, this expert knowledge, which the leader acquires in matters inaccessible, or almost inaccessible, to the mass, gives him a security of tenure which conflicts with the essential principles of democracy.

The technical competence which definitely elevates the leaders above the mass and subjects the mass to the leaders, has its influence reinforced by certain other factors, such as routine, the social education which the deputies gain in the chamber, and their special training in the work of parliamentary committees. The leaders naturally endeavor to apply in the normal life of the parties the maneuvers they have learned in the parliamentary environment, and in this way they often succeed in diverting currents of opposition to their own dominance. The parliamentarians are past masters in the art of controlling meetings, of applying and interpreting rules, of proposing motions at opportune moments; in a word, they are skilled in the use of artifices of all kinds in order to avoid the discussion of contro-

14. David Hume, *Inquiries Concerning the Human Understanding*: "Why is the aged husbandman more skilful in his calling than the young beginner but because there is a certain uniformity in the operation of the sun, rain, and earth towards the production of vegetables; and experience teaches the old practitioner the rules by which this operation is governed and directed?" (Clarendon Press edition, edited by Selby-Bigge, Oxford, 1902, p. 85.)

versial points, in order to extract from a hostile majority a vote favorable to themselves, or at least, if the worst comes to the worst, to reduce the hostile majority to silence. There is no lack of means, varying from an ingenious and often ambiguous manner of putting the question when the vote is to be taken, to the exercise on the crowd of a suggestive influence by insinuations which, while they have no real bearing on the question at issue, none the less produce a strong impression. As referendaries (*rapporteurs*) and experts, intimately acquainted with all the hidden aspects of the subject under discussion, many of the deputies are adepts in the art of employing digressions, periphrases, and terminological subtleties, by means of which they surround the simplest matter with a maze of obscurity to which they alone have the clue. In this way, whether acting in good faith or in bad, they render it impossible for the masses, whose "theoretical interpreters" they should be, to follow them, and to understand them, and they thus elude all possibility of technical control. They are masters of the situation.[15]

The intangibility of the deputies is increased and their privileged position is further consolidated by the renown which they acquire, at once among their political adversaries and among their own partisans, by their oratorical talent, by their specialized aptitudes, or by the charm of their intellectual or even their physical personalities. The dismissal by the organized masses of a universally esteemed leader would discredit the party throughout the country. Not only would the party suffer from being deprived of its leaders, if matters were thus pushed to an extreme, but the political reaction upon the status of the party would be immeasurably disastrous. Not only would it be necessary to find substitutes without delay for the dismissed leaders, who have only become familiar with political affairs after many years of arduous and unremitting toil (and where is the party which between one day and the next would be able to provide efficient substitutes?); but also it has to be remembered that it is largely to the personal influence of their old parliamentary chiefs that the masses owe their success in social legislation and in the struggle for the conquest of general political freedom.

15. It is interesting to note that the developing bourgeoisie of the seventeenth century found itself in relation to the monarchy in the same state of intellectual inferiority as that in which today are the democratic masses in relation to their leaders, and for very similar reasons. The ingenious Louis XIV expressed the point in the following words: In Franche Comté, "all authority is found, then, in the hands of Parliament which, like an assembly of simple bourgeois, would be easy either to fool or to frighten." (Trans. from Dreyss, *op. cit.*, vol. ii, p. 328).

The democratic masses are thus compelled to submit to a restriction of their own wills when they are forced to give their leaders an authority which is in the long run destructive to the very principle of democracy. The leader's principal source of power is found in his indispensability. One who is indispensable has in his power all the lords and masters of the earth. The history of the working-class parties continually furnishes instances in which the leader has been in flagrant contradiction with the fundamental principles of the movement, but in which the rank and file have not been able to make up their minds to draw the logical consequences of this conflict, because they feel that they cannot get along without the leader, and cannot dispense with the qualities he has acquired in virtue of the very position to which they have themselves elevated him, and because they do not see their way to find an adequate substitute. Numerous are the parliamentary orators and the trade-union leaders who are in opposition to the rank and file at once theoretically and practically, and who, none the less, continue to think and to act tranquilly on behalf of the rank and file. These latter, disconcerted and uneasy, look on at the behavior of the "great men," but seldom dare to throw off their authority and to give them their dismissal.

* * * * * *

## The struggle between the leaders and the masses

Those who defend the arbitrary acts committed by the democracy, point out that the masses have at their disposal means whereby they can react against the violation of their rights. These means consist in the right of controlling and dismissing their leaders. Unquestionably this defense possesses a certain theoretical value, and the authoritarian inclinations of the leaders are in some degree attenuated by these possibilities. In states with a democratic tendency and under a parliamentary regime, to obtain the fall of a detested minister it suffices, in theory, that the people should be weary of him. In the same way, once more in theory, the ill-humor and the opposition of a socialist group or of an election committee is enough to effect the recall of a deputy's mandate, and in the same way the hostility of the majority at the annual congress of trade unions should be enough to secure the dismissal of a secretary. In practice, however, the exercise of this theoretical right is interfered with by the working of the whole series of conservative tendencies to which allusion has previously been made, so that the supremacy of the autonomous and sovereign masses is rendered purely illusory. The dread by which Nietzsche was at one time so greatly disturbed, that every individual might become a functionary of the mass, must be completely dissipated in face of the truth that while all have the right to become functionaries, few only possess the possibility.

With the institution of leadership there simultaneously begins, owing to the long tenure of office, the transformation of the leaders into a closed caste.

Unless, as in France, extreme individualism and fanatical political dogmatism stand in the way, the old leaders present themselves to the masses as a compact phalanx—at any rate whenever the masses are so much aroused as to endanger the position of the leaders.

The election of the delegates to congresses, etc., is sometimes regulated by the leaders by means of special agreements, whereby the masses are in fact excluded from all decisive influence in the management of their affairs. These agreements often assume the aspect of a mutual insurance contract. In the German Socialist Party, a few years ago, there came into existence in not a few localities a regular system in accordance with which the leaders nominated one another in rotation as delegates to the various party congresses. In the meetings at which the delegates were appointed, one of the big guns would always propose to the comrades the choice as delegate of the leader whose "turn" it was. The comrades rarely revolt against such artifices, and often fail even to perceive them. Thus competition among the leaders is prevented, in this domain at least; and at the same time there is rendered impossible anything more than passive participation of the rank and file in the higher functions of the life of that party which they alone sustain with their subscriptions.[16] Notwithstanding the violence of the intestine struggles which divide the leaders, in all the democracies they manifest vis-à-vis the masses a vigorous solidarity. "They perceive quickly enough the necessity for agreeing among themselves so that the party cannot escape them by becoming divided."[17] This is true above all of the German social democracy, in which, in consequence of the exceptional solidity of structure which it possesses as compared with all the other socialist parties of the world, conservative tendencies have attained an extreme development.

When there is a struggle between the leaders and the masses, the former are always victorious if only they remain united. At least it rarely happens that the masses succeed in disembarrassing themselves of one of their leaders.

* * * * * *

There is no indication whatever that the power possessed by the oligarchy in party life is likely to be overthrown within an appreciable time. The independence of the leaders increases concurrently with their indispensability. Nay more, the influence which they exercise and the financial security of their position become more and more fascinating to the masses, stimulating the ambition of all the more talented elements to enter the privileged bureaucracy of the labor movement. Thus the rank and file becomes continually more impotent to provide new and intelligent forces capable of leading the opposition which may be latent among the masses.[18] Even today the masses rarely move except at the command of their leaders. When the rank and file does take action in conflict with the wishes of the chiefs, this is almost always the outcome of a misunderstanding. The miners' strike in the Ruhr

16. Similar phenomena have been observed in party life n America (Astrogorsky, *La Démocratie, etc.*, ed. cit., vol. ii, p. 196).

17. Trans. from Antoine Elisée Cherbuliez, *Théorie des Garantis constitutionelles*, Ab. Cherbuliez, Paris, 1838, vol. ii, p. 253.

18. Thus Pareto writes: "If B [the new élite] took the place of A [the old élite] by slow infiltration, and if the social circulation is not interrupted, C [the masses] are deprived of the leaders who could incite them to revolt." (Trans. from Vilfredo Pareto, *Les Systèmes socialistes*, Giard and Brière, Paris, 1892, vol. i, p. 35).

basin in 1905 broke out against the desire of the trade-union leaders, and was generally regarded as a spontaneous explosion of the popular will. But it was subsequently proved beyond dispute that for many months the leaders had been stimulating the rank and file, mobilizing them against the coal barons with repeated threats of a strike, so that the mass of the workers, when they entered on the struggle, could not possibly fail to believe that they did so with the full approval of their chiefs.

It cannot be denied that the masses revolt from time to time, but their revolts are always suppressed. It is only when the dominant classes, struck by sudden blindness, pursue a policy which strains social relationships to the breaking-point, that the party masses appear actively on the stage of history and overthrow the power of the oligarchies. Every autonomous movement of the masses signifies a profound discordance with the will of the leaders. Apart from such transient interruptions, the natural and normal development of the organization will impress upon the most revolutionary of parties an indelible stamp of conservatism.

* * * * * *

## The struggle among the leaders themselves

The thesis of the unlimited power of the leaders in democratic parties, requires, however, a certain limitation. Theoretically the leader is bound by the will of the mass, which has only to give a sign and the leader is forced to withdraw. He can be discharged and replaced at any moment. But in practice, as we have learned, for various reasons the leaders enjoy a high degree of independence. It is none the less true that if the Democratic Party cannot dispense with autocratic leaders, it is at least able to change these. Consequently the most dangerous defect in a leader is that he should possess too blind a confidence in the masses. The aristocratic leader is more secure than the democratic against surprises at the hands of the rank and file. It is an essential characteristic of democracy that every private carries a marshal's baton in his knapsack. It is true that the mass is always incapable of governing; but it is no less true that each individual in the mass, in so far as he possesses, for good or for ill, the qualities which are requisite to enable him to rise above the crowd, can attain to the grade of leader and become a ruler. Now this ascent of new leaders always involves the danger, for those who are already in possession of power, that they will be forced to surrender their places to the newcomers. The old leader must therefore keep himself in permanent touch with the opinions and feelings of the masses to which he owes his position. Formally, at least, he must act in unison with the crowd, must admit himself to be the instrument of the crowd, must be guided, in appearance at least, by its goodwill and pleasure. Thus it often seems as if the mass really controlled the leaders. But whenever the power of the leaders is seriously threatened, it is in most cases because a new leader or a new group of leaders is on the point of becoming dominant, and is inculcating views opposed to those of the old rulers of the party. It then seems as if the old leaders, unless they are willing to yield to the opinion of the rank and file and to withdraw, must consent to share their power with the new arrivals. If, however, we look more closely into the matter, it is not difficult to see that their submission is in most cases no more than an act of foresight intended to obviate the influence of their younger rivals. The submission of the old leaders is ostensibly an act of homage to the crowd, but in intention it is a means of prophylaxis against the peril by which they are threatened—the formation of a new élite.

The semblance of obedience to the mass which is exhibited by the leaders assumes, in the case of the feebler and the more cunning among them, the form of demagogy. Demagogues are the courtesans of the popular will. Instead of raising the masses to their own level, they debase themselves to the level of the masses. Even for the most honest among them, the secret of success consists in "knowing how to turn the blind impulsiveness of the crowd to the service of their own ripely pondered plans."[19] The stronger leaders brave the tempest, well-knowing that their power may be attacked, but cannot be broken. The weak or the base, on the other hand, give ground when the masses make a vigorous onslaught; their dominion is temporarily impaired or interrupted. But their submission is feigned; they are well aware that if they simply

19. Kochanowski, *Urzeitklänge, und Wetterleuchten Geschichtlicher Gesetze in den Ereignissen der Gegenwart*, Wagner, Innsbruck, 1910, p. 10.

remain glued to their posts, their quality as executants of the will of the masses will before long lead to a restoration of their former dominance. One of the most noted leaders of German socialism said in a critical period of tension between the leaders and the masses, that he must follow the will of the masses in order to guide them.[20] A profound psychological truth is hidden in this sarcasm. He who wishes to command must know how to obey.

* * * * * *

The struggle between the old leaders and the aspirants to power constitutes a perpetual menace to freedom of speech and thought. We encounter this menace in every democratic organization in so far as it is well ordered and solidly grounded, and in so far as it is operating in the field of party politics (for in the wider life of the state, in which the various parties are in continual reciprocal concussion, it is necessary to leave intact a certain liberty of movement). The leaders, those who already hold the power of the party in their hands, make no concealment of their natural inclination to control as strictly as possible the freedom of speech of those of their colleagues from whom they differ. The consequence is that those in office are great zealots for discipline and subordination, declaring that these qualities are indispensable to the very existence of the party. They go so far as to exercise a censorship over any of their colleagues whom they suspect of rebellious inclinations, forcing them to abandon independent journals, and to publish all their articles in the official organs controlled by the leaders of the majority in the party. The prohibition, in the German Socialist Party, of collaboration on the part of its members with the capitalist press, is in part due to the same tendency; whilst the demand that the comrades should have nothing to do with periodicals which, though socialist, are founded with private capital and are not subject to the official control of the party executive, arises solely from this suspicion on the part of the leaders.

In the struggle against the young aspirants, the old leader can as a rule count securely upon the support of the masses. The rank and file of the working-class parties have a certain natural distrust of all newcomers who have not been openly protected or introduced into the party by old comrades; and this is above all the case when the newcomer is derived from another social class. Thus the new recruit, before he can come into the open with his new ideas, must submit, if he is not to be exposed to the most violent attacks, to a long period of quarantine. In the German Socialist Party, this period of quarantine is especially protracted, for the reason that the German party has been longer established than any of the others, and because its leaders therefore enjoy an exceptional prestige. Many of them were among the actual founders of the party, and their personalities have been consecrated by the baptism of fire which they suffered during the enforcement of the anti-socialist laws. A socialist who has had his party card in his pocket for eight or ten years is often regarded in his branch as a "young" member. This tendency is reinforced by the respect for age which is so strong among the Germans, and by the tendency towards hierarchy of which even the democracy has not been able to divest itself. Finally, it may be added that the bureaucracy of the German labor movement, like every strongly developed bureaucracy, tends instinctively towards exclusivism. Consequently in the German social democracy, in contradistinction to other socialist parties which are less solidly organized, we find that not merely the recently enrolled member of the party (the so-called *Fuchs*), but also the ordinary member who does not live in the service and by the service of the party but has preserved his outward independence as a private author or in some other capacity, and has therefore not been incorporated among the cogwheels of the party machine, very rarely succeeds in making his influence felt. There can be no doubt that this fact plays a large part in the causation of that lack of a number of capable young men, displaying fresh energies, and not greatly inferior to the old leaders, a lack which has often been deplored. The annual congresses of the Socialist Party have even been spoken of as "congresses of the party officials." The criticism is not unjust, for among the delegates to the socialist congresses the percentage of party and trade-union officials is enormous. It is above all in the superior grades of the organization that the tendencies we are here analyzing are especially

20. "Ich bin ihr Führer, also muss ich ihnen folgen.' (Cf. Adolf Weber, *Der Kampf zwischen Kapital u. Arbeit*, ed. cit., p. 369.)

conspicuous. In Germany, the management of the Socialist Party is not entrusted to young men, as often happens in Italy, or to free publicists, as in France, but to old members, *des anciens*, elderly officials of the party. Moreover, the conservative psychology of the masses supports the aspirations of the old leaders, for it would never occur to the rank and file to entrust the care of their interests to persons belonging to their own proper sphere, that is to say, to those who have no official position in the party and who have not pursued a regular bureaucratic career.

Often the struggle between the old leaders in possession of power and the new aspirants assumes the aspects of a struggle between responsible and irresponsible persons. Many criticisms leveled by the latter against the former are beside the mark, because the leaders have grave responsibilities from which the aspirants are free. This freedom gives the aspirants a tactical advantage in their conflict with the old leaders. Moreover, precisely because they are irresponsible, because they do not occupy any official position in the party, the opponents are not subject to that simulacrum of democratic control which must influence the conduct of those in office.

In order to combat the new chiefs, who are still in a minority, the old leaders of the majority instinctively avail themselves of a series of underhand methods through which they often secure victory, or at least notably retard defeat. Among these means, there is one which will have to be more fully discussed in another connection. The leaders of what we may term the "government" arouse in the minds of the masses distrust of the leaders of the "opposition" by labeling them incompetent and profane, terming them spouters, corrupters of the party, demagogues, and humbugs, whilst in the name of the mass and of democracy they describe themselves as exponents of the collective will, and demand the submission of the insubordinate and even of the merely discontented comrades.

In the struggle among the leaders an appeal is often made to loftier motives. When the members of the executive claim the right to intervene in the democratic functions of the individual sections of the organization, they base this claim upon their more comprehensive grasp of all the circumstances of the case, their profounder insight, their superior socialist culture and keener socialist sentiment. They often claim the right of refusing to accept the new elements which the inexpert and ignorant masses desire to associate with them in the leadership, basing their refusal on the ground that it is necessary to sustain the moral and theoretical level of the party. The revolutionary socialists of Germany demand the maintenance of the centralized power of the executive committee as a means of defense against the dangers, which would otherwise become inevitable as the party grows, of the predominant influence of new and theoretically untrustworthy elements. The old leaders, it is said, must control the masses, lest these should force undesirable colleagues upon them. Hence they claim that the constituencies must not nominate parliamentary candidates without the previous approval of the party executive.

The old leaders always endeavor to harness to their own chariot the forces of those new movements which have not yet found powerful leaders, so as to obviate from the first all competition and all possibility of the formation of new and vigorous intellectual currents. In Germany, the leaders of the Socialist Party and the trade-union leaders at first looked askance at the Young Socialist movement. When, however, they perceived that this movement could not be suppressed, they hastened to place themselves at its head. There was founded for the guidance of the socialist youth a "Central Committee of Young German Workers," comprising four representatives from each of the three parties, that is to say, four from the executive of the Socialist Party, four from the general committee of trade unions, and four from the Young Socialists (the representatives of the latter being thus outnumbered by two to one). The old leaders endeavor to justify the tutelage thus imposed on the Young Socialists by alleging (with more opportunist zeal than logical acuteness) the incapacity of the youthful masses, if left to their own guidance, of wisely choosing their own leaders and of exercising over these an efficient control.

* * * * * *

## Final considerations

Leadership is a necessary phenomenon in every form of social life. Consequently it is not the task of science to inquire whether this phenomenon is good or evil, or predominantly one or the other. But there is great scientific value in the demonstration that every system of leadership is incompatible with the most essential postulates of democracy. We are now aware that the law of the historic necessity of oligarchy is primarily based upon a series of facts of experience. Like all other scientific laws, sociological laws are derived from empirical observation. In order, however, to deprive our axiom of its purely descriptive character, and to confer upon it that status of analytical explanation which can alone transform a formula into a law, it does not suffice to contemplate from a unitary outlook those phenomena which may be empirically established; we must also study the determining causes of these phenomena. Such has been our task.

Now, if we leave out of consideration the tendency of the leaders to organize themselves and to consolidate their interests, and if we leave also out of consideration the gratitude of the led towards the leaders, and the general immobility and passivity of the masses, we are led to conclude that the principal cause of oligarchy in the democratic parties is to be found in the technical indispensability of leadership.

The process which has begun in consequence of the differentiation of functions in the party is completed by a complex of qualities which the leaders acquire through their detachment from the mass. At the outset, leaders arise SPONTANEOUSLY; their functions are ACCESSORY and GRATUITOUS. Soon, however, they become PROFESSIONAL leaders, and in this second stage of development they are STABLE and IRREMOVABLE.

It follows that the explanation of the oligarchical phenomenon which thus results is partly PSYCHOLOGICAL; oligarchy derives, that is to say, from the psychical transformations which the leading personalities in the parties undergo in the course of their lives. But also, and still more, oligarchy depends upon what we may term the PSYCHOLOGY OF ORGANIZATION ITSELF, that is to say, upon the tactical and technical necessities which result from the consolidation of every disciplined political aggregate. Reduced to its most concise expression, the fundamental sociological law of political parties (the term "political" being here used in its most comprehensive significance) may be formulated in the following terms: "It is organization which gives birth to the dominion of the elected over the electors, of the mandataries over the mandators, of the delegates over the delegators. Who says organization, says oligarchy."

Every party organization represents an oligarchical power grounded upon a democratic basis. We find everywhere electors and elected. Also we find everywhere that the power of the elected leaders over the electing masses is almost unlimited. The oligarchical structure of the building suffocates the basic democratic principle. That which IS oppresses THAT WHICH OUGHT TO BE. For the masses, this essential difference between the reality and the ideal remains a mystery. Socialists often cherish a sincere belief that a new élite of politicians will keep faith better than did the old. The notion of the representation of popular interests, a notion to which the great majority of democrats, and in especial the working-class masses of the German-speaking lands, cleave with so much tenacity and confidence, is an illusion engendered by a false illumination, is an effect of mirage. In one of the most delightful pages of his analysis of modern Don Quixotism, Alphonse Daudet shows us how the "brav' commandant" Bravida, who has never quitted Tarascon, gradually comes to persuade himself, influenced by the burning southern sun, that he has been to Shanghai and has had all kinds of heroic adventures.[21] Similarly the modern proletariat, enduringly influenced by glib-tongued persons intellectually superior to the mass, ends by believing that by flocking to the poll and entrusting its social and economic cause to a delegate, its direct participation in power will be assured.

The formation of oligarchies within the various forms of democracy is the outcome of organic necessity, and consequently affects every organization, be it socialist or even anarchist. Haller long ago noted that in every form of social life relationships of dominion and of dependence are created by Nature herself.[22] The supremacy of the leaders in the democratic and revolutionary parties has to be taken into account in every historic situation present and to come, even though only a few and excep-

21. Alphonse Daudet, *Tartarin de Tarascon*, Marpon et Flammarion, Paris, 1887, p. 40.

22. Ludwig von Haller, *Restauration der Staatswissenschaften*, Winterthur, 1816, vol. i, pp. 304 *et seq.*

tional minds will be fully conscious of its existence. The mass will never rule except *in abstracto*. Consequently the question we have to discuss is not whether ideal democracy is realizable, but rather to what point and in what degree democracy is desirable, possible, and realizable at a given moment. In the problem as thus stated we recognize the fundamental problem of politics as a science. Whoever fails to perceive this must, as Sombart says, either be so blind and fanatical as not to see that the democratic current daily makes undeniable advance, or else must be so inexperienced and devoid of critical faculty as to be unable to understand that all order and all civilization must exhibit aristocratic features.[23] The great error of socialists, an error committed in consequence of their lack of adequate psychological knowledge, is to be found in their combination of pessimism regarding the present, with rosy optimism and immeasurable confidence regarding the future. A realistic view of the mental condition of the masses shows beyond question that even if we admit the possibility of moral improvement in mankind, the human materials with whose use politicians and philosophers cannot dispense in their plans of social reconstruction are not of a character to justify excessive optimism. Within the limits of time for which human provision is possible, optimism will remain the exclusive privilege of utopian thinkers.

The socialist parties, like the trade unions, are living forms of social life. As such they react with the utmost energy against any attempt to analyze their structure or their nature, as if it were a method of vivisection. When science attains to results which conflict with their apriorist ideology, they revolt with all their power. Yet their defense is extremely feeble. Those among the representatives of such organizations whose scientific earnestness and personal good faith make it impossible for them to deny outright the existence of oligarchical tendencies in every form of democracy, endeavor to explain these tendencies as the outcome of a kind of atavism in the mentality of the masses, characteristic of the youth of the movement. The masses, they assure us, are still infected by the oligarchic virus simply because they have been oppressed during long centuries of slavery, and have never yet enjoyed an autonomous existence. The socialist regime, however, will soon restore them to health, and will furnish them with all the capacity necessary for self-government. Nothing could be more antiscientific than the supposition that as soon as socialists have gained possession of governmental power it will suffice for the masses to exercise a little control over their leaders to secure that the interests of these leaders shall coincide perfectly with the interests of the led. This idea may be compared with the view of Jules Guesde, no less antiscientific than anti-Marxist (though Guesde proclaims himself a Marxist), that whereas Christianity has made God into a man, socialism will make man into a god.[24]

The objective immaturity of the mass is not a mere transitory phenomenon which will disappear with the progress of democratization *au lendemain du socialisme*. On the contrary, it derives from the very nature of the mass as mass, for this, even when organized, suffers from an incurable incompetence for the solution of the diverse problems which present themselves for solution—because the mass *per se* is amorphous, and therefore needs division of labor, specialization, and guidance. "The human species wants to be governed; it will be. I am ashamed of my kind," wrote Proudhon from his prison in 1850.[25] Man as individual is by nature predestined to be guided, and to be guided all the more in proportion as the functions of life undergo division and subdivision. To an enormously greater degree is guidance necessary for the social group.

From this chain of reasoning and from these scientific convictions it would be erroneous to conclude that we should renounce all endeavors to ascertain the limits which may be imposed upon the powers exercised over the individual by oligarchies (state, dominant class, party, etc.). It would be an error to abandon the desperate enterprise of endeavoring to discover a social order which will render possible the complete realization of the idea of popular sovereignty. In the present work, as the writer said at the outset, it has not been his aim to indicate new paths. But it seemed

23. Werner Sombart, *Dennoch!*, ed. cit., p. 90. Cf. also F. S. Merlino, *Pro e contro il Socialismo*, ed. cit., pp. 262 *et seq.*

24. Jules Guesde, *La Problème et la Solution*, Libr. du Parti Socialiste, Paris, p. 17.

25. Charles Gide et Charles Rist, *Histoire des Doctrines économiques depuis les Physiocrates jusquà nos jours*, Larose et Tenin, Paris, 1909, p. 709.

necessary to lay considerable stress upon the pessimist aspect of democracy which is forced on us by historical study. We had to inquire whether, and within what limits, democracy must remain purely ideal, possessing no other value than that of a moral criterion which renders it possible to appreciate the varying degrees of that oligarchy which is immanent in every social regime. In other words, we have had to inquire if, and in what degree, democracy is an ideal which we can never hope to realize in practice. A further aim of this work was the demolition of some of the facile and superficial democratic illusions which trouble science and lead the masses astray. Finally, the author desired to throw light upon certain sociological tendencies which oppose the reign of democracy, and to a still greater extent oppose the reign of socialism.

The writer does not wish to deny that every revolutionary working-class movement, and every movement sincerely inspired by the democratic spirit, may have a certain value as contributing to the enfeeblement of oligarchic tendencies. The peasant in the fable, when on his death-bed, tells his sons that a treasure is buried in the field. After the old man's death the sons dig everywhere in order to discover the treasure. They do not find it. But their indefatigable labor improves the soil and secures for them a comparative well-being. The treasure in the fable may well symbolize democracy. Democracy is a treasure which no one will ever discover by deliberate search. But in continuing our search, in laboring indefatigably to discover the undiscoverable, we shall perform a work which will have fertile results in the democratic sense. We have seen, indeed, that within the bosom of the democratic working-class party are born the very tendencies to counteract which that party came into existence. Thanks to the diversity and to the unequal worth of the elements of the party, these tendencies often give rise to manifestations which border on tyranny. We have seen that the replacement of the traditional legitimism of the powers-that-be by the brutal plebiscitary rule of Bonapartist parvenus does not furnish these tendencies with any moral or aesthetic superiority. Historical evolution mocks all the prophylactic measures that have been adopted for the prevention of oligarchy. If laws are passed to control the dominion of the leaders, it is the laws which gradually weaken, and not the leaders. Sometimes, however, the democratic principle carries with it, if not a cure, at least a palliative, for the disease of oligarchy. When Victor Considérant formulated his "democratico-pacificist" socialism, he declared that socialism signified, not the rule of society by the lower classes of the population, but the government and organization of society in the interest of all, through the intermediation of a group of citizens; and he added that the numerical importance of this group must increase *pari passu* with social development.[26] This last observation draws attention to a point of capital importance. It is, in fact, a general characteristic of democracy, and hence also of the labor movement, to stimulate and to strengthen in the individual the intellectual aptitudes for criticism and control. We have seen how the progressive bureaucratization of the democratic organism tends to neutralize the beneficial effects of such criticism and such control. None the less it is true that the labor movement, in virtue of the theoretical postulates it proclaims, is apt to bring into existence (in opposition to the will of the leaders) a certain number of free spirits who, moved by principle, by instinct, or by both, desire to revise the base upon which authority is established. Urged on by conviction or by temperament, they are never weary of asking an eternal "Why?" about every human institution. Now this predisposition towards free inquiry, in which we cannot fail to recognize one of the most precious factors of civilization, will gradually increase in proportion as the economic status of the masses undergoes improvement and becomes more stable, and in proportion as they are admitted more effectively to the advantages of civilization. A wider education involves an increasing capacity for exercising control. Can we not observe every day that among the well-to-do the authority of the leaders over the led, extensive though it be, is never so unrestricted as in the case of the leaders of the poor? Taken in the mass, the poor are powerless and disarmed vis-à-vis their leaders. Their intellectual and cultural inferiority makes it impossible for them to see whither the leader is going, or to estimate in advance the significance of his actions. It is, consequently, the great task of social education to raise the intellectual

26. Victor Considérant, *Principes du Socialisme. Manifeste de la Démocratie au xix Siècle*, Librairie Phalanstérienne, Paris, 1847, p. 53.

level of the masses, so that they may be enabled, within the limits of what is possible, to counteract the oligarchical tendencies of the working-class movement.

In view of the perennial incompetence of the masses, we have to recognize the existence of two regulative principles:—

1. The *ideological* tendency of democracy towards criticism and control;
2. The *effective* countertendency of democracy towards the creation of parties ever more complex and ever more differentiated—parties, that is to say, which are increasingly based upon the competence of the few.

To the idealist, the analysis of the forms of contemporary democracy cannot fail to be a source of bitter deceptions and profound discouragement. Those alone, perhaps, are in a position to pass a fair judgment upon democracy who, without lapsing into dilettantist sentimentalism, recognize that all scientific and human ideals have relative values. If we wish to estimate the value of democracy, we must do so in comparison with its converse, pure aristocracy. The defects inherent in democracy are obvious. It is none the less true that as a form of social life we must choose democracy as the least of evils. The ideal government would doubtless be that of an aristocracy of persons at once morally good and technically efficient. But where shall we discover such an aristocracy? We may find it sometimes, though very rarely, as the outcome of deliberate selection; but we shall never find it where the hereditary principle remains in operation. Thus monarchy in its pristine purity must be considered as imperfection incarnate, as the most incurable of ills; from the moral point of view it is inferior even to the most revolting of demagogic dictatorships, for the corrupt organism of the latter at least contains a healthy principle upon whose working we may continue to base hopes of social resanation. It may be said, therefore, that the more humanity comes to recognize the advantages which democracy, however imperfect, presents over aristocracy, even at its best, the less likely is it that a recognition of the defects of democracy will provoke a return to aristocracy. Apart from certain formal differences and from the qualities which can be acquired only by good education and inheritance (qualities in which aristocracy will always have the advantage over democracy—qualities which democracy either neglects altogether, or, attempting to imitate them, falsifies them to the point of caricature), the defects of democracy will be found to inhere in its inability to get rid of its aristocratic scoriæ. On the other hand, nothing but a serene and frank examination of the oligarchical dangers of democracy will enable us to minimize these dangers, even though they can never be entirely avoided.

The democratic currents of history resemble successive waves. They break ever on the same shoal. They are ever renewed. This enduring spectacle is simultaneously encouraging and depressing. When democracies have gained a certain stage of development, they undergo a gradual transformation, adopting the aristocratic spirit, and in many cases also the aristocratic forms, against which at the outset they struggled so fiercely. Now new accusers arise to denounce the traitors; after an era of glorious combats and of inglorious power, they end by fusing with the old dominant class; whereupon once more they are in their turn attacked by fresh opponents who appeal to the name of democracy. It is probable that this cruel game will continue without end.

FREDERICK W. TAYLOR

# Scientific Management

The writer has found that there are three questions uppermost in the minds of men when they become interested in scientific management.

*First.* Wherein do the principles of scientific management differ essentially from those of ordinary management?

*Second.* Why are better results attained under scientific management than under the other types?

*Third.* Is not the most important problem that of getting the right man at the head of the company? And if you have the right man cannot the choice of the type of management be safely left to him?

One of the principal objects of the following pages will be to give a satisfactory answer to these questions. . . .

Before starting to illustrate the principles of scientific management, or "task management" as it is briefly called, it seems desirable to outline what the writer believes will be recognized as the best type of management which is in common use. This is done so that the great difference between the best of the ordinary management and scientific management may be fully appreciated.

In an industrial establishment which employs say from 500 to 1000 workmen, there will be found in many cases at least twenty to thirty different trades. The workmen in each of these trades have had their knowledge handed down to them by word of mouth, through the many years in which their trade has been developed from the primitive condition, in which our far-distant ancestors each one practised the rudiments of many different trades, to the present state of great and growing subdivision of labor, in which each man specializes upon some comparatively small class of work.

The ingenuity of each generation has developed quicker and better methods for doing every element of the work in every trade. Thus the methods which are now in use may in a broad sense be said to be an evolution representing the survival of the fittest and best of the ideas which have been developed since the starting of each trade. However, while this is true in a broad sense, only those who are intimately acquainted with each of these trades are fully aware of the fact that in hardly any element of any trade is there uniformity in the methods which are used. Instead of having only one way which is generally accepted as a standard, there are in daily use, say, fifty or a hundred different ways of doing each element of the work. And a little thought will make it clear that this must inevitably be the case, since our methods have been handed down from man to man by word of mouth, or have, in most cases, been almost unconsciously learned through personal observation. Practically in no instances have they been codified or systematically analyzed or described. The ingenuity and experience of each generation—of each decade, even, have without

Reprinted from pp. 30–48, 57–60, in "The Principles of Scientific Management," from *Scientific Management* by Frederick Winslow Taylor, by permission of Harper & Row, Publishers. 

doubt handed over better methods to the next. This mass of rule-of-thumb or traditional knowledge may be said to be the principal asset or possession of every tradesman. Now, in the best of the ordinary types of management, the managers recognize frankly the fact that the 500 or 1000 workmen, included in the twenty to thirty trades, who are under them, possess this mass of traditional knowledge, a large part of which is not in the possession of the management. The management, of course, includes foremen and superintendents, who themselves have been in most cases first-class workers at their trades. And yet these foremen and superintendents know, better than any one else, that their own knowledge and personal skill falls far short of the combined knowledge and dexterity of all the workmen under them. The most experienced managers therefore frankly place before their workmen the problem of doing the work in the best and most economical way. They recognize the task before them as that of inducing each workman to use his best endeavors, his hardest work, all his traditional knowledge, his skill, his ingenuity, and his good-will—in a word, his "initiative," so as to yield the largest possible return to his employer. The problem before the management, then, may be briefly said to be that of obtaining the best *initiative* of every workman. And the writer uses the word "initiative" in its broadest sense, to cover all of the good qualities sought for from the men.

On the other hand, no intelligent manager would hope to obtain in any full measure the initiative of his workmen unless he felt that he was giving them something more than they usually receive from their employers. Only those among the readers of this paper who have been managers or who have worked themselves at a trade realize how far the average workman falls short of giving his employer his full initiative. It is well within the mark to state that in nineteen out of twenty industrial establishments the workmen believe it to be directly against their interests to give their employers their best initiative, and that instead of working hard to do the largest possible amount of work and the best quality of work for their employers, they deliberately work as slowly as they dare while they at the same time try to make those over them believe that they are working fast.[1]

The writer repeats, therefore, that in order to have any hope of obtaining the initiative of his workmen the manager must give some *special incentive* to his men beyond that which is given to the average of the trade. This incentive can be given in several different ways, as, for example, the hope of rapid promotion or advancement; higher wages, either in the form of generous piecework prices or of a premium or bonus of some kind for good and rapid work; shorter hours of labor; better surroundings and working conditions than are ordinarily given, etc., and, above all, this special incentive should be accompanied by that personal consideration for, and friendly contact with, his workmen which comes only from a genuine and kindly interest in the welfare of those under him. It is only by giving a special inducement or "incentive" of this kind that the employer can hope even approximately to get the "initiative" of his workmen. Under the ordinary type of management the necessity for offering the workman a special inducement has come to be so generally recognized that a large proportion of those most interested in the subject look upon the adoption of some one of the modern schemes for paying men (such as piece work, the premium plan, or the bonus plan, for instance) as practically the whole system of management. Under scientific management, however, the particular pay system which is adopted is merely one of the subordinate elements.

Broadly speaking, then, the best type of management in ordinary use may be defined as management in which the workmen give their best *initiative* and in return receive some *special incentive* from their employers. This type of management will be referred to as the management of "*initiative and incentive*" in contradistinction to scientific management, or task management, with which it is to be compared.

The writer hopes that the management of "initiative and incentive" will be recognized as representing the best type in ordinary use, and in fact he believes that it will be hard to persuade the average manager that anything better exists in the whole field than this type. The task which the writer has before him, then, is the difficult one of trying to prove in a thoroughly convincing way that there is

1. The writer has tried to make the reason for this unfortunate state of things clear in a paper entitled "Shop Management," read before the American Society of Mechanical Engineers.

another type of management which is not only better but overwhelmingly better than the management of "initiative and incentive."

The universal prejudice in favor of the management of "initiative and incentive" is so strong that no mere theoretical advantages which can be pointed out will be likely to convince the average manager that any other system is better. It will be upon a series of practical illustrations of the actual working of the two systems that the writer will depend in his efforts to prove that scientific management is so greatly superior to other types. Certain elementary principles, a certain philosophy, will however be recognized as the essence of that which is being illustrated in all of the practical examples which will be given. And the broad principles in which the scientific system differs from the ordinary or "rule-of-thumb" system are so simple in their nature that is seems desirable to describe them before starting with the illustrations.

Under the old type of management success depends almost entirely upon getting the "initiative" of the workmen, and it is indeed a rare case in which this initiative is really attained. Under scientific management the "initiative" of the workmen (that is, their hard work, their good-will, and their ingenuity) is obtained with absolute uniformity and to a greater extent than is possible under the old system; and in addition to this improvement on the part of the men, the managers assume new burdens, new duties, and responsibilities never dreamed of in the past. The managers assume, for instance, the burden of gathering together all of the traditional knowledge which in the past has been possessed by the workmen and then of classifying, tabulating, and reducing this knowledge to rules, laws, and formulæ which are immensely helpful to the workmen in doing their daily work. In addition to developing a *science* in this way, the management take on three other types of duties which involve new and heavy burdens for themselves.

These new duties are grouped under four heads:

*First.* They develop a science for each element of a man's work, which replaces the old rule-of-thumb method.

*Second.* They scientifically select and then train, teach, and develop the workman, whereas in the past he chose his own work and trained himself as best he could.

*Third.* They heartily cooperate with the men so as to insure all of the work being done in accordance with the principles of the science which has been developed.

*Fourth.* There is an almost equal division of the work and the responsibility between the management and the workmen. The management take over all work for which they are better fitted than the workmen, while in the past almost all of the work and the greater part of the responsibility were thrown upon the men.

It is this combination of the initiative of the workmen, coupled with the new types of work done by the management, that makes scientific management so much more efficient than the old plan.

Three of these elements exist in many cases, under the management of "initiative and incentive," in a small and rudimentary way, but they are, under this management, of minor importance, whereas under scientific management they form the very essence of the whole system.

The fourth of these elements, "an almost equal division of the responsibility between the management and the workmen," requires further explanation. The philosophy of the management of "initiative and incentive" makes it necessary for each workman to bear almost the entire responsibility for the general plan as well as for each detail of his work, and in many cases for his implements as well. In addition to this he must do all of the actual physical labor. The development of a science, on the other hand, involves the establishment of many rules, laws, and formulæ which replace the judgment of the individual workmen and which can be effectively used only after having been systematically recorded, indexed, etc. The practical use of scientific data also calls for a room in which to keep the books, records,[2] etc., and a desk for the planner to work at. Thus all of the planning which under the old system was done by the workman, as a result of his personal experience, must of necessity under the new system be done by the management in accordance with the laws of the science; because even if the workman was well suited to the development and use of scientific data, it would be physically impossible for him to work at his machine and

2. For example, the records containing the data used under scientific management in an ordinary machine-shop fill thousands of pages.

at a desk at the same time. It is also clear that in most cases one type of man is needed to plan ahead and an entirely different type to execute the work.

The man in the planning room, whose specialty under scientific management is planning ahead, invariably finds that the work can be done better and more economically by a subdivision of the labor; each act of each mechanic, for example, should be preceded by various preparatory acts done by other men. And all of this involves, as we have said, "an almost equal division of the responsibility and the work between the management and the workman."

To summarize: Under the management of "initiative and incentive" practically the whole problem is "up to the workman," while under scientific management fully one-half of the problem is "up to the management."

Perhaps the most prominent single element in modern scientific management is the task idea. The work of every workman is fully planned out by the management at least one day in advance, and each man receives in most cases complete written instructions, describing in detail the task which he is to accomplish, as well as the means to be used in doing the work. And the work planned in advance in this way constitutes a task which is to be solved, as explained above, not by the workman alone, but in almost all cases by the joint effort of the workman and the management. This task specifies not only what is to be done but how it is to be done and the exact time allowed for doing it. And whenever the workman succeeds in doing his task right, and within the time limit specified, he receives an addition of from 30 per cent to 100 per cent to his ordinary wages. These tasks are carefully planned, so that both good and careful work are called for in their performance, but it should be distinctly understood that in no case is the workman called upon to work at a pace which would be injurious to his health. The task is always so regulated that the man who is well suited to his job will thrive while working at this rate during a long term of years and grow happier and more prosperous, instead of being overworked. Scientific management consists very largely in preparing for and carrying out these tasks.

The writer is fully aware that to perhaps most of the readers of this paper the four elements which differentiate the new management from the old will at first appear to be merely high-sounding phrases; and he would again repeat that he has no idea of convincing the reader of their value merely through announcing their existence. His hope of carrying conviction rests upon demonstrating the tremendous force and effect of these four elements through a series of practical illustrations. It will be shown, first, that they can be applied absolutely to all classes of work, from the most elementary to the most intricate; and second, that when they are applied, the results must of necessity be overwhelmingly greater than those which it is possible to attain under the management of initiative and incentive.

The first illustration is that of handling pig iron, and this work is chosen because it is typical of perhaps the crudest and most elementary form of labor which is performed by man. This work is done by men with no other implements than their hands. The pig-iron handler stoops down, picks up a pig weighing about 92 pounds, walks for a few feet or yards and then drops it on to the ground or upon a pile. This work is so crude and elementary in its nature that the writer firmly believes that it would be possible to train an intelligent gorilla so as to become a more efficient pig-iron handler than any man can be. Yet it will be shown that the science of handling pig iron is so great and amounts to so much that it is impossible for the man who is best suited to this type of work to understand the principles of this science, or even to work in accordance with these principles without the aid of a man better educated than he is. And the further illustrations to be given will make it clear that in almost all of the mechanic arts the science which underlies each workman's act is so great and amounts to so much that the workman who is best suited actually to do the work is incapable (either through lack of education or through insufficient mental capacity) of understanding this science. This is announced as a general principle, the truth of which will become apparent as one illustration after another is given. After showing these four elements in the handling of pig iron, several illustrations will be given of their application to different kinds of work in the field of the mechanic arts, at intervals in a rising scale, beginning with the simplest and ending with the more intricate forms of labor.

One of the first pieces of work undertaken by us, when the writer started to introduce scientific management into the Bethlehem Steel Company, was to handle pig iron on task work. The opening of the Spanish War found some 80,000 tons of pig iron placed in small piles in an open field adjoining the works. Prices for pig iron had been so low that it could not be sold at a profit, and it therefore had been stored. With the opening of the Spanish War the price of pig iron rose, and this large accumulation of iron was sold. This gave us a good opportunity to show the workmen, as well as the owners and managers of the works, on a fairly large scale the advantages of task work over the old-fashioned day work and piece work, in doing a very elementary class of work.

The Bethlehem Steel Company had five blast furnaces, the product of which had been handled by a pig-iron gang for many years. This gang, at this time, consisted of about seventy-five men. They were good, average pig-iron handlers, were under an excellent foreman who himself had been a pig-iron handler, and the work was done, on the whole, about as fast and as cheaply as it was anywhere else at that time.

A railroad switch was run out into the field, right along the edge of the piles of pig iron. An inclined plank was placed against the side of a car, and each man picked up from his pile a pig of iron weighing about 92 pounds, walked up the inclined plank and dropped it on the end of the car.

We found that this gang were loading on the average about 12½ long tons per man per day. We were surprised to find, after studying the matter, that a first-class pig-iron handler ought to handle between 47 and 48 long tons per day, instead of 12½ tons. This task seemed to us so very large that we were obliged to go over our work several times before we were absolutely sure that we were right. Once we were sure, however, that 47 tons was a proper day's work for a first-class pig-iron handler, the task which faced us as managers under the modern scientific plan was clearly before us. It was our duty to see that the 80,000 tons of pig iron was loaded on to the cars at the rate of 47 tons per man per day, in place of 12½ tons, at which rate the work was then being done. And it was further our duty to see that this work was done without bringing on a strike among the men, without any quarrel with the men, and to see that the men were happier and better contented when loading at the new rate of 47 tons than they were when loading at the old rate of 12½ tons.

Our first step was the scientific selection of the workman. In dealing with workmen under this type of management, it is an inflexible rule to talk to and deal with only one man at a time, since each workman has his own special abilities and limitations, and since we are not dealing with men in masses, but are trying to develop each individual man to his highest state of efficiency and prosperity. Our first step was to find the proper workman to begin with. We therefore carefully watched and studied these seventy-five men for three or four days, at the end of which time we had picked out four men who appeared to be physically able to handle pig iron at the rate of 47 tons per day. A careful study was then made of each of these men. We looked up their history as far back as practicable and thorough inquiries were made as to the character, habits, and the ambition of each of them. Finally we selected one from among the four as the most likely man to start with. He was a little Pennsylvania Dutchman who had been observed to trot back home for a mile or so after his work in the evening about as fresh as he was when he came trotting down to work in the morning. We found that upon wages of $1.15 a day he had succeeded in buying a small plot of ground, and that he was engaged in putting up the walls of a little house for himself in the morning before starting to work and at night after leaving. He also had the reputation of being exceedingly "close," that is, of placing a very high value on a dollar. As one man whom we talked to about him said, "A penny looks about the size of a cart-wheel to him." This man we will call Schmidt.

The task before us, then, narrowed itself down to getting Schmidt to handle 47 tons of pig iron per day and making him glad to do it. This was done as follows. Schmidt was called out from among the gang of pig-iron handlers and talked to somewhat in this way:

"Schmidt, are you a high-priced man?"

"Vell, I don't know vat you mean."

"Oh yes, you do. What I want to know is whether you are a high-priced man or not."

"Vell, I don't know vat you mean."

"Oh, come now, you answer my questions. What

I want to find out is whether you are a high-priced man or one of these cheap fellows here. What I want to find out is whether you want to earn $1.85 a day or whether you are satisfied with $1.15, just the same as all those cheap fellows are getting."

"Did I vant $1.85 a day? Vas dot a high-priced man? Vell, yes, I vas a high-priced man."

"Oh, you're aggravating me. Of course you want $1.85 a day—everyone wants it! You know perfectly well that that has very little to do with your being a high-priced man. For goodness' sake answer my questions, and don't waste any more of my time. Now come over here. You see that pile of pig iron?"

"Yes."

"You see that car?"

"Yes."

"Well, if you are a high-priced man, you will load that pig iron on that car tomorrow for $1.85. Now do wake up and answer my question. Tell me whether you are a high-priced man or not."

"Vell—did I got $1.85 for loading dot pig iron on dot car tomorrow?"

"Yes, of course you do, and you get $1.85 for loading a pile like that every day right through the year. That is what a high-priced man does, and you know it just as well as I do."

"Vell, dot's all right. I could load dot pig iron on the car tomorrow for $1.85, and I get it every day, don't I?"

"Certainly you do—certainly you do."

"Vell, den, I vas a high-priced man."

"Now, hold on, hold on. You know just as well as I do that a high-priced man has to do exactly as he's told from morning till night. You have seen this man here before, haven't you?"

"No, I never saw him."

"Well, if you are a high-priced man, you will do exactly as this man tells you tomorrow, from morning till night. When he tells you to pick up a pig and walk, you pick it up and you walk, and when he tells you to sit down and rest, you sit down. You do that right straight through the day. And what's more, no back talk. Now a high-priced man does just what he's told to do, and no back talk. Do you understand that? When this man tells you to walk, you walk; when he tells you to sit down, you sit down, and you don't talk back at him. Now you come on to work here tomorrow morning and I'll know before night whether you are really a high-priced man or not."

This seems to be rather rough talk. And indeed it would be if applied to an educated mechanic, or even an intelligent laborer. With a man of the mentally sluggish type of Schmidt it is appropriate and not unkind, since it is effective in fixing his attention on the high wages which he wants and away from what, if it were called to his attention, he probably would consider impossibly hard work.

What would Schmidt's answer be if he were talked to in a manner which is usual under the management of "initiative and incentive"? say, as follows:

"Now, Schmidt, you are a first-class pig-iron handler and know your business well. You have been handling at the rate of 12½ tons per day. I have given considerable study to handling pig iron, and feel sure that you could do a much larger day's work than you have been doing. Now don't you think that if you really tried you could handle 47 tons of pig iron per day, instead of 12½ tons?"

What do you think Schmidt's answer would be to this?

Schmidt started to work, and all day long, and at regular intervals, was told by the man who stood over him with a watch, "Now pick up a pig and walk. Now sit down and rest. Now walk—now rest," etc. He worked when he was told to work, and rested when he was told to rest, and at half-past five in the afternoon had his 47½ tons loaded on the car. And he practically never failed to work at this pace and do the task that was set him during the three years that the writer was at Bethlehem. And throughout this time he averaged a little more than $1.85 per day, whereas before he had never received over $1.15 per day, which was the ruling rate of wages at that time in Bethlehem. That is, he received 60 per cent higher wages than were paid to other men who were not working on task work. One man after another was picked out and trained to handle pig iron at the rate of 47½ tons per day until all of the pig iron was handled at this rate, and the men were receiving 60 per cent more wages than other workmen around them.

The writer has given above a brief description of three of the four elements which constitute the essence of scientific management: first, the careful selection of the workman, and, second and third, the method of first inducing and then training and helping the workman to work according to the scientific method. Nothing has as yet been said about the science of handling pig iron. The writer trusts, however, that before leaving this illustration the reader will be thoroughly convinced that there is a science of handling pig iron, and further that this science amounts to so much that the man who is suited to handle pig iron cannot possibly understand it, nor even work in accordance with the laws of this science, without the help of those who are over him.

* * * * * *

The law is confined to that class of work in which the limit of a man's capacity is reached because he is tired out. It is the law of heavy laboring, corresponding to the work of the cart horse, rather than that of the trotter. Practically all such work consists of a heavy pull or a push on the man's arms, that is, the man's strength is exerted by either lifting or pushing something which he grasps in his hands. And the law is that for each given pull or push on the man's arms it is possible for the workman to be under load for only a definite percentage of the day. For example, when pig iron is being handled (each pig weighing 92 pounds), a first-class workman can only be under load 43 per cent of the day. He must be entirely free from load during 57 per cent of the day. And as the load becomes lighter, the percentage of the day under which the man can remain under load increases. So that, if the workman is handling a half pig weighing 46 pounds, he can then be under load 58 per cent of the day, and only has to rest during 42 per cent. As the weight grows lighter the man can remain under load during a larger and larger percentage of the day, until finally a load is reached which he can carry in his hands all day long without being tired out. When that point has been arrived at this law ceases to be useful as a guide to a laborer's endurance, and some other law must be found which indicates the man's capacity for work.

When a laborer is carrying a piece of pig iron weighing 92 pounds in his hands, it tires him about as much to stand still under the load as it does to walk with it, since his arm muscles are under the same severe tension whether he is moving or not. A man, however, who stands still under a load is exerting no horse-power whatever, and this accounts for the fact that no constant relation could be traced in various kinds of heavy laboring work between the foot-pounds of energy exerted and the tiring effect of the work on the man. It will also be clear that in all work of this kind it is necessary for the arms of the workman to be completely free from load (that is, for the workman to rest) at frequent intervals. Throughout the time that the man is under a heavy load the tissues of his arm muscles are in process of degeneration, and frequent periods of rest are required in order that the blood may have a chance to restore these tissues to their normal condition.

To return now to our pig-iron handlers at the Bethlehem Steel Company. If Schmidt had been allowed to attack the pile of 47 tons of pig iron without the guidance or direction of a man who understood the art, or science, of handling pig iron, in his desire to earn his high wages he would probably have tired himself out by eleven or twelve o'clock in the day. He would have kept so steadily at work that his muscles would not have had the proper periods of rest absolutely needed for recuperation, and he would have been completely exhausted early in the day. By having a man, however, who understood this law, stand over him and direct his work, day after day, until he acquired the habit of resting at proper intervals, he was able to work at an even gait all day long without unduly tiring himself.

Now one of the very first requirements for a man who is fit to handle pig iron as a regular occupation is that he shall be so stupid and so phlegmatic that he more nearly resembles in his mental make-up the ox than any other type. The man who is mentally alert and intelligent is for this very reason entirely unsuited to what would, for him, be the grinding monotony of work of this character. Therefore the workman who is best suited to handling pig iron is unable to understand the real science of doing this class of work. He is so stupid that the word "percentage" has no meaning to him, and he must consequently be trained by a man more intelligent than himself into the habit of working in accordance with the laws of this science before he can be successful.

The writer trusts that it is now clear that even in the case of the most elementary form of labor that is known, there is a science, and that when the man best suited to this class of work has been carefully selected, when the science of doing the work has been developed, and when the carefully selected man has been trained to work in accordance with this science, the results obtained must of necessity be overwhelmingly greater than those which are possible under the plan of "initiative and incentive."

FRITZ J. ROETHLISBERGER and WILLIAM J. DICKSON

# Human Relations

## An industrial organization as a social system

We shall now attempt to state more systematically than was possible in a chronological account the results of the research and some of their implications for practice. Each stage of the research contributed to the development of a point of view in terms of which the data could be more usefully assessed. In presenting the studies, this aspect of the research program was given primary emphasis and an effort was made to show how each successive step in the research resulted in the discovery of new facts which in turn brought forth new questions and new hypotheses and assisted in the development of more adequate methods and a more adequate conceptual scheme. The point of view which gradually emerged from these studies is one from which an industrial organization is regarded as a social system. In this chapter a statement of this point of view will be made. In the next chapter various management problems which have been discussed in connection with the various research studies will be restated in terms of this new point of view. In the concluding chapter the application of the concept of an industrial concern as a social system to problems of personnel practice will be considered.

The study of the bank wiremen showed that their behavior at work could not be understood without considering the informal organization of the group and the relation of this informal organization to the total social organization of the company. The work activities of this group, together with their satisfactions and dissatisfactions, had to be viewed as manifestations of a complex pattern of interrelations. In short, the work situation of the bank wiring group had to be treated as a social system; moreover, the industrial organization of which this group was a part also had to be treated as a social system.

By "system" is meant something which must be considered as a whole because each part bears a relation of interdependence to every other part.[1] It will be the purpose of this chapter to state this conception of a social system, to specify more clearly the parts of the social system of which account has to be taken in an industrial organization, and to consider the state of equilibrium which obtains among the parts.

### THE TWO MAJOR FUNCTIONS OF AN INDUSTRIAL ORGANIZATION

An industrial organization may be regarded as performing two major functions, that of producing a product and that of creating and distributing

Reprinted from *Management and the Worker*, pp. 551–68, by permission of the authors and publisher. 

1. "The interdependence of the variables in a system is one of the widest inductions from experience that we possess; or we may alternatively regard it as the definition of a system." Henderson, L. J., *Pareto's General Sociology*, Harvard University Press, 1935, p. 86.

satisfactions among the individual members of the organization. The first function is ordinarily called economic. From this point of view the functioning of the concern is assessed in such terms as cost, profit, and technical efficiency. The second function, while it is readily understood, is not ordinarily designated by any generally accepted word. It is variously described as maintaining employee relations, employee good will, cooperation, etc. From this standpoint the functioning of the concern is frequently assessed in such terms as labor turnover, tenure of employment, sickness and accident rate, wages, employee attitudes, etc. The industrial concern is continually confronted, therefore, with two sets of major problems: (1) problems of external balance, and (2) problems of internal equilibrium. The problems of external balance are generally assumed to be economic; that is, problems of competition, adjusting the organization to meet changing price levels, etc. The problems of internal equilibrium are chiefly concerned with the maintenance of a kind of social organization in which individuals and groups through working together can satisfy their own desires.

Ordinarily an industrial concern is thought of primarily in terms of its success in meeting problems of external balance, or if the problems of internal equilibrium are explicitly recognized they are frequently assumed to be separate from and unrelated to the economic purpose of the enterprise. Producing an article at a profit and maintaining good employee relations are frequently regarded as antithetical propositions. The results of the studies which have been reported indicated, however, that these two sets of problems are interrelated and interdependent. The kind of social organization which obtains within a concern is intimately related to the effectiveness of the total organization. Likewise, the success with which the concern maintains external balance is directly related to its internal organization.

A great deal of attention has been given to the economic function of industrial organization. Scientific controls have been introduced to further the economic purposes of the concern and of the individuals within it. Much of this advance has gone on in the name of efficiency or rationalization. Nothing comparable to this advance has gone on in the development of skills and techniques for securing cooperation, that is, for getting individuals and groups of individuals working together effectively and with satisfaction to themselves. The slight advances which have been made in this area have been overshadowed by the new and powerful technological developments of modern industry.

### THE TECHNICAL ORGANIZATION OF THE PLANT

In looking at an industrial organization as a social system it will first be necessary to examine the physical environment, for this is an inseparable part of any organization. The physical environment includes not only climate and weather, but also that part of the environment which is owned and used by the organization itself, namely, the physical plant, tools, machines, raw products, and so on. This latter part of the factory's physical environment is ordered and organized in a certain specified way to accomplish the task of technical production. For our purposes, therefore, it will be convenient to distinguish from the human organization this aspect of the physical environment of an industrial plant and to label it the "technical organization of the plant." This term will refer only to the logical and technical organization of material, tools, machines, and finished product, including all those physical items related to the task of technical production.

The two aspects into which an industrial plant can be roughly divided—the technical organization and the human organization—are interrelated and interdependent. The human organization is constantly molding and re-creating the technical organization either to achieve more effectively the common economic purpose or to secure more satisfaction for its members. Likewise, changes in the technical organization require an adaptation on the part of the human organization.

### THE HUMAN ORGANIZATION OF THE PLANT

In the human organization we find a number of individuals working together toward a common end: the collective purpose of the total organization. Each of these individuals, however, is bringing to the work situation a different background of personal and social experiences. No two individuals are making exactly the same demands of their job. The demands a particular employee makes depend not only upon his physical needs but upon his social needs as well. These social needs and the sentiments associated with them vary with his early personal history and social conditioning as well as with the needs and sentiments of people closely associated with him both inside and outside of work.

### THE INDIVIDUAL

It may be well to look more closely at the sentiments the individual is bringing to his work situation. Starting with a certain native organic endowment the child is precipitated into group life by the act of birth. The group into which the child is born is not the group in general. The child is born into a specific family. Moreover, this specific family is not a family in isolation. It is related in certain ways to other families in the community. It has a certain cultural background—a way of life, codes and routines of behavior, associated with certain beliefs and expectations. In the beginning the child brings only his organic needs to this social milieu into which he is born. Very rapidly he begins to accumulate experience. This process of accumulating experience is the process of assigning meanings to the socio-reality about him; it is the process of becoming socialized. Much of the early learning period is devoted to preparing the child to become capable of social life in its particular group. In preparing the child for social participation the immediate family group plays an important role. By the particular type of family into which the child is born he is "conditioned" to certain routines of behavior and ways of living. The early meanings he assigns to his experience are largely in terms of these codes of behavior and associated beliefs. As the child grows up and participates in groups other than the immediate family his meanings lose, although never quite entirely, their specific family form. This process of social interaction and social conditioning is never-ending and continues from birth to death. The adult's evaluation of his surroundings is determined in a good part by the system of human interrelations in which he has participated.

### THE SOCIAL ORGANIZATION OF THE PLANT

However, the human organization of an industrial plant is more than a plurality of individuals, each motivated by sentiments arising from his own personal and private history and background. It is also a social organization, for the members of an industrial plant—executives, technical specialists, supervisors, factory workers, and office workers—are interacting daily with one another and from their associations certain patterns of relations are formed among them. These patterns of relations, together with the objects which symbolize them, constitute the social organization of the industrial enterprise. Most of the individuals who live among these patterns come to accept them as obvious and necessary truths and to react as they dictate. Both the kind of behavior that is expected of a person and the kind of behavior he can expect from others are prescribed by these patterns.

If one looks at a factory situation, for example, one finds individuals and groups of individuals who are associated at work acting in certain accepted and prescribed ways toward one another. There is not complete homogeneity of behavior between individuals or between one group of individuals and another, but rather there are differences of behavior expressing differences in social relationship. Some relationships fall into routine patterns, such as the relationship between superior and subordinate or between office worker and shop worker. Individuals conscious of their membership in certain groups are reacting in certain accepted ways to other individuals representing other groups. Behavior varies according to the stereotyped conceptions of relationship. The worker, for example, behaves toward his foreman in one way, toward his first-line supervisor in another way, and toward his fellow worker in still another. People holding the rank of inspector expect a certain kind of behavior from the operators—the operators from the inspectors. Now these relationships, as is well known from everyday experiences, are finely shaded and sometimes become complicated. When a person is in the presence of his supervisor alone he usually acts differently from the way he acts when his supervisor's supervisor is also present. Likewise, his supervisor acts toward him alone quite differently from the way he behaves when his own supervisor is also there. These subtle nuances of relationship are so much a part of everyday life that they are commonplace. They are taken for granted. The vast amount of social conditioning that has taken place by means of which a person maneuvers himself gracefully through the intricacies of these finely shaded social distinctions is seldom explicitly realized. Attention is paid only when a new social situation arises where the past social training of the person prevents him from making the necessary delicate interpretations of a given social signal and hence brings forth the "socially wrong" response.

In the factory, as in any social milieu, a process of social evaluation is constantly at work. From this process distinctions of "good" and "bad," "inferior" and "superior," arise. This process of evaluation is carried on with simple and ready generalizations by means of which values become attached to individuals and to groups performing certain tasks and operations. It assigns to a group of individuals performing such and such a task a particular rank in the established prestige scale. Each work group becomes a carrier of social values. In industry with its extreme diversity of occupations there are a number of such groupings. Any noticeable similarity or difference, not only in occupation but also in age, sex, and nationality, can serve as a basis of social classification, as, for example, "married women," the "old-timer," the "white-collared" or clerical worker, the "foreign element." Each of these groups, too, has its own value system.

All the patterns of interaction that arise between individuals or between different groups can be graded according to the degree of intimacy involved in the relationship. Grades of intimacy or understanding can be arranged on a scale and expressed in terms of "social distance." Social distance measures differences of sentiment and interest which separate individuals or groups from one another. Between the president of a company and the elevator operator there is considerable social distance, more for example than between the foreman and the benchworker. Social distance is to social organization what physical distance is to physical space. However, physical and social distance do not necessarily coincide. Two people may be physically near but socially distant.

Just as each employee has a particular physical location, so he has a particular social place in the total social organization. But this place is not so rigidly fixed as in a caste system. In any factory there is considerable mobility or movement. Movement can occur in two ways: the individual may pass from one occupation to another occupation higher up in the prestige scale; or the prestige scale itself may change.

It is obvious that these scales of value are never completely accepted by all the groups in the social environment. The shop worker does not quite see why the office worker, for example, should have shorter hours of work than he has. Or the newcomer, whose efficiency on a particular job is about the same, but whose hourly rate is less than that of some old-timer, wonders why service should count so much. The management group, in turn, from the security of its social elevation, does not often understand what "all the fuss is about."

As was indicated by many of the studies, any person who has achieved a certain rank in the prestige scale regards anything real or imaginary which tends to alter his status adversely as something unfair or unjust. It is apparent that any move on the part of the management may alter the existing social equilibrium to which the employee has grown accustomed and by means of which his status is defined. Immediately this disruption will be expressed in sentiments of resistance to the real or imagined alterations in the social equilibrium.

From this point of view it can be seen how every item and event in the industrial environment becomes an object of a system of sentiments. According to this way of looking at things, material goods, physical events, wages, hours of work, etc., cannot be treated as things in themselves. Instead they have to be interpreted as carriers of social value. The meanings which any person in an industrial organization assigns to the events and objects in his environment are often determined by the social situation in which the events and objects occur. The significance to an employee of a double-pedestal desk, of a particular kind of pencil, or of a handset telephone is determined by the social setting in which these objects appear. If people with double-pedestal desks supervise people with single-pedestal desks, then double-pedestal desks become symbols of status or prestige in the organization. As patterns of behavior become crystallized, every object in the environment tends to take on a particular social significance. It becomes easy to tell a person's social place in the organization by the objects which he wears and carries and which surround him. In these terms it can be seen how the introduction of a technical change may also involve for an individual or a group of individuals the loss of certain prestige symbols and, as a result, have a demoralizing effect.

From this point of view the behavior of no one person in an industrial organization, from the very top to the very bottom, can be regarded as motivated by strictly economic or logical considerations. Routine patterns of interaction involve strong sentiments. Each group in the organization manifests its own powerful sentiments. It is likely that sometimes the behavior of many staff specialists which goes under the name of "efficiency" is as much a manifestation of a very strong sentiment—the sentiment or desire to originate new combinations—as it is of anything strictly logical.

This point of view is far from the one which is frequently expressed, namely, that man is essentially an economic being carrying around with him a few noneconomic appendages. Rather, the point of view which has been expressed here is that noneconomic motives, interests, and processes, as well as economic, are fundamental in behavior in business, from the board of directors to the very last man in the organization. Man is not merely—in fact is very seldom—motivated by factors pertaining strictly to facts or logic. Sentiments are not merely things which man carries around with him as appendages. He cannot cast them off like a suit of clothes. He carries them with him wherever he goes. In business or elsewhere, he can hardly behave without expressing them. Moreover, sentiments do not exist in a social vacuum. They are the product of social behavior, of social interaction, of the fact that man lives his life as a member of different groups. Not only does man bring sentiments to the business situation because of his past experiences and conditioning outside of business, but also as a member of a specific local business organization with a particular social place in it he has certain sentiments expressing his particular relations to it.

According to this point of view, every social act in adulthood is an integrated response to both inner and outer stimuli. To each new concrete situation the adult brings his past "social conditioning." To the extent that this past social conditioning has prepared him to assimilate the new experience in the culturally accepted manner, he is said to be "adjusted." To the extent that his private or personal view of the situation is at variance with the cultural situation, the person is called "maladjusted."

## THE FORMAL ORGANIZATION OF THE PLANT

The social organization of the industrial plant is in part formally organized. It is composed of a number of strata or levels which differentiate the bench-worker from the skilled mechanic, the group chief from the department chief, and so on. These levels are well defined and all the formal orders, instructions, and compensations are addressed to them. All such factors taken together make up the formal organization of the plant. It includes the systems, policies, rules, and regulations of the plant which express what the relations of one person to another are supposed to be in order to achieve effectively the task of technical production. It prescribes the relations that are supposed to obtain within the human organization and between the human organization and the technical organization. In short, the patterns of human interrelations, as defined by the systems, rules, policies, and regulations of the company, constitute the formal organization.

The formal organization of an industrial plant has two purposes: it addresses itself to the economic purposes of the total enterprise; it concerns itself also with the securing of co-operative effort. The formal organization includes all the explicitly stated systems of control introduced by the company in order to achieve the economic purposes of the total enterprise and the effective contribution of the members of the organization to those economic ends.

## THE INFORMAL ORGANIZATION OF THE PLANT

All the experimental studies pointed to the fact that there is something more to the social organization than what has been formally recognized. Many of the actually existing patterns of human interaction have no representation in the formal organization at all, and others are inadequately represented by the formal organization. This fact is frequently forgotten when talking or thinking about industrial situations in general. Too often it is assumed that the organization of a company corresponds to a blueprint plan or organization chart. Actually, it never does. In the formal organization of most companies little explicit recognition is given to many social distinctions residing in the social organization. The blueprint plans of a company show the functional relations between working units, but they do not express the distinctions of social distance, movement, or equilibrium previously described. The hierarchy of prestige values which tends to make the work of men more important than the work of women, the work of clerks more important than the work at the bench, has little representation in the formal organization; nor does a blueprint plan ordinarily show the primary groups, that is, those groups enjoying daily face-to-face relations. Logical lines of horizontal and vertical coordination of functions replace the actually existing patterns of interaction between people in different social places. The formal organization cannot take account of the sentiments and values residing in the social organization by means of which individuals or groups of individuals are informally differentiated, ordered, and integrated. Individuals in their associations with one another in a factory build up personal relationships. They form into informal groups, in terms of which each person achieves a certain position or status. The nature of these informal groups is very important, as has been shown in the Relay Assembly Test Room and in the Bank Wiring Observation Room.

It is well to recognize that informal organizations are not "bad," as they are sometimes assumed to be. Informal social organization exists in every plant, and can be said to be a necessary prerequisite for effective collaboration. Much collaboration exists at an informal level, and it sometimes facilitates the functioning of the formal organization. On the other hand, sometimes the informal organization develops in opposition to the formal organization. The important consideration is, therefore, the relation that exists between formal and informal organizations.

To illustrate, let us consider the Relay Assembly Test Room and the Bank Wiring Observation Room. These two studies offered an interesting contrast between two informal working groups; one situation could be characterized in almost completely opposite terms from the other. In the Relay Assembly Test Room, on the one hand, the five operators changed continuously in their rate of output up and down over the duration of the test, and yet in a curious fashion their variations in output were insensitive to many significant changes introduced during the experiment. On the other hand, in the Bank Wiring Observation Room output was being held relatively constant and there existed a hypersensitivity to change on the part of the worker—in fact, what could almost be described as an organized opposition to it.

It is interesting to note that management could draw from these studies two opposite conclusions. From the Relay Assembly Test Room experiment they could argue that the company can do almost anything it wants in the nature of technical changes without any perceptible effect on the output of the workers. From the Bank Wiring Observation Room they could argue equally convincingly that the company can introduce hardly any changes without meeting a pronounced opposition to them from the workers. To make this dilemma even more striking, it is only necessary to recall that the sensitivity to change in the one case occurred in the room where no experimental changes had been introduced whereas the insensitivity to change in the other case occurred in the room where the operators had been submitted to considerable experimentation. To settle this question by saying that in one case the situation was typical and in the other case atypical of ordinary shop conditions would be to beg the question, for the essential difference between the two situations would again be missed. It would ignore the social setting in which the changes occurred and the meaning which the workers themselves assigned to the changes.

Although in both cases there were certain informal arrangements not identical with the formal setup, the informal organization in one room was quite different from that in the other room, especially in its relation to the formal organization. In the case of the Relay Assembly Test Room there was a group, or informal organization, which could be characterized as a network of personal relations which had been developed in and through a particular way of working together; it was an organization which not only satisfied the wishes of its members but also worked in harmony with the aims of management. In the case of the Bank Wiring Observation Room there was an informal organization which could be characterized better as a set of practices and beliefs which its members had in common—practices and beliefs which at many points worked against the economic purposes of the company. In one case the relation between the formal and informal organization was one of compatibility; in the other case it was one of opposition. Or to put it in another way, collaboration in the Relay Assembly Test Room was at a much higher level than in the Bank Wiring Observation Room.

The difference between these two groups can be understood only by comparing the functions which their informal organizations performed for their members. The chief function of the informal group in the Bank Wiring Observation Room was to resist changes in their established routines of work or personal interrelations. This resistance to change, however, was not the chief function of the informal group in the Relay Assembly Test Room. It is true that at first the introduction of the planned changes in the test room, whether or not these changes were logically in the direction of improvement, was met with apprehension and feelings of uneasiness on the part of the operators. The girls in the beginning were never quite sure that they might not be victims of the changes.

In setting up the Relay Assembly Test Room with the object of studying the factors determining the efficiency of the worker, many of the methods and rules by means of which management tends to promote and maintain efficiency—the "bogey," not talking too much at work, etc.—were, in effect, abrogated. With the removal of this source of constraint and in a setting of heightened social significance (because many of the changes had differentiated the test room girls from the regular department and as a result had elevated the social status within the plant of each of the five girls) a new type of spontaneous social organization developed. Social conditions had been established which allowed the operators to develop their own values and objectives. The experimental conditions allowed the operators to develop openly social codes at work and these codes, unhampered by interference, gave a sustained meaning to their work. It was as if the experimenters had acted as a buffer for the operators and held their work situation steady while they developed a new type of social organization. With this change in the type of social organization there also developed a new attitude toward changes in their working environment. Toward many changes which constitute an unspecified threat in the regular work situation the operators became immune. What the Relay Assembly Test Room experiment showed was that when innovations are introduced carefully and with regard to the actual sentiments of the workers, the workers are likely to develop a spontaneous type of informal organization which will not only express more adequately their own values and significances but also is more likely to be in harmony with the aims of management.

Although all the studies of informal organization at the Hawthorne Plant were made at the employee level, it would be incorrect to assume that this phenomenon occurs only at that level. Informal organization appears at all levels, from the very bottom to the very top of the organization.[2] Informal organization at the executive level, just as at the work level, may either facilitate or impede purposive cooperation and communication. In either case, at all levels of the organization informal organizations exist as a necessary condition for collaboration. Without them formal organization could not survive for long. Formal and informal organizations are interdependent aspects of social interaction.

### THE IDEOLOGICAL ORGANIZATION OF THE PLANT

There is one aspect of social organization in an industrial plant which cuts across both the formal and informal organizations: the systems of ideas and beliefs by means of which the values residing in the total organization are expressed and the symbols around which these values are organized. Both the formal and informal organizations of a plant have systems of ideas and beliefs. Some are more capable of logical and systematic expression than others. Those of the formal organization in general are more logically explicit and articulate than those of the informal organization, but they are not for that reason more powerful in their effects than those of the informal organization. The sentiments underlying the beliefs and ideas of informal organizations are often very powerful determinants of overt behavior.

Some of these systems of ideas and beliefs represent what the organization should be; that is, what the relations of people to one another should be or

2. Barnard, C. I., *The Functions of the Executive*, Harvard University Press, 1938, pp. 223–24.

how people should behave. Some express the values of one part of the total organization, for each specialist tends to see the total organization from the point of view of the logic of his own specialty. Still others express the values residing in the inter-human relations of the different social groups involved.

Some of these ideas and beliefs represent more closely the actual situation than others. In all cases, however, they are abstractions from the concrete situation. In this respect they are to the concrete situation as maps are to the territories they represent.[3] And like maps these abstractions may be either misleading or useful. They may be misleading because sometimes the person using them fails to realize they are representing only one part of the total organization. Sometimes in the minds of certain individuals these abstractions tend to become divorced from the social reality and, in effect, lead an independent existence.

In their studies the investigators frequently ran into these different systems of ideas and beliefs. Although they were never made the object of systematic study, three general systems which seemed to cling together could be discerned.

*The logic of cost.* In the industrial plant there is a certain set of ideas and beliefs by means of which the common economic purposes of the total organization are evaluated. This we shall call the "logic of cost." Although the logic of cost is applied mostly to the technical organization, it is also sometimes applied to the human organization. When applied to the human organization it is frequently done under the label of "efficiency."

The word "efficiency" is used in at least five different ways, two of which are rather vague and not clearly differentiated: (*a*) sometimes when talking about a machine it is used in a technical sense, as the relation between output and input; (*b*) sometimes when talking about a manufacturing process or operation it is used to refer to relative unit cost; (*c*) sometimes when referring to a worker it is used to indicate a worker's production or output in relation to a certain standard of performance; (*d*) sometimes its reference becomes more vague and it is used as practically synonymous with "logical coordination of function"; (*e*) sometimes it is used in the sense of "morale" or "social integration."

We shall use the term "logic of cost" to refer only to the system of ideas and beliefs which are explicitly organized around the symbol of "cost" and are applied to the human organization from this point of view.[4] This logic represents one of the values of the formal organization: the system of ideas and beliefs which relates the human organization to the task of technical production.

*The logic of efficiency.* Closely associated with the logic of cost is another system of ideas and beliefs by means of which the collaborative efforts of the members of an organization are evaluated. This we shall call the "logic of efficiency."[5] This system of ideas and beliefs, which is organized around the symbol of "cooperation," represents another value of the formal organization. It is addressed primarily to the problem of how cooperation between individuals and groups of individuals can be effectively secured and is manifested in plans, such as wage payment plans, designed to promote collaboration among individuals.

A system of beliefs and ideas such as this is usually based upon certain assumptions about employee behavior. In the case of the wage payment plan in the Bank Wiring Observation Room, for example, it was assumed that the employee was a logical being and therefore could see the system, as its creators saw it, as a logical, coherent scheme which he could use to his economic advantage. It was assumed that, given the opportunity, the employee would act in such a way as to obtain the maximum of earnings consistent with his physical capacity. Carrying this basic assumption still further, it followed that the slower workers, who would interfere with the logical functioning of that system, would be disciplined by the faster workers and that daywork claims would be kept at a minimum. It was assumed that the division of labor would permit the employees to increase production through specialization. The possibility that division of labor might result in social stratification, which

3. This distinction has been borrowed from Korzybski, A., *Science and Sanity*, The Science Press Printing Co., New York, 1933.

4. According to this definition, "logic of cost" does not conform to any single one of the above uses of the word "efficiency" but conforms most closely to a combination of (*b*) and (*c*).

5. The "logic of efficiency" conforms most closely to a combination of uses (*c*), (*d*), and (*e*) of the word "efficiency" as given in the previous section.

in turn might generate nonlogical forces that would interfere with the logical functioning of that system, was unforeseen. Practically every aspect of the wage plan followed from the basic assumption that nothing would interfere with the economic motives. It is such assumptions as these that go to make up the "logic of efficiency."

*The logic of sentiments.* There is another system of ideas and beliefs which we shall give the label "the logic of sentiments." It represents the values residing in the interhuman relations of the different groups within the organization. Examples of what is meant here are the arguments employees give which center around the "right to work," "seniority," "fairness," "the living wage." This logic, as its name implies, is deeply rooted in sentiment and feeling.

*Management and employee logics.* At first glance it might seem that the logics of cost and efficiency are the logics of management groups, whereas the logic of sentiments is the logic of employee groups. Although in one sense this may be accurate, in another sense it is an oversimplification. All groups within the industry participate in these different logics, although some participate to a greater or less extent than others. One has only to interview a supervisor or executive to see that he has a logic of sentiments which is expressing the values residing in his personal interrelations with other supervisors or executives. Employee groups, moreover, are not unknown to apply the logic of cost.

However, it is incorrect to assume that these different logics have the same significance to different groups in an industrial plant. The logics of cost and efficiency express the values of the formal organization; the logic of sentiments expresses the values of the informal organization. To management groups and technical specialists the logics of cost and efficiency are likely to be more important than they are to employee groups. In form the logic of sentiments expressed by an executive is indistinguishable from that expressed by a worker, but in content it is quite different. As anyone knows who has had industrial experience, much time is spent in industry in debating the relative weights attaching to the logics of cost, efficiency, and sentiments when they are applied to a particular concrete situation.

DEFINITION OF TERMS

For convenience, it may be well to summarize the different parts into which the industrial plant as a social system can be divided and the way in which the labels attaching to them will be used in the two final chapters. The following outline will help the reader to see the levels of abstraction of the different parts of the system:

- 1 Technical Organization
- 2 Human Organization
  - 2.1 Individual
  - 2.2 Social Organization
    - 2.21 Formal Organization
      - 2.211 Patterns of Interaction
      - 2.212 Systems of Ideas and Beliefs (Ideological Organization)
        - 2.2121 Logic of Cost
        - 2.2122 Logic of Efficiency
    - 2.22 Informal Organization
      - 2.221 Patterns of Interaction
      - 2.222 Systems of Ideas and Beliefs (Ideological Organization)
        - 2.2221 Logic of Sentiments

1 The term "technical organization" will refer to the logical and technical organization of materials, tools, machines, and finished products, including all those physical items related to the task of technical production.

2 The term "human organization" will refer, on the one hand, to the concrete individual with his rich personal and social background and, on the other hand, to the intricate pattern of social relations existing among the various individuals and groups within the plant.

2.1 The term "individual" will refer to the sentiments and values which the person is bringing to the work situation because of his past social conditioning and present social situation outside of the plant; i.e., the past and present patterns of interaction in which he has participated or is participating outside of work.

2.2 The term "social organization" will refer to the actual patterns of interaction existing within and between employee groups, supervisory groups, and management groups in a plant here and now. It will include those relations that remain at a common human level (friendships, antagonisms, etc.), those that have been built up into larger social configurations (social codes, customs, traditions, routines, and associated ideas and beliefs), as well as those patterns of relations formally prescribed by the rules, regulations, practices, and policies of the company.

2.21 The term "formal organization" will refer to those patterns of interaction prescribed by the rules and regulations of the company as well as to the policies which prescribe the relations that obtain, or are supposed to obtain, within the human organization and between the human organization and the technical organization.

2.22 The term "informal organization" will refer to the actual personal interrelations existing among the members of the organization which are not represented by, or are inadequately represented by, the formal organization.

2.212 and 2.222 The term "ideological organization" will refer to the systems of ideas and beliefs by means of which the values of both the formal and informal aspects of the social organization are expressed and the symbols around which these values are organized.

2.2121 The term "logic of cost" will refer to that system of ideas and beliefs by means of which the common economic purposes of the total organization are evaluated.

2.2122 The term "logic of efficiency" will refer to that system of ideas and beliefs by means of which the collaborative efforts of the members of the organization are evaluated.

2.2221 The term "logic of sentiments" will refer to that system of ideas and beliefs which expresses the values residing in the interhuman relations of the different groups within the plant.

### A CONDITION OF EQUILIBRIUM

The parts of the industrial plant as a social system are interrelated and interdependent. Any changes in one part of the social system are accompanied bv changes in other parts of the system. The parts of the system can be conceived of as being in a state of equilibrium, such that "if a small (not too great) modification different from that which will otherwise occur is impressed on the system, a reaction will at once appear tending toward the conditions that would have existed if the modification had not been impressed."[6]

Some parts of the system can change more rapidly than others. The technical organization can change more rapidly than the social organization; the formal organization can change more rapidly than the informal; the systems of beliefs and ideas can change more rapidly than the patterns of interaction and associated sentiments, of which these beliefs and ideas are an expression. In the disparity in the rates of change possible there exists a precondition for unbalance which may manifest itself in many forms.

In their studies the investigators identified two such possibilities of unbalance. One was the disparity in the rates of change possible in the technical organization, on the one hand, and the social organization, on the other. This condition was manifested in the workers' behavior by distrust and resistance to change. This resistance was expressed whenever changes were introduced too rapidly or without sufficient consideration of their social implications; in other words, whenever the workers were being asked to adjust themselves to new methods or systems which seemed to them to deprive their work of its customary social significance. In such situations it was evident that the social codes, customs, and routines of the worker could not be accommodated to the technical innovations introduced as quickly as the innovations themselves, in the form of new machines and processes, could be made. The codes, customs, and traditions of the worker are not the product of logic but are based on deeply rooted sentiments. Not only is any alteration of the existing social organization to which the worker has grown accustomed likely to produce sentiments of resistance to the change, but too rapid interference is likely to lead to feelings of frustration and an irrational exasperation with technical change in any form.

Another possibility of unbalance lies in the relation of the ideological organization to the actual work situation. The logics of the ideological organization express only some of the values of the social organization. They frequently fail to take into account not only the feelings and sentiments of people within the plant but also the spontaneous informal social groups which form at all levels of the organization. Thus they tend to become

6. For a discussion of equilibrium, see Pareto, V., *The Mind and Society*, Harcourt, Brace & Co., New York, 1935, pp. 1435–42. The quotation used above is Dr. L. J. Henderson's adaptation of Pareto's definition of equilibrium.

divorced from the concrete situation and to lead an independent existence. As a result of failing to distinguish the human situation as it is from the way it is formally and logically represented to be, many human problems are stated either in terms of the perversities of human nature or in terms of logical defects in the formal organization. The facts of social organization are ignored, and consequently the result in terms of diagnosis or remedy is bound to be inadequate.

It became clear to the investigators that the limits of human collaboration are determined far more by the informal than by the formal organization of the plant. Collaboration is not wholly a matter of logical organization. It presupposes social codes, conventions, traditions, and routine or customary ways of responding to situations. Without such basic codes or conventions, effective work relations are not possible. In the chapters that follow, the implications of this point of view for management and personnel practice will be considered.

CHESTER I. BARNARD

# Cooperation

## The theory of formal organization

An organization comes into being when (1) there are persons able to communicate with each other (2) who are willing to contribute action (3) to accomplish a common purpose. The elements of an organization are therefore (1) communication; (2) willingness to serve; and (3) common purpose. These elements are necessary and sufficient conditions initially, and they are found in all such organizations. The third element, purpose, is implicit in the definition. Willingness to serve, and communication, and the interdependence of the three elements in general, and their mutual dependence in specific cooperative systems, are matters of experience and observation.

For the continued existence of an organization either *effectiveness* or *efficiency* is necessary;[1] and the longer the life, the more necessary both are. The vitality of organizations lies in the willingness of individuals to contribute forces to the cooperative system. This willingness requires the belief that the purpose can be carried out, a faith that diminishes to the vanishing point as it appears that it is not in fact in process of being attained. Hence, when effectiveness ceases, willingness to contribute disappears. The continuance of willingness also depends upon the satisfactions that are secured by individual contributors in the process of carrying out the purpose. If the satisfactions do not exceed the sacrifices required, willingness disappears, and the condition is one of organization inefficiency. If the satisfactions exceed the sacrifices, willingness persists, and the condition is one of efficiency of organization.

In summary, then, the initial existence of an organization depends upon a combination of these elements appropriate to the external conditions at the moment. Its survival depends upon the maintenance of an equilibrium of the system. This equilibrium is primarily internal, a matter of proportions between the elements, but it is ultimately and basically an equilibrium between the system and the total situation external to it. This external equilibrium has two terms in it: first, the effectiveness of the organization, which comprises the relevance of its purpose to the environmental situation; and, second, its efficiency, which comprises the interchange between the organization and individuals. Thus the elements stated will each vary with external factors, and they are at the same time interdependent; when one is varied compensating variations must occur in the other if the system of

1. Editors' note: "An action is effective if it accomplishes its specific aim . . . it is efficient if it satisfies the motives of that aim, whether it is effective or not, and the process does not create offsetting dissatisfactions. We shall say that an action is inefficient if the motives are not satisfied, or offsetting dissatisfactions are incurred, even if it is effective" (*The Functions of the Executive*, p. 20).

Reprinted from *The Functions of the Executive*, pp. 82–95, 165–71, by permission of the publisher. 

which they are components is to remain in equilibrium, that is, is to persist or survive.

We may now appropriately consider these elements and their interrelations in some detail, having in mind the system as a whole. In later chapters we shall consider each element in greater detail with reference to its variability in dependence upon external factors, and the interrelations of the elements as determining the character of the executive functions.

## I

### I. WILLINGNESS TO COOPERATE

By definition there can be no organization without persons. However, as we have urged that it is not persons, but the services or acts or action or influences of persons, which should be treated as constituting organizations, it is clear that *willingness* of persons to contribute efforts to the cooperative system is indispensable.

There are a number of words and phrases in common use with reference to organization that reach back to the factor of individual willingness "Loyalty," "solidarity," "*esprit de corps*," "strength" of organization, are the chief. Although they are indefinite, they relate to intensity of attachment to the "cause," and are commonly understood to refer to something different from effectiveness, ability, or value of personal contributions. Thus "loyalty" is regarded as not necessarily related either to position, rank, fame, remuneration, or ability. It is vaguely recognized as an essential condition of organization.

Willingness, in the present connection, means self-abnegation, the surrender of control of personal conduct, the depersonalization of personal action. Its effect is cohesion of effort, a sticking together. Its immediate cause is the disposition necessary to "sticking together." Without this there can be no sustained personal effort as a contribution to cooperation. Activities cannot be coordinated unless there is first the disposition to make a personal act a contribution to an impersonal system of acts, one in which the individual gives up personal control of what he does.

The outstanding fact regarding willingness to contribute to a given specific formal organization is the indefinitely large range of variation in its intensity among individuals. If all those who may be considered potential contributors to an organization are arranged in order of willingness to serve it, the scale gradually descends from possibly intense willingness through neutral or zero willingness to intense unwillingness or opposition or hatred. The *preponderance of persons in a modern society always lies on the negative side* with reference to any particular existing or potential organization. Thus of the possible contributors only a small minority actually have a positive willingness. This is true of the largest and most comprehensive formal organizations, such as the large nations, the Catholic Church, etc. Most of the persons in existing society are either indifferent to or positively opposed to any single one of them; and if the smaller organizations subordinate to these major organizations are under consideration the minority becomes of course a much smaller proportion, and usually a nearly negligible proportion, of the conceivable total.

A second fact of almost equal importance is that the willingness of any individual cannot be constant in degree. It is necessarily intermittent and fluctuating. It can scarcely be said to exist during sleep, and is obviously diminished or exhausted by weariness, discomfort, etc., a conception that was well expressed by the saying "The spirit is willing, but the flesh is weak."

A corollary of the two propositions just stated is that for any given formal organization the number of persons of positive willingness to serve, but near the neutral or zero point, is always fluctuating. It follows that the aggregate willingness of potential contributors to any formal cooperative system is unstable—a fact that is evident from the history of all formal organizations.

Willingness to cooperate, positive or negative, is the expression of the net satisfactions or dissatisfactions experienced or anticipated by each individual in comparison with those experienced or anticipated through alternative opportunities. These alternative opportunities may be either personal and individualistic or those afforded by other organizations. That is, willingness to cooperate is the net effect, first, of the inducements to do so in conjunction with the sacrifices involved, and then in comparison with the practically available net satisfactions afforded by alternatives. The questions to be determined, if they were matters of logical reasoning, would be, first, whether the opportunity to cooperate grants any advantage to the individual as compared with independent action; and then, if so, whether that advantage is more or less than the advantage obtainable from some other cooperative opportunity. Thus, from the viewpoint of the individual, willingness is the joint effect of personal desires and reluctances; from the viewpoint of organization it is the joint effect of objective inducements offered and burdens imposed. The measure of this net result, however, is entirely individual, personal, and subjective. Hence, organizations depend upon the motives of individuals and the inducements that satisfy them.

### II. PURPOSE

Willingness to cooperate, except as a vague feeling or desire for association with others, cannot develop without an objective of cooperation. Unless there is such an objective it cannot be known or anticipated what specific efforts will be required of individuals, nor in many cases what satisfactions to them can be in prospect. Such an objective we denominate the "purpose" of an organization. The necessity of having a purpose is axiomatic, implicit in the words "system," "coordination," "cooperation." It is something that is clearly evident in many observed systems of cooperation, although it is often not formulated in words, and sometimes cannot be so formulated. In such cases what is observed is the direction or effect of the activities, from which purpose may be inferred.

A purpose does not incite cooperative activity unless it is accepted by those whose efforts will constitute the organization. Hence there is initially something like simultaneity in the acceptance of a purpose and willingness to cooperate.

It is important at this point to make clear that every cooperative purpose has in the view of each cooperating person two aspects which we call (*a*) the cooperative and (*b*) the subjective aspect, respectively.

(*a*) When the viewing of the purpose is an *act of cooperation*, it approximates that of detached observers from a special position of observation; this position is that of the interests of the organization; it is largely determined by organization knowledge, but is personally interpreted. For example, if five men are cooperating to move a stone from A to B, the moving of the stone is a different thing in the organization view of each of the five men involved. Note, however, that what moving the stone means to each man personally is not here in question, but what he thinks it means to the organization *as a whole*. This includes the significance of his own effort as an element in cooperation, and that of all others, in his view; but it is not at all a matter of satisfying a personal motive.

When the purpose is a physical result of simple character, the difference between the purpose as objectively viewed by a detached observer and the purpose as viewed by each person cooperating *as an act of cooperation* is ordinarily not large or important, and the different cooperative views of the persons cooperating are correspondingly similar. Even in such cases the attentive observer will detect differences that result in disputes, errors of action, etc., even though no *personal* interest is implicated. But when the purpose is less tangible—for example, in religious cooperation—the difference between objective purpose and purpose as cooperatively viewed by each person is often seen ultimately to result in disruption.

We may say, then, that a purpose can serve as an element of a cooperative system only so long as the participants do not recognize that there are serious divergences of their understanding of that purpose as the object of cooperation. If in fact there is important difference between the aspects of the purpose as objectively and as cooperatively viewed, the divergencies become quickly evident when the purpose is concrete, tangible, physical; but when the purpose is general, intangible, and of sentimental character, the divergencies can be very wide yet not be recognized. Hence, an objective purpose that can serve as the basis for a cooperative system is one that is *believed* by the contributors (or potential contributors) to it to be the determined purpose of the organization. The inculcation of belief in the real existence of a common purpose is an essential executive function. It explains much educational and so-called morale work in political, industrial, and religious organizations that is so often otherwise inexplicable.

(*b*) Going back to the illustration of five men moving a stone, we have noted "that what moving the stone means to each man personally is not here in question, but what he thinks it means to the *organization as a whole*." The distinction emphasized is of first importance. It suggests the fact that every participant in an organization may be regarded as having a dual personality—an organization personality and an individual personality. Strictly speaking, an organization purpose has directly no meaning for the individual. What has meaning for him is the organization's relation to him—what burdens it imposes, what benefits it confers. In referring to the aspects of purpose as cooperatively viewed, we are alluding to the *organization* personality of individuals. In many cases the two personalities are so clearly developed that they are quite apparent. In military action individual conduct may be so dominated by organization personality that it is utterly contradictory of what personal motivation would require. It has been observed of many men that their private conduct is entirely inconsistent with official conduct, although they seem completely unaware of the fact. Often it will be observed that participants in political, patriotic, or religious organizations will accept derogatory treatment of their personal conduct, including the assertion that it is inconsistent with their organization obligations, while they will become incensed at the slightest derogation of the tenets or doctrines of their organization, even though they profess not to understand them. There are innumerable other cases, however, in which almost no organization personality may be said to exist. These are cases in which personal relationship with the cooperative system is momentary or at the margin of willingness to participate.

In other words we have clearly to distinguish between organization purpose and individual motive. It is frequently assumed in reasoning about organizations that common purpose and individual motive are or should be identical. With the exception noted below, this is never the case; and under modern conditions it rarely even appears to be the case. Individual motive is necessarily an internal, personal, subjective thing; common purpose is necessarily an external, impersonal, objective thing even though the individual interpretation of it is subjective. The one exception to this general rule, an important one, is that the accomplishment of an organization purpose becomes itself a source of personal satisfaction and a motive for many individuals in many organizations. It is rare, however, if ever, and then I think only in connection with family, patriotic, and religious organizations under special conditions, that organization purpose becomes or can become the *only* or even the major individual motive.

Finally it should be noted that, once established, organizations change their unifying purposes. They tend to perpetuate themselves; and in the effort to survive may change the reasons for existence. I shall later make clearer that in this lies an important aspect of executive functions.

### III. COMMUNICATION

The possibility of accomplishing a common purpose and the existence of persons whose desires might constitute motives for contributing toward such a common purpose are the opposite poles of the system of cooperative effort. The process by which these potentialities become dynamic is that of communication. Obviously a common purpose must be commonly known, and to be known must be in some way communicated. With some exceptions, verbal communication between men is the method by which this is accomplished. Similarly, though under crude and obvious conditions not to the same extent, inducements to persons depend upon communication to them.

The method of communication centers in language, oral and written. On its crudest side, motions or actions that are of obvious meaning when observed are sufficient for communication without deliberate attempt to communicate; and signaling by various methods is an important method in much cooperative activity. On the other side, both in primitive and in highly complex civilization "observational feeling" is likewise an important aspect of communication.[2] I do not think it is generally so

2. The phrase "observational feeling" is of my coining. The point is not sufficiently developed, and probably has not been adequately studied by anyone. I take it to be at least in part involved in group action not incited by any "overt" or verbal communication. The cases known to me from the primitive field are those reported by W. H. R. Rivers on pp. 94–97 of his *Instinct and the Unconscious* (2nd edition, Cambridge University Press, 1924), with reference to Polynesia and Melanesia. One case is summarized by F. C. Bartlett, in *Remembering* (Cambridge University Press, 1932), at p. 297. Rivers states in substance that in some of the relatively small groups decisions are often arrived at and acted upon without having ever been formulated by anybody.

I have observed on innumerable occasions apparent

recognized. It is necessary because of the limitations of language and the differences in the linguistic capacities of those who use language. A very large element in special experience and training and in continuity of individual association is the ability to understand without words, not merely the situation or conditions, but the *intention*.

The techniques of communication are an important part of any organization and are the preeminent problems of many. The absence of a suitable technique of communication would eliminate the possibility of adopting some purposes as a basis for organization. Communication technique shapes the form and the internal economy of organization. This will be evident at once if one visualizes the attempt to do many things now accomplished by small organizations if each "member" spoke a different language. Similarly, many technical functions could hardly be carried on without special codes; for example, engineering or chemical work. In an exhaustive theory of organization, communication would occupy a central place, because the structure, extensiveness, and scope of organization are almost entirely determined by communication techniques. . . .

## II

### I. EFFECTIVENESS OF COOPERATION

The continuance of an organization depends upon its ability to carry out its purpose. This clearly depends jointly upon the appropriateness of its action and upon the conditions of its environment. In other words, effectiveness is primarily a matter of technological processes. This is quite obvious in ordinary cases of purpose to accomplish a physical objective, such as building a bridge. When the objective is non-physical, as is the case with religious and social organizations, it is not so obvious.

It should be noted that a paradox is involved in this matter. An organization must disintegrate if it cannot accomplish its purpose. It also destroys itself by accomplishing its purpose. A very large number of successful organizations come into being and then disappear for this reason. Hence most continuous organizations require repeated adoption of new purposes. This is concealed from everyday recognition by the practice of generalizing a complex series of specific purposes under one term, stated to be "*the* purpose" of this organization. This is strikingly true in the case of governmental and public utility organizations when the purpose is stated to be a particular kind of service through a period of years. It is apparent that their real purposes are not abstractions called "service" but specific acts of service. A manufacturing organization is said to exist to make, say, shoes; this is its "purpose." But it is evident that not making shoes in general but making specific shoes from day to day is its series of purposes. This process of generalization, however, provides in advance for the approximate definition of new purposes automatically—so automatically that the generalization is normally substituted in our minds for the concrete performances that are the real purposes. Failure to be effective is, then, a real cause of disintegration; but failure to provide for the decisions resulting in the adoption of new purposes would have the same result. Hence the generalization of purpose which can only be defined concretely by day-to-day events is a vital aspect of permanent organization.

unanimity of decision of equals in conferences to quit discussion without a word to that effect being spoken. Often the action is initiated apparently by someone's rising; but as this frequently occurs in such groups *without* the termination of the meeting, more than mere rising is involved. "Observational feeling," I think, avoids the notion of anything "occult."

### II. ORGANIZATION EFFICIENCY

It has already been stated that "efficiency" as conceived in this treatise is not used in the specialized and limited sense of ordinary industrial practice or in the restricted sense applicable to technological processes. So-called "practical" efficiency has little meaning, for example, as applied to many organizations such as religious organizations.

Efficiency of effort in the fundamental sense with which we are here concerned is efficiency relative to the securing of necessary personal contributions to the cooperative system. The life of an organization depends upon its ability to secure and maintain the personal contributions of energy (including the transfer of control of materials or money equivalent) necessary to effect its purposes. This ability is a composite of perhaps many efficiencies and inefficiencies in the narrow senses of these words, and it is often the case that inefficiency in some respect can be treated as the cause of total failure, in the sense that if corrected success would then be possible. But certainly in most organization—social, political, national, religious—nothing but the absolute test of survival is significant objectively; there is no basis for comparison of the efficiencies of separate aspects.

. . . The emphasis now is on the view that efficiency of organization is its capacity to offer effective inducements in sufficient quantity to maintain the equilibrium of the system. It is efficiency in this sense and not the efficiency of material productiveness which maintains the vitality of organizations. There are many organizations of great power and permanency in which the idea of productive efficiency is utterly meaningless because there is no material production. Churches, patriotic societies, scientific societies, theatrical and musical organizations, are cases where the original flow of *material* inducements is toward the organization, not from it—a flow necessary to provide resources with which to supply material inducements to the small minority who require them in such organizations.

In those cases where the primary purpose of organization is the production of material things, insufficiency with respect to the nonmaterial inducements leads to the attempt to substitute material inducements for the nonmaterial. Under favorable circumstances, to a limited degree, and for a limited time, this substitution may be effective. But to me, at least, it appears utterly contrary to the nature of men to be sufficiently induced by material or monetary considerations to contribute enough effort to a cooperative system to enable it to be productively efficient to the degree necessary for persistence over an extended period.

If these things are true, then even in purely economic enterprises efficiency in the offering of noneconomic inducements may be as vital as productive efficiency. Perhaps the word efficiency as applied to such noneconomic inducements as I have given for illustration will seem strange and forced. This, I think, can only be because we are accustomed to use the word in a specialized sense.

The noneconomic inducements are as difficult to offer as others under many circumstances. To establish conditions under which individual pride of craft and of accomplishment can be secured without destroying the material economy of standardized production in cooperative operation is a problem in real efficiency. To maintain a character of personnel that is an attractive condition of employment involves a delicate art and much insight in the selection (and rejection) of personal services offered, whether the standard of quality be high or low. To have an organization that lends prestige and secures the loyalty of desirable persons is a complex and difficult task in efficiency—in all-round efficiency, not one-sided efficiency. It is for these reasons that good organizations—commercial, governmental, military, academic, and others—will be observed to devote great attention and sometimes great expense of money to the noneconomic inducements, because they are indispensable to fundamental efficiency, as well as to effectiveness in many cases.

The theory of organization set forth in this chapter is derived from the study of organizations which are exceedingly complex, although it is stated in terms of ideal simple organizations. The temptation is to assume that, in the more complex organizations which we meet in our actual social life, the effect of complexity is to modify or qualify the theory. This appears not to be the case. Organization, simple or complex, is always *an impersonal system of coordinated human efforts*; always there is purpose as the coordinating and unifying principle; always there is the indispensable ability to communicate, always the necessity for personal willingness, and for effectiveness and efficiency in maintaining the integrity of purpose and the continuity of contributions. Complexity appears to modify the quality and form of these elements and of the balance between them; but fundamentally the same principles that govern simple organizations may be conceived as governing the structure of complex organizations, which are composite systems.

* * * * * *

## The theory of authority

The necessity of the assent of the individual to establish authority *for him* is inescapable. A person can and will accept a communication as authoritative only when four conditions simultaneously obtain: (*a*) he can and does understand the communication; (*b*) *at the time of his decision* he believes that it is not inconsistent with the purpose of the organization; (*c*) *at the time of his decision*, he believes it to be compatible with his personal interest as a whole; and (*d*) he is able mentally and physically to comply with it.

*a*) A communication that cannot be understood *can* have no authority. An order issued, for example, in a language not intelligible to the recipient is no order at all—no one would so regard it. Now, many orders are exceedingly difficult to understand. They are often necessarily stated in general terms, and the persons who issued them could not themselves apply them under many conditions. Until interpreted they have no meaning. The recipient either must disregard them or merely do anything in the hope that that is compliance.

Hence, a considerable part of administrative work consists in the interpretation and reinterpretation of orders in their application to concrete circumstances that were not or could not be taken into account initially.

*b*) A communication believed by the recipient to be incompatible with the purpose of the organization, as he understands it, could not be accepted. Action would be frustrated by cross purposes. The most common practical example is that involved in conflicts of orders. They are not rare. An intelligent person will deny the authority of that one which contradicts the purpose of the effort as *he* understands it. In extreme cases many individuals would be virtually paralyzed by conflicting orders. They would be literally unable to comply—for example, an employee of a water system ordered to blow up an essential pump, or soldiers ordered to shoot their own comrades. I suppose all experienced executives know that when it is necessary to issue orders that will appear to the recipients to be contrary to the main purpose, especially as exemplified in prior habitual practice, it is usually necessary and always advisable, if practicable, to explain or demonstrate why the appearance of conflict is an illusion. Otherwise the orders are likely not to be executed, or to be executed inadequately.

*c*) If a communication is believed to involve a burden that destroys the net advantage of connection with the organization, there no longer would remain a net inducement to the individual to contribute to it. The existence of a net inducement is the only reason for accepting *any* order as having authority. Hence, if such an order is received it must be disobeyed (evaded in the more usual cases) as utterly inconsistent with personal motives that are the basis of accepting any orders at all. Cases of voluntary resignation from all sorts of organizations are common for this sole reason. Malingering and intentional lack of dependability are the more usual methods.

*d*) If a person is unable to comply with an order, obviously it must be disobeyed, or, better, disregarded. To order a man who cannot swim to swim a river is a sufficient case. Such extreme cases are not frequent; but they occur. The more usual case is to order a man to do things only a little beyond his capacity; but a little impossible is still impossible.

Naturally the reader will ask: How is it possible to secure such important and enduring cooperation as we observe if in principle and in fact the determination of authority lies with the subordinate individual? It is possible because the decisions of individuals occur under the following conditions: (*a*) orders that are deliberately issued in enduring organizations usually comply with the four conditions mentioned above; (*b*) there exists a "zone of indifference" in each individual within which orders are acceptable without conscious questioning of their authority; (*c*) the interests of the persons who contribute to an organization as a group result in the exercise of an influence on the subject, or on the attitude of the individual, that maintains a certain stability of this zone of indifference.

*a*) There is no principle of executive conduct better established in good organizations than that orders will not be issued that cannot or will not be obeyed. Executives and most persons of experience who have thought about it know that to do so destroys authority, discipline, and morale.[3] For

3. Barring relatively few individual cases, when the attitude of the individual indicates in advance likelihood of disobedience (either before or after connection with the organization), the connection is terminated or refused before the formal question arises.

It seems advisable to add a caution here against interpreting the exposition in terms of "democracy," whether in governmental, religious, or industrial organizations. The dogmatic assertion that "democracy" or "democratic methods" are (or are not) in accordance with the principles here discussed is not tenable. As will be more evident after the consideration of objective authority, the issues involved are much too complex and subtle to be taken into account in *any* formal scheme. Under many conditions in the political, religious, and industrial fields democratic

reasons to be stated shortly, this principle cannot ordinarily be formally admitted, or at least cannot be professed. When it appears necessary to issue orders which are initially or apparently unacceptable, either careful preliminary education, or persuasive efforts, or the prior offering of effective inducements will be made, so that the issue will not be raised, the denial of authority will not occur, and orders will be obeyed. It is generally recognized that those who least understand this fact—newly appointed minor or "first line" executives—are often guilty of "disorganizing" their groups for this reason, as do experienced executives who lose self-control or become unbalanced by a delusion of power or for some other reason. Inexperienced persons take literally the current notions of authority and are then said "not to know how to use authority" or "to abuse authority." Their superiors often profess the same beliefs about authority in the abstract, but their successful practice is easily observed to be inconsistent with their professions.

*b*) The phrase "zone of indifference" may be explained as follows: If all the orders for actions reasonably practicable be arranged in the order of their acceptability to the person affected, it may be conceived that there are a number which are clearly unacceptable, that is, which certainly will not be obeyed; there is another group somewhat more or less on the neutral line, that is, either barely acceptable or barely unacceptable; and a third group unquestionably acceptable. This last group lies within the "zone of indifference." The person affected will accept orders lying within this zone and is relatively indifferent as to what the order is so far as the question of authority is concerned. Such an order lies within the range that in a general way was anticipated at time of undertaking the connection with the organization. For example, if a soldier enlists, whether voluntarily or not, in an army in which the men are ordinarily moved about within a certain broad region, it is a matter of indifference whether the order be to go to A or B, C or D, and so on; and goings to A, B, C, D, etc., are in the zone of indifference.

The zone of indifference will be wider or narrower depending upon the degree to which the inducements exceed the burdens and sacrifices which determine the individual's adhesion to the organization. It follows that the range of orders that will be accepted will be very limited among those who are barely induced to contribute to the system.

*c*) Since the efficiency of organization is affected by the degree to which individuals assent to orders, denying the authority of an organization communication is a threat to the interests of all individuals who derive a net advantage from their connection with the organization, unless the orders are unacceptable to them also. Accordingly, at any given time there is among most of the contributors an active personal interest in the maintenance of the authority of all orders which to them are within the zone of indifference. The maintenance of this interest is largely a function of informal organization. Its expression goes under the names of "public opinion," "organization opinion," "feeling in the ranks," "group attitude," etc. Thus the common sense of the community informally arrived at affects the attitude of individuals, and makes them, as individuals, loath to question authority that is within or near the zone of indifference. The formal statement of this common sense is the fiction that authority comes down from above, from the general to the particular. This fiction merely establishes a presumption among individuals in favor of the acceptability of orders from superiors, enabling them to avoid making issues of such orders without incurring a sense of personal subserviency or a loss

processes create artificial questions of more or less logical character, in place of the real questions, which are matters of feeling and appropriateness and of informal organization. By oversimplification of issues this may destroy objective authority. No doubt in many situations formal democratic processes may be an important element in the maintenance of authority, i.e., of organization cohesion, but may in other situations be disruptive, and probably never could be, in themselves, sufficient. On the other hand the solidarity of some cooperative systems (General Harbord's army, for example) under many conditions may be unexcelled, though requiring formally autocratic processes.

Moreover, it should never be forgotten that authority in the aggregate arises from *all* the contributors to a cooperative system, and that the weighting to be attributed to the attitude of individuals varies. It is often forgotten that in industrial (or political) organizations measures which are acceptable at the bottom may be quite unacceptable to the substantial proportion of contributors who are executives, and who will no more perform their essential functions than will others, if the conditions are, to them, impossible. The point to be emphasized is that the maintenance of the contributions necessary to the endurance of an organization requires the authority of *all* essential contributors.

of personal or individual status with their fellows.

Thus the contributors are willing to maintain the authority of communications because, where care is taken to see that only acceptable communications in general are issued, most of them fall within the zone of personal indifference; and because communal sense influences the motives of most contributors most of the time. The practical instrument of this sense is the fiction of superior authority, which makes it possible normally to treat a personal question impersonally.

The fiction[4] of superior authority is necessary for two main reasons:

1) It is the process by which the individual delegates upward, or to the organization, responsibility for what is an organization decision—an action which is depersonalized by the fact of its coordinate character. This means that if an instruction is disregarded, an executive's risk of being wrong must be accepted, a risk that the individual cannot and usually will not take unless in fact his position is at least as good as that of another with respect to correct appraisal of the relevant situation. Most persons are disposed to grant authority because they dislike the personal responsibility which they otherwise accept, especially when they are not in a good position to accept it. The practical difficulties in the operation of organization seldom lie in the excessive desire of individuals to assume responsibility for the organization action of themselves or others, but rather lie in the reluctance to take responsibility for their own actions in organization.

2) The fiction gives impersonal notice that what is at stake is the good of the organization. If objective authority is flouted for arbitrary or merely temperamental reasons, if, in other words, there is deliberate attempt to twist an organization requirement to personal advantage, rather than properly to safeguard a substantial personal interest, then there is a deliberate attack on the organization itself. To remain outside an organization is not necessarily to be more than not friendly or not interested. To fail in an obligation intentionally is an act of hostility. This no organization can permit; and it must respond with punitive action if it can, even to the point of incarcerating or executing the culprit. This is rather generally the case where a person has agreed in advance in general what he will do. Leaving an organization in the lurch is not often tolerable.

4. The word "fiction" is used because from the standpoint of logical construction it merely explains overt acts. Either as a superior officer or as a subordinate, however, I know nothing that I actually regard as more "real" than "authority."

TALCOTT PARSONS

# Social Systems

For the purposes of this article the term "organization" will be used to refer to a broad type of collectivity which has assumed a particularly important place in modern industrial societies—the type to which the term "bureaucracy" is most often applied. Familiar examples are the governmental bureau or department, the business firm (especially above a certain size), the university, and the hospital. It is by now almost a commonplace that there are features common to all these types of organization which cut across the ordinary distinctions between the social science disciplines. Something is lost if study of the firm is left only to economists, of governmental organizations to political scientists, and of schools and universities to "educationists."

The study of organization in the present sense is thus only part of the study of social structure as that term is generally used by sociologists (or of "social organization" as ordinarily used by social anthropologists). A family is only partly an organization; most other kinship groups are even less so. The same is certainly true of local communities, regional subsocieties, and of a society as a whole conceived, for example, as a nation. On other levels, informal work groups, cliques of friends, and so on, are not in this technical sense organizations.

Reprinted from *Structure and Process in Modern Societies*, Chapter 1, "A Sociological Approach to the Theory of Organizations," pp. 16–19, 22–28, 41–47, 56–58, by permission of the author and The Macmillan Company. (©1960 by The Free Press of Glencoe.)

## The concept of organization

As a formal analytical point of reference, *primacy of orientation to the attainment of a specific goal* is used as the defining characteristic of an organization which distinguishes it from other types of social systems. This criterion has implications for both the external relations and the internal structure of the system referred to here as an organization.

The attainment of a goal is defined as a *relation* between a system (in this case a social system) and the relevant parts of the external situation in which it acts or operates. This relation can be conceived as the maximization, relative to the relevant conditions such as costs and obstacles, of some category of *output* of the system to objects or systems in the external situation. These considerations yield a further important criterion of an organization. An organization is a system which, as the attainment of its goal, "produces" an identifiable something which can be utilized in some way by another system; that is, the output of the organization is, for some other system, an input. In the case of an organization with economic primacy, this output may be a class of goods or services which are either consumable or serve as instruments for a further phase of the production process by other organizations. In the case of a government agency the output may be a class of regulatory decisions; in that of an educational organization it may be a certain type of "trained capacity" on the part of the students who have been subjected to its influence. In any of these cases there must be a set of consequences of the processes which go on within the organization, which make a difference to the functioning of some other subsystem of the society; that is, without the production of certain goods the consuming unit must behave differently, i.e., suffer a "deprivation."

The availability, to the unit succeeding the organization in the series, of the organization's output must be subject to some sort of terms, the settlement of which is analyzable in the general framework of the ideas of contract or exchange. Thus in the familiar case the economic producer "sells" his product for a money prize which in turn serves as a medium for procuring the factors of production, most directly labor services, necessary for further stages of the productive process. It is thus assumed that in the case of all organizations there is something analogous to a "market" for the output which constitutes the attainment of its goal (what Chester I. Barnard calls "organization purpose"); and that directly, and perhaps also indirectly, there is some kind of exchange of this for entities which (as inputs into it) are important means for the organization to carry out its function in the larger system. The exchange of output for input at the boundary defined by the attainment of the goal of an organization need not be the only important boundary-exchange of the organization as a system. It is, however, the one most directly involved in defining the primary characteristics of the organization. Others will be discussed later.

The existence of organizations as the concept is here set forth is a consequence of the division of labor in society. Where both the "production" of specialized outputs and their consumption or ultimate utilization occur within the same structural unit, there is no need for the differentiation of specialized organizations. Primitive societies, in so far as their units are "self-sufficient" in both economic and other senses, generally do not have clear-cut differentiated organizations in the present sense.

In its internal reference, the primacy of goal-attainment among the functions of a social system gives priority to those processes most directly involved with the success or failure of goal-oriented endeavors. This means essentially the decision-making process, which controls the utilization of the resources of the system as a whole in the interest of the goal, and the processes by which those responsible for such decisions can count on the mobilization of these resources in the interest of a goal. These mechanisms of mobilization constitute what we ordinarily think of as the development of power in a political sense.

What from the point of view of the organization in question is its specified goal is, from the point of view of the larger system of which it is a differentiated part or subsystem, a specialized or differentiated function. This relationship is the primary link between an organization and the larger system of which it is a part, and provides a basis for the classification of types of organization. However, it cannot be the only important link.

This article will attempt to analyze both this link and the other principal ones, using as a point of departure the treatment of the organization as a social system. First, it will be treated as a system which is characterized by all the properties which are essential to any social system. Secondly, it will be treated as a functionally differentiated subsystem of a larger social system. Hence it will be the other subsystems of the larger one which constitute the situation or environment in which the organization operates. An organization, then, will have to be analyzed as the special type of social system organized about the primacy of interest in the attainment of a particular type of system goal. Certain of its special features will derive from goal-primacy in general and others from the primacy of the particular type of goal. Finally, the characteristics of the organization will be defined by the kind of situation in which it has to operate, which will consist of the relations obtaining between it and the other specialized subsystems of the larger system of which it is a part. The latter can for most purposes be assumed to be a society.

* * * * * *

## The mobilization of fluid resources

The resources which an organization must utilize are, given the social structure of the situation in which it functions, the factors of production as these concepts are used in economic theory. They are land, labor, capital, and "organization" in a somewhat different sense from that used mainly in this paper. This possibly confusing terminological duplication is retained here because organization as a factor is commonly referred to in economic theory.

The factor of land stands on a somewhat different level from the other three. If we treat an organization, for purposes of analysis, as an already established and going concern, then, like any other social system, we can think of it as being in control of certain facilities for access to which it is not dependent on the maintenance of short-run economic sanctions. It has full ownership of certain physical facilities such as physical land and relatively nondepreciating or nonobsolescing building. It may have certain traditions, particularly involving technical know-how factors which are not directly involved in the market nexus. The more fully the market nexus is developed, however, the less can it be said that an organization has very important assets which are withdrawn from the market. Even sites of long operation can be sold and new locations found and even the most deeply committed personnel may resign to take other positions or retire, and in either case have to be replaced through the labor market. The core of this aspect of the "land" complex is thus a set of commitments of resources on value grounds.

The two most fluid factors, however, are labor and capital in the economic sense. The overwhelming bulk of personal service takes place in occupational roles. This means that it is *contracted for* on some sector of the labor market. It is not based on ascription of status, through kinship or otherwise, but depends on the specific terms settled between the management of the organization and the incumbent. There are, of course, many types of contract of employment. Some variations concern the agents involved in the settlement of terms; for example, collective bargaining is very different from individual bargaining. Others concern the duration of commitment, varying all the way from a casual relation terminable at will, to a tenure appointment.

But most important, only in a limiting case are the specific *ad hoc* terms—balancing specifically defined services against specific monetary remuneration—anything like exhaustive of the empirically important factors involved in the contract of employment. The labor market cannot, in the economic sense, closely approach being a "perfect market." It has different degrees and types of imperfection according to whether the employer is one or another type of organization and according to what type of human service is involved. A few of these differences will be noted in later illustrations. Here the essential point is that, with the differentiation of functionally specified organizations from the matrix of diffuse social groupings, such organizations become increasingly dependent on explicit contracts of employment for their human services.

Attention may be called to one particularly important differentiation among types of relation existing between the performer of services and recipients of the ultimate "product." In the typical case of manufacturing industry the typical worker works within the organization. The end result is a physical commodity which is then sold to consumers. The worker has no personal contact with the customer of the firm; indeed no representative of the firm need have such contact except to arrange the settlement of the terms of sale. Where, however, the "product" is a personal service, the situation is quite different; the worker must have personal contact with the consumer during the actual performance of the service.

One way in which service can be organized is the case where neither performer nor "customer" belongs to an organization. Private professional practice is a type case, and doctor and patient, for example, come to constitute a small-scale solidary collectivity of their own. This is the main basis of the sliding scale as a pattern of remuneration. A second mode of organization is the one which assimilates the provision of service to the normal pattern involved in the production of physical commodities; the recipient is a "customer" who pays on a value-of-service basis, with prices determined by commercial competition. This pattern is approached in the case of such services as barbering.

But particularly in the case of professional services there is another very important pattern, where the recipient of the service becomes an operative member of the service-providing organization. The school, university, and hospital are type cases illustrating this pattern. The phrase "member of the university" definitely includes students. The faculty are in a sense dually employed, on the one hand by their students, on the other by the university administration. The transition is particularly clear in the case of the hospital. In private practice the patient is unequivocally the "employer." But in hospital practice the hospital organization employs a professional staff on behalf of the patients, as it were. This taking of the customer *into* the organization has important implication for the nature of the organization.

In a society like ours the requirements of an organization for fluid resources are in one sense and on one level overwhelmingly met through financing, i.e., through the provision of money funds at the disposal of the organization (cf. Weber, *Theory of Social and Economic Organization* [1947], ch. iii). This applies both to physical facilities, equipment, materials, buildings, and to the employment of human services—indeed also to cultural resources in that the rights to use patented processes may be bought. Hence the availability of adequate financing is always a vital problem for every organization operating in a monetary economy no matter what its goal-type may be; it is as vital for churches, symphony orchestras, and universities as it is for business firms.

The mechanisms through which financial resources are made available differ enormously, however, with different types of organization. All except the "purest" charitable organizations depend to some extent on the returns they receive for purveying some kind of a product, be it a commodity, or a service like education or music. But even within this range there is an enormous variation in the adequacy of this return for fully meeting financial needs. The business firm is at one pole in this respect. Its normal expectation is that in the long run it will be able to finance itself adequately from the proceeds of sales. But even here this is true only in the long run; investment of capital in anticipation of future proceeds is of course one of the most important mechanisms in our society.

Two other important mechanisms are taxation and voluntary contributions. In a "free enterprise" economy the general principle governing financing by taxation is that organizations will be supported out of taxation (1) if the goal is regarded as important enough but organizations devoted to it cannot be made to "pay" as private enterprises by providing the service on a commercial basis, e.g., the care of large numbers of persons from the lower income groups who (by current standards) need to be hospitalized for mental illnesses, or (2) if the *ways* in which the services would be provided by private enterprise might jeopardize the public interest, e.g., the provision of military force for the national defense might conceivably be contracted out, but placing control of force to this degree in private hands would constitute too serious a threat to the political stability of the society. Others in these categories are left to the "voluntary" principle, if they are publicly sanctioned, generally in the form of "nonprofit" organizations.

It is important to note that financing of organizations is in general "affected with a public interest" and is in some degree to be regarded as an exercise of political power. This consideration derives from the character of an organization as a goal-directed social system. Every subgoal within the society must to some degree be integrated with the goal-structure of the society as a whole, and it is with this societal goal-structure that political institutions are above all concerned.[1]

## The concept of organization

The last of the four factors of production is what certain economists, notably Alfred Marshall, have called "organization" in the technical sense referred to above. This refers to the function of *combining* the factors of production in such ways as to facilitate the effective attainment of the organization's goal (in our general sense, in its "economic" or factor-consuming aspects). Its input into the organization stands on a level different from that of labor services and financing since it does not concern the direct facilities for carrying out defined functions in a relatively routine manner, but instead concerns readjustment in the patterns of organization itself. It is, therefore, primarily significant in the longer run perspective, and it is involved in processes of structural change in the organization. In its business reference it is in part what J. A. Schumpeter (cf. *The Theory of Economic Development* [1934]) referred to as "entrepreneurship." Organization in this economic sense is, however, an essential factor

1. This general thesis of the relation between financing and political power and the public interest has been developed by Parsons and Smelser, *Economy and Society* (1956), especially in chapters ii and iii.

in *all* organizational functioning. It necessarily plays a central part in the "founding" stages of any organization. From time to time it is important in later stages, since the kinds of adjustments to changing situations which are possible through the routine mechanisms of recruitment of labor services, and through the various devices for securing adequate financial resources, prove to be inadequate; hence a more fundamental structural change in the organization becomes necessary or desirable. This change would, in the present frame of reference, require a special input of the factor of organization in this technical sense.

The more generalized equivalent of the land factor is treated, except for the longest-run and most profound social changes, as the most constant reference point of all; its essential reference base is the stability of the value system in terms of which the goal of the organization is defined and the commitments involved in it are legitimized. It is from this reference base that the norms defining the broadly expected types of mechanism in the other respects will be derived, particularly those most actively involved in short-run operations, namely the recruitment of human services through the labor market and the financing of the organization.

* * * * * *

## The problem of power

As seen in the analysis in the first section of this paper, the development of organizations is the principal mechanism by which, in a highly differentiated society, it is possible to "get things done," to achieve goals beyond the reach of the individual and under conditions which provide a relative maximization of effectiveness, in Chester Barnard's sense. Subject to the over-all control of an institutionalized value system in the society and its subsystems, the central phenomenon of organization is the mobilization of *power* for the attainment of the goals of the organization. The value system *legitimizes* the organization's goal, but it is only through power that its achievement can be made effective.

Seen in these terms, power is the generalized capacity to mobilize resources in the interest of attainment of a system goal. The generation and utilization of power constitutes one of the fundamental functional imperatives of any social system. Like any other major system function, except in the simplest systems, power becomes the focus of a set of specialized mechanisms. So far as these mechanisms themselves become organized to constitute a distinct subsystem of the society, we can speak of the "polity" as the system oriented to the generation and allocation of power.[2] The polity in this sense is parallel to the economy as that concept is ordinarily used in economic theory.

The generation and exercise of power is most conspicuous in relation to a goal which is dramatically and unequivocally a common goal for a whole society, such as victory in war. But in more everyday terms, the goal of the society can be said to be to "get the things done" which are approved in terms of its values as "worth doing" (the term "worth" may, of course, signify varying degrees of urgency). Hence we may speak of power as a generalized societal resource which is allocated to the attainment of a wide range of subgoals and to organizations as the agents of the attainment of such subgoals. Power is comparable to wealth, which, as a generalized societal resource, is allocated to many different societal subsystems for "consumption" or for "capital" use.

The power exercised in and by an organization is generated both outside and within the organization. Every organization, whatever the nature of its functional primacy—for example, manufacturing, or medical care—is part of the polity and a generator of power, but is also a recipient of the power generated at higher echelons in the polity.

The generation of power on any given level depends, as we see it, on four fundamental conditions. The first condition is the institutionalization of a value system which legitimizes both the goal of the organization and the principal patterns by which it functions in the attainment of that goal. The second condition is the regulation of the organization's procurement and decision-making processes through adherence to universalistic rules

2. The polity in this sense is *not* identical with government, which we interpret to be a complex of *organizations*. Government has other than political functions, and other organizations participate in the polity. We conceive of the relation of polity and government as approximately parallel to that between economy and business. Cf. Talcott Parsons and Neil Smelser, *Economy and Society* (*op. cit.*) ch. ii.

and to such institutions as authority and contract. It is on these bases that the organization establishes generalized claims to the loyal cooperation of its personnel and of persons outside the organization on whose cooperation it depends. The third condition is the command of the more detailed and day-to-day support of the persons whose cooperation is needed. The fourth is the command of necessary facilities, of which the primary category in our society is financial.

In our society the first condition has frequently become formalized through the privilege and practice of incorporation. This establishes a direct positive link with government and the legal system. Organization for the purpose at hand is formally "authorized," and certain powers and privileges are thereby conferred. The second condition is partly met by the legal regulation of all organizational activity, and partly by an informal reputation for integrity and "good practice" which in itself often becomes an organizational asset. The third and fourth conditions are met by the operative mechanisms of procurement of resources and the operative code previously described. Certain variations in the mechanisms by which this occurs in different types of organizations will be discussed presently.

The mobilization and utilization of power is the central focus of the operation of organizations, but by virtue of the fact that an organization is a social system, it is also dependent on all the other exigencies of such a system. The value component has already been discussed. The other two components are economic resources (centering on the problem of financing) and the command of loyalties (which underlies efficiency in Barnard's sense). Power helps to *command* these essentials, but their availability is not a function only of power but also of the ways in which the cognate activities of the organization mesh with the relevant features of the situation in which it functions. Thus the organization always to some extent "produces" economically valuable goods or services; the marketability of these products constitutes one central set of conditions of its operation. Similarly, the organization is always, through "informal" organization and otherwise, a focus of the relatively noncontingent loyalties of its personnel. The extent to which this is true and the basis on which it rests form another essential condition of the organization's functioning. Power as a factor operates to exploit advantages on these levels and to make up deficits; power never operates alone.

The scheme we have presented is characterized by a certain formal symmetry. The value system of the organization is treated as defining and legitimizing its goal. Each of the other three aspects, the adaptive mechanisms and those mechanisms of operative goal-attainment and the integration of the organization, is regulated by subvalues governing each of these three aspects of organizational functioning. Each primary type of resource input is regulated by a type of contractual pattern, e.g., employment and investment. Each part of the operative code is governed in turn by an aspect of authority, and finally each context of institutionalization is a way of defining, for those participating, the extent of "loyalty" owing to the organization as compared with other commitments.

## Classification of types of organization

Organizations are of course always part of a larger social structure of the society in which they occur. There is necessarily a certain variability among organizations which is a function of this wider societal matrix; an American organization is never quite like a British one even though they are nearly cognate in function. Discounting this type of variability, however, organizations may in the first instance be classified in terms of the *type of goal or function* about which they are organized. The same basic classification can be used for goal types which has been used earlier in dealing with the functions of a social system. Thus we may speak of adaptive goals, implementive goals, integrative goals, and pattern-maintenance goals. The reference is always to function in the *society* as a system.

Seen in these terms the principal broad types of organization are:

1. *Organizations oriented to economic production:* The type case in this category is the business firm. Production should be understood in the full economic sense as "adding value"; it is by no means confined to physical production, e.g., manufacturing. It has been emphasized several times that every organization contributes in some way to every primary function (if it is well integrated in the society); hence we can speak only of economic *primacy*, never of an organization as being exclu-

sively economic. This applies also to the other categories.

2. *Organizations oriented to political goals*, that is, to the attainment of valued goals and to the generation and allocation of power in the society: This category includes most organs of government, but in a society like ours, various other organizations are involved. The allocation of purchasing power through credit creation is an exercise of power in this sense; hence a good part of the banking system should be treated as residing in primarily political organizations. More generally, it seems legitimate to speak of incorporation as an allocation of power in a political sense; hence the corporate aspect of formal organizations generally is a political aspect.

3. *Integrative organizations:* These are organizations which on the societal level, contribute primarily to efficiency, not effectiveness. They concern the adjustment of conflicts and the direction of motivation to the fulfillment of institutionalized expectations. A substantial part of the functions of the courts and of the legal profession should be classed here. Political parties, whose function is the mobilization of support for those responsible for government operations, belong in this category, and, to a certain extent, "interest groups" belong here, too. Finally, those organizations that are primarily mechanisms of social control in the narrower sense, for example hospitals, are mainly integrative.

4. *Pattern-maintenance organizations:* The principal cases centering here are those with primarily "cultural," "educational," and "expressive" functions. Perhaps the most clearcut organizational examples are churches and schools. (Pattern maintenance is not here conceived to preclude creativity; hence research is included.) The arts so far as they give rise to organization also belong here. Kinship groups are ordinarily not primarily organizations in our technical sense, but in a society so highly differentiated as our own the nuclear family approaches more closely the characteristics of an organization than in other societies. As such it clearly belongs in the pattern-maintenance category.

This primary basis of classification can be used as the point of departure for a more detailed one, by further subdividing each of the primary types into lower other subsystems. Thus in the economic case the main bases of subclassification would include specialization in adaptive functions for the economy (financing), in goal attainment (production and marketing in a narrower sense), etc. Similar considerations will apply in the cases of the other primary types. In each of these cases a primary determinant of the type of organization is the kind of boundary interchange operating between the societal system in which the organization is primarily anchored and the contiguous subsystem. Thus from the point of view of the economy, production and marketing are the sources of the ultimate production of goods and services to the consumer and of the input of labor services into the economy. Both consumer and worker are anchored in the first instance in the household as part of the pattern-maintenance system. Organizations oriented primarily to consumption interests are necessarily different from those oriented primarily to the financing of capital expansion.

* * * * * *

## Conclusion

The principal aim of this paper has been to relate the analysis of "formal organizations" more closely than is customary to some categorizations available in general sociological theory. There is a tendency in our society to consider different types of organizations as belonging in the fields allocated to different academic disciplines; thus students of business organization are likely to be economists, those of governmental and military organization, political scientists, and so forth. This tendency to divide the field obscures both the importance of the common elements, and the *systematic* bases of the variations from one type to another.

The procedure of this paper has been first to attempt to define an organization by locating it systematically in the structure of the society in relation to other categories of social structure. It seemed appropriate to define an organization as a social system which is organized for the attainment of a particular type of goal; the attainment of that goal is at the same time the performance of a type of function on behalf of a more inclusive system, the society.

It proved possible to bring to bear a general classification of the functional imperatives of social systems and with this to identify the principal mechanisms necessary to bring about the attainment of the goal or the organization purpose. The classification used has proved its applicability both for the level of the total society and for that of the small group. The present application to an intermediate level further increases confidence in its generality.

The classification distinguishes four main categories: the value system which defines and legitimizes the goals of the organization, the adaptive mechanisms which concern mobilization of resources, the operative code concerned with the mechanisms of the direct process of goal implementation, and finally the integrative mechanisms. These four categories are specifications of categories which, as noted, have been used in a variety of other contexts for the analysis of structural differentiation and phases of process over time in social systems.

These categories were first used to analyze the main components in the structure of an organization—its value system defining the societal commitments on which its functioning depends; its mechanisms of procurement of resources; its operative mechanisms centering about decision making in the field of policy, allocation, and integration; and its institutional patterns which link the structure of the organization with the structure of the society as a whole. It has proved possible to spell out these considerations in ways which link directly with the well-known ways of dealing with the problems of organization in the relevant literature.

The same basic classification of the functional problems of social systems was used to establish points of reference for a classification of types of organization, and the broadest outline of a proposed classification was sketched. The capacity of the conceptual scheme to account for variations in the important features of organizations was then tested in a preliminary, illustrative way by a rapid survey of some of the principal features of business, military, and academic organizations.

In the nature of the case this essay has been subject to severe limitations. Such limitations are partly involved in the space available. More important, however, is the fact that the essay constitutes a preliminary attempt to approach this range of problems systematically in terms of this order of general theoretical analysis. The results seem to justify the hope that carrying such analysis further will help to codify our knowledge of organizations more systematically than has been the case before, and to link it more closely with knowledge of other types of social systems and of the social environment within which formal organizations must operate in a society like our own.

# Part Two

# Current Theoretical Perspectives

To distinguish precisely between classical and current theoretical perspectives would be an obviously arbitrary act. Differences in perspectives emerge gradually. In order to avoid comparisons best made on hindsight and after the crucial test of time and use, we have ordered the five essays in the present section on the basis of date of publication.

Functional theory has long held a prominent and important place in sociological work. Beginning with Robert Merton's classic delineation of the functional paradigm, this theoretical perspective has been applied to the study of virtually every sociological problem. It is appropriate, therefore, that we begin this section with a discussion of functional theory, for the transition from classical to current theoretical perspectives is reflected in the controversy surrounding this approach (see, for example, N. J. Demerath III and Richard Peterson, eds., *System, Change and Conflict* [New York: The Free Press, 1967]).

In the first selection, Blau modifies and extends Merton's original formulation and illustrates its potential for the study of organizational problems. Blau's central thesis is that bureaucratic organizations continually create conditions that eventually modify these structures. Functional analysis directs attention to the functional, dysfunctional, and unanticipated consequences of various organizational patterns for the total system and thus indicates potential modifications in organizational structure. Blau is critical of Merton's distinction between "function" and "dysfunction," maintaining that it rests ultimately upon value judgments. Rather than abandon this approach, however, Blau argues that functional analysis should take values into account by determining not merely objective consequences but also their evaluative significance for the participants involved. This is especially important in the study of organizations because of the greater precision with which such values specify organizational goals or objectives. Hence, the explicit and formal objectives of bureaucratic organizations can greatly facilitate functional analysis.

In the second selection, March and Simon focus upon the organizational member as a decision-maker and problem-solver. Their thesis is that the basic features of organizational structure derive from the characteristics of human problem-solving and rational choice. Central to the argument is the concept of "performance program," which refers to a highly complex and organized set of responses evoked from the organizational member by some organizational stimulus. In such situations, search and choice processes involved in problem-solving are very much abridged (the example is given of the sounding of a gong in a fire station and the resulting responses on the part of the firemen). The importance of "performance programs" for understanding organizational behavior results from the fact that such situations are very common. They account for a very large part of the behavior of all organizational participants, particularly for those persons in lower level and relatively routine positions. March and Simon conclude that knowledge of the performance programs of organizations (which is relatively easily obtained through conventional research methods) permits one to understand and predict in considerable detail the behaviors of large segments of the organizational members.

In the third selection, Etzioni provides a classification of organizaion types based upon compliance relationships. The kinds of power applied by the organization to the lower-level participants and the kinds of involvement in the organization evidenced by these participants form the basis for the typology. Three main organizational types, the "congruent" types, are: (*a*) *coercive organizations*, in which coercion is the means of control and high alienation exists among the participants; (*b*) *utilitarian organizations*, in which remunerative power and calculative involvement are characteristic; and (*c*) *normative organizations*, in which normative power and high commitment among the participants are found.

This typology is important and useful in facilitating the comparative study of organizations because it employs theoretical distinctions in the classification of organizations that override common-sense labels. Moreover, in the larger work from which this selection is taken, Etzioni demonstrates that a large number of organizational characteristics are related empirically to the different organizational types.

In the next selection, Blau uses exchange theory to illustrate how complex forms of social structure can emerge from simple face-to-face interaction. Blau defines the basic principles underlying social exchange as follows: (*a*) a person who supplies rewarding services to another person obligates that person; (*b*) to discharge this obligation, the second person, in turn, must furnish benefits to the first; (*c*) if both persons value what they receive from one other, they are both motivated to supply more of their own service.

The interesting aspect of social exchange for our purposes derives from the situation in which one person needs something another has to offer, but has nothing the other needs in exchange. Blau argues that one alternative available to the person needing help is to subordinate himself to the other and comply with his wishes and in his way reward the other with power. The person with power over the other(s) can make "fair" or "unfair" demands upon the other(s). The unfair exercise of power may give rise to opposition and rebellion, but the fair exercise of power may give rise to social approval. If the person has power over a *group* of others, collective approval serves to *legitimate* that power. Blau argues that legitimate authority is the fundamental basis of organization.

The relevance of the above for understanding organizational behavior stems from the fact that power is a major and central element of organizational life. Persons with power over subordinates in organizations hold officially designated superior positions. Hence, formal power holders in organizations can use the principles of social exchange to extend the limits of their official (and limited) authority. They may do this by failing to utilize all of the power at their disposal and/or by providing services to subordinates. In this way, they relinquish some of their official power in exchange for social obligations from their subordinates. The rewards subordinates receive from this pattern of supervision obligate them to reciprocate by complying with the superior's directives and requests. In this way, formal authority can be greatly extended within the formal structure of the organization.

In the final selection, Katz and Kahn draw attention to an important and relatively neglected aspect of organizational functioning—the relationship between the organization and its environment. These authors argue that organizational theory should focus upon the input, output, and functioning of the organization as a system. Organizations are defined as open systems, that is, both the input of energies and the conversion of organizational output into further energic input involve transactions between the organization and the environment. Katz and Kahn are therefore critical of those traditional descriptions which view the goals or objectives of the organization as reflecting the conscious purposes of the group or its leaders. Open-systems theory, on the other hand, directs attention to the diversity of methods for achieving objectives, the nature and functions of feedback mechanisms, the extent to which organizations are dependent upon inputs from the environment, and the methods by which this dependency can and does produce changes in organizational structure.

PETER M. BLAU

# Functional Theory

Data do not speak for themselves but only answer questions the investigator puts to them. Conceptions of functional analysis are used to organize the data of this study, taking as a starting point the conceptual scheme developed by Robert K. Merton.[1] The basic tenet of this theoretical framework is that the social consequences of phenomena, not merely their origins, must be taken into account in sociological inquiry. Specifically, their contribution to and interference with adjustment or functioning in the social structure must be examined. This approach helps clarify the relationships between seemingly disparate observations and the processes of structural change.

The first concept, that of function, directs the researcher to ascertain the consequences of a given phenomenon and to evaluate their significance for the structure. For example, statistical records provided superior officials with accurate information about the operations of their subordinates in both agencies studied. They supplied a rational basis for supervision, which was intended to improve operations. Did they actually fulfill this function?

It is possible to answer questions like this one empirically because the main organizational objectives in these agencies were clearly defined. This is a peculiar advantage of the analysis of bureaucratic structures, not shared by investigations of institutions that have not been deliberately established, where it is often impossible to find unequivocal standards for deciding whether a given consequence enhances structural adjustment. But in the employment agency an exact criterion for determining the function of statistical records existed, since its major objective was officially specified as locating jobs for clients. The finding that the introduction of statistical records increased the proportion of clients placed in jobs therefore indicates that these records served the function of improving operations.

1. Robert K. Merton, *Social Theory and Social Structure* (rev. ed.; New York: Free Press, 1957), pp. 19–84. Émile Durkheim, in 1895, was the first to set forth principles of functional analysis in the social sciences. See *Rules of Sociological Method* (Chicago: University of Chicago Press, 1938), pp. 89–124. Although Weber explicitly rejected this approach (*op. cit.*, pp. 102–7), his discussion of bureaucracy is implicitly a functional analysis. For further formulations of this theory, parts of which are antithetical to that followed here, see Bronislaw Malinowski, "Culture," in *Encylopaedia of the Social Sciences*, IV (1931), 621–645, and "The Group and the Individual in Functional Analysis," *American Journal of Sociology*, 44 (1939), 939–964; A. R. Radcliffe-Brown, "On the Concept of Function in Social Science," *American Anthropologist*, 37 (1935), 349–402, and "On Social Structure," *Journal of the Royal Anthropological Institute of Great Britain and Ireland*, 70 (1940), 1–12; Clyde Kluckhohn, *Navaho Witchcraft*, in Papers of the Peabody Museum of American Archeology and Ethnology, Harvard University, Vol. 22, No. 2 (Cambridge, Mass.: Peabody Museum, 1944); Talcott Parsons, *Essays in Sociological Theory* (New York: Free Press, 1949), pp. 3–41; and Marion J. Levy, Jr., *The Structure of Society* (Princeton, N.J.: Princeton University Press, 1952).

**Reprinted from *The Dynamics of Bureaucracy*, pp. 6–13, by permission of the author and publisher.** 

The second functional consideration is: What are the mechanisms of processes through which a contribution is effected? Originally, it may have seemed that statistical records promoted efficiency because the better-informed superior can correct deficiencies more easily by giving the appropriate directives to his subordinates. Actually, however, more complex processes were involved. . . . It suffices to state here that the official's knowledge that statistical records provided his superior with accurate information on his operations induced him to improve his performance *without* direct intervention of the superior.

Third, latent functions are the unanticipated consequences of social behavior that contribute to structural adjustment. The discussion of mechanisms assumes new significance for the analyst sensitized by this concept. The existence of statistical records, since it constrained officials to improve their performance on their own initiative, enabled supervisors to criticize subordinates less often than their responsibility for operations would otherwise require. One of them put it aptly by saying, "I let the figures speak for themselves." With fewer criticisms, more cordial relations between supervisor and subordinates could develop, a latent function of performance records.

The tracing of unanticipated consequences is especially important for the understanding of unofficial practices that appear, at first, irrational and irrelevant to operations. Why did officials, though rushed for time, voluntarily perform tasks for which they were not responsible? Why did some white officials, no less prejudiced than others, treat Negro clients more impartially? Why did many officials ridicule clients when among themselves? Why did the very officials least familiar with regulations most strongly object to their being replaced by new regulations? The examination of latent functions provides answers to such questions.

The distinction between manifest and latent function raises the problem of the significance of awareness. What difference does it make whether a contribution is effected by deliberate effort or unintentionally? At several points in this study two different practices will be examined that had virtually the same function, but in one case participants were aware of this consequence of their behavior, and in the other they were not. These comparisons will indicate how recognition influences the way in which, and the extent to which, a given function is served.

Fourth, since behavior patterns have not only beneficial results, attention must also be paid to "*dysfunctions*, those observed consequences which lessen the adaptation or adjustment of the system."[2] The introduction of statistical records in the employment agency, for instance, generated competition among officials and made them reluctant to part with the job openings needed for serving clients. A group of specialists had no job openings of their own but were expected to serve their clients by obtaining openings from their colleagues. Competitive officials, however, tended to refuse such cooperation. This made it most difficult for the specialists to discharge their duties. Record-keeping was dysfunctional for the adjustment among officials and for providing employment service to the clients of the specialists.

The study of dysfunctions is of particular interest because they frequently are indicators of potential modifications of the structure. The distribution of specialized tasks in bureaucratic organizations makes each official responsible for the accomplishment of explicitly specified objectives.[3] In this context, a dysfunction that interferes with operations is experienced as a disturbance by certain members of the organization. The specialists, in the illustration cited, had to cope with the problem posed by the lack of cooperation of their colleagues in order to fulfill their responsibilities. A practice developed that seemed to be unrelated to this difficulty. Specialists voluntarily accepted the cases of the most unpopular clients of other officials. This put these officials under obligation to the specialists, constraining them, despite their competitive tendencies, to cooperate with specialists who looked for job openings. As a result, specialists were able to discharge their duty of providing employment service to their clients.

Dysfunctions often give rise to structural change. The disruption of operations consequent to the use of statistical records evoked new practices and interpersonal relations, in effect, a modification of the departmental structure. Similarly, performance records had been originally instituted in this

2. Merton, *op. cit.*, p. 50 (italics in original).

3. See on this point Herbert A. Simon, *Administrative Behavior* (New York: Macmillan, 1945), p. 172 and *passim*.

department in response to practices that interfered with employment service. The very innovation introduced to cope with one disturbance may in due course have consequences that create new problems and lead to new adjustments.

The central thesis of this study is that bureaucratic structures continually create conditions that modify these structures. In the study of larger social systems, it is now generally acknowledged that processes of social development must be taken into account, but bureaucracy is still too often regarded as a rigid equilibrium exempt from these processes. It, as well as other social structures, however, contains the seeds, not necessarily of its own destruction, but of its own transformation. The analysis of bureaucracies as organizations in flux is facilitated by the conceptions of functionalism. . . .

Functionalism was conceived by anthropologists as an alternative to the evolutionary approach. It was intended to substitute explanations of cultural phenomena on the basis of empirical evidence for interpretations in terms of speculations about historical origins and evolutionary progress.[4] This was an advance in scientific method. However, the limitations of the specific research situation—namely, that historical developments cannot be empirically traced in illiterate societies—were elevated into a scientific principle: past conditions are irrelevant for investigations of social systems. This ahistorical orientation and the parallel assumption of social equilibrium, which prevented systematic treatment of historical trends and social change, were serious deficiencies of functionalism.

Merton's paradigm constitutes a fundamental departure, which directs functional thinking toward problems of disequilibrium and social change. Empirical research benefits from these conceptions and simultaneously provides a testing ground for them. The concrete problems that arose in the analysis of the data of this study indicated some limitations of Merton's theoretical framework. There are insights that he does not make explicit and issues that he fails to consider, and these offer a challenge to extend his conceptual scheme.

4. See A. R. Radcliffe-Brown, "The Methods of Ethnology and Social Anthropology," *South African Journal of Science*, 1923, pp. 124–47, and "On the Concept . . .," *op. cit.*

By defining "function" as a type of *consequence* of a social pattern, Merton implicitly calls attention to the fact that social phenomena must be examined in the time sequence in which they occur. This requires the transformation of functional analysis from a synchronic into a diachronic approach, which is primarily concerned with the effects of patterns of social behavior on subsequent patterns. When specialists did favors for other interviewers, for example, this influenced the subsequent interaction between these two groups; the others became more cooperative. Of course, the expectation of the recurrence of favors was a main determinant of this cooperative behavior, but the doing of favors had preceded the emergence of these expectations as well as the cooperative practices. The recurrence of socially standardized acts obscures the time differential between antecedent and consequence, but it becomes apparent and can be empirically tested when the development of new patterns is examined.

Merton proposes to distinguish between functions and dysfunctions on the basis of whether consequences enhance or lessen "the adaptation or adjustment of the system."[5] This definition does not furnish precise criteria for making the distinction in empirical investigations. Whether a certain condition constitutes adjustment or maladjustment is by no means self-evident. The absence, or reduction, of social conflict is not a sufficient criterion of adjustment, as is apparent in cultures in which some types of competitive conflict are defined as socially desirable. It would be absurd to consider monopolistic practices as functional for a free-enterprise system, although they eliminate competitive conflicts. Indeed, the same social condition may be experienced as adjustment or as maladjustment, depending on the value-orientation of participants. Ultimately, therefore, the distinction between functions and dysfunctions rests on value judgments.

Of course, scientists should not introject their own values into scientific analysis. Quite the contrary, they must guard against the intrusion of their personal prejudices by recognizing that functional analysis involves value judgments and specifying the value criteria employed. Arbitrary standards are preferable to none, but they are not satisfactory. Consequences of social patterns are experienced by people in terms of their value orientations, and not

5. Merton, *op. cit.*, p. 51.

neutrally. Functional analysis takes this crucial aspect of social life into account by determining not merely the objective consequences of patterns but also their evaluative significance for participants. This necessitates that the values that prevail in the social system under consideration be ascertained and that they be used as criteria for defining function and dysfunction. The greater the precision with which value standards specify objectives, the greater their utility for scientific research. The explicit objectives of bureaucratic organizations, therefore, facilitate functional analysis.

Functions, then, can be defined as observed consequences of social patterns that change existing conditions in the direction of socially valued objectives or, more briefly, as consequences that contribute to the attainment of valued objectives. Dysfunctions, conversely, are those observed consequences of social patterns that change existing conditions in the direction opposite to socially valued objectives or consequences that interfere with the attainment of valued objectives.

Both functions and dysfunctions modify social conditions, but in opposite ways. The conditions *produced* by a dysfunctional pattern are identical, in one important respect, with those *relieved* by a functional pattern; both are experienced, in terms of prevailing values, as necessitating some improvement. Such conditions can be defined as social needs. Functions meet existing needs, whereas dysfunctions generate new needs.[6]

What happens if new social needs arise? There are three possibilities. First, the need may persist without being met. Many problems in bureaucratic organizations as well as in societies continue to require solutions for long periods of time. To be sure, if social needs were defined as prerequisites for survival, as they often are, it would be impossible to speak of needs that have not been met in an enduring social system. The advantage of the more limited concept adopted here is that it permits the empirical testing of functional hypotheses even when no information about extinct social systems is available.

To test the hypothesis that a pattern of behavior has a given function, it must be demonstrated that a condition necessitating improvement persists in structures in which this pattern does not occur, but does not exist in those in which it prevails. An alternative method is to show that the emergence of the pattern in a social structure eliminates this condition. Correspondingly, the test of a dysfunction of a social pattern requires evidence that a condition in need of improvement develops only in the presence of this pattern and not in its absence. In the study of prerequisites for survival, such comparisons have to be made between extinct social structures and enduring ones. Since this is rarely possible in the social sciences, functional imputations have often remained unproved assumptions. In the study of needs for the achievement of valued objectives, on the other hand, the comparison required is one between different surviving social structures which have attained a specific objective with varying degrees of success. Reliable data of this nature are much more readily accessible, which greatly increases the chances of being able to test functional hypotheses systematically.

A second possibility is that social needs disappear as a result of changes in value orientations. This involves more than becoming resigned to living under troublesome conditions, which indicates merely an adaptation to persistng needs. It means that situations that were once experienced as objectionable are now felt to be satisfactory because a new orientation has emerged. Learning is one of the processes through which such changes are brought about. As officials in the federal agency, for instance, learned to cope with the difficult problems of their work, their attitudes toward these problems changed, transforming them from disruptive threats into stimulating challenges.[7]

Finally, social needs may give rise to new social patterns that serve to meet them. Since this is only one of three alternatives, the existence of a need for improvement is not a sufficient condition for the development of such improvements. To explain their emergence, the conditions in social structures under which the need persisted and those under which it was met in a certain way must be contrasted. This analysis of structural constraints entails the comparison of historical developments

6. Often functions only reduce, and dysfunctions only intensify, social needs.

7. Conversely, changes in value orientations also produce new needs; conditions that were once considered satisfactory are defined by new objectives as necessitating improvement. . . .

in different structures, since past social experiences do, of course, influence present behavior.

A further specification of social needs and functions is important for this purpose, namely, an indication of the substructures particularly affected.[8] Which groups in a differentiated structure suffer from the existence of a given need, and which ones are relatively immune to it? Which groups benefit from the specific way a need is met, and which ones are not advantaged or are even disadvantaged? It is not possible to account for the persistence of needs, for practices that have serious dysfunctions, or for the fact that one pattern rather than another serves a given function, without inquiring into their differential effect on groups variously located in the power structure.

When a social pattern has a series of consequences, its dysfunctions may be looked upon as the social cost of its contributions. Presumably, once the cost outweighs the functions, the pattern will be abandoned. Often, however, social action is more constructive and less patient. People attack troublesome conditions, even if they cannot, or will not, eliminate the factors that produced them, and without waiting for a negative net balance of their consequences. We try to reduce highway accidents by means other than junking all cars and before their toll becomes so great that it would be preferable to give up motor transportation. Many emergent needs, in the two agencies studied, gave rise to social innovations that met the need without disturbing the pattern that had created it or the positive contributions of this pattern. The new practices, in turn, sometimes had dysfunctions as well as functions. Since the same social pattern that meets some needs frequently also generates others and since problems often lead to new solutions rather than to the elimination of their source, social structures continuously develop into different social structures.

8. See Merton, *op. cit.*, p. 52.

JAMES G. MARCH and HERBERT A. SIMON

# Decision-Making Theory

## The concept of rationality

How does the rationality of "administrative man" compare with that of classical "economic man" or with the rational man of modern statistical decision theory? The rational man of economics and statistical decision theory makes "optimal" choices in a highly specified and clearly defined environment:

1. When we first encounter him in the decision-making situation, he already has laid out before him the whole set of alternatives from which he will choose his action. This set of alternatives is simply "given"; the theory does not tell how it is obtained.

2. To each alternative is attached a set of consequences—the events that will ensue if that particular alternative is chosen. Here the existing theories fall into three categories: (*a*) *Certainty:* theories that assume the decision maker has complete and accurate knowledge of the consequences that will follow on each alternative. (*b*) *Risk:* theories that assume accurate knowledge of a probability distribution of the consequences of each alternative. (*c*) *Uncertainty:* theories that assume that the consequences of each alternative belong to some subset of all possible consequences, but that the decision maker cannot assign definite probabilities to the occurrence of particular consequences.

3. At the outset, the decision maker has a "utility function" or a "preference-ordering" that ranks all sets of consequences from the most preferred to the least preferred.

4. The decision maker selects the alternative leading to the preferred set of consequences. In the case of *certainty*, the choice is unambiguous. In the case of *risk*, rationality is usually defined as the choice of that alternative for which the expected utility is greatest. Expected utility is defined here as the average, weighted by the probabilities of occurrence, of the utilities attached to all possible consequences. In the case of *uncertainty*, the definition of rationality becomes problematic. One proposal that has had wide currency is the rule of "minimax risk": consider the worst set of consequences that may follow from each alternative, then select the alternative whose "worst set of consequences" is preferred to the worst sets attached to other alternatives. There are other proposals (e.g., the rule of "minimax regret"), but we shall not discuss them here.

### SOME DIFFICULTIES IN THE CLASSICAL THEORY

There are difficulties with this model of rational man. In the first place, only in the case of certainty does it agree well with common-sense notions of rationality. In the case of uncertainty, especially, there is little agreement, even among exponents of statistical decision theory, as to the "correct" definition, or whether, indeed, the term "correct" has any meaning here (Marschak, 1950).

Reprinted from *Organizations*, pp. 137–50, 169–71, by permission of the authors and publisher. 

A second difficulty with existing models of rational man is that it makes three exceedingly important demands upon the choice-making mechanism. It assumes (1) that all the alternatives of choice are "given"; (2) that all the consequences attached to each alternative are known (in one of the three senses corresponding to certainty, risk, and uncertainty respectively); (3) that the rational man has a complete utility-ordering (or cardinal function) for all possible sets of consequences.

One can hardly take exception to these requirements in a normative model—a model that tells people how they *ought* to choose. For if the rational man lacked information, he might have chosen differently "if only he had known." At best, he is "subjectively" rational, not "objectively" rational. But the notion of objective rationality assumes there is some objective reality in which the "real" alternatives, the "real" consequences, and the "real" utilities exist. If this is so, it is not even clear why the cases of choice under risk and under uncertainty are admitted as rational. If it is not so, it is not clear why only limitations upon knowledge of consequences are considered, and why limitations upon knowledge of alternatives and utilities are ignored in the model of rationality.

From a phenomenological viewpoint we can only speak of rationality relative to a frame of reference; and this frame of reference will be determined by the limitations on the rational man's knowledge. We can, of course, introduce the notion of a person observing the choices of a subject, and can speak of the rationality of the subject relative to the frame of reference of the observer. If the subject is a rat and the observer is a man (especially if he is the man who designed the experimental situation), we may regard the man's perception of the situation as objective and the rat's as subjective. (We leave out of account the specific difficulty that the rat presumably knows his own utility function better than the man does.) If, however, both subject and observer are men—and particularly if the situation is a natural one not constructed for experimental purposes by the observer—then it becomes difficult to specify the objective situation. It will be safest, in such situations, to speak of rationality only relative to some specified frame of reference.

The classical organization theory described in Chapter 2, like classical economic theory, failed to make explicit this subjective and relative character of rationality, and in so doing, failed to examine some of its own crucial premises. The organizational and social environment in which the decision maker finds himself determines what consequences he will anticipate, what ones he will not; what alternatives he will consider, what ones he will ignore. In a theory of organization these variables cannot be treated as unexplained independent factors, but must themselves be determined and predicted by the theory.

### ROUTINIZED AND PROBLEM-SOLVING RESPONSES

The theory of rational choice put forth here incorporates two fundamental characteristics: (1) Choice is always exercised with respect to a limited, approximate, simplified "model" of the real situation. We call the chooser's model his "definition of the situation." (2) The elements of the definition of the situation are not "given"—that is, we do not take these as data of our theory—but are themselves the outcome of psychological and sociological processes, including the chooser's own activities and the activities of others in his environment (Simon, 1947, 1955; March, 1955; Cyert and March, 1955, 1956; Newell, Shaw, and Simon, 1958).

Activity (individual or organizational) can usually be traced back to an environmental stimulus of some sort, e.g., a customer order or a fire gong. The responses to stimuli are of various kinds. At one extreme, a stimulus evokes a response—sometimes very elaborate—that has been developed and learned at some previous time as an appropriate response for a stimulus of this class. This is the "routinized" end of the continuum, where a stimulus calls forth a performance program almost instantaneously.

At the other extreme, a stimulus evokes a larger or smaller amount of problem-solving activity directed toward finding performance activities with which to complete the response. Such activity is distinguished by the fact that it can be dispensed with once the performance program has been learned. Problem-solving activities can generally be identified by the extent to which they involve *search*: search aimed at discovering alternatives of action or consequences of action. "Discovering" alternatives may involve inventing and elaborating whole performance programs where these are not already available in the problem solver's repertory (Katona, 1951).

When a stimulus is of a kind that has been experienced repeatedly in the past, the response will ordinarily be highly routinized. The stimulus will evoke, with a minimum of problem-solving or other computational activity, a well-structured definition of the situation that will include a repertory of response programs, and programs for selecting an appropriate specific response from the repertory. When a stimulus is relatively novel, it will evoke problem-solving activity aimed initially at constructing a definition of the situation and then at developing one or more appropriate performance programs.

Psychologists (e.g., Wertheimer, Duncker, de Groot, Maier) and observant laymen (e.g., Poincaré, Hadamard) who have studied creative thinking and problem-solving have been unanimous in ascribing a large role in these phenomena to search processes. Search is partly random, but in effective problem-solving it is not blind. The design of the search process is itself often an object of rational decision. Thus, we may distinguish substantive planning—developing new performance programs—from procedural planning—developing programs for the problem-solving process itself. The response to a particular stimulus may involve more than performance—the stimulus may evoke a spate of problem-solving activity—but the problem-solving activity may itself be routinized to a greater or lesser degree. For example, search processes may be systematized by the use of check lists.

### SATISFACTORY VERSUS OPTIMAL STANDARDS

What kinds of search and other problem-solving activity are needed to discover an adequate range of alternatives and consequences for choice depends on the criterion applied to the choice. In particular, finding the optimal alternative is a radically different problem from finding a satisfactory alternative. An alternative is *optimal* if: (1) there exists a set of criteria that permits all alternatives to be compared, and (2) the alternative in question is preferred, by these criteria, to all other alternatives. An alternative is *satisfactory* if: (1) there exists a set of criteria that describes minimally satisfactory alternatives, and (2) the alternative in question meets or exceeds all these criteria.

*Most human decision-making, whether individual[l] or organizational, is concerned with the discovery and selection of satisfactory alternatives; only in exceptional cases is it concerned with the discovery and selection of optimal alternatives.* To optimize requires processes several orders of magnitude more complex than those required to satisfice. An example is the difference between searching a haystack to find the *sharpest* needle in it and searching the haystack to find a needle sharp enough to sew with.

In making choices that meet satisfactory standards, the standards themselves are part of the definition of the situation. Hence, we need not regard these as given—any more than the other elements of the definition of the situation—but may include in the theory the processes through which these standards are set and modified. The standard-setting process may itself meet standards of rationality: for example, an "optimizing" rule would be to set the standard at the level where the marginal improvement in alternatives obtainable by raising it would be just balanced by the marginal cost of searching for alternatives meeting the higher standard. Of course, in practice the "marginal improvement" and the "marginal cost" are seldom measured in comparable units, or with much accuracy. Nevertheless, a similar result would be automatically attained if the standards were raised whenever alternatives proved easy to discover, and lowered whenever they were difficult to discover. Under these circumstances, the alternatives chosen would not be far from the optima, if the cost of search were taken into consideration. Since human standards tend to have this characteristic under many conditions, some theorists have sought to maintain the optimizing model by introducing cost-of-search considerations. Although we doubt whether this will be a fruitful alternative to the model we are proposing in very many situations, neither model has been used for predictive purposes often enough to allow a final judgment.

### PERFORMANCE PROGRAMS

We have seen that under certain circumstances the search and choice processes are very much abridged. At the limit, an environmental stimulus may evoke immediately from the organization a highly complex and organized set of responses. Such a set of responses we call a *performance program,* or simply a *program*. For example, the sounding of the alarm gong in a fire station initiates such a program. So does the appearance of a relief applicant at a social worker's desk. So does the appearance of an automobile chassis in front of the work station of a worker on the assembly line.

Situations in which a relatively simple stimulus sets off an elaborate program of activity without any apparent interval of search, problem-solving, or choice are not rare. They account for a very large part of the behavior of all persons, and for almost all of the behavior of persons in relatively routine positions. Most behavior, and particularly most behavior in organizations, is governed by performance programs.

The term "program" is not intended to connote complete rigidity. The content of the program may be adaptive to a large number of characteristics of the stimulus that initiates it. Even in the simple case of the fire gong, the response depends on the location of the alarm, as indicated by the number of strokes. The program may also be conditional on data that are independent of the initiating stimuli. It is then more properly called a *performance strategy*. For example, when inventory records show that the quantity on hand of a commodity has decreased to the point where it should be reordered, the decision rule that governs the behavior of the purchasing agent may call upon him to determine the amount to be ordered on the basis of a formula into which he inserts the quantity that has been sold over the past twelve months. In this case, search has been eliminated from the problem, but choice—of a very routinized kind, to be sure—remains.

We will regard a set of activities as routinized, then, to the degree that choice has been simplified by the development of a fixed response to defined stimuli. If search has been eliminated, but a choice remains in the form of a clearly defined and systematic computing routine, we will still say that the activities are routinized. We will regard activities as unroutinized to the extent that they have to be preceded by program-developing activities of a problem-solving kind.

## Performance programs in organizations

There are several ways to determine what programs a particular organization uses:

1. Observing the behavior of organization members. In relatively routine positions, where the same situations recur repetitively and are handled in terms of fairly definite programs, it is easy to infer the program from behavior. This is a common method for inducting new members of an organization into its procedures.

2. Interviewing members of the organization. Most programs are stored in the minds of the employees who carry them out, or in the minds of their superiors, subordinates, or associates. For many purposes, the simplest and most accurate way to discover what a person does is to ask him.

3. Examining documents that describe standard operating procedures. Programs may be written down, more or less completely and more or less accurately. The relation of a written operating procedure to the actual program that is carried out is complex, for the program may have been written down: (*a*) as an instruction to initiate a new program and communicate it to those who will carry it out; (*b*) as a description of an existing program to instruct new organization members; or (*c*) as an exposition (with or without amendments) of an existing program to legitimize or "formalize" it. There are other possibilities besides these three. In any event, when a document is used as a source of information about a program, the purposes for which it was prepared are relevant to its interpretation.

A person who has been trained in the observation of organizations can extract by these and other techniques a large part of the program that governs routine behavior. This is such a common-sense fact that its importance has been overlooked: Knowledge of the program of an organization permits one to predict in considerable detail the behavior of members of the organization. And the greater the *programming* of individual activities in the organization, the greater the *predictability* of those activities.

To be sure, prediction of behavior from the knowledge of a program has none of the element of "surprise" that we commonly associate with scientific prediction—any more than prediction of the lines that will be uttered by a Hamlet on the stage. It is no less important for its common-sense obviousness.

In general, we would anticipate that programs will be generated by past experience and in expectation of future experience in a given situation. Thus, the greater the *repetitiveness* of individual activities, the greater the programming. From this one would predict that programming will be most complete for clerical and factory jobs, particularly when the work is organized largely by process.

The prediction of behavior from a program when tasks are relatively simple and routine is illustrated by findings of Guetzkow and Simon (1955) using five-man experimental groups in the Bavelas network. Employing methods-analysis techniques, they were able to predict average trial times of groups to within 10 per cent from a knowledge of the methods the groups were using to perform the task.

If the program determines in some detail the behavior of individuals and groups performing relatively routine tasks, then we can predict behavior to the extent that we can answer the following questions: (1) What motivates members of the organization to accept a program as a determinant of their behavior? What processes, other than motivation, are involved in implementation of programs? This question has already been examined in earlier chapters. (2) What determines the content of a program? To what extent can the program be predicted uniquely from the requirements of the task? How are programs invented and developed, and what are the determinants of this process? (3) What are the consequences of programs, as developed and executed, for the goal and subgoal structure of the organization? (4) What are the predictors of behavior in areas that are not routinized and are unprogrammed? This question will be taken up in the next chapter.

We turn now to the second and third of these questions.

### PROGRAM CONTENT

The extent to which many human activities, both manual and clerical, can be programmed is shown by the continuing spread of automation to encompass a wider and wider range of tasks. In order to substitute automatic processes for human operatives, it is necessary to describe the task in minute detail, and to provide for the performance of each step in it. The decomposition of tasks into their elementary program steps is most spectacularly illustrated in modern computing machines which may carry out programs involving thousands of such steps. The capabilities of computers have now been extended to many tasks that until recently have been thought to be relatively complex, involving problem-solving activities of a fairly high order. Some examples are several existing computer programs for the automatic design of small electric motors and transformers, a program that enables a computer to discover proofs for certain kinds of mathematical theorems, and a program for translating languages.

Even on routine jobs, *program content* varies. We have already mentioned the extreme case: the detailed specification of output, methods, and pace in a man-paced assembly operation. But not all programs are of this type. They may not contain detailed time specifications (e.g., in typical machine-paced operations). In fact, programs usually specify the content of an activity more closely than its timing. They may specify the properties of the product (e.g., in blueprints, tolerances, etc.) rather than the detail of the methods to be used. We need propositions that will explain variations in program content along these dimensions:

*a*) The extent to which pacing rules are built into the program.
*b*) The extent to which work activities are detailed in the program.
*c*) The extent to which product specifications are detailed in the program.

Since performance programs are important aspects of the organizational system, their content will presumably tend to be related to the functions they perform. We can identify two major functions that such programs fulfill, or at least are intended to fulfill. First, they are a part of the control system in the organization. Organizations attempt to control employees by specifying a standard operating procedure and attaching organizational rewards and penalties to it. Second, performance programs are important parts of the coordination system in the organization. They help fulfill the needs for interdepartmental predictability (Blau, 1955).

Insofar as they are to function as controls, the programs must be linked to variables that are observable and measurable. We would expect program content to be a function of the *ease of observing job activities*, *the ease of observing job output*, and the *ease of relating activities to output*. Thus, we would predict that programs will contain activity specifications in preference to product specifications to the extent that: (*a*) the activity pattern is easily observed and supervised; (*b*) the quantity and quality of output are not easily observed and supervised; (*c*) the relations between activity pattern and output are highly technical, and are matters of scientific and engineering knowledge, better known to specialists in the organization than to the operatives (Ridley and Simon, 1938).

Conversely, programs will contain specifications of quality and quantity of output to the extent that: (*a*) the activity pattern is difficult to observe and supervise; (*b*) the quantity and quality of output are easily observed and supervised; (*c*) the relations between activity pattern and output are matters of common sense, are matters of skill in the specific occupation for which the operatives are trained, or are highly variable, depending upon circumstances of the individual situation that are better known to the operatives than to supervisors and specialists.

For performance programs to serve as coordinative devices, they must be linked to the coordination needs that are felt by the organization. Consequently, we would hypothesize that program content will be a function of the *need for activity coordination* and the *need for output coordination.* The more minutely other members of the organization need to synchronize or coordinate their activities with the activities of a particular member, the more completely will the program specify the activity pattern and/or the pacing of those activities. But to the extent that the activities of the former depend on the characteristics of the output of the latter, rather than on his activities, the program will specify product characteristics.

These propositions about program content are derived from the assumption that the program will be rationally adapted to the organization's objectives. To the extent that this assumption actually determines program, program content becomes a technological question in exactly the same way as the form of the production function is a technological question. In the experiment with the Bavelas network, mentioned previously, determining the most efficient program for performing the task is an exercise in methods study resting upon knowledge of human physiological constants—the times required to perform certain simple acts. If we assume that over some period of time an organization will actually arrive at an efficient program, we can predict its long-run behavior from our technical analysis.

Suppose, however, that we substitute for the maximizing assumption implicit in this method of prediction the assumption that behavior is rational in the more limited sense described earlier: that programs are sought that will operate "satisfactorily," and that the "best" program is not necessarily sought or found. In this case, predicting the program becomes more difficult. Which of the (presumably numerous) satisfactory potential programs the organization will adopt depends, under these circumstances, upon the procedures it employs to construct new programs and to improve existing ones. These procedures will provide the principal subject matter for the next chapter.

### THE STRUCTURE OF PROGRAMS

To illustrate further the structure of programs for handling recurrent events, we will describe some formal procedures often used by business concerns for controlling inventory. We will analyze first the common "two-bin" system of inventory control, then a more elaborate system.

In the two-bin system of inventory control, two quantities are established for each item kept in stock: (1) the order quantity (the amount to be purchased on a single order), (2) the buffer stock (the amount that should be on hand when a new order is placed). The program is very simple:

1. When material is drawn from stock, note whether the quantity that remains equals or exceeds the buffer stock. If not:
2. Write a purchase order for the specified order quantity.

Let us call the first step the "program-evoking" step, and the second step the "program-execution" step. The bifurcation is characteristic of programs—a program includes a specification of the circumstances under which the program is to be evoked. In the example just cited, the program specifies certain observations, which are to be made (whether the buffer stock is intact) whenever a certain event occurs (withdrawal of material from stock). A decision to act or not to act (to apply or not to apply the program) is based on the result of the observation.

The program-evoking step may involve only

observation auxiliary to some other activity (as in this example), or it may invoke systematic scanning of some part of the environment (e.g., the activity of a quality inspector). Further, a program-execution step by one member of an organization may serve as a program-evoking step for another member. In the example above, the receipt of a purchase order from the inventory clerk is a program-evoking step for the purchasing department.

In our very simple example, the program-execution step requires neither discretion nor problem-solving. In more complicated situations, the program will be a strategy; i.e., action will be contingent on various characteristics of the situation. For example, in a more elaborate inventory control scheme, the purchase quantity may depend on a forecast of sales. Then the program might look like this:

1. When material is drawn from stock, note whether the quantity that remains equals or exceeds the buffer stock. If not:
2. Determine from the sales forecast provided by the sales department the sales expected in the next *k* months.
3. Insert this quantity in the "order quantity formula," and write a purchase order for the quantity thus determined.

This program, although it is contingent on certain changing facts (the sales forecast), does not allow discretion to the person who executes it—at least in ordinary meanings of the word "discretion." If, however, the organization does not provide the inventory clerk with an official sales forecast, or does not establish a specific order quantity, we would say that the clerk's activity was, to that extent, discretionary. We might discover by observation and interview that the clerk was in fact following a very definite and invariable program, but one stored in his own memory and not recorded in official instructions.

### THE NATURE OF DISCRETION

The amounts and kinds of *discretion* available to the organizational participant are a function of his performance program and in particular the extent to which the program specifies activities (means) and the extent to which it specifies product or outcome (ends). The further the program goes in the latter direction, the more discretion it allows for the person implementing the program to supply the means-end connections. Compare the programs cited earlier with the following alternative program:

1. It is the duty of the inventory clerk to determine when each item should be recorded and in what quantity, and to place orders with the purchasing department. He should perform this function with attention to the costs of holding inventories, the costs of shortages, and the economies associated with bulk orders.

If we interpret the last sentence as enjoining the clerk to minimize the sum of the specified costs, we see that this program specifies a goal, but leaves the means undetermined. To construct a "rational" program starting from these premises requires the following steps: (1) defining the total cost function in specific terms; (2) estimating the coefficients that appear in the cost function; (3) deriving a formula or "strategy" that specifies the ordering rules as functions of : (*a*) the coefficients that appear in the cost function, (*b*) the sales forecasts (i.e., finding the policy that minimizes step 1), and (4) inserting in the formula the coefficients estimated in step 2, and the sales forecasts.

It is difficult to find a place for discretion within the framework of traditional theories of rational behavior. In the present theory, however, a whole host of phenomena fall under this heading.

First, when a program involves search activities, the actual course of action depends on what is found. We may regard the choice of a course of action after search as discretionary.

Second, when a program describes a strategy, application of the strategy to specific circumstances requires forecasts or other estimates of data. We may regard the application of the strategy to select a course of action as discretionary.

Third, a program may exist in the memory of the individual who is to apply it, having arrived there either as a result of extraorganizational training (e.g., professional training or apprenticeship), or as a product of learning from experience rather than as a result of formal instructions. Under these circumstances we often regard him as behaving in a discretionary fashion.

In all of the cases listed above, the decision process may in fact be highly routinized—the term "discretionary" referring in these instances to the form of the performance program or the source from which it was acquired. These cases need to be distinguished from a fourth meaning of "discretionary": A program may specify only general goals, and leave unspecified the exact activities to be used in reaching them. Moreover, knowledge of the means-ends connections may be sufficiently incomplete and inexact that these cannot be very well specified in advance. Then "discretion" refers to the development and modification of the performance program through problem-solving and learning processes. Although it is difficult to draw a perfectly sharp line between changing a program and changing a datum in applying a strategy, we have already argued that there is an important difference of degree here. With these several meanings of the term "discretionary" in mind, we do not need separate propositions about the amount of discretion, for these will be subsumed under the propositions already noted that specify the form, content, and completeness of programs.

### INTERRELATION OF PROGRAMS

A program, whether simple or complex, is initiated when it is evoked by some stimulus. The whole pattern of programmed activity in an organization is a complicated mosaic of program executions, each initiated by its appropriate program-evoking step.

Insofar as the stimuli that evoke programs come from outside the organization, the individual pieces of this mosaic are related to each other only in making claims on the same time and resources, and hence in posing an allocation problem. Nevertheless, if the goal of optimizing is taken seriously, this allocation problem will usually complicate the problem-solving process greatly, for it requires the marginal return from activity in response to any particular stimulus to be equated with the marginal return from activities in response to all other stimuli. Hence, all programs must be determined simultaneously.

When the goal is to respond to stimuli in a satisfactory, but not necessarily optimal, fashion, choice is much simpler; for the standards may be set at levels that permit a satisficing response to each stimulus without concern for the others. The organization, under these circumstances, normally has some slack that reduces the interdependence among its several performance programs.

Apart from resource-sharing, there may be other and more integral connections among programs. Program A may be a *higher-level* program, i.e., a problem-solving activity whose goal is to revise other programs, either by constructing new ones, reconstructing existing ones, or simply modifying individual premises in existing programs. In this case, the *content* of the lower-level programs that are related to A will depend on A. Or, program A may be a program one of whose execution steps serves as an initiating stimulus for program B.

The inventory example illustrates both possibilities. As to the first, program A may be a forecasting program, or a program for periodic revision of the coefficients in the cost function. As to the second possibility, the order that goes from the inventory clerk to the purchasing department serves to initiate one of the purchasing programs of the latter.

### PROGRAM AND ORGANIZATION STRUCTURE

In organizations there generally is a considerable degree of parallelism between the hierarchical relations among members of the organization and the hierarchical relations among program elements. That is to say, the programs of members of higher levels of the organization have as their main output the modification or initiation of programs for individuals at lower levels.

Any organization possesses a repertory of programs that, collectively, can deal in a goal-oriented way with a range of situations. As new situations arise, the construction of an entirely new program from detailed elements is rarely contemplated. In most cases, adaptation takes place through a recombination of lower-level programs that are already in existence. An important objective of standardization is to widen as far as possible the range of situations that can be handled by combination and recombination of a relatively small number of elementary programs.

Limitation of high-level action to the recombination of programs, rather than the detailed construction of new programs out of small elements, is extremely important from a cognitive standpoint. Our treatment of rational behavior rests on the proposition that the "real" situation is almost always far too complex to be handled in detail. As we move upwards in the supervisory and executive hierarchy, the range of interrelated matters over which an individual has purview becomes larger and larger, more and more complex. The growing complexity of the problem can only be matched against the finite powers of the individual if the problem is dealt with in grosser and more aggregative form. One way in which this is accomplished is by limiting the alternatives of action that are considered to the recombination of a repertory of programs (Simon, 1953).

We may again illustrate this point with the inventory example. Top management decides upon the total dollar inventories without controlling the distribution of inventories among individual items. Specific inventory control programs are found at lower levels of the organization.

* * * * * *

## Organization structure and the boundaries of rationality

It has been the central theme of this chapter that the basic features of organization structure and function derive from the characteristics of human problem-solving processes and rational human choice. Because of the limits of human intellective capacities in comparison with the complexities of the problems that individuals and organizations face, rational behavior calls for simplified models that capture the main features of a problem without capturing all its complexities.

The simplifications have a number of characteristic features: (1) Optimizing is replaced by satisficing—the requirement that satisfactory levels of the criterion variables be attained. (2) Alternatives of action and consequences of action are discovered sequentially through search processes. (3) Repertories of action programs are developed by organizations and individuals, and these serve as the alternatives of choice in recurrent situations. (4) Each specific action program deals with a restricted range of situations and a restricted range of consequences. (5) Each action program is capable of being executed in semi-independence of the others—they are only loosely coupled together.

Action is goal-oriented and adaptive. But because of its approximating and fragmented character, only a few elements of the system are adaptive at any one time; the remainder are, at least in the short run, "givens." So, for example, an individual or organization may attend to improving a particular program, or to selecting an appropriate program from the existing repertory to meet a particular situation. Seldom can both be attended to simultaneously.

The notion that rational behavior deals with a few components at a time was first developed extensively in connection with economic behavior by John R. Commons, who spoke of "limiting factors" that become the foci of attention and adaptation. Commons' theory was further developed by Chester I. Barnard, who preferred the term "strategic factor."

This "one-thing-at-a-time" or "*ceteris paribus*" approach to adaptive behavior is fundamental to the very existence of something we can call "organization structure." Organization structure consists simply of those aspects of the pattern of behavior in the organization that are relatively stable and that change only slowly. If behavior in organizations is "intendedly rational," we will expect aspects of the behavior to be relatively stable that either (*a*) represent adaptations to relatively stable elements in the environment, or (*b*) are the learning programs that govern the process of adaptation.

An organization is confronted with a problem like that of Archimedes: in order for an organization to behave adaptively, it needs some stable regulations and procedures that it can employ in carrying out its adaptive practices. Thus, at any given time an organization's programs for performing its tasks are part of its structure, but the least stable part. Slightly more stable are the switching rules that determine when it will apply one program, and when another. Still more stable are the procedures it uses for developing, elaborating, instituting, and revising programs.

The matter may be stated differently. If an organization has a repertory of programs, then it is adaptive in the short run insofar as it has procedures for selecting from this repertory a program appropriate to each specific situation that arises. The process used to select an appropriate program is the "fulcrum" on which short-run adaptiveness rests. If, now, the organization has processes for adding to its repertory of programs or for modifying programs in the repertory, these processes become still more basic fulcra for accomplishing longer-run adaptiveness. Short-run adaptiveness corresponds to what we ordinarily call problem-solving, long-run adaptiveness to learning.

There is no reason, of course, why this hierarchy of mechanisms should have only three levels—or any specified number. In fact, the adaptive mechanisms need not be arranged hierarchically. Mechanism A may include mechanism B within its domain of action, and vice versa. However, in general there is much asymmetry in the ordering, so that certain elements in the process that do not often become strategic factors (the "boundaries of rationality") form the stable core of the organization structure.

We can now see the relation between Commons' and Barnard's theories of the "limiting" or "strategic" factor and organization structure. Organization will have structure, as we have defined the term here, insofar as there are boundaries of rationality—insofar as there are elements of the situation that must be or are in fact taken as givens, and that do not enter into rational calculations as potential strategic factors. If there were not boundaries to rationality, or if the boundaries varied in a rapid and unpredictable manner, there could be no stable organization structure. Some aspects of structure will be more easily modified than others, and hence we may need to distinguish short-run and long-run structure.

In this chapter, we have been concerned mostly with short-run structure—with programs to respond to sequences of situations requiring adaptive action. The "boundaries of rationality" that have been the source of our propositions have consisted primarily of the properties of human beings as organisms capable of evoking and executing relatively well-defined programs but able to handle programs only of limited complexity.

## References

Blau, P. M. *The Dynamics of Bureaucracy*. Chicago, 1955.

Cyert, R. M., and J. G. March. "Organizational Structure and Pricing Behavior in an Oligopolistic Market." *American Economic Review* 45 (1955), 129–39.

———. "Organizational Factors in the Theory of Oligopoly." *Quarterly Journal of Economics* 70 (1956), 44–64.

Guetzkow, H., and H. A. Simon. "The Impact of Certain Communication Nets upon Organization and Performance in Task-oriented Groups." *Management Science* 1 (1955), 233–50.

Katona, G. *Psychological Analysis of Economic Behavior*. New York, 1951.

March, J. G. "An Introduction to the Theory and Measurement of Influence." *American Political Science Review* 49 (1955), 431–51.

March, J. G. "Rational Behavior, Uncertain Prospects, and Measurable Utility." *Econometrica* 18 (1950), 111–41.

Newell, A., J. C. Shaw, and H. A. Simon. "Elements of a Theory of Human Problem Solving." *Psychological Review* 65 (1958), 151–66.

Ridley, C. E., and H. A. Simon. *Measuring Municipal Activities*. Chicago, 1938.

Simon, H. A. *Administrative Behavior*, New York, 1947.

———. "Birth of an Organization: The Economic Cooperation Administration." *Public Administration Review* 13 (1953), 227–36.

———. "A Behavioral Model of Rational Choice." *Quarterly Journal of Economics* 69 (1955), 99–118.

AMITAI ETZIONI

# Compliance Theory

## A definition of compliance

Compliance is universal, existing in all social units. It is a major element of the relationship between those who have power and those over whom they exercise it (Simmel, 1896). Despite its universality, it has been chosen as a base for this comparative study because it is a central element of organizational structure. The emphasis on compliance within the organization differentiates the latter from other types of social units. Characteristics of organizations such as their specificity, size, complexity, and effectiveness each enhances the need for compliance. And in turn, compliance is systematically related to many central organizational variables.

*Compliance* refers both to a relation in which an actor behaves in accordance with a directive supported by another actor's power, and to the orientation of the subordinated actor to the power applied.[1]

By *supported* we mean that those who have power manipulate means which they command in such a manner that certain other actors find following the directive rewarding, while not following it incurs deprivations. In this sense, compliance relations are asymmetric (or "vertical"). But it is not assumed that the subordinates have no power, only that they have less.[2]

The power-*means*, manipulated to support the directives, include physical, material, and symbolic rewards and deprivations. Organizations tend to allocate these means systematically and strive to ensure that they will be used in conformity with the organizational norms.

The *orientation of the subordinated actor* can be characterized as positive (commitment) or negative (alienation). It is determined in part by the degree to which the power applied is considered legitimate by the subordinated actor, and in part by its congruence with the line of action he would desire. We refer to this orientation, whether positive or negative, as *involvement* in the organization. In sum, there are two parties to a compliance relationship: an actor who exercises power, and an actor, subject to this power, who responds to this subjection with either more or less alienation or more or less commitment.

The next task is to use compliance as here defined to develop an analytical base for the classification of organizations. This is done in three steps. First, three kinds of *power* are differentiated; then, three kinds of *involvement* are specified; and finally, the associations of kinds of power with kinds of involvement are indicated. These associations—which con-

1. For other usages of the term see Bendix (1947, pp. 502–7) and Zetterberg (1957). [Complete references appear at the end of the selection.]

2. See Parsons (1957, p. 139); cf. Dahrendorf (1954, p. 169).

**Reprinted with minor editorial adaptations from *A Comparative Analysis of Complex Organizations*, pp. 3–19, 23–33, 40–44, 55–59, 66–67, by permission of the author and The Macmillan Company.**

stitute *compliance relationships*—then serve as the basis of our classification of organizations.

## Three kinds of power: a comparative dimension

### A CLASSIFICATION OF POWER

*Power* is an actor's ability to induce or influence another actor to carry out his directives or any other norms he supports.[3] Goldhamer and Shils state that "a person may be said to have power to the extent that he influences the behavior of others in accordance with his own intentions" (p. 171). Of course, "his own intentions" might be to influence a person to follow others' "intentions" or those of a collectivity. In organizations, enforcing the collectivity norms is likely to be a condition determining the power-holder's access to the means of power.

*Power positions* are positions whose incumbents regularly have access to means of power. Statements about power positions imply a particular group (or groups) who are subject to this power. For instance, to state that prison guards have a power position implies the subordination of inmates. In the following analysis we focus on power relations in organizations between those higher and those lower in rank. We refer to those in power positions, who are higher in rank, as *elites* or as organizational *representatives*. We refer to those in subject positions, who are lower in rank, as *lower participants*.

Power differs according to the *means* employed to make the subjects comply. These means may be physical, material, or symbolic.[4]

*Coercive* power rests on the application, or the threat of application, of physical sanctions such as infliction of pain, deformity, or death; generation of frustration through restriction of movement; or controlling through force the satisfaction of needs such as those for food, sex, comfort, and the like.

*Remunerative* power is based on control over material resources and rewards through allocation of salaries and wages, commissions and contributions, "fringe benefits," services and commodities.

*Normative* power rests on the allocation and manipulation of symbolic rewards and deprivations through employment of leaders, manipulation of mass media, allocation of esteem and prestige symbols, administration of ritual, and influence over the distribution of "acceptance" and "positive response." (A more eloquent name for this power would be persuasive, or manipulative, or suggestive power. But all these terms have negative value connotations which we wish to avoid.)

There are two kinds of normative power. One is based on the manipulation of esteem, prestige, and ritualistic symbols (such as a flag or a benediction); the other, on allocation and manipulation of acceptance and positive response (Parsons, 1951, p. 108). Although both powers are found both in vertical and in horizontal relationships, the first is more frequent in vertical relations, between actors who have different ranks, while the second is more common in horizontal relations, among actors equal in rank—in particular, in the power of an "informal" or primary group over its members. Lacking better terms, we refer to the first kind as *pure normative power*, and to the second as *social power*.[5] Social power could be treated as a distinct kind of power. But since powers are here classed according to the means of control employed, and since both social and pure normative power rest on

3. See Parsons (1951, p. 121). See also Lasswell and Kaplan (1950, pp. 74–102); Easton (1952, p. 116); Dahl (1957); and Cartwright (1959).

4. We suggest that this typology is exhaustive, although the only way we can demonstrate this is by pointing out that every type of power we have encountered so far can be classified as belonging to one of the categories or a combination of them.

Boulding, Neuman, and Commons have suggested similar typologies. Boulding has developed a typology of "willingness" of persons to serve organizational ends which includes identification, economic means, and coercion. He suggests, however, that identification should be seen as an "economic" way of inducing willingness, a position which we believe is unacceptable to most sociologists (see Boulding, 1953, p. xxxi; and Niebuhr, "Coercion, Self-Interest, and Love," *ibid.*, pp. 228–44). Neuman has suggested that "three basic methods are at the disposal of the power group: persuasion, material benefits, violence" (1950, p. 168). Commons distinguishes among physical, economic, and moral power (1957, pp. 47–64). Janowitz analyzes international relations using the concepts of "economic resources, violence, and persuasion" (1960, p. 258). See also Deutsch (1953, pp. 218ff.).

5. This distinction draws on the difference between social and normative integration, referred to by Parsons, Bales, and Shils (1953, p. 182) as the distinction between the "integrative" and the "latent pattern maintenance" phases. In a volume in progress, Shils distinguishes between social and ideological primary groups (private communication). Coleman (1957, p. 255) has pointed to the difference between group-oriented and idea-oriented attachments.

the same set of means—manipulation of symbolic rewards—we treat these two powers as belonging to the same category.

From the viewpoint of the organization, pure normative power is more useful, since it can be exercised directly down the hierarchy. Social power becomes organizational power only when the organization can influence the group's powers, as when a teacher uses the class climate to control a deviant child, or a union steward agitates the members to use their informal power to bring a deviant into line.

Organizations can be ordered according to their power structure, taking into account which power is predominant, how strongly it is stressed compared with other organizations in which the same power is predominant, and which power constitutes the secondary source of control. . . .

### NEUTRALIZATION OF POWER

Most organizations employ all three kinds of power, but the degree to which they rely on each differs from organization to organization. Most organizations tend to emphasize only one means of power, relying less on the other two.[6] Evidence to this effect is presented below in the analysis of the compliance structures of various organizations. The major reason for power specialization seems to be that when two kinds of power are emphasized at the same time, over the same subject group, they tend to neutralize each other.

Applying force, for instance, usually creates such a high degree of alienation that it becomes impossible to apply normative power successfully. This is one of the reasons why rehabilitation is rarely achieved in traditional prisons, why custodial measures are considered as blocking therapy in mental hospitals, and why teachers in progressive schools tend to oppose corporal punishment.

Similarly, the application of remunerative powers makes appeal to "idealistic" (pure normative) motives less fruitful. In a study of the motives which lead to purchase of war bonds, Merton pointed out that in one particularly effective drive (the campaign of Kate Smith), all "secular" topics were omitted and the appeal was centered on patriotic, "sacred" themes. Merton asked a sample of 978 people: "Do you think that it is a good idea to give things to people who buy bonds?"

> Fifty per cent were definitely opposed in principle to premiums, bonuses and other such inducements, and many of the remainder thought it a good idea only for "other people" who might not buy otherwise. (1946, p. 47)

> By omitting this [secular] argument, the authors of her scripts were able to avoid the strain and incompatibility between the two main lines of motivation: unselfish, sacrificing love of country and economic motives of sound investment. (*Ibid.*, p. 45)

It is possible to make an argument for the opposite position. It might be claimed that the larger the number of personal needs whose satisfaction the organization controls, the more power it has over the participants. For example, labor unions that cater to and have control over the social as well as the economic needs of their members have more power over those members than do unions that focus only on economic needs. There may be some tension between the two modes of control, some ambivalence and uneasy feeling among members about the combination, but undoubtedly the total control is larger. Similarly, it is obvious that the church has more power over the priest than over the average parishioner. The parishioner is exposed to normative power, whereas the priest is controlled by both normative and remunerative powers.

The issue is complicated by the fact that the *amount* of each kind of power applied must be taken into account. If a labor union with social powers has economic power which is much greater than that of another union, this fact may explain why the first union has greater power in sum, despite some "waste" due to neutralization. A further complication follows from the fact that neutralization may also occur through application of the "wrong" power in terms of the cultural definition of what is appropriate to the particular organization and activity. For example, application of economic power in religious organizations may be less effective than in industries, not because two kinds of power are mixed, but because it is considered

6. In more technical language, one can say that the three continua of power constitute a three-dimensional property space. If we collapse each dimension into high, medium, and low segments, there are 27 possible combinations or cells. Our hypothesis reads that most organizations fall into cells which are high on one dimension and low or medium on the others; this excludes 18 cells (not counting three types of dual structures discussed below). On multidimensional property space, see Barton (1955, pp. 40–52).

illegitimate to use economic pressures to attain religious goals. Finally, some organizations manage to apply two kinds of power abundantly and without much waste through neutralization, because they segregate the application of one power from that of the other. The examination below of combat armies and labor unions supplies an illustration of this point.

We have discussed some of the factors related to the tendency of organizations to specialize their power application. In conclusion, it seems that although there can be little doubt that such a tendency exists, its scope and a satisfactory explanation for it have yet to be established.

## Three kinds of involvement: a comparative dimension

### INVOLVEMENT, COMMITMENT AND ALIENATION

Organizations must continually recruit means if they are to realize their goals. One of the most important of these means is the positive orientation of the participants to the organizational power. *Involvement*[7] refers to the cathectic-evaluative orientation of an actor to an object, characterized in terms of intensity and direction.

The intensity of involvement ranges from high to low. The direction is either positive or negative. We refer to positive involvement as *commitment*[8] and to negative involvement as *alienation*.[9] (The advantage of having a third term, *involvement*, is that it enables us to refer to the continuum in a neutral way.[10]) Actors can accordingly be placed on an involvement continuum which ranges from a highly intense negative zone through mild negative and mild positive zones to a highly positive zone.[11]

### THREE KINDS OF INVOLVEMENT

We have found it helpful to name three zones of the involvement continuum, as follows: *alienative*, for the high alienation zone; *moral*, for the high commitment zone; and *calculative*, for the two mild zones. This classification of involvement can be applied to the orientations of actors in all social units and to all kinds of objects. Hence the definitions and illustrations presented below are not limited to organizations, but are applicable to orientations in general.

*Alienative involvement.* Alienative involvement designates an intense negative orientation; it is predominant in relations among hostile foreigners. Similar orientations exist among merchants in "adventure" capitalism, where trade is built on isolated acts of exchange, each side trying to maximize immediate profit (Gerth and Mills, 1946, p. 67). Such an orientation seems to dominate the approach of prostitutes to transient clients (K. Davis, 1937, pp. 748–49). Some slaves seem to have held similar attitudes to their masters and to their work. Inmates in prisons, prisoners of war, people in concentration camps, enlisted men in basic

7. *Involvement* has been used in a similar manner by Morse (1953, pp. 76–96). The term is used in a somewhat different way by students of voting, who refer by it to the psychological investment in the outcome of an election rather than in the party, which would be parallel to Morse's usage and ours. See, for example, Campbell, Gurin, and Miller (1954, pp. 33–40).

8. Mishler defined *commitment* in a similar though more psychological way: "An individual is committed to an organization to the extent that central tensions are integrated through organizationally relevant instrumental acts." Cited by Argyris (1957, p. 202). See also Mishler (1953); Abramson, Cutler, Kautz, and Mendelson (1958, p. 16); H. P. Gouldner (1960, p. 469); and Becker (1960, pp. 35ff.).

9. We draw deliberately on the associations this term has acquired from its usage by Marx and others. For a good analysis of the idea of alienation in Marxism, and of its more recent development, see Bell (1959 and 1960, pp. 335–68). See also D. G. Dean (1960, pp. 185–89).

10. An example of empirical indicators which can be used to translate the involvement continuum into directly observable terms is offered by Shils and Janowitz (1948, pp. 282–83). They classify "modes of social disintegration" in the armed forces as follows: desertion; active surrender; passive surrender; routine resistance; "last-ditch" resistance. In the terms used here, these measures indicate varying degrees of involvement, from highest alienation (desertion) to highest commitment (last-ditch resistance).

Nettler (1958) has developed a 17-item unidimensional scale which measures alienation from society. It seems that a similar scale could be constructed for measuring alienation from or commitment to organizational power without undue difficulties. Kornhauser, Sheppard, and Mayer (1956, pp. 147–48) have developed a 6-item scale, measuring the orientation of union members to their organization, which supplies another illustration of the wide use and measurability of these concepts, which are central to our analysis (for some further specifications, see Chapter XII).

11. Several sociologists have pointed out that the relationship between intensity and direction of involvement is a curvilinear one: the more positive or negative the orientation, the more intensely it is held (Guttman, 1947, 1950, 1954, pp. 229–30; Suchman, 1950; McDill, 1959).

training, all tend to be alienated from their respective organizations.[12]

*Calculative involvement.* Calculative involvement designates either a negative or a positive orientation of low intensity. Calculative orientations are predominant in relationships of merchants who have continuous business contacts. Attitudes of (and toward) permanent customers are often predominantly calculative, as are relationships among entrepreneurs in modern (rational) capitalism. Inmates in prisons who have established contact with prison authorities, such as "rats" and "peddlers," often have predominantly calculative attitudes toward those in power (Sykes, 1958, pp. 87–95).

*Moral*[13] *involvement.* Moral involvement designates a positive orientation of high intensity. The involvement of the parishioner in his church, the devoted member in his party, and the loyal follower in his leader are all "moral."

There are two kinds of moral involvement, pure and social. They differ in the same way pure normative power differs from social power. Both are intensive modes of commitment, but they differ in their foci of orientation and in the structural conditions under which they develop. Pure moral commitments are based on internalization of norms and identification with authority (like Riesman's inner-directed "mode of conformity"); social commitment rests on sensitivity to pressures of primary groups and their members (Riesman's "other-directed"). Pure moral involvement tends to develop in vertical relationships, such as those between teachers and students, priests and parishioners, leaders and followers. Social involvement tends to develop in horizontal relationships like those in various types of primary groups. Both pure moral and social orientations might be found in the same relationships, but, as a rule, one orientation predominates.

Actors are means to each other in alienative and in calculative relations; but they are ends to each other in "social" relationships. In pure moral relationships the means-orientation tends to predominate. Hence, for example, the willingness of devoted members of totalitarian parties or religious orders to use each other. But unlike the means-orientation of calculative relationships, the means-orientation here is expected to be geared to needs of the collectivity in serving its goals, and not to those of an individual.

As has been stated, the preceding classification of involvement can be applied to the orientations of actors in all social units and to all kinds of objects. The analysis in this book applies the scheme to orientations of lower participants in organizations to various organizational objects, in particular to the organizational power system. The latter includes (1) the directives the organization issues, (2) the sanctions by which it supports its directives, and (3) the persons who are in power positions. The choice of organizational power as the prime object of involvement to be examined here follows from a widely held conception of organization as an administrative system or control structure. To save breath, the orientation of lower participants to the organization as a power (or control) system is referred to subsequently as *involvement in the organization.* When other involvements are discussed, the object of orientation—for example, organizational goals—is specified.

Organizations are placed on the involvement continuum according to the modal involvement pattern of their lower participants. . . .

## Compliance as a comparative base

### A TYPOLOGY OF COMPLIANCE

Taken together, the two elements—that is, the power applied by the organization *to* lower participants, and the involvement in the organization developed *by* lower participants—constitute the compliance relationship. Combining three kinds of power with three kinds of involvement produces nine types of compliance, as shown in the accompanying table.[14]

12. For a description of this orientation in prisons see Clemmer (1958, pp. 152ff.). Attitudes toward the police, particularly on the part of members of the lower classes, are often strictly alienative. See, for example, Banfield (1958). Illustrations of alienative orientations to armies are found in Norman Mailer, *The Naked and the Dead,* and Erich Maria Remarque, *All Quiet on the Western Front.*

13. The term moral is used here and in the rest of the volume to refer to an orientation of the actor; it does not involve a value-position of the observer (see Parsons and Shils, 1952, pp. 170ff.).

14. A formalization of the relationship between rewards-allocation (which comes close to the concept of power as used here) and participation (which, as defined, is similar to the concept of involvement) has been suggested by Breton (1960).

***A Typology of Compliance Relations***

| *KINDS OF POWER* | *KINDS OF INVOLVEMENT* | | |
|---|---|---|---|
| | *Alienative* | *Calculative* | *Moral* |
| Coercive | 1 | 2 | 3 |
| Remunerative | 4 | 5 | 6 |
| Normative | 7 | 8 | 9 |

The nine types are not equally likely to occur empirically. *Three*—the diagonal cases, 1, 5, and 9—*are found more frequently than the other six types.* This seems to be true because these three types constitute *congruent* relationships, whereas the other six do not.

*The congruent types.* The involvement of lower participants is determined by many factors, such as their personality structure, secondary socialization, memberships in other collectivities, and so on. At the same time, organizational powers differ in the kind of involvement they tend to generate. When the kind of involvement that lower participants have because of other factors[15] and the kind of involvement that tends to be generated by the predominant form of organizational power are the same, we refer to the relationship as *congruent*. For instance, inmates are highly alienated from prisons; coercive power tends to alienate; hence this is a case of a congruent compliance relationship.

Congruent cases are more frequent than noncongruent ones primarily because congruence is more effective, and organizations are social units under external and internal pressure to be effective. The effective application of normative powers, for example, requires that lower participants be highly committed. If lower participants are only mildly committed to the organization, and particularly if they are alienated from it, the application of normative power is likely to be ineffective. Hence the association of normative power with moral commitment.

Remuneration is at least partially wasted when actors are highly alienated, and therefore inclined to disobey despite material sanctions; it is also wasted when actors are highly committed, so that they would maintain an effective level of performance for symbolic, normative rewards only. Hence the association of remuneration with calculative involvement.

15. "Other factors" might include previous applications of the power.

Coercive power is probably the only effective power when the organization is confronted with highly alienated lower participants. If, on the other hand, it is applied to committed or only mildly alienated lower participants, it is likely to affect adversely such matters as morale, recruitment, socialization, and communication, and thus to reduce effectiveness. (It is likely, though, to create high alienation, and in this way to create a congruent state.)

*The incongruent types.* Since organizations are under pressure to be effective, the suggestion that the six less effective incongruent types are not just theoretical possibilities but are found empirically calls for an explanation. The major reason for this occurrence is that organizations have only limited control over the powers they apply and the involvement of lower participants. The exercise of power depends on the resources the organization can recruit and the license it is allowed in utilizing them. Involvement depends in part on external factors, such as membership of the participants in other collectivities (e.g., membership in labor unions[16]) basic value commitments (e.g., Catholic versus Protestant religious commitments[17]); and the personality structure of the participants (e.g., authoritarian[18]). All these factors may reduce the expected congruence of power and involvement.

*A dynamic hypothesis.* Congruent types are more effective than incongruent types. Organizations are under pressure to be effective. Hence, to the degree that the environment of the organization allows, *organizations tend to shift their compliance structure from incongruent to congruent types* and *organizations which have congruent compliance structures tend to resist factors pushing them toward incongruent compliance structures.*

Congruence is attained by a change in either the power applied by the organization or the involve-

16. On the effect of membership in labor unions on involvement in the corporation, see Willerman (1949, p. 4); L. R. Dean (1954); Jacobson (1951); and Purcell (1953, pp. 79, 146).

17. See W. F. Whyte et al. (1955, pp. 45–46). Protestants are reported to be more committed to the values of saving and productivity, whereas Catholics are more concerned with their social standing in the work group. This makes for differences in compliance: Protestants are reported to be more committed to the corporation's norms than Catholics.

18. For instance, authoritarian personality structure is associated with a "custodial" orientation to mental patients (Gilbert and Levinson, 1957, pp. 26–27).

ment of lower participants. Change of power takes place when, for instance, a school shifts from the use of corporal punishment to stress on the "leadership" of the teachers. The involvement of lower participants may be changed through socialization, changes in recruitment criteria, and the like.

Because the large majority of cases falls into the three categories representing congruent compliance, these three types form the basis for subsequent analysis. We refer to the coercive-alienative type as *coercive compliance*; to the remunerative-calculative type as *utilitarian compliance*; and to the normative-moral type as *normative compliance*. Students of organizational change, conflict, strain, and similar topics may find the six incongruent types more relevant to their work.

### COMPLIANCE AND AUTHORITY

The typology of compliance relationships presented above highlights some differences between the present approach to the study of organizational control and that of studies conducted in the tradition of Weber. These studies tend to focus on authority, or legitimate power, as this concept is defined.[19] The significance of authority has been emphasized in modern sociology in the past, in order to overcome earlier biases that overemphasized force and economic power as the sources of social order. This emphasis, in turn, has led to an overemphasis on legitimate power. True, some authority can be found in the control structure of lower participants in most organizations. True, authority plays a role in maintaining the long-run operations of the organization. But so does nonlegitimated power. Since the significance of legitimate power has been fully recognized, it is time to lay the ghost of Marx and the old controversy, and to give full status to both legitimate and nonlegitimate sources of control.

Moreover, the concept of authority does not take into account differences among powers other than their legitimacy, in particular the nature of the sanctions (physical, material, or symbolic) on which power is based. All three types of power may be regarded as legitimate by lower participants: thus there is normative,[20] remunerative, and coercive authority (differentiated by the kind of power employed, for instance, by a leader, a contractor, and a policeman).[21] But these powers differ in the likelihood that they will be considered legitimate by those subjected to them. Normative power is most likely to be considered legitimate; coercive, least likely; and remunerative is intermediate.

Finally, it is important to emphasize that involvement in the organization is affected both by the legitimacy of a directive and by the degree to which it frustrates the subordinate's need-dispositions. Alienation is produced not only by illegitimate exercise of power, but also by power which frustrates needs, wishes, desires. Commitment is generated not merely by directives which are considered legitimate but also by those which are in line with internalized needs of the subordinate. Involvement is positive if the line of action directed is conceived by the subordinate as both legitimate and gratifying. It is negative when the power is not

19. For various definitions and usages of the concept see Friedrich (1958). For a formalization of the concept in relation to power and to leadership, see Barton (1958). For a psychological discussion of legitimate power see French and Raven (1959, pp. 158–61).

20. The concept of "normative authority" raises the question of the difference between this kind of authority and normative power. There is clearly a high *tendency* for normative power to be considered legitimate and thus to form an authority relationship. The reason for this tendency is that the motivational significance of rewards and deprivations depends not only on the objective nature of the power applied, but also on the meaning attached to it by the subject. Coercive and remunerative means of control are considerably less dependent on such interpretations than normative ones. Most actors in most situations will see a fine as a deprivation and confinement as a punishment. On the other hand, if the subject does not accept as legitimate the power of a teacher, a priest, or a party official, he is not likely to feel their condemnation or censure as depriving. Since normative power depends on manipulation of symbols, it is much more dependent on "meanings," and, in this sense, on the subordinate, than other powers. But it is by no means necessary that the application of normative power always be regarded as legitimate.

A person may, for example, be aware that another person has influenced his behavior by manipulation of symbolic rewards, but feel that he had no right to do so, that he ought not to have such power, or that a social structure in which normative powers are concentrated (e.g., partisan control over mass media; extensive advertising) is unjustified. A Catholic worker who feels that his priest has no right to condemn him because of his vote for the "wrong" candidate may still fear the priest's condemnation and be affected by it.

21. For another classification of authority, which includes authority of confidence, of identification, of sanctions, and of legitimacy, see Simon, Smithburg, and Thompson (1959, p. 189).

granted legitimacy and when it frustrates the subordinate. Involvement is intermediate when either legitimation or gratification is lacking. Thus the study of involvement, and hence that of compliance, differs from the study of authority by taking into account the effects of the cathectic as well as the evaluative impact of directives on the orientation of lower participants.

## Lower participants and organizational boundaries

Before we can begin our comparisons, the following questions still remain to be answered. Why do we make compliance of lower participants the focus of the comparison? Who exactly are "lower participants"? What are the lower boundaries of an organization? In answering these questions, we employ part of the analytical scheme suggested above, and thus supply the first test of its fruitfulness.

### WHY LOWER PARTICIPANTS?

Compliance of lower participants is made the focus of this analysis for several reasons. First, the control of lower participants is more problematic than that of higher participants because, as a rule, the lower an actor is in the organizational hierarchy, the fewer rewards he obtains. His position is more deprived; organizational activities are less meaningful to him because he is less "in the know," and because often, from his position, only segments of the organization and its activities are visible.[22] Second, since we are concerned with systematic differences among organizations (the similarities having been more often explored), we focus on the ranks in which the largest differences in compliance can be found. An interorganizaitonal comparison of middle and higher ranks would show that their compliance structures differ much less than those of the lower ranks.

### WHO ARE LOWER PARTICIPANTS?

Organizational studies have used a large number of concrete terms to refer to lower participants: employees, rank-and-file, members, clients, customers, inmates.[23] These terms are rarely defined. They are customarily used to designate lower participants in more than one organization, but none can be used for all.

Actually, these terms can be seen as reflecting different positions on at least three analytical dimensions.[24] One is the *nature* (direction and intensity) of the actors' *involvement* in the organization. Unless some qualifying adjectives such as "cooperative" or "good" are introduced, *inmates* implies alienative involvement. *Clients* designates people with alienative or calculative involvement. *Customers* refers to people who have a relatively more alienative orientation than clients; one speaks of the clients of professionals but not ordinarily of their customers. *Member* is reserved for those who have at least some, usually quite strong, moral commitment to their organization. *Employee* is used for people with various degrees of calculative involvement.

A second dimension underlying these concrete terms is the degree to which lower participants are *subordinated* to organizational powers. Inmates, it seems, are more subordinated than employees, employees more than members, and members more than clients. A study in which subordination is a central variable would take into account that it includes at least two subvariables: the extent of control in each area (e.g., "tight" versus remote control); and the scope of control, measured by the number of areas in which the subject is subordinated. Such refinement is not required for our limited use of this dimension.

A third dimension is the amount of *performance* required from the participants by the organization: it is high for employees, low for inmates, and lowest for clients and customers.[25]

22. The term *visible* is used here and throughout this book as defined by Merton: "the extent to which the norms and the role-performances within a group are readily open to observation by others." (1957, pp. 319 ff.)

23. For one of the best discussions of the concept of participation, its definition and dimensions, see Fichter (1954, Part I, *passim*).

24. The difference between concrete and analytic membership in corporations has been pointed out by Feldman (1959).

25. Participants of a social unit might also be defined as all those who share an institutionalized set of role-expectations. We shall not employ this criterion since it blurs a major distinction, that between the organization as such and its social environment. Members of most groups share such role-expectations with outsiders.

A criterion of participation which is significant for other purposes than ours is whether lower participants have

Using concrete terms to designate groups of participants without specifying the underlying dimensions creates several difficulties. First of all, the terms cannot be systematically applied. Although "members" are in general positively involved, sometimes the term is used to designate lower participants with an alienative orientation. Archibald, for instance, uses this term to refer to members of labor unions who are members only *pro forma* and who see in the union simply another environmental constraint, to which they adjust by paying dues.

Most workers entered the yards not merely ignorant of unions, but distrustful of them. . . . They nonetheless joined the unions, as they were compelled to do, with little protest. They paid the initiation fees, averaging not more than twenty dollars, much as they would have bought a ticket to the county fair: it cost money, but maybe the show would be worth the outlay. As for dues, they paid them with resignation to the principle that all joys of life are balanced by a measure of pain (1947, pp. 131–32).

The term *customers* suggests that the actors have no moral commitments to their sources of products and services. But sometimes it is used to refer to people who buy from cooperatives, frequent only unionized barbers, and remain loyal to one newspaper—that is, to people who are willing to suffer some economic loss because they see in these sources of service something which is "good in itself"—people who, in short, have some moral commitments.

Any moral commitment on the part of mental patients, designated as *inmates*, is viewed either with surprise or as a special achievement of the particular mental hospital; on the other hand, members of labor unions are "expected" to show moral commitment and are labeled "apathetic" if they do not. The fact that some mental patients view their hospital as their home, and thus are positively involved, whereas labor union members may see their organization as a secondary group only, is hidden by the terminology employed. The same point could be made for differences in performance and in subordination.

Although the use of such concrete terms leads to overgeneralization, by implying that all lower participants of an organization have the characteristics usually associated with the label, they can also impede generalization. An illustration is supplied by studies of parishioners. Many of these studies focus on problems of participation, such as "apathy," high turnover, and declining commitment. But rarely are comparisons drawn, or insights transferred, from the study of members of voluntary associations and political organizations. Actually, all these organizations are concerned with the moral commitment of lower participants who have few performance obligations and little subordination to the organization.

formal or actual powers, such as those reflected in the right to vote, submit grievances, or strike.

Another advantage of specifying the analytical dimensions underlying these concepts is that the number of dimensions is limited, whereas the number of concrete terms grows continuously with the number of organizations studied. Thus the study of hospitals introduces patients; the analysis of churches brings up parishioners; and the examination of armies adds soldiers. Following the present procedure, we can proceed to characterize the lower participants of additional organizations by the use of the same three dimensions.

Specifying the underlying dimensions enables us not only to formulate analytical profiles of a large variety of lower participants, but also to compare them systematically with each other on these three dimensions. For instance, "soldiers" (in combat) are high on all three dimensions, whereas inmates are high on subordination and alienation but low on performance; employees are medium in involvement and subordination, but high on performance obligations. The import of such comparisons will become evident later.

Finally, whereas concrete terms tend to limit analysis to participants at particular levels, analytical terms such as alienative, calculative, and moral can be applied equally well to participants at all levels of the organizational hierarchy.

Ideally, in a book such as this, we should refer to lower participants in analytical terms, those of various degrees of involvement, subordination, and performance obligations. Since this would make the discussion awkward, the concrete terms are used, but only to refer to *typical* analytical constellations. *Inmates* are lower participants with high alienation, low performance obligations, and high subordination. The term will not be used to refer to other combinations which are sometimes found among lower participants in prisons. *Members* is used to refer only to lower participants who are highly committed, medium on subordination, and low on performance obligations; it is not used to refer to alienated lower participants in voluntary associations.

* * * * * *

## An analytical classification

All patterns of compliance exist in most organizations, but most organizations rely much more on one pattern than on the other two. Hence organizations are classified in this and the subsequent chapter according to their *predominant* compliance pattern as coercive, utilitarian, or normative. Within each category, organizations are ordered according to the *relative* emphasis given to the predominant pattern: thus some coercive organizations are found to rely heavily upon coercive compliance, whereas others, though also predominantly coercive, place considerably less stress on this pattern. When relevant, the secondary compliance pattern is also specified. The composite compliance distribution, of predominant and secondary patterns, is referred to as the *compliance structure* of the particular organizational rank (e.g., lower participants).

The categories for classification have been established. . . . Before we can begin the classification, however, we must specify the units to be classified.

## The units of classification

When comparative statements about organizations are made, concrete organizations are usually cited as instances of some common-sense "category." The United Automobile Workers is an instance of "trade unions," General Motors an instance of "corporations." Comparative statements are then formulated using these categories: for example, it is suggested that the members of the UAW have more power over their representatives than most stockholders of GM have over theirs, since in general union members are more involved in the union than stockholders are in the company.

The use of such common-sense categories as labor unions and corporations to isolate the units of comparison creates considerable difficulty. This method of classification tends to attach the same label to organizations which differ considerably, and to assign different names to organizations which are analytically similar in many significant ways, particularly in their compliance structure.

*Army*, *armed forces*, and *military organization*, for example, are labels in common use. Actually, they refer to a highly heterogeneous group. The terms comprise, for instance, both peacetime and combat units, which differ in their goals, social composition, training, disciplinary methods, socialization, communication networks, and compliance structure. Similarly, General Motors, restaurants (W. F. Whyte, 1948), and newspapers (Kreps, 1954) are all referred to as "industries";[26] the Communists as well as the Democrats and Republicans come under the heading of "political parties"; the term trade union is applied to both Soviet and American workers' organizations.

Again, it is generally assumed that the term *voluntary association* refers to a homogeneous category and that one may therefore generalize from findings concerning one voluntary association to the whole category. Actually, the category includes at least two distinct types. In one type, active participation and high commitment are conditions for the functioning of the association; fund-raising organizations such as the March of Dimes, religious orders, and political parties with strong ideological commitments fall into this subcategory. The other type—which also makes strong public claims for participation and commitment—can function effectively only so long as these claims are *not* met, or are met only on some occasions. Most labor unions, most political parties, stockholders' groups, and interest groups are of this type. Apathy, or lack of involvement—the central issue of many studies of voluntary associations—has thus a very different meaning for these two organizational types. For the first type, it means that a basic functional requirement is not fulfilled; for the second, it means that

26. On the problem involved in the use of common-sense classifications, especially with regard to the category "industry" as defined by dictionaries and by the Census Bureau, see Etzioni (1958*c*, p. 307). Part of the difficulty arises from the use of *industry* to designate any permanent investment of capital and labor, as well as a subcategory of this class—namely, the mechanical and manufacturing branches of producing activities as distinguished from agriculture, mining, and services.

the organization is operating smoothly, and possibly that one of the conditions necessary for its effective functioning is fulfilled.[27]

Some organizations covered by different names reveal more similarity than those grouped together under one name. Selznick (1952) has shown that the power structure, goals, means of communication, and role of primary groups of Communist parties resemble those of combat armies more than they do those of ordinary political parties. From some points of view, the quartermaster services of peacetime armies—classified as "military" organizations—have more in common with large-scale insurance offices and department stores, classified as "industry," than with other military units. Conversely, large insurance offices resemble peacetime armies more than they do mines, shipyards, and most factories, with which they are frequently grouped.

In our discussion, analytic attributes of organizations distinguish the units of classification. Unfortunately, we cannot follow the ideal procedure and classify each organization, because there are many hundreds of thousands of them. On the other hand, we have seen that common-sense classifications are of little use. We therefore take the middle way, breaking up the broad common-sense categories into subcategories. We shall not, for example, talk about military organizations, but about combat units and peacetime units. Similarly, we shall not classify all mental hospitals together, but distinguish between custodial hospitals and therapeutic hospitals. The differentiating criterion is the compliance structure of the various subcategories of organizations.

If all the organizations normally included in one common-sense category fall into the same compliance category, organizations are ordered within the category according to the relative stress on the predominant pattern. For example, many industries fall into the remunerative category, but differ according to how much stress they put on remuneration; blue-collar and white-collar industries, for example, differ in this respect.

The present classification is only a first approximation. As systematic information on organizations increases, new divisions in the categories and units of classification will have to be introduced, and some organizations will probably require reclassification. The present endeavor therefore should be viewed as a beginning, not an end. It should also be taken into account that this classification is designed to serve the study of compliance and its correlates. In all likelihood, other classifications are more useful for some other purpose.[28]

It should be emphasized that in the following pages we can devote only brief, schematic treatment to the examples discussed. There is an entire literature devoted to organizations; our task here is not to deal with all of it, but to place an organization in our scheme and to clarify certain problems which emerge from this classificatory endeavor. Occasionally, a somewhat more extensive discussion is needed to explore the difficulties a researcher might encounter in determining the nature of the compliance structure. In general, however, the reader must be referred to cited sources for a fuller treatment of the organizations briefly reviewed here.

Finally, a comment on indicators is necessary. We cannot hope to overcome the limitations of every secondary analysis: we are introducing *post hoc* concepts into studies conducted by other researchers with other concepts and procedures. We shall have to take whatever measures the study has used as our guide. Indicators of involvement illustrate the point. Sometimes these are holistic

27. A revised theory of apathy would have to be much more specific than can be suggested here in passing. It is vital, for instance, to distinguish between complete and partial apathy and to determine the type of members who are apathetic (e.g., elites as against rank and file). Some apathy is functional for almost all organizations, although they differ in the degree to which this is true. For a discussion of the functions of apathy, see W. H. M. Jones (1954).

28. It is more common to classify organizations according to the functions they fulfill for society. Parsons classifies organizations as: (1) oriented to economic production, (2) oriented to political goals, (3) integrative organizations, and (4) pattern-maintenance organizations (Parsons, 1956, pp. 228–29). This typology has been applied and elaborated by Eisenstadt (1958, pp. 116–17), Etzioni (1958*c*, pp. 208–10), Scott (1959, pp. 386–88), and Gordon and Babchuk (1959). Differentiation of organizations by goal or function is also used in a study of the technology and organizational structure of factories, mines, hospitals, and universities (Thompson and Bates, 1957); and in a study of "management of conflict" in "ideological organizations," "giant enterprises," and "local enterprises" (Thompson, 1960). Cf. the structural approach used by Moore (1957) in his comparative examination of management and unions, and by Stinchcombe (1959) in his comparison of bureaucratic and craft administration of production.

measures of the participants' general orientation to organizational power; sometimes they are more specific, as when attitudes toward only one aspect of power—for example, sanctions—are studied; and in still other cases, the only information available on involvement encompasses more than orientation to the control structure alone—for example, level of job satisfaction. In those few cases where the indicator is broader than the concept we are interested in, we are forced to use it nevertheless as a tentative clue to the nature of involvement in the organization. This kind of indicator is used only when the control structure constitutes the most salient of the involvement objects reported. Because the present study is an exploratory, proposition-formulating endeavor, this problem is not a crucial one. The material supplied illustrates the propositions; it does not, of course, validate them.

## Coercive organizations

Coercive organizations are organizations in which coercion is the major means of control over lower participants and high alienation characterizes the orientation of most lower participants to the organization. Typical cases are concentration camps, prisoner-of-war camps, the large majority of prisons, traditional "correctional institutions," and custodial mental hospitals. Forced-labor camps[29] and relocation centers[30] are also coercive organizations.

Force is the major means of control applied in these organizations to assure fulfillment of the major organizational task: keeping inmates in. Obviously, should the restraints on movement be lifted, hardly any inmate would stay inside. The accomplishment of all other tasks depends on the effective performance of this custodial task. The second major task of these organizations, keeping the inmates disciplined, is also attained through the potential or actual use of force, although here differences among various types of organization are greater.

Even when control relies directly on other means, indirectly it is based on force. An inmate may do many services for a guard in exchange for a cigarette, but this cannot be considered remunerative control since the special value of the cigarette and other such objects of satisfaction is derived from the segregation of the inmate from regular markets. This segregation is in turn based on force.

Organizations included in the coercive category may be arranged according to the relative weight of the coercive pattern. Concentration camps apply more coercion than regular prisons;[31] prisons apply more than "correctional institutions" for juvenile offenders, the latter being frequently the first to introduce various reforms (Ohlin, 1956, p. 13). Prisoner-of-war camps in modern democracies frequently apply only as much coercion as correctional institutions, or less.[32] It is reported that some North Korean prisoners of war were kept in a United Nations camp which did not have barbed wire (W. L. White, 1957, p. 8), and that "we had taken about 60,000 prisoners, so gentle that they could be marched to the rear in almost unguarded regiments" (*ibid.*, p. 34).

Assuming that we could control the effect of other factors, such as the degree of initial alienation the inmates bring with them to the various types of coercive organizations, we should expect to find higher alienation in those organizations that apply more coercion.[33] This seems indeed to be the case with one possible exception, that of concentration

29. For a personal account see Parvilahti (1960). There are several reports on such camps in a number of Soviet countries by the Mid-European Law Project, under the general title *Forced Labor and Confinement without Trial* (1952).

30. Leighton (1945, esp. chs. 6–10) deals with the relatively unsuccessful attempts to reduce coercion, develop self-government, and to avoid general social disorganization by means other than coercion in these camps. For another study of such camps see LaViolette (1948).

31. For studies of concentration camps see E. A. Cohen (1953, esp. ch. 1 and ch. 3) and Kogon (1950). Vaughan reports on the informal organization of the "Internees" in "Japanese camps in the Philippine Islands" and on the formal organization (1949, chs. 4 and 10, and ch. 7); for a report from the organizational viewpoint see the autobiography of Hoess (1960). See also Bondy (1943); Abel (1951); Adler (1958); and Jackman (1958).

32. For two of the few studies of POW camps which have sociological relevance, see I. Cohen (1917) and W. L. White (1957).

33. For an experimental study of the effects of mild versus severe punishment, and short versus prolonged and repeated punishment, as well as the effect of various combinations of these types on extinction of the punished behaviour, see Estes (1944, esp. pp. 37–38). The severe and prolonged punishment generated more alienating effects than the mild and short. Note, however, that all the subjects of the experiment were "albino rats from the Minnesota laboratory stock."

camps. Here, where the application of coercion reaches the highest level, instances of "utter indifference" and even commitment to the guards and wardens are reported (Bettelheim, 1943, pp. 448–51; Bloch, 1947, esp. p. 338; Kogon, 1950, pp. 274–77). Prolonged and extreme exposure to coercion may lead men to accept some of the power-holders' norms, to identify with them, and to deflect their alienation onto scapegoats. New inmates in concentration camps appeared to serve as such scapegoats, as did groups low in status by external stratification criteria (Cohen, 1953, pp. 26–28). Thus, in this extreme situation, the relationship between coercion and alienation seems to be reversed.

In all other coercive organizations the relationship seems to hold. If, for instance, one controls the degree of initial alienation, it seems that the alienation produced in the typical correctional institution is less than in the typical prison. Since the application of coercion for purposes of internal control (other than preventing escapes) is particularly small in POW camps administered by modern democracies, we would expect that the alienation produced in these camps is smaller than that produced in prisons.

Comparatively low alienation is reported by Leighton (1945) in his study of American "relocation centers" of civilians of Japanese ancestry. Control was exercised in part by recognizing strikes and grievances and by bargaining through mutual concessions. Force, the coercive organization's typical approach to inmate strikes, was not used. Other parts of Leighton's study also demonstrate the comparatively limited use of coercion for purposes of internal control.[34]

One way to determine empirically the place of an organization on the coercive continuum is to establish the typical punishment for the same kind of offense in various organizations. For instance, the punishment for attempting to escape from a concentration camp was often death or torture; from prisons, the extension of sentence, often by as much as a year; in "correctional institutions," an extension usually much shorter in duration. In American camps of German prisoners of war, the punishment was usually not more than two weeks on bread and water.[35] Similar comparisons can be made for other offenses.

Custodial mental hospitals are difficult to place in this manner, since in these organizations a different interpretation is given to the same offense, and since other forms of punishment—some seen by the staff as therapeutic measures—are available, such as electric shock, insulin injections, and the strait jacket.[36] To the degree that a comparison can be made, we suggest that custodial mental hospitals resemble correctional institutions for youthful offenders rather than prisons, to which they are often compared. It seems that youth and insanity mitigate the punitive orientation. People are committed to both organizations against their will, but the same deviant act brings shorter confinement when the offender is either young or legally defined as mentally ill. There is no capital punishment in either organization. Rehabilitation and therapy, limited as they may be, appear more often in these two organizational types than in prisons. Both fall in the relatively less coercive part of the coercive category.

The amount of relevant information on various types of coercive organization varies greatly. Prisons and mental hospitals, the two more common types, are studied rather frequently, and therefore the discussion of coercive organizations in subsequent chapters will focus on them. Information about compliance in concentration camps is very limited. For prisoners of war, we have some data on the compliance of soldiers from democratic societies in the camps of the enemy,[37] but little information about prisoners from totalitarian societies in the camps of democracies. More information on the latter would be required for a fuller analysis of variations in the exercise of coercion in modern democratic societies, the subject of our analysis.

If inquiry into concentration camps, POW camps, forced-labor camps, and similar coercive organizations is to be extended, special attention must be

34. Leighton (1945). On means of control see especially pp. 43, 155, 179; on the strike settlement, pp. 208–9. But compare the settlement of another strike, p. 244.

35. Private communication from two wardens of such camps.

36. For a discussion of the punitive use of electrical shock, see Belknap (1956, pp. 164, 191–94, 248).

37. For a report of the army studies of American prisoners of war in Korea, see Kinkead (1959). See also *The New Yorker* (Oct. 26, 1957, pp. 114–69); W. L. White, (1957).

paid to the pitfalls of value-laden labels. The Germans, for example, referred to Dachau and similar camps as "Arbeitslager," that is, work camps (E. A. Cohen, 1953, p. 19). The Japanese camp described in the Vaughan report is usually referred to as a concentration camp, although no violence was exercised except to keep "internees" in the camp.[38] Similar camps in the United States are referred to as relocation centers. On the other hand, the American Andersonville is described as a camp for prisoners of war, although 14,000 soldiers died there from starvation or disease, were maimed by bloodhounds, or were eaten by their crazed fellow prisoners.[39]

The following distinctions of usage may prove helpful: Organizations that serve as tools of mass murder should be called *concentration camps*, including some formally defined as camps for prisoners of war; organizations that serve merely to detain persons are *prisons*, including some so-called mental hospitals, "homes for the aged," and "intern" camps. Relocation centers in which people are involuntarily detained are a kind of prison; so are camps of forced labor, which have production as a secondary goal. Organizations that combine a strong emphasis on detention with some rehabilitation are *correctional institutions*.

## Utilitarian organizations

Utilitarian organizations are organizations in which remuneration is the major means of control over lower participants and calculative involvement (i.e., mild alienation to mild commitment) characterizes the orientation of the large majority of lower participants. Utilitarian organizations are commonly referred to as industries. But as we have seen, *industries* is one of those misleading common-sense labels. Although many industries are utilitarian organizations, some important subcategories have normative compliance structures. Thus, for our purposes, industries and divisions of industrial organizations can be classified into three main categories: those whose lower participants are predominantly *blue-collar* workers, such as most factories and mines; those whose lower participants are predominantly *white-collar* employees, such as offices, whether private (insurance companies and banks) or public (various governmental agencies); and those whose lower participants are *professionals*, such as research organizations, planning organizations, and law firms (these, as we will see, are normative organizations).

Statements made about one category of industry also hold, though to a lesser degree, for employees of the same type in subdivisions of other categories of organizations. Thus, statements about white-collar industries apply to office employees in factories; statements about professional organizations are also true for professional divisions in blue-collar industries, as in research and development divisions; and statements about blue-collar industries hold for janitors in a university. The statements hold "to a lesser degree" because the compliance of an organizational subdivision is affected not only by the type of work—manual, clerical, or professional—done by the subunit's employees, but also by the compliance pattern in the rest of the organization. Hospital attendants, who are doing blue-collar work in a normative organization, illustrate this point. We would expect them to be, as indeed they are, the most remunerative, least normative group of the hospital staff, but they are more normatively controlled than blue-collar workers in blue-collar industries. This fact is reflected in their moral commitment to the health of patients, in efforts to develop their professional self-image, in their comparatively high job satisfaction, and, of course, in their lower wages.[40]

Remunerative power—such as the manipulation of wages, salaries, commissions, fringe benefits, working conditions, and similar rewards—constitutes the predominant source of control in blue-collar industries. These sanctions also constitute the predominant means of control in white-collar industries, but they are less pronounced there than in blue-collar industries; and they constitute an important though secondary power in professional organizations. Normative controls play a relatively limited role in blue-collar industries; an important

38. "A woman was slapped across the face, another upon her back before a sober guard ordered the drunken ones away. In the history of the camp this was the only one of physical abuse by the Japanese." (Vaughan, 1949, p. 80).

39. For an early report close to the event see Roach (1865); for a recent publication see McElroy (1957).

40. On the professional self-image and intrinsic job satisfaction, see Simpson and Simpson (1959, p. 391).

though secondary role in white-collar industries; and they constitute the predominant means of control in professional organizations. In other words, professional organizations are not a remunerative but a normative "industry." . . .

The preceding statements can be specified further by differentiating within each of the major categories of industry. Blue-collar workers can be broken into unskilled, semiskilled, and skilled workers, or into industrial workers and craft workers. We would expect the unskilled industrial workers to be the most subject to remunerative controls, and the skilled or craft-oriented ones to be relatively more affected by normative controls.[41]

Similarly, white-collar employees can be divided into subgroups which consist, on the one hand, of lower-ranking personnel such as salesgirls, clerks, and tellers, and, on the other, somewhat higher-ranking personnel such as supervisory clerks or private secretaries, who have closer contact with management. The first are controlled by relatively more utilitarian means than the latter.[42] A comparison of typists in a large "pool" and single secretaries attached to "their" executive may illustrate the difference. Female workers, who constitute a large proportion of the lower-ranking white-collar employees, seem to be relatively more given to normative compliance than male white-collar employees.[43]

Finally, semi-professionals, such as engineers and laboratory technicians, seem to be less normatively controlled than full-fledged professionals.

Data on differences in alienation among these groups parallel those on differences in modes of control. Blauner (1960, pp. 342–43) has summarized a large number of studies which suggest that those who would choose the same kind of work if beginning their career again constitute about 20 per cent of the unskilled workers, about 30 to 40 per cent of the service employees, and 65 per cent or more of the professionals. Similar findings have been reported by Moore (1953) and by Morse and Weiss (1955, p. 197).[44]

* * * * * *

## Normative organizations

Normative organizations are organizations in which normative power is the major source of control over most lower participants, whose orientation to the organization is characterized by high commitment. Compliance in normative organizations rests principally on internalization of directives accepted as legitimate. Leadership, rituals, manipulation of social and prestige symbols, and resocialization are among the more important techniques of control used.

Although there are only two common types of coercive organizations (prisons and custodial mental hospitals), and two common types of utilitarian organizations (blue-collar and white-collar industries), there are at least nine frequently found types of normative organizations. In five of these the normative pattern is highly pronounced and other patterns are relatively minor. These are *religious* organizations, including churches, orders, and monasteries; a subcategory of *political* organizations, those which have a strong ideological program; *general hospitals*; *universities*; and *voluntary associations*, which, as we shall see, rely mainly on social powers and commitments. Less typical, in the sense that coercion plays an important secondary role, are *schools* and *therapeutic mental hospitals*. Also less typical are *professional* organizations, in which remuneration plays an important part. Finally, "*core*" organizations of social movements tend to have a normative compliance structure, though it is difficult to assess its exact nature.

The greater variety of normative organizations, and the fact that their compliance structure is less often discussed in professional literature, requires that we devote more space to them than to the other two types.*

41. The differences between the two types of workers are aptly described and analyzed by Warner and Low (1947, chs. 4 and 5).

42. For a discussion of the various types of white-collar employees, differences in their reward-structures, and differences in the degree of alienation generated, see Mills (1951, chs. 8 and 10).

43. Morse (1953, pp. 77ff.) studied involvement of white-collar workers in a company. She found the highest degree of involvement (53 per cent high) among semi-supervisory personnel, who are mostly women. This association holds when other factors, such as salaries, length of service' age, and education, are controlled.

44. See Chapter VIII, pages 197–98, on the problems involved in using job satisfaction as an indicator of involvement in the organization.

* Editors' note: Only the typical normative organizations are included in this excerpt.

TYPICAL NORMATIVE ORGANIZATIONS

*Religious organizations* must rely predominantly on normative powers to attain both acceptance of their directives and the means required for their operation.[45] No coercion is applied to a Mormon who does not pay his tithe (Webb, 1916, p. 116); he is punished by denial of access to religious services in the Temple.[46] Similarly, police will not arrest, nor will a court fine, a Catholic who is divorced or a nun who breaks her vows and leaves her order.[47] These and other breaches of discipline are major transgressions in the eyes of the various religions, but the impact of such a view depends on the ability of the church to influence the normative orientation of the parishioners. If the typical normative means of socialization in religious schools[48]—participation in religious rituals, sermons, and manipulation of various symbols—fail, there is little else the church can do.[49] Needless to say, remunerative powers cannot serve as the basis of religious compliance. Hence heavy reliance on normative means of control and moral commitments is mandatory for religious organizations.

The compliance structure of *political organizations*, such as political parties and labor unions, varies considerably. Some parties, especially on the local level and in particular among marginal groups such as farm hands and new immigrants, rely for the most part on patronage, allocation of spoils, and other nonsymbolic rewards ranging from distribution of coal to cancellation of parking tickets. But the majority of parties, in particular on the national level, have to rely predominantly on normative compliance. This is because no modern party can recruit the material means required to control a large and affluent electorate, and because normative appeals are more effective in maintaining party loyalties.

Labor unions in general are less normative than parties. . . . Business unions emphasize utilitarian compliance in "normal" (nonstrike) periods. Other unions make wide use of coercion for internal control purposes. Yet at least two kinds of unions are typical normative organizations: ideological unions, such as the Socialist and Communist unions in democratic societies, and social unions, which to a great extent rely for compliance on the social power of their *gemeinschaft* life.

*General hospitals* are tentatively classified as normative organizations, although there is little information concerning the ways in which patients are controlled.[50] A few unsystematic observations and interviews with physicians and hospital administrators suggest that the question of discipline comes up rarely, since the patient's need to comply is highly internalized. When doctors or nurses are asked, "What happens when a patient does not follow orders?" their immediate reply is typical of all contexts where only normative controls operate: "Nothing happens." Further probing shows that disobedience actually triggers a normative campaign whose scope and intensity depend on the seriousness of the consequences for the patient's health, as well as on the prestige of the professional who has been disobeyed and the degree to which the breach of discipline is visible to the various subgroups in the hospital community.

The following techniques of control are applied: (1) Informal talks with the patient by other staff members. A doctor may reinforce a nurse's orders, a chief surgeon those of his intern, a nurse may coax a patient to follow the doctor's orders. (2) The use of the hospital hierarchy to settle "disciplinary"

45. This might be an appropriate place to point out once more that our discussion centers on organizations in modern democratic societies.

46. Private communication with Ivan A. Vallier. For a theoretical discussion as well as a case analysis of the problems involved in the fulfillment of the "adaptive" (in Parsons' terminology) needs of systems emphasizing moral values, such as communes and religious organizations, see Vallier (1959). For another study of this problem see Doll (1951).

47. There are no sociological studies of convents. We do have the sober and authentic autobiographical account of Baldwin (1957) and the fictional account of Hulme (1956). Both books allow some insight into the compliance structure of nunneries. Note that in both cases, when it became evident that no normative power would hold the deviant nun, permission to leave was granted. See also Charques (1960).

48. For a report of socialization in these schools by an "insider," see Fichter (1958).

49. This is particularly true when the deviant is not an individual but a social group. It has been demonstrated, for example, that no one of the major religious organizations in the South—notwithstanding differences in hierarchical organizational controls—could overcome the resistance of its parishioners and part of the lower clergy to desegregation. See Campbell and Pettigrew (1959) and Zewe (1959).

50. For a descriptive report on the patients' involvement and perspective, see John (1935). See also H. L. Smith (1949) and Wessen (1951).

problems of patients. Burling, Lentz, and Wilson report: "The point is that the nurse must now adjust to him [the patient] almost as much as he is required to adjust to her and to hospital rules. When he becomes difficult to handle, the general-duty nurse calls upon the authority of the head nurse to bring about more cooperative relations. . . . Serious problems still go to the top [hospital administrator] but others are left to the head nurse for solution" (1956, p. 112). (3) Activation of relatives and friends to convince the patient, for example, to undergo an operation. (4) A visit by an outsider whom the patient respects, such as a pastor. (5) Asking the patient to sign a document releasing the hospital from responsibility for the consequences of his disobedience. This is usually seen as a legal act, which protects the hospital from possible damage suits. In addition, it frequently serves as part of the normative campaign, impressing the patient with the seriousness of his disobedience. Typically, it is used long before the hospital has really given up trying to convince the patient to follow orders. In general, only persons who do not have full legal rights, such as minors, inmates, and the mentally deficient, are treated through coercion.[51]

The diversity of *voluntary associations* is enormous. There is hardly a goal, from watching birds (the Audubon Society) to spacing births (the Planned Parenthood Federation of America) which has not been pursued by some association. It is not our task here to classify this large group according to goals, functions, or any aspect other than compliance.[52] From this viewpoint all voluntary associations have a similar structure: they are primarily social, using in addition varying degrees of pure normative power.[53] But the use of normative power rarely has the same significance as it does in religious, political, and educational organizations.

Fraternal associations, such as the Lions, Elks, Masons, Rotary, or Greek-letter societies on college campuses, which satisfy their members' gregarious needs through social activities, constitute a subcategory of voluntary associations which apply social power almost exclusively, building up social rather than moral commitments. In this type of organization, membership and degree of activity are so closely related to involvement[54]—while regulations and directives are so limited and open to individual interpretation—that disciplinary problems rarely arise. Social power is exercised mainly through informal sanctions (e.g., withdrawal of approval) and only infrequently through suspension or expulsion. Disapproval is either potent enough to generate conformity or abolishes the very motivation for belonging, since the gregarious needs remain unsatisfied.

Among the voluntary associations which build up moral as well as social commitments are fund-raising organizations such as the American Cancer Society, American Heart Association, United Cerebral Palsy, National Tuberculosis, the National Foundation, and the Community Chest.[55] These organizations tend to develop ideologies which build up the commitment of members and volunteer workers to the organization, and compensate them through symbolic rewards for their work and monetary contributions. It is probable that the feuds among some of these organizations have the latent function of building up such ideologies and membership commitments.[56]

* * * * * *

51. There are also some relevant differences in the treatment of paying patients and ward patients which have yet to be explored. Burling, et al. (1956, p. 112) report that the insured patients have a "more independent spirit."

52. Some of the best analyses of the functions of voluntary associations are unpublished Ph.D. dissertations. See Barber (1948); Axelrod (1953); S. D. Fox (1953); Goldsmer (1943). See the review of various approaches to the subject by Warner (1953, ch. 9); Chapple and Coon (1941, pp. 416–23); Rose (1954, pp. 72–115); Bottomore (1954); Chambers (1954); Henderson (1895). For an interesting classification see Gordon and Babchuk (1959, pp. 22–29).

53. Seventy per cent of the volunteers studied by Sills (1957, pp. 99–101) were either "Good Citizens" or "Joiners," both persons who join the Polio Foundation mainly for "social" reasons.

54. This is demonstrated for participation in a labor union by L. R. Dean (1954); for a fund-raising organization by Cornish (1960). For reviews of the research on determinants of participation see Barber (1950, pp. 481–84); and Komarovsky (1946, pp. 686–98). For two effective reviews and analysis of available evidence see Wright and Hyman (1958, pp. 284–94) and J. C. Scott, Jr. (1957, pp. 317–26).

55. For case studies of two of these associations, see Seeley, Junkers, Wallace, et al. (1957) and Sills (1957).

56. For an account of the public aspect of such an inter-organizational feud, see *The New York Times* (June 15–17, 1959). See also a study by Wiggins (1960); and Kohn, Tannenbaum, Weiss, et al. (1956). Rose (1955) studied the impact of inter-organizational conflict on the structure of voluntary associations. For an analysis of a large number of

## Dual compliance structures

So far we have examined organizations in which one compliance pattern is predominant. Some organizations, however, develop compliance structures in which two patterns occur with the same or similar frequency. We refer to these as *dual compliance structures*.

Earlier we presented some reasons why such a compliance structure would result in some waste of power resources through neutralization, and some loss of involvement because of the ambivalence of lower participants exposed to conflicting expectations (concerning their involvement) associated with the various types of power. Such ambivalence is generated, for example, when lower participants are expected to be calculatively and morally committed at the same time. We would therefore expect organizations with dual compliance structures either to be ineffective or to develop special mechanisms for reducing waste of power resources. The following examination of two dual types illustrates one major mechanism permitting the effective combination of two compliance structures.

In the remainder of this chapter, two dual structures are briefly examined: the balanced combination of normative and coercive compliance patterns in combat organizations, and the balanced combination of normative and utilitarian compliance patterns found in some labor unions.* Since these organizations have not yet been examined, other problems involved in determining their compliance classification are also discussed here.

There is relatively little information on a third dual type, the utilitarian-coercive combination. This seems to have existed in some of the earlier factories, especially in company towns where management had a private police force, or could use public enforcement agencies for disciplinary action such as strikebreaking and collecting forced debts (to the company store, company housing facilities, etc.). For example, Cash describes the impact of federal relief programs on cotton-growers in South Carolina during the Depression: Workers received more money on relief than they could earn picking cotton; so, to avoid losing their crops, landowners had recourse to the vagrancy laws "and the chief of police issued an ultimatum to the effect that anybody who could not satisfy him as to his means of support would have to accept a job picking cotton or go to jail and be farmed out to the landowners to pay his board bill. . . . In many districts threatened with the migration of labor to other places where higher wages were offered, armed patrols began to ride the roads to head off those who were leaving and drive them back to work at the prevailing wage" (1954, p. 407).[57] Compliance on ships in earlier centuries seems to have had such a compound structure, as evidenced, for example, in the formal right of the captain to arrest a disobedient sailor and the informal but well-established "right" of those higher in rank to beat those lower in rank—particularly that of the boatswain to flog young seamen. Since there is no systematic information on this type and an analysis of the two others will suffice to illustrate our main point, the utilitarian-coercive type will not be further discussed.

voluntary associations, other than fund-raising organizations, which have normative programs, see Hero (1960).

* Editors' note: The latter compliance structure is not included in this excerpt.

### NORMATIVE-COERCIVE STRUCTURE: THE CASE OF COMBAT UNITS

*Segregation in time.* In order to command the commitments required for effective realization of combat goals, modern combat units have to rely heavily on both normative and coercive powers. Peacetime armies rely on remunerative powers (secure salaries, fringe benefits, fines) and some coercion to control career soldiers;[58] they rely more exclusively on coercion to control draftees. These means would prove unsatisfactory as dominant mechanisms of control on the front lines.

Combat units must to some extent rely on normative powers because the deprivations inflicted by

57. For a description of the ways in which municipal police have been mobilized to prevent union organization of workers, see R. S. Lynd and H. M. Lynd (1937, p. 37 and ch. 2, *passim*). On the use of weapons, company police, and intimidation by corporations as well as close cooperation with local police forces to control labor, see Sutherland (1949, p. 141).

58. Janowitz supplies some information on the motivation of 113 military leaders in 1958. He shows that "those who see the military profession as a calling or a unique profession are outnumbered by a greater concentration of individuals for whom the military is just another job" (1960, p. 117). Uyeki supplies some information on the orientation of peacetime soldiers to their "job" (1958, pp. 7–8; 12). The calculative elements are stressed.

combat are such that no calculative involvement of the kind created by remuneration can compensate for them. No modern army can supply remuneration high enough to induce most lower participants to risk life and limb.[59] Even an attempt to compensate for other deprivations, such as separation from family and home, interruption of a career pattern, lack of amenities, and so on, would call for more funds than any modern organization could recruit.

Human beings can be made to follow highly depriving directives in two ways. They may come to believe it necessary to endure them, a feeling created when combat goals are internalized; or they may anticipate even worse deprivations if they seek to escape those of the front line.[60] Intensive moral involvement is created by officers who are leaders; by resocialization in basic training; in military schools; by educational or political officers; and through the influence of chaplains. Other expressive media and situations, such as the prayer before battle, heroes' funerals, and medals, have the same function (Marshall, 1947, pp. 138–56). Coercion is applied through confinement to the base, including the withdrawal of furlough privileges; the imprisonment or execution of deserters; and firing at retreating troops.

The application of the two powers, normative and coercive, is segregated in time in such a manner that the two powers conflict as little as possible. Normative power is applied first; only when this is or seems to be ineffective is there a resort to coercive power.

It is of interest to note that separation in time does not completely solve the problem created by two different types of control. Officers are often censured for misjudging the time for transition. They are considered poor officers (leaders) when they rely too much, and especially too soon, on coercion. On the other hand, if they become too involved with their men, or for some other reason continue to rely on normative powers when things get out of hand, they are considered "soft" and are subject to reprimands. Moreover, it is likely that the use of coercion at any time has some neutralizing effects on normative power and moral involvement even during the period in which coercion is not applied, despite the segregation in time.

*Social or pure normative compliance?* The significance of normative compliance in combat units is widely acknowledged, but it is less clear what kind of normative power plays the main role. Two well-known and often cited studies—one of the German *Wehrmacht* (Shils and Janowitz, 1948) and the other of American soldiers (Stouffer *et al.*, 1949; Merton and Lazarsfeld, 1950)—both conducted during World War II, raised the question of the relative importance of what, in our terms, are pure normative compliance and social compliance.[61] Several conclusions emerge from these studies. First, formal ideological communications (e.g., leaflet propaganda), when not absorbed and transmitted by leaders,[62] had little effect on the behavior of combat soldiers. However, more internalized values were very significant. The ideal of a "good soldier," of military honor, was one such factor. Shils and Janowitz report: "The code of soldierly honor and its ramifications took a deep root in the personality of the German soldiers of the line—even those who were totally apolitical. . . . For these people a military career was a good and noble one, enjoying high intrinsic ethical value" (1948, p. 296). Second, the importance of group solidarity or cohesiveness in controlling participants' behavior has been stressed in these studies; in fact, later interpretations of wartime studies have tended to overemphasize the role of cohesion in combat compliance. Both Shils and Janowitz have, in later writings, warned against such a tendency. Janowitz states: "Strategic issues and ideological images are elements of combat effectiveness and organizational control. The findings of sociologists

59. There were of course mercenary armies in earlier periods. But since they were much smaller, they could recruit their soldiers from the small groups of people whose relative attachment to life, money, and risk is quite different from the "normal."

60. ". . . the Nazis sought to counteract the fear of personal physical destruction in battle by telling the men that accurate records were kept on deserters and that not only would their families and property be made to suffer in the event of their desertion, but that after the war, upon their return to Germany, they, too, would be very severely punished" (Shils and Janowitz, 1948, p. 291).

61. For a bibliography and discussion of other studies see Janowitz (1959, pp. 64–82).

62. The significance of such "opinion leaders" for the "translation" of formal into informal communication, and hence for the effectiveness of formal communication, has been demonstrated in spheres other than combat. See Lazarsfeld, Berelson, and Gaudet (1948, second edition, esp. p. xxiii); Katz and Lazarsfeld (1955, ch. 2); and Katz (1957, pp. 61–78).

on the crucial importance of primary group cohesion in military morale do not overlook or eliminate the role of secondary identifications, although some of the enthusiasts of small group research seem to arrive at such a conclusion" (1959, p. 44). Shils has pointed out that "these data [supplied in *The American Soldier*] support the more complex hypothesis that primary group solidarity functions in the corporate body to strengthen the motivation for the fulfillment of substantive prescriptions and commands issued by the official agents of the corporate body, within the context of *a set of generalized moral predispositions or sense of obligation*" (1950, p. 22). Third, the various studies of combat behavior leave little doubt that the nature of the group's leadership determined to a considerable degree the combat commitment of soldiers (Grinkel and Spiegel, 1945, pp. 46–48). When the enlisted men in the *Wehrmacht* accepted the leadership of officers and noncommissioned officers, and when the leaders were devoted Nazis, the units were highly committed to combat goals as reflected in their combat effectiveness. When the leaders were not Nazis, or were rejected, the units were less effective. Furthermore, the higher the proportion of devoted Nazis in a given unit, the greater its combat effectiveness (Shils and Janowitz, pp. 286–88).

Thus two dimensions emerge from these studies which have to be carefully separated: the effect of leadership, and the effect of peer cohesion. In two subsequent chapters we shall examine closely the relationship of both factors to compliance.

To summarize, compliance in combat units rests on a balanced combination of two powers: normative and coercive. Neutralization or waste of those powers is minimized by temporal separation: Normative means are applied first, and only when these fail is coercion employed. Normative power may be either "pure" or "social." Many interpretations of studies describing combat units appear to have overemphasized the role of social power, or cohesion; obviously pure normative commitments, such as honor, prestige, and the leadership ideology, are also potent.

* * * * * *

## Summary of classification

Organizations in each category are listed according to the relative weight of the predominant compliance pattern in their compliance structure. Those giving the predominant pattern greatest weight are listed first.

1. *Predominantly coercive*
   - Concentration camps
   - Prisons (most)
   - Correctional "institutions" (large majority)
   - Custodial mental hospitals
   - Prisoner-of-war camps
   - Relocation centers
   - Coercive unions
   - Place in category undetermined: Forced-labor camps

2. *Predominantly utilitarian*
   - Blue-collar industries and blue-collar divisions in other industries
   - White-collar industries and white-collar divisions in other industries (normative compliance is a secondary pattern)
   - Business unions (normative compliance is a secondary pattern)
   - Farmers' organizations (normative compliance is a secondary pattern)
   - Peacetime military organizations (coercive compliance is a secondary pattern)

3. *Predominantly normative*
   - Religious organizations (including churches, orders, monasteries, convents)
   - Ideological political organizations
   - General hospitals
   - Colleges and universities
   - Social unions
   - Voluntary associations
     - *a*) fraternal associations (high social compliance
     - *b*) fund-raising and action associations (high social plus secondary emphasis on pure normative compliance)
   - Schools (coercion in varying degrees is the secondary pattern)
   - Therapeutic mental hospitals (coercion is the secondary pattern)
   - Professional organizations (including research organizations, law firms, newspapers, plan-

ning firms, etc.; utilitarian compliance is the secondary pattern)

Place in category undetermined: "Core" organizations of social movements

4. *Dual structures*

Normative-coercive: Combat units

Utilitarian-normative: Majority of unions

Utilitarian-coercive: Some early industries, some farms, company towns, and ships

## References


Abel, T. "The Sociology of Concentration Camps," *Social Forces*, 1951, 30: 150–55.

Abramson, E., Cutler, H. A., Kautz, R. W. and Mendelson, M. "Social Power and Commitment: A Theoretical Statement," *American Sociological Review*, 1958, 23: 15–22.

Adler, H. G. "Ideas Toward a Sociology of the Concentration Camp," *The American Journal of Sociology*, 1958, 63: 513–22.

Archibald, Katherine. *Wartime Shipyards*. Berkeley and Los Angeles: University of California Press, 1947.

Argyris, C. *Personality and Organization*. New York: Harper, 1957.

Axelrod, M. "A Study of Formal and Informal Group Participation in a Larger Urban Community." Unpublished doctoral dissertation, University of Michigan, 1953.

Baldwin, Monica. *I Leap over the Wall*. New York: Signet, 1957.

Banfield, E. *The Moral Basis of a Backward Society*. New York: The Free Press, 1958.

Barber, B. "Mass Apathy and Voluntary Social Participation in the United States." Unpublished doctoral dissertation, Harvard University, 1948.

———. "Participation and Mass Apathy in Associations," in A. W. Gouldner (ed.), *Studies in Leadership*. New York: Harper, 1950, pp. 477–504.

Barton, A. H. "The Concept of Property Space in Social Research," in P. F. Lazarsfeld and M. Rosenberg (eds.), *The Language of Social Research*. New York: The Free Press, 1955, pp. 40–53.

———. "Legitimacy, Power, and Compromise Within Formal Authority Structures—A Formal Model." Bureau of Applied Social Research, Columbia University, 1958, mimeo.

Becker, H. S. "Notes on the Concept of Commitment," *The American Journal of Sociology*, 1960, 66: 32–40.

Belknap, I. *Human Problems of a State Mental Hospital*. New York: McGraw-Hill, 1956.

Bell, D. "The 'Rediscovery' of alienation," *Journal of Philosophy*, 1959, 56: 933–52.

———. *The End of Ideology*. New York: The Free Press, 1960.

Bendix, R. "Bureaucracy: The Problem and Its Setting," *American Sociological Review*, 1947, 12: 493–507.

Bettelheim, B. "Individual and Mass Behavior in Extreme Situations," *Journal of Abnormal and Social Psychology*, 1943, 38: 417–52.

Blauner, R. "Alienation in Work: Industrial Variations and Industrial Trends." Mimeo, 1960.

Bloch, H. A. "The Personality of Inmates of Concentration Camps," *The American Journal of Sociology*, 1947, 52: 335–41.

Bondy, C. "Problems of Internment Camps," *Journal of Abnormal and Social Psychology*, 1943, 38: 453–75.

Bottomore, T. "Social Stratification in Voluntary Associations," in D. V. Glass (ed.), *Social Mobility in Britain*. New York: The Free Press, 1954, pp. pp. 349–82.

Boulding, K. E. *The Organizational Revolution*. New York: Harper, 1953.

Breton, R. "Reward Structures and Participation in an Organization." Paper presented to the Eastern Sociological Society, April 1960.

Burling, T., Lentz, Edith M. and Wilson, R. N. *The Give and Take in Hospitals*. New York: Putnam, 1956.

Campbell, A., Gurin, G. and Miller, W. E. *The voter Decides*. Evanston, Ill.: Row, Peterson, 1954.

Campbell, E. Q. and Pettigrew, T. F. *Christians in Racial Crisis*. Washington, D.C.: Public Affairs Press, 1959.

Cartwright, D. "A Field Theoretical Conception of Power," in D. Cartwright (ed.), *Studies in Social Power*. Ann Arbor: University of Michigan Press, 1959, pp. 183–220.

Cash, W. J. *The Mind of the South*. Garden City, N.Y.: Doubleday, 1954.

Chambers, Rosalind C. "A Study of Three Voluntary Organizations," in D. V. Glass (ed.), *Social Mobility in Britain*. New York: The Free Press, 1954, pp. 383–406.

Chapple, E. D. and Coon, C. S. *Principles of Anthropology*. New York: Holt, 1941.

Charques, Dorothy. *The Nunnery*. New York: Coward-McCann, 1960.

Clemmer, D. *The Prison Community*. New York: Holt, Rinehart, Winston, 1958.

Cohen, E. A. *Human Endeavor in the Concentration Camp*. New York: Norton, 1953.

Cohen, I. *The Ruhleben Prison Camp*. London: Methuen, 1917.

Coleman, J. S. "Multidimensional Scale Analysis," *The American Journal of Sociology*, 1957, 63: 253–63.

Commons, J. R. *Legal Foundations of Capitalism*. Madison: University of Wisconsin Press, 1957.

Cornish, Mary Jean. "Participation in Voluntary Associations." Unpublished report, Bureau of Applied Social Research, Columbia University, 1960.

Dahl, R. A. "The concept of power," *Behavioral Science*, 1957, 2: 201–15.

Dahrendorf, R. *Class and Class Conflict in Industrial Society*. Stanford, Calif.: Stanford University Press, 1959.

Davis, K. "The Sociology of Prostitution," *American Sociological Review*, 1937, 2: 744–55.

Dean, D. G. "Alienation and Political Apathy," *Social Forces*, 1960, 38: 185–89.

Dean, L. R. "Union Activity and Dual Loyalty," *Industrial and Labor Relations Review*, 1954, 7: 526–36.

Deutsch, K. W. *Nationalism and social communication*. New York: Wiley, 1953.

Doll, E. E. "Social and Economic Organization in Two Pennsylvania German Religious Communities," *The American Journal of Sociology*, 1951, 57: 168–77.

Easton, E. *The Political System*. New York: Knopf, 1952.

Eisenstadt, S. N. "Bureaucracy and Bureaucratization," *Current Sociology*, 1958, 7: 99–124.

Estes, W. K. "An Experimental Study of Punishment," *Psychological Monographs*, 1944, 57, No. 3.

Etzioni, A. "Industrial Sociology: The Study of Economic Organizations," *Social Research*, 1958, 25: 303–24.

Feldman, A. S. "The Interpenetration of Firm and Society." Paper presented at the International Social Science Council Round Table on Social Implications of Technical Change, Paris, March 1959.

Fichter, J. H. *Social Relations in the Urban Parish*. Chicago: The University of Chicago Press, 1954.

———. *Parochial School: A Sociological Study*. Notre Dame, Ind.: University of Notre Dame, 1958.

Fox, S. D. "Voluntary Association and Social Structure." Unpublished doctoral dissertation, Harvard University, 1953.

French, J. R. P., Jr. and Raven, B. "The Bases of Social Power," in D. Cartwright (ed.), *Studies in Social Power*. Ann Arbor: University of Michigan, 1959, pp. 150–67.

Friedrich, C. J. (ed.) *Authority*. Cambridge, Mass.: Harvard University Press, 1958.

Gerth, H. H. and Mills, C. W. (eds.), *From Max Weber: Essays in Sociology*. New York: Oxford University Press, 1946.

Gilbert, Doris C. and Levinson, D. J. "'Custodialism' and 'Humanism' in Staff Ideology," in M. Greenblatt D. J. Levinson and R. H. Williams, (eds.), *The Patient and the Mental Hospital*. New York: The Free Press, 1957, pp. 20–35.

Goldhamer, H. and Shils, E. A. "Types of Power and Status." *The American Journal of Sociology*, 1939, 45: 171–82.

Goldsmer, H. "Some Factors Affecting Participation in Voluntary Associations." Unpublished doctoral dissertation, University of Chicago, 1943.

Gordon, C. W. and Babchuk, N. "A Typology of Voluntary Associations," *American Sociological Review*, 1959, 24: 22–29.

Gouldner, Helen P. "Dimensions of Organizational Commitment," *Administrative Science Quarterly*, 1960, 4: 468–90.

Grinker, R. R. and Spiegel, J. P. *Men Under Stress*. Philadelphia: Blakiston, 1945.

Guttman, L. "The Cornell Technique for Scale and Intensity Analysis," *Educational and Psychological Measurement*, 1947, 7: 247–79.

———. "The Principal Components of Scale Analysis," in S. Stouffer *et al.*, *Measurement and Prediction*. Princeton, N.Y.: Princeton University Press, 1950, pp. 312–61.

———. "The Principal Components of Scalable Attitudes," in P. F. Lazarsfeld (ed.), *Mathematical Thinking in the Social Sciences*. New York: The Free Press, 1954, pp. 216–57.

Henderson, C. R. "The Place and Functions of Voluntary Associations," *The American Journal of Sociology*, 1895, 1: 327–34.

Hero, A. *Voluntary Organizations in World Affairs Communication*. Boston: World Peace Foundation 1960.

Hoess, R. *Commandant of Auschwitz*. New York: World, 1960.

Hulme, Kathryn. *The Nun's Story*. Boston: Little, Brown, 1956.

Jackman, N. "Survival in the Concentration Camp," *Human Organization*, 1958, 17: 23–26.

Jacobson, E. "Foreman and Steward, Representatives of Management and the Union," in H. Guetzkow (ed.), *Groups, Leadership, and Men*. Pittsburgh, Pa.: Carnegie Press, 1951, pp. 90–95.

Janowitz, M. *Sociology and the Military Establishment*. New York: Russell Sage Foundation, 1959.

———. *The Professional Soldier*. New York: The Free Press, 1960.

John, Gabriel (Sister). *Through the Patient's Eyes: Hospitals, Doctors, Nurses*. Philadelphia, Pa.: Lippincott, 1935.

Jones, W. H. M. "In Defense of Apathy," *Political Studies*, 1954, 2: 25–37.

Katz, E. "The Two-Step Flow of Communication: An Up-to-date Report on an Hypothesis," *Public Opinion Quarterly*, 1957, 21: 61–78.

——— and P. F. Lazarsfeld. *Personal Influence*. New York: The Free Press, 1955.

Kinkead, E. "The Study of Something New in

History," *The New Yorker*, Oct. 26, 1957, pp. 114–69.
Kinkhead, E. *In Every War But One*. New York: Norton, 1959.
Kogon, E. *The Theory and Practice of Hell: The German Concentration Camps and the System Behind Them*. New York: Farrar, Straus, 1950.
Kohn, R. L., Tannenbaum, A., Weiss, R., *et al.* "A Study of the League of Women Voters of the United States." Ann Arbor: University of Michigan, 1956, mimeo.
Komarovsky, Mirra. "Patterns of Voluntary Association Among Urban Working-class Families," *American Sociological Review*, 1946, 2: 686–98.
Kornhauser, A., Sheppard, H. L. and Mayer, A. J. *When Labor Votes*. New York: University Books, 1956.
Kreps, T. J. "The Newspaper Industry," in W. Adams (ed.), *The Structure of American Industry*. New York: Macmillan, 1954, pp. 485–504.
Lasswell, H. D. and Kaplan, A. *Power and Society*. New Haven: Yale University Press, 1950.
LaViolette, F. E. *The Canadian Japanese and World War II: A Sociological and Psychological Account*. Toronto: University Press, 1948.
Lazarsfeld, P. F., Berelson, B. and Gaudet, Hazel. *The People's Choice*. 2nd ed. New York: Columbia University Press, 1948.
Leighton, A. H. *The Governing of Men: General Principles and Recommendations Based on Experience at a Japanese Relocation Camp*. Princeton, N.J.: Princeton University Press, 1945.
Lynd, R. S. and Lynd, H. M. *Middletown in Transition*. New York: Harcourt, Brace, 1937.
McDill, E. L. "A Comparison of Three Measures of Attitude Intensity," *Social Forces*, 1959, 38: 95–99.
McElroy, J. *This Was Andersonville*. New York: McDowell, 1957.
Marshall, S. L. A. *Men Against Fire*. New York: Morrow, 1947.
Merton, R. K. *Mass Persuasion: The Social Psychology of a War Bond Drive*. New York: Harper, 1946.
———. *Social Theory and Social Structure*. Rev. ed. New York: The Free Press, 1957.
——— and Lazarsfeld, P. F. (eds.). *Continuities in Social Research*. New York: The Free Press, 1950.
Mills, C. W. *White Collar*. New York: Oxford University Press, 1951.
Moore, W. E. "Comment," *American Sociological Review*, 1953, 18: 397.
———. "Management and Union Organizations: An Analytical Comparison." In C. M. Arensberg *et al.*, *Research in Industrial Human Relations*. New York: Harper, 1957, pp. 119–30.
Morse, Nancy C. *Satisfactions in the White-collar Job*. Survey Research Center, University of Michigan, 1953.
——— and Weiss, R. S. "The Function and Meaning of Work and the Job," *American Sociological Review*, 1955, 20: 191–98.
Nettler, G. A. "A Measure of Alienation," *American Sociological Review*, 1957, 22: 670–77.
Neuman, F. L. "Approaches to the Study of Political Power," *Political Science Quarterly*, 1950, 65: 161–80.
Ohlin, L. E. *Sociology and the Field of Corrections*. New York: Russell Sage Foundation, 1956.
Parsons, T. *The Social System*. New York: The Free Press, 1951.
———. "Suggestions for a Sociological Approach to the Theory of Organizations," *Administrative Science Quarterly*, 1956, 1: 63–85, 225–39.
———. "The Distribution of Power in American Society," *World Politics*, 1957, 10: 123–43.
——— *et al.* (eds.). *Family, Socialization and Interaction Process*. New York: The Free Press, 1955.
——— *et al. Toward a General Theory of Action*. Cambridge, Mass.: Harvard University Press, 1952.
Parvilahti, U. *Beria's Gardens: A Slave Laborer's Experience in the Soviet Utopia*. Tr. by A. Blair. New York: Dutton, 1960.
Purcell, T. V. *The Worker Speaks His Mind on Company and Union*. Cambridge, Mass.: Harvard University Press, 1953.
Roach, Alva C. *The Prisoner of War and How Treated*. Indianapolis: Railroad City Publishers, 1865.
Rose, A. M. *Theory and Method in the Social Sciences*. Minneapolis: University of Minnesota, 1954.
———. "Voluntary Associations Under Conditions of Competition and Conflict," *Social Forces*, 1955, 34: 159–63.
Scott, Frances G. "Action Theory and Research in Social Organization," *The American Journal of Sociology*, 1959, 64: 386–95.
Scott, J. C., Jr. "Membership and Participation in Voluntary Associations," *American Sociological Review*, 1957, 22: 315–26.
Seeley, J. R., Junkers, B. H., Wallace, J. R., Jr., *et al.* *Community Chest*. Toronto: University of Toronto, 1957.
Selznick, P. *The Organizational Weapon*. New York: McGraw-Hill, 1952.
Shils, E. A. "Primary Groups in the American Army," In R. K. Merton and P. F. Lazarsfeld (eds.), *Continuities in Social Research*. New York: The Free Press, 1950, pp. 16–39.
——— and Janowitz, M. "Cohesion and Disintegration in the Whermact in World War II," *Public Opinion Quarterly*, 1948, 12 (2): 280–315.
Sills, D. L. *The Volunteers*. New York: The Free Press, 1957.
Simmel, G. "Superiority and Subordination as Subject-matter of Sociology," *The American Journal of Sociology*, 1896, 2: 167–89, 392–415.
Simon, H. A., Smithburg, D. W. and Thompson,

V. A. *Public Administration*. New York: Knopf, 1959.

Simpson, R. L. and Simpson, Ida H. "The Psychiatric Attendant: Development of an Occupational Self-image in a Low-status Occupation," *American Sociological Review*, 1959, 24: 389–92.

Smith, H. L. "The Sociological Study of Hospitals." Unpublished doctoral dissertation, University of Chicago, 1949.

Stinchcombe, A. L. "Bureaucratic and Craft Administration of Production: A Comparative Study," *Administrative Science Quarterly*, 1959, 4: 168–87.

Stouffer, S. A., *et al. The American Soldier*. Princeton, N.Y.: Princeton University Press, 1949.

Suchman, E. A. "The Intensity Component in Attitude and Opinion Research," in Stouffer *et al.* (1950), pp. 213–76.

Sutherland, E. *White Collar Crime*. New York: The Dryden Press, 1949.

Sykes, G. M. *The Society of Captives*. Princeton, N.Y.: Princeton University Press, 1958.

Thompson, J. D. "Organizational management of conflict," *Administrative Science Quarterly*, 1960, 4: 389–409.

——— and Bates, F. L. "Technology, organization, and administration," *Administrative Science Quarterly*, 1957, 2: 325–43.

Uyeki, E. S. "Sociology of the Cold-War Army." Paper presented to the American Sociological Society, Seattle, Wash., August 1958.

Vallier, I. A. "Production Imperatives in Communal Systems: A Comparative Study with Special Reference to the *Kibbutz* Crises." Unpublished doctoral dissertation, Harvard University, 1959.

Vaughan, Elizabeth M. *Community Under Stress*. Princeton, N.Y.: Princeton University Press, 1949.

Warner, W. L. *American Life*. Chicago: The University of Chicago Press, 1953.

——— and Low, J. O. *The Social System of the Modern Factory*. New Haven: Yale University Press, 1947.

Webb, R. C. *The Real Mormonism*. New York: Sturgis and Walton, 1916.

Wessen, A. F. "The Social Structure of a Modern Hospital." Unpublished doctoral dissertation, Yale University, 1951.

White, W. L. *The Captives of Korea: Our Treatment of Theirs; Their Treatment of Ours*." New York: Scribner, 1957.

Whyte, W. F. *Human Relations in the Restaurant Industry*. New York: McGraw-Hill, 1948.

——— *et al. Money and Motivation*. New York: Harper, 1955.

Wiggins, Belle. "Dynamics of Public Support of Volunteer Health and Welfare Associations." Unpublished report, Bureau of Applied Social Research, Columbia University, 1960.

Willerman, B. "Overlapping Group Identification in an Industrial Setting." Paper presented to the American Psychological Association, Denver, September 1949.

Wright, C. R. and Hyman, H. H. "Voluntary Association Memberships of American Adults: Evidence from National Sample Surveys." *American Sociological Review*, 1958, 23: 284–94.

Zetterberg, H. L. "Compliant Actions," *Acta Sociologica*, 1957, 2: 179–201.

Zewe, D. "The Functioning of Three Types of Church Structure in the School Integration Crisis." 1959. Unpublished.

PETER M. BLAU

# Exchange Theory

## The exchange of social rewards

By Honour, in its proper and genuine Signification, we mean nothing else but the good Opinion of others. . . .

The Reason why there are so few Men of real Virtue, and so many of real Honour, is, because all the Recompence a Man has of virtuous Action, is the Pleasure of doing it, which most People reckon but poor Pay; but the Self-denial a Man of Honour submits to in one Appetite, is immediately rewarded by the Satisfaction he receives from another, and what he abates of his Avarice, or any other Passion, is doubly repaid to his Pride. . . .

MANDEVILLE, *The Fable of the Bees*

Most human pleasures have their roots in social life. Whether we think of love or power, professional recognition or sociable companionship, the comforts of family life or the challenge of competitive sports, the gratifications experienced by individuals are contingent on actions of others. The same is true for the most selfless and spiritual satisfactions. To work effectively for a good cause requires making converts to it. Even the religious experience is much enriched by communal worship. Physical pleasures that can be experienced in solitude pale in significance by comparison. Enjoyable as a good dinner is, it is the social occasion that gives it its luster. Indeed, there is something pathetic about the person who derives his major gratification from food or drink as such, since it reveals either excessive need or excessive greed; the pauper illustrates the former, the glutton, the latter. To be sure, there are profound solitary enjoyments—reading a good book, creating a piece of art, producing a scholarly work. Yet these, too, derive much of their significance from being later communicated to and shared with others. The lack of such anticipation makes the solitary activity again somewhat pathetic: the recluse who has nobody to talk to about what he reads; the artist or scholar whose works are completely ignored, not only by his contemporaries but also by posterity.

Much of human suffering as well as much of human happiness has its source in the actions of other human beings. One follows from the other, given the facts of group life, where pairs do not exist in complete isolation from other social relations. The same human acts that cause pleasure to some typically cause displeasure to others. For one boy to enjoy the love of a girl who has committed herself to be his steady date, other boys who had gone out with her must suffer the pain of having been rejected. The satisfaction a man derives from exercising power over others requires that they endure the deprivation of being subject to his power. For a professional to command an outstanding reputation in his field, most of his colleagues must get along without such pleasant recognition, since it is the lesser professional esteem of the majority that defines his as outstanding. The joy the victorious team members experience has its counterpart in the disappointment of the losers. In short, the rewards individuals obtain in social

**Reprinted from *Exchange and Power in Social Life*, pp. 14–25, 199–223, by permission of the author and publisher.** 

associations tend to entail a cost to other individuals. This does not mean that most social associations involve zero-sum games in which the gains of some rest on the losses of others. Quite the contrary, individuals associate with one another because they all profit from their association. But they do not necessarily all profit equally, nor do they share the cost of providing the benefits equally, and even if there are no direct costs to participants, there are often indirect costs borne by those excluded from the association, as the case of the rejected suitors illustrates.

Some social associations are intrinsically rewarding. Friends find pleasure in associating with one another, and the enjoyment of whatever they do together—climbing a mountain, watching a football game—is enhanced by the gratification that inheres in the association itself. The mutual affection between lovers or family members has the same result. It is not what lovers do together but their doing it *together* that is the distinctive source of their special satisfaction—not seeing a play but sharing the experience of seeing it. Social interaction in less intimate relations than those of lovers, family members, or friends, however, may also be inherently rewarding. The sociability at a party or among neighbors or in a work group involves experiences that are not especially profound but are intrinsically gratifying. In these cases, all associates benefit simultaneously from their social interaction, and the only cost they incur is the indirect one of giving up alternative opportunities by devoting time to the association.

Social associations may also be rewarding for a different reason. Individuals often derive specific benefits from social relations because their associates deliberately go to some trouble to provide these benefits for them. Most people like helping others and doing favors for them—to assist not only their friends but also their acquaintances and occasionally even strangers, as the motorist who stops to aid another with his stalled car illustrates. Favors make us grateful, and our expressions of gratitude are social rewards that tend to make doing favors enjoyable, particularly if we express our appreciation and indebtedness publicly and thereby help establish a person's reputation as a generous and competent helper. Besides, one good deed deserves another. If we feel grateful and obligated to an associate for favors received, we shall seek to reciprocate his kindness by doing things for him. He in turn is likely to reciprocate, and the resulting mutual exchange of favors strengthens, often without explicit intent, the social bond between us.

A person who fails to reciprocate favors is accused of ingratitude. This very accusation indicates that reciprocation is expected, and it serves as a social sanction that discourages individuals from forgetting their obligations to associates. Generally, people are grateful for favors and repay their social debts, and both their gratitude and their repayment are social rewards for the associate who has done them favors.[1] The fact that furnishing benefits to others tends to produce these social rewards is, of course, a major reason why people often go to great trouble to help their associates and enjoy doing so. We would not be human if these advantageous consequences of our good deeds were not important inducements for our doing them.[2] There are, to be sure, some individuals who selflessly work for others without any thought of reward and even without expecting gratitude, but these are virtually saints, and saints are rare. The rest of us also act unselfishly sometimes, but we require some incentive for doing so, if it is only the social acknowledgment that we are unselfish.

An apparent "altruism" pervades social life; people are anxious to benefit one another and to reciprocate for the benefits they receive. But beneath this seeming selflessness an underlying "egoism" can be discovered; the tendency to help others is frequently motivated by the expectation that doing so will bring social rewards. Beyond this self-interested concern with profiting from social associations, however, there is again an "altruistic" element or, at least, one that removes social transactions from simple egoism or psychological hedonism. A basic reward people seek in their associations is

1. "We rarely meet with ingratitude, so long as we are in a position to confer favors." François La Rochefoucauld, *The Maxims*, London: Oxford University Press, 1940, p. 101 (#306).

2. Once a person has become emotionally committed to a relationship, his identification with the other and his interest in continuing the association provide new independent incentives for supplying benefits to the other. Similarly, firm commitments to an organization lead members to make recurrent contributions to it without expecting reciprocal benefits in every instance. The significance of these social attachments is further elaborated in subsequent chapters.

social approval, and selfish disregard for others makes it impossible to obtain this important reward.[3]

The social approval of those whose opinions we value is of great significance to us, but its significance depends on its being genuine. We cannot force others to give us their approval, regardless of how much power we have over them, because coercing them to express their admiration or praise would make these expressions worthless. "Action can be coerced, but a coerced show of feeling is only a show."[4] Simulation robs approval of its significance, but its very importance makes associates reluctant to withhold approval from one another and, in particular, to express disapproval, thus introducing an element of simulation and dissimulation into their communications. As a matter of fact, etiquette prescribes that approval be simulated in disregard of actual opinions under certain circumstances. One does not generally tell a hostess, "Your party was boring," or a neighbor, "What you say is stupid." Since social conventions require complimentary remarks on many occasions, these are habitually discounted as not reflecting genuine approbation, and other evidence that does reflect it is looked for, such as whether guests accept future invitations or whether neighbors draw one into further conversations.

In matters of morality, however, individuals have strong convictions that constrain them to voice their actual judgments more freely. They usually do not hesitate to express disapproval of or, at least, withhold approval from associates who have violated socially accepted standards of conduct. Antisocial disregard for the welfare of the in-group meets universally with disapprobation regardless of how immoral, in terms of the mores of the wider community, the norms of a particular group may be. The significance of social approval, therefore, discourages conduct that is utterly and crudely selfish. A more profound morality must rest not merely on group pressure and long-run advantage but primarily on internalized normative standards. In the ideal case, an individual unerringly follows the moral commands of his conscience whatever the consequences. While such complete morality is attained only by the saint and the fool, and most men make some compromises,[5] moral standards clearly do guide and restrain human conduct. Within the rather broad limits these norms impose on social relations, however, human beings tend to be governed in their associations with one another by the desire to obtain social rewards of various sorts, and the resulting exchanges of benefits shape the structure of social relations.

The question that arises is whether a rationalistic conception of human behavior underlies this principle that individuals pursue social rewards in their social associations. The only assumption made is that human beings choose between alternative potential associates or courses of action by evaluating the experiences or expected experiences with each in terms of a preference ranking and then selecting the best alternative. Irrational as well as rational behavior is governed by these considerations as Boulding has pointed out:

> All behavior, in so far as the very concept of behavior implies doing one thing rather than another, falls into the above pattern, even the behavior of the lunatic and the irrational or irresponsible or erratic person. The distinction between rational and irrational behavior lies in the degree of self-consciousness and the stability of the images involved rather than in any distinction of the principle of optimum.[6]

What is explicitly *not* assumed here is that men have complete information, that they have no social commitments restricting their alternatives, that their preferences are entirely consistent or remain constant, or that they pursue one specific ultimate goal to the exclusion of all others. These more restrictive assumptions, which are not made in the present analysis, characterize rationalistic models of human conduct, such as that of game theory.[7] Of

3. Bernard Mandeville's central theme is that private vices produce public benefits because the importance of social approval prompts men to contribute to the welfare of others in their own self-interest. As he put it tersely at one point, "Moral Virtues are the Political Offspring which Flattery begot upon Pride." *The Fable of the Bees*, Oxford: Clarendon, 1924, Vol. I, 51; see also pp. 63–80.

4. Erving Goffman, *Asylums*, Chicago: Aldine, 1962, p. 115.

5. Heinrich von Kleist's story "Michael Kohlhaas" is a pathetic illustration of the foolishness inherent in the insistence on rigid conformity with moral standards in complete disregard of consequences.

6. Kenneth Boulding, *Conflict and Defense*, New York: Harper, 1962, p. 151.

7. For a discussion of game theory which calls attention to its limitations, see R. Duncan Luce and Howard Raiffa, *Games and Decisions*, New York: Wiley, 1957, esp. chapters iii and vii. For other criticisms of game theory,

particular importance is the fact that men strive to achieve diverse objectives. The statement that men select the most preferred among available alternatives does not imply that they always choose the one that yields them the greatest material profit.[8] They may, and often do, choose the alternative that requires them to make material sacrifices but contributes the most to the attainment of some lofty ideal, for *this* may be their objective. Even in this choice they may err and select an alternative that actually is not the best means to realize their goal. Indeed, the need to anticipate in advance the social rewards with which others will reciprocate for favors in exchange relations inevitably introduces uncertainty and recurrent errors of judgment that make perfectly rational calculations impossible. Granted these qualifications, the assumption that men seek to adjust social conditions to achieve their ends seems to be quite realistic, indeed inescapable.

## Basic processes

To reward, is to recompense, to remunerate, to return good for good received. To punish, too, is to recompense, to remunerate, though in a different manner; it is to return evil for evil that has been done.

ADAM SMITH, *The Theory of Moral Sentiments*

The basic social processes that govern associations among men have their roots in primitive psychological processes, such as those underlying the feelings of attraction between individuals and their desires for various kinds of rewards. These psychological tendencies are primitive only in respect to our subject matter, that is, they are taken as given without further inquiry into the motivating forces that produce them, for our concern is with the social forces that emanate from them.

The simpler social processes that can be observed in interpersonal associations and that rest directly on psychological dispositions give rise to the more complex social processes that govern structures of interconnected social associations, such as the social organization of a factory or the political relations in a community. New social forces emerge in the increasingly complex social structures that develop in societies, and these dynamic forces are quite removed from the ultimate psychological base of all social life. Although complex social systems have their foundation in simpler ones, they have their own dynamics with emergent properties. In this section, the basic processes of social associations will be presented in broad strokes, to be analyzed subsequently in greater detail, with special attention to their wider implications.

Social attraction is the force that induces human beings to establish social associations on their own initiative and to expand the scope of their associations once they have been formed. Reference here is to social relations into which men enter of their own free will rather than to either those into which they are born (such as kinship groups) or those imposed on them by forces beyond their control (such as the combat teams to which soldiers are assigned), although even in these involuntary relations the extent and intensity of the association depend on the degree of mutual attraction. An individual is attracted to another if he expects associating with him to be in some way rewarding for himself, and his interest in the expected social rewards draws him to the other. The psychological needs and dispositions of individuals determine which rewards are particularly salient for them and thus to whom they will be attracted. Whatever the specific motives, there is an important difference between the expectation that the association will be an intrinsically rewarding experience and the expectation that it will furnish extrinsic benefits, for example, advice. This difference calls attention to two distinct meanings of the term "attraction" and its derivatives. In its narrower sense, social attraction refers to liking another person *intrinsically* and having positive feelings toward him; in the broader sense, in which the term is now used, social attraction refers to being drawn to another person for any reason whatsoever. The customer is attracted in this broader sense to the merchant who sells goods of a given quality at the lowest price, but he has no intrinsic feelings of attraction for him, unless they happen to be friends.

A person who is attracted to others is interested in proving himself attractive to them, for his ability

notably its failure to utilize empirical research, and an attempt to incorporate some of its principles into a substantive theory of conflict, see Thomas C. Schelling, *The Strategy of Conflict*, Cambridge: Harvard University Press, 1960, esp. chapters iv and vi.

8. See on this point George C. Homans, *Social Behavior*, New York: Harcourt, Brace and World, 1961, pp. 79–80; and Anatol Rapoport, *Fights, Games, and Debates*, Ann Arbor: University of Michigan Press, 1960, p. 122.

to associate with them and reap the benefits expected from the association is contingent on their finding him an attractive associate and thus wanting to interact with him. Their attraction to him, just as his to them, depends on the anticipation that the association will be rewarding. To arouse this anticipation, a person tries to impress others. Attempts to appear impressive are pervasive in the early stages of acquaintance and group formation. Impressive qualities make a person attractive and promise that associating with him will be rewarding. Mutual attraction prompts people to establish an association, and the rewards they provide each other in the course of their social interaction, unless their expectations are disappointed, maintain their mutual attraction and the continuing association.

Processes of social attraction, therefore, lead to processes of social exchange. The nature of the exchange in an association experienced as intrinsically rewarding, such as a love relationship, differs from that between associates primarily concerned with extrinsic benefits, such as neighbors who help one another with various chores, but exchanges do occur in either case. A person who furnishes needed assistance to associates, often at some cost to himself, obligates them to reciprocate his kindness. Whether reference is to instrumental services or to such intangibles as social approval, the benefits each supplies to the others are rewards that serve as inducements to continue to supply benefits, and the integrative bonds created in the process fortify the social relationship.

A situation frequently arises, however, in which one person needs something another has to offer, for example, help from the other in his work, but has nothing the other needs to reciprocate for the help. While the other may be sufficiently rewarded by expressions of gratitude to help him a few times, he can hardly be expected regularly to devote time and effort to providing help without receiving any return to compensate him for his troubles. (In the case of intrinsic attraction, the only return expected is the willingness to continue the association.) The person in need of recurrent services from an associate to whom he has nothing to offer has several alternatives. First, he may force the other to give him help. Second, he may obtain the help he needs from another source. Third, he may find ways to get along without such help.[9] If he is unable or unwilling to choose any of these alternatives, however, there is only one other course of action left for him; he must subordinate himself to the other and comply with his wishes, thereby rewarding the other with power over himself as an inducement for furnishing the needed help. Willingness to comply with another's demands is a generic social reward, since the power it gives him is a generalized means, parallel to money, which can be used to attain a variety of ends. The power to command compliance is equivalent to credit, which a man can draw on in the future to obtain various benefits at the disposal of those obligated to him.[10] The unilateral supply of important services establishes this kind of credit and thus is a source of power.

Exchange processes, then, give rise to differentiation of power. A person who commands services others need, and who is independent of any at their command, attains power over others by making the satisfaction of their need contingent on their compliance. This principle is held to apply to the most intimate as well as the most distant social relations. The girl with whom a boy is in love has power over him, since his eagerness to spend much time with her prompts him to make their time together especially pleasant for her by acceding to her wishes. The employer can make workers comply with his directives because they are dependent on his wages. To be sure, the superior's power wanes if subordinates can resort to coercion, have equally good alternatives, or are able to do without the benefits at his disposal. But given these limiting conditions, unilateral services that meet basic needs are the penultimate source of power. Its ultimate source, of course, is physical coercion. While the power that rests on coercion is more absolute, however, it is also more limited in scope than the power that derives from met needs.

A person on whom others are dependent for vital benefits has the power to enforce his demands. He may make demands on them that they consider fair and just in relation to the benefits they receive for submitting to his power. On the other hand, he may lack such restraint and make demands that appear

9. The last two of these alternatives are noted by Parsons (*The Social System*, New York: The Free Press, 1951, p. 252) in his discussion of a person's reactions to having his expectations frustrated by another.

10. See Parsons, "On the Concept of Influence," *Public Opinion Quarterly*, 27 (1963), 37–62, esp. pp. 59–60.

excessive to them, arousing feelings of exploitation for having to render more compliance than the rewards received justify. Social norms define the expectations of subordinates and their evaluations of the superior's demands. The fair exercise of power gives rise to approval of the superior, whereas unfair exploitation promotes disapproval. The greater the resources of a person on which his power rests, the easier it is for him to refrain from exploiting subordinates by making excessive demands, and consequently the better are the chances that subordinates will approve of the fairness of his rule rather than disapprove of its unfairness.

There are fundamental differences between the dynamics of power in a collective situation and the power of one individual over another. The weakness of the isolated subordinate limits the significance of his approval or disapproval of the superior. The agreement that emerges in a collectivity of subordinates concerning their judgment of the superior on the other hand, has far-reaching implications for developments in the social structure.

Collective approval of power legitimates that power. People who consider that the advantages they gain from a superior's exercise of power outweigh the hardships that compliance with his demands imposes on them tend to communicate to each other their approval of the ruler and their feelings of obligation to him. The consensus that develops as the result of these communications finds expression in group pressures that promote compliance with the ruler's directives, thereby strengthening his power of control and legitimating his authority. "A feeling of obligation to obey the commands of the established public authority is found, varying in liveliness and effectiveness from one individual to another, among the members of any political society."[11] Legitimate authority is the basis of organization. It makes it possible to organize collective effort to further the achievement of various objectives, some of which could not be attained by individuals separately at all and others that can be attained more effectively by coordinating efforts. Although power that is not legitimated by the approval of subordinates can also be used to organize them, the stability of such an organization is highly precarious.

11. Bertrand de Jouvenel, *Sovereignty*, University of Chicago Press, 1957, p. 87.

Collective disapproval of power engenders opposition. People who share the experience of being exploited by the unfair demands of those in positions of power, and by the insufficient rewards they receive for their contributions, are likely to communicate their feelings of anger, frustration, and aggression to each other. There tends to arise a wish to retaliate by striking down the existing powers. "As every man doth, so shall it be done to him, and retaliation seems to be the great law that is dictated to us by nature."[12] The social support the oppressed give each other in the course of discussing their common grievances and feelings of hostility justifies and reinforces their aggressive opposition against those in power. It is out of such shared discontent that opposition ideologies and movements develop—that men organize a union against their employer or a revolutionary party against their government.

In brief, differentiation of power in a collective situation evokes contrasting dynamic forces: legitimating processes that foster the organization of individuals and groups in common endeavors; and countervailing forces that deny legitimacy to existing powers and promote opposition and cleavage. Under the influence of these forces, the scope of legitimate organization expands to include ever larger collectivities, but opposition and conflict recurrently redivide these collectivities and stimulate reorganization along different lines.

The distinctive characteristic of complex social structures is that their constituent elements are also social structures. We may call these structures of interrelated groups "macrostructures" and those composed of interacting individuals "microstructures." There are some parallels between the social processes in microstructures and macrostructures. Processes of social attraction create integrative bonds between associates, and integrative processes also unite various groups in a community. Exchange processes between individuals give rise to differentiation among them, and intergroup exchanges further differentiation among groups. Individuals become incorporated in legitimate organizations, and these in turn become part of broader bodies of legitimate authority. Opposition and conflict occur not only within collectivities but also between them.

12. Adam Smith, *The Theory of Moral Sentiments* (2d ed.), London: A. Millar, 1761, p. 139.

These parallels, however, must not conceal the fundamental differences between the processes that govern the interpersonal associations in microstructures and the forces characteristic of the wider and more complex social relations in macrostructures.

First, value consensus is of crucial significance for social processes that pervade complex social structures, because standards commonly agreed upon serve as mediating links for social transactions between individuals and groups without any direct contact. Sharing basic values creates integrative bonds and social solidarity among millions of people in a society, most of whom have never met, and serves as functional equivalent for the feelings of personal attraction that unite pairs of associates and small groups. Common standards of valuation produce media of exchange—money being the prototype but not the only one—which alone make it possible to transcend personal transactions and develop complex networks of indirect exchange. Legitimating values expand the scope of centralized control far beyond the reach of personal influence, as exemplified by the authority of a legitimate government. Opposition ideals serve as rallying points to draw together strangers from widely dispersed places and unite them in a common cause. The study of these problems requires an analysis of the significance of social values and norms that must complement the analysis of exchange transactions and power relations but must not become a substitute for it.

A second emergent property of macrostructures is the complex interplay between the internal forces within substructures and the forces that connect the diverse substructures, some of which may be microstructures composed of individuals while others may themselves be macrostructures composed of subgroups. The processes of integration, differentiation, organization, and opposition formation in the various substructures, which often vary greatly among the substructures, and the corresponding processes in the macrostructure all have repercussions for each other. A systematic analysis of these intricate patterns, which will only be adumbrated in chapters ten and eleven, would have to constitute the core of a general theory of social structures.

Finally, enduring institutions typically develop in macrostructures. Established systems of legitimation raise the question of their perpetuation through time. The strong identification of men with the highest ideals and most sacred beliefs they share makes them desirous to preserve these basic values for succeeding generations. The investments made in establishing and expanding a legitimate organization create an interest in stabilizing it and assuring its survival in the face of opposition attacks. For this purpose, formalized procedures are instituted that make the organization independent of any individual member and permit it to persist beyond the life span or period of tenure of its members. Institutionalization refers to the emergence of social mechanisms through which social values and norms, organizing principles, and knowledge and skills are transmitted from generation to generation. A society's institutions constitute the social matrix in which individuals grow up and are socialized, with the result that some aspects of institutions are reflected in their own personalities, and others appear to them as the inevitable external conditions of human existence. Traditional institutions stabilize social life but also introduce rigidities that make adjustment to changing conditions difficult. Opposition movements may arise to promote such adjustment, yet these movements themselves tend to become institutionalized and rigid in the course of time, creating needs for fresh oppositions.

* * * * * *

## Legitimation and organization

A just ruler seems to make nothing out of his office; for he does not allot to himself a larger share of things generally good, unless it be proportionate to his merits; so that he labours for others, which accounts for the saying mentioned above, that "Justice is the good of others." Consequently some recompense has to be given him, in the shape of honour and dignity. It is those whom such rewards do not satisfy who make themselves tyrants.

ARISTOTLE, *The Nicomachean Ethics*

Organization involves the coordination of collective effort. Some form of social organization emerges implicitly in collectivities as the result of the processes of exchange and competition, in which the patterns of conduct of individuals and groups and the relations between them become adjusted. These processes have already been discussed. But other organizations are explicitly established for the purpose of achieving specified objectives, whether they are manufacturing goods that can be sold for a profit, participating in bowling tournaments, collective bargaining, or winning political victory. In these formal organizations, special mechanisms exist to effect the coordination of tasks of various members in the pursuit of given objectives. Such coordination of efforts, particularly on a large scale, requires some centralized direction. Power is the resource that makes it possible to direct and coordinate the activities of men.

Stable organizing power requires legitimation. To be sure, men can be made to work and to obey commands through coercion, but the coercive use of power engenders resistance and sometimes active opposition. Power conflicts in and between societies are characterized by resistance and opposition, and while the latter also occur within organizations, effective operations necessitate that they be kept at a minimum there and, especially, that members do not exhibit resistance in discharging their daily duties but perform them and comply with directives from superiors *willingly*. Only legitimate power commands willing compliance.

Legitimate power is authority, which Weber defines as "the probability that certain commands (or all commands) from a given source will be obeyed by a given group of persons." He adds that a basic criterion of authority "is a certain minimum of voluntary submission," although the specific motives for the obedience to commands may vary.[13] His analysis of three types of authority centers on the value orientations that cause people voluntarily to submit to orders from an authority they accept as legitimate.[14] What is left implicit in this analysis is the specific criterion in terms of which authority can be distinguished from other forms of influence to which individuals voluntarily submit. Indeed, the emphasis on voluntarism is misleading without further specification, since an authoritative command is one a subordinate cannot dismiss at will.

It may be suggested that the distinctive feature of authority is that social norms accepted and enforced by the collectivity of subordinates constrain its individual members to comply with directives of a superior. Compliance is voluntary for the collectivity, but social constraints make it compelling for the individual. In contrast to other forms of influence and power, the pressure to follow suggestions and orders does not come from the superior who gives them but from the collectivity of subordinates. These normative constraints may be institutionalized and pervade the entire society, or they may emerge in a group in social interaction. The latter emergent norms define leadership, which, therefore, is considered a type of authority. The authority in formal organizations entails a combination of institutionalized and leadership elements.

## Leadership

Furnishing needed contributions in a group empowers a man to effect compliance with his demands. The exercise of power exerts restraints, which are, in effect, inescapable if the need for the contributions is great and no alternative sources for them are available. Compliance is a cost that is judged on the basis of social norms of fairness. Excessive demands in terms of these social standards, though those subject to the power may not be able to refuse them, engender disapproval. A person whose demands on others are fair and modest relative to the great contribution he makes to their welfare, however, earns their approval. For example, a laboratory study of small groups found that the emergent leader was more apt to be liked by the rest if the initiative he took in social interaction was accompanied by a high rate of response from others, that is, by their frequently agreeing with him and turning to him with comments and questions, than if the rate of such feedback was low.[15] This may be interpreted to imply that excessive demands by a leader, as indicated by a low rate of feedback, create disapproval that make him less liked.

Compliance can be enforced with sufficient power, but approval cannot be forced regardless of

13. Max Weber, *The Theory of Social and Economic Organization*, New York: Oxford University Press, 1947, p. 324.

14. *Ibid.*, pp. 329–63.

15. Robert F. Bales, "Task Status and Likability as a Function of Talking and Listening in Decision-making Groups," in Leonard D. White, *The State of the Social Sciences*, University of Chicago Press, 1956, pp. 148–61.

how great the power. Yet the effectiveness and stability of leadership depend on the social approval of subordinates, as several studies have shown. Thus, the results of two experiments demonstrated that leaders who were accepted and approved by subordinates were more effective in exerting influence on them than superiors who were not.[16] A study of army leadership found that trainees who approved of their officers and noncommissioned officers were less likely to express various forms of aggression, such as going "AWOL" (absent without leave), "blowing their top," drunkenness, and gripe sessions, than those who described their superiors as arbitrary or weak.[17] The findings of another experiment indicated that group leaders whose suggestions and directives engendered a disproportionate amount of resistance and disagreement were relatively unstable, that is, they were more likely than others to be displaced as leaders in subsequent experimental periods.[18] The disapproval some leadership practices evoke among followers impede a leader's effectiveness because they create resistance, aggression, and possibly opposition that may lead to the downfall of an informal leader.

Collective approval, in contrast, legitimates leadership. The abilities that enable a person to make major contributions to the achievement of a group's goals command respect. The respect of others for him prompts them to follow his suggestion, since they expect to benefit from doing so more than from following the suggestion of someone whose abilities are less respected. The actual contributions to their welfare resulting from following his guidance not only validate the others' respect for such a person but also obligate them to comply with his directives regardless of whether doing so is in their personal self-interest. It is their obligation to comply with his directives, not simply their respect, that bestows leadership upon a person and empowers him to coordinate the activities of the members of a group, which involves directing individuals to do things that are not to their own immediate advantage. The effective coordination of effort produces rewards, and the leader's power enables him to exert a predominant influence on their distribution—how much of the honor and glory of the winning team will reflect on the rest rather than on himself, or how large a share of the material benefits goes to others and how much remains in his hands. It is this distribution of rewards that most directly effects the legitimation of leadership.

If the benefits followers derive from a leader's guidance exceed their expectations of a fair return for the costs they have incurred, both by performing services and by complying with directives, their collective approval of his leadership legitimates it. Their joint obligations for his contributions to their welfare and their common approval of his fairness, reinforced by their consensus concerning the respect his abilities deserve, generate group pressures that enforce compliance with his directives. These social pressures constrain individual group members who for personal reasons are inclined to resist the leader's guidance to submit to it lest they draw on themselves the social disapproval of their peers. Legitimate leaders command willing compliance, which obviates the need for sanctions to compel or induce others to comply with directives, because the group of subordinates exerts pressures on its members to follow the leader's orders and suggestions.

The social approval of followers that legitimates leadership is distinct from the respect they may have for the leader's abilities. Although the two go often together, a person in power may have abilities that command the respect of subordinates yet make oppressive demands on them to which they react with disapproval. Respect probably does, however, act as a catalyst of legitimate leadership, since it seems to make compliance with a person's directives less burdensome. Indirect support for this statement is provided by some findings from a study of sixty caseworkers in a welfare agency.[19] Generally, the factors that distinguished workers who were often consulted from those who were rarely consulted also distinguished those who were highly respected from those who were not. But some kinds of

16. John R. P. French, Jr., and Richard Snyder, "Leadership and Interpersonal Power," in Dorwin Cartwright, *Studies in Social Power*, Ann Arbor: Institute for Social Research, University of Michigan, 1959, pp. 118–49.

17. Hannan C. Selvin, *The Effects of Leadership*, New York: Free Press, 1960, chapter v.

18. Elihu Katz, Peter M. Blau, Morton L. Brown, and Fred L. Strodtbeck, "Leadership Stability and Social Change," *Sociometry*, 20 (1957), 36–50, esp. pp. 44–46.

19. Blau, "Patterns of Choice in Interpersonal Relations," *American Sociological Review*, 27 (1962), 41–55, sp. pp. 50–51, 55.

workers, such as oldtimers, were often consulted without being highly respected. The obligation incurred to consultants inhibited informal sociability with them if the consultants were not particularly respected, but it did not inhibit sociability if they were. This findng suggests that respect for a person legitimates the obligation to comply with his wishes and thus makes this obligation less of an impediment to informal intercourse with him.

Stable leadership rests on power over others and their legitimating approval of that power. The dilemma of leadership is that the attainment of power and the attainment of social approval make somewhat incompatible demands on a person. To achieve power over others requires not only furnishing services that make them dependent but also remaining independent of any services they might offer in return. To legitimate a position of power and leadership, however, requires that a leader be concerned with earning the social approval of his followers, which means that he does not maintain complete independence of them. An individual's refusal to accept offers of favors from others who are in his debt and his insistence on remaining entirely independent of them are usually experienced as rejections and evoke their disapproval. By asserting his dominance over the rest of the group in the process of becoming their leader and exercising his leadership, a person can hardly help antagonizing at least some of them, thereby endangering his chances of having his leadership legitimated by social approval. Conversely, preoccupation with the approval of followers interferes with a leader's ability to command their respect and compliance by making the greatest contribution to their welfare he can, because concern with being liked prevents him from basing his decisions consistently on criteria of effectiveness alone. Such preoccupation, in other words, induces a leader sometimes to refrain from making what is the best decision in his judgment for fear of antagonizing subordinates.

The dilemma of leadership can be epitomized by saying that its legitimation requires that a leader be magnanimous in the exercise of his power and in the distribution of the rewards that accrue from his leadership, but such magnanimity necessitates that he first mobilize his power and husband the group's resources, that is, act in ways that are the opposite of magnanimous. Once a man has attained much power, however, he can easily make demands that appear only moderate in view of his strength and capacity to supply benefits. In other words, extensive power facilitates obtaining legitimating approval for it.

Two different sets of expectations govern the process of legitimation, since the leader's general expectations define what is extensive or insufficient power, while those of the followers define what are moderate or unfair power demands. The less the leader expects to achieve with his power, the less power will be sufficient to meet his needs and the less demands he will make on those subject to his power. The reactions of the follower's to the leader's demands, in turn, are contingent on their normative expectations of how much a leader can fairly demand in return for his contributions. Small needs for power as well as great power make it easy for a man to exercise his power in ways that elicit legitimating approval from subordinates. The line between exploitative oppression and legitimate leadership is defined by the interplay between the expectations of the man in power that define his needs and the expectations of those subject to his power that define their needs and his complementary rights.

Power must be mobilized before it can be legitimated, because the processes involved in mobilizing it are not compatible with those involved in legitimating it. The dilemma of leadership is resolved by devoting different time periods to coping with its two horns, so to speak. This parallels the conclusion of Bales and Strodtbeck that the dilemma of group problem solving posed by the need for a cognitive orientation to the task and the need for a supportive orientation that reduces tensions, which are incompatible, is resolved by devoting different time phases to meeting these two needs.[20] The potential leader of a gang uses his physical strength first against the other members to assert his dominance over them. Only then can he organize their activities and lead

20. Bales and Strodtbeck, "Phases in Group Problem Solving," *The Journal of Abnormal and Social Psychology*, 46 (1951), 485–95. Another method for resolving the leadership dilemma is a division of labor within the leadership group, that is, having those leaders who exercise power and restraints supported by other leaders who do not and who command the approval and loyalty of followers; see Philip E. Slater, "Role Differentiation in Small Groups," *American Sociological Review*, 20 (1955), 300–310.

them in gang warfare, now using his strength and other resources in behalf of his followers against outsiders. If he is successful, his contributions to their welfare evoke legitimating approval of his leadership, which makes his continuing dominance independent of his use of physical sanctions against followers.

The situation of formal leaders in organizations is different from that of informal leaders who emerge in a group. Resources and institutionalized mechanisms place managers in organizations a priori in a dominant position over subordinates, thereby obviating the need for initially asserting their dominance and facilitating the development of legitimate authority.

## Legitimate authority

The employment contract into which the management of an organization enters with its members is a legal institution that obligates the members to furnish certain services and to follow managerial directives in exchange for a salary or wage.[21] These obligations are reinforced by institutionalized norms in our culture according to which employers have a right to expect their employees to comply with their directives as well as to perform specified duties faithfully. The ultimate source of these obligations, and thus of managerial power, are the organization's resources that enable it to buy the services of employees and to make them dependent on it for their livelihood, the degree of dependence being contingent on employees' investments in their jobs and the alternative employment opportunities available to them. (In organizations whose members are not employees, such as unions and political parties, the power of the leadership rests on the commitments of the members, the benefits they derive from membership, and—notably in the case of some organizations, such as armies—coercive force.) Management's power over dismissals and promotions, which is partly transmitted to lower managers and supervisors through mechanisms like periodic ratings of or *ad hoc* reports on their subordinates, makes the career chances of employees dependent on their performance and compliance.

A manager in an organization has some formal authority over subordinates, since they have accepted the contractual obligation to perform the tasks he assigns to them, and he has also considerable power over them, since he has official sanctions at his disposal through which he can affect their career chances. The managerial authority that is rooted in the employment contract itself is very limited in scope. It only obligates employees to perform duties assigned to them in accordance with minimum standards. This formal authority does not require them to devote much effort to their work, exercise initiative in carrying it out, or be guided in their performance by the suggestions of superiors. Effective management is impossible within the confines of formal authority alone. A manager may extend his control over subordinates by resorting to his sanctioning power to impose his will upon them, promising rewards for conformity and threatening penalties for disobedience. An alternative strategy a manager can use is to provide services to subordinates that obligate them to comply with his directives. His formal power over subordinates helps him to create joint obligations in part simply by refraining from exercising it. In this case, the manager relinquishes some of his official power in exchange for greater legitimate authority over subordinates.

The official position and power of the manager give him various opportunities to furnish important services to subordinates that obligate them to him. His superior knowledge and skill, on the basis of which he presumably was selected for his position, enable him to train newcomers and advise oldtimers. His formal status gives him access to top echelons and staff specialists in the organization, making it possible for him to channel needed information to subordinates and to represent their interests with the higher administration. While his official duties as manager *require* him to perform a minimum of these services for subordinates, the extra effort he devotes to benefit them beyond this minimum creates social obligations. Of special significance in this connection are the manager's status prerogatives and formal powers, for he can win the appreciation of his subordinates merely by not exercising these: by not insisting on the deference due his rank, by not enforcing an unpopular housekeeping rule, by ignoring how much time subordinates take for lunch as long as they perform

21. See John R. Commons, *Legal Foundations of Capitalism*, New York: Macmillan, 1924, pp. 284–86.

their duties. Every privilege the manager is granted and every rule he is empowered to enforce increase the capital on which he can draw to make subordinates indebted to him. By not using some of his power, he invests it in social obligations. The advantages subordinates derive from his pattern of supervision obligate them to reciprocate by complying with his directives and requests.

In this manner, managerial power is converted into personal influence, but the development of authority depends on a further transformation. A manager whose influence over subordinates rests on their *individual* obligations to him does not exercise authority over them, because authority requires social legitimation. Only the shared values of a collectivity can legitimate the power of a superior and thereby transform it into authority. Managerial practices that advance the *collective* interest of subordinates create *joint* obligations. When social consensus develops among subordinates that the practices of the manager contribute to their common welfare and that it is in their common interests to maintain his good will by discharging their obligations to him, shared feelings of loyalty and group norms tend to emerge that make compliance with his directives a *social* obligation that is enforced by the subordinates themselves. The subordinates' common approval of managerial practices that benefit them jointly gives rise to social norms that legitimate managerial authority.

Festinger's concept of cognitive dissonance can help explain the underlying process in the legitimation of authority.[22] If individuals must choose between two alternatives one of which is clearly superior, their decision entails no doubts and conflicts. But if the two alternatives are both attractive (or unattractive), the choice of one creates cognitive dissonance, that is, the cost incurred by having rejected an attractive opportunity produces doubts concerning the wisdom of the choice made, mental conflicts, and discomfort. Individuals often reduce this dissonance by changing their evaluations of the two alternatives after having committed themselves to one, that is, they resolve their disturbing doubts by inflating the value of the chosen and deflating the value of the rejected benefit. College students asked to choose one of two gifts they would receive for having participated in an experiment, for example, rated the chosen gift more highly and the rejected one less highly after having made the decision than they had done before.[23] Since social consensus on values serves to confirm the valuations of individuals, one would expect these tendencies to be particularly pronounced if they occur in a collective situation, as is the case when a group of subordinates is confronted by a superior who has power over them.

Cognitive dissonance arises only when a manager obligates subordinates to comply with his directives and not when a superior enforces compliance with his orders through sanctions. If a superior uses his coercive power to impose his will on subordinates, the serious cost of disobedience makes obedience unequivocally the preferable alternative. Although submission is unpleasant, subordinates have on doubt that the consequences of failure to submit would be more so. There is no cognitive dissonance and hence no basis for processes of dissonance reduction. But if a manager furnishes services that obligate subordinates to comply with his orders, noncompliance is a possible alternative that is not entirely unreasonable. The assumption is that the advantages of the services contingent on compliance outweigh its cost to subordinates, which is why they choose compliance over noncompliance. Nevertheless, doubts are likely to arise as to whether the benefits of the services are really worth the hardships entailed by following the orders of a superior, particularly in a democratic culture where equality and independence are highly valued. To resolve this cognitive dissonance, individuals are under pressure to appreciate the value of the benefits and depreciate the cost of compliance. They may extol the abilities of the superior and their respect for him and stress that following the guidance of such an expert is objectively the best course of action. They may emphasize that issuing directives is the manager's duty, not his privilege, and that their compliance with these directives does not constitute submission to his will but is simply part of their freely accepted responsibilities, just as issuing the directives is part of his.

These beliefs might be considered rationalizations through which individuals adapt to a subordinate position. Social processes, however, transform the

22. Leon Festinger, *A Theory of Cognitive Dissonance*, Evanston: Row, Peterson, 1957.

23. *Ibid.*, pp. 61–68.

individual rationalizations into common values. Subordinates who find themselves in the same situation are prone to discuss their justifications of their compliance with each other in order to have their doubts relieved and their justifying beliefs confirmed through social agreement. The social consensus that develops among subordinates in the course of their communication that it is right and proper and not at all degrading to follow managerial orders validates these beliefs and converts what might have been individual rationalizations into a common value orientation.

Authority, therefore, rests on the common norms in a collectivity of subordinates that constrain its individual members to conform to the orders of a superior. The joint obligations of subordinates for the benefits they derive from the superior's mode of supervision or leadership are at the roots of these normative constraints, which are reinforced by social values that justify compliance and lessen the onus of it. These norms, like social norms generally, are internalized by group members and socially enforced, with the result that even the potential deviant who for some reason does not feel personally obligated to the superior is under pressure to submit to his authority lest he incur the social disapproval of his peers. A man in authority does not have to enforce compliance with his orders, because the structural constraints that exist among subordinates do so for him. Authority entails voluntary compliance, in contrast to coercion, since the influence of the superior on subordinates rests on their own social norms. But authority entails imperative control, in contrast to persuasion and personal influence, since social norms and group sanctions exert compelling pressures on individual subordinates to follow the superior's directives. Compliance is voluntary from the perspective of the collectivity of subordinates, but it is compulsory from the perspective of its individual members. It is exactly as voluntary as conformity with social norms generally, for example, as our custom of wearing clothes.

The social norms and values of subordinates that legitimate the power of influence of a superior transform it into authority. Simultaneously, indirect processes of social exchange become substituted for the direct exchange transactions between the superior and individual subordinates. Before legitimating norms have developed, subordinates offer compliance with the superior's directive in exchange for services he furnishes, a process essentially similar to that in which consultants achieve compliance with their wishes in exchange for advice. The emergent social norms that legitimate authority give rise to two exchange processes that take the place of this one. Individual subordinates submit to the authority of the superior because group norms require them to do so and failure to conform evokes social disapproval. The individual exchanges compliance with the directives of the superior for social approval from his peers. The collectivity of subordinates exchanges prevailing compliance with the superior's orders, which it has to offer as the result of its social norms that enforce compliance, and which legitimates the superior's authority, for the contribution to the common welfare his leadership furnishes.

The question that arises is whether managerial authority has its ultimate source in the manager's leadership qualities and abilities to assist subordinates or in his official sanctioning power over them. To answer this question, let us assume that these two functions reside in two different persons; a supervisor who provides guidance and counsel but has no formal power of sanction, and an employer who does not guide the work of employees but evaluates its results and decides on promotions and dismissals in accordance with these evaluations. If the supervisor has the qualifications to furnish superior guidance and advice that improve and facilitate the work of subordinates, his contributions to their common welfare create joint obligations that serve as the basis of his authority over them. This situation corresponds essentially to informal leadership. If the employer distributes rewards and punishments purely in terms of objective criteria of performance, these sanctions would provide incentives to perform well but not to comply with his directives (except those specifying the parameters of adequate performance). If, however, he uses his sanctioning power to reward compliance and punish disobedience with his orders, employees may adapt to these conditions by developing social values and norms that justify and enforce their compliance and legitimate his authority. These considerations imply that both effective leadership and sanctioning power can become the sources of an authority structure, but sanctioning power does so at the cost of diverting the incentive system, at least in part, from its major function of encouraging optimum performance by using it to effect obedience. There can be little doubt that the reward systems in organizations are typically used in this manner as instruments of power and aids in the expansion of managerial authority.

Although managerial authority in organizations contains important leadership elements, its distinctive characteristic, which differentiates it from informal leadership, is that it is rooted in the formal powers and sanctions the organization bestows upon managers. Their official position and sanctioning power provide managers with tools that make it easy, even for those with only moderate leadership qualities, to broaden the scope of the limited authority initially invested in them through the employment contract, whereas informal leaders must rely on their own qualities and resources to command the willing compliance of followers. Effective authority, whether in formal organizations or outside, requires both power and legitimating approval, but the one is more problematical for the informal leader, and the other, for the formal leader in an organization.

The crucial problem for the formal leader, with undeniable power, is to win the loyalty and legitimating approval of subordinates, particularly since his power may tempt him to dominate them instead of winning their respect and willing compliance. In contrast, the crucial problem of the informal leader, whose position is evidence of the support and approval of his followers, is to mobilize his power of command and establish sufficient social distance to be able to direct effectively their activities. Fiedler's research indicates this difference.[24] He found that the informal leaders of such groups as basketball teams and surveying parties who manifested social distance toward followers were more effective than those who did not, that is, the performance of the groups under the former leaders was superior. The social distance of formal leaders toward subordinates, however, was not generally related to their effectiveness, except when they commanded the loyalty of subordinates and their social distance from subordinates was accompanied by some positive attitudes toward them.

Authority can *arise* only in social structures. The power or personal influence exercised in pair relations can never develop into legitimate authority. For only the common norms of a collectivity of subordinates can legitimate the controlling influence of a superior and effect willing compliance with his directives in the specific sense of making such compliance, since it is enforced by the subordinates themselves, independent of any inducements or enforcement actions of the superior himself. Once authority has become institutionalized and social norms of compliance have become part of the cultural heritage, however, it does find expression in isolated pair relations. A father exercises authority over an only child, because culturally defined role expectations shared by the entire community constrain him to control and guide the child and compel the child to obey him; failure to live up to these expectations draws community disapproval on both of them. Whereas authority typically *has its source* in the power of one individual over a group (or of a group over a larger collectivity), which subsequently becomes legitimated by their social approval and norms, institutionalized authority *is a source* of power, that is, it bestows power over others on individuals or groups occupying a given status.

The institutionalization of authority requires that the social norms that demand compliance with certain orders and the surrounding values that justify and reinforce this compliance become part of the common culture and be transmitted from generation to generation. Children internalize these cultural values and norms in the process of socialization, and the moral obligation to conform to commands from given sources remains part of their personality structure. Paternal, religious, and political authority rest on such cultural orientations. The normative standards underlying institutionalized authority do not emerge in the process of social interaction between superior and subordinates and among subordinates but rather in the process of socialization, to which each one of them is separately exposed in a common culture. The managerial ideologies that have developed in modern societies during the last centuries, which justify and fortify the power of management and the obligation of subordinates to submit to its directives, constitute

24. Fred E. Fiedler, *Leader Attitudes and Group Effectiveness*, Urbana: University of Illinois Press, 1958, esp. chapter iii.

such an institutionalized value orientation, which legitimates managerial authority in principle.[25] This value orientation, which employees in our culture bring to the organizational context, gives the employment contract salient meaning and serves as the foundation for the social processes in which the authority of specific managers over subordinates is legitimated and expanded. The institutional authority of management and the power its resources give it distinguish legitimating processes in organizations from those characteristic of the emergence of leaders outside an organizational framework.

Institutionalized authority in complex social structures, such as the political authority of a national government, has three distinctive characteristics. First, as just indicated, the people's obligation to comply with the authority's commands does not develop in social exchange as a result of the ruler's contribution to the common welfare but is a moral obligation inculcated by socializing agencies. Whereas disregard for an emergent leader is a sign of disloyalty, disregard for institutionalized authority is a sign of immorality. Second, the political authority is embodied in institutional forms that constitute a historical reality, such as the Congressional form of government in the United States. Third, the differentiated groups in complex structures make it likely that the institutionalized authority accepted by the major groups is not accepted by some entire subgroups and has to be enforced through external restraints on them. Although legitimate authority rests on the social norms and sanctions of the collectivity of subordinates, this does not mean that all groups in a society support institutionalized authority, or even that a majority do. The crucial factor is that important and powerful groups of subordinates enforce the commands of institutionalized authority, putting external pressures to comply on those groups who refuse to do so voluntarily. Governmental authority prevails if the groups who support and enforce it dominate the thinking as well as acting of the rest, so even the deviants recognize that their disobedience is illegitimate. In countries with autocratic traditions, there is, strictly speaking, no public opinion in the sense of all the people's opinion regarding matters of public concern, such as political authority,[26] and the elite's support of the ruler suffices to legitimate his authority as long as the *status quo* is accepted by the rest. It is only in countries where democratic values make the population at large concerned with political issues that the institutionalized authority of the legitimate government is in danger unless supported by the majority.

The authority of the government, then, rests on its acceptance as legitimate and its support by the dominant groups of subjects, that is, by the majority of those who participate in political life and are concerned with public matters, not necessarily a majority of the total population. The actual enforcement of the commands of political authority, furthermore, is usually delegated to special agents, such as military and police forces. The groups who support the government express their confidence in it by delegating the power to enforce its commands to agents under its own control. Generally, the political authority of a legitimate government consists of a grant of power "credit" by its supporters, which means that the government has the mandate to use powers vested in the community temporarily at its own discretion without having to account for every single decision.[27] The government that uses its mandate or credit of power to contribute to the welfare of its supporters tends to strengthen their legitimating approval of it, while the ruler who abuses his grant of power is likely to lose the political support that legitimates his rule, and with it his political dominance, unless he resorts to coercion to maintain it. The credit of political support and power on which legitimate governments can draw to enforce compliance, if needed, acts as a deterrent and fortifies their authority to command obedience, thereby having a multiplier effect and extending political control far beyond what could be achieved were it actually necessary to rely on the underlying coercive power.

## Organizing collective effort

An important function of legitimate authority is to organize collective effort on a large scale in the

25. See Reinhard Bendix, *Work and Authority in Industry*, New York: Wiley, 1956.

26. See Hans Speier, *Social Order and the Risk of War*, New York: Stewart, 1952, pp. 323–38.

27. See Talcott Parsons, "On the Concept of Influence," *Public Opinion Quarterly*, 27 (1963), 59–62, and James S. Coleman, "Comment," *ibid.*, pp. 72–77.

pursuit of ends commonly accepted. To be sure, this is not the only function of legitimate authority—paternal authority, for example, serves the function of socializing children and thus perpetuating the basic culture. But this is one of its major functions and the one that is manifest in formal organizations, whether they are political, economic, military, or some other kind. Using the term "voluntary association" quite broadly to refer to freely established collective organizations generally, de Jouvenel has stated: "By 'authority' I mean the faculty of gaining another man's assent. Or again it may be called, though it comes to the same thing, the efficient cause of voluntary associations. In any voluntary association that comes to my notice I see the work of a force: that force is authority.[28]

Commonly accepted ends are not necessarily common ends. Some organizations, such as unions, are designed to further the common objectives of the membership. The objectives of other organizations, such as business concerns, are those of the owners or of management. The majority of members whose services are bought in order to achieve these goals are expected to accept them as valid guides for operations, although they are not their own objectives. In either case, the members make contributions in exchange for rewards, but whereas the union member's rewards result from and are contingent on the achievement of the union's objectives, those of the firm's employee come from the salary he is paid for his services, which does not *directly* depend on the firm's profits, that is, on the achievement of the organization's objectives.

The difference between these two types of members of organizations corresponds to that between stockholders, who make investments in return for a share of the profits, as union members do, and bondholders, who receive a stipulated return for their investments, as employees do. The ideal expectation is that collective objectives are democratically decided on by the entire membership, while employees or bondholders are not expected to participate in deciding on objectives. In fact, however, objectives and policies are usually not democratically determined either by the union rank-and-file or by corporation stockholders, nor for that matter, by the membership of any large organization unless special mechanisms, such as a party system, facilitate democratic participation.

The establishment of an organization requires capital investments, often in the form of financial investments, always in the form of social investments.[29] Resources and efforts, which could be spent directly to obtain rewards, must be devoted to building the organization and developing its specialized structure, to recruiting members and contributors, to coordinating their activities and instituting normative standards for them to follow. Instead of pursuing their self-interests directly, the members of the organization make contributions to it in conformity with normative expectations and in anticipation of receiving rewards from it. All this entails postponement of gratifications in the hope of greater future gratifications, which requires a surplus of resources beyond those merely sufficient to meet current minimum needs. Hence, only individuals or groups with surplus resources can establish a business, organize a union, or create a political organization.[30]

Knight has emphasized that an organization's profits are the rewards for those who assume ultimate responsibility for entirely uncertain investments:

> Organization involves the concentration of responsibility, placing resources belonging to a large number of individuals under centralized control. Examination shows that the human functions in production involve making decisions, exercising control, but that this control is not final unless combined with assumption of the results of the decisions. The responsible decision relates to men rather than things; the ultimate manager is he who plans the organization, lays out functions, selects men for functions, and appraises their value to the organization as a whole, in competition with all other bidders in the market. For this ultimate management there is but one possible remuneration, the residuum of product remaining after payment is made at rates established in competition with all comers for all services of men or things for which competition exists. This residuum is profit. . . .[31]

28. Bertrand de Jouvenel, *Sovereignty*, University of Chicago Press, 1957, p. 29.

29. See George C. Homans, *Social Behavior*, New York: Harcourt, Brace and World, 1961, pp. 385–90.

30. For example, the workers who are most active in organizing unions and participating in them are not the poorest ones, who need unions most, but those with higher socioeconomic status, who have greater resources. See William Spinrad, 'Correlates of Trade Union Participation," *American Sociological Review*, 25 (1960), 237–44, esp. p. 239.

31. Frank H. Knight, *Risk, Uncertainty and Profit* (2d ed.), Boston: Houghton Mifflin, 1933, p. 308.

Leadership involves assuming responsibility for coordinating the work of others and for the consequences of the common endeavors. To the extent to which specific abilities of leaders make it possible to anticipate the achievements their guidance makes possible, uncertainty is removed. These administrative services of a leader or manager are remunerated by rewards established in competition, just as the rewards of employees are.[32] The leadership of men, however, entails a residue of uncertainty that defies prediction. Success in winning wars or negotiating for peace, in building empires or dominating a market, in consolidating unions or winning political campaigns cannot be predicted in advance with any degree of accuracy. The leaders who assumed ultimate responsibility for the decisions and guidance that brought these victories are the ones who reap the profits from them.

While a surplus is necessary to institute an organization, further surpluses are produced in it. The organization of collective effort replaces the free competition for and exchange of benefits among individuals by normatively regulated transactions, although within this framework of regulated transactions there also occur some direct exchanges, such as that of advice for status in work groups. Basically, members of organizations are not free to barter their services but are expected to conform to normative expectations, which involves furnishing services, and receive a return for doing so. The contributions made by employees of an organization, who are compensated for their services, tend to produce a surplus profit at the disposal of management, which it can use at its own discretion, and which is its return for having assumed responsibility for uncertainty by having guaranteed to employees returns for their services.

An organization whose members are not employees compensated for services, such as a union or any organization whose avowed purpose is to advance the common welfare of its membership in some way, also often obtains surplus profits from the contributions of its members. Whereas the members of such an organization are expected to receive this surplus in return for risking their contributions, the power vested in the leadership actually gives it the deciding voice on how to distribute the surplus. This situation is exactly parallel to that in a large corporation, whose stockholders are also expected to receive its surplus profits, but whose management has the power to distribute the surplus as it sees fit, subject only to the restriction that sufficient profits must be distributed to stockholders to attract all the needed capital. This is a severe restriction for weak corporations but not for strong ones, which can pay stockholders interests at a regular rate regardless of the actual profits made in any specific year, treating them, in effect, like bondholders.

Generally, the stronger an organization, the less are the restraints imposed on the leadership by the need to attract members who make contributions, and the greater is the surplus at the leadership's disposal. The leaders of strong unions or the bosses of strong political organizations can furnish sufficient rewards to members to assure their continuing contributions and still retain a surplus for use at their own discretion. This means that the leaders of strong organizations can and do treat members no differently from the way management treats employees, just as strong corporations can treat stockholders as if they were bondholders. For management, too, must distribute enough profits to employees to give them incentives for making contributions to the organization and can retain only the surplus left for its own use. In brief, an organization's great strength combined with its differentiated hierarchical structure tends to destroy the distinction between members, the furthering of whose welfare is presumably its purpose, and employees, whose services are purchased for this purpose. The paradox is that the great contributions made by a large membership, which make any member dispensable, are the very resources that empower the organization's leadership to treat members as if they were merely employees.

The ability to assume responsibility for complex decisions and tasks, which is important and highly prized in organizations, permits individuals to obtain great rewards at little cost to themselves. Jaques has suggested a quantitative measure for the level of responsibility of an organization member, namely, the inverse of the frequency with which his performance is reviewed by his superiors, which may be several times an hour for unskilled workers and once a year for top management.[33] The indivi-

32. See *ibid.*, pp. 285–87, 309.

33. Elliott Jaques, *Measurement of Responsibility*, London: Tavistock Publications, 1956, pp. 32–42.

dual's ability to stand uncertainty for extended periods of time governs the level of responsibility he can easily assume.[34] This ability, which depends on a person's technical competence and tolerance for ambiguity, determines, therefore, whether a certain responsibility is experienced as an enjoyable challenge, which is preferred to a more routine task, or whether it is perceived as an unpleasant threat, which engenders anxieties and a desire to escape from it. In short, the same amount of responsibility may be a gratifying reward for some and a punishing cost for others, and which of these it is determines the reactions of subordinates to supervision, on the one hand, and the power relations among managers, on the other.

Employees who experience their level of responsibility as an unpleasant burden will be grateful to a supervisor who readily offers counsel and guidance and reciprocate for his assistance by complying with his directives. Employees who find their responsibilities challenging, however, will define the same supervisory practices as too close supervision and as unjustified interference with their work rather than as help they appreciate. The manager who supervises his subordinates too closely continually makes demands on them, enabling them to discharge whatever obligations they have to him, whereas the one who does not supervise too closely, but lets subordinates come to him for advice or assistance, recurrently obligates them to reciprocate for his help by complying with his directives, thereby fortifying his authority over them.[35] In brief, the subordinates' orientation toward responsibility governs whether they consider given supervisory practices to be rewarding assistance or demanding interference and whether these practices strengthen or weaken the superior's authority.

Furthermore, a member of an organization who enjoys the challenge of responsibilities can relieve others of duties they dislike and thereby earn their appreciation as well as other rewards at little or no cost to himself. Thus, Crozier noted that the chief engineers in the plants of the bureaucratized French tobacco monopoly exercised more power than their official position warranted, because they were capable of assuming responsibility for maintenance problems with which no one else could cope.[36] Generally, men who discharge important responsibilities are rewarded by their fellows with great honor and power, and they typically make these gains at virtually no cost at all since they enjoy the challenge of their responsibilities.[37]

Risk is an essential element in responsibility, that is, assuming responsibilities entails making decisions whose outcome is uncertain. Frequent reviews of a man's decisions by his superior limit the uncertainty he must bear but do not entirely eliminate the risks he takes. His judgment may turn out to have been incorrect, and he must suffer the consequences when this is the case. According to Knight, only the entrepreneur who invests capital assumes responsibility for uncertainty and thus earns profits.[38] But in social life, at least, responsibility for uncertainty is not confined to the top of organizations but exists, in varying degrees, throughout their hierarchies. For taking these risks of making uncertain decisions, individuals expect to profit if they are successful, and the approval and power men typically earn for assuming responsibilities can be conceived of as constituting this profit.

The diverse comparisons of rewards between the many groups in a large and complex organization, finally, create special problems for management. The workers in each specialized group are eager to maximize the rewards they receive for their services,

34. *Ibid.*, pp. 85–106; see also Melville Dalton, *Men Who Manage*, New York: Wiley, 1959, pp. 243–48, 252–55.

35. Impersonal mechanisms of control, including such different kinds as assembly-line production and quantitative records of performance, promote the authority of superiors over subordinates in the organization, because these control mechanisms lessen the superior's need to make many demands on subordinates, and because they encourage subordinates to become obligated to their superior by coming to him with requests for help. See Blau, "Formal Organization," *American Journal of Sociology*, 63 (1957), 58–63.

36. Michel Crozier, *The Bureaucratic Phenomenon*, University of Chicago Press, 1964, pp. 112–74.

37. To be sure, rendering services entails costs in time, and the ability to provide complex services has been achieved at some investment costs. But given the requisite abilities, assuming greater responsibilities, instead of performing duties that involve lesser ones, does not entail a cost; on the contrary, it is rewarding. Although the social recognition and power men receive who exercise great responsibilities make doing so particularly gratifying, the challenge of responsibilities is inherently gratifying independent of any social rewards obtained for it, as illustrated by the fact that individuals who have the requisite abilities prefer working on difficult rather than easy crossword puzzles even when they are alone.

38. Knight, *op. cit.*, chapter x.

and they often engage in concerted union action for this purpose. As management yields to the pressures of one group to avert active opposition in the form of a strike or possible defections to other companies, or as it modifies a group's incentive system in ways that permit its members to increase their earnings, it satisfies the demands of one group but creates dissatisfaction in others. The members of other groups accustomed to comparing themselves with the one to whose demands management yielded experience relative deprivation as the result of the decline in the comparative level of their income and social status, although their absolute earnings and positions have remained the same. Such relative deprivation, no less than any other dissatisfaction, is likely to produce opposition and demands for improvements.[39] Indeed, once earnings have risen sufficiently above the minimum needed for a decent standard of living, relative standing tends to become as important for employees as absolute income. Homans has suggested that this produces a strange paradox for unions: "As for organized labor, the more successful it is in getting the general level of wages raised, the more likely it is to undermine its own unity; for then workers can begin to interest themselves not just in the absolute amount of wages but in wage differentials, and wage differentials are obviously apt to set one group of workers against another."[40]

Some conflict and opposition are inevitable in large organizations with many specialized subgroups, each of which is interested not only in raising its absolute volume of rewards but also its relative standing among others. To pacify the opposition of groups who have effective bargaining power, management may yield to their demands, and by doing so it often evokes the opposition of other groups. The unfavorable comparisons to which most members in large organizations are recurrently exposed create dissatisfaction and opposition that is directed not only against management but also against existing institutions in general. Empirical studies indicate that political radicalism is more pronounced and that work satisfaction is lower among workers in large plants than among those in small ones.[41] To be sure, the success of the enterprise and its expansion mitigate the internal conflicts by putting resources at the disposal of management, which make it possible to increase the benefits of all groups, just as an expanding economy lessens the class conflict in a society, as noted in chapter six. The significance of relative standing among groups, however, is likely to perpetuate conflict and opposition. As some groups gain advantages, the opposition of others is aroused, and as management solves some problems, the new conditions thereby introduced generate new ones. Hence, the process of change in organizations tends to assume a dialectical form,[42] and so does the process of change in social structures generally, as will be shown in subsequent chapters.

## Conclusions

The legitimation of patterns of social conduct and social relations requires that common values and norms put the stamp of approval on them and reinforce and perpetuate them. Legitimate organizations and social relations are those of which the community approves, whereas illegitimate ones violate the prevailing values in the community. Many social relations are neither explicitly legitimated by community values nor proscribed by community norms, because social standards only set wide limits within which a range of permissible relations may exist. This is true for exchange relations and power relations. Explicit legitimation entails not merely tolerant approval but the active confirmation and promotion of social patterns by common values, either pre-existing ones or those that emerge in a collectivity in the course of social interaction.

The exercise of power is judged in terms of social norms of fairness by those subject to it and by others witness to it. A powerful individual or group whose demands are moderate in terms of what these norms lead others to expect wins their social approval,

39. For a report on the reactions of workers to an increase in the earnings of another group of workers, see William F. Whyte, *Money and Motivation*, New York: Harper, 1955, chapter viii.

40. Homans, *op. cit.*, p. 393.

41. Seymour M. Lipset, Paul F. Lazarsfeld, Allen H. Barton, and Juan Linz, "The Psychology of Voting," in Gardner Lindzey, *Handbook of Social Psychology*, Cambridge: Addison-Wesley, 1954, Vol. II, 1139; and Sergio Talacchi, "Organization Size, Individual Attitudes and Behavior," *Administrative Science Quarterly*, 5 (1960), 398–420, esp. p. 409.

42. Blau, *op. cit.*, pp. 67–69.

which legitimates the authority and fortifies the controlling influence of the powerful. The exploitative use of power, in contrast, provokes social disapproval and opposition. A person who has much power is expected to make great demands, and he therefore can rather easily make demands others consider only fair and thus attain legitimating approval of his power. The conclusion that great power facilitates obtaining legitimating approval of the power must be qualified in two respects. First, if a person has very great needs for power, whether because of objective conditions or for psychological reasons, considerable power over others may still be insufficient for his needs and may not prevent him from using his power exploitatively rather than with moderation. Second, if social approval is irrelevant for a person, it will not restrain him from oppressing others. Legitimating approval is of great importance, however, for stable organizing power In the context of organized social endeavors, and particularly of formal organization, consequently, it is generally true that great power resources promote fairness in the exercise of power and thus legitimating approval of it, which is one reason why power tends to beget more power.

The dilemma of leadership is that it requires both power over others and their legitimating approval of that power, but the process of gaining ascendency over others and the process of winning their approval are in conflict. An individual who uses his resources to assert his dominance over a group and protects his dominant position by making them dependent on him while refusing to become dependent on them usually creates resentment and fails to earn general social approval. On the other hand, great concern with courting the approval of followers interferes with effective leadership, because it induces the leader to be governed by what followers like rather than by what most furthers the achievement of their common goals. The effective leader must be capable of restraining the immediate desires of individual followers for the sake of their long-run collective interests. Yet, unless he obtains their legitimating approval of his leadership, their desire to escape from his dominance makes his position precarious. Individuals who seek to become the leaders of groups tend to resolve this dilemma by mobilizing their power first and then using it in ways that win them the approval of followers, but as a result of the conflicts that occur in the process only a small proportion of the aspirants to positions of leadership succeed in attaining them. Efficient operations in formal organizations necessitate, however, that men appointed to managerial positions succeed in the majority of cases in establishing effective formal leadership over subordinates, and special mechanisms exist that greatly increase their chances of success in having subordinates accept their legitimate authority.

The institutionalization of the principle of managerial authority in modern societies and the sanctioning power of management which rests on the organization's resources that enable it to provide recurrent rewards to its members, greatly facilitate the individual manager's task of winning his subordinates' legitimating approval of his authority. A manager's outstanding abilities to contribute to the welfare of subordinates make him a particularly strong formal leader, as is the case for an informal leader, but his formal position and powers make it easy for a manager to benefit his subordinates even if his leadership qualities are limited, and in this respect his situation differs from that of the informal leader. The joint obligations of subordinates, which the manager's contributions to their common welfare have created, tend to find expression in group norms that demand compliance with his directives. These normative constraints of the collectivity of subordinates legitimate the superior's authority over them by effecting *voluntary* compliance with his commands in the specific sense of making such compliance independent of any enforcement action on his part.

Power is the resource that permits an individual or group to coordinate the efforts of many others, and legitimate authority is the resource that makes possible a stable organization of such coordinated effort on a large scale. The leadership of an organization makes contributions to the achievement of its objectives and expects to profit from these investments. The rewards other members receive must compensate them for two kinds of contributions, the instrumental services they render and their compliance with the leadership's directives (though in actual life these two frequently merge). Whereas employees are compensated for their services and are not entitled to a share of the surplus their contributions help to make, other members who risk their investments are expected to receive a share of the profits. This distinction, however, breaks down in very strong organizations, because its leaders can elicit the needed investments from members without giving them a proportionate share of the profits. This means that they treat members who have made investments in the organization, in fact, like management treats employees whose services it purchases. The powerless corporation shareholder and the powerless union rank-and-file are typical illustrations.

The organization of collective effort mobilizes power. The leadership's power over subordinates becomes the basis of the power at its disposal in relation to other segments of the society, and the successful exercise of its external power, in turn, increases its power within the organization. The exercise of power, however, generates conflict and opposition both within the organization and in its external relations. The frequent experience of relative deprivation resulting from the manifold comparisons between groups in large organizations is a source of dissatisfaction and opposition that exists to a lesser extent in small organizations. The commanding position of power leaders of strong organizations hold in the community, finally, is at the root of much social conflict and political opposition.

DANIEL KATZ and ROBERT L. KAHN

# Open-Systems Theory

The aims of social science with respect to human organizations are like those of any other science with respect to the events and phenomena of its domain. The social scientist wishes to understand human organizations, to describe what is essential in their form, aspects, and functions. He wishes to explain their cycles of growth and decline, to predict their effects and effectiveness. Perhaps he wishes as well to test and apply such knowledge by introducing purposeful changes into organizations—by making them, for example, more benign, more responsive to human needs.

Such efforts are not solely the prerogative of social science, however; common-sense approaches to understanding and altering organizations are ancient and perpetual. They tend, on the whole, to rely heavily on two assumptions: that the location and nature of an organization are given by its name; and that an organization is possessed of built-in goals—because such goals were implanted by its founders, decreed by its present leaders, or because they emerged mysteriously as the purposes of the organizational system itself. These assumptions scarcely provide an adequate basis for the study of organizations and at times can be misleading and even fallacious. We propose, however, to make use of the information to which they point.

The first problem in understanding an organization or a social system is its location and identification. How do we know that we are dealing with an organization? What are its boundaries? What behavior belongs to the organization and what behavior lies outside it? Who are the individuals whose actions are to be studied and what segments of their behavior are to be included?

The fact that popular names exist to label social organizations is both a help and a hindrance. These popular labels represent the socially accepted stereotypes about organizations and do not specify their role structure, their psychological nature, or their boundaries. On the other hand, these names help in locating the area of behavior in which we are interested. Moreover, the fact that people both within and without an organization accept stereotypes about its nature and functioning is one determinant of its character.

The second key characteristic of the common-sense approach to understanding an organization is to regard it simply as the epitome of the purposes of its designer, its leaders, or its key members. The teleology of this approach is again both a help and a hindrance. Since human purpose is deliberately built into organizations and is specifically recorded in the social compact, the by-laws, or other formal protocol of the undertaking, it would be inefficient not to utilize these sources of information. In the early development of a group, many processes are generated which have little to do with its rational purpose, but over time there is a cumulative

Reprinted from *The Social Psychology of Organizations*, pp. 14–29, by permission of the authors and publisher. 

recognition of the devices for ordering group life and a deliberate use of these devices.

Apart from formal protocol, the primary mission of an organization as perceived by its leaders furnishes a highly informative set of clues for the researcher seeking to study organizational functioning. Nevertheless, the stated purposes of an organization as given by its by-laws or in the reports of its leaders can be misleading. Such statements of objectives may idealize, rationalize, distort, omit, or even conceal some essential aspects of the functioning of the organization. Nor is there always agreement about the mission of the organization among its leaders and members. The university president may describe the purpose of his institution as one of turning out national leaders; the academic dean sees it as imparting the cultural heritage of the past, the academic vice-president as enabling students to move toward self-actualization and development, the graduate dean as creating new knowledge, the dean of men as training youngsters in technical and professional skills which will enable them to earn their living, and the editor of the student newspaper as inculcating the conservative values which will preserve the status quo of an outmoded capitalistic society.

The fallacy here is one of equating the purposes or goals of organizations with the purposes and goals of individual members. The organization as a system has an output, a product or an outcome, but this is not necessarily identical with the individual purposes of group members. Though the founders of the organization and its key members do think in teleological terms about organizational objectives, we should not accept such practical thinking, useful as it may be, in place of a theoretical set of constructs for purposes of scientific analysis. Social science, too frequently in the past, has been misled by such short-cuts and has equated popular phenomenology with scientific explanation.

In fact, the classic body of theory and thinking about organizations has assumed a teleology of this sort as the easiest way of identifying organizational structures and their functions. From this point of view an organization is a social device for efficiently accomplishing through group means some stated purpose; it is the equivalent of the blueprint for the design of the machine which is to be created for some practical objective. The essential difficulty with this purposive or design approach is that an organization characteristically includes more and less than is indicated by the design of its founder or the purpose of its leader. Some of the factors assumed in the design may be lacking or so distorted in operational practice as to be meaningless, while unforeseen embellishments dominate the organizational structure. Moreover, it is not always possible to ferret out the designer of the organization or to discover the intricacies of the design which he carried in his head. The attempt by Merton (1957) to deal with the latent function of the organization in contrast with its manifest function is one way of dealing with this problem. The study of unanticipated consequences as well as anticipated consequences of organizational functioning is a similar way of handling the matter. Again, however, we are back to the purposes of the creator or leader, dealing with unanticipated consequences on the assumption that we can discover the consequences anticipated by him and can lump all other outcomes together as a kind of error variance.

*It would be much better theoretically*, however, to start with concepts which do not call for identifying the purposes of the designers and then correcting for them when they do not seem to be fulfilled. The theoretical concepts should begin with the input, output, and functioning of the organization as a system and not with the rational purposes of its leaders. We may want to utilize such purposive notions to lead us to sources of data or as subjects of special study, but not as our basic theoretical constructs for understanding organizations.

Our theoretical model for the understanding of organizations is that of an energic input-output system in which the energic return from the output reactivates the system. Social organizations are flagrantly open systems in that the input of energies and the conversion of output into further energic input consist of transactions between the organization and its environment.

All social systems, including organizations, consist of the patterned activities of a number of individuals. Moreover, these patterned activities are complementary or interdependent with respect to some common output or outcome; they are repeated, relatively enduring, and bounded in space and time. If the activity pattern occurs only once or at unpredictable intervals, we could not speak of an organization. The stability or recurrence of activities can be examined in relation to the *energic input* into the system, the *transformation of energies within the system*, and the *resulting product or energic output*. In a factory the raw materials and the human labor are the energic input, the patterned activities of production the transformation of energy, and the finished product the output. To maintain this patterned activity requires a continued renewal of the inflow of energy. This is guaranteed in social systems by the energic return from the product or outcome. Thus the outcome of the cycle of activities furnishes new energy for the initiation of a renewed cycle. The company which produces automobiles sells them and by doing so obtains the means of securing new raw materials, compensating its labor force, and continuing the activity pattern.

In many organizations outcomes are converted into money and new energy is furnished through this mechanism. Money is a convenient way of handling energy units both on the output and input sides, and buying and selling represent one set of social rules for regulating the exchange of money. Indeed, these rules are so effective and so widespread that there is some danger of mistaking the business of buying and selling for the defining cycles of organization. It is a commonplace executive observation that businesses exist to make money, and the observation is usually allowed to go unchallenged. It is, however, a very limited statement about the purposes of business.

Some human organizations do not depend on the cycle of selling and buying to maintain themselves. Universities and public agencies depend rather on bequests and legislative appropriations, and in so-called voluntary organizations the output reenergizes the activity of organization members in a more direct fashion. Member activities and accomplishments are rewarding in themselves and tend therefore to be continued, without the mediation of the outside environment. A society of bird watchers can wander into the hills and engage in the rewarding activities of identifying birds for their mutual edification and enjoyment. Organizations thus differ on this important dimension of the source of energy renewal, with the great majority utilizing both intrinsic and extrinsic sources in varying degree. Most large-scale organizations are not as self-contained as small voluntary groups and are very dependent upon the social effects of their output for energy renewal.

Our two basic criteria for identifying social systems and determining their functions are (1) tracing the pattern of energy exchange or activity of people as it results in some output and (2) ascertaining how the output is translated into energy which reactivates the pattern. We shall refer to organizational functions or objectives not as the conscious purposes of group leaders or group members but as the outcomes which are the energic source for a maintenance of the same type of output.

This model of an energic input-output system is taken from the open system theory as promulgated by von Bertalanffy (1956). Theorists have pointed out the applicability of the system concepts of the natural sciences to the problems of social science. It is important, therefore, to examine in more detail the constructs of system theory and the characteristics of open systems.

System theory is basically concerned with problems of relationships, of structure, and of interdependence rather than with the constant attributes of objects. In general approach it resembles field theory except that its dynamics deal with temporal as well as spatial patterns. Older formulations of system constructs dealt with the closed systems of the physical sciences, in which relatively self-contained structures could be treated successfully as if they were independent of external forces. But living systems, whether biological organisms or social organizations, are acutely dependent upon their external environment and so must be conceived of as open systems.

Before the advent of open-system thinking, social scientists tended to take one of two approaches in dealing with social structures; they tended either (1) to regard them as closed systems to which the laws of physics applied or (2) to endow them with some vitalistic concept like entelechy. In the former case they ignored the environmental forces affecting the organization and in the latter case they fell back upon some magical purposiveness to account for organizational functioning. Biological theorists, however, have rescued us from this trap by pointing out that the concept of the open system means that we neither have to follow the laws of traditional physics, nor in deserting them do we have to abandon science. The laws of Newtonian physics are correct generalizations but they are limited to closed systems. They do not apply in the same fashion to open systems which maintain themselves through constant commerce with their environment, i.e., a continuous inflow and outflow of energy through permeable boundaries.

One example of the operation of closed versus open systems can be seen in the concept of entropy and the second law of thermodynamics. According to the second law of thermodynamics, a system moves toward equilibrium; it tends to run down, that is, its differentiated structures tend to move toward dissolution as the elements composing them become arranged in random disorder. For example, suppose that a bar of iron has been heated by the application of a blowtorch on one side. The arrangement of all the fast (heated) molecules on one side and all the slow molecules on the other is an unstable state, and over time the distribution of molecules becomes in effect random, with the resultant cooling of one side and heating of the other, so that all surfaces of the iron approach the same temperature. A similar process of heat exchange will also be going on between the iron bar and its environment, so that the bar will gradually approach the temperature of the room in which it is located, and in so doing will elevate somewhat the previous temperature of the room. More technically, entropy increases toward a maximum and equilibrium occurs as the physical system attains the state of the most probable distribution of its elements. In social systems, however, structures tend to become more elaborated rather than less differentiated. The rich may grow richer and the poor may grow poorer. The open system does not run down, because it can import energy from the world around it. Thus the operation of entropy is counteracted by the importation of energy and the living system is characterized by negative rather than positive entropy.

## Common characteristics of open systems

Though the various types of open systems have common characteristics by virtue of being open systems, they differ in other characteristics. If this were not the case, we would be able to obtain all our basic knowledge about social organizations through studying the biological organisms or even through the study of a single cell.

The following nine characteristics seem to define all open systems.

1. *Importation of energy*. Open systems import some form of energy from the external environment. The cell receives oxygen from the blood stream; the body similarly takes in oxygen from the air and food from the external world. The personality is dependent upon the external world for stimulation. Studies of sensory deprivation show that when a person is placed in a darkened soundproof room, where he has a minimal amount of visual and auditory stimulation, he develops hallucinations and other signs of mental stress (Solomon et al., 1961). Deprivation of social stimulation also can lead to mental disorganization (Spitz, 1945). Köhler's (1944, 1947) studies of the figural aftereffects of continued stimulation show the dependence of perception upon its energic support from the external world. Animals deprived of visual experience from birth for a prolonged period never fully recover their visual capacities (Melzack and Thompson, 1956). In other words, the functioning personality is heavily dependent upon the continuous inflow of stimulation from the external environment. Similarly, social organizations must also draw renewed supplies of energy from other institutions, or people, or the material environment. No social structure is self-sufficient or self-contained.

2. *The through-put*. Open systems transform the energy available to them. The body converts starch and sugar into heat and action. The personality converts chemical and electrical forms of stimulation into sensory qualities, and information into thought patterns. The organization creates a new product, or processes materials, or trains people, or provides a service. These activities entail some reorganization of input. Some work gets done in the system.

3. *The output*. Open systems export some product into the environment, whether it be the invention of an inquiring mind or a bridge constructed by an engineering firm. Even the biological organism exports physiological products such as carbon dioxide from the lungs which helps to maintain plants in the immediate environment.

4. *Systems as cycles of events*. The pattern of activities of the energy exchange has a cyclic character. The product exported into the environment furnishes the sources of energy for the

repetition of the cycle of activities. The energy reinforcing the cycle of activities can derive from some exchange of the product in the external world or from the activity itself. In the former instance, the industrial concern utilizes raw materials and human labor to turn out a product which is marketed, and the monetary return is used to obtain more raw materials and labor to perpetuate the cycle of activities. In the latter instance, the voluntary organization can provide expressive satisfactions to its members so that the energy renewal comes directly from the organizational activity itself.

The problem of structure, or the relatedness of parts, can be observed directly in some physical arrangement of things where the larger unit is physically bounded and its subparts are also bounded within the larger structure. But how do we deal with social structures, where physical boundaries in this sense do not exist? It was the genius of F. H. Allport (1962) which contributed the answer, namely, that the structure is to be found in an interrelated set of events which return upon themselves to complete and renew a cycle of activities. It is events rather than things which are structured, so that social structure is a dynamic rather than a static concept. Activities are structured so that they comprise a unity in their completion or closure. A simple linear stimulus-response exchange between two people would not constitute social structure. To create structure, the responses of A would have to elicit B's reactions in such a manner that the responses of the latter would stimulate A to further responses. Of course the chain of events may involve many people, but their behavior can be characterized as showing structure only when there is some closure to the chain by a return to its point of origin with the probability that the chain of events will then be repeated. The repetition of the cycle does not have to involve the same set of phenotypical happenings. It may expand to include more subevents of exactly the same kind or it may involve similar activities directed toward the same outcomes. In the individual organism the eye may move in such a way as to have the point of light fall upon the center of the retina. As the point of light moves, the movements of the eye may also change but to complete the same cycle of activity, i.e., to focus upon the point of light.

A single cycle of events of a self-closing character gives us a simple form of structure. But such single cycles can also combine to give a larger structure of events or an event system. An event system may consist of a circle of smaller cycles or hoops, each one of which makes contact with several others. Cycles may also be tangential to one another from other types of subsystems. The basic method for the identification of social structures is to follow the energic chain of events from the input of energy through its transformation to the point of closure of the cycle.

5. *Negative entropy*. To survive, open systems must move to arrest the entropic process; they must acquire negative entropy. The entropic process is a universal law of nature in which all forms of organization move toward disorganization or death. Complex physical systems move toward simple random distribution of their elements and biological organisms also run down and perish. The open system, however, by importing more energy from its environment than it expends, can store energy and can acquire negative entropy. There is then a general trend in an open system to maximize its ratio of imported to expended energy, to survive and even during periods of crisis to live on borrowed time. Prisoners in concentration camps on a starvation diet will carefully conserve any form of energy expenditure to make the limited food intake go as far as possible (Cohen, 1954). Social organizations will seek to improve their survival position and to acquire in their reserves a comfortable margin of operation.

The entropic process asserts itself in all biological systems as well as in closed physical systems. The energy replenishment of the biological organism is not of a qualitative character which can maintain indefinitely the complex organizational structure of living tissue. Social systems, however, are not anchored in the same physical constancies as biological organisms and so are capable of almost indefinite arresting of the entropic process. Nevertheless the number of organizations which go out of existence every year is large.

6. *Information input, negative feedback, and the coding process*. The inputs into living systems consist not only of energic materials which become transformed or altered in the work that gets done. Inputs are also informative in character and furnish

signals to the structure about the environment and about its own functioning in relation to the environment. Just as we recognize the distinction between cues and drives in individual psychology, so must we take account of information and energic inputs for all living systems.

The simplest type of information input found in all systems is negative feedback. Information feedback of a negative kind enables the system to correct its deviations from course. The working parts of the machine feed back information about the effects of their operation to some central mechanism or subsystem which acts on such information to keep the system on target. The thermostat which controls the temperature of the room is a simple example of a regulatory device which operates on the basis of negative feedback. The automated power plant would furnish more complex examples. Miller (1955) emphasizes the critical nature of negative feedback in his proposition: "*When a system's negative feedback discontinues, its steady state vanishes, and at the same time its boundary disappears and the system terminates*" (p. 529). If there is no corrective device to get the system back on its course, it will expend too much energy or it will ingest too much energic input and no longer continue as a system.

The reception of inputs into a system is selective. Not all energic inputs are capable of being absorbed into every system. The digestive system of living creatures assimilates only those inputs to which it is adapted. Similarly, systems can react only to those information signals to which they are attuned. The general term for the selective mechanisms of a system by which incoming materials are rejected or accepted and translated for the structure is coding. Through the coding process the "blooming, buzzing confusion" of the world is simplified into a few meaningful and simplified categories for a given system. The nature of the functions performed by the system determines its coding mechanisms, which in turn perpetuate this type of functioning.

7. *The steady state and dynamic homeostasis.* The importation of energy to arrest entropy operates to maintain some constancy in energy exchange, so that open systems which survive are characterized by a steady state. A steady state is not motionless or a true equilibrium. There is a continuous inflow of energy from the external environment and a continuous export of the products of the system, but the character of the system, the ratio of the energy exchanges and the relations between parts, remains the same. The catabolic and anabolic processes of tissue breakdown and restoration within the body preserve a steady state so that the organism from time to time is not the identical organism it was but a highly similar organism. The steady state is seen in clear form in the homeostatic processes for the regulation of body temperature; external conditions of humidity and temperature may vary, but the temperature of the body remains the same. The endocrine glands are a regulatory mechanism for preserving an evenness of physiological functioning. The general principle here is that of Le Châtelier (see Bradley and Calvin, 1956) who maintains that any internal or external factor making for disruption of the system is countered by forces which restore the system as closely as possible to its previous state. Krech and Crutchfield (1948) similarly hold, with respect to psychological organization, that cognitive structures will react to influences in such a way as to absorb them with minimal change to existing cognitive integration.

The homeostatic principle does not apply literally to the functioning of all complex living systems, in that in counteracting entropy they move toward growth and expansion. This apparent contradiction can be resolved, however, if we recognize the complexity of the subsystems and their interaction in anticipating changes necessary for the maintenance of an overall steady state. Stagner (1951) has pointed out that the initial disturbance of a given tissue constancy within the biological organism will result in mobilization of energy to restore the balance, but that recurrent upsets will lead to actions to anticipate the disturbance:

> We eat before we experience intense hunger pangs . . . energy mobilization for forestalling tactics must be explained in terms of a *cortica tension* which reflects the visceral-proprioceptive pattern of the original biological disequilibration. . . . *Dynamic homeostasis* involves the maintenance of tissue constancies by establishing a constant physical environment—by reducing the variability and disturbing effects of external stimulation. Thus the organism does not simply restore the prior equilibrium. A new, more complex and more comprehensive equilibrium is established. (p. 5)

Though the tendency toward a steady state in its simplest form is homeostatic, as in the preservation of a constant body temperature, the basic principle is *the preservation of the character of the system.* The equilibrium which complex systems approach is often that of a quasi-stationary equilibrium, to use Lewin's concept (1947). An adjustment in one direction is countered by a movement in the opposite direction and both movements are approximate rather than precise in their compensatory nature. Thus a temporal chart of activity will show a series of ups and downs rather than a smooth curve.

In preserving the character of the system, moreover, the structure will tend to import more energy than is required for its output, as we have already noted in discussing negative entropy. To insure survival, systems will operate to acquire some margin of safety beyond the immediate level of existence. The body will store fat, the social organization will build up reserves, the society will increase its technological and cultural base. Miller (1955) has formulated the proposition that the rate of growth of a system—within certain ranges—is exponential if it exists in a medium which makes available unrestricted amounts of energy for input.

In adapting to their environment, systems will attempt to cope with external forces by ingesting them or acquiring control over them. The physical boundedness of the single organism means that such attempts at control over the environment affect the behavioral system rather than the biological system of the individual. Social systems will move, however, towards incorporating within their boundaries the external resources essential to survival. Again the result is an expansion of the original system.

Thus, the steady state which at the simple level is one of homeostasis over time, at more complex levels becomes one of preserving the character of the system through growth and expansion. The basic type of system does not change directly as a consequence of expansion. The most common type of growth is a multiplication of the same type of cycles or subsystems—a change in quantity rather than in quality. Animal and plant species grow by multiplication. A social system adds more units of the same essential type as it already has. Haire (1959) has studied the ratio between the sizes of different subsystems in growing business organizations. He found that though the number of people increased in both the production subsystem and the subsystem concerned with the external world, the ratio of the two groups remained constant. Qualitative change does occur, however, in two ways. In the first place, quantitative growth calls for supportive subsystems of a specialized character not necessary when the system was smaller. In the second place, there is a point where quantitative changes produce a qualitative difference in the functioning of a system. A small college which triples its size is no longer the same institution in terms of the relation between its administration and faculty, relations among the various academic departments, or the nature of its instruction.

In fine, living systems exhibit a growth or expansion dynamic in which they maximize their basic character. They react to change or they anticipate change through growth which assimilates the new energic inputs to the nature of their structure. In terms of Lewin's quasistationary equilibrium the ups and downs of the adjustive process do not always result in a return to the old level. Under certain circumstances a solidification or freezing occurs during one of the adjustive cycles. A new base line level is thus established and successive movements fluctuate around this plateau which may be either above or below the previous plateau of operation.

8. *Differentiation.* Open systems move in the direction of differentiation and elaboration. Diffuse global patterns are replaced by more specialized functions. The sense organs and the nervous system evolved as highly differentiated structures from the primitive nervous tissues. The growth of the personality proceeds from primitive, crude organizations of mental functions to hierarchically structured and well-differentiated systems of beliefs and feelings. Social organizations move toward the multiplication and elaboration of roles with greater specialization of function. In the United States today medical specialists now outnumber the general practitioners.

One type of differentiated growth in systems is what von Bertalanffy (1956) terms progressive mechanization. It finds expression in the way in which a system achieves a steady state. The early method is a process which involves an interaction of various dynamic forces, whereas the later development entails the use of a regulatory feedback mechanism. He writes:

It can be shown that the *primary* regulations in organic systems, that is, those which are most fundamental and primitive in embryonic development as well as in evolution, are of such nature of dynamic interaction. . . . Superimposed are those regulations which we may call *secondary*, and which are controlled by fixed arrangements, especially of the feedback type. This state of affairs is a consequence of a general principle of organization which may be called progressive mechanization. At first, systems—biological, neurological, psychological or social—are governed by dynamic interaction of their components; later on, fixed arrangements and conditions of constraint are established which render the system and its parts more efficient, but also gradually diminish and eventually abolish its equipotentiality. (p. 6)

9. *Equifinality*. Open systems are further characterized by the principle of equifinality, a principle suggested by von Bertalanffy in 1940. According to this principle, a system can reach the same final state from differing initial conditions and by a variety of paths. The well-known biological experiments on the sea urchin show that a normal creature of that species can develop from a complete ovum, from each half of a divided ovum, or from the fusion product of two whole ova. As open systems move toward regulatory mechanisms to control their operations, the amount of equifinality may be reduced.

## Some consequences of viewing organizations as open systems

In the following chapter we shall inquire into the specific implications of considering organizations as open systems and into the ways in which social organizations differ from other types of living systems. At this point, however, we should call attention to some of the misconceptions which arise both in theory and practice when social organizations are regarded as closed rather than open systems.

The major misconception is the failure to recognize fully that the organization is continually dependent upon inputs from the environment and that the inflow of materials and human energy is not a constant. The fact that organizations have built-in protective devices to maintain stability and that they are notoriously difficult to change in the direction of some reformer's desires should not obscure the realities of the dynamic interrelationships of any social structure with its social and natural environment. The very efforts of the organization to maintain a constant external environment produce changes in organizational structure. The reaction to changed inputs to mute their possible revolutionary implications also results in changes.

The typical models in organizational theorizing concentrate upon principles of internal functioning as if these problems were independent of changes in the environment and as if they did not affect the maintenance inputs of motivation and morale. Moves toward tighter integration and coordination are made to insure stability, when flexibility may be the more important requirement. Moreover, coordination and control become ends in themselves rather than means to an end. They are not seen in full perspective as adjusting the system to its environment but as desirable goals within a closed system. In fact, however, every attempt at coordination which is not functionally required may produce a host of new organizational problems.

One error which stems from this kind of misconception is the failure to recognize the equifinality of the open system, namely, that there are more ways than one of producing a given outcome. In a closed physical system the same initial conditions must lead to the same final result. In open systems this is not true even at the biological level. It is much less true at the social level. Yet in practice we insist that there is one best way of assembling a gun for all recruits, one best way for the baseball player to hurl the ball in from the outfield, and that we standardize and teach these best methods. Now it is true under certain conditions that there is one best way, but these conditions must first be established. The general principle, which characterizes all open systems, is that there does not have to be a single method for achieving an objective.

A second error lies in the notion that irregularities in the functioning of a system due to environmental influences are error variances and should be treated accordingly. According to this conception, they should be controlled out of studies of organizations. From the organization's own operations they should be excluded as irrelevant and should be guarded against. The decisions of officers to omit a consideration of external factors or to guard against such influences in a defensive fashion, as if they would go away if ignored, is an instance of this type of thinking. So is the now outmoded "public be damned" attitude of businessmen toward the clientele upon whose support they depend. Open-system theory, on the other hand, would maintain that environmental influences are not sources of error variance but are integrally related to the functioning of a social system, and that we cannot understand a system without a constant study of the forces that impinge upon it.

Thinking of the organization as a closed system, moreover, results in a failure to develop the intelligence or feedback function of obtaining adequate information about the changes in environmental forces. It is remarkable how weak many industrial companies are in their market research departments when they are so dependent upon the market. The prediction can be hazarded that organizations in our society will increasingly move toward the improvement of the facilities for research in assessing environmental forces. The reason is that we are in the process of correcting our misconception of the organization as a closed system.

Emery and Trist (1960) have pointed out how current theorizing on organizations still reflects the older closed system conceptions. They write:

> In the realm of social theory, however, there has been something of a tendency to continue thinking in terms of a "closed" system, that is, to regard the enterprise as sufficiently independent to allow most of its problems to be analyzed with reference to its internal structure and without reference to its external environment. . . . In practice the system theorists in social science . . . did "tend to focus on the statics of social structure and to neglect the study of structural change." In an attempt to overcome this bias, Merton suggested that "the concept of dysfunction, which implied the concept of strain, stress and tension on the structural level, provides an analytical approach to the study of dynamics and change." This concept has been widely accepted by system theorists but while it draws attention to sources of imbalance within an organization it does not conceptually reflect the mutual permeation of an organization and its environment that is the cause of such imbalance. It still retains the limiting perspectives of "closed system" theorizing. In the administrative field the same limitations may be seen in the otherwise invaluable contributions of Barnard and related writers. (p. 84)

## Summary

The open-system approach to organizations is contrasted with common-sense approaches, which tend to accept popular names and stereotypes as basic organizational properties and to identify the purpose of an organization in terms of the goals of its founders and leaders.

The open-system approach, on the other hand, begins by identifying and mapping the repeated cycles of input, transformation, output, and renewed input which comprise the organizational pattern. This approach to organizations represents the adaptation of work in biology and in the physical sciences by von Bertalanffy and others.

Organizations as a special class of open systems have properties of their own, but they share other properties in common with all open systems. These include the importation of energy from the environment, the through-put or transformation of the imported energy into some product form which is characteristic of the system, the exporting of that product into the environment, and the reenergizing of the system from sources in the environment.

Open systems also share the characteristics of negative entropy, feedback, homeostasis, differentiation, and equifinality. The law of negative entropy states that systems survive and maintain their characteristic internal order only so long as they import from the environment more energy than they expend in the process of transformation and exportation. The feedback principle has to do with information input, which is a special kind of energic importation, a kind of signal to the system about environmental conditions and about the functioning of the system in relation to its environment. The feedback of such information enables the system to correct for its own malfunctioning or for changes in the environment, and thus to maintain a steady state or homeostasis. This is a dynamic rather than a static balance, however. Open systems are not at rest but tend toward differentiation and elaboration, both because of subsystem dynamics and because of the relationship between growth and survival. Finally, open systems are characterized by the principle of equifinality, which asserts that systems can reach the same final state from different initial conditions and by different paths of development.

Traditional organizational theories have tended to view the human organization as a closed system. This tendency has led to a disregard of differing organizational environments and the nature of organizational dependency on environment. It has led also to an overconcentration on principles of internal organizational functioning, with consequent failure to develop and understand the processes of feedback which are essential to survival.

## References


Allport, F. H. (1962). "A Structuronomic Conception of Behavior: Individual and Collective. I. Structural Theory and the Master Problem of Social Psychology." *Journal of Abnormal and Social Psychology*, 64: 3–30.

Bradley, D. F., and M. Calvin (1956). "Behavior: Imbalance in a Network of Chemical Transformations." *General Systems*. Yearbook of the Society for the Advancement of General System Theory, 1: 56–65.

Cohen, E. (1954). *Human Behavior in the Concentration Camp*. London: Jonathan Cape.

Emery, F. E., and E. L. Trist (1960). "Socio-Technical Systems." In *Management Sciences Models and Techniques*. Vol. 2. London: Pergamon Press.

Haire, M. (1959). "Biological Models and Empirical Histories of the Growth of Organizations." In M. Haire (ed.) *Modern Organization Theory*. New York: Wiley, 272–306.

Kohler, W., and D. Emery (1947). "Figural After-effects in the Third Dimension of Visual Space." *American Journal of Psychology*, 60: 159–201.

——— and H. Wallach (1944). "Figural After-effects: An Investigation of Visual Processes." *Proceedings of the American Philosophical Society*, 88: 269–357.

Krech, D., and R. Crutchfield (1948). *Theory and Problems of Social Psychology*. New York: McGraw-Hill.

Lewin, K. (1947). "Frontiers in Group Dynamics." *Human Relations*, 1: 5–41.

Melzack, R., and W. Thompson (1956). "Effects of Early Experience on Social Behavior." *Canadian Journal of Psychology*, 10: 82–90.

Merton, R. K. (1957). *Social Theory and Social Structure*, rev. ed. New York: Free Press.

Miller, J. G. (1955). "Toward a General Theory for the Behavioral Sciences." *American Psychologist*, 10: 513–31.

Solomon, P., *et al.* (eds.) (1961). *Sensory Deprivation*. Cambridge, Mass.: Harvard University Press.

Spitz, R. A. (1945). "Hospitalism: An Inquiry into the Genesis of Psychiatric Conditions in Early Childhood." *Psychoanalytic Study of the Child*, 1: 53–74.

Stagner, R. (1951). "Homeostasis as a Unifying Concept in Personality Theory." *Psychological Review*, 58: 5–17.

von Bertalanffy, L. (1940). "Der Organismus als physikalisches System betrachtet." *Naturwissenschaften*, 28: 521ff.

———. (1950). "The Theory of Open Systems in Physics and Biology." *Science*, 111: 23–28.

———. (1956). "General System Theory." *General Systems*. Yearbook of the Society for the Advancement of General System Theory, 1: 1–10.

# Part Three

# Methods of Study

The purpose of this section is to help pierce the mystery surrounding what sociologists actually do when they study the behavior of organizations. Obviously, we cannot present all of the methods of study used, but we can sample a broad range of techniques and demonstrate thereby the complex of problems and pleasures associated with each choice.

All students have participated as members of numerous organizations and therefore have the opportunity to put their sociological interests to work as lay participant-observers. Melville Dalton was in the unique position of being an employee of two of the organizations analyzed in his study. This allowed him the freedom to engage in detailed participant observation, to interview other organizational members, and provided him with some access to personnel files. Dalton also made extensive use of informants in the various organizations he studied and discussed the problems that resulted from their use. That Dalton's unorthodox methods were indeed successful in revealing important aspects of organizational life is evidenced in the selection from his work that appears later in this volume.

Lipset, Trow, and Coleman describe two different functions that a single case study can perform, their method of dealing with different units of analysis, and the shortcomings and advantages they feel accrue from their approach. The basic problem they confronted was how to make general statements about other organizations from an intensive internal analysis of only one. In a later section of this volume, a summary of the major substantive findings of their research on the International Typographer's Union is presented.

Blau suggests that comparative analysis of a large number of organizations is essential if one is interested in establishing valid relationships between organizational attributes. He describes three general approaches to the study of organization and argues that each approach is limited in the kinds of problems with which it is able to deal. He notes that organizations have attributes that do not pertain to the characteristics of their individual members, and that these attributes can be studied on their own without the time and effort required to survey organizational members.

Grusky and Churchill wanted to study a large number of organizations while being sure these organizations differed only in certain crucial theoretical variables. They dealt with this problem by creating seventy-two business organizations within the confines of the laboratory. One novel aspect of their method involved the use of confederates to aid in the manipulation of one of the independent variables. At the same time, a key element of succession, the other independent variable, namely, the confrontation of a leader with new subordinates in an ongoing organization, was real. The new manager and his assistants were actually strangers to one another. This technique, and other related approaches such as computer simulation and studies involving the use of various games, provide the advantages of rigorous control and are valuable additions insofar as they are applied to the study of meaningful organizational phenomena.

This section concludes with a highly personal and unusually candid account of how one investigator proceeded in formulating and executing his research on preindustrial work organizations. Two important aspects of research methods are dealt with in this selection. First, Udy indicates the importance of cross-cultural analyses of organizations and the problems associated with securing comparable data from more than one setting. Second, Udy's study is noteworthy in its creative use of the secondary analysis of published materials. Although encountering numerous problems, Udy was able to obtain useful data and produce a contribution to our knowledge of organizations from material already contained in the Human Relations Area Files.

MELVILLE DALTON

# Participant Observation

Influenced by the dogmatism of nineteenth century science[1] research methodology in the social and psychological sciences is now more cocksure than in the increasingly humble physical sciences. Even in the nineteenth century, celebrated discoveries were often achieved enigmatically. Kekule tortuously arrived at his theory of the benzene molecule; Davy blundered onto the anesthetic properties of nitrous oxide; Perkin's failure to produce synthetic quinine circuitously revealed aniline dyes; and Ehrlich tried 606 times before he succeeded in compounding salvarsan in 1910.

Today a mathematical biologist declares that "no scientist follows any cut-and-dried procedure. Intuition and idiosyncrasies probably play as important a part in the work of the scientist as they do in the work of the artist."[2]

Seeing the physicist's first task as one of establishing universal elementary laws, Einstein declares that "there is no logical path to these laws; only intuition, resting on sympathetic understanding of experience, can reach them. . . . There is no logical bridge between phenomena and their theoretical principles."[3]

This is not to attack method as such—and certainly it is not to say that unsupported "intuition" is *the* route—but to caution against letting method be a tail that wags the dog.[4] When treated as a fixed set of procedures, method ignores or obscures the researcher's frequent groping, fumbling, and setbacks. In current practice, the listing of fears, mistakes, and interpersonal problems in collecting data is likely to seem unorthodox and to be interpreted as a mark of ineptness. Yet these are accompaniments, and they may greatly influence what is seen, and how it is handled.

In the present research no explicit hypotheses were set up in advance but, as indicated in the Introduction, occupational involvements[5] usually

1. J. Bronowski, *The Common Sense of Science*, Wm. Heinemann, Ltd., London, 1955, pp. 124–27. As a physicist, Bronowski notes that "in the strict sense there are no exact sciences. There is science, and there is common sense; and both must learn to assimilate into their methods and basic ideas the underlying uncertainties of all knowledge" (p. 128).

2. Anatol Rapoport, *Operational Philosophy*, Harper and Brothers, New York, 1954, p. 48.

3. "Principles of Research," in *Essays in Science*, trans. by Alan Harris, Philosophical Library, New York, 1933, 1934, p. 4. See the similar but more elaborate remarks of another physicist, Harold K. Schilling, "A Human Enterprise," *Science*, 127 (No. 3310): 1324–1327, June 6, 1958.

4. Among the minority of people in the psychological and social sciences who give attention to the problem, see A. H. Maslow, "Problem-Centering vs. Means-Centering in Science," *Philosophy of Science*, 13: 326–31, October, 1946; Jessie Bernard, "The Art of Science," *American Journal of Sociology*, 55: 1–9, July, 1949.

5. In the main, I followed the guiding bias that "a subject becomes scientific not by beginning with facts, with hypotheses, or with some pet theory brought in *a priori*, but by beginning with the peculiar character of its particu-

Reprinted from *Men Who Manage*, pp. 194–217, by permission of the author and publisher. 

preceded questions and consciousness of problems to be studied.

Many questions and hunches originating in the experience at Milo and Fruhling were cross-fertilized by concurrent contacts at Attica and Rambeau.* Since no simultaneous systematic study could be made of all, and as Milo was the most accessible, that firm became the nucleus of inquiries and the continuing point of major effort. However, general questions and interpretations were increasingly influenced by study of the other firms, especially the factories. Common processes and similar recurring situations evoked interlocking questions which led to establishment of the problem areas. For example, why did grievers and managers form cross-cliques? Why were staff personnel ambivalent toward line officers? Why was there disruptive conflict between Maintenance and Operation? If people were awarded posts because of specific fitness, why the disparity between their given and exercised influence? Why, among executives on the same formal level, were some distressed and some not? And why were there such sharp differences in viewpoint and moral concern about given events? What was the meaning of double talk about success as dependent on knowing people rather than on possessing administrative skills? Why and how were "control" staffs and official guardians variously compromised? What was behind the contradictory policy and practices associated with the use of company materials and services? Thus the guiding question embracing all others was: what orders the schisms and ties between official and unofficial action?

Steps in getting answers to these and other changing questions can be discussed under (*a*) intimates, (*b*) techniques and sources of data, and (*c*) special problems.

## Intimates

In no case did I make a formal approach to the top management of any of the firms to get approval or support for the research. Several times I have seen other researchers do this and have watched higher managers set the scene and limit the inquiry to specific areas—outside management proper—as though the problem existed in a vacuum. The findings in some cases were then regarded as "controlled experiments," which in final form made impressive reading. But the smiles and delighted manipulation of researchers by guarded personnel, the assessments made of researchers and their findings, and the frequently trivial areas to which alerted and fearful officers guided the inquiry—all raised questions about who controlled the experiments. This approach was not suited to my purposes. Rather, by building on personal knowledge, I furthered the research through intimates—those who gave information and aid that, if generally known, would have jeopardized their careers. Though they knew of my general interest, I made no detailed statement of what I sought, and in all cases I indicated that my interest was broad information on "all kinds of personnel problems" from as many firms as possible. I usually supported this by asking informants questions about their earlier experiences. I hoped this would allay fear that *their* firm, or department, was of special interest. In some cases the procedure stimulated informants to insist on giving local details and drawing parallels with their earlier experiences (e.g., Kincaid, Chapter 5), which gave me leads and information.

The number and rank of intimates naturally varied in different firms.[6] At Fruhling, for example, where most of my attention was on a division of 3500, I was on close terms with 33 people, including Jessup and 18 other line personnel (13 foremen and 5 production workers), and 14 staff people.

Milo intimates totaled 81. Eleven were workmen, including 3 grievers; 24 first-line foremen; 14 general foremen; 6 line superintendents; 8 staff heads or assistants, and 18 staff supervisors or specialists. I directly or nondirectively interviewed 113 other persons in the Milo sample, and 27 hourly-paid foremen outside the sample.

Reynolds at Attica was merely a speaking acquaintance. However, I had the confidence of one of his secretaries,[7] two members of the grievance com-

lar problems." F. S. C. Northrop, *The Logic of the Sciences and the Humanities*, Macmillan, New York, 1947, p. 274.

* Editors' note: Milo, Fruhling, Attica, and Rambeau are fictitious names for the plants studied.

6. Number is of course less important than the individual person's reliability and knowledge, and the rapport achieved with him. More time was given to Milo and to cultivation of its personnel, hence the greater number of intimates in, and references to, that firm.

7. Several female secretaries and clerks were helpful in

mittee, and an engineer whom I had known earlier at Fruhling. I knew two of Reynolds' community intimates, and five former Milo workmen in the plant who supplemented my information about Attica's racial problems.

At Rambeau, I had but three associates—Nevers; the husband of one of Reynolds' secretaries; and the secretary herself, who was formerly employed there full time but now worked only during the evenings that Rambeau was open. Her friendship with the bureaucratic female department head (Chapter 7) was most helpful.

At Marathon Research Company my only informant was the chemist whom I had known earlier at Milo. At Argo Transit the top manager and three persons in his office supplied me with more information than I needed. The X-ray technician (Chapter 7) was my sole contact at his hospital. Four people whom I had earlier known at Fruhling gave me details of their activities under piecerate work at the unnamed cabinet factory (Chapter 7).

Intimates were invaluable not only as sources of information but for help in the research situation. Especially at Milo and Fruhling they occasionally served as what chemists would call "catalytic agents," because they accelerated reactions. In effect they sometimes initiated and pushed uncontrolled experiments for me. In the staff groups particularly, as well as in any situation where discussion was taking place and I knew in advance that I could be present and seemingly occupied with work, they introduced agreed topics and questions into the conversation. These stimuli were typically on issues in the problem areas. Usually "busy" over in a corner of the room, I was observing and taking notes on the remarks of one or more people. Some intimates developed an interest in this kind of study, and sketched events and conversations they thought relevant for me in my absence. These data were naturally evaluated before use. Such experimentation is of course regarded in some circles as "unethical," and would not be accepted as a "technique." But without note taking and careful assessment, this is a common and legitimate link in the fluid interchanges between the official and unofficial phases of organizational events. It seems no more unethical than the use of "visiting shoppers" in business or "projective techniques" in psychological research.

## Techniques and sources of data

Though often overlapping, because I expediently used any method that did not endanger the firm or personnel, my core efforts can be discussed under formal interviewing, work diaries, participant-observation, and socializing.

### FORMAL INTERVIEWS

I did little formal interviewing because of the obvious problem of explaining what I was doing, and the inadequacy of the approach for getting at unofficial activities—especially when other means were safer and more effective. In interviewing, I normally did not take notes,[8] but listened with relaxed intentness and then reconstructed the interview as soon as possible after it ended. This was done by first setting up a skeleton of key items remembered and then expanding by association to other parts and reworking until it seemed to be a facsimile. The results were relatively complete on topics covered and apparently accurate on grammar and speech mannerisms—judged by the occasional

the research. The potential contribution of persons in these roles is usually unappreciated. Several things fit them to aid research of this kind. They are probably more status conscious than males in the same roles, and quicker to note symbols of rank, differences in influence, and to spot certain of the factors involved. They are also more interested in events and social details and probably remember them better. Having this orientation and access to records and events, they are likely to possess considerable knowledge of unofficial activities and developing policy. Where his personal bent is a hindrance to clique participation, or his clique ties are fouled and he feels isolated, a manager confides more to his secretaries than to others and even relies on their judgment. (Research on the marriages of secretaries to their bosses in all walks of life would probably show that much more than physical proximity and sex attraction is involved.) It is trite to note that women have long played secondary formal roles, have had to use indirect approaches to win ends and have resented the condition. However, this may be relevant for the researcher. For where female secretaries are treated as intellectual menials, they are disposed to be communicative with those who show awareness of their insights and knowledge of affairs. At least this was true at Fruhling, Milo, and Attica.

8. Cowper (Chapter 6) however, in a tone indicating he had something of great weight to reveal, commanded me to take notes by asking, "Aren't you going to take any notes?" and handing me a pad.

read-backs I made to intimates of some of our discussions, and the checking of my notes with "catalysts" against what they believed had been said in group discussions involving people whose expressions and idioms they knew better than I did.

In the process of reconstructing interviews, I noted down emphases made, facial expressions, marks of concern and relief, and other gestures—aware that they could mislead—as possible clues to more basic things. When note-taking was essential and I could not keep up, I used abbreviations, *ad hoc* symbols, trade terms, or jargon as quickly decipherable recall crutches. The aim of such interviewing was usually to get a clear official statement, with as many rewarding slips as possible.

### WORK DIARIES

Through much of the period at Fruhling and Milo I recorded events, biographical information, gossip, and initial hypotheses in loose-leaf notebooks. For example, I outlined and dated "unusual" incidents (which in a flow of deviations might include a return to "usual" practices); questions to ask certain people; possible ties among events; signs of developing cliques; activities of cliques; out-of-role behavior; additions to biographical data; the search for and use of precedents by individuals and groups; contrary interpretations made of regulations with notes on who made them and leads to follow; overhead remarks made by people about each other—complimentary and not; threats and accusations in arguments; joking remarks that seemed to bear on events; provocative statistics and irregularities in reports as leads to follow or as related to established data; and marginal notes by various departments on work analysis sheets. Tentative answers were later incorporated with the questions; some questions were rephrased or dropped, and others introduced. Materials were later detached and grouped into logical categories. Periodically I sifted and reclassified data as accumulating evidence exposed errors of interpretation and emphasis. The "miscellaneous" category waxed and waned with progress, and with refinement of categories. Concern to miss nothing significant and knowledge that I was missing some things, obviously meant an accumulation of "irrelevant" data for the categories and problems settled on as most meaningful.

### PARTICIPANT-OBSERVATION[9]

My formal roles at Milo and Fruhling cannot be named without danger of exposing intimates to their superiors there. In both cases I was a member of staff groups which gave me—even required—great freedom of movement and wide contacts without raising questions.

This technique allowed me to spot and, aping line chiefs, utilize malcontents. These included members among first, my staff associates, then Catholics, minority ethnic groups, first-line foremen in general, and various individuals wherever I met them. Such persons were disposed to trust me and to speak more freely than were other initially non-intimates. Their information on past and developing events was most helpful, and constituted solid data one corrected for emotional distortions, such as the Catholic cry at Milo that "ninety-five per cent of management are Masons" and Sarto's allegation that no Italian could enter the hierarchy (Chapter 6). As fringe members of their groups, malcontents may distort from both ignorance and bias.

Of course (1) the carrying out of *line* assignments to find errors in inventories and the labeling and classification of raw materials; (2) the attendance of safety, union-management (low level), and other meetings; (3) the study and compilation of reports—including those that involved "government jobs" and "graphite analyses," job descriptions, and personnel assessments; and (4) the carrying out of unofficial assignments under an official title, were all important in getting at the similar activities of others and for judging the interplay and interconnections of official and unofficial action; for gaining access to personnel files, and for learning

9. See [the following] assessments of this controversial technique: John P. Dean, "Participant Observation and Interviewing," in John T. Doby, et al., *An Introduction to Social Research*, The Stackpole Co., Harrisburg, Pennsylvania, 1954, pp. 225–52; Morris Schwartz and Charlotte Green Schwartz, "Problems in Participant Observation," *American Journal of Sociology*, 60: 343–53, January, 1955; A. J. Vidich, "Participant Observation and the Collection and Interpretation of Data," *Ibid.*, 354–60; Jiri Kolaja, "A Contribution to the Theory of Participant Observation," *Social Forces*, 35: 159–63, December, 1956; Howard S. Becker and Blanche Geer, "Participant Observation and Interviewing: A Comparison," *Human Organization*, 16 (No. 3): 28–32, Fall, 1957, and Martin Trow, "Comment," *Ibid.*, pp. 33–35; Raymond L. Gold, "Roles in Sociological Field Observations," *Social Forces*, 36: 217–23, March, 1958.

what records were reliable as against those only "for the record."

Such functional intimacies naturally helped me to follow relations between Milo and the Office after the demise of the FWD. Lacking personal communication with the Office, I remained near the interplay by associating with (1) the few visiting representatives that I could; (2) some of the Milo personnel who had formerly been in the Office and continued to communicate with friends there; (3) a few Milo managers who made occasional trips to the Office; and (4) intimates who were critically involved in meeting expectations of the Office.

Grievance records reported for Fruhling (grouped with those of Attica and Milo) were compiled by the president of the local; those for Milo by the grievers themselves. The grievance steps, the grievances, and the decisions at Attica were transcribed by one of Reynolds' secretaries and confirmed by the grievance committee.

Access to Milo personnel files was arranged by two departments who were disputing about the merits of certain tests given to incoming personnel. It was decided that my academic training fitted me to extract "related information" from personnel files that a "clerk" might have trouble doing. Since some of the personnel who had taken the tests were managers and some were not, a powerful intimate in one of the staffs supported my suggestion that it would be helpful to examine the management file for the records of those who had taken the tests. Knowing vaguely of my intent, he cut me short, when I started to explain what I wanted and why, with the statement, "I trust you to be discreet, so I don't care what you plan to do, and I don't want to know anything about it!" In studying the files, I naturally extracted the data presented statistically in Chapter 6.

The subject of Masonry was so touchy at Milo that even some intimates shrank from having a hand in establishing precise membership and the number of Catholics who had become Masons. What seemed like a simple thing to accomplish, aroused fears, and alienated some of my fringe acquaintances whom I had mistakenly counted on for help, and whom I now saw as themselves worthy of more study. These people now avoided me and aroused my fear for success of the research. I learned later that they feared to aid me and feared not to, lest some of my intimates cause them trouble. (What should the researcher do when he disturbs the situation he would like to hold still?) Since the Masons were distributed among numerous lodges, to confirm membership I eventually had to submit lists of doubtful officers to seventeen intimates among the Masons.

Very close to people in Milo's FWD for over a year, I heard gossip from members who had been in various levels and divisions of the hierarchy; received an orientation to events of the preceding five years; studied mechanics of the FWD, and heard members analyze the department's interplay with line executives as I concurrently followed some developments in the shops. Later as a staff representative in the shops, in a role apart from the FWD, I was able to study events more connectedly while maintaining unofficial contacts with the FWD to learn of defenses that line chiefs were presenting there—without, of course, reporting anything but trivia of either side to the other.

Finally, participant-observation allowed what may be called conversational "interviewing." These efforts were verbal interaction, but not interviews in the usual sense. Since my relations with intimates often were already structured at the start of the research, any straining toward a detached manner, or pursuit of points with uncommon persistence would—and did until I learned better—defeat the purpose. Hence conversations dealing with an intimate's view of things were often broken and incomplete. In some cases utterances over a series of exchanges are tied together as one statement. The characteristic thing about them is that they were precipitated by events involving the intimate; they were "situation-centered" and often unguarded. Though most reported utterances were prompted by a question from me, or by an informal aide, some were parts of "noncatalytic" exchanges between others that I overheard in a shop or office. In other instances, comments were made as asides to me, in the shops, over an incident of the moment.

Some statements, such as the long outpourings by Geiger and Evans, in Chapters 4 and 6, respectively, were made at one time and without interruption by me. Geiger's remarks were in response to my question, "How did things go?" with reference to an exasperating cost meeting he had just left.

Usually expecting guarded talk, I sought when

possible to catch men in or near critical situations, and to learn in advance when important meetings were coming up and what bearing they would have on the unofficial aspects of various issues. Experiences with reneging informants (below) prompted me to get comments or gestures of some kind from certain people before their feelings cooled or they became wary. In "interviewing" I usually had in mind a schedule of points to follow. But when the respondent's talk uncovered events of seeming greater importance, I omitted or adapted my prepared questions. Then, or at a later meeting, when I had exhausted the planned questions for a given part of the research, and was sure of the intimate, I asked loaded questions in various directions and followed promising responses.

#### SOCIALIZING

Out-plant socializing enabled me to study activities at the Magnesia Yacht Club, which involved the community and leaders from many firms; to develop closer relations with the managers during their periods of relaxation; to attend the installation exercises for Masonic officers and to personally verify the membership of some of the managers; to continue contacts with people at Attica and Rambeau, and at Fruhling when I was no longer employed there.

In-plant socializing, especially on my days off, allowed the cultivation of foreign born and minority groups. Seen by these as one of the majority group, my initial approach was to talk with the foreign born about a topic unforgettable to them—their country of origin. Having a strong interest in European history and culture, I found this an easy way to establish rapport with natives of Britain, Germany, Poland, Italy, Spain, Greece, the Slovak and Baltic countries. Such ethnics were pleasantly surprised to find one of the usually condescending Americans interested in and having a small knowledge of the geography, show places, heroes, artists of various kinds, current political figures and interests, and accomplishments—including culinary skills—of their native countries, and wanting to know more. These persons cleared me with suspicious first-generation Americans. It was but a step from such pleasant beginnings to knowledge of (1) name-changing and associated attitudes, (2) leads to internal plant events that I could not possibly cover in person, (3) information not contained (or distorted) in the personnel records, etc. Since many of these persons, workers and managers, at Milo and Fruhling were Catholics, they also supplied leads and valid information on the Catholic-Masonic struggle in Milo and repercussions in the community. Some of the foreign born introduced me to the priests in Magnesia who helped me with additional details.

Discussions of sport, politics, and sex usually broke the ice with the American born.

### Special problems

These include (1) the obstacle of reneging informants; (2) the question of objectivity in covert research; (3) the researcher's predicament of knowing too much for his official role; and (4) the puzzle of escaping identification with any of the key groups under study.

#### RENEGING INFORMANTS

Obviously this is a chronic threat in every grapple with the unofficial. Moving in guarded areas, the researcher expediently seizes promising incidents and words, and comes to count on some informants more than others. But the play of events may dispose any informant to talk hot and cold. For example, a currently cooperative informant, caught in a troublesome situation, may fill a sympathetic ear today; but in a changed condition next week be cool, regret what he said, and indicate to the insensitive researcher that the latter's follow-up is in the wrong direction because he "misinterpreted" last week's remarks, etc. Since he hopes to conceal his withdrawal, this reneger offers no explanations. Presumably he thinks the researcher is too obtuse to detect the changed behavior, or he sees him as manageable or as one unable to or above taking reprisal. In dealing with such an informant a second researcher would probably get a different initial response from the first, and the first could not duplicate his earlier results.

In such cases I sought to hide my awareness of the change and my disappointment, and continued friendly relations to avoid arousing fears. However I used the informant's new stance as a clue to his probably changed involvements, and without discussing him I checked with others for possible hints of factors in his change. Drawing on these I naturally followed consistent leads, and utilized what had earlier seemed like contradictory data as they became consistent with the developing actions of this person's group or clique.

Renegers who openly withdraw as the inquiry deepens, threaten the research. Like the other type, they fear they will be labeled by their groups as persons who "talk out of turn," or that they will be punished. Apparently they fear the researcher less than their groups or other personnel, for they excuse the withdrawal, whether they explain fully or not.

Sometimes the researcher must assume blame for not having detected the informant's limits, for not more carefully preparing him and for having moved too rapidly. As with the other type of reneger, I continued on good terms. To reject the reneger is self-defeating and ignores the fact that he can feel friendship for the social analyst and still fear the larger network of ties in which both are caught. Attempts to understand the reneger are usually rewarding. He may add new angles, reveal disturbances he shares with others, and expose misinformation they have given. Though possibly shifting from the role of confidant, he continues as a subject for analysis, and a key to some areas of group feeling and action.

### OBJECTIVITY IN COVERT RESEARCH

Such situations obviously require careful and intimate contact. Studying them at a distance the investigator may be so "objective" that he misses his subject matter and cannot say just what he is objective about. Better, he alternately immerses himself in the areas he must know, steps out in the role of critic, reorients himself and re-enters. My greatest problem in these immersions and retreats was to distinguish purely official behavior (written or understood) from the more elusive and exciting unofficial phases. Since informalists were more successful in terms of reaching ends, escaping trouble, and maintaining relative poise, my impulse frequently was to slight the formal and to forget its guiding influence on the unofficial. Repeatedly I caught myself moralizing in terms of *my* definition of formal codes which were to others, as I saw later, implicit or so vague as not to fully warrant the meaning I was reading into some informal activities. For over a year, for example, I saw all unofficial use of materials and services (Chapter 7) purely as theft. It was only after developing close relations with Merza and Berger of Milo and Nevers of Rambeau, and after long reflection on the web of incidents which bound them to others, that I saw the oversimplification I was making and shifted from an interpretation of the too rigid and exclusive categories to a more realistic judgment about the whole.

### KNOWING TOO MUCH

The volume of unofficial activities, the revealing concealments to maintain essential appearances, and the official images personnel have of each other's roles—all can be brought out in time by the inquirer who labors from the screen of his formal (nonresearch) role. However, in his speculative prowling he is almost certain at times to forget that nonintimates see his formal function as embracing only a limited knowledge of unofficial events. Eager to learn more, he alarms some persons, even his fringe intimates, by accidentally disclosing bits of unofficial information they think it strange that he should have. Variously committed people misinterpret his slip, magnify what he knows, and fear that he will imprudently compromise them, or—in the changing scene—use his information for personal ends. In any case they are likely to treat him as a red light and to alert others.

Here the veiled scrutineer of things unofficial must map the total role knowledge and defenses peculiar to the different levels and functions of prospective informants. As he sensitizes himself to the role fronts of nonintimates and adapts his methods to them, he never forgets that he must simultaneously remain close to their view of his own role. Though his indirect actions are suspiciously similar to the "undercover" work of espionage agents, he is not that. He does not collect evidence to report to a control body in terms of a legal-illegal standard, nor does he seek to subvert or destroy any group. He is interested in feelings, motivations, and behavior as scientific, not criminal evidence. He does not regard his subjects as enemies of some norm he represents, and he conceals rather than reports identities. He observes to reach generalizations, not to fix moral responsibility.

### AVOIDING OBSTRUCTIVE IDENTIFICATIONS

Randall and others at Milo, and Jessup at Fruhling, were Masons who gave me valuable aid. In our conversations some of my actions were interpreted as showing a wish to affiliate with the Order. After I attended installation exercises at Randall's lodge, he specifically said, "You talk a good fight. Maybe you'd find out a lot more if you'd get to knowing how we do things." Taking such remarks as hints for more proof of where I stood, I feared that failure to respond to cues for closer identification might be interpreted as deliberate and thus endanger the inquiry. On the other hand I knew that entering the Order would alienate helpful Catholics. By chance I avoided the problem.

Escaping overidentification with any one group while maintaining some intimacy with all groups central to unofficial issues is a prime puzzle for the masquerading researcher. My own "solution" of minimum involvement for maximum findings was a compromise that undoubtedly restricted some specific data as the price for broader information. Knowing the deeper feelings of Masons who entered the Order for career purposes—and of members who were formerly Catholics—might have given important sidelights. The compromise assumes that this additional knowledge was not vital for the study as a whole, and that the cost of acquiring it probably would have hurt the research in other ways.

SEYMOUR M. LIPSET, MARTIN A. TROW, and JAMES S. COLEMAN

# Generalizing from a Case Study: Problems of Analysis

When an empirical analysis of a single case (in this instance, the typographical union's political system) is to be carried out, it can be of either of two general types, as follows:

*a*) Description and explanation of the single case, to provide information concerning its present state, and the dynamics through which it continues as it does. This may be called a *particularizing* analysis.

*b*) The development of empirical generalizations or theory through the analysis of the single case, using it not to discover anything about *it* as a system but as an empirical basis either for generalization or theory construction. This may be called a *generalizing* analysis.

The crucial element which distinguishes these two types of analysis is the way they treat general laws and particular statements about the single case. The first kind of analysis *uses* general laws or regularities in order to carry out the analysis of the particular case, much as a metallurgist utilizes his knowledge of general chemical properties in analyzing a sample of ore. That is, it uses previously known generalizations in order to help make particular statements. The second kind of analysis is just the reverse of this: much as a biologist focuses his microscope on a living and growing fruit fly in order to make generalizations about processes of growth, the social scientist in this kind of analysis attempts to utilize the particular case in developing general statements. The particular statement and the general law trade places in these two types of analysis. In the former, the law is used to aid in making particular statements; in the second, the particular statements are used to develop the law.

Both these kinds of analysis have long and honorable traditions in the social sciences, as they have in the natural sciences;[1] perhaps the best-known case of the first in social research is Max Weber's *Protestant Ethic*; a good example of the second is Michel's *Political Parties*.[2] In the former, Weber used general, well-accepted relations between values and behavior in order to partially explain the genesis of capitalism. In the latter, Michels examined many

Reprinted from *Union Democracy*, pp. 393–412, by permission of the authors and The Macmillan Company. (© The Free Press, A Corporation 1956.)

1. Some men have suggested that all of social science must be a particularizing or "idiographic" science, as contrasted to the generalizing or "nomothetic" natural sciences. The most influential of these was Wilhelm Rickert; many social philosophers since his time have spent much effort in refuting him. See, for example, Ernst Cassirer: *An Essay on Man*, New York, Doubleday, 1953, p. 235; and his *Substance and Function*, New York, Dover, 1953, pp. 226 ff.

2. Perhaps better examples of the second type can be given if the analyses under consideration are not restricted to a single case analysis, as we have restricted them. Durkheim in *Suicide* (New York, Free Press, 1951) used particular cases of suicide (or more accurately, rates of suicide) occurring in many social situations, and abstracted from those situations the properties which they held in common and which appeared to be relevant to suicide. This allowed him to make general statements about social organization and suicide, or more generally, certain kinds of deviant behavior.

aspects of the German Social Democratic Party over a period of time, not to make statements about that party, but to make statements about political parties in general.

The present analysis is not clearly in either of these categories; it always attempts to be in the second, though it sometimes goes no further than the first. Many statements refer to the ITU rather than to organizations in general, but at the same time there is usually implicit extension to organizations other than the ITU.

Since it is the second kind of analysis which is attempted here (though not always with success) several problems specific to this kind of analysis arise in the study.

## Multiple-level analysis: the problem of units and properties

In an analysis of the second kind, a generalizing one, several requirements arise which a particularizing analysis need not meet. An important one is the necessity of delineating *units* of analysis and characterizing the units according to certain general *concepts* or *properties*.

If, as is possible in a particularizing analysis, nothing more than a vivid picture is to be given of the system being analyzed, this problem need not arise. A faithful recording of events as they occur can fulfill the task of the particularizing analysis, much as a documentary film does, without once using general sociological concepts. But in order to make generalizations which may be applied to other organizations, general sociological concepts must be used. In the present analysis, this means characterizing several different "sizes" or "levels" of units. The man, his immediate social environment (e.g., his shop), the local, and the ITU as a whole are a minimum set of units which it is necessary to characterize. In this study the union as a whole was characterized in terms of certain structural and environmental properties: for example, the degree of stratification in the occupation, the political structure of the union, the issues which have existed at various times, the union's policies, the kind of employer attitudes toward the union.

It was necessary to characterize the New York local as well by these same kinds of variables. For example, the difference in types of policy problems at the local and international levels was documented, and this was related to an important difference in voting behavior of some men on the two levels (i.e., the predominance of wage-scale problems in local politics leads to interest voting which often unseats the incumbent).

Besides these properties of the New York union which are observable in the perspective of the union as a whole, the random sample allowed characterization of the New York union in terms of some parameters of the distribution of the men's attributes. The average age of printers, the number of men who have other printers as their best friends, and the proportion of men who work nights are examples of this. Such attributes characterize the union as a whole, even though they are based on data gathered from individual men. The interview data were used for characterizing an intermediate social unit as well, the man's direct social environment. His shop and his chapel chairman were both characterized by means of the sample data (and by the actual records of the shop's vote). Finally, the greatest amount of data characterized the man himself: his attitudes, his background, his behavior, etc.

The kinds of observations made and the properties by which the various units were characterized are indicated in Table 1, which summarizes the above discussion. In the cells of the table are listed the kinds of properties by which these units were characterized. This table suggests the complexity of the analysis, for properties in each cell must be related to those in other cells in propositions or generalizations.

This complexity raises a number of problems in the design of a study. Some of the most important of these, in the present study, were those related to the interview data. These data were perhaps the most important in the study. It was a primary means of characterizing at least three of the units in the analysis: (1) The population of the New York local union as a whole, in order to make statements like: "X per cent of the members have good friends among other printers off the job."[3] (2) The immediate social environment of the individual, including his shop, the clubs to which he belongs, his close

3. Such statements are ordinarily used in comparison of the union with another, or with itself at another time. If a comparative analysis (which will be discussed later) were being carried out, this would be a more important kind of statement than it is in this single-case analysis.

circle of friends, etc. Such characterizations are used in this study primarily for locating the effect of differing social environments on the individual. (3) The man, in order to determine relations between various properties of the man: his values and his vote, his background and his values, etc.

This study is weakest in its characterization of the immediate social environment. We could have attempted explicitly to characterize shops by interviewing all or almost all the men in them, and by asking questions more specifically directed toward finding the man's relation to his shopmates and to the employer. But such concentration would have been made at the expense of other gains: interviewing more men in each shop would have meant interviewing each man less thoroughly or else covering fewer shops, thus gaining knowledge about shops at the expense of knowledge about either individuals or the union as a whole.

What this really means is that not all values can be maximized at once, and that such studies as the present one must include in their design a decision as to what units it is most important to characterize with the interview data. As suggested above, the experience of the study suggests that in a single case analysis like this, it is more important to characterize the man and his immediate social environment than to characterize the union itself, that is, the single case being analyzed.

However, this is not the end of the sampling or design problems related to the interview data. Given some decision on the problem above, it is still necessary to decide whether some manner of random sampling is best (taking into account social environments, as indicated above, by two-stage sampling), or systematic sampling determined by the social or political structure of the union. We want to locate the elements which effect these men's political decisions. But do we consider all men's decisions equally important? Are not the decisions of some active men more important in influencing the outcome of union elections than are those of the followers? And is this criterion of "importance to the outcome" the optimum criterion for our purpose? These are questions which this study only begins to answer. At the same time, they are questions whose answers are important in the design of research.

One possible answer has been suggested in the analysis: to develop a provisional model of the political system, conceived as a structure of interlocking decisions (e.g., union officers, party leaders, convention delegates, voters), and to accurately measure the influences on each of these decisions.

***Table 1 – Types of Data Gathered, Types of Units Being Characterized, and Types of Resulting Properties***

| | *Kinds of Data* | | | | |
|---|---|---|---|---|---|
| | *TOTAL SYSTEM* | *INTERMEDIATE UNITS* | | *INDIVIDUALS* | |
| *Unit being characterized* | *Issues; Data on Occupation; Union Laws; Policies; Historical Data; Convention Reports* | *Local's Histories and Voting Records; Issues on Local Level; Size of Locals* | *Shop's Voting Records; Shop Size* | *Interviews with Leaders* | *Interviews of the Sample of Men* |
| ITU as a whole | Structural, environmental, behavioral properties | By inference: communication network (structural) | | | |
| Locals | Behavioral properties (militancy, etc.) | Behavioral properties, size | By inference: communication network (structural) | Structural, environmental, behavioral properties | Distributions of individual properties |
| Shops | | | Behavioral properties, and size | | Distributions of individual properties |
| Other immediate social environment of men | The social climate, by inference from dominant issues and election outcome | The social climate, by inference from dominant issues and election outcome | | | Chapel chairman's attributes; friends' attributes |
| Men | By inference: dominant values and interests | By inference: values, interests, and loyalties (e.g., to local over international) | By inference: values, interests, and loyalties (e.g., to shop over local) | By inference: values | Behavior, background, values, attitudes |

This would entail a rather complex research design, one which equalizes the accuracy with which each decision point in the system is analyzed.

## Multiple-level analysis: relations between different units

The second major problem concerning units at different levels is the problem of relating them by means of generalizations. This problem is an important one, for it is such generalizations which are the fruits of the analysis. The problem in its simplest aspects may be posed in this way: Certain properties of one unit (e.g., the total union) are determinants of behavior at another level (e.g., the individual). Yet how is it possible to really bridge the gap between the units? For example, to say that a certain political climate characterizes the union does not mean that this climate is felt by all printers alike. The climate makes itself felt more strongly by some men than others, depending upon their social and political locations.

When an analysis is not one of this multiple-level sort, then such a problem never exists: analysis relates an individual's political dispositions to his vote, or an organization's size to its bureaucratization. Both properties being related are attributes of the same unit (e.g., the individual, the organization), and there is no problem of bridging the gap between units at different levels.

We said above that relating two different levels is only the simplest case of the general problem. This certainly is so, for even if we succeed in relating properties of diverse social units to a man's vote decision, this is not at all the end of the analysis. The aim of this study is to be able to make statements about political systems as wholes, not statements about the determinants of individual vote decisions.

What we have done in focusing upon this individual vote decision has been to enter the system at a particular point and to work outward from there. . . .

But is this the best strategy for analyzing a social or political system? The point at which we entered is probably a very important one in the system, but would it have been better to proceed differently? For example, having a tentative *model* of the political system . . . the way is pointed to certain *variables* or concepts . . . and certain *processes* which seem important in the operation of the system. Only one of these processes concerns the vote decision; others concern the policy decisions of the administrative leaders, and the decision of the oppositionists or potential oppositionists. Perhaps the best mode of analysis, given that the aim is to analyze the system as a whole, would be to start with a crude model . . . and to focus upon each of the processes postulated in that model. An example of the way that such an analysis would be of aid is the following: The model indicates that one important decision point in the system is the president's policy decisions. In particular, it suggests that to know the constraints placed by the organization upon the president is important. Thus it directs one to ask such questions as: What restrained Scott (the ITU president) from sending in strikebreakers to New York in 1919? And why was George Berry, the Pressmen president (who did send in strikebreakers for the same strike by the printing pressmen) not restrained in the same way?

If we had focused in this study on the several decision points, and on the communication processes, rather than entering the system at a particular point, the results might have been far superior to those obtained. However, this is a matter as yet unresolved, and we intend only to raise the problem: What is the most advantageous way to carry out a study of the dynamics of a social or political system?

## The paradox: how to generalize from a single case

Another difficult problem arises in studies of organizations or social systems rather than individuals. Often, only a single case is analyzed, as is done here. This is in strong contrast to the usual statistical procedure with studies of individual behavior, where the number of cases is relatively great. The fact that the present study includes a sample of individuals from the union, and that part of the analysis is one of individual behavior, must not be allowed to confuse this issue. Clearly in this study these individuals are not themselves the focus of the analysis; it is the union as an organization which is the center of interest. This focus upon a single case rather than the statistical study of individual behavior implies a quite different kind of analysis. Perhaps some of the differences can be suggested by an analogy.

If a chemist is developing a theory or set of laws concerning the equilibrium system existing inside a test tube containing water, sodium hydroxide, and hydrochloric acid, he may utilize many kinds of data, but all from the single system which he has before him; tests of acidity, of electrical conductivity, examination of precipitate, and general knowledge about the reactivity of sodium, hydrogen, chlorine, and hydroxyl ions. He would not need to examine a thousand replications of this little test-tube system, but would analyze the internal dynamics of the single system, using these various types of data. From these he would build up knowledge about what reactions were taking place. He would conclude, among other things, that these chemicals reacted rather rapidly to form salt and water.

However, if the same chemist were concerned with finding the chemical properties of various metals and their relative positions on a scale of activity, he would need to carry out a comparative analysis, subjecting each of the metals to similar tests and noting the differences in their reactivity.

This analogy indicates that both internal analyses and comparative analyses have a place in research, and that neither is unilaterally superior. In the present study there was a choice between the two types: an intensive analysis of this single case, or an extensive and more superficial examination of many cases. The first was chosen and the latter discarded. Can we say anything about what was gained by this choice and what lost, that is, the differences between the two models of investigation?

The outcome of both such types of analysis is the same kind of generalizations. For example, "The more highly stratified an occupation is, the more intense and rigid will be its political cleavages if its union has democratic politics." A comparative analysis seeks to develop such generalizations in the obvious manner, by comparing occupations which differ with respect either to the independent or the dependent variable and then testing whether they also differ with respect to the other variable. The "internal analysis" attempts to establish the same generalization in one of two fashions:

1. It uses variations which occur *within* the system, either (*a*) over a period of time (e.g., at one time, there was stratification between a politically important group of Mailers and the majority, typographers; at the same time, rigid cleavage between these groups occurred); or (*b*) between different parts of the system (e.g., while there is little stratification within the union as a whole, there is economic stratification between officers and men; these create issues between the membership and the administration. . .). The internal analysis thus substitutes variations within the one system for variations between systems. This is in essence what an experimentalist does when he varies the conditions under which a particular system exists, or when he observes the evolution of an object over a period of time.

2. An internal analysis can operate in a different way. By going behind the over-all generalization to the processes through which it is presumed to exist, the internal analysis may validate the generalization by validating these processes. For example, the generalization above, relating economic stratification to the rigidity and intensity of political cleavage, can be either observed to hold true statistically or built up through more fundamental generalizations, to wit: (*a*) the economic motivation is an overriding one, which will be a very strong determinant of one's decision if economics are involved; (*b*) the policy decisions in a stratified union involved economic matters which will differentially affect persons at different economic levels. By proving that these two statements are true, one can prove, by inference, the original statement about stratifications and rigidity of cleavage. Thus internal analysis, which, in some cases, cannot directly prove a generalization, may prove it by indirection through proof of the generalizations underlying it.

An internal analysis will not ordinarily be as exhaustive of the important elements which affect a particular variable as will a comparative analysis, simply because certain things are invariant for the single system as a whole. Certain kinds of issues may never occur in this union, though they occur in others; certain aspects of the particular system are so invariant that situations common in other systems are simply absent in the ITU. These invariances can lead to overgeneralization; for example, some of Michels' generalizations from the German Social Democratic Party to organizations in general are seriously in error for certain kinds of organizations which diverge too much from the single case Michels examined.

But except for these difficulties, it seems that internal analysis has no great disadvantages with respect to comparative analysis. It may, in fact, have one important advantage: by taking simple comparative correlation out of the reach of the investigator, it focuses his attention upon the underlying processes which operate within the system. In this way the internal analysis may lead to a deeper explanation of the phenomenon and to generalization of a more fundamental kind.

But whether an internal analysis has more advantages or disadvantages with respect to a comparative analysis, it is important to realize that these two kinds of analyses of organizations both exist in social science, and a choice must be made between them in any research. The problem which begs for resolution here is the problem of spelling out the two different logics of analysis for these two methods, and of providing diagnostic indicators which will tell the relative merits of the two methods for a particular research problem.

These problems discussed above are three which seem to be of increasing importance as social research moves from description into analysis, and as it moves from focus upon individuals to a focus upon social units: voluntary organizations, the social system of communities, industrial plants, and so on. We have not attempted to give answers to the problems, but only to state them, in the hope that this will stimulate a search for the answers.

PETER M. BLAU

# The Comparative Study of Organizations

The comparative method, in the broadest sense of the term, underlies all scientific and scholarly theorizing. If we mean by theory a set of generalizations that explains courses of events or situations on the basis of the conditions and processes that produce them, every theory must rest on comparisons of contrasting cases; for to explain a state of affairs requires that the difference between it and some other state of affairs be accounted for—why democratic institutions developed in some countries but not in others, or what political processes distinguish democracies with multi-party systems from those with two-party systems. Usually, however, the term "comparative method" is used in a much narrower sense, though by no means a consistent one. Spencer and Durkheim, for example, referred by it to virtually opposite methodological principles. The former's comparative method involves collecting descriptions of the same institution in many different societies to demonstrate "laws" of social evolution,[1] whereas Durkheim, who rejected this procedure of the evolutionists, employed the same term to refer to the establishment of concomitant variations or correlations between two social phenomena.[2]

Although every analysis of organizations entails some explicit or implicit comparisons, the comparative method in the study of organizations is defined here more narrowly as the systematic comparison of a fairly large number of organizations in order to establish relationships between their characteristics. In short, the term is used here to refer to quantitative comparisons that make it possible to determine relationships between attributes of organizations, for example, what other differences are generally associated with variations in an organization's size, or the degree of its bureaucratization, or its functions. Lest this emphasis on quantitative research be misconstrued, let me hasten to add that it is not meant to imply a concern with mathematical models or advanced statistical techniques. These are not at all the focus of interest. The point made is rather that theoretical generalizations about organizations are necessarily rooted in comparisons of many that differ in relevant respects, regardless of how impressionistic the data on which the analysis is based. Since some quantitative comparisons are inherent in the method of constructing theories, such comparisons should be built into the research procedures from which the theories derive.

The distinctive nature of the comparative

1. See the discussion of Spencer's comparative method in Howard Becker and Harry E. Barnes, *Social Thought from Lore to Science*, 2nd ed., vol. 1 (Washington: Harren Press, 1952), pp. 748–49.

2. Emile Durkheim, *The Rules of Sociological Method* (Chicago: University of Chicago Press, 1930), pp. 125–40.

Reprinted from *Industrial and Labor Relations Review*, Vol. 18, No. 3 (April, 1965), pp. 323–38, by permission of the author and publisher. 

approach to the study of organizations, as defined, can be highlighted in juxtaposition with the case-study approach. Most empirical investigations in the field are case studies of single organizations. The rationale for this approach is that large modern organizations, which often contain many thousands of members, are too complex to permit studying more than one or two at a time. While this statement is obviously correct if the aim is to investigate the attributes and behavior of the individual members of organizations, it is highly questionable if the aim is to investigate the characteristics and operations of the organizations themselves. Many characteristics of organizations can be ascertained quite easily and without the time and effort required for a survey of a large part of the membership. In any case, to derive theoretical generalizations from the study of a single organization, either the conditions in this organization must be compared to those in others known from the literature, which means that most of the systematic information collected in the case study are ignored, or the analysis must center on internal comparisons of the various units within the organization.[3] The latter procedure tends to constrain the investigator to focus on principles about the structure of work groups and the behavior of individual members *within* organizations rather than on principles that govern the functioning and development *of* organizations. As a result of these tendencies, empirical studies in the field of organizations have contributed more to our knowledge of human relations and group structures in the context of organizations than to the theory of organizations as distinct social systems. To be sure, the intensive analysis of internal processes possible in case studies can greatly enrich the theory of organization, but only as a complement to inquiries based on comparative studies.

An organization is a system for mobilizing and coordinating the efforts of various, typically specialized, groups in the pursuit of joint objectives. Although an organization could not exist without the individuals who compose its membership, it has characteristics that do not pertain to characteristics of its individual members, such as its size, to name only the most obvious example. The sociological theory of organizations, the economic theory of the firm, and the political theory of the state or government constitute important potential links for interdisciplinary cross-fertilization and comparative research, inasmuch as they deal with diverse kinds of organizations, the organized government in a society being a particular kind of organization, namely, the one with the largest scope.[4] But there is actually little cross-fertilization on this level, in part because the theory of organization is in such a rudimentary state.

The objectives of this article are to conceptualize various dimensions that can be distinguished in the analysis of organizational life, to outline the comparative approach to the study of organizations, and to indicate the theoretical significance of this approach.

## Three foci of analysis

Three foci of analysis may be distinguished in organizational research, whether concern is with government agencies or industrial concerns, labor unions or political parties, armies or hospitals.[5] The focus of the analysis can be (1) the individual in his specific role as a member of the organization who occupies a certain position in it; (2) the struc-

3. On the method of internal comparison, see Seymour M. Lipset, *et al.*, *Union Democracy* (New York: Free Press, 1956), pp. 425–27.

4. This may well be at least as important a distinctive characteristic of the state as the usually emphasized monopoly over the use of force; see Max Weber, *The Theory of Social and Economic Organization* (New York: Oxford University Press, 1947), p. 156.

5. The conceptualization presented is a revision of one suggested in Blau, "Formal Organization," *American Journal of Sociology*, vol. 63, 1957, pp. 63–69. (Processes of development are not included as one of the three foci in the reconceptualized version because they belong to a different dimension which cuts across the three distinguished here, *not* because I consider them any less important.) A related schema of levels if analysis is presented in Stanley H. Udy, "The Comparative Analysis of Organizations," in James G. March, *Handbook of Organizations* (Chicago: Rand McNally, 1965), and a somewhat different schema is developed in W. Richard Scott, "Theory of Organizations," in Robert E. L. Faris, *Handbook of Sociology* (Chicago: Rand McNally, 1964). My ideas on this subject were clarified by the discussions of a work group in the Third Ford Seminar in the Social Science of Organizations, University of Pittsburgh, Summer 1964. The participants in this group were, in addition to Udy, Scott, and myself, Vaughn Blankenship, Tom Burns, Lyman W. Porter, and Stanton Wheeler, and I want to acknowledge the many stimulating ideas the discussion in this group provided for my reconceptualization.

ture of social relations among individuals in the various groups within the organization; or (3) the system of interrelated elements that characterizes the organization as a whole.

First, many studies carried out in organizations center attention on the attitudes and behavior of individual members insofar as they pertain to the functions of the organization. The application of survey techniques to research in organizations invites this focus, especially if representative samples are used, because sampling surveys make individuals the independent units of analysis. This type of analysis is illustrated by investigations of the attitudes of soldiers in combat, of the career patterns of civil servants and their implications for commitment to the organization, of the influence of the background characteristics of the labor force on performance of tasks and turnover, or of the conditions that promote work satisfaction. Studies of voting exemplify the same type in respect to the political organization of the government. These studies deal with processes that occur in the context of organizations and often show how the context modifies these processes—for instance, how the composition of work groups affects conduct—but they are not studies of organizations and the principles that govern their character and development. *The American Soldier* examines sociopsychological processes, such as those manifesting relative deprivation, but it tells us little about the organization of the army;[6] *Voting* analyzes political processes, such as the crystallization of voting decisions under cross pressure, but it has little to say about the ways in which governments are organized;[7] and *Management and the Worker* deals with behavior in work groups but not the organization of the factory.[8]

A second type of analysis focuses upon the structures of social relations that emerge in the groups and segments in the organization. Since interest centers on networks of social relations and characteristics of group structures in this case, data are typically obtained from every member of selected subgroups rather than from a sample of individuals dispersed throughout the organization. Examples of this type are studies of the informal organization of work groups (*Management and the Worker* being a pioneering one), of union solidarity among factory workers, of consultation among officials, or of the differentiation of informal status that emerges in social interaction. Here concern is with the social processes that govern the development of group structures and the effects of these structures on patterns of conduct. The aim is to discover the principles that characterize group life, and the organizational context within which the work groups exist is considered as a set of limiting conditions for the emergence of group structure. The conditions in the larger organization, therefore, are treated as given rather than as problematical; that is, they are not made the subject of the inquiry that needs to be explained.

Third, the analysis may focus on the attributes of organizations themselves, the interrelations between these attributes, and the processes that produce them. In order to determine the relationships between various characteristics of organizations, as an initial step in tracing the processes that give rise to them and explaining them, it is necessary to compare a large number of organizations which are similar in many respects but different in some. Studies on the connections between the size of organizations, their complexity, and the degree of bureaucratization within them illustrate this type, as do investigations of the impact of automation on the division of labor in factories, of the conditions that foster oligarchy in unions, of the implications of dispersed ownership for centralized control in corporations, or of the impact of the shape of the hierarchical pyramid on operations. The focus of interest now is the system of interrelated elements that characterize the organization as a whole, not its component parts. The aim is to discover the principles that govern the functioning system, although the processes and connections observed must often be inferred in the absence of detailed information on the internal structures and how they operate.

### IMPLICATIONS

It is evident that the three foci lead to the analysis of quite different, though by no means unrelated, problems. The phenomena that are made the cen-

6. Samuel A. Stouffer, *et al.*, *The American Soldier*, 2 vols. (Princeton: Princeton University Press), 1949.

7. Bernard R. Berelson, *et al.*, *Voting* (Chicago: University of Chicago Press, 1954).

8. F. J. Roethlisberger and William J. Dickson, *Management and the Worker* (Cambridge, Mass.: Harvard University Press, 1959).

tral subject of the inquiry in one kind of analysis are assumed to be given in the others. In the first case, the role attributes and performances of the individual members of organizations are investigated, and the context of the organization and even that of the work group are considered given conditions or stimuli that may affect the roles of individuals. In the second case, social relations and, particularly, the structures of social relations in groups are analyzed, and the characteristics of the individuals who compose these groups as well as the organizational context are treated as limiting conditions for the emergence of these social structures. In the third case, the combinations of attributes that characterize organizations as such and the development of these systems of organizing the efforts of various groups in joint endeavors are studied, and both the individual behavior and the group processes that underlie these systems are taken for granted.

The specific criterion for differentiating the three foci—role analysis, structural analysis, and organizational analysis—is whether the variables under consideration describe individuals, groups of interrelated individuals, or organized systems of interrelated groups. Thus, seniority, professional expertness, socioeconomic status, commitment to an organization, and political preference are attributes of individual human beings. But the strength of the cohesive bonds that unite group members and the extent of differentiation of status that emerges among them are variables that refer to groups as such and not to their individual members. Correspondingly, the division of labor among various groups, the degree of centralization of control in an organization, the age of the organization, and its size are characteristics of the organization as a whole that cannot be attributed either to its subgroups or to its individual members.

A complication arises, however, because the variables that *pertain* to a collectivity may be based on data *obtained* either by measuring a property of the collectivity itself or a property of all of its members. Lazarsfeld and Menzel have referred to the former as global properties, such as whether a factory is automated, uses assembly lines, or neither, and to the latter as analytical properties of collectivities, such as the proportion of older workers in a company.[9] The turnover rate in a factory, the average productivity of its labor force, and the proportion of its personnel in administrative positions are analytical properties that clearly refer to the organized collectivity but that are based on data derived from the behavior of individuals. For every analytical attribute that describes an organized collectivity there is a parallel attribute that distinguishes the members within it—the productivity of a worker, or whether an employee occupies an administrative position—but there are no such individual parallels for the global properties of collectivities—only factories can be distinguished by the degree of mechanization, not the individual workers within a factory. A simple illustration of this contrast is the difference between the age of a firm and the average age of its employees.

### FOCUS ON ORGANIZATIONAL ATTRIBUTES

The use of analytical properties—averages, proportions, or rates—as independent variables in organizational or structural analysis raises special problems. Let us assume that a comparative study of welfare agencies found that professionalization, that is, the proportion of caseworkers who have graduate training in social work, is associated with more extensive service to clients. Three interpretations of this finding are possible, depending on whether the focus is on roles, on group structures, or on the organization of the agencies. First, professionally trained individuals may provide more service to clients than untrained caseworkers. Second, the structure of work groups with a high proportion of professionals, perhaps by making informal status dependent on the way clients are treated, may encourage caseworkers, regardless of their own training, to extend more service to clients. Third, agencies with a high proportion of professionals on their staff may be better organized to serve clients, which would be reflected in improved service by individual caseworkers independent of these individuals' own training or the work groups to which they belong. To determine which one of these three different interpretations is correct, or whether more

9. Paul F. Lazarsfeld and Herbert Menzel, "On the Relation between Individual and Collective Properties," in Amitai Etzioni, *Complex Organizations* (New York: Holt, Rinehart and Winston, 1961), pp. 426–35. The other two types of properties they distinguish can be considered special cases of the two noted in the text.

than one or all three are, it is necessary to separate three distinct influences on treatment of clients, that of the individual's own training, that of the professional composition of his work group, and that of the professionalization of the agency in which he works. Statistical procedures for accomplishing this separation have been outlined elsewhere.[10]

It should be noted that the technical criterion by which organizational analysis is distinguished from the two other types is an analytical one that applies to all kinds of organized collectivities, not alone to formal organizations. Crosscultural comparisons or studies of the relationship between the stage of technological development and the stratification system in different societies involve organizational analysis in the technical sense, although they do not deal with formal organizations. To speak of a formal organization there must exist explicit procedures for organizing the subgroups in a collectivity to further some joint ends. On the basis of this definition, the political system in a society is a formal organization, while the stratification system is not, and neither is the economy, though a firm, of course, is one.

To advance the theory of formal organizations, a focus on organizational analysis is essential. This is not to say that role analysis and structural analysis of the members and work groups in organizations are unimportant, because they can supply evidence on the social processes that account for the systems that emerge in organizations, but this evidence can be used to explain organizational systems only in combination with comparative studies that focus on the relationships between various attributes of organizations themselves.

## Social processes in organizations

The study of social processes is often contrasted with the study of social structures or that of the interrelations between factors in a system, but it is not always entirely clear what the specific distinguishing marks of the analysis of social processes are. One implication of the term is that processes occur over time and that their investigation, therefore, must be diachronic rather than synchronic. Whereas the synchronic study of the interrelations between attributes in a system takes the emergence of these attributes for granted, the diachronic study of social processes traces the sequence of events or occurrences that led to the development of these attributes. An illustration of this difference would be an inquiry into the status structure in a group and the various characteristics associated with superior status, on the one hand, and an inquiry into the processes of differentiation that produced the status structure, on the other. Taking time into account, however, is only a necessary and not a sufficient condition for the analysis of social processes. Thus, panel studies that compare opinions or states of affairs at two points in time do not directly deal with social processes, although they make it easier to infer them than does research at a single point in time.

### ANALYSIS OF INTERVENING LINKS

The analysis of social processes requires the specification of a series of intervening links between an earlier state and a system or structure that subsequently develops. Thus, the investigation of the process of socialization seeks to trace the many steps that link the behavior and attitudes of parents to the internalized values and personalities that their children ultimately develop. Similarly, the investigation of the process of bureaucratization seeks to trace the sequence of typical events stimulated by the large size and complexity of an organization and eventuating in a formalized system of procedures and hierarchical authority. In brief, the examination of social processes entails the specification of intervening variables that connect initial conditions with their effects in a time sequence.

External as well as internal social processes affect organizations. Research on processes that occur outside the framework of organizations must not make organizations the unit of analysis but must find another more appropriate one. Thus, the study of the processes that give rise to technological advancements and the chain of implications of technological innovations must compare different cultures and not merely different organizations in one society. To investigate the processes that govern

10. Blau, "Structural Effects," *American Sociological Review*, vol. 25, 1960, pp. 178–93. The procedure there described for isolating the effects of social structure from those of role attributes can also be used to isolate the effects of organizational attributes from those of the other two.

career patterns, the occupational roles and career lines must be the focus of the analysis and the occupational experiences of individuals must be followed as they move into and out of various organizations. The student of organizations is not primarily concerned with these external processes but only with the results they produce, which constitute conditions that affect organizations, for instance, the limits set by the state of technological knowledge for organizational developments, or the influence career experiences have for the performance of organizational responsibilities.

The internal processes in organizations include the processes of social interaction among members that find expression in the emergent group structures and the processes through which the interrelated elements in the total system become organized. The analysis of processes of interaction may deal with the ways in which first impressions affect role expectations and how these in turn affect the conduct of interacting persons, with the exchanges of rewards in the form of advice, help, approval, and respect that shape the relations among group members, and with the modifications in these exchange patterns produced by differences in the complexity of the task or in the style of supervision. The aim of the analysis is to explain the differentiated social structures that arise as the result of these processes of interaction among individuals. Whereas this analysis exemplifies the structural focus, the organizational focus calls attention to such problems as the processes of increasing specialization, mechanization, professionalization, centralization, or bureaucratization, the conditions that give rise to these processes, and the interparlay between them. The aim here is to explain the systems of interrelated characteristics that evolve in various organizations. These are the processes that are of immediate concern to the student of organizations, because they constitute the intervening links that explain the connections between the inputs and outputs of the organizations, between the initial conditions and the system that develops.

### COMPASS OF SOCIAL SYSTEMS

Social systems are typically part of broader ones that encompass them and simultaneously constitute the environment of narrower systems they encompass. Work groups are the environment in which individuals act out their roles; the organization of the department is the context within which work groups develop their structure; the total organization sets limits to the ways in which departments can be organized; and the society, including the political order, other institutions, and the state of the technology, provides the social setting that conditions the character of the organizations in its boundaries. Whereas the larger system restricts the developments of those it encompasses, there are also feedback effects from the subsystems to the more encompassing ones, because subsystems are not infinitely pliable but tend to have a minimum of autonomy to which the encompassing system must adjust.[11] Thus, the occupational experiences and professional values of the members of an organization condition the performance of tasks, the informal structures of work groups modify the impact of the incentive system, and the professional requirements of the department of psychiatry set limits to the administrative requirements the hospital administration can impose on it.

Even in comparative studies only those characteristics of the units under consideration in respect to which they *differ* can be systematically investigated, whereas the characteristics all have in common must be allocated to the next higher level as part of the constant environment. If all work groups under investigation consist of six workers under a supervisor, size cannot be treated as a variable in the analysis of group structure but the existence of work units of this size must be considered part of the organizational context that conditions the emerging group structures. Similarly, if computers are used in some organizations but not in others, the significance of this aspect of mechanization for other characteristics of the organization can be examined, but if secretaries in all the organizations studied use typewriters, it must be inferred that this aspect of mechanization is part of the technological state of the society that is invariably reflected in its organizations. Whether this inference is correct or not depends on the representativeness of the organizations included in the sample. Regardless of whether the inference about all organizations is warranted, however, the fact

11. See Alvin W. Gouldner, "Reciprocity and Autonomy in Functional Theory," in Llewellyn Gross, *Symposium on Sociological Theory* (Evanston: Row, Peterson), pp. 254–66.

that a certain characteristic reveals no variation among all the organizations examined necessitates that it be treated as a given condition of organizational life in this particular research.

Whereas factors that cannot be explained within the framework of a specific investigation must be allocated to a more encompassing system, a full explanation of relationships between factors tends to involve references to a less encompsasing system. A theoretical interpretation of an observed relationship between two variables, an antecedent and its effect, entails subsuming it under a general proposition that connects two abstract concepts of which the observed variables are specific manifestations and, in addition, specifying intervening variables that account for the connection.[12] Thus, Durkheim explained the relationship between religion and suicide rates by suggesting that an individualistic belief system, by lessening social integration, promotes an egoistic mentality, which affords weak protection against crises.[13]

To explain the correlation between an independent and a dependent variable, the intervening processes that account for the connection are specified, and to explain the principles that govern these processes, intervening processes on a more fundamental level are indicated. For example, the relationship between the composition of a group and the status structure that develops in it is explained by taking into account the processes of social interaction that lead to differentiation of status, and patterns of social interaction and exchange are explained in terms of the psychological processes that underlie them. An explanation of psychological principles, in turn, refers back to the underlying physiological processes, and these physiological processes can be further explicated in terms of chemical ones. Serious scientific explanations typically confine themselves to adjacent levels and do not skip across many. Physiological principles do not help to account for group structures and social processes, and nuclear physics does not aid in clarifying learning theory, though there are undoubtedly indirect connections.

12. On the latter, see Particia L. Kendall and Lazarsfeld, "Problems of Survey Analysis," in Robert K. Merton and Lazarsfeld, *Continuities in Social Research* (New York: Free Press, 1950), pp. 147–62.

13. Durkheim, *Suicide* (New York: Free Press, 1951)' pp. 152–70.

CASE STUDY AND COMPARATIVE APPROACH

The aim of organizational analysis is to explain the systems of interrelated elements that characterze, various kinds of organizations. For this purposie the interdependence between different attributes of organizations must be established—their size, complexity, specialization, authority structure, professionalization, bureaucratization, and so forth. To clarify this constellation of attributes requires an understanding of the social processes through which the different attributes develop and the connections between them evolve. Since the structures of social relations among the members of the organization affect the processes of its development, a knowledge of these structures further contributes to the understanding of the development of the organizational system. Research has shown, for instance, that the informal organization of work groups exerts important influences on performance, the exercise of authority, and the significance of the incentive system for operations, which indicates that the study of the relationships between these and other factors must take the impact of informal structures into account.

A major contribution of case studies on organizations has been that they have called attention to these informal structures and investigated them intensively. This intensive investigation involved the analysis of the social processes through which the informal structures emerged, such as the process of cooptation that modifies the leadership structure,[14] the sanctioning processes in which output becomes regulated,[15] or the process of exchange of advice that gives rise to status differentiation.[16] Comparative studies of organizations, however, need not repeat such intensive analysis of informal processes, since it suffices for them to take account of the results of these processes that find expression in group structures. Indeed, even the role of informal structures will probably have to be inferred rather than directly investigated in most comparative studies of organizations, for systematic organizational analysis—analogous to all systematic analysis—cannot possibly take all factors that

14. Philip Selznick, *TVA and the Grass Roots* (Berkeley: University of California Press, 1949), pp. 85–213.

15. Roethlisberger and Dickson, *op. cit.*, pp. 379–524.

16. Blau, *The Dynamics of Bureaucracy*, 2nd ed. (Chicago: University of Chicago Press, 1963), pp. 121–64.

indirectly influence organizational life into account but must treat some as given conditions while inquiring into the interrelations of the basic features of organizations.

Theoretical interpretations of the relationships between antecedent conditions and their consequences remain inevitably somewhat inferential, it would seem, not only because they subsume relations under propositions on a higher level of abstraction that cannot be directly confirmed in research, but also because they typically conceptualize the connecting process as a series of links too complex for direct empirical testing. The proposition that the antecedent A promotes the occurrence B can be empirically confirmed, provided that operational measures for the two factors exist, by showing that B is more prevalent under condition A than under non-A. If the analysis of social processes means the specification of the intervening variables that link A and B in a time sequence, multivariate analysis should make it possible to test whether the process occurs as specified by ascertaining the relationships between A, all intervening variables, and B. Although this is correct in principle, it is usually impossible to implement such a test in actual practice, because so many intervening links tend to be indicated in process analysis that it is virtually impossible to examine the interrelations between all of them simultaneously.[17] Computers facilitate the simultaneous analysis of many variables, but the capacities of the human mind still limit the number of interrelated concepts that can be simultaneously taken into account in a theory.[18] Although theoretical explanations couched in terms of complex social processes cannot be directly tested, precise specification of these processes makes it possible to predict what combinations of organizational features the processes produce under varying conditions, and these predictions serve as indirect tests for the theory.

17. The principle is the same as that of a game in its normal form, as I understand it. Although game theory does not deal with processes or sequential steps but with single choices between strategies, sequential steps can be taken into account in advance by translating all possible sequences into a game in its normal form and then treating it as one choice between all these possibilities. In actual fact, however, the number of alternatives for games with any degree of complexity is virtually infinite, which makes the formalistic solution of translating successive steps into a game in its normal form useless for practical purposes.

18. It is, of course, much easier to clarify many successive situations, one at a time, than all of them simultaneously. Even a very good chess player can anticipate only a few moves ahead.

## Organizational theory

A theory of organizations, whatever its specific nature, and regardless of how subtle the organizational processes it takes into account, has as its central aim to establish the constellations of characteristics that develop in organizations of various kinds. Comparative studies of many organizations are necessary, not alone to test the hypotheses implied by such a theory, but also to provide a basis for initial exploration and refinement of the theory by indicating the conditions on which relationships, originally assumed to hold universally, are contingent. Strict impersonal detachment, for instance, may well promote efficiency only under some conditions and not at all under others.[19] Systematic research on many organizations that provides the data needed to determine the interrelations between several organizational features is, however, extremely rare. The main reason is that the investigation of the internal structure of a complex organization is so costly in time and effort to make the inclusion of many organizations in a single study design impracticable. One way out of this impasse is to study the major attributes of many organizations and sacrifice any detailed information on their internal structures.

The approach to comparative research on organizations proposed, therefore, would be explicitly restricted to those data that can be obtained from the records of organizations and interviews with key informants, without intensive observation or interviewing of most members, which would make it possible to collect the same data on one hundred or more organizations of a given type in one study. In other words, the research design sacrifices depth of information to achieve sufficient breadth to permit a minimum of quantitative comparison. The very limitation imposed by lack of extensive data on internal structures has a latent function, so to

19. See Eugene Litwak, "Models of Bureaucracy which Permit Conflict," *American Journal of Sociology*, vol. 67, 1962, pp. 177–84.

speak, inasmuch as it forces the investigator to focus on the neglected area of organizational analysis rather than on the repeatedly studied role relations and group structures within organizations. It is suggested that this approach, though prompted by methodological necessity, has the potential to contribute greatly to organizational theory. To illustrate the theoretical significance of the comparative approach to organizational research, let us examine how it could help refine Weber's theory of bureaucracy.[20]

### WEBER'S THEORY

Weber's analysis of bureaucracy is part of his general theory of types of political order and authority, and it is simultaneously a crucial case of the most pervasive theme in all his writings, namely, the increasing rationalization of modern life. The major characteristics Weber attributed to the typical bureaucracy will first be outlined, and his analysis of their functional interdependence will then be summarized.[21]

The large *size* of an organization and the great *complexity* of its responsibilities promote bureaucratization, according to Weber. One aspect of bureaucratization is the elaboration of the *administrative* apparatus in the organization. Bureaucracies also are characterized by a high degree of *specialization*, and their members are trained as specialized *experts* in the tasks assigned to them. Furthermore, official positions are organized in a *hierarchy* with clear lines of authority, th scope of which is precisely circumscribed by impersonal rules. Operations generally are governed by a consistent system of *rules* and regulations. *Impersonal* detachment is expected to prevail in the performance of duties and in official relations. Personnel and promotion policies, too, are governed by impersonal criteria, such as merit or seniority, which assures officials stable *careers* with some advancement in the organization. Weber held that this combination of characteristics tends to evolve because it is necessary for and furthers administrative efficiency.

In analyzing the processes that produce this interdepence among characteristics, Weber implicitly presents a functional analysis of bureaucracy, with rational decision making and administrative efficiency as the criteria of function. The requirement to discharge *complex* responsibilities effectively creates pressures to divide them into *specialized*, more easily manageable tasks and to appoint professionally qualified *experts* to perform the various specialized tasks. The pronounced division of labor, particularly in *large* organizations, creates special problems of coordination. An *administrative* apparatus tends to develop to maintain channels of communication and coordination, and a *hierarchy* of authority and responsibility is needed actually to effect the coordination of diverse tasks in the pursuit of organizational objectives by enabling superiors on successive levels to guide, directly or indirectly, the performance of increasingly wider circles of subordinates. But detailed supervision of all decisions by superiors is most inefficient and produces serious strains. The system of *rules* and official procedures is designed to standardize performance and restrict the need for direct supervisory intervention largely to extraordinary cases. Professional training and official rules notwithstanding, however, strong emotions or personal bias may interfere with rational decision making; the emphasis on *impersonal* detachment has the function of precluding the intrusion of such irrational factors into official decisions. Lest the strict impersonal discipline under which the members of a bureaucracy must operate alienate them, stable *careers* promote loyalty to the organization and counteract these burdens. In short, the problems created by one organizational feature stimulate processes that give rise to another, and many interdependent processes of this kind produce the constellation of features characteristic of the typical bureaucracy as conceptualized by Weber.

### OPERATIONAL MEASURES

Operational measures for the characteristics of bureaucratic organizations described by Weber can be obtained by the comparative method here advocated, and it would be sheer waste in most cases to employ more intensive methods to obtain these data. This is evidently the case for the *size* of an organization. Whether size is measured by number of employees of a factory, number of voters for a

20. Weber, *op. cit.*, pp. 324–41, and *From Max Weber: Essays in Sociological Theory* (New York: Oxford University Press, 1946), pp. 196–244.

21. Italics are used for the nine major concepts which are first presented, then related to one another, and finally operationalized.

party, number of beds in a hospital, or total assets of a firm, there is evidently no need to interview all members of the organization to ascertain this information. One index of *complexity* is the number of basic objectives or responsibilities of an organization—a university with graduate and professional schools has more complex responsibilities than a college without them—and another index of it is the number of different locations where the organization operates. Still another aspect of complexity is the degree of *specialization* in an organization, which might be measured by the number of different occupational positions, or by the distribution of the members among various occupational specialities, or by the number of functionally specialized departments. The amount of training required for various positions could serve as an indicator of professional *expertness*, as could the proportion of personnel with a given amount of professional education.

An index of bureaucratization that has been used in previous research is the relative size of the *administrative* component; that is, the proportion of personnel in administrative or staff positions.[22] Three related measures of the *hierarchy* of authority, which refer to the shape of the pyramid, would be the number of levels in the hierarchy, the average span of control, and the proportion of personnel in managerial positions. The extent to which procedures have been made explicit in formal *rules* is indicated by the existence and size of written procedure manuals and by the specificity of the prescriptions contained in them. Two other measures of an emphasis on uniform standards of performance are whether decisions are routinely reviewed for correctness and the amount of statistical information on operations that is kept in the organization as a basis for executive decisions. The use of such statistical records for the evaluation of the performance of subordinates can be considered an indication of *impersonality*, and so can precisely stipulated personnel policies, as exemplified by civil service regulations. The degree of *career* stability, finally, is manifest in membership turnover and average length of service.

This listing makes evident that the empirical data needed for research on the major characteristics of bureaucratic organizations included in Weber's theory are easily enough accessible to make it possible to obtain them for large numbers of organizations in brief visits to each. To be sure, to examine the various facets of each concept, as Weber does, would require more extensive data than those outlined. To cite only one example, an analysis of organizational authority should not be confined to the shape of the hierarchical pyramid but include other aspects of hierarchical control, such as the degree of centralization in the organization. There is no reason to assume, however, that additional measures suitable for comparative studies, which would complement the original ones and thus allow refinement of the analysis, cannot be devised; for instance, information could be obtained about the level in the hierarchy on which various important budgetary and personnel decisions are made to provide measures of centralization. The crucial point is that intensive investigations of internal structures and processes are neither needed not appropriate for obtaining the data that pertain most directly to theories of organization.

Empirical data of this kind about a fairly large sample of comparable organizations would make it possible to test numerous hypotheses implied by Weber's theory, such as that the processes of specialization, professionalization, and bureaucratization tend to occur together in organizations. Chances are that research findings would reveal that many hypotheses must be revised, thereby directing attention to needed reformulations and specifications in the theory. Thus, impressionistic observation leads one to suspect that increasing specialization is indeed accompanied by increasing professionalization in some types of organizations, such as hospitals, but that a high degree of specialization reduces the need for an expertly trained working force in other types, such as assembly-line factories. If this impression should be correct, it would raise the question of the conditions that determine whether or not an extensive division of

22. See, for example, Theodore R. Anderson and Seymour Warkov, "Organizational Size and Complexity," *American Sociological Review*, vol. 26, 1961, pp. 23–28; Alton W. Baker and Ralph C. Davis, *Ratios of Staff to Line Employees and Stages of Differentiation of Staff Functions* (Columbus: Bureau of Business Research, Ohio State University, 1954); Reinhard Bendix, *Work and Authority in Industry* (New York: Wiley, 1956), pp. 221–22; and Seymour Melman, "The Rise of Administrative Overhead in the Manufacturing Industries of the United States, 1899–1947," *Oxford Economic Papers*, vol. 3, 1951, pp. 64–66, 89–90.

labor is associated with a highly trained working force.

REFINING THEORY

Systematic exploration of the empirical relationships between organizational features would provide a basis for refining the theory of bureaucracy by indicating the conditions on which the concurrence of various bureaucratic characteristics is contingent, by helping to answer some questions Weber did not resolve, and by clarifying problems and issues his theory raises. For example, Weber considers both seniority and merit typical impersonal criteria of bureaucratic advancement. An important question which he never answers is what conditions determine whether promotions are largely based on seniority or primarily on merit, a difference that undoubtedly has significant implications for careers and for the organization. Properly designed comparative studies of organizations could help answer this question.

Whereas Weber implies that the large size of an organization as well as its complexity promotes bureaucratization, recent comparative research indicates that size is unrelated or inversely related to bureaucratization as measured by the proportion of the organization's personnel in administrative positions.[23] It appears that complexity is associated with a disproportionately large administrative apparatus, and large size often goes together with a high degree of complexity, but increasing size as such does not lead to a disproportionate expansion of the administrative apparatus. The question these conclusions raise is whether other aspects of bureaucratization, such as extensive written rules, detailed statistical controls, or impersonal personnel procedures, are associated with both size and complexity independently, in accordance with Weber's assumption, or only with one of the two or possibly with neither.

An important issue that has been raised concerns the relationship between professional competence and bureaucratic authority. Several authors, including notably Parsons, Gouldner, and Stinchcombe,[24] have criticized Weber's contention that professional expertness is a typical characteristic of bureaucracies which goes together with such other bureaucratic characteristics as strict lines of hierarchical authority that require disciplined compliance with the commands of superiors. It has been held that professional principles often conflict with the principles that govern hierarchical administration and that the two are not complementary, as Weber assumes, but rather alternative mechanisms of control and coordination. The empirical question is under which conditions professionalization and bureaucratization, especially as revealed in centralized hierarchical control, are associated in organizations and under which conditions they are not. Comparative research might explore, for instance, whether the association between professionalization and bureaucratization depends on the degree of specialization in the organization, because professional standards facilitate coordination among men in similar fields, reducing the need for bureaucratic mechanisms, whereas they make coordination between widely diverse fields more difficult, increasing the need for administrative mechanisms of coordination.

A related issue of even broader theoretical significance is posed by Weber's implicit assumption that strict hierarchical authority and discipline are universally most effective in achieving efficiency in administrative organizations. One might well wonder whether the Prussian army, which sometimes seems to have served Weber inadvertently as the prototype, is really the ideal model for all organizations, whatever the nature of their responsibilities, the composition of their personnel, and the culture in which they operate.[25] In a democratic culture where subordination under authoritative commands tends to be negatively valued, strict hierarchical control and close supervision may well be less effective methods of operation than delegating responsibilities and permitting subordinates some discretion in their exercise. The greater the professionalization of the staff, moreover, the less effective is control through directives from superiors

23. See references cited in preceding footnote.

24. Talcott Parsons, "Introduction," to Weber, *The Theory of Social and Economic Organization*, pp. 58–60 (fn.); Gouldner, *Patterns of Industrial Bureaucracy* (New York: Free Press, 1954), pp. 22–24; and Arthur L. Stinchcombe, "Bureaucratic and Craft Administration of Production," *Administrative Science Quarterly*, vol. 4, 1959, pp. 168–87.

25. According to Carl J. Friedrich, Weber's "very words vibrate with something of the Prussian enthusiasm for the military type of organization"; "Some Observations on Weber's Analysis of Bureaucracy," in Merton, *et al.*, *Reader in Bureaucracy* (New York: Free Press, 1952), p. 31.

likely to be. The most effective method for organizing an army, finally, is probably not identical with the most effective method for organizing a research laboratory. Comparative studies of organizations could throw some light on these broad issues too.

## Conclusions

Three foci of analysis have been distinguished in the study of organizational life: (1) role analysis is concerned with individual members of organizations, their attitudes, and their behavior; (2) structural analysis focuses upon groups of interrelated individuals in organizations and the patterns of social associations that develop in these groups and give them their form; (3) organizational analysis centers attention on systems of interrelated groups explicitly organized to achieve some joint ends and the constellations of attributes that characterize these organizations. The differentiating criterion is whether the unit of analysis whose characteristics are being compared, and of which, therefore, a fairly large number must be examined, is the individual member, the work group, or the entire organization.

In terms of this criterion, a case study of an organization cannot make the organization the unit of systematic analysis but only the structures of subgroups or the roles of individuals. By the same token, the study of the influence of the environment on organizations would have to employ a research design that includes organizations in a variety of different environments, and since hardly any studies do so, the complaint often heard that we know virtually nothing about the impact of the social setting on organizations is quite justified. Whereas more than three foci of analysis are possible—as just noted, the social setting could be the focus—the three outlined are the major ones in the study of organizational life. The most appropriate method for role analysis is the interviewing survey, for structural analysis, intensive observation of all members of selected groups, and for organizational analysis, the comparative study of many organizations.

A theory of organization seeks to explain the systems of relationships between elements in a structure that characterize organizations. Such explanations involve, like all theoretical explanations, subsuming observed relationships between characteristics under more general propositions and specifying the intervening processes responsible for the connections. A major contribution of case studies that investigate the internal structures of organizations is that they provide specific evidence on these underlying processes, which otherwise must be inferred in organizational analysis. But this is only a potential contribution to organizational theory as long as it stands by itself and is not yet a supplement to the data on constellations of organizational features provided by comparative studies of organizations, which must furnish the main foundation of such a theory. Only systematic comparisons of many organizations can establish relationships between characteristics or organizations and stipulate the conditions under which these relationships hold, thereby providing the material that needs to be explained by theoretical principles and important guides for deriving these principles. Although comparative research on a fairly large number of organizations is necessarily restricted to data easily accessible without time-consuming intensive investigations, these are the very data most relevant for organizational theory; for example, Weber's theory of bureaucracy.

OSCAR GRUSKY and LINDSEY CHURCHILL

# The Experimental Study of Organizational Variables

This paper describes in detail a new laboratory method created to study the effects of succession and organizational effectiveness under carefully controlled conditions.

The large bulk of research on organizations has consisted of field studies which, although invaluable as a source of new ideas, present the disadvantage of making it impossible to verify propositions systematically.[1] Since this technique has provided most of the data on succession and effectiveness, its methodological weaknesses need to be kept in mind. It is essential for the case study investigator to familiarize himself thoroughly with the organization and its key personnel. He must learn what the organization produces and how, its history, its formal structure, the nature of the informal alignments that have developed, and so on. Only after attaining an intimate involvement with the system, its members, and its operations, is the researcher able to complete his tasks. The process of field research on organizations is both taxing and time-consuming. Because it is wearing to study even one organization, the procedure can encourage a focus on unique events or on suborganizational variables and thereby make comparative analysis of organizational variables less feasible. Despite its limitations for testing hypotheses, the literature on formal organizations is dominated by case studies. Guest's research on succession, which compared a firm he studied with a gypsum plant studied by Gouldner, represented an advance, in part, because it went beyond the confines of a single case study.[2] Nevertheless, as the investigator realized, the comparisons were limited because the two firms were grossly different in numerous respects. Most important of all, the two case studies produced opposite findings on the effects of succession.

A fundamental problem in the study of organizational behavior has been the availability for research

1. This has been noted by W. Richard Scott, "Field Methods in the Study of Organizations," in James G. March, ed., *Handbook of Organizations* (Chicago: Rand McNally, 1965). For an excellent discussion of laboratory experimentation on organizations see in the same volume the chapter by Karl E. Weick.

This study was made possible by a grant from the National Science Foundation (GS-186) with the senior author as principal investigator. We are grateful to Professor George A. Miller for a critical reading of the manuscript, to Don Baker and Roy A. Hansen, research assistants on the project, to Professor Morris Zelditch, Jr., for advice and support, and Dr. Joan Lasko, Director of the Behavioral Science Laboratories of the Graduate School of Business Administration, UCLA. Although for convenience' sake we use the terms *experimental* and *laboratory* interchangeably, their differences might usefully be pointed out. The experimental method requires that the independent variable be manipulated by the investigator and its effects observed and measured. The laboratory approach specifies only the context within which the research takes place, that is, the setting is controlled by the investigator. Hence, a study may be considered properly to be a laboratory investigation although the experimenter does not manipulate the independent variable. Many of Bales' pioneer investigations of social interaction were laboratory but not experimental studies.

This article was especially prepared for this volume.

2. See Alvin W. Gouldner, *Patterns of Industrial Bureaucracy* (New York: The Free Press, 1954) and Robert H. Guest, *Organizational Change* (Homewood, Ill.: The Dorsey Press, 1962, and "Managerial Succession in Complex Organizations," *American Journal of Sociology*, 68, 1 (July, 1962), 47–54.

***Table 1***

| *Experimental Variations* | *Effectiveness of Division I Under Manager (Phase I)* | *Effectiveness of Division II Under Predecessor (Phase I)* | *Effectiveness of Division II After Succession (Phase II)* | |
|---|---|---|---|---|
| 1 | Low | High | Low | Decreasing Effectiveness |
| 2 | High | High | Low | |
| 3 | Low | Low | Low | Stable Effectiveness |
| 4 | High | Low | Low | |
| 5 | Low | High | High | |
| 6 | High | High | High | |
| 7 | High | Low | High | Increasing Effectiveness |
| 8 | Low | Low | High | |

of a sufficiently large sample of reasonably identical organizations to permit statistical analysis of relationships between clearly defined organizational characteristics. Some investigators such as Udy, Blau, Stinchcombe, and others have sought by ingenious techniques to deal with this problem. The present research sought to demonstrate further that the laboratory also can be one effective "solution" to this fundamental methodological dilemma.

In this study seventy-two identical, three-level, simulated business organizations were created in the laboratory. Although these systems had life histories averaging less than two hours each, all possessed the basic characteristics associated with formal organizations. We turn next to the experimental design which describes these characteristics.

## The method of study

The basic format consisted of setting up a simulated business firm having two identical component organizations, Division I and Division II. These organizations, which functioned independently of one another, were designed to resemble actual business firms. The subjects were taught their task responsibilities according to the position occupied and were observed as their organization was manipulated.

The experiment was designed to study simultaneously the effects of effectiveness and succession. Each experimental organization experienced two phases. Succession was created by transferring managers from one organization to another at the completion of the first phase and prior to the start of the second phase. Thus, managers learned their job in the first organization (Division) and were then transferred to the second organization as successors to the manager of that unit. In each phase, organizations were manipulated so as to be effective or ineffective. In this fashion, eight effectiveness variations were established, as shown in Table 1.

In addition, in order to examine the effects of succession independent of effectiveness, control groups without succession were run. Control groups were run for each of the four possible effectiveness conditions (see Table 2).

***Table 2***

| *Experimental Variation* | *Phase I* | *Phase II* |
|---|---|---|
| 1 | Low | Low |
| 2 | High | Low |
| 3 | Low | High |
| 4 | High | High |

## Subjects and experimental procedure

All subjects were male volunteers, predominantly undergraduates from the College of Letters and Science, University of California, Los Angeles. There were a total of 216 subjects, 150 in the experimental sessions and 66 in the control organizations. Seventy-two formal organizations were established, 50 experimental systems and 22 controls. When recruited subjects were told only that they would be members of simulated business organizations. All subjects were strangers to one another. The experimental sessions lasted from about an hour and one-half to two hours.

Confederates were also undergraduates from UCLA. Each organization consisted of seven positions, three filled by naive subjects and four by confederates. The latter were always workers, the former, managers. An organization chart, depicting the formal structure, was displayed in the managers' offices and in the room where the subjects received their instructions (see Figure 1).

As soon as the subjects arrived at the laboratory

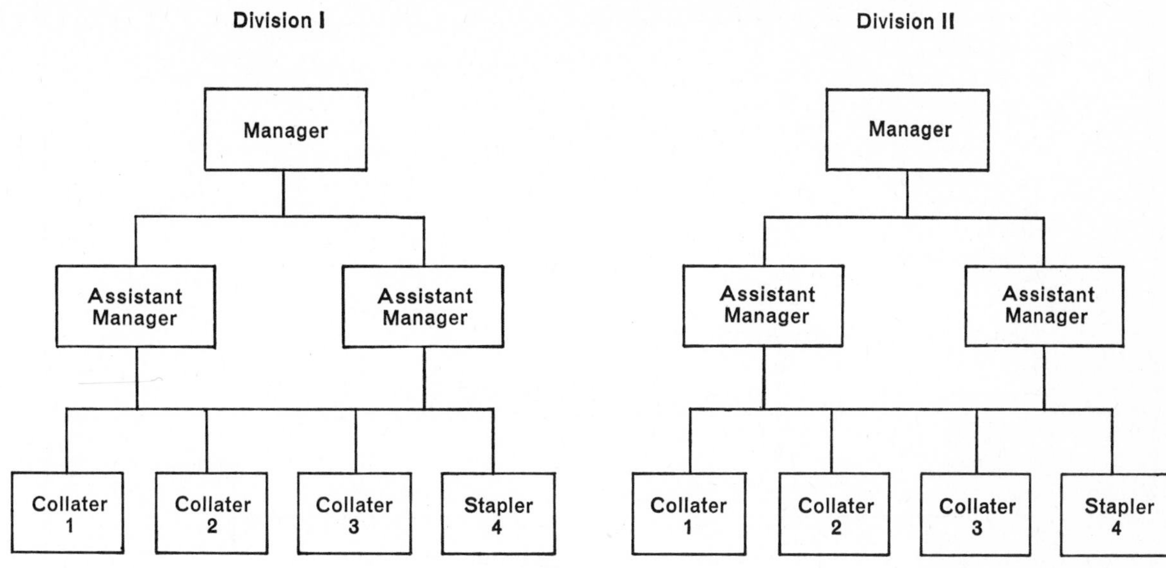


*Figure 1. Organization chart*

(see Figure 2 for the laboratory layout) they were given the "Short Form" of the Managerial Abilities Test, a test represented as one validated by a great deal of psychological research, and one that reputedly predicted accurately to managerial ability in business firms. In fact, the test was specially designed for the study. While the multiple-choice test was ostensibly being scored, the following instructions were given:

The basic purpose of this study is to see how well managers in large organizations are able to keep worker morale high enough to maintain productivity at a desirable level. To do this, we will establish a simulated business organization here in the laboratory. This organization will resemble as much as possible an average business firm. There will be an office for the managers of each Division, and a separate place for the workers to perform their job. There will be time pressures on production as in real production systems. Communication between the managers and the workers will be only by written memoranda—that is, it will be *impersonal* as in most large companies. Also, managers will be paid more and workers less, as in normal business organizations, because of the different degree of responsibility of the jobs.

The actual purpose of the organization will be the production of technical manuals for the Securities and Exchange Commission of the United States Government. The manuals will be in perfect order. The workers will assemble the manuals, the assistant managers will check them to see that they meet the required specifications, and the manager will carry ultimate responsibility for coordination and for maintaining high morale among the workers and assistant managers so that productivity is maximized.

The organization is like this (pointing to chart): There are one manager, two assistant managers, and four workers in each of two Divisions. The Divisions are identical. You will be assigned to positions on the basis of your score on the Managerial Abilities Test. The two highest scorers will be managers, the next four highest assistant managers, and the remaining eight will be workers.

Let me briefly explain your jobs.

First, let us look at the workers' job. This is the most routine task. Still, it is an essential position. Naturally, workers must *always* follow the instructions of the manager, even though these are written instructions. The workers are the ones who actually produce the manuals. Each Division has a separate work room for its workers. On tables in those large rooms are piles of mimeographed pages. (Experimenter points to work rooms, the doors of which are open and the material visible.) The workers must order the pages in the proper sequence and staple them together very carefully. Three workers, Nos. 1, 2, and 3 will collate, No. 4 will staple. One minute before the end of each six-minute work period, a short buzz will sound and one of the workers will collect the completed manuals and deliver them to the manager's office. One minute later a long buzz will sound, indicating the conclusion of that period and the beginning of the next one. Since communication is impersonal, the runner is not permitted to talk to the managers. There will be six six-minute work periods. The work group will start when the manager instructs them by memorandum to begin their job. Workers may send

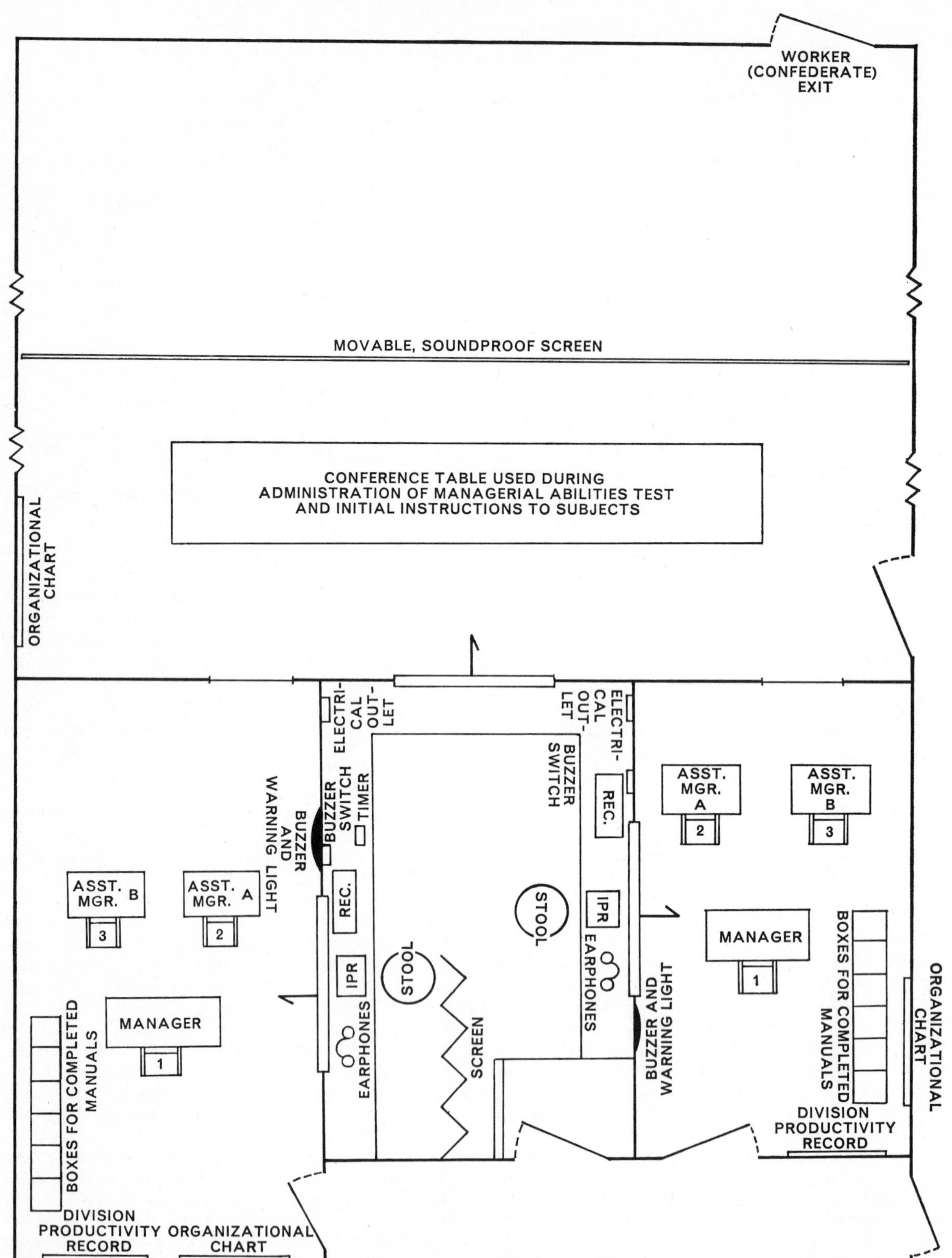


*Figure 2. Laboratory layout*

one message each period to the manager on the forms provided at the middle of each period. Workers may choose from among a set of fifty different messages in communicating to the managers. Hence, the messages are "canned," so as to maintain impersonal worker-manager relations. In order not to interfere with worker productivity, staff members will deliver the workers' messages. However, a worker will deliver the period's output.[3] Each worker will be paid one cent for each acceptable manual.

The assistant managers are responsible for supervising the job of the workers by checking their work. Assistant managers also must follow the instructions of the manager. The assistant manager goes over each manual checking for neatness of stapling, page sequence, and readability. He uses the Stapling Error Detection Device which is provided. At the end of the period, the assistant manager fills out an Error Report Form indicating how many errors were made and of what kind these were and hands the completed report to the manager. Assistant managers will be paid one and one-half cents for each acceptable manual. Here is a sample of an acceptable manual (passes out copies labeled "Sample").

At this point the two experimenters who left with the tests returned. The subjects' scores and organizational positions were then announced. In fact, selection to position was on a random basis, except on rare occasions. (If two persons had reported previously that they knew one another, and no substitute was available, they were assigned to different Divisions as assistant manager). All confederates, a total of eight for each session, were assigned positions as workers.

The instructions continued, as follows:

I have described the jobs of the workers and assistant managers. Now let me describe the job of manager. Managers have the *most* responsibility. Accordingly they are paid most—two cents for each acceptable manual. The manager has final authority for all decisions made. It is up to him to see that things move well and morale is high both among the assistant managers and the workers. This is not easy. He has several tasks:

1. First, distribute the manuals to the assistant managers for processing.
2. Keep the members informed of their productivity by putting the productivity results on the blackboard and sending a completed productivity form at the end of each period to the workers.
3. Send any morale messages to the workers he deems wise. The manager can write short comments to the workers which he believes will be most effective. The workers receive this message from the runner.
4. Advise the assistant managers when they need help.
5. If he thinks this is advisable, he may change the job of the stapler by sending a *Change-of-Job Notice*. It may be that shifting positions between the workers is desirable. The manager has this authority.
6. Finally, if he thinks it appropriate, he may permit the workers to take a one-minute rest period for every period after the first one. Whenever he feels worker morale would be helped by a short break, he may send a memorandum instructing the workers to relax for a short period. *As past studies have shown, the decisions that the manager makes are of considerable importance to the ability of the organization to operate at optimum morale and effectiveness.*

Gross output refers to the total number of manuals assembled. Net output is the number of *acceptable* manuals, that is, manuals that conform to specifications. We have found that *sixteen manuals* without error can *readily* be compiled in a six-minute period, *so this is the norm per period.* Remember, each of you earn only what you make on acceptable manuals, which shall be checked. There is no fixed payment of your time.

The workers (confederates) were then taken to their appropriate workrooms and the two groups of managers were led to their respective offices. As indicated in Figure 2, the following equipment was located in each office: small desks and chairs for each assistant manager, larger ones for the manager, signs on each desk indicating their position, appropriate business report forms for the manager, Stapling Error Detection Devices and report forms for the assistant manager, a chart of the organization, a Division Productivity Chart, a grease pencil, and bins for completed manuals delivered by the workers.

The manager was instructed to fill out immediately a Start Work Memorandum that started the first period for the workers. As soon as this was delivered, the experimenter returned, informed the subjects of the one-way mirror, and went over carefully the requirements of each position.[4] On

3. This was a new instruction added after Test No. 8. We found that credibility was enhanced by having a worker deliver the output. At the same time, we initiated the feature of leaving the doors of the workrooms open while the initial instructions were being given so that all the subjects could see the workrooms from where they sat.

4. It was, of course, standard procedure to inform the subjects of the tape recorder, the one-way mirror, and the fact that interaction process analysis was being employed. Responses to being observed naturally varied. The

the manager's desk was a list of duties of the manager for his ready reference.

Since the workers were confederates, all of their communications to the managers were easily standardized. A set of six messages, the first three worded in a slightly different fashion for each division so as to avoid suspicion after succession, were delivered to the managers (one each in the middle of Pre-period 1, Period 1, Period 2, Pre-period 4, Period 4, and Period 5). They were as follows:

*Division I*

1. "I'm tired of collating. Could I switch jobs?" Collator
2. "Things are kind of mixed up down here." Collator
3. "Our production line is running smoothly now." Collator
4. "We need a break." Stapler
5. "There's too much fooling around down here." Collator
6. "You deserve all the credit for our production." Collator

*Division II*

"I don't like stapling. How about another job?" Stapler
"Things are a little confused down here." Collator
"Things are going along better now." Collator

"We need a break." Stapler
"There's too much fooling around down here." Collator
"You deserve all the credit for our production." Collator

The same messages were used for all sessions, whether of high or low effectiveness.

## Success of the effectiveness manipulation

The two independent variables in this experiment were organizational effectiveness and succession. Effectiveness was controlled by manipulating the number of errors in the workers' (confederates') production. Table 3 describes the contrived output for the low and high effectiveness conditions.

The purpose of the company was to produce technical manuals. Each organization operated independently and identically in this process. The workers (ostensibly) collated and stapled prepared pages to make manuals, the assistant managers checked manuals for errors of assembly, and the managers supervised the whole operation. The work period in each organization consisted of eight six-minute periods, called Pre-period 1, Periods 1, 2, 3, Pre-period 4, Periods 4, 5, and 6. Pre-period 1 and Periods 1–3 ran continuously and constituted the first half of the work period. After Period 3 the experiment was interrupted to administer tests to the managers. Then Pre-period 4 and Periods 4–6 ran continuously and constituted the second half of the work period.

The workers made manuals (or so the subjects believed) during Pre-period 1 and Periods 1–2 in the first phase and during Pre-period 4 and Periods 4–5 in the second phase, while the assistant managers checked their output during Periods 1–3 and Periods 4–6, as indicated in Figure 3.

The independent variable of effectiveness was created by manipulating the number of errors in the prepared manuals. Two effectiveness conditions, high and low, prevailed throughout Periods 1–3 (Phase I) and throughout Periods 4–6 (Phase II). High effectiveness was created by sending in manuals that had few enough errors so that the number of acceptable manuals discovered by the managers would be above a stated norm (sixteen) in each of the three periods. Similarly, low effective-

***Table 3—Manipulation of Effectiveness***

| | PERIOD | | | | | | |
|---|---|---|---|---|---|---|---|
| | *Phase I* | | | | *Phase II* | | |
| | *I* | *II* | *III* | *(Transition)* | *IV* | *V* | *VI* |
| Gross Productivity | 17 | 19 | 18 | | 19 | 7 | 19 |
| Errors | 0 | 1 | 0 | | 1 | 0 | 1 |
| Net Productivity | 17 | 18 | 17 | | 18 | 17 | 18 |
| Norm | 16 | 16 | 16 | | 16 | 16 | 16 |

*Low-low effectiveness manipulation*

| | PERIOD | | | | | | |
|---|---|---|---|---|---|---|---|
| | *Phase I* | | | | *Phase II* | | |
| | *I* | *II* | *III* | *(Transition)* | *IV* | *V* | *VI* |
| Gross Productivity | 17 | 18 | 17 | | 17 | 18 | 17 |
| Errors | 5 | 7 | 6 | | 4 | 6 | 5 |
| Net Productivity | 12 | 11 | 11 | | 13 | 12 | 12 |
| Norm | 16 | 16 | 16 | | 16 | 16 | 16 |

*High-high effectiveness manipulation*

response of this subject seemed to be typical: "The fact that I knew people were on the other side of that mirror made me more serious. In fact, it was like in business. I would be very serious too in an actual business situation." However, we did not systematically study the effects of the one-way mirror.

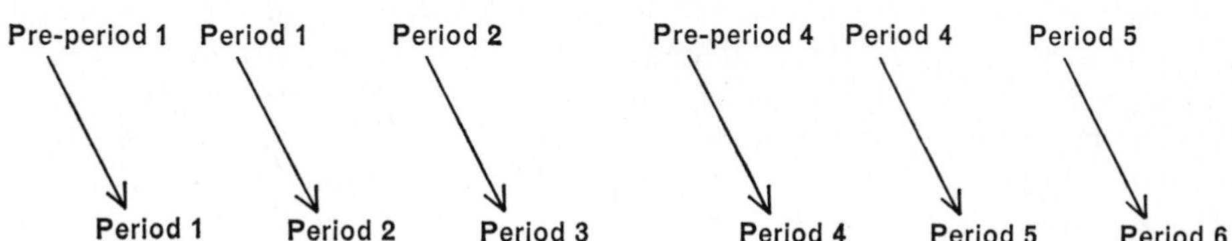


*Figure 3*

ness was created by sending in manuals during each period that had enough errors so that the number of acceptable manuals discovered would be well below the stated norm.[5] Output was varied for each type of manipulation so as to allay suspicion on the part of the subjects. The possibility existed that workers' errors would be overlooked by the assistant managers and hence the manipulated effectiveness level altered. In order to examine systematically this possibility, we compared the manipulated and perceived net productivities. Among the control organizations, the average net productivity for each period reported by the managers was 12.8 in the low-effectiveness condition ($N = 66$ periods) and 17.1 in the high-effectiveness periods ($N = 66$ periods). In the experimental organizations there was one group of assistant managers who were extraordinarily zealous in determining errors on the manuals. As a result, they transformed what was intended as a high-effectiveness manipulation into a low-effectiveness manipulation. For this group, we simply changed the manipulation to fit their perception. The average net productivity for each period reported by the managers was 12.8 in the low-effectiveness condition ($N = 149$ periods; in one case the manager did not make a written report) and 17.1 in the high-effectiveness periods ($N = 146$ periods; in four periods no report was made). The period by period correlation between perceived and objective (manipulated) net productivity was calculated separately for the experimental and control groups. In both cases it was extremely high and positive. The Pearson product-moment correlation for the two groups combined was $+ .90$ $p. < .0001$. Hence, the manipulated effectiveness level was effectively perceived as planned in both the experimental and the control groups.[6]

## The succession manipulation

At the conclusion of the third period each manager was taken to another room, tested, and interviewed. In the experimental sessions, the managers were brought together and told:

> It is common practice in large business organizations to rotate managers so as to broaden their experience. Therefore, you will now be manager of Division —— and you manager of Division ——.

Each manager was then taken to his new unit and the reason stated above for the rotation was explained to the assistant managers.

5. Effectiveness could conceivably have been manipulated in any of three ways: (1) by manipulating gross productivity; (2) by manipulating the number of errors; and (3) by manipulating both gross productivity and the number of errors. We favored the second method. However, the type of manipulation itself could have been a relevant variable. In general, we would expect greater managerial hostility to be directed toward the worker in the ineffectiveness conditions when the error rate was high than if gross productivity was low. Variations in gross productivity may be explained more readily by chance variations whereas frequent errors were more likely to be attributed directly to carelessness on the part of the workers. Particularly in the first phase, if a group is ineffective as a result of low gross productivity, the managers may very well direct their blame not at the workers but at the "unreasonableness" of the norms, an impersonal target of hostility. On the other hand, if the group is ineffective as a direct result of many errors, managerial hostility should be more likely to be directed primarily toward those making the errors, the workers. Also, it should be noted that our manipulation of effectiveness was not stable over the three periods involved. The low effectiveness condition involved a situation where the norm was never attained although there were varying degrees of closeness of the norm.

6. Despite considerable care there was some inevitable human error in the assembling of the manuals for the effectiveness manipulations. The correlation, we assume, would have been even higher if the manipulated productivity was, in fact, always what the schedule called for.

## Types of data

All subjects were given questionnaires, including sociometric items, and semantic differentials to complete at the end of the first phase and at the conclusion of the study. In addition, managers were interviewed privately at both times. Moreover, all sessions were monitored and tape-recorded.

Bales' twelve-category system of Interaction Process Analysis was modified by reducing it to the four categories labeled by Bales *A* (Observation Categories 1, 2, 3), Expressive–Integrative, Social–Emotional Area, Positive Reactions; *B* (Categories 4, 5, 6), Instrumental–Adaptive, Task Area: Solutions; *C* (Categories 7, 8, 9), Instrumental–Adaptive, Task Area: Questions; and *D* (Categories 10, 11, 12), Expressive–Integrative, Social–Emotional Area, Negative Reactions.[7]

Inter-rater reliability was assessed at four separate sessions during the experimental runs. The reliability across all acts for the four tests was: 0.98, 0.97, 0.97, and 0.98.[8] However, when inter-rater reliability was determined separately for each category of Act, *A*, *B*, *C*, and *D*, the averages across the four types of acts were reduced to: 0.83, 0.74, 0.73, and 0.77 for each test session. By far the lowest reliability was obtained for the *D* acts which included three types of behaviors: disagreement including passive rejection, tension and withdrawal, and antagonism. Inter-rater reliability for *D* acts considered separately in the four test sessions averaged only 0.504.

Each experimental session was concluded by discussing the general hypotheses of the research, answering the subjects' questions, and requesting that they maintain secrecy about the experiment. A pre-test revealed that subjects did not maintain secrecy about the effectiveness manipulation. Therefore, in most cases, the deception was maintained until a written report revealed it to them.

7. R. F. Bales, *Interaction Process Analysis* (Cambridge, Mass.: Addison-Wesley Press, 1950), pp. 190–93.

8. *N* was 28. Scores were recorded for each of four types of acts at the end of seven periods (six full periods plus the transition period between Phase I and Phase II). *N* was 7 for each type of act. Borgatta and Bales also report high between-observer reliability for skilled raters using the full twelve-category system. They also reported differences by category. See E. F. Borgatta and R. F. Bales, "The Consistency of Subject Behavior and the Reliability of Scoring in Interaction Process Analysis," *American Sociological Review*, 18 (1953), 566–69.

## Suspicion of the manipulation

Whenever possible we noted those subjects who were suspicious of the effectiveness manipulations. The findings reported were not affected significantly when suspicious subjects were omitted. For this reason, the decision to leave them in was made.

We decided to examine those subjects who it appeared were seeing through the manipulations. The most sensitive manipulation was, of course, that of effectiveness. When subjects were asked in the interview what they thought about their workers, they rarely stated that they did not believe in them. Further, subjects continued to behave as if the workers were actually producing the manuals even though they had expressed some suspicion in conversation during the experiment. For example, in one case the following exchange occurred at the beginning of the final period:

ASST. MGR. A. The errors have been introduced.
ASST. MGR. B. The errors have been just like they were in our first three ones [periods].
ASST. MGR. A. Yeah.

Yet the assistant managers worked during the remainder of the experiment as if there really were workers and no further indications of suspicion on their part were revealed.

At some points in the experiment, subjects voiced some questions about the reality of certain events, although typically in a passing way. In a short time, the subjects were caught up again in the activities of their tasks and failed to act on their suspicions in any observable fashion. Asch has reported a similar phenomenon.[9]

## Role of the experimenter

Although the formal structure of the organization depicted on the organization charts had only three levels of authority, a fourth level was established by selecting student subjects and by the demeanor of the professor-experimenters.[10] The result was to utilize the professor–student relationship so as to

9. S. Asch, "Effects of Group Pressure upon the Modification and Distortion of Judgments," in E. E. Maccoby, T. M. Newcomb, and E. H. Hartley (eds.), *Readings in Social Psychology* (New York: Henry Holt, 1958), p. 178.

10. For intensive studies of the effect of the experimenter, consult the following: R. Rosenthal, *Experimenter Effects in Behavioral Research* (New York: Appleton-

fit it into the organizational structure created in the laboratory. Hence, the interviews of the manager by the experimenter always began with questions concerning the subject's managerial performance. The experimenters thus assumed the positions of higher-level managers assessing the performance of lower-level ones.

The data revealed that the ability of the organization to produce at a high or low rate had a pronounced effect on the feelings of the managers. Despite the fact that the organization was simulated and of short duration, the manager's ego was nonetheless in most instances bound up in the performance of the organization. The manager did accept the delegated responsibility, which in this case was assigned to him by the experimenter and which in large-scale organizations is assigned to managers by comparable higher authorities.

Our data also suggested that the manager often felt that what he did as manager had specific consequences for the behavior of the organization. The managers believed that the changes they made were in fact responsible for the rise and fall in production. One manager of an ineffective division apologized to the interviewer with the comment: "I've never been in a managerial position like that." Another attributed the poor performance of his organization to his personal lack of confidence in himself and his lack of managerial experience: "I think that I'm not confident enough in my ability. I don't know much about business or managing people. I wish I were more confident in my personal life. I am too hesitant in doing things as a manager. But I think I am doing a reasonable job. I'm trying to, anyway."

These comments also indicated that the experimenters were successfully viewed (appropriate to their professional position) by student subjects as authority figures. Managers who felt they had performed poorly responded by attempting to justify their behavior just as managers in actual business firms may feel compelled to explain their performances in encounters with superiors. Hence, the experimenters' role as an authority appeared to contribute as planned to the attempt to simulate features of formal organizations in the laboratory.

## Conclusion

This paper has presented a complex simulation experimental design. The basic method consisted of setting up in the laboratory two simulated three-level business organizations having identical formal structures and technologies. Each organization consisted of seven coordinated positions, a manager, two assistant managers, and four workers. The organizations were designed to resemble actual business firms. For example, there was an official organizational goal, a hierarchy of authority, task specialization, a reward system, and differential communication control. Rank in the formal structure was tied to type of work, authority, and expertise (as measured by the Managerial Abilities Test), Access to information, freedom of communication. salary, and various status symbols such as desk size were also determined by level of position. The organization was designed to produce technical manuals. The workers (ostensibly) assembled the manuals, the assistant managers checked their output, and the managers were responsible for the administration of the total unit. The manager learned his job during his period in the first organization and was then transferred to the second. In this fashion, succession was manipulated. The effectiveness of the organization was manipulated by uisng confederates as workers. The preliminary results of the series of studies that have been conducted using this design are presented elsewhere.[11] Additional research applying the technique to a wide range of organizational problems is in progress.

Century-Crofts, Inc., 1966); M. T. Orne, "The Nature of Hypnosis: Artifact and Essence," *Journal of Abnormal and Social Psychology*, 58 (1959), 277–99; M. T. Orne, "On the Social Psychology of the Psychological Experiment: With Particular Reference to Demand Characteristics and their Implications," *American Psychologist*, 17 (1962), 776–83; M. T. Orne and F. J. Evans, "Social Control in the Psychological Experiment: Antisocial Behavior and Hypnosis," *Journal of Personality and Social Psychology*, 1 (1965), 189–200; T. M. Mills, "A Sleeper Variable in Small Groups Research; The Experimenter," *Pacific Sociological Review*, Spring, 1962.

11. See O. Grusky and L. Churchill, "Organizational Effectiveness and Managerial Role Strain: An Experimental Study," paper presented at the American Sociological Association Meeting, 1966; O. Grusky, "The Effects of Succession on Superior-Subordinate Relationships: An Experimental Study," paper presented at the American Sociological Association Meeting, 1967; O. Grusky, "Succession with an Ally," *Administrative Science Quarterly*, Vol. 14, 2 (June 1969); and O. Grusky, "The Effects of Inside versus Outside Succession on Communication Patterns," *Proceedings*, 77th Annual Convention, American Psychological Association, 1969.

STANLEY H. UDY, Jr.

# Cross-Cultural Analysis: A Case Study

A thesis topic, like greatness, is something which some students are born with, others achieve, and still others have thrust upon them. Since I was not so fortunate as to have been born with one, nor so unfortunate as to have had a topic thrust upon me, I was obliged to "achieve" one.

My approach to this perennial problem of the graduate student was to try consciously and systematically to choose that topic which combined the greatest number of my interests. After some exploration, the amalgam on which I settled was comparative social analysis, organization theory, industrial sociology, pleasure derived from reading ethnography, and curiosity about what one could do with the Human Relations Area Files. This combination (actually the result of putting together some works of Profs. Marion Levy, Wilbert Moore, and Melvin Tumin, under all of whom I had studied) suggested some kind of cross-cultural study of work organization in nonindustrial societies, assuming that such a study was possible and could be reasonably expected to contribute anything to organization theory.

I had read enough ethnography to be persuaded that some study along these lines was possible, but I did not yet know specifically what kind of study it should be or what particular questions it should attempt to answer. Furthermore, as yet I had no real justification—beyond the notion that it might be fun—for studying work organization cross-culturally. Why should that approach be used instead of some other one? In other words, is there some distinctive set of important problems in organization theory which not only can be studied cross-culturally but cannot readily be approached in any other way?

Let us begin to answer this question with a brief overview of the general relevance of cross-cultural analysis. Broadly speaking, cross-cultural analysis is appropriate to any research problem involving variables whose values differ from one society to another but remain more or less constant in any given society. Since most highly general institutional variables tend to be of this variety, one of the great advantages of the cross-cultural method is that it allows maximum variations in basic institutional structure to be introduced into the research design. Cross-cultural research is thus obviously relevant to the development of theories about basic institutions and entire societies. But cross-cultural analysis is also relevant at certain points to the development of theories about organizations that always appear in the context of some society. Inasmuch as such organizations are not self-contained but are dependent to some extent on the society within which they exist, the question eventually arises as to the degree to which their structural variations are accounted for by influences of the social setting, as opposed to pressures arising from

Reprinted from *Sociologists At Work* (ed. Phillip E. Hammond), pp. 161–83, by permission of the author and publisher. 

internal consistencies. In order to answer this question, one must use a design that allows the setting to vary. The most extreme variations can be achieved by comparing organizations in different societies, particularly in nonindustrial societies, since there is considerable reason to believe that industrial societies are substantially alike in many basic essentials.

But why do variations in the setting need to be so "extreme" as those afforded by a comparative study of nonindustrial situations? One can certainly introduce contextual variations in a comparative study of, say, work groups in American industry, or even work groups in the same plant. The value of studies which do this is undeniable. However, it is equally undeniable that organization theory has been carried to its greatest level of sophistication in its treatment of purely internal aspects of administrative operations with influences from the setting held constant. Part of the problem is that we do not really know what the major relevant dimensions of influence of setting on organizations are. Investigation of contextual influences on organizations is thus still pretty much at the exploratory stage; it is not a question of systematically introducing variations to test hypotheses but rather a question of discovering what the most strategic variables are and how they seem to operate. In such circumstances, there is great value in using data which may be expected to exhibit extreme variations, simply because extreme variations are more visible and hence more likely to be noticed in an exploratory study than are minute ones.

I thus became persuaded (1) that exploratory studies of relationships between organizations and their technical and social settings can contribute to organization theory and (2) that cross-cultural analysis, by reason of the relatively extreme variations which it permits one to introduce into one's design, would be one of the best ways to conduct such a study.

My purpose thus became the exploration of work organizations in different societies in order to discover the major relevant dimensions of influence of the setting on the organization. I took as my unit of investigation the *production organization*, defined as any social group manifestly engaged in carrying on one or more technological processes. My main working hypothesis—that the structure of any production organization is partly a function of the characteristics of the technological process which it is carrying on and partly a function of the nature of the social setting within which it exists—followed from the purpose of the study. The aim was to explore a number of different production organizations carrying on widely different kinds of technological processes in widely different social settings and to do so in such a way as to give specific content to the working hypothesis. In other words, my objective was to discover, insofar as possible, what particular characteristics of technology and what particular aspects of the social setting influence which specific elements of organization structure. And I proposed to do this by studying a number of different work organizations in a number of different societies.[1]

## Preliminary survey

According to the logic of research procedure, after one has defined the problem, one next draws a sample. But that is not what I did next, nor is it probably what any exploratory cross-cultural researcher would be likely to do next. I did not yet know how many societies I wanted to use. I had decided to attempt generalizations rather than purely descriptive "comparing and contrasting." But I did not know whether it would be better to study a few work organizations—say, eight or ten—"in depth" or to study specific features of the largest possible number of organizations. Also, I had not decided whether to do the whole thing in words or to use numbers and statistical techniques, though this issue was not a very important one at this stage. (In fact, a decision was not made on this score until rather late in the research.) But, above all, I was not yet sure just how much descriptive information was really available on nonindustrial work organizations.

Actually, many of my problems at this point resulted from my own background. I had been trained as a sociologist, rather than as an anthropologist, and thus was not systematically familiar with ethnological literature. I had read a considerable number of anthropological monographs—partly because I did, and still do, find them enjoy-

1. Stanley H. Udy, Jr., *Organization at Work: A Comparative Analysis of Production among Nonindustrial Peoples* (New Haven, Conn.: Human Relations Area Files Press, 1959), pp. 1–4.

able as well as instructive. In particular, I was familiar with the various works of Firth and Malinowski, especially as they deal with primitive economic systems, and with much of the literature on the Australian aborigines and the Plains and Northeastern American Indians. I also knew most of the standard works on primitive economics, such as those of Thurnwald and Herskovits. I had read Murdock's *Social Structure* in some detail.[2] I had also skimmed through, at one time or another, quite a few nineteenth-century works in the early "classical" comparative evolutionist tradition, and I must admit that I was greatly impressed by some of them, such as Julius Lippert's *Kulturgeschichte*.[3]

But that was it. I had read just about enough to be persuaded that this study was possible. So I tackled a list of representative ethnographic monographs, reading them, perforce, from a sociologist's point of view. I found out what anthropological journals and monograph series existed that I had not known about and began looking at them. At this point, I felt ready to survey the literature to find out if anyone had ever done what I had planned to do. My survey yielded Nieboer's *Slavery as an Industrial System* and Buxton's *Primitive Labour*, published in 1900 and 1924, respectively, as the only general works I could find which dealt directly with my topic.[4] And, although there was enough information in monographs to convince me that a study of nonindustrial work organization was possible, it nevertheless appeared impossible to study eight or ten organizations "in depth," largely because variations even on the most general level seemed so great that I had no way of deciding which eight or ten organizations to choose for purposes of generalization. I did not know what controls to make. It appeared that part of the purpose of the study would have to be to discover what types of work organizations would be strategic for a depth analysis. So I decided to use a large number of cases, to keep the analysis on a very general level, and to try to discover "what is going on here."

Having decided in a general way what I wanted to do and having gained at least a nodding acquaintance with the literature, I now needed to conceptualize my problem so that I would know what data to look for, how to classify it, and what to do with it after I had it, assuming I could get any. Professors of sociology seem particularly fond of telling students that one cannot just "go out and study something" without having some kind of conceptual framework. It is interesting that this is probably one of the most "okay" statements to make in our field, despite its palpable question-begging character where exploratory studies are concerned. It appears that one must know what variables are relevant in order to be able to explore data to find out what variables are relevant. This is, of course, not so, despite the fact that much of our methodological literature leads to this paradox. The problem is that such literature does not have much to say about the exploratory, "what is going on here" type of study, where the problem is more one of starting on a general level and working toward more detailed information through successive rounds of exploration." And one can begin on a very general level, indeed.

My main working hypothesis suggested three very broad categories: technology, organization, and social setting (i.e., the physical nature of the process being carried out, the structure of the organization doing the work, and external cultural influences on the organization). It also suggested a broad method of analysis, namely, to explore relationships between technology and organization, holding social setting constant, and to explore relationships between organization and social setting, holding technology constant. The exploratory problem emerges as a trial and error of various ways of subclassifying these categories in the context of this procedure.

Further reflection, aided by common sense, plus the literature on industrial sociology, suggested the desirability of a fourth broad category: reward systems. For one presumes that all motivation to work ultimately derives from goals held by organization members in the social setting, that rewards attached to work constitute one way of making organizational activities means to such goals, and that probably, therefore, certain things about reward systems will vary, depending on conditions in the social setting and the organization.[5]

2. George P. Murdock, *Social Structure* (New York: Macmillan, 1949).

3. Julius Lippert, *Kulturgeschichte der Menschheit* (Stuttgart: F. Enke, 1886–87).

4. H. J. Nieboer, *Slavery as an Industrial System* (The Hague: Martinus Nijhoff, 1900); L. H. D. Buxton, *Primitive Labour* (London, Eng.: Methuen, 1924).

5. Wilbert E. Moore, *Industrial Relations and the Social Order* (2nd ed., New York: Macmillan, 1951), pp. 253–70.

A fifth category suggested itself as a result of preliminary reading; namely, one which would include all activities other than production carried on by the organizations studied, including magical and ritual activities connected with work. Particularly in view of the work of Malinowski, it seemed advisable to keep track of such things separately from the outset, though this category is probably a special case of the "social setting" and, indeed, eventually proved to be analyzable in this manner. I felt that these five categories would be adequate for preliminary study and would also serve as a framework within which systematic exploration could take place later.

The next problem was to develop a system for searching the literature and recording data. I needed to be able to peruse ethnographic works, locate production organizations, and record data describing their internal structure, the technological nature of the tasks in which they were engaged, and those aspects of the social setting influencing their structure. I also wanted to be able to do all this rather quickly, since I was planning to use a large number of societies (I still did not know how many, or what kind of sample I would employ) and at the same time use uniform methods for all societies. Further, the data had to be compiled in such a way that they could be subsequently explored, not only for the purpose of discovering interrelationships among variables but also in many cases to discover what variables should be studied in the first place.

The cross-cultural researcher is fortunate in these regards, because a considerable part of this work has already been done for him, thanks to the Human Relations Area Files.[6] This facility represents an extremely ambitious effort to collect and classify all extant descriptive data relevant to social science on all known societies. Needless to say, this objective has not been reached and probably never will be; but fairly complete files exist at present on a surprisingly large number of societies, enough to make the files an indispensable research tool in any cross-cultural analysis involving a large number of societies. The societies in the files are classified in six major culture areas, with each such area subdivided into ten subareas. At the time of my work, the files contained too many gaps to enable them to be used directly in sampling. But, once a sample had been drawn on other grounds, I found that the files could be used wherever they were complete and that doing so saved unnumerable weeks of work.

The file on each society is divided into two parts. The first part consists of complete reproductions of all important source materials on the society in question, with a bibliography of materials not contained in the files. The second part consists of the same material classified in categories in such a way that material in the categories is comparable across societies—at least as comparable as possible, given the present state of ethnography and coding operations. It is thus apparent that the Human Relations Files can be of inestimable aid. To the extent that he can rely on the files, the researcher finds that the bibliographical work on each society has already been done and that the data have been collected and classified for him. All he needs is to go through the relevant categories in the files and run their contents against one another (whether verbally or statistically), and he will have a cross-cultural analysis.

Unfortunately, it is not that simple. The Human Relations Area Files are not like the *World Almanac*, despite the fact that one may be tempted to use them as such. One cannot just "look things up" in them, unless the categories relevant to his research happen to be the same as the categories used in the files. This is unlikely to be the case. I found that in order to use the files, I had to design a procedure for searching them and to do so in such a way as not to be bound in advance by the HRAF categories. This latter point was important for my purposes, as I was not yet sure what detailed categories I ultimately wanted to use.

I thus posed for myself the following problem. Assume I were to read an anthropological monograph on a particular society all the way through in detail and carefully retrieve any information from it dealing with work organization. What method of searching the files would result in my retrieving the same information with less time and effort? Accordingly, I procured from the library various ethnographic works on the Tikopia, Trobriand Islanders, Chukchee, and Crow. (I had no particular reason for choosing these societies, except that I wanted to include Firth, Malinowski, and

6. See George P. Murdock, C. S. Ford, *et al.*, *Outline of Cultural Materials* (New Haven, Conn.: Human Relations Area Files Press, 1950).

one older work—in this case, Bogoras on the Chukchee—and to take societies from roughly different parts of the world.)[7]

All the works I chose are also excerpted and classified in the Human Relations Area Files.

I then read these books carefully, recording all the production organizations reported in them and classifying the data on each such organization in the following broad categories: internal organization structure, technological characteristics of each production activity reported for each organization, other activities performed by the organization (including ritual and magic in connection with production), the system of rewards for work, and mutual influences between the organization and its setting. I then went to the Human Relations Area Files and tried various systematic search patterns to see if I could find one which would yield the same data with less time and effort. I did all this by trial and error, tempered with what I conceived to be a common-sense emphasis on those file categories which appeared obviously to be more relevant than others. As a result, I was able to devise a standard procedure which involved routinely searching the following categories:

22. Food Quest
23. Animal Husbandry
24. Agriculture
31. Exploitative Activities
32. Processing of Basic Materials
33. Building and Construction
342. Dwellings
62. Community
46. Labor
47. Business and Industrial Organization

Categories 22 through 342 represent those areas in which most of the organized work done in nonindustrial societies is carried on. Search of these categories therefore usually resulted in locating most of the production organizations and in finding any available information about their technological and internal structural characteristics. But the data contained in these categories proved only to allude in varying degree to the other matters on which I desired information. Such information, I found, could usually be obtained by searching Category 62 and "lining up" the information in it with the data previously obtained from the other categories. It was thus not ordinarily necessary to search all the institutional categories, since Category 62 proved to include most of the available information about interrelations of subgroups in the locality group. And due to the limited ambiences of nonindustrial peoples, this information was often sufficient. Where it was not, any other category that was clearly relevant in view of information obtained up to this point was consulted. The most frequently consulted ones were:

59. Kinship
60. Family
64. Government

These categories, however, were consulted only when clearly necessary.

Categories 46 and 47 were routinely searched as a check on the entire procedure, since in principle all production organizations are at least alluded to there. Any additional leads provided were followed up *ad hoc*. It had been my original intention to use these categories initially to locate production organizations and then follow them up as appropriate. But categories 46 and 47 proved to be too incomplete for such a procedure.[8]

In the four societies comprising my preliminary survey, I found that this search routine yielded the same information for my purposes as a complete reading of the monograph material and only consumed about 10 per cent as much time. I estimated that by this procedure I could "do" about four or five societies per day instead of one society every two days, assuming the societies in question to be included in the Human Relations Area Files.

## Sampling

I was now satisfied that a study of the kind I had in mind could be made and that it ought to proceed by exploring general relationships among a large number of cases. I had devised a broad conceptualization which, in view of my preliminary work, seemed to be a realistic and probably fruitful point of departure for an exploratory study. I had

7. Specifically, Raymond Firth, *We the Tikopia* (London: George Allen and Unwin, 1936); Bronislaw Malinowski, *Coral Gardens and Their Magic* (2 vols.; London: George Allen and Unwin, 1935); Waldemar Bogoras, *The Chukchee* (3 vols.; New York: G. E. Stechert, 1904, 1907, 1909); Robert H. Lowie, *The Crow Indians* (New York: Farrar and Rinehart, 1935).

8. Udy, *op. cit.*, pp. 4–9.

established the fact to my satisfaction that data could be collected and put into that conceptualization from existing ethnographic sources, and I had designed a routine for use with the Human Relations Area Files wherever use of the files proved possible. I could now confront the problem of collecting a sample of cases to compare.

Any research study of any type whatsoever which seeks to make generalizations beyond the material studied involves problems of sampling. It makes no difference what field the study is in, how many cases are analyzed, whether they are "in depth" or in general terms, whether the analysis is done with words or numbers, whether or not "statistical techniques" are employed, or whether or not the research is exploratory. In any of these instances, whenever the researcher proposes a generalization, he is implicitly identifying a larger population, of which his cases purport to be a representative sample, and contending that certain relationships observed in his sample could not have occurred there by chance. I say these things only because in some quarters impressions seem to exist to the contrary, particularly in connection with cross-cultural studies. It is simply not true that one can avoid sampling problems by proceeding in words instead of numbers or by avoiding the use of statistical techniques, though it is unfortunately true that by avoiding such methods one can often keep sampling problems from becoming explicit. To be sure, it is also unfortunate that the exploratory researcher is at something of a loss to be able to say definitively whether his relationships could or could not have occurred by chance. But this is not because he may be using numbers or statistical methods; it is because his research is exploratory, and he cannot solve this problem by being purposely vague about it and contending that because the research is exploratory, "anything goes."

Thus, it did not occur to me not to pay some attention to problems of representativeness, independence of cases, and randomization of choice where controls cannot be made. But it is admittedly frustrating to pay too much attention to such problems in a cross-cultural analysis, since one cannot really solve them. There is no reason, however, why one cannot endeavor to make the best of the situation and randomize sampling decisions whenever it is possible to do so. This is what I tried to do.

I had already decided to generalize to a population of all nonindustrial production organizations. Also, as explained earlier, I had decided to assume that production organizations in the same society are never independent events but that production organizations in different societies always are. These considerations suggested that I could draw a sample of nonindustrial societies and then draw one production organization from each society. The assumption that production organizations in the same society are not independent leads one into problems with larger societies which have discontinuous structures and hence, perhaps, afford the possibility of independent production organizations. But I could not devise any means of solving this problem which did not get me into other problems that seemed to be worse. Thus, I did not change this assumption, and as a result my sample was probably biased against production organizations in large societies.

The second assumption, that production organizations in different societies are always independent events, is probably one which, in retrospect, I would be inclined to change. If I were to do it over again, I think I would limit myself to a smaller number of cases drawn from different culture areas and thus be in a better position to argue their independence. My reason for not doing so initially was to maximize sample size for exploratory purposes, but in doing so I probably ran considerable risk of interaction.

It is obviously impossible to draw a random sample of all nonindustrial societies. One can, however, select a sample by design to represent the major culture areas of the world. On this basis, Murdock provides a guide for sample selection in cross-cultural research.[9] He divides the world's population into six basic ethnographic regions: Africa, Circum-Mediterranean, East Eurasia, the Insular Pacific, North America, and South America. He then subdivides each region into ten smaller areas which "insofar as possible" observe boundaries between recognized culture areas. Within each of these smaller areas, he lists from five to fifteen

9. George P. Murdock, "World Ethnographic Sample," *American Anthropologist*, LIX (1957), 664–87 (included in Frank W. Moore, ed., *Readings in Cross-Cultural Methodology* [New Haven: Human Relations Area Files Press, 1961], pp. 193–216).

societies, chosen so as to include those societies which (1) are the most populous, (2) are the best described, (3) exemplify each basic type of economy, (4) exemplify each linguistic stock or subfamily, (5) are relatively distinctive. He avoids selecting two societies from any area which are either geographically contiguous or characterized by mutually intelligible languages. The result is a list of 565 societies, more or less evenly distributed over the world.

Unquestionably, Murdock's selection, like everything else, is open to criticism. One might, for example, have preferred a grouping within regions which followed recognized culture areas more closely, rather than an insistence on dividing every region into ten parts. However, after tinkering for a while with various possible alternative procedures, I found that even when I thought I might have a better approach on purely technical grounds, I could not really evaluate it relative to Murdock's simply because I did not then, do not now, and am very unlikely ever to know as much about ethnography as he does. I thus decided to accept Murdock's sample as a base from which to work. For reasons already explained, I had decided to use the largest possible sample. But I could not use all 565 societies, because the particular material I desired was not available for all of them. In the interests of representativeness, however, I thought I had better end up with about the same number of societies in each of the six ethnographic regions and also space the societies in each region as evenly as possible over the ten areas. The size of my sample thus came to depend on the amount of data available for the most sparsely covered area.

At about this point, I joined the faculty of Yale University and met Prof. Murdock himself, who became extremely helpful. He advised me that material on South America was the most sparse, so I started there. I found that the largest minimum number of societies for which I could count on being able to get data consistently was two from each of the ten areas there. So I proceeded on this minimum basis, drawing two societies at random from those listed by Murdock under each area throughout his entire sample. I then looked at the ethnographic literature on each society to see whether the material I required was available. If it was not, I kept drawing at random until I found a society in the same area where it was. If I exhausted Murdock's list at any point, I substituted other societies from the same area, often making use of advice from Prof. Murdock, who was very helpful on this score, as in other ways. In only a very few instances was I unable to obtain data on at least two societies from the same region. The result was a sample of 120 societies.

The next step was to collect data on every production organization clearly reported in each of these societies. Using the Human Relations Area Files wherever possible, I did so, classifying the material according to the provisional scheme that I had decided on earlier, taking notes summarizing what the ethnographer said, and attempting no further coding at this stage. I took notes on all the organizations I could find because I thought my later explorations might require stratification of the sample in various ways which I could not at that time foresee exactly, and I wanted to make sure that I had enough material for such a purpose. At this point, I realized that as a minimum I wanted to be able to introduce gross variations in both technology and social setting, so I thought I had better check my sample to see if that was going to be possible. So I classified my organizations by type of technological process, using a traditional scheme of seven categories: tillage, hunting, fishing, collection, construction, animal husbandry, and manufacturing.

It turned out that I had relatively few construction and manufacturing organizations. I thus tried to add a few more societies offering information on construction and manufacturing (I succeeded with construction, but not with manufacturing), as well as some more societies which had centralized governments (another characteristic on which I thought I might wish to stratify). The net result was to throw the sample out of balance regionally, so I drew a few more societies at random in other regions to equalize the distribution as much as possible. Quite arbitrarily, I did not allow more than four societies to be included from any single area. The result was a final sample of 150 societies, from each of which I drew one production organization at random, except that I stratified the sample to yield approximately equal numbers of cases of each technological type. I felt that this sample would enable me to explore variations adequately in both technology and social setting, that in drawing it I had randomized my procedure as much as possible in the circumstances, and that where such was impossible I had tried to make my selection criteria explicit.

## Exploration, processing, and analysis

I now had a sample of 150 production organizations from 150 nonindustrial societies, for which I had assembled descriptions classified according to the provisional five-way breakdown already described. I now asked myself what the ultimate results would look like and how they would be presented, and I decided on something akin to Murdock's *Social Structure*. This implied systematic subclassification of my major categories such that I could count the frequencies in each category and cross-tabulate to show the various specific aspects of the relationships described by my original working hypothesis plus the further working hypothesis about reward systems. I thus faced the following steps: (1) exploring my existing data plus any relevant theoretical literature to suggest classification schemes and hypotheses; (2) analyzing and recoding all my data in terms of the resulting scheme; and (3) mechanically tabulating it. I decided not to "run everything against everything else" but to limit my runs to hypotheses either generated from the theoretical literature or previous studies or deduced from other hypotheses whose validity in my own sample had already been demonstrated. This did not make my procedure especially simon-pure, however, since the process of exploration automatically excluded inapplicable theoretical perspectives. The entire design of the study did not permit me to propose hypotheses and then accept or reject them on the basis of statistical tests; it simply permitted me to describe what I found.

Conceptually speaking, the final taxonomy involved seven concrete types of technological process crosscut by four aspects of any technological process; four concrete types of production organization crosscut by five aspects of organization structure, with each such aspect possessing anywhere from two to five subdimensions; at least three major relevant institutional areas in the social setting with each organizational type related to one or more of these three areas in up to seven different ways; and four kinds of reward systems. Ultimately, all these items were related to one another by sixty-four propositions, sixty-one of which described cross tabulations, one of which was an "existence theorem," and two of which were true by definition but did not seem obvious unless explicitly stated. It may seem a bit ridiculous to say that I frankly have trouble describing exactly how, by combining an exploration of my data with a study of the theoretical literature, I reached this elaborate conceptualization. But, however absurd that statement may seem, it is so, despite the fact that this process received my full-time attention for about seven months. I can, however, indicate in a general way what my approach was and describe some specific experiences I had in the course of the analysis.

Basically, it seems to me that there are three different ways by which one can arrive at relevant typologies from a mass of relatively undifferentiated verbal descriptive data and a virtually endless procession of theoretical works, all of varying relevance to one's problem. First, one can ransack the theoretical literature and try out all the existing typologies that one finds there. Graduate students, in particular, often seem to have a tendency to do this, and it is all right, as far as it goes. The trouble is that usually one's own research problem is not exactly like the problem discussed in the source one is using. At one point or another, the researcher will have to stop fishing and start cutting bait.

A second approach, particularly suited to "cutting bait" and starting from one's own data, has been termed "analytic induction."[10] Essentially, analytic induction is a piecemeal approach whereby one selects any two units that he is comparing and, on a purely descriptive level, makes all the general statements he can which apply to both units. He then takes a third unit and similarly compares it with the previous general statements, iterating this procedure until he finds a stable set of general statements, from which he then extracts a typology. Such an exploratory procedure can be extremely helpful, but it, too, suffers from various defects. First, unless the researcher is extremely cautious, he is quite likely to find himself straying from his original working hypotheses, since he is obliged to move "wherever the data take him." Second, analytic induction focuses on characteristics which

10. Florian Znaniecki, *The Method of Sociology* (New York: Farrar and Rinehart, 1934), pp. 235–331. Also see Donald R. Cressey, *Other People's Money* (New York: The Free Press, 1953), pp. 16–17.

are present rather than those which are absent and thus tends to yield a list of concrete attributes which everything has in common rather than a set of universally applicable variables or analytical categories. And finally, in a related vein, analytic induction says nothing about the process of generalization itself; it implies that one begins with a *tabula rasa*, which is impossible.[11] At best, analytic induction simply describes a way of going through one's material in conjunction with other methods.

The third type of exploratory procedure may seem to be a peculiar one to mention, but it is nevertheless an important one. That procedure is simply to sit and think about it. Before doing so, one should digest as much of his descriptive data as possible. Sometimes it is also a good idea to bear in mind a great deal of theoretical literature while doing so, because under those conditions one can usually better describe later where his ideas, if any, ultimately came from. At the risk of appearing either brutally frank or ridiculous, however, I must say that there were times in this study when I found it desirable to try to forget everything I knew about sociology and simply to ask myself how "any reasonable man" would go about attacking the problem. A case in point is the typology of reward systems which I employed. After repeated unsuccessful attempts to make any sense of the material in a way pertinent to my working hypotheses, I finally tried the following "common-sense" assumptions: (1) nobody will work unless he (*a*) is paid for it, (*b*) is forced to, or (*c*) feels very strongly that he ought to; (2) people who swap things around among themselves feel closer to one another than people who do not.

The first assumption suggested some hypotheses about relationships between the ways in which people are recruited for work and the strength of the reward system. The second assumption suggested in a vague way that the strength of the reward system might be estimated by variations in patterns of exchange of raw materials, produce, and the rewards themselves within the organization. It turned out that Max Weber discusses an analogous problem in connection with taxation, differentiating movements of goods and payments up and down the status hierarchy. I tried applying the same thing to production organizations, and it turned out, indeed, to provide at least a rough way of measuring the relative strength of different arrangements, although the over-all results were very crude.[12]

As one may infer from this example, I found it desirable to use a combination of the three exploratory methods described. I would usually start with one or the other in particular and then shift methods after I had carried the first one as far as I was able. After reaching a provisional classification via one method, I would then try retrospectively to see if I could also reach it starting with the two ways I did not use initially. This usually resulted in some revisions. Then, if I had not already done so, I would search the theoretical literature to see if I could, from that, justify what I was doing and also to find hypotheses about connections with other schemes in other relevant parts of the study.

In the case of technological processes, I used a standard concrete scheme directly from the anthropological literature (tillage, hunting, fishing, etc.), since it seemed that such a scheme involved types with widely different task problems. The next question was: along what principal, organizationally relevant dimensions do these types vary? At this point, I resorted to analytic induction to describe the major attributes of each of the seven types of processes. At the same time, I found a standard typology of division of labor used by many European economic historians of the early twentieth century and discovered that with some modifications in both I could generate that typology from a standard set of process dimensions derived from the contemporary industrial-engineering literature. I then—again with some mutual modifications—combined the result with the results of my earlier inductive analysis of my own data. This yielded four categories—work load, complexity, outlay, and uncertainty; indicated some subdimensions of complexity; and suggested some ways of measuring them in standard engineering terms.[13]

How did I know that this classification would be

11. See Marion J. Levy, "Some Basic Methodological Difficulties in Social Science," *Philosophy of Science*, XVII (1950), 294.

12. Udy, *op. cit.*, pp. 97–116; Max Weber, *General Economic History*, trans. by F. H. Knight (New York: The Free Press, 1950), pp. 95–336.

13. Udy, *op. cit.*, pp. 10–35; Carl Bücher, *Industrial Evolution*, trans. S. M. Wickett (New York: Henry Holt, 1912), pp. 83–149; Max Weber, *The Theory of Social and Economic Organization*, trans. A. M. Henderson and T. Parsons (New York: Oxford University Press, 1947), pp. 225–26; William G. Ireson and E. L. Grant, eds.,

better than some other scheme, that is, that I could predict more about organization structure by using it than some alternative taxonomy? I did not. One never does, for in principle there exists an infinite number of ways of classifying anything. However, I did know that two of its sources—the economic-historical and industrial-engineering schemes—had been found by other researchers to be related to organization structure, and by "working back" to these sources from my own I found that I could arrive at some hypotheses—as, for example, how complexity might be related to authority structure—which could be "translated" into my own framework and which also suggested some leads about relevant organizational categories. It also appeared to me that an argument could be made to the effect that the four categories which I had reached were special cases of Parsons' four functional problems of any social system, in that they seemed to represent four different ways in which technology posed adaptive problems for administrative structure (work load could be assigned to the goal-attainment cell, complexity to the integration cell, uncertainty to the latency cell, and outlay to the adaptation cell).[14] I simply took this possibility as evidence that these categories might be peculiarly relevant to administrative structure and made no further effort to carry out its implications systematically at that time.

The five aspects of organization structure—division of labor, authority, solidarity, proprietorship, and recruitment—were devised largely by starting with Levy's *Structure of Society* and sitting and thinking about how its contents might be applied to organization structure. Whatever one may think of the "functionalist" posture assumed by Levy, it does provide an orientation which I found quite useful from a practical standpoint in thinking up taxonomies. I would contend that once one has devised a taxonomy by this means, it must be justified on other grounds, but that does not alter the usefulness of "structural-functional requisite analysis" as an exploratory tool. While doing this, I also studied the industrial sociological literature and other theoretical writers, trying to "plug" any organization variables I could find into my nascent taxonomy and checking my data to see if I had enough information about them to use them. During this phase of the work, I "theorized" in the aforementioned fashion during the afternoon, read my data and checked it against the afternoon's results during the evening, slept on the outcome, and tried proposing hypotheses in the morning. I found it necessary purposefully to plan my time in this way to avoid being carried away by theory or getting bogged down in data.

As one may imagine, the ultimate result was wildly eclectic and contained some strange theoretical pedigrees. My dimensions of authority were for the most part straight from orthodox organization theory, whereas my five forms of recruitment represented the results of thinking about a combination roughly consisting of various works of Sir Henry Maine, Melvin Tumin, R. M. MacIver, Wilbert Moore, Melville J. Herskovits, and Richard Thurnwald in the afternoon, combined with analytic induction from my own data during the evening, plus efforts to see whether it worked the next morning.[15]

The "permanent versus temporary" aspect of solidarity I conceived to be obvious and a result of common sense, but my failure immediately to think of the equally obvious common-sense distinction between organizations which are autonomous as opposed to those which add and then drop auxiliary members from time to time resulted in a work standstill for about two months. I needed a typology of organizations based on recruitment to use as a bridge to considering influences of the social setting, but I simply could not seem to get my organizations to fit into any set of recruitment categories very well. The trouble was that in many cases different parts of the organization seemed to recruit in different ways. Finally, an almost chance passage from Weber's *Theory of Social and Economic Organization* suggested what was retrospectively obvious: divide the organizations into those with

*Handbook of Industrial Engineering and Management* (Englewood Cliffs, N.J.: Prentice-Hall, 1955), pp. 291–292.

14. Talcott Parsons and Neil J. Smelser, *Economy and Society* (New York: The Free Press, 1956), p. 199.

15. Sir Henry Maine, *Lectures on the Early History of Institutions* (New York: Henry Holt, 1889); Melvin M. Tumin, *Caste in a Peasant Society* (Princeton, N.J.: Princeton University Press, 1952); R. M. MacIver and Charles H. Page, *Society* (New York: Rinehart, 1949); W. E. Moore, *op. cit.*; Melville J. Herskovits, *Economic Anthropology* (New York: Alfred A. Knopf, 1952); Richard Thurnwald, *Economics in Primitive Communities* (Oxford, Eng.: Oxford University Press, 1932).

and without auxiliary members and classify the way the basic core of membership is recruited, separately from the mode of recruitment of auxiliary members.[16]

This procedure enabled me to move via recruitment into the realm of the social setting, with innumerable bouts like the ones I have described. I think there is no point in going into further details, except to note that I have said very little here about how I described hypotheses. This process is, I think, adequately described in the book itself, so I shall not treat it here.

This entire taxonomy-building process thus eventually resulted in a set of detailed categories—and even with a few honest-to-goodness variables, such as technological complexity. And inasmuch as analytic induction had been a part of the procedure at all points, all my categories were operational relative to my data, though, as we shall see presently, gaps in information existed in quite a few particular instances. Having completed the exploration, I could now formalize my procedure by coding my cases, counting frequencies, and cross-tabulating.

The coding operation proved to be very tedious "dog work," in the worst sense of the term. I had to do it all myself, and herein lies a basic defect of the study. Clearly, it would have been advisable to have other people do some coding so as to be able to check reliability. But this was impossible at the time. I also found that although I could code a great deal of the material from the notes I had taken—particularly where very general distinctions were involved—very frequently I had to have recourse to the original source materials. This took a great deal of time and was not very interesting, since I had been through all the material before and was now attempting to resist, rather than encourage, flights of imagination. I was also forced to make some decisions which were intellectually rather unsatisfying.

First, I had to assume that the ethnographer was always right. Researchers who use secondary sources are always open to the charge that they are cavalier and uncritical in their use of source materials, and cross-cultural analysis—particularly where large numbers of societies are used with information taken out of context—is particularly vulnerable to such criticism. I felt, however, that I had to face the fact that I did not know enough to be able to assess the validity of factual reporting by any ethnographer and that therefore I had to believe what he said if I were going to make this study. To decide otherwise would be to contend that ethnographers are inclined to be knaves or fools and that anthropology as a general discipline is hence useless. Needless to say, I cannot accept such a position.

Secondly, I had to accept the fact that there were gaps in the data about which I could do nothing. I would, for example, have liked to know more about the ideology of work and about prestige as a possible reward for labor. But I could not include them in my study. Also, I found that I could not use the entire sample of 150 for all my variables, for the same reason. Lastly, I had to decide how to handle situations where I wanted to classify something as being either present or absent under conditions where the ethnographer simply said nothing about it. Did this mean that the characteristic in question was really absent, or did it mean that the ethnographer had simply not investigated the matter? This is clearly a tricky question to decide, and I adopted the following convention. In cases of this sort, where my source was as a whole rather sketchy, I reported "don't know." This caused a great many South American societies to drop out of the analysis at various points, but there was nothing that I could do about them. In cases where two or more thorough and detailed sources were available, with neither reporting the characteristic in question, I reported the characteristic as "absent." Where only one source was available but was detailed and thorough, I read it carefully to see whether the ethnographer had discussed other closely related matters. If he had, I reported the unmentioned characteristic as "absent"; if not, I reported "don't know."[17]

The actual process of coding may be illustrated by the following example.

The *total complexity* of any process is defined as the number of *tasks* plus the maximum number of *specialized operations* ever present in any one task plus one or zero, depending on whether *combined effort* is ever present at any time in the process, or always absent, respectively. A *task* comprises all work

16. Weber, *The Theory of Social and Economic Organization, op. cit.*, p. 148.

17. Swanson, with more resources available, followed a superior procedure. See Guy E. Swanson, *The Birth of the Gods* (Ann Arbor: The University of Michigan Press, 1960), pp. 37–54.

performed during one period of organization assembly; an *operation* is any physical action which leaves raw material in such a condition that it can remain untended without further changes taking place during the time required by the task at hand; operations carried on simultaneously are *specialized*; *combined effort* is present whenever several persons work in unison according to some established rhythm. The coding problem is thus to discover the total complexity of any process ethnographically described, using these definitions. "Wet" ricefield cultivation among the Betsileo of Madagascar provides a good example.

*Tasks*. First, rice seed is planted and tended in a nursery. This appears to be a rather simple activity, and is carried out by the women of a residential family group. It is not clear whether one or two clearly differentiated tasks are involved (i.e., the extent to which planting shades over into tending). I coded this as a single task, as the differentiation over time did not appear to be clear. It is also not entirely clear whether there is any specialization or not in this task. I judged that there was not, on the ground that specialization seemed to be discussed in some detail elsewhere in the monograph. In any case, it seemed probable that there is less specialization in this task than in subsequent ones; if such is the case we do not need to know exactly how much occurs at this point for purposes of index construction.

Second, the ricefield proper is prepared and the rice shoots are transplanted from the nursery into the ricefield. This is done over a period of one very long day at maximum effort, with considerable specialization, as will be shown presently. This task involves getting an even flow of water into the field and controlling it by dikes; getting lumps out of mud in the field; removing plants from the nursery; transplanting them to the main field, and planting them.

Third (there may be some intervening tasks involving care of the crop), the rice is harvested. This too is done at maximum effort with considerable specialization, but not so much as is the case with preparation and planting.

Conservatively, I thus reported three tasks.

*Specialization of Operations*. The greatest degree of specialization appears to occur in the second task, that of preparing the ricefield, and transplanting shoots from the nursery into the ricefield. Five different operations are performed at once. The young men start across the field, driving cattle around in the mud to reduce the soil to an even consistency. Following immediately behind them are the middle-aged men with hoes who level the field and even it up. During this time the old women are digging up the plants from the nursery for transplanting and are transporting them to the younger women in the field. And the old men are repairing the dikes and regulating the water level around the side of the field. I thus reported five specialized operations.

*Combined Effort*. Combined effort clearly occurs in the third task, where the men manifestly reap in rhythm.

*Total Complexity* is thus coded as nine.[18]

The last step—apart from the actual writing—was the analysis of data. Since I had reached my "hypotheses" by a combination of verbal reasoning and ex post facto induction, the appropriate method in most cases appeared to me to be to array frequencies in fourfold tables, with controls as appropriate. This I did, proceeding from one hypothesis to another through a verbal chain of reasoning. I am now inclined to think that a more sophisticated approach might have been preferable. However, the nature of the study was such that this phase actually constituted a description rather than an analysis, properly so called. It seemed to me that any statistical devices used should be confined to those which were as close as possible to the verbal reasoning process which I actually employed. I did, however, at this point decide to present statistical tests, since it seemed to me that they accurately described the way in which I had actually been thinking about the material.[19] When anyone asserts that two things are related, he is implicitly saying that he has somehow been led to believe that the association which he has observed between them did not occur by chance. In other words, he is implicity comparing this association with a random model, regardless of whether he is using numbers or words. I took advantage of the fact that I had tabulated numerical frequencies, which fact enabled me to report explicitly what I had been doing.[20]

Such is the story of one cross-cultural analysis, which was subsequently written up and published.

18. H. M. Dubois, S. J. *Monographie des Betsileo* (Paris: Institut d'Ethnologie, 1938), pp. 434–40.

19. Andre J. Köbben, "New Ways of Presenting an Old Idea: The Statistical Method in Social Anthropology," *Journal of the Royal Anthropological Institute*, LXXXII (1952), 129–46 (included in F. W. Moore, *op. cit.*, pp. 175–92). I would agree with Köbben that there is nothing distinctive about "statistical methods." But it is important to recognize that there is nothing distinctive about other methods, either. Neither are the problems which he describes the result of using statistical methods nor can they be avoided by avoiding statistical methods. The advantages of statistical methods are twofold: (1) they tend to make problems visible which might otherwise be obscured by verbal discussion; (2) they make it easier to manipulate large amounts of data systematically.

20. For a critical discussion, see Harold E. Driver, "Introduction to Statistics for Comparative Research," in F. W. Moore, *op. cit.*, pp. 303–29.

If I were to do it again, there are many things that I would undoubtedly do differently. I have indicated some of these during the course of the discussion. I have, however, tried to describe as accurately as possible exactly what I did, even to the point of appearing rather farfetched at times and at the risk of sometimes providing a description of what not to do. I feel that there is much to be gained from cross-cultural research and that efforts to perfect its methodology are therefore well spent. I think I learned quite a bit from doing this study. I also enjoyed it.

# Part Four

# Selected Substantive Problems

As in every field of study, there is literally no end to a list of problems organization researchers define as of theoretical and empirical interest. Our selection of problems, however, is not entirely arbitrary. Some problems are more important than others at particular stages in the development of a discipline or subdiscipline. We used two major criteria for selecting the six problems to follow:

1. Generalizability of the problem. Does the problem present implications for the behavior of all organizations?

2. Personal interest and knowledge. Were we familiar with the main thrust of research in the area? The degree of specialization in the field of organizations is already so great that an intimate familiarity with research developments in particular subfields was essential.

The reader will observe also that the problems selected tend to shift from concern with structure to social process. In addition, a strong emphasis on recent studies prevails.

# Organizational Goals

The single feature of an organization that distinguishes this unit of study most clearly from other types of social systems is the centrality of a goal or set of goals around which the basic activities of the system are organized. The present section is designed to focus on some of the major theoretical and practical implications that flow from the "goal-orientedness" of organizations.

Etzioni compares the goal model, which confuses ideal with achievable objectives, with the system model, which takes a more appropriate conceptual base for analyzing organizational effectiveness. Next, he compares two different types of system models, one termed the "survival" and the other the "effectiveness" approach. A number of key assumptions attached to earlier evaluations of organizational goals are exposed. The intrinsic effects of the values associated with the theorists' point of view are revealed.

The second selection raises a crucial problem for all organizations: In what ways do organizations resist changes in their original objectives? Sills points to five theoretical sources of goal displacement and then systematically applies his framework to an examination of an unusually successful voluntary health organization, the National Foundation for Infantile Paralysis (now called the National Foundation).

The extraordinary success of the National Foundation provides a striking contrast to the clear failure of the Freie Gemeinde, a small-town Wisconsin free-thought organization studied by Demerath and Thiessen. This study, which smoothly integrates historical and contemporary data, emphasizes the role of the community environment in the process of reformulation of an organization's objectives.

Since all organizations must interact with their social environment, one may locate the sources of change mainly within the organization itself or in its relationships with other organizations, the community, or the wider society. The final selection by Blau returns to a primary concern with internal bureaucratic structure and its implications for goal change. The author provides an important corrective to the stereotypical view of bureaucracy as uniformly inhibiting adaptive social processes in organizations. The government agency studied revealed not only sources of opposition to the introduction of new policies and procedures, but, at the same time, a number of underlying bases of support for innovations in key areas. Hence, even highly bureaucratized organizations will not encounter stiff resistance to projected goal changes if such changes promise sufficient rewards for its members.

AMITAI ETZIONI

# Two Approaches to Organizational Analysis: A Critique and a Suggestion

Organizational goals serve many functions. They give organizational activity its orientation by depicting the state of affairs which the organization attempts to realize. They serve as sources of legitimation which justify the organization's activities and its very existence, at least in the eyes of some participants and in those of the general public or subpublics. They serve as a source for standards by which actors assess the success of their organization. Finally, they serve as an important starting point for students of organizations who, like some of the actors they observe, use the organizational goals as a yardstick with which to measure the organization's performance. This paper is devoted to a critique of this widespread practice and to a suggestion of an alternative approach.

## Goal model

The literature on organizations is rich in studies in which the criterion for the assessment of effectiveness is derived from organizational goals. We shall refer to this approach as the goal model. The model is considered an objective and reliable analytical tool because it omits the values of the explorer and applies the values of the subject under study as the criteria of judgment. We suggest, however, that this model has some methodological shortcomings and is not as objective as it seems to be.

One of the major shortcomings of the goal model is that it frequently makes the studies' findings stereotyped as well as dependent on the model's assumptions. Many of these studies show (a) that the organization does not realize its goals effectively, and/or (b) that the organization has different goals from those it claims to have. Both points have been made for political parties,[1] trade unions,[2] voluntary associations,[3] schools,[4] mental hospitals,[5] and other organizations. It is not suggested that these statements are not valid, but it seems they have little empirical value if they can be deduced from the way the study is approached.[6]

Goals, as norms, as sets of meanings depicting

I am indebted to William Delany, William J. Goode, Terence K. Hopkins, and Renate Mayntz for criticisms of an earlier version of this paper.

Reprinted from *Administrative Science Quarterly*, September, 1960, pp. 257–78, by permission of the author and publisher. 

1. Robert Michels, *Political Parties* (New York, 1949); Moise Ostrogorski, *Democracy and the Organization of Political Parties* (New York, 1902).

2. Michels, *op. cit.*; William Z. Foster, *Misleaders of Labor* (Chicago, 1927); Sylvia Kopald, *Rebellion in Labor Unions* (New York, 1924).

3. John R. Seeley *et al.*, *Community Chest* (Toronto, 1957).

4. A nonscientific discussion of this issue in a vocational school is included in E. Hunter's novel, *Blackboard Jungle* (New York, 1956).

5. Ivan Belknap, *Human Problems of a State Mental Hospital* (New York, 1956), esp. p. 67.

6. While such studies have little empirical value, they may have some practical value. Many of the evaluation studies have such a focus.

target states, are cultural entities. Organizations, as systems of coordinated activities of more than one actor, are social systems.

There is a general tendency for cultural systems to be more consistent than social systems.[7] There are mainly two reasons for this. First of all, cultural images, to be realized, require investment of means. Since the means needed are always larger than the means available, social units are always less perfect than their cultural anticipations. A comparison of actual Utopian settlements with descriptions of such settlements in the books by the leaders of Utopian movements is a clear, although a somewhat disheartening, illustration of this point.[8]

The second reason for the invariant discrepancy between goals and social units, which is of special relevance to our discussion, is that all social units, including organizations, are multifunctional units. Therefore, while devoting part of their means directly to goal activities, social units have to devote another part to other functions, such as the creation or recruitment of further means to the goal and the maintenance of units performing goal activities and service activities.

Looking at the same problem from a somewhat different viewpoint, one sees that the mistake committed is comparing objects that are not on the same level of analysis as, for example, when the present state of an organization (a real state) is compared with a goal (an ideal state) as if the goal were also a real state. Some studies of informal organizations commit a similar mistake when they compare the blueprint of an organization with actual organizational practice and suggest that an organizational *change* has taken place. The organization has "developed" an informal structure. Actually, the blueprint organization never existed as a social fact. What is actually compared is a set of symbols on paper with a functioning social unit.[9]

Measured against the Olympic heights of the goal, most organizations score the same—very low effectiveness. The differences in effectiveness among organizations are of little significance. One who expects a light bulb to turn most of its electrical power into light would not be very interested in the differences between a bulb that utilizes 4.5 per cent of the power as compared with one that utilizes 5.5 per cent. Both are extremely ineffective. A more realistic observer would compare the two bulbs with each other and find one of them relatively good. The same holds for organizational studies that compare actual states of organization to each other, as when the organizational output is measured at different points in time. Some organizations are found gradually to increase their effectiveness by improving their structure and their relations with the environment. In other organizations effectiveness is slowly or rapidly declining. Still others are highly effective at the initial period, when commitments to goals are strong, and less effective when the commitment level declines to what is "normal" for this organization. These few examples suffice to show that the goal model may not supply the best possible frame of reference for effectiveness. It compares the ideal with the real, as a result of which most levels of performance look alike—quite low.[10] Michels, for example, who applied a goal model, did not see any significant differences among the trade unions and parties he examined. All were falling considerably short of their goals.

When a goal model is applied, the same basic mistake is committed, whether the goals an organization claims to pursue (public goals) or the goals it actually follows (private goals) are chosen as a yardstick for evaluation of performance. In both cases cultural entities are compared with social systems as if they were two social systems. Thus the basic methodological error is the same. Still, when the public goals are chosen, as is often done, the bias introduced into the study is even greater.[11] Public goals fail to be realized not because of poor planning, unanticipated consequences, or hostile environment. *They are not meant to be realized.* If an organization were to invest means in public goals to such an

7. Talcott Parsons, *The Social System* (New York, 1951).

8. See Martin Buber, *Paths in Utopia* (Boston, 1958).

9. Actually, of course, in order for a blueprint to exist, a group of actors—often a future elite of the organization—had to draw up the blueprint. This future elite presumably itself had "informal relations," and the nature of these relations undoubtedly affected the content of the blueprint as well as the way the organization was staffed and so forth.

10. Paul M. Harrison, *Authority and Power in the Free Church Tradition* (Princeton, 1959), p. 6. Harrison avoids this pitfall by comparing the policy of the church he studied (The American Baptist Convention) at different periods, taking into account, but not using as a measuring rod, its belief system and goals.

11. Some researchers take the public goals to be the real goals of the organization. Others choose them because they are easier to determine.

extent that it served them effectively, their function, that is, improving the input-output balance, would be greatly diminished, and the organization would discard them.[12] In short, public goals, as criteria, are even more misleading than private ones.

## System model

An alternative model that can be employed for organizational analysis is the system model.[13] The starting point for this approach is not the goal itself but a *working model of a social unit which is capable of achieving a goal.* Unlike a goal, or a set of goal activities, it is a model of a multifunctional unit.[14] It is assumed *a priori* that some means have to be devoted to such nongoal functions as service and custodial activities, including means employed for the maintenance of the unit itself. From the viewpoint of the system model, such activities are functional and increase the organizational effectiveness. It follows that a social unit that devotes all its efforts to fulfilling one functional requirement, even if it is that of performing goal activities, will undermine the fulfillment of this very functional requirement, because recruitment of means,[15] maintenance of tools, and the social integration of the unit will be neglected.[16]

A measure of effectiveness establishes the degree to which an organization realizes its goals under a given set of conditions. But the central question in the study of effectiveness is not, "How devoted is the organization to its goal?" but rather, "Under the given conditions, *how close does the organizational allocation of resources*[17] *approach an optimum distribution?*" "Optimum" is the key word: what counts is a balanced distribution of resources among the various organizational needs, not maximal satisfaction of any one activity, even of goal activities. We shall illustrate this point by examining two cases; each is rather typical for a group of organizational studies.

### CASE I: FUNCTION OF CUSTODIAL ACTIVITIES

One function each social unit must fulfill is adjusting to its environment. Parsons refers to this as the "adaptive phase" and Homans calls the activities oriented to the fulfillment of this function "the external system." This should not be confused with the environment itself. An organization often attempts to change some limited parts of its environment, but this does not mean that adjustment to the environment in general becomes unnecessary. The changes an organization attempts to introduce are usually specific and limited.[18] This means that, with

12. Public goals improve the input-output balance by recruiting support (inputs) to the organization from groups which would not support the private goals. This improves the balance as long as this increase in input does not require more than limited changes in output (some front activities). An extreme but revealing example is supplied in Philip Selznick's analysis of the goals of the Communist party. He shows that while the private goal is to gain power and control, there are various layers of public goals presented to the rank and file, sympathizers, and the "masses" (*The Organizational Weapon* [New York, 1952], pp. 83–84).

13. Compare with a discussion of the relations between a model approach and a system approach in Paul Meadows, "Models, Systems and Science," *American Sociological Review*, 22 (1957), 3–9.

14. For an outline of a system model for the analysis of organizations see Talcott Parsons, "A Sociological Approach to the Theory of Organizations," *Administrative Science Quarterly*, 1 (1956), 63–85, 225–39.

15. The use of concepts such as goals, means, and conditions does not imply the use of a goal model as defined in the text. These concepts are used as defined on the more abstract level of the action scheme. On this scheme see Talcott Parsons, *The Structure of Social Action* (New York, 1937).

16. Gouldner distinguished between a rational model and a natural-system model of organizational analysis. The rational model (Weber's bureaucracy) is a partial model since it does not cover all the basic functional requirements of the organization as a social system—a major shortcoming, which was pointed out by Robert K. Merton in his "Bureaucratic Structure and Personality," *Social Theory and Social Structure* (rev. ed.; New York, 1957), pp. 195–206. It differs from the goal model by the type of functions that are included as against those that are neglected. The rational model is concerned almost solely with means activities, while the goal model focuses attention on goal activities. The natural system model has some similarities to our system model, since it studies the organization as a whole and sees in goal realization just one organizational function. It differs from ours in two ways. First, the natural system is an observable, hence "natural" entity, while ours is a functional model, hence a construct. Second, the natural system model makes several assumptions that ours avoids, as, for example, viewing organizational structure as "spontaneously and homeostatically maintained," etc. See Alvin W. Gouldner, "Organizational Analysis," in Robert K. Merton, Leonard Broom, and Leonard S. Cottrell, Jr., eds., *Sociology Today* (New York, 1959), pp. 401 ff.

17. "Resources" is used here in the widest sense of the term including, for example, time and administration as well as the more ordinary resources.

18. One way in which organizations can change their environment, which is often overlooked, is by ecological

the exception of the elements to be changed, the organization accepts the environment as it is and orients its activities accordingly. Moreover, the organization's orientation to the elements it tries to change is also highly influenced by their existing nature. In short, a study of effectiveness has to include an analysis of the environmental conditions and of the organization's orientation to them.

With this point in mind let us examine the basic assumptions of a large number of studies of mental hospitals and prisons conducted in recent years on the subject "from custodial to therapeutic care" (or, from coercion to rehabilitation). Two points are repeated in many of these studies: (1) The *goals* of mental hospitals, correctional institutions, and prisons are therapeutic. "The basic function of the hospital for the mentally ill is the same as the basic function of general hospitals . . . that function is the utilization of every form of treatment available for restoring the patients to health."[19] (2) Despite large efforts to transform these organizations from custodial to therapeutic institutions, little change has taken place. Custodial patterns of behavior still dominate policy decisions and actions in most of these organizations. "In the very act of trying to operate these institutions their *raison d'être* has often been neglected or forgotten."[20] Robert Vinter and Morris Janowitz stated explicitly:

> Custody and care of delinquent youth continue to be the goals of correctional agencies, but there are growing aspirations for remedial treatment. The public expects juvenile correctional institutions to serve a strategic role in changing the behavior of delinquents. Contrary to expectations, persistent problems have been encountered in attempting to move correctional institutions beyond mere custodialism. . . . Despite strenuous efforts and real innovations, significant advances beyond custody have not been achieved.[21]

The first question the studies raise is: What are the actual organizational goals? The public may change its expectations without necessarily imposing a change on the organization's goals, or it may affect only the public goals. As Vinter and Janowitz suggest, much of the analysis of these organizations actually shows that they are oriented mainly to custodial goals, and with respect to these goals they are effective.[22]

But let us assume that through the introduction of mental health perspectives and personnel—psychiatrists, psychologists, social workers—the organization's goal, as an ideal self-image, changed and became oriented to therapy. We still would expect Vinter and Janowitz's observation to be valid. Most prisons, correctional institutions, and mental hospitals would not be very effective in serving therapy goals. Two sets of reasons support this statement. The first set consists of internal factors, such as the small number of professionals available as compared to the large number of inmates, the low effectiveness of the present techniques of therapy, the limitations of knowledge, and so on. These internal factors will not be discussed here, since the purpose of this section is to focus on the second set, that of external factors, which also hinder if not block organizational change.

Organizations have to adapt to the environment in which they function. When the relative power of the various elements in the environments are carefully examined, it becomes clear that, in general, the sub-publics (e.g., professionals, universities, well-educated people, some health authorities) which support therapeutic goals are less powerful than those which support the custodial or segregating activities of these organizations. Under such conditions, most mental hospitals and prisons must be more or less custodial. There is evidence to show, for example, that a local community, which is both an important segment of the organizational environment and which in most cases is custodial-minded,

mobility, e.g., the textile industry moving to the less unionized South. But this avenue is open to relatively few organizations.

19. Quoted from M. Greenblatt, R. H. York, and E. L. Brown, *From Custodial to Therapeutic Patient Care in Mental Hospitals* (New York, 1955), p. 3; see also H. L. Smith and D. J. Levinson, "The Major Aims and Organizational Characteristics of Mental Hospitals," in M. Greenblatt, D. J. Levinson, and R. H. Williams, eds., *The Patient and the Mental Hospital* (New York, 1957), pp. 3–8.

20. Greenblatt, York, and Brown, *op. cit.*, p. 3.

21. Effective Institutions for Juvenile Delinquents: A Research Statement," *Social Service Review*, 33 (1959), 118.

22. R. H. McCleery, who studied a prison's change from a custodial to a partially "therapeutic" institution, pointed to the high degree of order and the low rate of escapes and riots in the custodial stage. See his *Policy Change in Prison Management* (East Lansing, 1957). See also Donald R. Cressey, "Contradictory Directives in Complex Organizations: The Case of the Prison," *Administrative Science Quarterly*, 4 (1959), 1–19; and "Achievement of an Unstated Organizational Goal: An Observation on Prisons," *Pacific Sociological Review*, 1 (Fall, 1958), 43–49.

can make an organization maintain its bars, fences, and guards or be closed.

> The [prison] camp has overlooked relations with the community. For the sake of the whole program you've got to be custodially minded. . . . The community feeling is a problem. There's been a lot of antagonism. . . . Newspapers will come out and advocate that we close the camp and put a fence around it.[23]

An attempt to change the attitudes of a community to mental illness is reported by Elaine and John Cumming. The degree to which it succeeded is is discussed by J. A. Clausen in his foreword to the study. "The Cummings chose a relatively proximate goal: to ascertain whether the community educational program would diminish people's feelings of distance and estrangement from former mental patients and would increase their feelings of social responsibility for problems of mental illness." They found that their program did not achieve these goals.[24] It should be noted that the program attempted by education to change relatively abstract attitudes toward *former* mental patients and to mental illness in general. When the rumor spread that the study was an attempt to prepare the grounds for the opening of a mental hospital in the town, hostility increased sharply. In short, it is quite difficult to change the environment even when the change sought is relatively small and there are special activities oriented toward achieving it.[25]

D. R. Cressey, addressing himself to the same problems, states: "In spite of the many ingenious programs to bring about modification of attitudes or reform, the unseen environment in the prisoner's world, with few exceptions, continues to be charged with ideational content inimical to reform."[26]

This is not to suggest that community orientation cannot be changed. But when the effectiveness of an organization is assessed at a certain point in time, and the organization studied is not one whose goal is to change the environment, the environment has to be treated as given. In contemporary society, this often means that the organization must allocate considerable resources to custodial activities in order to be able to operate at all.[27] Such activities at least limit the means available for therapy. In addition they tend to undermine the therapeutic process, since therapy (or rehabilitation) and security are often at least partially incompatible goals.[28] Under such circumstances low effectiveness in the service of therapeutic goals is to be expected.

This means that, to begin with, one may expect a highly developed custodial subsystem. Hence it seems justifiable to suggest that the focus of research should shift from the problem that, despite some public expectations, institutions fail to become primarily therapeutic to the following problems: To what degree are external and internal[29] organizational conditions responsible for the emphasis on security? Or are these conditions used by those in power largely to justify the elaboration of security measures, while the real cause for that elaboration is to be found in the personal needs or interests (which can be relatively more easily changed and for which the organization is responsible) of part of the personnel, such as guards and administrators? To what degree and in what ways can therapy be developed under the conditions given? Do external conditions allow, and internal conditions encourage, a goal cleavage, i.e., making security the public goal and therapy the private goal of the organization or the other way around?

We have discussed the effect of the two models the researcher uses to study the interaction between the organization and its environment. We shall turn now to examine the impact each model has on the

23. Oscar Grusky, "Role Conflict in Organization: A Study of Prison Camp Officials," *Administrative Science Quarterly*, 3 (1959), 452–72, quoted from p. 457. McCleery shows that changes in a prison he analyzed were possible since the community, through its representatives, was willing to support them, *op. cit.*, pp. 30–31.

24. See Elaine and John Cumming, *Closed Ranks* (Cambridge, Mass., 1957), p. xiv.

25. *Ibid.* It is of interest to note that the Cummings started their study with a goal model (how effective is the educational program?). In their analysis they shifted to a system model (p. 8). They asked what functions, manifest and latent, did the traditional attitudes toward mental health play for the community as a social system (ch. vii). This explained both the lack of change and suggested possible avenues to future change (pp. 152–58).

26. "Preface to the 1958 Reissue," in D. Clemmer, *The Prison Community* (New York, 1958), p. xiii.

27. Grusky, *op. cit.*; see also Cressey, "Foreword," to D. Clemmer, *op. cit.*

28. See Cressey, "Contrary Directives."

29. It seems that some security measures fulfill internal functions as well. They include control of inmates till the staff has a chance to build up voluntary compliance and safety of other inmates, of the staff itself, of the inmate in treatment, of the institutional property, as well as others. These internal functions are another illustration of the nongoal activities that a goal approach tends to overlook and that a system approach would call attention to.

approach to the study of internal structure of the organization.

CASE 2: FUNCTIONS OF OLIGARCHY

The study of authority structure in voluntary associations and political organizations is gradually shifting from a goal model to a system model. Michels' well-known study of socialist parties and trade unions in Europe before World War I was conducted according to a goal model.[30] These parties and unions were found to have two sets of goals: socialism and democracy. Both tended to be undermined: socialism by the weakening of commitments to revolutionary objectives and overdevotion to means activities (developing the organization) and maintenance activities (preserving the organization and its assets); democracy by the development of an oligarchic structure. A number of studies have followed Michels' line and supplied evidence that supports his generalizations.[31]

With regard to socialism. Michels claims that a goal displacement took place in the organizations he studied. This point has been extensively analyzed and need not be discussed here.[32] Of more interest to the present discussion is his argument on democracy. Michels holds that an organization that has *external* democracy as its goal should have an *internal* democratic structure; otherwise, it is not only diverting some of the means from goal to nongoal activities, but is also introducing a state of affairs which is directly opposed to the goal state of the organization. In other words, an internal oligarchy is seen as a dysfunction from the viewpoint of the organizational goals. "Now it is manifest that the concept *dictatorship* is the direct antithesis of the concept *democracy*. The attempt to make dictatorship serve the ends of democracy is tantamount to the endeavour to utilize war as the most efficient means for the defence of peace, or to employ alcohol in the struggle against alcoholism."[33] Michels goes on to spell out the conditions which make for this phenomenon. Some are regarded as unavoidable, some as optional, but all are depicted as distortions undermining the effectiveness of the organization.[34]

Since then it has been suggested that internal oligarchy might be a *functional* requirement for the effective operation of these organizations.[35] It has been suggested both with regard to trade unions and political parties that conflict organizations cannot tolerate internal conflicts. If they do, they become less effective.[36] Political parties that allow internal factions to become organized are setting the scene for splits which often turn powerful political units into weak splinter parties. This may be dysfunctional not only for the political organization but also for the political system. It has also been pointed out that organizations, unlike communities and societies, are segmental associations, which require and recruit only limited commitments of actors and in which, therefore, internal democracy is neither possible nor called for. Developing an internal political structure of democratic nature would necessitate spending more means on recruitment of members' interests than segmental associations can afford. Moreover, a higher involvement on the part of members may well be dysfunctional to the achievement of the organization's goals. It would make compromises with other political parties or of labor unions with management rather difficult. This means that some of the factors Michels saw as dysfunctional are actually functional; some of the factors he regarded as distorting the organizational goals were actually the mechanisms through which the functions were

30. Michels, *op. cit.*

31. See Oliver Garceau, *The Political Life of the American Medical Association* (Cambridge, Mass., 1941); R. T. McKenzie, *British Political Parties* (London, 1955). See also note [2].

32. Robert K. Merton, *Social Theory and Social Structure* (rev. ed.; New York, 1957), pp. 199–201; Peter M. Blau, *The Dynamics of Bureaucracy* (Chicago, 1955), see index; David L. Sills, *The Volunteers* (New York, 1957), pp. 62–69.

33. Michels, *op. cit.*, p. 401.

34. The argument over the compatibility of democracy and effectiveness in "private government" is far from settled. The argument draws from value commitments but is also reinforced by the lack of evidence. The dearth of evidence can be explained in part by the fact that almost all voluntary organizations, effective and ineffective ones, are oligarchic. For the most recent and penetrating discussion of the various factors involved, see Seymour M. Lipset, "The Politics of Private Government," in his *The Political Man* (Garden City, 1960), esp. pp. 360 ff. See also Lloyd H. Fisher and Grant McConnell, "Internal Conflict and Labor Union Solidarity," in A. Kornhauser, R. Dublin, and A. M. Ross, eds., *Industrial Conflict* (New York, 1954), pp. 132–43.

35. For a summary statement of the various viewpoints on the effect of democratic procedures on trade unions, see Clark Kerr, *Unions and Union Leaders of Their Own Choosing* (New York, 1957).

36. *Ibid.*

fulfilled, or the conditions which enabled these mechanisms to develop and to operate.

S. M. Lipset, M. A. Trow, and J. S. Coleman's study of democracy in a trade union reflects the change in approach since Michels' day.[37] This study is clearly structured according to the patterns of a system model. It does not confront a social unit with an ideal and then grade it according to its degree of conformity to the ideal. The study sees democracy as a process (mainly as an institutionalized change of the parties in office) and proceeds to determine the external and internal conditions that enable it to function. It views democracy as a characteristic of a given system, sustained by the interrelations among the system's parts. From this, a multifunctional theory of democracy in voluntary organizations emerges. The study describes the various functional requirements necessary for democracy to exist in an organization devoted to economic and social improvement of its members and specifies the conditions that have allowed these requirements to be met in this particular case.[38]

*Paradox of ineffectiveness.* An advantage of the system model is that it enables us to conceive of a basic form of ineffectiveness which is hard to imagine and impossible to explain from the viewpoint of the goal model. The goal approach sees assignment of means to goal activities as functional. The more means assigned to the goal activities, the more effective the organization is expected to be. In terms of the goal model, the fact that an organization can become more effective by allocating less means to goal activities is a paradox. The system model, on the other hand, leads one to conclude that, just as there may be a dysfunction of underrecruitment, so there may be a dysfunction of overrecruitment to goal activities, which is bound to lead to underrecruitment to other activities and to lack of coordination between the inflated goal activities and the depressed means activities or other nongoal activities.

*Cost of system models.* Up to this point we have tried to point out some of the advantages of the system model. We would now like to point out one drawback of this model. It is more demanding and expensive for the researcher. The goal model requires that the researcher determine the goals the organization is pursuing and no more. If public goals are chosen, they are usually readily available. Private goals are more difficult to establish. In order to find out how the organization is really oriented, it is sometimes necessary not only to gain the confidence of its elite but also to analyze much of the actual organizational structure and processes.

Research conducted on the basis of the system model requires more effort than a study following the goal model, even when private goals are chosen. The system model requires that the analyst determine what he considers a highly effective allocation of means. This often requires considerable knowledge of the way in which an organization of the type studied functions. Acquiring such knowledge is often very demanding, but it should be pointed out that (*a*) the efforts invested in obtaining the information required for the system model are not wasted since the information collected in the process of developing the system model will be of much value for the study of most organizational problems; and that (*b*) theoretical considerations may often serve as the bases for constructing a system model. This point requires some elaboration.

A well-developed organizational theory will include statements on the functional requirements various organizational types have to meet. These will guide the researcher who is constructing a system model for the study of a specific organization. In cases where the pressure to economize is great, the theoretical system model of the particular organizational type may be used directly as a standard and a guide for the analysis of a specific organization. But it should be pointed out that in the present state of organizational theory, such a model is often not available. At present, organizational theory is dealing mainly with general propositions which apply equally well but also equally badly to all organiza-

37. *Union Democracy* (New York, 1956). See also S. M Lipset, "Democracy in Private Government," *British Journal of Sociology*, 3 (1952), 47–63; "The Political Process in Trade Unions: A Theoretical Statement," in Morroe Berger *et al.*, *Freedom and Social Control in Modern Society* (New York, 1954), pp. 82–124.

38. Limitations of space do not allow us to discuss a third case of improved understanding with the shift from one model to another. Although apathy among members of voluntary associations as reflecting members' betrayal of their organizational goals and as undermining the functioning of the organization has long been deplored, it is now being realized that partial apathy is a functional requirement for the effective operation of many voluntary associations in the service of their goals as well as a condition of democratic government. See W. H. Morris Jones, "In Defense of Apathy," *Political Studies*, 2 (1954), 25–37.

tions.[39] The differences among various organizational types are great; therefore any theory of organizations in general must be highly abstract. It can serve as an important frame for specification, that is, for the development of special theories for the various organizational types, but it cannot substitute for such theories by serving in itself as a system model, to be applied directly to the analysis of concrete organizations.

Maybe the best support for the thesis that a system model can be formulated and fruitfully applied is found in a study of organizational effectiveness by B. S. Georgopoulos and A. S. Tannenbaum, one of the few studies that distinguishes explicitly between the goal and system approaches to the study of effectiveness.[40] Instead of using the goals of the delivery service organization, they constructed three indexes, each measuring one basic element of the system. These were: (*a*) station productivity, (*b*) intraorganizational strain as indicated by the incidence of tension and conflict among organizational subgroups, and (*c*) organizational flexibility, defined as the ability to adjust to external or internal change. The total score of effectiveness thus produced was significantly correlated to the ratings on "effectiveness" which various experts and "insiders" gave the thirty-two delivery stations.[41]

Further development of such system-effectiveness indexes will require elaboration of organizational theory along the lines discussed above, because it will be necessary to supply a rationale for measuring certain aspects of the system and not others.[42]

*Survival and effectiveness models.* A system model constitutes a statement about relationships which, if actually existing, would allow a given unit to maintain itself and to operate. There are two major subtypes of system models. One depicts a *survival model*, i.e., a set of requirements which, if fulfilled, allows the system to exist. In such a model each relationship specified is a prerequisite for the functioning of the system, i.e., a necessary condition; remove any one of them and the system ceases to operate. The second is an *effectiveness model.* It defines a pattern of interrelations among the elements of the system which would make it most effective in the service of a given goal.[43]

The difference between the two submodels is considerable. Sets of functional alternatives which are equally satisfactory from the viewpoint of the survival model have a different value from the viewpoint of the effectiveness model. The survival model gives a "yes" or "no" score when answering the question: Is a specific relationship functional? The effectiveness model tells us that, of several functional alternatives, some are more functional than others in terms of effectiveness. There are first, second, third, and *n* choices. Only rarely are two patterns full-fledged alternatives in this sense, i.e., only rarely do they have the same effectiveness value. Merton discussed this point briefly, using the concepts functional alternatives and functional equivalents.[44]

The majority of the functionalists have worked with survival models.[45] This has left them open to

39. The point has been elaborated and illustrated in Amitai Etzioni, "Authority Structure and Organizational Effectiveness," *Administrative Science Quarterly*, 4 (1959), 43–67.

40. "A Study of Organizational Effectiveness," *American Sociological Review*, 22 (1957), 534–40.

41. For a brief report of another effort to "dimensionalize" organizational effectiveness, see Robert L. Kahn, Floyd C. Mann, and Stanley Seashore, "Introduction" to a special issue on Human Relations Research in Large Organizations: II, *Journal of Social Issues*, 12 (1956), 2.

42. What is needed from a methodological viewpoint is an accounting scheme for social systems like the one Lazarsfeld and Rosenberg outlined for the study of action. See Paul F. Lazarsfeld and Morris Rosenberg, eds., *The Language of Social Research* (New York, 1955), pp. 387–491. For an outstanding sample of a formal model for the study of organizations as social systems, see Allen H. Barton and Bo Anderson, "Change in an Organizational System: Formalization of a Qualitative Study," in Amitai Etzioni, ed., *Complex Organizations: A Sociological Reader* (New York, 1961).

43. For many purposes, in particular for the study of ascriptive social units, two submodels are required: one that specifies the conditions under which a certain *structure* (pattern or form of a system) is maintained, another which specifies the conditions under which a certain level of activities or *processes* is maintained. A model of effectiveness of organizations has to specify both.

44. Robert K. Merton, *Social Theory and Social Structure* (rev. ed.; New York, 1957), p. 52; see last part of E. Nagel's essay, "A Formalization of Functionalism," in *Logic without Metaphysics* (New York, 1957).

45. One of the few areas in which sociologists have worked with both models is the study of stratification. Some are concerned with the question: is stratification a necessary condition for the existence of society? This is obviously a question of the survival model of societies. Others have asked: which form of stratification will make for the best allocation of talents among the various social positions, will maximize training, and minimize social strains? Those are typical questions of the effectiveness model. Both models have been applied in enlightening pebate over the function of stratification; see Kingsley Davis, "A Conceptual Analysis of Stratification," *American*

the criticism that although society or a social unit might change considerably, they would still see it as the same system. Only very rarely, for instance, does a society lose its ability to fulfill the basic functional requirements. This is one of the reasons why it has been claimed that the functional model does not sensitize the researcher to the dynamics of social units.

James G. March and Herbert A. Simon pointed out explicitly in their outstanding analysis of organization was based on a survival model:

> The Barnard-Simon theory of organizational equilibrium is essentially a theory of motivation—a statement of the conditions under which an organization can induce its members to continue participation, and hence assure organizational *survival*. . . . Hence, an organization is "solvent"—and will continue in *existence*—only so long as the contributions are sufficient to provide inducements in large enough measure to draw forth these conditions.[46] [All italics supplied.]

If, on the other hand, one accepts the definition that organizations are social units oriented toward the realization of specific goals, the application of the effectiveness model is especially warranted for this type of study.

## Models and normative biases

The goal model is often considered as an objective way to deal with normative problems. The observer controls his normative preferences by using the normative commitments of the actors to construct a standard for the assessment of effectiveness. We would like to suggest that the goal model is less objective than it appears to be. The system model not only seems to be a better model but also seems to supply a safety measure against a common bias, the Utopian approach to social change.

### VALUE PROJECTION

In some cases the transfer from the values of the observer to those of the observed is performed by a simple projection. The observer decides a priori that the organization, group, or public under study is striving to achieve goals and to realize values he favors. These values are then referred to as the "organizational goals," "public expectations," or "society's values." Actually they are the observer's values projected onto the unit studied. Often no evidence is supplied that would demonstrate that the goals are really those of the organization. C. S. Hyneman pointed to the same problem in political science:

> A like concern about means and ends is apparent in much of the literature that subordinates description of what occurs to a development of the author's ideas and beliefs; the author's ideas and beliefs come out in statements that contemporary institutions and ways of doing things do not yield the results that society of a particular public anticipated.[47]

Renate Mayntz makes this point in her discussion of a study of political parties in Berlin. She points out that the functional requirements which she uses to measure the effectiveness of the party organization are derived from *her* commitments to democratic values. She adds: "It is an empirical question how far a specific political party accepts the functions attributed to it by the committed observer as its proper and maybe noblest goals. From the point of view of the party, the primary organizational goal is to achieve power."[48]

There are two situations where this projection is likely to take place: one, when the organization is publicly, but not otherwise, committed to the same goals to which the observer is committed; the other, when a functional statement is turned from a hypothesis into a postulate.[49] When a functionalist

*Sociological Review*, 7 (1952), 309–21; Kingsley Davis and Wilbert E. Moore, "Some Principles of Stratification," *ibid.*, 10 (1954), 242–49; Melvin W. Tumin, "Some Principles of Stratification: A Critical Analysis," *ibid.*, 18 (1953), 387–94; Kingsley Davis, "Reply," *ibid.*, 394–97; W. E. Moore, "Comment," *ibid.*, 397. See also Richard D. Schwartz, "Functional Alternatives to Inequality," *ibid.*, 20 (1955), 424–30.

46. *Organizations* (New York, 1958), p. 84. See also Gouldner, *op. cit.*, p. 405, for a discussion of "organization strain toward survival." Theodore Caplow developed an objective model to determine the survival potential of a social unit. He states: "Whatever may be said of the logical origins of these criteria, it is a reasonable assertion that no organization can continue to exist unless it reaches a minimal level in the performance of its objective functions, reduces spontaneous conflict below the level which is distributive, and provides sufficient satisfaction to individual members so that membership will be continued' ("The Criteria of Organizational Success," *Social Forces*, 32 [1953], 4).

47. Charles S. Hyneman, "Means/Ends Analysis in Policy Science," *PROD*, 2 (March 1959), 19–22.

48. "Party Activity in Postwar Berlin," in Dwaine Marvick, ed., *Political Decision Makers* (New York, 1961).

49. On this fallacy, see Hans L. Zetterberg, *On Theory and Verification in Sociology* (New York, 1951), esp. pp. 26 ff.

states that mental hospitals have been established in order to cure the mentally ill, he often does not mean this as a statement either about the history of mental hospitals or about the real, observable, organizational goals. He is just suggesting that *if* the mental hospitals pursued the above goal, this *would be* functional for society. The researcher who converts from this "if-then" statement to a factual assertion, "the goal is . . . ," commits a major methodological error.

But let us now assume that the observer has determined, with the ordinary techniques of research, that the organization he is observing is indeed committed to the goals which he too supports; for instance, culture, health, or democracy. Still, the fact that the observer enters the study of the organization through its goals makes it likely that he will assume the position of a critic or a social reformer, rather than that of a social observer and detached analyst. Thus those who use the goal model often combine "understanding" with "criticizing," an approach which was recommended and used by Marx but strongly criticized and rejected by Weber. The critique is built into the study by the fact that the goal is used as the yardstick, a technique which, as was pointed out above, makes organizations in general score low on effectiveness scales.[50]

### EFFECTS OF LIBERALISM

The reasons why the goal model is often used and often is accompanied by a critical perspective can be explained partially by the positions of those who apply it. Like many social scientists, students of organizations are often committed to ideas of progress, social reform, humanism, and liberalism.[51] This normative perspective can express itself more readily when a goal model is applied than when a system model is used. In some cases the goal model gives the researcher an opportunity to assume even the indignant style of a social reformer.

Some writers suggested that those who use the system models are conservative by nature. This is not the place to demonstrate that this contention is not true. It suffices to state here that the system model is a prerequisite for understanding and bringing about social change. The goal model leads to unrealistic, Utopian expectations, and hence to disappointments, which are well reflected in the literature of this type. The system model, on the other hand, depicts more realistically the difficulties encountered in introducing change into established systems, which function in a given environment. It leaves less room for the frustrations which must follow Utopian hopes. It is hard to improve on the sharp concluding remark of Gresham M. Sykes on this subject:

> Plans to increase the therapeutic effectiveness of the custodial institution must be evaluated in terms of the difference between what is done and what might be done—and the difference may be dishearteningly small. . . . But expecting less and demanding less may achieve more, for a chronically disillusioned public is apt to drift into indifference.[52]

### INTELLECTUAL PITFALL

Weber pointed out in his discussion of responsibility that actors, especially those responsible for a system, such as politicians and managers, have to compromise. They cannot follow a goal or a value consistently, because the various subsystems, which they have to keep functioning as well as integrated, have different and partially incompatible requirements. The unit's activity can be assured only by concessions, including such concessions as might reduce the effectiveness and scope of goal activities (but not necessarily the effectiveness of the whole unit). Barnard made basically the same point in his theory of opportunism.

Although the structural position of politicians and managers leads them to realize the need to compromise, the holders of other positions are less likely to do so. On the contrary, since these others are often responsible for one subsystem in the organization, they tend to identify with the interests and values of their subsystem. From the viewpoint of the system,

50. One of the reasons that this fallacy does not stand out in organizational studies is that many are case studies. Thus each researcher discovers that his organization is ineffective. This is not a finding which leads one to doubt the assumptions one made when initiating the study. Only when a large number of goal-model studies are examined does the repeated finding of low effectiveness, goal dilution, and so on lead one to the kind of examination which has been attempted here.

51. A recent study of social scientists by P. F. Lazarsfeld and W. Thielens, Jr., demonstrates this point, *The Academic Mind* (New York, 1958). Some additional evidence in support of this point is presented in S. M. Lipset and J. Linz, "The Social Bases of Political Diversity in Western Democracies" (in preparation), ch. xi, pp. 70–72.

52. "A Postscript for Reformers," in his *The Society of Captives* (Princeton, 1958), pp. 133–34.

those constitute merely segmental perspectives. This phenomenon, which is sometimes referred to as the development of departmental loyalties, is especially widespread among those who represent goal activities. Since their interests and subsystem values come closest to those of the organization as a whole, they find it easiest to justify their bias.

In systems in which the managers are the group most committed to goal activities (e.g., in profit-making organizations), this tendency is at least partially balanced by the managers' other commitments (e.g., to system integration). But in organizations in which another personnel group is the major carrier of goal activities, the ordinary intergroup difference of interests and structural perspectives becomes intensified. In some cases it develops into a conflict between the idealists and the compromisers (if not traitors). In professional organizations such as mental hospitals and universities, the major carriers of goal activities are professionals rather than administrators. The conflict between the supporters of therapeutic values and those of custodial values is one case of this general phenomenon.[53]

So far the effect of various structural positions on the actors' organizational perspectives has been discussed. What view is the observer likely to take? One factor which might affect his perspective is *his* structural position. Frequently, this resembles closely that of the professional in professional organizations. The researcher's background is similar to that of the professionals he studies in terms of education, income, social prestige, age, language, manners, and other characteristics. With regard to these factors he tends to differ from managers and administrators. Often the researcher who studies an organization and the professionals studied have shared years of training at the same or at a similar university and have or had friends in common. Moreover, his position in his organization, whether it is a university or a research organization, is similar to the position of the physician or psychologist in the hospital or prison under study.[54] Like other professionals, the researcher is primarily devoted to the goal activities of his organization and has little experience with, understanding of, or commitment to, nongoal functions. The usual consequence of all this is that the researcher has a natural sympathy for the professional orientation in professional organizations.[55] This holds also, although to a lesser degree, for professionals in other organizations, such as business corporations and governmental agencies.

Since the professional orientation in these organizations is identical with the goal orientation, the goal model not only fails to help in checking the bias introduced by these factors but tends to enhance it. The system model, on the other hand, serves to remind one (*a*) that social units cannot be as consistent as cultural systems, (*b*) that goals are serviced by multifunctional units, and hence intersubsystem concessions are a necessary prerequisite for action, (*c*) that such concessions include concessions to the adaptive subsystem which in particular represents environmental pressures and constraints, and (*d*) that each group has its structural perspectives, which means that the observer must be constantly aware of the danger of taking over the viewpoint of any single personnel group, including that of a group which carries the bulk of the goal activities. He cannot consider the perspective of any group or elite as a satisfactory view of the organization as a whole, of its effectiveness, needs, and potentialities. In short, it is suggested that the system model supplies not only a more adequate model but also a less biased point of view.

53. Another important case is the conflict between intellectuals and politicians in many Western societies. For a bibliography and a recent study, see H. L. Wilensky, *Intellectuals in Labor Unions* (New York, 1956).

54. These similarities in background make communication and contact of the researcher with the professionals studied easier than with other organizational personnel. This is one of the reasons why the middle level of organizations is often much more vividly described than lower ranking personnel or top management.

55. Arthur L. Stinchcombe pointed out to the author that organizations whose personnel includes a high ratio of professionals are more frequently studied than those which do not.

DAVID L. SILLS

# Preserving Organizational Goals

## Introduction

The problem of maintaining membership interest, a problem common to all voluntary associations, was described in the previous chapter as stemming primarily from the process of delegating authority and functions *upwards* in an organization. A number of the Foundation's structural features which serve to alleviate this problem were indicated—of which the most important is undoubtedly the administrative separation of Chapter and March of Dimes organizations. The problem of preserving organizational goals, on the other hand, stems from the process of *downward* delegation, and is met in quite different ways.

The generic problem of goal preservation may be stated as follows: In order to accomplish their goals, organizations establish a set of procedures or means. In the course of following these procedures, however, the subordinates or members to whom authority and functions have been delegated often come to regard them as ends in themselves, rather than as means toward the achievement of organizations goals. As a result of this process, the actual activities of the organization become centered around the proper functioning of organization procedures, rather than upon the achievement of the initial goals.

This phenomenon of goal displacement is perhaps the most frequently noted pathological aspect of large-scale organizations. Philip Selznick, for example, calls it "the organizational paradox," and notes that because of this phenomenon organizational frustration is a persistent characteristic of our times.[1]

Practically every serious observer of large-scale organizations has noted instances of this tendency. Robert Michels, for example, in summarizing the tendencies toward oligarchy in socialist and labor organizations, noted that "from a means, organization becomes an end. . . . Henceforward the sole preoccupation is to avoid anything which may clog the machinery."[2] Walter Sharp's analysis of the French Civil Service led him to conclude that any bureaucracy faces "the constant danger that these routine operations will become sterilizing ends in themselves rather than the effective means to desirable ends."[3] Alvin Gouldner notes that a basic difference between two bureaucratic patterns he found in an industrial organization is that in "representative bureaucracies" obedience is given

Reprinted from *The Volunteers*, pp. 62–77, by permission of the author and The Macmillan Company. (Copyright by The Free Press, A Corporation 1957.)

1. Philip Selznick, "An Approach to a Theory of Bureaucracy," *American Sociological Review*, 8 (1943), p. 49.

2. Robert Michels, *Political Parties* (New York: Free Press, 1949), p. 373. Michels' analysis, however, was directed primarily toward organizations in which authority and functions are delegated upward by the members to the leaders, particularly the German Social-Democratic Party.

3. Walter R. Sharp, *The French Civil Service* (New York: Macmillan Co., 1931), p. 446.

to the rules because this would lead "to desirable consequences *beyond themselves*," while in "punishment-centered bureaucracies" the rule is treated "as an end in itself."[4] And Robert Merton, in his discussion of bureaucratic structure and personality, states that "adherence to the rules, originally conceived as a means, becomes transformed into an end-in-itself; there occurs the familiar process of *displacement of goals*. . . ."[5]

Arthur Davis has reported many instances of this phenomenon in the Navy Officer Corps in World War II. For example, he observed that the rule that communications in the Navy must follow the chain of command means that very simple messages sent from one officer to another often require the attention of eight to twelve persons over a ten-day period and that heavy-bomber crews on submarine patrol, in order to avoid being criticized by their superiors for errors in bombing missions, would often fly their patrols exactly as they were charted, even if this meant ignoring a suspicious object a few miles abeam. In short, he concluded, there is a "dysfunctional tendency of formal organizations to overemphasize their main instrumental devices. . . ."[6] S. D. Clark's study of the Salvation Army in Canada revealed that as the Army grew its leaders devoted increasing attention to the problems of maintaining the organization. They spent a disproportionate share of their energies on problems of administration and finance, for example, and even gave up evangelical work in areas where there was insufficient support for a strong local organization.[7] Finally, Philip Selznick, who has devoted more explicit attention to this phenomenon than any other student of large-scale organizations, has formulated the problem as follows:

> Running an organization, as a specialized and essential activity, generates problems which have no necessary (and often an opposed) relationship to the professed or "original" goals of the organization. The day-to-day behavior of the group becomes centered around specific problems and proximate goals which have primarily an internal relevance. Then, since these activities come to consume an increasing proportion of the time and thoughts of the participants, they are —from the point of view of actual behavior— *substituted* for the professed goals.[8]

This brief review of the attention which has been given to the problem of preserving organizational goals is perhaps sufficient to suggest its near-universality. In fact, the problem is mentioned so often, and the deleterious effects of goal displacement have been so frequently described, that the question inevitably arises as to how large-scale organizations are able to make progress toward their professed goals. The answer to this question of course is that organizations develop mechanisms of various kinds for minimizing the displacement of their goals. Before those mechanisms which the Foundation has developed are described, however, it is necessary to identify those specific sources of goal displacement which students of large-scale organizations have most frequently observed.

## Sources of goal displacement

The ultimate source of goal displacement is the process of delegation itself, since the individuals whose actions modify the goals of an organization are generally those to whom authority and functions have been delegated. The general process of goal displacement, in other words, takes place as a result of the actions of delegates coming to have an increasing *internal* relevance, rather than a direct relationship to the ultimate goals of the organization.[9] In more specific terms, the process may be observed by noting the actions of delegates which relate to (1) their status within the organization, (2) their interpretation of organizational rules, (3) their execution of organizational procedures, (4) their relationships with other participants, and (5) their relationships with the general public. Accordingly, the following discussion will focus upon each of these behavioral areas in turn. The major findings of previous research are summarized, and those aspects of the Foundation's formal structure which serve to preserve its goals are described.

4. Alvin W. Gouldner, *Patterns of Industrial Bureaucracy* (New York: Free Press, 1954), pp. 220–21.
5. Robert K. Merton, *Social Theory and Social Structure* (New York: Free Press, 1949), p. 155.
6. Arthur K. Davis, "Bureaucratic Patterns in the Navy Officers Corps," in Robert K. Merton, Ailsa P. Gray, Barbara Hockey, and Hanan C. Selvin (eds.), *Reader in Bureaucracy* (New York: Free Press, 1952), pp. 389–90.
7. S. D. Clark, *Church and Sect in Canada* (Toronto: University of Toronto Press, 1948), pp. 425–31.
8. Selznick, *op. cit.*, p. 48.
9. *Ibid.*, pp. 51–54.

### STATUS WITHIN THE ORGANIZATION

Discussions of large-scale organizations generally take it for granted that all the participants are employees of the organization. Max Weber, for example, included among the characteristics of an administrative staff the requirements that members be "remunerated by fixed salaries in money"; that "the office is treated as the sole, or at least the primary, occupation of the incumbent"; and that the office "constitutes a career . . . (with) a system of 'promotion' according to seniority or to achievement, or both."[10]

Most large-scale organizations meet Weber's requirements with respect to the character of their personnel. Accordingly, most discussions of the problem of goal displacement locate as one source of the phenomenon the desire of the employee to maintain his position and advance his career. According to Selznick, "[the employee's] interest in the ultimate purpose of the organization, or in the 'common good,' becomes subordinate to his preoccupation with the problems involved in the *maintenance* of his post."[11] And in his analysis of the prospects for democracy in trade unions, Martin Lipset has pointed out that a democratic turnover in office would demand "the institutionalization of movement from high to low status. . . ." Since this in turn would involve "the institutionalization of a major deviation from the dominant value of achievement," Lipset concludes that "the functional requirements for democracy cannot be met most of the time in most unions."[12] In order to maintain their high status and high salaried positions within the union, leaders often strive to minimize rather than maximize the effect of the democratic process.[13]

### THE INTERPRETATION OF ORGANIZATIONAL RULES

A fundamental characteristic of large-scale organizations is that the behavior of their membership is governed by a set of rules, rather than by traditions or by "devotion to the specific and exceptional sanctity, heroism or exemplary character of an individual person. . . .[14] Rules are of course necessary for the efficient day-to-day conduct of an organization. If every question had to be decided on its own merits, as happens quite frequently, for example, in such informal groupings as families or friendship cliques, an organization would be able to devote little attention to the conduct of its program.[15]

The rules which govern an organization, however, can also serve as a source of goal displacement. The underlying reason for this phenomenon is that the sentiments which are developed to buttress the rules are often more intense than is technically necessary. Strong sentiments surrounding obedience to rules are often necessary to protect the organization from the minority of irresponsible members, but these sentiments may cause other members of the organization to concentrate upon the details of behavior involved in abiding by the rules, rather than upon the aims of the organization. This phenomenon has been noted by most students of formal organizations; it has been described most fully by Merton (whose formulation of the problem has been followed here)[16] and by Peter Blau, who observed among some of the government employees he studied a tendency for the objectives of rules to be displaced by the techniques designed to achieve them.[17]

### THE EXECUTION OF ORGANIZATIONAL PROCEDURES

Without an organization a goal is merely a desired state of affairs; an organizational structure creates the conditions which allow concrete steps to be taken toward the realization of a goal. But the paradoxical fact is that the procedures involved in running an organization may come to assume greater importance than the initial goals them-

10. Max Weber, *The Theory of Social and Economic Organization.* Translated by A. M. Henderson and Talcott Parsons; edited by Talcott Parsons (New York: Oxford University Press, 1947), pp. 333–34.

11. Selznick, *op. cit.*, p. 52.

12. Seymour M. Lipset, "The Political Process in Trade Unions: A Theoretical Statement," in Morroe Berger, Theodore Abel, and Charles H. Page (eds.), *Freedom and Control in Modern Society* (New York: D. Van Nostrand Co., 1954), p. 121.

13. *Ibid.*, p. 96.

14. Weber, *op. cit.*, p. 328.

15. Efficiency is of course only one of the functions served by organizational rules. See Gouldner, *op. cit.*, pp. 157–80, for an extensive discussion of other functions which rules may serve.

16. Merton, *op. cit.*, pp. 154–55.

17. Peter M. Blau, *The Dynamics of Bureaucracy* (Chicago: University of Chicago Press, 1955), pp. 191–93.

selves. As Selznick has noted, in a passage cited earlier, these procedures come to be "*substituted* for the professed goals."

The substitution of proximate goals for professed goals is a phenomenon which can occur in a number of ways. Merton has noted that it may occur through a process which he calls *sanctification*:

> Through sentiment-formation, emotional dependence upon bureaucratic symbols and status, and affective involvement in spheres of competence and authority, there develop prerogatives involving attitudes of moral legitimacy which are established as values in their own right, and are no longer viewed as merely technical means for expediting administration.[18]

Davis, in his study of the Navy Officer Corps, notes the adverse impact of *ceremonialism* upon the manifest goals of the Navy. Ritual, which is particularly prevalent in the Navy, helps to maintain morale, but it also "may become an end in itself at the expense of the organization's capacity to perform efficiently its manifest functions."[19] Marshall Dimock has observed that *traditionalism* serves to impede an organization from selecting the most expedient procedures for achieving its goals:

> The older an institution becomes, the more settled its mould and procedures are likely to be. Traditions are hallowed. Ways of doing things take on a reverence which defies successful change, even when they may have been quite accidental in the first place or when better methods have been discovered. Institutions are conservative in the extreme.[20]

Numerous students of organizations have found that *red tape*, particularly as it involves obtaining approval or transmitting a communication through a chain of command, very often becomes an end in itself. Finally, Selznick has noted that *routinization* also often results in the displacement of goals; he suggests that the actual performance of the activities of an organization may become so routine that the underlying purposes of the activities tend to become obscured.[21]

### RELATIONSHIPS WITH OTHER PARTICIPANTS

The formal structure of an organization generally does not explicitly provide for the emergence of informal groupings among its participants, yet both everyday experience and systematic research furnish incontrovertible evidence that such groupings are inevitably developed. In fact, there is increasing official awareness of the fact that informal groups within an organization are necessary for the effective operation of the formal structure itself.[22] Selznick has summarized this necessity as follows:

> The informal structure will be at once indispensable to and consequential for the formal system of delegation and control itself. Wherever command over the response of individuals is desired, some approach in terms of the spontaneous organization of loyalty and interest will be necessary. In practice this means that the informal structure will be useful to the leadership and effective as a means of communication and persuasion. At the same time, it can be anticipated that some price will be paid in the shape of distribution of power or adjustment of policy.[23]

The present concern is of course with what Selznick calls the "price . . . paid in . . . adjustment of policy," that is, with the role primary groupings may play in the displacement of goals. Perhaps the best known study which demonstrates the existence of this possibility is the Roethlisberger and Dickson research into worker productivity. They found that the day-to-day practices of workers resulted in the emergence of an informal structure, which, among its other effects, led to the development of productivity norms. Since the professed goal of the organization was to maximize productivity, the restriction of output encouraged by these norms may be said to represent a displacement of goals.[24]

A second source of goal displacement generated by the informal structure is the sense of a common destiny which so often develops among fellow participants in a large-scale organization. Merton has noted that these sentiments may lead the participants "to defend their entrenched interests

18. Merton, *op. cit.*, p. 157.

19. Davis, *op. cit.*, p. 392.

20. Marshall E. Dimock, "Bureaucracy Self-Examined," in Merton, Gray, Hockey and Selvin, *op. cit.*, p. 401.

21. Selznick, *op. cit.*, p. 50.

22. A dramatic example of this increasing awareness is the recent attempt of the U.S. Army to encourage the emergency of informal groupings by establishing four-man teams which remain intact from basic training through assignment to an overseas unit. See Leonard Broom and Philip Selznick, *Sociology* (Evanston, Ill.: Row, Peterson and Co., 1955), p. 143.

23. Philip Selznick, *TVA and the Grass Roots* (Berkeley and Los Angeles: University of California Press, 1949), pp. 251–52.

24. F. J. Roethlisberger and William J. Dickson, *Management and the Worker* (Cambridge: Harvard University Press, 1943), pp. 379–548.

rather than to assist their clientele. . . ,"[25] and Davis has gone so far as to suggest that the inability of the Navy to perform properly at Pearl Harbor in 1941 was in part attributable to the "insulation of officers preoccupied with professional routine and Navy social life. . . ."[26]

The most extensive analysis to date of the effect of informal groupings upon the goals of an organization is Selznick's study of the T.V.A. One of his major findings concerns the consequences which resulted from the delegation of certain phases of the T.V.A.'s agricultural program to local organizations already existing in the T.V.A.'s area of operations. In order to make the program effective, these organizations were informally "co-opted" into the policy-making apparatus of the T.V.A. itself, and under the pressure of these "co-opted" organizations, the T.V.A. was deflected from the achievement of some of its primary goals.[27]

### RELATIONSHIPS WITH THE PUBLIC

All large-scale organizations which seek in any way to influence the behavior of outsiders, or which provide services for outsiders, must of necessity establish contact with members of the public. This is of course the most frequently delegated function, and one which is generally delegated to individuals on the lowest level of the organization. Post-office clerks, sales personnel, social workers, and campaign solicitors are ready examples of these types of positions.

Students of formal organizations have noted three characteristic problems which emerge from these interpersonal relationships and which may lead to the displacement of goals. First, there are problems which emerge from the *status* of the organizational member vis à vis the status of the people with whom he comes in contact. Merton has noted that—particularly in government organizations—the status of the official within the organization may not be commensurate with his status in relationship to the public. This situation may lead to an actually or apparently domineering attitude which interferes with the performance of his job.[28]

25. Merton, *op. cit.*, p. 156.
26. Davis, *op. cit.*, p. 392.
27. Selznick, *TVA and the Grass Roots*, pp. 217–46.
28. Merton, *op. cit.*, p. 158.

Second, problems may emerge from the fact that *impersonality* is usually supposed to govern relationships with the public. A bureaucratic organization, according to Weber, is governed by "a consistent system of abstract rules. . . ," and the activities of individual members "consist in the application of these rules to particular cases. . . ."[29] In applying these rules, the members should eliminate from their job "love, hatred and all purely personal, irrational, and emotional elements which escape calculation."[30] The need for impersonality in many situations is readily apparent, since the organizational member who comes into contact with the public is expected to act in the name of the organization, not on his own behalf. The possibility exists, however, that the minimization of personal relations and the resort to categorization may result in the disregard of the peculiarities of individual situations. If one of the purposes of the organization is to cope with peculiar cases, impersonality may lead to the displacement of goals.[31]

A third source of difficulty arising from relationships with the public is the violation of impersonalization, called *particularism*. Peter Blau, for example, in his study of two government agencies, noted that "some officials lost sight of the generic objective of raising the standard of living of American workers in the course of dealing with particular underpaid (or unemployed) individuals. . . . Although this particularistic orientation enhanced work satisfaction, it . . . created resistance in those situations where the interest of individual employees had to be set aside in the interest of the generic objectives of the agency. . . ."[32]

## The foundation and the problem of goal displacement

If we examine the record of achievement of the Foundation it is quite apparent that the organization has not been deflected from achieving its major goals. In fact, in the nearly two decades since its establishment it has sponsored research which has vastly increased medical knowledge of infantile

29. Weber, *op. cit.*, p. 330.
30. Max Weber, *Essays in Sociology*. Translated and edited by H. H. Gerth and C. W. Mills (New York: Oxford University Press, 1946), p. 216.
31. Merton, *op. cit.*, pp. 157–58.
32. Blau, *op. cit.*, pp. 191–92.

paralysis; it has brought about revolutionary changes in the methods of treating victims of infantile paralysis; it has introduced a completely new concept of how payment for medical and hospital bills may be shared by all the members of a community; it has sponsored the development of the Salk polio vaccine; and it is now on the threshold of achieving its major purpose—the elimination of epidemic infantile paralysis. It follows from this record of achievement that some provisions must have been incorporated into its formal structure which have served to minimize the displacement of its goals. This section is devoted to a description of those provisions which have served to mitigate the adverse effect of each of the sources of goal displacement previously described.

### STATUS WITHIN THE ORGANIZATION

Voluntary associations are inherently better protected than are other organizations against being deflected from their goals by the career interests of their members since the vast majority of their membership consists of unpaid volunteers for whom the activity is not their primary occupation. But a largely volunteer membership by no means provides complete immunity. In the first place, all large-scale voluntary associations employ some full-time professionals who carry out part of the day-to-day activity of the organization; in the second place, a volunteer member may be as interested as an employee in maintaining his position in the organization, and may accordingly orient his activities toward that end.

The formal structure of the Foundation provides several safeguards against the dangers inherent in the vested interests of individuals in maintaining their positions. In the first place, the ratio of professional employees to volunteer members is very low. The entire organization has fewer than 800 full-time employees, while more than 12,000 Volunteers are officers in local Chapters and many more Volunteers participate either in Chapter activities or in the March of Dimes. This reliance upon the volunteer membership for the performance of many functions is made feasible in two ways. First, unlike the situation which prevails in many national voluntary associations, there are no state societies which occupy an intermediate position between National Headquarters and local Chapters.[33] Since a state organization might require a minimum of perhaps ten or fifteen full-time employees, 400 to 600 positions are unnecessary. Second, the day-to-day program of the organization itself is such that it is possible for it to be performed for the most part by a few part-time Volunteers. This contrasts sharply with the situation which prevails in trade unions, for example, in which even the smallest local usually requires one or more employees to carry out the day-to-day responsibilities of the organization.

Another feature of the Foundation's formal structure which counterbalances the problems which arise from the desire of individuals to maintain their positions is the relative absence of status rewards associated with holding office. The professional employees have few opportunities to become widely-known outside of the organization and profession itself, and the officers of local Chapters generally do not hold widely coveted positions in the community. Furthermore, there are few opportunities for Volunteers to advance upward in the Foundation hierarchy. Paid personnel, for example, are only rarely ex-Volunteers, and the absence of state societies means that there are no higher positions within the Foundation toward which Volunteers can aspire. This situation contrasts sharply with that which prevails in organizations such as trade unions or the American Legion, where there is generally active competition for the position of local President or Post Commander, and active competition among these officers for state or national positions.

### THE INTERPRETATION OF ORGANIZATIONAL RULES

The rules which govern any organization are of two broad types. *Structural* rules specify how the organization is to be established, and include such items as qualifications for membership, the offices and committees which are authorized, and specific details concerning the delegation of authority and function. *Procedural* rules, on the other hand, specify how the activities of the organization are to be carried out, and consist largely of "do's" and "don't's."

33. As noted earlier, the Foundation's state offices are the headquarters of the State Representatives, not state organizations.

The rules which govern both the structure and the procedures of the Foundation's local Chapters are codified in the *Manual for Chapters*, which includes the *By-laws* of Chapters. Since Chapters are conceived as administrative units of the national organization, the *Manual* and the *By-laws* apply to all Chapters; they are established by the Board of Trustees and may not be changed except by the Board.[34]

Upon first inspection, the *Manual* and the *By-laws* seem very similar to those of any organization. They include such details as the name of the organization, its purpose, its qualifications for membership, its major activities, its financial procedures, and the like. But if an examination is made of those provisions of the rules which relate to the major activities of the local Chapter—granting financial aid to polio patients and raising funds through the annual March of Dimes—a significant fact emerges: practically none of the rules applies to these activities. This is particularly surprising with respect to the patient care program, since as any one who has had first-hand familiarity with assistance programs of any kind knows all too well, rules concerning such details as eligibility requirements are often worded in such a way that only an expert at finding "loopholes" can make the program truly effective. But the *Manual* has nothing to say concerning eligibility for financial aid, and stipulates only one prohibition: grants or expenditures in the aggregate amount of $2,000 or more cannot be made in one year for the benefit of any one person or institution without the written consent of National Headquarters. There are of course a number of absolute prohibitions upon expenses. A Chapter cannot, for example, purchase or erect hospitals or clinics, support research, or contribute to the educational expenses of polio patients. But the types of rules which lead to "overinterpretation" in any organization are seldom those which establish absolute prohibitions, but rather those which apply to judgments made in individual cases. Since the rules which govern the patient care program are not of this character, there is little opportunity for Volunteers to subvert the aims of the program by focusing undue attention upon legalisms.[35]

Very much the same situation holds with respect to the conduct of the March of Dimes. The broad outlines of the campaign are stipulated in the *Manual*: it is to be held in January, and it must be supported by each Chapter. But there is only one prohibition: no Chapter can engage in any fund-raising activity, either alone or in conjunction with another organization, other than the March of Dimes. Here again, it is difficult for Volunteers to displace the goals of the campaign by paying too strict attention to legalities.

### THE EXECUTION OF ORGANIZATIONAL PROCEDURES

An examination of the Foundation's formal structure reveals a number of implicit safeguards against the displacement of goals through undue emphasis upon procedures designed to achieve them. Perhaps of greatest importance is the division of responsibilities between National Headquarters and local Chapters. As described earlier, Chapters are responsible for granting financial assistance to polio victims in their area of responsibility, or informing the public about polio and the steps being taken to combat it, and for assisting to raise funds during the annual March of Dimes. Similarly, the responsibilities and activities of National Headquarters are described to Chapter Volunteers in specific terms:

1. It is currently engaged in support of research projects of great variety, nationally planned and coordinated. . . .
2. It investigates new methods of treatment offering promise, and facilitates their use when advisable.
3. It undertakes the training of physicians, nurses, physical therapists, health educators, medical social workers, medical record librarians and other professional workers. . . .
4. It aids schools, colleges and universities to expand their technical educational programs.
5. It engages in a widespread information program to the public, designed to present the facts about infantile paralysis, insure proper care and aid in dissipating panic.
6. It disseminates information to physicians, health departments, welfare agencies, to aid them in

34. National Foundation for Infantile Paralysis, *Manual for Chapters*, 1949 ed., p. 32.

35. The existence of only a few rules governing the patient-care program does not mean that Chapters are not provided with suggestions concerning how it may most effectively be carried out; in fact, an entire manual is devoted to this subject. See National Foundation for Infantile Paralysis. *Chapter Reference Book: Chapter Patient Care Program.*

programs in the care and rehabilitation of infantile paralysis patients.[36]

The most crucial aspect of this division of labor is that the sponsorship of scientific research—clearly the most directly goal-related activity of the Foundation—is confined to National Headquarters, while Chapters have major responsibility for patient care and fund-raising. This centralization of the function of sponsoring research serves of course the manifest function of making it possible to coordinate the research activities of hundreds of scientists more effectively. But the prohibition of Chapter sponsorship of research also serves an important unintended or latent function: it precludes the possibility that Chapters might neglect the research program in favor of the more immediately rewarding patient care program. Stated differently, it ensures that the ultimate goal (elimination of polio) will not be displaced by a proximate goal (caring for polio patients).

It is very significant in this connection that those national voluntary health associations which have corporate-type formal structures generally devote a much larger percentage of their budgets to research than do those with federation-type structures, expenditures which are for the most part made possible by the fact that the national headquarters of these organizations receive a larger share of the annual fund-raising proceeds.[37] The local units of voluntary health associations are generally reluctant, even when they are empowered to do so, to allocate funds for research, since other types of expenditures provide a more immediate return in terms of public response and personal satisfactions.

Since patient care is a proximate goal, and since the division of responsibility in the Foundation between National Headquarters and local Chapters ensures that patient care activities will not come to stand in the way of progress toward the ultimate goal, Volunteer attention to the needs of polio patients serves only the worthwhile function of making the program more effective; it does not, in short, serve as a possible source of goal displacement. Fund-raising, on the other hand, could easily become an end in itself, a development which would eventually react unfavorably upon the success of the fund-raising program. This possibility is clearly recognized by the Foundation; hence the oft-repeated admonition to Volunteers: "The National Foundation raises money to exist; it does not exist to raise money." But fund-raising is an activity which has such immediate and tangible rewards that some mechanism more effective than a verbal admonition is patently necessary to prevent local Chapters from focusing undue attention upon their fund-raising responsibilities. This mechanism is provided by the device of making fund-raising a Chapter *activity*, but one which is under the actual *direction* of National Headquarters.

Other features of the formal structure also serve to prevent a disproportionate emphasis upon procedures. *Sanctification* and *ceremonialism* are minimized by the fact that local Chapters are organized in such a way that Volunteers have few opportunities to devote attention to organization-related activities, at the expense of those which are goal-related. The headquarters for the Chapter is generally the business office or home of the Chairman; even in the case of large Chapters, the headquarters is simply a rented or donated small office. There is, in other words, no meeting place for the Chapter which can be invested with ceremonial sentiments. There are no initiation rites or investiture ceremonies and no uniforms or badges. With the exception of one or two meetings each year, the business of most Chapters is conducted over the phone and at small committee meetings over the lunch table or in the living room of one of the committee members. Similarly, the rigidities of *traditionalism* and *routinization* are largely avoided because the Foundation is a young organization, because the patient care and fund-raising programs are largely seasonal in nature, and, in the case of fund-raising, because the March of Dimes organization is reconstituted each year. There is, moreover, a strong tradition of informality which pervades all levels of the Foundation. As is the case with virtually every major feature of the Foundation, this tradition has its roots in the Georgia Warm Springs Foundation, which has since its inception prided itself upon its friendly and almost "family" atmosphere. This in turn had its origins

36. National Foundation for Infantile Paralysis, *Reference Book for Chapters*, pp. 202–3.

37. See the *Annual Reports* of the National Tuberculosis Association, the National Society for Crippled Children and Adults, the American Cancer Society, the American Heart Association, United Cerebral Palsy, and the National Multiple Sclerosis Association.

in the personality of President Roosevelt, who took pride in being the self-styled "Vice President in Charge of Picnics" at Georgia Warm Springs.[38]

RELATIONSHIPS WITH OTHER PARTICIPANTS

It was noted above that there are three quite different situations in which the relationships among participants may lead to the displacement of goals: the development of group norms which are incompatible with the organization's goal, the development of a sense of common destiny among participants, and the informal co-optation into the policy-making apparatus of outside groups which exert an adverse influence over the achievement of the original goals.

Consider first the emergence of group norms concerning how many polio patients should be helped, and how much assistance should be given. Every person residing in a Chapter's area of responsibility who contracts polio, and for whom the full payment of medical and hospital bills would constitute a major hardship, is eligible for aid. Since Chapter funds are limited, there is a natural desire of Volunteers to give aid only when it is actually needed. On the other hand, Chapter funds are intended precisely for this purpose, so there is nothing to be gained by withholding aid when it is needed. Accordingly, the scope of the patient care program within any one Chapter is governed in part by the incidence of polio and in part by the amount of funds available; since both polio incidence and March of Dimes success varies from year to year, the likelihood that a norm will emerge concerning how extensive the program should be is very slight.

The fund-raising program presents a somewhat different situation, since the possibility exists that a group norm might develop concerning how much money should be raised. Such a norm would violate Foundation policy, which is not to set quotas but to raise as much money as possible, since the needs of patients and the requirements of the research program have usually been in excess of the funds available.

Two mechanisms seem to prevent the emergence of such a norm. First, since the local Chapter receives for its own use only 50 per cent of all the funds it raises, which is often insufficient for local needs, and since the expenditure of these funds for patients is a source of satisfaction to individual Volunteers, the development of a quota would be against the better interests of the Chapter members. Second, as already noted, the March of Dimes is technically directed by National Headquarters, not by the local Chapters, and the national office technically appoints the local Campaign Director, who in many cases is not a member of the Chapter. This provision of the formal structure, which means that the Chapter supports but does not direct the March of Dimes, serves to minimize the possibility that Chapter members might be able—even if they so desired—to exert an influence over the amount of funds raised.

The major structural feature of the Foundation which mitigates against adherence to career interests is of course the over-whelmingly volunteer character of its personnel. Volunteers for the most part belong to many organizations, and their participation in Foundation activity is only part-time; accordingly, it is easier for them to maintain a goal orientation than it is for full-time employees of an organization whose career interests are inextricably bound up with the future of the organization itself.

Finally, the Foundation's structure precludes the possibility that outside groups will come to exert an untoward influence over its activities. An explicit feature of Foundation policy, it should be noted, is for Chapters to work in close cooperation with other community organizations—both official and private agencies concerned with health and welfare problems and voluntary associations which carry on a more general program. The purpose of this cooperation is three-fold. It avoids duplication of effort with respect to patient aid, it increases community recognition of the Chapter, and it enlists support for the March of Dimes. However, Chapters are not permitted to be sponsored by any other agency, nor are they permitted to delegate responsibility for the conduct of the entire fund-raising campaign. Rather, community organizations are informally asked to take over one specific phase of the campaign. The Parent-Teachers Association, for example, is often given major responsibility for the Mothers' March on Polio, and the Lions Club may

38. Turnley Walker, "Warm Springs," *Holiday*, 15 (February, 1954), p. 84. See also Turnley Walker, *Roosevelt and the Warm Springs Story* (New York: A. A. Wyn, 1953) for a vivid account of the informal atmosphere which prevails at Georgia Warm Springs.

take charge of Street Solicitation. Because responsibility is delegated piece-meal, as it were, rather than *en bloc*, the chances are slight that any cooperating organization could exert any influence over the policy of the March of Dimes.

### RELATIONSHIPS WITH THE PUBLIC

The provisions of the Foundation's formal structure which mitigate against relationships with the public, leading to a displacement of goals, may be stated very briefly. First, the character of local Chapter activities is such that Volunteers are never placed in a position of authority over members of the public. The patient care program involves a situation of helpfulness, not authority; the information program brings the Volunteer to the public as an expert on the problems of polio; and the fund-raising program puts him in the position of petitioner. In none of these situations is there any discrepancy between the Volunteer's role in the organization and his role with respect to the general public.

The patient care program involves making decisions with regard to individual cases, which is precisely the situation in which the adverse effects of both impersonalization and particularism are likely to take place. Two aspects of this situation, however, serve to reduce the possibility that these adverse effects will take place. First, since there are no rigid criteria on which the merits of individual cases are supposed to be judged, and since the number of cases concerning which decisions are to be made is small, it is possible for Volunteers to treat each case "on its own merits." Second, particularism is minimized by the fact that the relationship with patients is mediated through the medical profession. Since physicians are explicitly trained to strike a balance between impersonalization and particularism in their relationships with patients—an attitude of "detached concern" is considered the ideal[39]—Volunteers generally find it possible to adjust their own attitudes in this area to those of the medical profession, and thus avoid interfering with the over-all program.

39. The Bureau of Applied Social Research of Columbia University is currently undertaking a large-scale evaluation of medical school training. One of the problems being examined concerns the mechanisms through which the students learn to adopt an attitude of "detached concern" towards patients.

N. J. DEMERATH III and VICTOR THIESSEN

# On Spitting Against the Wind: Organizational Precariousness and American Irreligion

This paper offers a belated diagnosis of an organization that is currently in its death trance. The analysis follows the development and demise of a small-town Wisconsin free-thought movement or Freie Gemeinde which began in 1852, reached its zenith in the 1880's, and then began to atrophy with the pursuit of legitimacy. The study is intended as both a perverse chapter in the sociology of religion and a paragraph in the theory of organizational change. It has two primary justifications.

First, in focusing on irreligion it directs attention to a neglected phenomenon on the American religious scene. Although the sociology of religion has been born again, the sociology of irreligion remains in the womb[1] despite the current talk of secularization and the steady flow of theological amendments to nineteenth-century orthodoxy and despite the predictions of Weber, Marx, and Durkheim that the twentieth century would witness the decline of the religious establishment.[2] Certainly irreligion has failed to replace the churches. At the same time, studies of irreligion may provide insight into its difficulties and a new comparative basis for analysis of the churches themselves.

A second justification is more abstract. Irreligious groups are precarious by dint of their dissidence and their illegitimacy. Examination of this precariousness may inform the study of organizational dynamics generally. Most organizational analysis follows in the wake of Weber's concern with the bureaucratic monolith. While the topic of organizational growth is common, studies of organizational demise are rare. While the conservative organization has been compelling, the deviant organization

1. Organizational studies of irreligion are nonexistent, although there have been several surveys that tap irreligion in wider populations. See, e.g., Russell Middleton and Snell Putney, "Religion, Normative Standards, and Behavior," *Sociometry*, 25 (June, 1962), 141–52, and Putney and Middleton, "Ethical Relativism and Anomia," *American Journal of Sociology*, 68 (January, 1962), 430–38.

2. Max Weber, *The Protestant Ethic and the Spirit of Capitalism* (New York: Charles Scribner's Sons, 1958), pp. 181–83; *General Economic History* (New York: Collier Books, 1961), p. 270. Emile Durkheim, *The Elementary Forms of the Religious Life* (New York: Collier Books, 1961), pp. 427–29; *Professional Ethics and Civic Morals* (New York: Free Press, 1958), esp. pp. 55–56. See, e.g., Karl Marx, "Anti-Church Movement—Demonstration in Hyde Park," in *Marx and Engels on Religion* (New York: Schocken Books, 1964), pp. 127–34. Although all of these predictions are refuted in that the church remains strong, they are partially confirmed in the preconditions of that strength. Thus, the church has staved off irreligion by becoming increasingly secular and allowing room for potential irreligionists within its own ranks. The establishment may not have passed, but it certainly has changed.

This is an expanded version of a paper delivered at the American Sociological Association meetings in Chicago, September 1, 1965. We are indebted to the Danforth Study of Campus Ministries and to Dr. Kenneth Underwood for research support. We are grateful to the members of the Sauk City Freie Gemeinde for their patience, their candor, and their hospitality. Finally, we have profited from the suggestions of a number of colleagues, including Kenneth Lutterman, Roberta Goldstone, Gerald Marwell, Phillip Hammond, and Berenice Cooper.

Reprinted from *The American Journal of Sociology*, May, 1966, pp. 674-87, by permission of the author and publisher. (Copyright 1966 by The University of Chicago Press.)

is frequently ignored and often shunted to the less attended realm of collective behavior. There is, of course, a range of studies on religious sects[3] as well as the literature on political extremism[4] and social movements.[5] And yet the freethinkers have features that distinguish them from each of these.

Unlike religious sects, the free-thought movement lacks any crystallized doctrine and falls beyond the pale of American religious tolerance. Unlike political movements, the freethinkers have no sharply defined organizational goals, and pressures against them are more informal than the sanctions of the electorate or the courts. Finally, unlike the Townsend movement, the Women's Christian Temperance Union, or an educational reform group, irreligion has neither a natural population from which to recruit nor a set of values which are in any way consistent with the normative mainstream.

Because the Freie Gemeinde is peculiar in these and other respects it points to considerations that are largely mute in previous work. These include community structure and differentiation as they relate to expressed hostility; the effect of social class on the response to hostility; the difficulties of nurturing charisma as well as its importance in sustaining an illegitimate group; the problems of rallying commitment around a nihilistic doctrine and a goalless program; and the conflict between commitment and recruitment as organizational imperatives. Precisely because irreligion taxes previous frameworks without falling wholly outside of them, it should provide important additions to our current knowledge. Still, the study has no illusions of definitiveness. Since both irreligion and organizational precariousness have been little explored, our errors may be as instructive as our insights.

The paper comprises five sections. The first describes the study's methodology. The second offers a brief historical account of the group at issue. Third, we shall discuss some general characteristics of organizational precariousness and the range of adaptations to it. Fourth, we shall show how adaptation is influenced by external community factors. Fifth and finally, we shall discuss adaptation to dissidence and precariousness in the light of internal organizational characteristics.

## Methodology

The study invokes three methodological strategies: observation, historical records, and lengthy personal interviews. Although we intend more rigorous research in the future, this first study is undeniably "soft." Accordingly, we shall heed Howard S. Becker's advice[6] and present a chronology of the investigation as one slim basis for evaluation.

As is frequently the case in exploratory research, the analytic problem which finally emerged was not

3. For the classic statement on the religious sect, see Ernst Troeltsch, *The Social Teachings of the Christian Churches* (New York: Harper & Bros., 1960), I, 328–54. Several recent treatments include Bryan R. Wilson, "An Analysis of Sect Development," *American Sociological Review*, 24 (February, 1959); Benton Johnson, "On Church and Sect," *American Sociological Review*, 28 (August, 1963), 539–49; and Scott Grant McNall, "The Sect Movement," *Pacific Sociological Review*, 6 (Fall, 1963), 60–64. See also Leon Festinger, Henry W. Riecken, and Stanley Schachter, *When Prophecy Fails* (Minneapolis: University of Minnesota Press, 1956), for a more psychological analysis of a precarious religious cult.

4. Much of the literature on political extremism is more polemical than academic. Some of the better works include: Daniel Bell (ed.), *The Radical Right* (Garden City, N.Y.: Doubleday & Co., 1963); Irving Howe and Lewis Coser, *The American Communist Party: A Critical History* (New York: Praeger Books, 1962); Philip Selznick, *The Organizational Weapon* (New York: Free Press, 1960); Vladimir C. Nahirney, "Some Observations on Ideological Groups," *American Journal of Sociology*, 67 (January, 1962), 397–405; Egon Bittner, "Radicalism and Radical Movements," *American Sociological Review*, 28 (December, 1963), 928–40; and Neil J. Smelser, *Theory of Collective Behavior* (New York: Free Press, 1963), pp. 270–382.

5. The term "social movement" is, of course, a catchall. Several broad theoretical treatments include the divergent perspectives of Smelser, *ibid.*, and Hadley Cantril, *The Psychology of Social Movements* (London: Chapman & Hall, Ltd., 1941). Case studies include Burton R. Clark, "Organizational Adaptation and Precarious Values: A Case Study," *American Sociological Review*, 21 (June, 1956), 327–36; Joseph R. Gusfield, "Social Structure and Moral Reform: A Study of the Women's Christian Temperance Union, *American Journal of Sociology*, 61 (November, 1955), 221–32; Sheldon I. Messinger, "Organizational Transformation: A Case Study of a Declining Social Movement," *American Sociological Review*, 24 (February, 1955), 3–10; and C. Eric Lincoln, *The Black Muslims in America* (Boston: Beacon Press, 1961). Finally, for related treatments of delinquency and lower-class culture, see J. Milton Yinger, "Contraculture and Subculture," *American Sociological Review*, 25 (October, 1960), 625–45, and Lewis Yablonsky, "The Delinquent Gang as a Near-Group," *Social Problems*, 7 (Fall, 1959), 108–17.

6. Howard S. Becker, "Problems of Inference and Proof in Participant Observation," *American Sociological Review*, 23 (December, 1958), 652–60.

the one that launched the study. Our first information on the Freie Gemeinde included only its location in the small, predominantly Catholic community of Sauk City and its shrinking size. This suggested conflict between the group and its context, a conflict which was to be the focus of the research.

It took only a few visits to teach us otherwise. We soon discovered that actual conflict had seldom occurred and that even past hostility had evanesced as the group began to camouflage its principles and seek survival instead of reform. Thus, the study quickly shifted from static to dynamic. Rather than focus on the contemporary scene, we were led to the historical problem of a changing organization and its changing community relations.

This was the result of the research's first stage, involving lengthy conversations with strategic members of the organization. A second stage quickly followed and persisted. This involved "quasi-participant observation"[7] in the society's affairs, ranging from Sunday afternoon meetings held twice monthly to more informal gatherings. Third, we took advantage of the group's unique but dusty library to read and translate historical documents on nineteenth-century free thought. Fourth, we interviewed members of the movement more systematically. By this time we were aware of most of the key issues in the group's development. We had formed a number of hypotheses around which to probe for information.

Because the current membership is less than fifty, we decided to interview the entire population. But many members are no longer in the community, and others are so old as to be non-communicating. We completed interviews with twenty. Although these span all significant viewpoints within the group, there is no way of accurately assessing their representativeness. This together with the small number precludes statistical analysis and confines the yield to qualitative insights and illustration. In addition, we also interviewed apostates and non-affiliates in the community to gain a wider perspective. There was no formal community survey for fear of artificially reviving rancor and friction.

Finally, after the study was completed, we submitted drafts to several respondents for their comments. This revealed a few minor errors of fact, but all agreed that the basic theoretical points were sound, even those based on our own deductions rather than any direct mention in the interviews. Of course, acceptance of this sort may raise as many issues as it settles. It may be that our critics are too kind, especially to two outsiders who were giving them rare attention. It also may be that we suffered the analytic seduction that lurks for any observer. Nevertheless, these evaluations do confer one small stamp of validity, and validity is a precious commodity in a study of this sort.

## The Freie Gemeinde in historical review

As the analysis shifted from current conflict to organizational dynamics, history became a crucial ingredient. American irreligion has enjoyed more historical than sociological attention,[8] but even so, work on ethnic irreligion in the tradition of the Freie Gemeinde is sparse.[9] This brief chronology

7. Participant observation is not quite apt since we were conspicuous as outsiders and made no attempt to hide our research objectives. At the same time, we were graciously received, invited to every meeting, and witnessed no inhibitions. It is a commentary on the group itself, however, that it no longer discusses issues about which inhibitions might arise.

8. Most of this historical attention has been devoted to early American deists such as Jefferson, Franklin, and Paine, together with the East Coast offspring of Unitarianism, including the ethical-culture movement. See, e.g., Stow Persons, *Free Religion: An American Faith* (New Haven, Conn.: Yale University Press, 1947); Sidney Warren, *American Freethought: 1860–1914* (New York: Columbia University Press, 1943); and Martin Marty, *The Infidel* (New York: Living Age Books, 1961).

9. Most of the literature here was locally published in limited editions and in German. For the European background of the free-thought movement, see Friedrich Schuenemann-Pott, *Die Freie Gemeinde* (Philadelphia: B. Stephen Publishers, 1861), and Johannes Ronge, *Rede Gehalten beim Ersten Gottesdienste der Freien Christlichen Gemeinden zu Schweinfurt am Palm Sonntag* (Schweinfurt, 1849). For historical materials on the Wisconsin movement, see Karl Heinzen, *Deutscher Radikalismus in Amerika* (distributed by the "Verein zur Verbreitung radikaler Prinzipien," 1879); Max Hempel, *Was Sind die Freien Gemeinden von Nord-Amerika?* (Philadelphia, 1877); Friedrich Schuenemann-Pott (ed.), *Blaetter fuer Freies Religioeses Leben* (Wisconsin, 1855–71), Vols. 1–16; J. J. Schlichter, "Eduard Schroeter the Humanist," *Wisconsin Magazine of History* (December, 1944, and March, 1945); Freidenker Convention zu Milwaukee, *Blitzstrahlen der Wahrheit* (Milwaukee Freidenker, 1872). A good recent summary is provided in Berenice Cooper, "Die Freien Gemeinden in Wisconsin," *Wisconsin Academy of Science, Arts and Letters*, 53 (Fall, 1964), 53–65.

draws heavily upon personal recollections and untranslated documents. Some of the details await the theoretical discussion to follow.

The Freie Gemeinde emerged out of the religious and social unrest in Germany and Eastern Europe of the 1840's. Upon the excommunication of one Johannes Ronge for doubting the sacramental validity of a "holy robe" in Trier, a number of Catholics severed their ties with Rome and founded Free Christian or German-Catholic churches. The movement was neither united nor homogeneous. Ronge himself was anti-institutional rather than antidoctrinal. Yet some were more radical than others, and upon persecution, many fled the country. The emigration was accelerated by the German Revolution of 1848; hence the term "forty-eighters" to refer to this first major wave of German settlers.

The first Freie Gemeinde in the United States began in St. Louis in 1850. Other communities formed in Pennsylvania; California; Washington, D.C.; New York; Illinois; and Wisconsin. In Wisconsin there were some thirty groups by 1852 ranging from Milwaukee and Madison to Polktown and Koshkonong. The Sauk City group in question organized on October 24, 1852. Its declared purpose occurs in its articles of incorporation:

> The United German Free Congregation is our name for our organization, for we wish to unite the enemies of clericalism, official hypocrisy and bigotry, the friends of truth, uprightness and honesty to be found scattered among all religions, creeds, churches and sects.
>
> By means of such united strength we intend to erect a strong fortification against the pernicious power of the churches, sects and clericalism.
>
> The foundation of this organization is *reason*, which is defamed by the priests of all "revealed" religions, and the book of nature and world history, feared and repudiated by clericals, but loved and honored by the wise of all nations and all times.
>
> Obviously we do not recognize as "godless" those so called on account of their views (theoretical atheists) but rather the godless in fact—practical atheists, who behave as though there were no universal law to which they are obliged to submit, and no moral cosmic law to which they must conform. We dictate neither belief nor disbelief in God or immortality.[10]

Despite its stridency, the early Freie Gemeinde was a strong and cautiously respected element in the local community throughout the nineteenth century. Not only did they help to guide secular affairs, but they were often called in to mediate disputes within the churches themselves. The freethinkers were also an important cultural force. Their activities emphasized music, drama, poetry, ethics, and philosophy. Their periodic festivals drew capacity crowds and guest lecturers from all over the country.

All of this reached its zenith under the guidance of one leader in particular, Eduard Schroeter. He had received theological training in Germany but was later forced out of the country to the United States. From 1853 to his death in 1888, he was the rallying point for Wisconsin free thought. Not only was he the leader of the Sauk City group, but he also started the Milwaukee Freie Gemeinde and made yearly visits to many of the other free congregations.

At the time of Schroeter's death, the Sauk City organization had an active membership of over one hundred. Its militancy was pronounced. For example, one prominent freethinker bequeathed land for use as a cemetery and stipulated only that priests and ministers were never to set foot on the plot. A current member describes his grandfather this way: "He wasn't too tactful a person. He was a Bible scholar; he knew as much about religion as any preacher, and he'd just walk up to the preacher and argue with him about it. . . . I've seen some of the letters to the editor my grandfather wrote. I don't know of anyone now who would write things like that."

10. Clara Rung, "The Free Congregation of Sauk City" (unpublished manuscript, 1940), p. 11. Note that the statement is bitingly opposed to the church but somewhat ambiguous concerning doctrine. This Kierkegaardian syndrome was characteristic of early free thought, but two things are worth noting about its subsequent development in the Sauk City group. First, there is an ever widening gap between the statements of the organization and the beliefs of the individual members—perhaps an operationalization of both precariousness and bureaucracy. Confining ourselves to the former, the organization was forced to become more publicly accepting of both church and doctrine while its members increased their opposition to doctrine in particular. This leads to a second point. Over time the Kierkegaardian position has been reversed: the members' original hostility toward the church has ebbed, but their atheism has become more *pro*nounced if less *an*nounced. This tendency to accept the church while rejecting its doctrine has, of course, cut a swath through the religious establishment as well, accounting for the concomitant rise of both secularization and church participation.

Indeed, with Schroeter's death and the turnover from first to second generation members, the Freie Gemeinde began to lose its momentum. Gradually, its membership decreased, its activities grew less frequent, and its militancy subsided. The Freie Gemeinde began to cooperate more and condemn less. Its members began to attend the services of the orthodox churches whose own members were increasingly present at the Free Congregation's meetings. Some freethinkers began contributions to the Catholic church, and intermarriage increased. All of this is reflected in the group's changing constitution. Gradually it became less vindictive. The constitution drafted in 1917 lacks any polemic against the church, and a 1951 revision drops all reference to atheism. While nineteen of our twenty respondents are admitted atheists, organizational imperatives demand a less stigmatizing public stand.

Finally, consider the Sauk City group in contrast to its Milwaukee counterpart. Both were founded by the same man, at the same time, and with the same purpose. Yet the two are now estranged. The Milwaukee Freie Gemeinde has cleaved more closely to its original ideals and is more aggressive in pursuing them. To this end, it has joined the American Rationalist Federation (ARF): a lower-class, militant association that embraces Madályn Murray and *The Realist*,[11] together with rationalist societies in St. Louis, Philadelphia, New York, Baltimore, Cleveland, Chicago, and elsewhere. The ARF has repeatedly invited the Sauk City group to join. The invitations have never been answered. Instead Sauk City has chosen a different alliance. In order to legitimate itself and boost its recruitment potential, it became a member of the Unitarian-Universalist Fellowship in 1955. The move has had none of the salutary consequences expected and has even led to an unintended disruption. Recruitment and activities have remained at the same low ebb. The affiliation provoked sharp opposition from some members who felt betrayed and bolted to form a smaller but less compromising circle of their own. Hence this predominantly Catholic community of some 4,000 now hosts *two* irreligious groups. Although one is moribund and the other militant, the latter may very well follow the path of its predecessor. Free thought is neither big business nor aggressive associationalism.

11. Madalyn Murray is an outspoken and formidably aggressive atheist who has used her legal background to push for wider separation of church and state through the courts. Her recent moves from Baltimore to Hawaii and to Texas have left behind a cloud of legal proceedings and embittered former colleagues. *The Realist* is a magazine of free-thought satire that covers issues from homosexuality to foreign policy in the unflinching manner of a literary Lenny Bruce.

## Organizational precariousness and adaptive strategies

In a society in which a leading liberal politician can assert, "I don't care what a man's religion is as long as he believes in God," it is no surprise to consider the Freie Gemeinde a precarious organization. The term "precarious" is appropriate for any organization that confronts the prospect of its own demise. The confrontation need be neither intentional nor acknowledged. The important criterion is a threatened disruption of the organization such that achievement of its goals and the maintenance of its values are so obstructed as to bring on a loss of identity through deathly quiescence, merger, or actual disbandment.

There is no single source of precariousness. It may arise out of structural weaknesses concerning leadership, communication, compliance, or role differentiation. It may emerge from poor recruitment or from low commitment. It may stem from abrasive relations with a hostile environment, even relations that fall short of blatant conflict. The last is plainly the most conspicuous source for the precariousness of the dissident Freie Gemeinde. It is also a central factor in Burton Clark's insightful analysis of "precarious values."[12] Clark argues that a value may be precarious because it is undefined, because its functionaries are illegitimate, or because the value itself is "unacceptable to a 'host' population." All three of these conditions apply to the Freie Gemeinde at one time or another. And yet Clark's suggestion that groups with precarious value are led into strenuous social service in the search for acceptance is less apt. There are other forms of adaptations and other factors that govern the pressure to adapt in the first place.

In general the possible responses to a hostile environment may be ranged along a continuum. The alternatives move in two directions. On the one

12. Clark, *op. cit.*

hand, the group may follow Clark's scheme and pursue legitimation by changing or camouflaging its values, switching its functionaries and public spokesmen, or performing redeeming services for the community. Many groups attain stability in precisely this fashion. But for others the path may lead to organizational death. This is especially likely in groups like the Freie Gemeinde for whom dissidence itself was an original *raison d'être*.

On the other hand, a second adaptation involves increased militancy. Selznick, Nahirny, and Bittner have all pointed to the organizational gains that may be had by widening the gulf between the group and its context.[13] If membership commitment is a concern, one way to bolster it is to make commitment irrevocable by burning the members' bridges behind them and precluding competing allegiances to more legitimate organizations. Thus, a radical group's effectiveness may be judged by its ability to turn external hostility to an internal advantage. As we shall see, however, this ability is difficult to come by.

But is it necessary to adapt drastically in either direction? Certainly some organizations are able to compensate for hostility without radical shifts in either tactics or character. Some have no design on their context, and its hostility is therefore less urgent. Organizational structure and commitment may provide an imperviousness to opposition. Finally, the hostility itself may be poorly communicated, non-consensual, or effectively blunted. In short, there are really two issues involved in the adaptation to a hostile environment: is a major adaptation necessary and, if so, in which direction? To explore these questions further, let us return to the Freie Gemeinde in theoretical rather than historical relief. The problem is to account for the Sauk City group's adaptation in the direction of legitimacy. Possible solutions lie in two artificially distinguished clusters, one having to do with the community itself, the other relating to the group in particular.[14]

## Differentiation and the community context

There is perhaps no concept more central to community analysis than that of "differentiation." Yet there are at least two dimensions to this concept, both of which are important to the changing position of the Freie Gemeinde. First, one can speak of *vertical* differentiation, referring to social class and the ability to sustain calss distinctions and elites. Second, there is *horizontal* or "structural" differentiation,[15] referring to the degree of autonomy between various institutional spheres, including economics, politics, education, religion, and, indeed, irreligion.[16]

The relevance of vertical differentiation is discernible in two propositions. One is that strong elites may thwart the sentiments of the wider community by resisting or rechanneling their expression. Another is that a small town like Sauk City is unlikely to retain effective elites under the encroachments of the current "mass society."[17] In all of this, the contrast between the Sauk City group of 1865 and 1965 provides an illustration. Recalling the diatribe

13. See also the general literature on the sociology of conflict, including Lewis Coser, *The Functions of Social Conflict* (New York: Free Press, 1956), pp. 87–104, and Kenneth E. Boulding, *Conflict and Defense: A General Theory* (New York: Harper & Row, 1962), esp. pp. 162–64.

14. At this point it is instructive to compare the approach to follow with Smelser's landmark, *Theory of Collective Behavior*, *op. cit.* Although the Freie Gemeinde fits into Smelser's category of the "value oriented movement," it cannot be understood in Smelser's terms. Because of his emphasis on political revolutionism, Smelser puts a great deal of stress on repressive control by formally constituted authorities. He gives little attention to either informal control from the wider context or to "self-control" through internal organizational characteristics. Both of these are crucial to the free-thought movement, and this is one of a number of ways in which irreligion departs from previous cases and previous theories.

15. The theoretical literature on structural differentiation is burgeoning. For a critical exchange on its applicability to social change, see Talcott Parsons, "Evolutionary Universals in Society," *American Sociological Review*, XXIX (June, 1964), 339–57, and S. N. Eisenstadt, "Social Change, Differentiation and Evolution," *American Sociological Review*, XXIX (June, 1964), 375–85. For two discussions of its applicability to religion in particular, see Robert Bellah, "Religious Evolution," *American Sociological Review*, XXIX (June, 1964), 358–74, and Richard A. Peterson and N. J. Demerath III, "Introduction to Liston Pope," *Millhands and Preachers* (New Haven, Conn.: Yale University Press, 1942; 5th ed., 1965), pp. xxv–xxxii.

16. Note that differentiation can be seen *within* each of these spheres as well as *between* them. This is even the case for irreligion itself. Thus, St. Louis hosts both a strong Ethical Culture Society (middle class and church-like) and the headquarters of the ARF (lower class and more sect-like). The groups seldom communicate, and there is virtually no overlap in membership.

17. For a discussion of the role of elites in the contemporary small town, see Arthur J. Vidich and Joseph Bensman, *Small Town in Mass Society* (Garden City, N.Y. Doubleday & Co., 1960), esp. pp. 114–39, 287–89.

against the church in the Freie Gemeinde's original statement of principles, one might have expected countermeasures from the local Catholics. And yet the reciprocity was frustrated by an aristocratic class allegiance between the freethinkers and the most influential Catholics. Sauk City Catholics were originally polarized into two groups occupying the same church. The "old" Bavarian Catholics—wealthy, prominent, and educated—knelt in sharp contrast to the "new" Prussian Catholics who were lower rather than upper class and had migrated for economic rather than political reasons. One member of the Catholic church had this to say about the situation:

> There was more in common between the "Old Catholics" and the Freie Gemeinde than between the "Old Catholics" and the lower-class Catholics. . . . The freethinkers were a powerful force in the community. For many years they provided a cultural leadership. . . . The "Old Catholics" are contemptuous of many of the young priests who come in here who are ignorant, who have no real grasp of theology for all the preaching they do. So although the Catholics grew till they represented 70 per cent of the population of this community, they were never in a position to challenge the Freie Gemeinde. The bond between the "Old Catholics" and the Freie Gemeinde was too great.

Although the lower-class Catholics commonly had the priest as ally in their intended war against the freethinkers, the upper-class Catholics had the church coffers as a weapon in their opposition. As long as the elite retained its distinctive power in the church and community, the Freie Gemeinde was protected. By the turn of the century, however, this protective kinship had decreased. With acculturation and both upward and downward mobility, the Catholic church grew more homogeneous. Later we will note the downward mobility of the Freie Gemeinde itself. As both Catholics and freethinkers lost their upper-class character, pressure intensified and made an adaptive strategy necessary for the Freie Gemeinde.

But why a strategy of legitimation rather than increased militancy? Here the horizontal dimension of differentiation offers insight and Milwaukee offers a comparison. As a structurally differentiated urban center,[18] it affords its dissident groups both autonomy and a structured irrelevance. We would expect the Milwaukee Freie Gemeinde to choose the adaptive tack of militancy for several reasons. It not only must if it is to be heard, but it is allowed to since few are listening. Despite its bluster and intent, its disruptiveness is more threatened than real. Its militance is generally ignored because its activities do not impinge upon other community sectors or even upon the Milwaukee churches. But the less differentiated small town of Sauk City poses a different situation for its freethinkers. Because Sauk City forces an interpenetration of the activities of the Freie Gemeinde and every other institution, hostility increases and legitimation becomes a more likely response. In a small town, an irreligious group that occupies a prominent building on a large lot in the center of the community is more visible, more stigmatizing, and more consequential. Where this group is a dwindling minority, legitimation is the only recourse in the struggle for survival.

In all of this, there is a paradox and two tainted alternatives. In a differentiated community, the dissident group may be militant precisely because its militance goes unnoticed or ignored. In an undifferentiated community, the dissident group is much more noticed and, therefore, must put a damper on its pronouncements. Thus, one may have militancy at the cost of neglect or one may have attention at the price of legitimation. Of course, after a point, militancy may stimulate attention and legitimacy may bring on neglect. The latter is a major tactic of the Sauk City group. We mentioned earlier that the Freie Gemeinde joined the Unitarian-Universalist Fellowship to facilitate its recruitment by increasing its legitimacy. Even so, the group has qualms about risking a cultivated anonymity by launching a membership campaign of any sort. One member puts it this way: "If we ever battled for a member with one of the churches, then we might antagonize them. Our methods of obtaining members are far from the hard-sell type

18. For an account of the role of structural differentiation in urban centers, see Delbert C. Miller, "Decision-Making Cliques in Community Power Structures: A Comparative Study of an American and English City," *American Journal of Sociology*, 64 (November, 1958), 299–310; Robert A. Dahl, *Who Governs* (New Haven, Conn.: Yale University Press, 1961); Robert O. Schulze, "The Role of Economic Dominants in Community Power Structure," *American Sociological Review*, 23 (February, 1958), 3–9; and Linton Freeman *et al.*, "Locating Leaders in Local Communities," *American Sociological Review*, 28 (October, 1963), 796.

so that we don't antagonize any other group by trying to take members away from them." Of course, the churches have confronted the same problem among themselves. In many cases, they have evolved a complex set of recruitment boundaries to insure that every church has access to potential members without encroaching upon each other. The Freie Gemeinde is hardly eligible for the arrangement.

## Organizational characteristics and the pursuit of legitimacy

Other things being equal, a dissident group in an undifferentiated context will move toward legitimacy. But, of course, other things are seldom equal. Another set of factors that may mediate the influence of the community concerns internal characteristics of the dissident organization itself. Although we can assume that most groups would like to remain true to their original goals and values, we cannot assume that every group is up to the task.

Consider first the *social status of the membership*. In general, the higher the status of the members, the more militant a dissident group can be. This is so for several reasons. For one, the aura of prestige confers a certain license in itself. For another, high status often implies a crucial role in the community that redeems one's illegitimacy. For a third, high status makes the person more eligible for the support and tolerance of the community's wider elite. The early members of the Free Church had unequivocably high status in the community. In addition, they had power as editors of the local press, members of the community council, leaders of the local clubs, representatives on the village planning commission, and officers of the school board. We have already seen how these early freethinkers won the succor of the aristocratic Catholics. They also had leverage on the community as a whole, despite its hostility. A quote from Martin Marty's analysis of nineteenth-century Deism makes the point well for another irreligionist in another community: "Judge Driscoll could be a free thinker and still hold his place in society because he was the person of most consequence in the community, and therefore could venture to go his own way and follow his own notions."[19]

19. Marty, *op. cit.*, p. 76.

But, paradoxically, although the upper classes *can* be more militant they frequently opt not to be. Lacking the mutual reinforcement of the ethnic freethinkers, they may be concerned about overreaching the tolerance threshold and they may be coopted by conservative elements in the community. On the other hand, the lower classes are more militant in spite of the greater likelihood of arousing hostility. They have less to lose, and continued frustration may lead them to spurn rather than eat the pie in the sky. In all of this, it is the middle class that is most constrained. Here, occupations depend on the good will of the community. Insurance agents, small businessmen, barbers, and others in personal services cannot afford to antagonize their customers. One member of the Freie Gemeinde explained, "In a small town, a tradesman can't afford to be anti-anything." As this suggests, the Sauk City freethinkers are now more middle than upper class and this has been a factor in their increased pursuit of legitimacy. Of course, none of this is new or surprising. Homans comments on the license of high status;[20] middle-class constraint has become a sociological cliché; and Gusfield corroborates the relationship between dissidence and low status.[21]

Now, however, we turn to a more theoretically provocative area, that of *leadership*. Leadership is obviously crucial in a dissident group.[22] It is here that Weber makes some of his most important

20. George C. Homans, *Social Behavior: Its Elementary Forms* (New York: Harcourt, Brace, & World, 1961), pp. 349–55.

21. Gusfield, *op. cit.*

22. Yet there is a tentative qualification here concerning the relation between leadership and ideology. This is based on comparative observations of other irreligious groups, including the ethical movement and the ARF, together with the senior author's current analysis of civil rights organizations and their student volunteers. Where leadership is absent a strong ideology may fill the void by becoming doubly rigid and compelling. Where leadership and efficient organization occur, the ideology need be less compulsory and may be more flexible. The first case characterizes both the ARF and the Student Non-Violent Coordinating Committee. The second describes the ethical movement and the Southern Christian Leadership Conference.

23. Max Weber, *The Theory of Social and Economic Organization* (New York: Free Press, 1947), pp. 358–92. See also the critical piece based upon new evidence by Peter L. Berger, "Charisma and Religious Innovation: The Social Location of Israelite Prophecy," *American Sociological Review*, 28 (December, 1963), 940–50.

contributions to theories of social change. For Weber, charisma was a key factor in producing innovations and "breakthroughs" in the social order.[23] It was only by rallying around the magical that the membership could escape the mundane. And yet once the breakthrough had occurred, it was important to consolidate the gains. At this point, Weber discusses the shift from charismatic to non-charismatic authority as a way of stabilizing the movement and insuring its orderly march into future generations.

As apt as this theory may be for other groups, it must be amended for the Freie Gemeinde. Unlike the religious sect, irreligion provides poor soil for the nurturance of charisma. Weber puts strong emphasis on charisma's magical component, but freethinkers are vehemently oriented to science and rationality. Weber also stresses the importance of sacramental trappings for routinized charisma, yet freethinkers explicitly repudiate all ceremony let alone any doctrine resembling apostolic succession. This is a first instance of the way in which irreligious organizations are betrayed by irreligious tenets. Charisma is crucial to any dissident group's success, but free thought frustrates its development. Note, however, that the Freie Gemeinde did have an early approximation. Schroeter was charismatic in most respects save the magical. Indeed, his case points to several additional elaborations of Weberian theory.

It is important to recall that German immigrants had organized Wisconsin free thought *before* the emergence or arrival of a charismatic leader. This suggests that charisma is not always necessary for the inception of social movements. While charisma may be crucial in launching movements among an *indigenous* and rooted population, it may be less important for movements occurring among uprooted transplants or those who are sufficiently alien to band together without having to be rallied. Further, charisma may be more important in sustaining a militant movement than in starting it. Although a shift away from charisma may be salutary once a group has been *accepted* by its context, it may be fatal if the group remains stigmatized. Certainly Schroeter's primary contribution was to persistence rather than inception. With his death in 1888, the group began its slow demise. Although the current leader is responsible and efficient, he makes no pretense of serving charismatic functions. Unlike Schroeter, he lacks the glamour of previous persecution, and his work as an insurance salesman brands him as all too ordinary. He has no prophetic role and even avoids ethical or intellectual leadership. Here then is one more reason why the group has opted for legitimacy rather than militancy.

But note that once legitimation is pursued, the pursuit itself has further consequences for the leader. Under conditions of militancy and consequent duress, the leader's power is centralized and maximized. Under conditions of legitimation, he faces increasing difficulty in maintaining his authority since his decisions and programs are less urgent. Sensing the compromise of legitimation, the group is apt to hark back to the time when its original ideals were being forged and defended militantly. It may then idealize past rather than present leadership and confer a wishful "charisma in absentia" upon one long gone. This cultivation of the past has the best of both worlds. It reminds the group of its militant strain but locates this militancy safely in a bygone age where it can provoke no contemporary disruptions. In this regard it is important to note that although Schroeter was crucial to the Freie Gemeinde in both Milwaukee and Sauk City, he is given much less attention in the former. Milwaukee's militance has more nearly obviated such wistful glances into the heroic past.

A third organizational variable concerns values and goals or, more properly, their absence. As Clark has suggested, undefined values are one condition of precariousness. Unattainable or unrealistic goals may be another. Certainly conventional religious groups suffer on both counts since salvation is neither clear cut nor easily achieved. For this reason churches have long suffered from goal displacement or what could be termed the "means-ends inversion" in which means such as recruitment replace goals such as salvation. All of this underscores the importance of charisma; it may serve as an antidote by providing an alternative source of meaning and a more immediate rallying point. It is hardly surprising that religious groups have long outdistanced more pragmatic organizations in their production of charismatic types.[24]

24. Note the reference here to the "production of charisma." This is intended to suggest that charisma is often more imputed than claimed and that it relates more to group needs than to the psychology of leadership.

But if undefined and unattainable goals are a vulnerability of the churches, they are doubly so for the freethinkers. Here the problems escalate since values tend to be wholly relativistic and goals are rarely stipulated at all. The freethinker's high regard for individual autonomy makes an organizational creed anathema. The following quotations illustrate the members' amorphous conception of the Freie Gemeinde's purpose:

> Well, I think we're looking for something we can believe in.
>
> We try to educate people in cultural things, in anything that's above and beyond the average humdrum existence. When I talk about "above and beyond," I mean above and beyond our lives, the way we live now, where we came from and where we're going. . . . I think we all look for meanings; if there are any we hope to find them. We don't presuppose that there are meanings, however, that there are always answers. There may not be.
>
> We are a group of seekers rather than a body of believers. We think that through advancements of science the truth will change. We are prepared to accept this, and we can change our beliefs very easily, because if it follows the truth, then we believe we are right in changing it in contrast to other religions.

With such vague goals, passion dissipates. There are no concrete actions, no gauges by which to measure progress. There is little worth suffering for, and legitimacy is seductive to those who are dissident for no compelling reasons and with no measurable end in view.

Like the churches, then, the Freie Gemeinde has indeed witnessed an inversion of means and ends. Many respondents confessed that their participation was motivated more by social reasons than anything else. The combination of "mighty fine food" and German "egg coffee" has supplanted the reformist zeal of overturning the churches and emancipating their parishioners. Insofar as substantive issues occur, one member comments upon their deliberation as follows:

> In our meetings we never talk about the Freie Gemeinde as such, or try in any way to belittle the beliefs of others. We don't do anything except maybe we have a meditation or reading with the idea that they're not too strongly worded so that they won't cause any friction or hard feelings. Some ideas appeal to us more than others, but we don't use them because we don't want people to feel that we are trying to ram our ideas down their throats.

Part of this is due to the natural legacy of free thought; part of it is a redounding effect of legitimation. For whatever reason, irreligion has been replaced by areligion, and an organization has become a collectivity.

All of this leads in turn to the further factor of *commitment*. Obviously, membership commitment is another pre-condition to organizational militancy.[25] The commitment of most Sauk City members has flagged to the point where increased militancy would tax it beyond its breaking point. Nor does the decreasing strength of the organization bother them. One member shrugged and commented as follows:

> If the Free Church does disintegrate, fine, let it go; I've had it for fifty years, it's given me a lot of personal happiness. Let's make it pleasant for ourselves. I wouldn't want any people to join with very vehement feelings. . . . We had two or three who did that and everyone felt rather uncomfortable. It's a lot more pleasant just to let it go and not worry about it.

Certainly commitment is affected by the unattainability of goals above, but there are other factors as well. One is the generation of membership. Despite their differences, the Freie Gemeinde and the religious sect are similar in that second- and third-generation members are generally less sensitive to the original ideals and less militant in maintaining them.[26] One elderly freethinker recalled the change this way:

In this interpretation, Weber is hardly an advocate of the "great man theory of history." For an analysis in this vein, see Festinger *et al.*, *op. cit.*, and their implicit treatment of charisma as a response to collective dissonance.

25. The emphasis here is on the consequences of undercommitment for the pursuit of legitimation. And yet *overcommitment* is a pathology that may disrupt the militant group. Its symptoms are a penchant for the spectacular rather than the efficient and a tendency to grapple with the first task at hand instead of considering other tasks with more delayed but more important effects. Overcommitment is visible not only in the ARF as the most militant irreligious group but in civil rights organizations as well.

26. Clearly ethnic acculturation has taken its toll in this connection. Originally the Freie Gemeinde served an ancillary function in providing an island of old-world identity in the new-world sea. As ethnic lines blurred, the movement lost this role. Since then it has had to "make it" on the basis of irreligion alone. But, while this is an undeniable factor in the organization's decline, it is hardly a sufficient cause. Other ethnic free-thought movements in Milwaukee, St. Louis, and Philadelphia have maintained their militancy and conserved their strength in spite of acculturation.

> The Freie Gemeinde was more antichurch at that time because the people had come from Europe and were more opposed to it and were more eager to further their education. . . . Our forebears, when they first came, were getting away from something . . . there was something to fight for, there was much more. These things were fresh in their minds, and now there is an entirely different attitude.

Yet the members of later generations must not be confused with the convert. There is a difference between those whose membership is a family legacy and those who join out of independent conviction. Those respondents whose parents had *not* been members of the group were much more disgruntled with the current complacency. Most of them favored a more militant and more active program. However, as outsiders to a familistic organization, they lacked the influence to effect a change.

Finally, it is important to consider commitment alongside recruitment. One can relate the two hypothetically. Thus a militant group maximizes the commitment of its existing members but jeopardizes the recruitment of new adherents; a legitimizing group maximizes recruitment opportunities but minimizes commitment. In short, a dissident group cannot maximize commitment and recruitment at the same time. In order to secure commitment the group must adhere strongly to its dissident values, thereby alienating a flock of potential recruits who are not prepared to go so far. In order to enhance recruitment, the group must widen its appeal by reducing its dissidence, thereby betraying the allegiances of many of its original members.

The Freie Gemeinde offers a partial illustration. It is true that the group failed to take advantage of the recruitment opportunities afforded by their affiliation with the Unitarian-Universalist Fellowship. And yet merely securing the advantage at all had the predicted consequence of decreased commitment. Two lifelong members expressed their reactions as follows:

> I didn't like it very well, and I know that our forefathers wouldn't have agreed to it at all. I would rather that the group were like the way our forefathers had it.

> The Free Church now is a negative force—even in my youth it was still a positive force culturally . . . they are not a free church anymore; they are now a segment of the Unitarian church.

The dissension's denouement was a splinter movement that followed the classic path of the religious sect except that it moved to the radical left instead of the fundamentalist right. While the new group has only a dozen members, it is both more active and more militant. It also elicits envious reactions from older members of the parent Freie Gemeinde who did not make the jump but could understand it.

> One of the reasons they don't come anymore is that the *Freie Gemeinde* isn't as outspoken as it used to be. The group wasn't active enough to suit them. They became discouraged and therefore started a more active discussion group. . . . When Madalyn Murray was here last year, she was not invited to speak to the Free Church. She spoke to the other discussion group though, and many of us would have liked to talk to her.

## Summary

The preceding section isolated four distinct intra-organizational factors which inform adaptation to dissidence and precariousness: social status, leadership and charisma, organizational goals and values, and commitment and recruitment.[27] At this point it is worth considering their mutual relations. Although the four are intimately associated, this is not to say that they will always be consistent in leaning toward militancy or legitimation, growth or decline. Some organizations will maximize the conditions for growth in all four respects; some will maximize conditions in one factor but fall short on others; finally, there will be organizations like the Sauk City group that come a cropper on each. The Sauk City Freie Gemeinde's entire history reveals a succession of disasters as it systematically loses first one and then another factor in its favor. In its early phase it had an upper-class membership, a quasi-charismatic leader, a compelling goal in the revolt against the churches, and the high commitment of first-generation membership. Gradually each of these advantages fell away.

27. What is the basis of four factors, only four factors, and these four factors? They are not random choices, and they are recommended by two considerations. First, of course, they resonate in the interviews and documents that provide the data. Second, they articulate with broader theoretical schemes. E.g., there is a contrived but provocative parallel between status, leadership, commitment, and values, on the one hand, and A-G-I-L, on the other. Certainly Parsons' model can be employed in the analysis of precariousness and dissidence, as Smelser has indicated. Yet our present intentions is more to elucidate a single case than to engage in higher-order systematics.

Nor has the community been of recent help, as was seen in the section on differentiation and the external context. The early alliance between the Freie Gemeinde and the aristocratic Catholics has dissipated and there is no longer a defending elite. Sauk City has never had the structural differentiation of Milwaukee, and therefore the freethinkers have always had to contend with a hostile community sensitive to their actions and declarations. In all of this, it is no surprise that the Freie Gemeinde is on the verge of disbanding. It may have a fling at immortality in the continued existence of its splinter movement. But even this may soon follow the path of its forerunner and convert current militancy into proximate legitimacy and ultimate demise.

PETER M. BLAU

# Bureaucracy and Social Change

"Nobody can be at the same time a correct bureaucrat and an innovator. Progress is precisely that which the rules and regulations did not foresee; it is necessarily outside the field of bureaucratic activities."[1] This categorical conclusion does not seem warranted by its premises. To be sure, a member of a bureaucracy is restrained from changing procedures on his private initiative. But this means neither that precisely determined bureaucratic operations cannot be instrumental in instituting social change nor that they are immutable. On the contrary, bureaucratic structures are recurrently modified, as has been shown.

The fact that bureaucratic structures undergo modifications, however, does not necessarily indicate that they are compatible with social change. Studies of officials in administrative positions show that major organizational mutations result from the emerging "bifurcation of interest" of these officials. The identification of their career interest with the continued existence of the bureaucracy constrains administrators to disregard organizational objectives if their pursuit appears to threaten their tenure or the stability of the organization.[2] While this constitutes a basic modification of the structure, it is one that is antithetical to change in two respects. First, in the case of an organization that has the purpose of establishing institutional change (such as a union or a New Deal government agency), the administrator's willingness to compromise its objectives prevents the effective accomplishment of the intended reform. Second, identification with the existing bureaucratic apparatus creates a tendency to sanctify procedures and therefore to resist changes in them, even if conditions call for adjustments.

Among the *operating officials* studied, however, neither of these two bureaucratic trends was observed. That there was no rigid opposition to internal change is indicated by the emergence of unofficial adjustments and also by the reactions of these civil servants to the official innovations that were constantly instituted, particularly in the federal agency. Sometimes they objected to such innovations, but more often they welcomed them. Besides, far from having become alienated from the change-generating objectives of the organization, agents actually advocated new policies that would extend these objectives.

This chapter is concerned with attitudes of officials toward change, especially with the hypothesis that bureaucratic conditions engender favorable attitudes toward change, and not necessarily

1. Ludwig von Mises, *Bureaucracy* (New Haven, Conn.: Yale University Press, 1944), p. 67.

2. See Robert Michels, *Political Parties* (New York: Free Press, 1949), and Philip Selznick, "An Approach to a Theory of Bureaucracy," *American Sociological Review*, 8 (1943), 47–54.

Reprinted from *The Dynamics of Bureaucracy*, pp. 183–200, by permission of the author and publisher. (Copyright 1955 by The University of Chicago Press.)

resistance to change, as is often assumed. First, negative cases will be examined, situations in which officials opposed innovations. Next, ritualistic conformity will be contrasted with other forms of adaptation to the bureaucratic organization. Finally, an analysis will be presented of bureaucratic constraints that gave rise to demands for change. No claim is made that the tendencies found are typical of bureaucracies. Two cases cannot show what is typical, and, moreover, the federal agency belongs to the special class of innovating bureaucracies, having been established during the New Deal for the purpose of enforcing the adoption of new business practices. If this is a special case, it is also a crucial one, since Michels contends that precisely such organizations established to institute reforms depart from the pursuit of their objectives because officials become conservative and lose interest in accomplishing the reforms. The question raised here is: What conditions induced agents to continue to favor the New Deal objectives of their organization, even to advocate that it extend its innovating operations, and to welcome many changes in procedure?

## Fearful overconformity

Identification with the normative standards that govern bureaucratic operations furthers uniform and conscientious performance of official duties. It has been pointed out, however, that this very identification with procedures may also prevent effective operations:

> Adherence to the rules, originally conceived as a means, becomes transformed into an end-in-itself; there occurs the familiar process of *displacement of goals* whereby "an instrumental value becomes a terminal value." Discipline, readily interpreted as conformance with regulations, whatever the situation, is seen not as a measure designed for specific purposes but becomes an immediate value in the life-organization of the bureaucrat. This emphasis, resulting from the displacement of the original goals, develops into rigidities and an inability to adjust readily. Formalism, even ritualism ensues with an unchallenged insistence upon punctilious adherence to formalized procedures. . . . Thus, the very elements which conduce toward efficiency in general produce inefficiency in specific instances.[3]

3. Robert K. Merton, *Social Theory and Social Structure* (rev. ed.; New York: Free Press, 1957), pp. 199, 200 (italics in original).

The important question is, of course, under what conditions such inefficient rigidity occurs, since it is not typical of all bureaucrats in all situations. Indeed, in the two agencies studied, it seemed to be exceptional, but the exceptions are instructive. The following comment by a file clerk illustrates strict adherence to a trivial ruling of a superior that interfered with operations:

> You know how we tab the records of recent high-school graduates. We used red tabs for February graduates . . . and we decided to use black tabs for June graduates, because you can see that color well on the cards. [The department head] didn't know about that and sent around a memo saying they should be tabbed in yellow. Yellow you can't see at all. But since it had come down in writing, [the supervisor] refused to change it without permission from [the department head]. [The department head] had just arbitrarily chosen this color; it didn't make any difference. [The supervisor] could have changed it, but he didn't want to do it himself. [The department head] wasn't here, and we had to wait two days.

This instance of overconformity was clearly not due to the fact that ritualistic adherence to existing operating procedures had become an inescapable habit. The supervisor refused to set aside a recent order of the department head, although there were good reasons for doing so, because he worried about possible negative reactions of his superior, on whom his rating depended. Most other cases of overconformity observed could also be traced to fear of superiors and not to ingrained habits. The treatment accorded to mentally ill clients in the state agency exemplifies such tendencies in an entire group of officials.

The public employment agency was required by law to serve all clients who applied for service. Practically the only exceptions were clients with serious mental disorders. Like all handicapped applicants, mentally disturbed ones were handled by Section C. The members of this section, however, did not have the right to refuse service to them. The records of these clients with evidence of their illness and requests for discontinuing service (the so-called form 801) had to be sent to the superintendent. If she approved a request, she sent the case to a consulting psychiatrist, who made the final decision. This procedure was designed to protect an excitable client, for instance, from being refused service as a mentally ill person on the basis of a decision by an interviewer not trained to diagnose psychoses.

A few months before the observer came to the state agency, such a request had been disapproved by the psychiatrist, apparently with a reprimand for its having been made on the basis of insufficient evidence of mental illness. To forestall a repetition of this experience, the members of Section C ceased making these requests altogether. Yet obviously disturbed clients could not be referred to jobs without harming the agency's public relations. As a result of this cross-pressure, they were not referred, but neither was service to them officially discontinued. One official explained: "There are lots of applicants we tell little white fibs [claiming that no job openings are available], and we get around referring them this way, because we consider them nonreferable." This unofficial solution forced officials to continue to interview psychotic clients, a time-consuming and, sometimes, enervating task. Indeed, it became so difficult that the supervisor of Section C asked the superintendent for advice on dealing with emotionally disturbed persons. When the superintendent learned how seriously ill the clients under discussion were, she said that requests to discontinue service should be made. The exchange between her and the supervisor indicates the latter's reluctance to risk another disapproval of a request:

SUPERINTENDENT. I hate to see how much time has already been spent on her which shouldn't have been. You should have stopped seeing her months ago. Sure, you'll have a fight on your hands. It'll be unpleasant, but I'd rather have one fight than drag this on. . . .

SUPERVISOR. Don't you think we'll have to eat crow like on [the case where a request had been rejected]?

SUPERINTENDENT. I never let you down on that one. You know that the decision was made by someone above me.

SUPERVISOR. I know you didn't, but we still had to eat crow. . . .

SUPERINTENDENT. We agree that you'll write up those 801's earlier. I'll send them back to you if I don't think they are strong enough. You mustn't feel bad if I send them back to you.

SUPERVISOR. We've never been turned down before. Now we will. We'll spoil our record.

Literal compliance with the rule that specified the evidence required for discontinuing service to psychotic clients interfered with operations; it prevented the members of Section C from taking the official steps that would relieve them of the futile task of interviewing these clients. This rule had become all important, because past experience had impressed upon these officials that requests accompanied by insufficient evidence endangered their reputation with superiors. To protect themselves against this danger, they were willing to make difficult adjustments and to violate several other rules: they failed to request that service to a client be discontinued when they were expected to do so; they wasted time interviewing clients without providing employment or any other service; and they avoided referring clients by telling them "white fibs." It was not strong identification with rules in general but fear of censure by superiors that led these officials rigidly to adhere to a particular procedure.

If ritualistic conformity with established rules and regulations were a major value, resistance to any change in procedure would be expected. However, the fact that bureaucratic officials strongly oppose *some* innovations does not prove their rigid identification with the existing order; often it may be explained by more specific factors. For example, three of the four department heads in the clothing division of the state agency objected to a very minor and temporary innovation. Most clients were interviewed only if job openings were available for which they were qualified, but handicapped clients were interviewed whenever they came to the office. The agency administration proposed a survey to determine how many handicapped clients were mistakenly sent away because it was not known that they had a physical handicap. For one week the receptionists in all departments were to inquire of all clients whom they dismissed whether they had a handicap. Three department heads strongly opposed this survey. They argued that it would be too difficult to obtain this information from uneducated clients; many questions would have to be asked, clerks might not be qualified to ask the right questions, and, even if they could be taught, it would be time-consuming and delay the long lines of waiting clients. When the survey was made, it was found that it did not create the expected problems. In a two-hour lecture, clerks were taught how to ascertain this information, and the survey did not appreciably retard operations at the reception desk.

This looks, at first, like a clear case of resistance to an innovation motivated only by an exaggerated fear of any change. Indeed, the department head who had not opposed the survey interpreted the attitude of her colleagues in this way: "If you get a bunch of [department heads] together, they always think everything will be much harder." However, the same officials did not oppose many other changes in operations they were told to make. Their comments when they first heard of the proposed survey indicate the specific reasons for their objections to it. Two of them inquired whether it would be used to evaluate departmental operations. (They were told that this was not its purpose.) One said, half-jokingly, that his report will necessarily show no cases of handicapped clients being dismissed, since his clerks, whenever they discover a client to be handicapped, must not dismiss him but send him for an interview.[4] These administrators objected to this innovation because it might reveal imperfection in their departmental operations to their superiors, and not because they opposed change in general.

These findings suggest that ritualism results not so much from overidentification with rules and strong habituation to established practices as from lack of security in important social relationships in the organization. The instances of overconformity and resistance to change observed in the state agency were motivated by anxious concern with the attitudes and opinions of superiors. Two characteristics of bureaucratic structures, therefore, would be expected to have opposite effects on ritualistic tendencies. The hierarchy of authority relationships and sanctioning powers should foster them, since it makes officials highly dependent on their superiors. The relative employment security of civil servants, on the other hand, should lessen them, particularly if the development of a professional orientation neutralizes feelings of dependency. In the federal agency, where such an orientation was more pronounced than in the state agency, opposition to change was especially rare, and, when it did occur, it did not seem to be due to fear of superiors.

Occasionally, federal officials condemned an innovation instituted by the administration. The supervisor objected to the new evaluation procedure, as was pointed out in the last chapter, because it made it more difficult for him to justify his ratings to subordinates. Agents criticized a change in enforcement policy in such strong language as, "It stinks," and "Cockeyed! Crazy!" Since this new policy engendered serious conflicts with clients without furthering the objectives of the agency in any way, officials could hardly be expected to favor it.[5] The opposition to these two innovations, although it did not result from fear of superiors, illustrates the same principle, since both of them threatened the security of officials in important social relationships at work.

## Variations of displacement of goals

Displacement of goals does not necessarily assume the ritualistic form of indiscriminate resistance to change. In the federal agency it usually assumed different forms.

The laws administered by this agency had been enacted within the previous twenty years, and enforcement policies had not yet become firmly established. Legislative amendments, court decisions, and their administrative interpretations constantly required the alteration of regulations and the adoption of new ones. No month went by that did not see several changes in procedure.

Since change was a recurrent phenomenon, bureaucratic methods had been instituted to deal with it. Detailed procedures were designed to assure that new regulations became quickly and effectively incorporated into regular operating practices. Supervisors were briefed on innovations at weekly meetings of the administrative staff, and they explained new policies to agents and suggested techniques for enforcing them during the fortnightly departmental meetings. The problems en-

4. Of course, none of the department heads sabotaged the survey by failing to dismiss clients ready for dismissal if their handicap was discovered. However, the knowledge that the survey was taken probably induced clerks to be more careful before dismissing clients, making the figures of dismissed handicapped clients during that week unrepresentative. The division director believed that that was the case.

5. The implications of a Supreme Court decision compelled the bureau chief to adopt this policy. It was opposed by the administration of the agency, by both major political parties, by virtually all newspapers, and by employers as well as unions. Less than a year after its adoption, a congressional act reversed this policy.

countered in the enforcement of recently adopted regulations were fully discussed at these meetings. Pages with new and revised rulings were distributed to agents for insertion in the loose-leaf procedure manual, and supervisors always checked whether the insertion had been correctly made. This check on such a simple task, in sharp contrast to the discretion that agents generally exercised, served to emphasize the importance of new regulations.

Major policy changes were introduced in special, all-day conferences of the entire agency. Experts from bureau headquarters lectured on the new policy and illustrated its enforcement, and long periods of discussion served to arouse interest in the new task as well as to clarify problems. Whereas only a minority actively participated in these discussions, extended lunch periods on such occasions gave all agents an opportunity to discuss with colleagues the interesting problems posed by the new regulations.

Various devices focused attention on new procedures and furnished incentives for following them closely. For example, the first few cases that involved violations of an important new regulation had to be submitted to the district commissioner before final action was taken. This motivated agents to pay special attention to finding such violations, since doing so enabled them to attract the notice of the head of the agency, and it induced them to handle these cases, which the commissioner would himself examine, with great care. "Negative reporting" was another means of compelling agents to take cognizance of new regulations in their work. Usually they had to report only positive findings, that they had uncovered certain violations but not that other violations had not occurred. In the case of a major innovation, however, they also had to report the absence of a violation.

Statistical records of performance provided another mechanism for implementing changes in operations. The agent's interest required that he expend most effort on those tasks on which his evaluation depended. Agents could therefore be induced to change their operating practices by altering the weight given to the various statistical criteria in the evaluation. For instance, the administration wanted to complete an exceptionally large number of cases during a particular period. As was previously mentioned, the greater speed in operations needed for this purpose was effected by announcing that the interim rating for the next quarter would be based on the *number* of cases completed and not on the other criteria generally used for evaluation.

Recurrent change in procedure was part of the bureaucratic routine in this agency. New regulations frequently replaced old ones, but whatever regulations were in force at any one time constituted the law of the land, and strict compliance with them was mandatory. The system of evaluation and the exacting methods of instituting innovations constrained agents scrupulously to adhere to constantly changing normative standards. These conditions sometimes led to a legalistic orientation, a tendency to elevate into an end-in-itself, not specific rules, but the process of applying general regulations to particular cases.

Legalism is a form of displacement of the objectives of a law by the techniques designed to achieve them. A few officials were interested more in solving subtle legal problems than in the objectives their investigations were intended to attain. An administrative official contrasted this orientation with the prevailing one in these words:

> I imagine there are different kinds of people. Some are cold and factual, not too concerned with the social viewpoint. That type would prefer—would get more satisfaction out of the analysis and conclusion of the case, after the conference with the employer. Others think more of the social aspects of the law and the benefits for individuals. Their negotiations with employers would be a necessary evil to achieve a certain goal.

A legalistic orientation has some similarities with a ritualistic one: both engender strict conformity with regulations but reduce efficiency in situations not fully covered by regulations. Agents primarily concerned with legal problems were excellent investigators of complex cases, but they were not very successful in inducing employers to make voluntary adjustments. However, there is an important difference between the two orientations. Whereas a ritualistic identification with *specific* procedures interferes with adaptation to change in procedures, a legalistic interest in the niceties of law enforcement does not. On the contrary, new regulations provide more stimulating problems for the legalist.

Another form of displacement of goals, observed in both agencies, is the very opposite of legalism. Some officials lost sight of the generic objective of raising the standard of living of American workers in the course of dealing with particular underpaid (or unemployed) individuals. They were so concerned with the plight of the employees with whom they had contact that helping these specific persons became the major goal of their investigations and the main source of their work satisfaction. Thus one agent, after reminiscing about how this employee and that one had benefited as a result of his investigations, said: "You spread a little sunshine in this job. That's what I like. It's a very good job. It would be ideal if it were not for some little annoyances. I like the idea of helping people. For instance . . . she told me, I'm just like Santa Claus to her. That makes me feel good."

Although this particularistic orientation enhanced work satisfaction, it interfered with adaptation to bureaucratic conditions. A desire to help particular employees often made agents impatient with general rules that disregarded the welfare of specific persons. It created resistance in situations in which the interest of individual employees had to be set aside in the interest of the generic objectives of the agency—for example, when court action against an employer prohibited those adjustments that immediately benefited his employees. The three agents who were most concerned with helping particular individuals were not well adapted to their bureaucratic role; they failed to understand the abstract principles of law enforcement, and their performance was below average.

Evaluation on the basis of statistical records also generated the displacement of goals, as has already been mentioned in the discussion of the state agency. Since statistical indices influenced his rating, improving them became a major aim of the official. When an agent found a firm in perfect compliance with the law, he was disappointed (although the objectives of the agency had been met), because this lowered the proportion of cases in which he had found violations. Agents usually decided their work schedule in terms of their production record, as one of them explained: "There are certain cases where you know there won't be any problems. So you work on those if you feel you have to turn in additional cases." Many agents considered bookkeeping mistakes of a few dollars a violation. This was technically correct, but adjusting such mistakes was not part of their responsibilities. However, by classifying these errors as violations, they increased their "proportion of cases with violations." Concern with statistical records sometimes interfered with the rational performance of duties,[6] although it generally furthered operating efficiency. In any case, it did not inhibit changes in operations, since these records could be used to institute such changes.

Three variations of displacement of goals were observed, all of which differed from ritualism. Whereas these transformations of means into ends had certain dysfunctions for operations, they did not interfere with adaptation to new conditions. Of course, this still does not explain why most of these officials not only tolerated but often actually welcomed innovations in procedure. This positive attitude toward *bureaucratic* change should be kept distinct from another phenomenon, which also still awaits explanation, namely, the favorable attitude of most agents toward *external social* change, their great interest in seeing the New Deal objectives of the agency realized and even extended. There are some indications that individuals who had agreed with its objectives had been most likely to seek a job with this agency. This self-selection of personnel would account for their original identification with New Deal principles. However, why had these bureaucratic officials not become alienated from their progressive ideals, but continued to advocate them? Was their idealism beyond modification by bureaucratic conditions, or did, perhaps, bureaucratic constraints strengthen rather than weaken these very ideals?

## Succession of goals

The widely held belief that members of bureaucratic organizations necessarily resist change[7] rests

6. Refinements of statistical measures were designed to prevent officials from "manipulating" their records by taking all relevant aspects of operations into account. Thus the index that showed the amount of money involved in the violations discovered by each agent was little affected by the inclusion of small bookkeeping mistakes, but this index was given less weight than the number of violations found.

7. See, for instance, F. J. Roethlisberger and William J. Dickson, *Management and the Worker* (Cambridge, Mass.: Harvard University Press, 1939), pp. 525–68.

on the assumption that bureaucratic structures are characterized by a perfect state of equilibrium, which makes any alteration a disturbance. However, no such state of perfect adjustment and adaptation was observed in the two agencies studied. There seemed to exist at all times some conditions that created difficulties for officials and interfered with efficient operations, which constituted organizational needs that required adjustment *of* these conditions and not merely adaptation *to* them. Sometimes the needed innovations were officially introduced by superiors, such as the new evaluation system in the state agency designed to improve service to clients. At other times, adjustive modifications emerged in the process of operations, such as the consultation pattern, which reduced the anxiety of federal agents and thus contributed to effective operations. Difficulties that officials experienced in the course of performing their duties were responsible for the spontaneous development of unofficial practices and for their willing acceptance of many official innovations.

For example, the regulations that defined which occupations are exempt from the provisions of the federal law had become obsolete and contradictory. Determining which employees were exempt was a perplexing problem in many investigations because the regulations did not allow a clear interpretation as to whether a given job was exempt or not. When these troublesome regulations were replaced by new ones, agents warmly welcomed this official change, which facilitated their work.

The presence of irritating difficulties produced favorable attitudes toward innovations that eliminated the irritants. Hence agents not only readily accepted many changes in procedure but even advocated changes in policy that would remove persisting difficulties. For instance, they firmly indorsed the bureau chief's proposal to Congress to amend the law and empower the agency to compel employers to make retroactive adjustments. This policy would relieve agents of the arduous task of convincing employers that they must *voluntarily* make these adjustments, and it would avert the conflicts that this duty often created for enforcement officials.

However, agents also supported new policies that would not facilitate their work. Especially one extension of the law, which has since been enacted by Congress, was strongly advocated by all agents, although most of them realized that it would make their work more difficult. They explained that, since they believed in the agency's objective of raising the standard of living of underpaid workers, they favored changes in the law that would further the achievement of this objective, regardless of their effects on them personally. These idealistic attitudes were not so unrealistic as they may appear. The bureaucratic interest of these officials furnished a firm foundation for their ideological identification with such progressive goals.

To the extent to which an innovating agency has been successful in accomplishing its original purposes, they lose much of their earlier significance. Helping to implement some of the New Deal ideals had been an exciting and important task for officials who supported Roosevelt's program. In the pioneer days, as many officials told the observer, they had often worked until late into the night because they were so enthusiastic about enforcing the new law. Once most employers had accepted the new business practices that benefited workers—an indication that the operations of the agency had been effective—the job of the official became much less challenging, as one agent explained:

> There was lots more satisfaction when the law was first enacted, because there were sweatshops, etc. Generally, working conditions were so much worse then and were far below normal. When you enforced the law then, you saw you accomplished something. . . . The only satisfaction you can get now is from trying to get [the law] changed [so that new objectives can be accomplished].

The attainment of organizational objectives generates a strain toward finding new objectives. To provide incentives for its members and to justify its existence, an organization has to adopt new goals as its old ones are realized. Unions illustrate this transformation of ends into means. After a union establishes the right of collective bargaining, this original objective becomes a means for the accomplishment of new objectives, such as pensions and seniority rights for workers.[8]

This process, the reverse of displacement of goals,

8. The conceptualization of changes in union objectives as a transformation of ends into means was suggested by Wilbert E. Moore in a lecture at Wayne University in February, 1950.

can be called "succession of goals." Putting into effect profound changes in business practices against the prevailing sentiments of the business community had been a big assignment for the federal agency. Assuring continued compliance with the law, once it had been generally accepted, was a much narrower responsibility. This policing duty not only provided less gratification than the original mission, but it also could be fulfilled with a smaller staff. Indeed, reductions of personnel had already been ordered by Congress. If the agency assumed new responsibilities, the danger of future reductions of personnel would be averted and expansions might even become necessary. This would increase the job security of officials and the promotion chances of some of them, since a larger staff would require more supervisors. Extending the objectives of the agency was in the interest of the careers of its members. Their bureaucratic interest reinforced the identification of these officials with progressive ideals that justified the expansion of the agency.

The succession of organizational goals is most conspicuous in innovating organizations, since some of their initial objectives tend to become obsolete, but it is not confined to them. The careers of the members of other types of agencies will also benefit from an extension of their jurisdiction.[9] This encourages favorable attitudes toward new policies, as a comment by an interviewer in the state agency illustrates:

> Now they passed the Disability Pension law, but they made private insurance companies administer it. Of course, that's wonderful for these insurance companies. Many people thought that we would administer it. [Pause.] That would have been good for me, because then I would have gotten a promotion.
>
> (How come?) If we had administered it, the Service would have expanded, because there would have been so much more to do. Then they would have needed more supervisors, and I might have been promoted, since I'm on a promotion list.

The adoption of new policies furthers the economic interest of the members of an agency, but it also requires them to assume new duties, and this would seem to conflict with their interest in keeping their work free of hardships. When asked whether he did not worry about the additional work that the innovation he proposed would create, an agent said: "If I'm in agreement with the philosophy of the law and realize that [this innovation is necessary to achieve its objectives], the increased amount of work wouldn't matter too much. I would hand in fewer cases, possibly, that's all." Officials could magnanimously ignore how much effort the administration of a new policy they favored would involve, because they knew it would not increase their own work loads. The strict limitation of bureaucratic responsibility to forty hours of work a week, regardless of the amount of work the agency had, permitted officials to advocate new programs that would extend operations.

Of course, assuming new responsibilities, even if it did not create extra work for them, necessitated that agents make new adaptations and learn how to solve new problems. This very fact, surprisingly, made innovations particularly attractive to most officials. Although all of them disliked irksome difficulties, such as having to work with contradictory regulations, few agents preferred simple tasks to complex ones. Most objected to such simplicity as boring. Even complex tasks tended to become routine as they were fully mastered, and this also created a succession of goals, a desire for new challenges to make the job more stimulating again. Many agents welcomed frequent changes in procedure precisely because new problems made their work more interesting, as their statements indicate:

> Lots of us gripe about the fact that they change things all the time. But if I should be completely honest with you, although I also gripe about having to keep on learning new things, I really like it. That's what keeps the job interesting. I think this is a job in which you can't be successful unless you're alert and intelligent.
>
> The job would become stale, I imagine, if it weren't for the different phases of the law, the constant changes which make it a living thing. New interpretations are constantly coming out. That's what makes your job alive!

Not all agents, however, welcomed the challenge presented by changes in operations. Most of the less competent ones did not. Five of the fifteen members of Department Y[10] objected to, as one put it, "the myriad changes they always have, which are almost impossible to keep up with."

9. Expanding the jurisdiction of the organization is considered to be a major responsibility of the executive by Marshall E. Dimock (*The Executive in Action* [New York: Harper & Bros., 1945], pp. 53–68).

10. One of the sixteen agents was not interviewed.

Every one of these five belonged to the less competent half (seven) of the group, whereas none of the eight more competent agents opposed change. Preoccupied with and anxious about mastering the problems their duties presented, they experienced additional difficulties not as interesting challenges but as threatening obstacles to adequate performance. Ideologically and in terms of their interest as civil servants, these five officials were also identified with extending the objectives of the agency. Indeed, they, too, favored new policies, but their immediate worries over satisfactory performance overshadowed these more remote considerations when changes in operations actually occurred and made such changes objectionable to them.

This suggests that opposition to change in the organization, while apparently indicating perfect accommodation to existing conditions, is actually the result of insufficient adaption to them. Newcomers, who had not yet become adapted, as well as less competent officials, felt threatened by change, as the following account of an interviewer's experience when she first came to the state agency shows:

> I was terrifically frightened by this large office. . . . It took me a full year before I forgot myself. And procedure! It just floored me. As soon as you got used to something, they changed it. Now, you know what procedure is all about; you just know it, and are used to it. But I used to come home nights and worry about procedure all night. The whole situation was just a nightmare to me. . . . I felt very insecure about—my keeping the job, about being there, about everything. . . .
>
> When I first came here, I was terrified by the thought of having to work in another section. I was afraid. But I'm familiar with it now, and I wouldn't mind. It's just a matter of knowing what's what.

Officials who were secure in their knowledge of procedure and found security in the respect of their colleagues could enjoy the stimulation that new situations provided. They did not have to adhere rigidly to old established practices. Maladaptation, on the other hand, created anxiety, which made unmastered procedures appear like strange and complex external threats. This constrained an official to cling persistently to those aspects of the structure with which he had become familiar and to oppose change.[11] Strangely enough, officials who have most fully incorporated the existing normative structure into their own thinking can most easily depart from it.

## Conclusions

Bureaucratic conditions generated favorable attitudes toward change in several ways. First, the existence of irritating difficulties, such as cross-pressures between conflicting responsibilities, created positive attitudes toward innovations that removed the irritants. Second, the interest of civil servants identified them with new policies that required the expansion of the organization. In the federal innovating agency, this combined with a third factor, the progressive ideology of most officials, to engender the succession of goals. As the agency's original objectives were more or less achieved, the interest of its members strengthened their New Deal beliefs in extending the objectives of the organization. Fourth, the strict limitation of bureaucratic responsibility allowed officials to advocate new policies without fear that their adoption would occasion more work for them. Fifth, officials who had fully mastered their tasks welcomed the new problems produced by changes in operations, which made their work more interesting. But less competent officials tended to adhere rigidly to those parts of the existing procedure with which they were familiar. This made procedural changes objectionable to them, even though they also advocated changes in policy.

Studies of factory-workers—members of private bureaucracies—have often found that resistance to change prevailed among them. Most officials in the government agencies studied here, on the other hand, were favorably disposed toward change. The opposition of the insecure minority provides a clue for explaining this difference. Civil servants who were less competent and received a low rating felt insecure and objected to changes in operations. In general, the jobs of civil servants are much more

11. Insecurity produces rigidity in social relationships as well as in attitudes toward rules and regulations. It was reported in chap. viii that officials who had relatively more contacts with members of their own department also had a larger proportion of their contacts with members of other departments. Those who were least familiar with their immediate co-workers were, paradoxically, most likely to confine their interaction to them. (For the newcomer—but not for the isolate—this may serve the function of hastening his integration.)

secure than are those of factory workers.[12] The low employment security in most factories makes any change in the organization a portent of danger to workers and thus creates generic opposition to change, which even extends to situations where such opposition does not appear to be rational. The relative job security of civil servants, on the other hand, permits favorable attitudes toward change.

Social insecurity breeds rigidity, and this finds varied expressions. When officials were afraid of possible negative reactions of superiors, overconformity ensued. The less secure an agent's knowledge of existing procedures, the greater was his resistance to changes in them. The same principle seems to account for rigidity in social relationships. Officials whose position in their work group was least secure—who received few contacts from its other members—did not feel as free as others in their interaction with outsiders and, consequently, were less prone to extend their social relationships to the outgroup.

If insecurity pervades the work situation, risks must be avoided at all cost, and, since endeavors to find the best means for the achievement of given objectives always involves an element of risk, such endeavors will be abandoned. In this situation, one would expect officials to attempt to protect themselves against censure from superiors and their own feelings of insecurity by ritualistic displacement of goals. Contrary to prevailing assumptions, however, a secure position in the bureaucratic structure and strong identification with its normative standards do not lead to displacement of goals. Indeed, these conditions have the opposite effect: once the accomplishment of tasks becomes a mere matter of routine, officials will seek new fields to conquer in order to revitalize their work, and thus new goals will succeed the old ones.

The economic as well as psychological interests of the members of a bureaucratic organization require that it assume new responsibilities, since this would increase their work satisfaction and further their careers. To solve novel problems is most interesting; to help in the enforcement of new social legislation with which a person is identified is most exciting; promotion chances are best, and the danger of losing one's job is least, in the expanding agency. As tasks become routine, on the other hand, they become boring, and they can be accomplished by a smaller staff than before.

These social and psychological forces produce the succession of goals in organizations, the emergence of a concern with new objectives once the original ones have been largely attained and have lost much of their earlier significance. The ideals beyond the initial objectives suggest the nature of the new ones. This succession of goals has been observed in voluntary associations, for example, in the National Foundation after its own efforts had virtually conquered the scourge of infantile paralysis[13] and in labor unions,[14] as well as in the New Deal agency studied here.

It is the effective achievement of an organization's goals that stimulates the succession of more advanced ones. If an organization is frustrated in its endeavors to accomplish its basic mission and if its continued attempts to do so arouse opposition that threatens its very survival, the reverse process is likely to occur. The labor unions and socialist parties in imperial Germany that Michels studied were in precisely this kind of precarious situation, and it was the efforts of their officials to protect their survival in a hostile environment that led to a preoccupation with strengthening the administrative apparatus and to a retreat from the original radical objectives to more moderate reform goals.[15] The same interests of officials in their careers give rise to opposite developments, depending on the initial success of the organization. An interest in maintaining the organization promotes the displacement of goals if the original mission evokes intense hostility that endangers the organization's existence but it promotes the succession of goals if the original mission has been effectively accomplished, since this too would otherwise endanger the organization's continued existence.

12. Especially in a factory in which continuous layoffs occur during a depression and in which no union exists, as was the case in the factory studied by Roethlisberger and Dickson, *op. cit.*

13. David L. Sills explicitly applied this concept in his study, *The Volunteers* (New York: Free Press, 1957), pp. 254–264.

14. See, for example, C. W. M. Hart, "Industrial Relations Research and Social Theory," *Canadian Journal of Economics and Political Science*, 15 (1949), 53–73.

15. Michels, *op. cit.*

# Formal Structure

The set of norms or rules which establish the officially approved set of priorities obligations, and responsibilities of position occupants in organizations comprise the basic elements of formal structure. The four studies in this section are concerned with the various consequences of formal structure for member behavior.

Stinchcombe's comparative analysis of the administrative process and work requirements of mass production and construction industries provides the basis for a reformulation of Weber's traditional conceptions of bureaucracy. A close examination of the construction industry reveals the existence of skilled craftsmen rationally organized to attain the organization's objectives, but without several crucial features associated with bureaucratic forms. Stinchcombe's approach argues for the careful specification of the chief dimensions of bureaucratic structure. In addition, it suggests that the nature of the work process and the degree of professionalization of the members has important implications for formal structure.

Woodward's study also was concerned with the work process, but applied a different perspective. Technology refers to that part of formal structure devoted to those techniques employed in performing what the organization's norms define as work. This research accomplished two principal objectives. First, the necessity of detailed analysis of a wide range of industrial technical systems is demonstrated and a useful category scheme for their comparative study is devised. Second, a relationship between type of technology and degree of delegation and decentralization is established.

All organizations are political entities and therefore the complete analysis of formal structure must include the distribution and exercise of power. The second selection from *Union Democracy* applies and develops principles derived from Michels' classic analysis of *Political Parties*, an excerpt of which was presented earlier. The study of a deviant case—the International Typographers Union, a democratic labor union—raises this fundamental question: To what extent can an organization of any kind in a democratic society both attain its official objectives and meet the emergent political requirements of its members? Lipset, Coleman, and Trow's study confronts the problem of organizational democracy in a new and important fashion. The legitimacy of an opposition party within the organization's structure is shown to be one crucial structural element essential to the maintenance of the democratic process. The nature of large-scale organization itself and the learned orientations to power of its leaders, as well as the unique concatenation of historical events, are equally important.

The selection by Dalton examines the normative structure of business organization and reveals the intricate relationship between official and implicit understandings. The detailed analysis of theft not only demonstrates how the formal structure of the business system guides the particular pattern of theft behavior, but also shows how the organization's effectiveness can deteriorate under certain conditions if the system is unduly disturbed.

Thus, formal structure is shown to influence a broad range of behavior: the work of craftsmen, the process of industrial control, the political participation and perspectives of printers, and even the acts of theft of store and factory employees.

ARTHUR L. STINCHCOMBE

# Bureaucratic and Craft Administration of Production: A Comparative Study

Administration in the construction industry depends upon a highly professionalized manual labor force.[1] The thesis of this paper is that the professionalization of the labor force in the construction industry serves the same functions as bureaucratic administration in mass production industries and is more rational than bureaucratic administration in the face of economic and technical constraints on construction projects.

Specifically we maintain that the main alternative to professional socialization of workers is communicating work decisions and standards through an administrative apparatus. But such an apparatus requires stable and finely adjusted communications channels. It is dependent on the continuous functioning of administrators in official statuses. Such continuous functioning is uneconomical in construction work because of the instability in the volume and product mix and of the geographical distribution of the work. Consequently the control of pace, manual skill, and effective operative decision (the essential components of industrial discipline) is more economical if left to professionally maintained occupational standards.

After presenting evidence and argument for these assertions, we will try to show why work on large-scale tract construction of houses continues to be administered on a nonbureaucratic, craft basis. Tract housing turns out to be a major revision in the *marketing* of construction products, rather than a revision in the *administration of work*.

Our method will be to reanalyze certain published demographic and economic data for their administrative implications. Since the data were collected for other purposes, they fit the requirements of our problem only roughly. The gaps in the information and the gross character of the categories make it necessary, therefore, to use very rough statistical procedures and to limit the data to a suggestive role.

On the basis of the empirical findings, we will re-examine Max Weber's model of bureaucracy, showing that some elements of that model are not correlated with other elements. This will provide a basis for constructing a model of bureaucracy as a

1. "Professionalized" here means that workers get technical socialization to achieve a publicly recognized occupational competence. "Public recognition" involves preferential hiring (ideally to the point of excluding all others) of workers who have proved their competence to an agency external to the hiring firm or consumer. Often this agency is a professional association composed exclusively of qualified persons and more or less exhaustive of the occupation. This professional association itself often enforces preferential hiring rights of its members. The professional's *permanent labor market status* is not to be confused with permanent firm status (preferential hiring or continued employment of the current employees of a firm). This definition, therefore, differs somewhat from that of Nelson Foote in "The Professionalization of Labor in Detroit," *American Journal of Sociology*, 58 (1953), 371–80.

Reprinted from *Administrative Science Quarterly*, September, 1959, pp. 168–87, by permission of the author and publisher. 

subtype of rational administration, with professionalization another main subtype. A general model of rational administration will be built out of the common elements of these subtypes.

## Bureaucratic administration and craft administration

Craft institutions in construction are more than craft trade unions; they are also a method of administering work. They include special devices of legitimate communications to workers, special authority relations, and special principles of division of work, the "jurisdictions" which form the areas of work defining labor market statuses. The distinctive features of craft administration may be outlined by contrasting it with mass production manufacturing administration.[2] The object of this section is to show that craft institutions provide a functional equivalent of bureaucracy.

Mass production may be defined by the criterion that *both* the product *and* the work process are planned in advance *by persons not on the work crew*. Among the elements of the work process planned are: (1) the location at which a particular task will be done, (2) the movement of tools, of materials, and of workers to this work place, and the most efficient arrangement of these workplace characteristics, (3) sometimes the particular movements to be performed in getting the task done, (4) the schedules and time allotments for particular operations, and (5) inspection criteria for particular operations (as opposed to inspection criteria for final products).

In construction all these characteristics of the work process are governed by the worker in accordance with the empirical lore that makes up craft principles. These principles are the content of workers' socialization and apply to the jobs for which they have preferential hiring rights.

This concentration of the planning of work in manual roles in construction results in a considerably simplified communications system in the industry; but the simplification does not markedly reduce the number of people in administrative statuses. Administrative statuses are roughly equivalent to occupations in census categories: proprietors, managers, and officials; professional, technical, and kindred workers; and clerical and kindred workers.

The proportion of administrative personnel in the labor force in various fabricating industries does not vary widely. In construction the proportion of the labor force in the three administrative occupations is 15.5 per cent; in manufacturing as a whole it is 20.6 per cent; in iron and steel primary extraction, 15.5 per cent; motor vehicles and motor vehicle equipment, 17.6 per cent; in chemicals and allied industries, 33.4 per cent.[3] But these rough similarities in proportion of administrative personnel conceal wide differences in the internal structure of the communications system.

To provide a rough index of one of these differences in the internal structure of the authority systems, we have computed the proportion of clerical positions in the administration. This should provide an index of the proportion of people in administration who do not legitimate by their status the communications they process (e.g., typists, filing clerks, bookkeepers). They file the communications; they do not initiate them. Authority structures with special communications-processing positions may be called "bureaucratic" structures.[4] They provide for close control of the work process farther up the administrative hierarchy, and hence facilitate the control and planning of the work process in large enterprises. They decrease the dependence of the enterprise on empirical lore and self-discipline at the work level and allow technical and economic decisions to be concentrated. Finally, they allow the processing of information and communications from distant markets, enabling the enterprise to be less dependent on the geographical location of clients.

The proportion of administrative personnel who

2. This account of mass-production institutions is derived from Peter Drucker, *The New Society* (New York, 1950), and his *The Practice of Management* (New York, 1954), along with the work of David Granick, *Management of the Industrial Firm in the U.S.S.R.* (New York, 1954).

3. *Characteristics of the Population*, Part 1 (U.S. Summary) (*Census of the Population*, 2 [1950]), Table 134, pp. 290–91.

4. This takes one of Weber's criteria of bureaucratization as an empirical indicator, namely administration on the basis of files. I believe some of the other characteristics of bureaucracy named by Weber can be derived from this one, while some cannot. See Max Weber, *From Max Weber: Essays in Sociology*, tr. by H. H. Gerth and C. W. Mills (New York, 1946), pp. 196–98.

are clerks in various fabricating industries is presented in Table 1.

Clearly the proportion of all administrative personnel who are clerks is considerably greater in manufacturing generally than it is in construction, and the typical mass production industries tend to have even greater development of specialized communications processing structures. The centralized planning of work is associated with this development of filed communications, with specialized personnel processing them.

Another type of internal differentiation of authority structures (systems of originating and processing communications legitimately directing workers) concerns the status and training of the originators. In some authority structures in fabricating industries, people in authority are largely defined by ownership and contract institutions, while in others their status derives from professional institutions. That is, communications from a position in the authority system may be considered legitimate because of the special competence of the originator, a professional; or they may be legitimate because of the special responsibility of the originator, as owner or official, for economic decisions.

We may contrast administrations by the proportion of people in authority whose status derives from special education. This may be denoted as "the professionalization of authority." The proportion of all "top" administrative personnel (proprietors, managers, and officials; *and* professionals) who are professionals in the selected industries is presented in Table 2.

The contrast in the degree of professionalization of authority between manufacturing and construction, and more especially between mass production and construction, is just as clear as was the case with bureaucratization.

The engineering of work processes and the evaluation of work by economic and technical standards take place in mass production in specialized staff departments, far removed from the work crew in the communications system. In the construction industry these functions are decentralized to the work level, where entrepreneurs, foremen, and craftsmen carry the burden of technical and economic decision.

This decentralization of functions of the firm to the work level in construction, and the relative lack of information about and professional analysis of work processes at administrative centers, is accompanied by a difference in the types of legitimate communication.

In the construction industry, authoritative communications from administrative centers carry only specifications of the product desired and prices (and sometimes rough schedules). These two elements of the communication are contained in the contract; first, the contract between the client (with the advice of architects or engineers) and the general contractor,[5] and, second, between the general contractor and subcontractors. Subcontractors do the work falling within the "jurisdiction" of the trade they specialize in.

In mass production, where both the product and the work process are centrally planned, we find a system of legitimated advice on work and legitimate commands from line officials to foremen and workers to do particular work in particular ways. This more finely adjusted communications system depends on the development of specialized communications positions (clerks) and staff advice departments (professionals). These differences in administration are shown in Charts 1 and 2.

5. This step is omitted in the case of operative builders, but otherwise the authority structure is similar.

***Table 1—The Proportion of Administrative Personnel[a] Who Are Clerks in Selected Fabricating Industries, U.S., 1950***

| *Industry or industry group* | *Administrators, clerks* |
|---|---|
| Manufacturing | 53% |
| Motor vehicles and accessories | 63% |
| Iron and steel primary extraction | 60% |
| Chemicals and allied | 45% |
| Construction | 20% |

[a] Proprietors, managers, and officials; professional, technical and kindred workers. *Characteristics of the Population*, Part 1, pp. 290–91.

***Table 2—The Proportion of Top Administrators[a] Who Are Professionals in Various Industries, U.S., 1950***

| *Industry or industry group* | *Professional authority positions* |
|---|---|
| Manufacturing | 50% |
| Motor vehicles and accessories | 63% |
| Iron and steel primary extraction | 64% |
| Chemicals and allied | 65% |
| Construction | 31% |

[a] Proprietors, managers, and officials; and professional, technical and kindred workers. *Characteristics of the Population*, Part 1, pp. 290–91.

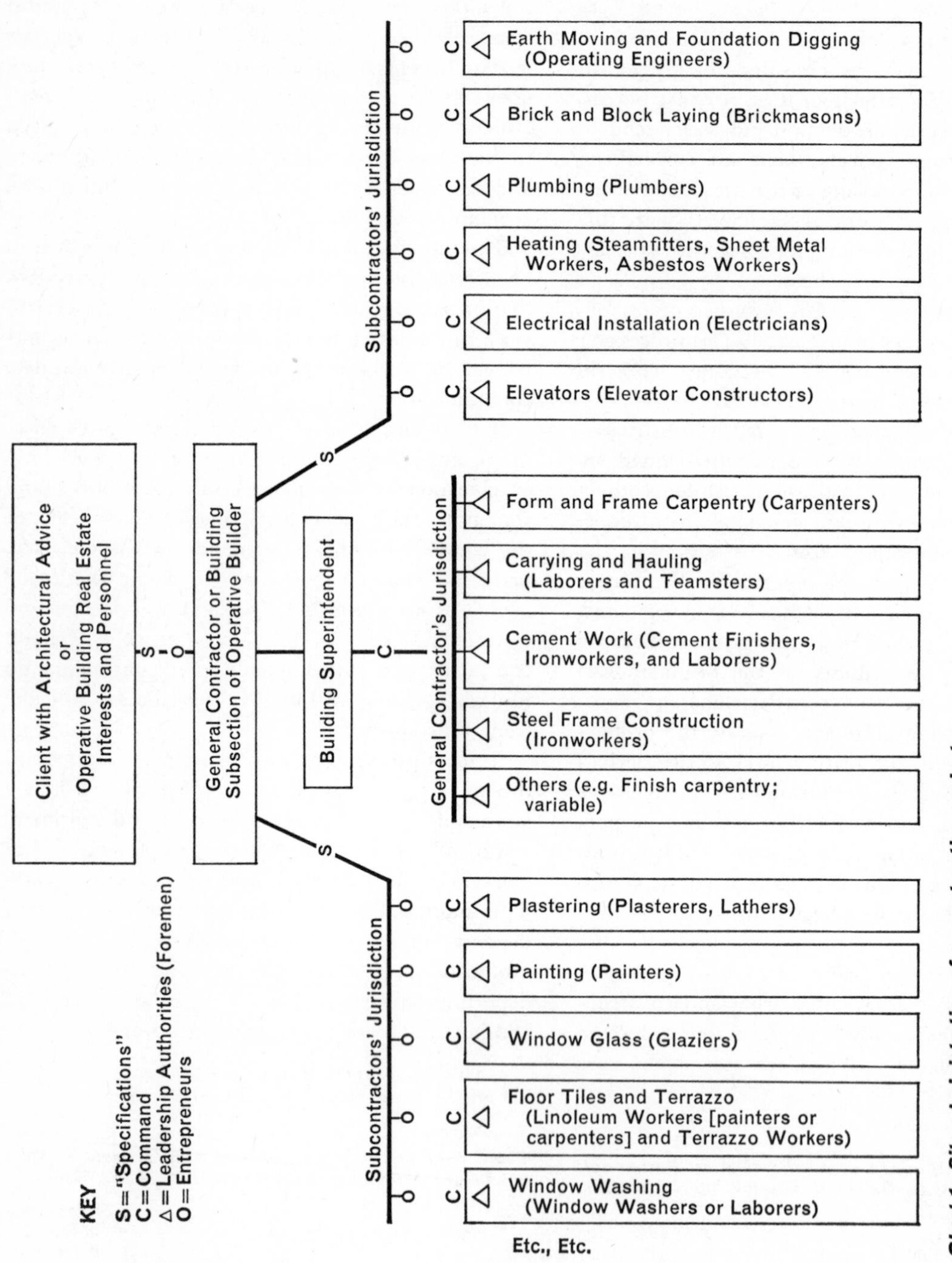

Client with Architectural Advice
or
Operative Building Real Estate
Interests and Personnel
S
O
General Contractor or Building
Subsection of Operative Builder
Building Superintendent
S
C
S
Subcontractors' Jurisdiction
Earth Moving and Foundation Digging
(Operating Engineers)
Brick and Block Laying (Brickmasons)
Plumbing (Plumbers)
Heating (Steamfitters, Sheet Metal
Workers, Asbestos Workers)
Electrical Installation (Electricians)
Elevators (Elevator Constructors)
General Contractor's Jurisdiction
Form and Frame Carpentry (Carpenters)
Carrying and Hauling
(Laborers and Teamsters)
Cement Work (Cement Finishers,
Ironworkers, and Laborers)
Steel Frame Construction
(Ironworkers)
Others (e.g. Finish carpentry;
variable)
Subcontractors' Jurisdiction
Plastering (Plasterers, Lathers)
Painting (Painters)
Window Glass (Glaziers)
Floor Tiles and Terrazzo
(Linoleum Workers [painters or
carpenters] and Terrazzo Workers)
Window Washing
(Window Washers or Laborers)
Etc., Etc.
KEY
S="Specifications"
C=Command
Δ=Leadership Authorities (Foremen)
O=Entrepreneurs

***Chart 1. Site administration of a construction project.***

Craft administration, then, differs from bureaucratic administration by substituting professional training of manual workers for detailed centralized planning of work. This is reflected in the lack of clerical workers processing communications to administrative centers and less complex staffs of professionals planning work. It is also reflected in the simplification of authoritative communications from administrative centers.

## Variability and bureaucratization

In this section we try to demonstrate that professionalization of manual labor is more efficient in construction because bureaucratic administration is dependent on stability of work flow and income, and the construction industry is economically unstable.

Bureaucratization of administration may be defined as a relatively permanent structuring of communications channels between continuously functioning officials. This permanent structuring of channels of legitimate communications, channels defined by the permanent official status of the originator of the communication and of its receiver, permits the development of routine methods of processing information upward and authoritative communication downward. That is, it permits administration on the basis of files and the economical employment of clerical workers.

Routine processing of administrative communications and information is economical only when the overhead cost of specialized information-processing structures is highly productive; this productivity will be high only if rules concerning the route of communication can be taught to clerks. Otherwise, if it is necessary to use discretion in the choice of the receiver of a communication, it is cheaper to rely on visual supervision and executive or professional discretion.

### THE CASE OF MASS PRODUCTION

Bureaucratization of administration depends therefore on the long-term stability of the administration. Of bureaucratic industrial administrations Peter Drucker says,

> The central fact of industrial economics is not "profit" but "loss"—not the expectation of ending up with a surplus . . . but the inevitable and real risk of ending up with an impoverishing deficit, and the need,

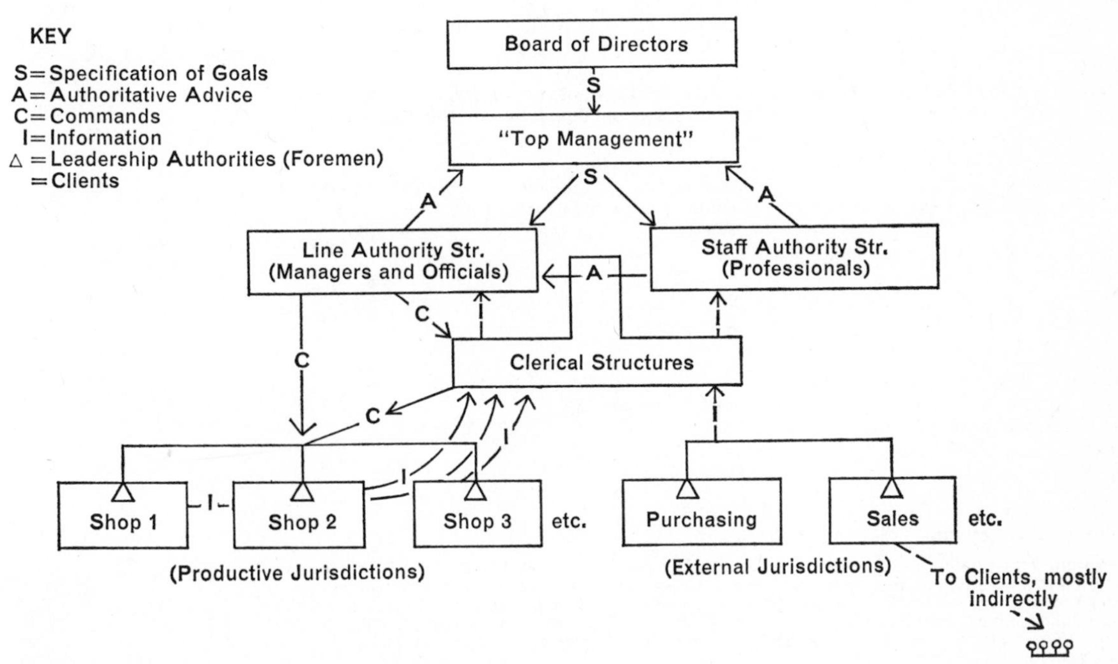


***Chart 2. Administration of a mass production firm.***

the absolute need, to avoid this loss by providing against the risks. . . . The economic activity of an industrial economy is not "trade" taking place in the almost timeless instant of exchange, but production over a very long period. *Neither the organization* (the human resources) nor the capital investment (the material resources) *are productive in the "here and now" of the present.* It will be years before the organization or the investment will begin to produce, and many more years before they will have paid for themselves.[6]

It is clear that he cannot be talking about construction organizations, which have to be productive "here and now."

This association between orientation to stability and large-scale bureaucratized firms reflects the social requirements of complex communications systems between designated officials. Administrations faced with critical problems of instability and flexibility, such as those in the construction industry, will not find it economical to teach clerks rules for channeling communications. For it is impossible to hire a clerk on the labor market who will know the firm's communications channels, so clerks have to be kept on even when they are not productive.[7] And it is difficult to specify rules for channeling communications in advance when volume, product mix, and work-force composition change rapidly, as they do in construction.

6. *The New Society*, p. 52 (our italics). Veblen said the same thing in a different moral vocabulary: "Under the changed circumstance [the replacement of the 'captain of industry'] the spirit of venturesome enterprise is more than likely to foot up as a hunting of trouble, and wisdom in business enterprise has more and more settled down to the wisdom of 'watchful waiting.' Doubtless this form of words, 'watchful waiting,' will have been employed in the first instance to describe the frame of mind of a toad who had reached years of discretion . . . but by an easy turn of speech it has also been found suitable to describe the safe and sane strategy of that mature order of captains of industry who are governed by sound business principles" (Thorstein Veblen, *The Portable Veblen* [New York, 1950], pp. 385–86).

### THE CASE OF CONSTRUCTION

The variability of the construction industry, its intimate dependence on variations in local markets, makes the development of bureaucracy uneconomical. Table 3 shows the relationship between one type of variability and the employment of clerks.

Data are for some types of construction firms, for all firms in Ohio large enough to have to report to the State Employment Office (those normally employing 3 or more persons). In the first column the mean size of firms in the branch is reported (computed here), and the branches are classified by

7. Also the class position of clerks makes it more difficult to hire temporary clerks.

***Table 3—The Relationship Between Mean Size of Firm, Seasonality of Employment, and the Percentage of Labor Force Clerks, for Branches of the Construction Industry***[a]

| *Type of contractor* | *Mean size of firms (1939)* | *Index of seasonality of employment (1926–1936)*[b] | *Per cent of clerks in labor force*[c] *(1939)* |
|---|---|---|---|
| More than 8 employees per contractor | | | |
| Street, road, and sewer | 12.3 | 73 | 4.8 |
| Sand, gravel, excavation | 9.9 | 43 | 7.6 |
| Ventilating and heating | 8.2 | 29 | 11.7 |
| 4–8 employees per contractor | | | |
| Brick, stone, and cement | 5.5 | 47 | 3.3 |
| General contracting | 6.9 | 43 | 5.2 |
| Sheet metal and roofing | 4.9 | 29 | 11.7 |
| Plumbing | 5.1 | 20 | 10.9 |
| Electrical | 6.3 | 13 | 12.5 |
| Less than 4 employees per contractor | | | |
| Painting and decorating | 2.5 | 59 | 3.9 |

[a] Taken from Viva Boothe and Sam Arnold, *Seasonal Employment in Ohio* (Columbus: Ohio State University, 1944), Table 19, pp. 82–87. Plasterers are omitted from this table, because the number employed was not large enough to give a reliable figure on seasonality of clerks' work, the original purpose of the publication. There were less than 50 clerks in plastering enterprises in the state. Consequently the needed figure was not reported in the source. Plasterers' employment is very unstable, so the omission itself supports the trend.
[b] See footnote 8.
[c] Excluding sales clerks.

mean size. In the second column is an index of seasonality of employment for the years 1926–36 (computed in the source[8]). In the last column the average proportion of the labor force who were clerks in 1939 is reported (computed here).

The relationship between the development of clerical statuses in administration and the stability of the work flow is clear from Table 3. The strength of the relationship within the industry can give us confidence in asserting that instability decreases bureaucratization. There are only two inversions, and these are of insignificant size: sheet metal and roofing should have been less bureaucratized than plumbing; and painters should have been less than brick, stone, and cement firms. This is a strong support for the hypothesis that the lack of bureaucratization in the construction industry is due to general instability.

We do not have space to document adequately the sources of variability in the work flow of construction administrations. The main elements may be outlined as follows:

1. Variations in the volume of work and in product mix in the course of the business cycle.[9]
2. Seasonal variations in both volume and product mix.[10]
3. The limitation of most construction administrations, especially in the specialty trades, to a small geographical radius. This smaller market magnifies the variability facing particular firms according to well-known statistical principles (individual projects can form a large part of a local market).[11]
4. The organization of work at a particular site into stages (building "from the ground up"), with the resulting variability in the productive purpose of any particular site administration.[12]

### SUMMARY OF EMPIRICAL PROPOSITIONS

It now seems wise to review the argument thus far. We are trying to show that the professionalization of the manual work force persists partly because it is a cheaper form of administration for construction enterprises than the bureaucratic form.

First we argued that bureaucracy and professionalized work force were real alternatives, that: (a) decisions, which in mass production were made outside the work milieu and communicated bureaucratically, in construction work were actually part of the craftsman's culture and socialization, and were made at the level of the work crew, (b) the administrative status structure of construction showed signs of this difference in the communications structure by relative lack of clerks and professionals, and (c) the legitimate communications in construction (contracts and subcontracts) showed the expected differences in content from the orders and advice in a bureaucracy. Contracts contained specifications of the goals of work and prices; they did not contain the actual directives of work, which, it seemed to us, did not have to be there because

8. The index of seasonality was computed in the source in the following way: The monthly index of employment in firms reporting was computed for each year of the ten-year period, to the base of the mean employment of that year. Then the ten indices (one index for each of the ten years) for each month were arrayed, and the median taken. The 12 monthly medians give an over-all picture of seasonality for the category for the ten years. Scatter diagrams of these monthly indices, standardized for the general level of employment during the year as outlined above, are presented in Viva Boothe and Sam Arnold, *Seasonal Employment in Ohio* (Columbus, 1944), Chart 16, pp. 83–86. Graphs of seasonality are presented by drawing lines through the median monthly indices. This procedure eliminates between-years (presumably cyclical) variations in employment level.

After this array of 12 monthly indices is found, the index of seasonality reported in Table 3 is computed by the formula:

$$\frac{\text{maximum} - \text{minimum}}{\text{maximum}} \times 100,$$

where the maximum is the largest median monthly index, and minimum the smallest. This gives an index ranging from zero (no seasonality) to 100, which would be the result of no employment at all in the minimum month. From the scatter diagrams, this might result in an under-estimation of the short-time instability only for electrical contracting firms. But other evidence indicates that electrical construction firms have very stable employment. See W. Haber and H. Levinson, *Labor Relations and Productivity in the Building Trades* (Ann Arbor, 1956), p. 54. They rank construction occupations by percentage working a full year. Electricians work less than proprietors but more than any other occupation, including "foremen, all trades."

9. Miles L. Colean and Robinson Newcomb, *Stabilizing Construction* (New York, 1952), pp. 18–20, 49–50, and Appendix N, pp. 219–42. Also Clarence Long, *Building Cycles and the Theory of Investment* (Princeton, 1940).

10. The data reported from Boothe and Arnold show both great seasonality and differential seasonality by trade. Their data show construction to be one of the most seasonal industries (*op. cit.*, pp. 23–27).

11. Colean and Newcomb, *op. cit.*, pp. 250–51, for the ecological limitations on administrative scope. For data on variations in volume in local areas, see U.S. Bureau of Labor Statistics, *Construction during Five Decades* (Bulletin no. 1146 [July 1, 1953]), pp. 22–25.

12. Gordon W. Bertran and Sherman J. Maisel, *Industrial Relations in the Construction Industry* (Berkeley, 1955), pp. 3–5.

they were already incorporated in the professionalized culture of the workers.

Secondly, we argued that the bureaucratic alternative was too expensive and inefficient in construction because such administration requires continuous functioning in organizational statuses. But continuous functioning is prevented by the requirement that construction administrations adapt to variability in both volume and product mix. Using the employment of clerks as an index of bureaucratization, a close relation was found between seasonality in branches of construction and bureaucratization. This strong relationship was combined with knowledge of the general instability of construction to support the contention that bureaucracy was inefficient in construction.

## The implications of marketing reform

There is a good deal of careless talk about the bureaucratization of construction and the introduction of mass production by operative building of tract homes. The central innovation of operative building is in the field of marketing and finance rather than in the administration of production. The similarity of productive administration in operative building and in other large-scale building is well summarized by Sherman Masiel:

> Many popular assumptions about subcontracting—that it lowers efficiency, raises costs, and leads to instability—are contradicted by our study in the Bay area of the reasons for subcontracting and its efficiency relative to its alternatives. Building appears to be one of the many industries where vertical disintegration increases efficiency and lowers costs without lessening stability. The fact that most large [operative housebuilding] firms have tried integrating various of the processes normally subcontracted but have usually returned to subcontracting them, is of great importance because it shows that the present prevalence of subcontracting is the result of a policy deliberately adopted by builders after testing alternative possibilities. . . .
>
> The logic of trade contracting has developed as follows: (1) Efficiency reaches its maximum effectiveness under specialized labor. (2) Specialized labor reaches its maximum effectiveness when applied regularly on many units. . . . (3) The problem of sustaining specialized jobs as well as the coordination of the movement of men among them requires special supervision, usually performed by trade contractors. . . .
>
> Given a need for specialized mechanisms, the builder gains greater flexibility and a decrease in the problems of supervision through subcontracting.[13]

The central limitation on supervision is the increase in overhead when mediated communication is introduced. "A disproportionate increase takes place [in overhead in the largest construction firms] because production has spread beyond the area of simple visual control by the owner or owners [of the firm]."[14]

In fact, the characteristic of mass-production administration, increasing specialization of tools and other facilities at a planned work place, does not take place with increasing size. Most machinery added in large firms consists of hand power tools and materials-handling machinery.[15]

The low development of distinctively bureaucratic production-control mechanisms, such as cost accounting, detailed scheduling, regularized reporting of work progress, and standardized inspection of specific operations, is outlined by Maisel.[16] What happens instead of centralized planning and bureaucratic control of work is an increase in the fineness of stages on which crews of workers are put. This results in the development of more efficient, but still quite diversified, skills. And most important, these skills still form a component of a labor market rather than an organizational status system.

Operative decisions are still very important at the work level, rather than being concentrated in production engineering and cost-accounting departments. Modification of tools for special purposes is done by workers (e.g., the making of templates which provide guides for standardized cutting operations, or the construction of special scaffolds for the crew.) There is no large element in the administration with the specialized task of planning technological innovation in the work process. And stable communications between work crews and decision centers are poorly developed.

The central consideration is that variability of work load for the administration is not very much reduced, if at all, by operative building. And it is not necessarily economical to take advantage of

13. *Housebuilding in Transition* (Berkeley and Los Angeles, 1953), pp. 231–32.
14. *Ibid.*, p. 102.
15. *Ibid.*, p. 103.
16. *Ibid.*, pp. 123–30.

what reduction there is, when the subcontracting system and structured labor market are already in existence.

What is changed, what makes the economies possible, is the place of the goal-setting function. The productive goals in the past were set by clients with architectural advice, who quite naturally did not set goals in such a way as to maximize productive efficiency. In operative building productive goals are set autonomously by the administration. This means that they can choose, among the products they might produce, those which are technically easier. The main reduction of costs, of course, comes from the planning of the construction site so as to minimize transportation and set-up costs. Sites next to each other minimize costs of moving men, materials, and equipment to the site. Warehousing of materials can be planned to fit the individual site, rather than burdening builders' supply places. Uniformity of design reduces the complexity of materials distribution, reduces design costs, and so forth.

The main innovation, then, is the planning of the *product* for ease of production, rather than in the planning of the *productive process*. This is the introduction of the conceptions of Eli Whitney on *standardized parts* into construction, rather than of Henry Ford's innovation of *standardized tasks*.

## Rational administration and bureaucracy

Since Weber, there has been a tendency to regard rational administration as identical with bureaucratic administration. This tendency has been especially strong among sociologists. We have chosen to define bureaucracy as a special type of rational administration and to discuss the social sources of an alternative method of institutionalizing rationality, namely, professionalization.

The central point of this analysis is that the components of Weber's ideal type do not form an inherently connected set of variables. Some of the components of the ideal type are relatively uncorrelated with others, while some are highly correlated.

We have called craft production unbureaucratized, although it does involve "the principle of fixed and official jurisdictional areas, which are generally ordered by rules."[17] The rules in this case are to be found in the jurisdictional provisions of trade unions, in the introductory sections of collective contracts, and in state licensing laws for contractors. The duties in construction are "distıibuted in a fixed way as official duties"[18] through legally binding contracts. "The authority to give the commands required for the discharge of these duties is distributed in a stable way."[19] The sanctions, especially firing, are stably allocated to contractors and subcontractors on the particular project.

The principal difference comes in the criterion: "Methodical provision is made for the *regular and continuous* fulfillment of these duties and for the execution of the corresponding rights."[20] It is not the rules governing jurisdiction and authority which we take to be characteristic of bureaucracy, but the regularity and continuity of work and status within an administrative system. We have shown that regularity and continuity are in fact correlated with our operational criterion of bureaucratization, the proportion of clerks among administrators.

Secondly, we have argued that "the principles of office hierarchy . . . in which there is supervision of the lower officer by the higher ones,"[21] is dependent on stable communications structures, provided we differentiate *goal setting* from *supervision*. In construction there is no possibility of "appealing the decision of a lower office [subcontractor] to its higher authority [the general contractor or client]."[22] The goals of subcontractors are set by "higher authorities." But their work is not supervised, nor are their decisions appealable. Office hierarchy in the command-advice sense, then, is correlated with regularity and continuity in official statuses. Goal-setting arrangements can be changed drastically (e.g., from the client to the operative building corporation) without changing the administration of work in a bureaucratic direction.

The other main criterion Weber proposes concerns the stable structuring of communication (files), which we have taken as the empirical indicator of stable, rule-governed communication channels among official statuses.

17. Max Weber, *op. cit.*, p. 196.
18. *Ibid.*
19. *Ibid.*
20. *Ibid.* (our italics).
21. *Ibid.*, p. 197.
22. *Ibid.*

These last three elements of Weber's ideal type (continuity, hierarchy, and files), then, are functionally interrelated; they are found together in mass-production administration but are absent in construction administration. But the first three elements (stable jurisdictions, official duties, and authority) are found in both construction and mass production, so they cannot be highly correlated with the elements of continuity, hierarchy, and files.

Weber draws from his ideal type certain implications concerning the position of the official. Some of these are derived from distinctive characteristics of bureaucracy as we have defined it, and some are derived from general requirements of rationality. Characteristics common to bureaucracies *and* non-bureaucratic rational administrations include:

1. Positions in the organization are separated from the household. Positions in construction as workers, foremen, and entrepreneurs involve the separation of work from home life, firm accounts from household accounts, firm and trade promotions from family ties.[23]
2. Rational administration requires the allocation of work to those who are competent. This often involves hiring on the basis of formal training, certification, and examination. Not only civil servants, but also craftsmen, and private legal and medical practitioners, have to pass examinations or possess certificates of formal training. The main difference is that professional examinations allocate work throughout a labor market, while civil service examinations recruit only to organizational statuses.
3. To a large extent pecuniary compensation, regulated by the status of the worker, characterizes rational administration, as well as bureaucracy. At least, wage rates for each occupational status in construction are negotiated.

A characteristic of bureaucratic officials not found in construction is permanent appointment. Authorities on a construction project are appointed by subcontracts only for the duration of the project. The basis of responsibility for leadership duties is the contract for specific work (and the contractors' reputations) rather than generalized loyalty to the administration. Payment to authorities is not salary determined by the status of the official but payment for performance set by competitive bidding. Finally the career of the worker in construction is structured not by administrative regulation but by status in a structured labor market. These differences also distinguish private professional practice from bureaucratic administration.

We would construct an ideal type of functionally interrelated characteristics of bureaucracy as follows: The defining criterion would be stable, rule-ordered communications channels from and to continuously occupied statuses. This criterion implies: (1) development of files and employment of clerks, (2) hierarchical command-advice authority structures, and (3) career commitment to an *organizational* rather than a labor market or *occupational* status system.

Bureaucracy thus defined is a subtype of rational administration. Rational administration requires the government of work activity by economic and technical standards and hence requires:

1. Differentiation of the work role from home life (and other deep interpersonal commitments).
2. The organization of work statuses into some sort of career, in which future rights and duties depend on present performance according to specified standards.
3. A stable allocation of work to persons formally identified as able and willing to work and subject to discipline by understood work standards, and payment by the administration only when such workers are "productive."
4. A stable legitimate way of communicating at least the goals to be reached by subordinates and of seeing that these goals are accomplished.

This means that we take Weber's observations on the "Presuppositions and Causes of Bureaucracy"[24] to be mainly about the presuppositions and causes of any kind of rational administration. The presuppositions of bureaucracy are conditions facilitating continuous operation of an organizational status system, either continuity of work load and returns or institutionalized legitimacy of the status system itself (e.g., the military).

Continuity in status in a labor market, instead of an organization, we take to be the defining characteristic of professional institutions. Both the traditional professions and crafts in construction have

23. Not that being a contractor's son doesn't give a competitive advantage; it is only that positions are not inherited, but awarded on a competitive basis. A contractor's son still has to meet occupational standards. On the advantage of sons of *Handwerker* in various trades in Germany, see Heinz Lamprecht, "Über die soziale Herkunft der Handwerker," *Soziale Welt*, 3 (Oct., 1951), 42, 52.

24. *Op. cit.*, pp. 204–9.

professional institutions in this sense. These are characterized by (roughly) occupationally homogeneous organizations seeking control of the rights and duties associated with doing work within a defined jurisdiction. By this control they assure competence discipline. Both professions and crafts, then, guarantee labor market rights and enforce labor market duties which make up a professional status.

## Conclusion

Concepts in organizational theory, such as bureaucracy, tend to take on a nebulous character because research in this area has consisted largely of case studies of particular organizations. An industrial firm engaged in mass production may certainly be bureaucratic, but not all the characteristics of the organization are distinctive of bureaucracy. Case studies cannot, ordinarily, sort out the inherent from the ephemeral connections among organizational characteristics. Systematic comparisons of different types of organizations, which we have attempted here, can refine our conceptual apparatus by defining complex concepts comprised of elements that hang together empirically.

The concept of bureaucracy developed here is not merely a descriptive one; it contains propositions about the connection between its elements. Such a concept can be refined either by proving new elements to be necessarily connected to those already incorporated or by disproving the hypothesized connection between elements. Similar definition is needed for other complex concepts in the social sciences: the city, sovereignty, the firm.

A definition of the firm, for example, should include those characteristics inevitably found in social units producing goods for markets. Such a definition of the firm would be not merely a category to put concrete organizations into, but a set of propositions about the relations between markets and social groups. Such propositional definitions can be best derived from the systematic comparative study of organizations.

JOAN WOODWARD

# Technology and Organization

## Systems of production

One interesting characteristic of classical management theory, the concepts and formulas of which formed the basis of analysis in the previous chapter, is that it was developed in a technical setting but independently of technology. In general the formulas are closely linked with the personalities of those who worked and wrote in this field. It is true that several of the people concerned, including Taylor himself, were engineers with a technical background who had practiced successfully in manufacturing industry. But they tended to generalize on the basis of their experience, and the expedients they found effective in practice were often given the status of fundamental truths or general laws by those attracted to their ideas. The result was that the assumption first put into words by Follett (1927)[1] that "whatever the purpose towards which human endeavor is directed, the principles of that direction are nevertheless the same" became an accepted part of management theory. There has been a tendency to develop ideas about the administrative process independently of technical considerations, and the technical backgrounds of the people who practiced successfully as managers tend to have been overlooked or forgotten in the evaluation of their work.

Sociologists who turned their attention to problems of either administration or industrial behavior, from Weber and Veblen onwards, took a different point of view in theory, assuming that the technological circumstances, either of a society in the wider sense or of a social system such as a factory was a major variable in the determination of its structure and behavior. For example, the assumption that technical change has a profound effect on social relationships underlies the industrial relations studies undertaken by the Department of Social Science of the University of Liverpool.[2] Trist and his colleagues of the Tavistock Institute of Human Relations have done a good deal of interesting and exciting work on the basis of a similar assumption. The phrase "a socio-technical system" was coined and has been used extensively to explain the interplay of social and technical factors in the work situation.[3]

1. Mary Parker Follett in *Papers on Dynamic Administration*, given at the annual conference of the American Bureau of Personnel Administration 1924–28. The majority of these reports are reproduced in a memorial volume entitled *Dynamic Administration* edited by Henry Metcalfe, and L. Urwick (Management Publication Trusts Ltd., West Willow and Harper Bros., New York).

2. W. H. Scott, J. A. Banks, A. H. Halsey, and T. Lupton, *Technical Change and Industrial Relations* (Liverpool University Press, 1956).

3. One of the earliest articles published on this theme was that which appeared in *The Manager* in December 1955: "Some Contrasting Socio-Technical Production Systems," by A. T. M. Wilson.

Reprinted from *Industrial Organization: Theory and Practice*, pp. 35–44, 50–67, by permission of the author and publisher.

Dubin (1959)[4] went so far as to contend that technology is the most important single determinant of working behavior. He also defined his use of the word technology by subdividing it into two major phases; first, the tools, instruments, machines, and technical formulas basic to the performance of the work, and secondly, the body of ideas which express the goals of the work, its functional importance, and the rationale of the methods employed. Indeed, a considerable part of the literature of industrial sociology in the last five years is concerned with the relationship between behavior and technology at either the "tool" or the "control" level.

Having reached negative conclusions from the initial analysis of their material, the research workers turned almost automatically to their technological data. Was it possible to systematize this data in such a way as to show whether there was any relationship between organizational characteristics and technology? A difficulty immediately arose, for although the existence of a link between technology and behavior is more or less taken for granted by social scientists, the technical variables on which the differences in structure and behavior depend, have not yet been isolated. Except in relation to specific case studies the concept of a socio-technical system remains largely an abstraction and is therefore of little value as a predictive tool in the study of industrial behavior.

What was needed by the research workers at this point in the analysis was a natural history of industry, something in the nature of a botanist's "flora" that they could use to identify in technological terms the firms they had studied. Without a precise instrument of this kind all that could be done was to group together on a rough and ready basis all the firms in which manufacturing processes and methods appeared to be similar. The first point of interest to emerge from this grouping was that Dubin's two phases of technology are closely related. It soon became obvious that firms with similar goals and associated manufacturing policies had similar manufacturing processes—the range of tools, instruments, machines, and technical formulas was limited and controlled by manufacturing policy. For example, a firm restricting itself to the manufacture of bespoke suits was not able to use the same advanced techniques of production as a firm making mass-produced men's clothing.

Indeed, the first important breakdown of the firms studied was between those where production was of the "one off" kind, to meet customers' individual requirements, and those where production was standardized. Firms making products on a "one off" basis were further subdivided according to the nature of these products. Some were simple from a technical point of view (like the bespoke suits referred to above); others were more complex—for example prototypes of electronic equipment. The size of the unit product was important too; large equipments such as radio transmitting stations had to be fabricated in stages, the manufacturing methods differing considerably from those used in the production of smaller prototypes.

Firms making standardized products could also be subdivided; in some, production went on continuously, in others it was interrupted at more or less frequent intervals. Furthermore, whereas in some firms there was considerable diversity of products, in others there was relatively little flexibility in production facilities.

Another possible way of dividing firms was to differentiate between those making integral products and those making dimensional products measured by weight, capacity, or volume. Firms making integral products are sometimes referred to collectively as manufacturing industry, and firms making dimensional products as process industry. Dimensional products are normally manufactured in chemical plants. Here again, in analysing the data a distinction could be drawn between the multipurpose plant in which production was intermittent and the single-purpose plant in which production was continuous, stopping only in the event of a breakdown or for a complete overhaul.

It soon became obvious to the research workers that there were so many variations in manufacturing methods that every situation which they examined was to some extent unique. Nevertheless, if an attempt was to be made to assess the effect of technology upon organization, some system would have to be devised for dividing the firms studied into sections and for classifying firms with technical characteristics in common within each section. It was felt that the system of division normally used

4. Robert Dubin, "Working Union-Management Relations," *The Sociology of Industrial Relations* (Prentice Hall, Englewood Cliffs, N.J.).

by production engineers into the three categories of jobbing, batch, and mass production was inadequate for this purpose, as each of these headings covered a very broad field. On the other hand it had to be borne in mind that the research data related to a hundred firms only. Thus too many categories would make the numbers in each too small to reveal trends or relationships.

In the final analysis, therefore, production systems were grouped into the eleven categories illustrated in Figure 1. It will be seen that in eighty firms a single system of production predominated, while in a further twelve, two systems were combined into one process of manufacture. These combinations were of two main kinds; one, agricultural engineering, for instance, consisted of the production of standard parts subsequently assembled into diverse products. The other, found in such industries as pharmaceutical chemical manufacture, combined the manufacture of a product in a plant with its subsequent preparation for sale by packaging. Dimensional products, measured by weight or volume, became integral products after further processing; a quantity of acetylsalicylic acid, for example, became a number of aspirin tablets.

Eight firms could not be fitted into any of the eleven categories: one was a Remploy factory operating under special conditions, another was concerned mainly with storage and servicing operations. In a further four production was extremely mixed, and the other two were in transition, radical technical changes bringing them out of one category into another.

## Production systems and size

Having devised a system for classifying production systems, it was important to ensure that something more than merely reclassifying firms on a basis of size had been done; production systems were therefore related to size. As Figure 2 shows, however, there appeared to be no significant relationship; both large and small firms were found in each production category.

## Increasing technical complexity

It will be seen that the first nine systems of production given in Figure 1 form a scale; they are listed in order of chronological development, and technical complexity; the production of unit articles to customers' individual requirements being the oldest and simplest form of manufacture, and the continuous-flow production of dimensional products, the most advanced and most complicated. Moving along the scale from Systems I to IX, it becomes increasingly possible to exercise control over manufacturing operations, the physical limitations of production becoming better known and understood. Targets can be set and reached more effectively in continuous-flow production plants than they can in the most up-to-date and efficient batch production firms, and the factors likely to limit performance can be allowed for. However well-developed production control procedures may be in batch production firms, there will be a degree of uncertainty in the prediction of results. Production proceeds by drives and a continuous attempt is made to push back physical limitations by setting ever higher targets. The difficulties of exercising effective control, particularly of prototype manufacture, are greatest in unit production. It is almost impossible to predict the results of development work either in terms of time or money.

In general it is also true to say that prediction and control are easier in the manufacture of dimensional production than in the manufacture of integral products.

The fact that a firm was placed in one of the more technically advanced categories did not necessarily mean that it was a progressive firm in the more generally accepted sense as used by Carter and Williams (1958).[5] The attitude of a firm towards technical or administrative innovation is not always reflected in its production system. Firms in which production systems were basically the same differed considerably in the extent to which they had tried to rationalize their production, in their awareness and interest in technical developments, and in their use of techniques such as work study, methods engineering, and operations research. But there did seem to be a relationship between progressiveness and the production system, for, as already indicated, the production system limited and controlled the extent to which a firm could go. Progressiveness can therefore be defined as a willingness to do every-

5. P. Carter and B. Williams, *Industry and Technical Progress* (Oxford University Press).

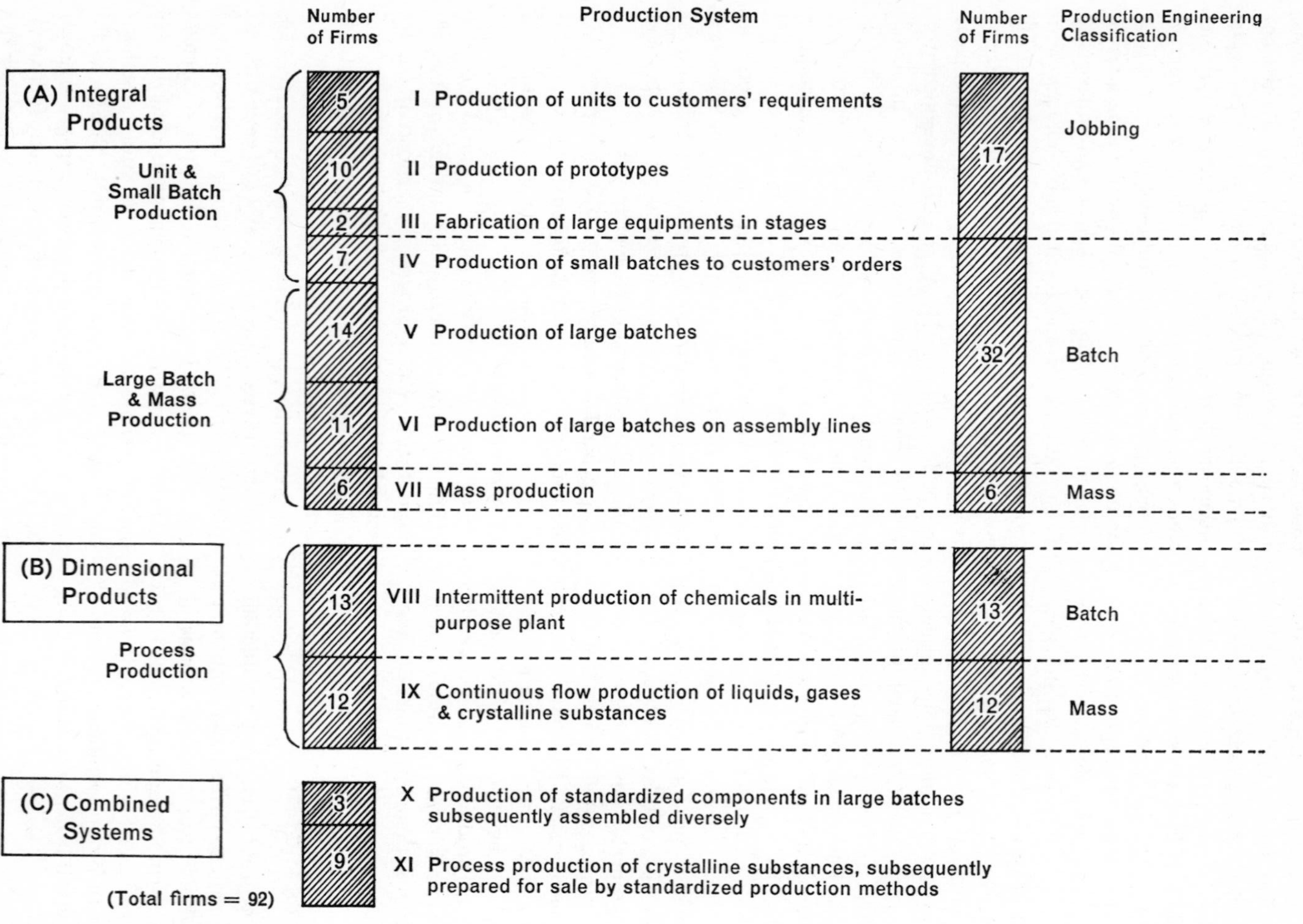


*Figure 1. Production systems in South Essex industry.*

thing possible within the limits set by objectives and technology, to increase effectiveness and extend control over manufacturing operations.

Moreover, the development of newer and more effective methods of manufacture does not necessarily mean that the older systems of production become outmoded. Each of the systems of production listed in Figure 1 has its own applications and limitations, and each is appropriate to the achievement of specific objectives. Continuous-flow production methods originally confined to the manufacture of liquids, gases, and crystalline substances are being increasingly introduced into the manufacture of solid shapes. Steel, paperboard, millboard, and some engineering parts are among the products concerned. But it is not easy to foresee their application to manufacture involving the assembly of large numbers of different components.

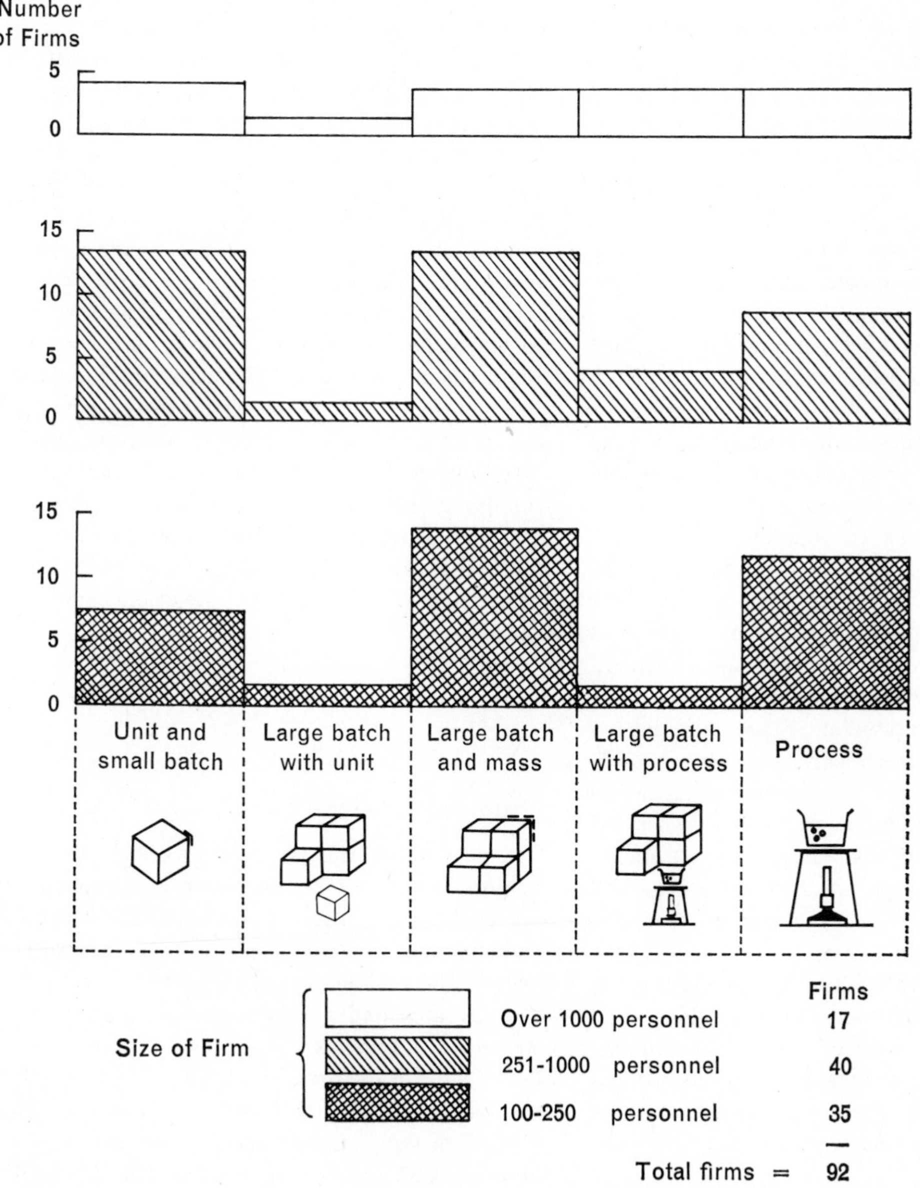


*Figure 2. Production systems analyzed by number employed.*

Unit production, the simplest system, will continue as long as large items of equipment have to be fabricated and in industries where development proceeds at too rapid a rate to make standardization of products possible. Some firms also will probably continue to cater for individual idiosyncrasies.

Industrial administration theorists tend to be intolerant of individual idiosyncrasies. Urwick (1943)[6] says: "to allow the individual idiosyncrasies of a wide range of customers to drive administration away from the principles on which it can manufacture most economically is suicidal—the kind of good intention with which the road to hell or bankruptcy is proverbially paved." Standardization, specification, and simplification are the ideals on which modern manufacturing methods are based, and it is, of course, true that our increased standard of living depends upon standardized production. It is also true that increases in the standard of living are likely to result in greater demands for goods manufactured to customers' individual requirements; more people will want and be able to afford such things as bespoke suits or gold-plated limousines. Thus the number of firms catering for individual idiosyncrasies is more likely to increase than decrease; unit production will probably be with us for many years to come.

As has already been pointed out, some firms seemed less explicitly aware of their primary tasks and manufacturing objectives than others. The history of these firms suggests that means had sometimes been allowed to determine ends. An enthusiasm for a new technique of manufacture or for a more elaborate system of programming or control would lead to a modification in manufacturing policy without those responsible for its determination being consciously aware of what was happening. The effects of the innovation on quality standards or on the type of customers served had not always been thought out in advance.

One such firm employing approximately 500 people was concerned with batch production; it made large batches of standardized products, and small batches of customers' individual requirements. Management consultants had been brought in, their brief being the rather general one of increasing the firm's efficiency. The first thing the consultants had done was to introduce a better system of cost accounting, demonstrating to the management how unit costs could be progressively reduced by increases in batch size. They recommended that the firm should reduce the variety of its production and concentrate on a small number of standard lines. The firm did this and then found that their customers were not particularly interested in the standard lines. The retailers said they had accepted them only because the firm was prepared to make smaller quantities of special products to customers' individual requirements. Sales dropped when those special facilities were withdrawn, and the firm lost ground to one of the larger industrial organizations operating in the same field.

6. L. Urwick, *Elements of Administration* (Pitman, London).

The research workers visited this firm about a year later. A drop in sales had forced the firm—incidentally, one of the oldest in the area—to declare redundant workers who had been with them for many years and for whom no alternative employment was available locally. It then decided to revert to its earlier practice of catering for individual requirements on demand. The decision caused some heart-burning, for the management was now more sophisticated about the costs of such production. Nevertheless the firm survived and continued to fulfill a useful social function, thus demonstrating that there is still a place for a firm prepared to cater for individual idiosyncrasies in an industry where production methods are on the whole more advanced.

* * * * * *

## Organizational trends

The next step in the survey was to relate the information about the way firms were organized and operated to the technical framework. This was done, and for the first time in the analysis patterns became discernible: firms with similar production systems appeared to have similar organizational structures. There were, of course, differences between some of the firms placed in the same production category, but the differences inside each category were not, on the whole, as marked as those between categories. The figures relating to the various organizational characteristics measured tended to cluster around medians, the medians varying from one category to another.

Therefore the main conclusion reached through this research project was that the existence of the link between technology and social structure first postulated by Thorstein Veblen (1904)[7] can be demonstrated empirically. It is not suggested that the research proved technology to be the only important variable in determining organizational structure, or that such factors as the history and background of a firm and the personalities of the people who built it up and subsequently managed it were unimportant. For example, the research workers soon became aware, going from firm to firm, that individual managers differed considerably in their willingness and ability to delegate responsibility for decision-making to their subordinates. Nevertheless, in spite of individual differences, there was more delegation and decentralization in process industry than in large batch and mass production industry.

Technology, although not the only variable affecting organization, was one that could be isolated for study without too much difficulty. The patterns which emerged in the analysis of the data indicated that there are prescribed and functional relationships between structure and technical demands. Trends in organization appeared to be associated with an increasing ability to predict results and to control the physical limitations of production. These trends were of two kinds, for whereas some organizational characteristics were directly and progressively related to the scale of technical advance formed by the first nine systems of production listed in Figure 1 others formed a different pattern; the production systems at each end of the scale resembled each other, while the greatest divergences were between the extremes and the middle ranges.

## The direct relationship

Among the organizational characteristics showing a direct relationship with technical advance were: the length of the line of command; the span of control of the chief executive; the percentage of total turnover allocated to the payment of wages and salaries, and the ratios of managers to total personnel, of clerical and administrative staff to manual workers, of direct to indirect labor, and of graduate to nongraduate supervision in production departments.

Figure 3 shows how the number of levels of management in direct production departments increased with technical advance, the longest lines being found in process industry. This diagram indicates clearly the way in which inside each production group statistics relating to organization tended to cluster around the median. Included here are only the firms in which a single system of production predominated. It was found that in firms where two systems of production were combined there was a tendency to organize each system independently. In eight of the nine firms combining process production with mass production there were more levels of management on the process side of manufacture than in the departments where the products were prepared for sale, and a higher proportion of managers to operators. In the three firms where the production of components was associated with diverse assembly there were more levels on the components side than on the assembly side, and also a much higher ratio of operators to supervisors.

Technical factors also seemed to explain the wide variations in the span of control of chief executives, the people responsible to the policy-forming body for the conduct of their firm's business. In unit production firms the number of people directly responsible to the chief executive ranged from two to nine, the median being four; in large batch and mass production firms the range was from four to thirteen, the median being seven, and in process production firms the range was from five to nineteen, the median being ten.

The information obtained indicated that not only the span of control of a chief executive but also the role and functions were modified by technical factors. "Management by committee" was more common in process industry than in the less complex systems. Twenty of the twenty-five process production firms had management committees or executive boards, whereas the figures for large-batch and mass production were ten out of thirty-one, and for small-batch and unit production three out of twenty-four. This meant that in many process industries the chief executive functioned more as

7. Thorstein Veblen, *The Theory of Business Enterprise* (Scribner).

the chairman of a decision-making body than as an authoritarian decision-maker.

As already pointed out, the variations in the number of levels of management made it difficult to compare the size of the spans of control at the intermediate levels in detail. The figures that were obtained, however, suggested that these too varied with the degree of technical complexity. In direct contrast to the span of control of the chief executive, which grew larger with technical advance, spans of control at middle management levels grew smaller. The small spans of control and the long lines of command characteristic of process industry meant that in this type of industry management structure could be represented by a long and narrowly based pyramid. In unit production the pyramid was short and broadly based.

As Figure 4 shows, the proportion of total turnover allocated to the payment of wages, salaries, and related expenditure was another characteristic varying with the type of production, the proportion becoming smaller with technical advance.

It can be seen from Figure 4 that the biggest difference in labor costs was between firms making integral products and firms making dimensional products. In firms making integral products, the decrease in labor costs associated with increasing technical complexity was relatively small. Labor costs in unit production firms tended to be largely development costs, whereas in large-batch produc-

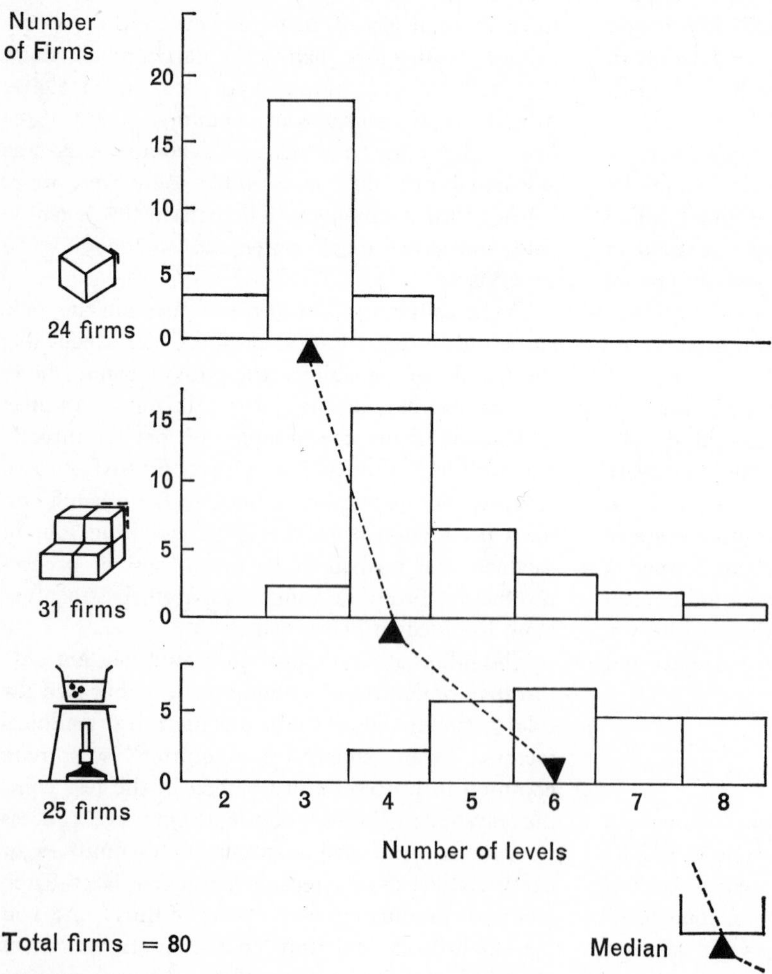


*Figure 3. Levels of management.*

tion they tended to be production costs. Moreover, inside each production category the range was wide, the percentage distribution of costs being affected by a number of variables, the most important of which was the price of the raw materials used. The firms in the process production categories not only had very much lower labor costs, but were also more homogeneous as far as their cost structure was concerned. Moreover, there was a more direct relationship with technical complexity. Labor costs were lower in single-purpose continuous-flow plants than in multipurpose plants producing batches of dimensional products.

It was interesting to find that the ten firms in which labor costs were less than $12\frac{1}{2}$ per cent of total turnover spent the greatest amount per head on employee welfare and services. There was also a tendency for firms in which labor costs were low to spend more money on the employment of specialists in the personnel management and human relations fields. Of the ten low-labor-cost firms, seven had high-status personnel departments covering all the accepted functions of personnel management, and a further two had welfare departments with more limited status and functions. Four of these nine firms employed fewer than 250 people.

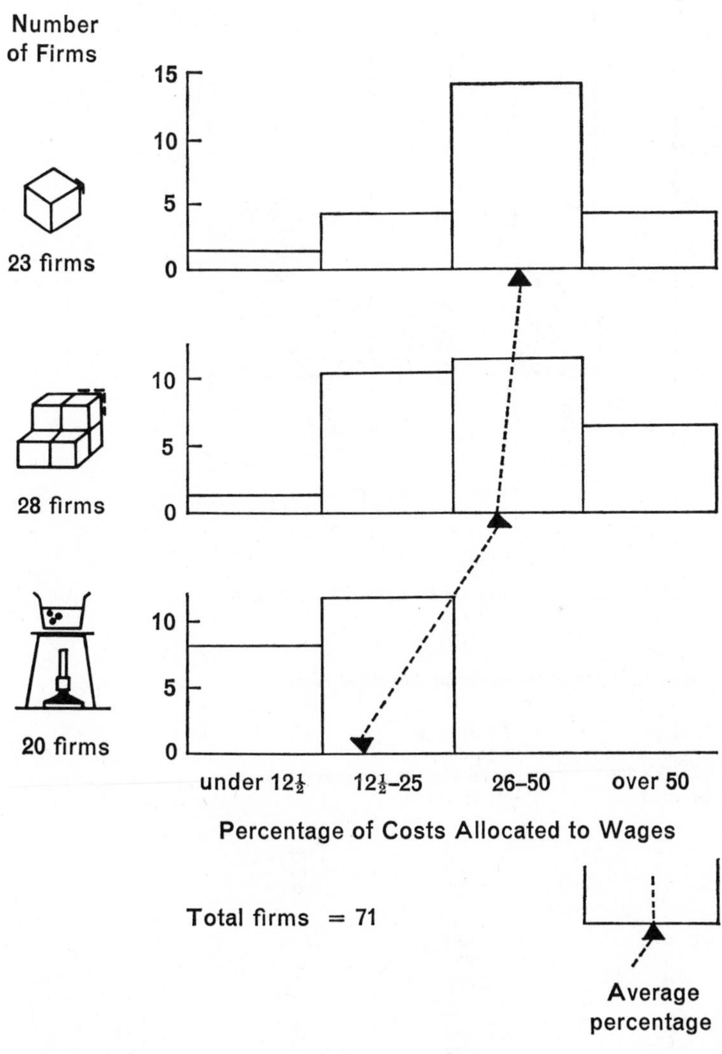


*Figure 4. Labor costs.*

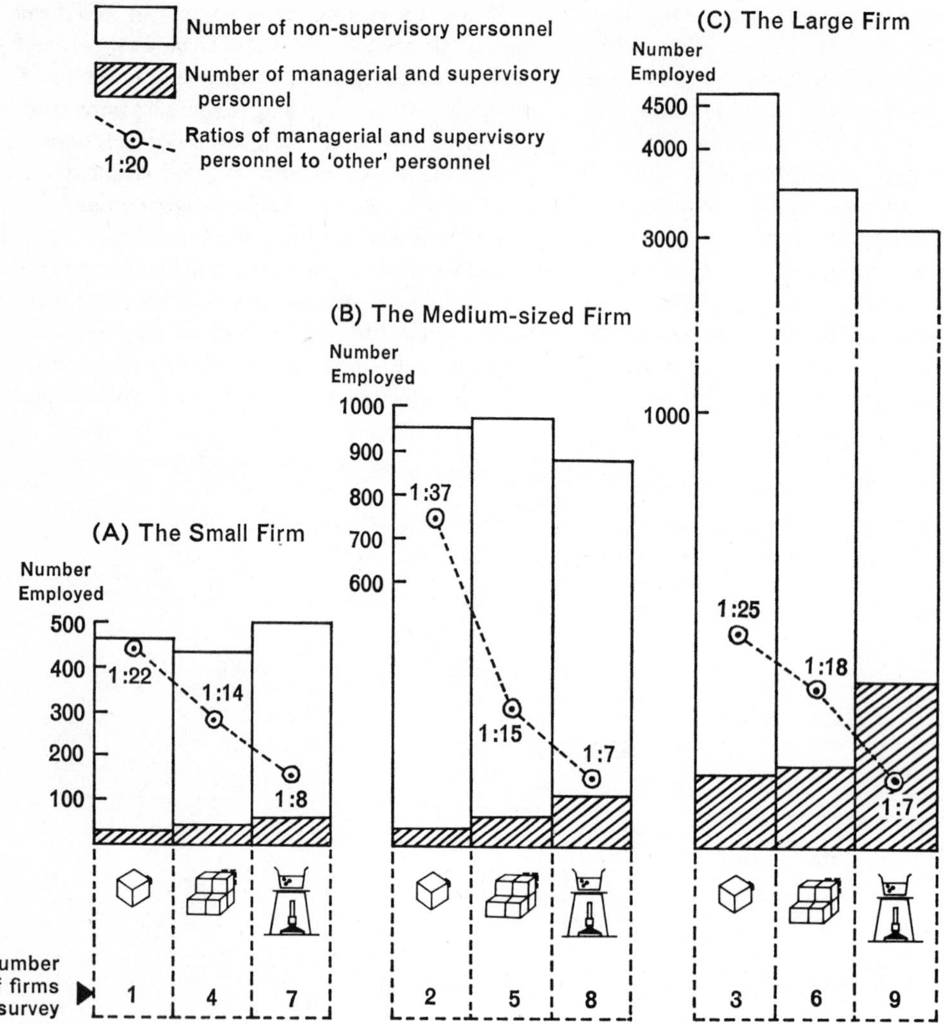


*Figure 5. Ratio of managers and supervisory staff to total personnel in selected firms (analyzed by size).*

***Table 1 – Ratios of Managers and Supervisory Staff to Total Personnel in Selected Firms (analyzed by technology)***

| *Production system* | *Total number employed* | *Number of managerial and supervisory personnel* | *Number of non-supervisory personnel* | *Ratio* |
|---|---|---|---|---|
| Unit and small batch | | | | |
| Firm 1 | 455 | 20 | 435 | 1 : 22 |
| Firm 2 | 948 | 25 | 923 | 1 : 37 |
| Firm 3 | 4,550 | 175 | 4,325 | 1 : 25 |
| Large batch and mass | | | | |
| Firm 4 | 432 | 30 | 422 | 1 : 14 |
| Firm 5 | 975 | 60 | 915 | 1 : 15 |
| Firm 6 | 3,519 | 180 | 3,329 | 1 : 18 |
| Process | | | | |
| Firm 7 | 498 | 55 | 443 | 1 : 8 |
| Firm 8 | 888 | 110 | 778 | 1 : 7 |
| Firm 9 | 3,010 | 375 | 2,635 | 1 : 7 |

The obvious explanation was that firms in which labor costs were low and which were not so concerned with labor economies could afford the more highly paid specialists that function in the personnel management field. Industrial relations certainly seemed to be better in process industry than in large-batch and mass production, but it is not safe to assume that the good relationships were due to the large number of specialist staff employed. As will be seen later, there were a number of contributory factors: less tension and pressure, smaller working groups, and smaller spans of control, for instance. In fact the firms that could afford these specialists may have needed them least.

There was also a link between a firm's technology and the relative size of its management group, the ratio of managers and supervisors to nonsupervisory personnel increasing with technical advance. The sixteen firms shown earlier as having one supervisor to between five and nine nonsupervisory personnel were all process production firms. On average in this type of industry the ratio was 1:8, whereas in large-batch and mass production it was 1:16, and in unit and small-batch production 1:23.

In Table 1 (Figure 5) the numbers are given for three firms in each main production group, these firms having been selected as representative of small, medium, and large firms respectively.

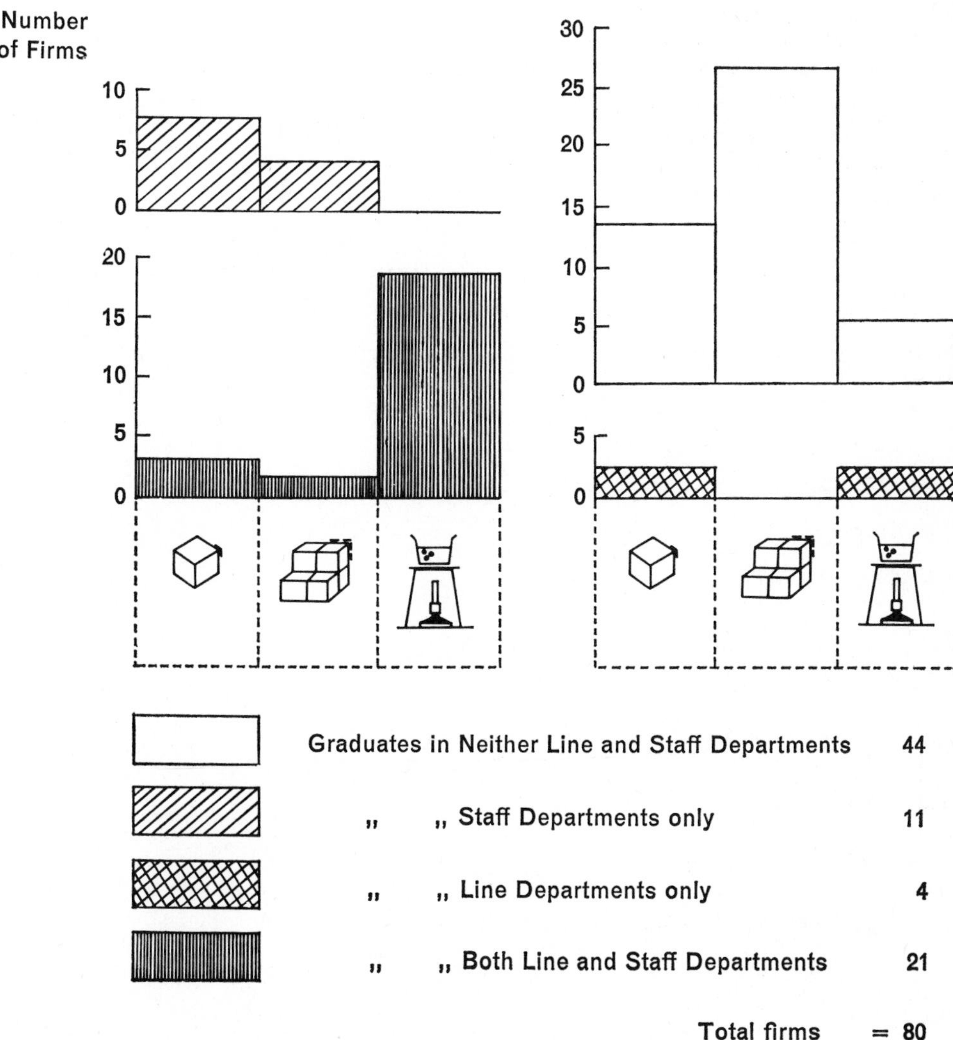


*Figure 6. Employment of graduates.*

The figures are interesting; they show how labor structure is affected by technology, and they give an indication of the additional demand for managerial and supervisory skills likely to arise from technical change. Provision will have to be made in South Essex for the training of more technical and managerial personnel to meet the demands likely to arise from . . . technical changes. . . .

The research workers came to the conclusion that the size of the management group gave a better indication of the "bigness" of a firm than the total number of employees. Some of the firms studied, although employing relatively few people, had all the other characteristics of large companies; including a well-developed management structure, considerable financial resources, long-term planning, generous employee services, and a highly-paid executive staff. This was particularly true of process production firms. It was found, for example, that Firm 7 of Table 1 employed 55 managers out of a total labor force of 498; in all the above respects it resembled Firm 5, which had 60 managers to a total labor force of 975. The status and prestige of the two firms was also similar; they were represented on the same local committees and equally influential in local politics.

Not only were there relatively more managers and supervisors in process industry but they were also better qualified; the degree of technical complexity being related to the number of graduates employed on production management. As Figure 6 shows, twenty process firms employed graduates on line management, whereas only two unit production firms and one mass production firm did so.

Moreover, twelve of the fifteen firms operating regular and systematic management training courses were process firms; so were twenty of the thirty firms whose policy was to fill managerial posts almost exclusively by promotion from within. Most of the process production firms studied seemed to take in a group of graduate trainees each year and then promote from this group.

It will be seen from Figure 6 that there were seven unit and small-batch production firms and

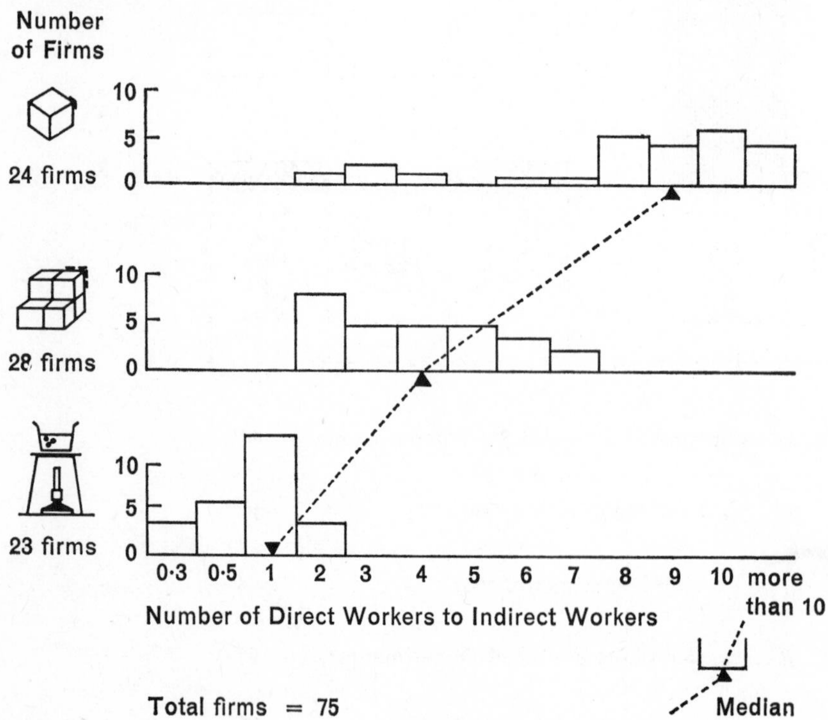


*Figure 7. Ratio of direct to indirect labor in different systems of production.*

four mass and large-batch production firms in which all the graduates employed were in staff departments. The majority were concerned with research and development or inspection functions, and their firms were those whose products themselves, rather than the methods of manufacturing, were technically complex.

In Figure 7 the information given in an earlier figure is broken down on a basis of production system. The clerical and administrative group, like the management and supervisory group, grows larger with technical advance. In the unit and small batch system of production, however, the range is wider than in the other systems. This is because the different types of unit production varied considerably; the firms making technically complex products, both prototypes or large equipments, had a higher ratio of clerical and administrative staff to hourly-paid than those making simple products to customers' individual requirements, either as unit articles or in small batches.

Figure 8 . . . shows that the ratio of indirect workers to direct workers gets larger with technical advance. It is process industry that employs a majority of indirect workers, many of whom are responsible for the maintenance of plant and machinery.

## Similarities at the extremes

Turning now to the figures that rose to a peak in the middle of the technical scale, the first discernible trend of this kind related to the size of the span of control of the first-line supervisors in production departments. Figure 9 shows the average number of hourly-paid workers controlled by first-line supervisors in the different systems of production, the highest averages being in the large-batch and mass production firms. Figure 10 gives the averages for individual firms and shows clearly the similarity between the extremes of the technical scale.

The small spans of control in unit production and process production were an indication of the breakdown of the labor force into small primary working groups. As a result, the relationship between the group and its immediate superior was more intimate and informal in these types of production than in

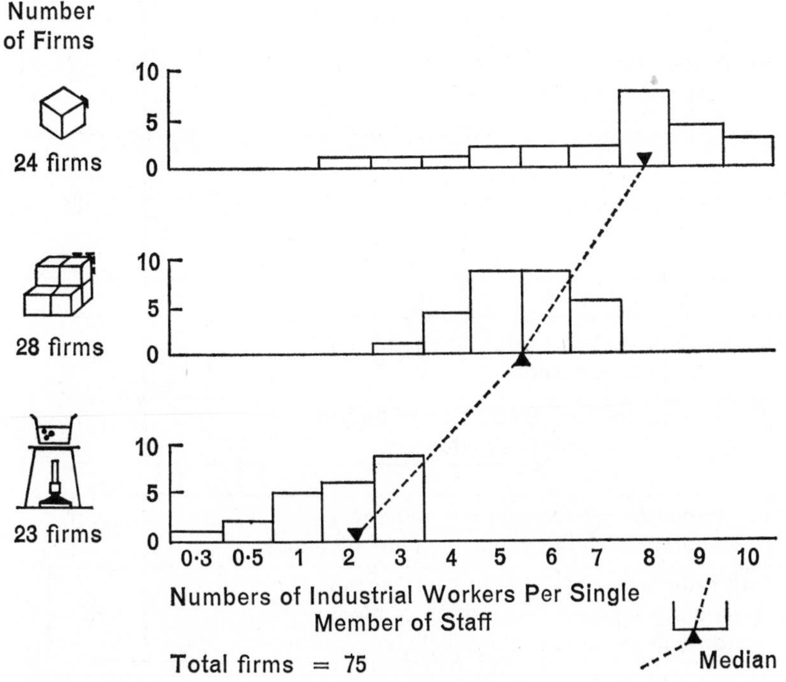


*Figure 8. Ratio of staff to industrial workers analyzed by production system.*

the large-batch and mass production firms studied; this was probably a contributory factor to better industrial relations.

Another resemblance between unit production and process production was that it employed a large number of skilled workers in comparison with large-batch and mass production; there were nineteen firms in which skilled workers outnumbered semiskilled workers, nine of them being unit production firms and ten process production firms. In all the large-batch and mass production firms, the skilled workers were the smallest group. The skilled

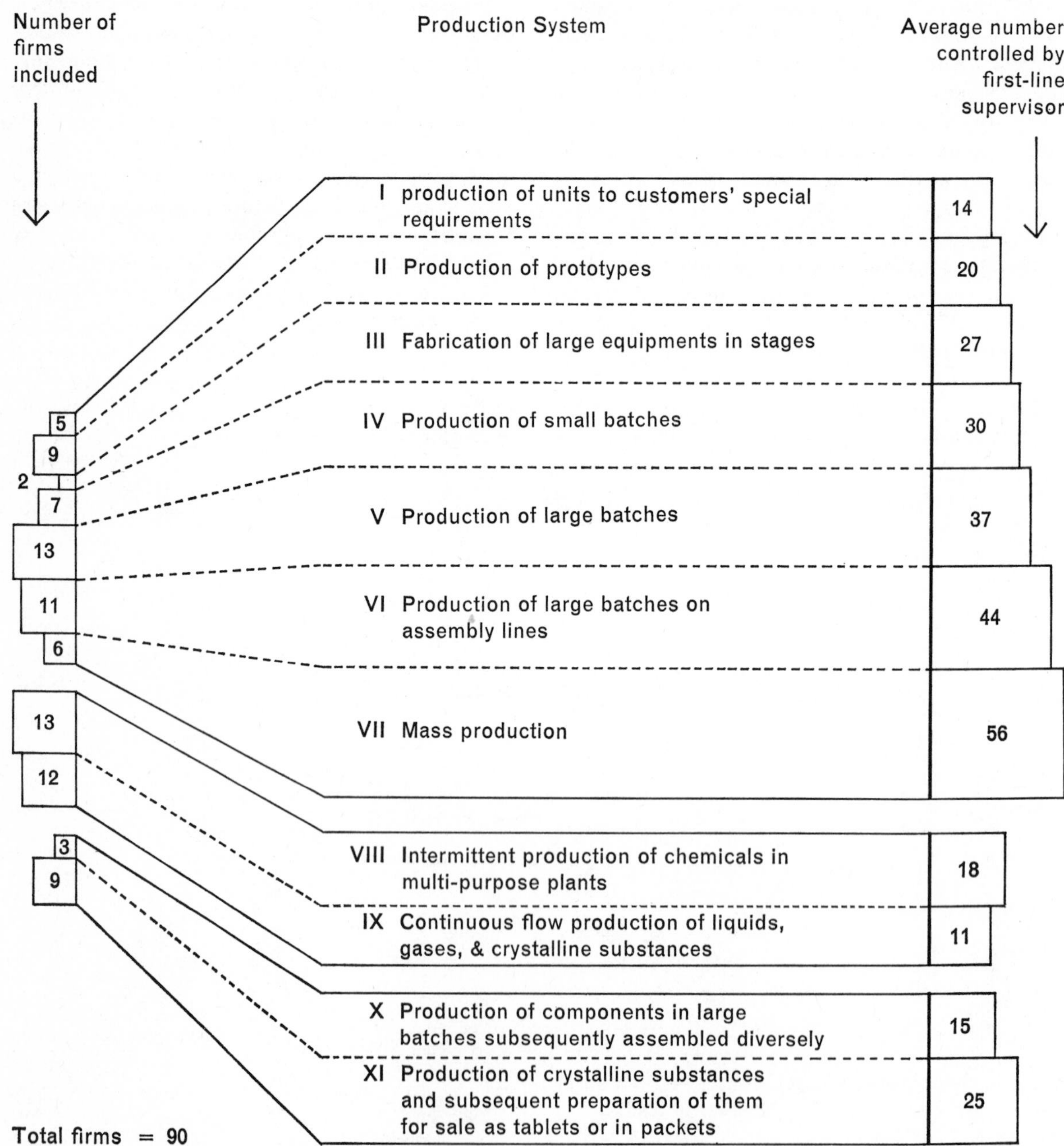


*Figure 9. Average number controlled by first-line supervisors in the different systems of production.*

workers employed in unit production firms were concerned directly with production, the more mechanical parts of their job being delegated to semiskilled workers, while unskilled workers serviced the craftsmen and fetched and carried for them. Occupational status was linked not only with numerical superiority and high pay, but also with a close identification with the immediate production objective. All the elements of skill, conceptual and perceptual, as well as the manual and motor, were brought together in the work of the craftsmen.

In the large-batch and mass production firms studied, the semiskilled workers not only outnumbered the craftsmen but were also the people actually responsible for production, the skilled men being in the main the indirect labor responsible for the maintenance of tools and plant. The unskilled workers did very much the same kind of job as they did in unit production, except that they were concerned more with the servicing of sections or departments than individuals. Standardized production and all that it implied had taken the perceptual and conceptual elements of skill out of the main production task, although much of the work still required a fair degree of motor skill and manual dexterity. In most of the large-batch and mass production firms studied, the patterns of behavior were no longer determined by the skilled men. Moreover, in the firms which ran incentive schemes, their earnings were hardly higher than those of the semiskilled production workers.

It was interesting to notice how the role and functions of the draughtsmen differed from one production system to another. In unit and small batch production the draughtsman was a bridge between the development function and the produc-

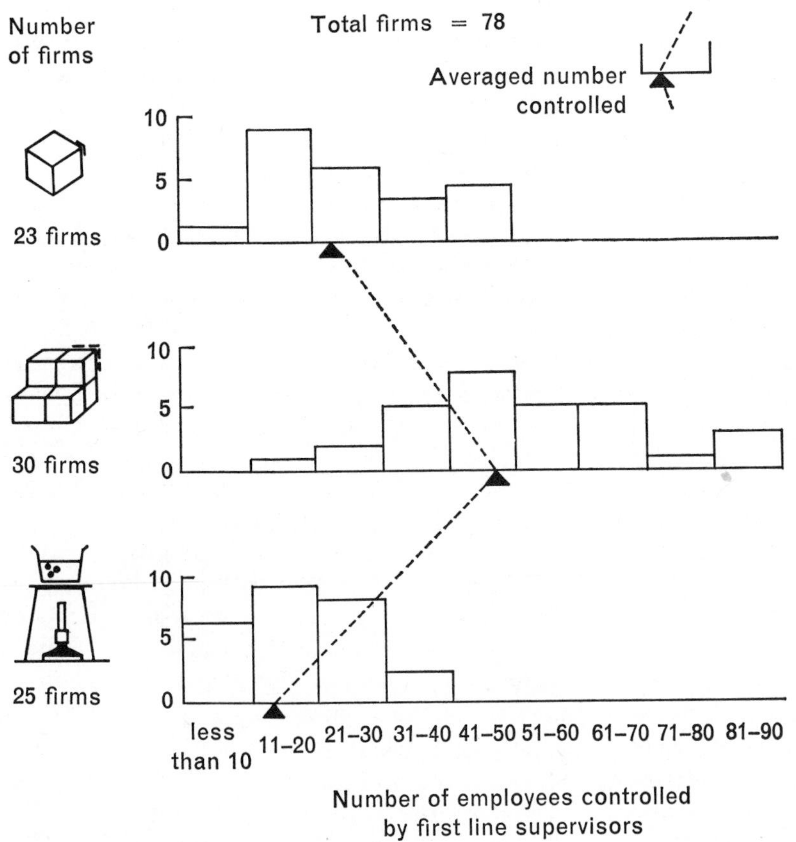


*Figure 10. Size of the span of control of first-line supervisors in three main types of production.*

tion function; a main channel both of communication and control. In large-batch and mass production he no longer filled this dominant role; he was merely one of a number of intermediaries who had some part to play in bridging the gap between the design of a product and its manufacture.

In process production, although the organization of work was basically the same as in large-batch and mass production, the skilled men were the indirect labor force responsible for the servicing and maintenance of plant. The maintenance function was of great importance, the maintenance department being the largest single department in most firms. Thus the skilled men were able to influence the situation more than their counterparts in mass production, and were in a more dominant position.

The main problem in this type of industry appeared to be establishing the occupational status of the plant operators; these men, although often highly skilled, were not formally recognized as skilled outside their own firm. The traditional differentiation between the skilled and the semiskilled worker does not allow for a situation in which the manual and motor elements of skill have been taken out of the main production task, while the conceptual and perceptual elements remain.

The skill of a plant operator is of the perceptual and conceptual kind in that over a period of time he has to learn to absorb a great deal of information and to act on it continuously. But, this skill not being recognized formally, the plant operator has to be recruited as a semiskilled worker at a comparatively low rate of pay. Several firms felt that this created difficulties for them, as in the competitive labor situation of the area it was very difficult to find and keep men of sufficiently high caliber at this low figure. A job in which the emphasis is laid more on the intellectual elements of skill, and which calls for articulation in both speech and writing, can attract only those with the minimum educational qualifications.

Firms at the top and bottom of the technical scale resembled each other in a number of ways, not so easy to illustrate by reference to figures. First, there was a tendency for organic management systems to predominate in the production categories at the extremes of the technical scale, while mechanistic systems predominated in the middle ranges. Clear-cut definition of duties and responsibilities was characteristic of firms in the middle ranges, while flexible organization with a high degree of delegation both of authority and of the responsibility for decision-making, and with permissive and participating management, was characteristic of firms at the extremes. There was less "organization consciousness" at the extremes; it was the firms in the middle ranges which found it easier to produce organization charts.

The second trend was for the line-staff type of organization to be more highly developed in the middle ranges of the scale. The two firms in which there was functional organization and fifteen of the firms in which line organization predominated were process production firms. The other line organization firms were in the unit production categories.

In unit production firms, where relatively few specialists were employed inside production departments, the line supervisors themselves had to be technically competent. Their technical competence was, in most cases, of the kind acquired by long practical experience, and was based on "know-how" rather than professional training. It was interesting to find that in this type of production, supervisors and managers were on average about ten years older than their counterparts elsewhere.

In each of the three firms in which unit production had recently been superseded by standardized production of parts and subsequent diverse assembly, the number of specialists employed had increased by about 25 per cent as a result of the reorganization.

Firms in the large-batch production categories employed the largest number of specialists. In many cases the managerial and supervisory group broke down into two distinct subgroups, general managers comprising one and specialists the other; these subgroups had differing and sometimes conflicting objectives and ideologies. In these firms too there was the most rigid application of line-staff organization. On paper, at least, there was a clear-cut distinction between executive and advisory responsibility. On the organization charts some positions were linked with continuous lines and others with dotted lines, indicating line and staff roles respectively.

In process industry, it was extremely difficult to distinguish between executive and advisory responsibility. Not only was organization more flexible but in many cases it was also changing. The tendency seemed to be for firms to move away from the line-staff type of organization towards either functional or predominantly line organization. In some firms the line of command seemed to be disintegrating, executive responsibility being conferred on specialist staff. Eight of the twelve firms in which the status and prestige of the specialists were so high that it was impossible, in practice, to distinguish between advice, service, and control on the one hand, and executive responsibility on the other, were process production firms. In the other process production firms, specialist skills and knowledge were being increasingly incorporated in the line. In these firms, as in the unit production firms studied, stress was laid on the importance of the line managers being technically competent. Here, of course, the technical competence required was of a different kind; it was intellectual rather than intuitive and based on qualifications and knowledge rather than on long experience and "know-how." In comparison with the managers in unit production, those employed in process production were young. In one process production firm a hundred of the hundred and twenty managers and supervisors were under thirty-five.

It was interesting to find that two oil refineries, approximately equal in size and situated in the same area, were moving away from line-staff organization in opposite directions. In one, specialist skills were being incorporated into the line, line management being technically competent and of high status. In the other the line managers had limited status and were not professionally qualified, their functions being no more than the routine supervision of production operations. They worked alongside highly trained specialist staff who, although nominally advisory, did in effect make executive decisions.

Even in those process production firms with an organizational pattern of the line-staff type there was not the same dichotomy between general managers and specialists as in large-batch and mass production firms. There were no clear-cut distinctions between the objectives and ideologies of the two kinds of management. The main reason for this seemed to be that in most of these firms line managers and specialists were interchangeable. Firms tended to recognize "specialisms" rather than specialists: the laboratory chemist of today could become the line manager of tomorrow. In some cases this interchangeability extended as far as the personnel management staff. A number of the personnel managers and officers in the process production firms included in the survey were scientists and engineers with general management experience, who expected to return to general management after a period in the personnel department.

Another distinction that was most clear-cut in the middle of the technical scale was that between production administration and the supervision of production operations. It was here too that production control procedures were most elaborate and sanctions most rigorously applied. At the bottom of the technical scale the difficulties of controlling production and predicting results appeared to be so great that few firms were prepared to attempt the task. On the other hand, the exercise of control in process production firms was such a relatively simple matter that conflict or stress was rarely associated with it; in many cases the mechanism for exercising control was built into the manufacturing processes themselves.

It would not be true to say that all the firms in the middle ranges of the scale had introduced equally elaborate production control procedures. Some of them still seemed to rely almost entirely on the clinical judgements of their line supervision. This meant that there was greater variation in the way in which production operations were planned and controlled between firms in the middle ranges of the scale than between firms at the extremes.

A similar pattern emerged in relation to communication methods. As might have been expected, the production control procedures in operation in the middle ranges of the scale gave rise to a considerable amount of paper work. Even allowing for this, however, it was interesting to find that in firms at the extremes of the scale communications between managers and departments tended to be verbal, while in the middle ranges they tended to be written. The amount of paper work—interdepartmental memoranda, operating instructions, and policy directives—increased as technology advanced, reaching a peak in assembly-line production firms. As technology advanced beyond this point, however, the amount of paper work began to decrease, and in process production, communications were almost entirely verbal again.

The research workers got the impression that this tendency to communicate in writing in the middle ranges of the scale was linked with the pressures and stresses arising from batch production. The reduction in the area of discretion of line supervision, and the conflicts that arose between them and the specialist personnel encouraged them to safeguard themselves by communicating in writing. They felt it necessary to be able to produce copies of the memoranda they had sent to other managers so that they could clear themselves in the event of a dispute. Life in firms in the middle ranges of the technical scale was therefore less pleasant and easygoing than in firms at the extremes. The research workers themselves soon became aware of this, for they found that it was easier and less arduous to obtain information in unit production and process production firms than in large-batch and mass production firms.

SEYMOUR M. LIPSET, MARTIN A. TROW, and JAMES S. COLEMAN

# Why Democracy in the ITU?

In spite of the detailed nature of our analysis the reader may still legitimately raise the question: Why democracy in the ITU? Is it really a necessary consequence of the structural factors which have been examined? Is it not possible that even if a union possesses all the attributes that the ITU has, it will not develop nor sustain a democratic political system? To what extent could matters have developed differently in the ITU if certain events had occurred differently, or if at some crucial periods in its existence ruthless and powerful men had been at the helm of the union and had been willing to risk destruction of the union rather than lose power? In a real sense, these questions cannot be answered, for in the context of the study of a single case it is impossible to isolate completely all the potentially relevant factors and then specify which factors, either individually or in combination, account for the differences in internal political organization between the ITU and most other unions. We know, for example, that the particular pattern of ITU politics is not repeated in other printer unions in Europe, although there is evidence which suggests that as a group they are more democratic and less centralized than unions in other occupations.

## Historical analysis

The sociological analysis with which most of the book is concerned is an analysis of the factors which contribute to the continuation of the democratic political system at the present time. But it is important to recognize that this analysis gives only a static picture, a description which shows the processes at work within the going system, but not the processes which enabled the system to reach more or less stable equilibrium. At any point in time, the political system of an organization or a society has a certain degree of stability. That is, it has a certain probability of continuing in its present form, and a certain probability of changing. The political system of the ITU is always being supported by some factors and undermined by others. By thus viewing the system as being in an equilibrium which at any point in time has a certain stability, but which could have moved in different directions if some of the factors in the situation had occurred differently, we can see the need to deal with historical materials. It remains for the historical analysis of events which were unique to the ITU to indicate which factors favored the emergence and stability of ITU democracy at different points in time, and to specify the crucial junction points at which new elements entered the situation.

In this way we see that the existence of democracy in the ITU is largely the result of the convergence of a set of events, each of which contributes to or detracts from the continuing stability of the system. If some one event in the early history had turned the other way, then present-day democracy in the

Reprinted from *Union Democracy*, pp. 393–412, by permission of the authors and The Macmillan Company. (© The Free Press, A Corporation 1956.)

union would have been less likely. The existence of democracy at present may be likened to a series of successive outcomes of casting dice, dice which are with each favorable throw more heavily loaded toward a favorable outcome on the next throw.[1] Democracy in the ITU was thus no necessary consequence of a particular set of static factors, but rather was favored from the beginning by numerous factors and even more strongly favored as time went on and numerous events added to the system's stability.

The answer to our original question, Why democracy in the ITU? can be found only by combining the structural and historical analyses to determine the system's stability at each point in time. Thus, in conclusion we would like to examine again some of the crucial turning points in the union's early history.

Many of the factors which contribute to ITU's democracy were present when the union was organized. The printers' strong identification with the craft of printing, probably more pronounced then than now, meant that they were more likely to be involved in the affairs of their organization than workers in other occupations. This same identification, together with other factors such as the high status and irregular work hours of printing, also fostered a strong occupational community. This occupational community, in turn, stimulated the desire of printers to participate in their union. The borderline or marginal status of printing between the middle class and the working class insured the value cleavage which provided the content of politics and evenly split the union into "radical" and moderate camps. Perhaps most important of all at this period was the fact that a large proportion of the printing trades was organized before the creation of a strong international union with a large treasury and paid full-time officials. Thus, the various large city locals of the ITU had a long history of complete autonomy and resisted efforts to create a centralized international structure.

The significance of this factor in the history of the union may be seen by comparing the implications of two ideal-type patterns through which organizations are created. One is organization from the top down, where the group which originally starts the association organizes other individuals and branches into a larger structure. In such a situation we may expect the existence from the start of a formal bureaucratic structure with the new subordinate officials and groups deriving their authority from the summits of the organization. On the other hand, a large national organization may come into existence as a federation through the combination of a number of existing groups. In such a federation the creation of a one-party bureaucratic hierarchy requires the reduction of once independent locals or groups of leaders to subordinate power and status position.

While the ITU illustrates the second pattern, which obviously has greater potential for internal conflict and politics, the International Printing Pressmen and Assistants' Union, the other large printing trades union, exemplifies the first pattern. There, George Berry became president of the union while it was a small, weak organization, and organized the bulk of the trade into a highly centralized and dictatorial organization.[2] Thus the way in which the ITU came into existence and the late development of full-time international officers was not only a factor making for early democracy in the union, but also helped insure that the next throw of the dice would be loaded in favor of democracy and decentralization.[3]

1. See Max Weber: *The Methodology of the Social Sciences*, New York, Free Press, 1949, pp. 182–85, for a similar discussion, including this "dice-throwing" analogy.

2. See Carolyn A. Taylor: *The Emergence and Stabilization of Oligarchy in the International Printing Pressmen and Assistants Union of North America*. M.A. thesis, Columbia University, Department of Sociology, 1952.

3. A somewhat similar variation in organizational history accounts in large part for the differences in the political history of the United Automobile Workers and the United Steel Workers, two unions formed about the same time and affected by similar structural conditions. The Steel Workers was originally formed by the Steel Workers Organizing Committee under Philip Murray. With few exceptions, almost every local of this union was created *after* the initial power structure was established. From its inception there have been no serious factional disputes in the union which have given the members the right to choose among rival candidates for office. Any local center of disturbance was eliminated by Murray. On the other hand, the United Automobile Workers was formed out of an amalgamation of a number of existing automobile unions, and a number of its other local units were organized independently of national control and with relatively little aid from the national body. The subsequent bitter factional fights in the union have in part been a consequence of the attempt of various national administrations to set up

A second important event affecting ITU politics was the formation of the secret societies which over the years endeavored to control both union offices and foremen's jobs. These societies, which were the first major challenges to the democracy of the printers' locals, contributed important elements to the union's democratic system. The autonomy of the locals, referred to above, helped prevent the secret societies from completely dominating the union, for the existence of local administrations opposed to the dominant secret society gave the ordinary printers a nucleus of organization and helped to expose the activities of the society. Also important is the fact that the intense identification of printers with their craft meant that the norms of brotherhood engendered by this identification made membership in an exclusive clique illegitimate in the eyes of many secret-society members as soon as the society lost its early legitimate function of protecting the union.

Thus the stability of ITU democracy was tested and found strong even before the institutionalization of the party system. The struggle over the secret societies, however, added another element which served to preserve the union. Large numbers of printers had a deep personal interest in the fight, since it affected their personal security of employment and opportunity to get work. At least two major cliques or factions developed in most locals, the adherents and the opponents of the secret societies, and these cleavages resulted in deep personal conflicts. The struggle, consequently, could not simply be solved by the victory of one group in an election and the subsequent disappearance of the defeated faction, a frequent development in other unions where the factionalism has not deeply involved the interests or values of the large majority of the members. In the ITU the opposing factions had their roots in a basic cleavage among the members themselves, a cleavage which outlived the tenure in office of a given group and provided the basis for continuing opposition.

a single bureaucratic hierarchy. Most of the factional leaders in the UAW were leaders in the early organizational period of the union, and the different factions have largely been coalitions of the groups headed by these different leaders jointly resisting efforts to subordinate them to the national organization. In spite of the fact that the structural conditions in a large industrial union like the UAW are not favorable to internal democracy and large-scale rank-and-file participation, it has taken close to two decades to approach a one-party structure, and the process is still not completed.

Again, it is difficult to state why such secret societies developed only within the ITU; but one guess is that the factors making for an occupational community helped to sustain the secret societies. These groups (and their opponents as well) were not just power-politics groups, but social clubs which fulfilled many of the same functions as other clubs in the printers' community. The fact, however, that secret political societies were formed cannot be explained by the tendency of printers to mingle with fellow craftsmen, but rather must be seen as a fortuitous reaction to a crisis in the union's relation with employers. Had the union not required such instruments of defense in the 1870's, there was no necessary reason for the emergence of these groups nor for the subsequent development of bitter struggles to abolish them.

The struggle over the secret societies also facilitated the democratization of the ITU's political structure through providing a rationale (*a*) for making the election of international officers a popular election, replacing the then existing system of election-by-convention, which is more easily controllable by the administration even in the ITU; (*b*) for reserving the decision on many matters to popular referendum; and (*c*) for providing an easy method of rank-and-file initiation of referenda. These measures in turn enabled the ITU membership to hold down the salaries of their officers, since increases could only be secured with the approval of the membership in referenda, approval which usually was not given. The fact that the fight against the secret societies was defined as a struggle against domination by visible organized minority cliques, and not simply as a fight against an incumbent administration, helped give the membership a sophisticated awareness of structural dangers to democracy. Thus were instituted important legal elements which support the stability of ITU democracy today.

Again, the pressmen may be used as a comparative case. Although that union underwent a factional struggle early in its history which resulted in the overthrow of the incumbent administration in 1907, factionalism was not institutionalized and perpetuated. The Pressmen's Union had a typical factional fight organized around a specific issue—the conservative collective-bargaining policy followed by the union. Once the old administration was defeated, factionalism practically vanished, since it did not take on the deep intralocal and personal character of the early ITU fights. The new president, George Berry, was able to use his victory to change the constitution in ways which solidified the power of the administration.

These two important points in the early history of the ITU are part of a pattern of "favorable dice throws." Another example, the permanent institutionalization of a rigid priority system in the ITU, was a result of the desire by the members to restrict one of the sources of power of the secret societies and was made possible largely by the existence of the referendum. Without the secret societies and the referendum, the ITU might never have developed a rigid priority system, and one of the factors which safeguard the members' activity in politics against the administration would never have developed. The pressmen, for example, have never adopted a priority system, and its absence has been one of the major resources of the oligarchic rulers of that union.

One additional turning point in the ITU's history deserves mention because it involves the first coming to power of the opposition party. The institutionalization of the practice of gracefully giving up office to an opposition without attempting to use illegitimate means to retain office is one of the most important aspects of a democratic society, which those living in such a society take for granted, while citizens of many states and members of many trade unions know that it is not a simple and regular event. In many unions, administrations on the verge of defeat have resorted to various means, such as the expulsion of the opposition or its leaders, in order to retain power. It is not inconceivable that the Wahneta administration of 1919–1920 might have done the same thing. One factor, however, which served to prevent this from happening was the fact that the Progressives captured only one of the executive offices, the presidency, in the election, while the Administration Party retained its hold over the rest of the major offices and the Executive Council. Given its long-term rule of the union, it is clear that it expected to regain the presidency and retain control of the union once the temporary crisis occasioned by the 1919 New York strike was over. But the union remained more or less evenly divided between the two parties from 1920 to 1928. During these years each party could well hope that the next election would give it complete power. Thus, democratic practices continued through this critical period. Comparison may again be made with the Pressmen's Union, where evidence would suggest that George Berry was on the verge of defeat in the 1920's. He averted such a result by expelling opposition locals and leaders.

The 1920 election was important for the continuation of ITU democracy for another reason. As we pointed out earlier, Marsden Scott, the Wahneta president of the ITU, attempted to break the "vacationist" strike of the New York union. Had this not led to a defeat for Scott, primarily because the New York local voted overwhelmingly against him, the autonomy of the large locals would have been seriously impaired. The international officers would have felt free to manipulate the large locals at will. As it was, this event marked the first major victory of the Progressives, and served as a warning to future international officers not to treat lightly the wishes of large locals. This occurrence also may serve as another illustration of the way in which previous events help load the dice in one direction. The 1919 strike was a joint action of the New York pressmen and typographer locals against the orders of their internationals. When the IPP local disobeyed, Berry expelled the entire New York membership and brought in strikebreakers from outside the city. Scott limited his actions to calling publicly upon the men in Big Six to ignore their local leaders and return to work. Perhaps one reason why Berry and Scott acted differently was that the political consequences of their actions were predictably different. The pressmen's constitution, drawn up by Berry before he faced internal opposition, provided for elections through an electoral-college system in which large locals such as New York have a maximum of six votes while every small local has at least one electoral vote. Thus six locals with less than two hundred members among them, which supported Berry, could balance out the vote of the entire New York membership against him. In the ITU, however, every member votes individually. Scott, therefore, had to try to retain some support in New York if he hoped to be re-elected, and this fact may have operated to restrain his strikebreaking activities. The fact that the ITU decided in 1896 to elect officers by referendum may have been a crucial element in preserving its democracy in 1919–1920.

Without discussing other events chronologically, it is worth mentioning in this context the way in which the existence of an institutionalized party system operates to preserve and extend democratic institutions. At various points in ITU history the constitution has been amended at the initiative of the opposition or by a party just returned to office, in ways designed to weaken the power of the incumbents. The right of all candidates to print statements in the *Typographical Journal*, various elaborate controls over the spending of union monies, the creation of independent auditors elected in staggered six-year terms, and other similar legislation are examples of the ways in which ITU democracy has become incorporated in the law and mores.

These examples of different historical events which have strengthened the base for ITU democracy should serve to illustrate the point that social structure—using the term in this case to refer to the social system comprising the occupation, the industry, and union—defines the probabilities that given historical events can result in an enduring institutional pattern such as a two-party system. Social structure thus constitutes a *potential* for democracy, a potential which, however, may be realized only under certain historical circumstances. This potential can exist without bearing fruit if the initiating events do not occur, or if other abortive events happen. The history of the Pressmen's Union is perhaps a case in point. More often in American unions, one can find a pattern of events which might have initiated a party system had it not occurred in an organization whose social structure offered barren ground for democratic institutions. The United Automobile Workers is perhaps a case in point here.

## Implications for organizational democracy

Observers have called the ITU an anachronism, much like some of the small Swiss cantons which still preserve the direct citizen-assembly control of government, and there is much truth in that view. The major trends in our society are all toward further rationalization of industry, the further concentration and centralization of economic units, and the increasing division of labor, with the substitution of automatic machine operations for skilled craftsmen. Technological developments in the printing industry point in the same direction, with the introduction of new mechanical processes which require little more than the skills of the typist. Although the union is resisting efforts on the part of the employers to divide composing work into two skill levels, many union leaders and members are privately pessimistic about their ability to maintain the centuries-old principle of printers that every worker who sets type should have the same training and be regarded as of equal skill level. The threats to the union posed by new mechanical devices, plus the growing importance of international union policies which meet the need to protect past rights challenged by government legislation, seem to be gradually resulting in a decline of the autonomy of the larger locals. Identification with the craft, and the isolation of printers from interaction with people in higher or lower status levels than themselves also appears to be lessening with changes in the American status structure, and the evidence would seem to indicate that the occupational community of the late forties and early fifties, while still strong, is weaker than it was before World War II. The ITU is still one of the most powerful unions in America and may for some time absorb or cushion the impact of technological developments on the status, income, and skill definition of printing. But major changes in the structure of the industry such as are occurring could conceivably destroy the political system of the union by changing the social system in which it is rooted.

There are mitigating factors, however. The decline of democracy in the ITU is a prediction for the long run, and as John Maynard Keynes has said, in the long run we are all dead. In the meantime, those political institutions which were institutionalized as a consequence of the social conditions making for democracy may prolong for a considerable period the democracy which exists. The normative and legal safeguards to the stability of democracy which developed throughout the union's history can act to preserve democracy long after some of the factors which gave rise to them have vanished. Perhaps the most important democratic defense mechanism which has been institutionalized in the ITU is the two-party system itself. The sheer existence of a two-party system provides one of the principal opportunities and stimulations for participation in politics by the members of an organization or community. If one compares a party conflict to contests between different athletic organizations, one can see how this process operates in areas other than politics. In a city which has two baseball clubs, or two high-school football teams, many individuals who have no great interest in sports are exposed to pressures to identify with one or the other team by the fans of each one. Such identification once made and reinforced by personal relations with committed fans seems to lead many people to become strongly interested in who wins a given sports contest. Political identification, while more complicated, nevertheless takes on some of the aspects of team identification. Political parties, once in existence, attempt to activate the apathetic in order to keep alive and win power. This process undoubtedly leads more people to become interested and involved in the affairs of the community or organization than when no political conflict exists.[4]

As long as some men feel strongly about union issues and others are desirous of securing or retaining the status derivative from the role of union political leader, the party organizations will be maintained in the ITU, since they are the institutionalized mechanisms through which such men can express themselves.

In a one-party structure, on the other hand, politically interested or ambitious men have only one outlet for their activity, and that is involvement in the activities sponsored by the administration. In the absence of a democratic political arena in which men may learn the skills of politics outside the administration, union officers are usually faced with a paucity of skilled and capable prospective subordinate officials, and are usually willing and even anxious to coopt capable union activists into the administrative structure. In such one-party unions, apathy on the part of the membership is functional to the stability of the incumbent machine. The less the members know or desire to know about policy, the more secure the leaders are. The single-party organization in a trade union consequently acts to dampen participation, while in the ITU, membership interest and activity are the lifeblood of the party.[5]

This brief comparison of some of the ways in which one-party and two-party systems, once institutionalized, operate to perpetuate the existing system demonstrates again the link between the historical and the sociological levels of analysis. The historical analysis explains how the system, in this case two-party democracy, came into existence, while the sociological analysis accounts for the ways in which structural factors, either those existing in the situation or those created by specific historical developments, operate to maintain it. The latter factors, those which are created by a unique series of events, may over the years turn out to be even more important in explaining why the system continues. An example drawn from economic history may help to illustrate the general significance of this methodological point.

Max Weber, in his classic studies of the relations between economic behavior and cultural values, attempted to demonstrate that the emergence of a unique cultural ethos in certain Protestant sects

4. Various election studies show that the closer the contest in a given electoral unit, the higher the rate of voting participation. See Herbert Tingsten, *Political Behaviour*; D. E. Butler: *The British General Election of 1951*, London, The Macmillan Co., Ltd., 1951; H. F. Gosnell: *Why Europe Votes*, Chicago, University of Chicago Press, 1930; and V. O. Key, *Southern Politics*.

5. There is one important exception to the generalization that leaders of one-party unions or dictatorships will not attempt to stimulate membership participation. In totalitarian states and in Communist-controlled labor unions, extreme efforts are made to secure the participation of citizens or members. The totalitarian leader is concerned with having his followers attend meetings, read political or union literature, listen to broadcasts, and engage in other similar activities, since this means that he can reach them with his point of view and attempt to indoctrinate them. If the members or citizens are not "politically" active, they are also removed from the influence of the controlling power. As a general hypothesis, one might suggest that the greater the changes in the structure of the society that a governing group is attempting to introduce, or the greater the changes in the traditional functions of unions that a union leadership is attempting to effect, the more likely a leadership is to desire and even require a high level of participation by citizens or members. The radical changes that accompany social revolution, or on a smaller scale, the transformation of a trade union into a political weapon, put severe strains on group loyalties and create the potential for strong membership hostility toward the leadership. A high level of controlled and manipulated rank-and-file participation is perhaps the only effective way, given the leadership's purposes, of draining off or redirecting the discontent which violent changes in traditional patterns and relationships engender.

provided the effective set of economic values which made possible the development of a rational capitalist economic system.[6] Ascetic Protestantism, especially Calvinism, so defined the situation for its followers as to require their concentration on the maximization of economic wealth so as to assure themselves that they were predestined to go to heaven. The specific Protestant *religious* ethos has disappeared, however, in many countries in which the economic "spirit of capitalism" still exists. The religious system is no longer necessary in the United States, for example, to support the economic ethos of a going industrial society. Any attempt today to explain the continued existence of a secular "Protestant ethic," must locate the relationship between that ethic and the functional requirements of a going capitalist economic system. Such an analysis might point to the fact that in a capitalist social system the dominant roles through which social status is secured are best achieved or maintained by men acting in accordance with the "spirit of capitalism." Here we have an interdependent system in which status achievement requires adhering to certain values, and adhering to these values facilitates status achievement. Such a functional analysis, however, will not explain why this system is best developed in countries with an ascetic Protestant background rather than in Catholic or non-Christian countries. To deal with this problem, it would be necessary to go back to an analysis of the conditions under which the new system first came into existence.

## Conclusions

The conclusions derived from theoretical analyses of the possibilities for democracy inherent in the structure of large-scale voluntary organizations, from empirical descriptive analysis of what actually goes on in most trade unions and other voluntary organizations, and from specifying the conditions which are related to democracy in the most democratic large voluntary association, the International Typographical Union, suggest that the functional requirements for democracy cannot be met most of the time in most unions or other voluntary groups.

To recapitulate the major points in this analysis:

1. The structure of large-scale organization inherently requires the development of bureaucratic patterns of behavior. The conditions making for the institutionalization of bureaucracy and those making for democratic turnover in office are largely incompatible. While bureaucracy reduces the area which is political—the area subject to discussion and choice among the members—it also gives an incumbent administration great power and advantage over the rank and file or even an organized opposition. This advantage takes such forms as control over financial resources and internal communications, a large, permanently organized political machine, a claim to legitimacy, and a near monopoly over political skills.

2. The normal position of the trade-union member in modern urban society makes it likely that few individuals will ordinarily be actively interested in the affairs of the union. Leisure-time activities are centered around home and neighborhood rather than around one's vocation. The absence of membership participation facilitates the existence of one-party oligarchy.

3. While the power inherent in bureaucratic social organization and lack of membership participation would be enough to account for the absence of democracy in trade unions, various pressures on trade-union leaders act as further forces making them seek means of reducing democracy in their unions. In the trade-union movement, democracy—the possibility that an official can be defeated for re-election—means that the leader must be willing to move from a position of high status, power, and income to a much lower one if he is still to remain within the union. The institutionalization of such movement from high to low status would require the union leader to accept as probable a future sharp decline in his position in society. Given the great emphasis placed by the social structure on achieving and maintaining high status, it is clear that the norms of democracy in trade unions and those of achievement in the larger society are often in sharp conflict. This may help account for the fact that democracy is found mostly in unions in high-status

6. See Max Weber: *The Protestant Ethic and the Spirit of Capitalism*, New York, Charles Scribner's Sons, 1930; *The Religion of China*, New York, Free Press, 1950; and *Ancient Judaism*, New York, Free Press, 1952; also see Talcott Parsons: *The Structure of Social Action*, New York, Free Press, 1949, for a discussion of Weber's method. Weber's conclusions have been challenged by many economic historians. In citing this example, however, we are not interested in who is right in this controversy, but rather in the method of analysis.

occupations or in small local organizations in which the status differentiation between leaders and followers is very small. Where the status gap is large, the leader is under strain from his position to institutionalize dictatorial mechanisms which will reduce the possibility that he may lose his office.[7]

Our analysis of the factors related to democracy in the ITU has pointed to conditions under which democracy may be institutionalized in large-scale private governments. Basically, however, it does not offer many positive action suggestions for those who would seek consciously to manipulate the structure of such organizations so as to make the institutionalization of democratic procedures within them more probable. We have shown that there is much more variation in the internal organization of associations than the notion of an iron law of oligarchy would imply, but nevertheless, the implications of our analysis for democratic organizational politics are almost as pessimistic as those postulated by Robert Michels.

It may be, however, that like Michels, we are too hard on trade unions and voluntary associations. Perhaps viewing such organizations in other perspectives may justify more optimistic conclusions. Before closing therefore, we should like to examine some of the alternative conceptions of the democratic potential inherent in trade unions.

One school of thought, the Marxist, has for obvious reasons been much concerned with the problem of oligarchy in labor organizations. Those Marxists who have written on the problem have tended to agree with Michels that trade unions are oligarchic, but have suggested that some of the factors making for oligarchy are inherent in the capitalist system of social relations, and that under a new social structure of socialism or communism, some of the factors making for oligarchy will be reduced, while those making for democracy will increase. Perhaps the most sophisticated presentation of this approach can be found in a book by Nikolai Bukharin, one of the major pre-Stalinist theoreticians of communism. Bukharin recognized the problem and even acknowledged that after the working class comes to power, "There will inevitably result a *tendency* to 'degeneration,' i.e., the excretion of a leading stratum."[8]

The answer to the problem posed by a "stratum of leaders" who would seek to control the institutions of a socialist society is, according to Bukharin, that "what constitutes an eternal category in Michels' presentation, namely, the 'incompetence of the masses' will disappear, for this incompetence is by no means an attribute of every social system; it likewise is a product of the economic and technical conditions, expressing themselves in the general cultural being and in the educational conditions. We may state that in the society of the future there will be a colossal overproduction of organizers, which will nullify the *stability* of the ruling groups."[9] Thus, interestingly, Bukharin posits that one of the conditions which will develop under socialism is similar to one which we have suggested already exists in the ITU, namely, a large group of men who are educated and skilled in the ways of politics, a group which is too large to be encompassed in the governing apparatus and which constitutes the base for an organized opposition to the dominant faction. On a theoretical level, however, Bukharin could not recognize that control over a "leading stratum" required an organized opposition group, a second party, since Marxian dogma prescribed that parties could only reflect class antagonism and within the working class there could be no such antagonism.[10]

We would be foolhardy to reject the possibility that major changes in the social structure will increase the potential for democracy within the labor movement. In fact, a number of the changes which are an outgrowth of the efforts for a more socialist or equalitarian society do point in the direction of reducing the factors making for oligarchy within the

7. Instead of suggesting that power corrupts in all situations, this analysis suggests that such corruption is a consequence of specific social structures, where *conformity to one norm necessarily involves violation of another norm.* Cf. R. K. Merton: *Social Theory and Social Structure,* New York, Free Press, 1949, Chap. 4, "Social Structure and Anomie."

8. Nikolai Bukharin, *Historical Materialism,* pp. 310–11.

9. *Loc. cit.* (Bukharin's emphasis).

10. Friends of Bukharin have reported that, following his defeat by Stalin, he did recognize the need for a second party in the Soviet Union. It is interesting to note that even in 1923 when he first wrote this book, Bukharin, although a leading member of the ruling group in Russia, could write that the question of whether there would be a socialist democracy or the dictatorship of the leading stratum was not a settled question. "The outcome will depend on which tendencies turn out to be the strongest." *Ibid.,* p. 311.

labor movement. Perhaps the most important of these are the efforts in Great Britain and the Scandinavian countries to reduce the income and presumably consequent status differentiation attached to various levels of skill. In addition, as trade unions assume the power to affect major national political questions such as foreign policy, national wage policy, local planning, and many others, the battles traditionally fought at the ballot box in democratic countries are increasingly becoming questions of controversy within British trade unions. Aneurin Bevan, for example, has recently threatened to work directly within the trade unions to challenge their leadership on issues which are far removed from collective-bargaining policies. Consequently the crucial way in which the emergence of socialism improves the conditions for democracy within labor unions is by legitimating internal controversies within labor organizations that are conducted on ideological lines and involve more than the bread-and-butter questions of "business unionism." By stating that a union should be concerned with matters beyond collective bargaining, socialist union leaders are unwittingly encouraging the possibility of political factionalism within their organization.

Conversely, it should be noted that business unionism, as a set of ideas justifying the narrowest definitions of a union's role in society, also helps to legitimate one-party oligarchy, for it implies that union leadership is simply the administration of an organization with defined, undebatable goals: the maximization of the member's income and general welfare. The more narrowly an organization defines its functions as fulfilling limited and specific needs, the narrower the range there is for controversy.[11] No one has attempted either a qualitative or quantitative analysis of the relationship between diffuse political or specific business-union ideologies and the presence or absence of political conflict within trade unions. The general proposition may be suggested, however, that the more diffuse the ideology of a trade union, the greater the likelihood of internal factionalism. Consequently, the more directly unions are involved in politics and the more important their political decisions are to power in the total society, the more likely that national political ideologies and movements will affect the internal politics of labor. This pattern might have developed in a more clear-cut fashion than it has if a part of the left wing of the labor movement had not been captured by a totalitarian political movement, the Communist Party. Before the emergence of the Communist Party, many European labor unions and socialist parties were divided between left and right wings, which battled for influence and power according to the rules of democracy, much as do supporters of Aneurin Bevan and Hugh Gaitskell in the present-day British Labour Party. The Communists, by refusing to play the democratic game, help to break down or prevent the institutionalization of internal democratic procedures within the more political European labor movement. It is, however, possible that a democratic socialist society, somehow blessed with the

11. It should also be noted that limiting the functions of an organization helps to reduce the likelihood that a member will feel the need to participate in and influence the policies of the organization. People may belong to many organizations, such as the American Automobile Association, a local consumer's cooperative, a medical plan, a bowling congress, a national stamp club, and many others, without feeling any obligation to participate actively in the internal operations of the group and without feeling coerced by the fact that decisions are made without their having been consulted. In large measure, each of the various voluntary associations to which people may belong is judged on the basis of the ability to satisfy a limited need of its individual members. On the other hand, the more diffuse the functions of a group or organization, the more likely an individual is to find sources of disagreement with and desire to participate actively in its operation.

Applying the above analysis to trade unions, the union which simply operates as a business union may be placed in the category of specific, one-function organizations. Outside of the shop organization where there is normally the largest participation by workers, the single major task of the business union, collective bargaining, does not take place oftener than once a year, and in many unions only once every two or three years. The day-to-day administration of union affairs need not concern the average member any more than do the day-to-day activities that go into running a veterans' group or a medical plan. It is of course true that a union deals with the individual in his occupational role, and we might expect it to call forth more of his interest and concern than other voluntary organizations to which the individual relates through his less important roles. Nevertheless, the generalization should hold within the labor movement; the more specific the functions of the union, the less involvement of members; and the more diffuse its relations to the members, the more involvement. The latter situation may be a by-product either of an occupational community, as in the case of the ITU, or of a political ideology which widens the definition of the role of the union as occurs in many European countries.

absence of the Communists, will have more democratic trade unions than now exist.

A second school of thought, found most generally among supporters of existing trends in the labor movement, challenges the definition of democracy used by Michels and would presumably reject the one used in this book. These observers argue that trade unions are democratic in the sense that they represent the interests of their members in a struggle with the employers, regardless of whether internal opposition can exist within them. As V. L. Allen has put it:

> It has been argued by some that a voluntary society must provide for membership participation and install the checks and brakes on authority in the manner undertaken by the State in order to achieve and maintain democracy. This contention is misleading, for a voluntary society is not a State within a State; nor does it operate on the same scale or undertake the same functions. Its end and its means are different from those of the State. The government operates the supreme coercive power within a State and the necessity of preventing the use of that power contrary to the interests of the community is of immense over-riding importance in a political democracy. . . . None of this holds for voluntary societies, which by definition, cannot impose punitive measures on their members and which have no means of enforcing their regulations other than by persuasion and sound common sense. There is not in a voluntary society "the organized force which is the distinctive mark of the state (and which) so alters the nature of the political problems as to make any analogy between democracy in politics and in non-political societies only misleading."
>
> It is the voluntary nature of organizations within a State which is essential for the preservation of democracy within those organizations. . . .
>
> It is contended here, however, that trade union organization is not based on theoretical concepts prior to it, that is on some concept of democracy, but on the end it serves. In other words, the end of trade-union activity is to protect and improve the general living standards of its members and not to provide workers with an exercise in self-government.[12]

It is the general assumption of exponents of this school that trade unions, even when oligarchic and dictatorial, are representative of their members' interest in the general socio-economic struggle in the same sense that political parties, although not directly controlled by the social groups which give them electoral support, nevertheless represent these social groups in the government. Presumably unions or political parties which ceased to represent their constituents or members would lose their allegiance. In the most general sense of the term "represent," this assumption is probably valid. One can show that even the most dictatorial trade-union leaders must be somewhat responsive to the economic needs of their members. A union oligarchy which does not defend the economic interests of the rank and file may find its membership disappearing either into another union or into nonmembership in any union, as John L. Lewis did in the twenties and early thirties. Lewis, then a trade-union as well as a political conservative, almost lost the United Mine Workers. Only after adopting the militant tactics for which he is now famous was he able to rebuild the union. A trade union which is not an economic defense organization has no function and will not long remain on the scene.

To recognize this fact does not involve declaring that a trade union is necessarily representative of its members' interests, or must be considered a democratic organization. Control over the organizational machinery enables the officialdom of a union to define the choices available to the organization and its members. Without a sophisticated organized opposition, the members have no way of discovering for themselves what is possible. A union may, for example, present a contract as containing substantial gains by engaging in statistical double talk, as the United Steel Workers did recently. The failure of the printing pressmen to win a priority system cannot be presented as the will of the membership in that completely dictatorial union. The divergencies in the national political action of the Amalgamated Clothing Workers and the International Ladies Garment Workers are clearly a product of the political ambitions and viewpoints of Sidney Hillman and David Dubinsky, not of the membership of the two unions. Communist-led unions have on occasion engaged in prolonged strikes which were unjustifiable by any collective-bargaining criteria, while other conservative unions have attempted to avoid strikes under almost all conditions. Some union leaders have engaged in programs to rationalize their industry, even though this meant a great decline in the total number of

12. V. L. Allen: *Power in Trade Unions*, London, Longmans, Green and Company, Ltd., 1954, pp. 10–11, 15. The quotation is from A. D. Lindsay, *The Essentials of Democracy*, p. 49.

man-hours of work available to their members, while others have fought efforts to institute labor-saving devices. The West Coast longshoremen have instituted a rigid sharing of the work according to a numerical list, while the East Coast longshoremen have retained the shape-up system of hiring, which permits hiring bosses to discriminate among the men.[13] In the face of these differences, it would be hard to assert that unions represent their members' interests when the members have little control over policy formation.

The lack of internal democracy also tends to reinforce a factor which makes for both oligarchy and unrepresentativeness: the widening of the salary and status gap between the members and leaders. Without the presence of opposition groups, most American union leaders have raised their salaries far above those of the members. The history of the United Automobile Workers is a good example of this phenomenon. While major factional groups existed in the union, national officers, including the president, received less than $10,000 a year. Once Reuther consolidated his power, the salaries of officers gradually increased. Perhaps even more important than salaries, however, is the union officers' opportunity to receive perquisites in the form of expense accounts, union-purchased automobiles, vacation expenses, and the like, which do not appear in the records. In recent years, union welfare funds have provided a new source of extra income for some union leaders, their families or friends, through new pay rolls and insurance commissions. In the ITU or any union with an organized opposition, such financial manipulations would be impossible, since the opposition would make them an election issue.

As union leaders secure higher financial rewards from their jobs, their sense of identification with the men and the urgency of their problems must inevitably suffer. Hence lack of opposition makes for unrepresentative action both in the form of union policies which the membership probably would not approve if they had the power to affect them, and also by diminishing the leaders' sense of importance of members' economic problems.

The principal premise in the argument that oligarchic unions may be regarded as democratic rests, as Allen makes clear, on the assumption that trade unions are voluntary associations which members may leave much as they may quit a stamp club when they object to what it is doing. This assumption clearly does not apply to most American trade unions, although it may be applicable to many British and European labor organizations. Under the closed shop, and more recently the union shop, men cannot legally quit their union without losing their jobs. Where the union has power, even the legal right to resign from the union and keep one's job is relatively meaningless, since the union can effectively blacklist a man either by having the cooperation of the employer who seeks to keep on good terms with the union leadership, or through sanctions imposed by men who remain in the union. The development of union welfare funds has proved to be a new restriction on the rights of workers to choose their union. Recently, a minority group in the United Textile Workers, CIO, attempted to secede from that union and join the AFL textile union. A number of locals which were sympathetic with the secession move found that their welfare funds were tied up with the international union and that they would lose them if they left the CIO.[14]

The fact, therefore, that unions must to some extent represent their members' interests in the market must not be allowed to conceal the fact that union leaders possess great power to do things which would never be approved if a democratic choice were available. As Howe and Widdick have pointed out:

> There is one decisive proof of democracy in a union (or any other institution): oppositionists have the right to organize freely into "parties," to set up factional machines, to circulate publicity and to propagandize among the members. . . . The presence of an opposition . . . is the best way of insuring that a union's democratic structure will be preserved. . . . To defend the right of factions to exist is not at all to applaud this or that faction. But this is the overhead (well worth paying) of democracy: groups one considers detrimental to the union's interest will be formed. The alternative is dictatorship.[15]

13. This system was legally abolished in 1954 by the states of New Jersey and New York, after the union refused to abolish it.

14. It should be noted that Allen makes an exception in his argument about union democracy for unions which have compulsory membership.

15. Howe and Widdick, *The UAW and Walter Reuther*, pp. 262–63.

The emphasis in this book on the undemocratic character of most labor unions is not designed to negate the general proposition of the political pluralists that trade unions, like many other internally oligarchic organizations, serve to sustain political democracy in the larger society.[16] As many political observers have made clear, many internally dictatorial organizations operate to protect the interests of their members by checking the encroachments of other groups. Democracy in large measure rests on the fact that no one group is able to secure such a basis of power and command over the total allegiance of a majority of the population that it can effectively suppress or deny the claims of groups it opposes. The labor movement in particular has played a major role in fostering the institutions of political democracy in the larger society and in fostering the ideology of equalitarianism. Workers today can live and act with much less fear of the consequences of their acts than was generally true even three decades ago. There are few, although unfortunately some, unions which have as much potential power over the lives of their members as employers once held over their workers. In large measure, the chance that the collectivist society which is developing in most countries will be democratic rests on the possibility that trade unions, although supporters of socialist objectives, will maintain their independence of the state, and will act to protect their members and the citizenry in general against the tremendous state power inherent in a collectivist society. The behavior of the trade unions of the British Commonwealth and Scandinavian countries furnishes real evidence that trade unions, regardless of their internal structure, will continue to play the role of defenders of democracy and equalitarianism under collectivism.

Nevertheless, the extension of democracy in an industrial society requires the extension of control by men over those institutions they depend on. To the sympathetic student of the labor movement, the ITU stands as a model of the trade union in a democratic society. In the ITU he sees the image of the democratic processes he prizes in the national body politic, in the organization through which printers exercise some control over the conditions of their livelihood. Although the events and conditions which have given rise to and sustained democracy in the ITU are unique and are rarely found in trade unions or other voluntary large social organizations generally, it would be foolhardy to predict that democratic processes cannot develop elsewhere. The specific factors which underlie ITU democracy are not likely to be duplicated elsewhere; but the very great variety of factors present in the situation suggests that democratic processes may develop under quite different conditions and take quite different forms.

If it is not to serve as a model, the ITU may well serve as a touchstone against which the internal political processes of other unions and of other voluntary groups, such as the American Legion or the American Medical Association, may be appraised and criticized. As Robert K. Merton has said in another connection:

> In the world laboratory of the sociologist, as in the more secluded laboratories of the physicist and chemist, it is the successful experiment which is decisive and not the thousand-and-one failures which preceded it. More is learned from the single success than from multiple failures. A single success proves it can be done. Thereafter, it is necessary only to learn what made it work. This, at least, is what I take to be the sociological sense of those revealing words of Thomas Love Peacock: "Whatever is, is possible."[17]

The ITU and its democratic political system *is*: to know what makes and has made it what it is may help make possible the development of organizational democracy elsewhere. Democracy, whether in national society or in private organizations, is not achieved by acts of will alone; but men's wills, through action, can shape institutions and events in directions that reduce or increase the chances for the development and survival of democracy. For men of good will, there is much to learn in the history, institutions, and arguments of American printers.

16. Cf. Franz L. Neumann: "Approaches to the Study of Political Power," *Political Science Quarterly*, 65:161–80 (June, 1950).

17. Robert K. Merton: *Social Theory and Social Research*, New York, Free Press, 1949, pp. 194–95.

MELVILLE DALTON

# The Interlocking of Official and Unofficial Reward

Use of materials and services for personal ends, individual or group, is, of course, officially forbidden, for in both plant theory and popular usage this is *theft*. But our concern to pinpoint the informal phases of administration where possible requires scrutiny of this generally known but taboo subject.

Such practices are as delicate to discuss as they are to apply. For as long as rivalries can generate "reasons" there will be double talk around the concept of "reward," especially in organizations that stress "fair-dealing," "job evaluation," "merit-rated salaries," etc. The dynamics of individual and group action do not require that one agree fully with those who say that no word[1] ever has the same meaning twice, but they do demand that one recognize the difficulties of assigning absolute meanings to terms describing the kinds of situations we are dealing with.[2] What in some sense is theft, may, in the context of preserving the group and solving present problems, lose much or all of its odious overtones. We only need note the gradations of terms referring to theft to suspect this. As theft requires more ingenuity, becomes larger in amount, and is committed by more distinguished persons (whose power is often related to their importance in the operation of society), its character is correspondingly softened by such velvety terms as *misappropriation*,

1. S. I. Hayakawa, *Language and Thought in Action*, Harcourt, Brace and Co., New York, 1949, pp. 60–62.

2. Even in the physical sciences there are disputes about the definition, perception, and nature of matter. See the comments of two *physicists*: Martin Johnson, *Art and Scientific Thought*, Columbia University Press, New York, 1949; and J. Bronowski, "Science and Human Values," *The Nation*, 183: 550–66, December 29, 1956, and *The Common Sense of Science*, Wm. Heinemann, Ltd., London, 1951, especially chaps. 6–8. Disputes increase in the biological sciences. For example, because they combine both plant and animal characteristics, we find such organisms as *Euglena viridis* and the slime-fungi studied by both zoologists and botanists. Books from satirical to scientific levels debate the nature of *truth, fact*, and *meaning*. In the opening pages of his *Ethics*, Aristotle notes the difficulty of expecting a mathematician to see facts as *probable*, or a politician to see them as *precise*. For himself he believed that different subject matters admit of different degrees of precision in handling. See also the two works of T. V. Smith, "In Accentuation of the Negative," *The Scientific Monthly*, 63: 463–69, December, 1946 and *The Ethics of Compromise*, Starr King Press, Boston, 1956; and the numerous articles in L. Bryson et al., *Symbols and Values*, Harper and Brothers, New York, 1954, *Symbols and Society*, Harper and Brothers, New York, 1955; Anthony Standen, *Science Is a Sacred Cow*, E. P. Dutton and Co., New York, 1950; S. I. Hayakawa, ed., *Language, Meaning and Maturity*, Harper and Brothers, New York, 1954; H. Hoijer, ed., *Language in Culture*, University of Chicago Press, 1954; E. A. Burtt, *The Metaphysical Foundations of Modern Science*, Doubleday and Co., Garden City, N.Y., 1955; Howard Becker, *Through Values to Social Interpretation*, Duke University Press, Durham, N.C., 1950; Boris B. Bogoslovsky, *The Technique of Controversy*, Harcourt, Brace and Co., New York, 1928, especially chaps. 4–9; Kenneth Burke, *Attitudes Toward History*, 2 vols., The New Republic, New York, 1937, especially vol. 2, pp. 52–256.

**Reprinted from *Men Who Manage*, pp. 194–217, by permission of the author and publisher. (Copyright 1959 by John Wiley and Sons, Inc.)**

*embezzlement*, and *peculation*, which often require special libraries to define. To spare the living[3] and some of the recent dead, and to ignore differences in time and place, we can point to Cellini—and remember Pope Paul III's judgment of him that "men like Benvenuto, unique in their profession, are not bound by the laws"—Aretino, Casanova, and even Voltaire. These men were all scoundrels of a kind who, nevertheless, were esteemed for their commendable contributions to society.

Always there are genuine transitional nuances, with debatable margins, between covert internal theft and tacit inducement or reward. Immemorially the esteemed personality who also performs unique services can move closer to "theft" than others without censure.

## Managerial motivation

To talk of rewarding is to talk of motivation, and students declare, and show by their disagreement, that little is known of managerial motivation.[4] Distinguished executives and specialized students admit that the whole subject of reward is so dynamic that attempts either rigidly to define motivation,[5] or specifically to reward managers[6] are both likely to go amiss.

Our data have shown that what is a reward for one man is not for another[7] . . ; that the rank a manager craves at one time, he rejects at another . . . ; that the same inducements cannot be given to all on a given level because of differences in ability and demand for reward . . . ; uses of the office of assistant-to, etc.;[8] that the organization's contact with the community may demand greater reward for some managers than for others; that "power struggles" are forbidden but do occur and must be disguised;[9] and that more than financial reward is necessary.[10] We know that some managers are more venturesome and more inclined to "play the game" than others are.[11] This may mean unexpected errors, losses, and gains for the organization. In any case such managers must have greater resources and rewards than rigid planning will allow.[12] We saw . . . that Milo managers were concerned to maintain social as well as productive mechanisms, and that, in addition to the use of materials and services for this purpose, they juggled accounts to (*a*) allow full and part-time employment of the friends and relatives of plant and community associates, to (*b*) justify plush offices stemming from their rivalries, and to (*c*) keep a margin, or kind of "slush fund," in the naval sense, for emergencies—social and mechanical.

Although these practices may vary among cultures and inside a given culture,[13] and with the size, age and financial state of a firm,[14] as well as by

3. See Edwin H. Sutherland, *White Collar Crime*, The Dryden Press, New York, 1949; *The Autobiography of Lincoln Steffens*, Harcourt, Brace and Co., New York, 1931; John T. Flynn, *Graft in Business*, The Vanguard Press, New York, 1931, pp. 103–6.

4. Summer Slichter, "Report on Current Research: Economics," *Saturday Review*, 36: 24, April 4, 1953; Arthur H. Cole, "An Approach to the Study of Entrepreneurship," *Journal of Economic History* 6, Supplement 1–15 (1946); Robert A. Gordon, *Business Leadership in the Large Organization*, Brookings Institution, Washington, D.C., 1945; Clare E. Griffin, *Enterprise in a Free Society*, R. D. Irwin, Chicago, 1949, chap. 5; John K. Galbraith, *American Capitalism*, Houghton Mifflin, Boston, 1952; Albert Lauterbach, *Man, Motives and Money*, Cornell University Press, Ithaca, New York, 1954; George Katona, *Psychological Analysis of Economic Behavior*, McGraw-Hill Book Co., New York, 1951; *Business Week*, "A Tempo Shapes a Type," April 25, 1953, pp. 56, 58, 60; C. C. Abbott, J. D. Forbes, L. A. Thompson, *The Executive Function and Its Compensation*, Graduate School of Business Administration, The University of Virginia, Charlottesville, 1957.

5. C. I. Barnard, *Functions of the Executive*, Harvard University Press, Cambridge, 1938, pp. 138–60.

6. P. F. Drucker, *The Practice of Management*, Harper and Brothers, New York, 1954, p. 152; Abbott, Forbes, and Thompson, *op. cit.*, pp. 46–55.

7. See also Morris S. Viteles, *Motivation and Morale in Industry*, Norton, New York, 1953; Kornhauser, in Kornhauser, Dubin, and Ross, *op. cit.*, pp. 59–85; W. F. Whyte *et al.*, *Money and Motivation*, Harper and Brothers, New York, 1955.

8. Also see C. I. Barnard, "Functions and Pathology of Status Systems in Formal Organizations" in W. F. Whyte, ed., *Industry and Society*, McGraw-Hill Book Co., New York, 1946, pp. 207–43.

9. The various struggles of Milo and Fruhling with their Offices. Also see Galbraith, *American Capitalism*, Houghton Mifflin, Boston, 1952, p. 28.

10. Barnard, *op. cit.*, pp. 139–60.

11. Griffin, *op. cit.*, chap. 5; Gordon, *op. cit.*, pp. 305–12. Geiger's "free-wheeling" bent is suggested by his remark that "The engineers aren't practical. They want everything to be exact. They can't see that in operation you've got to lie and steal and cheat a little." See also W. H. Knowles, *Personnel Management: A Human Relations Approach*, American Book Co., New York, 1955, p. 130; Robert B. Fetter and Donald C. Johnson, *Compensation and Incentives for Industrial Executives*, Indiana University, Bloomington, 1952, p. 57.

12. Abbott, Forbes, and Thompson, *op. cit.*, p. 41.

13. Lauterbach, *op. cit.*, chap. 1.

14. Katona, *op. cit.*, chap. 9.

industry,[15] they nevertheless occur widely and point to further problems for the manager who deals with other firms or other plants of his own corporation; we have but to recall Geiger's problems from having his unit compared with that of the Colloid plant.

As a result of these gaps between the inherent limitations of formal reward and the obscure complex of activities that must be rewarded, an organization's services and materials, designed for its official functioning, are repeatedly drawn on to fill the breach. Used injudiciously, this may lead to plunder.

## Theft: Real and questionable

Before we present cases, let us admit the probably universal existence of internal theft, individual and organized, that is more damaging than helpful to the firm and that would strain the term to be called reward for specific contributions. Various informants report almost incredible cases of empire-building with minimum functions or contributions for many members; of favors and perquisites granted to some for no obvious important service in return; organized pilfering rights—including regular paid frolics for some of the company's members as "representatives" or "spokesmen" at some "event"; and the purely personal use of plant resources under the guise of "community relations," and sometimes not honored with a pretext. This is reported as common in some of the large firms doing contracted work for various governmental bodies where . . . the pressure for economy is less.

There is, of course, widespread individual theft in which tools, clerical supplies, home fixtures, etc., are taken for personal use without the knowledge of superiors or concern for one's group or the organization, and which could not be justified in case of detection. Similar internal theft by subgroups and cliques, with lifting-license tied so closely to rank that stealing beyond one's station is punished by death, can occur even in sacred organizations.[16] Civic bodies of antiquity were similarly tapped by members.[17]

Theft may also be enforced in the group and occur systematically over a long period. For example, in a small cabinet factory in the Mobile Acres region, the employees of one department, on piece-rate pay, regularly turned in more pieces than they actually completed, and coerced newcomers to do the same to protect old hands.

Between theft and informal reward is the gray-green practice of expense-accounting, which is also related to rank. "Theft" is softened to "abuse of privilege," but the feeling of some companies is clear in their demands for explanations. Others, however, including those sensitive to the tax factor, see large accounts as "part of the man's compensation," or as necessary to "attract and hold top men," or as a practice comparable to the "employee medical program."[18]

One organization reflects this attitude in its contract with a well-known top executive. After defining his duties and authority, the company says that:

> During the continuance of the employment of [the executive] hereunder he shall be paid a weekly salary of Twenty-five Hundred ($2500) Dollars, and in addition a weekly general expense allowance of Five Hundred ($500) Dollars which shall not include travelling expenses or other items generally related thereto, which shall also be paid by the Company. There shall be no abatement or diminution of the compensation or expense allowance of [the executive] during such time, if any, as he may fail to perform the services required to be performed by him hereunder solely because of illness or physical incapacity even though such illness or incapacity may prevent the performance by him of any duties whatsoever for a period up to six consecutive months. . . . [If the executive shall be required to change headquarters around the Company operating areas he shall receive] such suitable office accommodations and such clerical and other assistance as shall, from time to time, be reasonably required by him, and of such type, character and extent as shall be consistent with the position of Chief Executive Officer of the Company. . . . [He] shall receive fair and reasonable vacations with pay, commensurate with the position and duties undertaken by him hereunder.[19]

15. *Business Week*, April 25, 1953, pp. 56, 58, 60.

16. Will Durant, *The Renaissance*, Simon and Schuster, New York, 1953, p. 401.

17. Article "Aqueducts," *Encyclopaedia Britannica*, vol. 2, 14th edition, 1932, p. 161.

18. *Newsweek*, "Those Big-Figure Expense Accounts," vol. 41, No. 20, pp. 87, 90–92, May 20, 1957; Seymour Mintz, "Executive Expense Accounts and Fringe Benefits: A Problem in Management, Morality and Revenue," *Journal of Taxation*, 1: 2–9, June, 1954; Abbott, Forbes, and Thompson, *op. cit.*, p. 41.

19. See various responses (public documents) to form 10-K of the Securities and Exchange Commission, Washington, D.C., for the Fiscal Year ended August 21, 1956.

Coercion in expense-accounting can function as in the cabinet factory cited above. An informant from an optical company reports that lower-ranking, and obviously less imaginative, employees who rarely used expense accounts were not permitted by higher-ranking members to list their costs exactly. Rather they were forced to inflate the report, sometimes very much, so as not to "show-up the fat accounts" of the habitual users. Internal coercion to protect one's own masquerade might at times be justified, but apparently was not in this case.

Though parallel cases only at times, featherbedding by labor, and the various professional and managerial practices embracing pay-backs, split-fees and rebates,[20] also lie in this twilight area.

## Unofficial incentives

In crossing the middle ground between understood theft of materials and their controlled use as inducements and rewards, one must always fight the sheep-or-goat concept of truth. Responsible persons who succeed in this apparently broaden the system of rewards and are able to stimulate those not lured by standard appeals, or who also require other[21] incentives for greater effort.

### INDIVIDUAL

Because of the tacit stress on flexibility and supplementation of the more common inducements, unofficial reward is naturally directed more toward specific contributions and situations than toward rank as such. But obviously if such reward is not confidential, or if it is known and not justified in the minds of others, it is likely to follow formal rank and become systematic theft of the kind we noted above.

Although informal reward ideally is given for effort and contribution beyond what is expected of a specific rank, it is also granted for many other purposes, often unexpected and formally taboo yet important for maintaining the organization and winning its ends. For example, it may be given (1) in lieu of a promotion or salary increase that could not be effected; (2) as a bonus for doing necessary but unpleasant or low-prestige things; (3) as an opiate to forget defeats in policy battles or status tiffs; (4) as a price for conciliating an irate colleague or making, in effect, a treaty with another department; (5) as a perquisite to key persons in clerical or staff groups to prevent slowdowns, and to bolster alertness against errors during critical periods; (6) as a frank supplement to a low but maximum salary; (7) for understandng and aid in the operation, and the defense, of the unofficial incentive system; (8) for great personal sacrifices. There are, of course, more subtle supports which may not be articulated but are intuitively recognized and rewarded where possible. These include: ability to maintain morale in the group or department; skill in picking and holding good subordinates; habitual tacit understanding of what superiors and colleagues expect but would not in some cases want to phrase, even unofficially; and expertness in saving the face of superiors and maintaining the dignity of the organization under adverse conditions. This last may be aptness in masking and supporting the fictions essential for regulation of error, and in perpetuating symbols considered necessary by the dominant group.[22]

These performances are not exhaustive and may overlap in the same person. There is no fixed tie either, of course, between services rendered and the kind of material reward or privilege granted. Though we are confining our discussion to positive rewards, there are also negative ones, such as exemptions from rules binding on others, which . . . was but one in the first-line foreman's repertory of inducements for production workers.

Though his general contributions were great, the Milo foreman, Kustis . . . illustrates the privileges given for personal sacrifice. Kustis dropped his Catholicism, from choice but with suffering, to become a Mason and thus demonstrate his fealty and fitness. . . . But with the knowledge of his superiors, he built a machine shop in his home, largely from Milo materials. He equipped his drill press, shaper, and lathe with cutters and drills from Milo. He supplemented these with bench equipment, such

20. Fred H. Colvin, *The Industrial Triangle*, Columbia Graphs, Columbia, Connecticut, 1955, pp. 95–96; Benjamin Aaron, "Governmental Restraints on Featherbedding," *Stanford Law Review*, 5: 680–721, 1953.

21. See the theory of Abbott, Forbes, and Thompson, *op. cit.*, pp. 34–38.

22. See Havelock Ellis, *The Dance of Life*, The Modern Library, New York, 1923, pp. 89–98, and Robert Dubin, *Human Relations in Administration*, Prentice-Hall, New York, 1951, pp. 336–45.

as taps, reamers, dies, bolts and screws. Finally, piece by piece and day by day he removed a retired grinder from his shop. Normally such tools were sent to another department or unit of the corporation.

Ted Berger, officially foreman of Milo's carpenter shop, was *sub rosa* a custodian and defender of the supplementary reward system. Loyal beyond question, he was allowed great freedom from formal duties and expected, at least through the level of department heads, to function as a clearing-house for the system. His own reward was both social and material, but his handling of the system unintentionally produced a social glue that bound together people from various levels and departments. Not required to operate machines, Berger spent a minimum of six hours daily making such things as baby beds, storm windows, garage windows, doll buggies, rocking horses, tables, meat boards, and rolling pins. These objects were custom built for various managers. European-born,[23] Berger was a craftsman and eager to display his skills. However, his American-born associates with their folklore of "one good turn deserves another," often gave him a "fee" for his work. Since everyone knew his thirst, these gifts[24] were usually wines, ranging from home-made "Dago Red" to choice imported varieties. But he also accepted dressed fowl, preferably duck and turkey. In some cases he made nothing, but used his influence to aid with a problem. In other cases he found a place in his department for the summer employment of someone's son, and again usually he received some unspoken favor. The transfer effect of these exchanges needs no elaboration.

Jim Speier, one of Peters' (formal chart) foremen, gave Peters great support in the latter's conflicts with Taylor. An understanding foreman and bulwark of the unofficial directorate, he made great use of both the structural and carpenter shops with Blanke's approval. He had a wood and steel archway for his rose garden prefabricated in the plant, and removed it piecemeal. Incentive-appliers estimated that exclusive of materials[25] the time spent on this object would have made its cost at least $400, in terms of the hourly charging rate. Also in Berger's shop, Speier had fourteen storm windows made, and a set of wooden lawn sprinklers cut in the form of dancing girls and brightly painted. For use on his farm, Speier had a stainless steel churn made that cost over a hundred and fifty dollars by the charging rate. In the same shop Speier had several cold-pack lifting pans made, also of stainless steel. According to self-styled experts on such matters, the design and workmanship of these pans was superior to anything obtainable on the market. Incentive-appliers declared that the welding, brazing, grinding, and polishing costs made the pans "worth their weight in gold."

Pete Merza, a general foreman in Springer's division, was given enough freedom in the use of building materials that his reward was seen by some —ignorant of his unofficial contributions—as approaching theft. Like Kustis, he had withdrawn from the Church to become a Mason, but this was more a gesture than a personal sacrifice for him. An inimitably warm and helpful person acceptable to all factions, he was really rewarded as Milo's peacemaker in the clashes between Operation and Maintenance. Informants stated that he "carried out several hundred dollars worth" of bricks and cement and used Milo bricklayers on company time to build much, or most, of his house.

In another Milo case, reorganization dropped two general foremen to the first-line level. At that time, salary decreases followed automatically. Since the two men did not wish to continue at Milo as first-line foremen, they were put in charge of warehouses as positions there opened. They understood that

23. In a study of production workers on piece rate in a plant of Mobile Acres, I earlier indicated some of the differences in feeling for craftsmanship between European-apprenticed and American-born workers. See "Worker Response and Social Background," *Journal of Political Economy*, 55: 323–32, August, 1947.

24. A colleague suggests that this "looks like bribery." It is hardly that. Rather these gifts were gestures of good will, and in some cases substitutes for favors due that could not be exchanged in the course of carrying out regular duties. One can argue that people were being persuaded to violate their official duties. With no more casuistry one can also argue that "bribes" of this kind contribute to the carrying out of official duties, and that, inside varying and debatable limits, they are a legitimate cost for the maintenance of solidarity. This is not to deny that bribery occurs in industry, as elsewhere (Flynn, *Graft in Business*, The Vanguard Press, New York, 1931, pp. 55–76), or that bestowal of gifts cannot be bribery. See "Should Companies Give?" *Newsweek*, December 24, 1956, pp. 59–60.

25. No estimate was made of the cost of materials, since many of these came from the scrap pile and would have been discarded anyway.

discreet use of nails, paint, brushes, plumbing and electric fixtures, safety shoes, etc., was acceptable as long as inventories balanced.

Unofficial rewards are of course given for uncovering *pure* theft and misuse of materials. But this calls for internal espionage, which is a harrowing and impossible role for some people. This informal role of theft intelligencer is essential in many organizations. House detectives, various guards, and company police are the conventional guardians in business and industry. But this official role advertises itself. Everyone knows who to watch, and many resent the implications of being watched. Those who play the formal role of guard and investigator are not only likely to be compromised in various ways (see below), but they cannot function at the expected level of efficiency. For as they begin to accomplish official purposes they become the focus of informal attack and are made aware that they can be put in a bad light. . . . The theft intelligencer compensates for this defect. Simultaneously filling a formal role,[26] he must be one who has the tact and address to conceal his role of developing intimacies to discover misuse of materials.

At Milo, such investigations were usually carried on by selected persons in both staff and line. However as rule-makers and refiners who had to justify their existence, staff groups were especially eager to avoid blots on their professional escutcheons. Meeting this inherent perspective of the staff role limited the means of unofficially rewarding staff people. Materials and services would usually be inconsistent as a reward. Hence the staff agent who successfully carried out "intelligence" assignments was usually given his next promotion six months early, which admirably fitted *his* needs, and job logic.

Some inducements were both rewards and rights, but for different people. For example, what was at first a reward to some younger officer grew with his rank and seniority into a right which he in turn doled out judiciously as a reward to demanding subordinates.[27] Services and materials from the company garage, and long distance telephone calls were among the items spread along this axis of reward-rights. Line officers in good standing above the level of general foreman, and certain anointed staff figures including Rees at Milo and Reynolds at Attica, frequently, if not regularly, filled their gas tanks from company stock and received car servicing including washing and waxing. Rank was exercised, with the understanding for all that interference with garage personnel and use of materials culminating in defective operation or tie-up of company trucks and tractors, or accidents of any kind attributable to such interference, would threaten or even cut off reward-rights. As the balance of rewards and rights became too heavy with rights, inevitable crackdowns cut the rights and led higher executives to call on skilled machinists from the shops, instead of garage personnel, to give tune-ups, minor repairs, etc. Machinists in a sense shared these rewards and rights by (*a*) escape from repetitive work; (*b*) association with superiors whom they never met socially and seldom officially; (*c*) the privilege of taking Lincolns and Cadillacs out of the plant for "trialspins" after tune-ups, and driving home "on company time" to take their wives shopping and "be seen." All time of machinists in such activity was of course charged to their regular jobs.

The axis of reward-right has another common phase: some executives ambiguously feel a "right" to use materials and services whether granted or not, and if questioned would defend their practice as a due reward. These are the managers who put in much overtime (emergencies, meetings, etc.) without extra compensation, and who resent the time-and-a-half overtime pay of hourly-paid workers, and who assist in compiling and circulating lists of these workers whose annual incomes exceed, say, six thousand dollars. Frequently these are also the officers who angrily agree that the organization owns them and in turn, quite within the range of normal madness, protest a counter ownership of its resources. These managers would say, sociologically, that unofficial demands call for unofficial rewards.

26. In diplomacy, the old role of papal *legatus a latere* was similar in the sense that a formal role, usually that of cardinal, embraced a confidential unofficial function.

27. Naturally, friendship was sometimes a consideration in meeting pressure from below. But where demands were made without significant contribution—and in the tone of "a right to share"—the "reward" given was sometimes a disguised penalty. At Attica one such aggressive person demanded a "share" of the house paint he knew others had received. He was given all the usual bulk-purchased and unmixed ingredients—except the drying fluid. Elated, he mixed and applied the paint. When it did not dry, the accumulations of dust and insects ruined his work. He became a laughing-stock without recourse.

Where people have been "oversold" by higher management's attempt to win their identification, they may of course expect greater reward than they receive and resort to supplementation.

Use of materials to supplement low salary is apparently rather common in some of the smaller firms that are less formalized and less able to pay incomes comparable to those of larger companies. In the Argo Transit Company, a firm of two hundred employees, several of the office force were variously rewarded to keep them from moving elsewhere. One individual who had reached the top pay bracket, was given an extra day off each week with pay. Another person, considered as an indispensable secretary, was each week given any halfday off she desired with pay. Since she sewed much for her family and was the only secretary in that office, she did most of her handwork there in connection with sewing. She also did all her letter writing on the job and used company materials and stamps. Use of stamps at Christmas time amounted to a bonus. As she was expected to conceal her unofficial pay and to guard the box from other employees, she evidently also received a certain psychic reward. As a practice this is of course not new. Saintly Charles Lamb, known to have hated his job at the East India Company, used his employer's time and materials and franked letters to his friends, whom he requested to write collect to him. This was probably understood and acceptable, and was not a positive reward as in the case above.

An X-ray technician—of unknown quality—in a general hospital reported that his salary was so low he was "expected to steal hams and canned food" from the hospital supplies to supplement it. Though not in the same hospital, this may be related to the Midwestern hospital thefts nationally reported in October, 1953. There many additional items were taken, but the thefts may have started as an internal reward system and then have grown to a pilfering right extending to outside persons. The typical internal use of materials is suggested by the defense of one of the hospital attendants who allegedly said she had "never seen a hospital where they didn't take things," and the hospital administrator's apparent knowledge of the thefts and reluctance to intervene.

Evidently leaks of information at the technician's hospital transformed the plan of salary supplementation into a problem of theft. For one person rewarded by the informal plan was also unofficially paid for his suggestion for keeping the system in bounds. Despite its obvious complications, his proposal that nurses leave the hospital by the rear exit was accepted. As they passed through this door their clothing and bundles were inspected. But professional indignation and the rights of rank ended the inspection when one nurse objected that she had worked there "twenty years only to be reduced to sharing the scrub woman's entrance!"

### UNOFFICIAL INCENTIVES FOR THE GROUP

Berger's remarks above indicated the private use of work groups by some Milo managers. As one of those referred to, Hardy's worth to the firm was unquestioned. Presumably Stevens knew of his more overt use of materials and services, which included the necessary labor and supplies for building a fireplace in his home under construction. Through Milo offices he also ordered a plate glass for his picture window and removed the glass from Milo on Sunday. He may have paid part of the cost of the glass since one reward-right in many firms is to allow elect members to buy through the company at wholesale prices, and less.

A recently retired Milo executive, who was a bird lover, had an eleven unit aviary built in Milo shops and installed on his large rear lawn. Each spring he sent carpenters from the plant—and continues to receive this service possibly as a phase of his pension—to remove, recondition, renovate, and re-install the bird houses. This person, who started the emphasis on Masonry as an unannounced requirement, frequently used the same carpenters for redecorating his home. Lack of comparable maintenance skills apparently checked this practice at Attica, but it occurred at Fruhling though documentary support is inadequate for that plant. As with the use of materials alone, this double employment of facilities and stores obviously may become abused "rights" that blur the line between theft and reward. However, managers in both firms raised defenses that fluctuated between double talk and sound argument. My bantering of intimates raised certain questions. For example, when unavoidable emergencies, errors in planning, and market changes made work shortages, was it better to let "idle" men be seen by those who were busy, to reduce the work force, or to take the idle men out of the plant to do something else, something that was usually a lark for them? Management argued that unrest is promoted by "task inequities," and that men with nothing to do are pleased with a break in the monotony. Inquiries to Beemer, Brady, Spencer, and various maintenance workers usually elicited strong approval of this last alternative. For example, it was pointed out that "you get to sit down for twenty to forty minutes both ways" in traveling to and from an executive's home. Beemer saw this as equivalent to "several coffee breaks." Furthermore, the executive's wife "always gives us a lot of good eats." The president of the Milo union local supported the practice and held that it prevented layoffs. Management said essentially the same thing in noting that training costs and turnover were reduced, and at the same time there was no surplus of employees, for many of those "used on odd jobs" had to put in overtime at other periods. As with the machinists called on to service executive cars, those employees sporadically retained for out-plant work with some executive, derived both imponderable and concrete satisfactions. However, some first-line foremen and some workers saw the practice as "dirty," "unfair," and "taking advantage of your authority." And some people will call the practice high-level rationalization or collusion, but . . . it is more likely to be expediency periodically reclothed with new protective fictions.

Theft overlaps with reward-right where lower groups, foremen or workers, draw on plant resources, and higher management knows but dares not interfere, as in the hospital scandal. A European informant tells me of maintenance workers in railroad shops who drive their cars into the plant, rather than park outside as in our cases, and repair each other's cars on company time with company supplies. The cars are few and old and serve as busses as well as private vehicles. The practice is known to all, but since there is no fixed lunch hour, workers give the pretext if questioned that they work on the cars only during their lunch periods. Sometimes five to eight workers will be around one car for two or three hours at a stretch. With a short labor supply, and the practice apparently universal, management may officially protest, but usually looks the other way for fear the workers will seek jobs elsewhere.

The force of materials and services as unofficial incentives—internally for the company and externally for its ties with the community—was clearly visible in the activities of Magnesia's Yacht Club. As we saw in the preceding chapter, at least one hundred and fourteen members of Milo, and an unknown number from Fruhling, were active participants in the Club, at an individual annual fee of $50. Building additions to the Club and maintenance of its plant, as well as of privately owned boats, drew on the stores and services of Milo and Fruhling. Repair work was charged to various orders, which . . . was done with some regular work. Propeller shafts, bushings, fin keels, counterweights, pistons, hand railings, and the like, were made and/or repaired for boat owners among the managers as well as their friends in the community.

All of this was tied in with the prevailing practice here, and throughout industry, of doing "government jobs." These include original, as well as repair, work of many kinds usually done by maintenance forces—with plant materials and equipment on job time—as a "favor" for employees at all levels. At Milo, workers were singled out to aid the Club by doing miscellaneous government jobs. This was a compliment to their skills and a gesture of acceptance by higherups that appealed to the impulse to serve others, however weak this urge is according to cynics, or overpowering according to some theorists. Praise and minor perquisites were accepted as abundant rewards. And for some, inside and across all job divisions, old rifts born in the heat of past emergencies were often healed by shared work on these unofficial assignments. The opportunities offered by such work for exchange of obligations, for establishing warm understandings, and for blurring differences in official reward, needs no comment. Bureaucratic rationality is progressively, if unwittingly, reduced through these invasions by community recreational life. It can be argued that government jobs aid the survival of Maintenance, which is normally at conflict with Operation in their official functions.

We need more study on the ramifications of government jobs[28] and unofficial services, apart from understood rewards.

28. At least one large company outside this study sees government jobs as a problem unless limited to certain employees and done by specific people during given hours.

### THE AUDITOR'S DILEMMA

Together, theft and socially consumed materials cut into a firm's substance sufficiently to alarm auditors and staffs, committed as they are to compiling the statistics for detection, analysis, and control of all departures from the ideal, and to warrant their own pay.[29]

Above Milo's divisional level, concern was always shown when inventories turned up losses. The usual reaction was to state that nonsupervisory employees were to blame, and to order plant police to be more vigilant in their inspection of lunch buckets, bags, and bulging coats of outgoing personnel at the four gates.

The volume of materials "lost" was not known exactly. But cost analysts totaled and classified all incoming materials, then removed from the compilations all items, about 85 per cent of the total, that "could not possibly" be taken from the plant by persons on foot without detection. According to one analyst:

> It's not right on the nose, but about $15,000 of every $100,000 worth of material that *could* be taken out disappear—and never can be accounted for. Books can be juggled on some things but not much on this. Besides it's too damn constant. There's no question that it's carried out. If it's not, where the hell does it go to?

Some of the Milo managers and police suspected each other of carrying out materials or of collusively working with others to that end. Voicing his suspicions, the police chief was notified that his distrust was unfounded and insulting. On its side, management pointed to "statistical evidence" of police laxity. In delivering materials and removing the product, outside truckers had somehow sandwiched in forty-seven of some six hundred motors stored in an empty bay before the theft was discovered by the police. Management suspected some of the guards of bribed collaboration. Hardy set up a plan for unsystematic rotation of police around the circuit of gates. He believed this would prevent collusion between them and outsiders. Rotations were made monthly, but instead of moving all the men from one gate to the next nearest gate, only one man moved at a time and not in any sequence of gates or period of the month. This theory was not based on what had happened, and it was faulty in assuming that the major "nonproductive" consumption of materials was pure theft and was confined to production workers. Both in underestimating the ingenuity of lower ranking employees and in not seeing the nature of human association, the scheme did not prevent production workers from carrying out materials.

First, the theft of motors was accomplished by collusion of a few laborers with the truckers, but was concealed to protect a night supervisor. The suspected laborers were officially laid off for other reasons. The police were not participants. Second, we have seen that the major unofficial consumption of materials was by management itself, and in many cases was not pure theft. Finally, the theory ignored both the backgrounds of the police and the significance of government jobs. The police were not overpaid, and as company watchdogs they were, of course, persons for production workers to stand in well with. But as ex-workers, in most cases, the police also knew plant life and had need of government jobs for which they, too, were prepared to exchange favors. For example, when one of the gate guards knew that a friend wished to carry something from the plant, he told the friend which gate he was tending. At the gate, with a guard on each side, the friend making his exit approached his confidant who simulated an inspection and sent him through with a clap on the back.

### IN DEPARTMENT STORES

The use of internal materials and services as spurs and requitals of course is not confined to factories. Department stores, with their range of commodities, are a rich field for research in the use of implicit rewards.[30] The Rambeau Mart, member of a state chain, was one of the most flourishing department

In this case, only salaried people may take such work to a shop set up for that purpose which operates between 6 P.M. and 10 P.M., Monday through Friday.

29. Probably all organizational groups demand the stimulus of extra reward whether it be more of what they are already receiving or a greater share of those things having prestige value. The perquisite of staffs is usually the less material one of late arrival, early departure, and more socializing on the job, though additionally they, too, may participate in small government jobs.

30. For an intensive study of twenty salesgirls in the setting of a large department store, see George F. F. Lombard, *Behavior in a Selling Group*, Harvard University, Graduate School of Business Administration, Boston, 1955.

stores in the Mobile Acres area, and probably owed much of its solidarity to its flexible unofficial incentives.

Rambeau had a total of three hundred and seventy employees including the clerical force and three levels of management: the store chief and his assistants, the division heads, and the department heads. The store had the usual official structure—an auditing department with appropriate specialists, a quadruplicate reporting system, explicit rules against personal use of materials and services, and a budget allowance of ten per cent to cover shoplifting. Two store detectives supplemented the controls. They were gatetenders of a kind in seeing that only employees entered the store before opening time, and in checking the parcels of outgoing employees, at quitting time only, to see that they bore sales slips and the signature of a department head. Yet the managers of Rambeau tacitly adapted its resources to individual orientations, and in a showdown clearly approved the practice.

The unofficial incentive system took various forms. When conditions allowed, and within limits, some department heads privately altered the price of merchandise to fit the local market and to satisfy their own needs. Also, department heads aided each other, but in all cases they worked inside the dual requirement of having to show a profit and to pass the scrutiny of an annual audit. The latitude that ingenuity could establish inside these limitations showed that a brand of individual enterprise still exists and is rewarded in organizations that, at least unofficially, accent individual as well as group effort.

A common practice by department heads was to take items they wanted that were "shopworn" or "damaged" and mark them down "reasonably" for their own purchase. Some female heads regularly, but discreetly, gave certain items a "damaged" appearance. Division chiefs unofficially knew of this, and set no limit to the markdown that could be made, other things equal. However, those department heads who shrank from the ambiguities of exercising their authority and asked a division manager the limit for a markdown were usually told "30 per cent."

Heads of the various men's departments usually clothed themselves from each other's stocks at little or no cost. This might be accomplished, for example, by selling a bargain stock of two thousand pairs of socks not at the agreed 59 cents per pair, but at 69 cents, which accumulated to a fund of $200 above profit requirements. A given head could draw from this to cover the suits, shoes, shirts, etc., essential for his proper grooming. The markup, like the kind and volume of stock, might vary.

Normally, merchandise control demanded that each item, even when the stock and price were uniform, have its individual stock number and price tag. But as in the case of the socks, some commodities might be thrown on a table, without their separate labels, under one posted price. This of course allowed inclusion of some lower-priced items of similar quality which, as with the socks, contributed to the private trading fund. Detailed records of what he removed for himself or others in the inter-departmental trading, and careful balancing of the dollar value of total merchandise withdrawn against the dollar value of unofficial markups enabled the department chief to meet the inventory. If emergencies prevented this, he reported his stock as larger than it was at the time of inventory; for instance, he might report thirty suits on hand, when he had only twenty-seven. Help from assistants in the inventory allowed this, but no help could postpone judgment day beyond the next inventory when this particular stock would be double-checked. To prevent abuse of this elastic incentive, there was always the threat that auditors from another unit would be present to assist at some inventory.

Department heads reciprocated in their mark-down of items sold to each other. When the transaction had to be written up, the heads sometimes used a fictitious name, or the names of their new employees as customers. This utilized the fact that the employees themselves were as yet still naive, and their names were still strange in the auditing and shipping departments. Obviously intended in part to forestall such practices, the quadruplicate form requiring a name and address meant little in these cases until the employee became widely known. Where the women in these interchanges usually got only clothing, the men fully utilized the system. For example, Joe, in plumbing, wanted furniture, so he talked with Bill, head of furniture, to see what Bill wanted in plumbing of about the same value that could be exchanged. The total of their trades and adjusted records, however, did not prevent them from showing a profit in the annual audit. Where such persons work together for years this becomes simple and so unofficially acceptable that it seems natural.[31] Like the skeletons in every family closet, these practices are not for public consumption but serve to unify the firm, as the skeletons do the family.

However, two department heads were dropped from this unit of Rambeau because of their use of company resources. Officially, one was released because of theft; the other, L. Nevers, because he wanted to transfer to another unit of the firm. The first head flagrantly took money from the tills of his salesmen, so that the following morning their cash and sales tallies did not match. This person was fired outright before he had taken a hundred dollars. But in Nevers' case light is thrown on what the internal use of materials and services meant in the context of incentives.

Nevers followed the procedures we have sketched and added his own refinements. In his accounting he was aided by one of his saleswomen whom he regularly befriended by ringing his sales on her cash drawer. However, her friendly relations with a saleswoman in another department led her to report Nevers' accounting methods and use of merchandise to the store manager and to name it as theft and malfeasance. Nevers' saleswoman, a "rate-buster," had worked with the other woman for years at Rambeau and elsewhere. Her friend's husband, shortly to return from the armed forces, had been head of a Rambeau department before being drafted. However there was uncertainty about his getting his old position back. So his wife, seeing the interpretation that could be made of Nevers' bookkeeping, and the consequences, hoped to have him fired and have her husband succeed him. She persuaded Nevers' saleswoman to report him in as bad a light as possible. The officially ignorant general manager knew roughly of Nevers' techniques and regarded him as "too good a man for the organization to lose." Forced to defend procedural dignity, he simulated a release but gave Nevers his choice of workplace among the statewide units, vigorously recommended him, and aided him in the successful transfer.

31. Favor-trading and adaptation of official procedures are likely to rise above any control. Even the outside organizations called in to assist in guaranteeing a certain conduct among given employees are similarly used by cliques to protect the group and to maintain the informal status of its individual members. For example, Rambeau subscribed to the service of "Willmark," an organization that checks on the selling behavior of clerks. This is done by confidentially sending representatives to make purchases from employees and then formally scoring and reporting each person's sales behavior to the store office. However, at Rambeau—and doubtless elsewhere—when the "shoppers" registered in the manager's office, an upper member of the grapevine heard of it and whispered the phrase "shoppers today" to an intimate on the selling floor who passed the word. But only insiders were alerted; they in effect commanded deference and aid from new and fringe members of the sales force by tacit threat of not notifying them.

Two common merchandising policies encourage the use of goods as a supplementary incentive. First, the department head, as in other organizations, is expected to interpret policy. Second, all items are age-coded and regarded as having an approximate life expectancy. Some items of women's clothing may be "old" in less than four months, whereas some merchandise in hardware has an indefinite life. The age-code, or purchase date of items, is recorded at inventory. If too old, this advertises both the department head's poor judgment in making the original purchase, and his failure to "move" the goods. Hence in part to escape discredit he marks down older items for disposal among employees. Of course, he simultaneously sets up counter claims. In the phraseology of Rambeau department heads these items were "odds and ends of merchandise lying around in the way that can't be sold anyhow." One of these heads declared that the "paper and handling costs" of storing or returning some items for disposal elsewhere exceeded the worth of the merchandise many times over and were, therefore, a drain on the firm.

The conditions attending demotion of a female department head support the existence of these policies. This person originally gained the post through her brother's office at state headquarters. She "worried the life out of" the division heads because only rarely could she "make decisions on her own." She, too, desired "shopworn" items, including jewelry with chipped stones, but she called on the merchandising chief for judgments on the markdown she should make and was repeatedly given the official "30 per cent." Knowing that others more than doubled this figure, she caused trouble by her gossip and insinuations. She was eventually demoted on the pretext that "store policy" demanded placement of a returning veteran—actually from another unit of Rambeau—and that hers was the logical post. Aware that the conditions of her original employment were contrary to Rambeau's merit system, she offered no resistance and was even "glad to get away from all that crazy paper work."

Thus inside the same unit, officially bureaucratic Rambeau could adjust its incentives to satisfy both its enterprising and its less ambitious managers. But in environments of this kind, the person who fits the ideal of believing that his pay matches or exceeds his worth to the firm becomes a potential isolate and requires special attention, though his contribution is valued and utilized. Higher managers naturally wish to reward this attitude, but since the employee may misinterpret any concrete informal reward as unacceptable "favoritism," the question is how? Rambeau had a female department head of this type. Of all the departments, her inventory came nearest to the expected dollar value. It would have been perfect except for the small surplus from single sales of three-for-a-price items. (The surplus also indicated departmental alertness against shoplifting.) Since she was a known devotee of bureaucratic procedure, her department in effect selected personnel like herself, and acquired a reputation for this. When new heads for the candy counter were required they were drawn from this woman's department because of the likelihood that they would not be "free-loaders," nor tolerant of such people among other employees. The only informal reward that Rambeau chiefs could give this person and her kind was deference, and praise before others.

Rambeau's rule-devotee had a counterpart in one unit of a drugstore chain near Mobile Acres. She managed the drugstore's soda fountain. A problem arose from her consistently having the highest percentage of profits among the chain's soda fountain managers. The matter was an issue among fountain heads in neighboring units of the chain, who were in personal rivalry with her. Her success was officially honored, for the situation was competitive and fountain supervisors received a percentage of profits above a given level. But a typical condition —which some students may mistakenly call "institutionalized theft"—existed among all the other units and worked to adversely interpret her achievement. Volume of business on the fountains was comparable in cities near the same size as was the seating capacity, facilities, and the margin of profits among all but the one fountain. The chief difference between practices in this fountain and the others—covertly charged by the woman and admitted by some of the store managers and pharmacists—was that the other fountain heads gave food and confections free to relatives and close friends, drinks to fountain employees, and variously bartered with nonfountain employees in much the manner of department heads at Rambeau. Unofficial reward, in the form of meals, to fountain employees was, of course, encouraged by the chain's wage rate which, while comparable to that of the local stores, was no higher than the minimum industrial rates. Most of the fountain heads covertly rewarded their "good workers" in this way to hold them.

The practices were engaged in up to the point of maintaining at least a narrow margin of profit for the store if not for the fountain heads. The latter were apparently guided more by concern to show a small profit for the fountain—which they did not share—than by a wish to achieve the higher departmental margin that would allow them a percentage of money profits from the fountain. Prices to the public, set by the chain's state-wide committee, were uniform throughout the system. Excepting the one, all fountain managers discreetly helped themselves to canned foods, dairy products, and meats from the departmental stock, with the knowledge of the store manager who received free meals, and coffee at any time. The one fountain chief allowed no gratis consumption to employees, friends, relatives, or herself. She kept the refrigerators locked and closely supervised the handling of stock. When emergencies prevented her from shopping for her family and she took a loaf of bread from the fountain stock, she deposited the price in the cash register. Married to a farmer-factory worker, she stressed loyalty to the store chief, customer service, and money profits for herself. Her superior could not condemn this, but he was disturbed by her boasting of her standing in the chain, and by the innuendoes from other store managers about her "pencil work." To minimize the woman's behavior, he backed his half-hearted praise of her with the logic that fountains are only a supplement to drug and cosmetic services, and that in total store profits his unit was sometimes second or lower in state rankings. But the resentment of other fountain managers—and of his own nonfountain employees against the woman's opposition to the perquisites usually allowed such personnel—forced him openly to check her records, to imply that she was making errors, and to withhold the praise she obviously craved. Higher chain officials also asked her to explain her unique performance and hinted that she could not be that much superior to other fountain managers. After two years of mounting resentments, she quit the firm. The store manager regarded her as a failure because she did not understand what he could not tell her—that her margin of profits was too high and that some social use of materials, not theft, was expected. In his mind, she was too little concerned with the system's internal harmony, and too devoted to formalities.

These practices at Rambeau and in the drugstore chain are doubtless common in many stores, but they are not made obvious to the students responsible for theory about organizational roles, job structure, resources, and pay. And they mean different things to the people involved.

## Summary and comment

The diversity and range of contributions required of an administrative or functional group cannot be exactly reflected in the official system of rewards. This is an inherent, not a diabolical, shortcoming. It springs largely from (1) the assumption that the total duties and essential skills for a given job are boxed in and paid for, and from (2) the impossibility of officially recognizing some of the extraordinary contributions made by various members—often out of role—during crises.

On the first point, not only must compensation be planned to maintain minimum harmony among personnel, but the limited resources of every firm require it. On the second point, open recognition of some essential contributions would advertise conditions that should not exist, promote rivalries,[32] hurt official dignity, and encourage disrespect for regulations. Hence recourse is had to semi-confidential use of materials and services as a supplement. This can be both inducement and requital to those who must receive great recognition to do their best, and to those who would move elsewhere without the increment.

Supplementation may be accompanied by abuse to the extent (1) that the reward becomes habitual and is unrelated to contribution; (2) that it is shared by those who make no unusual contribution; or (3) that it expands and becomes coerced theft. The changing line between reward and abuse may be difficult to find and hold, but nothing can be done until the problem is faced. Evading it disposes nonparticipating personnel and the public to label all use of materials and services in this sense as theft. This cynicism cannot be eliminated by allocating 10 to 15 per cent of the budget to cover "shoplifting" by nonsupervisory employees and the public. Such allocation may of course enable some managers and subordinates to hide their own theft up to this limit. But it fails to distinguish theft from essential maintenance of the social mechanism. The problem is pervaded by our tradition of political spoils,[33] and our logic that service to the organization must have a one-to-one relation to rank and explicit compensation. We must note that absence of this neat balance induces supplementation, and inflicts moral suffering among members inversely to their capacity for automatic hypocrisy.

It is unlikely that a universally applicable system of informal rewards can be set up, but it is certain that where abuse of the practice develops it will not be eliminated by moral exhortations, elaborate paper forms, or rigid policing. These restraints all help, but as we all know, those who make and apply controls may be like Cellini. If so, their close

32. We earlier noted Barnard's analysis of democratic rivalries, and the need in decision making to anticipate and avoid their consequences. In the 1830's an acute French visitor commented on the always smoldering envy among Americans. Here officially to study our prison system, he remarked that "the hatred which men bear to privileges increases in proportion as privileges become more scarce . . . so that democratic passions . . . seem to burn most fiercely . . . when they have least fuel." Americans, then as now, "dread all violent disturbance . . . and love public tranquillity." But in their mania for equality they attribute the success of an *equal* "mainly to some one of his defects" rather than "to his talents or virtues." For to do otherwise "is tacitly to acknowledge that they are themselves less virtuous and talented." See Alexis de Tocqueville, *Democracy in America* (trans. by Henry Reeve), 2 vols., The Cooperative Publication Society (The Colonial Press), New York, 1900, vol. 1, p. 229; vol. 2, pp. 307–8.

33. Walter Lippmann, *A Preface to Politics*, The Macmillan Company, New York, 1913, chap. 1; Charles A. and Mary Beard, *The Rise of American Civilization*, 2 vols. in one, The Macmillan Co., New York, 1937, vol. 1, pp. 547–57; V. O. Key, Jr., *Politics, Parties, and Pressure Groups*, 2nd edition, Thomas Y. Crowell Co., New York, 1947, pp. 316–39.

associates are likely to share their privileges[34] and echo the general lament of abuse by "others."

Admitting the potential disruptiveness of implicit rewards, can we assure the full commitment of all abler members without them? And since we dare not preach what we practice, how do we know that we would have less disturbance and as much or more contribution without supplementation and some abuse? Can we show that the cost of, say 15 per cent, to cover theft and unofficial reward is excessive in lieu of other inducements which also cost? This is not to say that what exists is good, but to say that we do not know how bad it is until we can see it more closely.

Abuse is indefensible, but for the sake of a sharper focus on the issue let us say that as varieties of supplementation and limited abuse sap one brand of company resources, they protect other assets. For example, do they not in many cases also reduce disruptive conflict, break the monotony of routine, allow more personal expression, ease the craving for spontaneity, and to some extent catch up all levels of personnel in a system of mutual claims so that aid can be requested and hardly denied?

However, even with revision of the sheep-or-goat outlook, the problem must mark time until serious students are able in many contexts to at least look at (1) the elusive nature of organization that requires unofficial performances; (2) the relation of reward to informal services given; and (3) the relation of all reward to organizational resources, material and social.

Those who regard this chapter as merely a series of episodes on theft have missed the point. Our study of unofficial rewards is not an attempt to justify internal plunder or to say that theft by membership is inevitable. Both "theft" and "reward" derive their meaning from the social context. To insist that this context is constant—so that we can preserve the admitted convenience of fixed definitions—is to pervert meaning, block the issue, and deny that there are ethics in reward.

To repeat, the aim has been to show that however well defined official tasks may be, and however neatly we think we have fitted our personnel to these roles, the inescapably fluid daily situation distorts expected working conditions. Circumstances require various out-of-role and unplanned actions. Regardless of formal rankings, which are often only nominally based on potential for such action, some personnel more aptly do what is essential than do others. Tacitly or not, both they and their rewarders are aware of who solves problems and sustains the organization. Through time they are compensated as resources and situations allow. The process may seem to overlap with theft, or it may escape control and become theft, but able executives both utilize and contain unofficial rewards.

34. Again speaking timelessly, but referring to earlier Americans, de Tocqueville declared that, "Whatever may be the general endeavor of a community to render its members equal and alike, the personal pride of individuals will always seek to rise above the line, and to form somewhere an inequality to their own advantage." *Op. cit.*, vol. 2, p. 226.

# Organizational Control

Organization implies coordination over specialized activities that require some mode of control. When persons become organizational members, they recognize and accept that some limits and controls upon their behavior will be exercised by the organization. Of course, organizations differ in the types and degrees of organizational control they manifest.

In the first selection, Peabody reviews previous discussions of authority in terms of four distinct types of authority. He then examines empirically the perceptions of authority relations in three public service agencies—a welfare department, a police department, and an elementary school. The question of interest in this research is whether the analytical distinctions concerning types of authority are also perceived by the members in these organizations as bases of authority. Peabody finds that the analytical distinctions do in fact differentiate among the three types of organizations studied, suggesting the importance of comparative research and refinements in theory for understanding problems involving authority relations in organizations.

In the second selection, Scheff shows how subordinates in a mental hospital exert control over organizational policy concerning treatment goals. He finds that the staff members had many means of control available to them, including the withholding of information, the manipulation of patients, disobedience, and the withholding of cooperation. Scheff's research demonstrates that these subordinates formed a stable and highly organized group who were able to extend their control over organizational policy to the extent that a new program of social reform was successfully stifled.

The next two selections deal with the important relationship between the supervisor and his subordinates. Brewer is interested in accounting for the diversity of various styles of supervision commonly reported in the literature. He argues that the particular style of supervision adopted by the supervisor is determined by the type of compliance he must obtain from his subordinates in order to perform his own role effectively. Brewer is able to show that both complex organizational tasks and dangerous and isolated work tasks force the supervisor to go beyond the formal requirements of his role if he is to achieve initiative and compliance from his subordinates. Thus, Brewer suggests that special aspects of the work situation may lead to the debureaucratization of authority relations.

In the final selection, Day and Hamblin present experimental evidence describing the effects of two contrasting styles of supervision upon subordinate behavior and attitudes. The authors experimentally created two levels of "closeness" of supervision and two levels of "punitive" supervision among twenty groups of workers. Their findings show that workers expressed aggression towards one another and little or no aggression toward the supervisor under the condition of close supervision. The opposite pattern was observed under the condition of punitive supervision. Here the workers expressed aggression toward the supervisor and little aggression toward one another. Day and Hamblin are also able to show that the relationship between style of supervision and aggression among subordinates is further conditioned by the level of self-esteem manifested by the workers.

This section, then, illustrates both the complexity and the importance of organizational control. Not only are there differing bases of authority in different types of organizations, but control over major organizational goals may come from subordinates. Moreover, the specific nature of the work situation effects the particular style of supervision adopted, and different styles of supervision have contrasting effects upon subordinates.

ROBERT L. PEABODY

# Perceptions of Organizational Authority: A Comparative Analysis

Authority relations are an integral component of organizational behavior. Clarification of the concept of authority would seem to be essential to the development of systematic organization theory.[1] Despite numerous attempts at conceptual clarification and a growing body of empirical inquiries focusing on organization behavior, Herbert A. Simon could conclude in 1957 that "there is no consensus today in the management literature as to how the term 'authority' should be used."[2] For Simon, the source of the difficulty lay in the failure of many writers to distinguish between "(1) a specification of the set of behaviors to which they wish to apply the term 'authority'; and (2) a specification of the circumstances under which such behaviors will be exhibited."[3] The first problem, one of definition, or the way in which the term "authority" will be used, continues to plague students of administration.[4] There seems to be considerable agreement, however, on an important facet of the second problem, namely, identification of the bases of authority that facilitate its acceptance. This paper briefly summarizes this apparent consensus in the literature and reports some tentative findings developed from an exploratory study of authority relations in three public service agencies: a branch office of a county welfare department, a municipal police department, and a suburban elementary school.

1. This article is based on the author's doctoral dissertation at Stanford University entitled "Authority in Organizations: A Comparative Study" (1960). The research was financed in part by a grant from the Stanford University Committee on Research in Public Affairs. Further revision was made possible by a Brookings Institution Research Fellowship for 1960–1961. For helpful comments on earlier versions of this paper I am indebted to Heinz Eulau and Robert A. Walker of Stanford University, James D. Thompson of the University of Pittsburgh, and F. P. Kilpatrick, Milton Cummings, and M. Kent Jennings of the Brookings Institution.

2. *Administrative Behavior* (2d ed.; New York, 1957), pp. xxxiv–xxxv. For criticism of Simon's "operational definition" of authority and Simon's rejoinder see Edward C. Banfield, "The Decision-making Schema," *Public Administration Review*, 17 (1957), 278–85, and Simon "'The Decision-making Schema': A Reply," *ibid.*, 18 (1958), 60–63.

Reprinted from the *Administrative Science Quarterly*, March, 1962, pp. 463–82, by permission of the author and publisher. 

3. *Administrative Behavior*, p. xxxv.

4. For a more recent unsuccessful attempt at an operational definition, see Daniel J. Duffy, "Authority Considered from an Operational Point of View," *Journal of the Academy of Management*, 2 (Dec. 1959), 167–75. For a more traditional viewpoint of authority see Merten J. Mandeville, "The Nature of Authority," *Journal of the Academy of Management*, 3 (Aug. 1960), 107–18. While numerous definitions of authority occur in the literature of administration and organization theory, a review of these writings reveals considerable variation, vagueness, and ambiguity. For extended comment, see the author's review of the literature of organizational authority (cited in note 1) and a closely parallel review of leadership theories by Warren G. Bennis, "Leadership Theory and Administrative Behavior: The Problem of Authority," *Administrative Science Quarterly*, 4 (1959), 259–301.

## The bases of authority

This study is focused upon organizational authority in its several forms. Although authority is initially based on formal position, legitimacy, and the sanctions inherent in office, its acceptance is conditioned by several additional factors. In analyzing such related phenomena as professional competence, experience, and leadership, which modify and condition the exercise of formal authority, several different approaches could be taken. Some sociologists, for example Robert K. Bierstedt, would clearly distinguish between authority, competence, and leadership, reserving the label "authority" for hierarchical status relationships between incumbents of formal positions in organizations.[5] Other students of administration, notably Herbert A. Simon and Robert V. Presthus, would broaden the meaning of authority to include additional bases beyond formal position and the sanctions inherent in office.[6] Everyday usage of the word and much of the interview data of this inquiry seem to support the more inclusive interpretations of Simon and Presthus. However, the development of a science of administration may necessitate either a restriction of the term "authority" to a more precise technical meaning or an abandonment of the term for purposes of rigorous theory building.[7] Which of these two usages of the term is finally adopted is not as important as making clear the implications of each. The bases of *formal* authority—legitimacy, position, and the sanctions inherent in office—need to be distinguished from the sources of *functional* authority, most notably, professional competence, experience, and human relations skills, which support or compete with formal authority.[8]

Rather than attempt an exhaustive review of the literature, five contributors to the study of authority relations in organizations—Max Weber, Lyndall F. Urwick, Herbert A. Simon, Warren G. Bennis, and Robert V. Presthus—will be singled out as illustrative of a growing consensus as to the importance of several bases of authority which condition its acceptance. While not all these social scientists have placed emphasis on the same sources of authority and while they have frequently used different words to convey similar meanings, the essential points of agreement can be classified under four broad categories: (1) authority of legitimacy; (2) authority of position, including the sanctions inherent in position; (3) authority of competence, including both technical skills and experience, and (4) authority of person, including leadership and human relations skill (see Table 1).

### AUTHORITY OF LEGITIMACY

Unlike the related concepts of power and influence, the concept of authority has implicit in it the notion of legitimacy or ethical sanctification. Philosophers have long struggled with the complex and continuing problems of political authority, couched in the language of social contract theories and doctrines of

5. "The Problem of Authority," Morroe Berger, Theodore Abel, and C. H. Page eds., *Freedom and Control in Modern Society* (New York, 1954), pp. 67–81. In an earlier paper, Bierstedt defined authority as "institutional power," which appears to be a concept of authority somewhat broader than formal status relationships ("An Analysis of Social Power," *American Sociological Review*, 15 [1950], 736).

6. Simon, "Authority," in C. M. Arensberg *et al.*, *Research in Industrial Human Relations* (New York, 1957), pp. 104–6; Herbert A. Simon, D. W. Smithburg, and V. A. Thompson, *Public Administration* (New York, 1950), pp. 189–201; Presthus, "Authority in Organizations," *Public Administration Review*, 20 (1960), 86–91.

7. "In the initial stages of scientific inquiry, descriptions as well as generalizations are stated in the vocabulary of everyday language. The growth of a scientific discipline, however, always brings with it the development of a system of specialized, more or less abstract, concepts and of a corresponding technical terminology." See Carl G. Hempel, "Fundamentals of Concept Formation in Empirical Science," *International Encyclopedia of Unified Science* (Chicago, 1952), II, No. 7, p. 1.

8. In general, functional authority supports formal authority. In a given superior-subordinate relationship, it is the superior's lack of functional authority or the subordinate's possession of greater competence, experience, or personal skills which tends to undermine formal authority. Competition may also occur between incumbents of equal formal rank, but different task or specialist orientations, as for example between the controller and the merchandise manager of a department store. Finally, competition between functional and formal authority may occur where hierarchical channels are ambiguous, a condition frequently characteristic of staff-line relationships. Cf. Victor A. Thompson's distinction between hierarchical and nonhierarchical authority, "Hierarchy, Specialization, and Organizational Conflict," *Administrative Science Quarterly*, 5 (1961), 499. See also, Melville Dalton, "Conflicts between Staff and Line Managerial Officers," *American Sociological Review*, 15 (1950), 342–51; O. Glenn Stahl, "The Network of Authority," *Public Administration Review*, 18 (1958), ii–iv; O. Glenn Stahl, "More on the Network of Authority," *Public Administration Review*, 20 (1960), 35–37; Robert T. Golembiewski, "Toward the New Organization Theories: Some Notes on 'Staff,'" *Midwest Journal of Political Science*, 5 (1961), 237–59.

political obligation.[9] The employment relationship, evolving out of the relationship between master and servant, has frequently been phrased in the same language.[10] Those in authority have the *right* to demand obedience; those subject to authority have the *duty* to obey.[11] Max Weber, whose influence permeates almost all studies of bureaucracy, classifies the types of authority "according to the kind of claim to legitimacy typically made by each."[12] While both traditional authority and charismatic authority are owed to a *person*, the chief or charismatic leader, "in the case of legal authority, obedience is owed to the legally established impersonal order."[13] As Parsons and Gouldner have pointed out, Weber sets forth but does not elaborate on several additional bases of legal-rational authority, for example, hierarchical office and technical knowledge and experience.[14] Other writers, most notably Simon and Presthus, have further developed these concepts of the underlying bases of authority. While Simon uses "authority of legitimacy" in the narrower sense utilized here, Presthus extends the concept of "legitimation" to include all processes by which authority is accepted, reserving the concept of a "generalized deference to authority" (which in turn reflects the process of individual socialization), for this narrower sense of ethical sanctification.[15] For Simon, it is through the

9. See, for example, Carl J. Friedrich, ed., *Authority* (Cambridge, Mass., 1958), or Bertram de Jouvenel, *Sovereignty* (Chicago, 1957).

10. Reinhard Bendix, *Work and Authority in Industry* (New York, 1956).

11. Simon, Smithburg, and Thompson, *op. cit.*, p. 180.

12. *The Theory of Social and Economic Organization*, A. M. Henderson and Talcott Parsons, trans., Talcott Parsons, ed. (New York, 1947), p. 325.

13. *Ibid.*, p. 328.

14. Parsons, in *ibid.*, n. 4, pp. 58–60; Gouldner, "Organizational Analysis," in Robert K. Merton, Leonard Broom, and Leonard S. Cottrell, Jr., eds. *Sociology Today* (New York, 1959), pp. 400–23.

15. Presthus, *op. cit.*, n. 8, p. 88.

***Table 1—The Bases of Authority***

| | *FORMAL AUTHORITY* | | *FUNCTIONAL AUTHORITY* | |
|---|---|---|---|---|
| | *Legitimacy* | *Position* | *Competence* | *Person* |
| Weber[a] | Legal . . . . . . . . . . | | Rational authority | Traditional authority |
| | Legal order | Hierarchical office | Technical knowledge, experience | Charismatic authority |
| Urwick[b] | | Formal, conferred by the organization | Technical, implicit in special knowledge or skill | Personal, conferred by seniority or popularity |
| Simon[c] | Authority of legitimacy, social approval | Authority of sanctions | Authority of confidence (technical competence) | Techniques of *persuasion* (as distinct from authority) |
| Bennis[d] | | Role incumbency | Knowledge of performance criteria | Knowledge of the human aspect of administration |
| Presthus[e] | Generalized deference toward authority | Formal role or position | Technical expertise | Rapport with subordinates, ability to mediate individual needs |

[a] Max Weber, *The Theory of Social and Economic Organization*, A. M. Henderson and Talcott Parsons, trans., Talcott Parsons, ed. (New York, 1947), pp. 328, 339.

[b] L. Urwick, *The Elements of Administration* (London, 1944), p. 42.

[c] Herbert A. Simon, "Authority," in Conrad M. Arensberg, *et. al.*, eds., *Research in Industrial Human Relations* (New York, 1957), pp. 104–6; H. A. Simon, D. W. Smithburg, V. A. Thompson, *Public Administration* (New York, 1950), pp. 189–201.

[d] Warren G. Bennis, "Leadership Theory and Administrative Behavior: The Problem of Authority," *Administrative Science Quarterly*, 4 (1959), 288–89.

[e] Robert V. Presthus, "Authority in Organizations," *Public Administration Review*, 20 (1960), 88–91.

indirect mechanism of social approval from the particular reference group that the motive of legitimacy obtains its greatest force.[16] But whether used in the broad or narrow sense, authority of legitimacy is inextricably fused in reality with a second source or base frequently discussed in the literature, that is, authority of position.

### AUTHORITY OF POSITION

As Robert K. Merton restates Weber's classic treatment of authority based on hierarchical office: "Authority, the power of control which derives from an acknowledged status, inheres in the office and not in the particular person who performs the official role."[17] That is to say, when a person becomes a member of an organization he is already predisposed to accept orders given to him by persons acknowledged to be his superiors by their position in the formal organizational chart. As March and Simon make this point:

> In joining the organization [the employee] accepts an authority relation; i.e., he agrees that within some limits (defined both explicitly and implicitly by the terms of his employment contract) he will accept as the premises of his behavior orders and instructions supplied to him by the organization.[18]

Although their language has been different, writers such as Urwick, Bennis, and Presthus all have had reference to much the same thing when they discussed formal authority, role incumbency, and formal position.

Simon, among others, has given the authority of position an extended interpretation in his discussion of the authority of rewards and sanctions inherent in office. His assertions that "the most important sanctions of managers over workers in industrial organizations are (*a*) power to hire and fire, (*b*) power to promote and demote, and (*c*) incentive rewards," are equally true of public organizations.[19] Both participants in a superior-subordinate relationship are aware of the disparities in sanctions which support the relationship. However, while the subordinate is subject to the commands of the superior, the superior is dependent on the subordinate to get the job done. The supervisor engages in periodic ratings of his workers, ratings which affect promotion, pay raises, and even the chances of keeping the job. But if subordinates take no initiative, solve no problems for themselves, do everything the superior asks them, but *no more*, the superior will soon be faced with the impossible task of trying to do every job in the organization by himself.[20] On the other hand, as long as subordinates know that a superior controls ultimate sanctions to compel obedience if his orders are resisted, authority cannot be defined solely in terms of acceptance or consent.[21] But even this advantage possessed by the superior is not without its costs. As Peter M. Blau points out, the continued use of sanctions, or threat of their use, will in the long run undermine authority. "This is the dilemma of bureaucratic authority: it rests on the power of sanction but is weakened by frequent resort to sanctions in operations."[22] One consequence of this relationship of mutual dependency with disparate sanctions is that the superior must broaden the base of his authority if he is to secure the active cooperation of his subordinates in order to achieve organizational goals. Formal authority flowing from legitimacy and organizational status almost invariably must be supported by authority based on professional competence and human relations skills.

### AUTHORITY OF COMPETENCE

While the authority of competence is not limited to formal hierarchical relationships, and indeed frequently cuts across the formal channels of communication, possession of experience and appropriate technical skills by the superior obviously greatly enhances the acceptance of his formal authority by his subordinates. In general, authority based on technical knowledge and authority based on experience are closely related, although distinctions can be made between these two subtypes of the authority of competence. Familiarity with certain operations can only be gained from day-to-day confrontation of problems. What may be a crisis for the beginner is

16. "Authority," *op. cit.*, p. 106.
17. *Social Theory and Social Structure* (rev. ed.; New York, 1957), p. 195.
18. *Organizations* (New York, 1958), p. 90.
19. "Authority," *op. cit.*, p. 104.
20. Harold J. Leavitt, *Managerial Psychology* (Chicago, 1958), pp. 150–51.
21. Robert V. Presthus, "Toward a Theory of Organizational Behavior," *Administrative Science Quarterly*, 3 (1958), 57.
22. *Bureaucracy in Modern Society* (New York, 1956), pp. 76–77.

routine to the old hand. Technical knowledge, in contrast with experience, is more apt to come from professional training, for example, specialized graduate education. Indeed, when promotional opportunities arise, seniority may frequently compete with technical proficiency; therefore the prerequisites for most supervisory positions stress both professional training and experience.

There remains, however, a more fundamental ambivalence regarding bases of authority in organizations. As Gouldner asserts, "one of the deepest tensions in modern organizations, often expressed as a conflict between the line and staff groups, derives from the divergence of . . . two bases of authority"—authority legitimized by incumbency in office and authority based on professional competence.[23] Not only do subunits of organizations differ as to the importance attached to these two bases of authority, but different kinds of organizations,[24] over different time periods,[25] and within different cultures[26] also seem to emphasize one or the other of these bases of authority. While a number of writers have commented upon an increasing tendency toward reliance on professional competence with an attending decline in the perceived legitimacy of hierarchical authority, evidence suggests that the strategic location and influence of those in hierarchical roles often enables them to resist specialist claims. As Victor A. Thompson shows, control of the organization's distribution system remains in hierarchical hands:

> Above what might be considered a market minimum, the satisfactions which the organization has to offer are distributed according to hierarchical rank. They include, in addition to money, deference, power, interesting activities and associations, conveniences, etc. Because these goods are distributed according to status rank, and access to any rank is controlled by . . . hierarchical position, these positions acquire great power. . . .[27]

The tension between positional and specialist authority, which appears to be endemic in hierarchical organizations, may sometimes be mediated by a fourth basis of authority, authority of person.

### AUTHORITY OF PERSON

Authority based on legitimacy, position, and competence can be analytically distinguished from the authority of person. Such a distinction takes a number of forms in the literature. As already suggested, Weber makes use of the distinction between authority based on office and authority based on personal attributes to differentiate the first of his three pure types of authority,—legal-rational authority (itself containing seeds of other bases of authority) from his second and third types—traditional and charismatic authority.[28] Both Henri Fayol and Chester Barnard make similar distinctions between what Fayol referred to as "official authority" and "personal authority" and what Barnard described as "authority of position" and "authority of leadership."[29] A number of social scientists, including Bierstedt, Blau, Gibbs, Selznick, and Urwick, have made analytical distinctions between authority and leadership.[30] The focus in this study is not so much on personal or informal leader-follower relations, but rather on the *fusion* of leadership skills—be it charisma or routinized human relations skills—in a person who *also* occupies a position of authority; not on leadership as personal quality, but on leadership as an organizational

23. *Op. cit.*, p. 414. See Thompson, *op. cit.*, for an extended analysis of conflict arising from growing inconsistencies between specialist and hierarchical roles.

24. James D. Thompson and Frederick L. Bates, "Technology, Organization, and Administration," *Administrative Science Quarterly*, 2 (1957), 332–34; Amitai Etzioni, "Authority Structure and Organizational Effectiveness," *Administrative Science Quarterly*, 4 (1959), 43–67.

25. Morris Janowitz, "Changing Patterns of Organizational Authority: The Military Establishment," *Administrative Science Quarterly*, 3 (1959), 473–93; Bendix, *op. cit.*

26. Walter B. Miller, "Two Concepts of Authority," *American Anthropologist*, 57 (1955), 271–89; Stephen A. Richardson, "Organizational Contrasts on British and American Ships," *Administrative Science Quarterly*, 1 (1956), 189–207; Elliot Jaques *The Changing Culture of a Factory* (London, 1951), p. 254; Heinz Hartmann, *Authority and Organization in German Management* (Princeton, 1959), pp. 5–7.

27. *Modern Organization* (New York, 1961), p. 65.

28. Weber, *op. cit.*, p. 328.

29. Fayol, *General and Industrial Management*, Constance Storrs, trans. (London, 1949), pp. 19–21; Barnard, *The Functions of the Executive* (Cambridge, Mass., 1937), p. 173.

30. Bierstedt, *op. cit.*, pp. 70–71; Peter M. Blau, *The Dynamics of Bureaucracy* (Chicago, 1955), p. 178; Cecil A. Gibbs, "Leadership," in Gardiner Lindzey, ed., *Handbook of Social Psychology* (Reading, Mass., 1954), II, 882; Philip Selznick, *Leadership in Administration* (Evanston, Ill., 1957), p. 24; L. F. Urwick, *Leadership in the Twentieth Century* (New York, 1957), p. 37.

function.[31] Thus, as Bennis, Presthus, and others have suggested, "the knowledge of the human aspect of administration," "the ability to mediate individual needs," and the possession of certain leadership traits by a superior enhance the frequency and extent of acceptance of formal authority on the part of his subordinates.[32]

Before reporting some results from an empirical inquiry of authority relations which seems to support a fourfold typology of authority, several assumptions underlying the selection of field setting, working hypotheses, and methodology of this study should be made explicit.

## Field setting and methodology

Three local public service organizations were selected as the field setting in which working hypotheses relating these analytical types of authority could be explored. Before stating these hypotheses more explicitly, several characteristics of the organizational environment, size, and hierarchy need to be set forth. These three organizations—a branch office of a large county welfare department, a police department in a council-manager city of some 25,000 population, and an elementary school in a suburban school district—share roughly the same broad cultural setting in that all three public agencies are located within a ten-mile radius of one another and operate from overlapping or analogous political, social, and economic bases. The welfare office with twenty-three members, the police department with thirty-three members, and the elementary school with twenty-one members, were roughly comparable in size. The hierarchical structure of the police department consisted of five formal ranks (chief, lieutenant, sergeants-inspectors, patrolmen, and dispatchers-clerical staff), the welfare office had four (district director, supervisors, social workers, and clerical staff), and the elementary school had three (principal, teacher, and supporting staff).

The police department was selected as an organization that, at least outwardly, seemed to epitomize reliance on authority of position as exemplified by such characteristics as clear-cut distinctions between ranks and within ranks, the wearing of uniforms, and the use of strict sanctions for disciplinary purposes. In contrast, it was expected that schoolteachers and social-welfare workers would, at least in theory, place greater emphasis on professional standards with a consequent diffusion of authority throughout the hierarchical structure. A further index of the differing emphasis on hierarchy in the three organizations was the ratio of supervisory personnel to rank-and-file workers, ranging from one to five in the police department, one to six in the welfare department, and one to seventeen in the elementary school.[33]

In attempting to relate the four analytical types of authority based on legitimacy, position, competence, and person, the most appropriate index to authority of position was obvious, namely, the incumbent's occupancy of formal office, including job title, in the organization. For the purposes of this study it was assumed that authority of legitimacy would be attributed to position until further inquiry revealed otherwise. Given this assumption, several working hypotheses relating authority of competence and authority of person to this composite authority of position were advanced:

1. Authority of position is strongest when supported by both authority of competence and authority of person.
   1.1 If the immediate superior or superiors are not perceived as a source of professional advice and assistance (authority of competence), then authority of position is weakened.
   1.2 If the immediate superior or superiors are not preceived as good leaders in the organization (authority of person), then authority of position is weakened.
2. Conversely, if the immediate superior or superiors are perceived neither as a source of professional advice nor as good leaders, then the absence of these bases of authority will result in a breakdown of authority of position and the loss of authority of legitimacy attributed to that position.

An eighteen-question interview schedule was designed to investigate related perceptions of authority in organizations.[34] Formal interviews were held with seventy-six of the seventy-seven members of the three organizations. Interviews ranged from

31. Alex Bavelas, "Leadership: Man and Function," *Administrative Science Quarterly*, 4 (1960), 491.

32. Bennis, *op. cit.*, pp. 283–87; Presthus, "Authority in Organizations," p. 91.

33. The school principal shared supervisory responsibilities with central office personnel over the office secretary, custodian, and school nurse (part-time).

34. Responses to the following two questions were used

twenty minutes to over three hours, averaging about an hour in length. The information gained from the use of a structured interview schedule was supplemented by customary research materials, including informal discussions, the observation of routine and crisis operations within the organizations, and the analysis of manuals, charts, procedures, policy statements, personnel records, and newspaper accounts. In addition, some twenty relatively unstructured interviews were held with key administrative and staff personnel in the parent organizations: the county manager's office and central office of the welfare department; the city manager's office; and the central office of the school district.

The limitations of the exploratory approach adopted here should be clearly noted, however. This research was not aimed at describing total organizational behavior, nor was it designed to test hypotheses consisting of causal relationships between clearly defined and carefully controlled variables. A research design having minimization of bias and maximization of the reliability of the evidence as its principal objectives seemed premature.[35] Instead, maximum flexibility permitting the broadest consideration of as many different aspects of authority relations as possible seemed preferable. No claims are made as to the representativeness of the three organizations under study; therefore, generalizations are hazardous. Only in a limited sense can the interview data be construed as any sort of "proof" of the working hypotheses which guided this study. A final note of caution should be sounded about cultural and temporal qualifications. The field phase of this study was carried out in several adjacent suburban community settings in one western state in the United States during a five-month period from late November, 1959, to early April, 1960. This, then, was an exploratory study aimed at clarifying the concept of organizational authority, illustrating some of the bases which condition its acceptance, and establishing guidelines for further investigation.

## Empirical results

What are the underlying bases of authority which facilitate its acceptance in organizations? Four types of authority based on legitimacy, position, competence, and person have been abstracted from the literature of administration and organization theory. While these analytical distinctions seem to facilitate understanding of complex organizational relations, do members of organizations also perceive these as important bases of authority?[36]

In response to the question, "What does authority mean to you?"[37] all but about one-fifth of the members in each of the three organizations specified one or more sources from which authority sprang. A summary of these reported bases of authority is presented in Table 2. The various sources of authority were classified according to the four analytical types developed from the literature.

as indices of authority of competence and authority of person, respectively:

"14. When you need some professional advice or assistance, where do you get it?
  14a) In particular, what persons do you go to?
  14b) Why do you go to him (or her, or them?)
  14c) If he (or she, or they) doesn't have the answer, then who do you go to?"

"17. More specifically, who do you think is a good leader in [name of organization]?"

Question 17 followed a question about the qualities or traits making for a "good leader" in the particular organization.

35. Claire Selltiz, Marie Jahoda, Morton Deutsch, and Stuart W. Cook, *Research Methods in Social Relations* (rev. ed.; New York, 1959), p. 50.

36. "The constructs of the social sciences are, so to speak, constructs of the second degree, namely, constructs of the constructs made by actors on the social scene, whose behavior the social scientist has to observe and to explain in accordance with the procedural rules of his science" (Alfred Schutz, "Concept and Theory Formation in the Social Sciences," *Journal of Philosophy*, 51 [1954], 267).

37. Question 5, which was primarily designed to elicit perceptions of internal authority, was preceded by a brief introduction:

"5. In the study of organizations one hears a lot about 'authority' and 'responsibility.' Now these are pretty broad terms, but I'm interested in trying to pin down the meaning of some of these words. What is your definition of these words? What does authority mean to you?

After the respondent replied to this open-ended question, he was asked to compare his authority with that of other positions in the organization, by way of the following two questions:

"5a) In comparison with other positions in [name of organization] would you say you had
  — a great deal of authority
  — somewhat above average authority
  — an average amount of authority
  — somewhat below average authority
  — no authority at all.

"5b) What leads you to say that?"

Despite the diversity of responses, which was characteristic of all three organizations, the tendency to localize the source of authority in the top internal executive, immediate supervisor, or the worker's own position, was particularly apparent. Representative excerpts from the interviews, some of which convey more than one source in a single response, illustrate the more specific classifications.

A number of members emphasized legitimacy or called more specific attention to legislation, manuals, or governmental institutions as bases of authority:

When I work any place I feel that whatever they want, I give 'em. It's as simple as that. Whoever the boss is . . . [shrugs shoulders].

Authority to me is something you're bound to obey. It's something that I respect.

A lot of authority is in the manual—it's the law.

Authority as far as I'm concerned is the rights we have as a policeman to do certain things. There is a certain authority given to us by the courts, by the state government. . . .

Several comments illustrate the many references to authority inherent in the position or in the persons occupying certain ranking positions:

The person with the rank has the final say. Whether you agree with him or not you go along with him.

My understanding of authority is that it is more or less part of a job, something which you have to accomplish, particularly as a supervisor or a director.

Authority in reference to the ranking officers, the sergeants, the lieutenant, the chief? It's a sign or symbol to the average patrolman or average citizen that that man is in authority. He has, how would you put it? . . . a little more power than the average patrolman within the police department.

Authority is mostly our supervisor and grade-II supervisor.

Others emphasized professional competence or experience as the source of authority:

I have the final word in licensing. There is no written law as to what a good foster home or what a bad foster home is, except as we have defined it in our experience and knowledge. We have the authority to deny the license entirely. And it's based on this knowledge and experience rather than the manual.

Well, my authority is completely within my class-

***Table 2—Perceptions of the Bases of Authority in Three Public Service Organizations***

| *Bases of authority* | *Police department (N = 33)* | *Welfare office (N = 23)* | *Elementary school (N = 20)* |
|---|---|---|---|
| Authority of legitimacy | %[a] | %[a] | %[a] |
| Generalized legitimacy | 12 | 9 | 10 |
| Law, state legislation, city ordinances, the state, county, city | 15 | 17 | 15 |
| Administrative codes, rules, regulations, manuals | 0 | 17 | 0 |
| Governing boards, policies of board | 0 | 0 | 10 |
| Authority of position | | | |
| Top *external* executive or executives, organization as a whole[b] | 0 | 17 | 15 |
| Top *internal* executive, ranking officers, administration as a whole[c] | 27 | 13 | 30 |
| Immediate supervisor | 9 | 39 | 0[d] |
| Inherent in position or job characteristics | 30 | 26 | 15 |
| Authority of competence | | | |
| Professional or technical competence, experience | 15 | 22 | 45 |
| Authority of person | | | |
| Personal characteristics or way in which authority is exercised | 42 | 13 | 15 |
| Other sources | 6 | 4 | 0 |
| No source specified | 18 | 22 | 15 |

[a] Percentages total more than 100 per cent because some respondents indicated more than one base of authority.

[b] The category of "top *external* executive" included the chief executives of the parent organizations, for example, the county manager, director of public welfare, city manager, and school superintendent.

[c] The category of "top *internal* executive" included the police chief, the district director, and the principal.

[d] Coded as "top *internal* executive" in the case of the elementary school.

room, and I'm given a great deal of authority there. And I'm appreciative of this. I'm given a complete rein. I can use my own philosophy, mainly because it's the philosophy of the district. With a good teacher, that's O.K. With a bad teacher, it's not.

The source of authority was also seen to depend on the way authority was exercised and certain underlying personal traits:

Authority in general? Oh, I don't know. I've never objected to people having authority over me, if I felt they were competent. They don't have to be an intellectual or sharp-looking, but they should at least be on an equal with me as far as mental and physical ability. If not, I'd object to it. I had some bosses back home, which I didn't go for. I still did the work. Maybe not as hard and not as efficiently, but I did it.

Authority is based on someone to lead . . . so a person in authority would have to be a leader. He would have to have the ability to command and other traits of leadership. My favorite one is this: "They should back up their men." I hate a person who says out in front of everyone, "You did that wrong." He should stick up for his men.

Finally, authority might be seen as coming from other sources as mundane as a uniform—"Actually, I have no authority to the other men, but the police uniform gives you a certain authority out in the public"—or from such "ultimate" sources as the social worker who saw authority as "God-given," or the police officer who expressed the view that authority was derived from "the people as a whole."

### SOME TENTATIVE GENERALIZATIONS

In Table 2 we saw that authority of position was emphasized in the police department, particularly the authority delegated from the chief of police or incorporated in all ranking officers of the organization. In an organization where formal rank—epitomized by uniforms, insignia, and militarylike courtesy—plays such an important part in day-to-day activity, it could hardly be otherwise. The amount of authority attributed to sergeants and inspectors (theoretically of the same rank) varied extensively, but each of these officers was well aware that he had more formal authority than a patrolman, if less than the lieutenant or police chief. What was somewhat surprising, however, was the importance attached to authority of person. Not only were human relations skills singled out more frequently than any other basis of authority, but police officers placed much greater emphasis on the possession of such skills than did social workers or elementary school teachers. In part, of course, this was a reflection of the type of activity that differentiates these jobs as well as the kind of person attracted to them. These findings also seem to support Janowitz's conclusions that in military-like establishments, skill in interpersonal relations rather than technical competency is emphasized as the basis of authority.[38] As younger, career-oriented police officers with college training in police administration replace older, "small-town cops," the importance attached to authority of competence in this police department will probably increase.

Another unexpected finding was the extent to which social workers, in contrast to police officers and elementary school teachers, singled out authority of position. Approximately 40 per cent of the twenty-three members of the public welfare branch office mentioned their immediate supervisor as a source of authority. Authority inherent in their own position was the second most frequently mentioned basis of authority, followed by authority of competence (Table 2). In part, the social workers' emphasis on the authority of their immediate supervisor reflected the matriarchal role assumed by one of the three line supervisors, an older woman who had played an instrumental role in creating the branch office and who felt responsible for its entire operation. Workers who rejected her authority or served under other supervisors, were more likely to mention the authority implicit in their jobs, or to cite administrative manuals or regulations. The relatively low degree of importance attributed to authority of competence may have been a function of the lack of graduate professional training characteristic of all but three members of the staff.

Perhaps the most striking contrast between these three public service agencies was the relative importance attached to authority of professional competence in the elementary school. Almost half of the twenty-member school staff singled out this basis as compared with 22 per cent of the welfare workers and only 15 per cent of the police officers. In part, this was related to the fact that 75 per cent of the school staff had had graduate training, including nine teachers with the equivalent of master's degrees or beyond. Furthermore, all school

38. *Op. cit.*, p. 492.

staff members except the secretary and the custodian belonged to two or more professional organizations, as compared with about half the members of the police department and about one-quarter of the welfare workers who belonged to one or more professional organizations. While the principal of this school played a more passive "democratic" leadership role than either the police chief or the district director, his position or the school administration as a whole was the next most frequently mentioned source of authority in the school. The diffusion of authority which seemed to characterize this school may be the dominant pattern of authority relations in such highly professionalized organizations as research institutions, psychiatric and medical clinics, and universities.[39]

Earlier in this paper it was suggested that functional authority based on technical and human relations skills might serve to bolster formal authority based on legitimacy and position. In the course of these interviews with public service employees, however, numerous examples were cited which seem to suggest a basic ambivalence, if not an inherent conflict, between these different bases of authority. Approximately 40 per cent of the members in each of these three organizations responded to a question on whether or not they ever received conflicting instructions from above with either a concrete example of authority of competence taking precedence over authority of position, or acknowledged the supremacy of authority based on technical skills within certain spheres of their work.[40] The following quotation from an interview with a veteran patrolman illustrates a situation in which authority based on technical knowledge supersedes a higher ranking officer's authority of position:

> Last Tuesday a man came out of the . . . Bar with another man chasing him, carrying a rifle. He fired three shots and then left. The guy being shot at told us the story. I picked up a .22 short shell on the property. The [ranking officer] came out and said, "Make it up as a 417." That's displaying a weapon in a rude and unlawful manner. It's only a misdemeanor. It would have meant I couldn't have arrested him, and yet he fired three shots at somebody That's assault with a deadly weapon at a minimum. a felony. They should throw the book at that guy! A misdemeanor? Ridiculous. And I told the [ranking officer] so. I finally got him to change it to my way, and finally a day later I did arrest the man.

A more typical reaction to conflicting instructions from above in the police department and the welfare office, and to a lesser extent in the elementary school, was acquiescence to authority of position, particularly among the less experienced members.

## Summary

A survey of the bases of authority posited by five contributors to organizational theory—Weber, Urwick, Simon, Bennis, and Presthus—reveals considerable consensus, despite different terminology. From writings of these and other social scientists, four analytical types of authority relations have been developed: (1) authority of legitimacy, (2) authority of position, (3) authority of competence, and (4) authority of person. This typology also seems to be useful for ordering perceptions of authority by seventy-six members of three public service agencies: a branch office of a county welfare department, a municipal police department, and a suburban elementary school. Interactions between superiors and subordinates contain elements of all four types of authority, although the relative importance of each would seem to vary from person to person as well as from organization to organization. While the interview data must be interpreted with caution, the following generalizations can be derived from this study of the bases of authority in these three organizations. Over one-third of the members of all three organizations, particularly welfare department employees, emphasized legitimacy and position as important bases of authority. In addition, police officers stressed authority of person, while school employees emphasized authority of competence. Authority relations need to be examined in a number of different types of organizations within one culture and in several cultural settings at different periods in order to develop generalizations as to what types of authority lead to what consequences for different kinds of organizations under a variety of stable and crisis situations.

39. Etzioni, *op. cit.*, p. 67.
40. This question was worded as follows:
"7. Do you ever get instructions from above which seem to conflict with what you as [job title] feel you should do?
7a) (If yes) Can you give me an example?
(if no) If you did get such instructions, what would you do?
7b) What did you do then?
7c) How does this work out?"

THOMAS J. SCHEFF

# Control over Policy by Attendants in a Mental Hospital

A central problem in the study of organizations is the extent of participation in policy decisions by organization members. On one extreme are autocracies, in which policy is formed almost completely within the superior group; on the other, examples of dominance or control by subordinate groups: "bureaucratic sabotage" in government, and restriction of production by work groups in industry are two examples. Whether the situation is that of autocracy, control by subordinate groups, or "codetermination," these different modes of policy formation may be used to illustrate the social bases which underlie decision processes in complex organizations.

## Problem and method

The question raised is: How is it possible for subordinate groups in an organization to exert control over organization policy? This question is particularly relevant in the United States to custodial organizations such as prisons and mental hospitals, since there are concerted efforts underway to find an effective method of changing the traditional policies of these organizations. The data of this study are based on participant observation in a large state mental hospital. The administration of this hospital had launched a vigorous and ambitious program of reform in the hospital in 1957. Despite the administration's energetic efforts, the program was largely frustrated by the lower staff, particularly by the attendants.[1] How did this come about?

The explanation given here is in terms of the system of social control operative in the hospital. In order for a subordinate group to exert control over organization policy, it must, first, exact compliance from the superior group and, then, maintain discipline and a united front among its own members. These two requirements imply a system of social control which is effective between and within groups in the organization.

Any system of social control has two components: one, overt actions (sanctions), the other, verbal statements (rationalizations). Considering one special type of sanction in their discussion of the stability of governments, political scientists have noted that force by itself is usually incapable of maintaining a stable system of control. Power must be converted into authority through legitimation by the persons ruled. Like force, social sanctions used by a group are usually accompanied by rationalizations which legitimate its own practices and "neutralize" (deny the legitimacy) of those of its opponents.[2] Social

Reprinted from the *Journal of Health and Human Behavior*, 2 (1961), pp. 93–105, by permission of the author and publisher. 

1. For a case study of staff reaction to a similar program in a prison, cf. Richard McCleery, *Policy Change in Prison Management* (East Lansing: Governmental Research Bureau, Michigan State University, 1957).

2. Rationalization is not used here in the disparaging sense of fictional excuses, but in the neutral, social psychological sense of "definition of the situation."

control, then, arises out of the interplay of sanctions and rationalizations.[3]

CONTROLS BY A SUBORDINATE GROUP: HOSPITAL ATTENDANTS

In the hospital observed, a subordinate group was influential in shaping hospital policy (1) through the vulnerability of the administration to control by its physicians, (2) the techniques used by the attendants to control the physicians, and (3) the techniques employed to maintain a united front within the attendant group. These techniques can be understood better in the light of the situation in the hospital at the time of this study.

"Western State," as it will be called, is a 4,000-bed state mental hospital located in a middle-sized Western city. It is relatively old, dating back over a hundred years. Early in 1957, the administration of this hospital initiated a program which was intended to change radically the character of the hospital.

The central feature of the new program, as seen by the staff, was the ward meeting, which was called "the T.C." (Therapeutic Community) by the staff and patients.[4] The administration hoped that this meeting would: (1) function as a treatment procedure for individual patients, like an enlarged group therapy session and, more importantly, (2) serve to break down traditional staff practices by providing channels of communication between patients and ward staff, supervisors, and physicians. It was thought that custodial practices could be eliminated and replaced by "social treatment."

Meetings were not begun on all wards in the hospital; the adoption of the meeting was left up to each ward staff. Three wards volunteered initially. After a one-year trial, by the end of 1957, there were some nine wards out of a total of forty-four holding meetings. The administration had hopes that meetings would be adopted on all wards throughout the hospital. To further these hopes, it had conducted a series of intensive lectures and demonstrations for the entire hospital staff, to convince the staff of the benefits of the program.

The reaction of the staff to the new program was largely negative, however. The attendants, particularly, who were by far the largest staff group (about six hundred persons), reacted strongly against the program, deeming it impractical, fraudulent, and immoral. At the time the present study began, in the early part of 1958, the furor of discussion and condemnation of the new program had reached a peak. At times, the reactions of the staff were visible even in public meetings. One incident at a hospital-wide meeting provides an example.

The meeting was part of the series of demonstrations of the "Therapeutic Community." A period had been left for questions, with the superintendent in charge. Initially, staff members were slow to raise questions, but after the early minutes had passed, questions came rapidly. The rejection of the program soon became evident from the character of the questions. Toward the end of the hour, the meeting nearly broke up when one staff member asked if it were true that the administration condoned intimate contacts between male and female patients. The superintendent answered that the administration did not condone improper behavior, but the phrasing of his answer was not direct enough to satisfy the audience. In what was virtually a demonstration, the audience jeered and hooted the superintendent.

By the last part of 1958, it was clear that the new program was not going to be adopted by the entire hospital in the near future, if at all. Although the administration's program was carefully conceived and implemented, the resistance of the staff was so

The use of the term "neutralize" follows Gresham M. Sykes and David Matza, "Techniques of Neutralization: A Theory of Delinquency," *American Sociological Review*, 22 (1957) 774–840.

3. The pervasive influence of social control, when control occurs through both sanctions and rationalizations, was first noted by Emile Durkheim. In *The Elementary Forms of the Religious Life*, he suggested that religious practices and religious beliefs were mutually sustaining elements in the survival of religious institutions. For a critical exposition, see Talcott Parsons, *The Structure of Social Action* (New York: McGraw Hill, 1937), Chapter 10.

4. Another aspect of the new program was the encouragement of outside research in the hospital. This report was made possible through the cooperation and financial support of the hospital administration. The author was attached to the hospital staff as a research sociologist, and permitted to follow his own research interests. Free from formal duties, he was able to spend from four to six hours a day in the wards in informal discussions with staff and patients, and in attending staff and ward meetings, for a period of six months. The report on the larger study of which this paper is a part is *Staff Resistance to Change in a Mental Hospital* (Unpublished doctoral dissertation, University of California, Berkeley, 1960). The observations reported here were made largely on four wards: two receiving wards and two "chronic" wards.

determined as to force the abandonment of sections of the program. The staff's victory was manifested at a later meeting, when in response to staff questions, the superintendent announced that "Therapeutic Community" was not necessary for every ward; it was just one more technique added to the hospital's battery of treatment procedures. This was the announcement that the conservative staff had waited to hear: like all earlier innovations, the ward meetings could also be absorbed into the traditional hospital structure. What had begun as a revolutionary new program ended as only one more treatment procedure.

One factor in this result was the vulnerability of the administration to control by the staff.

### VULNERABILITY OF THE WARD PHYSICIAN

The focal point of staff control over the administration was the ward physician. The ward physician was the sole representative of the administration in most wards in the hospital. In this capacity, the physician was responsible for the treatment of the ward patients, and for insuring staff obedience to hospital regulations. The ward physician found it difficult to carry out his duties as the representative of the administration, however. Typically, the doctor facing the ward staff was in a weak position, relative to the staff, because of his short tenure on the ward and his lack of training and interest in administration. The problem of the length of tenure of ward physicians will be considered first.

During this study, the modal length of stay of a physician on a ward was approximately two and one-half months. Complaints about the turnover of physicians were raised in several ward meetings. One "charge" (supervisory attendant) stated: "Just about the time we have them broken in to our ward, off they go to somewhere else." The high turnover rate of ward physicians was due to the large number of separations from the hospital and to the administrative practice of periodic changes in assignments.

Separations from the hospital were frequent among the physicians. Five out of the hospital's total of thirty left during the study period of six months. According to informants, this high rate of separation (33p er cent per year) was not unusual for the physician group.

Had turnover been due solely to separation, only one ward in three would have been affected during any given year. In actuality, the turnover due to separation was magnified by the administrative policy of reassignment. During the year, a physician was likely to be transferred within the hospital from two to five times. At times, transfers were made for training purposes; the administration tried to expose a doctor in training to a variety of wards.

More frequently, the administration appeared to be juggling the particular skills and interests of the physicians against the special demands of the various wards. On one occasion, in a hospital policy meeting, a replacement was being discussed for a receiving ward physician who was leaving the hospital. One administrator suggested the name of a staff physician. Another said, "Oh, no, not him. We need a 'live one' for this ward." The final outcome of this discussion was that five physicians were transferred: one to replace the physician who was leaving, one to replace the replacement, and so on. This practice magnified the effect of separation many times.

As a result of these conditions, the typical ward physician was a newcomer. The ward staff, in contrast, was all but rooted to the ward. The supervisory staff of many wards had been as long as five years in the same assignment. Although the rank-and-file attendants were moved more frequently, even the most mobile of them usually had more seniority on the ward than the physician.

The typical ward physician was not only a newcomer, but also, as far as most ward problems were concerned, an amateur. By training, the physician is prepared to give medical treatment to individual patients. Yet the demands of the ward physician's role are for a ward administrator and leader. The making of ward policy and the command of the ward staff and patients were duties which pressed for immediate attention. None of the physicians was prepared for these duties by their training.

The physicians were not only unprepared for administrative duties, they were also apt to look upon them with distaste. Oriented toward the individual patient, many considered time spent outside of psychotherapy or medical treatment as an irritating distraction from their "real" job.[5] One psychiatrist, a respected young resident, said:

5. The Cummings noted the same phenomena in the hospital they studied. Cf. Elaine Cumming and John

I've spent three years in medical school, and two years as a psychiatric resident, yet I could have done as well in this job (ward physician) after the first six months of medical school. There is practically no time for psychotherapy here. The best we can offer is a social cure.

Another ward physician made a similar comment. "I seldom use anything I learned in medical school. Practically all I do is go to meetings."

By its emphasis on individual treatment, the physician's training had focused his attention and interest elsewhere, making it difficult for him to learn from experience on the ward. In a mental hospital ward, preparation for private practice comes very close to being a "trained incapacity" for ward leadership.

Without training or interest in administration, the new physician was confronted by a ward staff which was relatively permanent and well-organized. Given this situation, the doctor was in the position described by Weber, that of the "political amateur" leading a bureaucracy.[6] Lipset notes this condition in his discussion of a governmental succession:

The new ministers, like most politicians, were amateurs in their respective departments. None of them had ever had administrative experience in a large organization.[7]

This condition, Lipset believes, is the typical setting for "bureaucratic sabotage." In it the reform aims of the succeeding government easily become enmeshed in the traditional pattern of bureaucratic operation, and are transformed or replaced.

According to Weber, the amateur successor quickly becomes dependent on his staff, to the point that he is partially or completely captured. In many cases capture took place in the mental hospital ward. If the doctor too readily took the side of the patients in the ward meetings, or sought to advance the administrative position, the staff had procedures available to control the doctor. Often these procedures were successful because of the physician's impossible span of control.

The ward physician, even if assigned to only one ward, had many other duties besides those in his ward. Admission and physical examination, conferences on various administrative levels, and in-service training and workshops made demands on his time. In the back wards, a physician might be assigned as many as four wards. Most physicians, therefore, were present on their wards a maximum of three or four hours a day.

### TECHNIQUES USED TO CONTROL THE ADMINISTRATION: SANCTIONING OF THE PHYSICIAN

One type of sanction was withholding information. During the physician's absence of twenty or more hours during the day, and on weekends, he was dependent on the staff for reports of the behavior of the patients who were in his care. If the doctor was too demanding of the ward staff, he found that the information he needed to evaluate his patients was not forthcoming, or given only in part. One physician, for example, complained bitterly that his ward staff told him only halftruths.

A second type of sanction used by the staff involved the manipulation of patients. One of the traditional duties of the ward staff was to allow only patients with appointments to see the doctor. The writer has witnessed occasions on both a back ward and on a front ward which were very nearly mob scenes. Patients who would have ordinarily been shunted away from the doctor were encouraged by staff members to accost him with their requests. This tactic apparently had developed out of dissatisfaction with the doctor's performances in ward meetings earlier in the same week. In such a situation, the physician, whose time on the ward was limited, found it difficult to get off the ward gracefully.

A third type of sanction was outright disobedience. This tactic was used with some physicians, but more usually, against psychologists and social workers. On one front ward, a psychologist had begun daily group psychotherapy sessions with a small group of patients. He found, however, that he could not get the cooperation of the nursing staff:

Every day at the specified time I went to start the session. The attendants would say, "Oh, is it two o'clock already!" I would have to round up the patients myself. Patients would then leave or be

Cumming, "The Locus of Power in a Large Mental Hospital," *Psychiatry*, 19 (1956), 371–83. See particularly the first paragraph on page 364.

6. Max Weber, *The Theory of Social and Economic Organization* (New York: Oxford University Press, 1947), p. 128.

7. Seymour M. Lipset, *Agrarian Socialism* (Berkeley and Los Angeles: University of California Press, 1950), p. 262.

taken from the group while I was getting the others. I finally gave up the session for patients. We'll have to work on the staff first.

The fourth, and probably the most important, sanction was available chiefly to the supervisory personnel: the withholding of cooperation. The ward physician is legally responsible for the care and treatment of each ward patient. This responsibility requires attention to a host of details. Medicine, seclusion, sedation, and transfer orders, for example, require the doctor's signature. Tranquilizers are particularly troublesome in this regard since they require frequent adjustment of dosage in order to get the desired effects. The physician's order is required to each change in dosage. With 150 patients under his care on tranquilizers, and several changes of dosages a week desirable, the physician could spend the major portion of his ward time in dealing with this single detail.

Given the time-consuming formal chores of the physician, and his many other duties, he usually worked out an arrangement with the ward personnel, particularly the charge (supervisory attendant), to handle these duties. On several wards, the charge called specific problems to the doctor's attention, and the two of them, in effect, would have a consultation. The charge actually made most of the decisions concerning dosage change in the back wards. Since the doctor delegated portions of his formal responsibilities to the charge, he was dependent on her good will toward him. If she withheld her cooperation, the physician had absolutely no recourse but to do all the work himself.

Of course, the ward doctor could buck the ward staff and seek to rely upon his own devices. In this situation, he must stay on the ward virtually all of his waking hours in order to keep up with his responsibilities. This happened only once at Western State, to the writer's knowledge. In this case the doctor flouted the traditional routine of the staff and sought to impose reform on the ward under his personal direction. He found his position on the ward untenable, however, and was transferred at his own request.

The physician was caught, then, between administrative and ethical imperatives, on the one hand, and the demands of the staff, on the other. There appeared to be two common resolutions to this dilemma. The first resolution occurred often among the psychiatrists and younger physicians. The encroachments of the ward staff on the doctor's prerogatives, and the atmosphere of resistance strengthened their resolve to be quit of the hospital as soon as possible. Their feeling was that they could easily find a job involving higher pay, use their medical skills, and find a more appreciative and cooperative staff. Thus, the role dilemma of the physician, which arose in part from the high separation rate of the physicians, became a cause of further separations, creating a vicious circle.

The second solution to the physician's role conflict was to reach a tacit understanding with the staff. To the extent that the physician sided with the staff, he found his relations with the staff improving, and that he was able to leave the ward after a reasonable expenditure of time. The physician new to the ward soon got the point, and arrived at a working arrangement which involved the continuation of much of the old ward system in return for cooperation from the staff.

Although the working arrangement between staff and physician brought relief to the physician from some of the strains in his role, this resolution was not completely free of tension. In yielding to the demands of the ward staff, he was in some danger of reprimand by the administration. The administration did not go too far, however, in its censure of physicians. For the past several years, the hospital has been unable to fill its vacant posts for physicians. The administration treated its physicians, therefore, with deference. This is not to say that the administration was improperly lenient with physicians. It simply did not seek trouble with the psysicians, in order to keep the staff it had.

A second source of embarrassment for the physicians who compromised with the staff was in the ward meeting itself. Patients with grievances against staff members told all to the new ward doctor in the staff meeting. For example, on one back ward, a patient stated heatedly in ward meeting that she had been held and choked by three staff members. Even though the staff members named resolutely denied everything, and made countercharges against the complaining patient, the situation was somewhat embarrassing to the doctor. As a representative of the administration, and as a professional, he should take action to find the truth of the matter. But since he had arrived at an understanding with the staff, such action would jeopardize his relationship with the staff. The way in which this impasse was handled by the doctor and the staff was characteristic of the hospital, and will be treated now in detail.

### RATIONALIZATIONS USED AGAINST THE ADMINISTRATION

There was a strong feeling of solidarity among the staff in the hospital in the face of attack from the administration. "Whitecoats stick together" was a motto of the attendants. The feeling of solidarity was so strong that it was difficult, even in a staff meeting in which no outsiders were present, for any criticism of a staff member to be voiced. Even the reform-oriented staff members felt this imperative. As a result, ward problems were virtually never discussed directly and forthrightly. They were transformed, rather, into problems of patients.[8]

Because of this convention, the misbehavior of single patients was discussed for days running. Often the breach of the rules seemed rather trivial in comparison with the extended and heated argument that resulted from it. The outsider, who is unaware of the conflicts within the staff, is apt to be puzzled by the seemingly endless discussion of a negligible offense by a patient.

On one occasion in a back ward, the question of demoting a patient, Jenny White (pseudonyms are used for all patients and staff) from her position as clothesroom helper, lasted four days, and crowded what seemed to be pressing problems from discussion. The argument centered about the question of whether this patient was faking seizures in order to avoid the heavy work connected with the clothesroom. The final result of this extended discussion was that the patient was transferred to another ward.

Curious about the heated argument, the writer questioned several of the staff members in private about the patient. It was stated that this patient was the center of a dispute between two ward factions. Her supporters, a group of older attendants, had made her a favorite among the patients, and treated her with small indulgences. For instance, they allowed her to keep her clothes and cosmetics in the clothesroom in excess of the space allotted to the other patients. A group of younger attendants, on the other hand, felt that Jenny was the "pet" of the older group and that the indulgences were unfair.

The writer asked one informant if arguments between these two staff groups had occurred over other "pets." The answer was in the affirmative; there had been many similar frustrating discussions about other "pets." The writer asked if the problem was actually the conflict between the staff groups, and not the patients. The informant seemed surprised, but said that might be the case. The writer then asked why the difference in the points of view of the staff groups were not discussed. The informant appeared embarrassed. She said:

> "You can't talk about things like that around here."
> "Why not?"
> "It's not right." (said with conviction)
> "Why not?"
> "Oh, you can't talk about that in front of the doctor and everybody."
> "What about when there's no one there but the attendants?"
> "Oh, I don't know. We don't do it then either. Nobody wants to start."

By transforming the ward's problems into problems of patients, the staff protected the legitimacy of traditional practices.[9] With this technique,

8. Caudill called attention to what may have been the same techniques: "The tendency to focus on a particular patient as the source of a problem, rather than also utilizing knowledge about the wider context in which the problem occurs, seems to be a very general phenomenon in a psychiatric hospital." William A. Caudill, *The Psychiatric Hospital as a Small Society* (Cambridge: Harvard University Press, 1958), pp. 322–23.

9. The transformation of the problems of the staff into problems of patients was a process which pervaded staff discussion to the point where most staff meetings would have been incomprehensible to the listener unless he understood this technique. The process of transformation may be germane to a proposition suggested by Stanton and Schwartz. Alfred H. Stanton and Morris S. Schwartz, *The Mental Hospital* (New York: Basic Books, 1954), pp. 342–66. They propose that the "disturbed behavior" of a patient might be caused by covert conflict among members of the staff over that patient. In a subsequent study, this proposition was not supported. See Anthony F. C. Wallace and Harold A. Rashkis, "The Relation of Staff Consensus to Patient Disturbance in Mental Hospital Wards," *American Sociological Review*, 24 (1959) 829–36. If the same kind of transformation described here occurred in the small hospital they studied, it is possible that it is not "disturbed behavior" that arises from covert conflict, but *staff discussion* of the patient's "disturbed behavior." Since disturbances are relatively frequent in mental hospital wards, it is possible that Stanton and Schwartz inadvertently selected only those

the ward doctor and the staff, in collaboration, dealt with the impasse in ward meetings mentioned earlier, when the patient complained of mistreatment by a staff member. This staff member resolutely denied the charge, and made counter-charges against the patient. Other staff members joined in, making the patient's charges an occasion for recalling the history of the patient's past misdeeds. In the general confusion, the doctor and still other staff members found it easy to obscure the issue further by asking misleading and obfuscating questions of the complaining patient. The patient saw the futility of his complaints in this situation and sat down.

After several weeks of such behavior by a doctor, the patients no longer turned to him in staff meetings. An outsider, if one was present, or other staff members, was addressed instead. On several occasions the writer has seen patients stating a complaint, turning from staff member to staff member, as he spoke, as if seeking a sympathetic listener.

The other important type of rationalization was neutralizing the claims to legitimacy of an opponent. This technique was used effectively against the reforms urged by the administration. One technique was to characterize all reforms as coming from "outside," and not really part of the hospital. Gouldner noticed the same device in the factory, as an aspect of "mock" bureaucracy.[10] Thus, with no justification, many of the staff identified the 1957 reforms solely with the acting-superintendent, rather than with the superintendent himself, who was on a short leave. One staff member stated: "All this nonsense will stop when our superintendent gets back." This feeling persisted in spite of the fact that the superintendent had been present when the reforms were initiated, and had expressed himself as strongly in favor of the changes.

The theme of outsiders arose continually in ward discussion. The psychologists and social workers were favorite targets for ridicule as outsiders. One typical comment was their lack of acquaintance with ward problems. On one occasion an attendant complained about the social worker attached to the ward:

> Always criticizing our doctor. She doesn't understand what it's really like here. You can't handle these patients as if they were ordinary people.

At times the maneuver to neutralize opposing policies was subtle. One of the back wards had a series of techniques of defense against an outsider, differentiated according to the length of time he was on the ward. The one-day visitor was given the "tour," arranged so that the more creditable aspects of the ward were shown. If an observer was to be on the ward for any length of time, emphasis shifted from misleading to discrediting him. On one occasion a social worker was asked his opinion of a matter being discussed in staff meeting. Since the worker had been on the ward only a week at the time, he was flattered to be brought into the discussion. He proceeded to give his opinion. He later learned that he had been taken in by a ruse. He was purposely asked a question about a problem which the staff knew to be an intricate one, in the hope that he would make a fool of himself.

### TECHNIQUES OF CONTROL WITHIN THE STAFF: SANCTIONS

Perhaps the most pressing problem faced by the staff in its maneuvers was keeping discipline among its own members. A sizable minority of the staff was in sympathy with the administration's program. Particularly with the advent of the ward meeting, coalitions between dissidents and reforming physicians were possible. Other workers were tempted to break ranks in their sympathetic treatment of particular patients. Yet in spite of these possibilities, most of the staff were kept in their place. How was this accomplished?

The system of social control which operated within the staff had both direct and subtle aspects. One potent set of practices stemmed from the ward supervisors, the attendant charges. These leaders had control over work assignments and influence in promotions. The control exercised by the leadership has been described by Belknap, and will not be discussed here.[11]

Other practices were more subtle. One procedure was to control the staff through sanctioning of patients. The system of patient control operated in the back wards with a clarity and force that was

disturbances which were called to their attention by protracted staff discussion.

10. Alvin W. Gouldner, *Patterns of Industrial Bureaucracy* (New York: The Free Press, 1954), pp. 182–83.

11. Ivan Belknap, *Human Problems of a State Mental Hospital* (New York: McGraw-Hill, 1956), pp. 180–90.

somewhat puzzling. The vigor with which patients were controlled seemed excessive relative to the patient behavior which supposedly called it forth. By far the greatest number of the patients were quite abject in their relations to the staff. From time to time, one of a small group, consisting of not more than six or seven patients, behaved insolently, or was insubordinate toward a staff member. Such behavior was unusual, even in this group. Moreover, the control activities were not centered on this "insubordinate" group, but extended to most of the patient population.

Also puzzling was the relationship of the most outspoken of the conservative members of the staff toward the patients. Although these staff members raised their voices against the patients at almost every opportunity, in their personal relations with patients, they were often cordial; their behavior often seemed to belie the contempt for patients they expressed publicly. The longer the author stayed in back wards, the more obvious the paradoxical nature of the control measures became. How can these discrepancies be accounted for?

The explanation of the intensity of the sanctions in the back wards lay in the fact that the control of the patients was only one aspect of a larger system of control. The sanctions which kept the patients in their place also operated indirectly upon the staff members. The intensity and inconsistency of the staff behavior mentioned above arose because the patients were not their main target. The target was those staff members who would allow the patients to forget their place. By disparaging the patients in forceful terms, these staff members were warning the reform-oriented members of the staff and, indirectly, attacking them.

Of the sanctions which controlled staff behavior, the coercive measures used by the leaders figured largely. Control through formal leaders was only an aspect of the system of control, however. The operation of informal measures such as gossip and ridicule, which found all staff members participants, was also important. One example was the use of ridicule in staff meetings. The bitter invective which was aimed at patients also implied the unworthiness of a staff member who would fraternize too closely with the patients. On several occasions, several members were accused of being "soft" with the patients. This pattern of reproach is similar to the use of stinging epithets by Southern whites against those who would break the "color lines." "Nigger-lover" is one such term. These terms pose a scarcely veiled threat to the person's reputation and self-esteem, and are therefore potent measures of control.

Often the control measures were more covert. Reformist staff members occasionally ventured to suggest trials of various aspects of the administration's program. On several of these occasions, conservative staff members, rather than attacking the program or its advocates directly, brought the discussion around to descriptions of the current behavior of some of the ward patients. By their accurate descriptions of the behavior of these patients, they undercut the suggestions of the reformers on the staff. The assumption of the reform program was that patients as a group are worthy of the time and effort required to transform the hospital. By implying the unworthiness, repulsiveness and contemptible nature of the patients as a group, the conservative staff members effectively attacked this assumption, and easily won the argument, since the reformers were unable to answer these hidden attacks.

A final example of the operation of sanctions within the staff is provided by a situation which occurred frequently in one of the back wards. It was the custom of the afternoon shift attendants to sit together before the entrance to the ward office during a quiet period of the day. With the exception of two of the attendants who manned an outer office, and the afternoon "charge," who often was inside the office, the entire afternoon shift sat in a semicircle, guarding the office. Sitting in this position, they talked among themselves and watched the patients. If the doctor was in the office, they kept the patients from seeing him. Very few patients approached this barrier. A patient who did come to this group, with a request for a dental appointment, for example, was usually teased or taunted until she gave up. Under these conditions a civil conversation between patient and staff members was impossible.

All of the shift participated in this activity, including the most reform-oriented staff members. In order to honor a patient's request in a situation like this, a staff member would have had to oppose, however gently, another staff member in the presence of a patient. Since this was counter to one of the unspoken rules of the staff, it seldom occurred.

Similar kinds of control are exercised in groups of adolescent boys. All of the boys, not only the leader, use the epithet "chicken" for the person who does not conform. Staff members on the afternoon shift, similarly, kept each other from consorting with patients, even when the shift leader was absent.

### RATIONALIZATIONS USED WITHIN THE STAFF

Staff members were controlled through the operation of sanctions such as those used by the leadership, and through informal measures such as gossip and censure in face-to-face interaction. Of greater importance than sanctions in the control of the staff, however, were rationalizations that were shared by the staff members. Unlike the patients, the staff members were not overwhelmed by the operation of sanctions; staff members could themselves strike back against the shift leadership if provoked. That they seldom did so was the result not only of the power of the leadership, but also of the fact that the bulk of the staff was caught up in the system of rationalizations which prevented organized opposition. Even in wards where a stable reform group existed, the actions of the group were highly variable and inconsistent. The rationalizations which kept this group and similar groups on other wards captive are discussed below. Three types of rationalization will be considered: patient labels, ridicule of patients, and fictions concerning patients.

*The use of labels.* The use of convenient labels for the patients operated to justify and maintain traditional hospital practices. Terms such as "vegetable" (a withdrawn patient) which were at once an attack on the patient's moral worth, and a justification of inactivity of the staff, were used by most of the staff in referring to a patient, rather than the more neutral psychiatric term.[12] This particular term, "vegetable," was no longer used openly, since its use had been forbidden by the administration. In the informal discussions in which most ward business was conducted, however, it was still used.

There were two main reasons for its continued use. The nursing staff had little training in the use of psychiatric terminology. Mainly, however, they felt that the diagnostic terms were pretentious and irrelevant to hospital problems, with some justification. Although an official diagnosis was attached to each patient, little use was made of it in the entire course of treatment.[13] The nursing staff thought of diagnosis as one more of the hospital formalities which had little relation to actual hospital practices.

Rather than using psychiatric terminology, the nursing staff described patients either in terms of organic conditions, or in terms of their ward behavior. Examples of the former usage were "ep" (epileptic), and "lobotomy" (as in the statement by one of the reform group: "You will never get anywhere with her, she's a lobotomy." That is, the patient was brain-damaged and therefore permanently unresponsive). Further examples were: "feebie" (feeble minded), "luie" (luetic: a patient with syphilis), "drug addict," and "alcoholic." Examples of labels based on behavior were: "pest," "nuisance," "manic," "suicide," "untidy" (incontinent), "promiscuous," "runaway," "hebie" (hebephrenic-silly), "queen bee" (referring to patients who tried to keep themselves attractive through the use of cosmetics, dress and so on. Usually this term had the connotation of persons who thought themselves superior to the other patients), "withdrawn," and "combative."

All of these terms carried disparagement, both for the individual patients, and for the patients as a group. Often, however, these terms were used not to disparage, but simply for convenience. The ward culture possessed no other generally accepted terms which did not disparage. In these cases, the patient's

12. Even the supposedly neutral psychiatric terms often carry disparagement. Caudill noted what appears to be a similar technique in the hospital he studied (*op. cit.*, p. 62):

". . . Some thought was given to the meaning of diagnosis as a security operation. Within a hospital, diagnosis may be thought to serve two functions: on the one hand, it is a useful way of classifying a patient in terms of the etiology and symptoms of his illness; but, on the other hand it is also a way of disposing of a patient by labeling him. For example, if a patient's behavior comes to be continually explained by the 'fact' that he 'has' schizophrenia, then the chance of the patient being relegated to a chronic hospital career are increased. In this latter case, diagnosis may be thought of as a security operation, meaning that uncertainty about a patient is removed by labeling him and that many communications from him may now be safely ignored."

For a speculative but more general discussion of the moral condemnation implicit in psychiatric terminology, see Sebastian de Gratzia, *Errors of Psychotherapy* (Garden City: Doubleday, 1952).

13. The relative unimportance of the official classifications of patients was noted by Belknap in "Southern State Hospital," see Belknap, *op. cit.*, p. 128.

low status was reaffirmed even when there was no intention to do so.

*Ridicule of patients.* There is a great deal of nervous laughter in the mental hospital ward. Staff members faced with a constant array of immediate, yet recurring, problems frequently tell jokes at the patients' expense. The types of humor considered here are: "identity" jokes, ridicule of patients, and other humor.[14]

Identity jokes refer to real or pretended mistaken identities, mistaking a patient for a staff member, or vice versa. In the staff dining room an attendant who was first in line with a group of attendants said to the staff food-handlers: "I get so tired of taking these people (i.e., patients) to eat." Jokes about letting staff members and others on and off a locked ward with a key are frequent. These sometimes have a hostile edge. On the author's first visit to a men's ward, when he asked to be let off the ward, one attendant said: "These people come in and then they want to get out right away." The other attendant said: "You have to go through the (disposition) clinic if you want to get out, just like the others."

Staff members often complained that the dress of some of the physicians made it impossible to distinguish them from the patients. This declaration was usually met by a smile or laughter from other staff members present, as if it were malicious to admit such a mistake for someone with so high a status as a doctor. The humor in this situation was based on the unstated assumption of the lowly, undesirable status of the patient. The fact that staff members laughed at jokes like these was an inadvertent affirmation of these underlying assumptions.

Ridicule occurred, even on front wards, when a patient's record was read to the staff for the first time in ward "intake" conferences. Some typical situations which occurred in a front ward "intake," where the physician in charge was an extremely conscientious psychiatrist:

1. *Doctor:* "We have a liberal dose of psychosis this morning. This patient has always thought she was Honeybear Warren. Better write to Warren and tell him he is a bigamist." (Laughter).

*Attendant:* "Married to a women 35 years and then . . ." (she laughs) The patient was brought in. She told her story and was taken out. Turning to the social worker after the patient left, the physician said: "Would you check on this?" (Laughter).

2. *Another patient, an American Indian.* The physician read from her record: "She was doing a war dance on Highway 99. (Laughter) She was heading West on the wrong side of the road."

*Attendant:* "All good Indians go West." (She laughed).

3. *Another patient:* the doctor read from her record: "She sets off fire alarms." (Laughter) "She thought her hotel was full of rubber snakes and some of them weren't rubber." (Laughter).

4. *This patient* was a middle-aged woman with her hair in ring curls. The patient had finished her story of plots on television to "get her," men watching her doing her wash, and planning earthquakes when she dried her clothes. At this point in her story, she interjected: "Things like that would make most people mentally ill. Thank God I'm not crazy." At this point, staff members coughed, covered their mouths, and took other steps to avoid laughing out.

5. *After the "intake"* was over, during which one patient had said that she was Greg Sherwood, an attendant said to another: Do you think Pat Boone looks you in the eye when he's on TV?" (They both laughed).[15]

*The power of fiction.* In the back wards there was a large body of beliefs about patients which was based partly on experience, but depended mostly on being transmitted from employee to employee. Some of these beliefs were stated frequently and openly: (1) Epileptics have a very bad disposition—there is an "epileptic" personality consisting of being willful, stubborn, changeable and deceptive, and so on. (2) A series of beliefs were related to the notion that patients are like children; and that patients are happy. (3) Female patients are wilder and stronger than male patients. (4) Persons lose all sense of morality when they become mentally ill. This conviction was related to staff beliefs about patients' sexuality. Other convictions were held firmly, but seldom discussed openly. Two examples will illustrate the tenor of a large body of similar beliefs.

14. For a bibliography of studies of humor as an instrument of social control, see Russell Middleton and John Moland, "Humor in Negro and White Subcultures: A Study of Jokes Among University Students," American Sociological Review, 24 (1959) 61–69.

15. Goffman reports instances of the "discrediting" of patients which involve subtle ridicule, in his study of St. Elizabeth's Hospital. Cf. Erving Goffman, "The Moral Career of the Mental Patient," *Psychiatry*, 22 (1959), 136–37.

One attendant stated that the reason there was so much incontinence was that when a person becomes mentally ill, he loses control of the sphincter. She said that the doctor would agree to that. Author: "Why is it, then, that there is so much incontinence here and so little on some of the other wards?" Attendant: "Because our patients are so much sicker."

A front-ward attendant, a person who was an unusually competent nurse and was sympathetic with the patients when in actual contact with them (although she "talked tough" with the other attendants) stated, as an aside from the main topic of conversation, that all mental patients have a distinctive odor: "You get in the showers with them sometimes. It just pours off them."

On back wards such beliefs were firmly held by most of the staff. Since practically all of the staff shared these beliefs, they were validated by consensus. On front wards, however, these beliefs were much more of an individual matter, so that the staff member was much less certain of their validity.

Of all the aspects of patients' behavior discussed by the staff, the most prominent was the patients' sex life. The nursing staff had the strong belief that patients' sex life was abnormal and should be strictly regulated. In one staff conference, the misbehavior of a patient on the grounds was the topic of discussion. A number of rumors of misbehavior by this patient had been discussed. The argument appeared to be resolved, however, when a student nurse indicated that she was an eye-witness to the incident.

STUDENT NURSE. "Lola was carrying on with a male patient near the tennis court." (Said with rolling of eyes and gestures indicating a serious offense).

SOCIAL WORKER. "What was she doing?"

ATTENDANT. "That's just like Lola. I wouldn't put it past her." At this point there was a great deal of tsk-tsking, nodding of heads, and giggling. Staff members began to whisper to each other about other aspects of the "patient sex problem."

SOCIAL WORKER. "Just exactly what was she doing? Were they having intercourse?"

STUDENT NURSE. "No." (This came as a surprise, since everyone had assumed that had been what she meant.) "They were just kissing, but Lola was the aggressor; he was trying to bring her back to the ward, and she kept dragging him back."

SOCIAL WORKER. "Maybe she was out of line, but there was nothing terribly wrong about what you saw, which is the idea you gave us at first."

STUDENT NURSE. "I guess what she was doing was all right, *but not for a patient in a State Mental Hospital*."

The student nurse felt, and the other staff strongly concurred, that such behavior was inappropriate for a person with the status of a patient. Although patients occasionally were promiscuous, there was no factual basis for most of the stories that circulated through the staff.

The cumulative result of the stream of rationalizations, the labels, ridicule, and fictions was that an image of the patient was created and maintained in the ward, an image that was congruent with traditional practices. The administration sought to break up this image in its training of the attendants, and in its formal presentations. But the image offered by the administration was vague in outline, and heard infrequently on the back wards.

The circumstance which sealed off the possibility of escape from the ward frame of reference was the condition of the patients. The administration program rested on the assumption that patients were worthy human beings, yet the evidence afforded by the staff's own eyes seemed to belie the assumption. Most of the patients on back wards were pitiful in appearance, at best, living under crowded and harrowing conditions. Without adequate clothing and washing conveniences, cut off from support from the outside community, abandoned by their relatives, they were a sorry picture to the staff. Under the impact of the ward rationalizations, the staff was selectively sensitized to only the worst features of the patients, and often overlooked the courage and decency that accompanied these features. In these circumstances, the rationalizations presented in staff discussions seemed to be confirmed daily, and the administration's program seemed Utopian and fanciful.

With the combined impact of sanctions and rationalizations, the members of the neutral and conservative groups were kept firmly in their place as traditional staff members. Even the members of the reform group, who had their own defenses against these controls, were not able to act consistently to further hospital reform. These staff members had no "place to stand" psychologically, because of their isolation. Because of the continual, but disguised verbal assaults on the patients, in which they occasionally participated, they were unable to maintain their ideological bearings, and drifted back and forth in their opposition to traditional ward practices.

## Summary

This analysis of the reaction of the staff of a large mental hospital to an administrative program of change has revolved around the question: How was the staff able to resist the program introduced by the administration? It suggests that the answer lay in the differing structures of the administrative and staff groups.

The staff of the hospital was a stable and highly organized community. Within this community, over the years, an informal system of sanctions and rationalizations had evolved. These techniques were described. They enabled the staff to exert control over the administration and to keep discipline within its own ranks. The system of social control was sufficiently effective to stalemate a vigorous program of reform introduced by the administration. The system was also so pervasive that even the sizable group within the staff who wished to participate in hospital reform were confused or neutralized.

The administrative and medical personnel, by contrast, were highly mobile and lacking in the training and interest necessary to provide leadership in the staff community. Due to the shortages of personnel and resources, and the nature of the physicians' training, the administration relied largely on formal controls, without the informal system of controls which usually supports changes in organizations.[16] In this situation, the defensive tactics of the staff were effective to the point that the program did not reach completion.

Assuming that the shortages of personnel and resources that the administration faced will not be greatly changed in the near future, the problem of planning change in existing mental hospitals and similar custodial organizations becomes a problem of understanding the informal techniques of control used by the staff, and of counter-techniques to be used in instituting new programs.

16. Cf. Chester Barnard, *The Functions of the Executive* (Cambridge: Harvard University Press, 1938). According to Samuel A. Stouffer, *et al.*, *The American Soldier: Combat and Its Aftermath* (Princeton: Princeton University Press, 1949), Vol. 2, p. 114:

"One important function of the existence of formal sanctions was that when imposed they called into *automatic* (italics mine) operation informal sanctions, both social and internalized. The existence of these informal sanctions gave the formal sanctions much of their force."

This quotation illustrates the importance of the informal system of control. However, it is questionable whether the informal sanctions are *automatically* called into operation to support the rule. They may, as has been pointed out here, subvert it. The conditions under which the informal system supports or subverts the formal system can only be answered through empirical investigation.

JOHN BREWER

# Organizational Patterns of Supervision: A Study of the Debureaucratization of Authority Relations in Two Business Organizations

## Introduction

There has been a great deal of research on supervision in formal organizations, particularly business organizations. The bulk of it has been concerned with the effects of different styles of supervision upon subordinates' productivity and morale. However, this study is concerned with supervision in business organizations in a different sense. Instead of taking as the major question the consequences of different supervisory styles for organizational effectiveness and efficiency, the research focuses upon the diversity of supervisory styles itself and asks what the social processes within organizations are that produce this diversity. It undertakes, first, to investigate two propositions current in the literature which relate the pattern of supervision that develops in an organization to the nature of the task in which the organization is engaged. The two propositions set forth conditions which are thought to bring about the debureaucratization of authority relations. Second, in an attempt at theoretical consolidation, it suggests a theory of the social processes that shape supervision which will explain these two propositions and presumably others as well. *The theory states, in brief, that a superior's style of supervision is determined by the type of compliance that he must get from his subordinates in order to perform his own organizational role successfully.* It is formulated and empirically tested in relation to less inclusive rival theories that have been put forth to explain each of the propositions separately. The study is based upon quantitative case studies of supervision in several departments of two large business organizations. As a part of the research, a set of categories was devised to describe supervision as a process of social interaction. The major data on supervision were collected by systematically observing and classifying the interaction between superiors and subordinates in these organizations using these categories.

## A theoretical overview: Debureaucratization and compliance

Perhaps because of the overriding concern with its practical consequences, supervision has not often been treated within the framework of general sociological theories of formal organization. However, the two major propositions that are investigated here explicitly conceptualize supervision in terms of bureaucratic theory.[1] Moreover, they are of particu-

I am especially grateful to Peter M. Blau of the University of Chicago for his advice and encouragement throughout. For a detailed description of the methods and findings of this research, see my "Organizational Patterns of Supervision: A Study of Superior-Subordinate Interaction in Two Business Organizations," unpublished Ph.D. dissertation, University of Chicago, 1968.

This article was written especially for this volume.

1. Max Weber, *The Theory of Social and Economic Organizations*, A. M. Henderson and Talcott Parsons (trans.) and Talcott Parsons (ed.), New York: Oxford University Press, 1947. And Hans Gerth and C. Wright Mills, *From Max Weber: Essays in Sociology*, New York: Oxford University Press, 1946.

lar interest because they deal with a relatively neglected aspect of bureaucratic theory, namely, with debureaucratization or the tendency for organizational authority relations to become less bureaucratic. *The first proposition states that as organizational goals and the formal structure and technology employed to achieve these goals become more complex, the relations between superiors and subordinates are apt to become less marked by strict hierarchical control and impersonality, which are the major criteria of bureaucratic supervision.* This proposition has been suggested in both theoretical works and comparative studies of organizations, such as Janowitz's study of the traditional and modern military, Blauner's study of industries using different technologies, and Zald's study of correctional institutions with custodial and treatment goals.[2] *The second proposition states that debureaucratization is encouraged by dangerous or unusual tasks that are carried out in units which are isolated from the rest of the organization and from outside contacts.* The proposition was advanced by Katz and Eisenstadt to account for a number of cases of extreme debureaucratization that have been reported in studies of combat units in World War II, night-working printers, gypsum miners, a naval unit on a Pacific island, navy disbursing officers, and in their own studies of Israeli bureaucrats and new immigrants.[3]

An analysis of the literature from which these two propositions were derived suggests that both can be explained by the compliance theory of supervision. *The theory states that the style of supervision which a superior adopts is the result of the kinds of compliance that he must elicit from subordinates in order to perform his own role successfully. The theory is based on the assumptions that a strong motivation for supervisors' behavior is the need to perform their roles successfully, that a major factor in successful supervisory-role performance is gaining subordinates' compliance, that styles of supervision are important determinants of the kinds of compliance which subordinates are able and willing to give, and that compliance needs vary among organizations and organizational subunits.* It is argued that complex tasks and dangerous, isolated tasks require different kinds of compliance than their simpler, more routine counterparts. It is also argued that these tasks require types of compliance that are not considered in bureaucratic theory.

*Bureaucratic theory assumes that the major compliance need of organizations is disciplined compliance with explicitly stated official directives and rules which specify the activities required for effective organizational operations.* The bureaucratic exercise of authority emphasizing strict hierarchical control and impersonality is thought to insure this compliance by seeing to it that the proper directives are issued, by checking that they are obeyed and correctly carried out, and by preventing personal feelings from interfering with the control process. However, task complexity makes it extremely difficult for superiors to supervise closely more than a fraction of their subordinates' work or to formulate sufficiently extensive or detailed rules. This means that in many instances subordinates must be relied upon to take appropriate action on their own initiative to handle important operating problems. Under these circumstances, a supervisory style that encourages rote compliance will not result in highly effective supervisory role performance. Similarly, dangerous and isolated tasks seem often to require more than just rote compliance with routine directives and rules. This type of task is more likely than others to produce crisis situations in which superiors and subordinates must perform their roles in unofficial ways in order to avert consequences costly to the organization. Bureaucratic theory assumes that the regularly required activities of the organization are assigned as official duties. However, where crises are frequent the assumption may often be invalid, pushing the superior to go beyond the bureaucratic exercise of authority to find ways of motivating compliance with unofficial or informal directives. It is suggested then that complex tasks and dangerous, isolated ones constrain superiors to supervise so as to encourage, respectively, initiative and informal compliance among subordinates. The literature suggests that nonbureaucratic supervision is

2. Morris Janowitz, "Changing Patterns of Organizational Authority: The Military Establishment," *Administrative Science Quarterly*, 3 (1959), pp. 473–93. Robert Blauner, *Alienation and Freedom*, Chicago: University of Chicago Press, 1964. Mayer N. Zald, "Organizational Control Structures in Five Correctional Institutions," *American Journal of Sociology*, 68 (1962), pp. 335–45. See also Eugene Litwak, "Models of Bureaucracy Which Permit Conflict," *American Journal of Sociology*, 67 (1961), pp. 177–84.

3. Elihu Katz and S. N. Eisenstadt, "Some Sociological Observations on the Response of Israeli Organizations to New Immigrants," *Administrative Science Quarterly*, 5 (1960), pp. 113–33.

more likely to promote initiative and informal compliance than more strictly bureaucratic styles.

For neither proposition is the compliance theory the only possible explanation. In each case, a major alternative explanation is suggested by the literature. The relationship between complexity and debureaucratization might be explained by what may be called the administrative-load theory of supervision. This theory suggests that it becomes all the more difficult for a superior to exercise close hierarchical control with the increasing number of different items to which he must give his time, attention, and energy. This is basically an extension of the familiar span of control theory to include items other than the number of subordinates. It can be argued that complex tasks impose a heavier administrative load upon superiors than simple ones. So too, the relationship between danger, isolation, and debureaucratization might be explained not by the special compliance needs created by danger and isolation but instead by what Katz and Eisenstadt call role-impingement. They argue that the conditions of danger and isolation lead superiors and subordinates to become dependent upon one another for rewards that are more appropriate to other, extra-organizational role relationships and that as a result they come to relate to one another in nonbureaucratic ways. In other words, nonbureaucratic roles impinge upon bureaucratic ones.

A major focus of the research is testing empirically the different and contradictory predictions that can be made from these theories of debureaucratization. There are two major predictions of this kind. First, the compliance explanation of the relationship between complexity and debureaucratization suggests that, in order to encourage initiative among subordinates, supervisors will be less bureaucratic in terms of both hierarchical control and impersonality. The administrative-load theory, on the other hand, leads to the prediction that control and impersonality will be inversely rather than directly related. The demands of a heavy administrative load should not only make close supervision difficult but should also encourage greater detachment. Second, the role-impingement theory of debureaucratization suggests that debureaucratization should be accompanied by reduced supervisory effectiveness, since it basically involves the subversion of organizational roles by extra-organizational roles. The compliance theory suggests the opposite: that superiors debureaucratize in order to gain the compliance needed to perform their roles more effectively.

## The research findings: Supervision in two business organizations

The research to investigate these ideas was carried out in several departments of an insurance company and an electric light and power company. From the study in the insurance company, data are presented on eight superintendents and their subordinates in two of the company's home-office underwriting departments, which are referred to here as Departments A and B. These departments were charged with the responsibility of regulating the underwriting activities in particular lines of insurance of the company's branch offices and agencies throughout the country. The underwriters and their superintendents were middle-management officials in the company. From the study in the electric company, data are presented on eleven crew leaders and seven roving foremen from two of the company's construction departments. This work was performed by crews of from two to four men (the same size as work groups in the insurance departments). Each crew was supervised by a crew leader, who was a "working supervisor." This means that he was expected to spend a large part of his time working with his men as well as supervising. The crew leaders were considered to be part of the "bargaining unit" rather than part of management and were members of the union like their men. The crew leaders were themselves supervised by roving foremen, who were the lowest-level management officials. Each foreman had about four crews under his control. The crews usually worked at different locations and on different jobs, so that the foremen spent much of the day driving from one work location to the next. The technology of electrical construction is basically craft technology, and the electrical construction workers received training similar in type and amount to that received by members of the electrical craft unions. However, electrical construction is not a traditional craft but is what may better be called a bureaucratized craft. The union serves mainly to represent the workers in dealings with management. The company primarily provides training, certifies workers' competence for their positions, and decides upon work methods and standards.

Supervision is, of course, basically a process of social interaction between an organizational superior and his subordinates. As such, the most direct way to measure styles of supervision is through the systematic, quantitative observation of this interaction, making use of methods similar to those used in laboratory studies of small groups. However, these methods have not been widely used for this purpose. Most of the observational studies have been impressionistic, and most of the systematic, quantitative studies have used either questionnaires or interviews. Fortunately, it was possible in this study to observe firsthand the daily on-the-job interactions of the superiors and their subordinates in each organization and to classify and analyze systematically the interaction to derive measures of supervisory style. A category system, which is a considerably modified version of Bales' system of interaction process analysis categories, was especially devised for this purpose as a part of the research.[4] The categories are shown in Table 1. Scoring in terms of Bales' units, 8,399 separate interactions were observed and classified for the eight superintendents and their subordinates in the insurance underwriting departments and 14,245 interactions for the eighteen crew leaders and foremen and their subordinates in the electrical construction departments. Background data and data on variables other than supervision were obtained through interviews, impressionistic observation, and by consulting organizational records and publications.

The variable of central interest in the study is the extent to which relations between superiors and subordinates are bureaucratic. Bureaucratic authority relations are seen as having two major dimensions: the hierarchical control of task activities and impersonality. Empirical indices of the degree of bureaucratization are derived from the categories in the system. The categories in Section I of the system describe the control of task activities. The categories in Section II describe the expression of sentiments. Each unit of interaction was classified in both sections. The same categories are used to classify superiors' and subordinates' interaction, but the implications of the categories for measuring control and impersonality are clearly different for superiors and subordinates. Therefore, separate indices of control and impersonality were necessary

4. Robert F. Bales, *Interaction Process Analysis*, Cambridge, Mass.: Addison-Wesley, 1950.

***Table 1—Categories for Observing Supervisor-Subordinate Interaction***

I. Control of Task Activities

1. *General directives*: Orders, suggestions, and requests that assign work objectives only in broad outline.
2. *Specific directives*: Orders, suggestions, and requests that assign a very specific work objective or that specify how a job is to be done or how a work problem is to be solved.
3. *Opinions*: Statements that are evaluative, interpretative, or conjectural.
4. *Information*: Statements of fact and statements to orient the other person to the process of interaction.
5. *Reports on own future work*: Statements in which the person suggests or announces plans for his own future activities.
6. *Reports on own past work*: Statements in which the person tells what he has already done.
7. *Agreement, support, praise.*
8. *Disagreement, criticism and argument.*
9. *Checking*: Questions asking for reports of past work or plans for future work.
10. *Testing*: Questions to elicit discussion and test the other person's competence.
11. *Questions*: Requests for information, opinions, directives, or help in general.
0. *Purely social or expressive forms of interaction.*

II. Expression of Sentiments

A. *Solidarity*: Interaction implying friendship, informality, consideration, sympathy, strong approval, or satisfaction.
B. *Superordination and hostility*: Interaction implying authoritarianism, antagonism, disrespect, lack of sympathy or consideration, dislike, or strong disapproval.
C. *Dependency*: Interaction implying deference, submission, or recognition of another person's social or personal superiority.
D. *Stress*: Interaction implying diffuse tension, anxiety, nervousness, embarrassment, or frustration.
E. *Neutrality*: Interaction with no overt emotional implications.

for the two. Essentially, these indices measure the extent to which superiors and subordinates interact in the categories that are appropriate to their hierarchical roles. With regard to control, this means for the superior the extent to which he concentrates upon giving directives, opinions, and information, and upon checking, testing, and criticizing subordinates (categories 1, 2, 3, 4, 8, 9, and 10). For the subordinate, it means the extent to which he concentrates upon giving reports, agreeing, and asking questions (categories 5, 6, 7 and 11). With regard to impersonality, taking the appropriate role means the extent to which the superior's interaction is free of overt expression of sentiments other than superordination (category B) and the extent to which the subordinate's interaction is free of the overt expression of sentiments other than deference and dependency (category D).

The insurance underwriters in Department A and the electrical construction crews provide nearly model cases for studying the impact of complexity and danger and isolation upon supervision. The work of the underwriting department was technically complex, requiring more training and experience to perform than that in any of the other underwriting departments. The work of the department was also functionally complex; the department handled numerous lines of insurance, and the branches and agencies that it regulated were located throughout the country. In addition to being complex internally, the department was part of a complex organization. This makes it possible to study the effect on supervision of complexity as a contextual variable. It is thought that being part of a complex organization alters traditional supervision by making it necessary as a condition of successful operation to maintain more extensive coordination with other organization units than is otherwise required. This means that much more time must be spent on external contacts by both superiors and subordinates, thereby creating both a heavier administrative load and greater needs for initiative. The work of the construction crews was both dangerous and unusual and to a large degree isolated them from the rest of the organization. They worked on or near high-voltage electrical equipment, and often had to climb and work from tall utility poles. They worked outdoors in severe weather, and most public emergencies (storms, fires, etc.) required their services. Their work sites were in the field, away from the main office, and their only regularized contact with the parent organization was through the brief daily visits of the foremen.

A direct test of the hypotheses studied here would require a comparative study in which these two units could be compared to other organizational units that differ in terms of the crucial variables of complexity and danger and isolation but are similar with regard to other extraneous variables. This was not possible here, however. Instead, an alternative research design was used. Taking these two cases as the starting point, the study employs the research strategy that Lipset, Trow, and Coleman call internal analysis.[5]

The first proposition was tested by comparing supervision in organizational subunits that were judged to differ in task complexity. First, Department A was compared to the electrical construction crews. The task supervised by the crew leaders was probably no less technically complex than that of the insurance superintendents, but there was a clear difference in functional complexity. The crew leaders supervised men all working on one job at one location. The insurance superintendents supervised men who worked on different jobs that overlapped in time and frequently required travel to different branches and agencies. And while both were parts of complex organizations, the crews were more insulated from the demands of complexity than the underwriters, because it was the duty of the foremen to coordinate the activities of the crews with those of other units. Therefore, the crew leaders could concentrate more upon the internal affairs of their work groups. By contrast, the insurance supervisors and the underwriters spent more of their time in contacts with other units than they did with each other. When the indices of hierarchical control and impersonality were compared for the two groups, it was found that the insurance superintendents were less bureaucratic in terms of control but more bureaucratic in terms of impersonality, thus supporting the administrative-load theory.

There were, of course, many other differences between the insurance superintendents and the crew leaders besides complexity that might account for these findings, including differences in methods

5. Seymour M. Lipset, Martin A. Trow, and James S. Coleman, *Union Democracy*, New York: The Free Press, 1956, pp. 425–27.

of collecting data in the two organizations. Therefore, it was desirable to supplement this comparison with others that were not subject to the influence of the same extraneous differences. Two such comparisons were made. In the insurance company, Department A was compared to Department B. Department B's work was less technically complex (its personnel needed less training and experience to qualify for their positions), less functionally complex (it handled fewer lines of insurance and was responsible for fewer branches and agencies), and much less time was spent in contacts with other units. This comparison too supported the administrative-load theory. In the electric company, the crew leaders were compared to the roving foremen. The foremen supervised different crews on different jobs at different locations, handled the more technically complex problems that confronted the crews, and were responsible for coordination with other units. The foremen were found to supervise less closely than the crew leaders, but little difference was found in impersonality. In summary then, these two comparisons substantiated the findings of the initial comparison that *complexity is associated with less close hierarchical control*, but with regard to impersonality they are less clear. Therefore, a further test was needed to help differentiate between the compliance and administrative-load explanations of the variations in hierarchical control. It consisted of examining the relationship between the control and impersonality components of bureaucratization within each unit. The compliance theory suggested that they would be directly related, the administrative-load theory that they would be inversely related. The findings supported the compliance theory.

To investigate the second proposition a different strategy had to be used. Since no comparison between the construction crews and other units was available where the difference in danger and isolation was not confounded with a difference in task complexity, the analysis had to rely upon comparisons among the crew leaders themselves. The focus of the analysis was upon verifying the processes that are thought to underlie the original proposition and in this way indirectly verify the proposition itself. To validate the compliance theory it was necessary at the minimum to demonstrate that informal compliance was necessary for effective role performance and that nonbureaucratic supervisors were better able to get informal compliance and were thereby made more effective in performing their roles.

It was also necessary to show that this theory explained the facts of nonbureaucratic supervision better than the role-impingement theory. The role-impingement explanation of debureaucratization in conditions of danger and isolation suggests that debureaucratization occurs because these conditions lead superiors to become dependent upon their subordinates for personal rewards as the result of their involvement with them in extra-organizational role relations. This explanation leads to the predictions that those superiors who are most involved with their subordinates outside of their work roles will be the least bureaucratic and that the less bureaucratic supervisors will be the less effective. *The data show that the less bureaucratic crew leaders are indeed more likely to be involved with subordinates outside of work roles, but it also shows that they are judged to be the most effective by their superiors.* They are also found to have more involvements with peers and superiors as well. It is suggested that this may keep them from becoming personally dependent upon subordinates.

Impressionistic observation suggested that an important criterion for judging the effectiveness of crew leaders was their ability to handle organizational crises and that an important part of this ability was the capacity to induce subordinates to perform their roles in unofficial ways. An outstanding example of this was the way some crew leaders were able informally to transform their own roles as working supervisors so that they actually rarely worked with their men but instead spent most of their time in planning the work and in contacts with other units. This kind of role transformation required considerable informal cooperation or compliance from the crew leaders' subordinates. Theories of social exchange and observation of specific instances in which crew leaders sought informal compliance suggested the hypothesis that this compliance was secured by supervising in a lenient, nonbureaucratic manner, thereby creating informal social obligations which constrained subordinates to cooperate with the crew leader in transforming his role.

This interpretation was supported by the findings that the less bureaucratic crew leaders were less likely to complain about the adequacy of their formal authority, that the more effective crew leaders were most likely to have transformed their roles, and that the crew leaders who had transformed their roles were less bureaucratic in their supervision than those who had not done so. Furthermore, the interpretation that it was not nonbureaucratic supervision per se that led to greater effectiveness but the role transformation that it made possible is supported by the finding that while nonbureaucratic supervision and role transformation are associated, nonbureaucratic supervision is less highly associated with effectiveness than is role transformation.

One possibility was that the less bureaucratic supervision of the high-role transformers was due to the heavier administrative load imposed by the transformed role. This was tested by examining separately the control and impersonality components of the indices of bureaucratization. The nonbureaucratic high-role transformers were found to be less impersonal than the bureaucratic low-role transformers. This finding supports the compliance rather than the administrative-load explanation.

The compliance theory does not predict that all organizational compliance needs will be met. Instead, it predicts that those compliance needs are met which are important to successful supervisory role performance. This point was illustrated by examining instances of unmet organizational compliance needs in the construction departments. Nor does it predict that all superiors will supervise so as to meet compliance needs. It suggests instead that their behavior will vary with their role-performance motivation. This is supported by the finding that the more ambitious crew leaders were the most likely to transform their roles. The data suggest that this was a more important factor than relations with the foreman, because disloyal crew leaders (i.e., those who indicated they would not choose their present foreman if given free choice) were found to be no less likely to transform their roles than those who were loyal to their foremen.

## Conclusion

This study examined the two propositions that complex organizational tasks and dangerous, isolated tasks lead to the debureaucratization of authority relations. In general, the data that were reported from studies of supervision in two business organizations supported the two propositions, although the comparisons of complex and simple organizational units suggested that increased complexity may well be associated with increased impersonality. Alternative theories of debureaucratization were formulated and tested for each proposition. It was argued that the compliance theory of supervision might explain both propositions. The study of the electrical construction crews suggested that debureaucratization in a unit engaged in a dangerous, isolated task could indeed be explained better by the compliance theory than by the alternative role-impingement theory. However, the findings from the comparisons of supervision in complex and simple units were less clear. Comparisons between units supported the administrative-load theory, but the study of variations in supervision within units supported the compliance theory. These contradictory findings may be due to systematic differences among the units in the formal power and status of the supervisors.

ROBERT C. DAY and ROBERT L. HAMBLIN

# Some Effects of Close and Punitive Styles of Supervision

## Introduction

Close supervision was originally isolated and studied as a style or dimension of supervision by teams of researchers connected with the Survey Research Center at the University of Michigan and led by Daniel Katz.[1] In an early study of female workers in a large metropolitan insurance firm, Morse reported that workers subjected to a close supervision style were less satisfied with the supervisor's ability to handle people, less satisfied with the reasonableness of her expectations, and generally less satisfied with the rules she enforced.[2] These findings suggest a specific hypothesis that aggressive feelings are instigated by close supervision. Katz and Kahn reported finding this relationship between close supervision and aggressive feelings of workers in a tractor plant.[3] Furthermore, if lowered productivity is taken as a form of retaliatory aggression toward the supervisor, data reported earlier by Katz and his associates[4] are also consistent with this hypothesis. Gouldner produced evidence, from an illuminating study of a gypsum factory, that further supports the close supervision-aggression hypothesis.[5]

In the present study, close supervision is conceptualized as one end of a continuum that describes the degree to which a supervisor specifies the roles of the subordinates and checks up to see that they comply with the specifications. However, there are two other points of this continuum worth noting. The opposite extreme to close supervision might appropriately be termed "anomic supervision," as it would involve no specifications (that is, no expectations or norms) and no checkups. Somewhere in the midde area of this theoretical continuum, the general style of supervision can be

1. D. Katz and R. L. Kahn, "Some Recent Findings in Human-Relations Research in Industry," in G. E. Swanson, T. M. Newcomb, and E. L. Hartley (eds.), *Readings in Social Psychology* (2d ed.; New York: Henry Holt & Co., 1952), pp. 650–65; D. Katz and R. L. Kahn, "Leadership Practices in Relation to Productivity and Morale," in D. Cartwright and A. Zander (eds.), *Group Dynamics* (2d ed.; Evanston, Ill.: Row, Peterson Co., 1960), pp. 554–70; D. Katz, N. Maccoby, G. Gurin, and Lucretia G. Floor, *Productivity, Supervision and Morale among Railroad Workers* (Ann Arbor: Survey Research Center, University of Michigan, 1951); and D. Katz, N. Maccoby, and Nancy C. Morse, *Productivity, Supervision and Morale in an Office Situation*, Part 1 (Ann Arbor: Survey Research Center, University of Michigan, 1950).

2. Nancy C. Morse, *Satisfactions in the White Collar Job* (Ann Arbor: Survey Research Center, University of Michigan, 1953).

3. Katz and Kahn, "Leadership Practices . . . ," *op. cit.*

4. Katz and Kahn, "Some Recent Findings . . . ," *op. cit.*

5. A. W. Gouldner, *Patterns of Industrial Bureaucracy* (New York: Free Press, 1954).

**This research was supported in part by a contract with the Office of Naval Research Nonr 816 (11), and the computer analysis was supported in part by a grant from the National Science Foundation, No. G-22296. The authors also wish to thank Professor Alvin W. Gouldner for his encouragement, suggestions, and criticisms.**

**Reprinted from *The American Journal of Sociology*, March, 1964, pp. 499–510, by permission of the authors and publisher. (Copyright 1964 by The University of Chicago Press.)**

postulated; it involves a moderate number of specifications and checkups, at least enough to let the workers know what they are supposed to do. Thus, in close supervision the attempt is to structure completely the workers' behavior, and in general supervision, to structure it only to the point where the worker does not feel at a loss as to what to do; in anomic supervision no attempt is made at all to structure the behavior. Although it would have been interesting, anomic supervision was not included in the present investigation because of the limits of time.

To account for the relationship between close supervision and aggressive feelings or actual aggression, a softened version of the frustration-aggression hypothesis can be used,[6] since close supervision apparently is frustrating to the subordinate. To the extent that it is frustrating, then, the subordinate should be instigated to aggress against the supervisor as the agent of frustration and, in some cases, perhaps actually to translate his impulses into direct aggression, such as angry words, or indirect aggression, such as a conscious retaliatory slowdown in productivity.

However, an important point to grasp here is that close supervision is not in itself aggression. For to be aggression, a manifest intention in applying it would necessarily be to hurt or injure the subordinate. But as Gouldner has suggested, the manifest intention involved in using the close style of supervision is probably to increase productivity.[7] The supervisor may not even be aware that his close supervision is frustrating, thus producing psychological pain or injury. In terms of intention or awareness, the close style of supervision may be contrasted with a second style, "punitive" supervision, which involves the intentional, conscious use of aggression to gain the compliance of subordinates.

To the extent that a supervisor enforces work specifications or rules by aggressing against those subordinates who depart from or violate the rules, he is using a punitive style of supervision. When the punitive supervisor uses aggression (most often in the form of angry, ego-lacerating reprimands), he is attempting to reinforce the avoidance of behavior that violates work rules. Thus, he is usually aware that his aggression is painful to the subordinate, and is in effect saying to him, "I know this hurts, but it is your own doing. If you want to avoid it in the future, follow my rules." Because it is so painful, he is probably aware that his aggression instigates subordinates to counteraggress, but because of his authority to hire, fire, promote, or demote, he evidently also assumes ultimate victory in any aggressive exchange. Furthermore, since the workers are aware of his superior power, he counts upon their not wanting to start an aggressive exchange by counteraggressing.

Yet, unresolved tensions have a way of being channeled into more subtle forms of indirect aggression that are not easily detected or eliminated, as, for example, when workers channel their aggressive impulses into conscious, retaliatory slowdowns in production. If artfully practiced, this form of aggression can hurt the supervisor badly while making it most difficult for him to fix blame or take active corrective measures. This evidently happened with railroad section gangs studied by Katz and his associates, who found that foremen of low-producing gangs tended to use a punitive style of supervision.[8]

Thus far, we have postulated that aggression is the over-all result of both the close and the punitive styles of supervision because both styles, whether intentionally or not, are painful to subordinates. Specifically, we have mentioned two forms of aggression: angry words and a conscious, retaliatory slowdown in production. But these may not be the only manifestations of aggression that result from the frustrations inherent in the close and punitive styles of supervision. Negative emotions often become displaced, and consequently could magnify out of proportion the aggression that sometimes accompanies routine conflicts among workers. Furthermore, these emotions might also be displaced to magnify any incipient dissatisfaction with the work situation itself. Thus, in hypothesizing that both the close and the punitive styles of supervision result in increased aggression, we are actually predicting that they both result in (1) an increase in the amount of verbal aggression toward the supervisor, (2) a decrease in productivity, (3) an increase in verbal aggression toward co-workers, and (4) an increase in dissatisfaction with the work situation.

6. N. E. Miller, "I. The Frustration-Aggression Hypothesis," *Psychological Review*, 48 (1941), 337–42.

7. *Op. cit.*

8. Katz, Maccoby, Gurin, and Floor, *op. cit.*

However, in making our predictions we should note that Pepitone and Reichling found that relationships based on displacement are usually weaker than the others.[9]

Although the close supervision-aggression hypothesis has been generally supported in a number of investigations, evidently the strength of the relationship is quite variable. Again, if lowered productivity is taken as an indication of indirect aggression, the data reported by Katz and his associates in 1950 show that a strong relationship exists where the close versus general styles are used by second-line supervisors in their relations with section heads, but only a moderate relationship in relations between section heads and their subordinates.[10] Data from a second study in 1951 by Katz and associates indicate no relationship at all between close versus general supervision and worker aggression.[11] These variations seem to indicate that a third variable mediates the relationship between close supervision and aggression. In this instance, the mediator is probably a characteristic of the subordinate that influences the amount of frustration he experiences when he is subjected to close and perhaps punitive supervision. The rationale for suggesting self-esteem as the mediating variable is best understood in the context of Goffman's dramaturgical theory of social behavior.[12]

Using the theoretical metaphor extensively, Goffman views the behavior of persons in social contexts as a sequence of carefully guided performances serving to create a "front" or an impression. In attempting to create and maintain a satisfactory self-image, the individual tries to define the situation in such a way that he is able to guide and control the impressions that others obtain of him in the situation. The individual's concern, then, is to put his act over successfully, to maintain by various techniques a favorable, creditable self-image. Thus, in a bureaucratic situation the workers may be viewed as striving to project a self-image to the supervisor and to co-workers, "and the characteristic issue, the crucial concern, is whether it [the self-image] will be credited or discredited."[13]

From the assumption that the workers are attempting to project a creditable self-image, it follows that the close and punitive styles of supervision would be frustrating for two reasons. First, the styles imply a lack of competence, a lack of skill on the part of the worker. Second, they imply a lack of motivation on his part to do the right thing or, in fact, a kind of malicious motivation to do the wrong thing. Thus, when a subordinate is subjected to either of these two styles of supervision, his self-image may be discredited severely. Furthermore, he may be able to do very little to change the situation so that he can create a more favorable impression.

However, and this is the critical assumption, not all subordinates may be equally concerned with maintaining the front, with presenting a creditable self-image. Specifically, our assumption is that some individuals have such strong, favorable self-images, such high *self-esteem*, that they are relatively *unconcerned* with impression management, whereas other individuals have such ambiguous, ambivalent self-images, such low *self-esteem*, that they are *highly concerned* with impression management, with maintaining a front and thus projecting a creditable self-image. If so, the amount of frustration an individual experiences when subjected to close or punitive supervision should vary inversely with his self-esteem. Furthermore, since the strength of the postulated relationship between either style of supervision and aggression should be a function of the amount of frustration experienced,[14] the strength of the relationship should also be a function of the self-esteem of subordinates. Perhaps a simpler statement is: The association between the two styles of supervision and the various aggression variables should be relatively weak among subordinates who have high self-esteem, but relatively strong among those with low self-esteem.

## Method

### THE EXPERIMENTAL GROUPS

Twenty-four groups, each consisting of four women

9. A. Pepitone and G. Reichling, "Group Cohesiveness and the Expression of Hostility," *Human Relations*, 8 (1955), 327–37.

10. Katz, Maccoby, and Morse, *op. cit.*

11. Katz, Maccoby, Gurin, and Floor, *op. cit.*

12. We wish to express our appreciation to Alvin W. Gouldner for suggesting Goffman's theory as the conceptual context in which to discuss self-esteem as a mediating variable (E. Goffman, *The Presentation of Self in Everyday Life* [Garden City, N.Y.: Doubleday & Co., 1959]).

13. *Ibid.*, p. 253.

14. Miller, *op. cit.*

recruited from undergraduate classes and dormitories at Washington University, were used in the experiment. Controls were applied for age (seventeen to nineteen years) and years of schooling (Freshmen and Sophomores).

### THE EXPERIMENTAL SITUATION

At an appointed time each group arrived at the laboratory and was ushered into an experimental room designed to simulate reasonably well an industrial work station. Here the subjects were given a pre-experimental questionnaire and then task instructions. After these were completed, each group worked at the task for a period of forty minutes, and then completed a postexperimental questionnaire. The forty-minute experimental session included ten-minute periods with a supervisor (a trained member of the experimental staff) in the room and two intervening five-minute periods during which the supervisor left the room for the expressed purpose of evaluating the workers' production. Her absence, however, was designed to give the subjects a chance to be alone and thereby some freedom to express any aggressive feelings toward the supervisor or the experiment. Her exits and entrances were timed precisely with a stopwatch that she held in her hand and that, in addition to accurate timing, provided a note of precision and authority. As in a factory setting, an impersonal buzzer was used to signal the beginning and end of the work period.

The task consisted of assembling models of molecules using pegs, springs, and various colored balls provided in Sargent Kits, which are often used in university chemistry classes. Drawings of elaborate, complicated molecular structures were provided as "blueprints" for molecule construction. These models seemed to be novel and complex enough to interest and involve the subjects for the required forty-minute work period. The fact that the task was complex and naturally suited for assembly-line procedures contributed to making this a natural situation where various styles of supervision could be used. (In any experiment it is important that the manipulation not be external to the situation and thus relatively obvious to the subjects, who usually are interested in guessing "what they're after." The general assumption is, of course, that subjects cannot systematically fake behavioral effects unless the goals of the experimenters are obvious.) In addition to providing a natural environment for the manipulations, the kits for molecule construction afforded a rather simple but reliable quantitative measure of productivity.[15]

To simulate an industrial setting, the member of the experimental staff who took the role of supervisor was introduced simply with, "This is Miss Bradshaw, your supervisor during the work period." To heighten the impersonality of the situation, subjects were not introduced to the supervisor, but were addressed by numbers conspicuously displayed at each of their work stations. In addition, words such as "supervisor," "worker," "blueprint," "material bin," "work efficiency," "production unit," "sub-assemblies," and "production line" were used to convey the atmosphere of an industrial situation. However, in order to promote interaction, the situation was designed to be different from the usual production line in one important way: The subjects were stationed around an oval table that permitted each subject to view all co-subjects during the work period.

### THE EXPERIMENTAL DESIGN

Technically, the experiment involved a two-by-two factorial design with high-low manipulations of the two independent variables, that is, the close and punitive styles of supervision. Using a table of random numbers, six of the twenty-four groups were assigned to each of the four "cells," as shown in Figure 1.

To operationalize the four styles of supervision, two lists of remarks were drawn up for use by the supervisor. To operationalize closeness of supervision, a set of clear, concise instructions (role

15. Several considerations went into the decision to set up a production line. First, it was desirable to standardize and keep constant the overall sequence of operations for all groups. To this end, subjects were given definite subtasks to perform; that is, the groups did not determine their own division or non-division of labor. Second, it was undesirable either for the final combinations of operations to be so inefficient or slow that tension would be generated by the task itself, or for each worker to be allowed to proceed to construct whole models by herself in relative isolation, with no interdependence with the others. Although the latter procedure would have maximized productivity in the time allotted to the task, intersubject conflict would have been virtually absent even in high-tension situations. Consequently, although the sequence of operations chosen was efficient enough to keep frustrations at a minimum, it included enough interdependence among subjects to make some conflict inevitable.

definitions) was developed. In the general supervision situations, the eight most essential of these instructions were used by the supervisor to give a minimum definition of the situation. In the close supervision situations, forty instructions were used; also, certain amounts of obvious hovering and watching as well as repetitions of previous instructions were used as checkup techniques.

To operationalize the punitive style in both the close and general situations, a list of sarcastic, negative, status-deflating remarks was developed for the supervisor to use as punitive sanctions. In the high-punitive situation, she made forty such remarks; in the low-punitive situation, she made none at all.

Two members of the staff who observed verbal aggression by the subjects also counted the supervisor's punitive remarks. The experimenter kept a count of the instructions and checkups, and a system of lights informed the supervisor when she had given the required number of remarks for each situation.

Fourteen practice sessions were required to standardize and internalize the multiple facets of the supervisor's role.[16] All extraneous remarks had to be identified and inhibited, and important non-verbal gestures (facial and body) had to be standardized. She had to learn to recognize and "control" subjects who were skilled at becoming dependent on the supervisor through asking for support. To help the supervisor control and minimize support-giving, observers registered all supportive remarks by the supervisor during this training period. Finally, she had to practice giving instructions that were devoid of aggressive connotations.

16. The supervisor's role demanded a person who could combine a certain ability to act with emotional stability, maturity, and general interpersonal insightfulness. The role was taken by a recent graduate in nursing who had a major in psychiatric nursing and whose past experience in therapeutic role-playing with mental patients and hospital-ward supervision constituted an excellent background for the job.

| | Close Supervision | General Supervision |
|---|---|---|
| High Punitive Style | 6 Groups | 6 Groups |
| Low Punitive Style | 6 Groups | 6 Groups |

*Figure 1.*

MEASUREMENT

*Self-esteem.* The measure of self-esteem used in this experiment was developed by de Charms and Rosenbaum[17] and was based in part on an earlier measure by Janis.[18] The subjects were instructed to choose an answer ranging from "strongly agree" through "strongly disagree" that best characterized their usual reactions. (In listing these and other items in this section, the numbering and order are appropriate to this presentation and consequently depart from the format used in the questionnaire.)

1. I feel capable of handling myself in most social situations.
2. I seldom fear my actions will cause others to have a low opinion of me.
3. It doesn't bother me to have to enter a room where other people have already gathered and are talking.
4. In group discussions I usually feel that my opinions are inferior.
5. I don't make a very favorable first impression on people.
6. When confronted by a group of strangers, my first reaction is always one of shyness and inferiority.
7. It is extremely uncomfortable to accidentally go to a formal party in street clothes.
8. I don't spend much time worrying about what people think of me.
9. When in a group, I very rarely express an opinion for fear of being thought ridiculous.
10. I am never at a loss for words when I am introduced to someone.

Agreement with items 1, 2, 3, 8, and 10 and disagreement with items 4, 5, 6, 7, and 9 probably indicate high self-esteem or self-confidence and little concern with the presentation of self, that is, with the management of the image presented to others. On the other hand, opposite responses to these items indicate low self-esteem and low self-confidence and a great deal of concern and anxiety about the presentation of self in everyday situations.

*Aggressive feelings.* To measure covert aggressive

17. R. de Charms and M. E. Rosenbaum, "Status Variables and Matching Behavior," *Journal of Personality*, 28 (1960), 492–502.

18. I. L. Janis, "Personality Correlates of Susceptibility to Persuasion," *Journal of Personality*, 22 (1954), 504–18.

feelings toward the supervisor, that is, those aggressive feelings which did not erupt into overt behavior, the following items were used:

1. How often did you become annoyed with the supervisor?
2. How often did you become irritated with the supervisor?
3. If you were to participate in this group again, how would you feel about having the supervisor replaced?

On the first two items, the subjects were asked to make responses on a six-point scale ranging from "continually" to "never"; for the third item, a seven-point scale was used ranging from "extremely favorable" to "extremely unfavorable." The responses provided an estimate of the frequency with which each subject experienced aggressive feelings toward the supervisor during the work period.

Two sets of items similar to these were used to measure aggressive feelings toward co-workers and dissatisfaction with the task. The first set was identical with the above items except that the term "co-workers" was substituted for "supervisor." The response alternatives were the same except for the third item; here the subjects were asked to indicate the actual number of co-workers they would prefer to have replaced. In measuring dissatisfaction with the task, only the first two of the above items were used, but they were used twice, first with the term "molecules" and second with the phrase "job in general" substituted for the term "supervisor." Ranging from "continually" to "never," the response alternatives were the same as before.

*Overt aggression.* As may be recalled, we assumed that overt aggression might be expressed directly as verbal aggression or indirectly as a conscious slowdown in production. Two rather complex measures thus were required.

After two female observers had reached a level of competence where they could reliably code verbal aggression as it occurred during the experimental-work period, they independently entered marks on forms each time a subject (*a*) antagonistically criticized the supervisor or used indirect sarcasm with definite negative content in reference to the supervisor; (*b*) antagonistically criticized or used sarcasm about her co-worker; or (*c*) antagonistically criticized or joked about the task or the experimental situation. In general, the observers were asked to perceive and evaluate each remark simultaneously along two dimensions: objective content and affective content. All remarks that were negative in objective meaning were counted as verbal aggression regardless of affective content. Remarks that were not objectively negative but tended to carry negative affective connotations were more difficult to categorize reliably. However, 85 per cent agreement of two observers was obtained throughout the experiment on items, not just cell totals.

The production-line arrangement of work required to encourage interdependence in interaction among subjects virtually precluded the possibility of taking accurate or even meaningful measures of each subject's production rate. Consequently, a measure based on the group's total production was used. This was calculated as the sum of the model components (the colored balls, pegs, and springs) completed per forty-minute work period, minus errors and omissions.

*Factor analysis.* Data from each of the scales administered in the pre- and post-experimental questionnaires were factor-analyzed using the principal axis method. The obtained factor weights were used, together with standardized scores for each of the subjects, to obtain indexes for each of the above-mentioned dimensions[19] (Table 1).

19. These procedures are outlined in detail in M. J. Hagood and D. O. Price, *Statistics for Sociologists* (New York: Henry Holt & Co., 1952), pp. 526–30.

***Table 1—Factor Analysis Weights[a] for Pre- and Post-Experimental Questionnaire Scales***

| Scale | ITEM NUMBER 1 | 2 | 3 | 4 | 5 | 6 | 7 | 8 | 9 | 10 |
|---|---|---|---|---|---|---|---|---|---|---|
| 1. Self-esteem | 0.77 | 0.42 | 0.74 | −0.50 | −0.42 | −0.75 | −0.35 | 0.38 | −0.65 | 0.58 |
| 2. Aggressive feelings, supervisor | .94 | .96 | .78 | | | | | | | |
| 3. Aggressive feelings, co-workers | .97 | .95 | .64 | | | | | | | |
| 4. Dissatisfaction, task | 0.90 | 0.89 | 0.88 | 0.92 | | | | | | |

[a] These weights were extracted using the principal axis method. A separate analysis was done for each scale, and in each case the weights given are those obtained on the first factor.

## Results

Analysis of the results began with group data and the testing of basic hypotheses for the stable effects. Then individual scores and a smaller number of independent variables selected on the basis of the initial analysis were used to test the more complex hypotheses involving the mediating variable, that is, the psychological dimension of self-esteem.

### THE BASIC HYPOTHESES TESTED WITH GROUP DATA

Results relevant to the basic hypotheses are presented in Tables 2 and 3. For all the basic hypotheses, the analysis-of-variance results in Table 2 give significance as well as explained variance. In Table 3 the means are given where significant relationships were found.

From Tables 2 and 3 it is apparent that close supervision produced a significant and large increment in aggressive feelings toward the supervisor. The data also indicate a moderate and near-significant increment in aggressive feelings toward co-workers. On the other hand, close supervision was not significantly related to dissatisfaction with the task, to verbal aggression against the supervisor or co-workers, or to verbal dissatisfaction with the task. Finally, the data indicate that close supervision results in a significant and rather substantial decrease in productivity.

Tables 2 and 3 also indicate that the punitive style of supervision resulted in a large, significant increment in aggressive feelings toward the supervisor. However, in this case the relationships between punitive supervision and aggressive feelings toward co-workers or dissatisfaction with the task are both small and insignificant, as are the relationships between punitiveness and verbal aggression toward co-workers or verbal dissatisfaction with the task. Unlike close supervision, however, punitive supervision resulted in a large, significant increase in verbal aggression toward the supervisor. Finally, it is

***Table 2—Summary of Two-Way Analysis of Variance Using Data Tabulated by Groups***

| Dependent variable | *CLOSE SUPERVISION* | | *PUNITIVE SUPERVISION* | | *INTERACTION* | |
|---|---|---|---|---|---|---|
| | *F-value*[a] | *Explained variance*[b] | *F-value* | *Explained variance* | *F-value* | *Explained variance* |
| 1. Aggressive feelings, supervisor[c] | 10.3 | .24 | 10.9 | .25 | 3.0 | .07 |
| 2. Aggressive feelings, co-workers | 4.0 | .16 | 0.0 | .00 | 0.4 | .02 |
| 3. Dissatisfaction, task | .6 | .03 | 0.2 | .01 | 0.1 | .01 |
| 4. Verbal aggression, supervisor | 1.8 | .04 | 20.3 | .48 | 0.9 | .02 |
| 5. Verbal aggression, co-workers | 2.8 | .11 | 2.2 | .09 | 0.1 | .00 |
| 6. Verbal dissatisfaction, task | 2.0 | .09 | 1.4 | .06 | 0.0 | .00 |
| 7. Productivity | 5.2 | .17 | 4.2 | .14 | 1.1 | .04 |

[a] Results are significant at the 0.10 level if $F$ is equal to or greater than 3.0; at the 0.05 level if $F$ is equal to or greater than 4.4.

[b] The measure of explained variance is $n$.

[c] Using Bartlett's test, the variance of all dependent variables was tested for homogeneity. All variances were homogeneous except for this particular variable. To achieve homogeneity, the scale was transformed using the following formula: $\frac{1}{4}(X - 100/50)$. We wish to thank Keith Miller for helping us find this and other transformations used later.

***Table 3—Cell Means for Two-Way Analysis of Variance***

| Dependent variable | *MEANS* General nonpunitive style | Close nonpunitive style | General punitive style | Close punitive style |
|---|---|---|---|---|
| 1. Aggressive feelings, supervisor[a] | 0.73 | 1.14 | 1.15 | 1.27 |
| 2. Aggressive feelings, co-workers[a] | 1.84 | 2.07 | 1.70 | 1.84 |
| 3. Dissatisfaction, task[a] | 1.90 | 2.06 | 1.64 | 2.01 |
| 4. Verbal aggression, supervisor[b] | 0 | 4.5 | 10.8 | 11.7 |
| 5. Verbal aggression, co-workers[b] | 5.2 | 14.0 | 15.2 | 19.2 |
| 6. Verbal dissatisfaction, task[b] | 9.3 | 17.8 | 16.5 | 24.5 |
| 7. Productivity[c] | 335 | 252 | 258 | 226 |

[a] These measures of aggressive feelings are based on standard scores which have little obvious meaning. However, the means are included here to give an idea of the relative magnitude of the effects of close and punitive supervision.

[b] All of these verbal measures are in terms of the number of aggressive or negative remarks.

[c] In terms of the number of correct connections of the pegs, springs, and balls completed during the work period.

evident that punitive supervision also resulted in a relatively large decrease in productivity—a decrease which, because of a small $N$, is of borderline significance.

Thus far the data have not supported all of the basic hypotheses. The results with respect to direct verbal aggression and the displacement of aggressive feelings toward co-workers and the task were variable. Consequently, the more detailed analysis will be limited to two dependent variables: aggressive feelings toward the supervisor and productivity.

### HYPOTHESES INVOLVING SELF-ESTEEM AND ANALYSIS IN TERMS OF INDIVIDUAL SCORES

The results relevant to the mediating hypotheses are found in Tables 4, 5, and 6. Table 4 gives the results of an analysis of variance, with significance levels and explained variance; Tables 5 and 6 show the means involved in the significant interactions. Before turning to these interactions, note that the relationships between punitive or close supervision, on the one hand, and aggressive feelings toward the supervisor or productivity, on the other, are much stronger in this than in the preceding analysis. This reflects the difference between group and individual data—largely the difference between an $N$ of 24 (groups) and an $N$ of 96 (individual subjects).

In Table 4 the findings indicate a significant interaction between closeness of supervision and self-esteem with respect to feelings of aggression toward the supervisor, but not with respect to productivity. In Table 5, the means indicate that this significant interaction is precisely the one that was predicted. The relationship between close supervision and aggressive feelings toward the supervisor is much stronger among subjects with low than among subjects with high self-esteem. In fact, the difference between the means for subjects with high self-esteem is nil. In other words, the overall relationship observed between closeness of supervision and aggressive feelings toward the supervisor is due primarily to the subjects with low self-esteem. Yet, at the level of indirect aggression apparently no difference existed, since the interaction between close supervision and self-esteem with respect to productivity involved very little variance and was insignificant as well. In the close supervision

**Table 5—Means Involved in Significant Interaction between Close Supervision and Self-esteem with Respect to Aggressive Feelings toward Supervisor**

| *Means* | *Aggressive feelings, supervisor* |
|---|---|
| General style, low self-esteem | 1.54 |
| Close style, low self-esteem | 1.74 |
| General style, high self-esteem | 1.64 |
| Close style, high self-esteem | 1.66 |

**Table 6—Means Involved in Significant Interaction between Close and Punitive Supervision with Respect to Productivity**

| *Means* | *PRODUCTIVITY* No. of units | *PRODUCTIVITY* Percentage reduction |
|---|---|---|
| General style, nonpunitive | 84 | 100 |
| Close style, nonpunitive | 63 | 75 |
| General style, punitive | 65 | 77 |
| Close style, punitive | 56 | 67 |

**Table 4—Summary of Three-Way Analysis of Variance Involving Close Supervision, Punitive Supervision, and Self-esteem, Using Data Tabulated in Terms of Individual Scores**

| *Source of variation* | *AGGRESSIVE FEELINGS, SUPERVISOR*[a] *F-value*[b] | *Explained variance*[c] | *PRODUCTIVITY* *F-value* | *Explained variance* |
|---|---|---|---|---|
| 1. Close supervision | 9.3 | .08 | 23.7 | .17 |
| 2. Punitive supervision | 11.3 | .10 | 18.0 | .13 |
| 3. Self-esteem[d] | 0.3 | .00 | 0.1 | .00 |
| Close style × punitive style | 2.7 | .02 | 4.0 | .03 |
| Close style × self-esteem | 5.0 | .04 | 1.1 | .01 |
| Punitive style × self-esteem | 1.0 | .01 | 0.7 | .00 |
| 1×2×3 | 0.0 | .00 | 0.7 | .01 |

[a] Using Bartlett's test, the variance of this dependent variable was tested for homogeneity with negative results. The unhomogeneous variance was corrected using a log $x$ transformation.

[b] Results are significant at the 0.10 level if $F$ is equal to or greater than 2.79; at the 0.05 level if $F$ is equal to or greater than 3.96.

[c] The measure used for explained variance is $n$.

[d] Because of unequal cells, the approximate method for analysis of variance was that presented in Helen M. Walker and Joseph Lev, *Statistical Inference* (New York: Henry Holt & Co., 1953).

variations, the subjects with high self-esteem evidently engaged in indirect aggression through lowered productivity as readily as did those with low self-esteem. The difference apparently was in their emotional state; that is, whether or not aggressive feelings, perhaps anger, accompanied their decision to decrease productivity. However, it should be noted that this pattern could be an artifact of the group productivity scores.

In Table 4 it is apparent that the interactions between punitive supervision and self-esteem with respect to both aggressive feelings and productivity are insignificant. Apparently the experience of being aggressed against in the form of punitive supervision produces aggressive feelings as well as indirect aggression equally in subjects with high and low self-esteem. We can make this assumption with some confidence because the variance involved in the relevant interactions is very low and because we have seen that the measure of self-esteem is sensitive enough to detect rather precise effects.

Finally, are the effects of the two supervisory styles a simple additive function? If they are, the interactions between close and punitive supervision with respect to any of the aggression variables will be insignificant. It is apparent in Table 4 that the interaction between the close and punitive styles of supervision with respect to aggressive feelings toward the supervisor only approaches significance at the 10 per cent level. However, the interaction with respect to productivity is significant, even though a modest amount of variance is involved. This result, of course, implies something more than a simple additive effect with respect to productivity. Apparently the effects of punitive and close supervision with respect to productivity are less than would be expected on the basis of the effects of close supervision alone and punitive supervision alone. As can be noted in Table 6, close supervision by itself reduces productivity by 25 per cent and punitive supervision reduces it by 23 per cent. Together they do not reduce it by 48 per cent as would be expected if the effects were a simple additive function, but only by 33 per cent. Since the decrease in productivity, indicating as it does an increase in aggression, is less than might be anticipated, we will refer to the phenomenon apparent in this interaction as the dampened-increment effect.

This dampened-increment effect might have occurred for one of two reasons. First, productivity in the experimental situation might have been very difficult to reduce below some minimal level regardless of aggressive feelings or impulses to reduce it still further. Second, the aggressive feelings themselves might not have been additive. In other words, double frustration may not lead to double aggressive feelings, but to something much less than double. As can be seen from the first line in Table 3, the data are consistent with this latter interpretation. The scores indicating aggressive feelings toward the supervisor are increased (from .73) 41 points by close supervision alone and 42 points by punitive supervision alone. Together, however, they increase the score only 54 points, as compared with an increment of 83 points that would be predicted if the effects were not dampened. These data, showing as they do a dampened-increment effect, are remarkably consistent with the data in the previous paragraph which showed a similar effect with respect to productivity.

## Discussion

Overall, the results present an interesting pattern that is laden with implications. The lack of support for a number of the hypotheses matters very little, as these involved displacement which usually vitiates the strength of aggressive phenomena. But the interesting thing is that in the close supervisions situations a certain amount of displacement evidently did occur. The subjects by and large expressed more than usual aggressive feelings against one another as co-workers. It is this tendency to displace, plus the absence of verbal aggression toward the supervisor, which distinguishes the close from the punitive supervision situations. In the latter, the tendency to displace aggressive feelings was conspicuously absent and verbal aggression toward the supervisor conspicuously present. Why should such a difference obtain?

A number of explanations are possible, but the one that suggests itself involves the generic distinction between close and punitive supervision made in the theoretical section, that of intention. Our argument there was that with close supervision the *intention* is simply to increase production; the resulting psychological pain is unanticipated, unintentional, and possibly even an unknown consequence. Therefore, close supervision was characterized as frustrating rather than aggressive. On the other hand, with punitive supervision, the pain-producing activities are used intentionally because the pain presumably reinforces the desired avoidance responses. Since activities used with the intention of producing pain or injury are by definition aggression, we pointed out that punitive supervision is a form of aggression. Thus, at a more generic level, the close supervision-aggression hypotheses tested here are simply variants of the basic frustration-aggression hypotheses, whereas the punitive supervision-aggression hypotheses are basically aggression-aggression hypotheses. Phrased this way, these hypotheses may appear to be circular, but they are not. What really is meant is: "To the extent that A frustrates B, B will be instigated to aggress against A," and "To the extent that A aggresses against B, B will be instigated to aggress against A." In other words, genuine causal relationships are involved in the hypotheses because the hypotheses involve an exchange between two individuals.

If this distinction is valid, then the difference in response patterns to close and punitive supervision may actually represent a more generic difference in response patterns to frustration and aggression. Evidently, when A either frustrates B or aggresses against B, the unvarying result is the instigation of aggressive feelings in B. Furthermore, if an indirect avenue of aggression is available, such as decreasing productivity, then in either case B will use this indirect aggression against A. However, a basic difference evidently arises at the level of direct verbal aggression. Although they recognized that the pain they felt was not intended, those subjects who were frustrated by the close supervision practices had a difficult time expressing their aggressive feelings directly at the verbal level, whereas those subjects who felt the aggression inherent in punitive supervision, perhaps because they recognized it as intentional, retaliated openly in kind. Apparently because the latter subjects were able to verbalize their aggressive feelings directly, they were not led into displacing the feelings as were the subjects who experienced the frustrations of close supervision.

Before concluding, we must pay tribute to the women who were subjects in this investigation. While their behavior was not predicted precisely, it was not entirely unpredictable, as we sometimes feared it would be. They probably reacted to the various styles of supervision in much the same way as men would have reacted; most differences probably would be a matter of degree. However, our empirical impression is that women suppress their tendencies to overt aggression, particularly verbal aggression, more than do men. Rather than express their negative feelings in words, they tend to express them more in nervous laughter, or alternatively to withdraw more than do men. In other words, if the experiment were duplicated using men, we think any change in results would be with respect to verbal aggression: verbal aggression would be much more frequent in the punitive situation, and a significant relationship might obtain between close supervision and verbal aggression.

# *Informal Adaptations*

Organizations are complex social systems composed of both formal and informal structures. The early industrial studies revealed that the behavior of workers could not be adequately understood without considering the informal organization of the group. Research documented the existence of explicit norms governing work and the relationships among the workers. Soon, concepts like "restriction of output," "make-work," and "bootlegging" began to appear. While such adaptations occur in all organizations, this section focuses upon informal adaptations in total institutions. It is in organizations like the military, the prison, and the mental hospital where organizational control and formal structure are most manifest and where informal adaptations appear most clearly and in their most interesting forms.

In the first selection, Little shows that buddy relations were the basic element of infantry social organization during the Korean conflict. His analysis shows clearly that primary group relations had an important effect upon combat motivation and the effectiveness of military organization. Two deviant roles, the "dud" and the "hero," defined the minimum and maximum standards of performance for the members. Although the norms of the buddy system defined the limits of military effectiveness, the solidarity that developed enabled the organization to maintain control at the level of greatest risk. Thus, Little is able to show that although buddy relations were often at odds with the official authority system, this informal system nevertheless contributed to the overall military goals of combat.

The next two selections provide important correctives and extensions to theory and research dealing with inmate social systems in prisons and correctional institutions. Both studies are critical of traditional descriptions which view the inmate social system as one of "solitary opposition" to the official system. Street brings a comparative perspective to bear on differences in the structures of correctional organizations for juveniles. He shows the importance of variations in type of social control and type of organizational goal for the nature of the informal social structure that develops. His research shows that differences between custodial and treatment goals are related to inmate norms and attitudes toward the prison, their social relationships, and the types of leadership evident among the prisoners.

Giallombardo compares the complex of social roles of female prisoners with those usually reported for male prisoners and finds great differences between the two. She finds, for example, a large number of homosexual roles available for women in prison as evidenced by such roles as "penitentiary turnout," "stud broad," "chippies," "cherries," and "kick partners." Giallombardo argues that these differences are not a function of deprivations and frustrations resulting from imprisonment, but are due to general cultural definitions ascribed to male and female roles in the larger society which are imported into the prison.

In the final selection, Goffman provides ethnographic data describing the forms of secondary adjustments made by mental patients which constitute part of the "underlife of social establishments." Goffman first specifies the organizational conditions necessary for the existence of this underlife and then describes such techniques as "working the system," "make-do's," "places," "stashes," and "removal activities."

ROGER W. LITTLE

# Buddy Relations and Combat Performance

Infantrymen in combat frequently refer to one another as "buddies." Some with long experience would even say that "it takes a buddy to cover the ground." By this they mean that their social relations are equal in importance to their tasks in the organization. A sociologist, pausing briefly among men like those in the Korean Conflict, would be likely to assume that they referred to specific members of their squad or platoon, easily charted on a sociogram. If he lived among them long enough, however, he would learn that the term "buddy" had two distinct meanings. In a singular sense, the buddy relationship was intensely personal and intimate, fostered by conditions of actual and expected stress. But the word was also used as a general term to describe all the men in the same unit with whom one shared the risks and hardships of combat. Although often at odds with the authority system, the network of inter-personal relationships formed by buddies contributed to operational effectiveness by establishing and enforcing upper and lower limits to role performance.

It was important, of course, that buddies, as primary groups, supported the organization because they comprised its foundation. A study of military organization would be incomplete without a projection of the meaning of these relationships to the larger organization.

Reprinted from *The New Military* (edited by Morris Janowitz), pp. 195–219, by permission of the author and publisher. (Copyright 1964 by Russell Sage Foundation.)

Primary group solidarity does not automatically ensure that an organization will perform effectively. This has been long recognized by students of organization. Studies of industrial organization have noted that cohesive primary groups can at times supply the basis for group opposition to the goals of management. Such a response is dramatically encountered in the correctional institution where solidary inmate groups are organized in opposition to the authorities. Thus the focus of this paper is not on the detached analysis of primary group relations in the military context. To the contrary, it is concerned with how the buddy system, as encountered in the Korean situation, articulated with the structure and goals of military command. In this case, we are dealing with two very different environmental situations: that of combat and that of the reserve rear area. The task is to understand why in combat the primary group relations—the buddy system—operated to support organizational goals to a greater extent than in the reserve areas.

Several sociologists have reported on primary groups in military organization since World War II, but few had opportunity for continuous observation of a single combat unit in the field. The author was able to make such a study while living with a rifle company from November, 1952, through February, 1953. His role was that of an observer of technical aspects of combat operations.[1]

1. R. W. Little, "Collective Solidarity and Combat

The combat conditions encountered by this company, as well as its composition in terms of personnel and equipment, were the same as any other rifle company in Korea during that time. The period of observation covered three consecutive tactical situations: (1) a reserve bivouac with intensive patrol activity in forward areas; (2) a defensive position on the forward edge of the battle area with intermittent patrolling; and (3) withdrawal into reserve for retraining and the reception of replacements.

Combat activity at this time was relatively passive compared to earlier periods of the Korean conflict. Enemy contacts took the form of brief, sharp engagements, interrupting a longer time perspective of standing guard at dug-in positions ("fighting bunkers") with a persistent expectation of enemy infiltration. Offensive combat actions by Americans were primarily in the form of patrols to the forward edge of the enemy battle area for the purpose of detecting changes in deployment. An awareness of the presence of a real enemy with a potential for destruction was maintained by frequent, sudden, and saturating mortar barrages.

In at least three specific ways the composition of combat units in Korea differed from those of World War II. First, there was a higher degree of youthful homogeneity among these troops. Ninety per cent of the platoon that the author observed were twenty-three years of age or less. Sixty-one per cent were in the age group from eighteen to twenty-one years. Only one man was a college graduate (and he was an enlisted man who had volunteered for assignment to a rifle company after being rejected for intelligence duties). Three others (including the officer platoon leader) had attended college for two years or less. Thirty per cent were high-school graduates, and the remainder had less than a high-school education.

Second, the duration of membership in the organization was determined by a concrete measure of individual experience rather than a national goal (such as "Victory" in World War II). "Rotation" was a policy of the Department of the Army designed to require periods of service in Korea in inverse proportion to the degree of risk and hardship to which individuals were exposed. The policy was implemented by establishing zones of relative risk and crediting each individual with "constructive months of service" (commonly referred to as "points") for the period that his unit was located in a specific zone. Men assigned to infantry battalions on the line received the maximum of four points compared to men at stations in Japan, for example, who received the base credit of one point for each month of service.

Thus when two or more men joined the company together, their rotation status would be the same as long as they remained with the company. The number of points was not affected by promotion awards, punishments, transfers, or any factor other than the individual's period of service with the company, or larger unit, within the same zone of risk. This policy provided every man with an individual goal which could be achieved without activities involving greater risk than that to which all other members of the company were exposed.

Third, almost one fourth of the platoon consisted of native Korean soldiers. The "ROKs" (for "Republic of Korea") were originally assigned during a period of shortage of American replacements, but remained after the need was filled.[2] They were distributed among the four squads. An American soldier was assigned as a sponser to each Korean with the expectation that the ensuing relationship would be comparable to that of American buddies, but this kind of friendship rarely developed. The sponsor relationships were adhered to only on guard posts or when the American was reporting to an officer from a command level higher than the company.

The ROKs constituted a social system of their own, distinct from that of the Americans in the unit to which they were assigned. Rigid policies from higher echelons restricted their activity to specific combat tasks which tended to make their roles more specialized than those of the Americans. The Koreans were not required to go on patrols, they did not "pull K.P." when the company was in reserve, nor were they ever assigned as assistants on the automatic rifle. They segregated themselves in the chow line. On work details they exchanged tools

Role Performance" (unpublished Ph.D. dissertation, Michigan State University, 1955).

2. R. E. Appleman, *South to the Naktong, North to the Yalu: U.S. Army in the Korean War.* (Washington: Office of the Chief of Military History, Department of the Army, 1960), pp. 385–89.

with one another but rarely with an American unless the latter initiated the exchange. The Americans seldom differentiated them by name, and never mentioned them as specific "buddies." When the squad moved as an integral unit, the Koreans walked at the rear of the column.

There were, however, major similarities between the U.S. Army in the Korean conflict and in World War II. The basic organization of infantry units was the same as in World War II with only minor changes made in weaponry. Tactical formations were identical. The conditions of infantry life—harsh, primitive, and "close to the ground"—were the same as in World War II. The faces had changed but the story remained much the same.

The methods used by the author were very simple. He selected one platoon in order to get to know the members as individuals and to recognize them in the chow line or on work details. He talked to each one alone at least twice, and subsequently in the presence of his companions at their positions, in the bunkers, or at chow. In the solitary interviews, he encouraged each man to talk about his "best friends" and asked him which, if any, he considered a buddy. The men were reluctant to designate one or more specific persons as a buddy. Once they had made a choice, however, they talked extensively about him, although the man designated rarely reciprocated the choice. Next, an attempt was made to find pairs of men who consistently went to chow together, or exchanged tools more frequently on work details, assuming that such observations would validate their choices in the interviews.

The data on buddy choices indicate the following. Of thirty-nine men in the platoon, nine were Korean soldiers and not interviewed; thirty men were interviewed and observed. Twenty-one men designated only one other person as a buddy. Four men made no choices. Five men designated two other persons as buddies. Of these five, three designated each other or reciprocated one another's choice.

Thus it appeared that a primary aspect of the social system of the platoon was a network of interpersonal linkages. Everyone was a buddy, but one man was usually more so. The one man toward whom the choice was directed, however, did not usually return the choice verbally. Buddy choices were private decisions and consequently never threatened the solidarity of the squad or platoon. The resulting relationships were thus a molecular or granular type of primary group.

But an interview or conversation about "buddies" always elicited additional comments about a context of solidarity in which distinctions among individuals did not appear. Even though a buddy choice was not reciprocated, there was another level of significance at which everyone in the squad seemed to have a centripetal effect, tending to draw all members into a system of consensus. Thus buddies also constituted a status group at a specific echelon of risk and involved by implication the larger organization to which they were assigned.

## The context of buddy choices

The buddy role was an expectation of mutual loyalty and reciprocity attributed to another person at the same relative level in the organization. Behavior in the buddy role could be observed when opportunities existed for free choice of companions. These opportunities were limited by the "Table of Organization."

The formal positions men held in relation to one another comprised a scheme of interaction that would occur if the platoon moved as an integral unit, as in a parade. The pattern would also be used in an attack formation, a factor frequently mentioned as a basis for restricting buddy choices to the same squad.

There were other occasions when companions could be chosen freely, the most spontaneous occurring in the "chow line." Platoon integrity was maintained in reporting for meals but it was possible to exchange places in line with a man from another squad. Work details (digging and building field fortifications) were performed by squads, but within the squad it was possible to exchange tools more frequently with one man than another. Although patrols were composed of men drawn from all squads of the platoon, the buddy of a man designated by the platoon leader could volunteer to accompany the man selected. And finally, a man from one squad could visit a man in another squad at night when the unit was in reserve, although this was more difficult when the squads were on the line.

Buddy choices were always made in a situation of stress which provided opportunities for the offering or acceptance of help. "Old men" offered help as a sponsor, coach, or as the companion of another "oldtimer" who had been through the same combat experiences. "New men" accepted help as novices or as companions of other new men.

Here are some of the ways buddy choices were made.[3]

As a companion to another new man:

I was in the 1st Squad when I made my first buddy. I was sent to the command post to get him. We were both new guys, and it's easier for two new guys to buddy than to get in with the old ones. The first few nights we pulled listening posts together. We were so close that we would read each other's letters. That way we got to feel that we were in the same family. I think that what really made us buddies, though, was that we were new men together.

As a novice sponsored by an "old man":

Camp introduced me to everyone in the squad, and stayed with me that night because I was a new man. He told me a lot about each man in the squad, about the Chinese and their tricks. Then he told me that there would be days when we would feel like brothers, other days that we would hate each other, but that feeling that way was all just part of the job.

As a sponsor:

From the first time that I saw Dion on Sandbag, I liked him. That night I volunteered to take his place on listening post because he was a little jumpy. I wasn't being a hero; I just felt that I'd rather go myself than let someone go who was jumpy. Now no matter what happened he'd still be my buddy.

As a companion for another "old man":

When I joined the squad, Baum was *it*. Now he's the only one who was with us at Sandbag Castle. We depend on each other. I don't think that he would bug out, but if he did, it wouldn't make much difference. The only thing that would break us up would be if one of us was killed or left the company. Bell has been buddying with us but he's still a new man and hasn't been through any of the things that Baum and I have been through.

## Norms of the buddy relationship

From comments of these men and others, and the way they behaved, a set of norms that seemed to guide the behavior of buddies can be formulated.

3. Names used in interview material are pseudonyms, allocated as follows: Those beginning with "A" to platoon headquarters, "B" to 1st Squad, "C" to 2nd Squad, "D" to 3rd Squad, and "E" to 4th Squad.

First, a buddy had to "understand" in a deeply personal sense. Buddies became therapists to one another. Infantrymen were most likely to encounter situations provoking unusual and deviant emotional reactions. One man said of another whom he had chosen as a buddy, "Our minds seem to run together."

A buddy understands you and is interested in your story. Some big mouths talk as if everyone is interested in their story but they're not. You've got to find a guy you like and he likes you, then you're buddies and you know he'll listen to you when you want to talk. A buddy shares everything; if you don't get mail, he lets you read his.

The more one buddy told another, the more each depended on the other. And whatever buddies heard or learned of each other, they kept to themselves.

Second, although one man might think of another as a buddy, he seldom stated it publicly or boasted of the attachment. Only when the chips were down would his choice be displayed.

You've got to make every man in the squad your buddy to get things done. You've got to get down and work with them and get them to feel that they can depend on you to stick by them. But I can never show that one man is my buddy because a lot of guys may think that I'm a buddy.

This norm recognized that the nature of the battlefield was such that he might need another buddy when the publicly designated one was not available. The rule tended to unite buddies subjectively with the squad or platoon as an integral unit, as it would be required to function in a combat formation.

Third, buddies did not boast of individual combat skills or compare combat proficiency. To do so was to suggest that obligation to the organization was more important than loyalty to one another.

In the bunker the men don't talk much about combat. When they do the old men like Camp and Chap call them "war daddy" and they shut up. Clay is like that. Most of the time they talk about places back in the States or incidents around the company. It's a lot better to talk about things like that until you've really had some combat behind you.

The man who often boasted or expected recognition for his combat skills was considered the one most likely to forget, in a combat crisis, that he had a buddy and that buddies had to depend on each other.

Fourth, buddies never put one another on the spot by demanding a choice between loyalty as a buddy and obligation to the organization as an infantryman. One man did not volunteer for a patrol unless he had first obtained the concurrence of the person he considered his buddy, and then both volunteered at the same time. Usually one had been selected and the other felt compelled to volunteer because, on patrols, events were most likely to occur in which they would need each other.

> Buddies have to talk when they get the chance, and you're never sure when you'll get the chance. When on a patrol all the sweat is on the way out, when you're spread out and can't say anything to anyone. When you get to the objective you can say something to your buddy. Maybe you were afraid on the way out. You feel better after you've told someone. It could happen to anyone, and your buddy would understand even if no one else did.

Finally, in a crisis and if forced to make a choice, a man would think first of his loyalty to a buddy, and second of his obligations to the organization. If a man was wounded he expected his buddy to care for him until the "medic" arrived, even though the buddy had been taught to continue in the attack. "Bugging out" was an even more extreme form of deviating from the organizational task; deserting the field and leaving one's companions to continue in the fight. The attitudes of most men toward "bugging out" were expressed like this:

> I always wanted to shoot the guy who bugged out on me, and I would anybody but my buddy, Dion. Lots of times fellows do things when they're scared that they don't do at any other time. But I don't like to think of that happening.

Of the twenty-six men who made buddy choices in the platoon, twenty stated that even if the buddy should "bug out," they would remain buddies without any change in the relationship. Of the remaining six men, three stated that they were not sure that it would make a difference, while only three were certain that it would break the relationship. (Four men made no buddy choices.)

## Deviant roles: The dud and the hero

In each platoon there were two deviant roles which some men assumed. Usually it was enough to have one dud and one hero to a platoon, because the role itself was more important than the number of men occupying it. They were extreme types in their contribution to the organization. The hero did too much. The dud contributed the minimum necessary to get by. Men who were classified as duds or heroes could not make buddies, or lost them quickly.

The dud was a person who refused to do his share. He was not called a dud because he lacked skill, or was awkward, or nervous. To such men the others always gave more help and attention. The dud was deliberately undependable, and would not try. Indeed, he was crafty in avoiding the tasks that had to be performed together or not at all. He knew how to hide by lingering in the chow line, or by dallying on the work detail. He was rarely available when a patrol was being selected. In each case he made more work for the others. They had to do his share, not because the dud lacked ability, but because he refused to use it.

Frequent attendance at sick call was often interpreted as characteristic of the dud:

> When a man goes on sick call a lot, he misses out on things that happen to the squad. Then when he comes back he can't talk about it as if he had been with us. When he's gone someone else has to take his place, and that means more work for everyone else and no sweat for him. When he does come back, if the doctor didn't do anything for him, the guys think that he's been aping off. Crum just can't get close to the guys anymore, but he doesn't care because he has so many points and will rotate soon.

The dud had a rough time until one of two things happened. Sometimes he came around and began to do his share, yielding to the pressures exerted on him, but he never lived down his past. He could become an acceptable member of the squad—and be a buddy—only at the price of living with his old record, and being constantly reminded of it with jokes and nicknames. When the bitterness and rejection were gone, the reformed dud continued to serve a useful purpose; new men learned, from his reputation, that "aping off" was more easily forgiven than forgotten.

More often, however, the dud became increasingly isolated from the other men in the squad. He was seldom present when the squad worked together on a patrol, or on detail. Consequently, he had little to say when such activities were being discussed. He often became the butt of jokes in the bunker or chow line. Eventually he would abandon any pretense of being a member of the squad and direct all of his efforts toward getting a transfer. The irony of it was that when he did "get out," he was transferred to the rear as a driver or a cook's helper, at an echelon of less risk and more comfort.

The opposite role was that of the "hero." Unlike the dud, the hero wanted to do *more* than his share for the organization. In doing so he made it necessary for others to follow, or at least to expose themselves to additional risk.

> A guy who is just trying to show that he's not scared and sometimes trying to show up the other men. He's not braver. You shouldn't stick your neck out unless you have to. If someone gives me an order, we'll do it but we aren't going to take any unnecessary chances. If a guy gets a medal for doing his job it's O.K. But if he's taken a chance or exposed his men, he's no hero because he's made it more risky for everyone.

The hero frequently boasted of his courage and aggressiveness. He clamored for intensive combat. Like the dud, the hero appeared to be thinking first of himself, and only secondarily of the other members of the squad or platoon. No more than the dud could he be depended upon to act as one bound by his loyalty to a buddy.

Although buddies used the term "hero" in a negative sense, the organization provided a special, positive meaning for the term. From the organization point of view a hero was a person whose action had been officially recognized as making an exceptional contribution to the mission of the organization. A decoration or an award was the organization's mark for a hero, to be perceived by the recipient's peers as a reward for a deed well done and an inspirational symbol toward which others might strive.[4]

4. A valorous act and an award for the act were separated by an administrative process which often appeared arbitrary. First, getting an award was dependent on being "put in" for it by the company commander, usually at the suggestion of the platoon leader. Hence, whether or not the act was recognized by the organization depended on whether it was defined by someone in the chain of command as exceptional behavior. The intervening administrative process often discouraged the submission of names for awards. Second, quotas of awards were often allocated by the organization for the purpose of stimulating the recognition of valor. However, the quota system resulted in a monthly redefinition of valor. When such awards were presented in ceremonies they were described as being "handed out" with the implication that it was a routine distribution.

But a man who received an award often seemed to feel an obligation to deny that he had "earned" the medal. For example:

> Sergeant Alex was calling Earl out of his bunker to give him orders every five minutes. Earl objected and Sergeant Alex called him "our little hero" because he got the Bronze Star on Sandbag Castle. Earl got mad and said that he had never asked for it; they *gave* it to him. He told me that he wished that he'd been someplace else when it happened.

Although the hero was as isolated from his peers as the dud, it was easier for the hero to "reform" and become acceptable. It usually happened as a matter of course that he boasted less of combat experiences. As the number of "old men" in the platoon dwindled, he assumed the role of an "old-timer" himself and found that role more satisfying. As he took on their sentiments, he volunteered less frequently. Sometimes the hero found this change too difficult. When the tactical situation failed to provide opportunities for him to live up to his ideals, he tended to withdraw, apparently into a world of his own.

The range of behavior defined by the roles of dud and hero has an implication for the larger organization. The role of the dud defined the minimal performance standards of a member. Below those limits, his failure to perform involved a distortion of the functional integrity of the unit. The negative definition of the hero's role tended to discourage episodes of reckless, aggressive behavior which would exceed the support capability of the larger organization, and enabled it to function with predictable routines.

## Combat role motivation

Despite the defensive value system which they developed, the tendency to restrict the aggressive activities of one another and to deprecate the symbols of the organization, the fact remains that buddies performed their roles effectively. They might have talked about what they would do if one of them bugged out, but no one ever did. They endured life in this harsh and primitive environment. What made them do it?

There are three major explanations of the way men perform in combat roles.

The first asserts that their performance is motivated by identification with some formal symbols of a particular organization or its traditions. For these men, however, the Army began with their buddies and extended little farther than the platoon and company. Beyond these levels the organization was as meaningless as it was complex. Men from one company seldom made contacts with men from other companies—even other platoons of their own company—so that their uniqueness in terms of unit identifications rarely came into play.

It may be that at some remote point in history (a favorite explanation of military historians) this condition was different, especially when outfits had fewer members, and units bivouacked and fought in close proximity. Then men of one company became acquainted with men of another, and their membership in different units would be one of the distinctions they made. Even the men of this company, who expressed or displayed no identification with the regiment while with the company, would be heard boasting of their membership, wearing the regimentals, and using distinctive calls, while in the rear or in Japan at rest centers. But while actually in combat, at this time and place in the Korean Conflict, membership in a particular unit appeared to have little effect on combat performance.

A second explanation would contend that men behave in a particular way in combat to "live up" to the code of "being a man." In these terms the man most respected in combat was the one who typically acted independently, aggressively, and with great enthusiasm. The least masculine person would be totally dependent on his fellows and least likely to act independently or with initiative. But this conception of masculinity did not operate either. This is certainly not to say that buddies did not "act like men," but that they had a different conception of masculinity, developed under constant threat to their lives. They thought of the man who acted independently as one who could not be depended upon in a combat skirmish. The hero exposed others to unnecessary risk, thought of himself (if anyone) first, and his buddies second, and forgot that buddies must fight together or not at all.

A third explanation is in terms of abstract values or the symbols of the larger society, such as patriotism, the flag, or "our way of life." It may be true that these factors have some inspirational influence when used by themselves in attempts to motivate the combat soldier. But such values and symbols were never talked about directly nor were they used to account for the failures of some men to perform adequately. A man accepted his position in the outfit as a matter of fate—it was "the way the ball bounced" —rather than a citizen's duty.

There is one way in which this explanation may have even greater validity. We can say that an important motivating force in the combat role was the soldier's relationship to some meaningful element of the large society, especially his family. Real and symbolic activities of the organization based on this relationship were effective. It was not enough that he heard about patriotism, the flag, and our way of life in the abstract and general way of indoctrination. He had to hear about them from persons who represented those values to him intimately, persons whose evaluations of his behavior as good or bad were of great significance to him.

## The primary group and combat roles

These explanations all failed to identify personal relationships as having an independent significance in military organization. The point of departure was an assumption that all members of the organization shared the same norms and sentiments, a consistency attributed to habituation and leadership. However, following World War II, one military observer and sociologists, generally, accorded greater prominence to the significance of the primary group.

Marshall, a military historian, discerned a deviant pattern in the reluctance of riflemen to fire. From interviews with combat infantrymen assembled in rear areas after the event, he concluded that only 15 per cent of the participants in a combat event had fired their weapons at either enemy positions or personnel. He noted that the most active firers were usually in small groups working together. However, he attributed this deviance to personality characteristics rather than recognizing it as a normative standard of organized deviance.[5]

5. S. L. A. Marshall, *Men Against Fire* (New York: William Morrow and Co., 1947), especially pp. 54–56. Marshall does not take into consideration two factors that could be of major practical significance in restricted firing behavior. First, the conditioning effect of marksmanship training, with emphasis on hitting a specific target with a limited number of rounds (cartridges). Second, the prob-

Stouffer and his colleagues in *The American Soldier* presented a systematic and extensive collection of studies of the attitudes of individuals representing the social relations and activities of many combat units.[6] The discrepancy between the sentiments of officers and enlisted men as status groups was thoroughly demonstrated, although an inadequate effort was made to analyze the social structure within which these attitudes were generated. The responses were also generalized over a period of time and not related to specific combat events. These studies represent an excellent general description of the military population of World War II and of their attitudes toward salient features of their experiences with military organization.

The function of the primary group under the stress of combat was more specifically defined by Shils and Janowitz in an analysis of the effects of Allied psychological warfare on the *Wehrmacht*. Continued effectiveness of the individual combat soldier was concluded to be a function of his immediate primary group, to the extent that it "met his basic needs, offered him affection and esteem from both officers and comrades, supplied him with a sense of power, and adequately regulated his relations with authority. . . ." The acceptance of secondary symbols was of significance only "to the extent that these secondary symbols became directly associated with primary gratifications." There was also recognition of the significance to the primary group of the continued functioning of top command and supply echelons.[7]

Popular literature of World War II also contained significant descriptions of primary group situations. Notable among these was the work of Mauldin, the cartoonist, whose characters, Willie and Joe, became stereotypes of the infantryman, as well as objects of identification. Prominent among the sentiments depicted was the mitigating effect that risk had on differences between status groups. Willie and Joe were consistently closer to their company commander than they were to their status peers at battalion headquarters.[8]

Thus at the beginning of the Korean conflict the significance of the primary group for combat role motivation was well established. However, isolated from the relational context in which it developed, the conception of the primary group tends to be broad and undifferentiated. Within such a context, the term "buddy" has two levels of meaning. Specifically, it identifies interpersonal choices and primary group relationships. Generally, it describes status group peers in military organization. The conception of buddies as status group peers can be extended to an explanation of military organization as a social system.

## Solidarity and the social system

Buddy relationships were established and maintained within the context of military organization as a social system. In this system, one aspect—the chain of command or system of authority—was the primary point of reference. All important offices in the chain of command beyond the squad were occupied by officers; officers and authority being frequently thought of together. The chain of command is a system of positions, however, and the authority is in the position.

Thus only a person who had a command relationship with another "in the performance of duty" could legitimately require compliance with an order. An officer could not "prefer charges" against a subordinate who was not under his command. He could merely make a written complaint to the subordinate's commander, who would then decide whether an offense had been committed, and if so, administer the punishment or refer the complaint to a higher echelon for determination. A staff officer or a first sergeant had legitimate authority only insofar as it was derived from their commanding officers. Hence authority was an element of the position, not of the social rank of the person who occupied the position.

The chain of command is, however, a deceptively simple scheme of the operation of the company. Division of all members into two status groups, and the distribution of rank corresponding to position held, tended to reinforce the chain of command.

lem of ammunition resupply in an attack. Rounds expended can only be replaced by personnel who move out of dug-in defensive positions, or by risking the chance that ammunition bearers will not catch up with the assault.

6. Samuel A. Stouffer, and others, *The American Soldier: Studies in Social Psychology in World War II* (Princeton, N.J.: Princeton University Press, 1949).

7. Edward A. Shils, and Morris Janowitz, "Cohesion and Disintegration in the Wehrmacht in World War II," *Public Opinion Quarterly*, 12 (Summer, 1948), pp. 280–315.

8. Bill Mauldin, *Up Front* (New York: Henry Holt and Co., 1945).

Increasing the risk to which all members of the company were exposed weakened the chain of command.

The battlefield situation was the prototype relationship between officers and enlisted men throughout military organization. Dominating all else was the probability that in a combat event and as a result of the officer's command, some members of the formation would be killed or wounded. Second, in the intensive system of interpersonal relationships existing among those who moved out in the attack, was a potential for collective defiance of the task demanded by the organization. Third, there was the problem of adequate reward for those who conformed and moved forward in the assault. Survival, the greatest reward, was a chance of the situation rather than something to be dispensed by the commander. The organization could offer nothing more than symbols of compliance in the form of decorations for valor.

The platoon leader occupied the lowest position of all officers in the chain of command. As the degree of risk increased, the intensity and frequency of the platoon leader's interaction with enlisted men increased, and, correspondingly, significant interaction with status peers decreased. The more he participated in their activities, the more he tended to share the sentiments of the men he commanded, and his willingness to use the sanctions available to him diminished correspondingly.

Yet the situations in which his authority was required were more crucial than those encountered by commanders at higher echelons. First, the chances were greater that the men he commanded would deviate from his orders because the risks of compliance were greater. Second, he was intimately associated with the men he commanded. Third, the sanctions at his disposal were of no immediate value if defiance occurred in the assault. The rifleman who refused to advance could only be punished by repeated threats of sanctions to be imposed when the battle was over.[9]

Besides these problems in using authority, the commander had to make punishment appear more unpleasant than the risks of combat. For a rifleman, tried by a Summary or Special Court Martial, only a fine would have been a penalty. If there was a sentence of confinement, the offender would be transferred to a rear echelon stockade to serve out his sentence, and this would be a reward rather than a penalty. The result was to make sanctions and courts-martial more effective in prospect than in deed.

Authority was thus likely to fail if used alone. It worked only because it was supported by "manipulations:" indirect or symbolic acts which induced implicitly the desired behavior.[10] Such acts had the objective of creating a condition of generalized individual compliance with the ideals of the organization. They may have taken the form of an elaborate ritual such as a parade. They may have been as subtle as occasional breaches in the rigid limits of the social order by visits to the sick, or informal welfare inquiries while on formal inspection tours. They might have been as pointed as the presentation of an award for an exceptionally aggressive action, or for a wound incurred in the organization's battle.

The elaborate system of regulations and conventions applicable to officers as a status group functioned as a resource for manipulation. We have mentioned that authority was invested in positions, not in the status group attributes of the occupants. However, the association between status group membership and degree of authority was reinforced by permitting only officers to occupy significant positions in the chain of command. Thus even if a platoon had no officer, the platoon sergeant could not be the platoon leader unless he was made an officer. If there were no officers in the company, the first sergeant would command but he would not be the company commander. Hence there was a consistent relationship between the authority of these positions and their monopolization by officers as a status group.

There were procedures to ensure that the officer viewed himself—and was perceived by enlisted men —as having a relatively greater investment in the larger organization than in his platoon and the men

9. Collective defiance most often occurs in combat as a passive refusal to move. It is legitimated when the organization describes a unit as being "pinned down." At this point the organization recognizes a collective definition of the probability of survival as being less than the chances of death and wounding, and the futility of invoking sanctions.

10. Morris Janowitz, "Changing Patterns of Organizational Authority: The Military Establishment," *Administrative Science Quarterly*, 3 (March, 1959), pp. 473–93.

with whom he lived. These procedures began when he arrived in the Division and continued until he reached his platoon. At each echelon he was introduced to his superior commanders personally and indoctrinated with the values of the organizational level through which he was passing. Even while isolated from his peers and living on the line with his platoon, the protocol of inspections maintained his identification with the larger organization.

When officers were together, as in the reserve period, their sentiments were the ideals of the organization. They were more intimately involved in the ceremonial activity of the organization, referring often to the traditions or abstract symbols of the organization. Technical competence was identified with status group solidarity. Initiative, aggressiveness, and tactical proficiency were the attributes they used in evaluating one another and the enlisted men.

The effect of continued solidarity with the superior status group was to develop in the officer a conception of himself as having "status potency," that is, the capacity to induce compliance by virtue of his status group affiliation alone. Although officers were provided with the right to invoke more severe sanctions than noncommissioned officers, ideally the "good officer" (among officers) was one who could get results without employing any sanctions. So long as his status potency was recognized he was seldom required to administer punishment.

When status potency failed and sanctions were required, he was sensitive to the evaluations of his status group peers. So long as he could contain the offense and punishment to his own unit, the apparent loss of his status potency was not recognized. Serious offenses, however, required that he relinquish his responsibility to a higher echelon. The subsequent trial procedure entailed an investigation by colleagues and a consequent evaluation of the effectiveness of his status attributes. Status potency and attempts to maintain the image of the good officer thus tended to mitigate the use of the sanctions actually available.

The mobility pattern among officers also fostered identification with the larger organization, for they rarely remained in the rifle company throughout their tour of duty in Korea. Enlisted men usually remained in their initial assignment and rarely moved to positions of less risk except within the company. Officers were initially assigned to a rifle platoon, then moved to the weapons platoon, where they did not have to lead patrols. The next step was to company executive officer and the management of supply and administration. One officer might become company commander, but the others would probably move to a staff position or service unit to complete their tours.

The battlefield situation itself often provided a manipulative resource in the form of the "status legend," an exaggerated descriptive narrative of a combat experience, varying according to the status vantage point of the observer. Status legends were confined to battalion or more remote commanders. The legend originated in a context of ambiguous feelings toward the commander, then an event occurred that structured the men's attitudes toward the commander even though he might not have recognized the event as important. His behavior during the event was subsequently evaluated and elaborated by persons at varying status levels. Thus formulated, the story was passed on from oldtimer to replacement, becoming a durable element in the sentiments of the unit, surviving long after the commander's departure and the membership of the unit had changed completely.

Positive status legends often referred to the commander's democratic eccentricities, his concern for human life, or his tolerance of deviations from the policies of the larger organization. Such positive legends assured the commander of warm, affectionate responses and willing cooperation from his subordinates. Other legends, however, tended to create an aura in which the commander's every step was critically and negatively evaluated. Whether positive or negative, the status legend expressed the troops' conception of their commander in battle, in an extension of behavior expected in his position.

The differentiation of officers as a status group was the organizational response to a problem of control. In the rifle platoon—the point at which control was crucial—there was a tendency for the effectiveness of specific sanctions to be dissipated. The willingness of officers to use the sanctions available to them was compromised by their solidarity with the men under their command. Traditions and procedures which reinforced the officer's solidarity with other officers ensured his fidelity to the norms of the larger organization.

### RANK AND AUTHORITY

Within the chain of command the relative importance of each position was indicated by the rank stipulated for the position. Thus each squad leader should have been a sergeant, the platoon sergeant a master sergeant, and the company commander a captain. Rank also carried perquisites as rewards for the persons who occupied such positions to ensure their fidelity to the organization at a cost of increasing the social distance between themselves and men with relatively less rank.

The lowest position in the chain of command was the squad leader. His fidelity, like that of the platoon leader, had to be maintained; but unlike the platoon leader, he was an enlisted man. At this time, in Korea, squad leaders did not have enough rank to differentiate them from other members of the squad. There were time-in-grade requirements which few men were able to meet before they rotated. Occasionally men with the stipulated grade but without combat experience came in as replacements and were assigned as squad leaders. Then the acting squad leader was "bumped" and had to move down a notch as did everyone else in the squad. The effect was to reduce the significance of formal social ranking within the squad and platoon and to increase the informal importance of seniority.

Many men were reluctant to accept positions of increased authority when they knew that the organization could not give them rank with the positions. The prospect that an acting squad leader would be "bumped" by a replacement squad leader also limited his effectiveness in the role. An acting leader's relationships with his peers was always threatened when he attempted to exert the authority of the position without the corresponding rank. Hence, few men were motivated to move up to higher positions when mobility involved little probability of reward but almost certainly the weakening of relationships with the peers to whom they might be compelled to return.

The uncertainty of rank tended to exaggerate the significance of the position held within the squad. Although the rank for the job might not be available, the job had to be done. In the order of rank formally prescribed by the organization the squad leader was followed by his assistant, then in descending order, the automatic rifleman and his assistant, and six riflemen. But members of the squad thought of this sequence as indicating the order of seniority and the mobility pattern within the squad rather than a hierarchy of rank or skill.

Although the grade did not "count for much" in the platoon or company, it was expected to be a source of prestige in the larger society, through the family and the work group. Promotion disappointment became increasingly severe as the rotation date approached. The rank held at discharge was expected to affect civilian employment opportunities. Men who had been performing in a higher position had frequently written letters to family and friends, describing their responsibilities and mentioning the stipulated rank as a measure of the importance of their positions. Some received letters addressed to them in the grade of the position to which they had been temporarily assigned. Their apprehension was expressed as an expectation that, if one should return home as a private, "they'll think that I've been giving them a line all the time."

Among officers rank was as uncertain as it was for enlisted men. Although the stipulated rank for the position of company commander was that of captain, in this company the commander was a first lieutenant. The only requirement for promotion to first lieutenant was eighteen months in the grade of second lieutenant. Officers were distinguished not by their relative rank, which was not so different, but the positions they held. When this company commander left the company area and the persons who identified him with his position, he was recognized only by the insignia of his rank, which was that of a very junior member of his status group. The mobility pattern among officers also tended to emphasize positions rather than rank. Just as the arrival of a new man in the platoon initiated a process of mobility, the assignment of a new officer to the regiment made it possible for a company commander or a senior platoon leader to move to battalion or regimental headquarters, as the new officer was assigned to the lowest vacancy created.

In summary, because rank so rarely corresponded with the position for which it was stipulated, it became a random factor and position was correspondingly exaggerated in significance. Authority appeared to be derived exclusively from the position occupied rather than supported by the rank of the occupant which contributed to a further deterioration in the significance of rank.

RISK, RESERVE, AND RITUAL

The location of the rifle platoon and company in relation to the larger organization fostered the development of a defensive value system. Spatially, they were exposed to maximum risk. Socially, they were the ultimate recipients of most orders issued by higher echelons. Their value system was defensive in the sense that most of the norms that could be articulated justified resistance to the demands of the organization. Their norms tended to discourage the aggressive kind of behavior that was the ideal of the organization, and deprecated the symbols that the organization bestowed to reward such behavior. Thus united, members of the platoon comprised a group with a potential for collective action independent of orders given by the designated leaders of the chain of command.

The longer a unit was "on the line" directly confronting the enemy, the more intensive their relationship became, and the more their behavior deviated from the norms of the organization. Even the officers who lived with their platoons tended to think like their men, and to minimize their own contacts with higher echelons. Relations between the company commander and the platoon leaders became increasingly contentious. The probable response of the latter in executing orders in situations involving great risk was accordingly uncertain.

When an organization reached this stage, it was described as having "low morale" and withdrawn into reserve for "retraining." This is not to say that the senior commander would withdraw a unit for this reason, but that such conditions were usually present at the time the unit was withdrawn. The relief of a unit depended on many other factors, including the very practical one of having another unit in reserve to replace the unit withdrawn.

The reserve situation was a time for maximum impact from the larger organization with all members in range of continuous surveillance by the company and senior commanders. They were far enough away from combat to line up in parade formations, in the ideal shape of the Table of Organization. Dwelling arrangements were such that men lived together as squads or platoons, rather than as *ad hoc* formations determined by the size of the "living bunker" on the line. The officers lived together as a group rather than sharing bunkers with the men of their platoons, as they had done on the line.

Administrative activity predominated through the day. Property shortages were accounted for, replacements received and assigned. Improvised personnel situations which had been kept loose and flexible on the line were now brought up for reconsideration and if affirmed, became solid arrangements. A training program was carried on which stressed adherence to correct tactical doctrine as compared to improvised solutions to real combat events mentioned by members of the unit.

Withdrawal to reserve also limited the commander's range of judgment. On the line, the commander was relatively isolated from controls by the larger organization. He was expected to make decisions in terms of his personal judgment, without reference to the higher echelon. Since he controlled the channels of communication to other units and echelons, negative information about his decisions could be effectively contained. But in reserve, as in garrison, units were in close and constant contact with each other. A decision by one commander with respect to a particular form of delinquency immediately became a factor in his evaluation by superiors and status peers. Accordingly, his area of discretion was sharply reduced.

This spatial arrangement enabled the next higher echelon to impose on the company a condition of "command saturation." The shortened lines of communication permitted more detailed stipulation of organizational activities in the form of standard operating procedures, routine compliance reports, and official policies. In the place of the environment of creative freedom existing on the line, the commander was now required to become a manager, executing in mechanical routine the decisions originally formulated by higher echelons. His competence here was evaluated in terms of his knowledge of a large number of routine operations and gimmicks, and a general avoidance of ambiguous situations in which the rules could not be applied.

In this environment a ceremonial combat emerged in the form of the garrison *contest*. The norms guiding competing commanders were derived from real combat situations, and the ideals of the organization remained those of the combat crisis. But the measures of achievement were the only ones available in the reserve location. Two or more commanders were confronted with an opportunity to be comparatively evaluated by a higher commander. Extraordinary judgment or effort, analogous to their behavior in a combat crisis, was presumed necessary to excel other commanders. Members of the unit, in turn, had to be induced by persuasive techniques to provide the commander with material that could be used as measures of competence. The situations utilized for the contest were typically those in which only manipulative techniques were appropriate, such as athletic events or contributions to charities.

Each subordinate commander assumed that a relative superiority in the outcome of the contest would be evaluated by the higher commander as evidence of greater competence in inducing collective effort among the members of his unit, although such an assumption was rarely stated explicitly. The event was represented to members of the unit as an opportunity to demonstrate collective superiority over competing units. Since the subordinate commander represented his unit to superior commanders, the collective achievements of the unit became a measure of the competence of the subordinate commander.

The move from positions on the line to the reserve location was accompanied by a shift from instrumental to expressive or ceremonial activities. An awareness of their relationship to combat activity was maintained only by such rituals as the parade formation, while actual experiences in combat were evaluated as good or bad in terms of the degree to which they coincided with tactical doctrine. The intensity of interpersonal relationships declined with the removal of risk and the need for mutual dependency, and because of transfers within the company. The solidarity of the company as a whole declined when they lost their identity and distinctive activity by merger with the larger organization.

### SOLIDARITY AND THE LARGER ORGANIZATION

Contacts between the company and higher echelons were intensified in the reserve location, but even on the line the company was almost completely dependent on the larger organization for supplies. The sentiments regulating the use and disposal of supplies or "property" differentiated between the company as a component unit and as a social system.

The organization itself provided two kinds of supplies: those which were used up rapidly ("expendable") such as food and fuel, and those used by a succession of persons, such as weapons and vehicles. The second type, referred to as "property," was strongly identified with authority, in the sense that it belonged to the organization and was only "lent" to the person using it. This identification was fostered by making the commander personally responsible when property was lost or damaged. Officers were graded on efficiency reports in terms of their "cost consciousness."

When some items of property could not be accounted for, the responsible officer had two possible courses of action. First, he could attribute the loss to the negligence of the user and require that the cost of the item be deducted from the enlisted man's pay. The advantage of this method was that the "Statement of Charges" did not pass through command channels. After signature by the man admitting responsibility for the loss, it was merely forwarded to the personnel officer at the division rear echelon where the necessary action was taken. Second, the responsible officer could originate a "Report of Survey." Such action ordinarily used for major expensive items, or when individual responsibility could not be fixed, indicated that the loss was attributed to combat action or other "fair wear and tear."

The Report of Survey was a last resort, however, because it passed through command channels, involving an investigation by an officer from a higher headquarters and an explicit evaluation of the responsible officer's behavior in relation to property. Usually the investigating officer determined that the property was lost without negligence. The company commander was then excused from responsibility and replacement items issued. Less frequently but always possibly, the company commander could be found responsible because of the inadequate supervision of supply accounts, lack of good judgment in property utilization, or "poor leadership," because men had abandoned their equipment wantonly. Thus the Report of Survey was a risky venture in relation to the larger organization. The objective became one of minimizing deficiencies in supply accounts, not because this was in conformity with the organization's ideals, but because it reduced the chances of involvement with the next higher echelon.

The enlisted man primarily responsible for property within the company was the supply sergeant. He was the only person who left the company area frequently, meeting supply sergeants of other companies at supply points and depots. These colleagues were united by a system of "scrounging." Whenever the company moved into a new area, items abandoned by the previous unit were recovered and turned into the supply room. In traveling from one unit to another he found other apparently discarded or carelessly guarded equipment. When a property discrepancy developed in his own company, he had a "barter bank" with which to approach the supply sergeants of other units.

"Scrounging" was illegal. It violated procedures stipulated by the organization for revealing discrepancies and for disposing of surpluses. It protected supply sergeants as colleagues from having to reveal a shortage to their company commanders. Since the exchanges always took place between supply sergeants as enlisted men, the chain of command was not involved. However, company commanders tolerated and often encouraged scrounging because it was a simple way to keep the supply accounts in good condition for inspections by higher echelons and reduced the need for initiating Reports of Survey.

There was a contrasting set of attitudes toward "personal property." The contrast originated in the fact that organization property was identified with the chain of command and could be "shared" only in a very formal sense. The physical environment of the company on the line, dominated by proximity to enemy observation and fire, necessarily limited the amounts and kinds of personal possessions that could be retained. There were few sources for such goods with no post exchange or native store regularly available. New items of a personal nature could be obtained only from home, or by bringing them back from Japan.

Formal rules against theft of personal property were reinforced by an elaborate system of attitudes regulating the use and disposal of all such possessions regardless of their value. These items either had to be carried by the owner, or left unguarded in his bunker. The only protection for such property was the honor of every person who had access to it.

Opposed to this conception of personal property, however, was the norm of "sharing," generated in a bleak environment where possessions were scarce. Packages from home derived their unique significance from the fact that they were so easily shared. Packages symbolized all personal property and formed the basis for the development of a ritual relating it to the combat situation.

For example, one man said:

> If a guy didn't share, maybe someday he'd be in a tough spot and the buddy would remember it and think about when you didn't make an offer. You don't always have a chance to do a favor in combat, but if you share everything, you can be pretty sure that your buddy will remember it if you need help.

Another man, who had been identified by others as a "dud," said:

> Even though a guy has been treating you pretty rough, he'll offer you something from his package and it helps you forget what he said about you. Just like at home, you'd try to make up with a guy by buying him a beer. When you pass a package around you show that everyone is your buddy.

The discrimination between organization and personal property reflected a differentiation between the chain of command and the system of buddy relations. Organization property was considered an aspect of the authority system which could be manipulated to defend the company from intervention by higher echelons. Personal property was associated with the norm of sharing and strengthened the system of interpersonal relationships.

## Solidarity and military effectiveness

What was the relationship between solidarity and military effectiveness?

The primary basis for solidarity in the platoon and company was the recognition of mutual risk. A set of norms so regulated their behavior as to minimize that risk. On this basis buddy relationships were established and maintained. The effectiveness of the sanctions available to the chain of command depended on their meaning in a context of risk. Officers as a status group maintained their independence insofar as they could remove or protect themselves from the consensus induced by mutual risk.

Traditional explanations which neglected the significance of risk were examined. Thus individual identification with the larger unit did not appear to enhance effectiveness because there was little awareness of the existence of such a relationship. Nor was effectiveness increased by peer emulation of persons who had received awards for conforming to organizational ideals. Such attributes of masculinity as aggressiveness and initiative also appeared to have minimal influence on effectiveness.

At this point it would appear that solidarity and the effectiveness demanded by the organization were not compatible. There were, however, some aspects of solidarity which converged with the objectives of the organization and promoted effectiveness.

First, the organization permitted the norms of the buddy system to define the limits of effectiveness. The minimum contribution was that which fell below the standards exemplified by the dud. The maximum effort was that of and beyond the actions of the hero. Within this range of expected behavior, the larger organization was able to function within predictable limits.

Second, events which reinforced the soldier's relationship to some meaningful element of the larger society—especially his family—correspondingly strengthened his relationship to the organization. In a sense, the infantryman communicated with his family through the organization. The symbols understood by the family were those of the organization (such as rank), not of the buddy system. The organization also provided symbolic evidence of the soldier's career in the unit, factors which would be of greater significance to his peers in the larger society than among his buddies in the organization. This may be one reason that "mail call" is of such critical importance in combat, and to a lesser extent, in military service generally. Letters represent the soldier's major contact with the social unit that reinforces his desire to serve faithfully and under great hardship. The conception of his role as a citizen of a community or member of a family was influenced by the letters written him by persons whose evaluations of him were very important, or by the clippings they enclosed with their letters. When the time for rotation approached and he anticipated the reaction of his family and civilian friends, he became increasingly aware of the symbols that he had previously deprecated with his peers.

Third, status group solidarity enabled the organization to maintain control at the level of greatest risk: the rifle platoon. On the line, officers were isolated from their status peers. When sharing the risks and hardships of their men they tended to develop solidarity with them and to support deviations from the norms of the larger organization, although their ultimate loyalty to the organization was effectively maintained. Technical competence as commanders was identified with status group solidarity. Concrete and ceremonial evidence of their affiliation with the organization as a whole was continuously provided. Since the duration of their exposure was limited, acts of valor and dedication to the ideals of the organization could be expected to enhance their chances of moving to positions of less risk.

DAVID STREET

# The Inmate Group in Custodial and Treatment Settings

Previous accounts of correctional institutions generally have portrayed these organizations as handicapped by the informal inmate system. This system, it has been said, invariably is built around norms and values of solidary opposition to the official system and to staff, and its objectives are to minimize interference and maximize accommodations from staff, to enhance inmates' access to both official and unofficial values, to exert vigorous control over communication between inmates and staff, and to sanction an ideal model of behavior in which the inmate becomes a master at "playing it cool." So far as this system succeeds, inmates released from the institution may leave more "prisonized" than rehabilitated. Such a description often has been treated as universally valid for adult institutions,[1] and the same account appears in generally accepted descriptions of juvenile institutions.[2]

Applicable as this image of the inmate system

1. For example, Sykes and Messinger, reviewing over 35 studies of correctional organizations, conclude that "Despite the number and diversity of prison populations, observers of such groups have reported only one strikingly pervasive value system . . . [which] commonly takes the form of an explicit code . . . The maxims are usually asserted with great vehemence . . . and violations call forth a diversity of sanctions ranging from ostracism to physical violence . . . The chief tenets . . . [include] those maxims that caution: *Don't interfere with inmate interests*, which center of course in serving the least possible time and enjoying the greatest possible number of pleasures and privileges in prison. The most inflexible directive [is] *Never rat on a con* . . . The prisoners must present a united front against their guards no matter how much this may cost in terms of personal sacrifice." (Gresham M. Sykes and Sheldon L. Messinger, "The Inmate Social System," in Richard A. Cloward, *et al.*, *Theoretical Studies in Social Organization of the Prison*, New York: Social Science Research Council, 1960, pp. 5–8.)

2. For example, Lloyd E. Ohlin and William C. Lawrence, "Social Interaction among Clients as a Treatment Problem," *Social Work*, 4 (April, 1959), pp. 3–14. Similar treatments of the inmate group in juvenile correctional organization are found in Richard A. Cloward, "The Correctional Institution for Juveniles: A Discussion of Selected Problems," paper read at the New York School of Social Work seminar on juvenile institutions, 1956; and George P. Grosser, "The Role of Informal Inmate Groups in Change of Values," *Children*, 5 (January–February, 1958), pp. 25–29. Other analyses suggesting that the inmate system in these institutions operates principally to oppose or circumvent the organization's aims include Howard Polsky's study of a cottage in a treatment institution, reported in "Changing Delinquent Subcultures: A Social Psychological Approach," *Social Work*, 4 (October, 1959), pp. 3–16, and *Cottage Six—The Social System of Delinquent Boys in Residential Treatment*, New York: Russell Sage Foundation, 1962; and Lloyd Ohlin's observations on a training school for girl delinquents, "Reduction in Role Conflict in Institutional Staff," *Children*, 5 (March–April, 1958), pp. 65–69.

An earlier version of this paper was read at the meetings of the Midwest Sociological Society, Milwaukee, Wisc., April, 1963. This research was carried out in part under a predoctoral fellowship from the National Institute of Mental Health, Public Health Service, and was done in close association with a comprehensive study of juvenile correctional institutions directed by Robert D. Vinter and Morris Janowitz and supported by NIMH grant M-2104. Not only the data from this project but also the ideas and criticisms of the participants were of great help.

Reprinted from *American Sociological Review*, February, 1965, pp. 40–55, by permission of the author and publisher. (Copyright 1965 by the American Sociological Association.)

may be to many penal institutions, it has several deficiencies as a general description and analysis. First, most of the research on which it is based involves case studies and unsystematic observation and has lacked adequate methods to assess similarities and differences between organizations or even to make satisfactory estimates of any variability in inmate orientations within the single population studied. Yet, the notion that inmate attachment to oppositional groups and culture varies has been at least implicit in much of this research,[3] and it is clearly explicit in recent systematic research such as the Wheeler and Garabedian studies of socialization in the prison.[4]

Second, the "solidary opposition" account fails to consider adequately the consequences for the inmate social system of changes in the larger organization, particularly the introduction of modern treatment ideology and technology.[5] Treatment programs, if they go beyond the simple insertion of psychotherapeutic counseling into the institutional program, require fundamental alterations in staff behavior toward inmates. The distinctive sociological character of the correctional institution and the deviant background predispositions of the inmates may indeed give rise to certain patterns of group development in all correctional organizations, but it is equally probable that variations in the institutional context generate changes in the inmate system.

Third, applied *a priori* to juvenile correctional institutions, the generally accepted account ignores important differences between these organizations and those for adults, including the relatively short stay and presumed lesser criminality of the juveniles and the possibility that many of the social forms that constitute severe deprivation and degradation in the adult correctional institution, where men are treated like children, may not be so degrading in the juvenile institution.

Finally, many researchers in the correctional field, lacking comparative methods, have been insufficiently sensitive to a significant theoretical question: under what organizational conditions do the members of an organization collectively become committed to or alienated from the official objectives of the organization?[6] By stressing the impact of deprivation and degradation on the inmates and

3. Variation in inmate attitudes and behavior underlies the whole notion of prisonization. See Donald Clemmer, *The Prison Community*, New York: Rinehart, 1958, and the various studies of social types in the prison, for example, Clarence Schrag, "Social Types in a Prison Community," unpublished M.A. thesis, University of Washington, 1944, and his "Leadership among Prison Inmates," *American Sociological Review*, 19 (February, 1954), p. 42, in which he writes of "a number of dissentient minorities [which] resist, at least to some extent, the dominant influence of the typical leader group."

4. Stanton Wheeler, "Socialization in Correctional Communities," *American Sociological Review*, 26 (October, 1961), pp. 697–712, and Peter C. Garabedian, "Social Roles and Processes of Socialization in the Prison Community," *Social Problems*, 11 (Fall, 1963), pp. 139–52, and "Legitimate and Illegitimate Alternatives in the Prison Community," *Sociological Inquiry*, 32 (Spring, 1962), pp. 172–84. See also the discussion of the inmate society as made up of three subcultures dependent on latent identities, in John Irwin and Donald R. Cressey, "Thieves, Convicts, and the Inmate Culture," *Social Problems*, 10 (Fall, 1962), pp. 142–55, along with the contributions by Wheeler, Schrag, and Donald L. Garrity to Donald Cressey (ed.), *The Prison: Studies in Institutional Organization and Change*, New York: Holt, Rinehart, & Winston, 1961.

5. The major empirical works directly addressing the problems of the inmate group but taking exception to the general view of it are studies of treatment-oriented camps for young offenders by Oscar Grusky, "Organizational Goals and the Behavior of Informal Leaders," *American Journal of Sociology*, 65 (July, 1959), pp. 59–67, and Bernard Berk, "Informal Social Organization and Leadership among Inmates in Treatment and Custodial Prisons," unpublished Ph.D. dissertation, University of Michigan, 1961. Other writings deriving from the same study as the present report, and directly relevant to many parts of it, include Robert Vinter and Morris Janowitz, "Effective Institutions for Juvenile Offenders: A Research Statement," *Social Service Review*, 33 (June, 1959), pp. 118–31; Mayer Zald, "The Correctional Institution for Juvenile Offenders: An Analysis of Organization 'Character,'" *Social Problems*, 8 (Summer, 1960), pp. 57–67, and "Comparative Analysis and Measurement of Organizational Goals: The Case of Correctional Institutions for Delinquents," *Sociological Quarterly*, 4 (1963), pp. 206–30; Rosemary Conzemius Sarri, "Organizational Patterns and Client Perspectives in Juvenile Correctional Institutions," unpublished Ph.D. dissertation, University of Michigan, 1962; Juvenile Correctional Institutions Project, *Research Report*, Ann Arbor: University of Michigan, 1961; and David Street, "Inmate Social Organization: A Comparative Study of Juvenile Correctional Institutions," unpublished Ph.D. dissertation, University of Michigan, 1962.

6. After considerable study and discussion, informal groups have come to be viewed as neither wholly reflective of the larger structure nor wholly determinative of it; rather, the role of these groups in the attainment of organizational ends varies according to the organizational context. Students of industrial plants generally have stressed the negative impact of informal groups on productivity (for example, see the classic discussions of informal relations and structures in F. J. Roethlisberger and W. J. Dickson, *Management and the Worker*, Cam-

the ways in which the inmates defend themselves, these researchers have developed a plausible hypothesis: that the inmate group serves the function of alleviating its members' deprivation and degradation.[7] Yet, they have failed to go farther and inquire into the effects of varying levels of deprivation or analyze the conditions necessary to stimulate, permit, and sustain the successful use of such a group solution to the problems of deprivation.

In contrast, this paper will treat inmate group patterns as problematic, bringing a comparative perspective to bear on data from several juvenile institutions. This analysis should have implications for the general proposition that the characteristics and functions of informal groups vary with the larger organizational context. Hypotheses linking the larger organization to the informal inmate system were developed by considering first, the implications of variations in goal emphasis among juvenile institutions, and second, the characteristics of the inmate group, conceived as a problem-solving system.

## Goals and institutions

Goals may usefully be regarded as the conception of the organization's tasks held by the members whose positions make their definitions of events authoritative. Their conception of task is expressed in their views of the organization's desired end product, the "materials" it must work with, the ideal and practical requirements of the task, and the organization's distinctive competencies for it. The goals imply and set limits upon the organizational technologies seen as appropriate. Thus, goals define as required, or preferred, alternative sets of social relations between staff and inmates.

Analysis of the goals of correctional institutions provides a basis for classifying these organizations along a rough custodial-treatment continuum. This classification reflects the relative emphasis on containing the inmates as against rehabilitating them. More analytically, the continuum incorporates two dimensions of the staff conception of the organization's task: the staff members' view of the actual rehabilitational potential of the inmates, and their concept of the "materials" they have to work with and the implicit "theory of human nature" they apply to these materials.[8] At the custodial extreme, major emphasis is placed on the need to protect the community by containing the inmates within the institution. The inmates are seen as simple, similar, and relatively unchangeable creatures who require simple, routine, conventional handling. To succeed here, the inmate must conform. At the treatment extreme, community and containment are comparatively unimportant, and stress is put on changing the inmate's attitudes and values by increasing his insight or otherwise altering his psychological condition. The inmate's social identity is viewed as problematic, and the inmates are seen as relatively complex beings who need complex, individualized, flexible handling—an attitude that sometimes requites such departures from conventional morality as tolerance of "acting out." To succeed here, the inmate must indicate intra-psychic change. These variations in organizational goals are accompanied by variations in the distribution of power in the organization: as institutions become more treatment-oriented, power to define events flows into the hands of a highly educated and professionalized "clinic staff."

bridge: Harvard University Press, 1941, and Orvis Collins, Melville Dalton and Donald Wray, "Restrictions on Output and Social Cleavage in Industry," *Applied Anthropology*, 5 (1946), pp. 1–14), while sociologists who have studied military organization have traced the positive functions of such groups (Samuel A. Stouffer, *et al.*, *The American Soldier*, Princeton: Princeton University Press, 1949, Vol. II, pp. 130–49; Edward A. Shils, "Primary Groups in the American Army," in Robert K. Merton and Paul F. Lazarsfeld (eds.), *Continuities in Social Research: Studies in the Scope and Method of "The American Soldier,"* New York: Free Press, 1950, pp. 19–22; and Edward A. Shils and Morris Janowitz, "Cohesion and Disintegration of the Wehrmacht in World War II," *Public Opinion Quarterly*, 12 (1948), pp. 280–315). For a recent conception of this problem in general terms, see Amitai Etzioni, *A Comparative Analysis of Complex Organizations*, New York: Free Press, 1961.

7. The inmate system is seen as providing new, deviant standards that allow the inmates to assuage guilt by "rejecting their rejectors" (Lloyd W. McCorckle and Richard Korn, "Resocialization within Walls," *The Annals*, 293 (May, 1954), pp. 88–98), to achieve compensatory status and to benefit from contraband and illegitimate activities (Ohlin and Lawrence, *op. cit.*), and to defend against aggression and exploitation by other inmates (Sykes and Messinger, *op. cit.*). The latter authors, even though they seem to assume that the inmate group is inevitably cohesive and opposed to official goals, also suggest that the extent of deprivation and degradation might predict the inmate group's response (p. 19).

8. On the theory of human nature, see Erving Goffman, "On the Characteristics of Total Institutions: Staff-Inmate Relations," in Cressey, *op. cit.*, p. 78.

These characterizations of the custodial and treatment types of institution are supported by a wide variety of data from the institutions we studied. The institutions were selected non-randomly to insure variation in goals and other dimensions. Each was studied intensively through observation, interviewing, analysis of documents and file data, and administration of questionnaires to virtually all staff members and inmates.[9] Two of the institutions stressed custody; the other two, treatment. Ranked from more custodial to more treatment-oriented and identified by mnemonic labels, they were:

*Dick* (Discipline)—a large (200–250 inmates) public institution which had no treatment program, whose staff felt no lack because of this, and which concentrated on custody, hard work, and discipline.

*Mixter* (Mixed Goals)—a very large (375–420 inmates) public institution with poorly integrated "mixed goals" of custody and treatment. Some treatment was attempted, but this was segregated from the rest of the activities, and for most boys the environment was characterized by surveillance, frequent use of negative sanctions, and other corollaries of an emphasis on custody.

*Milton* (Milieu Therapy)—a fairly large (160–190 inmates) public institution using not only individual therapy but a range of other treatment techniques. This institution resembled Mixter in its bifurcation between treatment and containment staffs and activities, but by and large the clinicians were in control, used treatment criteria, and influenced the nonprofessional staff to allow the inmates considerable freedom.

*Inland* (Individual Therapy)—a small (60–75 inmates) private "residential treatment center" in which the clinicians were virtually in complete control, allowing much freedom to the inmates while stressing the use of psychotherapeutic techniques in an attempt to bring about major personality change.

Limitations of space preclude full analysis and documeatntion of these differences between organizations, which in any case are presented elsewhere,[10] but some indication of their nature may be conveyed by data on staff-inmate ratios and contacts (Table 1), and by data from the staff questionnaire (Table 2). Higher ratios of staff, especially social service staff, to inmates, and higher inmate-social service contacts characterize the treatment institutions. The questionnaire results show that in the more treatment-oriented institutions staff members are more likely (1) to see the organization's goal as producing change in attitudes, values, and insights; (2) to value treatment programs more highly than custodial considerations; (3) to believe that inmates can be rehabilitated; and (4) to believe that adults can have trusting, close, and understanding relations with inmates, the development of such relationships being part of the staff's task. In contrast, staff members in the more custodial organizations are more likely (5) to stress order, discipline, and the use of powerful negative sanctions; (6) to insist on inmate conformity to institutional rules, including immediate response to staff members' demands; (7) to believe in universalistic application of rules; and (8) to have negative attitudes toward informal relations among the inmates, believing that the inmates should keep to themselves. Such attitudinal differences between institutions hold up among cottage parents and in other groups when the respondent's staff position and his education are controlled,[11] and, further, the implied differences in behavior toward the inmates are confirmed by observations made in the institutions of the use of physical punishment, for example. To see how these different institutional environments affect the inmates, let us consider the inmate social system.

## The inmate group

Informal group structure grows out of primary relations among inmates in all institutions, and it

9. Here I shall report findings principally on the four "closed" institutions studied intensively in the juvenile corrections project. Near the end of this paper I shall refer to findings on three additional institutions, not as directly comparable for the problems discussed here. For details of questionnaire administration and other research techniques, see Street, *op. cit.*, pp. 198–202.

10. See especially Juvenile Correctional Institutions Projects, *op. cit.*

11. *Ibid.*, chs. 7 and 9.

***Table 1—Inmate-staff Ratios and Contacts***

| | *CUSTODIAL* | | *TREATMENT* | |
|---|---|---|---|---|
| | *Dick* | *Mixter* | *Milton* | *Inland* |
| Inmate-Staff Ratio | 3.9 | 2.3 | 1.7 | 1.5 |
| Inmate-Social Service Staff Ratio | 125.0 | 45.9 | 22.2 | 15.0 |
| Frequency of Inmate-Social Service Contact[a] | .13 | .47 | .76 | .85 |

[a] Proportion of respondents to inmate questionnaire reporting two or more contacts with social service staff in the last month.

can be assumed to have a significant role in socializing and relating the inmate to the institution, in defining informal norms of inmate behavior and approved sets of values and beliefs, and in defining and allocating valued objects (e.g., contraband) among the inmates. Given the inmate group as a system potentially oriented toward ameliorating its members' deprivation, two major environmental factors could condition its response: (1) variations in the balance of gratifications and deprivations, and (2) variations in the conditions under which the group must attempt to solve its problem—that is, in the patterns of control and authority that the staff exercise over inmate action and behavior.

1. *Variations in the balance of gratifications and deprivations.* By limiting the available supply of rewards and thus creating a high ratio of deprivation to gratification the institution sets the stage for the development of a system for obtaining and distributing scarce values, both licit (e.g., choice job assignments) and illicit (contraband). Development of such a system presupposes that some inmates have access to values in short supply, and that inmates are sufficiently interdependent to set up a system of allocation and stabilize it in role expectations. Continuing access to the valued objects, and various forms of mutual aid, require a division of labor, which in turn is likely to produce a leadership structure reflecting differential power with regard to values within the system. Norms of reciprocity are likely to develop, to limit the advantages of those powerful enough to monopolize scarce values, but the latter nevertheless form a leadership cadre in which power is relatively highly centralized. To the extent that the system is deeply involved in the secretive and illicit transactions of contraband allocation, these leaders may have, at least covertly, very negative attitudes toward the staff and institution. Such leadership cadres might influence the group and make it more hostile to the official system than it otherwise would be.

2. *Variations in staff patterns of control and*

***Table 2—Perspectives of Staff Members, by Institution***[a]

| *Percentages of staff who:* | *CUSTODIAL* | | *TREATMENT* | |
|---|---|---|---|---|
| | *Dick* | *Mixter* | *Milton* | *Inland* |
| 1. Perceive the executive's view of organizational purpose as bringing change in inmate attitudes, values, and insight | 10 | 19 | 38 | 51 |
| 2. Say they would approve of sacrificing custodial security in order to introduce a new treatment program | 41 | 53 | 76 | 80 |
| 3. Say you can change most inmates | 56 | 39 | 72 | 78 |
| 4a. Believe you can trust and have close relationships with delinquents (3-item scale) | 68 | 53 | 79 | 78 |
| 4b. Think staff are expected to develop close relationships with inmates | 19 | 23 | 46 | 54 |
| 4c. Say understanding is important in working with delinquents (3-item scale) | 16 | 32 | 63 | 83 |
| 5a. Think staff must keep order at all times | 58 | 45 | 13 | 14 |
| 5b. Believe delinquents need much discipline (5-item scale) | 76 | 67 | 34 | 15 |
| 5c. Say they would invoke strong sanctions for a wide variety of inmate misbehaviors (5-item index) | 61 | 68 | 24 | 10 |
| 6a. Believe the best way for an inmate to get along is "don't break any rules and keep out of trouble" | 58 | 46 | 8 | 3 |
| 6b. Believe inmate must do what he is told and do it quickly | 92 | 75 | 44 | 16 |
| 7. Believe all inmates should get the same discipline for rule-breaking | 85 | 50 | 30 | 30 |
| 8a. Believe informal inmate groups always or usually have a bad influence | 96 | 26 | 4 | 5 |
| 8b. Believe inmates should keep to themselves | 40 | 38 | 15 | 3 |
| Numbers of Respondents | (57–62) | (115–170) | (105–108) | (37–40) |

[a] Differences in proportions between staff of the two custodial and two treatment institutions are statistically significant at or beyond the .05 level on every item.

*authority.* Rigid and categorical practices of control and authority are likely to facilitate the inmates' recognition of a common fate and their potentialities for collective problem-solving. Differences in authority, general status, age, and often social class, between staff and inmates, generally lead inmates to see each other as members of the same category in all institutions, but the authority structure and its impact vary among institutions. Frequent scheduling of mass activities in the company of other inmates, group punishment, and administering physical punishment before groups of inmates enhance the probability that inmates identify strongly with one another against staff. When, in addition, staff maintain domineering authority relationships and considerable social distance, inmates further perceive themselves as members of a group opposed to staff, and divergent interests between these groups are more fully recognized.

Staff patterns of control and authority also limit inmate association and group elaboration. Thus at the same time that rigorous practice of control and authority stimulate recognition of a common problem and the use of group solutions, they also make such solutions more difficult to achieve. Although only extreme techniques, such as keeping the inmates locked in separate rooms, effectively prevent the emergence of social relations among the inmates,[12] rigorous control could severely limit and structure opportunities for interaction and group formation—particularly the formation of groups covering the entire institution. In this situation, group activities must be conducted on a covert level, involving norms of secrecy and mutual defense against the staff.

## Hypotheses

These two dimensions, gratification-deprivation and patterns of control and authority, link the institutional goals with the responses of the inmate group; both vary between the custodial and treatment settings. On the first of these dimensions, treatment institutions place much less emphasis on degradation ceremonies, the use of powerful sanctions, and denial of impulse gratification, and much greater emphasis on providing incentives, objectives, and experiences that the inmates consider desirable. On patterns of control and authority, treatment institutions place much less stress on surveillance, control over inmate association, restrictions of freedom, rigid conformity to rules, and domination and high social distance in authority relations. The simultaneous effects of these dimensions on informal groups in each type of setting should be as follows:

*The custodial setting.* Because of the high level of deprivation, the group is organized to allocate legitimate and illicit values and provide mutual aid. These functions reflect and generate relatively negative and "prisonized" orientations toward the institution and staff. Although staff control and authority practices increase the need for inmate group solutions, they also handicap interaction and group formation, so that integration and solidarity are relatively underdeveloped. The leaders, highly involved in illicit and secret activities, tend to have a negative orientation toward the institution.

*The treatment setting.* The inmate group is organized more voluntaristically, around friendship patterns. Since the level of deprivation is lower, mutual aid is less necessary, and any ameliorative system tends to lose its market. The group is involved in the allocation of values among its members, but these are positive rewards, more consonant with staff definitions of merit. Staff gives much freer rein to inmate association, so that primary group integration and norms of group solidarity are at a higher level than in the custodial setting. This cohesiveness does not necessarily imply opposition to staff, however, for the inmate group emphasizes more positive norms and perspectives and greater commitment to the institution and staff. Leaders' orientation is also more positive.

Finally, the more positive character of staff behavior toward inmates and the positive orientation of the inmate group generates more positive attitudes toward self among the inmates of treatment institutions than among those in custodial organizations.

Data are not available to test all features of the foregoing contrasts, but a reasonably satisfactory test can be made of the following specific hypotheses:

12. Even this technique is not necessarily effective. See Richard McCleery's account of an adult maximum security unit, "Authoritarianism and the Belief Systems of Incorrigibles," in Donald Cressey (ed.), *The Prison: Studies in Institutional Organization and Change, op. cit.*, pp. 260–306.

1. In the custodial institutions, the dominant tone of the inmate group will be that of opposition and negative, "prisonized" norms and perspectives with regard to institution, staff, and self; in the treatment institutions, positive, cooperative norms and perspectives will dominate.
2. Inmate groups in the custodial institutions will display somewhat lower levels of primary relations and weaker orientations of solidarity than will groups in the treatment institutions.
3. Relatively uncooperative and negative leaders will emerge in the inmate groups of the custodial institutions; relatively cooperative and positive leaders will emerge in the treatment institutions.

## Findings

The hypotheses will be tested here by analyzing results of the inmate questionnaire. The inmates' responses, shown by institution in Table 3, convey the dominant tone of inmate group norms and perspectives.[13]

Findings on all but one of these items support the hypotheses.[14] Inmates in the treatment-oriented institutions more often expressed positive attitudes toward the institution and staff, non-prisonized views of adaptation to the institution, and positive images of self change. The exception is that on the index of "ratting to staff" no difference between custodial and treatment institutions appeared.

*Background attributes and length of stay.* Ques-

13. Indices were derived partly from the results of a factor analysis of inmate responses. For details of this analysis and of the construction of indices, see Street, *op. cit.*, pp. 213–24.

14. I have used statistical tests of difference between groups of respondents heuristically, to help decide whether to deny predicted differences between the custodial and treatment types of organization. Although the non-random selection of institutions, the clustering of all respondents in four organizations, and the sampling of entire institutional populations make use of the word "test" in its strict sense illegitimate, no more appropriate bases for decision-making are available. Note, too, that because the tests (as well as the measures of association presented below) combine the data for each of the pairs of institutions, to highlight the differences between the custodial and treatment types, the results may obscure differences within pairs. Important within-type variation will be discussed in the text.

***Table 3—Inmate Perspectives, by Institution***

| | *CUSTODIAL* | | *TREATMENT* | | |
|---|---|---|---|---|---|
| *Percentage of inmates who:* | *Dick* | *Mixter* | *Milton* | *Inland* | *Statistical significance*[a] |
| Score high positive on summary index of perspectives on the institution and staff[b] | 42 (209) | 44 (364) | 58 (155) | 85 (65) | $p < .01$ |
| Score high on cooperation with staff on summary index of "ratting"[c] | 54 (209) | 46 (364) | 49 (155) | 54 (65) | N.S. |
| Gave a "prisonized" response to question about the best way to get along[d] | 74 (202) | 73 (348) | 55 (151) | 45 (60) | $p < .01$ |
| Gave a "prisonized" response to question about ways to receive a discharge or parole[e] | 59 (187) | 47 (352) | 27 (140) | 13 (65) | $p < .01$ |
| Score positive on self-image index[f] | 38 (188) | 42 (327) | 51 (143) | 79 (60) | $p < .01$ |

[a] Significance refers to the difference between the inmates of the two custodial institutions combined and those of the two treatment institutions.

[b] The specific items summarized by this index were (paraphrased): (1) Is this a place to help, send, or punish boys? (2) Rather be here or in some other institution? (3) Summary: Did you think this would be a good or bad place, and what do you think about it now? (4) Agree that the adults here don't really care what happens to us. (5) Agree that the adults are pretty fair. (6) Agree that adults here can help me. (7) How much has your stay here helped you?

[c] The specific items summarized in this index followed a presentation of hypothetical situations, and were (paraphrased): (1) Should a boy warn an adult that boys plan to rough up his friend? (2) Should he warn an adult that inmates plan to beat up a staff member? (3) Would you tell an adult which boys were stealing from the kitchen, when group punishment was being used? (4) Would you try to talk a boy out of running?

[d] The question was "Regardless of what the adults here say, the best way to get along here is to . . ." ("stay out of the way of the adults but get away with what you can" and "don't break any rules and keep out of trouble" were classified as "prisonized" responses, and "show that you are really sorry for what you did" and "try to get an understanding of yourself," as "non-prisonized").

[e] The question was "*In your own words,* write in what you think a boy has to do to get a parole or discharge from here" (responses of conformity, avoidance of misbehavior, "doing time," and overt compliance were coded as "prisonized").

[f] Those classified as "positive" on the index of self-image said that they had been helped by their stay a great deal or quite a bit and that the way they have been helped was by having "learned something about myself and why I get into trouble," rather than having "learned my lesson."

***Table 4—Percentages of Inmates Positive on Index of Perspectives on Institution and Staff, by Selected Background Characteristics and Institution*[a]**

| | CUSTODIAL | | TREATMENT | |
|---|---|---|---|---|
| | *Dick* | *Mixter* | *Milton* | *Inland* |
| Seriousness of major offense[b] | | | | |
| Less serious | 38 (66) | 52 (75) | 57 (67) | 82 (45) |
| More serious | 42 (140) | 43 (286) | 60 (84) | 90 (20) |
| Number of offenses | | | | |
| Less than 3 | 42 (161) | 52 (40) | 51 (43) | 87 (54) |
| 3 or more | 40 (48) | 43 (307) | 60 (112) | 73 (11) |
| Number of times returned to this institution[c] | | | | |
| None | 44 (156) | 47 (283) | 62 (135) | 84 (63) |
| One or more | 31 (52) | 38 (78) | 29 (17) | 100 (2) |
| Previous institutionalization of any kind[d] | | | | |
| None | 42 (191) | 48 (295) | 61 (118) | 94 (16) |
| Some | 33 (15) | 33 (66) | 50 (34) | 83 (6) |
| Age | | | | |
| Under 16 | 34 (94) | 50 (204) | 56 (121) | 85 (41) |
| 16 and over | 47 (114) | 40 (160) | 62 (34) | 83 (24) |
| Race | | | | |
| White | 43 (181) | 47 (245) | 62 (104) | 82 (55) |
| Non-white | 24 (25) | 40 (116) | 48 (48) | 100 (10) |
| I. Q.[e] | | | | |
| 90 and below | 30 (44) | 45 (120) | 58 (41) | 80 (5) |
| 91 and above | 37 (38) | 43 (203) | 64 (56) | 85 (55) |
| Family situation | | | | |
| Intact, no problems | 46 (95) | 49 (204) | 62 (42) | 80 (39) |
| Not intact, or problems | 36 (111) | 40 (157) | 56 (108) | 92 (26) |
| Rural-urban origin[f] | | | | |
| "Rural" | 41 (208) | 50 (126) | 55 (107) | 100 (3) |
| "Urban" | ... (0) | 43 (235) | 64 (45) | 85 (60) |
| Occupation of father or other head of house-household | | | | |
| White collar | 22 (18) | 71 (21) | 63 (8) | 78 (18) |
| Blue collar or not in labor force | 42 (179) | 44 (330) | 58 (141) | 85 (34) |

[a] Data were obtained from institutional files. The index of perspectives on institution and staff is described in Table 3.

[b] The "more serious" category includes arson, forgery, sex offenses, breaking and entering, and crimes of violence, but excludes truancy, "incorrigibility," "maladjustment," theft, and vandalism.

[c] The Milton figures underestimate the actual number of returnees to some unknown degree because ordinarily only those who are re-committed to the institution, after having been supervised for several months following release by another state agency, are entered in institutional records as returnees. Others, returned during the period of supervision, generally are not so classified.

[d] Information on the majority of cases at Inland was missed due to coding error.

[e] The majority of inmates at Dick were not tested.

[f] "Urban" inmates are from counties with at least one city of 90,000 or more; "rural" inmates come from counties that do not have such a city.

tion immediately arises as to whether these differences in perspectives on the institution and staff, adaptation, and self might not reflect variations in inmates' predispositions rather than variations in the institutional setting. A careful analysis of the impact, by institution, of delinquency history, past institutional record, age, race, IQ, family situation, urban-rural background, and social class indicates a negative answer to this question.[15]

Table 4 shows that the direction of the effect of each of the background variables on perspectives varies from institution to institution, and that the custodial-treatment differences in perspective hold up when background attributes are controlled. In nearly every instance, the inmates of both treatment institutions were more likely to have positive perspectives on staff and institution than the inmates of either custodial institution. The three exceptions to this predicted pattern were: (1) among those with fewer offenses, Mixter inmates (51 per cent positive) did not differ from those in Milton (50 per cent positive); (2) disproportionately few (29 per cent) of the Milton inmates classified as returnees had positive perspectives; and (3) a disproportionately large number of positive responses came from Mixter inmates with white-collar backgrounds.

The first of these exceptions suggests that a portion of the relatively negative over-all response at Mixter may be a result of its heavy recruitment of inmates with many offenses. But this would not explain why those with three or more offenses are so negative compared with similar inmates at Milton and Inland. The second exception is probably a result of the fact that the Milton returnees, as indicated in the note to the table, are not directly comparable with the others, apparently constituting an especially "hard core." The last exception may simply reflect the small number of "white-collar" inmates at both Mixter and Milton. Altogether, these exceptions do not challenge the conclusion that these background attributes cannot explain the observed differences between types of institution.

Similarly, interinstitutional variations were not simply a reflection of the fact that the treatment institutions usually keep their inmates longer. Data on this point may also be used to assess the degree to which the prisonization model or one of its variants "fits" these institutions.[16] Figure 1, graphing positive perspectives on the institution and staff against length of stay, indicates that differences between types of institution cannot be accounted for by differences in average length of stay. Inmates of the treatment institutions are more likely to express positive perspectives at almost every point in time. Within the custodial institutions, the overall trend is for the proportion negative to increase with length of stay. Although this tendency toward increasing negativism in the custodial institutions is akin to what one would predict under the prisonization model, attitude changes in the treatment institutions are in the opposite, positive direction. In these institutions, the proportion expressing positive perspectives increases rapidly over time in the early months and, after a downturn, increases further in the later months.[17]

*Effects of Primary Group Integration on Perspectives.* Data on integration into the inmate group provide a more adequate test of the hypothesis about the dominant tone of the inmate group if one assumes that when those who are better integrated express more positive perspectives, it is because their group exerts a positive influence, and when the better-integrated are more negative, it is because their group exerts a negative influence. Operationally, the better-integrated inmates are those who said they had two or more friends in the institution.[18]

The findings clearly indicate that positive attitudes are more closely associated with primary group integration in the treatment institutions than in the custodial institutions (Table 5). Results on

15. Street, *op. cit.*, pp. 75–83.

16. Clemmer, *op. cit.*, Wheeler, "Socialization . . . ," *op. cit.*, and Garabedian "Social Roles . . . ," *op. cit.*

17. Institutional records show that average stay before release is: Dick, 10 to 11 months; Mixter, 7.5 months; Milton, 15 months; and Inland, 11.5 months, with an average of 18 months for those who complete the institution's program.

18. The question was: "How about *close* friends? Some boys have close friendships with other boys here and some boys don't. How many of the other boys here are close friends of yours?" We assumed that a respondent who reported one or no friends was not really integrated into the group, having at best only a single "buddy." While this definition of integration is subject to questions regarding the probable reporting error and the relation of this "primary relations" interpretation to other meanings of the concept, it provides an empirically profitable starting point for analyzing the consequences of integration.

the four indices significantly related to integration consistently display the predicted pattern. Thus integration into the inmate group was more strongly associated with positive perspectives on the institution and staff in the treatment setting than in the custodial environment. Further, despite the fact that custodial and treatment settings did not differ with respect to scores on the "ratting" index (see Table 3), integration and cooperation with staff are positively associated in the treatment but not in the custodial setting. (This finding principally reflects the strong positive association in Milton; in Inland and in both custodial institutions, it was relatively weak.) Finally, in the treatment institutions integration was inversely associated with the prisonized view of adaptation and positively related to a positive self-image, while in the custodial institutions there was little or no association with these indices.

An analysis of the joint impact of integration and length of stay on these attitudinal measures indicated that variations in length of stay did not

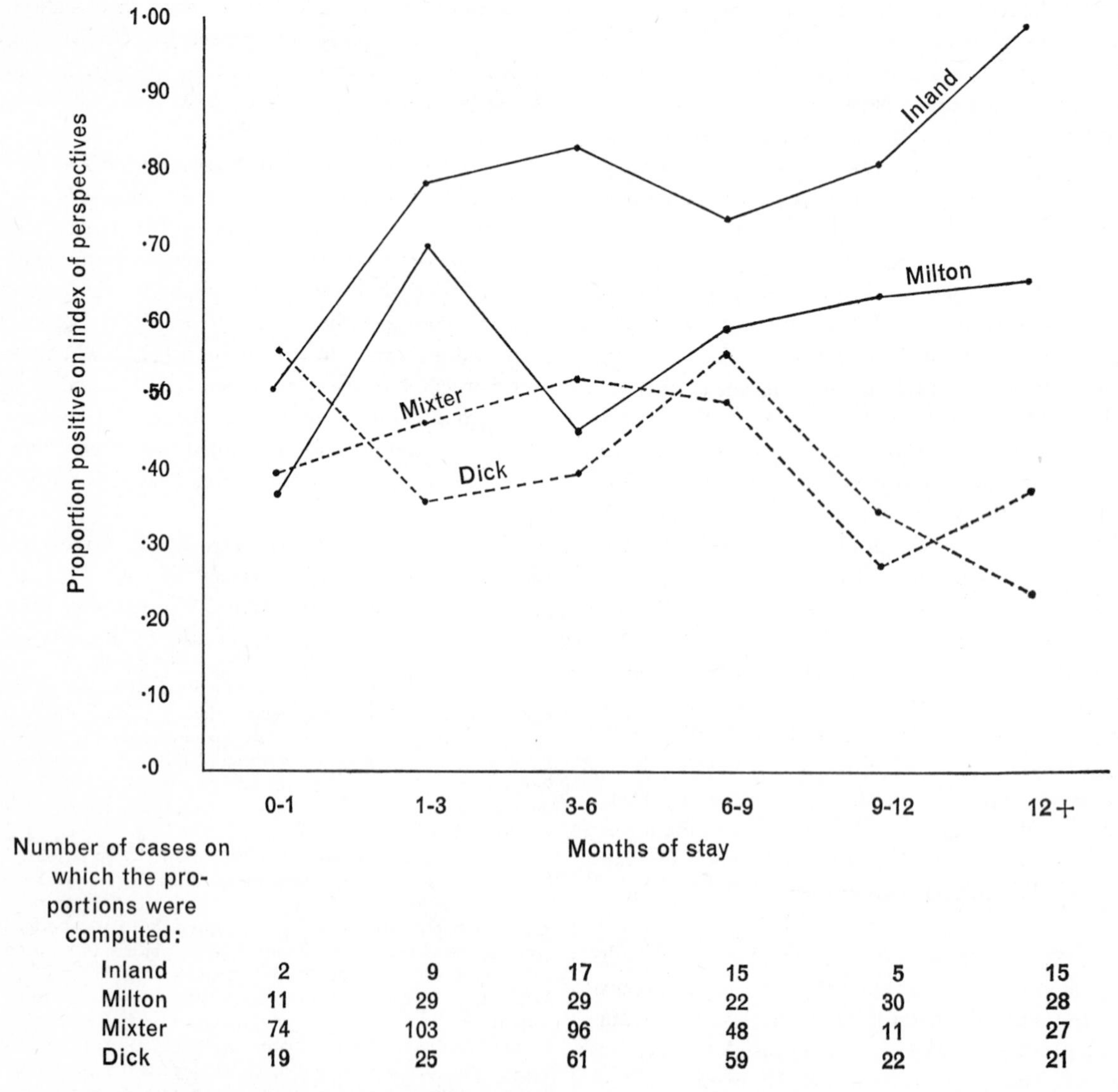


| Number of cases on which the proportions were computed: | 0-1 | 1-3 | 3-6 | 6-9 | 9-12 | 12+ |
|---|---|---|---|---|---|---|
| Inland | 2 | 9 | 17 | 15 | 5 | 15 |
| Milton | 11 | 29 | 29 | 22 | 30 | 28 |
| Mixter | 74 | 103 | 96 | 48 | 11 | 27 |
| Dick | 19 | 25 | 61 | 59 | 22 | 21 |

*Figure 1. Length of stay and perspectives on institution and staff.*

account for these variations in the relation between integration and attitudes.

*Levels of inmate primary relations and solidarity.* A variety of findings consistently support the second hypothesis, that inmates in the treatment setting have more highly developed primary relations and stronger orientations of solidarity (Table 6).[19] In-

19. The specific questions asked were: (1) "Do you usually hang around here with several guys, a few, mostly with one boy, or with none?" (2) The integration question (see note 18); (3) "How many of the boys you have met here would you like to see again after you get out?" (4) "Suppose you had been feeling sad for several days and are very upset about a personal problem. Are there any *boys* here you would go to and talk about the things that made you sad?" (5) "Some boys say that you have to be pretty careful about what you say or do around the other boys here, or else they may give you a rough time. What do you think about this?" (6) Summary of responses to "How much of the time do you think most of the boys here really stick together, and are loyal to each other?" And "Regard-

***Table 5—Inmate Perspectives, by Integration Into the Inmate Group***[a]

| Percentages of inmates who: | CUSTODIAL Dick | | Mixter | TREATMENT Milton | | Inland |
|---|---|---|---|---|---|---|
| Score high positive on index of perspectives on institution and staff | | | | | | |
| Non-integrated | 36 (62) | | 36 (115) | 31 (26) | | 55 (11) |
| Integrated | 44 (146) | | 49 (247) | 64 (126) | | 89 (52) |
| | | $p<.05$ Q = .22 | | | $p<.01$ Q = .61 | |
| Score high cooperation on "ratting" index | | | | | | |
| Non-integrated | 48 (62) | | 48 (115) | 23 (26) | | 46 (11) |
| Integrated | 56 (146) | | 44 (247) | 55 (126) | | 56 (52) |
| | | N.S. Q = .01 | | | $p<.01$ Q = .49 | |
| Give prisonized response on question about best way to get along | | | | | | |
| Non-integrated | 73 (62) | | 73 (110) | 72 (25) | | 60 (10) |
| Integrated | 76 (139) | | 74 (238) | 51 (123) | | 44 (48) |
| | | N.S. Q = .04 | | | $p<.05$ Q = −.39 | |
| Are positive on index of self-image | | | | | | |
| Non-integrated | 31 (52) | | 37 (101) | 35 (23) | | 44 (9) |
| Integrated | 41 (135) | | 44 (225) | 55 (119) | | 86 (49) |
| | | N.S. Q = .16 | | | $p<.01$ Q = .50 | |

[a] Kendall's Q is used to measure the association between integration and the score or response indicated.

***Table 6—Inmate Social Relations, by Institution***

| Percentages of inmates who: | CUSTODIAL Dick | Mixter | TREATMENT Milton | Inland | Statistical significance[a] |
|---|---|---|---|---|---|
| Hang around with three or more boys | 59 | 71 | 78 | 91 | $p<.01$ |
| Have three or more close friends (integration index) | 70 | 68 | 83 | 83 | $p<.01$ |
| Want to see all or most inmates again after release | 27 | 14 | 35 | 27 | $p<.01$ |
| Would talk to other inmates about a personal problem | 58 | 50 | 66 | 76 | $p<.01$ |
| Say you don't have to be careful around the other boys | 14 | 18 | 21 | 27 | $p<.05$ |
| Are high on index of solidary orientation | 27 | 28 | 31 | 55 | $p<.01$ |
| Numbers of Respondents | (202–208) | (356–363) | (152–155) | (62–64) | |

[a] Refers to differences between the custodial and treatment organizations.

mates of the treatment institutions more frequently reported "hanging around" with other inmates, having several friends, and (reflecting the difference between Mixter and Milton) wanting to see other inmates again after release. In addition, the treatment inmates more frequently indicated a willingness to talk with other boys about a personal problem and more often rejected the view that you "have to be pretty careful what you say or do" around other inmates.

Finally, scores on an index of solidarity orientation, here defined as emphasis on general loyalty to the group beyond primary ties with particular others, show a similar pattern. In the treatment settings, especially Inland, inmates were more likely to express such an orientation than were those in the custodial institutions. In neither setting was solidary orientation related to a statistically significant degree to perspectives toward the institution and staff or to scores on the "ratting" index.[20]

*Leadership.* Data bearing on the third hypothesis, that the attitudes of inmate leaders would be relatively positive in the treatment setting and relatively negative in the custodial environment, also tend to follow the predicted pattern. Boys who were nominated four or more times as having the most "influence" in the institution were classified as leaders.[21] On three attitudinal indices, statistically significant differences between leaders and non-leaders were found in either the custodial or treatment setting (Table 7). Leadership is more strongly associated with positive perspectives on staff and institution in the treatment environment than in the custodial setting, reflecting the strongly positive association at Milton. The same finding emerges on the self-image index—again the Milton leaders are highly positive. On the index of "ratting," leadership and cooperation with staff tend to be negatively associated in all institutions, but the association is

less of how much the boys actually do stick together now, how much do you think they *should* stick together?" Respondents who answered both questions positively were scored high on the solidarity orientations index.

20. That these differences in social relations actually follow from organizational control practices is suggested by responses to a question asking for agreement or disagreement with the statement that "You have to be careful about the boys you get friendly with around here. To stay out of trouble with the adults you have to keep to yourself." Considerably higher proportions of inmates rejected this statement in the treatment setting (79 per cent in Inland and 52 per cent in Milton) than in the custodial institutions (30 per cent in both Mixter and Dick).

21. The specific question was "What three boys are best at getting other boys to do what they want them to do—that is, which three have the most influence among the boys? Think of the boys that you know in your cottage, in school, and in the work program, or recreation."

***Table 7—Leadership and Perspectives Toward the Institution and Staff[a]***

| Percentages of inmates who: | CUSTODIAL Dick | | CUSTODIAL Mixter | TREATMENT Milton | | TREATMENT Inland |
|---|---|---|---|---|---|---|
| Are positive on index of perspectives toward the institution and staff | | | | | | |
| Non-leaders | 42 (177) | | 45 (318) | 53 (130) | | 83 (48) |
| Leaders | 37 (32) | | 48 (46) | 80 (25) | | 88 (17) |
| | | N.S. Q = −.005 | | | p<.01 Q = .52 | |
| Are highly cooperative on index of "ratting" | | | | | | |
| Non-leaders | 56 (177) | | 47 (318) | 51 (130) | | 56 (48) |
| Leaders | 38 (32) | | 37 (46) | 44 (25) | | 47 (17) |
| | | p <.01 Q = −.26 | | | N.S. Q = −.14 | |
| Are positive on index of self-image | | | | | | |
| Non-leaders | 39 (162) | | 41 (287) | 47 (120) | | 75 (44) |
| Leaders | 32 (25) | | 53 (40) | 74 (23) | | 87 (16) |
| | | N.S. Q = .09 | | | p<.01 Q = .53 | |

[a] Q measures the association between leadership and the score or response indicated.

stronger in the custodial than in the treatment institutions. Thus, findings on all three indices support the hypothesis that leaders have more positive perspectives in the treatment environment.

A separate analysis indicates that these differences among leaders characterize both "integrated" and "non-integrated" leaders. And other data, on inmate perceptions of leadership in general, support the characterization of leaders in the treatment settings as having more positive attitudes.[22]

These and the other findings reported here indicate a difference between the two treatment institutions, Milton and Inland. On the one hand, data on inmate perspectives, effects of length of stay, and social relations clearly indicates that inmates have more positive attitudes and more highly developed primary relations at Inland. On the other hand, group involvement, as measured by integration and leadership, was more closely associated with positive perspectives at Milton than at Inland. Milton is a "milieu" institution; perhaps this finding reflects its conscious attempt to manipulate the inmate group.

*Data from Additional Institutions.* Data on inmate groups in three other institutions for juvenile offenders, studied less thoroughly than the four organizations just analyzed, shed additional light on the custodial-treatment differences I have reported. The first of these units, *Maxwell* (Maximum Security) was a geographically and administratively separate part of Mixter, established to handle the "most difficult" inmates of the parent institution shortly before the end of our field work. The other units, *Regis* (Religious) and *Bennett* (Benign), were small private institutions that were "open," sending their charges away from the institution every day for ordinary public or parochial schooling. In their goals and in the staff's behavior toward the inmates, these two open institutions seemed to fall between the custodial and treatment types; their goal might be characterized as "training." The inmate is viewed as changeable, but such simple techniques as altering skills and habits are considered appropriate. Within this training model, Regis stressed constant work and recreation activities along with indoctrination and enforcement of obedience and religiosity, while Bennett emphasized the creation of a home-like environment with staff serving as parental surrogates.

22. Street, *op. cit.*, pp. 116–19.

Results from these three units are represented by findings on the association between integration into the inmate group and responses to four attitudinal items (Table 8). These data, together with those from the major institutions (Table 5), show, first, that integration is negatively associated with positive perspectives on the institution and staff, cooperativeness with staff in "ratting," and self-image in Maxwell but not in the custodial or treatment institutions, and that a direct association between integration and "prisonized" response to the third item occurs only at Maxwell. Second, patterns in the two open institutions are generally inconsistent: Regis resembles Maxwell on the first two items, Bennett resembles the treatment institutions on all items, and in both institutions the association between integration and self-image is positive, as it is in the treatment institutions.

***Table 8 – Inmate Perspectives, by Integration into the Inmate Group, in Maximum Security and Open Units[a]***

| | *MAXIMUM SECURITY* | *OPEN* | |
|---|---|---|---|
| *Percentages of inmates who:* | *Maxwell* | *Regis* | *Bennett* |
| Score high positive on index of perspectives on institution and staff | | | |
| Non-integrated | 64 (11) | 84 (19) | 36 (11) |
| Integrated | 54 (33) | 63 (38) | 91 (23) |
| | Q = −.19 | Q = .17 | |
| Score high cooperation on "ratting" index | | | |
| Non-integrated | 45 (11) | 47 (19) | 27 (11) |
| Integrated | 21 (31) | 32 (38) | 35 (23) |
| | Q = −.51 | Q = −.15 | |
| Give prisonized response on question about best way to get along | | | |
| Non-integrated | 60 (10) | 72 (18) | 60 (10) |
| Integrated | 73 (33) | 71 (38) | 45 (22) |
| | Q = .28 | Q = −.14 | |
| Are positive on index of self-image | | | |
| Non-integrated | 56 (9) | 40 (15) | 33 (9) |
| Integrated | 60 (30) | 58 (31) | 71 (21) |
| | Q = .09 | Q = .49[b] | |

[a] Q measures the association between integration and the score or response indicated.
[b] Difference in proportions significant at the .05 level.

These findings and other results suggest that in Maxwell—which, with its stringent security regulations, resembles the traditional adult prison more than any of the other institutions—the "solidary opposition" model fits the inmate group reasonably well. Only in this institution was the relation between scoring high on the index of solidary orientations and strong opposition to staff on the "ratting" index statistically significant ($p < .05$ and $Q = .75$). Our data collection took place only three months after the unit was opened, however, and after several crises of organizational birth, when the inmates may have had a special *esprit de corps* because they were the first group considered incorrigible enough to be sent there. We have no evidence, therefore, that the "solidary opposition" model will continue to fit inmate groups in this type of setting.

Despite the fact that Regis and Bennett were open, allowing their inmates considerable freedom away from the institution, this milieu did not consistently generate as positive a response as did the closed treatment setting. On the other hand, the fact that on some dimensions, e.g., self-image, the association with integration is positive, and as strong as in Milton and Inland, suggests that a relatively benign, open environment might make it possible to achieve some of the benefits of treatment without the expense of a treatment program.

## Discussion

These findings generally support hypotheses about differences between custodial and treatment settings with regard to inmate norms and perspectives, social relations, and leadership and therefore clearly challenge the general applicability of the "solidary opposition" model of the inmate group, at least to juvenile institutions. Variation in organizational goals gave rise to differences in inmate orientations and characteristics of the inmate group, and only in the limited data from a new maximum security unit was there any consistent indication that the "solidary opposition" model was appropriate. By treating the balance of gratification and deprivation and patterns of staff authority and control as variables affecting the inmates, I have replaced the assumption that inmates form solidary and oppositional problem-solving groups with the assumption that under different conditions, different patterns of orientations, social relations, and leadership occur among the inmates. This more open perspective should be applicable to the study of adult institutions, too.

Although we were unable to obtain comparable data on recidivism for the various institutions, our findings indicate tentatively that both custodial and treatment organizations tend to accomplish their proximate goals. By stressing covert opposition and "playing it cool," the custodial inmate group encouraged behavior consistent with the custodial goals of containment and conformity. Thus, the level of "prisonized" orientations was higher among the custodial than among the treatment inmates. Similarly, the treatment inmate group seemed to produce in its members an orientation consistent with the goal of achieving change. Evaluating outcomes with reference to goals is more difficult in the treatment case, of course, for the nature of the most appropriate technology for rehabilitation is undiscovered. Under the current treatment technologies, however, a minimally positive orientation toward the agents of change, e.g., the counselors, is clearly a necessary pre-condition to successful rehabilitation. The inmate groups in the treatment settings more frequently encouraged a positive orientation, and less often encouraged the development of a negative self-image, apparently, than in the custodial institutions.

Finally, this research suggests that the study of correctional institutions would be substantially improved if researchers more frequently recognized the generality of the concept of social control and the variety of devices used to maintain control. All correctional organizations exercise a great deal of control over their inmate members, but while custodial organizations emphasize formal and severe sanctions directed at ordering and containing the inmates, treatment institutions are more likely to rely on informal, personal sanctions and incentives directed at behavior perceived as relevant to inmate change. The implementation of a treatment program in a previously custodial environment implies a shift not to less control, but rather to *different types of control* exercised on the bases of different criteria. As numerous writers have pointed out, humanitarian pressures have already limited severely the use of the most repressive (and perhaps most effective) custodial techniques in American juvenile institutions, even though most of them still are predominantly custodial. Under continuing humanitarian pressure, and faced with evidence that custodial techniques are incompatible with other organizational goals, these institutions are very likely to alter their patterns of authority and control in the coming decades. Researchers interested in the question of implementing successful rehabilitation programs in correctional settings might do well to consider and investigate more fully a variety of combinations of different social control and rehabilitation techniques. Perhaps the treatment model represented in this research is the only really viable model, or perhaps other models, e.g., some form of the "training" model, could combine order-keeping and rehabilitation successfully and in a manner more compatible with the budgets and present commitments of most institutions today.

ROSE GIALLOMBARDO

# Social Roles in a Prison for Women

A neglected area in deviance studies of the adult prison setting concerns female forms of deviation. The study of deviance in the prison setting has typically been concerned with male forms of deviation. Indeed, with the exception of Harper's analysis of the "fringer" role[1] and the recently reported study of a women's prison by Ward and Kassebaum[2] which describes the homosexual adaptation of female inmates, scientific description and analysis of the informal organization of the adult female prison have been overlooked.[3] In the present paper, inmate social roles and social organization in a women's prison will be described in some detail; comparisons of this informal social structure will be made with relevant literature on the social roles assumed by male prisoners; and the social structure inside the prison setting will be viewed in relation to the external environment.

Previous accounts of the male prison have taken the view that the most important features of the inmate culture emerge as a response to the conditions of imprisonment. The features of this system are well known and need not be repeated here.[4] The

1. Ida Harper, "The Role of the 'Fringer' in a State Prison for Women," *Social Forces*, 31 (October, 1952), pp. 53–60.

2. David A. Ward and Gene G. Kassebaum, "Lesbian Liaisons," *Transaction*, 1 (January, 1964), pp. 28–32. Also David A. Ward and Gene G. Kassebaum, "Homosexuality: A Mode of Adaptation in a Prison for Women," *Social Problems*, 12 (Fall, 1964), pp. 159–77. In this institution, the authors found little evidence of the differentiated social types or of inmate solidarity that is typical of the male prison.

3. In this connection, it should be pointed out that in addition to the aforementioned studies of the adult women's prison, there are several reports of institutions for juvenile girls which reveal homosexual practices and/or the presence of "family" groups among the delinquent girls. These reports are unsystematic investigations and impressionistic reports. See, for example, Charles A. Ford, "Homosexual Practices of Institutionalized Females," *Journal of Abnormal and Social Psychology*, 23 (January–March, 1929), pp. 442–44; Margaret Otis, "A Perversion Not Commonly Noted," *Journal of Abnormal Psychology*, 8 (June–July, 1913), pp. 112–14; Lowell S. Selling, "The Pseudo Family," *The American Journal of Sociology*, 37 (September, 1931), pp. 247–53; Seymour L. Halleck and Marvin Hersko, "Homosexual Behavior in a Correctional Institution for Adolescent Girls," *American Journal of Orthopsychiatry*, 32 (October, 1962), pp. 911–17; Sidney Kosofsky and Albert Ellis, "Illegal Communication Among Institutionalized Female Delinquents," *The Journal of Social Psychology*, 48 (August, 1958), pp. 155–60; Romolo Toigo, "Illegitimate and Legitimate Cultures in a Training School for Girls," *Proceedings of the Rip Van Winkle Clinic*, 13 (Summer, 1962), pp. 3–29. Ward and Kassebaum, however, reported that there were no indications of family groups in the prison they studied; *Social Problems, op. cit.*

4. See esp. Gresham M. Sykes and Sheldon L. Messinger, "The Inmate Social System" in *Theoretical Studies in Social Organization of the Prison*, New York: Social Science Research Council, March, 1960, pp. 5–19;

The complete study is reported in *Society of Women: A Study of a Women's Prison*, New York: John Wiley and Sons, 1966. The writer is indebted to Richard D. Schwartz and Paul J. Bohannan for their critical reading and comments of an earlier version of this paper. Acknowledgment is also made to Eliot Freidson for his constructive criticism and invaluable suggestions.

Reprinted from *Social Problems*, Winter, 1966, pp. 268–88, by permission of the author and publisher. (Copyright 1966 by The Society for the Study of Social Problems.)

point to be stressed, however, is that the functional interpretation which is made for the emergence of the inmate system typically views the culture that forms within the prison as a response to the problems found in the internal world of the prison and the crucial ways in which it differs from the external world. It is argued that while the prisoner cannot completely eliminate the pains of imprisonment, a cohesive inmate system which has group allegiance as its dominant value provides the inmate with a meaningful reference group that may reinstate the inmate's self-image, or in some sense neutralize the deleterious effects of its loss. This formulation derives from case studies of single institutions, and, therefore, it is extremely difficult to ascertain the validity of the conclusions drawn as previous writers have not explored systematically the interaction of the external culture with the conditions for survival faced by the prison aggregate. Nor has anyone assessed several adult prisons simultaneously so that a comparative analysis could be made.[5] I think we are just beginning to understand the variability of one prison from another as they are affected by organizational goals, the composition of staff and inmates. Indeed, recent systematic studies of socialization in the male prison by Wheeler and Garabedian call into question the solidary opposition model of inmate culture even within single institutions, as these scholars found that prisoners varied in their support of the inmate culture over time and according to type of prisoner.[6]

Moreover, Irwin and Cressey have advanced the thesis that there are three subcultures in the prison which they maintain reflect the presence of different types of prisoners. These differences presumably are a reflection of the values and attitudes particular inmates bring into the prison and are related to latent identities.[7] Similarly, Schrag attempts to account for inmate deviants with respect to internalization of inmate culture and support of the inmate code in terms of their preprison characteristics and identities.[8] Thus, the developing theoretical considerations tend to emphasize values and attitudes learned by inmates prior to entering the prison.

The present findings from a case study of a women's prison bear on this matter. In the adult female prison which the writer studied, it was found that in order to cope with the major problems of institutional living, the female inmates have also labeled the reactions of prisoners according to the mode of response exhibited by the inmate to the prison situation and the quality of the inmate's interaction with other inmates and staff. However, although the deprivations of imprisonment were present and felt keenly by the female prisoners, the female argot roles differ in structural form and in the sentiment attached to them from the roles assumed by male prisoners. In addition, it should be pointed out that homosexual dyads cast into marriage alliances, family groups, and other kinship ties formed by the inmates integrate the inmates into a meaningful social system and represent an attempt to create a substitute universe within the prison.[9]

Gresham M. Sykes, *The Society of Captives*, Princeton, N.J.: Princeton University Press, 1958; Erving Goffman, "On the Characteristics of Total Institutions: Staff-Inmate Relations," in Donald R. Cressey (ed.), *The Prison: Studies in Institutional Organization and Change*, New York: Holt, Rinehart and Winston, 1961, chs. 1 and 2; Richard A. Cloward, "Social Control in the Prison," *Theoretical Studies in the Social Organization of the Prison*, *op. cit.*, pp. 20–48. See also Donald Clemmer, *The Prison Community*, New York: Holt, Rinehart and Winston, 1958 (reissue of the 1940 edition); Morris G. Caldwell, "Group Dynamics in the Prison Community," *Journal of Criminal Law, Criminology and Police Science*, 46 (January–February, 1956), pp. 648–657; Norman S. Hayner, "Washington State Correctional Institutions as Communities," *Social Forces*, 21 (1943), pp. 316–22; Norman S. Hayner and Ellis Ash, "The Prison as a Community," *American Sociological Review*, 5 (August, 1940), pp. 577–83; Hans Reimer, "Socialization in the Prison Community," *Proceedings of the American Prison Association*, 1937, pp. 151–55.

5. It is interesting that an analysis of variations in organizational goals and an examination of data on the inmates of several juvenile correctional institutions for boys call into question the "solidary opposition" model of the inmate group. See David Street, "The Inmate Group in Custodial and Treatment Settings," *American Sociological Review*, 30 (February, 1965), pp. 40–55.

6. Stanton Wheeler, "Socialization in Correctional Communities," *American Sociological Review*, 26 (October, 1961), pp. 696–712; Peter C. Garabedian, "Social Roles and Processes of Socialization in the Prison Community," *Social Problems*, 11 (Fall, 1963), pp. 139–52.

7. John Irwin and Donald R. Cressey, "Thieves, Convicts, and the Inmate Culture," *Social Problems*, 10 (Fall, 1962), pp. 142–55.

8. Clarence Schrag, "Some Foundations for a Theory of Correction," in Donald R. Cressey (ed.), *The Prison: Studies in Institutional Organization and Change*, New York: Holt, Rinehart and Winston, 1961, pp. 309–57.

9. Marriage, family, and kinship in the female prison will be discussed in a forthcoming paper. However, in this context it might be worthwhile pointing out that the

The empirical evidence to be presented supports the thesis that differences in the informal social structure in male and female prison communities can be understood in terms of the differential cultural definitions ascribed to male and female roles in American society. More specifically, it is suggested that the prison structure incorporates and reflects the *total* external social structure in that the differential cultural definitions ascribed to male and female roles in the external world influence the definitions made within the prison, and function to determine the direction and focus of the inmate cultural system.

### CULTURAL EXPECTATIONS OF MALE AND FEMALE ROLES

Are sex roles so sharply differentiated in American society that we would expect wide variations in behavior patterns to be found in the two prison communities? There are a number of areas in which American society differentiates male and female roles. In the main, it may be said that in contrast to the male, who is expected to prepare for an occupational role, and whose prestige rank is established by the nature of his life work, the female's life goal is achieved through marriage and child-rearing. Although the "career woman" is an important social type,[10] the percentage of women who pursue uninterrupted careers is very small in our society. So long as women bear children, there must be some social arrangement to ensure that the functions of nurturing and training during the period of dependency are fulfilled.

And we may point to other areas in which American culture tends further to differentiate male and female roles. It does not discourage and accepts a public display of affection between two women such as the use of terms of endearment, embracing, holding hands, and kissing. Such behavior on the part of the male, however, would immediately be defined as homosexual. Moreover, women are said to be more dependent, emotional, less aggressive, and less prone to violence than men. It is said that women generally show less initiative in openly defying authority, whereas men have been defined as independent, violent, and aggressive.[11] This *generalized popular culture* persists for women on another level—the woman-to-woman popular culture. In this vein, the mass media perpetuate the stereotype that a "woman's worst enemy is another woman." Because of the female's orientation to the marriage market, it is argued that she tends to see other women as rivals.[12] This view finds its significance and signature underscored in the highly stylized type of the best friend "betrayed." A similar theme is operative when we find that working women state preferences for male supervisors rather than female supervisors.

To the extent that this generalized popular culture persists in the prison setting, a situation of calculated solidarity may be said to obtain between the female inmates. Calculated solidarity is defined as a social unity based not upon automatic conformity to a set of common norms perceived to be morally binding, but, rather, a unity which is subject to constant interpretation by the inmate as she perceives each situation from the point of view of her own interests. Common responsibility in any particular situation, then, exists only to the extent that the individual perceives her own interests to be served.[13] Unless the formal organization can supply the inmates with all of their wants, then perforce inmates must turn to one another for the satisfaction of those needs which are attractive and agreeable to

differentiation of sex roles is crucial as it structures at the outset many other roles which the inmate may legitimately play. Once an inmate has adopted a sex role, it automatically closes off some family roles, while at the same time it opens up legitimate avenues for other roles.

10. Robin M. Williams, Jr., *American Society* (rev. ed.), New York: Alfred A. Knopf, 1960, pp. 64–65. Although many married women at one time or another do some kind of work outside the home for which they earn a salary, marriage and family are the primary goals for most American women. Indeed, despite the marked increase in the number of married women in the labor market, the worker role of women continues to be regarded by society as secondary to the traditional role of women as mothers and homemakers.

11. Indeed, the architecture of the male prison has been historically oriented upon the general belief that the male criminal is aggressive and dangerous.

12. Simone de Beauvoir, *The Second Sex*, trans. and ed. by H. M. Parshley, New York: Bantam Books, 1961, p. 514. She argues that the marriage market from one age period to another is very unstable for the female. Consequently, the process of acquiring a husband becomes an urgent matter, and this concern is often destructive of feminine friendships, for the young girl sees rivals rather than allies in her companions. In this connection, Jules Henry has stated that the self-orientation of the female begins at an early age; see *Culture Against Man*, New York: Random House, 1963, pp. 150–55.

13. As Malinowski has cogently pointed out, however,

them, and which cannot be fulfilled by the formal organization. Clemmer's finding is relevant here. In response to questionnaire items, seventy per cent of his subjects concluded that "friendships in prison result from the mutual help man can give man rather than because of some admired trait."[14] However, if the popular culture on the woman-to-woman level is imported into the prison environment, then we would expect that violations of much tabooed behavior may not be severely punished, or may be overlooked, as the very nature of the case implies that expectations of behavior cannot be consistent. Possible latent dysfunctions of the popular culture, then, would be to neutralize deviant acts.

### METHOD OF STUDY

I was fortunate to have the opportunity to undertake field work for a period of one year in a large women's prison in a correctional system generally regarded as one of the most progressive. Data were gathered by personal observation of the inmates as they participated in formally scheduled inmate activities: work assignments, vocational and avocational classes, group counseling sessions, academic educational classes, recreational and religious activities. At all inmate functions, the observer sat with the inmates. Other sources of data were obtained by personal observation of informal interaction patterns in the cottage units and on the grounds. During the year it was possible to get to know all the inmates who were at the prison when the study began, approximately 650, and, also, many of the inmates who were committed during the course of the year as well. Interviews of one hour to three hours in length were held with these inmates. These interviews provided basic information on the nature and meaning of the cultural experiences and activities of the group, as well as the social values attached to them. The sociological characteristics of the inmate population were obtained by an examination of the record files of 653 inmates who were confined at the same time.

Other data were obtained by attendance at classification and subclassification meetings; the disciplinary court; meetings of the lieutenants and correctional officers; and other scheduled staff meetings. Informal interviews with correctional officers, prison administrators, and other staff members provided additional data. During the last week of the study, an anonymous questionnaire was administered to all the correctional officers to obtain data on the sociological characteristics of the correctional officers and perceptions of their role function.

### THE DEPRIVATIONS OF IMPRISONMENT

Sykes has noted in his study of the Trenton prison that the pains of imprisonment for the modern prisoner are not rooted in physical brutality, but rather may be seen as attacks on the psychological level.[15] The "residue of apparently less acute hurts," he argues, such as the deprivation of liberty, goods and services, heterosexual relations, autonomy, and security, "may indeed be the acceptable or unavoidable implications of imprisonment, but we must recognize the fact that they can be just as painful as the physical maltreatment which they have replaced."[16]

What would constitute deprivations for women? Interview data revealed that although the perception of the female inmates vary from one another in this regard depending upon the stage of the inmate's prison career, one's former commitment history,[17] and/or the relative ease with which the individual may adjust to the inmate social system, there is nevertheless a "hard core of consensus" among the female prisoners that prison life *is* depriving and frustrating.

In the female institution studied, it is quite true that in some areas the deprivations of imprisonment are less harsh. The physical surroundings are cer-

automatic conformity does not exist empirically. But we may conceive of automatic conformity and lawlessness as ideal types with the prison approximating calculated solidarity. See Bronislaw Malinowski, *Crime and Custom in Savage Society*, New York: Harcourt, Brace, 1932, esp. chs. 3, 4, and 5.

14. Donald Clemmer, *The Prison Community*, *op. cit.*, p. 123.

15. Gresham M. Sykes, *The Society of Captives*, *op. cit.*, p. 64.

16. *Ibid.*, p. 64.

17. On a selected day the records revealed that 52.1 per cent had been previously jailed or imprisoned. The commitment age of the inmates ranged from fifteen to sixty-seven years, with a mean of 32.2 and a median of 30.5. Fifty-six per cent of the inmate population were white and 44 per cent were Negro. The marital status of the inmates indicated that 27.1 per cent were single; 31.5 per cent were married; 20.7 per cent were separated; 16.4 per cent were divorced and slightly over 4 per cent were widows.

tainly more pleasant; the cottages although starkly simple are clean and provide the inmate with adequate physical living conditions; with some ingenuity and mutual aid, the inmates enjoy limited opportunity for variety in the matter of dress.[18] The list could doubtless be expanded.

In spite of the mitigation of the pains of imprisonment, however, the differences cited are merely peripheral to the major concerns of prison life. The problems to be solved by the female inmate in this institution are the same conditions for survival as those which the male prisoner has found it necessary to provide solutions in order to survive psychically in the prison environment. These problems have their basis in the disorientation resulting from the abrupt termination of the individual's freedom: the lack of opportunity for heterosexual relations—the fracturing of every influence favorable to the cultivation of emotional reciprocity as a result of being cut off from family and friends; withholding of material goods; attacks on the self through the humiliating experiences incidental to a prison commitment; the loss of autonomy and responsibility to which life in a prison inevitably leads; and the lack of security and privacy.

The loss of liberty and autonomy are among the most uniformly felt deprivations of imprisonment among the female inmates. Restraints on the inmate's freedom are keenly felt, and the transition from liberty to rigidly restricted movement is a matter with which the female must come to terms in order to survive psychically in the prison world.

Whatever the material circumstances may have been for the individual inmate in civil society, the punishing aspect of denying the inmate ownership of personal goods in prison is that it removes the last resource the inmate possesses to express individuality, and, therefore, the abrupt removal of personal effects tends to destroy the inmate's self-image. The stripping and mortifying process[19] occurs immediately after the inmate's entrance into the prison; the personal clothing and other possessions of the inmate are replaced by the prison issue which is fairly uniform, certain to have been worn by generations of prisoners, and to be either sizes too large or sizes too small. When one recalls that it is always open season on women's fashions, it is not surprising to learn that the attack on the individual's self-image with reference to clothing is particularly acute for the female inmate. The strategies employed by some of the inmates in the admission and orientation unit to individualize the prison issue by monograms, embroidery, or the strategic placement of pleats on a surplus WAC jacket in an attempt to make them "more like free world clothes" are all evidence of the subtlety of deprivation.

For the male prisoner, it has been pointed out that lack of heterosexual intercourse is frustrating and depriving, and the evidence indicates that the same holds true for the great majority of the female inmates. Most inmates have enjoyed the company of men outside, and sex constitutes a major problem of adjustment for almost every inmate. Women do not choose to live their lives entirely apart from men, and the necessity of doing so in prison is frustrating for the individual.[20] Indeed the situation for the imprisoned female may, perhaps, be seen to be more serious than for the male. "[American] culture," writes Jules Henry, "gives women no firm role except an erotic one."[21] In this regard, Parsons has discussed three broad categories of adjustment for the American female: (1) the "good companion" role; (2) the "glamour girl" role; and (3) the

18. Yarn may be purchased at the commissary store. Knitted items such as socks and sweaters provide another means by which the loss of goods may be mitigated.

19. Stripping and mortifying practices are discussed in Erving Goffman, *Asylums*, New York: Doubleday, 1961; see esp. pp. 14–25. In the prison, no clothing may be kept by the inmates except girdles (if they are not the panty type), brassieres, and shoes of simple (relatively low-heeled) closed styles. Medals, simple style earrings and wedding rings which are not studded with precious or semiprecious stones may be kept by the inmate, as well as wrist watches which are valued under fifteen dollars.

20. The obvious exceptions to this, of course, are the homosexuals who have practiced homosexuality in the free community. Approximately 5 per cent of the inmate population fall into this category. For this group, it cannot be said that this aspect of imprisonment is depriving. In a sense, the imprisonment of the homosexual—whether male or female—is ironical, for the loss of liberty, except in a few countries, is always accompanied by the denial of contact with the opposite sex so as to increase the burden of punishment. The homosexual in prison, however, is actually in a favored position, because the competition of the opposite sex has been excluded.

21. Jules Henry, *op. cit.*, p. 61; also cf. Margaret Park Redfield, "The American Family: Consensus and Freedom," *The American Journal of Sociology*, 52 (November, 1946), p. 182. "Beyond the roles of glamour girl and nursemaid, the part to be played by women is but vaguely defined in our society."

"domestic" role.[22] Thus, with the closing of the prison gate, the female prisoner finds herself cut off from the structure of American society conducive to the cultivation of a female role which is the avenue through which she achieves self-respect and status.

The evidence, however, suggests that the other major deprivation suffered by the male prisoner, namely, the loss of security,[23] occurs on another level of experience for the female inmate, which is consistent with the popular culture. In the words of the inmates: "The hardest part of living in a prison is to live with other *women*." Commonly expressed attitudes of the nature of women are: "You can't trust another woman"; "Every woman is a sneaking lying bitch." Hence, it is not so much the constant fear of violence or sexual exploitation such as is the case for the male prisoner which creates a hardship for the female inmates, but, rather, the strain involved in being in the forced company of women who are believed to be untrustworthy, capable of predatory tactics. Thus, the female inmate is apt to fear the consequences of aroused jealousy transformed into vitriolic verbal attacks;[24] and she suffers acute insecurity in confronting and handling the frequent attacks of *penitentiary darby*—gossip which takes place at all times and on all sides within the prison. Moreover, there is enough differentiation among the inmates so that some women experience insecurity in adjusting to living in the forced company of others whom they consider to be socially inferior; some of the white women, for example, find living in close proximity with Negroes to be distasteful; others feel repulsion at having to associate with prostitutes, women who are untidy in their personal habits, or who use vulgar language.[25]

22. Talcott Parsons, "Age and Sex in the Social Structure of the United States," *American Sociological Review*, 7 (October, 1942), pp. 610–13.

23. Sykes, *op. cit.*, p. 78.

24. This is not to say, however, that there are no fights which take place among the inmates, but the real violence that occurs in the prison, however, tends to be in connection with a homosexual triangle. And in this connection the great fear is not so much for one's life, as the fear of *disfigurement*—the fear that an inmate "out to get" another will use razor or scissors to disfigure one's face. It is worthwhile noting that the prison officials issue scissors to each inmate; the blades are fairly blunt, but, nevertheless, this indicates the widely held belief of women as nonaggressive types.

25. Types of contaminative exposures have been discussed by Erving Goffman in *Asylums, op. cit.*, pp. 25–35.

As does the male prisoner, the female prisoner soon discovers that escape routes in prison are few. Psychological and physical withdrawal are not significant modes of adaptation to mitigate the pains of imprisonment for the inmates in this institution. What follows now is a description of the informal social structure which provides a complex of clearly defined social roles for the female prisoners and sets the limits of mutual accommodation.

## The social roles

### SNITCHERS AND INMATE COPS OR LIEUTENANTS

Communication across caste lines is strictly forbidden in the female prison studied except for matters of urgent business, and all such interaction is expected to be handled with swift dispatch. Indeed, to violate the ban placed on legitimate communication flowing from inmates and staff is considered to be a very serious matter. The female inmates argue that no inmate should jeopardize the successful execution of activities based upon the common interests of the inmates in connection with the performance of illegal functions to relieve the pains of imprisonment; and secondly, supplying information to officials may result in the withdrawal of privileges or other forms of punishment, thereby adding to the pains of imprisonment for the inmate.

In the female prison, the role of the *snitcher* is the female counterpart to the "rat" in the male prison. To accuse an inmate of snitching is the most serious accusation which one inmate may hurl at another because it clearly signifies the division of loyalty between the staff and the inmates. The importance placed upon the "no snitching" norm is apparent as it covers every range of behavior and is put in the imperative to the new inmate or the deviant: "See and see nothing! Hear and hear nothing!"

Although the female prisoners agree that inmates should never give any information concerning an inmate to the staff, any prisoner, according to the female inmates, may occasionally engage in snitching when it is believed to serve the individual's interest. Moreover, the female's self-orientation and the tendency to see one another as rivals both function to decrease general expectations of rigid alliance from one another. Consequently, the female inmate rarely expresses any surprise when she suspects another inmate of deviating from the norm prohibiting communication of inmate affairs across caste lines—only a kind of bitterness that the status of inmate is not sufficient to bind and solidify the inmates completely into a cohesive group. The popular culture, then, in connection with the extent to which any female may be trusted, functions to neutralize many deviant acts in the prison. As a result, many deviant acts are overlooked, or are not severely punished; in contrast to the situation in the male prison, we find that violation of the "no snitching" norm does not often result in violence. In the words of one prisoner: "A lot is said about what will be done if you catch a snitch, but you know women! They talk loud, draw a crowd, and that's as far as it goes. When it comes to a showdown, they chicken out." This does not mean, however, that negative sanctions are not imposed. Panning and signifying are common modes of punishment to control behavior in the female inmate community.

*Panning* is general derogatory gossip about an inmate when the inmate is not physically present. *Signifying*, on the other hand, is a more compelling negative sanction because the offending inmate is physically present. A group of inmates will discuss a deviant act in considerable detail with biting sarcasm, scorn, and mimicry; the inmate's name is not at any time mentioned, but little doubt is left as to the inmate's identity. Both panning and signifying are extremely effective modes of social control. But sanctions need not always be so obvious to be effective. The fact that the prison is isolated,[26] of course, makes the prisoners extremely dependent upon one another for emotional reciprocity, and this in itself serves to check much continued deviant dehavior. In the words of an inmate: "It's rough when the group ignores you." Inflection in one's voice, then, pretense that one has not seen another, and turning the head to avoid a greeting, can be exquisite punishment in the prison community, and can often be quite as devastating as the more pointed panning and signifying.

Inmates who violate the ban on communication are watched closely and pertinent information concerning their activities is circulated quickly to other inmates. The snitcher, in short, is *persona non grata* in the prison community, and any common cause with an inmate assuming this role would in all certainty hurt one's reputation and close off interaction with the great majority of inmates. The snitcher is condemned by the female inmates because she denies the cohesion of the inmate community and jeopardizes the successful execution of the many illegal activities that take place in the prison to mitigate the pains of imprisonment. And the fact that the snitcher is disloyal to the inmate group adds to the burden of imprisonment.

The behavior subsumed under "center man" in the male prison finds expression in the role of *inmate cop* or *lieutenant*. The inmate cop is a prisoner who is in a position of authority over other inmates, and in the process of executing her work function will issue orders to other inmates or report infractions of rules in connection with work. The prison experience is considered to be the "great equalizer"[27] and inmates resent taking orders from other inmates. As one prisoner said contemptuously: "She tries to act just like an officer. She forgets that she came through that gate and she's got five numbers across her chest just like the rest of us. She's an officer without a uniform, and she tries to tell another inmate what to do. They're always in the officer's face. . . ." The inmate cop or lieutenant in effect takes the role of the officer and thereby violates an important tenet of the inmate code: she denies the egalitarian ethos of the inmates.

The inmate cop's disloyalty is despised not only because it is open to view, but also because it is often flaunted in the face of other inmates. Here is an open and shut case of identification with staff values, and the inmate cop's actions deny the solidarity of the inmate body and weaken the bonds of interdependence which bind them together. Moreover, the inmate cop is apt to rationalize her actions in terms of noncriminal values which according to the inmate code have no place in the prison. Unless this inmate can be persuaded to "see the light" through socialization into the inmate culture, she cannot be reasoned with or bought. In this sense she poses a real threat to the inmate community,

26. Most women, as a matter of fact, serve their entire sentence without a visit from the outside world. In the year 1962, for example, an examination of the records revealed that seventy-nine inmates or about 12 per cent of the inmate population received visits during the entire year.

27. Cf. Judge M. Murtagh and Sara Harris, *Cast the First Stone*, New York: Cardinal, 1958, p. 244.

because the inmate cop is an added bulwark to the staff's forces, and the fact that an inmate is adding to the pains of imprisonment by joining forces with the staff makes her doubly despised.

### SQUARES AND JIVE BITCHES

Along with the snitchers and the inmate cops, the *squares* are truly the pariahs of the inmate community. "Square" is a derisive label pinned on inmates who are considered to be accidental criminals. The behavior of the square in the prison community clearly betrays her alien status, as she is oriented to the prison administration and tends to possess "anti-criminal" loyalties. Degrees of "squareness" are recognized by the female inmates ranging from the inmate who is said to be "so square that she's a cube" to the inmate designated as a "hip square." The "cube square" is very definitely oriented to societal values and the prison administration, whereas the "hip square" tends to sympathize with the inmate code and adheres to some of its principles, sometimes going so far as to *pin*—act as a lookout—for other inmates. Her sympathy tends to take the form of stated tolerance for inmate activities. The distinguishing characteristic of the "hip square," however, is that she does not engage in homosexual activity, as well as the fact that she is oriented to the administration and societal values. In the female prison studied, it should be pointed out that anyone who does not engage in homosexual activities in the prison in one form or another is automatically labeled a square.

Not only are *squares* outside the main stream of inmate activities—excluded and ostracized by the inmate population—but more important for the inmate social system, squares are pitied. It is said that squares "don't know any better," and, further, it is widely believed that the square is not "woman enough" to commit a crime. "They're suckers and fools—gullible without even knowing it." And herein lies the key to understanding the threat that the square poses for the inmate community. Like the inmate cop or lieutenant, the square tends to identify with the institutional officials. In the case of squares, however, association is considered to be doubly hazardous, for in their presumed gullibility squares may unwittingly divulge information to the officials. It is for this reason that squares are apt to be "fed with a long-handled spoon," that is, information concerning inmate activities is carefully sifted and censored.

While the deviance of the square is often the consequence of an artless simplicity—and presumably leaves open the possibility that induction into the inmate culture may remedy the situation (indeed, the pressures applied are so great that this frequently does occur)—the deviance of the *jive bitch*, on the other hand, is a deliberate, calculated strategy to cause conflict. In short, the *jive bitch* is a troublemaker whose strategy often involves a distortion of the facts, as in the case, for example, when she is interested in breaking up an established homosexual relationship: she will often volunteer information about *kites* (prison letters) and illicit rendezvous to the injured party who, in many cases, would prefer not to be the recipient of such information—as it will mean that ignorance is no longer bliss—and who may be goaded into terminating an affair, which although perceived not to be perfect may be felt to be better than none.

Moreover, the jive bitch can't be trusted to keep her word when she gives it, indicating her disloyalty to the inmate group. Although female inmates claim that women are not trustworthy, it is normatively demanded that once you give your word to a prisoner, you should keep it—particularly in connection with matters concerning mutual aid. An example of a jive bitch supplied by an inmate follows:

> You're out of cigarettes, and you go to a girl and say, "Look, I'm out of cigarettes, and I won't have any money until next week. When you go to Commissary, would you buy me a carton, and I'll pay you back next week?" She says, "Sure, baby, sure. I'll get them for you on Friday." When Friday comes, you go to her house to get the cigarettes and when you say, "Did you get the cigarettes?" she opens her mouth like she's surprised and maybe slaps her cheek and she looks at you and says, "Oh, baby, I forgot all about it. I'm sorry, baby, honest!" That's a jive bitch 'cause she had no intention of getting you those cigarettes in the first place.

The jive bitch, in short, is an example *par excellence* of the woman-to-woman popular culture translated into role behavior. And the fact that she cannot be depended upon weakens even the bonds of calculated solidarity which exist among the female inmates.

### RAP BUDDIES AND HOMEYS

While no inmate trusts another woman completely—"You pick your people and even then you only go so far"—within the limitations imposed by this definition of the situation, an inmate may single out another prisoner as a special friend. She is one with whom an inmate can converse easily, and, further, assume reasonably that the conversation will be mutually binding as secret. Any two people who find one another compatible in this way may become *rap buddies* to one another. This relationship is dissolved if the expectations concerning the relationship are not honored by either of the incumbents of the rap buddy role; or if the relationship develops into a homosexual relationship, the inmates become a "couple" and assume the obligations relevant to a homosexual relationship.

The *homey* role is probably as close to "blood" relationship that one comes to in the female prison, and the relationship holds a special place in the lexicon of the inmates. Technically speaking, even if conflict ensues between homeys, the relationship still holds. The homey is the inmate who is from another inmate's home town or nearby community. Homeys may or may not have known one another before incarceration; but whatever the case, within the prison these inmates become homeys to one another. Contact is made as soon as the presence of a homey becomes known; information is usually obtained from inmate orientation helpers or inmate office workers. Inquiries as to whether a homey's needs in the orientation unit have been met are immediately made: cigarettes, soap, toothpaste, facial tissues, and any other commissary items which she needs will somehow be routed to her. The special bond of reciprocity which is established between homeys is of a vastly different degree of intensity than that between rap buddies, and is expected to cover a wide range of behavior; homeys have the right to turn to one another when material need arises, and the further expectation exists that if economically possible, the merchandise is to be returned at a later date.

Although superficially the rap buddy and homey roles may appear to be quite similar, the basis for the allocation of these roles and functions is quite different. What is the basis for allocation of functions with respect to the homey role? While there is a special relationship that exists between homeys, significantly the homey relationship excludes homosexuality. Indeed, an inmate will express great indignation if the suggestion—however lightly veiled—is made that a homosexual relationship exists between her and a homey. "That's my homey. I wouldn't do that to her," certainly suggests the exploitative evaluation many inmates have of the homosexual relationship. But when we examine other aspects of the role this explanation adds little to our understanding of the function the role plays in the lives of the female inmates.

A significant aspect of the homey relationship lies in the fact that inmates sharing this status address and refer to one another by the term "homey," emphasizing to the incumbents of the role and the inmate community alike the nature of the special relationship involved. Indeed, a novitiate who calls a homey by her given name is promptly corrected by other inmates. One is quite reasonably led to ask why it is that mutual aid and mode of address are patterned between homeys and not, for example, between rap buddies. Does the answer lie in the fact that they are from the same geographical area? Given the self-orientation of the female, it is not very likely that this would seem to be a plausible explanation. Actually the occupants of the homey role are, as it were, buying insurance for the future. The extension of mutual cooperation between homeys insures both role occupants that the possibility will not arise that a homey will "read" her—that is, speak derogatively of her behavior in prison to anyone in civil society. Presumably, the inmate who resides in the same geographical area would most likely be in a favored position to do so.

The homey relationship is a splendid example of the refinement in social roles which takes place in the female community to solve the special problems of the inmates stemming from the cultural definition females have of one another.

### CONNECTS AND BOOSTERS

The fifteen dollars which inmates are permitted to spend per month at the commissary store is not a large sum when one takes into account that it covers almost all purchases, including cigarettes.[28] Furthermore, even this modest sum is beyond the reach of most inmates. Few legitimate channels are open to

28. It is possible to make special withdrawals for yarn purchases.

the female inmates to improve their economic lot in the prison. Like the male prisoners, the female inmates also find it necessary to exploit the environment in order to improve their material circumstances. Here it takes the form of stealing from institutional supplies. Significantly, a role based upon aggressive physical tactics such as the "gorilla" reported by Sykes who takes what he wants from other inmates by force does not emerge in the female inmate community. By contrast, in the female prison the *connect* is any inmate with a "good job" who will cooperate in the procurement of scarce goods and/or information. Connects are also those inmates who are in a position to negotiate with other inmates to obtain information or goods, that is, acting both as middleman and distributor. Thus, this role includes the procurement of both goods and services.

In this connection, the inmates draw a sharp line between the connect, who often takes a dual role, and the *booster* whose exploitation of the environment consists solely of stealing from official stores and carries on a successful business enterprise. Of course, it should be made clear that stealing from the officials is universal at the prison. Even inmates designated by sister inmates as squares and inmate cops declare they will sometimes take a pot of coffee out of the dining room "on principle." Inmates, however, make a clear distinction between the petty boosting which is engaged in by all the inmates—say a few teaspoonfuls of sugar placed in a napkin, a sandwich, and the like, while in the dining room—and the stealing engaged in by the booster. The difference lies mainly in the source of supply, the regularity with which the goods may be procured, and the purpose for which the items are stolen. Items stolen sporadically for individual consumption tend to be classified under the category petty boosting. The booster is the inmate who is in a position to steal desired objects regularly and in fairly large quantities.

Now in the male prison, regardless of the source of supply, giving and sharing is normatively demanded by the inmate code—especially if the materials have been stolen from the officials. The "pedlar" or "merchant" has been described as "a man so alienated from other prisoners, so selfish in his pursuit of material advantage, that he is willing to thrive on the misery of his companions. He places his own well-being above the well-being of the inmates as a whole. He does not share the goods in short supply but exploits, instead, the needs of others."[29] Interestingly, the same behavior for which the "merchant" is despised in the male prison is that which receives words of praise from female inmates. To "get a good thing going," that is, to engage in a successful enterprise is to draw forth admiration from the inmates. It is held: "If you can get a little racket going, more power to you." And yet at the same time inmates rationalize many of their actions by saying, "If I don't get there first, someone else will," which clearly indicates the self-orientation of the inmates. In a real sense, boosters are inmates who have "gotten there first," and for this feat there is admiration—albeit tinged with not a little envy. In addition, inmates tend to feel gratitude to the booster, for it is recognized that the booster's role involves a certain amount of risk. Whatever recompense is necessary to enjoy the pleasure of making a cup of coffee at odd hours of the day is thought to be well worth the price. The inmates will gladly exchange a carton of cigarettes for a pound of coffee,[30] and if this transaction can be made a weekly matter, prison life is made more tolerable.

In contrast to the male prisoner, no sharp line is made by the female inmates between selling and giving, except between *homeys*, inmates participating in a homosexual marriage, and other "family" members. Who are the inmates that become the clients for the supply of illicit goods? All prisoners do not have an opportunity to enjoy these luxury items, regardless of their financial situation. Low caste inmates, such as snitchers, squares, and inmate cops or lieutenants, of course, lie outside the boundary of legitimate giving, as these inmates have deviated from the inmate code and, therefore, have roped themselves off from the privilege of sharing in the scarce goods that circulate about the prison. They are in the same boat as "rats," "center men," "weaklings," and "fish" in the male prison. Apart from the pariahs in the female prison, mutual aid is greater near the locus of high intensity of emotional reciprocity. As intensity of emotional reciprocity decreases, mutual aid decreases proportionately.

29. Sykes, *op. cit.*, p. 94.

30. Cigarettes are the most important nexus of exchange among the inmates.

PINNERS

Since complete elimination of detection is never possible in the performance of many illicit activities, the female inmates find it necessary to minimize the risk of being detected by the prison officials. For this reason, the role of *pinner* is very crucial in the prison.

The pinner in the female prison is a lookout, stationed as a sentry to prevent a surprise attack upon inmates engaging in illicit activities from all unauthorized persons—whether they be staff or inmates. With discovery always imminent and punishment a certainty, the pinner's role is not one to allocate to amateurs or to inmates whose loyalty is in doubt. The pinner must be an inmate who can be trusted, stand up under pressure, and she must be "in the know." Depending upon the task at hand, sometimes the female inmates find it necessary to mobilize a team of pinners—each of whom must share the responsibility that the task at hand be carried out successfully. The interdependence of the inmates requires the cooperation of other inmates in order to carry out their activities successfully. In the words of an inmate:

> Even if you wanted to go it alone, it's almost impossible to do. The situation is such that you need the help of other inmates. For example, if you're makin' it with someone, you need a pinner. This means initiating the aid of a third party—maybe more. And you might be called up to help two other people in the same situation. . . . The way pinning works is this—maybe I've got two friends who are involved with each other. O.K., well, I'll go into the office and keep the officer busy for an hour talking about a problem I have or I make one up. She can't be in two places at one time, so usually this is a safe procedure. Or a girl will stand at the foot of the stairs with a tin can in her hands. If the officer or a person known to be a snitcher goes up the stairs, she drops the can, or she whistles loudly. These signals are understood.

Now while it is important to the female inmates that the pains of imprisonment be mitigated, it is also imperative that in the process of doing so their deviant actions do not result in disciplinary action which will increase the burden of punishment. The pinner, therefore, is a valued individual, as she imparts a measure of reasonable security to the inmates that their deviant performances will not result in loss of days or other forms of punishment.

THE HOMOSEXUAL CLUSTER: PENITENTIARY TURNOUTS, LESBIANS, FEMMES, STUD BROADS, TRICKS, COMMISSARY HUSTLERS, CHIPPIES, KICK PARTNERS, CHERRIES, PUNKS, AND TURNABOUTS

The problems and concerns of the female inmates in adjusting to deprivation of heterosexual relationships are revealed by the number of roles channeled into homosexual behavior. Moreover, the female inmate's *role refinement* with respect to the categories of homosexual activity illustrates its function as both a motivating force in the lives of the inmates and as an organizing principle of social organization.

The inmates apply a number of labels to homosexual behavior in the prison depending upon the specific role assumed, the adeptness with which the assumed role is played, or the motivation for the behavior. Broadly speaking, the inmates differentiate between penitentiary turnouts and lesbians. The *penitentiary turnout* is the prisoner who resorts to homosexuality in the prison because heterosexual relationships are not available; in contrast, the *lesbian prefers* homosexual relations in the free community. In this respect she resembles the "fag" in the male prison. The *lesbian* is labeled as a sick person by the inmates because it is argued that the preference and selection of homosexual relations in a situation where choice is possible clearly constitute a true perversion. It is only in the penitentiary world where men are unavailable that the values and norms regarding homosexual behavior are redefined by the inmates and—within the limits imposed by this definition—accepted as a temporary substitute for heterosexual relations.

Stylized symbolic devices make it possible for the female inmates to attach new meanings to a culturally defined sex *role* representation seen as a variation of a sex *type* based upon biological attributes. The institutionalized character of the differential sex roles orders the behavior of the inmates and defines the limits of permissible behavior and regulates the interaction between the inmates.

The *femme*[31] or *mommy* is the inmate who plays the female role in a homosexual relationship. The femme role is a highly sought-after role in the prison because most of the inmates want to continue to play the feminine role in a meaningful way in

31. This role is also reported in Ward and Kassebaum, *op. cit.*, p. 169.

the prison. Cast in the context of a "marital" relationship, the femme continues to act out many of the functions assigned to the role of wife in civil society. The complementary role to the femme is the *stud broad*[32] or *daddy* who assumes the male role. The stud broad is accorded much prestige by other inmates for these reasons: first, the stud is said to provide the prison with the male image; secondly, the role is considered to be a more difficult one for an inmate to assume and sustain over a period of time, because it is thought to be "unnatural" for a female to assume the guises of the male. Moreover, the role is considered to be difficult because studs not only assume certain external symbols of sex differentiation, but in addition are expected to incorporate into role behavior the many social expectations of the male role.

As far as homosexual relations are concerned, the evidence is consistent with that reported by Ward and Kassebaum; that is, homosexual relations are established voluntarily between the principals involved. No physical coercion is applied in obtaining a homosexual partner.[33] In seeking a solution to the problem engendered by the lack of heterosexual relations, interpersonal relations in connection with homosexuality play a major part in the lives of the female inmates. Cast in the context of a "marital" relationship, the homosexual dyad is viewed by the inmates as a meaningful personal and social relationship. From the mass of interview data it is clear, however, that this mode of adjustment (with the exception of homosexuals who practice homosexuality in the free community) would be repugnant for most prisoners, but the uniqueness of the prison situation compels the inmate to redefine and attach new meanings to this behavior within the prison structure.[34]

The inmates are not able to resolve their sense of isolation within the formal organization, and, therefore, develop relationships and behavior patterns within an informal structure. For the vast majority of the inmates, adjustment to the prison world is made by establishing a homosexual alliance with a compatible partner as a marriage unit. Although we cannot discuss the dynamics of mate selection, courtship, and marriage in this paper, it should be pointed out that when a stud and femme have established a homosexual alliance, they are said to be "makin' it" or to be "tight"; that is to say, they are socially recognized as constituting a legitimate married pair. Since one of the important goals in establishing a homosexual marriage alliance is to strive for what is referred to as a "sincere" relationship, which is translated to mean a stable relationship and one based upon romantic love, the *trick* is held in low esteem by the inmates because she allows herself to be exploited, rather than to develop a relationship that is sincere. And the trick permits exploitation in a variety of ways—usually economically and as a source of labor. Any individual who allows herself to be exploited in this manner is considered "weak." Moreover, tricks are regarded as "suckers" and "fools" because they may be kept dangling with promises.

Who are the inmates who utilize exploitative tactics? The *commissary hustler* is so labeled as an individual who establishes a single homosexual alliance with an inmate who lives in the same cottage, but in addition establishes relationships with one or more inmates in other cottages for economic purposes. This is called "mating for commissary reasons," and any femme other than the inmate who lives in the stud's cottage is labeled as a trick in the relationship. The commissary hustler presents a commissary list to the tricks scattered throughout the prison, and they, in turn, supply the commissary hustler with needed material items. The function of all the tricks in this "polygynous" system is an economic one. The "wife" in the cottage takes precedence over all others. She shares in the bounty and usually knows of the existence of other femmes, i.e.,

32. Cf. the role of the butch in Ward and Kassebaum, *ibid.*, pp. 168–69.

33. Ward and Kassebaum, *ibid.*, p. 171.

34. Estimates of the number of inmates who are involved in homosexuality vary. Inmates who are very much involved in this phase of inmate culture place the figure at 90 or 95 per cent. The Associate Warden (treatment) estimated that 80 per cent of the inmates were involved in homosexual relations. Correctional officers tended to set the figure at 50 or 75 per cent, which agrees with the usual estimates I obtained from squares. Some officers and other staff members set the figure at 100 per cent. At one point in the study, I made a cottage count of inmates assuming the male role, and the studs totaled 215 inmates. The number of "males" in the prison tends to vary slightly from day to day depending upon inmate releases and individual role choice. And the same is equally true of the inmates playing the femme role. At this time, there were 336 femmes out of a total of 639 inmates. At any rate, it is apparent that femmes are competing for a scarce commodity.

tricks. Indeed, if the "couple" is in serious economic difficulty, she may suggest to her stud that this role be assumed. Or the stud may consult the femme in arriving at a decision to "work a few tricks."

So long as the "wife" shares the same household as the stud, the existence of other femmes (tricks) in the relationship is tolerable. As the inmates put it: "The nearest is the dearest, and the closest gets the mostest." In addition, it should be pointed out that the "wife" who lives in the same household as the stud also derives security from the public recognition of the relationship as legitimate. They are recognized as a "couple." The additional wife (or wives) merely serves an economic function. One would be well advised to ask why an inmate enters into a trick role. The stud population is outnumbered by the femme population, and competition for studs is very keen. Actually, each trick in this situation anticipates and plans for the day when the relationship will become a permanent one; each trick anticipates displacing the cottage "wife" in the affections of the stud. And since the trick is, after all, an inmate with a commissary account, the possibility that this might occur is a good one. While it is more or less understood that she wait for an invitation to move to the stud's cottage, sometimes a trick may lose patience and forego prison etiquette. Such cottage moves present complicating triangular situations, often leading to violence.

The role of commissary hustler is one which requires a certain amount of adroitness to carry out successfully. The inmates argue that in the free community, the commissary hustler would tend to exploit men, but since there are no men in prison, they exploit women. Although there may be individual personality factors involved, there are structural features in the prison which precipitate this role. Every inmate is not compensated for work performed in the prison, and the role of commissary hustler provides an avenue whereby an inmate may solve her economic needs.

The dyad configuration cast into the framework of a marital relationship covers a wide range of behavioral expectations. The commissary hustler, although in some respects exploitative, nevertheless does maintain a stable and sincere relationship with the femme who shares the same cottage. However, when the individual exploits *each* situation with a partner for its unique possibilities, whether it be sexual gratification or material, the inmate is said to occupy a *chippie* role. This role differs from the commissary hustler in a very important way. Although the commissary hustler actually establishes one sincere relationship and exploits other inmates in order to provide for the femme in the relationship, the chippie establishes no single relationship of this type. Chippies are said to be "makin' it," but not to be "in love" with any individual. The chippie, in the inmates' eyes, is the prison prostitute. The inmate who "chippies from one bed to another"—i.e., terminates affairs too quickly—is held in scorn by the inmates, as her behavior is held to be promiscuous. This behavior draws forth words of scorn from the inmates because the ideal cultural pattern in the prison is to establish a permanent relationship. The chippie clearly deviates from the ideal pattern, as the affairs of this inmate are characterized by their striking temporary quality.

The female inmates distinguish clearly between homosexual activity that is considered to be promiscuous and that which is engaged in solely for sexual gratification. Although *kick partners* are also not involved as "lovers," there is, nevertheless, a predictable permanence in the relationships maintained between kick partners, but the motivation for entering into the partnership is clearly understood to be solely for physical gratification. There is usually no economic exchange in this relationship, and the inmates exhibit no jealousy. An inmate is apt to enter such a relationship when she does not wish to assume the responsibilities that a more permanent tie would entail. The object of this relationship is to release sexual tension. Kick partners sometimes consist of a group of several women among whom partners are exchanged and friendly relations exist between all members concerned. To the extent that kick partners are "discreet," the behavior is not looked down upon by the inmates.

Every society has a reserve of members from which potential mates may be obtained. When resources are limited, or because of cultural prescriptions, mates may be drawn from other groups. In the female prison, the kick partner is an individual who may be drawn into a permanent tie. And there is also the possibility that the square will in time come to "see the light" and enter into the inmate social organization. But there is one category of inmates in prison, namely, those labeled *cherries*, who constitute an uncommitted sizable reserve for potential mates, as they are the inmates who have never been "turned out"—initiated into homosexual practices. Cherries, however, are not squares. Often they are young and first offenders, and they are usually initiated by older women. Cherries in this context are "hep" individuals, i.e., know what the score is from the point of view of the prisoners, but for one reason or another have not engaged in homosexuality. Sometimes a short sentence may be the deciding factor; a preference not to become emotionally involved; or it may be that the individual decides that this mode of adjustment may not be desirable.

One who assumes a false part or assumes a character other than the real is despised for his hypocrisy both within and without the prison gates. Within the female prison, the *punk* is despised for pretense and deceit. In the male prison, it will be recalled that the "punk" is an inmate who plays the submissive part in a homosexual relationship because he is coerced into doing so. In this respect it is said that "punks" differ and may be distinguished from "fags," who it is said are "born" not "made." In a sense, "fags" resemble the lesbians for it is said by the inmates that they are "born that way," or "something happened to them in their childhood."

The punk in the female prison, on the other hand, is the inmate so designated because she acts like a female, that is, takes on the coquettish mannerisms of a woman when the expected behavior is that of the male. The behavior of the punk elicits a combination of anger and ridicule from the inmates. The tendency is to heap blame upon the punk, because the punk's "impotence" is not a constitutional failure, but, rather, is due to incomplete role learning. Responsibility, therefore, is placed upon the individual. Punks are, as it were, self-proclaimed studs without substance—unconvincing sexual deviates. The punk is despised and ridiculed by the inmates.

While the punk is guilty of incomplete role learning, the *turnabout*, on the other hand, claims expertise at playing both male and female roles. As a matter of fact, she not only describes herself glowingly in terms of her versatility, that is, "good either way," but stands ready to put her boasted skill to the test. Such protean versatility, however, is viewed with amused contempt by the inmates. As a prisoner put it, "There's a lot of talk, but not the right kind of talk. She should know what she is and stay that way. And we tell them, 'Get yourself together and find out what you are!' "

The female inmates prefer a structured situation in their prison world, and inmates playing male roles one day and female roles the next confuse the issue greatly, especially for the inmate who may be planning a strategy of conquest. In addition, anything which tends to decrease the "male" population in the prison is apt to be alarming to the inmates. It is not surprising, therefore, that the turnabout is held in low esteem.

## Conclusion

The social roles as distinguished and labeled by the female inmates constitute the basic structure of social relationships formed by the inmates in response to the problems of a prison commitment. While it is apparent from the previous discussion that some argot roles are mutually exclusive, other roles clearly are not. Furthermore, an inmate may assume one role soon after commitment, for example, such as square, but may assume many other roles at a later point in time if drawn into the inmate social organization.

In addition to the comparisons with the male prison community that have already been made, there are other important differences that may be pointed out at this time. Consistent with the cultural definition of the female as nonaggressive, the roles of violence that emerge in the male prison, namely, those of "wolf," "tough," "gorilla," "hipster," and "ball buster," are notably absent among the female inmates. Also significant is the fact that a role resembling the structure of the "right guy" who is such a dominant figure in the male prison does not emerge in the female prison. Concepts such as "fair play," "courage," and the like—which are consistent with the concepts of endurance, loyalty, and dignity associated with the "right guy"—are not meaningful to the female. Although it is true that the norm of inmate loyalty exists in the prison world, the popular culture of women as untrustworthy is imported into the prison world and serves both to neutralize many deviant acts and to furnish the rationale for their commitment.

The need to assert or defend one's femininity, in the same way that the male inmate must prove his masculinity in the group if his manhood is called into question, clearly does not arise for the female inmate. This is a reflection of the self-orientation of the female, and the fact that the female validates her femininity by proving she can attract men. In other words, it appears that general features of American society in connection with the cultural definitions ascribed to male and female roles are imported into the prison and are reflected in the structure of social relationships formed by the inmates. Nowhere is this more dramatically revealed than in the extraordinary function of the homey role with its extended implications for the reentry of the inmate into civil society. From the same vantage point, we saw that the function of the pinner's role serves to control the physical distance between inmates engaging in illicit activities on the one hand, and the snitcher on the other, in order to make it possible for the female inmates to avoid discovery and punishment.

The number of roles clustered about homosexual behavior clearly reveals the problems and concerns of the female inmates in connection with adjustment to deprivation of heterosexual relationships. Moreover, the distinctions made by the inmates as to motivation, role assumed, adeptness with which the assumed role is played, and so on, indicate the values and expectations of the inmates with respect to this behavior. But the rights and obligations attached to a legitimate "marital" relationship automatically close off much interaction among the inmates, as inmates assuming this type of relationship must account for all of their contacts with members of the "opposite sex." As the inmates move closer to legitimate relationships in the prison, then, the refinement of roles becomes necessary in order to control and to account for the behavior of every inmate in the system.

The cultural orientation of males, however, precludes legitimate marriage and family groupings as a feasible alternative solution for the male prisoners, as the serious adoption of a female role is contrary to the definition of the male role as masculine. Hence, family groups do not emerge in the male prison. It is noteworthy that in the male prison the "fags" and "punks" are both held in derision by the vast majority of male inmates as it is felt that they have sacrificed their manhood, but the homosexuality of "wolves" is looked upon as a temporary adjustment to sexual tensions generated by the prison setting. The absence of sentiment and the aggressive behavior of the "wolf" is consistent with the cultural definition of the *masculine* role, and thus homosexuality loses the taint of femininity in the prison that male homosexuality tends to carry in civil society. In addition, the cultural orientation of the male role with respect to demonstrations of affection toward another member of the same sex clearly precludes the adoption of legitimate feminine roles by male inmates in informal kinship groupings such as those found among the female inmates. The ease with which women may demonstrate acts of affection, both verbally and physically, toward members of the same sex, perhaps may provide a *predisposition* to widespread homosexuality and its ready acceptance under the extreme conditions of isolation in the prison setting. This fact alone, however, is not enough to account for the emergence of the female inmate social system.

Why do these remarkable differences in inmate culture emerge in the two prison communities? Two theoretical positions have already been posed. The first of these is the typical structural-functional analysis of total institutions which asserts that behavior systems of various types of inmates are a result of the conditions of imprisonment. However, when we consider that the deprivations of imprisonment were found to be present in the female prison studied and keenly felt by the female prisoners—yet the typical cultural system which emerges in the adult male prison is not present—we must conclude that the differences in structural form found in the two prison communities are inadequately explained by current functional analysis *solely* as a response to the deprivations of imprisonment. The deprivations may provide necessary conditions for the emergence of an inmate system, but they are not in themselves sufficient to account for the structural *form* that the inmate social system assumes in the male and female prison communities.

The second interpretation views inmate culture as somehow imported into the prison world from the external world by the inmates who compose that culture, through the particular attitudes and values which inmates learned prior to entering the prison. This position has been most forcibly suggested by Schrag, Irwin, and Cressey, and calls our attention to the thesis that the behavior patterning of inmates is influenced by pre-prison experiences, social identities, and cultural background. Simply stated, the behavior patterns in the prison are the result of the inmates' relations in the external world; however, the external world is important only in providing the particular cultural elements that the inmates learn. Inasmuch as the individuals who enter the prison world are not a random sample of the population, the values and attitudes brought into the prison do not comprise a random sample of elements of outside culture; hence, prison culture differs—especially by the presence of increased hostility, violence, and traffic in illicit goods. The three subculture groups (thief, convict, and legitimate) in Irwin and Cressey's typology presumably demonstrate this thesis,[35] as these authors maintain that their three subculture groups share learned behaviors which are common and peculiar to them in or out of prison. Elsewhere, it has been cogently pointed out that Irwin and Cressey do not demonstrate that this is so.[36] Nevertheless, they have called attention to the important thesis that the behavior patterning of inmates may be influenced by social identities and cultural backgrounds.

We suggest, rather, that the culture that forms within the prison by males and females can be understood in these terms: the prison inmate social system is not an intrinsic response to the deprivations of imprisonment, although the deprivations of imprisonment may be important in precipitating inmate culture; nor can inmate culture be viewed as a mere reflection of the values and attitudes inmates bring into the prison world. The evidence presented here suggests that the male and female inmate cultures *are* a response to the deprivations of prison life, but the nature of the response in both prison communities is influenced by the differential participation of males and females in the external culture. The culture that emerges within the prison structure may be seen to incorporate and reflect the total external social structure; that is, the way in which roles are defined in the external world influence the definitions made within the prison. General features of American society with respect to the cultural definitions and content of male and female roles are brought into the prison setting and they function to determine the direction and focus of the inmate cultural system. These general features I have suggested are those concerned with the orientation of life goals for males and females; second, cultural definitions with respect to dimensions of passivity and aggression; third, acceptability of public expression of affection displayed toward a member of the same sex; and, finally, perception of the same sex with respect to what I have called the popular culture.

It is the *system* of roles and statuses that is imported into the prison setting, and not merely the values and attitudes of the individuals who enter the prison world. It is in these terms that the importance attached to the female role, marriage ties, and family groups can be understood as salient elements of prison culture in the female prison community, but not in the male prison community. It would seem, then, that there is greater unity between the inner and outer worlds than has heretofore been thought. Accordingly, greater understanding of the prison communities may be accomplished by focusing our attention on the relationship of the external and internal cultures rather than trying to understand the prison as an institution isolated from the larger society.

35. Irwin and Cressey, *op. cit.*, esp. pp. 148–53.

36. Julian Roebuck, "A Critique of 'Thieves, Convicts, and the Inmate Culture,'" *Social Problems*, 11 (Fall, 1963), pp. 193–200. It should be pointed out that Schrag's analysis also remains unclear, for at one point he comments: "Juxtaposed with the official organization of the prison is an unofficial social system originating within the institution and regulating inmate conduct with respect to focal issues, such as length of sentence, relations among prisoners, contacts with staff members and other civilians, food, sex, and health, among other things." This suggests that all inmates face a number of common problems of adjustment as a result of incarceration and that social organization develops to provide solutions. See Clarence Schrag, "Some Foundations for a Theory of Correction," in Cressey (ed.), *The Prison*, *op. cit.*, p. 342.

ERVING GOFFMAN

# The Underlife of a Public Institution: A Study of Ways of Making Out in a Mental Hospital

An "instrumental formal organization" may be defined as a system of purposely coordinated activities designed to produce some overall explicit ends. The intended product may be material artifacts, services, decisions, or information, and may be distributed among the participants in a great variety of ways. I will be mainly concerned with those formal organizations that are lodged within the confines of a single building or complex of adjacent buildings, referring to such a walled-in unit, for convenience, as a social establishment, institution, or organization.

Some qualifications might be suggested to my traditional approach. Formal organizations may have a multiplicity of conflicting official goals, each with its own special adherents, and some doubt as to which faction is to be the spokesman for the organization. Further, while a goal like cost reduction or asepsis can be objectively applied as a detailed standard for many of the minor activities occurring within some organizations, other establishments, such as some clubs and community recreation centers, do not have the kind of goals that provide a clear-cut standard against which to examine details of life within the establishment. In still other formal organizations the official goal may be of small importance, the main issue being the conservation or survival of the organization itself. Finally, physical boundaries such as walls may in the last analysis be an incidental feature of organizations, not an analytical one.[1]

Walled-in organizations have a characteristic they share with few other social entities: part of the individual's obligation is to be *visibly* engaged at appropriate times in the activity of the organization, which entails a mobilization of attention and muscular effort, a bending of oneself to the activity at hand. This obligatory engrossment in the activity of the organization tends to be taken as a symbol both of one's commitment and one's attachment, and, behind this, of one's acceptance of the implications of participation for a definition of one's nature. Any study, then, of how individuals adapt to being identified and defined is likely to focus on how they deal with exhibiting engrossment in organizational activities.

An instrumental formal organization survives by being able to call forth usable contributions of activity from its members; stipulated means must be employed, stipulated ends must be achieved. However, as Chester Barnard has suggested, an organization, acting through its management, must recognize limits upon the degree to which a member can be relied upon to contribute suitable activity.[2]

Reprinted from *Asylums*, pp. 175–80, 188–93, 201–3, 207–12, 227–30, 248–51, 298–300, 308–12, 318–20, by permission of the author and publisher, Doubleday and Company, Inc., 1961.

1. Amitai Etzioni has suggested this argument in personal conversation.

2. Chester Barnard, *The Functions of the Executive* (Cambridge: Harvard University Press, 1947), ch. xi, "The Economy of Incentives."

The human vessel is defined as notoriously weak; compromises must be made, consideration must be shown, protective measures must be taken. The particular way in which these limitations to the use of participants are formulated in a given culture would seem to be a very important characteristic of it.[3]

Our Anglo-American imagery for delineating these limits appears to be something like the following, as expressed from the point of view taken here, which identifies an organization with its managers.

First, the participant is granted certain "standards of welfare" while he is engaged in the activity of the organization, these being above the minimum required to keep the human organism going. Standards here pertain to: levels of comfort, health, and safety; limits on the kind and amount of effort required; consideration for the member's participation in other organizations that have a legitimate claim upon him; rights regarding retirement and vacations; expression of grievances and even legal review; and, at least at the level of public pronouncements, a right to dignity, self-expression, and opportunities for creativity.[4] These standards of welfare clearly acknowledge that a human being is something more than just a member of the particular organization.

Second, the imagery of our society suggests that the member of an organization may voluntarily cooperate because of "joint values" through which the interests of the organization and the individual member coalesce, intrinsically as well as strategically. In some cases it is presumably the individual who identifies himself with the organization's goals and fate, as when someone takes personal pride in his school or place of work. In other cases the organization appears to become involved in the personal fate of a particular member, as when a hospital staff becomes genuinely excited over a patient's recovery. In most organizations some of both kinds of joint value serve to motivate the member.

Third, it is sometimes recognized that "incentives" may have to be provided, these being rewards or side payments that frankly appeal to the individual in his capacity as someone whose ultimate interests are not those of the organization.[5] Some of these incentives are externally relevant, being rewards that the recipient can carry off the premises and use at his own discretion without implicating other members of the organization; money payments, training, and certification are the three principal instances. Some incentives are internally relevant, being perquisites that require the organization's own stage setting for their realization; important here are increases in rank and improvement in one's allotment of institutional conveniences. Many incentives carry both types of relevance, as in the case of occupational titles such as "executive."

Finally, it is perceived that participants may be induced to cooperate by threats of punishment and penalty if they do not. These "negative sanctions" can involve an eventful decrease in usual rewards or in usual levels of welfare, but something other than mere reduction in reward seems to be involved. The notion that punishment can be an effective means of calling forth desired activity is one that requires assumptions about the nature of human nature different from those needed to account for the motivating effect of incentives. Fear of penalization seems adequate to prevent the individual from performing certain acts, or from failing to perform them; but positive rewards seem necessary if long-range, sustained, personal effort is to be obtained.

In our society, then, as presumably in some others, a formal instrumental organization does not merely use the activity of its members. The organization also delineates what are considered to be officially appropriate standards of welfare, joint values, incentives, and penalties. These conceptions expand a mere participation contract into a definition of the participant's nature or social being.

3. For economic institutions this has recently been summarized by Talcott Parsons and Neil J. Smelser, *Economy and Society* (New York: The Free Press, 1956), ch. iii, "The Institutional Structure of the Economy." A detailed treatment regarding industrial organizations may be found in Reinhard Bendix, *Work and Authority in Industry* (New York: Wiley, 1956).

4. Bendix, *op. cit.*, "Managerial Conceptions of 'The Worker,'" pp. 288–97.

5. Our way of thinking easily distinguishes between organizational goals and payments to employees, when in fact these may coincide. It is possible to define the goal of the organization as the allocation of privately consumable rewards to its employees, the janitor's pay having the same status as an organizational goal as the stockholder's profits. See R. M. Cyert and J. G. March, "A Behavioral Theory of Organizational Objectives," in Mason Haire, ed., *Modern Organization Theory* (New York: Wiley, 1959), p. 80.

These implicit images form an important element of the values which every organization sustains, regardless of the degree of its efficiency or impersonality.[6] Built right into the social arrangements of an organization, then, is a thoroughly embracing conception of the member—and not merely a conception of him *qua* member, but behind this a conception of him *qua* human being.[7]

We can readily see these organizational conceptions of man in those radical political movements and evangelical religious groups that stress Spartan standards of welfare and joint values that are at once intense and pervasive. Here the member is expected to place himself at the disposal of the current needs of the organization. In telling him what he should do and why he should want to do this, the organization presumably tells him all that he may be. There will be many ways of backsliding, and even where backsliding does not occur frequently, concern that it may happen may be great, clearly pointing to the question of identity and self-definition.[8]

* * * * * *

## Primary and secondary adjustments

A concept can now be introduced. When an individual cooperatively contributes required activity to an organization and under required conditions—in our society with the support of institutionalized standards of welfare, with the drive supplied through incentives and joint values, and with the promptings of designated penalties—he is transformed into a cooperator; he becomes the "normal," "programmed," or built-in member. He gives and gets in an appropriate spirit what has been systematically planned for, whether this entails much or little of himself. In short, he finds that he is officially asked to be no more and no less than he is prepared to be, and is obliged to dwell in a world that is in fact congenial to him. I shall speak in these circumstances of the individual having a *primary adjustment* to the organization and overlook the fact that it would be just as reasonable to speak of the organization having a primary adjustment to him.

I have constructed this clumsy term in order to get to a second one, namely, *secondary adjustments*, defining these as any habitual arrangement by which a member of an organization employs unauthorized means, or obtains unauthorized ends, or both, thus getting around the organization's assumptions as to what he should do and get and hence what he should be. Secondary adjustments represent ways in which the individual stands apart from the role and the self that were taken for granted for him by the institution. For example, it is currently assumed in America that prisoners are persons who should have library facilities, the minds of prisoners being something that can and ought to be allowed to profit from reading. Given this legitimate library activity, we can anticipate Donald Clemmer's finding that prisoners often order books not for self-edification but to impress the parole board, give trouble to the librarian, or merely receive a parcel.[9]

There are sociological terms that refer to secondary adjustments, but these also refer to other things. The term "informal" might be used, except that an organization can formally provide a time and place where members can be officially on their own, to create and enjoy recreational activity of their own choosing while exercising a behavioral style of locker-room informality: morning recess at school is an example. Informality here is part of primary adjustment. The term "unofficial" might be used, except that this concept tends to pertain only to what would ordinarily be the official part of activity in the organization, and in any case the term "unofficial" can properly be applied to those tacit understandings and uncodified activities through which the official aims of the organization can be furthered and the participants attain whatever primary adjustment is possible in the situation.[10]

6. For a consideration of the value tasks of economic organizations, see Philip Selznick, *Leadership in Administration* (Evanston, Ill: Row, Peterson & Co., 1957).

7. For a case study see Alvin Gouldner, *Wildcat Strike* (London: Routledge & Kegan Paul, 1955), especially "The Indulgency Pattern," pp. 18–22, where he outlines workers' moral expectations of the organization which are not an official part of the work contract.

8. This is nicely portrayed in Isaac Rosenfeld's story, "The Party," *The Kenyon Review*, Autumn, 1947, pp. 572–607.

9. Donald Clemmer, *The Prison Community* (reissue; New York: Rinehart, 1958), p. 232.

10. In the classic Hawthorne study of informal or unofficial work groups, the main function of worker solidarity seems to have been to counter management's view of what workers ought to do and what they ought to be, in which case secondary adjustments and informal adjustments would refer to the same thing. However,

I want to mention here some difficulties in using the concept of secondary adjustments. There are some secondary adjustments, such as a worker's practice of supplying his family's needs for the product he helps produce, that become so much an accepted part of the workings of an organization that they take on the character of "perquisites," combining the qualities of being neither openly demanded nor openly questioned.[11] And some of these activities are not merely ones that are soon to be made legitimate but rather ones that must remain unofficial if they are to be effective. As Melville Dalton has shown, special capacities of a participant may have to be underwritten with rewards that no one else of his category receives. And what the courted participant may see as something he is getting away with—a secondary adjustment—may be deliberately allowed him by a conscientious official acting solely from a desire to see the over-all efficiency of the organization sustained.[12] Further, as previously suggested, there may be little agreement as to who are the spokesmen of the organization, and, where there is agreement, the spokesmen may be doubtful in their own minds as to where to draw the line between primary and secondary adjustments. For example, in many American colleges it would be considered a wrongheaded view of the nature of the student to curb too much the extracurricular "social" part of college experience. This is in line with current views as to the necessity of having "all-round" or "well-rounded" students. But there is less consensus about exactly how the student's time is to be divided between academic and extracurricular work. Similarly, it is understandable and widely accepted that some female students will meet their future husbands at college and, once married, feel it more appropriate to drop out of school than to complete work for a degree. But college deans show varying degrees of concern when a female student switches her major each year upon playing out the field of men that the courses made accessible. Similarly, the managers of a commercial office may be clear about feeling it permissible for clerks and secretaries to select one another for personal relationships—provided that not too much working time is wasted in this way—and just as clearly disapprove of trainees who stay only long enough to check through the courting possibilities before going on to a fresh office and a new pasture. But management may be much more vague as to where between these two extremes the

later studies illustrated the fact that informal cliques at work might sustain activities perfectly compatible with, and even supportive of, the role established by management for workers. See Edward Gross, "Characteristics of Cliques in Office Organizations," *Research Studies*, State College of Washington, 19 (1951), especially p. 135; "Some Functional Consequences of Primary Controls in Formal Work Organizations," *American Sociological Review*, 28 (1953), pp. 368–73. Obviously, a choice of "substantive" rationality over "formal" rationality—the selective pursuit of some official goals over other conflicting official goals—may be exhibited by management as well as by subordinates. See, for example, Charles Page, "Bureaucracy's Other Face," *Social Forces*, 25 (1946), pp. 88–94; A. G. Frank, "Goal Ambiguity and Conflicting Standards: An Approach to the Study of Organization," *Human Organization*, 17 (1959), pp. 8–13. See also the very remarkable study by Melville Dalton, *Men Who Manage* (New York: Wiley, 1959), for example, p. 222: ". . . informal action may work for many ends: to change and preserve the organization, to protect weak individuals, punish erring ones, reward others, to recruit new personnel, and to maintain dignity of the formal, as well as, of course, to carry on power struggles, and to work for ends we would all frown on."

11. See, for example, the discussion by Paul Jacobs, "Pottering about with the Fifth Amendment," *The Reporter*, July 12, 1956.

12. Dalton, *op. cit.*, especially ch. vii, "The Interlocking of Official and Unofficial Reward." Dalton argues (pp. 198–99) that, in industry, corresponding to a wide range of unofficial rewards there is a very wide range of unofficial services that the executive must somehow call forth from his men if the organization is to function smoothly:

"Although informal reward ideally is given for effort and contribution beyond what is expected of a specific rank, it is also granted for many other purposes, often unexpected and formally taboo yet important for maintaining the organization and winning its ends. For example, it may be given (1) in lieu of a promotion or salary increase that could not be effected; (2) as a bonus for doing necessary but unpleasant or low-prestige things; (3) as an opiate to forget defeats in policy battles or status tiffs; (4) as a price for conciliating an irate colleague or making, in effect, a treaty with another department; (5) as a perquisite to key persons in clerical or staff groups to prevent slowdowns, and to bolster alertness against errors during critical periods; (6) as a frank supplement to a low but maximum salary; (7) for understanding and aid in the operation, and the defense, of the unofficial incentive system; (8) for great personal sacrifices. There are, of course, more subtle supports which may not be articulated but are intuitively recognized and rewarded where possible. These include: ability to maintain morale in the group or department; skill in picking and holding good subordinates; habitual tacit understanding of what superiors and colleagues expect but would not in some cases want to phrase, even unofficially; and expertness in saving the face of superiors and maintaining the dignity of the organization under adverse conditions."

line is to be drawn separating the legitimate incidental use of an establishment as a convenience from illegitimately making a convenience of an institution.

Another problem associated with the distinction between primary and secondary adjustments is that these two modes of adaptation do not exhaust the possibilities; to get a rounded picture we may have to introduce another possibility. In whatever direction management presses the participants, it is possible for the participants to show more commitment and attachment to the entity than has been asked for or, sometimes, than is desired by management. A parishioner may try to live too much in and for the church; a housewife can keep her domain too clean; a junior officer can insist on going down with the ship. I do not think we have a major social problem here, except perhaps for those inmates of jails, mental hospitals, barracks, colleges, and parental homes who decline to use their discharge; analytically, however, we must see that just as there will always be persons who are felt not to embrace sufficiently a social entity to which they belong, so we will always find at least a few who may embarrass an organization by embracing it too warmly.

Finally, as we shall see later, the official doctrine according to which an institution is run may be so little honored in practice, and a semi-official perspective may be so firmly and fully established, that we must analyze secondary adjustments relative to this authorized-but-not-quite-official system.

* * * * * *

We can begin to look at secondary adjustments—at the practices comprising the underlife of social establishments—by noting that they occur with different frequency and in different forms according to the location of the practitioner in the hierarchy of the organization. Persons at the bottom of large organizations typically operate in drab backgrounds, against which higher-placed members realize their internal incentives, enjoying the satisfaction of receiving visible indulgences that others do not. Low-placed members tend to have less commitment and emotional attachment to the organization than higher-placed members. They have jobs, not careers. In consequence they seem more likely to make wide use of secondary adjustments. Although people toward the top of organizations are likely to be appreciably motivated by joint values, their special duties as representatives of the organization are also likely to lead to travel, entertaining, and ceremonials—that special class of secondary adjustments recently publicized in descriptions of the "expense account" round of life. Perhaps secondary adjustments are least found in the middle range of organizations. It is here, perhaps, that people most closely approach what the organization expects them to be, and it is from here that models of good conduct can be drawn for the edification and inspiration of those lower down.[13]

At the same time, of course, the character of primary adjustments will differ according to rank. Workers at the bottom may not be expected to throw themselves into the organization or "take it home" with them, but high officers are likely to have these identificatory obligations. For example, an attendant in a state mental hospital who leaves work as soon as his shift is over may be acting in a way that has been legitimated for him, expressing the nature the organization accords him; if a head of a service gives this nine-to-five impression, however, he may be considered dead wood by management—someone who is not living up to the standards of devotion expected of a real doctor. Similarly, an attendant who reads a magazine during working hours on the ward may be considered within his rights as long as no immediate duty calls him; a nurse who thus conducts herself is more likely to offend because this is "unprofessional" conduct.

The undergrowth of secondary adjustments also differs in extent according to the type of establishment.

Presumably the shorter the period of continuous time that a given category of participant spends on the premises, the more possible it will be for management to maintain a program of activity and motivation that these participants accept. Thus, in those establishments whose purpose is the sale of a minor standardized item such as cigarettes, customers will usually complete the purchase cycle without deviating very far from the role programmed for them—except, perhaps, in demanding or declining a moment's sociability. Establishments

13. Suggested by Paul Wallin.

that oblige the participant to "live in" will presumably be rich in underlife, for the more time that is programmed by the organization, the less likelihood of successfully programming it.

So also in those organizations where recruitment is involuntary, we can expect that, at least initially, the recruit will not be in harmony with the self-definitions officially available for persons like himself and will therefore orient himself to unlegitimized activities.

Finally, as previously suggested, establishments that do not provide appreciable external incentives, not having made their peace with what is seen as the Adam in man, are likely to find that some external incentives are unofficially developed.

All of the conditions that are likely to promote active underlife are present in one institution that is receiving considerable attention today: the mental hospital. In what follows I want to consider some of the main themes that occur in the secondary adjustments I recorded in a year's participant observation study of patient life in a public mental hospital of over 7000 patients, hereafter called "Central Hospital."

* * * * * *

## Sources

I turn now to consider the sources of materials that patients employ in their secondary adjustments.

The first thing to note is the prevalence of *make-do's*. In every social establishment participants use available artifacts in a manner and for an end not officially intended, thereby modifying the conditions of life programmed for these individuals. A physical reworking of the artifact may be involved, or merely an illegitimate context of use, in either case providing homely illustrations of the Robinson Crusoe theme. Obvious examples come from prisons, where, for example, a knife may be hammered from a spoon, drawing ink extracted from the pages of *Life* magazine,[14] exercise books used to write betting slips,[15] and cigarettes lit by a number of means—sparking an electric-light outlet,[16] a homemade tinderbox,[17] or a match split into quarters.[18] While this transformation process underlies many complex practices, it can be most clearly seen where the practitioner is not involved with others (except in learning and teaching the technique), he alone consuming what he just produced.

In Central Hospital many simple make-do's were tacitly tolerated. For example, inmates widely used freestanding radiators to dry personal clothing that they had washed, on their own, in the bathroom sink, thus performing a private laundry cycle that was officially only the institution's concern. On hard-bench wards, patients sometimes carried around rolled-up newspapers to place between their necks and the wooden benches when lying down. Rolled-up coats and towels were used in the same way. Patients with experience in other imprisoning institutions employed an even more effective artifact in this context, a shoe.[19] In transferring from one ward to another, patients would sometimes carry their belongings in a pillow slip knotted at the top, a practice which is semi-official in some jails.[20] The few aging patients fortunate enough to have a private sleeping room would sometimes leave a towel underneath their room washstand, transforming the stand into a reading desk and the towel into a rug to protect their feet from the cold floor. Older patients who were disinclined or unable to move around sometimes employed strategies to avoid the task of going to the toilet: on the ward, the hot steam radiator could be urinated on without leaving too many long-lasting signs; during twice-weekly shaving visits to the basement barbershop, the bin reserved for used towels was used for a urinal when the attendants were not looking. Back-ward patients of all ages sometimes carried around paper drinking cups to serve as portable spittoons and ash trays, since attendants were sometimes more concerned about keeping their floors clean than they were in suppressing spitting or smoking.[21]

14. Cantine and Rainer, *op. cit.*, p. 42.

15. Frank Norman, *Bang to Rights* (London: Secker and Warburg, 1958), p. 90.

16. *Ibid.*, p. 92.

17. George Dendrickson and Frederick Thomas, *The Truth About Dartmoor* (London: Gollancz, 1954), p. 172.

18. *Ibid.*, pp. 172–73.

19. Compare the naval equivalent (Melville, *op. cit.*, p. 189): ". . . the hard, unyielding, and ponderous man-of-war and Navy regulation tarpaulin hat which, when new, is stiff enough to sit upon, and indeed, in lieu of his thumb, sometimes serves the common sailor for a bench."

20. For a British example, see Dendrickson and Thomas, *op. cit.*, p. 66.

21. In Central Hospital many patients remained entirely

In total institutions make-do's tend to be focused in particular areas. One area is that of personal grooming—the fabrication of devices to facilitate presenting oneself to others in a seemly guise. For example, nuns are said to have placed a black apron behind a window pane to create a mirror—a mirror being a means of self-examination, correction, and approval ordinarily denied the sisterhood.[22] In Central Hospital, toilet paper was sometimes "organized"; neatly torn, folded, and carried on one's person, it was apologetically used as Kleenex by some fastidious patients. So, too, during the hot summer months a few male patients cut and tailored their hospital-issue khaki pants into neat-appearing summer shorts.

The simple make-do's I have cited are characterized by the fact that to employ them one need have very little involvement in and orientation to the official world of the establishment. I consider now a set of practices that imply somewhat more aliveness to the legitimated world of the institution. Here the spirit of the legitimate activity may be maintained but is carried past the point to which it was meant to go; we have an extension and elaboration of existing sources of legitimate satisfactions, or the exploitation of a whole routine of official activity for private ends. I shall speak here of "working" the system.

Perhaps the most elementary way of working the system in Central Hospital was exhibited by those patients on back wards who went on sick call or declined to comply with ward discipline in order, apparently, to trap the attendant or physician into taking notice of them and engaging them in social interaction, however disciplinarian.

Most hospital techniques for working the system did not seem to be closely connected with mental illness, however. An example of such techniques is the elaborate set of practices associated with food-getting. For example, in a large cafeteria where the 900 patients of a male chronic service[23] ate in shifts, some would bring their own condiments so as to season their own food to their own taste; sugar, salt, pepper, and catsup were brought in for this purpose in small bottles carried in jacket pockets. When coffee was served in paper cups, patients sometimes protected their hands by inserting their cup in a second paper cup. On days when bananas were made available, a few of the patients would spirit away a cup of milk from the jug meant for those who required milk on their diet, and would cut their bananas up in slices, put on some sugar, and expansively eat a "proper" dessert. On days when the food was both liked and portable, for example when frankfurters or liver were served, some patients would wrap up their food in a paper napkin and then go back for "seconds," taking the first serving back to the ward for a night snack. A few patients brought empty bottles on days when milk was served, taking some of this back to the ward, too. If more of a given item on the menu was desired, one device was to eat just that item, dump the remainder of one's serving in the slop pail, and return (when this was allowed) for a full course of seconds. A few of the paroled patients assigned to eat in this cafeteria would, for the evening meal in summer, put their cheese between two slices of bread, wrap up what had now become a sandwich, and eat in peace outside the patient canteen, buying a cup of coffee. Patients with town parole would sometimes top this off by buying pie and ice cream at the local drugstore. In a smaller dining room in a different hospital service, patients who (rightly) feared that seconds would not be available for long

mute, were incontinent, hallucinated, and practiced other classic symptoms. However, very few patients, as far as I could see, had the temerity purposely and persistently to drop ashes on the linoleum floor, just as few declined to line up for food, take their shower, go to bed, or get up on time. Behind a ward show of frank psychosis was a basic ward routine that was quite fully adhered to.

22. Kathryn Hulme, *The Nun's Story* (London: Muller, 1956), p. 33. Norman, *op. cit.*, p. 87, states that during Christmas-day relaxation of discipline at the British prison, Camp Hill, homosexuals made their faces up with white tooth powder and reddened their lips with dye obtained by wetting the covers of books.

23. Residentially speaking, American mental hospitals are typically organized officially by wards and services. A ward usually consists of sleeping quarters (which often can be locked off), a day room, a nurses' station with a view of the day room, various maintenance and administrative offices, a row of isolation cells, and sometimes a dining-room area. A service consists of a set of these wards filling one or more separate buildings, involving a common administration, and having some basis of patient homogeneity—age, sex, race, chronicity, etc. This homogeneity allows the service to evolve wards of differentiated character and function, roughly providing a ladder of privilege, up and down which any patient in the service can be shifted with minimum bureaucratic effort. The hospital as a whole tends to repeat through its services what, in miniature, each service does through its wards.

would sometimes take their portion of meat from their plate, put it between two pieces of bread, leave this by their place, and immediately return to the line to get seconds. These farsighted patients would sometimes return to their places to find that a fellow inmate had made off with the first serving, cheating the cheaters at the cost of very little effort.

In order to work a system effectively, one must have an intimate knowledge of it;[24] it was easy to see this kind of knowledge put to work in the hospital. For example, it was widely known by parole patients that at the end of charitable shows at the theater hall cigarettes or candy would probably be given out at the door, as the patient audience filed out. Bored by some of these shows, some patients would come a few minutes before closing time in order to file out with the others; still others would manage to get back into the line several times and make the whole occasion more than ordinarily worthwhile. Staff were of course aware of these practices, and latecomers to some of the hospital-wide patient dances were locked out, the assumption being that they timed their arrival so as to be able to eat and run. The Jewish Welfare women apparently served brunch after the weekly morning service and one patient claimed that "by coming at the right time you can get the lunch and miss the service." Another patient, alive to the little-known fact that the hospital had a team of seamstresses to keep clothes in repair, would take his own clothes there and get shirts and pants tailored to a good fit, showing his gratitude by a package or two of cigarettes or a small sum of money.

* * * * * *

## Places

Some of the elementary sources of material for secondary adjustments in Central Hospital have been considered. I turn now to the question of the setting, for if these activities of underlife are to occur, they must occur in some place or region.[25]

In Central Hospital, as in many total institutions, each inmate tended to find his world divided into three parts, the partitioning drawn similarly for those of the same privilege status.

First, there was space that was off limits or out of bounds. Here mere presence was the form of conduct that was actively prohibited—unless, for example, the inmate was specifically "with" an authorized agent or active in a relevant service role. For example, according to the rules posted in one of the male services, the grounds behind one of the female services were out of bounds, presumably as a chastity measure. For all patients but the few with town parole, anything beyond the institution walls was out of bounds. So, too, everything outside a locked ward was off limits for its resident patients, and the ward itself was off limits for patients not resident there. Many of the administrative buildings and administrative sections of buildings, doctors' offices, and, with some variations, ward nursing stations were out of bounds for patients. Similar arrangements have of course been reported in other studies of mental hospitals:

> When the charge [attendant] is in his office, the office itself and a zone of about 6 square feet outside the office is off limits to all except the top group of ward helpers among the privileged patients. The other patients neither stand nor sit in this zone. Even the privileged patients may be sent away with abrupt authority if the charge or his attendants desire it. Obedience when this order occurs—usually in a parental form, such as "run along, now"—is instantaneous. The privileged patient is privileged precisely because he understands the meaning of this social space and other aspects of the attendant's position.[26]

Second, there was *surveillance space*, the area a patient needed no special excuse for being in, but where he would be subject to the usual authority

24. Knowledge of a guard's routine figures in many fictional escape stories. Desperation and knowledge of routines are also linked in real experience as Kogon (*op. cit.*, p. 180) illustrates in discussing the response of Buchenwald prisoners to reduction and withdrawal of rations: ". . . When an inmate had died in the tents, the fact was concealed and the dead man was dragged or carried by one or two men to the bread issue point, where the ration was issued to the 'helpers.' The body was then simply dumped anywhere in the roll-call area."

25. The study of the social use of space has recently been restimulated by the work of animal ethologists such as H. Hediger and Konrad Lorenz. See, for example, the very interesting paper by Robert Sommer, "Studies in Personal Space," *Sociometry*, 22 (1959), pp. 247–60, and H. F. Ellenberger, "Zoological Garden and Mental Hospital," *Canadian Psychiatric Association Journal*, 5 (1960), pp. 136–49.

26. Ivan Belknap, *Human Problems of a State Mental Hospital* (New York: McGraw-Hill, 1956), pp. 179–80.

and restrictions of the establishment. This area included most of the hospital for those patients with parole. Finally, there was space ruled by less than usual staff authority; it is the varieties of this kind of space that I want to consider now.

The visible activity of a particular secondary adjustment may be actively forbidden in a mental hospital, as in other establishments. If the practice is to occur, it must be shielded from the eyes and ears of staff. This may involve merely turning away from a staff person's line of vision.[27] The inmate may smile derisively by half-turning away, chew on food without signs of jaw motion when eating is forbidden, cup a lighted cigarette in the hand when smoking is not permitted, and use a hand to conceal cigarette chips during a ward poker game when the supervising nurse passes through the ward. These were concealment devices employed in Central Hospital. A further example is cited from another mental institution:

> My total rejection of psychiatry, which had, after coma, become a fanatical adulation, now passed into a third phase—one of constructive criticism. I became aware of the peripheral obtuseness and the administrative dogmatism of the hospital bureaucracy. My first impulse was to condemn; later, I perfected means of maneuvering freely within the clumsy structure of ward politics. To illustrate, my reading matter had been kept under surveillance for quite some time, and I had at last perfected a means of keeping *au courant* without unnecessarily alarming the nurses and attendants. I had smuggled several issues of *Hound and Horn* into my ward on the pretext that it was a field-and-stream magazine. I had read Hoch and Kalinowski's *Shock Therapy* (a top secret manual of arms at the hospital) quite openly, after I had put it into the dust jacket of Anna Balakian's *Literary Origins of Surrealism*.[28]

In addition, however, to these temporary means of avoiding hospital surveillance, inmates and staff tacitly cooperated to allow the emergence of bounded physical spaces in which ordinary levels of surveillance and restriction were markedly reduced, spaces where the inmate could openly engage in a range of tabooed activities with some degree of security. These places often also provided a marked reduction in usual patient population density, contributing to the peace and quiet characteristic of them. The staff did not know of the existence of these places, or knew but either stayed away or tacitly relinquished their authority when entering them. Licence, in short, had a geography. I shall call these regions *free places*. We may especially expect to find them when authority in an organization is lodged in a whole echelon of staff instead of in a set of pyramids of command. Free places are backstage to the usual performance of staff-inmate relationships.

* * * * * *

In everyday life, legitimate possessions employed in primary adjustments are typically stored, when not in use, in special places of safekeeping which can be gotten to at will, such as footlockers, cabinets, bureau drawers, and safe deposit boxes. These storage places protect the object from damage, misuse, and misappropriation, and allow the user to conceal what he possesses from others.[29] More important, these places can represent an extension of the self and its autonomy, becoming more important as the individual forgoes other repositories of selfhood. If nothing can be kept only for oneself, and everything one uses is used by others, too, then little protection from social contamination by others is possible. Further, some of the things one must give up are those with which one has become especially identified and which one employs for self-identification to others. It is thus that a man

27. An American prison example may be cited from Alfred Hassler's *Diary of a Self-Made Convict* (Chicago: Regnery, 1954), p. 123: "A few minutes later the guard makes his 'count,' at which time each man is supposed to be standing, fully dressed, at his door. Since the hack simply glances in at the window, however, it is a simple enough matter to slip one's shirt on and, by standing close to the door, give the desired impression."

28. Carl Solomon, "Report from the Asylum," in G. Feldman and M. Gartenberg, eds., *The Beat Generation and the Angry Young Men* (New York: Dell Publishing Co., 1959), pp. 177–78.

29. Personal places of safekeeping are, of course, known in cultures not our own. See, for example, John Skolle, Azalaï (New York: Harper & Bros., 1956), p. 49: "The Tuareg carried all their possessions in leather bags. Those containing valuables they would lock with their native *cadenas*, three keys sometimes being required to work the combination. The system seemed singularly ineffectual as a measure of precaution because every man carried a dagger and anyone who so desired could ignore the lock and slash the leather bag. But no one thought of doing this. The lock was universally respected as a symbol of privacy."

in a monastery may be concerned about his one privacy, his letterbox,[30] and a man on a frigate about his canvas clothes bag.[31]

Where such private storage places are not allowed, it is understandable that they will be illicitly developed. Further, if one is to possess an object illicitly, then the place in which it is stored may itself have to be concealed. A personal storage space that is concealed and/or locked not merely to thwart illegitimate interlopers but also legitimate authority is sometimes called a *stash* in the criminal and near-criminal world, and will be called this here.[32] It may be noted that these illicit storage places represent a more complex matter, organizationally, than do simple make-do's, since a stash can ordinarily safeguard more than one kind of illicit possession. I would like to add that one important object that may be stashed is the human body (dead or alive), giving rise to special terms such as hideout, stowaway, laying low, and to one of the inevitable scenes of detective fiction.

When patients entered Central Hospital, especially if they were excited or depressed on admission, they were denied a private, accessible place to store things. Their personal clothing, for example, might be stored in a room that was beyond their discretionary use. Their money was kept in the administration building, unobtainable without medical and/or their legal agents' permission. Valuables or breakables, such as false teeth, eyeglasses, wrist watches, often an integral part of body image, might be locked up safely out of their owners' reach. Official papers of self-identification might also be retained by the institution.[33] Cosmetics, needed to present oneself properly to others, were collectivized, being made accessible to patients only at certain times. On convalescent wards, bed boxes were available, but since they were unlocked they were subject to theft from other patients and from staff, and in any case were often located in rooms locked to patients during the day.

If people were selfless, or were required to be selfless, there would of course be a logic to having no private storage place, as a British ex-mental patient suggests:

> I looked for a locker, but without success. There appeared to be none in this hospital; the reason soon abundantly clear; they were quite unnecessary—we had nothing to keep in them—everything being shared, even the solitary face cloth which was used for a number of other purposes, a subject on which my feelings became very strong.[34]

But all have some self. Given the curtailment implied by loss of places of safekeeping, it is understandable that patients in Central Hospital developed places of their own.

It seemed characteristic of hospital life that the most common form of stash was one that could be carried around on one's person wherever one went.[35] One such device for female patients was a large handbag; a parallel technique for a man was a jacket with commodious pockets, worn even in the hottest weather. While these containers are quite usual ones in the wider community, there was a special burden placed upon them in the hospital: books, writing materials, washcloths, fruit, small valuables, scarves, playing cards, soap, shaving equipment (on the part of men), containers of salt, pepper, and sugar, bottles of milk—these were some of the objects sometimes carried in this manner. So common was this practice that one of the most reliable symbols of patient status in the hospital was bulging pockets. Another portable storage device

30. Thomas Merton, *The Seven Storey Mountain* (New York: Harcourt, Brace and Company, 1948), p. 384.

31. Melville, *op. cit.*, p. 47.

32. An American prison example may be cited from Hassler, *op. cit.*, pp. 59–60:

> "Directly across from me is the dormitory's most illustrious tenant—"Nocky" Johnson, erstwhile political boss of Atlantic City and, if my memory serves, concessionaire for most of the more sordid activities in that resort. Nocky is a tall, heavily built man in his sixties. His standing in the prison hierarchy is evident, at first glance, in the half-dozen fine woollen blankets stacked on his cot (the rest of us have two of much poorer quality) and the lock on his tin cabinet—definitely *de trop* among the lesser fry. My embezzler neighbor tells me the hacks never examine Nocky's possessions as they do everyone else's. The glimpse I had of the interior of his cabinet showed it to be jammed with cartons of cigarettes—the principal medium of exchange in this moneyless sanctuary.

33. It should be clearly stated that there are many strong clinical and administrative arguments for denying particular patients their personal possessions. The question of the desirability of such denials is not here at issue.

34. Johnson and Dodds, *op. cit.*, p. 86.

35. In the light literature on criminal activity there are well-known portable stashes: false heels, false-bottomed suitcases, anal suppositories, etc. Jewels and narcotics are the favorite items stashed in this manner. More fanciful stashes are described in espionage fiction.

was a shopping bag lined with another shopping bag. (When partly full, this frequently employed stash also served as a cushion and back rest.) Among men, a small stash was sometimes created out of a long sock: by knotting the open end and twisting this end around his belt, the patient could let a kind of moneybag inconspicuously hang down inside his trouser leg. Individual variations of these portable containers were also found. One young engineering graduate fashioned a purse out of discarded oilcloth, the purse being stitched into separate, well-measured compartments for comb, toothbrush, cards, writing paper, pencil, soap, small face cloth, toilet paper—the whole attached by a concealed clip to the underside of his belt.

* * * * * *

I want to raise two general questions about underlife in Central Hospital.

First, it should be clear that a description of underlife in an institution can provide a systematically biased picture of life in it. To the degree that members confine themselves to primary adjustments (whether out of satisfaction or incapacity to build a different world), underlife may be unrepresentative and even unimportant. Moreover, the secondary adjustments most easily observed may be ones that are elaborate and colorful, and these, as in the case of Central Hospital, may be practised mainly by a handful of well-connected informal leaders. Their conduct may be of great importance to the student if he wants to learn how the particular institution can be worked and how institutions in general might be worked; but in searching for the range and scope of secondary adjustments, the student may fail to see how the average member lives. This report necessarily focuses on the activity of manipulative paroled patients, giving an over-rosy view both of the life of patients as a whole in Central Hospital and of the efficiency of their techniques for unofficially altering their life conditions.

The second general question I want to raise has to do with social control and bond formation.

The social arrangements which make economic and social exchange possible obviously function to ensure that the individual will be able to incorporate into his own plan of action the efforts of others, increasing many times the efficacy of secondary adjustments he makes by himself on his own behalf. Now it is plain that if these social arrangements are to be sustained, some form of social control will have to be exerted to keep people in line, to make them live up to their bargains and their obligation to perform favors and ceremonies for others. These forms of social control will constitute secondary adjustments of a very special class—a class of adjustments which underlie and stabilize a vast complex of other unofficial, undercover practices. And from the point of view of inmate underlife in total institutions, these controls will have to be exerted over both inmates and staff.

Inmate control of staff in total institutions takes traditional forms, for example: arranging for "accidents" to occur to a staff person,[36] or the massed rejection of a particular item of food,[37] or the slowing-down of work production, or the sabotaging of plumbing, lighting, and communication systems, all of which are readily vulnerable to inmate action.[38] Other inmate sanctions of staff may take the form of "collective" or individual teasing and more subtle forms of ritual insubordination, such as the military technique of saluting a troublesome officer from too great a distance, or with too much precision, or with too slow a tempo. A staff threat to the whole system of undercover arrangements may be answered with extreme action such as strikes or riots.

* * * * * *

Of the many different kinds of secondary adjustment, some are of particular interest because they bring into the clear the general theme of involvement and disaffection, characteristic of all these practices.

One of these special types of secondary adjustment is "removal activities" (or "kicks"), namely, undertakings that provide something for the individual to lose himself in, temporarily blotting out all sense of the environment which, and in which, he must abide. In total institutions a useful exemplary

36. For example, Dendrickson and Thomas, *op. cit.*, p. 130.

37. Cantine and Rainer, *op. cit.*, p. 4.

38. *Ibid.*, p. 10.

case is provided by Robert Stroud, the "Birdman," who, from watching birds out his cell window, through a spectacular career of finagling and make-do, fabricated a laboratory and became a leading ornithological contributor to medical literature, all from within prison.[39] Language courses in prisoner-of-war camps and art courses in prisons[40] can provide the same release.

Central Hospital provided several of these escape worlds for inmates.[41] One, for example, was sports. Some of the baseball players and a few tennis players seemed to become so caught up in their sport, and in the daily record of their efforts in competition, that at least for the summer months this became their overriding interest. In the case of baseball this was further strengthened by the fact that, within the hospital, parole patients could follow national baseball as readily as could many persons on the outside. For some young patients, who never failed to go, when allowed, to a dance held in their service or in the recreation building, it was possible to live for the chance of meeting someone "interesting" or remeeting someone interesting who had already been met—in much the same way that college students are able to survive their studies by looking forward to the new "dates" that may be found in extracurricular activities. The "marriage moratorium" in Central Hospital, effectively freeing a patient from his marital obligations to a nonpatient, enhanced this removal activity. For a handful of patients, the semi-annual theatrical production was an extremely effective removal activity: tryouts, rehearsals, costuming, scenery-making, staging, writing and rewriting, performing—all these seemed as successful as on the outside in building a world apart for the participants. Another kick, important to some patients—and a worrisome concern for the hospital chaplains—was the enthusiastic espousal of religion. Still another, for a few patients, was gambling.[42]

Portable ways of getting away were much favored in Central Hospital, paper-back murder mysteries,[43] cards, and even jigsaw puzzles being carried around on one's person. Not only could leave be taken of the ward and grounds be taken leave of through these means, but if one had to wait for an hour or so upon an official, or the serving of a meal, or the opening of the recreation building, the self-implication of this subordination could be dealt with by immediately bringing forth one's own world-making equipment.

Individual means of creating a world were striking. One depressed, suicidal alcoholic, apparently a good bridge player, disdained bridge with almost all other patient players, carrying around his own pocket bridge player and writing away occasionally for a new set of competition hands. Given a supply of his favorite gumdrops and his pocket radio, he could pull himself out of the hospital world at will, surrounding all his senses with pleasantness.

In considering removal activities we can again raise the issue of overcommitment to an establishment. In the hospital laundry, for example, there was a patient worker who had been on the job for several years. He had been given the job of un-

39. Gaddis, *op. cit.*

40. J. F. N., *op. cit.*, pp. 17–18.

41. Behind informal social typing and informal group formation in prisons there is often to be seen a removal activity. Caldwell, *op. cit.*, pp. 651–53, provides some interesting examples of prisoners on such kicks: those involved in securing and using drugs; those focused on leatherwork for sale; and "Spartans," those involved in the glorification of their bodies, the prison locker room apparently serving as a muscle beach; the homosexuals; the gamblers, etc. The point about these activities is that each is world-building for the person caught up in it, thereby displacing the prison.

42. Melville, *op. cit.*, devotes a whole chapter, ch. lxxiii, to illicit gambling aboard his frigate.

43. The getaway role of reading in prison is well described in Behan, *op. cit.;* see also Heckstall-Smith, *op. cit.*, p. 34: "The prison library offered a fairly good selection of books. But as time went by I found myself reading merely to kill time—reading everything and anything I could lay my hands on. During those first weeks, reading acted as a soporific and on the long early summer evenings I often fell asleep over my book."

Kogon, *op. cit.*, pp. 127–28, provides a concentration-camp example:

"In the winter of 1942–43 a succession of bread thefts in Barracks 42 at Buchenwald made it necessary to establish a nightwatch. For months on end I volunteered for this duty, taking the shift from three to six o'clock in the morning. It meant sitting alone in the day room, while the snores of the comrades came from the other end. For once I was free of the ineluctable companionship that usually shackled and stifled every individual activity. What an experience it was to sit quietly by a shaded lamp, delving into the pages of Plato's *Dialogues*, Galsworthy's *Swan Song*, or the works of Heine, Klabund, Mehring! Heine? Klabund? Mehring? Yes, they could be read illegally in camp. They were among books retrieved from the nation-wide wastepaper collections."

official foreman, and, unlike almost all other patient workers, he threw himself into his work with a capacity, devotion, and seriousness that were evident to many. Of him, the laundry charge attendant said:

> That one there is my special helper. He works harder than all the rest put together. I would be lost without him.

In exchange for his effort, the attendant would bring from home something for this patient to eat almost every day. And yet there was something grotesque in his adjustment, for it was apparent that his deep voyage into the work world had a slightly make-believe character; after all, he was a patient, not a foreman, and he was clearly reminded of this off the job.

Obviously, as some of these illustrations imply, removal activities need not be in themselves illegitimate; it is the function that they come to serve for the inmate that leads us to consider them along with other secondary adjustments. An extreme here, perhaps, is individual psychotherapy in state mental hospitals; this privilege is so rare in these institutions,[44] and the resulting contact with a staff psychiatrist so unique in terms of hospital status structure, that an inmate can to some degree forget where he is as he pursues his psychotherapy. By actually receiving what the institution formally claims to offer, the patient can succeed in getting away from what the establishment actually provides. There is a general implication here. Perhaps every activity that an establishment obliges or permits its members to participate in is a potential threat to the organization, for it would seem that there is no activity in which the individual cannot become overengrossed.

* * * * * *

It would be easy to account for the development of secondary adjustments by assuming that the individual possessed an array of needs, native or cultivated, and that when lodged in a milieu that denied these needs the individual simply responded by developing makeshift means of satisfaction. I think this explanation fails to do justice to the importance of these undercover adaptations for the structure of the self.

The practice of reserving something of oneself from the clutch of an institution is very visible in mental hospitals and prisons but can be found in more benign and less totalistic institutions, too. I want to argue that this recalcitrance is not an incidental mechanism of defense but rather an essential constituent of the self.

Sociologists have always had a vested interest in pointing to the ways in which the individual is formed by groups, identifies with groups, and wilts away unless he obtains emotional support from groups. But when we closely observe what goes on in a social role, a spate of sociable interaction, a social establishment—or in any other unit of social organization—embracement of the unit is not all that we see. We always find the individual employing methods to keep some distance, some elbow room, between himself and that with which others assume he should be identified. No doubt a state-type mental hospital provides an overly lush soil for the growth of these secondary adjustments, but in fact, like weeds, they spring up in any kind of social organization. If we find, then, that in all situations actually studied the participant has erected defenses against his social bondedness, why should we base our conception of the self upon how the individual would act were conditions "just right"?

The simplest sociological view of the individual and his self is that he is to himself what his place in an organization defines him to be. When pressed, a sociologist modifies this model by granting certain complications: the self may be not yet formed or may exhibit conflicting dedications. Perhaps we should further complicate the construct by elevating these qualifications to a central place, initially defining the individual, for sociological purposes, as a stance-taking entity, a something that takes up a position somewhere between identification with an organization and opposition to it, and is ready at the slightest pressure to regain its balance by shifting its involvement in either direction. It is thus *against something* that the self can emerge. This has been appreciated by students of totalitarianism:

44. Of approximately 7000 patients in Central Hospital, I calculated at the time of the study that about 100 received some kind of individual psychotherapy in any one year.

In short, Ketman means self-realization *against* something. He who practices Ketman suffers because of the obstacles he meets; but if these obstacles were suddenly to be removed, he would find himself in a void which might perhaps prove much more painful. Internal revolt is sometimes essential to spiritual health, and can create a particular form of happiness. What can be said openly is often much less interesting than the emotional magic of defending one's private sanctuary.[45]

I have argued the same case in regard to total institutions. May this not be the situation, however, in free society, too?

Without something to belong to, we have no stable self, and yet total commitment and attachment to any social unit implies a kind of selflessness. Our sense of being a person can come from being drawn into a wider social unit; our sense of selfhood can arise through the little ways in which we resist the pull. Our status is backed by the solid buildings of the world, while our sense of personal identity often resides in the cracks.

45. Czeslaw Milosz, *The Captive Mind* (New York: Vintage Books, 1955), p. 76.

# *Succession and Mobility*

The necessities of survival induce all social systems, small groups, formal organizations, communities, and even nation-states, to establish some techniques for coping with the loss of their members and their replacement with new ones. Administrative succession refers specifically to the social processes associated with the treatment of this problem in organizations, where the basic unit is the position or office. How do organizations deal with changes in occupants of offices? What are the consequences of these changes for the organization, its subsystems, and for the community and society? The four selections are addressed to these general problems.

Weber's approach to succession involved a focus on its implications for organizational control via the transfer of authority to the new leader. Gouldner's intensive case study of succession in a gypsum plant extends Weber's formulations although still based on the assumption that ". . . the adaptation of an organization to a threat is mediated and shaped by powerful individuals" (p. 436). A number of new and important problems are highlighted: the effects of succession on the relationship between the new man and his subordinates, the problems of legitimacy that beset the new leader, the origin of challenges to his legitimacy, the importance of commitments of the new man to higher-level management, and the relevance of changes in style of supervision.

Grusky's approach to succession differs from Gouldner's both in underlying assumptions and in method. Here the focus is on the effects of turnover at all management levels and not only that of the top leaders. Also, the concern is with the rate of succession in the system as a whole; the unit of study is the organization rather than the superior-subordinate role relationship. By comparing two markedly different types of organizations, one military and one business, the effects of rate of succession on executive homogeneity, organizational control, commitment, and community involvement, are studied. By broadening the latter perspective even further to include nonmanagement personnel, the study of succession and that of career mobility combine to produce a set of mutually relevant organizational problems.

The ways in which organizations function to facilitate or impede the career mobility of their members is the shared concern of the remaining pair of selections, that by Clark and by Goldner and Ritti. Clark analyzes the role of the junior college in American society by means of the application of Merton's means-ends schema which notes the disjuncture between major cultural goals and the institutionally acceptable means of attaining them. He describes the organizational processes by which the junior college student is "cooled-out" by a redefinition of his failure in a gradual, step-by-step, and therefore less anxiety-arousing fashion.

Goldner and Ritti are concerned with the relationship between professionalization and mobility. By examining the career patterns of professional engineers and salesmen, among others, they show the professional ladder to be not as it is officially presented, but instead as a means by which management "cools out" its less acceptable members and, at the same time, by providing alternative goals, seeks to utilize their contributions and maintain their commitment. Hence, both investigations converge on a single problem—the organization's attempt to restructure the hopes and aspirations of its members.

ALVIN W. GOULDNER

# Succession and the Problems of Bureaucracy

With Peele's promotion to plant manager, the growth of bureaucratic organization became pronounced. How can this be explained? As a first step, though by no means as a complete answer, it is helpful to consider Peele as a man playing a peculiar role—the role of a "successor." Instead of examining Peele's unique personality, let us begin by identifying the kinds of pressures and problems which beset him because of this role. Peele's psychological "traits" will be considered only to the extent that they relate to conditions of sociological importance.

Before proceeding further, however, one other feature of Peele's behavior deserves emphasis; these are the changes which he made among middle management personnel. As already shown, Peele brought in a new personnel director, Jack Digger, from the "outside." Digger had come from the plant at which Peele formerly had been manager, a plant also owned by the Company. Beyond this, four other replacements were made to supervisory positions which had been newly opened. This rapid change in supervisory personnel, following a succession, is so common that it should be given a distinctive label—we shall call it "strategic replacements."

The problem of the present chapter can now be formulated as follows: In what ways does the role of a successor conduce to increasing bureaucratization and to an increased rate of strategic replacements?

## The successor's sentiments

Before being handed the reins at the Oscar Center plant, Peele was called to the main office for a "briefing." The main office executives told Peele of his predecessor's shortcomings, and expressed the feeling that things had been slipping at the plant for some time. They suggested that Old Doug, the former manager who had recently died, had grown overindulgent with his advancing years, and that he, Peele, would be expected to improve production. As Peele put it, "Doug didn't force the machine. I had to watch it. Doug was satisfied with a certain production.[1] But the Company gave me orders to get production up."

With the renewed pressure of postwar competition, the main office expected things to start humming; traditional production quotas were about to be rationalized. A "briefing," it will be seen, does more than impart technical data. It also serves to

1. Roethlisberger and Dickson have emphasized the tendency of informal cliques of workers to limit their output in a traditionalistic way, through their beliefs concerning a "fair day's work." But restriction of output, or "sabotage" as Veblen referred to it, is not manifested solely by operatives; it is found also among managerial personnel. Veblen, of course, has long since noted this; he tended, however, to focus on the rational motives for "sabotage" among managers, neglecting the traditionalistic component.

Reprinted from *Patterns of Industrial Bureaucracy*, pp. 70–101, by permission of the author and The Macmillan Company. 

crystallize *attitudes* toward an assignment and to raise the salience of *values* considered appropriate to the situation.

Peele, therefore, came to the plant sensitized to the rational and impersonal yardsticks which his superiors would use to judge his performance.

As a successor, Peele had a heightened awareness that he could disregard top management's rational values only at his peril, for his very promotion symbolized the power which they held over him. Since he was now on a new assignment, Peele also realized that he would be subject to more than routine observation by the main office. As a successor, he was "on trial" and, therefore, he was anxious, and anxious to "make good." Comments about Peele's anxiety were made by many main office personnel, as well as by people in the plant, who spoke repeatedly of his "nervousness."

In turn, this anxiety spurred Peele to perform his new role according to main office expectations. As one of the main office administrative staff said, "Peele is trying hard to arrive. He is paying more attention to the plant." Peele also accepted top management's view of the plant out of *gratitude* for having been promoted from the smaller plant at which he had been, to the larger one at Oscar Center. "I appreciate their confidence in me," he said, "and I want to show it."

By virtue of his succession, Peele was, at the very least, new to his specific position in the Oscar Center plant's social system. As it happened, he had come from the "outside' and was new to the entire plant. He was all the more a stranger among strangers, as yet untied by bonds of friendship to people in his new plant. He was, therefore, able to view the plant situation in a comparatively dispassionate light and was, further, freer to put his judgments into practice. Unhampered by commitments to the informal understandings established in the plant, the successor came with a sharpened propensity for rational, efficiency-centered action.

Even before setting foot in the plant, then, Peele had an intimation that there would be things which needed "correction." He began to define the plant as one needing some "changes," changes oriented to the efficiency-maximizing values of top management, and he tentatively began shaping policies to bring about the requisite changes.

## The old bunch

When a successor's promotion is announced, he may, however, be subjected to pressures which can introduce another, potentially conflicting, element into his frame of reference. On his way up, he is likely to have incurred obligations and to have made some friends whose loyalty and help expedited his ascent. Since a succession is often a time of promotion and enhanced power, it becomes the moment of reckoning awaited by friends, when their past favors to the successor can be reciprocated.

In a succession entailing a promotion, such as this, the successor is subjected, therefore, to somewhat contradictory pressures. On the one hand, his superiors expect him to conform to rational values and to act without "fear or favor" for any individuals in accomplishing his new mission. His old friends, however, are simultaneously exerting counterpressures, expecting him to defer to their claims for personal preferment. The outcome of these conflicting pressures cannot be predicted without considering the distinctive problems that succession engenders for the new manager.

It might be imagined that the successor would quickly resolve this conflict in favor of the demands and outlook of top management. After all, the main office has far more power over him than his friends can muster. Moreover, the successor might evade his old obligations if he is no longer among the friends to whom he owes them. (He might say, as the newly crowned Henry the Fifth said to Falstaff, "I know thee not, old man: fall to thy prayers . . . Presume not that I am the thing I was . . .")

But when the successor enters and tries to become a part of his new plant, he faces another difficulty which soon leads him to look with favor upon the claims of his old friends. The difficulty is that, as a new manager, he is left with a heritage of promises and obligations that his *predecessor* has not had an opportunity to fulfill. For example, when a mechanic was asked about his chances of becoming a foreman, he answered unhappily:

> I don't know what the chances are here. I wasn't approached last time. But when Doug was here, he asked me, and I said I would like it very much and would appreciate it . . . He asked me, but then he died and we got this new man, Mr. Peele.

The successor finds that his predecessor has left

behind him a corps of lieutenants who were personally close and loyal to him. When the old lieutenants find that the successor, either because of ignorance or deliberate decision, fails to respect these old obligations and their informally privileged position, they begin to resist.[2]

One expression of this was found in the behavior of the old office manager, Joe Cook. Cook had been with Doug for a long while and had worked closely with him. When Peele came, Cook continued on as office manager. But to Cook, Peele was not the man that Doug had been, and he proceeded to make Peele "look bad" in the eyes of the main-office executives.

For example, when the main office would telephone the plant, Cook frequently would take the call in Peele's absence. When asked to put Peele on the phone Cook would make some effort to find him, but would finally report that he couldn't contact Peele. Instead of "*covering up*" for Peele—as he had for Doug—by pretending that Peele was in some inaccessible part of the mine, Cook would intimate that Peele had not let him know where he could be found. The main office was allowed to draw the inference that Peele was acting irresponsibly.

Since they are often placed in strategic positions, the old lieutenants are able to do substantial damage to the successor—if they want to. Another of the reasons why they were willing to do so was the old lieutenants' belief that the new manager was not the legitimate heir. In this plant, there was a widespread conception of the proper line of succession to the position of plant manager; the supervisor of the "board building" was commonly viewed as "next in line" for promotion to manager. The old lieutenants, therefore, considered one of their own group, Johnson, the board building super, as the legitimate heir to the managership. When deprived of what he felt to be his just aspirations, Johnson became disaffected and hostile to Peele.

On one occasion, for example, Peele had to be hospitalized during a heated siege of wage negotiations. Johnson was then appointed as acting plant manager, with responsibility for conducting discussions with the union. From management's point of view, he played an extremely ineffectual role in the negotiations, not attempting to "handle" or "control" the situation even when it headed toward a strike. For these reasons, Peele became particularly critical of Johnson, disparaging him as the "least strict" of all the supervisors in the plant.

The old lieutenants are, also, often in a position to mobilize rank and file sentiment against the successor. An illustration of this involved Ralph Byta. Byta was a neighbor of Doug and had been induced by him to come to work at the plant. Doug had promised Byta quick advancement which, because of Doug's sudden death, did not materialize.

About four months after Peele's arrival, Byta was elected president of the plant's union. Byta's new position was now much more invulnerable than those of the other old lieutenants who held supervisory offices. He could not be replaced or fired, but had to be "dealt with." As Byta stated with disarming frankness:

> The good men know that a union's the best way to get ahead. You can't walk into the Company and ask them for a raise for yourself. It's different, though, if you represent 150 men. *Then, too, if the Company sees you're a leader—and the Company sees it!—well, maybe you can get yourself a raise.*

Nor was Byta's expectation a fanciful one; it had solid justification in the Company's previous actions. As a member of the main-office staff explained:

> Some of our foremen are ex-union presidents . . . The union can pick out a good man for president. If you want a good man, pick the president of the union. If you have good morale, the men elect responsible people to union leadership.

When first elected, Byta played the role of a militant and was characterized by management as "bitter." Some months following his election Peele had a "man to man" talk with him, after which Byta was viewed by management as much more "reasonable." Byta's case, then, is another example of the resistance of the old lieutenants to the succes-

2. Other industrial studies have also emphasized that succession periods often induce widespread tensions. For example, "A new boss inevitably disrupts (established informal understandings) . . . The employees feel held off and frustrated in trying to find out what is wanted and in trying to secure the customary satisfaction of their wants. Inevitably this prevents them from relying with confidence upon a new superior . . ." *Technology and Labor*, by Elliott Dunlap Smith with Richmond Carter Nyman, Yale University Press, New Haven, p. 125. Instead of dealing only with the responses of "employees" in general to the successor, we have found it useful to distinguish the responses made by rank and file operatives, on the one hand, and the "old lieutenants" or supervisory staff, on the other.

sor. For his part, Peele quickly detected this mounting resistance. As he put it:

> Every foreman had set ways. When I wanted to make some changes (in procedure), the supervisors told me, "Doug used to do this and that." I didn't make many changes and I'm satisfied with the changes I've made. The foremen are getting smoothed off now.

Peele needed to bring the resisting old lieutenants "into line" in some way; it is partly for this reason that the successor's old friends cease to be a source of embarrassment to him and become, instead, a reserve of possible allies. For it is among them that he first looks for loyal and willing subordinates with whom he can replace the intractable old lieutenants. If he fulfills his friends' claims, he can now justify this as a means of securing personnel enabling him to satisfy top management's demands for heightened efficiency.

## The workers' resistance

The old lieutenants' resistance finds its counterpart among rank and file operatives, when the successor's new measures are put into effect. As the discussion of the "Rebecca Myth" will indicate later, the operatives resist because they resent the dissolution of their old prerogatives and the crumbling of the indulgency pattern.

Like their supervisors, the workers too may challenge and deny the legitimacy of the new manager. Whether or not this occurs depends, in part, on the specific yardsticks used to evaluate a manager's "right" to hold office. In general, though, a succession provides a suitable occasion when threatening questions about the legitimacy of a successor will be generated and entertained most readily. In a society such as ours, with its accent on achieved, rather than ascribed, status, especially in the industrial sphere, the manner in which a manager obtains and then uses his office is a crucial measure of his legitimacy. In this plant, if a manager accepted workers' traditional privileges, if he did not "act superior," workers were disposed to accept his authority as legitimate. If, moreover, the manager showed a readiness to "stand on his own feet," without obsequious dependence on the main office, he would, all the more quickly, be taken to the workers' hearts.

Influenced by his main office briefing, however, the successor prejudged some of the workers' established privileges as impediments to efficiency. He was, too, inclined to wait for the main office to resolve the plant's problems. Main office administrators recognized that Peele's dependent and procrastinating behavior was, in some measure, compelled by his status as a successor. As one of them said, "A new plant manager is more prone to lean on the top administration than a more experienced one."

Workers viewed this pattern of behavior as "unmanly." It created a situation in which they did not know where they stood, and in which they felt powerless. For example, a mechanic remarked:

> The main office reads the labor law for its own benefit and Vincent Peele doesn't dare to read it any other way. The workers get hooked in any deal like this. *We got nobody out here to give you a down-and-out yes and no. Nobody here has any say-so.*

A supervisor concurred, saying:

> Vincent is a stickler for running the plant according to the main office. Vincent says that if that's the way they want it, that's the way they get it.

These were almost exactly the words of Digger, Peele's new aide:

> I'm not interested in what went on before. The way the Company wants it, that's the way it's going to be.

A union officer summed up the workers' contemptuous feelings about Peele's behavior by saying:

> Peele can't do too much without getting Lakeport permission . . . The saying around here is that Vincent can't take a s—— without calling Lakeport first. We come in and ask him for something and he tells us to *wait* while he thinks it over. Then we come back in *several days* and he has the answer. He's telephoned Lakeport in the meanwhile.

For these reasons, therefore, workers challenged Peele's legitimacy. Since any human relationship is stable to the extent that the behavior of each party is adjusted to the expectations of the other, and "rewarded" by his responses, it is clear that the succession had shaken the stability of the worker-manager relationship at its very foundations. For by virtue of his preoccupation with *top management* expectations, the successor acted with little regard for the expectations of the *workers in his plant.* Since the successor primarily sought the approval of the main office, the workers' ability to "control" him and influence their relationship was impaired. If, in effect, the successor would not accept the workers' approval as "legal tender," it became necessary for them to buy what they wanted from him, namely the restoration of the indulgency pattern, by minting a more compelling coin, disapproval and resistance.

## The Rebecca myth

A common indication of the degree and source of workers' resistance to a new manager is the prevalence of what may be called the "Rebecca Myth." Some years ago Daphne DuMaurier wrote a novel about a young woman who married a widower, only to be plagued by the memory of his first wife, Rebecca, whose virtues were still widely extolled. One may suspect that many a past plant manager is, to some extent, idealized by the workers, even if disliked while present.

Bill Day, for example, had made many complimentary remarks about Old Doug, but another supervisor who had overheard him, said sourly:

Sure, that's today. But you should have heard Day talk when Doug was *here*. My wife used to know his, and the things Day's wife used to say were plenty.

Day's idealized image of Doug was typical of many; for the workers' reminiscences about the regime of "Old Doug" were scarcely less than a modern version of "Paradise Lost."[3]

Though the world of mythology has a weakness for heroes all shining, and villains all fearsome, nonetheless, even myths are instructive things. For the many-threaded stereotypes of Doug and Peele, which the workers wove, reveal the sharp impact which the successor's policies had upon them.

Almost to a man, workers in the plant were in the spell of a backward-looking reverie. They overflowed with stories which highlighted the differences between the two managers, the leniency of Doug and the strictness of Peele. One tale contrasted the methods which Peele and Doug used to handle the problem of absenteeism. In the words of one worker:

Among other things, Vincent is cracking down on absenteeism. He really lays the law down on this issue. Usually there are some who take off after payday for a day or so; mostly among the miners. But Vincent doesn't stand for it anymore. Doug used to go right out and get the men. It was funny. If a man or a couple of men were out, the foremen called Doug about it. He would hop into his car, drive down to their house and tell the men that he needed them. And nine times out of ten, they would go back with him. Vincent doesn't stand for it, and he has let it be known that any flagrant violations will mean that the man gets his notice.

An edge man complained about Peele's method of "checking up" on workers:

Some of the men were saying that he was snooping around at three in the morning, but what probably happened was that he broke up a crap game . . . Old Doug never used to come around much and when he did, you could just see him puffing to get back to the office.

"Peele's the opposite of Doug," said a laborer.

He's always around checking on the men and standing over them. As long as production was going out Doug didn't stand over them. Peele is *always around* as though *he doesn't have faith* in the men like Doug.

Peele's impersonal attitudes were widely thought to be inappropriate. An electrician put it this way:

When Doug was here, it was like one big happy family. Peele is *all business*.

A car operator in the mine adds:

Doug was a little more *intimate* with his men. Peele is a little stricter.

In other words, Peele's withdrawal from informal interaction with the workers was experienced as a deprivation. A foreman, fumbling for words, explains:

I don't mean that Vincent wouldn't stop and pass the time of day with a man in the shop, if they should happen to meet. But it was different with Doug. All the men liked Doug, but most of them don't get very *close* to Vincent.

A car trimmer in the mine also said:

Doug was more friendly. Every time he'd see me he'd say, 'Hi'ya, Jack.' Doug was more friendly than Peele.

3. In another connection the Lynds have commented on this phenomenon. "Middletown is wont to invoke old leaders against new leaders who threaten to leave the 'safe and tried middle of the road.'" Robert S. Lynd and Helen M. Lynd, *Middletown in Transition*, New York, 1937; cf., W. Lloyd Warner and J. O. Low, *The Social System of the Modern Factory*, New Haven, 1947, for a pithy account of the functioning of the Rebecca Myth during a strike.

"I'll give you an illustration about the difference between Doug and Peele," said another worker:

> When Doug was here, all you had to say to Doug was, "Say, Doug, I need some board for the house." "Take a truck or a box car and fill 'er up," he would say. "But git it the hell out of here." With Peele, you have to pay for any board you take.

Nor did the men feel that Peele gave them a "second chance." Even one of the mine foremen recognized this:

> Doug and Vincent just had entirely different ways. Doug always gave the men more of a chance in the plant. If he had any problems he wanted straightened out, he would go down to the mine and ask them what they thought about it . . . He wouldn't go directly to the foremen like Vincent does . . . Vincent backs up the foremen, doesn't deal with the men.

A catalogue of Doug's virtues reads as follows: Never came around much; "ran the plant by phone"; gave the workers free board; related to everyone in a friendly and personal way; didn't punish men for their absences; but he was especially appreciated, perhaps, because he "knew how to handle the front office." The men noticed that he had entertained and had been on "drinking terms" with the president of the Company. They chuckled over stories that Doug used his deafness as a cover-up, pretending he couldn't hear things, when he did not want to take the main office's advice.

The men saw that Peele, by contrast, was "nervous" in his dealings with the Lakeport office; they felt he was stingy, coldly impersonal or "businesslike," and much too strict about the rules.

This, then, was the content of the "Rebecca Myth" at the Oscar Center Plant. The myth seems to have served as a means of demonstrating that Doug had accepted the workers' criteria of a "good plant" and of expressing the grievances which Peele's behavior had aroused. Since, as seen earlier, so many of the workers' standards of a good plant were of dubious validity, it would not be easy to complain openly of their violation. The myth of Old Doug was an effort to legitimate the indulgency pattern; by transforming Peele's attack on the indulgency pattern into an attack on Old Doug, the workers' grievances could be given voice. The issue need no longer be "This is what *we* want"; it could be stated, "Old Doug did thus and so, and he was a good man."

The "Rebecca Myth" also had bearing on the bureaucratic system which was developing in the plant. As shown, the very things for which Doug was extolled were his informality, his lack of emphasis on formal hierarchy and status, his laxness with the rules, his direct interaction with the workers. These, typically, are traits which are the antithesis of bureaucratic administration. The one unfriendly comment heard about Doug came from a mechanic who remarked:

> Doug used to say that any fellow was a mechanic to some extent . . . and he didn't want maintenance to come in on a thing until the men had tried to fix it . . .

This, though, only reinforces the picture; for Doug's rejection of distinctly separated and limited spheres of competence also violates bureaucratic principles of organization. On the other hand, the nicest compliments heard about Peele were that he "comes to the point" and was "businesslike"—in other words, that he behaved with bureaucratic impersonality.

## "Sits not so easy on me"

The new manager was caught in a tangle of interrelated problems: (1) Implementation of the efficiency goals set for him by top management and which he himself accepted. (2) As a necessary condition for solution of this first problem, he needed to control or eliminate the resistance to his plans by the "old lieutenants"; in Peele's words, "straightening out shirkers." (3) As another condition for successful solution of the first problem, he needed to handle the resistance developing among rank-and-file workers. (4) Finally, Peele experienced a problem, more accurately, perhaps, a diffuse "tension," on a totally different, a psychological, level. This was the necessity to cope with his mounting anxiety, which, situationally aroused by the definition of his succession as a "test," was exacerbated by the resistance he met.

Broadly speaking, the successor had two major avenues of solution available to him: (a) He could act upon and through the informal system of relations. (b) He could utilize the formal system of organization in the plant. Stated differently, Peele could attempt to solve his problems and ease his tensions either by drawing upon his resources as a "person," or by bringing into operation the authority invested in his status as plant manager.

To consider the first tactic, the utilization of informal relations in the plant: Peele could have attempted to mobilize informal solidarity and group sentiment and harness them to his goals. Such an approach might be exemplified by the appeal, "Come on, men, let's all pitch in and do a job!" He could offer his friendship to the men, or at least pretend to,[4] hoping that in return the workers would support his program. Peele did, for example, take pains to contact the men. "I talk with them," he explained, "I congratulate them about births and things like that, *if I can only get an inkling of it. Personal touches here and there help.*"

But in this case, mobilization of the informal system was a difficult, if not impossible, task for several reasons:

1) The very program for which Peele sought to enlist the aid of informal relations by his "personal touches" was a program that violated the workers' informal sentiments. He could not very well use the informal system to uproot customs that it was organized to express and defend.

Informal solidarity premises a greater consensus of ends and sentiments than existed. Because of his role as a successor, Peele was particularly concerned with cutting costs and raising productivity. The workers, though, were much less interested in these ends and were more concerned about defending the old indulgency pattern. Peele was oriented to the future and indifferent to the past; he symbolized the initiation of new and better ways. The workers, however, stood for the preservation of the old and time-honored paths. It is difficult to maintain, and especially to create, informal solidarity in pursuit of ends which are so differently valued by group members.

2) Even if a successor is wise to the ways of manipulation and pretended friendship, he is tongue-tied by his sheer *ignorance*. As Peele indicated, in his last comment above, his efforts to be friendly with the men were snarled by his inability to get "an inkling" of the things which personally concerned them. Successful manipulation of the informal network requires knowledge of the intimate events and sentiments which they communicate. Peele, though, was a successor knowing little of the subtle, but all too concrete, arrangements and understandings comprising the plant's informal system; because he was ignorant of the magic words of condolence and congratulation, the doors to the informal system remained unyielding. In fact, he even had grave difficulties with the informal group nearest his own level, the "old lieutenants."

The new manager, therefore, found that he had no social "connective tissue," that is, no informal social relations, between himself and the lower echelons. As he became more isolated at this point, he was increasingly aware of his own inadequate supply of news and information. A communication problem, to be considered in the next chapter, is added to those he already had.

## The successor's defenses

These cumulated pressures channeled Peele's anxiety, focusing it into a suspicion of what was happening down below. One worker assessed the situation acutely:

> When Doug was here, it was all like one big happy family . . . Why, Doug could *get on the phone*, call up the foremen and have the situation well in hand. *Peele has to come around and make sure things are all right*. Maybe that's why he's bringing in his own men.

These remarks suggest that "strategic replacement" served to bridge the communication gap between Peele and the rest of the plant and, thereby, to alleviate his own suspicions and anxieties. They also indicate another mechanism used to mend poor upward communications; Peele goes out and "sees for himself," and engages in "close supervision."[5]

## Close supervision

Peele's practice of flitting around the plant released a vicious cycle which only intensified his problems; for the men resented his continual presence, feeling

4. This, in brief, is Robert K. Merton's concept of "pseudo-gemeinschaft." That is, "the feigning of personal concern with the other fellow in order to manipulate him the better." *Mass Persuasion*, by Robert K. Merton with the assistance of Marjorie Fiske and Alberta Curtis, Harper and Bros., New York, 1946, p. 142.

5. This term is borrowed from Daniel Katz and Robert L. Kahn, "Human Organization and Worker Motivation," in *Industrial Productivity*, edited by L. Reed Tripp, Industrial Relations Research Association, 1951.

it to be an expression of distrust. A sample worker stated this succinctly:

Doug *trusted* his men to do a job. Vincent doesn't. Doug didn't come around so much. He *relied* on the men.

Close supervision, which served as a substitute for informal upward communication, violated workers' beliefs that they should be little checked upon, and resulted in even greater exclusion of the successor from the informal system and its communication networks. Mere visitations to the plant, though, did little to dissolve Peele's tensions. He was well aware that the men modified their behavior upon his approach. Peele, therefore, soon took to showing up at what he hoped would be unexpected times and places. In a mechanic's words:

Peele is like a mouse in a hole. You don't know when he will pop out.

But Peele could not be truly ubiquitous; try as he might, he could not be everywhere at once personally checking up on everyone. He was compelled, therefore, to resort to methods more congruent with his role. Although as a successor he had no secure position in the system of informal relations and communications, and could not infuse it with his goals, he still had unimpaired use of his official powers as plant manager. He could, therefore, make changes in the formal organization of the plant and move about, or remove, certain of the key personnel.

## Strategic replacements

Peele could deal with the problem of the resistant "old lieutenants" in a limited number of ways: (1) He might get rid of the "old lieutenants" and replace them with his own; (2) he could open up new or additional supervisory posts which he could staff, thereby affecting the "balance of power" among the middle managers; or (3) he might decide to "pay off" the inherited obligations to the "old lieutenants."

These three solutions are not equally useful to the successor, nor are they all equally available to him. If, for example, the new manager employs the last tactic, the "old lieutenants" may simply view this as "squaring accounts." The "old lieutenants" may feel that the successor has only given them something which they had long since earned and they, therefore, may believe they owe him nothing in return.

Thus, when Peele did promote some of the older men in the plant to new supervisory positions, they were not especially appreciative. "They don't feel very good about it," said a supervisor:

You see they have felt that *their having worked here for a long time should have earned them promotions anyhow* . . . They feel that they are being given the jobs now only because there are no experienced men left to take them. They are taking them all right, but there is still that tongue-in-cheek feeling against the higher-ups.

This "ungrateful" reaction, among men who feel entitled to their rewards, directs the successor away from choosing replacements who would be legitimate, and hence acceptable, supervisors, in terms of the plant workers' values. By the very nature of the case, the legitimate replacements will often feel that they have merely been given their due, and will not tend to respond as the new manager hopes.

The successor finds himself constrained, therefore, to choose as replacements those whose appointment is more likely to make the workers resentful. The pressures are such that he inclines toward replacements either from among plant workers whose claim to advancement is not strongly legitimate, or else from among men he has known outside the plant. As a result, he tends to handle his problems by replacing the recalcitrant supervisors or by opening up new supervisory positions.

The successor's ability to create new positions is, however, definitely limited. As a new manager he is especially hesitant to initiate anything that would require main office approval, particularly if it entails increased costs. Yet this is involved in opening up new supervisory positions.

An escape from the above difficulty is possible if new equipment and machinery are being installed in the plant. The simultaneous introduction of new machinery and new managers probably occurs with a frequency greater than that due solely to chance.[6]

6. This is partially supported by the findings of Smith and Nyman, *ibid*. For example, "An extensive labor-saving installation commonly involves the elimination of some unfit employees and even executives" (p. 68). In this case Peele's succession was due to Doug's death; it just so happened, however, that new machinery was also introduced shortly prior to Doug's death and heightened main-office concern with efficiency, in order to make the new machinery pay.

In this plant, about a million and a half dollars worth of new equipment was being installed in the board building, at just this time. With the anticipated increase in scope and speed of operations, a case was made out, in pure efficiency terms, to expand the supervisory staff. For example, it was pointed out that the increased speed of the new machines made for greater waste if a breakdown occurred, and thus more supervisors were needed to prevent this. The addition of "know-how" and "do-how" foremen was justified in this way.

It is not being suggested that the successor merely "rationalized" his status-generated needs for additional supervisors in terms made convenient by the technological innovations.[7] Regardless of the new manager's motives for requesting additional supervisors, the introduction of new machinery did allow for the expansion of the supervisory staff, which consequently helped the successor to handle the "old lieutenants."

The gains which accrue to the successor, if he solves the problem of the "old lieutenants" by replacing them with new ones, are now clear. No budgetary increase is required and, in consequence, main office sanction, if needed at all, is less complicated. It is hard for the main office to judge from its distance whether or not a man at a local plant deserves to be fired; it is comparatively easy for them to estimate whether an increased dollar outlay is justified. A decision about the former problem is, for this reason, more likely to be left to the discretion of the plant manager. Thus replacement of the old with new supers, as a method of handling the "old lieutenants," is a more reliable and controllable solution for the successor.

Nor need he replace the entire group of "old lieutenants," even if this were feasible; for by firing some he creates anxiety among those who remain and extracts conformity from them. As Peele noted when asked:

*You had some difficulty with the supervisors . . . ?*
Yes, I had some trouble straightening out shirkers. Some of them thought they were going to get fired. *I could work on these guys*. But others, who didn't expect to get fired, were. Each foreman is just a little bit *on edge* now. They don't know whether they're doing right. A new plant manager is going to make some changes—to suit my own way. I had to watch them. I made those changes.

In short, the use of replacements enables the successor to accomplish several things: (1) He gets rid of some of those who were "shirking"; (2) he silences others and forces acquiescence from them, and (3) he can create new lieutenants, from among those he brings up, who will be grateful and loyal to him. This can be seen from an interview with one of Peele's replacements:

*Who was the plant manager at the time you began working here?*
Why, Fier was top man then and after him Farr, Doug Godfrey, and now Vincent.
*How would you compare the four men as bosses?*
They were all good men if you did the job.
*Would you say any was a little more strict than the other?*
Oh, maybe a little, one way or the other, but you expect that. Vincent comes around more than Godfrey did, but none of them was really strict.
*How would you say the men generally felt about them?*
I don't think there was any feelings against any of them. I've never heard a word against Vincent.
*Would you say then that the men feel the same way about Vincent as they did about Doug?*
I think that maybe the men think a little *more* of Vincent because he really sticks up for the men, and I don't mean only the foremen, but all the men.

Unlike his references to the preceding plant managers, this supervisor called Peele by his first name; he was reluctant to give voice to the near-universal criticisms of Peele's strictness; he imagined that Peele was better liked than Doug. Evidently his appointment to a supervisory position by the successor made him a staunch adherent of the new manager.[8]

7. The role of technological and market pressures in inducing tensions will be examined in *Wildcat Strike*, Yellow Springs, Ohio: Antioch Press, 1954.

8. The connection between succession and strategic replacements has not gone unnoticed by other industrial sociologists. There has, however, been a tendency to explain strategic replacements primarily as a consequence of efficiency needs and the technical inadequacy of the old supervisors. For example: "The new manager did all in his power to develop sufficient ability in the supervisory force to measure up to the new requirements. But as these requirements were raised, first one supervisor then another proved incapable of being developed to meet them . . . (Therefore) in the long run nearly the entire original staff was dismissed . . ." Smith and Nyman, *ibid.*, p. 128. This analysis omits consideration of two things which we have held focal: (1) The function of strategic replacements in resolving the new manager's status problems, which are generated by his role as a *successor*; (2) the existence of certain elements in the situation which

## The new informal group

In obligating new lieutenants to himself, through the use of strategic replacements, the successor establishes extra-formal ties with them which he can draw upon to implement his goals. In effect, strategic replacement enables the new manager to form a new informal social circle, which revolves about himself and strengthens his status. It provides him with a new twoway communication network; on the one hand, carrying up news and information that the formal channels exclude; on the other hand, carrying down the meaning or "spirit" of the successor's policies and orders.[9] Beyond its purely communication functions, the new informal group also enables the successor to control the plant more fully; for the new lieutenants can be depended on to enforce the new manager's changes and punish deviations from them.

Finally, the new informal group also served to ease Peele's personal anxieties. A new manager commonly becomes very friendly with one of his strategic replacements. This became Digger's role and, soon after his arrival, he was known to be Peele's confidant. Digger and Peele's relationship was widely resented in the plant and became one of the men's most outspoken grievances. Disturbed by Peele's failure to establish friendly connections with them, the workers, with more than a touch of envy, complained: "Digger and Peele are as thick as thieves."

Digger provided Peele with an opportunity to unburden himself at a time when few men wanted to have anything to do with him. Digger gave Peele support and approval when most of those near to him "hated his guts." In this way, Digger played an important cathartic function for Peele, serving to ease his fears and anxieties. Digger helped Peele, but at the cost of heightening the workers' awareness of Peele's impersonal and unfriendly behavior toward them. Moreover, since he felt confident of Peele's favor, Digger could behave in an "arrogant" manner, leading the workers to complain that "he acted as if he owned the plant." This, in turn, only swelled the workers' hostility toward Peele.

## Succession and bureaucracy

Disposing of the "old lieutenants" takes time. If the new manager is at all sensitive to what is going on, he does not wish to be accused of failing to give the "old lieutenants" a "chance," nor of seeking to install his favorites with indecent haste. He has to spend some time looking for possible allies and lining up replacements. In the meanwhile, the breakdown of upward communications to the new manager grows more acute. It is, in part, as an outgrowth of this crisis that the successor elaborates the system of "paper reports," the better to "keep his finger on things," and to check up on the unreliable "old lieutenants."

At this time, he also began to introduce and emphasize adherence to the "rules." Barred from effective use of the informal system of controls, the successor was compelled to rely more heavily upon the formal system. As an observant main office executive noticed: "Peele will follow along in *organizational* lines, while Doug handled things on a *personal* basis." The comments of the Company's labor relations director provide a clue about the role of succession in this change:

> *New* managers always tend to rely more on the rules. They call us up and ask us if we have lists of rules which they can use. *They are unsure of themselves and they need something to lean on.* After they're on the job somewhat longer they're less worried about the rules.

These remarks tend to reinforce the contention that there is a close connection between succession and a surge of bureaucratic development, particularly in the direction of formal rules.

To appreciate why this is so, it is necessary to consider another of the dilemmas in which the successor finds himself. It has been shown that the

constrain the successor to meet his problems by dismissing the old supervisors, rather than utilizing other problem solutions. Smith and Nyman recognize that "to attempt to meet the situation by replacement is perilous. Extensive or unjust discharges cause the remaining management and employee body to fear the changes and in secret to work against it" (*ibid.*, p. 129). If this is typically or at least frequently the case, as Smith and Nyman suggest, then strategic replacements frustrate the intended improvement of efficiency. We must, therefore, attempt to account for the repeated coincidence of succession and strategic replacements in terms other than the utilitarian emphasis on efficiency consequences.

9. This last point deserves emphasis, for, no matter how model a bureaucratic structure the successor may finally create, its formal rules will be enmeshed in and in need of reinforcement by a framework of supporting sentiments and attitudes. Cf., Reinhard Bendix, "Bureaucracy: The Problem and Its Setting," *American Sociological Review*, Oct., 1947, for a discussion of this point.

new manager's role disposes him to a great dependence on the main office. Yet his position is such that he must attempt to conceal this dependence, and attempt to act with a semblance of autonomy.

Some of the latter pressures stem from workers' feeling that a manager should "stand on his own feet." The main office staff, too, is ambivalent about the successsor's dependence on them. The main office prefers a manager who will heed its advice on matters of major policy; but within these limits they want a manager to be independent. "We have about twenty-five plants to handle," explained a Lakeport administrator. "We just can't spend all of our time on any one plant." Nor does the main office especially esteem a manager who "doesn't talk back once in a while."

Thus the new manager must, somehow, seek techniques whereby he can be sure that his decisions are in conformity with main-office expectations; techniques which will, at the same time, allow him to make these decisions with a minimum of contact with main office people, quickly, and with the appearance of independence. These appear, in part, to be the specific functions performed by the rules which the successor seeks from his main office. Once he has the rules, he need no longer telephone it about every problem that arises in the plant. The rules, further, provide a framework which he can use to justify his decisions should the main office ever examine or challenge them.

Nor are the rules useful only in the successor's dealings with the main office; they also help to make his behavior a bit more palatable to people in the plant. When Peele did something which he knew the workers would not like, he often justified it as due to main office requirements. The workers would then criticize the main office for the new pattern, blaming Peele only because he "didn't have guts enough to fight back." Thus one worker commented:

> . . . it has always been the plant policy not to have men who are relations, especially father-and-son teams. But while Doug was here we did that quite a bit. He was pretty easygoing on that. But now that Vincent is here, it isn't being done.
>
> *Why do you suppose that this is so?*
>
> Vincent is more strict on conforming to Company rules than Doug was.

In other words, Peele was seen as bringing the plant into line with established Company rules. Some of the aggression that would have been directed at Peele was thereby deflected onto the main office. In general, the Lakeport office was aware of this and accepted it as a way of relaxing relationships between plant workers and local management, encouraging the latter to "put the blame on us."

Like all other solutions which Peele adopted to handle the problems of his succession, the development of formal rules also had an anxiety-allaying function. The rules define the new situation into which the successor has entered, allowing him to make decisions with a minimum of uncertainty and personal responsibility. Moreover, there is reason to believe that the rules had, more specifically, a guilt-relieving role for Peele. Some of the things which Peele had done could not be easily condoned, even by himself. His failure to give Day a warning before he demoted him, or an explanation afterwards, involved the infraction of values which Peele had never deliberately set out to violate, and to which he was still oriented. The belief that he was only doing what he must, softened Peele's doubts about his own behavior. As he remarked:

> Some of the men probably think I'm a mean cuss, but I've got to follow our Company policy like everyone else. If I don't, someone else will.

## The rate of succession

The Oscar Center plant had about six managers from the time of its inception, an average of about one for every four years of its existence. These changes suggest the importance of another specific dimension of succession, the rate of turnover among plant managers. In a case study such as this, however, since it extends over only a small period in the plant's lifetime, it is impossible to do more than allude to the possible significance of varying rates of succession and their effects on patterns of administration.

Even a cursory contrast with previous societies suggests that the rate of succession in the modern factory is "high." In part, this high rate of succession, particularly in the pinnacles of authority, is made possible by the development of the corporative form.[10] In fact, the corporation was, in some

10. It is interesting to note that the problem of succes-

measure, deliberately designed to enable business organizations to persist beyond the life of their founders.

Where authority may have to be transferred frequently, personalized loyalties to those in office may impede succession, as noted in the discussion of the "Rebecca Myth." Contrariwise, it is easier to transfer authority when workers' loyalties are attached to the office, and the rules of which it is composed, rather than to the person who occupies the position. Bureaucratization is, therefore, functional to a group subjected to an institutionally compelled "high" rate of succession while, in turn, a high rate of succession operates as a selecting mechanism sifting out or disposing to bureaucratic modes of organization.[11]

As this was a plant with a history of some twenty-five years, it was not totally lacking in bureaucratic procedures. Nor was Peele devoid of bureaucratic intentions prior to his arrival. On the contrary, the plant had experienced a degree of bureaucratization before Peele came. Moreover, the new manager was oriented to values which might, in any event, have led him in a bureaucratic direction, regardless of the circumstances of his succession.

The role of a successor, however, confronted Peele with distinctive problems. He had to solve these problems if he wished to hold his job as manager. In the process of solving them, the successor was compelled to use bureaucratic methods. Peele intensified bureaucracy not merely because he wanted to, not necessarily because he liked bureaucracy, nor because he valued it above other techniques, but also because he was constrained to do so by the tensions of his succession.

sion in strategic offices appears to be becoming a matter of conscious and public interest among business executives. Apparently, though, pressures are being exerted to define this problem primarily in terms of its pecuniary consequences, rather than in its impact on the organization as a social system. Thus in the November, 1949, *Fortune*, The Mutual Benefit Life Insurance Company had the following advertisement:

> "Am I really that old?" was my first thought.
>
> "Jim, you're too valuable to lose. The firm's going to insure your life. . . ."
>
> "Don't let these gray hairs fool you, J. D.," I quipped half-heartedly.
>
> 'They don't, Jim," he reassured me. "But this is a special kind of insurance that's going to do both of us a lot of good. . . . This plan protects our company against the loss of valuable key men like yourself. It provides cash to attract a capable replacement, and it cushions our possible losses while he's breaking in."

11. Some of John Commons' writings suggest the connection between the rate of succession and rules on a more general level; he spoke, for example, of the "set of working rules which keep on working regardless of the incoming and outgoing of individuals." *The Legal Foundations of Capitalism*, Macmillan Co., 1932, New York, p. 135.

## Underlying assumptions

The assumptions underlying the analysis thus far can be summarized as follows: Bureaucratic behavior was conceived of as a problem-solving type of social action. This led to an inquiry about the nature of these problems; how were they conceived or formulated? We then had to specify who formulated these problems; that is, what was this person's status, and how did his status influence his formulation of problems and choice of problem-solutions?

Since groups possess forms of stratification, it cannot be tacitly assumed that all individuals, or all positions in the system of stratification, exert equal influence on those decisions from which bureaucratization emerges as planned or unanticipated consequence. Pedestrian as this point is, Weber's analysis of bureaucracy largely ignores it. But bureaucratic behavior in a factory must either be initiated by the manager, or at least finally ratified by him or his superiors. What has here been essayed is an analysis of some institutionally derived pressures, convergent on the position of a new plant manager, which made him accept and initiate bureaucratic patterns.

Thus the relevance of *status*-generated tensions and perspectives is accentuated. Instead of assuming that bureaucracy emerged in direct response to threats to the *organization as a homogeneous whole*, the analysis proceeded from a different premise; namely, that the adaptation of an organization to a threat is mediated and shaped by powerful individuals. It was assumed, further, that to the degree these powerful individuals perceived the "needs" of the organization, they became "problems" which were molded in specific ways by status tensions. As a result, the adaptive efforts which are made may be divergent from the "needs" of the organization as a whole.

Peele's bureaucratic innovations cannot be understood in terms of their contribution to the stability of the plant as a whole. Nor were "strategic replacements" or "close supervision" mechanisms that brought the entire plant into equilibrium. At the very least, each of these three defense mechanisms did as much to disturb, as to defend, the integration of the plant. These paradoxical consequences were explained by taking into account the dilemmas and tensions engendered by the peculiar role of a successor.

## Growing points

If Peele's bureaucratic behavior, especially his development of bureaucratic rules, is usefully viewed as a problem-solution, what was the nature of the problem as he perceived it? A brief recapitulation of the plant situation, as Peele first came upon it, will reveal this.

When he arrived, Peele found that some workers preferred to punch in early and accumulate a little overtime, or punch out early on special occasions. He discovered that the miners believed that a certain amount of absenteeism was permissible, and, in fact, was a customary way of showing that "down here we are our own bosses." The resistance to Peele grew wider and more acute when he attempted to eliminate these practices.

As his "mouse-in-the-hole" behavior attests, Peele began to lose "faith" in workers and middle management, commencing to "check up" closely on both groups. He did not "trust" his subordinates, and he doubted whether they would perform their roles in accordance with his expectations. In fact, as he said explicitly of the "old lieutenants," they were "shirkers."

So much, for the present, concerning the orientation and outlook of those who initiate or ratify bureaucratic measures. Aside from this point of departure, analysis of the succession process also brought into view certain aspects of the organizational *situation* out of which the bureaucratic patterns grew. These, too, provide growing points for subsequent expansion, indicating a range of specific variables important in the later discussion.

From the standpoint of their effects on the plant as a social system, the following seem to be the most crucial tension-provoking features of the succession situation:

1) *Interaction of bearers of different values:* The successor was oriented to rational, efficiency-enhancing values, while workers were oriented mainly to the traditional, custom-honored sentiments of the indulgency pattern. The successor's outlook was structured by the main office's emphasis on rational administration; thus there was a value-cleavage emerging along status lines, that is, between top managers and the workers.

2) *Ambiguous canons of legitimacy:* Whether or not the expectations held by workers were legitimate, or were properly applicable to the plant situation, was uncertain even in the workers' view. They were not so sure that their expectations were a solid and justifiable basis for action.

3) *Unrequited expectations:* The workers expected the new manager to conform to the indulgency pattern, even though unsure that this expectation was legitimate. The successor, though, was more concerned about his superiors' efficiency-centered expectations and, therefore, was not responsive to subordinates.

4) *Decline of informal interaction across status lines:* The new manager had fewer personal ties with workers.

5) *Hiatus in the chain of command:* The successor could not rely upon the "old lieutenants" in supervisory positions to support and enforce his new policies.

6) *Shortcircuited communications:* Because of the inaccessibility of the informal system to the successor, as well as the hiatus in the chain of command, the new manager's sources of information were meager.

7) *Challenge to managerial legitimacy:* Both the "old lieutenants" and the rank and file of workers doubted the legitimacy of the successor. They did not merely resist him because they thought they could get away with it, that is, on purely expedient grounds, but because they felt that he was not a "proper" manager and did not *deserve* to be supported.

8) *Degeneration of motives for obedience:* Both supervisors and workers had fewer sentiments of loyalty to Peele than they had to Doug. They resisted his program of changes and the policies he formulated.

OSCAR GRUSKY

# The Effects of Succession: A Comparative Study of Military and Business Organization

The problem of succession is the organizational equivalent of the larger societal problem of generations.[1] The replacement of personnel in complex organizations is a continuous process, just as the cycle of life and death is an inevitable feature of human existence. This study is concerned with a comparative analysis of the effects of succession on a military installation and a large business firm.

The study of succession, sometimes called occupational or administrative succession, has been pursued from two vantage points. One approach locates the problem exclusively at the top of the organization hierarchy.[2] Such a viewpoint offers the distinct advantage of a focus upon those elites that are generally most accountable for the direction and implementation of organizational objectives. A second approach emphasizes that the proper study of succession should be broadened to include the effects of personnel circulation through positions at all levels in the hierarchy.[3] By this approach the concepts of occupational mobility and administrative succession tend to be fused and career mobility in an organizational setting is seen not only as essential for leadership development, but, at the same time, as creating problems of organizational continuity in the performance of its critical functions. Succession, as we shall use the term, is meant to refer to the processes associated with the movement of members out of the organization and their replacement by new members.

Comparative analysis of military and industrial organization suggests that military organization has reached a stage of bureaucratic development which seemingly anticipates the future movement of other complex systems. Concepts now commonly applied in industry, such as line of command, staff-line, the

1. Karl Mannheim, *Essays on the Sociology of Knowledge* (New York: Oxford University Press, 1952), pp. 276–80.

2. A. W. Gouldner, *Patterns of Industrial Succession* (New York: The Free Press, 1954); R. H. Guest, "Managerial Succession in Complex Organizations," *American Journal of Sociology*, 68 (July, 1962), pp. 47–54; R. H. McCleery, *Policy Change in Prison Management* (East Lansing, Mich.: Governmental Research Bureau, Michigan State University, 1957); Ernest Dale, "Du Pont: Pioneer in Systematic Management," *Administrative Science Quarterly*, 2 (June 1957), pp. 25–29; Oscar Grusky, "Administrative Succession in Formal Organization," *Social Forces*, 39 (December, 1960), pp. 105–15.

3. W. L. Warner, and J. C. Abegglen, *Occupational Mobility in American Business and Industry*, 1929–1952 (Minneapolis: University of Minnesota Press, 1955); Bernard Levenson, "Bureaucratic Succession" in Amitai Etzioni, editor, *Complex Organizations: A Sociological Reader* (New York: Holt, Rinehart, and Winston, 1961), pp. 362–75.

I regret that I cannot name the Air Force officers whose overall aid and attempts to educate me about the base and about the military establishment as a whole were virtually indispensable. I am also grateful to the officers and managers who provided the basic data for the research. Most of the data on business managers were gathered during the tenure of a Ford Foundation Faculty Research Fellowship in Social Science and Business. I wish to thank Don Baker for research assistance. Morris Janowitz first suggested that I make this study and provided continuing intellectual stimulation.

development of oral briefing, and others, were derived from military experience. It is already evident that the highly bureaucratized patterns of career succession in the military have spread to large industrial corporations. Still, the degree of bureaucratization of careers is greater in military than in business organization. Four factors have contributed to the extensive organizational control of the military over officer career patterns: the nature of its mission, its size, complexity, and geographical dispersion. The intense political and social implications involved in the management of violence require careful control over the training particularly of those in executive positions. The distribution of goods and services for profit does not require the same degree of close control. The sheer size of a centralized military establishment necessitates control by extensive rules and regulations. There were about 2,450,000 men under arms and 343,000 officers on active duty in 1962. Research indicates that large size in itself may not require an unusually large administrative apparatus, but size is positively related to complexity of organization and the more complex the system the greater the demand for a large administrative staff.[4] The many component parts of the military mission and the related necessity for locating military units all over the world combine to emphasize the overall complexity of the United States military establishment. However, it should be kept in mind that because the military is both a unified and highly centralized system it is not strictly comparable to business organization. Rotation in the military is from one unit to another within a single establishment. The business executive may either transfer from one unit to another within the corporation or move to another firm. Hence in business two different modes of succession exist whereas there is one in the military. We have assumed arbitrarily that the military base may be considered to be equivalent to the business firm. We justified this decision on the grounds that both units of study have clear and, we think, parallel organizational identities within their respective institutional contexts as well as within the local community in which they are situated. Interdepartmental transfers, either in the military base or business organization, were not considered in this study. Instead, our focus was on movement into and out of the military base and the business firm.

Assuming that "Military career lines are highly standardized, as compared with other professions,"[5] and some comparative data will be presented to test this contention, what are the effects of this bureaucratization? Two independent studies have shown that large, and therefore more bureaucratized, organizations have greater rates of executive succession than small organizations.[6] Kriesberg has pointed out that this may mean that career patterns are different in the small and large systems. The small organization is more likely to be manned by "home-guards" or "locals," whose careers are characterized by relatively little movement from place to place. Larger organizations are more likely to be dominated by executives who are "itinerants," moving frequently from organization to organization.[7] Military systems are of theoretical significance to organization theory because all those of executive rank are, of necessity, itinerants. Thus military systems are desirable objects of investigation for the student of succession because they represent a relatively extreme career situation. Military rotation policies require officers to change their assignments after a given period of time. This period may be one year in hardship areas, but more typically two, three, four, and at times, five years. Hence executive succession at all military installations is highly routinized and frequent.[8]

4. T. R. Anderson, and Seymour Warkov, "Organizational Size and Functional Complexity: A Study of Administration in Hospitals," *American Sociological Review*, 26 (February, 1961), pp. 23–28.

5. Janowitz, Morris, *The Professional Soldier: A Social and Political Portrait* (New York: Free Press, 1960).

6. See Oscar Grusky, "Corporate Size, Bureaucratization, and Managerial Succession," *American Journal of Sociology*, 67 (November, 1961), pp. 261–69; and Louis Kriesberg, "Careers, Organization Size, and Succession," *American Journal of Sociology*, 68 (November, 1962), pp. 355–59.

7. E. C. Hughes, *Men and Their Work* (New York: The Free Press, 1958), p. 129; A. W. Gouldner, "Cosmopolitans and Locals: Toward an Analysis of Latent Social Roles—I," *Administrative Science Quarterly*, 2 (December, 1957), pp. 281–306.

8. Hanson W. Baldwin reports this study: "An informal survey made last spring of a 20 per cent random sample of officers in each grade assigned to Headquarters, First United States Army, on Governors Island, indicated that the average officer had 17 years of commissioned service, acquired eight military occupational specialties, made 12 PCS (permanent changes of station), had 26 major

A number of studies of small organizations have indicated that succession is disruptive, typically producing low morale and conflict among the staff.[9] It is likely that in highly bureaucratized organizations such as the military where succession is closely regulated, these disruptive responses are muted. By standardizing career experiences the organization systematically prepares the manager for future moves. Comparisons of business firms and military installations facilitate the study of the effects on succession of differential degrees of organizational control.

Three problems formed the central interest of our study. First, we were concerned with the structural context in which succession takes place. What are the organizational correlates of the two types of succession, bureaucratic and less bureaucratic? Second, we were interested in the consequences of succession for organizational commitment. How does rotation influence the orientation of the military officer to his present organizational assignment? Third, we were interested in adjustment to community life. How does the military officer adapt to the transient nature of his family life? Is he truly "rootless" or does his behavior reflect an alteration in the conventional patterns of integration found in stable settings?

No single unit could hope to be typical of either industrial or military organization, although military organizations have a common format. In both cases, it was the cooperation on the part of the host institution in permitting the study, and, to a lesser extent, geographical location, that dictated our choices. It is probably unnecessary to say that access for research purposes to either of the two types of organization is not always readily available. The data on the industrial firm were collected in 1960; that on the military installation in 1962. In both instances the research techniques applied were diverse. They included exploratory interviews, observation, perusal of official documents, and questionnaires. The latter represented the source of the most systematic data.

A questionnaire was distributed to all 2,198 managers (as defined by the firm) of the United Utility Corporation (a fictitious name), the largest single enterprise of a major public utility holding company in the United States. Approximately 75 per cent, or 1,649 usable, signed schedules were returned. A comparison by salary, sex, and position of the distributions of the sample with that of the total population of managers in the firm revealed a very close correspondence.

On the basis of observation, a six-level corporate hierarchy was initially distinguished, as follows: I. Top Management; II. Upper-Middle Management; III. Middle Management; IV. Lower-Middle Management; V. Lower Management; VI. First-Line Supervisors. The last group consisted almost completely of females, who were not included in the present study. Two managers in the firm (one Level III, and the other Level IV) independently placed each of the 318 management positions in the corporation on one of the six levels, applying the criterion of amount of official authority associated with the position.[10]

The United Utility Corporation has several branches, most of which are located within the confines of a single metropolitan area, a format that increases its relevance for comparison with the military base. The largest proportion of managers are situated in a single building, the general headquarters. Length of time with the organization, which we shall use as a measure of succession, refers in most cases to service within the numerous departments of the United Utility Corporation. The large majority of the managers (84.7 per cent) started in nonmanagement positions and worked up the hier-

assignments (not including minor additional duties), and made at least 16 moves (combat zones excluded) that required uprooting of his family," *New York Times*, Western Edition, October 21, 1963.

9. Gouldner, *op. cit.* (note 2); W. F. Whyte, "The Social Structure of the Restaurant Industry," *American Journal of Sociology*, 54 (January, 1949), p. 304; Oscar Grusky, "Role Conflict in Organization: A Study of Prison Officials," *Administrative Science Quarterly*, 3 (March, 1959), pp. 463–67.

10. Interrater reliability was .904 ($p < .0001$). When the raters were brought together to examine disagreements, none of which deviated by more than one level, complete agreement was arrived at when the criterion was restated and the duties of the position discussed. Corporate level was related both to salary (Cramer's $V = .58$, $p < .0001$ and perceived authority $V = .21$ $p < .0001$). A description of Cramer's V may be found in H. M. Blalock, Jr., *Social Statistics* (New York: McGraw-Hill, 1960), p. 230. Since the study of the military installation and the business firm were both based on a nonrandom sample, the application of statistical tests is problematical. Our interpretations of the findings are based on patterns of differences and not on statistical tests. In every case our interpretations should be viewed as highly tentative.

archy. In this respect, as in others, the firm may not be typical of most large business enterprises.

The military installation was a United States Air Force base. Although not of the combat type, it was adequate for our purposes with respect to its overall form. Specifically, the rotation problems of the base were characteristic of military installations. Hence we could properly assess the effects of these on officer behavior. Of the 629 questionnaires distributed to the entire complement of officers, 11 were returned as unreceived and 556, or almost 90 per cent, were completed and returned.[11] A comparison by military rank and aeronautical rating of the questionnaire sample and the total officer population revealed a close correspondence. Such an unusually high rate of return, exceeding even the high return of the business managers, may have been partly a function of the endorsement of the study by the Commanding Officer. Such support was unquestionably more effective than the corresponding support by the President and Board Chairman of United Utility, reflecting perhaps an important difference between civilian and military authority systems. The fact that the military questionnaire could not be signed may also have facilitated a higher rate of return.[12]

There is some limited evidence that organizations with markedly different authority structures may respond in different ways to executive personnel changes.[13] A comparison of the authority structure of the industrial firm and the military installation was therefore desirable. Table 1 presents such a comparison. In order to have a sufficient number of cases in each category we found it necessary to combine top executives and upper-middle management (both to be called Top Executives) on the one hand, and Generals and Colonels on the other. Moreover, lower management and supervisors (to be called First-Level Management), and Captains, First and Second Lieutenants were combined for the sake of convenience. The business organization had a higher proportion of top managers and middle managers than the Air Force base. On the other hand, the latter had considerably more lower level management. Nevertheless, as shown in Table 1, there was overall similarity in the two structures, considering the fundamental differences in their official objectives.

Further indication of structural similarity was revealed from the questionnaire data. The business managers and Air Force officers were asked: "In general, how much do you personally have to say about how things are decided in your department?" The responses permitted were: "I have a great deal to say," "I have some say," or "I have no say at all!"

In one sense, in both settings, there is an overall pattern of similarity (Table 2). The order in the percentage responding, "I have a great deal to say" was not markedly different between the two hierarchies; for the military, at the top the percentage was 92 and at the bottom 21 per cent; by comparison the range for the business firm was from 82 per cent at the top to 34 per cent at the bottom. However,

11. In both samples, questionnaires were distributed by the institution but mailed on completion directly to the University of California, Los Angeles.

12. Pelz found that identification of response by code on a questionnaire did not produce more cautious responses than when the respondent was anonymous. See D. C. Pelz, "The Influence of Anonymity on Expressed Attitudes," *Human Organization*, 18 (Summer, 1959), pp. 88–91.

13. Amitai Etzioni, "Authority Structure and Organizational Effectiveness," *Administrative Science Quarterly*, 4 (June, 1959), pp. 43–67.

***Table 1—Military Versus Business Organization: Hierarchy of Authority Levels***

| *MILITARY INSTALLATION 1962* | *Per cent* | *BUSINESS FIRM 1960* | *Per cent* |
|---|---|---|---|
| Generals | .5 | Top executives | 1.6 |
| Colonels | 4.6 | Upper-middle management | 6.7 |
| Lt. Colonels | 10.0 | Middle management | 14.4 |
| Majors | 23.5 | Lower-middle management | 40.2 |
| Captains | 55.3 | Lower management | 36.3 |
| First Lieutenants | 4.8 | First-line supervisors | .8 |
| Second Lieutenants | 1.3 | | |
| Total | 100.0 | Total | 100.0 |
| *Number of cases* | *631* | *Number of cases* | *1,240* |

the pattern of gradation was not without differences. In the case of the military a sense of authority was closely linked to rank, and increased rank by rank. For the business firm, while first level of rank was slightly higher than the comparable level in the military, it was comparable to the next, the lower-middle management level. In fact, the third, the middle management, was only slightly higher. In short, the pattern of the business firm showed limited spread at the lower and middle ranks and a larger gap to the top level. Thus the military revealed a greater degree of hierarchicalization, and since degree of hierarchicalization of authority is one index of bureaucratization, these data may be taken as support for the assumption of greater bureaucratization in military than in business organization.

## The structure of succession

Two ends of a continuum describing rates of succession have been suggested. On one end, the maximum rates of succession in an organization would be represented by the hypothetical case in which all the members of the system are replaced daily, hourly, or even more rapidly. The French Army in the middle of the eighteenth century approximated this extreme. Because of an abundance of officers, practices were created that encouraged rapid succession and minimum effectiveness. The historian Walter L. Dorn, described the situation thus: "The incredible number of officers with their elaborate baggage and servants, who frequently became entangled with marching columns, reduced the mobility of the army in the field. The Quartermaster-General had often to mobilize the resources of an entire city to provide for them. Actual service occupied only a small proportion of the officers. To create opportunities for all of them, one struck upon the expedient of rotating Lieutenant-Generals and Marshalls 'du jour,' just for the day. The commands of the line and the flanks were passed on from one officer to another from one day to the next."[14] The other extreme form would be represented by an organization in which the members remain throughout their lifetimes. Among industrial organizations, the Japanese factory is illustrative of an extremely low rate of succession at all levels in the hierarchy. Abegglen notes that in the Japanese factory, unlike its American counterpart, the employee commits himself and the firm correspondingly feels committed to him for a lifetime relationship.[15] A factory employing 4,250 persons in Osaka was described by the author. In this firm only five or six persons, or about one per thousand, leave the company each year, and these for extreme behavior, such as habitual thievery.[16] Most organizations, naturally, would be situated somewhere between these two radical types.

Table 3 compares the rates of managerial succession among business managers and officers of the military installation studied. It is readily apparent that their differences were considerable. Almost half (45.5 per cent) of the Air Force officers had been at their base a year or less, while only slightly more than 2 per cent (2.1 per cent) of the business managers had been with the firm for a comparable

14. W. L. Dorn, *Competition for Empire, 1740–1763* (New York: Harper and Row, Publishers, 1963), pp. 86–87.

15. J. C. Abegglen, *The Japanese Factory* (New York: The Free Press, 1958), pp. 11–25.

16. *Ibid.*, p. 12.

***Table 2—Military Versus Business Organization: Perceived Authority of Executives at Various Levels of the Hierarchy***

| *Per cent responding: "I have a great deal to say."* | *MILITARY INSTALLATION* | | *BUSINESS FIRM* | |
|---|---|---|---|---|
| | *Per cent* | *Number of cases* | *Per cent* | *Number of cases* |
| Colonels and Generals (Top executives) | 92 | *26* | 82 | *101* |
| Lt. Colonels (Middle management) | 65 | *55* | 44 | *174* |
| Majors (Lower-middle management) | 49 | *138* | 32 | *492* |
| Captains and Lieutenants (First-level management) | 21 | *332* | 34 | *455* |

[a] Item: "In general, how much do you personally have to say about how things are decided in your department?"

period of time. Correspondingly, almost nine out of ten of United's managers had at least five years of service with the Corporation, while only about one officer in twenty (5.6 per cent) staioned at the military installation had a similar length of service.

Both the high rate of succession of the Air Force base and the low rate of the business corporation maintained themselves at every major hierarchical level. At the top executive level, all but 7 per cent of the business managers had at least five years' service with the firm, while only one-third of the Colonels and Generals had equivalent experience with their organization (Table 4). The Chairman of the Board of the business firm had been with the firm for thirty years and had occupied his present position or that of President for thirteen years. In contrast, the Commanding Officer of the Air Force base had a three-year tour of duty. A similar situation prevails at most military installations, although normal tours of duty occasionally may be slightly greater.

Continuing with our comparison of the succession rates of our two research sites, Table 4 indicates that the discrepancy between the two institutions on this variable can be found at the lower levels of management as well as at the higher ones. Considering for the moment only those business executives with five years of service or more, we found that at every hierarchical level over eight out of ten of the managers held the maximum of organizational experience. If the criterion of organizational experience is raised to fifteen years or more with the firm, hierarchical differences among business managers emerge clearly. Almost half (48 per cent) of the top level executives of United had been with the company that length of time. This reduced to 22 per cent for middle management and 16 and 17 per cent for each of the two lower-level strata. A greater proportion of senior officers, that is, Colonels and Generals, were likely to have had five or more years' experience at the base than officers of lower rank. Whereas one-third of the top level officers (N = 9) had this amount of experience at the base, fewer than 2 per cent of the company grade officers, Captain and below, had equivalent experience. Moreover, it was at the lowest rank level that the largest percentage of officers had one year or less experience. Hence two propositions were supported

***Table 3—Military Versus Business Organization: Length of Time in the Organization of Executives***

| *Length of time in the organization* | *Military installation* | *Business firm* |
|---|---|---|
| | *(Percentages)* | |
| 1 year or less | 45.5 | 2.1 |
| 2 years | 18.8 | 2.0 |
| 3 years | 15.7 | 3.9 |
| 4 years | 14.4 | 4.6 |
| 5 years or more | 5.6 | 87.5 |
| Total | 100.0 | 100.1 |
| *Number of cases* | *554*[a] | *1,219*[b] |

[a] 2 cases were not ascertained.
[b] 21 cases were not ascertained.

***Table 4—Military Versus Business Organization: Length of time in the Organization of Executives at Various levels of the Hierarchy***

| *Length of time at various levels of hierarchy* | *Military installation* | *Business firm* |
|---|---|---|
| | *(Percentages)* | |
| Colonels and Generals (Top executives) | | |
| 1 year or less | 33 | 4 |
| 2 years | 26 | 1 |
| 3 years | 4 | 2 |
| 4 years | 4 | — |
| 5 years or more | 33 | 93 |
| Total | 100 | 100 |
| *Number of cases* | *27* | *99* |
| Lt. Colonels (Middle management) | | |
| 1 year or less | 36 | 2 |
| 2 years | 20 | 1 |
| 3 years | 24 | 2 |
| 4 years | 15 | 6 |
| 5 years or more | 5 | 89 |
| Total | 100 | 100 |
| *Number of cases* | *55* | *175* |
| Majors (Lower-middle management) | | |
| 1 year or less | 30 | 4 |
| 2 years | 17 | 2 |
| 3 years | 20 | 5 |
| 4 years | 23 | 6 |
| 5 years or more | 10 | 82 |
| Total | 100 | 100 |
| *Number of cases* | *138* | *494* |
| Captains and Lieutenants (First-level management) | | |
| 1 years or les | 54 | — |
| 2 years | 19 | 2 |
| 3 years | 14 | 2 |
| 4 years | 12 | |
| 5 years or more | 1 | 933 |
| Total | 100 | 100 |
| *Number of cases* | *334* | *447* |

by our analysis thus far: (1) The military installation studied was confronted with more rapid succession than the business firm at every level of the management hierarchy. (2) In both types of organization, the rate of succession tended to be somewhat lower among the top executives of the organization. (However, the small number of top-level officers at the military base gave us considerably less confidence in the second proposition than the first.)

The purpose of showing that the two research sites were different with respect to their rates of succession was to prepare the way for our primary concern, the consequences of the bureaucratization of succession. Effects in two areas were indicated, organizational homogeneity and strength of executive control.

*Rapid succession is associated with greater homogeneity among organizational members.* Bureaucratic control involves the widespread application of rational, universalistic criteria in dealing with members of the system. Hence general indexes of bureaucratization are the extensiveness of rules, the degree of hierarchicalization, impersonality, and the focus on managerial expertise.[17] The opposite type of control, the nonbureaucratic, implies the absence of those factors. In the less bureaucratic form, social control is more personal and the uniqueness of the organization and its chief administrators is paramount.

The more rapid succession of officers at the military installation meant that the *range* of executive experience in the organization was much less among this group than among the business managers. Most of the officers at the Air Force base had two years or less experience, while most of the business managers had at least five years' experience in the organization and almost half of the top level managers had at least fifteen years. Therefore it appears that a concomitant of rapid succession may be decreased executive homogeneity with respect to experience in a particular organizational setting. But the military officer rotates through an establishment which has a basic format and a high degree of organizational standardization. At the same time, the socialization for higher position of all managers, business and military, requires constant exposure to a large number of organizations. The crucial difference would seem to be this: The business executive is more likely than his military counterpart to be able to count on staying with an organization for a long enough period to implement major innovations.

In general, rapid succession encourages executive homogeneity with respect to universalistic criteria. Data on age and seniority may be cited illustratively. Table 5 represents the age distribution of executives of the United Utility Corporation and the officers of the Air Force base. Because of military retirement policies, the officers were, on the whole, much younger than the business managers. In general, age and rate of executive succession should be directly related.[18] Thus the finding that the military installation had a higher rate of succession than the business firm may actually tend to underestimate slightly the true relationship to be found were age to be adequately controlled.

Table 6 compares the age distribution of executives of the military and business organization at each level of the authority structure. A greater proportion of older executives, that is, those fifty-five and older, was found consistently in the business firm.[19] Also relevant is the finding that the Air Force officers were considerably more homogeneous with respect to age than the business executives. Note that 80 per cent of the Captains and Lieutenants were under thirty-five, almost nine out of ten (88.3 per cent) of the Majors and Lieutenant Colonels were in the same thirty-five to forty-four

17. For a statement that applies these four factors, see P. M. Blau, *Bureaucracy in Modern Society* (New York: Random House, 1956), p. 19.

18. Grusky, *op. cit.*

19. The youth of the Air Force Officers, a favorite gibe during World War II, cannot match that of the French Army of the middle of the eighteenth century where the colonel of fourteen or sixteen was not at all rare. See Dorn, *op. cit.*, p. 88.

***Table 5—Military Versus Business Organization: Age Distribution of Executives***

| *Age distribution* | *Military installation* | *Business firm* |
|---|---|---|
| | *(Percentages)* | |
| Under 35 years | 49.4 | 33.4 |
| 35 to 44 years | 45.3 | 43.8 |
| 45 to 54 years | 4.9 | 14.7 |
| 55 years and over | .4 | 8.1 |
| Total | 100.0 | 100.0 |
| *Number of cases* | *554*[a] | *1,226*[b] |

[a] 2 cases were not ascertained.
[b] 14 cases were not ascertained.

of homogeneity at any level in their structure of authority. Reflected strongly in these data is the systematic selection and promotion policies typical of the present American military system. Military recruitment is tied closely to age, and promotion up to field grade rank is linked just as closely to length of service.[20] Data from United Utility Corporation indicated that here, too, length of employment with the firm was positively related to amount of upward age bracket, and finally, about three-fourths of the top-level officers (71.4 per cent) were similarly located in a single age category. The business executives failed to approach this exceptional degree career mobility.[21] Table 7 examines the relationship between hierarchical position and seniority (the number of years of service in the corporate or military establishment) for the two samples.[22] It is evident that the military sample is more homogeneous than the business managers at *every* hierarchical level. One hundred per cent of the

20. Janowitz, *op. cit.*, pp. 6–64.

21. See my "Career Mobility and Organizational Commitment," *Administrative Science Quarterly*, *10*, 4 (March 1966), 488–503.

22. Seniority in business in order to be properly equated with military seniority ought to be construed as meaning total length of time in the business world. Actually, as we noted, it refers in this case to its customary reference, number of years in the employ of the corporation.

***Table 6—Military Versus Business Organization: Age Distribution of Executives at Various Levels of the Hierarchy***

| *Age distribution at various levels of hierarchy* | *Military installation* | *Business firm* |
|---|---|---|
| | *(Percentages)* | |
| Colonels and Generals (Top executives) | | |
| Under 35 years | — | 9 |
| 35 to 44 years | 74 | 41 |
| 45 to 54 years | 22 | 32 |
| 55 years and over | 4 | 18 |
| Total | 100 | 100 |
| *Number of cases* | *27* | *101* |
| Lt. Colonels (Middle management) | | |
| Under 35 years | — | 27 |
| 35 to 44 years | 85 | 48 |
| 45 to 54 years | 13 | 18 |
| 55 years and over | 2 | 7 |
| Total | 100 | 100 |
| *Number of cases* | *55* | *175* |
| Majors (Lower-middle management) | | |
| Under 35 years | 5 | 40 |
| 35 to 44 years | 88 | 42 |
| 45 to 54 years | 7 | 13 |
| 55 years and over | — | 5 |
| Total | 100 | 100 |
| *Number of cases* | *137* | *495* |
| Captains and Lieutenants (First-level management) | | |
| Under 35 years | 80 | 34 |
| 35 to 44 years | 19 | 45 |
| 45 to 54 years | 1 | 12 |
| 55 years and over | — | 9 |
| Total | 100 | 100 |
| *Number of cases* | *335* | *455* |

***Table 7—Military Versus Business Organization: Seniority of Executives at Various Levels in the Hierarchy***

| *Seniority at various levels of hierarchy* | *Military installation* | *Business firm* |
|---|---|---|
| | *(Percentages)* | |
| Colonels and Generals (Top executives) | | |
| 0 to 4 years | — | 7 |
| 5 to 9 years | — | 5 |
| 10 to 14 years | — | 40 |
| 15 years or more | 100 | 48 |
| Total | 100 | 100 |
| *Number of cases* | *27* | *99* |
| Lt. Colonels (Middle management) | | |
| 0 to 4 years | — | 11 |
| 5 to 9 years | — | 13 |
| 10 to 14 years | 4 | 54 |
| 15 years or more | 96 | 22 |
| Total | 100 | 100 |
| *Number of cases* | *55* | *175* |
| Majors (Lower-middle management) | | |
| 0 to 4 years | — | 19 |
| 5 to 9 years | 1 | 16 |
| 10 to 14 years | 43 | 49 |
| 15 years or more | 56 | 16 |
| Total | 100 | 100 |
| *Number of cases* | *135* | *494* |
| Captains and Lieutenants (First-level management) | | |
| 0 to 4 years | 14 | 7 |
| 5 to 9 years | 48 | 21 |
| 10 to 14 years | 37 | 55 |
| 15 years or more | 1 | 17 |
| Total | 100 | 100 |
| *Number of cases* | *334* | *447* |

senior military executives had fifteen or more years of seniority compared to only 48 per cent of their business counterparts. At the middle management level, the comparison is 96 per cent to 22 per cent in the maximum seniority category. Among those we have termed lower middle management, we find 99 per cent of the officers grouped in the two highest seniority categories compared to only 65 per cent of the business managers in the same group. The degree of homogeneity among the military officers at the first level of management is brought out most clearly if this group is differentiated more sharply by rank. Seven out of seven Second Lieutenants had four years or less of military service, 78 per cent of the First Lieutenants were in the same category, and 93 per cent of the Captains had either between five or nine or ten through fourteen years of seniority. This close relationship between rank and seniority was not matched by the business managers.

A comparatively slow rate of succession in the business firm studied seemed to function to produce homogeneity through shared experiences in the organization. The significance of leadership homogeneity for administration has been noted by Selznick: "Another developmental problem is that of creating an initial homogeneous staff. The members of this core group reflect the basic policies of the organization in their own outlooks. They can, when matured in this role, perform the essential task of indoctrinating newcomers along desired lines. They can provide assurance that decision-making will conform, in spirit as well as letter, to policies that may have to be formulated abstractly or vaguely. The development of derivative policies and detailed applications of general rules will thus be guided by a shared general perspective."[23] Such functions, essential to business organization, ostensibly are replaced in military systems by bureaucratic forms.

The high rate of succession in the military installation militated against the creation of homogeneity through shared experiences in the particular organization of which the officer is a part. Instead, the bases for homogeneity would seem to lie with the similarity of the officers' military training, social values, the hierarchy of authority, age, sex, and other nonparticularistic factors. In the military, the nature of the particular installation is less important to administration than the fundamental similarities of each base. Rapid succession may be both a cause and a product of organizational uniformity.

*Rapid succession is associated with limitations on executive control.* It is frequently argued that in an organization where few executives can anticipate long periods of service and most can look forward to relatively short tenures in that particular organization, the ability of the executive to implement major policy changes is greatly weakened. By contrast, failure to rotate creates powerful barriers to innovation by entrenching traditionalistic perspectives. Continuous rotation clearly fashions the pattern of organizational innovations in military systems, especially at the operational level. All too frequently, the first year of a three-year tour of duty is spent familiarizing oneself with the idiosyncrasies of the base, the second in implementing a number of relatively limited rule changes, the third in setting the base in order in anticipation of departure. Moreover, where civilian employees have long tenures and military officials are frequently rotated, we would expect the former group to tend to absorb a disproportionate amount of influence on the implementation of policy and policy-making. Nor is such a situation conducive to identification with the commanding officer of a military base. The performance of General Curtis E. LeMay in welding the Strategic Air Command into a highly effective and adaptable force was undoubtedly related to the fact that he was left in command for over eight years rather than the normal shorter tour of duty.[24]

When asked: "What officer of General rank, past or present, do you admire most?" the 497 military officers who responded selected 118 different generals. Less than one per cent selected their own commanding officer. For these officers, the system of rotation produced attachments not so much to one well-known leader but to one of many lesser known leaders. It is only in the small unbureaucratized organization or in the large complex system unified through a single overriding objective, as in combat, that a specific leader is closely identified with the organization as a whole.[25]

23. Philip Selznick, *Leadership in Administration* (Evanston, Ill.: Row, Peterson and Co., 1957), p. 105.

24. Huntington, S. P., *The Common Defense* (New York: Columbia University Press, 1961), p. 311.

25. Business novels provide some illustrations. These comments were ascribed to Avery Bullard, chief executive of Tredway Corporation, in Cameron Hawley's famous

One concrete aspect of the consequences of rotation can be seen in the data linking length of service in the organization and perceived authority; that is, the amount of authority the person believes he has. These data are presented in Table 8, which reveal differences between the military and the business setting. When officers who had been stationed at the base for more than two years were compared with officers at the base for less than two years, a greater proportion of the former felt that they had a "great deal of authority." This held true for all ranks, perhaps most clearly among the uppermost ranks. Although the small number of cases compels qualifying our comments, it appears that knowledge of the military base plus the integration of the officer into its organizational structure, served to strengthen perceived authority. In the business organization, the same relationship was present, but it operated more selectively with respect to the rank structure. At the very top level of management, perceived authority did not increase with length of service, nor were the differences very great at the bottom level. It was only in the middle ranks that there was a marked increase in perceived authority with length of service. Hence, it would appear that frequent succession conditions personal executive authority. The highly bureaucratized system, by routinizing the succession process, modifies the authority of the person through reliance on the authority of the total complex organization.

novel, *Executive Suite*: "When he did come for lunch, there was no man in Millburgh, even the president of the Susquehanna National Bank, who could escape the temptation of bragging to his wife that he had lunched that day at the table next to Avery Bullard's." And one of Bullard's vice-presidents described him as ". . . a great man . . . He was the greatest man I've ever known." See *Executive Suite*, Houghton-Mifflin Co., Boston, 1952, p. 31.

## Succession and organizational commitment

Two "types" of succession have thus far been described. The first, represented by the business firm, is characterized by a comparatively slow rate of succession, particularly among the top executives. The integration of the top-level group, as well as to a lesser extent, the lower-level stratum, is encouraged through shared experiences that take place within the context of a single corporation. The second kind of succession, typified by the military installation, is defined by continuous and regular changes among occupants of all of the positions in the system. Military organization is viewed as a collection of separate and structurally identical installations and a military career may be defined as a journey, with regularly spaced intervals, from one fundamentally equivalent bureaucratic organization to another.

The resulting career patterns should yield different types of commitment to the organization and to its subunits. The present study permitted us to compare the degree of commitment of the officials of the two organizations. We assumed tentatively that differences in commitment might be attributed, in part, to differences in succession experiences. By commitment we refer to the nature of the affective

***Table 8—Military Versus Business Organization: Length of Time in the Organization and Perceived Authority at Various Levels of the Hierarchy***

| *Per cent responding: "I have a great deal to say."* | *Length of time in the organization* | | | |
|---|---|---|---|---|
| | *LESS THAN 2 YEARS* | | *2 YEARS OR MORE* | |
| *Military installation* | *Per cent* | *Number of cases* | *Per cent* | *Number of cases* |
| Colonels and Generals | 75 | *8* | 100 | *17* |
| Lt. Colonels | 55 | *20* | 71 | *35* |
| Majors | 49 | *41* | 50 | *96* |
| Captains and Lieutenants | 17 | *179* | 26 | *152* |

| | *LESS THAN 5 YEARS* | | *5 TO 14 YEARS* | | *15 OR MORE YEARS* | |
|---|---|---|---|---|---|---|
| *Business firm* | *Per cent* | *Number of cases* | *Per cent* | *Number of cases* | *Per cent* | *Number of cases* |
| Top executives | 83 | *7* | 80 | *45* | 83 | *47* |
| Middle management | 25 | *20* | 43 | *116* | 51 | *39* |
| Lower-middle management | 13 | *91* | 31 | *324* | 56 | *79* |
| First-level management | 31 | *32* | 34 | *340* | 35 | *75* |

relationship of the member toward the organization as a whole and toward the department. Commitment was measured in these areas by means of two three-item Guttman scales.[26]

26. The Guttman scale of Attitude toward the Organization was based on three items worded as follows: (1) "Do you feel that the men who ran the Base (Company) recognize your ability and what you are able to do?" (2) "How well do you feel that the men who run the Base (Company) understand your problems and needs?" (3) "In general, how well do you think the Base (Company) is run?" The responses were dichotomized. The coefficient of reproducibility for the business managers was .96 and for the Air Force officers .94. For the items comprising the Guttman scale of Attitude toward the Department, the term "department" was substituted for Base or Company. The coefficient of reproducibility for the business managers was .95 and for the Air Force officers also .95.

Tables 9 and 10 present the major findings. The outstanding differences between the two institutions were the consistently stronger commitment of the officers and the differential effects of organizational experience. When controls for numerous variables were applied, such as education, age, and rank, these differences remained.

We have already suggested that bureaucratic career patterns tend to produce a limited identification with the chief executive. The present findings suggest that affect is transferred from the leader to the organization. Bureaucratic career patterns emphasize the influence of the organization and the profession rather than that of the individual. Accordingly, we find in Table 9 that length of service in the organization was not directly related

***Table 9—Military Versus Business Organization: Relationship Between Length of Time in the Organization and Two Indexes of Commitment***

| | *Length of time in the organization* | | | | | | | |
|---|---|---|---|---|---|---|---|---|
| | *LESS THAN 2 YEARS* | | *2 TO 3 YEARS* | | *4 YEARS OR MORE* | | | |
| *Military installation* | *Per cent* | *Number of cases* | *Per cent* | *Number of cases* | *Per cent* | *Number of cases* | | |
| a) Favorable attitude toward the organization | 53 | *252* | 52 | *191* | 57 | *111* | | |
| b) Favorable attitude toward the department | 67 | *252* | 62 | *191* | 68 | *111* | | |
| *Business firm* | *0 TO 4 YEARS* | | *5 TO 9 YEARS* | | *10 TO 14 YEARS* | | *15 YEARS OR MORE* | |
| a) Favorable attitude toward the organization | 29 | *149* | 29 | 193 | 34 | *613* | 48 | *231* |
| b) Favorable attitude toward the department | 40 | *147* | 51 | 194 | 50 | *613* | 55 | *236* |

***Table 10—Military Versus Business Organization: Indexes of Executive Commitment at Various Levels of the Hierarchy***

| | *MILITARY INSTALLATION* | | *BUSINESS FIRM* | |
|---|---|---|---|---|
| *Indexes of executive commitment* | *Per cent* | *Number of cases* | *Per cent* | *Number of cases* |
| Colonels and Generals (Top executives) | | | | |
| a) Favorable attitude toward the organization | 67 | *27* | 65 | *97* |
| b) Favorable attitude toward the department | 81 | *27* | 56 | *97* |
| Lt. Colonels (Middle management) | | | | |
| a) Favorable attitude toward the organization | 69 | *55* | 42 | *170* |
| b) Favorable attitude toward the department | 74 | *55* | *49* | *173* |
| Majors (Lower-middle management) | | | | |
| a) Favorable attitude toward the organization | 61 | *139* | 28 | *486* |
| b) Favorable attitude toward the department | 68 | *139* | 42 | *484* |
| Captains and Lieutenants (First-level management) | | | | |
| a) Favorable attitude toward the organization | 47 | *335* | 34 | *448* |
| b) Favorable attitude toward the department | 62 | *335* | 58 | *452* |

to strength of commitment to the military installation. Those officers with more than four years of organizational experience on the base were as strongly committed to the organization and to their department as those officers with less than two years' experience. On the other hand, the pronounced lower rate of career succession of the business managers may have been responsible for the strength of their commitment increasing steadily with length of time in the organization. Only 29 per cent of the business managers with less than five years' experience compared with almost half (48 per cent) of those with fifteen or more years' experience in the organization had favorable attitudes toward the firm. Likewise, positive commitment to the department was on the whole positively related to length of time in the organization.

Three major findings are shown in Table 10: (1) It presents additional support for the previously reported stronger commitment of the Air Force officers. In all comparisons a greater proportion of military officers than business managers were favorably oriented toward the organization and subunit. (2) It suggests the greater importance for strength of commitment of hierarchical position in the military than in the business firm. Although by no means unimportant to business organizations, hierarchicalization in the military setting was more uniform and hence more closely predictive of attitudes. (3) In both institutions, commitment to the subunit (department) was considerably greater than commitment to the organization. (See also Table 9.) The lone exception was among the top business executives.

The data presented, which demonstrated a stronger organizational commitment among military officers than among business managers, may challenge the assertions of those military analysts who have maintained that the rapid rate of military succession has led to declining officer morale.[27] Succession in a highly bureaucratized context may, in most cases, call forth a highly adaptive series of responses. Rather than always disrupt social relations, rapid succession, if routinized, may be associated with the emergence of new patterns of adaptation.

## Succession and involvement in community affairs

Theorists of mass society have insisted appropriately on the importance of community associations as mediating links between the nation-state and the otherwise alienated, powerless citizen.[28] According to some, C. Wright Mills was the most prominent proponent of this view, the rising importance of bureaucratic organization threatens to atomize the middle class and thereby weaken their social power.[29] In fact, however, the new middle classes do not lessen their participation in voluntary associations. On the contrary, as W. H. Whyte has suggested, Organization Man may be more likely than his predecessor to be involved in community life.[30]

Our research situation enabled us to examine these apparent effects of bureaucratization by comparing the community participation of military officers and business managers. Two approaches to the effects of succession on community involvement may be distinguished. The first, which sees succession as socially disruptive, argues that the high rate of succession associated with the bureaucratic career pattern prevents the manager from planting his roots in the community. Rapid succession should militate against frequent participation in voluntary associations because it promotes a transient orientation toward such involvement. Therefore, by this approach, officers of the military installation should be less likely to be involved in community affairs than the business managers of the firm studied. An alternative orientation, stemming from the theory of bureaucracy, leads to the opposite hypothesis. Frequent succession, a standard attribute of the bureaucratic career pattern, is highly routinized and therefore normally anticipated. The anticipation of

27. Baldwin states: "There are far too many transfers and shifts—so many that a great many service officers feel that they never stay long enough at any one job to master it properly." He cites illustratively the case of a Major Wood who resigned ostensibly because of the rapid succession he experienced—thirty-three moves in thirteen years. *New York Times*, Western Edition, October 21, 1963.

28. William Kornhauser, *The Politics of Mass Society* (New York: The Free Press, 1959); R. A. Nisbet, *The Quest for Community* (New York: Oxford University Press, 1953).

29. C. Wright Mills, *The Power Elite* (New York: Oxford University Press, 1951), p. 262.

30. W. H. Whyte, Jr., *The Organization Man* (Garden City, N.Y.: Doubleday Anchor Books, 1957), chaps. 20 and 21.

change enables the highly mobile manager to deal with his transiency by means of a series of adjustive responses.[31] We speculated that one such response was to quickly become a part of the local community in a new assignment by joining voluntary associations. In effect, awareness of transiency generates a strong desire to become socially involved. Hence, the hypothesis that military officers would be more likely to be involved in community affairs than business managers.

Our measure of community involvement was the number of memberships in various community voluntary associations.[32] Data were collected from both samples pertaining to four types of organizations: church groups, fraternal organizations, neighborhood clubs, and sports clubs. In three of these four the Air Force officers demonstrated a greater overall proportion of memberships: church groups, 33 to 29 per cent, neighborhood clubs, 54 to 47 per cent, and sports clubs, 42 to 29 per cent. The business managers were more likely, to a slight extent, to be members of one or more fraternal organizations, 30 to 28 per cent. (Officers are not permitted to be members of political clubs while on active duty.[33] Hence, comparisons of this type were not feasible.) Sixty-one per cent of the total military sample belonged to three organizations or more, while only 31 per cent of the business managers reported memberships in an equivalent number of organizations. Table 11 indicates that when length of time in the organization was controlled, the same pattern of differences was maintained. Of 15 comparisons that could be made, 13 were in the direction supporting the proposition that a greater proportion of military officers than business managers were likely to be members of voluntary associations. Wright and Hyman's report of the Denver study of associational membership showed no systematic relationship between length of time in the community and incidence of membership in voluntary associations.[34] Contrary to this report, and con-

31. Eugene Litwak, "Voluntary Association and Neighborhood Cohesion," *American Sociological Review*, 25 (February, 1960), pp. 258–71; Phillip Fellin, and Eugene Litwak, "Neighborhood Cohesion Under Conditions of Mobility," *American Sociological Review*, 28 (June, 1963), pp. 364–76. Our findings are consistent with those of Litwak, who found that bureaucratic managers were more likely than entrepreneurs to integrate quickly into a neighborhood.

32. Respondents were asked to list the names of associations to which they currently belong. Associations to which only their wives belonged were not solicited. Examples of each type of organization were provided. Unfortunately, we had no measure of extent of involvement in each association.

33. Of course, this is not unique to the United States military system. Alfred Vagts quotes Lorenz von Stein, noting that in 1868 members of the English army were not allowed "to institute or take part in any meetings, demonstrations, or processions for party or political purposes in barracks, quarters, camps, or elsewhere." *A History of Militarism*, W. W. Norton and Co., New York, 1937, p. 169.

34. This is an oversimplification and should be qualified. Although there is a marked difference in associational memberships between urban residents and rural *farm* residents, the reported differences between urban and rural *non-farm* residents were not great when degree of urbanization of the county was controlled. However, relevant to the present case, Wright and Hyman found that the more urbanized the county in which the urban resident was located the smaller the proportions of persons with no

***Table 11—Military Versus Business Organization: Length of Time in the Organization and Participation in Voluntary Associations***

| | *Length of time in the organization* | | | | | |
|---|---|---|---|---|---|---|
| | *LESS THAN 2 YEARS* | | *2 TO 3 YEARS* | | *4 YEARS* | |
| *Members of one or more organizations* | *Military installation* | *Business firm* | *Military installation* | *Business firm* | *Military installation* | *Business firm* |
| | *(Percentages)* | | *(Percentages)* | | *(Percentages)* | |
| Church groups | 27 | 24 | 31 | 29 | 43 | 30 |
| Fraternal organizations | 26 | 32 | 23 | 20 | 22 | 32 |
| Neighborhood clubs | 40 | 24 | 54 | 29 | 63 | 50 |
| Sports clubs | 35 | 24 | 49 | 29 | 50 | 30 |
| Political clubs | —[b] | 4 | — | 9 | — | 5 |
| Three organizations or more | 52 | 28 | 71 | 16 | 81 | 33 |
| *Number of cases* | *153* | *25* | *111* | *71* | *68* | *128* |

[a] The overall proportion of memberships in each type of association was as follows (military organization first): Church groups, 33 per cent and 29 per cent; fraternal organizations, 28 per cent and 30 per cent; neighborhood clubs, 54 per cent and 47 per cent; sports clubs, 42 per cent and 29 per cent; political clubs, business managers only, 6 per cent; three organizations or more, 61 per cent and 31 per cent. Number of cases was slightly different for each type of association.

[b] No data on this item were collected from the military officers.

sistent with Zimmer's findings, the data reported in Table 11 indicated that among military officers such a relationship did exist.[35] The pattern suggests clearly that frequency of affiliation was positively related to length of time in the specific military organization (and hence in the community). Only fraternal organizational memberships violated the overall trend. The pattern was less clear among business managers. While church, neighborhood, and sports group memberships increased with length of time with the firm, fraternal and political club memberships did not, nor did overall frequency of total memberships.

One among several problems in comparing our two samples lay in the relationship between length of time in the organization and length of time in the community. Among the military officers, this problem could be ignored as the two variables were perfectly and positively correlated. Not so with the businessmen. A manager may have been with his present firm a short time, but still be a long-time community resident. Fortunately, however, this factor should have worked against the pattern reported of greater community participation among officers than among business managers.

Several studies have demonstrated a positive relationship between social stratification and incidence of affiliation with voluntary associations.[36] Position in the system of stratification of the association is positively correlated with position in the community's stratification system, as Table 12 demonstrates. Class self-conceptions were determined by this item: "If you were asked to use one of these names (upper, upper middle, middle, lower middle, working, and lower class), to which social class would you say you belonged?" In both samples, the proportion of persons identifying themselves as members of the upper and upper middle classes increased directly with level in the organizational hierarchy. Once again the greater importance of the rank hierarchy in the military setting was revealed. The converse proposition, namely, that the proportion of persons identifying themselves as members of the lower and working classes was inversely correlated with hierarchical level, held in perfect order only for the military population. Parenthetically, Table 12 also revealed a consistent tendency for military officers at every rank level to identify themselves as members of higher class levels. Although the differential decreased with downward movement in the hierarchy, military officers were more likely than business managers to place themselves in the upper and upper middle classes. Despite the fact that our sample of military officers did not suggest any narrow social class alignment, it nevertheless pointed toward a greater homogeneity of perspective in the military than in the business firm studied.

associational memberships. See C. R. Wright, and H. H. Hyman, "Voluntary Association Memberships of American Adults: Evidence from National Sample Surveys," *American Sociological Review*, 23 (June, 1958), pp. 284–94.

35. B. G. Zimmer, "Participation of Migrants in Urban Structures," *American Sociological Review*, 20 (April, 1955), pp. 218–24.

36. These are reviewed in Wright and Hyman, *op. cit.*, pp. 288–89.

***Table 12—Military Versus Business Organization: Social Class Self-Conceptions at Various Levels of the Hierarchy***

| *Social class self-conceptions* | *Military installation* | *Business firm* |
|---|---|---|
| | *(Percentages)* | |
| Colonels and Generals (Top executives) | | |
| Upper and upper middle class | 52 | 38 |
| Middle class | 41 | 57 |
| Lower and working class | 7 | 5 |
| Total | 100 | 100 |
| *Number of cases* | *27* | *99* |
| Lt. Colonels (Middle management) | | |
| Upper and upper-middle class | 48 | 31 |
| Middle class | 44 | 59 |
| Lower and working class | 8 | 9 |
| Total | 100 | 99 |
| *Number of cases* | *54* | *174* |
| Majors (Lower-middle management) | | |
| Upper and upper-middle class | 43 | 17 |
| Middle class | 51 | 64 |
| Lower and working class | 6 | 19 |
| Total | 100 | 100 |
| *Number of cases* | *137* | *490* |
| Captains and Lieutenants (First-level management) | | |
| Upper and upper-middle class | 36 | 9 |
| Middle class | 55 | 59 |
| Lower and working class | 9 | 32 |
| Total | 100 | 100 |
| *Number of cases* | *327* | *448* |

Table 13 compared voluntary association memberships in the two samples within social class groupings. In ten of thirteen comparisons, a greater proportion of military officers than business managers were members of voluntary associations. Two of three exceptions again referred to fraternal organizations. Memberships in this type of association seem to be stressed more heavily in business.[37] On the other hand, the greater stress in the military on physical fitness undoubtedly accounts in part for the officers' more frequent memberships in athletic organizations.

The relationship between hierarchical level and participation in voluntary associations is shown in Table 14. The greater community involvement of the military sample was once again sustained in seventeen of twenty comparisons. (It was impossible because of the limitation in number of cases to control simultaneously for socio-economic level, rank, and length of time in the organization.) It should be noted that executives of United Utility Corporation were actively encouraged by superiors to join community associations. In this sense, United resembled the absentee-owned corporation in "Bigtown," a community studied by Pellegrin and Coates.[38] In this study, the authors observed that "Executives are expected to belong to civic organizations and serve on committees as part of their jobs."[39] A comparable policy encouraging affiliation with local organizations was not discovered at the military installation. The clearest association between corporate level and associational membership was found for political organizations. Only the top business executives, to any significant extent, belonged to political clubs.[40]

37. For example, see Melville Dalton, *Men Who Manage: Fusions of Feeling and Theory in Administration* (New York: John Wiley and Sons, 1959), pp. 178–81.

38. R. J. Pellegrin, and C. H. Coates, "Absentee-owned Corporations and Community Power Structure," *American Journal of Sociology*, 61 (March, 1956), pp. 413–19.

39. *Ibid.*, p. 416.

40. Rossi found that business executives in Mediana (a fictitious name) tended to avoid any community participation where possible community conflict might be involved. He observed: "Participating in political affairs is acceptable only when the element of hostility and possible opposition are moved from the scene, preferably in advance." See P. H. Rossi, "The Organizational Structure of an American Community" in Amitai Etzioni, editor, *Complex Organizations*, p. 306.

***Table 13—Military Versus Business Organization: Voluntary Association Memberships, Social Class Self-Conceptions Controlled***

| *Members of one or more organizations* | *Military installation* | *Business firm* |
|---|---|---|
| | *(Percentages)* | |
| Upper and upper-middle class | | |
| Church groups | 37 | 35 |
| Fraternal organizations | 30 | 41 |
| Neighborhood clubs | 61 | 52 |
| Sports clubs | 48 | 26 |
| Three organizations or more | 68 | 44 |
| *Number of cases*[a] | *214* | *214* |
| Middle class | | |
| Church groups | 31 | 29 |
| Fraternal organizations | 28 | 30 |
| Neighborhood clubs | 53 | 48 |
| Sports clubs | 41 | 32 |
| Three organizations or more | 58 | 31 |
| *Number of cases* | *162* | *716* |
| Lower middle, lower, or working class | | |
| Church groups | 30 | 25 |
| Fraternal organizations | 27 | 24 |
| Neighborhood clubs | 45 | 48 |
| Sports clubs | 34 | 26 |
| Three organizations or more | 54 | 24 |
| *Number of cases* | *44* | *250* |

[a] Number of cases for each type of group varied slightly.

***Table 14—Military Versus Business Organization: Executive Participation in Voluntary Associations at Various Levels in the Hierarchy***

| *Members of one or more organizations* | *TOP EXECUTIVES* | | *MIDDLE MANAGEMENT* | | *LOWER-MIDDLE MANAGEMENT* | | *FIRST-LEVEL MANAGEMENT* | |
|---|---|---|---|---|---|---|---|---|
| | *Military installation* | *Business firm* | *Military installation* | *Business firm* | *Military installation* | *Business firm* | *Military installation* | *Business firm* |
| | *(Percentages)* | | *(Percentages)* | | *(Percentages)* | | *(Percentages)* | |
| Church groups | 42 | 32 | 33 | 31 | 43 | 32 | 30 | 24 |
| Fraternal organizations | 31 | 45 | 35 | 29 | 31 | 30 | 26 | 27 |
| Neighborhood clubs | 58 | 51 | 75 | 52 | 70 | 47 | 45 | 45 |
| Sports clubs | 56 | 30 | 48 | 36 | 45 | 27 | 40 | 32 |
| Political clubs[a] | — | 16 | — | 4 | — | 4 | — | 4 |
| Three organizations or more | 85 | 53 | 62 | 35 | 76 | 32 | 54 | 25 |
| *Number of cases*[b] | *26* | *102* | *52* | *178* | *138* | *497* | *332* | *459* |

[a] No data were collected on this item from the military officers.
[b] Number of cases for each type of group varied slightly.

Thus, the pattern of involvement in local community affairs differed consistently in the two research sites. Officers apparently responded to their assignments, which were of brief duration, by quickly tying themselves into local community activities. Rapid succession, instead of producing a withdrawal from community life, was associated with an active and continuing search for extensive social involvement.

## Summary and conclusions

Although we have deliberately focused on differences between military and business organization, it is apparent that all organization officials in our society share certain characteristics. They occupy well-defined positions in a hierarchy; interpersonal skills are critical to their career advancement; they are concerned with salary and prestige as measures of worth; and they seek to maintain ties to the local community and to the society as a whole. However, these many similarities ought not obscure the fact that organizations have markedly different objectives and structures and that these necessarily produce different patterns of behavior among their executives.

We have assumed that bureaucratic career patterns were more typical of military than business organization. And we did find that rapid succession, typical of highly bureaucratized systems, characterized the military installation to a much greater extent than it did the business firm. Moreover, not surprisingly, we found consistent evidence of greater hierarchicalization in the military site.

It was the consequences of rapid succession, however, which concerned this exploratory study most of all. How do organizations and their members respond to highly routinized and rapid succession? The limited evidence was examined in four problem areas: executive homogeneity, control, commitment, and community involvement.

Because bureaucratic control necessitates the extensive application of rational criteria for selection and promotion of personnel, homogeneity among executives with respect to numerous social characteristics tends to result. Accordingly, we found at each rank level greater uniformity in age, length of time in the organization, and seniority among the military officers than among business managers.

Routinized succession conditions the exercise of organizational control. Rapid succession in the military inhibits strong identification with the chief executive. The data collected for this study indicated that length of tenure at the military base increased the perceived authority of the officers, including those at the highest ranks. Length of tenure also increased perceived authority in the business setting, but not at the top ranks. Thus it appears that in the military, bureaucratic forms of rotation, regardless of the organizational objectives they serve, weaken personal executive power and encourage the development of a general orientation toward organizational authority.

More favorable orientations toward the organization and the specific department were found in the military setting than in the business organization. In the military system, and unlike the business firm studied, length of experience in the particular installation was not systematically related to the strength of these attitudes. Instead, the more favorable orientations to the organization and the subunit could be seen as tied closely to the greater standardization of assignment and greater strength of professional commitment in the military.

Evidence supporting the hypothesis that frequent succession inhibits extensive participation in community life was not found. Instead, the opposite pattern prevailed. Military officers, despite their short time in the community, were found more likely to be members of various community voluntary associations than were business managers. The findings were viewed as suggestive of a pattern of adaptation to bureaucratic succession. Military officers, knowing full well that their assignment to a given base was temporary, apparently responded by rapidly integrating themselves into the local community through memberships in numerous voluntary associations.

BURTON R. CLARK

# The "Cooling-Out" Function in Higher Education

A major problem of democratic society is inconsistency between encouragement to achieve and the realities of limited opportunity. Democracy asks individuals to act as if social mobility were universally possible; status is to be won by individual effort, and rewards are to accrue to those who try. But democratic societies also need selective training institutions, and hierarchical work organizations permit increasingly fewer persons to succeed at ascending levels. Situations of opportunity are also situations of denial and failure. Thus democratic societies need not only to motivate achievement but also to mollify those denied it in order to sustain motivation in the face of disappointment and to deflect resentment. In the modern mass democracy, with its large-scale organization, elaborated ideologies of equal access and participation, and minimal commitment to social origin as a basis for status, the task becomes critical.

The problem of blocked opportunity has been approached sociologically through means-ends analysis. Merton and others have called attention to the phenomenon of dissociation between culturally instilled goals and institutionally provided means of realization; discrepancy between ends and means is seen as a basic social source of individual frustration and recalcitrance.[1] We shall here extend means-ends analysis in another direction, to the responses of organized groups to means-ends disparities, in particular focusing attention on ameliorative processes that lessen the strains of dissociation. We shall do so by analyzing the most prevalent type of dissociation between aspirations and avenues in American education, specifying the structure and processes that reduce the stress of structural disparity and individual denial. Certain components of American higher education perform what may be called the cooling-out function,[2] and it is to these that attention will be drawn.

**Revised and extended version of paper read at the Fifty-fourth Annual Meeting of the American Sociological Association, Chicago, September 3–5, 1959. I am indebted to Erving Goffman and Martin A. Trow for criticism and to Sheldon Messinger for extended conceptual and editorial comment.**

**Reprinted from *The American Journal of Sociology*, May, 1960, pp. 569–76, by permission of the author and publisher. (Copyright 1960 by The University of Chicago Press.)**

1. "Aberrant behavior may be regarded sociologically as a symptom of dissociation between culturally prescribed aspirations and socially structured avenues for realizing these aspirations" (Robert K. Merton, "Social Structure and Anomie," in *Social Theory and Social Structure* [rev. ed.; New York: Free Press, 1957], p. 134). See also Herbert H. Hyman, "The Value Systems of Different Classes: A Social Psychological Contribution to the Analysis of Stratification," in Reinhard Bendix and Seymour M. Lipset (eds.), *Class, Status and Power: A Reader in Social Stratification* (New York: Free Press, 1953), pp. 426–42; and the papers by Robert Dubin, Richard A. Cloward, Robert K. Merton, and Dorothy L. Meier, and Wendell Bell, in *American Sociological Review*, 24 (April, 1959).

2. I am indebted to Erving Goffman's original statement of the cooling-out conception. See his "Cooling the Mark Out: Some Aspects of Adaptation to Failure," *Psychiatry*, 15 (November, 1952), 451–63. Sheldon Messinger called the relevance of this concept to my attention.

## The ends-means disjuncture

In American higher education the aspirations of the multitude are encouraged by "open-door" admission to public-supported colleges. The means of moving upward in status and of maintaining high status now include some years in college, and a college education is a prerequisite of the better positions in business and the professions. The trend is toward an ever tighter connection between higher education and higher occupations, as increased specialization and professionalization insure that more persons will need more preparation. The high-school graduate, seeing college as essential to success, will seek to enter some college, regardless of his record in high school.

A second and allied source of public interest in unlimited entry into college is the ideology of equal opportunity.[3] Strictly interpreted, equality of opportunity means selection according to ability, without regard to extraneous considerations. Popularly interpreted, however, equal opportunity in obtaining a college education is widely taken to mean unlimited access to some form of college: in California, for example, state educational authorities maintain that high-school graduates who cannot qualify for the state university or state college should still have the "opportunity of attending a publicly supported institution of higher education," this being "an essential part of the state's goal of guaranteeing equal educational opportunities to all its citizens."[4] To deny access to college is then to deny equal opportunity. Higher education should make a seat available without judgment on past performance.

Many other features of current American life encourage college-going. School officials are reluctant to establish early critical hurdles for the young, as is done in Europe. With little enforced screening in the pre-college years, vocational choice and educational selection are postponed to the college years or later. In addition, the United States, a wealthy country, is readily supporting a large complex of colleges, and its expanding economy requires more specialists. Recently, a national concern that manpower be fully utilized has encouraged the extending of college training to more and different kinds of students. Going to college is also in some segments of society the thing to do; as a last resort, it is more attractive than the army or a job. Thus ethical and practical urges together encourage the high-school graduate to believe that college is both a necessity and a right; similarly, parents and elected officials incline toward legislation and admission practices that insure entry for large numbers; and educational authorities find the need and justification for easy admission.

Even where pressures have been decisive in widening admission policy, however, the system of higher education has continued to be shaped partly by other interests. The practices of public colleges are influenced by the academic personnel, the organizational requirements of colleges, and external pressures other than those behind the open door. Standards of performance and graduation are maintained. A commitment to standards is encouraged by a set of values in which the status of a college, as defined by academicians and a large body of educated laymen, is closely linked to the perceived quality of faculty, student body, and curriculum. The raising of standards is supported by the faculty's desire to work with promising students and to enjoy membership in an enterprise of reputed quality—college authorities find low standards and poor students a handicap in competing with other colleges for such resources as able faculty as well as for academic status. The wish is widespread that college education be of the highest quality for the preparation of leaders in public affairs, business, and the professions. In brief, the institutional means of the students' progress toward college graduation and subsequent goals are shaped in large part by a commitment to quality embodied in college staffs, traditions, and images.

The conflict between open-door admission and performance of high quality often means a wide discrepancy between the hopes of entering students and the means of their realization. Students who

3. Seymour Martin Lipset and Reinhard Bendix, *Social Mobility in Industrial Society* (Berkeley: University of California Press, 1959), pp. 78–101.

4. *A Study of the Need for Additional Centres of Public Higher Education in California* (Sacramento: California State Department of Education, 1957), p. 128. For somewhat similar interpretations by educators and laymen nationally see Francis J. Brown (ed.), *Approaching Equality of Opportunity in Higher Education* (Washington, D.C.: American Council on Education, 1955), and the President's Committee on Education beyond the High School, *Second Report to the President* (Washington, D.C.: Government Printing Office, 1957).

pursue ends for which a college education is required but who have little academic ability gain admission into colleges only to encounter standards of performance they cannot meet. As a result, while some students of low promise are successful, for large numbers failure is inevitable and *structured.* The denial is delayed, taking place within the college instead of at the edge of the system. It requires that many colleges handle the student who intends to complete college and has been allowed to become involved but whose destiny is to fail.

## Responses to disjuncture

What is done with the student whose destiny will normally be early termination? One answer is unequivocal dismissal. This "hard" response is found in the state university that bows to pressure for broad admission but then protects standards by heavy drop-out. In the first year it weeds out many of the incompetent, who may number a third or more of the entering class.[5] The response of the college is hard in that failure is clearly defined as such. Failure is public; the student often returns home. This abrupt change in status and in access to the means of achievement may occur simultaneously in a large college or university for hundreds, and sometimes thousands, of students after the first semester and at the end of the freshman year. The delayed denial is often viewed on the outside as heartless, a slaughter of the innocents.[6] This excites public pressure and anxiety, and apparently the practice cannot be extended indefinitely as the demand for admission to college increases.

A second answer is to sidetrack unpromising students rather than have them fail. This is the "soft" response: never to dismiss a student but to provide him with an alternative. One form of it in some state universities is the detour to an extension division or a general college, which has the advantage of appearing not very different from the main road. Sometimes "easy" fields of study, such as education, business administration, and social science, are used as alternatives to dismissal.[7] The major form of the soft response is not found in the four-year college or university, however, but in the college that specializes in handling students who will soon be leaving—typically, the two-year public junior college.

In most states where the two-year college is a part of higher education, the students likely to be caught in the means-ends disjuncture are assigned to it in large numbers. In California, where there are over sixty public two-year colleges in a diversified system that includes the state university and numerous four-year state colleges, the junior college is unselective in admissions and by law, custom, and self-conception accepts all who wish to enter.[8] It is tuition-free, local, and under local control. Most of its entering students want to try for the baccalaureate degree, transferring to a "senior" college after one or two years. About two-thirds of the students in the junior colleges of the state are in programs that permit transferring; but, of these, only about one-third actually transfer to a four-year college.[9] The remainder, or two out of three of the professed transfer students, are "latent terminal students": their announced intention and program of study entails four years of college, but in reality their work terminates in the junior college. Constituting about half of all the students in the California junior

5. One national report showed that one out of eight entering students (12.5 per cent) in publicly controlled colleges does not remain beyond the first term or semester; one out of three (31 per cent) is out by the end of the first year; and about one out of two (46.6 per cent) leaves within the first two years. In state universities alone, about one out of four withdraws in the first year and 40 per cent in two years (Robert E. Iffert, *Retention and Withdrawal of College Students* [Washington, D.C.: Department of Health, Education, and Welfare, 1958], pp. 15–20). Students withdraw for many reasons, but scholastic aptitude is related to their staying power: "A sizeable number of students of medium ability enter college, but . . . few if any of them remain longer than two years" (*A Restudy of the Needs of California in Higher Education* [Sacramento: California State Department of Education, 1955], p. 120).

6. Robert L. Kelly, *The American Colleges and the Social Order* (New York: Macmillan Co., 1940), pp. 220–21.

7. One study has noted that on many campuses the business school serves "as a dumping ground for students who cannot make the grade in engineering or some branch of the liberal arts," this being a consequence of lower promotion standards than are found in most other branches of the university (Frank C. Pierson, *The Education of American Businessmen* [New York: McGraw-Hill Book Co., 1959], p. 63). Pierson also summarizes data on intelligence of students by field of study which indicate that education, business, and social science rank near the bottom in quality of students (*ibid.*, pp. 65–72).

8. Burton R. Clark, *The Open Door College: A Case Study* (New York: McGraw-Hill Book Co., 1960), pp. 44–45.

9. *Ibid.*, p. 116.

colleges, and somewhere between one-third and one-half of junior college students nationally,[10] these students cannot be ignored by the colleges. Understanding their careers is important to understanding modern higher education.

## The reorienting process

This type of student in the junior college is handled by being moved out of a transfer major to a one- or two-year program of vocational, business, or semi-professional training. This calls for the relinquishing of his original intention, and he is induced to accept a substitute that has lower status in both the college and society in general.

In one junior college[11] the initial move in a cooling-out process is pre-entrance testing: low scores on achievement tests lead poorly qualified students into remedial classes. Assignment to remedial work casts doubt and slows the student's movement into bona fide transfer courses. The remedial courses are, in effect, a subcollege. The student's achievement scores are made part of a counseling folder that will become increasingly significant to him. An objective record of ability and performance begins to accumulate.

A second step is a counseling interview before the beginning of the first semester, and before all subsequent semesters for returning students. "At this interview the counselor assists the student to choose the proper courses in light of his objective, his test scores, the high school record and test records from his previous schools."[12] Assistance in choosing "the proper courses" is gentle at first. Of the common case of the student who wants to be an engineer but who is not a promising candidate, a counselor said: "I never openly countermand his choice, but edge him toward a terminal program by gradually laying out the facts of life." Counselors may become more severe later when grades provide a talking point and when the student knows that he is in trouble. In the earlier counseling the desire of the student has much weight; the counselor limits himself to giving advice and stating the probability of success. The advice is entered in the counseling record that shadows the student.

A third and major step in reorienting the latent terminal student is a special course entitled "Orientation to College," mandatory for entering students. All sections of it are taught by teacher-counselors who comprise the counseling staff, and one of its purposes is "to assist students in evaluating their own abilities, interests, and aptitudes; in assaying their vocational choices in light of this evaluation; and in making educational plans to implement their choices." A major section of it takes up vocational planning; vocational tests are given at a time when opportunities and requirements in various fields of work are discussed. The tests include the "Lee Thorpe Interest Inventory" ("given to all students for motivating a self-appraisal of vocational choice") and the "Strong Interest Inventory" ("for all who are undecided about choice or who show disparity between accomplishment and vocational choice"). Mechanical and clerical aptitude tests are taken by all. The aptitudes are directly related to the college's terminal programs, with special tests, such as a pre-engineering ability test, being given according to need. Then an "occupational paper is required of all students for their chosen occupation"; in it the student writes on the required training and education and makes a "self-appraisal of fitness."

Tests and papers are then used in class discussion and counseling interviews, in which the students themselves arrange and work with a counselor's folder and a student test profile and, in so doing, are repeatedly confronted by the accumulating evidence—the test scores, course grades, recommendations of teachers and counselors. This procedure is intended to heighten self-awareness of capacity in relation to choice and hence to strike particularly at the latent terminal student. The teacher-counselors are urged constantly to "be alert to the problem of unrealistic vocational goals" and to "help students to accept their limitations and strive for success in other worthwhile objectives that are within their grasp." The orientation class was considered a good place "to talk tough," to explain in an *impersonal* way the facts of life for the overambitious student. Talking tough to a whole group is part of a soft treatment of the individual.

10. Leland L. Medsker, *The Junior College: Progress and Prospect* (New York: McGraw-Hill Book Co., 1960), chap. iv.

11. San Jose City College, San Jose, Calif. For the larger study see Clark, *op. cit.*

12. San Jose Junior College, Handbook for Counselors, 1957–58, p. 2. Statements in quotation marks in the next few paragraphs are cited from this.

Following the vocational counseling, the orientation course turns to "building an educational program," to study of the requirements for graduation of the college in transfer and terminal curriculum, and to planning of a four-semester program. The students also become acquainted with the requirements of the colleges to which they hope to transfer, here contemplating additional hurdles such as the entrance examinations of other colleges. Again, the hard facts of the road ahead are brought to bear on self-appraisal.

If he wishes, the latent terminal student may ignore the counselor's advice and the test scores. While in the counseling class, he is also in other courses, and he can wait to see what happens. Adverse counseling advice and poor test scores may not shut off his hope of completing college; when this is the case, the deterrent will be encountered in the regular classes. Here the student is divested of expectations, lingering from high school, that he will automatically pass and, hopefully, automatically be transferred. Then, receiving low grades, he is thrown back into the counseling orbit, a fourth step in his reorientation and a move justified by his actual accomplishment. The following indicates the nature of the referral system:

> *Need for Improvement Notices* are issued by instructors to students who are doing unsatisfactory work. The carbon copy of the notice is given to the counselor who will be available for conference with the student. The responsibility lies with the student to see his counselor. However, experience shows that some counselees are unable to be sufficiently self-directive to seek aid. The counselor should, in such cases, send for the student, using the Request for Conference blank. If the student fails to respond to the Request for Conference slip, this may become a disciplinary matter and should be referred to the deans.
>
> After a conference has been held, the Need for Improvement notices are filed in the student's folder. *This may be important* in case of a complaint concerning the fairness of a final grade.[13]

This directs the student to more advice and self-assessment, as soon and as often as he has classroom difficulty. The carbon-copy routine makes it certain that, if he does not seek advice, advice will seek him. The paper work and bureaucratic procedure have the purpose of recording referral and advice in black and white, where they may later be appealed to impersonally. As put in an unpublished report of the college, the overaspiring student and the one who seems to be in the wrong program require "skillful and delicate handling. An accumulation of pertinent factual information may serve to fortify the objectivity of the student-counselor relationship." While the counselor advises delicately and patiently, but persistently, the student is confronted with the record with increasing frequency.

A fifth step, one necessary for many in the throes of discouragement, is probation: "Students [whose] grade point averages fall below 2.0 [C] in any semester will, upon recommendation by the Scholarship Committee, be placed on probationary standing." A second failure places the student on second probation, and a third may mean that he will be advised to withdraw from the college altogether. The procedure is not designed to rid the college of a large number of students, for they may continue on probation for three consecutive semesters; its purpose is not to provide a status halfway out of the college but to "assist the student to seek an objective (major field) at a level on which he can succeed."[14] An important effect of probation is its slow killing-off of the lingering hopes of the most stubborn latent terminal students. A "transfer student" must have a C average to receive the Associate in Arts (a two-year degree) offered by the junior college, but no minimum average is set for terminal students. More important, four-year colleges require a C average or higher for the transfer student. Thus probationary status is the final blow to hopes of transferring and, indeed, even to graduating from the junior college under a transfer-student label. The point is reached where the student must permit himself to be reclassified or else drop out. In this college, 30 per cent of the students enrolled at the end of the spring semester, 1955–56, who returned the following fall were on probation; three out of four of these were transfer students in name.[15]

This sequence of procedures is a specific process of cooling-out;[16] its effect, at the best, is to let down hopes gently and unexplosively. Through it students who are failing or barely passing find their occupa-

13. *Ibid.*, p. 20.

14. Statement taken from unpublished material.

15. San Jose Junior College, "Digest of Analysis of the Records of 468 Students Placed on Probation for the Fall Semester, 1956," September 3, 1956.

16. Goffman's original statement of the concept of cooling-out referred to how the disappointing of expecta-

tional and academic future being redefined. Along the way, teacher-counselors urge the latent terminal student to give up his plan of transferring and stand ready to console him in accepting a terminal curriculum. The drawn-out denial when it is effective is in place of a personal, hard "No"; instead, the student is brought to realize, finally, that it is best to ease himself out of the competition to transfer.

## Cooling-out features

In the cooling-out process in the junior college are several features which are likely to be found in other settings where failure or denial is the effect of a structured discrepancy between ends and means, the responsible operatives or "coolers" cannot leave the scene or hide their identities, and the disappointment is threatening in some way to those responsible for it. At work and in training institutions this is common. The features are:

1. *Alternative achievement.* Substitute avenues may be made to appear not too different from what is given up, particularly as to status. The person destined to be denied or who fails is invited to interpret the second effort as more appropriate to his particular talent and is made to see that it will be the less frustrating. Here one does not fail but rectifies a mistake. The substitute status reflects less unfavorably on personal capacity than does being dismissed and forced to leave the scene. The terminal student in the junior college may appear not very different from the transfer student—an "engineering aide," for example, instead of an "engineer"—and to be proceeding to something with a status of its own. Failure in college can be treated as if it did not happen; so, too, can poor performance in industry.[17]

2. *Gradual disengagement.* By a gradual series of steps, movement to a goal may be stalled, self-assessment encouraged, and evidence produced of performance. This leads toward the available alternatives at little cost. It also keeps the person in a counseling milieu in which advice is furnished, whether actively sought or not. Compared with the original hopes, however, it is a deteriorating situation. If the individual does not give up peacefully, he will be in trouble.

3. *Objective denial.* Reorientation is, finally, confrontation by the facts. A record of poor performance helps to detach the organization and its agents from the emotional aspects of the cooling-out work. In a sense, the overaspiring student in the junior college confronts himself, as he lives with the accumulating evidence, instead of the organization. The college offers opportunity; it is the record that forces denial. Record-keeping and other bureaucratic procedures appeal to universal criteria and reduce the influence of personal ties, and the personnel are thereby protected. Modern personnel record-keeping, in general, has the function of documenting denial.

4. *Agents of consolation.* Counselors are available who are patient with the overambitious and who work to change their intentions. They believe in the value of the alternative careers, though of lower social status, and are practiced in consoling. In college and in other settings counseling is to reduce aspiration as well as to define and to help fulfil it. The teacher-counselor in the "soft" junior college is in contrast to the scholar in the "hard" college who simply gives a low grade to the failing student.

5. *Avoidance of standards.* A cooling-out process avoids appealing to standards that are ambiguous to begin with. While a "hard" attitude toward failure generally allows a single set of criteria, a "soft" treatment assumes that many kinds of ability are valuable, each in its place. Proper classification and placement are then paramount, while standards become relative.

## Importance of concealment

For an organization and its agents one dilemma of a cooling-out role is that it must be kept reasonably away from public scrutiny and not clearly perceived or understood by prospective clientele. Should it become obvious, the organization's ability to perform it would be impaired. If high-school seniors and their families were to define the junior college

tions is handled by the disappointed person and especially by those responsible for the disappointment. Although his main illustration was the confidence game, where facts and potential achievement are deliberately misrepresented to the "mark" (the victim) by operators of the game, Goffman also applied the concept to failure in which those responsible act in good faith (*op. cit., passim*). "Cooling-out" is a widely useful idea when used to refer to a function that may vary in deliberateness.

17. *Ibid.*, p. 457; cf. Perrin Stryker, "How To Fire an Executive," *Fortune*, 50 (October, 1954), 116–17 and 178–92.

as a place which diverts college-bound students, a probable consequence would be a turning-away from the junior college and increased pressure for admission to the four-year colleges and universities that are otherwise protected to some degree. This would, of course, render superfluous the part now played by the junior college in the division of labor among colleges.

The cooling-out function of the junior college is kept hidden, for one thing, as other functions are highlighted. The junior college stresses "the transfer function," "the terminal function," etc., not that of transforming transfer into terminal students; indeed, it is widely identified as principally a transfer station. The other side of cooling-out is the successful performance in junior college of students who did poorly in high school or who have overcome socioeconomic handicaps, for they are drawn into higher education rather than taken out of it. Advocates of the junior college point to this salvaging of talented manpower, otherwise lost to the community and nation. It is indeed a function of the open door to let hidden talent be uncovered.

Then, too, cooling-out itself is reinterpreted so as to appeal widely. The junior college may be viewed as a place where all high-school graduates have the opportunity to explore possible careers and find the type of education appropriate to their individual ability; in short, as a place where everyone is admitted and everyone succeeds. As described by the former president of the University of California:

> A prime virtue of the junior college, I think, is that most of its students succeed in what they set out to accomplish, and cross the finish line before they grow weary of the race. After two years in a course that they have chosen, they can go out prepared for activities that satisfy them, instead of being branded as failures. Thus the broadest possible opportunity may be provided for the largest number to make an honest try at further education with some possibility of success and with no route to a desired goal completely barred to them.[18]

The students themselves help to keep this function concealed by wishful unawareness. Those who cannot enter other colleges but still hope to complete four years will be motivated at first not to admit the cooling-out process to consciousness. Once exposed to it, they again will be led not to acknowledge it, and so they are saved insult to their self-image.

In summary, the cooling-out process in higher education is one whereby systematic discrepancy between aspiration and avenue is covered over and stress for the individual and the system is minimized. The provision of readily available alternative achievements in itself is an important device for alleviating the stress consequent on failure and so preventing anomic and deviant behavior. The general result of cooling-out processes is that society can continue to encourage maximum effort without major disturbance from unfulfilled promises and expectations.

18. Robert Gordon Sproul, "Many Millions More," *Educational Record*, 39 (April, 1958), 102.

FRED H. GOLDNER and R. R. RITTI

# Professionalization as Career Immobility

## Introduction

The purpose of this paper is to examine the relationship between professionalism in large organizations and career mobility. The rapid increase in the industrial employment of professionals along with the proliferation of specialist units in industrial organizations has led to a number of organizational problems. For example, these specialist groups bring to the organization a set of career aspirations that comes into conflict with existing career paths. The accepted definitions of success that accompany these existing career paths are challenged by the development of specialist careers.

New organizational forms and relationships have been produced to accommodate these problems.[1] We shall attempt to describe some of the factors related to this process of accommodation by focusing on one of the particular organizational arrangements that has been produced in adapting to new specialist careers—the dual ladder. We shall be especially concerned with its use in providing alternative career paths for engineers and salesmen.

The dual ladder refers to the side-by-side existence of the usual ladder of hierarchical positions leading to authority over greater and greater numbers of employees and another ladder consisting of titles carrying successively higher salaries, higher status, and sometimes greater autonomy or more responsible assignments.[2]

Much of the literature discusses the dual ladder as an incentive provided by the organization in response to various pressures from professionals working within it.[3] Our research indicates that the dual ladder can also be created by management. While organizational members often do aspire to professionalism, management frequently imposes such a definition on specialists. And in many of the cases where professionalism is sought after, it is only by those who have failed to be promoted.

Organizations require the continued productive efforts of experienced specialists who will remain in their specialties. Management thus attempts to

1. For an account of these accommodations see William Kornhauser with the assistance of W. O. Hagstrom, *Scientists in Industry: Conflict and Accommodation* (Berkeley: University of California Press, 1962). The best theoretical discussion of these problems is presented in Victor A. Thompson, *Modern Organization* (New York: Alfred A. Knopf, Inc., 1961).

Fred H. Goldner was supported in this work by the Faculty Research Fund of the Columbia University Graduate School of Business. We would like to thank D. Caplovitz, R. Colvard, W. Hagstrom, S. Klein, C. Perrow, and G. Sjoberg for their comments on an earlier draft.

Reprinted from *The American Journal of Sociology*, March, 1967, pp. 489–502, by permission of the authors and publisher. (Copyright, 1967, by The University of Chicago Press.)

2. For a review of the literature on the dual ladder see the chapter on "Professional Incentives in Industry" in Kornhauser, *op. cit.*, pp. 137, 143–49. See also Bertram Schoner and Thomas W. Harrell, "The Questionable Dual Ladder," *Personnel*, 42 (1965), 53–57.

3. Kornhauser, *op. cit.*, pp. 204–5, Schoner and Harrell, *op. cit.*, p. 53; and Bernard Barber, "Some Problems in the Sociology of the Professions," *Daedalus* (Fall, 1965), p. 681.

impose professionalism[4] as a definition of success within the organization in order to maintain commitment on the part of those specialists who would ordinarily be considered failures for not having moved into management. Identification as professional has become a way to redefine failure as success. It will be our claim that professionalism is often synonymous with career immobility in many of the emerging specialist occupations.

## The professional ladder: Some false assumptions

A common explanation for the problems that result when professionals enter industrial organizations is that their goals clash with the reward of promotion into management which serves as one incentive for employees to perform tasks required by the organization. Success in most organizations is defined as movement into management. This route, however, leads the professional away from the practice of his chosen specialty. Engineers, for example, are reported as having a dislike of working with people—preferring the handling of "things."[5] In addition to requiring a different set of incentives, professionals are also assumed to have stronger loyalties to their profession than to the organization employing them.[6] A professional is said to care little for organizational matters that do not impinge upon his area of specialty.[7] The ideology of professionalism, as stated, implies a trade-off between specialist autonomy and power in the organization. All of these portraits embody the notion that upward mobility in the organizational hierarchy is of little importance to the professional. Furthermore, mobility aspirations are seen as antithetical to the true values of a profession.

These beliefs led to the development of what has been referred to as the dual ladder or, as we shall refer to it, the professional ladder:[8] "in simplest terms, the problem appears to be to find a way of rewarding scientists for good scientific performance without removing them from scientific work."[9] This is to be done by "rewarding them with prestige, freedom, and job luxuries (special parking spaces, comfortable offices, secretaries, private laboratories, etc.)."[10] The connection between incentives and the professional ladder was made clear by Kornhauser: "Insofar as the traditional system of incentives in organizations prevails, motivation for a career in science or engineering will be dampened. Industry is becoming aware of this, and recently has been experimenting with "professional ladders," whereby scientists and engineers can secure advances in salary and status without taking on administrative duties. Instead of greater authority, they are rewarded with greater freedom to engage in their specialties."[11]

The professional ladder makes no pretense in the direction of increasing the authority of title-holders. It is based on the same assumptions that support an ideology of professionalism, assumptions stating that upward mobility in the power hierarchy is of no importance compared to autonomy in the practice of one's special competence and that success for the professional is independent of such mobility.

These assumptions are incorrect when applied to

4. The term "professional" and its variations are generally used rather loosely—especially in popular usage. We will use "professionalism" to indicate the possession of some of the attributes of a profession. We will use "professionalization" to indicate a process of acquiring some degree of these attributes. Whenever we think one of these terms describes a group possessing so few of these attributes that the terms would only be used thusly by a "layman," we will try to indicate this by using quotation marks. We would agree with Vollmer and Mills about the disutility of arguing whether a group is or is not a profession and about the usefulness of professionalization as a concept. However, we would go beyond them and maintain that even the professionalization concept has severe limitations in helping to understand the effects of the emergence of new occupational groups in organizations and in society. The concept offers little aid in understanding large, complex technical organizations that contain a work force increasingly composed of college-educated specialists who carry with them myths and ideologies that only pertain to independent professionals. See Howard M. Vollmer and Donald L. Mills (eds.), *Professionalization* (Englewood Cliffs, N.J.: Prentice-Hall, Inc., 1966), pp. v–ix.

5. James A. Davis, *Great Aspirations* (National Opinion Research Center Report No. 90, March, 1963), p. 283.

6. George Strauss, "Professionalism and Occupational Associations," *Industrial Relations*, 2 (1963), 7–31. See especially pp. 8 and 9.

7. *Ibid.*, p. 25.

8. We refer to the ladder as a professional one because it has been set up specifically to accommodate professionals. While it has been called the dual ladder by some, we feel this is not appropriate because there are already dual ladders in organizations that have both general management and functional management (e.g., engineering or marketing management).

9. Herbert A. Shepard, "The Dual Hierarchy in Research," *Research Management*, 1 (1958), 179.

10. *Ibid.*, p. 182.

11. Kornhauser, *op. cit.*, p. 205.

most engineers.[12] And it is primarily for engineers that the professional ladder has been instituted. Engineers generally enter industry with nonprofessional goals. The goals of recent engineering graduates are oriented toward entrance into positions of power and participation in the affairs of the organization rather than simply the practice of their original specialties. From the start of their business careers many engineers have personal goals that coincide with the business goals of the corporation (see Table 1).[13] These data indicate that most of the engineers in our sample display few, if any, characteristics of professionals. They strongly identify with the organization and its goals, and they want to participate in decisions that affect their area. In contrast, the professional values of communication of results and of basing reputations on technical contributions seem to be of little importance.[14]

Even while they are still in engineering school they seem more business than professionally oriented. For example, 60 per cent of the seniors from a large engineering school agreed with the statement that the goal of most engineers is to become a member of management.[15] Sixty-nine per cent expressed optimism over this possibility by agreeing with the statement that, "more and more, industry is realizing that engineers make the best executives." On the other hand, only 25 per cent agreed with the statement that "a staff engineer's important work is on his own technical projects; he leaves the organization of others' efforts to management."

The replies of 205 engineering seniors who accepted a job offer from Company A[16] in 1965 further contradict the notion that engineers, as professionals, identify more with their specialty than with their company. When asked, "To what extent do you think of your job as a career in (Company A) rather than as a career in your field of specialty?" 6 per cent replied, "primarily or solely as a career in my specialty" as opposed to 41 per cent replying "primarily or solely as a career in (Company A)." (Thirty-four per cent indicated "somewhat more"

12. For this discussion it is important to differentiate between scientists and engineers. Strauss, *op. cit.*, p. 22, takes note of such differences, as does Kornhauser at times. We intend to treat these differences more fully in a forthcoming publication.

13. These data come from 1964 and 1965 anonymous opinion surveys of engineers who have received offers of employment from Company A. Those who accepted the offer of employment constitute roughly half the sample in both years. Responses to these items were given on a 0–10 scale anchored at "of no importance whatsoever" and "of utmost importance." An item checked 8, 9, 10 was scored as being an important goal for the respondent. Importance scores for the total group who rejected the employment offer correlate .98 (1964) and .95 (1965) with the scores for the total group accepting. Furthermore, similarity in percentage levels indicates no sizeable bias attributable to trying to "look good."

14. For recent similar evidence from a large national sample of employed engineers see: William K. LeBold, Robert Perrucci, and Warren Howland, "The Engineer in Industry and Government," *Journal of Engineering Education*, 56, No. 7 (March, 1966), 237–73.

15. From an unpublished study by R. R. Ritti of Purdue University engineers in 1957. See Harold L. Wilensky, "The Professionalization of Everyone?" *American Journal of Sociology*, 70 (September, 1964), 137–58 for a discussion of the role of the training school in the process of the professionalization of a specialty. We would expect seniors about to graduate from the professionalizing institution to best exhibit the professional value system. Wilensky's data indicate engineers to be the least professionally oriented of the groups he considers.

16. Company A is a large electronics company employing engineers who work on the development of electrical and electronic systems as well as on the mechanical components that serve these systems. The resulting systems can be classified as "highly engineered" and require large project groups. Approximately 3 per cent of the engineers have Ph.D.'s, 23 per cent have a master's degree, and 63 per cent have a bachelor's degree. Ten per cent are classified as "professionals" through experience.

***Table 1—Relative Importance of Different Personal Goals for Nationwide Sample of Engineering Seniors Who Received Job Offers from Company A***

| *Personal goal* | *Percentage indicating goal is important* |
|---|---|
| Participate in decisions that set the direction of technical effort in the company | 68* |
| Participate in decisions that affect the future business of the company | 64* |
| Have the opportunity to help the company increase its profit | 57* |
| Become a first-line manager in your line of work | 56 |
| Advance to a policy-making position in management | 55* |
| Work on projects that have a direct impact on the business success of your company | 47 |
| Establish a reputation outside the company as an authority in your field | 41** |
| Communicate your ideas to others in your profession through papers delivered at professional meetings | 21 |
| Publish articles in technical journals | 20** |
| Be evaluated *only* on the basis of your *technical* contribution | 14 |

*Note.* Results shown above are from surveys in 1964 ($N = 629$) and 1965 ($N = 447$) and include electrical and mechanical engineers only. Items used in 1964 are asterisked. Double asterisked items represent the composite percentages for items used in both 1964 and 1965. All other items are from 1965.

as a career in the company, and 19 per cent "somewhat more" as a career in their specialty.)

From these data, it is quite clear that the professional ladder is based on erroneous notions about the goals of engineers. Perhaps this is the reason why commentators and analysts, after ten years of writing about it, still refer to the professional ladder as an experiment.[17]

## Work activities and the involvement of power

The failure of these assumptions about engineers casts doubt on the ability of the professional ladder to fulfil its function of providing the desired incentives of increased status, increased money, and more freedom for individual research. Indeed, there have been comments about its lack of success, but these comments have focused on the ladder's inability to provide enough of the first two incentives of status and money.[18] We believe, however, that the third item of freedom or autonomy is more central to its lack of success. If we examine the possibility of such freedom it will become apparent that the professional ladder must be judged in terms of power as well as just its incentive value.

Professionalism is commonly defined as having the four ingredients of (1) specialized competence, (2) autonomy in exercising the competence, (3) commitment to a career in this competence, and (4) influence and responsibility in the use of the special competence.[19] The professional ladder only partially meets these requirements. It does provide a career solely within the specialty, but it fails to provide the autonomy considered so important—except in a few isolated cases where the nature of the work makes autonomy possible for a few individuals. And by definition the professional ladder fails to provide the influence and responsibility that is part of professionalism.

If progress up the professional ladder is supposed to include greater freedom over what one does, it becomes crucial to inquire whether the work can be done by an *individual.* If so, that individual can be rewarded by letting him spend all or a significant part of his time on work of his own choosing—with the hope that there might be a payoff for the employing organization. However, if the work can only be done in cooperation with others, or if one person can only do part of a project, then a need for some coordinated group effort remains. And if this is so, then the larger freedom, freedom to set the course of work activities, can be had only by project groups—not by individuals in those groups. In fact, freedom to pursue individual work may simply mean withdrawal from the crucial work of the field.

But the professional ladder was never meant to provide this freedom for professional *groups*—only for individuals. It is a mechanism to satisfy the personal goals of individual professionals within the constraints of their containing organizations. It is most definitely not a mechanism to reduce strains resulting from conflict between organizations and the *profession as an institution.* In any particular case then, a number of questions must be asked about the actual work—whether it can be done in isolation, done with resources also used by others, done with resources not obtainable on one's own, or done with others.

A consideration of whether or not solo work is possible also leads us to question some of the assumptions about freedom as a source of strain between professionals and the organization. For example, Kornhauser puts it as a prime source: "The scientific community places a very high value on its freedom from outside control, and on the autonomy of the individual scientist. The ideal form of professional control is advice and consultation among colleagues, leaving the final responsibility for professional judgment to the individual. This procedure is subject to considerable pressure from the organization."[20] The ideal of "leaving the final responsibility for professional judgment to the individual' is dependent not so much on the extent to which a group or an individual meets criteria of professionalism but on whether the work can be done alone or must be done with others. Although individual work is more possible among scientists

17. John J. Beer and W. David Lewis, "Aspects of Professionalization of Science," *Daedalus*, 92 (1963), 776; Kornhauser, *op. cit.*, p. 205.

18. Schoner and Harrell, *op. cit.*, p. 57; Kornhauser, *op. cit.*, p. 146. Shepard, *op. cit.*, p. 184, in listing the weaknesses of the dual ladder mentions power but does not develop his argument further.

19. Kornhauser, *op. cit.*, p. 11.

20. William Kornhauser, "Strains and Accommodations in Industrial Research Organizations," *Minerva*, 1 (1962), 34.

than engineers, Kornhauser evidently considered teamwork among scientists so important that he found it necessary to discuss the differences between scientific work teams organized along functional lines and those along project lines.[21]

The bulk of the engineering carried on by large industrial employers is group effort. It is programmatic rather than individualistic. Few, if any, engineering projects can be accomplished by one man. There is a complex division of labor resulting from, among other things, the need for specialized skills and the time pressures created by market competition. In turn specialization means that individuals with different skills are required to perform complementary assignments. Complex engineering efforts can easily involve several years of effort on the part of hundreds of engineers. The ability to coordinate this kind of program is a premium skill, and it is the program administrator who must pre-empt much of the decision-making power of individuals. Clearly, not everyone can have the powers that go with the managerial role. If the only question, then, is whether this administrator happens to be a fellow scientist or professional rather than a layman, the important distinction is not between superordinate control and colleague (peer) control but whether the control is by knowledgeable and sympathetic people.[22]

We contend that the work done in many fields commonly called professions is not done in isolation and, therefore, requires varying amounts of coordination. And, if this is true, then the professional ladder is not a viable alternative to having the kind of power over one's work usually associated with being a professional. More than that, as we discuss below, there are areas other than one's own immediate professional work where control is desired.

## Professors and professionals misleading analogues

An analogy between the professional ladder and professorial rank has frequently been made as has the inference that the university setting provided the example that industry followed.[23] It is implied that those on titled ladders have the same relation to managers as do professors to university administrators. The analogy is false—it ignores consideration of power.

Questions related to power and control are crucial on the campus; professors maintain power over what is important to them. Conflicts take place over the kind of people to recruit, curriculums, socialization processes, what constitutes acceptable research, and the methodologies that are appropriate.[24] Those things that are not the sole prerogative of the academic department are frequently acted upon by committees composed of peers in other departments rather than administrators. Professors are even able to control the affairs of other groups in the university, such as students.

The professional ladder does not provide an organizational arrangement for a share of the power necessary in controlling professions and scientific disciplines. That is its major fault. Conflicting issues are as prevalent in industry as on the campus. Whenever there are scarce resources, there will be an evaluatory and an allocative process that requires control.[25] The view of a clash between the organization and the "independent" or "autonomous" professional conceals the many power struggles that take place over issues such as those cited in the preceding paragraph.

The lack of power in the professional ladder comes not so much from the lack of supervisory responsibility over others as from a lack of involvement in the decision-making and power processes of the organization. Promotions to higher positions in organizations customarily are accompanied by getting more power within the organization and getting confidential information—in brief, a change in organizational style of life.

21. *Ibid.*, pp. 50–56. See also Herbert A. Shepard, "Nine Dilemmas in Industrial Research," *Administrative Science Quarterly*, 1 (1956), 300–303.

22. For a detailed discussion of superordinate as opposed to colleague control in research organizations see Simon Marcson, "Organization and Authority in Industrial Research," *Social Forces*, 40 (1961), 72–80.

23. Beer and Lewis, *op. cit.*, p. 777.

24. For examples see the excellent book by Warren O. Hagstrom, *The Scientific Community* (New York: Basic Books, Inc., 1965). For an example of an academic tenure conflict involving some of these questions, see the article on the Yale Philosophy Department: *New York Times*, March 10, 1965, p. 52.

25. This might not be true of the independent professional, but he hardly exists outside of the old prototype of the family doctor—and that is who really runs the American Medical Association. Most professionals are engaged in working with other professionals, for example, in universities, medical schools, hospitals, law firms.

The professional ladder leads away from desired and required power. Status and money accrue to those with power, and, hence, the ladder cannot provide enough to those who have chosen to work with things rather than with people.[26] It is not, then, primarily a form of incentive demanded by those who do not desire or have not the capability to go up the normal managerial ladder with its "onerous" administrative duties. For example, one Company A engineering manager, describing his duties with some distaste, pointed to the crucial "trade-off" between power and professionalism.

MANAGER. I spend (about 50 per cent) of the time in planning, managerial problems and a lot of just plain "hand-holding."

INTERVIEWER. Which type of work do you prefer, then, the purely technical or the type of job you've just described?

MANAGER. Oh! The kind of job I've got now.

INTERVIEWER. Why is this?

MANAGER. Power! To be brutally frank, power! You see in this position I have some say in policy decisions. As a technical engineer I would have to stick strictly to design problems.[27]

The importance of power in its relation to the professional ladder is indicated by the change in the attitude of engineers from the time they enter the organization until they learn something about the world of work. Before making a choice (or having it made for them) about the route they wish to travel, they view the professional ladder as relatively attractive. Once on the ladder, they come to recognize that power is an essential ingredient of success and that the ladder does not provide it (see Tables 2 and 3).[28] Our data indicate that most beginning

26. Engineers may not place a high value on working with people, but they are evidently willing to do it to secure other goals. The study by Davis, *op. cit.*, pp. 282–97, bears out that student engineers are less interested in working with people but that they are as interested as any in money. He did not present the alternative goal of working only with "things."

27. For more examples of this issue see R. R. Ritti, "Engineers and Managers: A Study of Engineering Organization" (unpublished Ph.D. dissertation, Cornell University, Ithaca, N.Y., 1960).

28. These data come from a company-wide survey of engineers in Company A taken in 1964. Responses of those on the managerial ladder were almost the same (within 3 percentage points) as those on the professional ladder.

***Table 2—Percentage Distribution for Engineering Employees of Company A, by Hierarchical level, on Replies to the Question, "How Do You Think Most Technical People View a Promotion from Associate Level to Staff Level as Compared to a Promotion from Associate Level to (Equivalent Manager) Level?"***

| | *PERCENTAGE SAYING* | | *TOTAL* | |
|---|---|---|---|---|
| *Level* | *Promotion to manager is much or slightly bigger* | *Promotions are about the same or promotion to staff is bigger* | *Per cent* | *N* |
| Professional ladder (staff level) | 86 | 14 | 100 | 324 |
| Preladder: | | | | |
| Associate level | 71 | 29 | 100 | 782 |
| Entry (beginning) level | 45 | 55 | 100 | 154 |

*Note.* The staff level represents positions on the professional ladder that correspond on organization charts to managerial levels. The preladder levels of Associate and Entry precede promotion to either the professional or managerial ladder.

***Table 3—Percentage Distribution for Engineering Employees of Company A, by Hierarchical Level, on Replies to the Question, "To What Extent Does the Managerial Job Differ from the Equivalent Staff Professional Job in the Chance to Make Important Technical Decisions?"***

| | *PERCENTAGE SAYING* | | *TOTAL* | |
|---|---|---|---|---|
| *Level* | *Manager much or slightly more chance* | *About the same or staff more chance* | *Per cent* | *N* |
| Professional ladder (staff level) | 56 | 44 | 100 | 332 |
| Preladder: | | | | |
| Associate level | 42 | 58 | 100 | 792 |
| Entry (beginning) level | 33 | 67 | 100 | 161 |

engineers see promotion onto the professional ladder as at least equal to a promotion onto the managerial ladder. As they advance in the company this percentage declines. While it seems reasonable that individuals would adjust their views of "where they stand" in a favorable direction, those already on the professional ladder overwhelmingly see the promotion they have received as being smaller than the one onto the managerial ladder. The same pattern occurs with responses to a question about the respective opportunities of the two groups to make important technical decisions. The preladder engineers see those above them on the professional ladder as having more chance to make such decisions than those on the managerial ladder. Those who have already gone onto the professional ladder see the managers as having more chance.[29]

The inadequacy of the professional ladder to provide the kinds of power required even in technical fields is indicated by 1961 questionnaire data from a small engineering research laboratory in Company B (another large electronics equipment manufacturing company). The company merged

29. Another indication of lack of influence in professional positions is the fact that propensity toward union membership increases with length of time in the company. See James W. Kuhn, "Success and Failure in Organizing Professional Engineers," *IRRA Proceedings* (December, 1963), pp. 200–201.

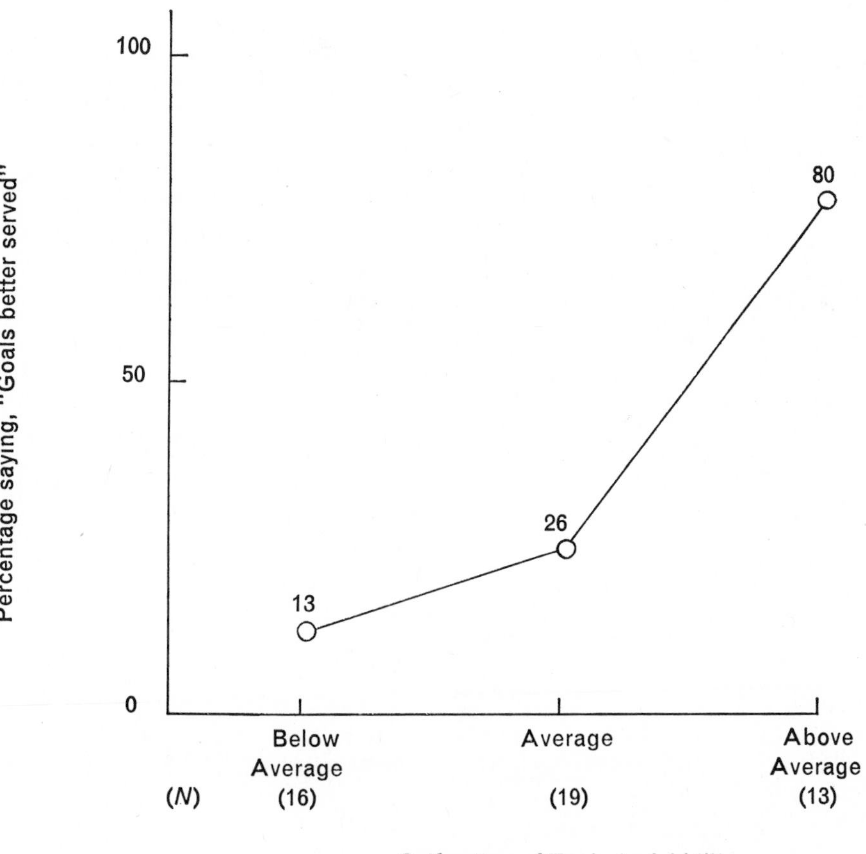


*Figure 1. Relationship of attitudes toward the merging of professional and managerial ladders to relative self-rating of technical ability. Attitudes were indicated by answers to the question, "With respect to your personal goals, do you feel that the new organizational structure will make much difference?" Respondents rated themselves on a percentile scale of technical ability relative to others of similar age and training. These ratings have been combined into three approximately equal groups around the average of the ratings.*

the two sides of a dual ladder into a single management hierarchy. Those who had been on the professional ladder were placed on the merged ladder just below positions that were supposed to have been equivalent to their positions on the professional ladder. Even though they got lower formal positions they were evidently pleased to be where it was possible to have power. Fifty-four per cent of them said that their goals were better served by the change, and only 15 per cent felt that they had lost ground. They now attended policy-making management meetings and shared authority and status with those in supervisory management. On the other hand, those who had been the sole occupants of the managerial ladder were much less pleased by the merger. Thirty-seven per cent of them said they had lost ground, and 25 per cent answered that their goals were better served.

The relevance of power to even the technically oriented engineer is shown by the very favorable responses to the new arrangement by those in Company B's laboratory who were most concerned with technical expertise. Figures 1 and 2 indicate that the more importance one accorded to being a technical authority and the higher one rated himself in technical ability, the more he thought his goals were better served by the change away from a professional-ladder structure.

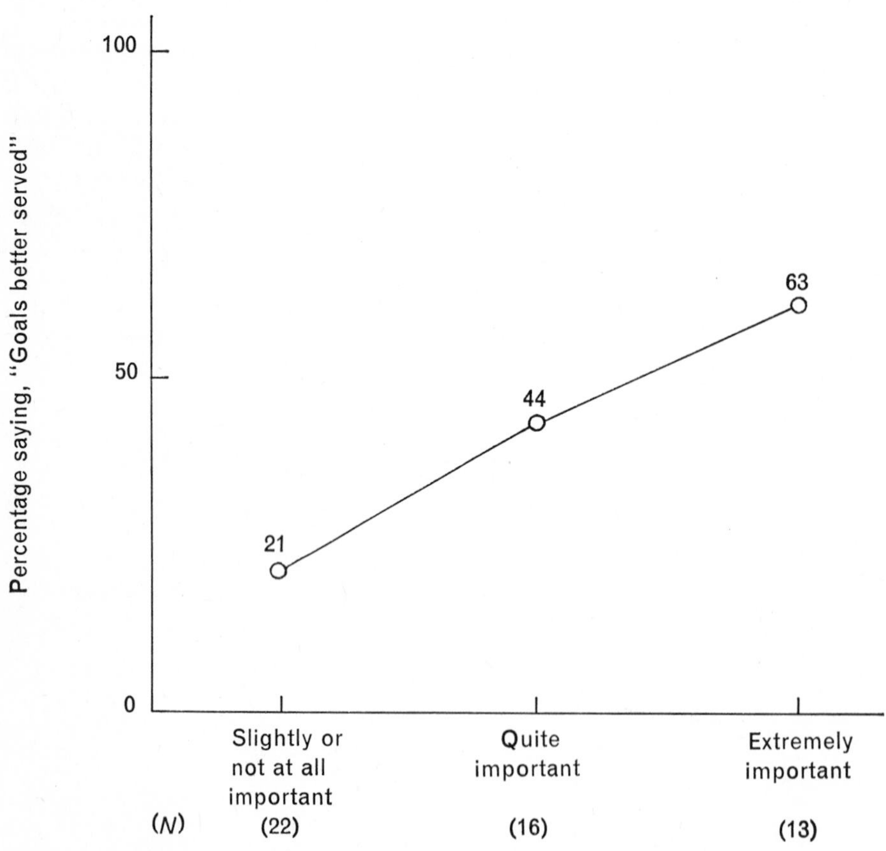


*Figure 2. Relationship of attitudes toward the merging of professional and managerial ladders to importance of being an authority in a technical field. Percentages based on answers to same question as in Figure 1.*

## Professionalism and definitions of success and failure

What, then, is the professional ladder all about? On the surface, it appears that the professional ladder is nothing more than an attempt by management to cool out[30] those who have not made it into management—an attempt to maintain the commitment of those who can no longer retain normal organizational aspirations. And those organizations whose work consists of mental performance are dependent on retaining the commitment of employees—a commitment that might be lost if employees do not achieve expected successes.

But this is too simple a description of the processes we have been discussing. It is not just a process of cooling out those who do not reach a goal but is an attempt to make alternative goals viable. Employees who might otherwise be considered failures by other organizational members are provided with alternative definitions of success.[31] Also, anxiety caused by the disjunction between goal and opportunity is alleviated by reducing or changing the goals. Sociologists have long been concerned with deviance that arises from the failure to achieve success in a society.[32] In organizations, however, the structure of success is different—for unlike society—an organization can deliberately create new definitions of success.[33]

Instead of dealing with various adaptations to failure, we are discussing a process whereby situations that have formerly been defined as failures are redefined as success experiences. This is accomplished by creating new sets of expectations so that there will be no need for a cooling-out process.[34] It has become not an "after-the-fact" adjustment but a "before-the-fact" one.

Definitions of success and failure vary by society, as well as by reference groups within societies.[35] One of the most persistent themes in the literature on professionals in organizations deals with the claim that scientists, engineers, or other technical specialists are "usually more concerned about securing recognition from their professional colleagues than from the company where they happen to be working."[36] But this is not at all inconsistent with movement into management being defined as "success." If most of the "good" people (defined in terms of competence in the specialty) do, in fact, move up and the "bad" ones are left behind, then moving up or staying behind will be defined by specialist groups as success or failure as they are defined by those in the rest of the organization.

Those who are thoroughly professionalized before entrance into the organization are likely to have established notions of success and failure as related to the practice of their specialized competence. However, undergraduate and graduate engineering schools do not provide such specific definitions of success and failure in technical-engineering endeavors. Instead, success is characterized by most engineering students (even at the graduate level) in such general terms as advancement, getting ahead in the organization—getting into "management."[37] The definitions of success, in a professional sense, must thus emerge from the organizational context in which engineers find themselves. Without a firm prior definition they will be influenced by their current peers. The professional ladder is thus one way of attempting to redefine success for a whole group so that the new definition will be accepted by any individual who uses this specialist group as his reference group.

The professional ladder is an attempt to provide engineers with a new set of expectations about their future careers—expectations that will serve as

30. Erving Goffman, "On Cooling the Mark Out: Some Adaptions to Failure," *Psychiatry*, XV (1952), 451–63.

31. The power of ambiguity to confuse definitions of failure is indicated in Fred H. Goldner, "Demotion in Industrial Management," *American Sociological Review*, 30 (1965), 714–24.

32. Robert K. Merton, *Social Theory and Social Structure* (New York: Free Press, 1957), chap. iv.

33. This is of course an overstatement. As societies do this, they become more like organizations.

34. For examples of prior adaption processes see Goldner, *op. cit.*

35. For example, see Samuel A. Stouffer, Edward A. Suchman, Leland C. De Vinney, Shirley A. Star, and Robin M. Williams, Jr., *The American Soldier: Adjustment during Army Life* ("Studies in Social Psychology during World War II," Vol. I [Princeton, N.J.: Princeton University Press, 1949]).

36. Schoner and Harrell, *op. cit.*, p. 53; For a fuller account of the claim about the importance of colleague recognition see Simon Marcson, *The Scientist in American Industry* (Princeton University Industrial Relations Section Report No. 99, 1960), chap. vi.

37. H. S. Becker and J. Carper, "Identification with an Occupation," *American Sociological Review*, 21 (1956), 341–48. More recently see Walter Barlow, "Discontent among Engineers," *Journal of College Placement*, 25 (1965), 24, 25, 72, 74, 76.

acceptable alternatives to the possession of power. It is at least partially successful in this respect, because engineers are specialists who are generally acknowledged as professionals. But the professional ladder is increasingly held out to other groups of specialists and thus operates as a force for professionalization.

## The creation of the "professional": from above

Management may attempt to thrust the definition of "professional" upon a group in order to turn failure into success. The use of the professional ladder has not been confined to scientists and engineers. Organizations have used these ladders in an attempt to professionalize other occupational groups. The logic runs something like this. (1) If organizations have to provide success experiences to serve as incentives to employees, then the organizations must be prepared to handle a number of failures. (2) In order to serve as an incentive, success must be distinguished from something—from failure. (3) One of the ways of dealing with failure is to try to provide alternative modes of success that might appeal to those who have not succeeded along conventional lines. As one Company A sales manager put it:[38] "We have to cultivate in the company the idea that there is a future for those who don't make management. In the 1950's we hired on the notion that if you don't make management, you are a failure. This has to be reversed."

This organization has attempted to create the notion of "professional salesmen" in order to maintain the effectiveness of older salesmen[39] who have not made it onto the managerial ladder. In an organization where there is a heavy emphasis on rising into management (as indicated in the above quotation), those who do not rise become labeled, in time, as failures. In order to forestall subsequent self-identification as a failure, the organization will try to provide alternative definitions that have some currency in society. Identification as a "professional" is a ready-made alternative. As a sales manager said: "I have a guy who was [one of the top salesmen in the company] and everybody says, how can we get him promoted? He says he wants it but I can talk of professional salesmen and convince him the other way."

There are many salesmen who prefer to remain salesmen because of the nature of the work, the lack of responsibility, and the good pay but who buckle under the pressure of being labeled as failures because they did not pursue the more generally preferred management career. They get lumped together with those who wanted to but could not move up. And both of these groups find themselves thrown together with much younger and less experienced men who have not yet exhausted the possibility of moving into management.

The company has attempted to solve this problem by creating a professional ladder for salesmen with appropriate titles, status symbols, and special territories. They have attempted to create enough differences between these salesmen and the younger ones to reduce the stigma of failure to become a manager. The need was acknowledged by one manager because: "We need Indians. I have thirteen salesmen and four are promotable [into management]. It is a good percentage. We need professional salesmen." *This last sentence was an equating of "professional" with those who failed to move up into management.*

This same technique was used in this company with another occupational group—those who repair and maintain the company's products in the customer's office. It was called a "career program." One executive even maintained that the new position levels were not the creation of the company but a direct result of the achievements of the technicians themselves.

## The creation of the "professional": from below

We do not maintain that all attempts to professionalize specialist groups are initiated from above. We acknowledge that many individuals identify themselves as professionals prior to their entrance into an organization and that they may desire no other role. In addition, many employees attempt to become professionals—not only by joining an estab-

38. Unless specifically indicated otherwise, all managers and salesmen referred to or quoted are from Company A.

39. Older salesmen in this case were frequently those in their late thirties who were operationally defined as older because they no longer were looked at as candidates for promotion and had been in the business about fifteen years.

lished profession but by professionalizing their own occupation.[40]

It has been pointed out in another study[41] that an attempt to professionalize an occupation was one of the reactions to blocked mobility even among those already in management. Thus, a safety director of Rock Product Corporation was quoted: "Mobility possibilities can be limiting. It's not a real deterrent. Safety is a real profession as good as any of them. We can't all be chiefs. . . . I have lots of contacts with other companies. I belong to two societies and also panels, and community organizations."[42]

This professional identification sustains many in a position of blocked mobility by providing them both with a reason for their lack of mobility and an alternative chance to advance within their "profession"—on a plateau within the management organization. This same kind of reaction was reported by Peter Blau, who found that "the system that prevents civil servants from deriving satisfaction from hopes of spectacular advancements probably also constrains them to find gratification in their work and thus invites a professional attitude toward it."[43]

If blocked mobility leads to attempts to become professionalized, there may be some who see the causal relationship going in the opposite direction. For example, managers in the Rock Product's labor-relations department not only rejected a professional identity but also rejected attempts to have it thrust upon them. They made it a big point to proclaim that one could not prepare for this kind of job through formal schooling.[44] This group, unlike those in safety and other areas of personnel, already had power within the organization and had aspirations of moving into general management. As they approached the top of their specialist hierarchy, they entertained notions of moving into whatever would afford further opportunities of promotion. To be identified as part of a "profession" would preclude concurrent identification as general management. Their rejection of professionalization was an attempt to prevent part of a dual ladder from being identified as a professional ladder. *From this perspective we again see professionalization identified as synonymous with immobility.*

Professionalization pressure from below has also come from the salesmen discussed above. It comes not only from the immediate fact of their blocked mobility but also from the way this blockage structures their relations with customers. Permanent salesmen evidently become more attached to the customer relationship than to the relationship with those above them in the organization. Salesmen become more dependent on their customers than on their bosses when they forsake promotion into management. They frequently take the customer's point of view. They see him as a client, and the more specialized and complicated the product they sell the more they must develop a service relationship with the customer. They feel they are involved in a professional-client relationship. As one put it: "I look upon it [selling] as a service we are doing to an individual that will be of value to him. I feel as though we are more or less professional in filling the need we may create for an individual. We speak with people who are on the management level most of the time and aren't trying to con people but doing them a service. There are times we actually don't recommend our equipment—that is professionalism."

## Conclusion and implications

Our studies of engineers and salesmen, and observations of other kinds of work, indicate that, although in a "real" profession (one that meets the original criteria of a profession) positions on a professional ladder may indicate success, the use of such positions in a "profession" imbedded in the context of a larger non-professional organization is an indication of failure.[45]

40. There is a good deal that has been written about occupational groups—outside of organizational contexts—attempting to become professionalized. For one of the more recent and better studies see Wilensky, *op. cit.*

41. Fred H. Goldner, "Industrial Relations and the Organization of Management" (unpublished Ph.D. dissertation, University of California, Berkeley, 1961).

42. *Ibid.*, pp. 206–7.

43. Peter Blau, *The Dynamics of Bureaucracy* (Chicago: University of Chicago Press, 1963), p. 258.

44. Goldner, *op. cit.*, p. 226.

45. While his imagery is somewhat obsolete technologically, Hughes makes the point well. "In a considerable number of professions the basic techniques and intellectual skills are becoming something one learns as a condition of getting on the ladder of mobility. The engineer who, at forty, can still use a slide rule or logarithmic table, and make a true drawing, is a failure." (Everett C. Hughes,

The established professional within an organization does not covet the professional ladder—it offers him little; he already has status in the wider society, and the ladder leads away from power. The employee in a specialty occupation, blocked from further promotion, seeks professionalism and the professional ladder to gain status. At this stage, he not only is without power but is in no position to aspire to it.

The strain between organizations and the new professions has been misunderstood as one of obtaining traditional professional rewards such as autonomy and not wanting administrative or supervisory duties. The conflict between superordinate and collegiate authority is *real*, but there has been confusion about it. The professional ladder was never an answer to that problem. Professionalization continues apace, but the new professions within organizations are different from the autonomous professions of old.

The proliferation of specialties has resulted in a pluralistic system of contending groups. And that struggle is not simply between a professional group and the "organization"; it is between that professional group and other groups in the organization.

The use of the term "professional" says too much and not enough. The term has lost much of its meaning because of the proliferation of meanings. If we cannot use it except in its pure form, then some new terms are necessary. We can use the concept of professionalization to understand the processes at work and to examine changes that have occurred in organizational form. But this is not enough. We need new concepts to describe what is and has been emerging from the process of professionalization. But what new terms, and to describe what? Many have used the term "profession" as synonymous with staff. That really obscures the issues. We will have to start by asking what, in fact, is *management* as opposed to *professional*? The term "management" itself has also lost much of its meaning. It includes more than those who supervise others, for it must include those involved in actively allocating the resources of the company and involved in the decision-making process.

In summary then, the professional ladder has been used as a means of providing an alternative definition of success in order to prevent an otherwise failure from opting out of the system. However, it has not really provided the status and money of "equivalent" managerial positions. It does not provide these because it does not provide the power to allocate limited resources or to pursue alternative goals, and this power is intrinsic to traditional prestigious and successful professional performance.

The very existence of the professional ladder is evidence that those in power—top management—define the "professional" as a person who cannot be moved up the main ladder. Recognition of the same definition can be seen in efforts to professionalize work—initiated, not from above, but from below by people who are blocked in any further mobility up the management ladder.

But professional ladders remain and are still being constructed because the problem is still an emergent one. The proliferation of new functions and the development of entire work forces composed of highly trained specialists (all college educated) have taken most of the meaning from our old definition of management as simply one of supervision. The professional ladder is not an answer to these new problems, but it is part of the adaptive process. We are on our way to radically different organizations.[46] The uncritical use of the old concept of profession or even the use of the concept of professionalization, can only obscure the process.

*Men and Their Work* [New York: Free Press, 1958], p. 137).

46. Questions of the relationship between new organizational forms and professionalism have been raised in Wilensky, *op. cit.*, pp. 157–58.

# *Professionalization and Commitment*

All organizations face the important problem of securing from their members the commitment, loyalty, and cooperation necessary for effective goal attainment. This problem is particularly relevant for professional personnel. This is so because professionals have commitments and loyalties to a reference group composed of other professionals and to a definite set of normative standards governing their work, besides their commitment to the organization. These differing sets of commitments are often contradictory and may result in organizational conflicts. This section deals with some of the problems and consequences of professionalization for organizational functioning.

In the first section, Gouldner discusses two important latent social identities that are common to a large number of different types of organizations. Latent social identities involve criteria for classifying people that are not officially prescribed by the organization but that nevertheless are often used and that exert pressures upon the manifest organizational roles. The "cosmopolitans" are persons who are more committed to their job and professional reference group than to the employing organization. "Locals," on the other hand, are more committed to the employing organization than to an outside reference group. Gouldner shows that these two different orientations have consequences for organizational problems involving promotion, evaluation of performance, and organizational role behavior.

Wilensky offers a useful method of distinguishing between occupations and professions and argues against the practice of describing many occupations as if they were becoming "professionalized" by carefully specifying the typical process by which professions have become established. He then discusses the major organizational threats to professional autonomy and the service ideal as well as the effects of organizational employment upon differing orientations (latent social identities) of professors, lawyers, and engineers. From this analysis he concludes that bureaucracy may endanger the service ideal more than it threatens professional autonomy, and that organizational employment is not a necessary barrier to professional commitment.

The last two selections relate structural features of the organization to alienation from work among professionals. Miller shows that differences in organizational control and professional incentives are strongly related to the degree of work alienation exhibited by industrial scientists and engineers. These relationships are then shown to be affected by the length and type of professional training received and the nature of the organizational unit in which the professional performs his work activity.

Aiken and Hage, in a comparative study of sixteen welfare agencies, show how centralization and formalization are related both to alienation from work and alienation from expressive relations among social workers. These investigators find that both types of alienation are related to lack of participation in organizational decisions by professionals and to the existence of strict rules governing professional work.

Thus, professionalization has important consequences for traditional bureaucratic principles of organization. Commitment to both the organization and to the profession vary greatly depending upon the type of organizations in which professionals are employed.

ALVIN W. GOULDNER

# Cosmopolitans and Locals: Toward an Analysis of Latent Social Roles

Sociologists have long since documented the empirical utility of role theory. It may be, however, that concepts stagnate when small theoretical investments yield large empirical dividends. The very currency of role concepts may invite complacency concerning their theoretical clarity.

Although the larger theory of social roles could doubtless profit from serious recasting and systematic reappraisal,[1] this is not the place for so ambitious an undertaking. All that will be essayed here are some limited questions relating to role analysis. In particular, an attempt will be made to develop certain distinctions between what will be termed "manifest" and "latent" identities and roles.

1. Such an overhauling seems well begun in the recent volume by S. F. Nadel, *Theory of Social Structure* (New York, 1957). Efforts moving in a similar direction may also be found in Marion J. Levy, Jr., *The Structure of Society* (Princeton, 1952), pp. 157–66, and in Robert K. Merton, *Social Theory and Social Structure* (New York, 1957), pp. 368–80, 415–20.

The author wishes to thank the Social Science Research Council and the Research Board of the University of Illinois for funds which made possible completion of the analysis of the data. During the course of the research Helen P. Gouldner, Esther R. Newcomb, Henry Bobotek, and Ruth Landman assisted in various parts of the work. Carol Tucker guided the factor analysis through the Illiac. Raymond Cattell, Percy Tannenbaum, and George Suci were generous in allowing consultation with them in connection with the factor analyses. Particular thanks are due Robert K. Merton and Paul F. Lazarsfeld for a painstaking reading of a first draft and for numerous cogent suggestions. Needless to say, responsibility for all errors is entirely the author's.

Reprinted from the *Administrative Science Quarterly*, December, 1957, pp. 281–92, by permission of the author and publisher.


Since role theory already encompasses a welter of concepts,[2] the introduction of new concepts requires firm justification. Concepts commend themselves to social scientists only as tools with which to resolve problematic situations. Unless this criterion is insisted upon, there inevitably eventuates a sterile formalism and a needless proliferation of neologisms. We must therefore justify the proposed distinction between manifest and latent roles by indicating the theoretic context from which it emerged and by showing its use in various studies.

## Theoretical considerations

A social role is commonly defined as a set of expectations oriented toward people who occupy a certain "position" in a social system or group. It is a rare discussion of social role that does not at some point make reference to the "position" occupied by a group member. Despite its frequent use, however, the notion of a social "position" is obscure and not likely to provide cleancut directives for social research. Often, it is used as little more than a geometrical metaphor with little value for guiding the empirical studies of behavioral scientists.

It seems that what is meant by a "position" is the social identity which has been assigned to a person

2. The variety of these role concepts is well displayed in Erving Goffman, *The Presentation of Self in Everyday Life* (Edinburgh, 1956), and is discussed with great cogency in Joseph R. Gusfield, "General Education as a Career," *Journal of General Education*, 10 (Jan. 1957), 37–48.

by members of his group. That is, group members may be regarded as acting in the following manner: (1) They observe or impute to a person certain characteristics; they observe certain aspects of his behavior or appearance which they employ as clues to enable themselves to answer the question "Who is he?" (2) These observed or imputed characteristics are then related to and interpreted in terms of a set of culturally prescribed *categories* which have been learned during the course of socialization. Conversely, the culturally learned categories focus attention upon certain aspects of the individual's behavior and appearance. (3) In this manner the individual is "pigeonholed"; that is, he is held to be a certain "type" of person, a teacher, Negro, boy, man, or woman. The process by which the individual is classified by others in his group, in terms of the culturally prescribed categories, can be called the assignment of a "social identity." The types or categories to which he has been assigned *are* his social identities. (4) When this assignment of identity is consensually or otherwise validated in the group, people then "ask themselves" what they know about such a type; they mobilize their beliefs concerning it. Corresponding to different social identities are differing sets of expectations, differing configurations of rights and obligations. In these terms, then, a social role is a shared set of expectations directed toward people who are assigned a given social identity.

Obviously the people in any one group have a variety of social identities. In a classroom, for example, there are those identified as "students," but these same people are also identified as men, women, young, mature, and so on. In the classroom situation, it is primarily their identity as students that others in the group regard as central and properly salient. It is also the expectations congruent with this salient identity that are most appropriately activated and have the fullest claim to application. But while the expectations congruent with the student identity are most institutionally relevant and legitimately mobilizable, it is clear that in various ways certain of the other identities do "intrude" and affect the group's behaviour in sociologically interesting ways. For example, there is usually something happening between the students that is influenced by their sexual identities.

It is necessary to distinguish, then, between those social identities of group members which are consensually regarded as relevant to them in a given setting and those which group members define as being irrelevant, inappropriate to consider, or illegitimate to take into account. The former can be called the *manifest* social identities, the latter, the *latent* social identities. Let us be clear that "social identities," manifest or latent, are not synonymous with the concept of social status. Social identities have to do with the way in which an individual is in fact *perceived* and classified by others in terms of a system of culturally standardized categories. Social statuses, however, refer to the complex of culturally standardized categories to which individuals in a group may be assigned; they are sometimes also defined as the hierarchical "position" of the individual in relation to others, as well as the culturally prescribed expectations directed toward those in this position.[3]

Expectations which are associated with the manifest social identities can be termed the manifest social *roles*, while expectations oriented toward the

3. The terminological disparities with respect to the definition of "status" barely fall short of being appalling. Among the varying definitions which may be found are the following: (1) "a position in the social aggregate identified with a pattern of prestige symbols . . ." D. Martindale and E. D. Monachesi, *Elements of Sociology* (New York, 1951), p. 540; (2) the "successful realization of claims to prestige . . . the distribution of prestige in a society . . ." H. Gerth and C. W. Mills, *Character and Social Structure* (New York, 1953), p. 307; (3) "a measure of the worth or the importance of the role," R. Freedman, A. H. Hawley, W. S. Landecker, and H. M. Miner, eds., *Principles of Sociology* (New York, 1952), p. 148; (4) "the rank position with respect chiefly to income, prestige, and power—one or all of these," G. Knupfer in R. O'Brien, C. C. Shrag, and W. T. Martin, *Readings in General Sociology* (New York, 1951), p. 274; (5) "a collection of rights and obligations . . ." R. Linton, *The Study of Man* (New York, 1945), p. 113; (6) a "complex of mutual rights, obligations, and functions as defined by the pertinent ideal patterns," T. Parsons, *Essays in Sociological Theory Pure and Applied* (New York, 1949), p. 42; (7) "a position in the general institutional system, recognized and supported by the entire society . . ." K. Davis, *Human Society* (New York, 1949), p. 87. One could go on. That these varying definitions are not necessarily contradictory is small consolation and certainly no guarantee that they all refer to the same things. Nowhere do these definitions become more opaque than when—as they frequently do—they refer to a status as a "position" in something. The ready familiarity of the word position seems to induce paralysis of the analytic nerve. Needless to say such terminological confusion begets efforts at neologistic clarification which may then only further becloud the field. We can only hope that this has not happened here.

latent identities can be called the latent social roles. Just as others can be oriented toward an individual's latent identities, so, too, can the individual himself be oriented to his own latent identities. This is, of course, to be expected in the light of Mead's role theory, which stresses that an individual's self-conception is a function of the judgments and orientations which significant others have toward him.

At the present time, little systematic attention is given to the functioning of either latent identities or roles. It is too easy to focus on the more evident manifest identities and roles in a group. As a result, even in a world on which Freudian theory has made its impact, many sociologists give little indication of the fact that the people they study in offices, factories, schools, or hospitals are also males and females. The sociologist's assumption often seems to be that the latent identities and roles are as irrelevant as the people whom they are studying conventionally pretend. The fact seems to be, however, that these do affect group behavior.

This is, of course, obvious from the most commonplace of questions. For example: Are the career chances of industrial workers affected by their ethnic identity? Are "old-timers" in a group more or less friendly toward each other than with those of less tenure? Do college professors take note of and behave somewhat differently toward members of the college football team who are taking their courses? Do Unitarian ministers sometimes refer to their "Jewish" parishioners?

While it is obvious that individuals in a group have a variety of social identities, and not merely one, we need conceptual tools that firmly distinguish between different types of social identities and facilitate analysis of the varying ways in which they influence group behavior. While it is obvious that a group member may have many social identities, it needs to be stressed that not all of them are regarded as equally relevant or legitimately activated in that group. This is precisely the point to which the concepts of latent identities and roles direct attention.

This implies that when group members orient themselves to the latent identities of others in their group, they are involved in a relationship with them which is not culturally *prescribed* by the group norms governing their manifest roles. It implies, also, that they are utilizing reference persons or groups which are not culturally prescribed for those in their roles. Thus the concepts of latent identities and roles focus research on those patterns of social interaction, and lines of orientation, which are not prescribed by the group under study. It would also seem clear that latent identities and roles are important because they exert pressure upon the manifest roles, often impairing conformity with their requirements and endemically threatening the equilibrium of the manifest role system. In contrast, the concept of manifest roles focuses on the manner in which group norms yield *prescribed* similarities in the behavior and beliefs of those performing the same role.

The role of "elders" in a gerontocratic society, with the deference and respect due them by their juniors, is in these terms a manifest role. For, in this case, the rights and obligations of elders are culturally prescribed. Here to be an "elder" is a societally relevant identity. Note, however, that even in the American factory elders may also receive some special consideration and similar if not equal deference from their juniors. Here, however, the role of the elder is a latent one, being based upon an assignment of identity which is not regarded as fully legitimate or as clearly relevant in the factory, even if fully acknowledged in the larger society.

This distinction between manifest and latent roles directs us to search out and specify the latent identities, and the expectations corresponding to them, which crosscut and underlie those which are culturally prescribed in the group under study. The concept of latent roles suggests that people playing *different* manifest roles may be performing *similar* latent roles and, conversely, that those performing the *same* manifest role may be playing *different* latent roles. The concept of latent role may then aid in accounting for some of the differences (in behavior or belief) among those in the same manifest role or for some of the similarities among those having different manifest roles. Neither the similarities nor the differences mentioned above need be due to the intrusion of "personality" factors or other individual attributes. They may derive from the nature of the latent roles, that is, from the responses to the latent identities of group members, which yield culturally unprescribed yet structured interactions and orientations with others.

The problem that will be explored in the following analysis is whether there are latent identities and roles of general significance for the study of the modern complex organization. That is, can we discern latent identities and roles which are common to a number of different complex organizations? In this connection, we will explore the possibility that, as distinguished from and in addition to their manifest identities, members of formal organizations may have two latent social identities, here called "cosmopolitan" and "local."[4] Development of these concepts may enable organizational analysis to proceed without focusing solely on the relatively visible, culturally differentiated, manifest organizational identities and roles, but without confining analysis to an undifferentiated blob of "bureaucrats." There are of course other latent identities which are of organizational significance....

## Concerning cosmopolitans and locals

A number of prior researches have identified certain role-playing patterns which appear convergent with each other and which, further, seem to be commonly based upon those latent identities which will be called "cosmopolitans."

In a study of a factory,[5] "The General Gypsum Company," I noted a type of company executive which I called the "expert." Experts tend to be staff men who never seem to win the complete confidence of the company's highest authorities and are kept removed from the highest reaches of power. Much like staff men in other companies, these experts can advise but cannot command. They are expected to "sell" management on their plans, but cannot order them put into effect. It is widely recognized that these experts are not given the "real promotions." The expert is under pressure to forego the active pursuit of his specialty if he wishes to ascend in the company hierarchy. Among the reasons for the experts' subordination may be the fact that they are less frequently identified as "company men" than others in the executive group. The "company man," a pervasive category for the informal classification of industrial personnel, is one who is regarded as having totally committed his career aspirations to his employing company and as having indicated that he wishes to remain with it indefinitely. In effect, then, company personnel were using a criterion of "loyalty to the company" in assigning social identities to members of their organization. A company man is one who is identified as "loyal."

Experts are less likely to be identified in this manner in part because their relatively complex, seemingly mysterious skills, derived from long formal training, lead them to make a more basic commitment to their job than to the organization in which they work. Furthermore, because of their intensive technical training, experts have greater opportunities for horizontal job mobility and can fill jobs in many different organizations. As E. C. Hughes would say, they are more likely to be "itinerants." Consequently, experts are less likely to be committed to their employing organization than to their specialty.

The expert's skills are continually being refined and developed by professional peers outside of his employing organization. Moreover, his continued standing as a competent professional often cannot be validated by members of his own organization, since they are not knowledgeable enough about it. For these reasons, the expert is more likely than others to esteem the good opinion of professional peers elsewhere; he is disposed to seek recognition and acceptance from "outsiders." We can say that he is more likely to be oriented to a reference group composed of others not a part of his employing organization, that is, an "outer reference group."

Leonard Reissman's study of the role conceptions of government bureaucrats provides another case in point.[6] Among these is the "functional bureaucrat"

4. These terms are taken from Robert K. Merton, "Patterns of Influence, Local and Cosmopolitan Influentials," in Merton, *op. cit.* Merton's terms are used with respect to types of roles within communities rather than in connection with formal organizations, as they are here. Moreover, Merton's focus is on the conjunction between influence and cosmopolitans-locals, whereas our analysis applies cosmopolitan and local orientations to role players apart from considerations of their influence. Note, also, the similarity between my own discussion of "latent" identities and roles and that of R. Linton, in T. N. Newcomb and E. L. Hartley, eds., *Readings in Sociology* (New York, 1947), p. 368.

5. Alvin W. Gouldner, *Patterns of Industrial Bureaucracy* (New York, 1954). It may be worth mentioning that the research published here represents an effort at deliberate continuity and development of some of the conceptions that emerged in the *Patterns* volume.

6. Leonard Reissman, "A Study of Role Conceptions in Bureaucracy," *Social Forces*, 27 (1949), 305–10.

who is found to be oriented toward groups outside of his employing bureaucracy and is especially concerned with securing recognition from his professional peers elsewhere. If he is an economist, for example, he wants other economists to think well of him, whether or not they are his organizational associates. The functional bureaucrats are also more likely to associate with their professional peers than with their bureaucratic colleagues. They are less likely than other types of bureaucrats to have sentiments of loyalty to their employing bureaucracy. Finally, more than other bureaucrats their satisfaction with their job depends upon the degree to which their work conforms with professional standards, and they seem to be more deeply committed to their professional skills. In short, Reissman's "functional bureaucrat" is much the same as our "expert," insofar as both tend to manifest lesser organizational loyalty, deeper job commitment, and an outer reference group orientation, as compared with their colleagues.

A third study, by Vernon J. Bentz,[7] of a city college faculty, again indicates the interrelationship of these variables and suggests their relevance in another organizational setting. Bentz divided the college faculty into two groups, those who publish much and those publishing little or nothing. Publication as such is not of course theoretically interesting, but it becomes so if taken as an index of something else. The difficulty is that it is an ambiguous index. Within limits, it seems reasonable to treat it as an index of the degree of commitment to professional skills. However, "high" publication might also indicate a desire to communicate with other, like professionals in different organizations. The high publisher must also take cognizance of the publications which others elsewhere are producing. Thus high publication may also be an index of an outer reference group orientation. High publishers also tend to deemphasize the importance which their own college department had to them and to express the feeling that it had comparatively little control over them. This might be taken to imply a lower degree of commitment or loyalty to that particular group.

Although Bentz's research findings are less direct than the others examined, they do seem to point in the same direction, indicating similarities between the high publisher, the functional bureaucrat, and the expert. They were also particularly useful to my own later study of a college by suggesting indices for some of the significant variables.

These three cases suggested the importance of three variables for analyzing latent identities in organizations: (1) loyalty to the employing organization, (2) commitment to specialized or professional skills, and (3) reference group orientations. Considerations of space do not permit this to be developed here, but each of these studies also found role-playing patterns polar to those discussed. This led us to hypothesize that *two* latent organizational identities could be found. These were:

1) *Cosmopolitans:* those low on loyalty to the employing organization, high on commitment to specialized role skills, and likely to use an outer reference group orientation.

2) *Locals:* those high on loyalty to the employing organization, low on commitment to specialized role skills, and likely to use an inner reference group orientation.

Cosmopolitans and locals are regarded as *latent* identities because they involve criteria which are not fully institutionalized as bases for classifying people in the modern organization, though they are in fact often used as such. For example, "loyalty" usually tends to be taken for granted and is, under normal circumstances, a latent social identity in a rational bureaucracy. For example, it may be preferred, but it is not usually prescribed, that one should be a "company man." While loyalty criteria do become activated at irregular intervals, as, for example, at occasional "testimonial dinners" or during outbursts of organizational conflict and crisis, other criteria for identifying personnel are routinely regarded as more fully legitimate and relevant. For example, skill and competence or training and experience are usually the publicly utilized standards in terms of which performances are judged and performers identified.

While organizations are in fact concerned with the loyalty of their personnel, as indicated by the ritual awarding of gold watches for lengthy years of "faithful service," the dominant organizational orientation toward rationality imposes a ban of pathos on the use of loyalty criteria. Organiza-

7. Vernon J. Bentz, "A Study of Leadership in a Liberal Arts College" (Columbus: Ohio State University, 1950; mimeo.).

tional concern with the skill and competence of its personnel exerts pressure against evaluating them in terms of loyalty. Indeed, one of the major dilemmas of the modern organization is the tension between promotions based on skill versus promotions based on seniority, the latter often being an informal index of loyalty. Despite the devotion to rational criteria in the modern organization, however, considerations of loyalty can never be entirely excluded and loyalty criteria frequently serve as a basis for assigning latent identities. In some measure, loyalty to the organization often implies the other two criteria, (1) a willingness to limit or relinquish the commitment to a specialized professional task and (2) a dominant career orientation to the employing organization as a reference group. This linking of organizational criteria is only barely understood by the group members. Thus cosmopolitans and locals are also latent identities because the *conjunction* of criteria involved is not normatively prescribed by the organization.

Each of the other two criteria involved may, however, become an independent basis for assigning organizational identities. For example, in the modern organization people tend to be distinguished in terms of their commitment to their work as well as to their employing organization. A distinction is commonly made between the "cynics" and "clock watchers" or those who are just "doing time," on the one hand, and those who "believe in" or are "fired up" by their task.[8] This distinction is based on the common, if not entirely documented, assumption that the latter are likely to be superior role performers.

It is, however, relatively difficult to know how a person feels about his job; it is easier, and is therefore frequently regarded as more important, to know how he *does* it. Performance rather than belief more commonly becomes the formal criterion for assigning organizational identity. Nonetheless, belief is never totally neglected or discarded but tends, instead, to become a basis on which more latent identities are assigned.

While the significance of reference group orientation varies from one type of organization to another, it remains a commonplace if somewhat subtle criterion for assigning latent identities. In colleges, groups distinguish between "insiders" and "outsiders," sometimes using such informal indices as whether or not individuals orient themselves to certain "schools of thought" or people, share familiarity with a prestigious literature, or utilize certain styles of research. In trade unions, different identities may be assigned to those who orient themselves to political movements or to professional peers in other types of organizations and to those who are primarily oriented to the more limited goals of the union—the "union men." Such identities are not fully institutionalized or legitimated, although they may obliquely impinge on promotions, election to office, and evaluation of performance.

8. For a broader discussion of this problem, see Howard S. Becker and Blanche Geer, "The Fate of Idealism in Medical School" (unpublished paper, available from authors at Community Studies, Inc., Kansas City, Mo.).

HAROLD L. WILENSKY

# The Professionalization of Everyone?

Many occupations engage in heroic struggles for professional identification; few make the grade. Yet there is a recurrent idea among students of occupations that the labor force as a whole is in one way or another becoming professionalized.[1] In a worthy effort to uncover similarities among all occupations, many sociologists have succumbed to the common tendency to label as "professionalization" what is happening to real estate dealers (realtors) and laboratory technicians (medical technologists). Personal service functionaries like barbers, bellboys, bootblacks, and taxi drivers, it appears, are also "easily professionalized."[2]

## Defining profession

What are the differences between doctors and carpenters, lawyers and autoworkers, that make us speak of one as professional and deny the label to the other? The best way to approach the problem is to assess critically the argument that labor is becoming professionalized (see Chart 1).

If, as Chart 1 suggests, specialization, the ultimate application of theory, transferability of skill, stability of employment or attachment to firm, and the existence of work rules do not help in defining a "profession," what does?

Any occupation wishing to exercise professional

1. The Webbs early predicted that "the Trade Unions of the Workers . . . will more and more assume the character of professional associations." Representing crafts based on "expert specialization" validated by "public opinion," they wrote, "Each Trade Union will find itself, like the National Union of Teachers, more and more concerned with raising the standard of competency in its occupation, improving the professional equipment of its members, 'educating their masters' as to the best way of carrying on the craft, and endeavoring by every means to increase its status in public estimation" (S. and B. Webb, *Industrial Democracy* [London: Longmans, Green & Co., 1902], pp. 825–26. Cf. R. H. Tawney, *The Sickness of an Acquisitive Society* [London: Fabian Society and George Allen & Unwin, 1920], chap. vii). Discussion of the professionalization of management has continued for decades. See, e.g., L. D. Brandeis, *Business—a Profession* (Boston: Small, Maynard & Co., 1914). And more recently, talk of the professionalization of labor has been revived (see N. Foote, "The Professionalization of Labor in Detroit," *American Journal of Sociology*, 58 [January, 1953], 371–80; and A. L. Stinchcombe, "Bureaucratic and Craft Administration of Production: A Comparative Study," *Administrative Science Quarterly*, 4 [September, 1959], 168–87).

2. T. Caplow, *The Sociology of Work* (Minneapolis: University of Minnesota Press, 1954), pp. 48, 139.

This paper is a general development and test of ideas about the professionalization of social welfare occupations in H. L. Wilensky and C. N. Lebeaux, *Industrial Society and Social Welfare* (New York: Russell Sage Foundation, 1958), chap. xi, and of hospital administration in my "The Dynamics of Professionalism," *Hospital Administration*, 7 (Spring, 1962), 6–24. It owes much to the work of E. C. Hughes, *Men and Their Work* (New York: Free Press, 1958), and R. K. Merton *et al.* (eds.), *The Student-Physician* (Cambridge, Mass.: Harvard University Press, 1957). . . . I am grateful to the National Institute of Mental Health (M-2209, 1958–63), the Department of Sociology of the University of Michigan, and the Center for Advanced Study in the Behavioral Sciences for generous support, and to Albert J. Reiss, Jr., and Erving Goffman for critical readings of an early draft.

Reprinted from *The American Journal of Sociology* (September, 1964), pp. 137–58, by permission of the author and publisher. (Copyright 1964 by The University of Chicago Press.)

authority must find a technical basis for it, assert an exclusive jurisdiction, link both skill and jurisdiction to standards of training, and convince the public that its services are uniquely trustworthy. While this traditional model of professionalism, based mainly on the "free" professions of medicine and law, misses some aspects of the mixed forms of control now emerging among salaried professionals, it still captures a distinction important for the organization of work and for public policy. In the minds of both the lay public and professional groups themselves the criteria of distinction seem to be two: (1) The job of the professional is *technical*—based on systematic knowledge or doctrine acquired only through long prescribed training.[3] (2) The professional man adheres to a set of *professional norms*.

To say "technical" is not to say "scientific." For the basis of the claim to exclusive competence varies according to the distinctive features of each profession's functions and background. Contrast, e.g., two of the oldest professions—medicine and the ministry. Medicine, since its "reform" in the United States some sixty years ago, has emphasized its roots in the physical and natural sciences along with high, rigorously defined, and enforced standards of training designed to impart that body of knowledge. Among the dominant denominations in the ministry, rigorous standards of training are also stressed, and doctrines are well codified and systematized, providing a technical base for practice—a base less secure than that of medicine, but still within the scope of the definition.

These two cases tell us not only that both scientific and nonscientific systems of thought can serve as a "technical" base for professionalism but that the success of the claim is greatest where the society evidences strong, widespread consensus regarding the knowledge or doctrine to be applied. In modern societies, where science enjoys extraordinary prestige, occupations which shine with its light are in a good position to achieve professional authority. Thus, while medicine has had its sectarian dissenters (chiropractors, osteopaths, and at one time psychoanalysts), it enjoys more acceptance than the ministry, whose doctrines are anchored in conflicting religious communities. There is clearly more consensus about the products of applied science than about spiritual values; the best way to avoid smallpox is more certain than the best way to achieve salvation. Nevertheless, in some places the ministry comes close to science-based professions in its monopoly of recognized skill while carpentry does not; many of us might construct a homemade bookcase, few would forgo a clergyman at the grave. The key difference is that the clergy's tasks and tools, unlike the carpenter's, belong to the realm of the sacred—which reinforces a jurisdictional claim grounded in formal training and indoctrination. Occupations which successfully identify themselves with the sacred may achieve as much of a mandate for monopoly as those which identify themselves with science. University teaching throughout modern history has combined both strategies. And the legal profession is based on moral doctrines only slightly modified by systematic empirical research.[4] We have perhaps made too much of the difference between an occupational mandate derived from science and sanctioned by law (medicine) and one derived from morality or religion and sanctioned by public opinion or by the supernatural (the priesthood). Science, as Durkheim noted, cannot combat popular opinion if it does not have sufficient authority "and it can obtain this authority only from opinion itself."[5]

The criterion of "technical" is not enough, however. The craftsman typically goes to a trade school, has an apprenticeship, forms an occupational association to regulate entry to the trade, and gets

3. An operational test for "technical" is that preference in hiring is given to those who have proved competence to an agency external to the hiring firm or consumer (cf. Stinchcombe, *op. cit.*). Again what counts is training for practice in an exclusive occupational jurisdiction; there is no notion that it can all be learned on the job.

4. In a sense social work has vacillated between the ministry (doctrine-oriented social reform) and medicine (science-oriented clinical practice) as models for the professional thrust.

5. E. Durkheim, *The Elementary Forms of the Religious Life* (New York: Free Press, 1947 [first ed.; London: G. Allen & Unwin, 1915]), p. 208. The consensus of client publics regarding the knowledge base of an occupation is both cause and consequence of the degree of professionalization. Perhaps occupational groups which serve mainly high-status clientele (e.g., Presbyterian and Episcopalian clergy) are pressured into organizing themselves professionally. The members, many themselves professionals with long training and rationalized work, expect high standards of preparation and performance from those who serve them. At the same time, once an occupation has secured an institutional basis for practice (a professional school, strong organization, legal protection, etc.), it is easier for it to develop, disseminate, and claim exclusiveness for its knowledge; it can "enforce" the notion that it is "technical."

legal sanction for his practice. But the success of the claim to professional status is governed also by the degree to which the practitioners conform to a set of moral norms that characterize the established professions. These norms dictate not only that the practitioner do technically competent, high-quality work, but that he adhere to a service ideal—devotion to the client's interests more than personal or commercial profit should guide decisions when the two are in conflict.

Despite the temptation to adopt C. Wright Mills's cynicism,[6] the norm of selflessness is more than lip-service. It is probably acted out in the established professions at a somewhat higher rate than in other occupations. Among the reasons are the following: (1) The belief that the professions offer superior opportunity for service is widespread; it is one of the motives accounting for the excess of aspirants over entrants to these occupations—and there may be a self-selection of the service-motivated. (2) The client is peculiarly vulnerable; he is both in trouble and ignorant of how to help himself out of it. If he did *not* believe that the service ideal were operative, if he thought that the income of the professional were a commanding motive, he would be forced to approach the professional as he does a car dealer—demanding a specific result in a specific time and a guaranty of restitution should mistakes be made. He would also refuse to give confidences or reveal potentially embarrassing facts. The service

6. C. W. Mills, *White Collar* (New York: Oxford University Press, 1956), chap. vi.

***Chart 1—Is There a Professionalization of Labor?***

| *Labor Becoming Professional*[a] | *Labor Not Becoming Professional* |
|---|---|
| 1. More manual jobs involve a *specialized technique* supported by a body of *theory*—mathematical, physical, chemical, even physiological and social-psychological. Systematic on-the-job training leads to *upgrading* of machine tenders. "Almost every employee in the plants of Detroit will be an engineer of one kind or another." | 1. Specialization is no basis for professional authority. High degrees of specialization prevail at every skill level, both in jobs which can be done by almost anyone (assembler in auto plant) and in jobs done only by the trained (surgeon).<br>The link between manual work and theory is tenuous. While ultimately all labor is rooted in theory, the civil engineer who designs a bridge may know some laws of physics, the workers who build the bridge do not.<br>If by upgrading we merely mean ability to learn by virtue of previous experience and challenge, then IQ becomes the criterion for professional. |
| 2. *More manual jobs involve transferable skills.* | 2. *Transferability of skills* is limited in most manual jobs outside of the traditional crafts; much of the new technology requires training for the specific system or machine in the particular workplace. Such transferability is often absent in the established professions anyway. E.g., the house counsel and other staff experts have skills which are bound to a particular organization; their knowledge concerns the traditions, personalities, and procedures unique to that organization. |
| 3. More manual jobs now provide *careers* regulated and supported by a colleague group. Unions try to "reconstruct industry so as to assure to every man a career." The evidence is in union demands for:<br>*a) Seniority in promotions*—to assume that everyone will wait his turn and so eventually reach "a job which matches his highest powers—one object of a career." Like the system of rank and pay of the professor.<br>*b) Demand for continuous income*—wage and work guaranties, pension and welfare programs, salaried status. | 3. No evidence that colleague control of manual jobs is increasing. The pace of technological change is fast; the changes are administered mainly by employers. This makes it unlikely that manual jobs, comprising a declining fraction of the labor force, will provide stable "careers" in any sense of the term.[b]<br>Most of these ways to increase the job security of high-seniority workers are traditional; they have not prevented the wiping out of obsolete crafts or unstable employment among low-seniority men. If salaried status were a criterion of professionalism, we would have to call the fee-taking doctor non-professional and the office clerk professional. If stable attachment to the enterprise is the criterion, this goes with a decline in colleague control. |
| 4. *An objective and fair set of rules and standards* enforced by grievance procedures and arbitration under union contract is the *equivalent of professional codes of ethics* supported by public trust. Moreover, unions show an increasing responsibility toward the consumer—a new concern with the impact of wages on prices, laws to protect consumers, etc. | 4. Negotiated plant rules are not focused mainly on quality of product or of work performance; they are overwhelmingly and properly concerned with protection of employees rather than the public. The public-relations programs of both unions and management should not be mistaken for their hard-core policies in contracts and daily life. |

[a] The arguments are adapted from Nelson Foote, *op. cit.*, who states them in their sharpest form. Quotations are from Foote.
[b] H. L. Wilensky, "Orderly Careers and Social Participation: The Impact of Work History on Social Integration in the Middle Mass," *American Sociological Review*, 26 (August, 1961), 521–39.

ideal is the pivot around which the moral claim to professional status revolves.

Supporting the service norm are several additional ideas which influence relations with clients and colleagues but which distinguish professional occupations in only minor degree. For instance, norms covering client relations dictate that the professional be *impersonal* and *objective* (limit the relationship to the technical task at hand, avoid emotional involvement) and *impartial* (not discriminate, give equal service regardless of personal sentiment).[7] However, these norms do not provide a clear demarcation between professional and non-professional occupations, for many crafts and commercial establishments foster similar work rules; such statements describe customer-clerk relations in established department stores almost as much as doctor-patient relationships.

In the area of colleague relations, two norms seem especially well developed in established professions: (1) "Do what you can to maintain professional standards of work" (e.g., professionals tend to honor the technical competence of the formally qualified, avoid criticism of colleagues in public, condemn unqualified practitioners, avoid too much or too little work if it lowers standards, etc.); (2) "Be aware of the limited competence of your own specialty within the profession, honor the claims of other specialties, and be ready to refer clients to a more competent colleague."[8] Both norms can be viewed as essential conditions for the maintenance of the master norm—the technical service ideal.

In short, the degree of professionalization is measured not just by the degree of success in the claim to exclusive technical competence, but also by the degree of adherence to the service ideal and its supporting norms of professional conduct.

## Is there a process of professionalization?

While there may be a general tendency for occupations to seek professional status, remarkably few of the thousands of occupations in modern society attain it. Perhaps no more than thirty or forty occupations are fully professionalized—an estimate that moves up or down depending upon how many of the scores of engineering and scientific specialties we include. An obvious difficulty here is the overlap between a scientific discipline (psychology, physics) and a profession (the practice of clinical psychology, aerospace science). A science, in contrast to a profession, has no clients except, in an ultimate sense, society; and bosses, if any, are often indeterminate. The main public for the scientist is fellow scientists, who are in a position to judge competence; the main public for the professional is clients or employer-clients, who usually cannot judge competence. The ambiguity arises from the fact that the scientist as teacher or employee may come to view his students or other groups as clients and reduce his sensitivity to colleagues, while the professional may have a high degree of sensitivity to his colleagues and reduce his openness to influence from clients or bosses. The typical case in the professional world of the future (assuming a larger percentage of salaried professionals and more scientific practice) may combine elements from each model. At any rate, the scientist's disinterested search for truth is the functional equivalent of the professional's technical service ideal, and where a scientific discipline has a substantial segment of its adherents fully engaged in applied work, the requisites of a profession are generally met.

Which occupations have gone how far in professionalizing? Established solidly since the late Middle Ages have been law, the clergy, university teaching (although the church did dominate universities, medieval faculty were by no means all clergy), and to some extent medicine (especially in Italy). During the Renaissance and after, the military provided professional careers for a dispossessed aristocracy. Officer cadres in the standing armies of Europe from the sixteenth to the nineteenth centuries developed a professionalism based on a sense of brotherhood in a self-regulating fraternity dedicated to codes of honor and service.[9] Dentistry, architecture, and some areas of engineering (e.g., civil engineering) were professionalized by the early 1900's; certified public accounting and several

7. Cf. T. Parsons, *The Social System* (New York: Free Press, 1951), pp. 433–39, 454 ff., and *Essays in Sociological Theory* (New York: Free Press, 1949), chap. viii.

8. Wilensky and Lebeaux, *op. cit.*, pp. 303–8.

9. A. Vagts, *The History of Militarism* (rev. ed.; Greenwich: Meridian Books, 1959), pp. 43–54. Cf. M. Janowitz, *The Professional Soldier* (New York: Free Press, 1960).

scientific and engineering fields came along more recently. Some are still in process—social work correctional work, veterinary medicine, perhaps city planning and various managerial jobs for nonprofit organizations—school superintendents, foundation executives, administrators of social agencies and hospitals. There are many borderline cases, such as schoolteaching, librarianship, nursing, pharmacy, optometry. Finally, many occupations will assert claims to professional status and find that the claims are honored by no one but themselves. I am inclined to place here occupations in which a market orientation is overwhelming—public relations, advertising, and funeral directing.[10] The barriers to their professionalization are discussed below.

Can a comparison of the few occupations which are clearly recognized and organized as professions tell us anything about the process of professionalization? Is there an invariant progression of events, a path along which they have all traveled to the promised professional land? Do the less-established and marginal professions display a different pattern?

Such students of the sociology of work as Everett Hughes have pictured a "natural history" of professionalism.[11] Their studies are suggestive, but to establish anything firm here we need both detailed social histories of occupations and more systematic comparison of the cases in hand. Table 1 attempts such comparison. It sum... of eighteen occupations for wh... information could be obtained and sequence that best fits the development of ... lished professions in the United States; it suggests some necessary elements in the professional package and confirms the idea that there is a typical sequence of events. While that sequence is by no means invariant, the table shows that only 32 of 126 dates for crucial events in the push toward professionalization deviate from the following order:

1. An obvious first step is to *start doing full time the thing that needs doing.* The sick were always nursed, but technical and organizational developments created nursing as an occupation. Hospitals have always been managed, more or less, but the development of the modern hospital created the occupation of hospital administration. At this early stage, the practitioners come, of necessity, from other occupations.[12]

2. The question of training soon arises. The early recruits, or a client public or, less often, a professional association press for *establishment of a training school.* The first teachers, Everett Hughes suggests, are enthusiastic leaders of a movement (like municipal reform among the city managers) or protagonists of some new technique (casework among social workers), or both (probation officer is a new occupation based both on the prison-reform movement and on a new technique).

If these training schools do not *begin* within universities, as they do in the case of hospital administration, city planning, and accounting, they always eventually seek contact with universities, and there is a steady development of standard terms of study, academic degrees, and research programs to expand the base of knowledge. A corps of people who teach rather than practice is an inevitable accompaniment. Higher standards increase the length and cost

10. Among discussions of the forces promoting and impeding professionalization, see M. Lieberman, *Education as a Profession* (Englewood Cliffs, N.J.: Prentice-Hall, Inc., 1956); J. L. Colombotos, "Sources of Professionalism: A Study of High-School Teachers" (unpublished Ph.D. dissertation, University of Michigan, 1961); W. J. Goode, "The Librarian: From Occupation to Profession?" *Library Quarterly*, 31 (October, 1961), 306–20; M. L. Fiske, *Book Selection and Censorship* (Berkeley: University of California Press, 1958); R. W. Habenstein and E. A. Christ, *Professionalizer, Traditionalizer, and Utilizer* (Columbia: University of Missouri, 1955), a study of general-duty nurses; L. Reissman and J. H. Rohrer, *Change and Dilemma in the Nursing Profession* (New York: Charles Putnam's Sons, 1957); T. H. McCormack, "The Druggists' Dilemma: Problems of a Marginal Occupation," *American Journal of Sociology*, 61 (January, 1956), 308–15; L. H. Orzack and J. R. Uglum, "Sociological Perspectives of the Profession of Optometry," *American Journal of Optometry and Archives of American Academy of Optometry*, 35 (August, 1958), 407–24; and R. W. Habenstein, "The American Funeral Director" (unpublished doctoral dissertation, University of Chicago, 1954).

11. Hughes, *op. cit.*, pp. 133–37. Cf. A. M. Carr-Saunders and P. A. Wilson, *The Professions* (Oxford: Clarendon Press, 1933), and Caplow, *op. cit.*, pp. 139–40.

12. As recently as 1948, e.g., a study done by the American College of Hospital Administrators of the careers of 1,000 members showed that they were recruited from 131 diverse occupational backgrounds and varied greatly in education, age, and viewpoint (*Hospital Administration: A Life's Profession* [Chicago: American College of Hospital Administrators, 1948]; C. E. Prall, *Problems of Hospital Administration* [Chicago: Physicians' Record Co., 1948]). The recruitment base for welfare-agency executives was once heterogeneous: public administration, business administration, law, politics. Similar data on urban planners have been reported by Harry Gold in an unpublished study sponsored by the American Institute of Planners.

**Table 1—The Process of Professionalization**[a]

| | Became full-time occupation | First Training school | First university school | First local professional association | First national professional association | First state license law | Formal code of ethics | No. of errors | No. of ties | Per cent error, by groups[b] |
|---|---|---|---|---|---|---|---|---|---|---|
| Established: | | | | | | | | | | |
| Accounting (CPA) | 19th cent. | *1881*[c] | *1881*[c] | 1882 | 1887 | 1896 | 1917 | 0 | 1 | |
| Architecture | 18th cent. | 1865 | 1868 | 1815 | 1857 | 1897 | 1909 | 2 | 0 | |
| Civil engineering | 18th cent. | 1819 | 1847 | 1848 | 1852 | 1908 | *ca.* 1910 | 0 | 0 | |
| Dentistry | 18th cent. | 1840[d] | 1867 | 1844 | 1840[d] | 1868 | 1866 | 3 | 1 | |
| Law | 17th cent. | 1784 | 1817 | 1802 | 1878 | 1732 | 1908 | 2 | 0 | |
| Medicine | *ca.* 1700[e] | 1765 | 1779 | 1735 | 1847 | Before 1780 | 1912 | 2 | 0 | 21 |
| Others in process, some marginal: | | | | | | | | | | |
| Librarianship | 1732 | 1887 | 1897 | 1885 | 1876 | Before 1917 | 1938 | 2 | 0 | |
| Nursing | 17th cent. | 1861 | 1909 | 1885 | 1896 | 1903 | 1950 | 1 | 0 | |
| Optometry | .............. | 1892 | 1910 | 1896 | 1897 | 1901 | *ca.* 1935 | 1 | 0 | |
| Pharmacy | 1646 | 1821[d] | 1868 | 1821[d] | 1852 | 1874 | *ca.* 1850 | 2 | 1 | |
| School teaching | 17th cent. | 1823 | 1879 | 1794 | 1857 | 1781 | 1929 | 3 | 0 | |
| Social work | 1898(?) | 1898 | 1904 | 1918 | 1874 | 1940 | 1948 | 1 | 0 | |
| Veterinary medicine | 1803 | 1852 | 1879 | 1854 | 1863 | 1886 | 1866 | 3 | 0 | 27 |
| New: | | | | | | | | | | |
| City management | 1912 | 1921 | 1948 | After 1914 | 1914 | None | 1924 | 2 | 0 | |
| City planning | 19th cent. | *1909*[c] | *1909*[c] | 1947 | 1917 | 1963 | 1948 | 2 | 1 | |
| Hospital administration | 19th cent. | *1926*[c] | *1926*[c] | ...... | 1933 | 1957 | 1939 | 2 | 1 | 29 |
| Doubtful: | | | | | | | | | | |
| Advertising | 1841 | 1900(?)[f] | 1909(?)[f] | 1894 | 1917 | None | 1924 | 1 | 0 | |
| Funeral direction | 19th cent. | *ca.* 1870 | 1914 | 1864 | 1882 | 1894 | 1884 | 3 | 0 | 29 |
| | | | | | | | Total errors | 32 | | 25 |

[a] Dates concern only events in the United States. Among the sources: *Occupational Licensing in the States* (Chicago: The Council of State Governments, 1952); *Encyclopaedia of Associations* (3d ed.; Detroit: Gale Research Co., 1961); L. E. Blauch (ed.), *Education for the Professions* (Washington, D.C.: Government Printing Office, 1955); *Encyclopedia of the Social Sciences* and other encyclopedias; J. W. Kane, *Famous First Facts* (New York: H. W. Wilson Co., 1950); professional association journals, newsletters, and yearbooks; and specialized histories, official or not. In cases of disagreement, precedence was given to a competent history—e.g., R. W. Habenstein and W. M. Lamers, *The History of American Funeral Direction* (Milwaukee, Wis.: Bulfin Printers, 1955)—or to a date supplied by a professional association cross-checked by one other independent source. I am grateful to Anne Mooney, Ted Cooper, and the headquarters of the dominant professional associations for assistance.

[b] The total number of dates out of order in group divided by total possible entries in group. The errors for the whole table are 25 per cent of possible entries.

[c] Dates in italics in the same row designate the same event.

[d] Two dates in the same row marked (*d*) designate associated events.

[e] Only three or four physicians are known to have resided in the Colonies prior to 1700. From 1607 to 1730 Colonial medical practice was relatively primitive (R. H. Shyrock, *Medicine and Society in America: 1660–1860* [Ithaca, N.Y.: Cornell University Press, 1962], pp. 7, 18).

[f] "(?)" designates best inference from available information.

of training and force earlier commitment among recruits. In the successful case, the standardized training is requisite to entering the occupation.

It should be noted that in four of the six established professions in Table 1, university training schools appear on the scene before national professional associations do. In the less-established professions, the reverse pattern is typical. This underscores the importance of the cultivation of a knowledge base and the strategic innovative role of universities and the early teachers in linking knowledge to practice and creating a rationale for exclusive jurisdiction. Where professionalization has gone farthest, the occupational association does not typically set up a training school; the schools usually promote an effective professional association.

3. Those pushing for prescribed training and the first ones to go through it *combine to form a professional association.* Activists in the association engage in much soul-searchng—on whether the occupation is a profession, what the professional tasks are, how to raise the quality of recruits, and so on. At this point they may change the name of the occupation. In this way hospital superintendents have become hospital administrators; relief investigators, caseworkers; newspaper reporters, journalists. The change in label may function to reduce identification with the previous, less-professional occupation. Many, of course, are unsuccessful in this effort. Thus funeral directors or morticians have not escaped the public image of undertaker, and salvage consultants are, alas, still confused with junk dealers.

All this is accompanied by a campaign to separate the competent from the incompetent. This involves further definition of essential professional tasks, the development of internal conflict among practitioners of varying background, and some competition with outsiders who do similar work.

*a*) It is in the *further self-conscious definition of the core tasks* that a pecking order of delegation occurs. The doctor allocates much of his job to less-trained nurses and laboratory and X-ray technicians; the nurses, as they seek to professionalize, allocate much of their less attractive work to practical nurses, aides, and nurse assistants; and these, in turn, allocate some of their chores to ward helpers. A similar tendency exists among all professional groups in short supply—dentists, teachers, engineers, scientists, and social workers, all of whom are redefining their functions upward and at the same time are sloughing off their dirty work, that is, their less technical or less-rewarding tasks.

At the same time that the long process of defining and redefining the area of competence goes on, and entry is gradually restricted to those willing to go through the prescribed training, problems of internal morale and interprofessional conflict develop.

*b*) *The contest between the home guard who learned the hard way and are committed to the local establishment, on the one hand, and the newcomers who took the prescribed course and are committed to practicing the work wherever it takes them* (these newcomers tend to job-hop a bit more in search of better working arrangements)[13]—this age-old conflict comes to a head. The newcomers see the oldtimers as a block to successful professionalization; the latter see the former as upstarts. If hiring and firing is out of the hands of the professional association, this remains a sore spot, for those who recruit take their choice and may prefer old experience to new training.

*c*) What is true of internal conflict is also apparent in external relations: *hard competition with neighboring occupations seems to go with these later stages of professionalization.* All occupations in the human-relations field have only tenuous claims to exclusive competence. This results not only from their newness, uncertain standards, and the embryonic state of the social and psychological sciences on which they draw, but also from the fact that the types of problems dealt with are part of everyday living. The lay public cannot recognize the need for special competence in an area where everyone is "expert."

The competition among clinical psychology, psychiatry, and other brands of psychotherapy for the right to practice therapy is typical. But even more clearly technical occupations, like medicine, find themselves doing battle with marginal practitioners—with peaceful absorption as one outcome (osteopathy) and all-out war as another (chiropractic).

4. There will be persistent *political agitation* in order to win the *support of law* for the protection of the job territory and its sustaining code of ethics.

13. Studies of nurses (Habenstein and Christ, *op. cit.*, pp. 87, 134) and of labor union staff experts (H. L. Wilensky, *Intellectuals in Labor Unions: Organizational Pressures on Professional Roles* [New York: Free Press, 1956], pp. 133 ff.) show that those with the strongest professional commitments tend to be the most mobile.

Where the area of competence is not clearly exclusive, legal protection of the title will be the aim (certified psychologist, registered engineer); where definition of the area of competence is clearer, then mere performance of the act by someone outside the fraternity may be declared a crime (medical practice laws).

Licensing and certification as weapons in the battle for professional authority are the least important of these events—although legal protection is a hot issue in some newer professions such as social work and clinical psychology. In Table 1 the first state licensure law usually comes toward the end of the process, but the professions clearly cannot claim this as a unique feature of their development: for some time egg-graders have been licensed in Indiana, well-diggers in Maryland, horseshoers in Illinois, plumbers and midwives in many places, notaries public everywhere.

Two lessons may be inferred: the turn toward legal regulation may be an expedient of an occupation "on the make," where internal debate persuades members that it will enhance status or protect jobs; or it may be forced on an occupation by some clear and present danger where public debate persuades lawmakers to protect the layman (e.g., from forged documents or quack "cures"). Medicine, law, and optometry, for instance, were licensed either before they established a university connection or before they formed a national professional association. Legal protection is apparently not an integral part of any "natural history" of professionalism.

5. Eventually rules to eliminate the unqualified and unscrupulous, rules to reduce internal competition, and rules to protect clients and emphasize the service ideal will be embodied *in a formal code of ethics*. Among new or doubtful cases this may appear at the beginning of a push for professional status (e.g., city management, hospital administration, funeral direction), but in ten of thirteen established professions or professions in process it comes at the end (civil engineering, law, medicine).

In sum, there is a typical process by which the established professions have arrived: men begin doing the work full time and stake out a jurisdiction; the early masters of the technique or adherents of the movement become concerned about standards of training and practice and set up a training school, which, if not lodged in universities at the outset, makes academic connection within two or three decades; the teachers and activists then achieve success in promoting more effective organization, first local, then national—through either the transformation of an existing occupational association or the creation of a new one. Toward the end, legal protection of the monopoly of skill appears; at the end, a formal code of ethics is adopted.

Power struggles and status strivings common to all occupations help to explain deviations from the sequence. The newer and more marginal professions often adopt new titles, announce elaborate codes of ethics, or set up paper organizations on a national level long before an institutional and technical base has been formed. Note, for instance, that the first national professional association comes before the first university school in all seven of the occupations "in process" but in only two of the established professions (dentistry and architecture). There is a hint, too, that newer professions make contact with universities earlier in their careers (the first training school *is* the university-affiliated school in the cases of hospital administration and city planning). Finally, the tactical and strategic situation of an occupation, old *or* new, may demand early licensure or certification whatever the actual level of development of the technique, training, or association. Indeed, in a culture permeated by the idea of professionalism but little touched by its substance, many occupations will be tempted to try everything at once or anything opportunity and expediency dictate. The "professionalization" of labor, management, and commerce is largely of this kind.

## Barriers to professionalization

Those technical occupations that have gone through the above process and that to some extent adhere to professional norms have acquired extraordinary autonomy—the authority and freedom to regulate themselves and act within their spheres of competence. Elaborate social arrangements, formal and informal, sustain this autonomy.

One might argue that such control as these professions have exercised will decline—or at least that very few additional occupations will acquire the label, "established." For there are some major barriers to professionalization: organizational contexts which threaten autonomy and the service ideal, and bases of knowledge which threaten exclusive jurisdiction. The future of professionalism depends on developments in the organization of both work and knowledge.

### ORGANIZATIONAL THREATS TO AUTONOMY AND THE SERVICE IDEAL

It is commonly assumed that bureaucracy, or more accurately, complex organization, clashes with professionalism. It is sometimes assumed that a client- or customer-orientation is incompatible with a professional orientation. Both assumptions contain truth; both deserve critical examination.

An increasing percentage of professionals work in complex organizations (scientists, engineers, teachers, architects, even lawyers and physicians). These organizations develop their own controls; bosses, not colleagues, rule—or at minimum, power is split among managers, professional experts, and lay boards of directors. The salaried professional often has neither exclusive nor final responsibility for his work; he must accept the ultimate authority of non-professionals in the assessment of both process and product. For instance, compare the fee-taking doctor in general practice with the salaried industrial scientist in product development. The scientist can be bypassed if his company chooses to buy up licenses or subcontract the work to outside laboratories; his work can be terminated, expanded, cut back, or disposed of according to the judgments of laboratory directors responding to outside units or higher-ups; his power and status, reflected in salaries and tables of organization, are lower than those of the men he serves. In contrast, the doctor's authority and responsibility, often exercised under emergency conditions, is typically final (we speak of "doctor's orders"); he stands at the top of the income-prestige ladder in the medical "industry"; diversification of clients frees him from dependence on any one.[14]

The matter of autonomy is, of course, not that simple. Our scientist may be in a laboratory run by a scientist-administrator and a firm run by former members of the laboratory staff, all of whom pursue administrative policies aimed at preserving his professional autonomy. Or he may simply be in a good market position, his services so much in demand, his mobility chances so great, that his superiors tread lightly when they reject his advice or make suggestions about his work. A study of top staff experts in labor unions found that the men who had received serious outside job offers since their employment in the union had more influence on union decisions than those without such offers.[15] The crux of the issue of autonomy for salaried professionals is whether the organization itself is infused with professionalism (as measured, say, by a large percentage of professionally trained employees and managers) and whether the services of the professionals involved are scarce (as measured by a large number of attractive job offers from the outside). If the answer is "yes" in both instances, the salaried professional may have more autonomy in his work than those self-employed professionals whose relatively low income forces them to scramble for many clients or who depend on the patronage of a few powerful clients.

Does complex organization threaten the service ideal? The cases of professors and clergymen suggest the difficulties in arriving at an answer. Here are two ancient professions, practiced traditionally in well-organized bureaucratic contexts in which service motives have been strongly institutionalized. Are professors less committed to the disinterested search for truth than lawyers are to their clients' rights? Are ministers less concerned about the spiritual and social welfare of their parishioners than doctors are about the health of their patients? We lack the necessary evidence. It is true that one of the main centers of resistance to Nazi terror in Germany between 1933 and 1939 was a bureaucratic profession—personified by Pastor Niemöller of the Protestant Confessional Church and some of the leading Catholic clergy.[16] But it is also true that many salaried professors in Nazi Germany prostituted their scholarship to ends

14. Cf. W. Kornhauser, *Scientists in Industry* (Berkeley: University of California Press, 1962). A comparison of the organization of "craft production" and "mass production" leads to similar conclusions: in mass production both product and process are planned in advance by persons not on the work crew, while in craft production centralized planning of tasks is abandoned in favor of decisions made by the work crew based on their training and occupational culture (Stinchcombe, *op. cit.*).

15. Wilensky, *Intellectuals . . .*, *op. cit.*, pp. 227 ff.

16. E. K. Bramstedt, *Dictatorship and Political Police* (New York: Oxford University Press, 1945), pp. 192–204.

which they knew were false. Teachers generally were among the earliest and most enthusiastic recruits for the Nazi party. At the same time, however, fee-taking lawyers were subverting the rule of law and fee-taking physicians were conducting bizarre "medical experiments" in the concentration camps. "Bureaucratic" or "free," professionals in a totalitarian context do not come out well—especially when, as in the Germany of the early 1930's, their careers are threatened by unemployment and political crises.

How do salaried professionals compare with their independent colleagues in a pluralist society—especially when their services are in demand and they have frequent occasion to choose between self-interest and the interests of their clients? That commercial contexts for professional practice such as real estate agencies, advertising firms, and banks frequently put the establishment's interests before the client's requires no notice. But such non-profit service workshops as schools, universities, hospitals—alike in their broad community base and ideology—also acquire a life of their own and that life is not always fully described by the technical service ideal.

The image of rational, technical work routines aimed solely at client welfare is difficult to sustain in many service establishments, whatever the occupation. Medical occupations in hospitals highlight the dilemma. Some hospitals are operated frankly for the profit of their owners. And in all hospitals, patients come to feel that much of what goes on is dictated by non-medical considerations—that many rules for patient management are designed for the convenience and comfort of the staff. The feeling is strongest where the disease is chronic and the stay in the hospital long.[17]

The difficulty of sustaining the fiction that all effort is bent toward technical service is particularly apparent in the mental hospitals described by Erving Goffman,[18] and the problems of maintaining professional status for any of the personnel are accordingly intensified. Even where the inside view made possible by long-term incarceration does not give the patient the impression that medical care is sometimes a subordinate aim of the hospital, the point may be dramatized in (1) the inevitable conflict between the needs of patients and the needs of teaching and research programs; and (2) the restriction of communication intrinsic to all status systems ("I'm not going to call Dr. Smith," says the nurse to the nurse's aide, as the patient gasps for breath. "It'll be my neck if nothing's wrong with her").

All this is not to say that the hospital should be geared for full-speed production: this would mean more examinations, tests, conferences, more irregular work (examinations and surgery would bunch up), less leisure, even less sleep, perhaps lowered staff morale and increased labor turnover. It does imply, however, that service workshops, profit and non-profit private and public, organize their work in ways that protect the income, security, and well-being of their most valued personnel—and that where such institutional considerations are prominent, the technical service ideal will be threatened, whatever the anxious effort to preserve it.

In brief, perhaps bureaucracy enfeebles the service ideal more than it threatens professional autonomy. Both salaried *and* self-employed professionals are vulnerable to loss of autonomy when demand for service is low and dependence on powerful clients or bosses unreceptive to independent professional judgment is high. But where comfortable organizational routines take command, the salaried professional (or the fee-taking professional affiliated with a service workshop) may lose sight of client needs more quickly than his solo brother.

### THREATS TO EXCLUSIVE JURISDICTION

A major barrier to the professionalization of many occupations "on the make," aside from organizational threats to autonomy and the service ideal, is the nature and structure of their base of knowledge and doctrine. If the technical base of an occupation consists of a vocabulary that sounds familiar to

17. A sensitive study of TB hospitals that focuses on what is urgent to the patient, his timetable of progress, notes that crucial decisions to discharge the patient, schedule him for surgery, promote him to a new activity classification, when made on Friday, are commonly not reported to the patient until Monday. If an X-ray is defective, physicians at a discharge conference will not order another but will instead put off the decision in this case until the next routine conference. Surgery, of course, may be put off for weeks, even months, for the sake of maintaining a regular schedule for the surgeon (J. A. Roth, *Timetables* [Indianapolis: Bobbs-Merrill Co., 1963]).

18. *Asylums* (Garden City, N.Y.: Doubleday & Co., 1961), pp. 321–86.

everyone (social science and the arts of administration) or if the base is scientific but so narrow that it can be learned as a set of rules by most people, then the occupation will have difficulty claiming a monopoly of skill or even a roughly exclusive jurisdiction. In short, there may be an optimal base for professional practice—neither too vague nor too precise, too broad nor too narrow.

Many new or aspiring professions face this barrier because they are grounded mainly in human-relations skills or some program of reform. The search of social work for a technical base illustrates the dilemma of most "human-relations professions"—knowledge which is at once too broad and too vague.[19] *Paradoxically, knowledge at the other extreme—narrowly restricted, very precise—is also a poor foundation for professonial jurisdiction.* When we are able to break a skill down into component elements, prescribe sequences of tasks in a performance, leaving little to the judgment and understanding of the worker, we have a job that can be taught to most people, often in a short time—indeed, a job which is ripe for elimination through programming on a computer. We also have a system of procedures which by its very accessibility is open to critical examination and debate by all comers—and is therefore vulnerable to quick displacement. It is by its nature anti-traditional, never "established."

Professional knowledge, like all knowledge, is to some extent tacit; and it is this that gives the established professions their aura of mystery. As Michael Polanyi reminds us,[20] "there are things that we know but cannot tell": the doctor's recognition of the characteristic appearance of a disease, the taxonomist's recognition of the specimen of a species—these are like our everyday recognition of the identity of a person, the mood of a face; they are acts of understanding complex entities which we cannot fully report. Both experimental evidence (on "sublimal perception") and everyday life (placing a physiognomy) confirm that we can know how to discriminate a complex pattern of things without being able to specify by what features we discriminate it.

The expert may be defined as a man who knows so much that he can communicate only a small part of it. Taxonomist and doctor alike acquire much diagnostic knowledge that they do not learn from books. This element of tacit knowledge in the sciences and professions helps explain their achievement of exclusive jurisdiction; it also helps explain their traditionalism. The client public sees a mystery in the tasks to be performed, a mystery which it is not given to the ordinary man to acquire.[21] Since tacit knowledge is relatively inaccessible, it is also less subject to direct criticism and quick change. The tacit component of their knowledge base is a seldom-recognized cause of the tenacious conservatism of the established professions.

While the nature of the knowledge base is the main reason for the aura of mystery, mysteriousness may also be deliberately used as a tactical device, a means of building prestige and power. The legal profession is a case in point. Like primitive medicine-men who cultivated the occult knowledge of the supernatural, lawyers have always sedulously cultivated the myth of the majesty and the mystery of the law. "The client has to have confidence in the law and the lawyer," a general counsel for a union once told me. "It builds [the top officer's] confidence in the lawyer when he sees us in action. He gets the idea we know what we're talking about."[22] Ferdinand Lundberg, pointing to such metaphysical constructs as "corporate entity," "property rights," "fair value," "conspiracy," "proximate cause," "good faith, bad faith," and "malice,"[23] observes that the law must still be classified with theology and lawyers as political theologians.

In short, the optimal base of knowledge or doctrine for a profession is a combination of intellectual and practical knowing, some of which is explicit (classifications and generalizations learned from books, lectures, and demonstrations), some implicit ("understanding" acquired from supervised practice and observation). The theoretical aspects of professional knowledge and the tacit elements in both intellectual and practical knowing combine to make long training necessary and to persuade the

19. For details on the traditions of social reform and social science on which social work practice is based, see Wilensky and Lebeaux, *op. cit.*, pp. 283–334.

20. "Tacit Knowing: Its Bearing on Some Problems of Philosophy," *Reviews of Modern Physics*, 34 (October, 1962), 601.

21. Archaic usages of the noun "mystery" include "occupation," "craft," "art," "calling," and "skill."

22. Wilensky, *Intellectuals . . .*, p. 234.

23. "The Priesthood of the Law," *Harper's Magazine*, 178 (December, 1938–May, 1939), 515–26.

public of the mystery of the craft. If an occupation is based on knowledge or doctrine which is too general and vague, on the one hand, or too narrow and specific, on the other, it is not likely to achieve the exclusive jurisdiction necessary to professional authority.

In assessing the barriers to a claim of exclusive jurisdiction, I have so far focused on the technical underpinnings of professional practice, without reference to the changing character of the clientele which must honor the claim. What does the rising educational level of the population imply for professionalism? The facts present a paradox: with education come (1) greater sophistication about matters professional, more skepticism about the certainties of practice, some actual sharing in professional knowledge (the mysteries lose their enchantment); but at the same time (2) more willingness to *use* professional services.[24] The question is open whether a population prone to greater use of professional service which is at the same time more critical and less deferential will mean greater pressure for high standards of technical and ethical performance or an increasing skepticism, a discounting of professional claims, even a tendency to see in the professional just another commercial vendor. We lack the necessary data on the perspectives of potential clients varying in education, information, troubles, and experience with various professions.

## New forms of professionalism

There is another way to view what is happening to professionalism: it is not that organizational revolution destroys professionalism, or that the newer forms of knowledge (vague human-relations skills at one extreme, programmed instructions at the other) provide a poor base for professionalism, but simply that all these developments lead to something new. The culture of bureaucracy invades the professions; the culture of professionalism invades organizations.[25]

To understand the future of professionalism we must grasp the diversity of orientations that now prevail among men with high levels of training and link these orientations to specific attributes of occupation and workplace. If interpenetration of various "bureaucratic" and "professional" cultures is taking place, the individual role orientations appropriate to each should also merge; mixed cultures should be reflected in mixed attitudes of professional people.

### DATA ON THE CLASH OF PROFESSIONAL CAREERIST, MISSIONARY, AND CLIENT ORIENTATIONS

Several observers of occupational life—in contexts as diverse as the Wisconsin civil service, the Office of Naval Research, big national labor unions, general hospitals in Missouri, a liberal arts college, and university social science departments—have independently come to very similar conclusions about the types of orientations professional and executive personnel have toward their work (orientations variously labeled "career commitments," "role concepts," "role orientations," "job identifications," or "reference groups").[26] The diversity of these orientations suggests modifications of stereotypical portraits of the Organization Man or of the glad-handing, other-directed characters who people the pages of *The Lonely Crowd*. Chart 2, based on these previous studies, outlines the principal types and suggests hypotheses about how they develop.[27]

This research suggests that one of three major types emerging is the professional service expert, whose professional training and commitment to an outside colleague group at once give him motive and strength to resist the demands of the employing organization and, where his orientation is accommodated, make him useful as a source of flexibility,

24. E. Friedson, *Patients' Views of Medical Care* (New York: Russell Sage Foundation, 1961), provides some evidence on the first point. What separates the educated patient from the less educated is the former's critical attitude toward the services he is in a position to demand. The less educated do not make trouble for the doctor; they are typically docile and appreciative of what they get.

25. Cf. T. H. Marshall, "The Recent History of Professionalism in Relation to Social Structure and Social Policy," *Canadian Journal of Economics and Political Science*, 5 (August, 1939), 325–40.

26. L. Reissman, "A Study of Role Conceptions in Bureaucracy," *Social Forces*, 27 (March, 1949), 305–10; D. Marvick, *Career Perspectives in a Bureaucratic Setting* (Ann Arbor: University of Michigan Press, 1954); Wilensky, *Intellectuals* . . . ; Habenstein and Christ, *op. cit.*; A. Gouldner, "Cosmopolitans and Locals," *Administrative Science Quarterly*, 2 (1957–58), 281–306, 444–80; and P. Lazarsfeld and W. Thielens, Jr., *The Academic Mind* (New York: Free Press, 1958).

27. Cf. Wilensky, *Intellectuals* . . . , pp. 111–74, 313–17.

innovation, and reliable intelligence. However, each complex organization, having multiple functions, requires its own distribution of role orientations; and each man's biography is in some respects unique. We would therefore expect diverse workplaces to display central tendencies toward one or another role orientation. Among individuals—recruitment, training, and indoctrination being everywhere imperfect, man and job never fitting precisely—we would further expect mixed orientations to be frequent.[28]

28. In a recent study of industrial scientists and engineers, Kornhauser (*op. cit.*) shows that professional orientations are most frequent among producers of research, "organizational" orientations are most common among men who administer the conditions under which research is produced, and mixed orientations typify men who apply and communicate research. The earlier studies mentioned above are consistent, although every one of them turned up large numbers who combine elements from each type.

In order to test these ideas in three professional groups, I devised an index of *professional-discipline orientation* and another of *careerist orientation.*[29] The indexes are based on the following:

29. The analysis is based on detailed interviews with probability samples or universes of six professional groups stratified for various characteristics. The interviews took place in the first half of 1960. Only white males who were in the labor force and who were currently or previously married were interviewed. All had college degrees. The special selection criteria follow (an initial phone contact screened in the eligible lawyers and engineers): (1) *Lawyers.* Selected randomly from the Michigan State Bar Roster and the Martindale-Hubbell Law Directory. Age: 30–55. Family income: at least $8,000 in one of the past five years. All have law degrees and derive half or more of total income from law. (*a*) *Solo lawyers.* A pure type including only individual practitioners or two-man family partnerships in the Detroit area. May be associated with other lawyers but does not share clientele on any permanent basis. $N = 100$. (*b*) *Firm lawyers.* Selected from the nineteen Detroit firms with ten or more partners and associates. House counsel were excluded. $N = 107$

***Chart 2—Social Structure, Life-History, and Role Orientation***

| *Type of Role Orientation* | *Roots in Structure* | *Roots in Biography* |
|---|---|---|
| *Professional service* (or discipline). Highly identified with profession; oriented toward outside colleague group; wants to give competent, objective, technical service of which outside colleagues would approve; accents full use of skills. | Role is technical, demands formal grad. training. Structure is managed by men with professional training and job histories.<br>Org. interests impinge on large no. of outside groups, org. is public relations-sensitive, so it hires specialists in accommodative techniques who can deal with government agencies and others professionally staffed. | Origins: high status categories—e.g., upper-middle class, Protestant.<br>Education: many years of college—esp. professional or graduate school built on undergraduate liberal arts degree. Orderly career.<br>Participates in professional affairs. |
| *Careerist* ("Organization Man"). Highly identified with incumbent leadership of his org.; oriented toward career within workplace hierarchy. No ideological commitments, no dilemma-producing non-organizational goals; little professional identification. Wants chance for social mobility, rewards recognized in local community—money, promotions, security. | Role carries prestige in community.<br>Structure provides opportunity for much job progression; career climb associated with residential mobility.[a] | Origins: middle mass; medium to low status ethnic-religious groups (esp. Catholics).<br>Education: college dropout or 4-year grad. with low exposure to liberal arts; weak graduate training, if any. Less orderly career (e.g., several tries before got on present ladder).<br>Little participation in professional affairs, more in local community. |
| *Missionary.* Oriented toward some abstract concept of a social movement; highly identified with an outside political or religious-political group. Sees organization as vehicle for social change fitting private goals—goals derived from past or present participation in social movement. | Role created as end product of social movement (e.g., labor movement→staff of unions; good govt. movement→city managers; political movements→staff of parties, govt. agencies; humanitarian reform movement→welfare occupations, correctional officers, nurses.<br>Role not clearly defined (new because org. is new, new unit in established org., or org. has diffuse purposes), provides chance for innovator. | Origins: marginal (e.g., minority groups such as Jews and Negroes; families often entrepreneurial, broken, or unusually intellectual).<br>Education: broad (via favored colleges, big-city colleges, or self-teaching).<br>Career: includes "ideological occupations" (e.g., journalism or adm. or organizational work in reform adm., political party, or little magazines; campus radical).<br>Participation: professional and social action. |

[a] H. L. Wilensky, "Work, Careers, and Social Integration," *International Social Science Journal*, 12 (Fall, 1960), 555–56.

1. A ranking of reference groups on a card, with appropriate variations in phrasing for lawyers, engineers, and professors: "Here are some groups that inevitably judge the quality of professional performance (*show card*). Whose judgment should count most when your overall professional performance is assessed?" "Are there any others on this list whose judgments should count?" Table 2 shows the percentage mentioning each reference group as most important.

2. Free responses to the question, "Different people want different things out of their jobs. What are the things you yourself feel are most important in a job?"

3. A question concerning those professional journals read regularly: "Generally speaking, would you say you read your professional journals thoroughly, partially, or do you just glance through them?"

Responses were scored as shown in Table 1 (respondents' total scores ranged from a high of 8 to a low of 1 on professionalism and 5 to 1 on careerism).

(2) *Professors.* Full-time faculty of arts and sciences colleges in two universities. Rank: assistant professor and up. Age: 29–55. Disciplines: physical sciences (including mathematics) and the humanities. All professors who fit these criteria were interviewed. Excluded: the social sciences and professional schools. Both institutions are large, but not eminent: (a) "*Church U.*" Church-controlled. $N = 31$. (b) "*Urban U.*" A fast-growing state university. $N = 68$. (3) *Engineers.* Had an engineering degree or its equivalent. Age: 30–55. Family income: at least $8,000 in one of the past five years. Generally research and development specialists, supervisors, or executives. Two large enterprises: (*a*) "*Unico.*" A unit making one main product subject to great fluctuations in demand. Reputation: a dead end for engineers. $N = 91$. (*b*) "*Diversico.*" A unit with diversified operations and a history of stable growth. Reputation: recruiting ground for top executives in central headquarters. $N = 93$.

As expected, the two indexes are negatively correlated ($r = -.27$, $p < .01$).* Men who score very high on professionalism seldom score high on careerism; men who rate very high on careerism seldom rate high on professionalism. Taking account of the entire range, however, this inverse relationship is not strong, which suggests that mixed types of orientation are typical, consistent with the idea of the interpenetration of bureaucratic and professional cultures.

Where is professionalism most likely to flourish? Table 4 shows that Urban University professors lead (six in ten are high on professionalism), Church University professors and lawyers as groups are medium, and engineers are low (only one in ten comes through strong on professionalism).

These findings again emphasize that (1) bureaucracy is not a necessary bar to professional commitments (e.g., recruitment and administrative policies encourage professionalism at Urban University, not at Church University); (2) occupational training is generally more important than workplace indoctrination as a source of role orientation (e.g., despite contrasting organizational contexts, firm and solo lawyers are similar in professionalism; and engineers, the occupational group with least professional training, are by far the most careerist and least professional). Thus, organizational threats to colleague control, which have received so much

* Editors' note: The reader is directed to the exchange between Professor Richard J. Hill and the author regarding this relationship. See "Letters to the Editor," *The American Journal of Sociology*, 71 (July, 1965), 84–86.

***Table 2***

| Lawyers | Per cent | Engineers | Per cent | Professors | Per cent |
|---|---|---|---|---|---|
| a) Clients | 43 | The consumer of the product or service | 34 | Students | 9 |
| b) Executives or heads of firms (if lawyer is not self-employed) | 8 (of firm men) | Immediate superiors in one's company | 47 | The administration | 2 |
| | | | | The department chairman | 6 |
| c) Colleagues—other lawyers familiar with one's work | 51 | Fellow engineers in one's specialty | 16 | Colleagues in one's own department | 24 |
| | | | | Colleagues in one's discipline, whatever their affiliation | 56 |
| d) Community leaders | — | Community leaders | 0 | Community leaders active in educational affairs | 0 |
| e) Bar association leaders | 0 | Leaders of professional engineering associations | 2 | | |
| | | | | The college faculty as a whole | 1 |

attention in debate about the rise and fall of professionalism, are attenuated by occupational training and organizational purpose.

Perhaps more subversive of autonomy and the service ideal are pressures from the non-organizational users of service—where the client is not a boss but just a customer. "The quack," Everett Hughes suggests, "is the man who continues through time to please his customers but not his colleagues."[30] In any work context where the professional lacks strong colleague constraints, the customer's complaints, real or imaginary, are likely to receive prompt and costly attention; his real problems, if they require professional skill, may be overlooked. In the extreme case, the client-oriented practitioner makes a point of maligning the techniques and motives of his professional competitors and, like the proverbial ambulance chaser, solicits work where no work needs doing.

In order to pin down this clash between colleague control and client control, I constructed an index

30. *Op. cit.*, p. 98.

***Table 3***

| *PROFESSIONAL-DISCIPLINE ORIENTATION* | *CAREERIST ORIENTATION* |
|---|---|
| *Whose Judgment Should Count* | |
| 3. One of the following is *most* important *and* mentions the second: colleagues in own department or discipline for professors; colleagues or bar association leaders for lawyers; fellow engineers, leaders of engineering associations for engineers. | 3. One of the following is *most* important: department chairman or administration for professors; heads of firms for lawyers; immediate superiors for engineers. (Solo lawyers not scored here; score adjusted by weighing things most important in a job twice.) |
| 2. Mentions one as most important, not the other. | 2. Mentions one but not as most important. |
| 1. One or both mentioned but not as most important. | |
| 0. None of above. | 0. None of above. |
| *Things Most Important in a Job* | |
| 3. Mentions technical tasks *and* autonomy or service *and* recognition from colleagues, profession, or discipline as things most important. | 3. Mentions income or economic security, mobility and status, *and* recognition from superiors as things most important. |
| 2. Technical tasks, *and either* autonomy, service, *or* recognition, etc. | 2. Income or economic security *and either* of others but not both. |
| 1. Technical task but neither of the others. | 1. Income or economic security but neither of the others. |
| 0. Mentions none of above. | 0. Mentions none of above. |

*Thoroughness of Reading Professional Journals*

3. Thorough.
2. Partial.
1. Glances through.
0. Reads none regularly.

***Table 4—Occupation Counts More than Workplace as a Source of Professionalism and Careerism; Solo Practice Encourages a Client Orientation (per cent)***

| | *PROFESSORS* | | | *LAWYERS* | | | *ENGINEERS* | | | *GRAND TOTAL* |
|---|---|---|---|---|---|---|---|---|---|---|
| | *Urban U.* (*N* = *68*) | *Church U.* (*N* = *31*) | *Total* (*N* = *99*) | *Firm* (*N* = *107*) | *Solo* (*N* = *100*) | *Total* (*N* = *207*) | *Diversico* (*N* = *93*) | *Unico* (*N* = *91*) | *Total* (*N* = *184*) | (*N* = 490) |
| Index of professional orientation: | | | | | | | | | | |
| High (6–8) | 60% | 32 | 51 | 27 | 24 | 25 | 13 | 8 | 11 | 25 |
| Medium (4–5) | 36 | 48 | 39 | 50 | 57 | 53 | 57 | 52 | 55 | 51 |
| Low (0–3) | 4 | 19 | 9 | 24 | 19 | 22 | 30 | 39 | 35 | 24 |
| Total | 100% | 99 | 99 | 101 | 100 | 100 | 100 | 99 | 101 | 100 |
| Index of careerist orientation: | | | | | | | | | | |
| High (4–5) | 1 | 6 | 3 | 7 | 6 | 6 | 25 | 24 | 25 | 12 |
| Medium (2–3) | 67 | 51 | 62 | 39 | 41 | 40 | 62 | 59 | 60 | 52 |
| Low (0–1) | 31 | 42 | 34 | 55 | 53 | 54 | 13 | 17 | 15 | 35 |
| Total | 99 | 99 | 99 | 101 | 100 | 100 | 100 | 100 | 100 | 99 |
| Index of client orientation: | | | | | | | | | | |
| Medium-High (1–2) | 31 | 29 | 30 | 41 | 61 | 51 | 30 | 39 | 35 | 41 |
| Low (0) | 69 | 71 | 70 | 59 | 39 | 49 | 70 | 60 | 65 | 59 |
| Total | 100 | 100 | 100 | 100 | 100 | 100 | 100 | 99 | 100 | 100 |

of client orientation, using the questions mentioned above. To receive a high score the respondent must spontaneously give client-oriented responses in "things most important in a job" (i.e., recognition or appreciation from clients, chance to serve clients, enjoy working with clients, or good quality of clientele) *and* rank clients as "most important" in judging the quality of professional performance. A medium score indicates one of the two, a low score, neither.

The results confirm the conflict between client and colleague orientations. The negative correlation between professionalism and client orientation ($r = -.33$, $p < .01$) is somewhat stronger than that between professionalism and organizational careerism. Eighty-four per cent of those who score high (6–8) in professionalism score low (0) in client orientation; 32 per cent of those high in client orientation are low (0–3) in professional orientation and the rest are medium (4–5).

The variations by occupation and work setting are also consistent with the hypothesis. Table 2 shows that lawyers, the most "independent" of the three professional groups, are medium on professionalism but high on client orientation—a product perhaps of medium-long professional training but weak colleague constraints on the job. Professors rank high on professionalism, low on client orientation—a product perhaps of longer training and stronger colleague constraints. Most important, solo lawyers, while average in professionalism and low in careerism, have a strong edge in client orientation; six in ten score medium or high compared to about three or four in ten of other groups. Anchored in neither organization nor colleague group, the sensitivity of the solo professional gravitates naturally to the customer.

Will the clash of client and colleague diminish or increase in the future? One could argue that the increasing fraction of the labor force in the tertiary sector—service occupations in which client and customer contact is prominent—implies that a client orientation will be an increasing threat to professionalism. Insofar as self-employment encourages a client orientation, however, the professional segments of the service sector are becoming less vulnerable, as they become more salaried. On balance, the *organizational* threat to professionalism, to the extent that it is a threat, is the one that will grow in influence. The interpenetration of organizational controls and professional controls, careerist and professional orientations, remains the central problem for analysis in assessing the future of professionalism. The occasional rise of social movements spawning new occupational groups and missionary orientations is also worth further attention. I will return to these problems below.

### POWER STRUCTURE AND PROFESSIONAL CONTROLS

Just as the clash of professional, careerist, missionary, and client orientation results in a mixed picture so the interpenetration of professional and nonprofessional controls leads to new structural forms. A preview of these mixed forms of control may be seen in some of the newer, marginal, or would-be professions—first, in occupations which share control with social establishments where careers may lead to managerial positions (e.g., engineering, teaching, librarianship, social work); second, in occupations in which careers do not lead to management but where control is split among professionals, laymen, and administrators (e.g., the many occupations ancillary to medicine such as hospital administration, nursing, pharmacy). The crucial question concerns how much weight professionals, bosses, laymen, or clients carry in decisions regarding standards of entry, performance, reward, and promotion.

In librarianship and teaching, salaried professionals face powerful lay boards who appoint supervisors and administrators from professional ranks. The dominant voices are lay and managerial. Trade unions (the American Federation of Teachers AFL–CIO) have a small percentage of the membership; the leading occupational associations (the National Education Association) include administrators (school principals), emphasize public relations, and eschew collective bargaining. However, where trade unions share jurisdiction with professional associations, there is a tendency for each to copy the organizational forms and strategies of the other. Thus, the AFT has long officially stated that it is against strikes, and the NEA has recently set negotiating goals and indorsed tactics short of the strike—ranging from complaints to the press to national sanctions like withholding contracts for the coming school year.

Among engineers and foremen the same situation

prevails, but here an overwhelmingly dominant managerial group, in active opposition to unionism and hostile to autonomous professional groups, has usually prevented the full development of either.[31] Of course, management domination is sometimes attenuated and, as I have suggested above, a professional group in great demand, with a firm base of independent training, may acquire considerable autonomy even in command-conscious sectors such as industry and the military establishment.[32] And in Europe it is common for management to share control with white-collar unions, some of which have a semi-professional character.

Instead of facing a powerful lay board, or a powerful managerial group, an aspiring occupation may face an entrenched profession. A large number of the quasi-professions which have strived mightily to expand their professional status—pharmacists, nurses, hospital administrators—find themselves in the stultifying shadow of medicine. The doctor is still officially a guest of the hospital, but, like the Man Who Came to Dinner and stayed for several months, he carries heavy weight and indeed, upon occasion, has full charge of the management of daily affairs. In seeking autonomy in the technical performance of their work, hospital administrators, like pharmacists, must travel a rocky road. By legal and informal means medicine resists encroachment on its authority.

This fact reflects a common dilemma in organizational life: the simultaneous necessity of giving autonomy to highly trained specialists and yet giving some occupations the authority to coordinate the specialists. Two outcomes seem typical: the layman gets control, as in teaching and librarianship; or professionals administer, as social workers in welfare agencies, clergy in churches, or professors in universities. Hospital administration may be something new: professionals and laymen together hire administrators who then must struggle for the authority to do their coordinating job. If the hospital administrator decides to intervene in such touchy matters as the use and payment of salaried medical specialists, the control of the quality of surgery, a death from a new drug or anesthetic, or sometimes even in more routine matters such as scheduling of operations and admissions or the use of proper techniques of sterilization, he is likely to be lectured about interfering with the "sacred doctor-patient relationship."[33] It seems clear that ancillary medical occupations will arrive at an autonomy befitting professional status only at the expense of control now in the hands of physicians and board members who will not readily yield.

All these cases point up the importance of the pre-existing power structure as a barrier to full professionalization and as a determinant of the mixed forms of organization that professional aspirants adopt. To the degree that professionalization is the expedient adoption of professional forms in a struggle for prestige and income, the fact that someone—layman, manager, or professional—got there first is central.

## Conclusions and implications

If the marks of a profession are a successful claim to exclusive technical competence and adherence to the service ideal, the idea that all occupations move toward professional authority—this notion of the professionalization of everyone—is a bit of sociological romance. Many occupations which aspire to become professional are in organizational contexts that threaten autonomy and the service ideal: some are overcrowded occupations of low rank where the work is supervised by men without professional training or sympathy; some are practiced in service establishments which, in their concern with the comfort and morale of their most valued personnel, lose sight of client needs; others are so commercialized that talk of the service ideal is nonsense. Many occupations rest on a base of knowledge or doctrine which is (1) too general and vague or (2) too narrow and specific for achievement of the exclusive jurisdiction and autonomy of a profession. The first is epitomized by the personnel men, salesmen, junior social workers, and other human-relations specialists

31. See the symposium on professional workers in industry in *Industrial Relations*, 2 (May, 1963), especially G. Strauss, "Professionalism and Occupational Associations," and E. J. Dvorak, "Will Engineers Unionize?"

32. Commenting on kickback practices in the buying operations of auto manufacturers a purchasing agent said, "Management at Chrysler was able to tell Purchasing from whom to buy and look at the scandal. I bet they couldn't get away with telling a professional accountant to falsify the books" (Strauss, *op. cit.*; cf. Janowitz, *op. cit.*).

33. Cf. T. Burling, E. M. Lentz, and R. N. Wilson, *The Give and Take in Hospitals* (New York: G. P. Putnam's Sons, 1956).

who are products of American general education at the college level; the second, by the scores of engineering specialties in the Soviet Union where the regime finds it easy to train and control its technicians by continual narrowing and redivision of traditional engineering curriculums.[34]

Another clue to the obstacles to any marked growth of professionalism is in the difference between the process by which the established professions have achieved their position and the process pursued by occupations aspiring to professional status. In the recent history of professionalism, the organization push often comes before a solid technical and institutional base is formed; the professional association, for instance, typically precedes university-based training schools, and the whole effort seems more an opportunistic struggle for the rewards of monopoly than a "natural history of professionalism."

This is not to say that many occupations which fail to fit the professional model are not developing higher levels of training and performance, an increasingly sober, dutiful dedication to the task, and even some standards of honorable dealing—what T. H. Marshall calls "a modern type of semi-professionalism"[35] and what Shils sees as a happy integration of professional and civil culture.[36] It may also be true that the empirical, critical, rational spirit of science finds its way into an increasing number of occupations. This should not lead us to mistake the rhetoric of professionalism for its substance or to ignore the distinctive features of professional life that sort out the established professions from new and different organizational forms.

The occupational group of the future will combine elements from both the professional and bureaucratic models; the average professional man will combine professional and non-professional orientations; the typical occupational association may be neither a trade union nor a professional association. Mixed forms of control, hybrid organizations—not a straight-line "professionalization of labor"—are the likely outcomes.

Occupational structures now emerging have their individual correlates. As the data above suggest, the role orientations of many professionals reflect a resolution of the clash between the requirements of profession, organization, and social movement. Most obvious, professional orientations rooted in a colleague group will increasingly be found mixed with careerist orientations rooted in a workplace hierarchy. This is one of the costs of specialization and bureaucratization noted by Carr-Saunders as he laments, "no one speaks any more of the learned professions."[37] Less obvious but no less important, the neutral and objective advice of the "technician professional" will be mixed more and more with a sense of program, of long-run goals and possibilities. In many a corner of the bureaucratic machinery of modern society, one finds what I have elsewhere labeled the "program professional"—the specialist in depth (e.g., experts in social insurance, rehabilitation, public assistance, public finance, housing, race relations, labor disputes settlement) whose professional competence and commitment are beyond question, but whose commitment to particular programs and policies (e.g., health insurance) is just as strong. By virtue of his technical prowess, he makes himself indispensable as a policy adviser. In his job moves—between government and private agencies, civic organizations, foundations, universities—he follows the programs to which both his skills and his social philosophy are bound.[38] The labor staff expert striving to "keep Labor left" supplies ideology and programs for community relations and national political action, the caseworker or groupworker who becomes a supervisor or administrator broadens his ties to the larger community of pressure groups and politicians, and can thereby engage in social action on behalf of his profession. These have their counterparts among

34. N. De Witt (*Education and Professional Employment in the U.S.S.R.* [Washington, D.C.: Government Printing Office, 1961], pp. 228 ff.) reports that there are programs for metallurgical engineering specialists in copper and alloy, in lightweight metals or in ferrous metallurgy; for mining engineering specialists in the drilling of petroleum and gas wells or in the exploration of coal deposits; for civil engineering specialists in bridge design, in building large-scale hydrotechnical structures or in erecting industrial buildings. "This fragmentation," he says, "is characteristic of every field of engineering."

35. Marshall, *op. cit.*, p. 338.

36. E. Shils, "Demagogues and Cadres in the Political Development of the New States," in L. Pye (ed.), *Communications and Political Development*, (Princeton, N.J.: Princeton University Press, 1963), pp. 68–69, 76.

37. A. M. Carr-Saunders, "Metropolitan Conditions and Traditional Professional Relationships," in R. M. Fisher (ed.), *The Metropolis in Modern Life* (Garden City, N.Y.: Doubleday & Co., 1955), p. 286.

38. Wilensky, *Intellectuals . . .*, pp. 129–43.

lawyers working for minority defense agencies and civil liberties organizations, social scientists working for government agencies, political parties, and congressional committees. End products of broad movements of social reform, these men combine professional standards of work with programmatic sense and constitute an important link between professional culture and civil culture, the man of knowledge and the man of power. As we assess the mixed organizational forms and mixed role orientations of the future, we must attend not only to the barriers to the professionalization of newer occupations, but to the emergence from existing professions of such policy-minded staff experts.

GEORGE A. MILLER

# Professionals in Bureaucracy: Alienation Among Industrial Scientists and Engineers

Etzioni has said that most of us are born in organizations, educated by organizations, work for organizations, and spend much of our leisure time paying, playing, and praying in organizations.[1]

The modern scientist and engineer represent dramatic examples of the incorporation of professionals into organizations. At present, nearly three-fourths of all scientists in the United States are employed by industry and government, with the greatest proportion of these in industry.[2] Previous research findings show that businessmen are increasingly dependent upon the scientist and engineer for ideas necessary for the accomplishment of their organizational goals[3] and that the amount of research conducted by staff scientists in industrial organizations is an important factor differentiating the dynamic from the more stagnant industries.[4] The employment of scientists and engineers in industry is not increasing at the same rate in all types of industry—as evidenced by the increase in the numbers of these professionals who are employed in the aerospace industry.[5] Moreover, the aerospace industry itself has become more and more dependent upon the federal government as an increasing proportion of its research and development is supported directly by the National Aeronautics and Space Administration and the Department of Defense.[6]

This growing interdependence has created conflicts for both the professional and his employing organization. Blau and Scott have shown that, although professional and bureaucratic modes of organization share some principles in common, they rest upon fundamentally conflicting principles as well.[7] Kornhauser concludes that most conflicts between the scientist or engineer and his employing organization stem from the basic organizational dilemma of autonomy vs. integration. These professionals must be given enough autonomy to enable

1. Amitai Etzioni, *Modern Organizations*, Englewood Cliffs, N.J.: Prentice-Hall, 1964, p. 1.
2. William Kornhauser, *Scientists in Industry: Conflict and Accommodation*, Berkeley: University of California Press, 1962, p. 10.
3. Simon Marcson, *The Scientist in American Industry*, New York: Harper and Brothers, 1960, p. 5.
4. Arthur L. Stinchcombe, "The Sociology of Organization and the Theory of the Firm," *Pacific Sociological Review*, 13 (Fall, 1960), p. 80.
5. National Science Foundation, *Scientific and Technical Personnel in Industry* 1960, Washington, D.C.: Government Printing Office, 1961, p. 20.
6. National Science Foundation, *Research and Development in Industry* 1960, Washington, D.C.: Government Printing Office, 1963, p. 64.
7. Peter M. Blau and W. Richard Scott, *Formal Organizations*, San Francisco: Chandler Publishing Company, 1962, p. 60.

This investigation was supported in part by a Public Health Service Fellowship from the National Institutes of Health. The author is greatly indebted to L. Wesley Wager, University of Washington, for aid and criticism in the formulation of this research and to Samuel J. Surace, Warren D. TenHouten, and Ralph H. Turner for their many helpful comments on an earlier draft of this paper.

Reprinted from *American Sociological Review*, October, 1967, pp. 755–67, by permission of the publisher. (Copyright 1967 by the American Sociological Association.)

them to fulfill their professional needs, yet their activity must also contribute to the overall goals of the organization.[8]

The professional who experiences such conflicts in his work may become alienated from his work, the organization, or both. This research examines work alienation as one major consequence arising from the professional-bureaucratic dilemma for industrial scientists and engineers.

Although it is clear that conflicts exist between professionals and their employing organizations, it is also clear that organizational administrators are not unaware of the problems and conflicts inherent in the employment of professional personnel. The research to date suggests that these organizations are attempting to become more professional and flexible. One method for alleviating conflicts is to modify the organizational structure by providing more *professional incentives* and lessening the degree of *organizational control* for the professional employee.[9]

However, these changes in the organizational structure may not be made available to all professionals. This paper will suggest that structural modification in professional incentives and organizational control will vary by (1) the length and type of training received by the professional, and (2) the type of organizational unit in which the professional performs his work activity.

### PROFESSIONAL TRAINING

Orth describes the importance of professional training for the scientist or engineer who enters a bureaucratic organization, as follows:

> Professional training in itself, whether it be in medicine, chemistry, or engineering, appears to predispose those who go through it to unhappiness or rebellion when faced with the administrative process as it exists in most organizations. Scientists and engineers *cannot* or *will not* . . . operate at the peak of their creative potential in an atmosphere that puts pressure on them to conform to organizational requirements which they do not understand or believe necessary.[10]

Kornhauser contends that the strength of professional loyalty and identification can be expected to vary by the *type* of training received by the professional. He notes that professions differ in their selectivity of recruitment, intensity of training, and state of intellectual development and that all of these factors affect the nature of the person's orientation.[11] Becker and Carper in a study of three groups of students found differences between those majoring in engineering and those majoring in physiology and philosophy. The engineers felt that their future lay somewhere in the industrial system. For many, a broad range of positions within an organization was thought acceptable, including such "unprofessional" positions as manager or research supervisor.[12] Similarly, Clovis Shepherd found differences between scientists and engineers concerning their goals, reference groups and supervisory experiences. Engineers were typically more "bureaucratic" in their orientation, whereas scientists were more "professional." Shepherd attributes this difference to the more intensive training received by the scientists.[13] Goldner and Ritti also contend that engineers are more concerned with entrance into positions of power and participation in the affairs of the organization than with professional values and goals. They argue that engineers recognize power as an "essential ingredient of success" for them.[14]

In addition to differences in type of professional training, differences in the *length* of training are important. Those professionals who receive the Ph.D. degree should develop stronger professional loyalties and identifications than those persons with M.A. or M.S. degrees. This greater length of training also represents a greater investment on the part of the professional. It is reasonable to assume that he will *expect* higher rewards from the organization in return for his services. Moreover, if these rewards are not forthcoming, professionals with advanced degrees are in a better position to market their skills

8. Kornhauser, *op. cit.*, pp. 195–96.

9. These are two of the four areas of conflict identified and discussed by William Kornhauser. See Kornhauser, *op. cit.*, p. 45.

10. Charles D. Orth, "The Optimum Climate for Industrial Research," in Norman Kaplan, ed., *Science and Society*, Chicago: Rand McNally, 1965, p. 141.

11. Kornhauser, *op. cit.*, p. 138.

12. Howard S. Becker and James Carper, "The Elements of Identification with an Occupation," *American Sociological Review*, 21 (June, 1956), pp. 341–48.

13. Clovis Shepherd, "Orientations of Scientists and Engineers," *Pacific Sociological Review*, 4 (Fall, 1961), pp. 79–83.

14. Fred H. Goldner and R. R. Ritti, "Professionalization as Career Immobility," *The American Journal of Sociology*, 72 (March, 1967), pp. 491–94.

and find employment in an organization that does offer such rewards.

Some evidence exists for these assumptions. For example, Wilensky found that top staff experts in labor unions who had received serious job offers since their employment had more influence on union decisions than did those without such offers.[15] Paula Brown found that "key" scientists and engineers in a governmental laboratory were given "special considerations" by their administrators, were highly respected by them, and were able to "control" the laboratory to a considerable extent. Brown argues that professionals with less national prestige would not have been given the same treatment nor have been able to control the organization as effectively.[16] Pelz's and Andrews' findings parallel those reported earlier in a study undertaken by the Princeton Opinion Research Corporation. In both studies, those professionals with the Ph.D. degree and those trained as scientists participated most often in decisions regarding their work, had more individual freedom, and enjoyed more professional incentives.[17]

However, the "match" between organizational structure and the professional's length and type of training is seldom perfect. As Etzioni notes:

> If personalities could be shaped to fit specific organizational roles, or organizational roles to fit specific personalities, many of the pressures to displace goals, much of the need to control performance, and a good part of the alienation would disappear. Such matching is, of course, as likely as an economy without scarcity and hence without prices.[18]

The above line of reasoning serves as the basis for the following hypotheses to be explored in this paper: (1) degree of alienation from work should be positively associated with degree of organizational control and negatively associated with number of professional incentives for all professional personnel; (2) the above relationships should be stronger for those professionals with the Ph.D. degree and those professionals trained as scientists than for professionals with the M.A. or M.S. degree and professionals trained as engineers.

### ORGANIZATIONAL UNIT

An equally important conditioning variable is the type of organization in which the professional performs his work. Comparative organizational research shows that the greater the organization's dependence upon research, the more the organization will manifest high professional incentives and low organizational control.[19]

Structural variations *within* an organization may also be apparent. One instance where structural variation might be expected in an organization employing scientists and engineers is between those areas where application and development are the primary goals and those areas where the primary goal is pure or basic research. Most aerospace companies are engaged in both types of activity, but the basic research aspect is usually carried out in a special laboratory that is separated from the larger organizational unit.

This research allows for a comparison of these two very different types of organizational units and thus permits a further evaluation of the hypothesized relationship between organizational structure and work alienation. Specifically, there should be less organizational control and more professional incentives in the laboratory than in the larger unit. Therefore, less alienation from work should be experienced by professionals employed in the laboratory than by professionals employed in the larger organizational unit.

## Method

Data were gathered during the summer of 1965 from scientific and engineering personnel employed in two divisions of one of the largest aerospace companies in the United States. The organization, at the time of the study, employed over 100,000 persons within its five operating divisions and had separate facilities in four states and subsidiaries in Canada. The company is engaged in the manufac-

15. Harold L. Wilensky, *Intellectuals in Labor Unions: Organizational Pressures on Professional Roles*, New York: The Free Press, 1956.

16. Paula Brown, "Bureaucracy in a Governmental Laboratory," *Social Forces*, 32 (March, 1954), pp. 259–68.

17. Donald Pelz and Frank M. Andrews, "Organizational Atmosphere, Motivation and Research Contribution," *The American Behavioral Scientist*, 6 (December, 1962), pp. 43–47. See also, *The Conflict Between the Scientific and the Management Mind*, Princeton: Opinion Research Corporation, 1959.

18. Etzioni, *op. cit.*, p. 75.

19. Kornhauser, *op. cit.*, pp. 148–49.

ture of military aircraft, commercial airliners, supersonic jet transports, helicopters, gas-turbine engines, rocket boosters for spacecraft, intercontinental ballistic missiles, and orbiting space vehicles.

The largest of the five divisions is the Aero-Space Group, containing a missile production center and a space center. Included within the Aero-Space Group are a variety of independent laboratories, testing facilities, manufacturing areas, and the world's largest privately-owned wind tunnel. Shortly after this study was undertaken, a large space-simulation laboratory was completed.

In 1958 the company established a Basic Science Research Laboratory which operates independently from all other laboratories and divisions of the company. The principal product of the Laboratory is the scientific and engineering information made known to other divisions of the company by means of consultation and publication programs. The laboratory has three major objectives: (1) to carry on research programs that will put the company into direct and effective communication with the larger scientific community; (2) to choose and maintain a staff of competent specialists who will provide consulting advice in their chosen fields of specialization; and (3) to engage in exploratory and basic research in fields where new discoveries will be of value to the company's overall operations.[20]

The two divisions thus represent a sharp contrast in the nature of the work situation for the professionals involved. Professionals in the Basic Science Laboratory share an environment more like that of the university, whereas professionals in the Aero-Space Group are more representative of persons engaged in traditional research and development work and function primarily as staff personnel within the division.

Subjects for this study are non-supervisory scientists and engineers selected from the Aero-Space Group and the Basic Science Laboratory. All subjects held the degree of M.A., M.S., or Ph.D. in science, engineering, or mathematics. A listing of all employees meeting the above criteria was provided by the company and the selection of respondents was made from this listing. Twenty different types of engineers were represented, ranging from aerospace to electrical to nuclear engineers. Scientists included astronomers, chemists, and physicists. General, applied and theoretical mathematicians were included. Respondents within the two divisions were selected by the following criteria:

1. All Basic Science Laboratory personnel (N = 66),
2. All persons in the Aero-Space Group with the degree of Ph.D. (N = 74),
3. All persons in the Aero-Space Group with the degree of M.A. or M.S. in science or mathematics (N = 164),
4. A 50 percent random sample of all persons in the Aero-Space Group with the degree of M.A. or M.S. in engineering (N = 236).

In the analysis to follow, those persons with degrees in mathematics are included with those having degrees in science and both are labeled "scientists." The engineering personnel are treated as a separate group of "engineers." Because of the sampling design, the engineering group is under-represented in terms of their actual proportion in the organization although their proportion in the sample is greater than for any other professional specialty.

Data were gathered by means of a mailback questionnaire sent to the homes of the study participants. The questionnaire was anonymous and a postcard was included for the respondents to sign and return after they had returned their questionnaires. This procedure allowed for subsequent follow-ups in the case of nonrespondents and two such follow-ups were undertaken.

Seventeen of the original 540 subjects had either moved from the area or the addresses provided by the company were incorrect, leaving 523 potential subjects. Of this total, 84 per cent returned the questionnaires and 80 per cent (N = 419) were completed sufficiently to be used in this analysis.

## Measures

### WORK ALIENATION

The work of professionals, as contrasted with the work of non-professionals, is characterized by high intrinsic satisfaction, positive involvement, and commitment to a reference group composed of other professionals.[21] In addition, as Orzack has

20. These objectives were emphasized by the director of the laboratory in conversations with the author and appear in various company documents.

21. Amitai Etzioni, *A Comparative Analysis of Complex Organizations*, New York: The Free Press, 1961, p. 53.

demonstrated, the work of professionals plays a much more important role in their life than it does for the non-professional worker.[22]

For a scientist, the importance of and devotion to a particular style of life and work was best described by Weber. In his essay concerning science as a vocation, he indicates the importance of "inward calling" for the scientist:

> . . . whoever lacks the capacity to put on blinders, so to speak, and to come up to the idea that the fate of his soul depends upon whether or not he makes the correct conjecture at this passage of his manuscript may as well stay away from science. He will never have what one may call the "personal experience" of science. Without this strange intoxication, ridiculed by every outsider; without this passion, this "thousands of years must pass before you enter into life and thousands more wait in silence"—according to whether or not you succeed in making this conjecture; without this, you have *no* calling for science and you should do something else. For nothing is worthy of man as man unless he can pursue it with passionate devotion.[23]

The scientist who is unable to find "self-rewarding work activities to engage him," who does not experience an "intrinsic pride or meaning in his work," and who "works merely for his salary" or other remunerative incentives is experiencing the type of alienation described by Melvin Seeman as self-estrangement.[24] As defined, self-estrangement is *not* the same as dissatisfaction with one's job. As Mills and others have pointed out, a person may be alienated from his work yet still be satisfied with his job.[25]

The measure of work alienation employed is a five-item cumulative scale consisting of statements referring to the intrinsic pride or meaning of work. Three statements were developed by the author and two were selected from Morse's scale of "intrinsic pride in work."[26] The statements are:

1. I really don't feel a sense of pride or accomplishment as a result of the type of work that I do.
2. My work gives me a feeling of pride in having done the job well.
3. I very much like the type of work that I am doing.
4. My job gives me a chance to do the things that I do best.
5. My work is my most rewarding experience.

Response categories provided for each statement were: (1) Strongly Agree; (2) Agree; (3) Disagree; and (4) Strongly Disagree. The response distribution to each item was dichotomized between those agreeing and those disagreeing with the statement. This procedure yielded a Guttman scale with the following characteristics: Coefficient of Reproducibility (Goodenough technique) = 0.91; Minimum Marginal Reproducibility = 0.70; Coefficient of Scalability = 0.69; and Coefficient of Sharpness = 0.69.[27]

The scale scores were trichotomized to obtain three levels of work alienation. Persons with a scale score of "0" (30 per cent) were classified as low, those with scale scores of "1" or "2" (40 per cent) were classified as medium, and those with scale scores of "3," "4," or "5" (30 per cent) were

22. L. H. Orzack, "Work as a Central Life Interest of Professionals," *Social Problems*, 7 (1959), pp. 125–32.

23. Hans H. Gerth and C. Wright Mills, eds., *From Max Weber: Essays in Sociology*, New York: Oxford University Press, 1946, p. 135.

24. Melvin Seeman, "On the Meaning of Alienation," *American Sociological Review*, 24 (December, 1959), p. 790.

25. Mills argues that to equate alienation with what is commonly measured as "job dissatisfaction" by psychologists and sociologists is to misunderstand Marx. See C. Wright Mills, *The Marxists*, New York: Dell Publishing Company, 1962, p. 86. Harold Wilensky makes the same point and has developed a measure specifically directed toward ascertaining the social-psychological aspects of alienation from work within a framework of role-self analysis. See Harold L. Wilensky, "Work as a Social Problem," in Howard S. Becker, editor, *Social Problems: A Modern Approach*, New York: John Wiley and Sons, 1966, pp. 138–42. However, there does not appear to be agreement concerning this point. Aiken and Hage, for example, have recently developed a measure of alienation from work based on a factor analysis of items concerned with the "degree of satisfaction with various aspects of the respondents' work situation." See Michael Aiken and Jerald Hage, "Organizational Alienation: A Comparative Analysis," *American Sociological Review*, 31 (August, 1966), p. 501.

26. Nancy Morse, *Satisfactions in the White Collar Job*, Ann Arbor: University of Michigan Press, 1953.

27. The best description of the Goodenough technique is Allen L. Edwards, *Techniques of Attitude Scale Construction*, New York: Appleton-Century-Crofts, 1957, pp. 184 ff. Edwards states that, unlike the C. R. produced by the Cornell technique, the C. R. produced by the Goodenough technique *accurately* represents the extent to which individual responses can be reproduced from scale scores. The Coefficient of Scalability is described in Herbert Menzel, "A New Coefficient for Scalogram Analysis," *Public Opinion Quarterly*, 17 (Summer, 1953), pp. 268–80. The Coefficient of Sharpness is described by James A. Davis, "On Criteria for Scale Relationships," *The American Journal of Sociology*, 63 (January, 1958), pp. 371–80.

classified as high in experiencing alienation from work.[28]

ORGANIZATIONAL CONTROL

Organization implies the coordination of diverse activities necessary for effective goal achievement. Such coordination requires some mode of control over these diverse activities. Traditional bureaucratic modes of control differ significantly from the mode of control deemed appropriate by professionals. Whereas organizations tend to be structured hierarchically, professions tend to be organized in terms of a "colleague group of equals" with ultimate control being exercised by the group itself.[29] Hence, bureaucratic control violates the profession's traditional mandate of freedom from control by outsiders.[30]

One specific area where the nature of the organizational control structure becomes manifest is in the type of supervisor-employee relationship. This is a major source of conflict for the professional as it is for other types of organizational participants. In this respect, Baumgartel suggests that three styles of supervision (or leadership) can be identified, based upon rates of interaction, degree of influence, and decision-making. The three styles of supervision are: *Directive* (low rate of interaction and unilateral decision-making by the supervisor); *Participatory* (high rate of interaction and joint decision-making by supervisor and researcher); and *Laissez-Faire* (low rate of interaction, with the researcher making most of the decisions).[31]

In his study of scientists and supervisors in the National Institutes of Health, Baumgartel found that research performance, job satisfaction, and positive attitudes toward the supervisor were highest for Participatory, lowest for Directive, and intermediate for Laissez-Faire supervisors. These findings differ sharply from those reported by Argyris. Eighty-seven per cent of the foremen studied by Argyris report that in order to be effective, they must try to keep everyone busy with work that guarantees a fair take-home pay, to distribute the easy and tough jobs fairly, and *to leave the employees alone as much as possible*. Argyris concludes that a successful foreman, from the point of view of both foremen and employees, is neither directive nor is he an expert in human relations.[32]

To determine the types of supervision evident in the present organization, the following question was asked:

Which of the following statements most nearly represents the type of work relationship that exists between you and your immediate supervisor?

1. We discuss things a great deal and come to a mutual decision regarding the task at hand.
2. We discuss things a great deal and his decision is usually adopted.
3. We discuss things a great deal and my decision is usually adopted.
4. We don't discuss things very much and his decision is usually adopted.
5. We don't discuss things very much and I make most of the decisions.

Persons responding with statement number 4 above were classified as working for a Directive type supervisor (16 per cent), those responding with statement number 5 above were classified as working for a Laissez-Faire type (45 per cent), and those responding with statements 1, 2, or 3 above were classified as working for a Participatory type supervisor (39 per cent).

The second empirical indicator of organizational control concerns the professional's freedom to choose or select the types of research projects in which he is implicated. Leo Meltzer found that scientists in industrial organizations usually have

28. Response categories were reversed in the first item to make them consistent with the others. Persons disagreeing or strongly disagreeing with each item were coded as "1" and those agreeing or strongly agreeing were coded as "0." Thus, a scale score of 5 means that the person "disagreed" with all five items and a scale score of 0 means that he "agreed" with all five items.

29. Etzioni, *Modern Organizations*, *op. cit.*, p. 80.

30. See for example, Eliot Freidson and Buford Rhea, "Knowledge and Judgment in Professional Evaluations," *Administrative Science Quarterly*, 10 (June, 1965), pp. 107–8, Ernest Greenwood, "Attributes of a Profession," *Social Work*, 2 (July, 1957), pp. 45–55, and Everett C. Hughes, *Men and Their Work*, New York: The Free Press, 1958.

31. Howard Baumgartel, "Leadership, Motivations, and Attitudes in Research Laboratories," *Journal of Social Issues*, 12 (1956), p. 30, and "Leadership Style as a Variable in Research Administration," *Administrative Science Quarterly*, 2 (December, 1957), pp. 344–60.

32. Chris Argyris, *Understanding Organizational Behavior*, Homewood: The Dorsey Press, 1960, p. 94. Italics added. Aiken and Hage found that rule observation, which implies close supervision by superiors, was the single best predictor of alienation from expressive relations. See Aiken and Hage, *op. cit.*, p. 506.

ample funds and facilities for research but very little freedom in the selection of research projects. Conversely, scientists in universities are usually short on funds but have freedom to do what they wish. Both freedom and funds were found to be correlated with publication rate, but were negatively correlated with each other. Meltzer concludes that freedom to choose research projects is representative of other variables which facilitate the intrinsic satisfactions which scientists derive from the actual content of their work.[33]

To ascertain the degree of freedom accorded professionals in this study, the following question was asked:

In general, how much choice do you have concerning the types of research projects in which you are involved?
1 . . . Almost no choice 3 . . . Some
2 . . . Very little 4 . . . A great deal

Persons responding "Almost no choice" or "Very little" were classified as low (38 per cent), those indicating they had "Some" choice were classified as medium (40 per cent), and those indicating they had "A great deal" of choice were classified as high (22 per cent) in freedom to choose research projects.

### PROFESSIONAL INCENTIVES

Previous research findings describe the incentives most sought after by scientists and engineers as (1) freedom to publish the results of their research, (2) funds for attending professional meetings, (3) freedom and facilities to aid in their research, (4) promotion based upon technical competence, and (5) opportunities to improve their professional knowledge and skills.[34] It is more common, however, for industry to slight professional incentives in favor of organizational incentives, such as promotions in the line, increases in authority, and increases in salary. This is the case because organizational incentives have proved satisfactory for other employees in the past and differing incentive structures are viewed as competing sources of loyalty.[35]

Two empirical indicators of the professional incentive structure are utilized in this research. The first, *Professional Climate*, is a general index of the professional incentives made available to the professional by the organization and is composed of two items:

1. (Company) provides us with many opportunities to obtain professional recognition outside the company.
1 . . . Strongly disagree 3 . . . Agree
2 . . . Disagree 4 . . . Strongly agree

2. In general, how much time are you provided to work on or pursue your own research interests?
1 . . . Almost none 3 . . . Some
2 . . . Very little 4 . . . A great deal

The response distribution for each item was dichotomized between responses 2 and 3. Persons agreeing with the first statement and persons responding "some" or "a great deal" to the second question were classified as high. These two dichotomies were then cross-classified to obtain three levels of perceived professional climate: those high on both dimensions (28 per cent), those high on one dimension (34 per cent), and those low on both dimensions (38 per cent).

A second indicator, *Company Encouragement*, attempts to discern the organization's encouragement of specific professional incentives. Three items comprise this index:

1. (Company) encourages us to publish the results of our research.
2. (Company) encourages us to attend our professional meetings.
3. (Company) encourages us to further our professional training by attending special lectures and/or classes at academic institutions.

Response categories provided for each question were Strongly Disagree, Disagree, Agree, and Strongly Agree. The response distribution for each item was dichotomized between those who agreed and those who disagreed with the statement. Those disagreeing with all or two of the statements were classified as low (35 per cent), those agreeing with two of the statements were classified as medium (28 per cent), and those agreeing with all three state-

33. Leo Meltzer, "Scientific Productivity in Organizational Settings," *Journal of Social Issues*, 12 (1956), pp. 32–40.

34. See, for example, John W. Riegal, *Intangible Rewards for Engineers and Scientists*, Ann Arbor: University of Michigan Press, 1958, pp. 12–13, and Todd LaPorte, "Conditions of Strain and Accommodation in Industrial Research Organizations," *Administrative Science Quarterly*, 10 (June, 1965), pp. 33–34.

35. Kornhauser, *op. cit.*, p. 135. The dependence of staff on line is discussed in Melville Dalton, *Men Who Manage*, New York: John Wiley and Sons, 1959.

ments (37 per cent) were classified as perceiving high encouragement from the company.

## Results

The first hypothesis states that alienation from work will be positively associated with degree of organizational control and negatively associated with number of professional incentives. Table 1 shows support for this general hypothesis.

There are fairly large differences between those professionals working for Directive and Participatory supervisors in the proportions with differing degrees of alienation. However, the proportions of those with differing degrees of work alienation who work for Participatory and Laissez-Faire supervisors are almost identical. Thus, the major difference in the degree of alienation experienced by these professionals occurs between those who work for a Directive Supervisor and those working for *either* of the other types.

The relationship between company encouragement and work alienation is much the same. Differences exist between those professionals with low and high company encouragement who experience alienation; however, the proportions of those experiencing differing degrees of alienation with medium and low company encouragement are very similar.

### LENGTH OF PROFESSIONAL TRAINING

The original relationships just examined are expected to be conditional relationships. It was hypothesized that the relationships should be stronger for those professionals with advanced training. Table 2 shows strong support for this expectation.

The relationship obtained in each partial is consistent in direction with that expected and the degree of association is much stronger for those professionals with the Ph.D. degree. In addition, the form of the relationships involving type of supervisor and company encouragement differs in the two partials.

The importance of length of professional training on the relationship between type of supervisor and work alienation is clear. The relationship obtained for those with the M.A. degree is similar to the original relationship. For those with the Ph.D. degree, however, type of supervisor is important and is reflected in the differences in degree of work alienation evident among professionals working for the three types of supervisors. The proportions with various degrees of alienation are about the same for both Ph.D.'s and M.A.'s who work for a Directive supervisor. However, the Ph.D.'s differ from the M.A.'s with respect to the importance of the other two supervisor types. While there is no difference among those M.A.'s who experience high alienation, there is a 17 per cent difference among the Ph.D.'s. Conversely, for those experiencing low alienation there is a 10 per cent difference between those working for the two supervisor types. In fact, 56 per cent of those with the Ph.D. degree experience low alienation under a Laissez-Faire supervisor as compared with only 27 per cent of those with the M.A. degree.

The relationships obtained between company encouragement and work alienation are similar. As with type of supervisor, the partial obtained for those with the M.A. degree is very similar to that observed in the original relationship, with little difference in degree of alienation evident for those with low and medium company encouragement. However, for the Ph.D.'s, these differences are more apparent and the degree of association is very different in the two partials. For the Ph.D.'s, the

***Table 1—Relationship between Work Alienation and Four Indicators of Organizational Control and Professional Incentive Structures***

| Control-incentive structure | WORK ALIENATION Low | Med. | High | N |
|---|---|---|---|---|
| Supervisor type | | | | |
| Directive | .10 | .33 | .57 | 63 |
| Participatory | .32 | .42 | .26 | 158 |
| Laissez-faire | .35 | .42 | .23 | 176 |
| | Gamma = −.30 | | | |
| Research choice | | | | |
| Low | .11 | .34 | .55 | 150 |
| Med. | .32 | .48 | .20 | 158 |
| High | .56 | .40 | .04 | 87 |
| | Gamma = −.64 | | | |
| Professional climate | | | | |
| Low | .15 | .34 | .51 | 155 |
| Med. | .29 | .45 | .26 | 133 |
| High | .51 | .43 | .06 | 106 |
| | Gamma = −.55 | | | |
| Company encouragement | | | | |
| Low | .20 | .39 | .41 | 142 |
| Med. | .26 | .38 | .36 | 107 |
| High | .42 | .44 | .14 | 144 |
| | Gamma = −.35 | | | |

difference between those perceiving low and high company encouragement who experience high work alienation is 37 per cent as compared with only 12 per cent for those with the M.A. degree. Conversely, the same difference for those experiencing low alienation is 34 per cent for the Ph.D.'s and only 14 per cent for the M.A.'s.

### TYPE OF PROFESSIONAL TRAINING

The strength of the original relationships is also expected to vary with type of professional training. Specifically, the relationships should be stronger for those trained as scientists than for those trained as engineers. Table 3 shows only partial support for this expectation.

The relationship between type of supervisor and work alienation again remains consistent in direction but differs greatly in magnitude between the two partials. In the partial obtained for the engineering personnel, the relationship is similar to that observed in the original relationship and among professionals with the M.A. degree. Working for a Directive supervisor is associated with high alienation but little difference is evident in the degree of alienation between those persons working for Participatory and Laissez-Faire supervisors. In the partial obtained for the scientific personnel, however, there is clearly a difference in the degree of alienation experienced by professionals working for all three types of supervisors. Working for a Directive supervisor leads to high alienation, but 11 per cent more scientists experience high alienation under Participatory supervisors than under Laissez-Faire supervisors (as compared with a difference of only 4 per cent for the engineering group).

Thus, the relationship between type of supervisor and degree of work alienation is conditional with respect to type and length of professional training. For those professionals with M.A. degrees or who have been trained as engineers, the major differences in alienation appear between those working for a Directive as opposed to *either* a Participatory or Laissez-Faire supervisor. For those persons with the Ph.D. degree or who were trained as scientists, however, the less the supervision (as all three types are differentiated), the less the degree of alienation from work.

The relationship between company encouragement and work alienation is consistent in direction with that obtained in the original relationship but is much stronger for scientists than for engineers. For the scientists, the difference between those who

***Table 2—Relationship Between Work Alienation and Four Indicators of Organizational Control and Professional Incentive Structures: By Length of Professional Training***

| | *Length of professional training* | | | | | | | |
|---|---|---|---|---|---|---|---|---|
| | *M.A. DEGREE WORK ALIENATION* | | | | *PH.D. DEGREE WORK ALIENATION* | | | |
| *Control-incentive structure* | *Low* | *Med.* | *High* | *N* | *Low* | *Med.* | *High* | *N* |
| Supervisory type | | | | | | | | |
| Directive | .10 | .30 | .60 | 52 | .11 | .33 | .56 | 9 |
| Participatory | .28 | .47 | .25 | 124 | .46 | .24 | .30 | 33 |
| Laissez-faire | .27 | .47 | .26 | 122 | .56 | .31 | .13 | 52 |
| | Gamma = −.25 | | | | Gamma = −.40 | | | |
| Research choice | | | | | | | | |
| Low | .11 | .36 | .53 | 131 | .17 | .17 | .66 | 18 |
| Med. | .33 | .50 | .17 | 127 | .33 | .34 | .33 | 27 |
| High | .42 | .53 | .05 | 38 | .67 | .31 | .02 | 49 |
| | Gamma = −.59 | | | | Gamma = −.71 | | | |
| Professional climate | | | | | | | | |
| Low | .17 | .34 | .49 | 132 | .09 | .32 | .59 | 22 |
| Med. | .26 | .50 | .24 | 107 | .48 | .22 | .30 | 23 |
| High | .38 | .55 | .07 | 58 | .67 | .29 | .04 | 48 |
| | Gamma = −.45 | | | | Gamma = −.68 | | | |
| Company encouragement | | | | | | | | |
| Low | .18 | .42 | .40 | 117 | .29 | .29 | .42 | 24 |
| Med. | .21 | .42 | .37 | 79 | .41 | .22 | .37 | 27 |
| High | .34 | .48 | .18 | 100 | .63 | .32 | .05 | 41 |
| | Gamma = −.29 | | | | Gamma = −.48 | | | |

perceive high and low company encouragement who experience high alienation is 38 per cent, as compared with a difference of only 14 per cent for the engineers. Conversely, there is little difference in degree of alienation among engineers who perceive low as opposed to high company encouragement. For the scientists, however, there is a corresponding difference of 38 per cent.

Thus, the relationship between company encouragement and alienation from work is consistent with the general hypotheses. The greater the company encouragement, the less the feelings of work alienation among professionals. This relationship is stronger for those with the Ph.D. degree and for those trained as scientists than for those with the M.A. degree and for those trained as engineers.

Type of professional training *does not* appear to be an important conditioning factor in the relationships involving freedom of research choice or professional climate. The relationships obtained are strong but similar in both partials. These two variables were most strongly associated with work alienation in the original relationships. The degree of association remained high in the partials when length of professional training was controlled (although the relationships were stronger for the Ph.D.'s than for the M.A.'s, as expected). Unlike the relationships obtained with type of supervisor or company encouragement, however, the relationship between these variables and work alienation remain very strong and about the same for both scientific and engineering personnel.

This unanticipated finding suggests that these two aspects of the organizational structure are important to *both* scientists and engineers. Moreover, since these relationships also remained strong when length of professional training was controlled, it may be concluded that having freedom to choose research projects and working in a professional atmosphere are more important than type of supervisor or amount of company encouragement as these aspects of the organizational structure are related to the experiencing of work alienation among professionals.

### ORGANIZATIONAL UNIT

As previously described, the goals of the Laboratory are more concerned with pure or basic scientific research whereas the goals of the Aero-Space Group are more concerned with traditional research and development work. Therefore, the Laboratory should be characterized by less organizational con-

***Table 3—Relationship Between Work Alienation and Four Indicators of Organizational Control and Professional Incentive Structures: By Type of Professional Training***

| | *Type of professional training* | | | | | | | |
|---|---|---|---|---|---|---|---|---|
| | *ENGINEERS WORK ALIENATION* | | | | *SCIENTISTS WORK ALIENATION* | | | |
| *Control-incentive structure* | *Low* | *Med.* | *High* | *N* | *Low* | *Med.* | *High* | *N* |
| **Supervisory type** | | | | | | | | |
| Directive | .09 | .35 | .56 | 32 | .10 | .28 | .62 | 29 |
| Participatory | .30 | .42 | .28 | 90 | .34 | .42 | .24 | 67 |
| Laissez-faire | .21 | .47 | .32 | 89 | .51 | .36 | .13 | 85 |
| | Gamma = −.12 | | | | Gamma = −.49 | | | |
| **Research choice** | | | | | | | | |
| Low | .10 | .38 | .52 | 92 | .14 | .28 | .58 | 57 |
| Med. | .26 | .52 | .22 | 89 | .43 | .40 | .17 | 65 |
| High | .59 | .37 | .03 | 27 | .55 | .42 | .03 | 60 |
| | Gamma = −.61 | | | | Gamma = −.60 | | | |
| **Professional climate** | | | | | | | | |
| Low | .16 | .31 | .53 | 89 | .15 | .37 | .48 | 65 |
| Med. | .20 | .53 | .27 | 74 | .43 | .34 | .23 | 56 |
| High | .41 | .50 | .09 | 46 | .59 | .38 | .03 | 60 |
| | Gamma = −.49 | | | | Gamma = −.58 | | | |
| **Company encouragement** | | | | | | | | |
| Low | .21 | .42 | .37 | 87 | .19 | .35 | .46 | 54 |
| Med. | .23 | .35 | .42 | 60 | .30 | .40 | .30 | 46 |
| High | .24 | .53 | .23 | 62 | .57 | .45 | .08 | 79 |
| | Gamma = −.13 | | | | Gamma = −.55 | | | |

trol and more professional incentives than the Aero-Space Group. In addition, since alienation from work is related to differences in organizational structure, professionals working in the Laboratory should experience less alienation than professionals working in the Aero-Space Group.

Table 4 shows striking differences in the control and incentive structures of the two organizational units. In each of the four comparisons, there is less control and more incentives in the Laboratory than in the Aero-Space Group.

That these differences in organizational structure are reflected in differences in the degree of work alienation experienced by the professionals is shown in Table 5. In the Laboratory, only 4 per cent experienced high work alienation as compared with 34 per cent of those persons in the Aero-Space Group. Moreover, 63 per cent of those in the Laboratory experienced low alienation as compared to only 25 per cent of those in the Aero-Space Group. Thus, type of organizational unit is clearly related to degree of work alienation in the expected direction.

A question may arise concerning this interpretation. It is clear that the properties of the organizational structure dealt with here are defined empirically in terms of the professional's *perception* of the type of structure in which he is employed. Therefore, a question may arise as to whether the respondents are *accurately* perceiving the structure or merely perceiving it in such a manner as to be *consistent* with their previous training.

This question is a crucial one since all of the previous findings rely upon empirical indicators which ask the respondent to describe the structure as he perceives it. Thus, these relationships may reflect an association between the way these persons perceive the structure and work alienation rather than an association between organizational structure and work alienation. Moreover, it is clear from inspection of the previous tables that there is a "hidden" association between length and type of professional training and work alienation. Therefore, it is possible that the differences in degree of work alienation observed between the two organizational units is simply a result of the differing *composition* of the members within each unit with respect to length and type of professional training. To answer this question, it is necessary to examine the relationship between organizational unit and degree of work alienation while controlling for length and type of professional training.[36]

36. This type of analysis controls for the compositional effect in terms of the similarity in length and type of professional training of the professionals employed by each unit. It should be indicated that differences in recruitment

***Table 4—Respondents' Perceptions of Organizational Control and Professional Incentive Structures: By Organizational Unit***

| Control-incentive structure | *Organizational unit* AERO-SPACE GROUP Per cent | Number | BASIC LABORATORY Per cent | Number |
|---|---|---|---|---|
| Supervisor | | | | |
| Directive | 17 | (64) | 2 | (1) |
| Participatory | 43 | (158) | 20 | (10) |
| Laissez-faire | 40 | (145) | 78 | (38) |
| Research choice | | | | |
| Low | 42 | (151) | 8 | (4) |
| Med. | 44 | (162) | 6 | (3) |
| High | 14 | (51) | 86 | (43) |
| Professional climate | | | | |
| Low | 44 | (158) | 0 | (0) |
| Med. | 38 | (136) | 10 | (5) |
| High | 18 | (64) | 90 | (45) |
| Company encouragement | | | | |
| Low | 40 | (142) | 4 | (2) |
| Med. | 28 | (100) | 20 | (10) |
| High | 32 | (112) | 76 | (37) |
| Total | 100 | (369) | 100 | (50) |

Tables 6 and 7 show the partials obtained when length and type of professional training are controlled. It will be noted that the direction of association remains consistent across the four partials. The difference between Aero-Space Group and Basic Laboratory personnel in experiencing low work alienation is over 30 per cent in all four partials, with Laboratory personnel experiencing much less alienation than Aero-Space personnel. Moreover, the difference between personnel with high work alienation in the two units is also 30 per cent in three of four partials. This finding, then, lends additional support to the findings concerning the effects of organizational structure on feelings of work alienation among professional personnel.

procedures, in professional ability, and in type of work actually engaged in by the professionals may also yield differences in the kinds of professionals employed by each unit and thus affect the relationship between their perceptions of the organizational structure and degree of work alienation.

***Table 5—Degree of Work Alienation in Aero-Space and Basic Laboratory Organizational Units***

| | *WORK ALIENATION* | | | |
|---|---|---|---|---|
| *Organizational unit* | *Low* | *Med.* | *High* | *N* |
| Aero-space group | .25 | .41 | .34 | 349 |
| Basic laboratory | .63 | .33 | .04 | 49 |
| | Gamma = −.69 | | | |

## Summary and conclusions

This study examined the relationship between the type of organizational structure in which the professional performs his work activity and his experiencing feelings of alienation from work. This relationship was explored for each of four empirical indicators of organizational structure for all professionals, and separately for professionals differing in length and type of professional training and for professionals working in two very different organizational units.

In general, the findings of this research support the hypothesis that alienation from work is a consequence of the professional-bureaucratic dilemma for industrial scientists and engineers. Differences in type of supervision, freedom of research choice, professional climate, and company encouragement were associated with degree of work alienation in the expected manner.

The conditioning effects of length and type of professional training on the above relationships were only partially supported by these data. Alienation from work was more strongly associated with type of supervisor and degree of company encouragement among scientists and professionals with advanced training than for engineers and professionals with less advanced training. Freedom of research choice and professional climate were

***Table 6—Degree of Work Alienation in Aero-Space and Basic Laboratory Organizational Units: By Length of Professional Training***

| | *Length of professional training* | | | | | | | |
|---|---|---|---|---|---|---|---|---|
| | *M.A. DEGREE WORK ALIENATION* | | | | *PH.D. DEGREE WORK ALIENATION* | | | |
| *Organizational unit* | *Low* | *Med.* | *High* | *N* | *Low* | *Med.* | *High* | *N* |
| Aero-space group | .23 | .44 | .33 | 288 | .36 | .29 | .35 | 59 |
| Basic laboratory | .54 | .46 | .00 | 13 | .67 | .28 | .05 | 36 |
| | Gamma = −.48 | | | | Gamma = −.59 | | | |

***Table 7—Degree of Work Alienation in Aero-Space and Basic Laboratory Organizational Units: By Type of Professional Training***

| | *Type of professional training* | | | | | | | |
|---|---|---|---|---|---|---|---|---|
| | *ENGINEERS WORK ALIENATION* | | | | *SCIENTISTS WORK ALIENATION* | | | |
| *Organizational unit* | *Low* | *Med.* | *High* | *N* | *Low* | *Med.* | *High* | *N* |
| Aero-space group | .21 | .43 | .36 | 199 | .31 | .38 | .31 | 147 |
| Basic laboratory | .58 | .42 | .00 | 12 | .65 | .30 | .05 | 37 |
| | Gamma = −.75 | | | | Gamma = −.62 | | | |

strongly associated with work alienation for all professionals. Moreover, these relationships remained strong when length and type of professional training were controlled.

This unanticipated finding is important when it is recalled that the largest group of professionals employed by the organization are engineers with M.A. or M.S. degrees. These data suggest, therefore, that research freedom and professional atmosphere are more important to the majority of professional personnel than are type of supervision and specific professional incentives (as these factors are related to the experiencing of work alienation).

Although the relationships involving research freedom and professional atmosphere are *similar* for both scientists and engineers, these professionals may be experiencing work alienation for *different* reasons. Freedom of research choice, "having time to pursue one's own research interests," and having "opportunities to obtain professional recognition outside the company" may be interpreted by these professionals in terms of different goals and reference groups. If scientists and engineers differ in their professional goals, then the alienation manifested by engineers may result from their lack of power and participation in organizational affairs whereas the alienation manifested by scientists may reflect their lack of autonomy to pursue their work with the passion Weber described. This interpretation is consistent with the findings obtained in the relationships involving company encouragement and type of supervisor. That these relationships were stronger for the scientists and for those with advanced training may reflect the facts that the specific incentives comprising the company encouragement index are more important for the attainment of scientific than organizational goals, and that working for Participatory supervisors reflects participation in the decision-making process for engineers and violation of professional freedom for scientists who prefer to be left alone as much as possible.

Striking differences were found in the organizational structures of the Aero-Space Group and the Basic Science Laboratory. In addition, degree of work alienation was found to be highly related to type of organizational unit, with Laboratory personnel experiencing a very low degree of alienation as compared with Aero-Space personnel. This relationship remained consistent with respect to direction and degree when length and type of professional training were controlled.

The very different organizational structures evident in the Laboratory and the Aero-Space Group, as well as the effect of such structures upon work alienation for different types of professionals within these units, raise questions concerning the empirical generality of many studies to date which have focused on the Laboratory rather than the larger unit in their analysis. This research suggests that caution should accompany attempts to generalize across units within an organization. Studies of Laboratory personnel may yield findings very different from those obtained from professionals working in the larger organization—where most professional scientists and engineers are in fact employed.

MICHAEL AIKEN and JERALD HAGE

# Organizational Alienation: A Comparative Analysis

A persistent theme both in contemporary novels and in commentaries about modern life is the alienation of modern man.[1] Social scientists have also become enamored, and perhaps inebriated, with the idea of alienation in modern society and have attempted to forge indices of man's sense of malaise. One major fault of most of these discussions is that alienation has been defined, measured, and discussed as if it represented some "free floating" human condition irrespective of specific social contexts which produce such mental states.[2]

Our concern in this paper is to examine the relationship between two dimensions of organization—centralization and formalization—and two types of alienation—alienation from work and alienation from expressive relations. For this purpose sixteen welfare organizations, staffed largely by professional workers, were compared on these dimensions.

Alienation from work reflects a feeling of disappointment with career and professional development, as well as disappointment over the inability to fulfill professional norms. Alienation from expressive relations reflects dissatisfaction in social relations with supervisors and fellow workers. These two types of alienation can be compared with two of those discussed by Marx, namely, alienation from the process of production and alienation from fellow workers.[3]

1. For example, see Erich Fromm, *Marx's Concept of Man*, New York: Frederick Ungar, 1961; Morton Grodzins, *The Loyal and the Disloyal*, Chicago: University of Chicago Press, 1956; Eric and Mary Josephson (eds.), *Man Alone: Alienation in Modern Society*, New York: Dell, 1962; Eric Kahler, *The Tower and the Abyss*, New York: George Braziller, 1957; Herbert Marcuse, *One Dimensional Man*, Boston: Beacon Press, 1964; Robert Nisbet, *The Quest for Community*, New York: Oxford University Press, 1953; Fritz Pappenheim, *The Alienation of Modern Man*, New York: Monthly Review Press, 1959; and Gerald Sykes (ed.), *Alienation*, New York: George Braziller, 1964.

2. See, for example, Dwight G. Dean, "Alienation: Its Meaning and Measurement," *American Sociological Review*, 26 (October, 1961), pp. 753–58; Gwynn Nettler, "A Measure of Alienation," *American Sociological Review*, 22 (December, 1957), pp. 670–77; John P. Clark, "Measuring Alienation Within a Social System," *American Sociological Review*, 24 (December, 1959), pp. 849–52; Jan Hajda, "Alienation and Integration of Student Intellectuals," *American Sociological Review*, 26 (October, 1961), pp. 758–77; Melvin Seeman, "On the Meaning of Alienation," *American Sociological Review*, 24 (December, 1959), pp. 783–91. Recently John Horton has emphasized the failure of many researchers to specify the content in which alienation occurs. See John Horton, "The Dehumanization of Anomie and Alienation: A Problem in the Ideology of Sociology," *British Journal of Sociology*, 15 (December, 1964), pp. 283–300.

3. See *Karl Marx: Early Writings*, T. B. Bottomore (ed.), New York: McGraw-Hill, 1963, pp. 120–34. For a

This investigation was supported in part by a research grant from the Vocational Rehabilitation Administration, Department of Health, Education, and Welfare. We are also indebted to the National Science Foundation and the University of Wisconsin Computing Center for their research support. A special note of gratitude is owed to Jack Ladinsky, Anthony Costonis, Paul E. Mott, Jerry Marwell, and James Hudson for their critical comments on an earlier draft of this paper.

Reprinted from *American Sociological Review*, August, 1966, pp. 497–507, by permission of the authors and publisher. 

By *centralization* we mean the degree to which members participate in decision-making. Our concept of centralization is similar in part to that of Pugh and his associates. They define centralization as "... the locus of authority to make decisions affecting the organization."[4] But there are two important aspects of centralization. First, organizations vary in the extent to which members are assigned tasks and then provided with the freedom to implement them without interruption from superiors; we call this the degree of hierarchy of authority.[5] A second, and equally important, aspect of the distribution of power is the degree to which staff members participate in setting the goals and policies of the entire organization; we call this the degree of participation in decision-making.[6]

The findings of a number of studies suggest that highly centralized organizations—those with little autonomy over individually assigned tasks and little participation in agency-wide decisions—are likely to have high rates of work alienation. Blauner argues that workers have strong feelings of powerlessness in industries such as textiles and automobiles in which the workers have little control over the conditions of employment (with respect to both company-wide policies and the individual worker's immediate process).[7] Pearlin noted greater alienation among nurses if the authority structure was too rigid and impersonal.[8] Still other studies suggest that organizations characterized by a rigid hierarchy of authority have little cohesion among workers.[9] This lack of cohesion should be reflected in a high degree of alienation from fellow workers.

The potential for both types of alienation in organizations with an unequal distribution of power should be even greater in those that have a professional staff than in those that lack such a staff.[10] Professionals have advanced training and normally adopt codes of professional behavior that foster norms of autonomy and expectations of involvement in shaping the goals of the organization.[11] If they

discussion of the pre-Marxian uses of the concept of alienation, see Nathan Rotenstreich, "On the Ecstatic Sources of the Concept of Alienation," *Review of Metaphysics*, 16 (March, 1963), pp. 550–55.

4. D. S. Pugh, D. J. Hickson, C. R. Hinings, K. M. Macdonald, C. Turner and T. Lupton, "A Conceptual Scheme for Organizational Analysis," *Administrative Science Quarterly*, 8 (December, 1963), pp. 289–315. See also Jerald Hage, "An Axiomatic Theory of Organizations," *Administrative Science Quarterly*, 10 (December, 1965), pp. 289–321.

5. What we have called hierarchy of authority has been referred to by some researchers as "closeness" or "tightness" of supervision. See, for example, Peter M. Blau and W. Richard Scott, *Formal Organizations*, San Francisco: Chandler Publishing Company, 1962, pp. 140–64.

6. The work of Tannenbaum and his associates reflects a concern with what we have called centralization. See, for example, Arnold S. Tannenbaum, "The Concept of Organizational Control," *The Journal of Social Issues*, 12 (1956), pp. 50–60; Arnold S. Tannenbaum, "Control Structure and Union Functions," *American Journal of Sociology*, 61 (May, 1956), pp. 536–45; Arnold S. Tannenbaum, "Control and Effectiveness in a Voluntary Organization," *American Journal of Sociology*, 67 (July, 1961), pp. 33–46; and Arnold S. Tannenbaum and Basil S. Georgopoulos, "The Distribution of Control in Formal Organizations," *Social Forces*, 36 (October, 1957), pp. 44–50.

7. Robert Blauner, *Alienation and Freedom*, Chicago: University of Chicago Press, 1964.

8. Leonard Pearlin, "Alienation from Work: A Study of Nursing Personnel," *American Sociological Review*, 27 (June, 1962), pp. 314–26.

9. Blauner, *op. cit.*; Arthur J. Kover, "Reorganization in an Advertising Agency," *Human Organization*, 22 (Winter, 1963–64), pp. 252–59; Michel Crozier, *The Bureaucratic Phenomenon*, Stanford: Stanford University Press, 1963; Tom Burns and G. M. Stalker, *The Management of Innovation*, London: Travistock Publications, 1961. The latter work characterized organizations as having either an organic structure (high integration, low centralization, and low formalization) or a mechanical structure (low integration, high centralization and high formalization). Integration is measured not only by the frequency of interaction but also by the number of different social positions that interact. See also Stanley H. Udy, Jr., "The Comparative Analysis of Organizations," in *Handbook of Organizations*, James G. March (ed.), Chicago: Rand McNally, 1965, especially pp. 702–5.

10. Etzioni has suggested the distinction between professional, semi-professional, and nonprofessional organizations. The social casework agencies in our study are examples of what he calls semi-professional organizations while psychiatric hospitals are examples of what he calls professional organizations. The rehabilitation organizations in our study are more difficult to classify because of the variations in professionalism of their staffs. We consider it less useful to employ such a typological approach than to regard the degree of professionalism as a variable and then to relate this to other organizational properties. See Amitai Etzioni, *Modern Organizations*, Englewood Cliffs, N.J.: Prentice-Hall, 1964, pp. 75–93.

11. See Mary E. W. Goss, "Physicians in Bureaucracy: A Case Study of Professional Pressure on Organizational Roles," (unpublished doctoral dissertation) Columbia University, 1959, chapter 1, a discussion of the various pressures against the exertion of control over professionals. For a review of the conflicts between professionals and managers see William Kornhauser, *Scientists in Industry*, Berkeley: University of California Press, 1962, chapter 1; and Peter Blau and W. Richard Scott, *Formal Organizations, op. cit.*, pp. 60–74.

are denied access to the seat of power, they are likely to become dissatisfied with their jobs. Job alienation may spill over into other aspects of organizational life. Thus organizations in which expectations of decision-making are violated may also have less communication among staff members, and alienation from fellow workers may increase.

Another tradition of research in industrial relations has been concerned with the correlates of worker morale. In a review of the literature, Herzberg *et al.* summarized studies which demonstrate that quality of supervision is highly related to worker morale.[12] This tradition of research is obviously tapping some of the same dimensions of organizational life that we have attempted to capture. However we have chosen to conceive of dissatisfaction with work situation in terms of alienation. Few of the studies reported by Herzberg looked at organizational characteristics as they relate to morale; most were psychologically oriented.

This discussion leads us to hypothesize that both alienation from the job and alienation from fellow workers will be greater in highly centralized organizations than in decentralized ones.

By *formalization* we mean the degree of work standardization and the amount of deviation that is allowed from standards. Blau and Scott have described bureaucratic formalization as:

"... official procedures ... which prescribe the appropriate reactions to recurrent situations and furnish established guides for decision-making."[13]

A high degree of formalization implies not only a preponderance of rules defining jobs and specifying what is to be done, but also the enforcement of those rules.[14] The two French public agencies described by Crozier had an almost obsessive reliance on routines and procedures, and these organizations were characterized not only by workers' dissatisfaction with the conditions of employment, but also by little worker solidarity.[15] In a study of an air force tracking station Gross noted that the great emphasis on rules in the organization resulted in workers feeling that the work was meaningless.[16] Worthy found that an increase in supervisory pressures brought about a decline in worker morale.[17] Such findings would lead us to expect alienation from work and from expressive relations to be greater in organizations which place too much reliance on codification of tasks and observation of rules. The nature of professional social welfare work simply does not lend itself to easy codification of jobs or reliance on rules without numerous exceptions. We therefore hypothesize that the degree of alienation from work and from fellow workers will vary comcomitantly with the degree of formalization of an organization.

## Study design and methodology

The data upon which this study is based were gathered in sixteen social welfare agencies located in a large midwest metropolis in 1964. Ten agencies are private; six are either public or branches of public agencies. These agencies are all of the larger welfare organizations that provide rehabilitation and psychiatric services or services for the mentally retarded as defined by the directory of the Community Chest. The agencies vary in size from twelve to several hundred. Interviews were conducted with 314 staff members of these sixteen organizations. Respondents within each organization were selected by the following criteria:

12. Frederick Herzberg, *et al.*, *Job Attitudes: Review of Research and Opinion*, Pittsburgh: Psychological Service of Pittsburgh, 1957, pp. 37–93.

13. Blau and Scott, *op. cit.*, p. 240.

14. Organizational researchers such as Udy have argued for the conceptualization of organizations as a system of variables rather than as ideal-typical categories such as formal or informal. We agree with Udy on this point of view, but we have chosen to retain the concept "formalization" as a variable reflecting the degree to which rules obtain that restrict behavior as well as the degree to which rules are enforced. Udy also says that informal (as opposed to formal) is often used to refer to aspects of organization which are not part of the rationally conceived organizations. We are not implying the latter use of the concept "formalization." See Stanley H. Udy, Jr., "'Bureaucracy' and 'Rationality' in Weber's Organizational Theory: An Empirical Study," *American Sociological Review*, 24 (December, 1959), pp. 791–95. In a later writing, Udy has used the concept "specificity of the job" to refer in part to what we have called job codification; he has no exact counterpart for what we have called rule observation. See Udy, "The Comparative Analysis of Organizations," *op. cit.*, p. 793.

15. Crozier, *op. cit.*

16. Edward Gross, "Some Functional Consequences of Primary Controls in Formal Work Organizations," *American Sociological Review*, 18 (August, 1953), pp. 368–73.

17. James C. Worthy, "Organizational Structure and Employee Morale," *American Sociological Review*, 15 (April, 1950), pp. 169–79.

a) All executive directors and department heads;
b) In departments of less than ten members one half of the staff selected randomly;
c) In departments of more than ten members, one-third of the staff selected randomly.

Nonsupervisory administrative and maintenance personnel were not interviewed.

This sampling procedure divides the organization into levels and departments. Job occupants in the upper levels are selected because they are most likely to be key decision-makers and determine organizational policy; job occupants in the lower levels are selected randomly. The different ratios within departments ensure that smaller departments are adequately represented. Professionals, such as psychiatrists, social workers, and rehabilitation counselors, are included because they are intimately involved in the achievement of organizational goals and are likely to have organizational power. Non-professionals, such as attendants, janitors and secretaries, are excluded because they are not directly involved in the achievement of organizational goals and have little or no power. The numbers of interviews varied from seven in the smallest to forty-one in one of the larger agencies.

The units of analysis in this study are organizations and not individuals in the organizations. Information obtained from respondents is pooled to reflect properties of the sixteen organizations. These properties are then related to one another.[18] Aggregating individual data in this way presents methodological problems for which there are as yet no satisfactory solutions. For example, if all respondents are equally weighted, undue weight is given to respondents lower in the hierarchy. Yet those higher in the chain of command—not those lower in the chain of command—are most likely to make the decisions which give an agency its ethos.[19]

We attempted to compensate for this by computing an organizational score from the means of social position within the agency.[20] A social position is defined by the level or stratum in the organization and the type of professional activity. For example, if an agency's professional staff consists of psychiatrists and social workers, each divided into two hierarchical levels, the agency has four social positions: supervisory psychiatrists, psychiatrists, supervisory social workers and social workers. A mean is then computed for each social position in the agency. The organizational score for a given variable is determined by computing the average of all social position means in the agency.

Computation of means for each social position has the advantage of avoiding the potential problem created by the use of two sampling ratios. In effect, responses are standardized by organizational location—level and occupation—and then combined into the organizational score. Computation of means of social position also has the major theoretical advantage of focusing on the sociological perspective of organizational reality.[21] An organization is a

18. The measurement of organizational properties has variously been referred to as contextual analysis, structural-effects analysis, or compositional-effects analysis. See, for example, Paul F. Lazarsfeld and Herbert Menzel, "On the Relation between Individual and Collective Properties," in Amitai Etzioni (ed.), *Complex Organizations: A Sociological Reader*, New York: Holt, Rinehart and Winston, 1961, pp. 422–40; and James S. Coleman, "Research Chronicle: *The Adolescent Society*," in *Sociologists At Work*, Phillip E. Hammond (ed.), New York: Basic Books, 1964, pp. 184–211. Additional discussion of the problem is found in Peter M. Blau, "Formal Organization: Dimensions of Analysis," *American Journal of Sociology*, 63 (July, 1957), pp. 58–69; Peter M. Blau, "Structural Effects," *American Sociological Review*, 25 (April, 1960), pp. 178–93; James A. Davis, Joe L. Spaeth and Carolyn Huson, "A Technique for Analyzing the Effects of Group Composition," *American Sociological Review*, 26 (April, 1961), pp. 215–25; and Arnold S. Tannenbaum and Jerald G. Bachman, "Structural versus Individual Effects," *American Journal of Sociology*, 69 (May, 1964), pp. 585–95. Here we are primarily concerned with relating structural or compositional effects to each other, *i.e.*, we take the organization as the unit of analysis, but we do not attempt to separate individual from structural effects.

19. Blau's techniques are subject to this criticism. Selvin and Hagstrom also suggest giving equal weight to individual respondents regardless of social position. However, in the college residence groups that they studied, the problem did not arise because there were few discernible social positions. See Hanan C. Selvin and Warren O. Hagstrom, "The Empirical Classification of Formal Groups," *American Sociological Review*, 28 (June, 1963), pp. 399–411.

20. The two procedures produce very similar results. Product-moment correlation coefficients between them are as follows:

| | |
|---|---|
| Hierarchy of authority | .70 |
| Rule observation | .88 |
| Actual participation in decisions | .90 |
| Job codification | .68 |
| Alienation from work | .89 |
| Alienation from expressive relations | .88 |

21. Despite the frequency with which the concept of social position is found in sociology texts, it is rarely used

collection of social positions rather than an aggregate of individuals; sociological properties are more than a summation of psychological properties.

The two types of alienation discussed in this paper were measured with an index of work alienation and an index of alienation from expressive relations. Alienation from work was computed on the basis of responses to the following six questions:

1. How satisfied are you that you have been given enough authority by your board of directors to do your job well?
2. How satisfied are you with your present job when you compare it to similar positions in the state?
3. How satisfied are you with the progress you are making towards the goals which you set for yourself in your present position?
4. On the whole, how satisfied are you that (your superior) accepts you as a professional expert to the degree to which you are entitled by reason of position, training and experience?
5. On the whole, how satisfied are you with your present job when you consider the expectations you had when you took the job?
6. How satisfied are you with your present job in light of career expectations?

Alienation from expressive relations was computed on the basis of responses to the following two questions:

1. How satisfied are you with your supervisor?
2. How satisfied are you with your fellow workers?[22]

There was a strong relationship between these two indices of alienation ($r = 0.75$).

The two aspects of centralization were measured by an index of hierarchy of authority and an index of participation in decision-making. The index of hierarchy of authority was computed by first averaging the replies of individual respondents to each of the following five statements:

1. There can be little action taken here until a supervisor approves a decision.
2. A person who wants to make his own decisions would be quickly discouraged here.
3. Even small matters have to be referred to someone higher up for a final answer.
4. I have to ask my boss before I do almost anything.
5. Any decision I make has to have my boss' approval.

Responses could vary from 1 (definitely false) to 4 (definitely true). The individual scores were then combined into an organizational score as described above.[23]

The index of participation in decision-making was based on the following four questions:

1. How frequently do you usually participate in the decision to hire new staff?
2. How frequently do you usually participate in decisions on the promotion of any of the professional staff?
3. How frequently do you participate in decisions on the adoption of new policies?
4. How frequently do you participate in the decisions on the adoption of new programs?

Respondents were assigned numerical scores from 1 to 5 depending on whether they answered "never," "seldom," "sometimes," "often," or "always," respectively, to these questions. An average score on these questions was computed for each respondent, and then the data were aggregated into organizational scores as described above.

The index of hierarchy of authority shows the extent of reliance upon supervisors in making decisions about individually assigned tasks. The

in research. An interview schedule seldom asks a respondent to report what he does as an occupant of a particular social position. Even less common is the interview schedule that asks a respondent to report characteristics of his social position, such as the proportion of time spent in particular activities or the frequency of interaction vis-à-vis other social positions.

22. The items in these indices were selected on the basis of a principal components solution factor analysis of thirteen items concerning the degree of satisfaction with various aspects of the respondents' work situation. The original battery of 13 items was taken from Neal Gross, Ward Mason and Alexander McEachern, *Explorations in Role Analysis*, New York: John Wiley, 1958, Appendix B. In their research they used a split-half reliability test while we used a factor analysis to determine unidimensionality. Etzioni called this latter concept "cohesion." See Amitai Etzioni, *A Comparative Analysis of Complex Organizations*, New York: The Free Press, 1961, pp. 196–98.

23. The items in this index were selected on the basis of a principal components solution factor analysis of 21 items in a "hierarchy of authority" battery and a "rules" battery, as reported by Richard H. Hall in "An Empirical Other of Bureaucratic Dimensions and Their Relation to Study Organizational Characteristics," unpublished Ph.D. dissertation, Ohio State University, 1961. See also Richard H. Hall, "The Concept of Bureaucracy: An Empirical Assessment," *American Journal of Sociology*, 69 (July, 1963), pp. 32–40. Our factor analysis indicated that there were several discrete dimensions among Hall's hierarchy of authority and rules batteries, including the index of job codification and the index of rule observation—indicators of formalization that are discussed below. We chose to base our analysis on the factor analytic structure of these items, to assure us of discrete measures, rather than to retain Hall's scales for sake of comparability.

index of participation in decision-making reflects the relative degree of participation in decisions affecting the entire organization, such as those involving the adoption of new programs, new policies, and the hiring and promotion of personnel. There is a strong inverse relationship between these two measures of centralization, as shown in Table 1.

The two aspects of formalization were measured with two scales: the index of job codification and the index of rule observation. The index of job codification was based on the following five questions:

1. I feel that I am my own boss in most matters.
2. A person can make his own decisions without checking with anybody else.
3. How things are done here is left up to the person doing the work.
4. People here are allowed to do almost as they please.
5. Most people here make their own rules on the job.

Replies to these questions were scored from 1 (definitely true) to 4 (definitely false), and then each respondent's answers were averaged. Organizational scores were then aggregated as described previously.

The index of rule observation was computed by averaging, as described previously, responses to the following two statements:

1. The employees are constantly being checked on for rule violations.
2. People here feel as though they are constantly being watched, to see that they obey all the rules.

The index of job codification reflects the degree to which job incumbents must consult rules in fulfilling professional responsibilities; the index of rule observation reflects the degree to which employees are observed for rule violations. These measures are not related. (See Table 1.)

## Findings

### CENTRALIZATION AND ALIENATION

These professionalized and semi-professionalized social welfare organizations in our study have little hierarchy of authority, although there is considerable variation in the index of participation in decision-making. The organizational scores on the index of hierarchy of authority vary from 1.50 to 2.10 (where the possible scores range from a low of 1.00 to a high of 4.00). In a possible range of scores on the index of participation in decision-making from 1.00 (low participation) to 5.00 (high participation), these agencies had scores of 1.68 to 3.69.

Litwak has suggested that organizations performing primarily non-uniform tasks are more likely to be decentralized.[24] All of our organizations, because they provide physical and social rehabilitation services, perform relatively non-uniform tasks. The sixteen organizations are skewed in the direction of decentralization (as measured by the index of hierarchy of authority), although they tend to be more centralized on the index of participation in decision-making. There is still considerable variation among these agencies in their degree of centralization, however, and such variations have important implications for the degree of alienation.

There is a correlation of 0.49 between the degree

24. Eugene Litwak, "Models of Bureaucracy Which Permit Conflict," *American Journal of Sociology*, 67 (September, 1961), pp. 177–84.

***Table 1—Product-Moment Correlations Between Measures of Centralization and Formalization, for Sixteen Welfare Organizations***

| *Measures of centralization and formalization* | *CENTRALIZATION* | | *FORMALIZATION* | |
|---|---|---|---|---|
| | *Hierarchy of authority* | *Participation in decision-making* | *Job codification* | *Rule observation* |
| Centralization | | | | |
| Hierarchy of authority | . . . | −.55 | .14 | .43 |
| Participation in decisions | . . . | . . . | −.12 | −.26 |
| Formalization | | | | |
| Job codification | . . . | . . . | . . . | −.03 |
| Rule observation | . . . | . . . | . . . | . . . |

Note: The units of analysis are the sixteen organizations in our study, not the 314 individual respondents. With so few cases, product-moment correlation coefficients are highly sensitive to even slight modifications of numerical scores. Since these sixteen organizations constitute a universe of organizations, tests of statistical significance are inappropriate.

of hierarchy and alienation from work as shown in panel A of Table 2. The relationship between degree of hierarchy and alienation from expressive relations is approximately the same (0.45). Organizations that rely heavily on hierarchical arrangements are likely to be characterized by both work alienation and alienation from expressive relations. These more centralized authority structures also have less cohesion among staff members. One way to explain these results is that a strict hierarchy of job authority reduces the opportunities for communication among the members of the organization; the consequence of reduced communication is alienation from fellow workers.

The lack of participation in agency decision-making is strongly related to alienation from work ($r = -0.59$), as shown in panel A of Table 2. Thus alienation is higher in those organizations in which staff members have a small voice in agency-wide decisions. Limited participation in decision-making has less of an effect on alienation from expressive relationships ($r = -0.17$).[25]

These results are broadly consistent with the generalizations derived from the Human Relations school of organizational behavior. A high degree of centralization as measured by participation in organization-wide decisions and degree of control over assigned tasks is related to the presence of work alienation and disenchantment with expressive relations, especially with superordinates.

### FORMALIZATION AND ALIENATION

The agencies in our study were found to have relatively little formalization. On the index of job codification, which may range from 1.00 (low formalization) to 4.00 (high formalization), the scores of our agencies were between 2.22 and 2.70. On the index of rule observation, the second indicator of formalization, our 16 organizations had organizational scores of 1.11 to 1.90 on a scale which may range from 1.00 (low rule observation) to 4.00 (high rule observation).

As shown in panel B of Table 2, there is a direct relationship between the degree of job codification and both alienation from work ($r = 0.51$) and alienation from expressive relations ($r = 0.23$). The former relationship is much stronger than the latter. This means that there is great dissatisfaction with work in those organizations in which jobs are rigidly structured; rigidity may lead to strong feelings of work dissatisfaction but does not appear to have such a deleterious impact on social relations in the organization.

There is a strong direct relationship between the index of rule observation and both alienation from work ($r = 0.55$) and alienation from expressive relations ($r = 0.65$). Organizations in which rules are strictly enforced have high degrees of both work alienation and alienation from expressive relations. The relationship between rule observation and the latter type of alienation is slightly greater than with alienation from work, suggesting that disruptions in social relations may be more likely to occur under conditions of strict enforcement of rules while work alienation may be more likely to occur under conditions of highly structured jobs.[26]

25. One could argue that a low degree of participation in decision-making may have a different impact on satisfaction with relations with supervisors than with fellow workers. When we separated these two components, we found that there was a moderately strong inverse relationship between participation in decisions and alienation from supervisors ($r = -0.40$) but a direct relationship between participation and alienation from fellow workers ($r = +0.23$). This finding suggests that greater participation in organizational decisions is associated with positive affect towards supervisors but with negative affect towards fellow workers. Other relationships discussed in this paper were unaffected by analyzing the two components of this index separately.

26. Some might argue that such relationships as these might simply be a function of various environmental factors such as age of the organization, auspices (whether private or public), size of the organization, and major function (limited commitment to clients—as in social casework agencies, or high commitment to clients—as in sheltered workshops and psychiatric hospitals). This will be the subject of a forthcoming paper; preliminary analysis suggests that the relationships discussed in this paper remain essentially unchanged when these factors are controlled.

***Table 2—Product-Moment Correlations Between Measures of Alienation and Measures of Centralization and Formalization, for Sixteen Welfare Organizations***

| Measures of centralization and formalization | MEASURES OF ALIENATION: Alienation from work | Alienation from expressive relations |
|---|---|---|
| A. Centralization | | |
| Hierarchy of authority | .49 | .45 |
| Participation in decisions | −.59 | −.17 |
| B. Formalization | | |
| Job codification | .51 | .23 |
| Rule observation | .55 | .65 |

MULTIVARIATE ANALYSIS OF CENTRALIZATION, FORMALIZATION, AND ALIENATION

One of the problems confronting the social scientist is determining the effect of a variable independently of all others. The relationship between variables such as hierarchy of authority and work alienation may be merely the accidental consequence of their relationships with a third variable, such as participation in decision-making. In an attempt to determine the net effect of independent variables we employed partial and multiple regression analyses.

The first question concerns the two measures of centralization—hierarchy of authority and participation in decision-making—and their relationships with alienation from work and alienation from expressive relations. Panel A of Table 3 shows that participation in decision-making is more closely associated with work alienation than hierarchy of authority when the effect of each is controlled. While the partial correlation coefficients of each with work alienation is less than the zero-order correlation, the partial correlation of participation in decisions ($r_{Y2.1} = -0.45$) is greater than that of hierarchy of authority ($r_{Y1.2} = 0.24$). The beta weights show a similar relationship. On the other hand, hierarchy of authority is more strongly related to alienation from expressive relations than participation in decision-making when the effect of the latter is controlled. The partial correlation of hierarchy of authority with alienation from expressive relations, controlling for participation in decisions, is essentially the same as the zero-order relationship ($r_{Z1.2} = 0.43$). The relationship between participation in decisions and alienation from expressive relations is still weak, and reversed, ($r_{Z2.1} = 0.10$) when the effect of hierarchy is controlled. Again, the beta weights show similar results. It seems that work alienation depends more on the degree to which staff members participate in agency-wide decision-making, while alienation from fellow workers depends more on the degree to which supervisors must be consulted in fulfilling individually assigned tasks. Thus disruptions in social relations seem to emerge from the closeness of interaction implicit in little autonomy in decisions about individual tasks. Decisions about the allocation of agency resources should—and do—have little effect on the nature of social relations.

Both rule observation and job codification, our two measures of formalization, have strong and independent relationships with work alienation as shown in Panel B of Table 3. The partial correlation coefficients of each with alienation from work, controlling for the influence of the other, are 0.66 and 0.63 respectively. In each case the partial correlation is slightly greater than the zero-order correlation. The presence of either or both of these aspects of formalization in an organization appears to be associated with a high degree of work alienation. This is not the case with respect to alienation from expressive relations, however. The degree of rule observation has a much stronger relationship with alienation from expressive relations than the degree of job codification as shown in Panel B of Table 3. The relationship between job codification and alienation from expressive relations is slightly in-

***Table 3—Coefficients of Partial Correlation and Beta Weights Indicating Relative Importance of Measures of Centralization and Formalization in Affecting Alienation, for Sixteen Welfare Organizations***

| | *Measures of alienation* | | | | | |
|---|---|---|---|---|---|---|
| | *ALIENATION FROM WORK (Y)* | | | *ALIENATION FROM EXPRESSIVE RELATIONS (Z)* | | |
| *Measures of centralization and formalization* | *Coefficients of partial correlation* | | *Beta weights*[a] | *Coefficients of partial correlation* | | *Beta weights*[a] |
| A. Centralization | | | | | | |
| 1. Hierarchy of authority | .24 | | .234 | .43 | | .511 |
| 2. Participation in decisions | −.45 | | −.465 | .10 | | .107 |
| Multiple correlation | | .63 | | | .46 | |
| B. Formalization | | | | | | |
| 3. Job codification | .63 | | .522 | .32 | | .244 |
| 4. Rule observation | .66 | | .569 | .68 | | .660 |
| Multiple correlation | | .76 | | | .70 | |

[a] Regression coefficients in standard measure.

creased when the influence of rule observation is removed, however.

Having considered the relative influence of the indicators of centralization and formalization separately, we now ask which of these organizational properties is most importantly associated with our two types of alienation. As shown in Table 4, the degree of participation in decision-making ($r_{Y2.134} = -0.57$), the degree of rule observation ($r_{Y4.123} = 0.63$), and the degree of job codification ($r_{Y3.124} = 0.67$) have strong and independent effects on alienation from work. In fact, each of the two indicators of formalization has a slightly higher relationship with work alienation than participation in decision-making when the effect of the other variables is removed, but the differences are small. Thus, we could infer that the presence of a high degree of either aspect of formalization or a low degree of participation in organizational decisions is likely to induce work alienation. Among the four structural properties examined in this analysis, rule observation still has the strongest relationship with alienation from expressive relations when the effect of other variables is controlled ($r_{Z4\cdot 123} = 0.61$). Both hierarchy of authority and job codification have some independent and adverse effect on social relationships in these organizations, but the degree of rule observation is much more strongly related to alienation from expressive relations than either of these two factors.

Participation in decisions that shape the organization's direction, relatively unstructured jobs, and freedom from the restraints of enforced rules are important conditions for a climate of high work morale. Professionals in welfare organizations, by virtue of their advanced training, can make legitimate claims to involvement in policy formulation as well as demands for freedom from excessive constraints of rules; it is in those organizations where professionals are denied access to power or denied such freedom, or both, that work alienation is greatest. It is rule observation—a dimension of formalization—that is most highly associated with alienation from expressive relations. Rule observation is more highly related to this form of alienation than is either job codification or the two measures of centralization. As suggested earlier, rule observation implies close supervision by superiors which leads to disruptions in supervisor-staff member relations; this disruption in social ties evidently spills over into social relations with fellow workers.

## Summary and conclusions

In this study, we used the organization as the unit of analysis relating variation in several dimensions of agency structure to two kinds of alienation. This conceptualization is in the tradition of Marx's attempt to relate conditions of work to feelings of alienation. While Marx was primarily interested in the economic organization of total societies and its relationship with alienation, this study indicates that the problem of alienation also occurs in welfare agencies, schools and hospitals, both private and public.

We have shown that highly centralized and highly formalized organizational structures are characterized by greater work alienation and greater aliena-

***Table 4—Coefficients of Partial Correlation and Beta Weights Indicating Relative Importance of Measures of Centralization and Formalization in Affecting Alienation, for Sixteen Welfare Organizations***

| | *Measures of alienation* | | | |
|---|---|---|---|---|
| | *ALIENATION FROM WORK (Y)* | | *ALIENATION FROM EXPRESSIVE RELATIONS (Z)* | |
| *Measures of centralization and formalization* | *Coefficients of partial correlation* | *Beta weights*[a] | *Coefficients of partial correlation* | *Beta weights*[a] |
| Centralization | | | | |
| 1. Hierarchy of authority | −.01 | −.005 | .27 | .245 |
| 2. Participation in decisions | −.57 | −.421 | .17 | .141 |
| Formalization | | | | |
| 3. Job codification | .67 | .470 | .30 | .225 |
| 4. Rule observation | .63 | .460 | .61 | .591 |
| Multiple correlation | | .86 | .72 | |

[a] Regression coefficients in standard measure.

tion from expressive relations. Specifically, these two types of alienation are related to the absence of staff opportunities to participate in decisions concerning organizational policies and individually assigned tasks, and they are manifested where there are strict rules governing jobs and where rules are rigidly enforced. These findings confirm the position that it is indeed important—as Marx suggested more than a century ago—to consider different types of alienation. It is also important to consider the different aspects of organizational structure which give rise to distinctive forms of alienation. We have found that participation in decision-making—an aspect of centralization—as well as a high degree of both job codification and rule observation—aspects of formalization—have strong and independent effects on the degree of work alienation, while the degree of rule observation—an aspect of formalization—is the single best predictor of alienation from expressive relations. Excessive supervision was found to be associated with both types of alienation, but other structural properties were also associated with alienation from work. Future research should attempt to locate those structural properties that are associated with other types of alienation.

While a few previous research studies have explored the relationship between organizational structure and alienation, most prior organizational studies have not. Those which have were either: (1) case studies of single organizations which permitted only limited comparisons; or (2) studies which used the individual as the unit of analysis, relating individual perceptions of organizational structure to other individual reactions.

This research was done in social welfare organizations in which most staff members had some type of professional training. An organizational structure which restricts workplace freedom and participation in setting the goals of the organization was found to be associated with feelings of work alienation even among the members of professions—those individuals who have relatively high pay and prestige in our society.[27]

Variations in other aspects of organizational structure such as the degree of stratification, the relative emphasis on quality or quantity of client services, or the number and types of effective channels of communication may induce different types of alienation in an organization—perhaps types of alienation other than those discussed in this report. These results clearly indicate the importance of comparative organizational analysis.

27. Such findings are consistent with others which stress the importance of the content of the job in leading to work satisfaction. See, for example, Nancy C. Morse and Robert S. Weiss, "The Function and Meaning of Work and the Job," *American Sociological Review*, 20 (April, 1955), pp. 191–98.

# Part Five

# Organizations in Other Industrial Societies

In *The Rules of the Sociological Method*, Durkheim asserts that comparative sociology *is* sociology, that it is fundamental to the discipline. In this section the application of the comparative approach to the cross-national study of organizations is highlighted.

It is essential to an adequate understanding of organizations to consider fully the cultural and the organizational context within which they are embedded. The implications of this axiom are brought out by each of the five selections in different ways. By restricting our selections to highly industrialized societies it is possible to accent the importance of cultural differences for organizational structure and functioning. The five nations represented still differ considerably in degree of industrialization, even though they are comparatively homogeneous. The Soviet Union, France, the United States, Japan, and the United Kingdom are among the small elite group of the wealthiest and largest nations on earth. It was mainly to emphasize the differences between even the most highly industrialized nations that led us to omit organizational studies of the less-developed societies.

The essay by Bendix was chosen to lead this section for several reasons. Bendix is among the few organization theorists who have developed and applied a comparative frame of reference. He focuses on ideology, a key aspect of culture, as a means of differentiating industrial societies from one another. A theoretical perspective is presented that permits systematic comparison of the same societies over time and between a wide range of societies. In the larger study from which the selection was taken, England, Russia, the United States, and East Germany are distinguished analytically by their unique combinations of these characteristics: the extent to which entrepreneurs and managers form an autonomous class, the extent to which entrepreneurs and managers are controlled by the government, the existence of entrepreneurial ideologies when industry began, the nature of the ideologies of management in the nation's large-scale business enterprises. This study provides an historical context for viewing two nations, England and Russia, that are also represented in two problem-oriented studies.

The four remaining selections differ in scope and intent from the first. Richardson's analysis of a British and an American cargo ship reveals some of the consequences of differing cultural orientations toward authority for organizational structure. The greater deference toward authority of the British sailors allowed for the development of a control structure that was based on impersonal rules to a much lesser extent than in the American case.

It has become traditional in organizational research in the United States to assume that informal groups inevitably emerge. Crozier's study challenges this culture-bound generalization by demonstrating how French values, which stress individualism and personal autonomy, produced important effects on the extent and the nature of informal work groups in bureaucratic settings. Berliner's study turns our attention to an examination of the social pressures on the manager rather than the worker. The analysis of "storming" in Soviet enterprises suggests the importance of the nation's overall economic and political structure for managerial behavior. Berliner's research not only reveals the key role of cultural and political values, but in addition demonstrates the intricate interdependence with the environment especially characteristic of factory organizations in a highly centralized economic structure.

The final study of the Japanese factory by Abegglen raises a number of questions, the most important ones centering on the effects of the introduction of modern industry in other societies. As Abegglen notes: "The Japanese case suggests that these experiences and the organizational system used in the West are not necessary to the introduction of industry into another social system." All sciences seek to establish universal propositions. Cross-cultural analysis of organizational structure and development, like the method of comparative study of organizations within a single society, serves the important function of raising the fundamental question of the universality of the relationship in question.

REINHARD BENDIX

# The Impact of Ideas on Organizational Structure

## Major themes

This study deals with the role of ideas in the management of economic enterprises. Wherever enterprises are set up, a few command and many obey. The few, however, have seldom been satisfied to command without a higher justification even when they abjured all interest in ideas, and the many have seldom been docile enough not to provoke such justifications. This study deals with the ideas and interests of the few who have managed the work force of industrial and business enterprises since the Industrial Revolution. It is particularly concerned with ideas which pertain to the relations between workers and employers or their agents. Such ideas have been expressed by employers, financiers, public-relations men, personnel specialists, general managers, engineers, economists, political theorists, psychologists, government officials, policemen, political agitators, and many, many others. All these men have had in common a direct concern with the problems of industrial organization, whether or not they have worked in some managerial capacity themselves.

Industrialization has been defended in terms of the claim that the few will lead as well as benefit the many. It has been attacked in terms of the assertion that both the exploiting few and the exploited many are made to suffer, body and soul. The most rapidly advancing industrialized nations, the United States and Soviet Russia, are heir to these conflicting ideological antecedents. Since this conflict is the point of departure for the present study, it is appropriate to formulate at the beginning the common core of the two entrepreneurial or managerial ideologies which have been used in the advance of industrialization.[1]

Reprinted from *Work and Authority in Industry*, pp. 1–5, 13–21, by permission of the author and publisher. 

1. I shall use the phrase "ideologies of management" as the generic designation. All ideas which are espoused by or for those who exercise authority in economic enterprises, and which seek to explain and justify that authority, are subsumed under this phrase. "Entrepreneurial ideologies" will refer to such ideas in the early phase of industrialization and "managerial ideologes" will refer to the analogous ideas in modern industries. The term "industrialization" is used to refer to the process by which large numbers of employees are concentrated in single enterprises and become dependent upon the directing and coordinating activities of entrepreneurs and managers. (By "large numbers" I refer to any number of employees in excess of that which still permits a face-to-face relationship between employer and employee.) The terms "industrial enterprise" and "economic enterprise" will be used as interchangeable synonyms with the understanding that reference is made to all income-producing enterprises in which large numbers of employees work under managerial direction. No effort is made to distinguish between owners, employers, entrepreneurs, managers, or leaders of economic enterprises; these terms are used interchangeably to refer to all those engaged in coordinating and directing the work of employees in economic enterprises. However, the leaders of enterprises during the early phase of industrialization will on occasion be distinguished from the leaders of modern industry; in such cases the terms: "entrepreneur" and "manager" will be used.

In the West industrialization has been defended by ideological appeals which justified the exercise of authority in economic enterprises. Qualities of excellence were attributed to employers or managers which made them appear worthy of the position they occupied. More or less elaborate theories were used in order to explain that excellence and to relate it to a larger view of the world. The exercise of authority would also be justified in terms of the "naturally" subordinate position of the many who obey. To this a further reference to the social order was usually added, holding out a promise to the many who with proper exertion might better themselves or even advance to positions of authority. These ideas appear to lack humane appeal. A creed which expounds the identity of virtue and success will strengthen the conviction of those who are convinced already. And the related admonition to the "poor" to exert themselves as their "betters" have, will be reassuring to those who have arrived. Such appeals express the interests of a group of men, whose power and social position are more or less secure by virtue of their successful leadership of economic enterprises. But it is probable that these ideas have also had a strong appeal for those who spend their daily life under the authority of the very employers whose achievements are celebrated. Indeed that authority has been defended on the ground that each man is free to enjoy what he can acquire on his own, and the promise of freedom based on exertion has excited the human imagination. But this position has also been attacked on the ground that the few are rewarded while the many are deprived, that the promise of freedom is spurious as long as it implies the risk of starvation as well as each man's dependence upon an irrational market and an inhuman machine. Still, the ideological defense of industrialization has helped to structure our image of the social world—within the orbit of Anglo-American civilization. The following study examines this ideological defense, first at the inception of industrialization, and then in its contemporary setting.

In Soviet Russia industrialization has been advanced by ideologies of management, which originated as a critique of industry. That critique pointed to two disastrous consequences which society must avoid or undo. Through their pursuit of gain men had been alienated from their fellows; the relations among them had come to depend upon the cash-nexus. And through the division of labor industrialism had subjected the individual producer to the degrading domination of the machine, depriving him of the satisfaction which the craftsmen enjoyed. To undo these consequences it was necessary to afford all men the opportunity of doing their work as participants in a common undertaking. Accordingly, the commands of managers and the obedience of workers should receive their justification from the subordination of both groups to a body which represented managers and workers so that each man would obey policies he had helped to formulate. Hence, the exercise of authority by the few and the subordination of the many would be justified by the service each group rendered to the achievement of goals determined for it. And the relations between employers and workers would be regulated in conformity with an authoritative determination of the role of each.

If the Western spokesmen of industry can be identified by the expression of material interests, their opponents in Russia may be identified by the assertion that their interests are identical with the higher interests of mankind. Communism has owed its strength to the articulation of grievances against the industrial way of life. The belief that the pursuit of gain alienates men from their fellows, that the rich are depraved and the poor are deprived, constitutes a potent appeal to the dissatisfactions of the many and facilitates identification with humanity. Yet this attack has been incorporated in a managerial ideology, which combines these negative appeals with the ideal of collective ownership and planning. Karl Marx had capped his attack upon capitalism with the proposal to restore "real" freedom. Men "should consciously regulate production in accordance with a settled plan" so that they would carry on their work with the means of production in common.[2] All should own and plan as well as work, so that all might be free. These ideas have been defended on the ground that men can find personal fulfillment only when they own their tools and consciously direct their own activity. They have been attacked on the ground that such personal participation in collective ownership and planning is nominal only, that the promise of personal fulfill-

2. See Karl Marx, *Capital* (New York: Modern Library, Inc., 1936), pp. 92–93.

ment is spurious as long as each must carry on his work in accordance with dictates and in the absence of privacy. This, then, is the other ideology which this study examines, again at the inception of industrialization and in its contemporary setting. For we are confronted with the paradox that the ideas with which the effects of industry were condemned have been incorporated in ideologies of management which today prevail within the orbit of Russian civilization. . . .

During the early phase of industrialization a new way of life is in the making and an old way of life is on the defensive. In this respect I shall compare England and Russia during the eighteenth and nineteenth centuries. For those who initiate the development of industry must overcome the opposition of many groups, and the ideas they advance concerning the relations between employers and workers will appear as part of the whole effort to gain acceptance for, and to facilitate, the development of industry.

While the initiation of industry involves everywhere a break with the past, it also involves quite dissimilar patterns of developments. In taking my cue from the present division of the world into East and West, I have chosen two such patterns of industrialization. These may be distinguished in the sense that English industrialization resulted principally from the struggle of a rising entrepreneurial class, while in Russia the interaction among social classes which was connected with industrialization was continually subject to autocratic intervention and bureaucratic controls.

This contrast between a society in which those who govern industry form a more or less autonomous social class, and a society in which entrepreneurs are subordinate to governmental controls, has endured till the present day; but the internal organization of economic enterprise has undergone profound changes, which have consisted, broadly speaking, in the multiplication of technical and administrative tasks as well as in the lengthening of the rank-order of authority in industrial organizations. As a result the tasks of management have increased in number and complexity, and the ideas concerning the relations between employers and workers have become a part of the effort to solve these managerial tasks more successfully. Accordingly, the outline of this study may be represented by the following schematic representation:

| | Entrepreneurs and managers form an autonomous class | Entrepreneurs and managers are subordinate to government control |
|---|---|---|
| Entrepreneurial ideologies at the inception of industry | England | Russia |
| Managerial ideologies in large-scale economic enterprises | United States | East Germany |

* * * * * *

## Industrialization and entrepreneurial ideologies in sociological perspective

All economic enterprises have in common a basic social relation between the employers who exercise authority and the workers who obey. And all ideologies of management have in common the effort to interpret the exercise of authority in a favorable light. At this most general level it is largely a matter of finding arguments in support of two related contentions. One of these refers to those in authority who are alternately shown not to rule at all, or to rule only in the interest of large numbers. The other refers to the many who obey orders, and who are alternately shown to obey only when they consent to do so, or because such obedience provides them with the greatest opportunities of advancement. Apparently, such ideologies interpret the facts of authority and obedience so as to neutralize or eliminate the conflict between the few and the many in the interest of a more effective exercise of authority. To do this, the exercise of authority is either denied altogether on the ground that the few merely order what the many want; or it is justified with the assertion that the few have qualities of excellence which enable them to realize the interests of the many. This is the common theme which makes ideologies of management comparable despite the different patterns of industrialization and despite the variety of specific interpretations.

The most general contrast between the civilizations of Russia and the West has to do with the extent to which social relations are free from, or are affected by, political decisions and governmental controls. In the context of this study I am concerned with two interrelated aspects of industrialization which underlie the formulation of ideologies of management. Employers or their agents exercise authority over their workers, and this shared position and function may give rise to common interests and actions. An individual entrepreneur, for example, may join other entrepreneurs, in order to formulate the interests that are common to the group and to implement these common aspirations by appropriate collective action. But the act of joining with others and the formulation of common aspirations and their implementation through collective action are not necessarily a by-product of the fact that industrialists are by and large men who have a social position and economic interests in common.[3] The unity of thought and action among employers is necessarily provisional, depending as it does upon their several practical interests. And the ideologies of management which are formulated on this basis are likely to reflect whatever diversity of practical interests exists among the members of this social class.[4]

These statements apply by and large to the industrial history of England and the United States as well as of other countries of western Europe. They do not apply, however, to the industrialization of Russia, for they presuppose that employers are free to exercise authority over their workers and to join together in order to pursue their common interests. To some extent such freedom existed in Russia as well, but the distinctive feature of the Russian development is that the employers' exercise of authority and their collective actions and ideas have been subordinated throughout to the principle of governmental supremacy. While actual administrative intervention in industrial relations has been sporadic, the important point is that the relations between employers and workers have been interpreted throughout as affecting the public interest. Ideologies of management have been formulated, therefore, in the course of interaction between employers and government officials.

There is a significant difference between men who pursue their economic interests and officials who do their appointed task. The unity of thought and action among these two groups arises either on the basis of shared interests or on the basis of authoritative directives. Social classes become effective agents of collective action to the extent that shared social and economic characteristics give rise to organizational cohesion. Bureaucracies become effective agents of collective action to the extent that their hierarchical organizations give rise to shared social and economic characteristics among the officials. And if officials are called upon to superintend the pursuit of practical interests by employers, then the organization of industry and the management of labor become subordinate to the maintenance and advancement of superordinated administrative hierarchies.[5] These distinctions are frequently blurred in practice, since the officials may support industry for political reasons; but even

3. This distinction between the social and economic conditions of a social class and the collective actions by the united members of that class is important and has been neglected. In his introduction to *Das Kapital* Marx pointed out that he did not attribute the evils committed by the class of capitalists to capitalists as individuals. Yet the polemical style of the literature which Marx initiated quickly obscured this distinction between individual members of a class and the class as an acting group, and hence the distinction between the economic interests of individuals and their readiness to participate in collective action. Cf. Reinhard Bendix and S. M. Lipset, "Karl Marx' Theory of Social Classes," in Reinhard Bendix and S. M. Lipset, eds., *Class, Status and Power* (The Free Press, 1953), pp. 26–35.

4. It is awkward but unavoidable to speak of "members" of a social class. Strictly speaking, individuals merely share certain social and economic characteristics, and those who do are therefore "members" of a class only in the classificatory sense; but such individuals may also join to act in common and only then are they members without quotation marks. Since most references to social class, however, relate the shared characteristics of individuals to their capacity and actual readiness for collective action, it is not possible to keep the two meanings verbally separated.

5. This subordination of economic actions to political considerations did not remain confined to Tsarist Russia. It is equally prominent in Lenin's theory of the labor movement. His essay "What is to be done?" contains the most important modern formulation of the conflict between group action based upon political as against economic principles. Its major thesis is that workers by themselves develop "only a trade-union consciousness," a term which stands for their concern with an improvement of wages and working conditions. But these economic interests of the workers are, according to Lenin, not "historical" interests of their class. The workers must rather be educated to recognize these class interests and the historic mission which they imply. And the educators of the working class must be a band of professional revolutionaries, whose intellectual comprehension of history and whose organizational discipline will place them in the vanguard of the labor movement.

where the interests of employers and officials coincide, the rival principles of organization remain.[6] And these rival principles are reflected in the different ideologies of management which have developed in Russian and in Anglo-American civilization. . . .

### ENGLAND

Industrialization in England was initiated by a rising class of entrepreneurs. The formation of a social class may be analyzed in terms of the position its members occupy in the society, and in terms of the ideas by which they achieve a measure of self-identification or class consciousness. In late eighteenth-century England the position of the entrepreneurial class was circumscribed by the activities of its members in the promotion of economic enterprises. While the social origin and the education of the early entrepreneurs will be discussed, major emphasis will be placed upon the development of class consciousness. The early entrepreneurs were welded into a social class, in part because they were caught up in an emerging mass excitement concerning the promise of technology. Moreover, their class consciousness grew because they resented the prevailing aristocratic prejudices against people who engaged in commerce and industry. The opposition of ruling groups in English society to the rising entrepreneurs was an important stimulus to the formation of this social class, for this opposition was strong enough to be experienced as a frustration but not strong enough to suppress the development of collective actions and ideas.

The growth of economic enterprise in the late eighteenth century stimulated the demand for labor. The dislocations associated with this increased demand made the place of the laborer in English society problematic. The traditional life of the worker was disrupted despite his strong reluctance to leave his accustomed work and residence and despite his aversion to factory discipline. Moreover, his poverty was made to appear not as a burden, but as a sign of idleness and sin at a time when his employers became rich, when his own standard of living rose somewhat, and when ideas concerning personal rights became widely known. In this way industrialization coincided with institutional and ideological changes which caused the worker to become aware of his position as a second-class citizen. The traditional subordination of the "lower classes" had always been attributed to forces beyond human control; now, the worker was held personally responsible for the poverty from which he suffered. Thus, the disruption of a traditional way of life coincided with the denial that the worker had a legitimate place in society, for a poverty which resulted from defects of character rather than from inscrutable forces tended to stigmatize the worker and undermine his self-respect.

In England this social isolation of the emerging working class was opposed in many ways. The prevailing view of the English aristocracy was to assert that the "higher classes" were obliged to think for, and to protect, the "poor" while the latter had to be submissive, depending entirely upon their "betters." This view was put into practice in a good many industrial enterprises; aristocratic owners, members of dissenting sects, and entrepreneurs in areas of labor scarcity were among those who managed their work force in the traditional manner. Also, management by subcontractors and foremen encouraged the retention of traditional relations between employers and workers, though this relation could be tyrannical as well as benevolent. Even where traditional practices were abandoned, the belief in them was frequently retained.

Indeed, the assertion that the "higher classes" are responsible and that the "lower classes" may depend upon them, became a matter of conscious agitation. Evangelical preaching reflected preconceptions with which portions of the ruling groups sought to meet the challenge of industrialization. As the rising entrepreneurial class broke with traditionalism ideologically, evangelism increased its efforts to inculcate morality in masses of the people. And although the immediate effect of the evangelical movement was to facilitate the subordination and improve the work habits of the people, its long-run significance was that it succeeded along with the Methodist revival in overcoming the worker's social isolation and restoring his self-respect.

6. Karl Wittfogel has criticized Marx for his failure to consider the role of bureaucracy, but Wittfogel himself fails to make any distinction between a "ruling class" and a "ruling bureaucracy." This distinction is likely to be obscured whenever all political actions and organizations are treated as by-products of "basic" economic changes. Cf. Karl Wittfogel, "The Ruling Bureaucracy of Oriental Despotism," *The Review of Politics*, 25 (1953), pp. 350–59.

Ideologically, there was considerable tension between evangelical preaching and the beliefs of the early entrepreneurs. The masses of the people were said to be immoral, their distress the result of indolence and sin. No educational or institutional device would improve their evil habits; only hunger could accomplish that. Meanwhile arguments were adduced to show that the rich could do nothing to relieve the distress of the poor. And the laws of nature and of nature's God were employed to show that the poor must help themselves. All the means for their relief, namely, moral conduct and the postponement of marriage, were within their power and within their power alone. Eventually, this demand for a reform of the habits of the poor was implemented in a manner which seemed to give to the equation of poverty with immorality the sanction of a public institution. Yet shortly thereafter, in conjunction with the demand for free trade, an entrepreneurial ideology was developed which appealed to the worker as a member of the community, which praised his independence where his insubordination had been condemned, and which preached a gospel of work and hope in lieu of the earlier gospel of work and despair. The English entrepreneurial class had found an ideological basis, on which it could exercise its authority within economic enterprises without condemning the workers to a position of social isolation.

### RUSSIA

Industrialization in Russia was initiated by an autocratic ruler, whose centralized power precluded the existence of autonomous social groups. Prior to the eighteenth century the duties of each group had been legally defined: the peasants were bound to the land, and the government exacted specific services from townspeople and landowners. The development of urban centers and of industrial production was greatly retarded. The governmental promotion of economic growth reflected these legacies. Enterprises were set up with state funds. Labor was made available through forced recruitment. The bulk of the products was sold to the government, and management was entrusted to employers who were duty-bound to serve the state and whose "rights" merely consisted in privileges designed to facilitate that service. Under Peter the Great the landed aristocracy stood in a similar relationship to the state. Consequently, conflicts of interest between social groups, such as that between the aristocracy and middle-class employers, consisted in the competition for privileges from the Tsar.

During the eighteenth century the relations among the several social groups changed significantly. After the death of Peter the Great (1725) the obligations of the landed aristocracy were gradually reduced while its privileges were increased. This changing position of the aristocracy had several significant repercussions. The privileges previously granted to merchants and manufacturers were withdrawn. Productive activities increased on the landed estates, as aristocrats were more frequently exempted from military or administrative services and as they encouraged their peasant serfs to engage in trade and production. The greatly improved position of the aristocracy was not, however, a token of its increasing power in the state. Rather, the Tsars, and especially Catherine II, utilized the privileges granted to the aristocracy as a means of keeping it out of power. And the power of the Tsar was strengthened by the growing antagonism among aristocrats, middle-class employers, and the working masses.

This intensification of class differences became especially manifest in the relations among the Tsar, the aristocracy, and the serfs. The privileges of the aristocracy were increased along with the exploitation of the peasantry; but in a predominantly agricultural country income was primarily derived from the work of the peasants, so that the revenue of the state as well as the wealth of the aristocracy depended upon it. Hence, Tsarist officials and aristocratic landowners made competing claims upon the peasantry. In the relations between the landowners and the peasantry this development led to a "moral estrangement between the classes." The increasing exploitation of the peasants was made possible by increased privileges, which had been granted to the aristocracy at a time when that aristocracy was generally exempted from the military or administrative services which had justified its privileges previously. The relations between the Tsar and the peasantry were also transformed, but in a different way. The Tsars retained ultimate authority over the peasant serfs; yet in their efforts to satisfy the aristocracy without giving it power, they increased the landowners' authority over the serfs. Hence, the Tsars' claim to ultimate authority contrasted with their inability and unwillingness to control the landowners' exercise of power over the serfs. In the unavailing but persistent attempts to make their lot more tolerable, the peasant serfs utilized this situation by appealing to the Tsar for relief from their exploiters, and rumors of the Tsar's real intentions were used to justify sporadic rebellions. By such actions the peasants unwittingly upheld the ultimate authority of the Tsars even when the latter failed to do so themselves.

Though primarily related to agriculture, this setting determined the relations between employers and workers and the development of entrepreneurial ideologies in all forms of economic enterprises. Peasants and workers were regarded as beasts of burden, whose complete subordination was essential to the established social order, and whose labor was regarded as a token of their submission. No other moral demand was made upon them, since the authority relations between masters and serfs were modeled after the authority relations between the Tsar and his subjects. In practice this approach led to many difficulties. Tsarist control over labor relations in economic enterprises gave all possible support to the owners and aided them in the exploitation of the serfs. Yet the authorities repeatedly asserted the Tsar's benevolent protection of all his subjects. When the exploitation of workers and peasants by the landowners finally provoked rebellions, the government frequently took over the operation of the enterprise to safeguard order and secure the supplies to the government.

In the case of middle-class employers, moreover, the government sought to achieve the same ends by administrative regulation and police inspection. And its regulation of the so-called possessional enterprises vacillated between an official support of the employer's control over the work force and occasional attempts to control the actions of the employers as well. The Tsarist regime overwhelmingly favored the employers in its effort to uphold the social order. Yet, the regime could never undo the basic principle of its own authority, in accordance with which the Tsar superintended *all* relations among social groups in Russian society. Hence, workers continued to look to the government for protection against their employers, just as the latter looked to the government for support against their workers.

The more rapid development of economic enterprises during the second half of the nineteenth century did not change these relationships, though it made them increasingly tenuous. In the past the government had been very reluctant to interfere with the landowner's power over his serfs; but the emancipation of the serfs in 1861 necessitated more rather than less governmental control of landowners and peasants. Similarly, the growth of economic enterprises from the 1840's on was accompanied by a "hands-off" policy: the Tsarist government lent its support to the authority of the employer and intervened only when disturbances among workers became unmanageable. Yet some Tsarist officials and some employers continued to advocate more regulations. And the prevailing system of taxation and police registration made some governmental regulation of the employers and the workers necessary in any case: it perpetuated the rural residence of industrial workers which resulted in high labor turnover and in a division of control over the work force between the employers and the government. Hence, employers *and* workers continued to look to the government for intervention on their behalf, despite the "hands-off" policy. When such intervention became necessary toward the end of the nineteenth century, Tsarist officials sought to control the relations between employers and workers by prescribing the actions of both groups and, in addition, by seeking to control the workers from within their own ranks.[7] This superimposition of governmental controls, however, implied that every protest against employers was a protest against the government. When the government failed to act in its proclaimed role as a defender of the workers' interests, economic grievances became transformed into a revolution against the prevailing social order.

This brief synopsis of the English and the Russian development may be formulated in more general terms. Where industrialization is the work of a rising entrepreneurial class, that class is likely to seek social recognition from the ruling groups at the

7. This conception of governmental authority, which supplements the stipulation and enforcement of rules with attempts to organize compliance with the rules from within the ranks of labor or of management, has become the model after which the practices and ideologies of labor management have been fashioned in Soviet Russia.

same time that its ideas and economic activities challenge the traditions of the ruling groups at many points. These activities lead to the creation of a nonagricultural work force under conditions of great economic distress. While poverty is not a new experience for this rising working class, factory discipline and the disruption of a traditional way of life are. By their ideological appeals the new entrepreneurs may aggravate that new experience by making the workers personally responsible for the distress which industrialization imposes upon them. This social isolation of the workers, which results from the activities of the rising entrepreneurial class, is resisted by the workers and the older ruling groups. Both tend to combat it by clinging fast to the practices and to the ideal images of the preindustrial society. By so doing the older ruling groups seek, in effect, to restore the working class to an accepted position within society. The workers' quest for an accepted if subordinate place in the new society may take the form of radical demands, but these often derive their strength from an insistence upon traditional rights. The nature of these traditional ideas and practices helps to determine whether and in what manner the "reincorporation" of the workers in the new industrial society is achieved. In England the precepts of evangelism and the Methodist revival among the workers were instrumental both in serving the interests of the entrepreneurs and in aiding this reintegration of the workers. And when a new entrepreneurial ideology was formulated, shortly after the ideological break with traditionalism was complete, the new ideology further contributed to this reintegration. For it is significant that in England the workers adopted many middle-class values in the process of attaining for themselves a recognized position within the industrial society.

When industrialization occurs in a country with a centralized, autocratic regime, then an entrepreneurial class will seek recognition for its economic activities from the government, especially in the form of privileges that will facilitate these activities. Competition with the ruling social groups may be keen, but it is not likely to challenge the principal buttress of this social order: that the government is the ultimate arbiter of conflicting claims by virtue of its control over the distribution of privileges. Essentially the same point applies to the position of the peasants and workers. The government continues to proclaim itself the ultimate authority and the guardian of the people. The peasants and workers continue to act upon this view in seeking redress for their grievances against their masters. Hence, in theory, the subordinate but accepted position of peasants and workers in Russian society remained unchanged, but the emancipation of the serfs and the increased mobility incident to a rising industrial work force altered that subordinate position in fact. The people continued to call upon the government to protect them against exploitation and to grant them the rights which had been withheld in the past, while the government continued to claim ultimate authority but failed to act accordingly. In the end the people rebelled against the Tsar's failure to fulfill his acknowledged obligation to the people, as they interpreted it. That is, they sensed and eventually rebelled against their social isolation from the society after the emancipation of the serfs and industrialization in the second half of the nineteenth century had partly terminated their old subordination, and after the government had opened up and then withdrawn previously unknown opportunities of social recognition.

STEPHEN A. RICHARDSON

# Organizational Contrasts on British and American Ships

To be effective, an organization must have a structure appropriate for the particular purpose and the resulting necessary tasks. At the same time, the form of organization and the values and needs of its members must be adapted to one another. Variations in organization, then, can be expected to follow from variations of the cultures from which members of an organization are drawn. The effects of cultural factors can be seen in comparing organizations which function in a wide variety of countries and have identical purposes and similar environments.

The social organization on British and United States merchant ships was selected for study because cargo ships have identical purposes, closely comparable environments, and a set of conditions as near to the research ideal as is likely to be found in a natural setting without experimental manipulation. Cargo ships or freighters of approximately seven thousand tons, carrying crews of forty men, were selected for study.

We will first describe the purpose and environment which are common to foreign-going cargo ships of all nationalities. Then we will describe how British and United States seamen arrange their shipboard lives to meet these common conditions. For the purposes of this paper the description will be limited to some differences found between the two nationalities in training, social control, and stratification.[1]

## Methods used in collecting data

In evaluating a study it is helpful for the reader to know something about the methods used in carrying out the study. The author had firsthand experience for nine years on British and United States merchant ships, from 1937 to 1946. He sailed in all deck department ranks from able-bodied seaman's apprentice to chief officer and holds a British master mariner's certificate. The author kept a daily diary during this nine-year period. In 1947 the author returned to sea in connection with this study. Two passages were made, one as chief officer of a British ship and one as an able-bodied seaman on an American ship. Detailed daily observations were made and recorded.

In 1948 seventy-two interviews were conducted

Gratitude and thanks are expressed to an American seaman, Professor G. C. Homans of Harvard University, for his advice, criticism, and encouragement during the fieldwork and writing of this study, and to the many Maritime Union officials and seamen who generously gave their time and provided the material and many of the ideas that appear in this study.

Reprinted from *Administrative Science Quarterly*, September, 1956, pp. 189–207, by permission of the author and publisher. (Copyright 1956 by The Graduate School of Business and Public Administration, Cornell University.)

1. This study was completed in 1949, as an honors thesis for the Bachelor of Arts degree, in the Department of Social Relations at Harvard University. A full report can be found in S. A. Richardson, *The Social Organization of British and United States Merchant Ships*. Mimeographed copies are available through the New York State School of Industrial and Labor Relations, Cornell University.

in port with men of all ranks in the deck department of British and American ships and with American union officials. Because of the conditions under which interviewing took place, a flexible procedure was used. A set of topics for the interviews was developed from the personal experiences of the author and from documentary sources. The set of topics was memorized and used as a guide, but none of the actual questions asked were preformulated.

Various drafts of the larger study were read by seamen and union officials of both nationalities, and the subsequent evaluations and discussions were taken into account in revising the final report.

## Common purpose and environment

A merchant ship's purpose is to transport cargo and passengers. This demands three main focuses of work for the crew: (1) aiding and facilitating the loading and discharging of cargo and passengers; (2) bringing the ship and her contents safely to her appointed destination, and (3) throughout the life of the ship, maintaining and repairing her so that she will give efficient service.

A ship and her contents are a large capital investment. She is exposed frequently to such hazards as storms, collision, fire, and shipwreck. The safety of the ship depends in large measure upon the quick judgments and actions of experienced and skillful seamen. The social organization of the crew must therefore have a clearly designated hierarchy of responsibility and must make provision for rapid communication and execution of orders. Because potential hazards to the ship exist at all times, the organization must function continuously.

A ship's movements impose limitations as to when a member of the crew may form and sever connection with the ship. A seaman joins a ship when it is in his country and reasonably close to his home. With few exceptions, he must remain with the ship until it returns to his home country. This period may be from a month to two years. During the voyage, the crew therefore has a smaller turnover than any comparable organization ashore.

Members of the crew spend their working hours and leisure time at sea, isolated from other people. In foreign ports the friendships they can form ashore are limited by the brief duration of the ship's stay and by the limited channels that may be used to establish social contacts. Life at sea has in most cases been found unsuitable for families. Members of the crew must therefore be separated from their families for the duration of the voyage.

## The social system of merchant ship crews

To fulfill the purpose of a ship and to adapt the seaman to the environment which has been described, a clearly defined social system has been evolved through centuries of experience. This system must be sufficiently clear so that a new crew made up of men who have never before met can immediately coordinate the complex task of running a ship.

Before describing and analyzing some of the differences found in the social system on British and American merchant ships, we will outline the organization of the crews of both nationalities and the way in which the crews function. The crew is divided into four departments which work in close cooperation: deck, engineering, stewards, and radio. In this article, attention will be focused on the deck department, with other departments discussed only in relation to this department. Figure 1 shows the manning and basic working organization which with little variation is typical of British and United States cargo ships of about seven thousand tons (e.g., World War II liberty ships).

There are two main categories of work for the crew while the ship is at sea. These are:

*Navigating and propelling the ship:* While at sea, a ship is continuously under way, and most members of the crew are divided into three shifts, or watches. Each watch alternates four hours on duty with eight hours off duty. A watch on deck is made up of one officer, two able-bodied seamen, and an ordinary seaman.[2] Although the deck watch-keeping officers are in full charge, the captain is at all times responsible for the safety of the ship and is on call if an unusual situation is suspected or special vigilance is required. The chief engineer is at all times responsible to the captain for the ship's machinery. Radio officers receive and transmit mes-

2. Able-bodied seaman is a rank obtained after a man has spent three years in the deck department and has passed the required examination. The rank of ordinary seaman is given men in the deck department when they first go to sea.

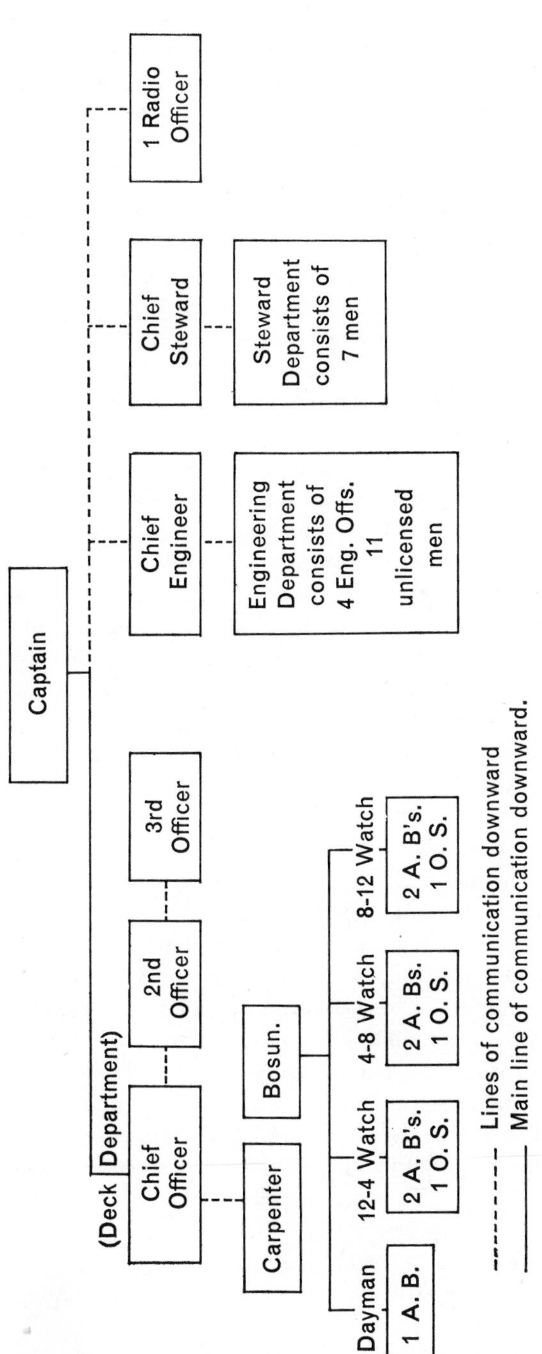


*Figure 1. Typical manning and formal organization of crew of a 7,000-ton-gross United States or British merchant ship. Total number of men in crew is forty.*

sages at internationally agreed-upon times. Competence of all officers is tested by a governmental examination system. The watch-keeping routine at sea is broken only in extraordinary circumstances. The entire crew is trained in the procedures to be adopted in case of emergency.

*Ship's maintenance:* During the day, the carpenter works on his own, and the bosun[3] works with any able-bodied seamen who are on day work and do not keep watch, and with the two watch members not steering the ship. Since this gives the bosun only three or four men, if any large job has to be done extra men are called out during their time off watch and paid overtime. On occasion, the bosun may be supervising ten to twelve men. Planning and supervising the deck-department work is done by the chief officer (often called the mate) during his time off watch. The captain rarely participates in this supervision but may do so if he wishes.

### THE EFFECTS OF THE UNIONS ON THE ORGANIZATION OF THE CREW

British and American officers and men are represented by unions, and collective bargaining between the shipping companies and unions is well accepted. While at sea, the crew must determine the administration and interpretation of the agreements without assistance from shore officials. On British ships this task is left to traditional informal practices, and the unions do not require any organized activity while the crew is aboard the ship. On United States ships, however, unions representing the unlicensed personnel require a number of types of activity while at sea. Because of the widespread effects that union activity has had on American ships these will be described first.

At the beginning of the voyage, a meeting is called which is obligatory for all members not on duty. At the meeting, the deck, engine-room, and stewards departments each elect a delegate. The types of qualifications looked for are sea experience, education, thorough knowledge of the contract, fluency of speech, and the ability to stay sober at the pay-off at the end of the voyage. The department delegates act as official union spokesmen to the head of their department. A ship's delegate or chairman is also elected to coordinate the departments and act as delegate to the captain for all unlicensed personnel when matters arise involving more than one department. The chairman and departmental delegates constitute the ship's committee. Delegates check up on members' subscriptions, hold meetings which must be attended, educate the membership about union policies and rules, watch over members' interests, and maintain union solidarity and discipline (see Figure 2). The unions believe that any hierarchy within their ranks aboard ship might decrease their unity and strength in action; therefore union educational policies stress that all members are equals and brothers. This also tends to prevent delegates from exploiting their position for personal or political ends.

Union activity at sea is instigated mainly by the ship's committee. The union headquarters offers a wide range of suggestions and facilities, which are reflected in the agenda for union meetings of the crew. The agenda includes union business, reports from the ship's committee on the handling of complaints, education, political action, and "good and welfare." Any matter can be brought to the floor by crewmen in the form of a motion. Under the heading of "good and welfare," it is said that "everyone gets a chance to blow his top."[4] While political and educational activities take place only on some ships, the ship's committee always handles complaints, watches over living conditions, and serves a policing function in seeing that members live up to the terms of the agreement and behave in a manner which will give the shipping company no grounds for withdrawing any part of the gains won by the union. The National Maritime Union summarizes the aim of union activity aboard ship as follows: "Everyone has his special job and keeps checking with everyone else. The same policy, the same method of handling problems, the same rights apply to all. That's what makes a happy, livable, workable ship."[5]

Union activity can have an important effect on the informal structure of the unlicensed personnel.

3. The position of bosun is analogous to that of foreman. It requires an able-bodied seaman's rating and sufficient sea experience and supervisory ability (as judged by competent seamen) to be responsible to the chief officer for the work of the able-bodied and ordinary seamen.

4. National Maritime Union, Pilot, Education and Publicity Department Publication No. 16, *Heart of the Union* (November 1947).

5. *Ibid.*

It provides a number of positions that give prestige and leadership and an opportunity to participate in group activities. It tends to bring together the unlicensed men in the three departments, maintains union interests, gives a sense of solidarity and distinction, and provides meaningful activity in a restricted environment where men have few facilities for entertainment when not at work.

Both British and United States officers have their own unions, which have no organized activity aboard the ships while at sea.

## Differences between the social system on British and United States ships

For the effective maintenance and survival of the social system on a ship there are two important requirements: (1) a continuous supply of trained men and (2) ways to control deviance from normative or ideal patterns of behavior if the degree of deviance becomes a threat to the functioning of the system. We will now focus attention on some of the national differences that appear in the way these requirements are met.

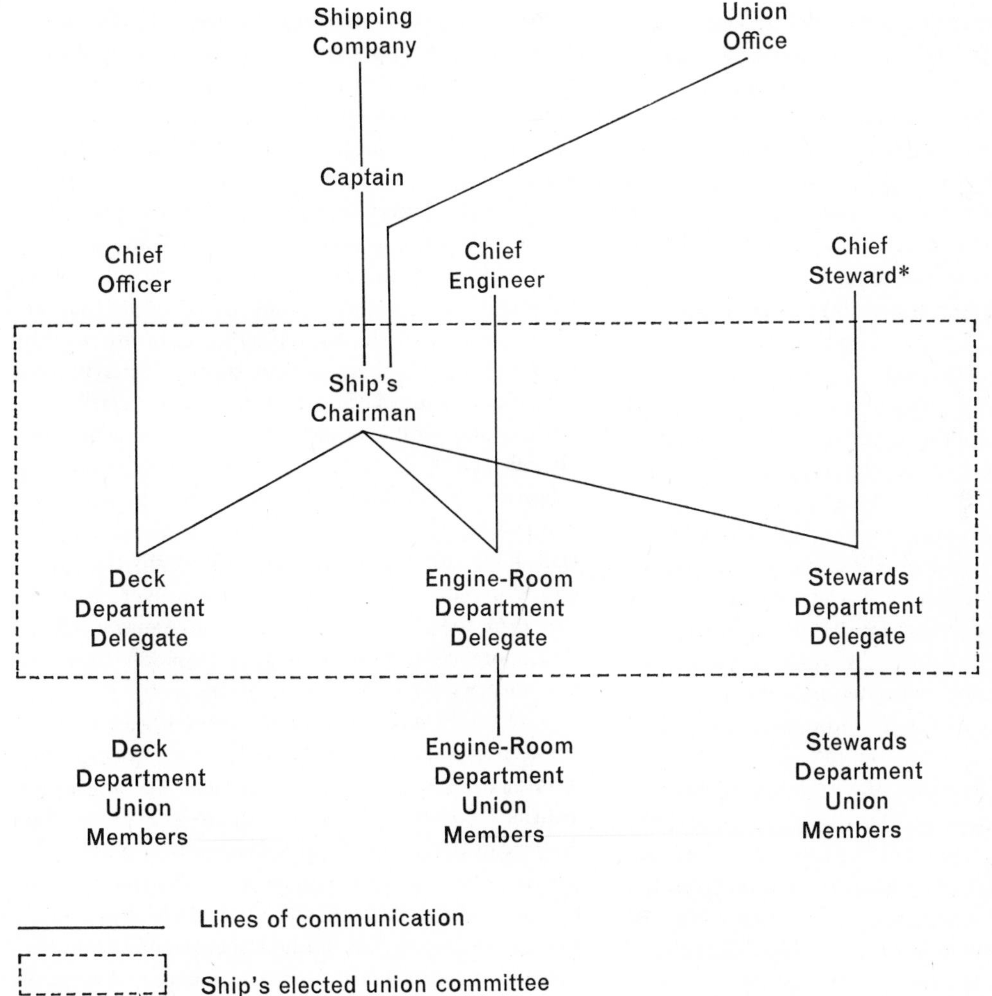


*Figure 2. Union organization of unlicensed personnel on United States ships.*

TRAINING OF DECK DEPARTMENT OFFICERS

On British ships, the four-year apprenticeship for youths intending to become officers is generally spent with one company. This training begins at age sixteen or seventeen, and the company takes the responsibility of teaching the apprentice the business of a seaman and the duties of a navigating officer. The apprentice "binds and obliges himself . . . to faithfully serve [the company] and any shipmaster . . . and obey their and his lawful commands [perform various duties] . . . nor absent himself from their service without leave nor frequent taverns or alehouses, nor play at unlawful games."[6] About three-fourths of British Merchant Service officers receive their training as apprentices or cadets, and the remainder put in the required sea time as ordinary seamen and able-bodied seamen.

In the American Merchant Marine, a man is required to have three years of training before he can become an officer. Youths who train as cadets spend two of their three years at a shore-based maritime academy and two six-month periods at sea, either in maritime-academy training ships or in regular merchant ships. Training begins at eighteen or nineteen years of age.

Only about 10 per cent of the officers in the American Merchant Marine are trained as cadets. The remaining 90 per cent sail as ordinary seamen and able-bodied seamen and then take the examination for their license.

Among British officers, primary loyalty is found to be to the shipping companies, and to be a "company man" is considered advantageous. Among American officers, primary loyalty is found to be to the unions. For them the expression "company man" has disparaging connotations, the most important of which is its use as an opposite to "union man."

A number of factors in the training of officers suggest an explanation for this difference in loyalty. A youth sixteen to seventeen years old is in the process of gaining emotional emancipation from his parents, and is doing so through increased membership in peer groups outside his family. When the British boy goes to sea as an apprentice, he is separated from his family and his friends and placed in a social structure composed almost entirely of adult men. Here the peer group is limited to one or two somewhat older apprentices, since he is not allowed to associate with able-bodied seamen or ordinary seamen. However, the captain as shipping-company representative has certain responsibilities to the youth and plays a role closely analogous to that of a father. Because the youth is in need of stability, a sense of belonging, and friendship to replace what he has lost, he is highly motivated to use the captain, who represents the company, as a substitute for his father. The company is interested in training its apprentices in its ways and follows the youth's training and development with interest because it is likely that if he shows promise he will remain with the company throughout his career. Although the apprentice is given a great deal of work that is normally done by the unlicensed personnel, he is trained to identify himself with the officers even though he does not hold officer's status.

The few American officers who are trained as cadets have little or no connection with any shipping company. Two thirds of their training takes place ashore in schools which they enter when they are older than British apprentices, and where they associate mainly with a peer group. This type of training precludes the possibility of a relationship with a shipping company such as exists between British companies and officers. Although the majority of American officers go to sea at a somewhat older age than British seamen, they still have to make the difficult transition from shore to ship life. They have, however, a wider range of men with whom they may make friends and more chance of finding persons of their own age with whom they may associate.

The union and its elected representatives in the crew provide guidance and training for youths coming to sea as ordinary seamen. In return the youths develop a strong loyalty to the union. For American deck officers who first go to sea as ordinary seamen, the union plays a role comparable to that played by the company for British apprentices. When American able-bodied seamen become officers, it is natural for their allegiance to be transferred to the officer's union rather than to the companies, which they have been trained to consider as more unfriendly than friendly to the seaman.

6. Indentures to Anchor Line Ltd., Glasgow.

Among the unlicensed personnel, the difference in loyalty may be explained in part by the greater militancy and youth of the American unions. The American union-controlled hiring halls, the union-organized activity at sea, and the union discipline, as compared to the British jointly controlled company-union hiring halls and the lack of union activity and discipline at sea result in different attitudes toward the companies and the unions.

### MECHANISMS OF CONTROL USED BY UNLICENSED SEAMEN

An intricate set of checks and counterchecks are continuously in play between the mate, bosun, and deck crowd.[7] The captain and officers' interest and responsibility is to initiate the work and see that it gets done. The deck crowd's interest is to control authority which is not customarily acceptable or is illegitimate. Only the differences in the kinds of controls used by the deck crowd will be examined here.

*British ships.* When the able-bodied seamen or ordinary seamen think the mate has infringed on an official regulation (e.g., not kept an accurate check of the number of hours overtime) the offended person will generally enlist the sympathy of the deck crowd, since there is close identity of interest and a tendency to stand together for mutual protection. The first formal move generally is to take the complaint to the bosun, although this is often little more than a gesture to prevent any comeback from him that would occur if he were ignored. The deck crowd often feels that the bosun is on the chief officer's side. A direct approach to the department head would probably meet with refusal and an order to see the bosun. This was well described in two interviews:

> The bosun is rather suspect, because he works so close with the mate. The men are afraid he can be too easily called [talked around by the mate]. He is more used to acting for the mate than the men, so he may not be a good spokesman.
>
> [British able-bodied seaman]

7. On U.S. ships the term "deck gang" is used. These terms, used by the men themselves, have no derogatory connotation.

> Often the men try the bosun to get him to clear up the trouble and he has failed. [British second officer]

If the complaint is not settled by the bosun himself or by his referring the matter to the mate, the second step is for the aggrieved individual, a spokesman, or a delegation to go to the mate. There is no formal way of selecting a spokesman, but one appears in almost every deck crowd. The ability to talk well and think fast seems to be the prerequisite. In interviews, an able-bodied seaman said a delegation was sent to accompany the spokesman "for moral support," and the second officer explained that the delegation was sent "to give him moral courage and to see he says his piece."

If the complaint cannot be settled with the chief officer, the delegation may then go to the captain. The use of delegations for giving moral courage is evidenced by the more common usage of a delegation for the captain than for the chief officer. Omitting some of these steps may be done intentionally as a sign of hostility to or disparagement of a disliked bosun or mate.

*United States ships.* The unions have laid down rules for handling complaints against infringement of rules. The elected union delegate handles all grievances. This arrangement reinforces the union structure aboard the ship since it allows the ship's committee to have control and to interpret communications, and it prevents individual members from taking complaints directly to the captain and heads of departments. The discussion of any grievance centers around the interpretation of the union contract, which describes in great detail the rules and conditions of work. Having all complaints handled by the union delegate has the advantages of saving time and having an experienced man handle the disputes. It also ensures consistency in the treatment of comparable disputes. There is the disadvantage, however, that the chief officer receives complaints at secondhand and has no opportunity to gauge the feelings underlying the complaint, to learn how widely those feelings are shared, and in some cases to know who instigated the complaint. The delegate system also makes it difficult for the chief officer to give a man more overtime than he has earned, a procedure sometimes used by British chief officers to reward better workers.

An American bosun has described how the procedure affects the bosun, if it is functioning well:

The bosun likes the system of having the delegate handle all the beefs with the mate. The delegate gets the dirt and leaves the bosun clear of being involved in friction with the mate. As the bosun is clear of beefs he [is] in a more favorable position in handling the men. He keeps in touch with all beefs as these are aired at the union meetings. If the deck crowd are dissatisfied with anything the bosun does, he is talked to by the delegate and they try to straighten it out. If this is not possible the delegate takes the beef to the mate. The delegate would not go over the bosun's head.

The success of this procedure depends on its acceptance by the chief officer and on the willingness of the bosun to work in cooperation with the union. The bosun is in a difficult position, however, if the chief officer resists the union form of communication. If the chief officer is antiunion, he can weaken the union structure on board by discouraging the delegate and by encouraging communication through the bosun. In one way this strengthens the bosun's position, especially if his actions are fully backed by the chief officer, since then he is working on the side of the officers. He is, however, a union member, and by working with the officers, who tend to be identified with the company, he may antagonize the men, thus losing their support and incurring the strong controls that the union can apply to deviant members. If the bosun resists the chief officer's attempt to undermine the union communication procedure, the bosun will antagonize the chief officer. This places him in a difficult position since close cooperation between chief officer and bosun is essential in the smooth running of the crew. The difficulty of the bosun has been increased as the result of the loss of some of his traditional status symbols. Whereas he used to eat separately from the deck crowd, he now eats in the same messroom; and whereas he used to have a single cabin, he now tends to share a cabin with the deck maintenance crew. This, together with his membership in the same union as the men he supervises, has made his status less well defined and increased the difficulties of his position as "football" in the communication struggle.

It is probable that, as a result of increased experience with the union system of communication, its operation will become smoother.

The American unions have also developed a set of formal rules governing the role the deck-crowd union members should play in exercising self-regulatory controls. An able-bodied seaman outlined the delegate's job in this way:

The delegate's job is to keep the guys in line. Charges may be brought against fellow union men for inefficiency, not cooperating, refusing work, drunkenness, being antiunion, stealing from a shipmate, pulling knives. . . . The crew tries to take care of what happens. I think the Old Man likes the men to straighten out their own troubles. All the delegates may go to the Old Man and straighten things out with him. Then the delegates will call a meeting for the membership to endorse action or decide what should be done.

Some practical difficulties which lie in the way of the delegate's carrying out his job were raised by a second officer:

Discipline hardly lies with the union delegate. Union education is good on this matter, but one or two troublemakers are enough to wreck this. The delegate has got to live with the men, and if the trouble starts in Singapore, it is a long time for him to swim against the tide [until the end of the voyage].

The formal system of handling complaints has focused interest on the problem of formal and informal control. The subject was more often brought up by Americans than British and was spoken of at greater length. Controlling deviant behavior is a problem of great importance because it is conceived of not as a personal but as a union-owner issue. From the union's point of view, this approach has value in maintaining members' interest in the union. From the point of view of the chief officer, bosun, and deck crowd, a lack of agreement in interpreting the formal grievance rules leads to caution in adopting a flexible give-and-take system, and sometimes a struggle ensues between the chief officer and the deck crowd for the bosun's allegiance.

### INFORMAL CONTROLS ON BRITISH AND UNITED STATES SHIPS

It is possible for behavior to deviate widely from expected or ideal forms of behavior without technically infringing upon any written agreement. To counteract such deviations by officers, a number of informal controls are commonly used by crews on British and United States ships.

*Work slowdowns.* Close supervision of most of the work on deck is difficult, especially if the bosun is party to the slowdowns. Slowdowns have to be very marked before the captain or chief officer can find grounds for action—great ingenuity can be exercised in doing nothing, and doing it industriously. A slowdown is most commonly used to counteract too close supervision by the mate or too rigid application of working rules without allowing for any flexibility or give-and-take. It is also used to prevent the chief officer from deviating far from the role expected of him in his relations with the men.

*Quality of work.* Reduction in the quality of the work on deck serves the same purpose as work slowdowns, and these two forms of control are generally used together. Within certain limits, it is difficult for the chief officer to obtain sufficient evidence of poor workmanship, especially where the work is of such a nature or in such a position as to be difficult to check with periodic inspection.

*Misuse of ship's equipment.* This may take the form of misusing equipment or dumping overboard small articles not easily checked. The degree to which this is done will depend largely on how well equipment is watched by the chief officer. Misuse of equipment is a more destructive reaction than work slowdowns and is likely to lead to further deterioration of relations, whereas slowdowns and poor work can vary in seriousness, and any sign of improved relations instigated by the chief officer can be encouraged by increased output and quality of work.

*Leaving the ship.* If the work relationship has been poor between the deck officers and the men, and if the men's complaints have met with little or no satisfaction from the captain, a great deal of hostility accumulates. This is often harmlessly dissipated at the end of the voyage, but the men may all leave the ship or make a formal complaint to the union if there are grounds for action against the captain or chief officer. A complete turnover of the crew at the end of a voyage, especially if this happens on several consecutive voyages, may indicate to the shipping company's officials that the cause may be a captain or officer. The men leaving the ship spread the information of the cause for leaving, and it may in extreme cases reach the stage where the shipping company has trouble in getting a new crew so long as the officer causing the difficulty remains on the ship. A formal complaint achieves the same purpose directly.

## Effects of social stratification on patterns of behavior

If the social structure of the crew is conceived as occupying a vertical scale with the captain at the top and a first-voyage ordinary seaman at the bottom, it should be possible to place all crew members on this scale and to determine the range within which groups form. This grouping may be called social stratification, and the distance along the scale may be called social distance. There are a number of indicators of social stratification and distance which are recognized implicitly or explicitly by members of British and American crews. These include wages, qualifications formally required for holding an office (such as examinations and length of sea service), number of persons supervised, food and living conditions, and such behavior as the use of titles in addressing people. Together these indicators influence the behavior of every member of the crew with respect to every other member, providing pressures toward maintaining approved patterns of behavior.

Comparison of British and American crews on indicators of social stratification and distance showed that American seamen consistently play down behavioral and physical symbols that strengthen status and social distance. Some examples of the differences will now be given.

### FOOD AND THE DIVISION OF THE CREW AT MEALS

The value of the eating arrangements aboard ship as a measure of social stratification was recognized by Herman Melville in *White Jacket* when he observed that "the dinner table is the criterion of rank in our man-of-war world."[8]

The British crews have more divisions than the American. The British bosun and carpenter eat with the engine-room supervisory men; this group is often called the petty officers. The American bosun and carpenter and other petty officers eat with the able-bodied seamen and ordinary seamen, but generally at a separate table. Interviews showed a close positive relationship between status and the quality of food on British ships. The same was true of American ships in an earlier period, until unions

8. *The Romances of Herman Melville* (New York, 1931), p. 1126.

won the right of equal food for all. This right is carefully guarded by unlicensed personnel, whose delegates compare the quality of food being served officers and men. The British able-bodied seamen and ordinary seamen collect their meals from the cook, carry food to their messroom, and after eating do their own cleaning up. American able-bodied seamen and ordinary seamen are provided with a steward, who takes orders from the men, acts as waiter, and afterward cleans up the utensils and messroom. Both British and American officers are served at meals. Whereas on British ships only officers have tablecloths at meals, on American ships tablecloths are provided for all hands.

Although union membership has had little effect on status on British ships, the American union organization among unlicensed personnel at sea has tended to decrease social distance between fellow union members of different status, because the union teachings of brotherhood and equality are in contradiction to the official social hierarchy. Social pressures are applied to the bosun, chief steward, and carpenter to make them work in close cooperation with, and give their loyalty to, the able-bodied and ordinary seamen rather than form a separate petty-officer group. Through union efforts, the pay differential and differences in living conditions have been reduced between bosun, carpenter, chief steward, and the able-bodied and ordinary seamen.

On American ships the consistent playing down of symbols that strengthen status and social distance as compared with British practice appears to be closely related to the sentiments the men have toward social distance and authority. While interviewing, I found a consistent difference between British and American seamen in the degree of awareness and acceptance of social distance between statuses. On American ships, early in the interviews, I met such expressions as:

> The bosun, he's one of the boys. He's just another fellow. [Able-bodied seaman]

> The mates, they just act big because they don't do no lousy jobs, and walk up and down the bridge doing nothing. I'm as good a man as any of them. [Able-bodied seaman]

As the interviews developed, seamen did give various reasons why there was a need for social distance, and these explanations would often be accompanied by surprise, as if these were ideas they had never before explicitly recognized.

On British ships, in contrast, social distance was accepted as a matter of course, and it was stressed among the men that one of the reasons that officers and men for the most part kept separate was that the men had no wish to mix with the officers and preferred companions from their own or a similar status.

## Conclusion

The description of the purpose and environment of a ship showed that it was necessary to have a clearly designated hierarchy of authority to meet the hazards and emergencies which the ship may encounter at any time. During nonemergency activities which account for most of the routine aboard ships, the full measure of vested authority remains latent, and a form of authority more suited to nonemergency routine work and living is manifest. There is always the possibility, however, that the powers necessary for emergency action may be misused by the captain and officers for dealing with nonemergency issues. Comparison of British and American crews suggests that the British realize and accept the authority of competent persons and are not as fearful of the misuse of authority as Americans. This acceptance of authority is closely related to acceptance of social stratification and the symbols of these differences. Status symbols function as cues for self-regulation, in conformity with the status and role requirements of the ship. British seamen are conditioned before coming to sea to accept authority, and consequently the change in attitudes required when a man becomes a seaman is slight. Acceptance of authority, by trainees, facilitates training and a willingness to rely largely on informal and traditional practices for dealing with behavior of the captains and officers which they consider deviant.

Among American crews a far greater fear and suspicion of authority appears to exist. Social stratification is not widely accepted and is often denied. Many symbols of social stratification and authority have been removed, and, because they are suspect, the remaining symbols do little to enhance self-regulation of the men in conformity with the status and role demands of the ship's social organization. If the symbols of social stratification are ineffective, alternative procedures are necessary for training Americans for the requirements of life at sea and for maintaining the necessary social system. The alternative procedure has been a far greater formalization of the social system than the British. Greater formalization is evident in training men for the system, in maintaining the expected patterns of behavior, and especially in placing constraints upon authority.

Examples given have included the formalization of working conditions through a detailed union contract, formalizing the system of handling complaints, and the training of officers and men to a far greater degree than the British through specialized shore-based training institutions. The unions have played an important part in this process of formalization. The cultural differences between the British and Americans operating through their beliefs and attitudes have, then, important effects in the operation and maintenance of a social system developed to meet an identical purpose and similar environment.

MICHEL CROZIER

# The French Bureaucratic System of Organization

## The problem of interpersonal and intergroup relationships

Interpersonal and intergroup relationships present some characteristic, and rather similar, traits in the Clerical Agency and in the Industrial Monopoly. These traits—the isolation of the individual, the predominance of formal over informal activities, the isolation of the strata, and their struggles for privileges—play an important role in our model of a bureaucratic system of organization. Strata isolation, especially, is a key point for the development of the vicious circle which is the basis of our scheme of interpretation. Yet all these traits may also be considered as permanent French cultural traits.

Let us examine our data carefully. We noticed how few informal relationships there were among the employees of the Clerical Agency. Girls remained isolated, although this entailed hardship for many of them who were strangers in the city and had been abruptly severed from families and friendship ties. They reported that they very rarely had friends in the agency. They reiterated that they preferred having their friends outside. Even among those who had friends, the friendships seemed never to develop into articulate groups. There were very few associations of any sort—no cultural, educational, or leisure joint activities worth mentioning. Trade unions were more active; but for the average girl, whether or not she belonged to one, they remained rather formal affairs in which she did not participate. On the whole, we were left with the impression of a significant lack of informal groups. No clans or cliques of any sort were able to exist for long, and none of them was ever able to cut across different categories.

More friendships were reported in the Industrial Monopoly, but they did not develop into cliques or even into stable informal groups. Cliques were viewed with great disfavor, and groups that could cut across several categories were inconceivable.

These patterns contrast strongly with the usual picture of the American industrial shop climate as it has been portrayed since the first experiences of the Hawthorne testroom. They contrast also with reports on American public agencies,[1] such as those of Peter Blau, and of Roy Francis and R. C. Stone.[2]

These peculiarities fit very well with the rationale of the strata system that we have analyzed. In a bureaucratic system of organization, the individual

Reprinted from *The Bureaucratic Phenomenon*, pp. 214–24, by permission of the author and publisher. (Copyright 1964 by The University of Chicago Press.)

1. Peter Blau, *The Dynamics of Bureaucracy* (Chicago: University of Chicago Press, 1955); Roy G. Francis and Robert C. Stone, *Service and Procedure in Bureaucracy* (Minneapolis: University of Minnesota Press, 1956).

2. One can contend that the French industrial shop climate is also characterized by many informal group activities, but the evidence for this is not so conclusive as it at first appears. We have shied away from such discussion for lack of relevant empirical data. See Jacques Barbichon, "Etats d'insatisfaction, la vie parallèle dans l'entreprise et dans les loisirs," *Peuple et Culture, XIIème Congrès National*, 1956.

is adequately protected by the abstract formal group[3]—i.e., the stratum or ranking category—to which he belongs. The rules of seniority prevent interference by outside authorities and impose a strict equality among all the members of the group. As a consequence, the individual does not need the protection of an informal group. In addition, he knows that separate informal activities are likely to threaten the cohesion of the formal category to which he is bound, and he is vulnerable to the pressure of this whole formal category against such activities. Cliques that cut across categories are especially objectionable, since they inevitably foster *favoritism*, the system's cardinal sin.

Thus, in a world where conformity is achieved through the joint influence of impersonal rules that apply to all, and of group pressure that polices behavior within each category, the formal group takes precedence over the informal, and the individual remains isolated. This mechanism, which was especially obvious in the Industrial Monopoly,[4] is directly linked with the disappearance of formal and informal hierarchical pressure. Instead of the usual pattern of subordinates' developing informal groups to resist the pressure of the superordinate system, we have a very different pattern. Here, the superordinate system has been stripped of its potential of discrimination by being too well formalized, and isolated individuals control and check each other in order to maintain the formalism that protects them.

The precedence of the formal group over the informal, the tight control of each stratum over its members—these are associated with the isolation of the strata, the difficulty of promotion from one stratum to another, the difficulty of communicating across strata, and the development of ritualism. We have analyzed the importance of the formal peer group as a direct consequence of strata isolation and an indirect consequence of the pressure to impose impersonal rules, in order to eliminate the discretionary will of any individual.

But it can also work the other way around. If they already exist as distinct cultural patterns, such traits as the isolation of the individual and the lack of informal activities may act as powerful incentives for the development of this kind of bureaucratic system of organization. In any case, they will be important elements for understanding the success of certain patterns of organization within a given cultural context.

These traits indeed appear, to a large extent at least, to be rather well-established French cultural traits. We cannot rely, unfortunately, upon neat comparative tests, since empirical comparative studies remain to be made. But most observers have pointed out the low state of free group activities in France and the difficulty that Frenchmen experience in cooperating on a formal basis.

The few serious anthropological studies made provide significant and concordant details in the same direction. Lucien Bernot and René Blancard, in their thorough study of a village near Paris, note, for example: "Already, among children, one discovers one of the characteristic features of Nouville's life, the absence of groups. One does not find among the children any gang or clique within the village."[5] The same thing, they tell us, prevails among adults, and even among the industrial workers of the nearby factory, who do not develop lasting ties although, or perhaps because, they live in the same close community. The only group that exists in the village is a group of youngsters who have a significantly higher status than the rest of their peers; but their group, which has no leader, is not very successful. If the Catholic priest and the schoolteachers were to leave, "the very small amount of collective life or organized leisure would disappear because of the apathy of a youth group that does not dare to take the risks of responsibility."[6] The political field is the exact image of this apathy, although a good part of the votes will go to the extreme left in a general election.

There is rather more activity in the sunny village in the Vaucluse that Lawrence Wylie discusses.[7] However, the insightful remarks of the author indicate that the situation is basically the same. People tend to remain aloof; they have the same difficulties in co-operating. No organized activities are allowed to disrupt the theoretical equality between the vil-

3. It is abstract, in the true sense, for the technical engineer who never sees his own colleagues.

4. It will be remembered that production workers and maintenance men conformed rigorously to the norms of their group in all strategic areas and that the official line took precedence in a public encounter over individual personal opinions.

5. *Nouville, un village français* (Paris: Institut d'Ethnologie, 1953), p. 148.

6. *Ibid.*, p. 169.

7. *Village in the Vaucluse* (Cambridge, Mass.: Harvard University Press, 1958).

lagers. Anyone who shows initiative is likely to be accused of trying to boss the others.

In a study of a rural community under the impact of drastic change (flooding of the area for the erection of a big dam), Jean Dubost[8] documents the same amazing lack of constructive organized activities. Leadership emerged only in the last extremity —and then on a temporary basis and for a negative purpose.

In the past history of France, there is abundant testimony to the persistence of these patterns over long periods of time. None is more eloquent than this short statement of Turgot, the most famous reform minister of the late Monarchy, as quoted by de Tocqueville: "A French parish is a congeries of huts and countryfolk as inert as their huts."[9]

The most penetrating analyst of these traits is de Tocqueville himself. He explains at length how the municipal policy, and especially the fiscal policy, of the kings in the seventeenth and eighteenth centuries had quelled all possibility of spontaneous organized activities, especially at the lower levels:

> Such was the system of taxation that every taxpayer had an urgent and unfailing motive for spying on his neighbours and promptly notifying the Collector of any increase in their means.[10]

He sees clearly the link between the isolation of the individual and the lack of collective spirit, on the one side, and the isolation of the different strata and their perennial fight for rank and status, on the other:

> Each group was differentiated from the rest by its right to petty privileges of one kind or another, even the least of which was regarded as a token of its exalted status. Thus they were constantly wrangling over questions of precedence, so much so that the Intendant and the courts were often at a loss for a solution of their differences. "At last an order has been passed that the holy water is to be given to the judges of the presidial court before being given to members of the town corporation. The parlement had been unable to come to a decision, so the King took the matter up in Council and had decided it himself. It was high time, too, as the whole town was in a ferment." When a group was not given the precedence it claimed in the general assembly of notables, it ceased to attend, preferring to withdraw from public affairs altogether rather than to stomach such an affront to its dignity.[11]

Leadership and constructive activities could have merged only if groups cutting across ranks had developed. However, their development was prevented by the continuous policy of the royal administration, which preferred failure to the risk of competition:

> Any independent group, however small, which seemed desirous of taking action otherwise than under the aegis of the administration filled it with alarm, and the tiniest free association of citizens, however harmless its aims, was regarded as a nuisance. The only corporate bodies tolerated were those whose members had been hand-picked by the administration and which were under its control. Even big industrial concerns were frowned upon. In a word, our administration resented the idea of private citizens' having any say in the control of their own enterprises, and preferred sterility to competition.[12]

The privileges and particularisms of the *ancien régime* have gone. But the same patterns—individual isolation and lack of constructive cooperative activities on the one side, strata isolation and lack of communication between people of different rank on the other—have persisted.

The persistence of strata isolation was especially well analyzed in the 1920's by a shrewd observer of the French bourgeois pattern of living, the philosopher Edmond Goblot. According to Goblot, bourgeois society in France was ruled by two great principles, which he called "the barrier" and "levelling."[13] "The barrier" refers to all the kinds of obstacles raised by the bourgeoisie to prevent people from achieving bourgeois status. "Levelling" refers to the theoretical equality conferred to each person once he has crossed over. Goblot's study consists mainly of analyses of all the different and indirect kinds of obstacles and the rationalizations used to justify them. Classical culture as sanctioned by the baccalaureate, professional ethics, fashion,

8. Jean Dubost, "Commissariat General du Plan, Paris" (unpublished paper).

9. Alexis de Tocqueville, *The Old Régime and the French Revolution* (New York: Doubleday, 1955), Book II, chap. 3, p. 121.

10. *Ibid.*, Book II, chap. 12, p. 183.

11. *Ibid.*, Book II, chap. 9, p. 157.

12. *Ibid.*, Book II, chap. 6, p. 132. For an analysis of the persistence of this spirit in contemporary France see Arnold Rose, "Voluntary Associations in France," in *Theory and Method in the Social Sciences* (Minneapolis: University of Minnesota Press, 1954).

13. Edmond Goblot, *La Barrière et le Niveau, étude sociologique de la bourgeoisie française moderne* (Paris: Alcan, 1925), pp. 126–27.

and art have provided ways of isolating the bourgeoisie from the common man. But whatever the obstacles, they are conceived as restrictive for those who are outside and in an equalitarian way for those inside. Here again, we see the link, emphasized several times already, between equalitarianism and stratification.

Finally, echoing de Tocqueville, Goblot insists on the social and collective aspect of the barrier. It does not vanish because individuals can cross it. On the contrary, it becomes even more humiliating.[14]

Individual isolation and lack of constructive activities have been studied more recently by an American sociologist, Jesse R. Pitts. Pitts has presented a new and interesting interpretation of this pattern of action.

According to Pitts, informal activities are not absent in the French way of life. However, they are negative, instable, and never expressed openly. To characterize them, Pitts has coined the suggestive term, the "delinquent community," which he used first in an analysis of the children's activities at school.[15] It suggests a kind of implicit solidarity among all members of the same rank, which can be tapped when necessary but can never appear in the open. This is a negative kind of solidarity, directed against superiors and against other groups. It is extremely successful in preventing any attempt at leadership within the group. For Frenchmen, the delinquent community is the model of all collective activities in which they participate.[16] In a recent paper, Pitts summarizes its importance as follows:

> The school peer group is the prototype of the solidarity groups which exist in France beyond the nuclear family and the extended family. They are characterized by jealous equalitarianism among the members . . . conspiracy of silence against superior authority, incapacity to take any initiative outside of the interpretations and accommodations with the directives of superior authority, in an effort to create for each member a zone of autonomy, of caprice, of creativity.[17]

This analysis of the "finishing school of the French citizen" fits very well with our own observations of the girls and their supervisors in the Clerical Agency, and of the production and maintenance workers in the Industrial Monopoly. The delinquent community, in those cases, is the implicit pact of defense of all the members of the formal group, and its meaning is narrow but clear. If and when a member asks for help from another member of his formal peer group, for the protection of his zone of independence and free activity, any other member is required to assist him, whatever the former's feelings toward him may be.

## The problems of authority and the avoidance of face-to-face relationships

The specific patterns of action of the French peer group as described by Pitts, the isolation and lack of initiative of the individual as described in the remarks of Bernot, Blancard, and Wylie, the protective role of the strata which Goblot analyzed, and the long tradition of apathy in public affairs that de Tocqueville and Taine emphasized, correspond to the patterns of interpersonal and intergroup relations that we observed in our case studies. At the same time, it seems quite clear that all these traits finally revolve around the basic difficulty of facing conflict and developing acceptable leadership at the level of the primary group. They directly raise the problem of the cultural aspect of basic authority relationships.

This is apparent in each case. The "delinquent community" is a protective device against external authority—whether that of the teacher, that of the state, or that of the boss—and at the same time an indirect but extremely efficient way of making it impossible for an individual member of the group to become its leader. Groups described by Bernot, Blancard, and Wylie are extremely anxious to prevent any one of their members from raising himself above the others. If a group member shows initiative, he risks being deserted by his fellows and being deeply humiliated. Apathy, the refusal to partici-

14. De Tocqueville himself said about the French nobility: "But the barriers between the French nobility and the other classes, though quite easily traversed, were always fixed and plain to see; so conspicuous, indeed, as to exasperate those against whom they were erected. For once a man had crossed them he was cut off from all outside the pale by privileges injurious both to their pockets and their pride." (De Tocqueville, *op. cit.*, Book II, chap. 9, p. 152.)

15. Jesse R. Pitts, "The Bourgeois Family and French Economic Retardation" (Ph.D. diss., Harvard University, 1957), pp. 329–31.

16. *Ibid.*, pp. 338–43.

17. Jesse R. Pitts, in *In Search of France* (Cambridge, Mass.: Harvard University Press, 1963).

pate, as we have argued in the preceding chapter, is a rational response if people want, above all, to evade conflict situations and to escape dependence relationships. Strata isolation, focusing on rank and status, and the impossibility of informal grouping across strata, all stem from the same difficulties. All these traits ultimately refer to the basic cultural conditions predetermining the possible scope of authority relationships.

We should like, at this point, to review the data, remarks, and analyses of other social scientists and writers who have studied this central relationship. Unfortunately, authority has been a neglected field —at least, authority as a modern cultural pattern. We have little reliable information about it, and nothing comparable to the greater amount of material on interpersonal and intergroup relationships. The works of philosophers and essayists who have studied the peculiarities of French rationalism and Cartesianism as a basis of French culture cannot be too helpful.[18] The work of the study group on contemporary cultures inspired by Margaret Mead,[19] and the cultural analyses of the characteristic plays and movies of a period as performed by Wolfenstein and Leites,[20] may be more interesting, but much consists of anecdotes and is often debatable. We can point out, however, that the descriptions of the classroom by Wylie, and to some extent by Bernot and Blancard, confirm the scheme Rhoda Métraux and Margaret Mead propose in *Themes in French Culture*.[21] Furthermore, there is no contradiction between this scheme and our model. But the field is still so unexplored that one cannot make too much of these correspondences.

We shall thus have to be content with a more modest endeavor. We shall elaborate a working hypothesis, starting with our observations in our two case studies, and discuss the extent to which it fits with the recorded experiences of the functioning of other organizations.[22]

In both cases we analyzed, there is a central and recurrent pattern. Direct face-to-face authority relationships are avoided as much as possible. Open conflicts appear only between groups that do not directly confront each other. Partners appear just like the children described by Wylie, or the famous characters of the Pagnol folk plays, who shout insults at each other only in situations where they do not run any physical risk. Authority is converted, as much as possible, into impersonal rules. The whole structure is so devised that whatever authority cannot be eliminated is allocated so that it is at a safe distance from the people who are affected.

We wish to suggest the following hypothesis. This pattern of human relations may provide an adequate answer to the problems raised by the functioning of modern organizations. It is its "bureaucratic," or one of its "bureaucratic," answers. But at the same time it is also specifically French. Face-to-face dependence relationships are, indeed, perceived as difficult to bear in the French cultural setting. Yet the prevailing view of authority is still that of universalism and absolutism; it continues to retain something of the seventeenth century's political theory, with its mixture of rationality and *bon plaisir*.[23] The two attitudes are contradictory. However, they can be reconciled within a

18. One may, however, propose some subtle indirect analogies in the works of such astute observers as Ernst Robert Curtius, *Essai sur la France* (Paris: Grasset, 1941); Paul Distelbarth, *La personne France* (Paris: Alsatia, 1942); and Salvador de Madariaga, *Anglais, Français, Espagnols* (Paris: Gallimard, 1930).

19. Rhoda Métraux and Margaret Mead, *Themes in French Culture* (Stanford, Calif.: Stanford University Press, 1954); Margaret Mead and Martha Wolfenstein (eds.), *Childhood in Contemporary Cultures* (Chicago: University of Chicago Press, 1955); see also the valuable study of Erik Erikson on Germany, in his *Childhood and Society* (New York: Norton, 1950).

20. Martha Wolfenstein and Nathan Leites, *Movies: A Psychological Study* (New York: Free Press, 1950). Recently, Nathan Leites has moved forward again in that direction, discussing, in a very brilliant although still anecdotal manner, the basic cultural traits of French society and of its elite. See Nathan Leites, "La Règle de jeu" and "L'Obsession du mal" (mimeographed reports; Paris: Ecole Pratique des Hautes Etudes, 1960 and 1961).

21. According to these authors, it will be remembered, French education "is characterized by a tight control and a repression of movement and physical aggression, a great pressure of the outside world with socialization achieved by shaming and nagging and a reliance on oral aggression as a way of relief."

22. In the next chapter we shall use this hypothesis as a scheme for analyzing a number of characteristic patterns of action in other walks of life—thus putting the model to a kind of test.

23. *Bon plaisir* ("good pleasure," i.e., the arbitrary will of the ruler) was the official term for legitimating the king's order at the time of absolutism. In Parsonian categories, the French conception of authority should be considered as diffuse, in contrast to a more modern "specific" conception. In this perspective, the main contradiction of French society, made possible by the permanence of a bureaucratic system of organization, is the coexistence of universalistic traits with diffuse, non-specific ones.

bureaucratic system, since impersonal rules and centralization make it possible to reconcile an absolutist conception of authority and the elimination of most direct dependence relationships. In other words, the French bureaucratic system of organization is the perfect solution to the basic dilemma of Frenchmen about authority. They cannot bear the omnipotent authority which they feel is indispensable if any kind of cooperative activity is to succeed. It can even be argued that this dilemma has been perpetuated by the long tradition of the French bureaucratic patterns, whose strength comes from their meeting two contradictory and equally potent aims, preserving the independence of the individual and insuring the rationality of collective action.

*Bon plaisir* is the law of formal apparatus. Authority at each echelon is conceived of as absolute. There are no checks and balances. There is not so much respect for due process as in Anglo-Saxon countries.[24] But although subordinates are not protected by law and are thus more vulnerable to arbitrary procedures, they benefit from another and equally strong protection—the counter-pressure of the peer group.[25] *Bon plaisir*, however, is not completely imaginary. It is expressed in the symbols and paraphernalia of the ranking system. It bears on the status rewards received from membership in each of the strata. Finally, it may become operative during a crisis, when people must overcome their *amour-propre* and cooperate to achieve common ends.[26]

Individual isolation and strata isolation, on the other hand, allow some part of *bon plaisir* to everyone, although largely in a negative sense. People are protected against interference from above. They do not have to yield to someone's pressure; what they do, they do of their own accord. Work tends to be done without any obligation or pressure. People do not work because they have to, but because they want to.[27] This freedom from interference—this independence—is, therefore, another form of the absolutist conception of authority. To compromise, to make deals, to adjust to other people's claims is frowned upon; it is considered better to restrict oneself and to remain free within the narrower limits one has fixed or even those one has had to accept.

This insistence on personal autonomy and this pattern of restriction are old in France. They were, and to some extent remain, one of the main elements of the value system of traditional French peasantry. The terms in which de Tocqueville, among others, has characterized these feelings are meaningful: "On the other hand the small landowner's motive for action comes from himself alone; within his narrow sphere he moves freely." This is to be understood in contrast to "la petite fortune moblière" despised by the French, with which "one is dependent almost always, more or less, on the whims and fancies of someone else. One must bow before the rules of an association or the will of another man."[28]

A bureaucratic system of organization of the French type makes it possible to retain something of the independence of another time within the framework of modern organization. One always obeys the rules, but one need not submit to other men's whims. This is, however, a negative advantage; on the positive side, one does not gain so much. Each member of a superordinate group is given a judicial function over some members of the subordinate strata. It is still an absolute and awe-inspiring function, and he may enjoy it if he does not care too much for actual power.

Privileges, strategic individual and group influences working everywhere within the organization, only reflect the impossibility of isolation from the outside world. They are the dark spots in an

24. This analysis, of course, would have to be qualified in many ways. Good observers have contended that in no other country were subordinates as well protected against arbitrary action as in the French public service. Yet the government public administration theoretically disposes of a great number of discretionary powers and only administrative courts can review their acts. See Brian Chapman, *The Prefects and Provincial France* (London: Allen & Unwin, 1955).

25. This relative helplessness of central authority enables us to understand why it is so desperately attached to maintaining arbitrariness when applying the rules. This is the only way for it to retain some influence over subordinates otherwise impossible to cope with.

26. This may be one of the reasons why people are so fascinated by crises and why crises are so frequent.

27. This is, of course, in many cases a figure of speech; yet there are frequent instances of careers completely divorced from achievement at work, and situations in which people are rather free to choose whether to give or to refuse their personal co-operation at work.

28. Freely translated from de Tocqueville, *L'ancien régime et la Révolution* (Paris: Gallimard, 1952), p. 52.

otherwise perfect rationalistic system of organization. But they, as we noted earlier, actually reinforce it. They give the system its short-run dynamism. The issue of equality and resistance to favoritism is kept alive by the persistence and constant reappearance of privileges. From this viewpoint, French public administration must not be considered as a static organization. It is always in the process of rationalizing, eliminating abnormal situations, undue interference, and undue competition, and, above all, it is constantly chasing privileges.[29]

To conclude: To the French, a bureaucratic system of organization seems the best way to afford some participation in *bon plaisir* to the greatest number of persons. Its development may be analyzed as a process of granting new strata adequate status and the concomitant guarantees of participation in the game. Certain of the lowest subordinate groups do not participate very much as yet, as, e.g., the girls of the Clerical Agency. But even these employees have some leeway, and, in any case, they are supposed to be there only for a few years and may accept their lot because they have the prospect of future rewards.

29. One can see a paradox in the contrast between the relentless egalitarian claims one always hears in all French bureaucratic organizations, and the relative lack of favoritism that really occurs compared to other countries' patterns of action. From this point of view, the difference between private and public organization may be smaller than is usually expected.

JOSEPH S. BERLINER

# A Problem in Soviet Business Administration

Soviet industrial organization has long been plagued by a number of nagging little problems. They have not prevented the state from achieving a considerable success in its prime objective of getting its salaried managers, the men who run the nation's business, to turn out impressive quantities of goods and services. But there remain certain things which the state, with all its power, has not been able to get its managers to do. The intractable is always intriguing, and one wonders why these persistent thorns have not been eliminated.

Holders of power can rarely expect to achieve a perfect compliance with their wishes, and it is to be expected that Soviet industrial organization would have its share of defects. What is interesting, however, is the particular form they assume. Like the pathology of an organism, an examination of a characteristic defect of a system of organization may be expected to provide an insight into the nature of that system. It is with this end in view that we turn to an inquiry into one such defect in the case of the Soviet industrial enterprise.[1]

Conveniently for us, the leaders of the Soviet state deliver from time to time very candid reports on the state of the nation's industry to the governing bodies of the Communist party. These reports constitute a set of fairly comparable documents which lend themselves to an analysis of the persistent and the changing features of industrial organization over a period of time.[2] In February 1941, G. M. Malenkov delivered to the Eighteenth Party Conference a report which, as it turned out, proved to be a summing up of the state of industry at the end of the prewar period. Among the many matters which he considered important enough to call to the attention of the assembled party leaders was the following:

> Now, Comrades, matters stand thus; in most of our enterprises the output of finished production is carried out unevenly, in spurts, and is concentrated as a rule at the end of the month. Enterprises lack a firm, previously worked-out schedule of production.
>
> Here are some typical examples.
>
> The Kolomensk Machinery Works in Moscow

1. The Soviet industrial enterprise may be thought of roughly as mill or factory under the management of a director and his administrative staff. The director is primarily responsible to a minister or one of his assistants. The minister is part of the executive arm of the state. The broad decisions as to what is to be produced are made by the state and transmitted to the enterprises through the ministries.

2. The three reports referred to may be found in *Izvestiia*, Feb. 16, 1941, pp. 1–3 (the Malenkov 1941 report); Leo Gruliow, ed., *Current Soviet Policies* (New York, 1953), pp. 106–16 (the Malenkov 1952 report); *Current Digest of the Soviet Press*, 7 (Aug. 24, 1955), 3–20 (the Bulganin 1955 report).

The author wishes to thank Dr. Richard Axt of the National Science Foundation and Hans Heymann of the RAND Corporation for their valuable comments.

Reprinted from *Administrative Science Quarterly*, (June, 1956, pp. 86–101, by permission of the author and publisher. (Copyright 1956 by The Graduate School of Business and Public Administration, Cornell University.)

County worked this way in 1940: in the first ten days of every month it produced 5 to 7 per cent of its output, in the second ten days, 10 to 15 per cent, and in the third ten days, 75 to 80 per cent.

The Karl Marx-Leningrad Plant, in December 1940, produced 2 per cent of its monthly output in the first ten days, 8 per cent in the second ten days, and 90 per cent in the third ten days.

In the Moscow Pump and Compressor Plant, in December 1940, 3.4 per cent of the month's output was produced in the first ten days, 27.5 per cent in the second ten days, and 69.1 per cent in the third ten days.

We must put an end to this lack of planning, to this uneven rate of production, to this storming in the work of enterprises. We must achieve a day-to-day fulfillment of the production program according to a previously worked-out schedule, by every factory, mill, mine, and railroad.

In October 1952, at what proved to be the last party congress of the Stalin era, Malenkov was again accorded the honor of delivering the official report. Eleven years of war and reconstruction had elapsed, during which time the preceding generation of industrial managers must have been largely replaced by a new generation. But again, surveying the broad canvas of Soviet industrial achievements and problems, he lashed out against the same old problem. "The Party has more than once drawn our industrial executives' attention to this defect," he said. "Nevertheless many enterprises continue to work in spurts, producing almost half the month's program during the final ten days of the month."

A few months later Stalin died, an uncomfortable collegial form of government emerged, industrial ministries were suddenly combined into a very small number and subsequently decentralized once more, Malenkov fell from the peak of power, and on the next occasion that a major report on the economy was made, it was delivered by Premier N. A. Bulganin. In preparing this first great pronouncement of the new regime on the subject of industrial organization, before a plenary session of the Central Committee of the party in July 1955, Bulganin chose to call attention to the same matter:

A very serious shortcoming in the work of our industry is the lack of rhythm in production, and the resulting uneven output of industrial production.

Here are three factories. . . . The average fulfillment of the monthly plan at these factories by ten-day periods during the first quarter of 1955 is as follows: first ten days—Russian Diesel, 5 per cent; Spirit of the Revolution, 3 per cent; Kolomna plant, 6 per cent. Second ten days—Russian Diesel, 23 per cent; Spirit of the Revolution, 26.6 per cent; Kolomna plant, 23.3 per cent. Third ten days—Russian Diesel, 72 per cent; Spirit of the Revolution, 70.4 per cent; Kolomna plant, 70.7 per cent. How can one talk of rhythm in the work of these plants when nearly three quarters of the month's work is being carried out in the third ten days? . . .

Much has already been written and said about the lack of rhythm in work, and decisions have been made. However, it must be admitted that we have been unable to achieve any substantial improvement in this matter.

This practice of "storming" leads to a number of uneconomic consequences. States of emergency constantly arise; men and equipment are subject to periods of unnecessary idleness; during the days of storming the rate of spoilage increases, overtime pay mounts up, the machines suffer from speed-up, and customers' production schedules are interrupted. It is certainly a practice which the state would wish to eliminate if it could. Yet storming does not occupy a top position on the list of problems facing the state. If it did, perhaps the leaders would have been willing to take the measures necessary to eliminate it. It has not been the object of a major "campaign," the technique whereby the state attacks a bothersome problem by mobilizing all its propaganda and police resources and focusing them upon that problem. For this very reason, the practice of storming serves our purpose best by providing a case study of a normal problem in the administration of economic activity.

In examining the reports cited above, one is struck by the absence of an explanation of the causes of storming. Only Bulganin offered a feeble sort of explanation. "The principal cause," he said, "is lack of order in the supplying of materials and equipment to industry. . . . Customers usually are sent the major part of their requirements during the second half of the month, and especially during the last ten days." Now this indeed does explain why the customer has to speed up his rate of production at the end of the month, but it does not explain why the supplier failed in the first place to deliver the required materials in the early part of the month, that is, why the supplier engaged in storming. In effect, storming in one enterprise is caused by storming in another enterprise. This does explain how storming is propagated through the system once it is caused somewhere, but it obviously does not explain why it is caused.

The explanation must be cast in terms of the objectives of enterprise managers and the conditions of the economic milieu within which these objectives must be achieved. The prime obligation of managers is the fulfillment of the monthly output plan. The plan is the document in which the state translates its broad economic objectives into specific production instructions for each of the many thousands of enterprises which make up the industrial system. At the highest level, the National Economic Plan is a listing of the annual production targets for the whole economy, with supplementary targets of investment, increases in labor productivity, reduction of production costs, and so on. On the basis of the National Economic Plan, each of the industrial ministries receives its set of annual targets, subdivided into quarters of the year. The ministries' quarterly targets are then translated into monthly targets for each of their enterprises, which carry out the actual production work.

If the economic objectives of the state are to be achieved, enterprises must meet their production targets in the proper quantities and at the proper times. For this reason, the whole system of incentives which the state has fashioned for the purpose of recruiting high-quality people into managerial positions and motivating them to do their jobs well is geared to fulfillment of the monthly plan, particularly the production target of the plan. First and most immediate is the ample money bonus. Depending upon the importance of the industry and the size of his enterprise, the manager earns a bonus of 30 to 100 per cent of his base salary every month in which he just fulfills his plan.[3] For each percentage overfulfillment of his plan he earns an additional bonus of 2 to 10 per cent of his base salary. The opportunities of adding to an already substantial base salary are thus quite appealing. The director of a coal mine, for example, whose base salary may be about 10,000 rubles a month, would earn a total of 25,000 rubles in any month in which he overfulfilled his plan by 5 per cent.

One need not be a *homo economicus* to be profoundly motivated by such income possibilities. Moreover, the state has seen to it that this money incentive is not in conflict with, but is rather reinforced by, other incentives which may motivate a Soviet manager. Personal advancement, public recognition, and all the prestige which the state can officially confer or channel are available to the manager who regularly fulfills his plans. Demotion is the usual lot of a manager who proves incapable of meeting production targets.

The point is that the state has quite successfully met the problem of eliciting a high level of managerial effort. Soviet managers work hard, not only in terms of their hours of work but in the energy and worry they devote to their jobs. And the focus of their efforts is the fulfillment of the monthly plan.

But fulfilling the monthly plan is no easy matter, and this is the second point to be made. The state has succeeded in organizing a system of establishing plan targets which is calculated to maintain the targets at a high level. Among the various devices developed to achieve this aim is one based on the "ratchet" principle. According to this principle, when an enterprise overfulfills a plan target, the plan target for the following period must be raised. That is, if an enterprise overfulfills its plan of a million rubles' worth of output in one period, the plan for the following period must be greater than a million.[4] In combination with a powerful motivation for managers to overfulfill their plans, the ratchet principle provides an ever-rising floor beneath which output plans cannot fall. The abundant bonuses induce managers to overfulfill their plans, the ratchet snaps the catch, as it were, beneath the new level of output achieved, and the manager must then exert even greater effort to overfulfill the raised target. This would seem to be a very efficient mechanism for securing the state's objective of an ever-increasing rate of output.

What we have just described is, to be sure, an

3. A. Vikent'ev, *Ocherki razvitiia sovetskoi ekonomiki v chetvertoi piatiletke* ("Essays on Soviet Economic Development in the Fourth Five Year Plan") (Gosplanizdat, 1952), p. 175.

4. The ratchet principle is not an explicit principle of planning but a generally understood rule among managers and planners. In the published sources one catches glimpses of it in the criticism of planners who apply it overzealously (*Stroitel'naia gazeta*, July 27, 1955, p. 2), and in criticisms such as that by Malenkov in his 1941 report, directed against "commissariats which not only did not fulfill their 1940 plans but actually reduced their output below 1939." Usually the ratchet principle operates over yearly periods, occasionally over quarterly periods.

abstract model of a real process. In fact, managers have been forced to adopt certain methods of defense against the working of this mechanism. Awareness of the action of the ratchet principle causes the prudent manager to beware of overfulfilling his plan by too large an amount, a practice which is contrary to the intentions of the state. Similarly, managers take pains to preserve a "safety factor" in their production targets, so that they can overfulfill their plans and yet not exhaust their real production potential.[5] But, in general, the effect of the mechanism is to maintain plan targets at a level high enough that the margin of fulfillment is perilously close for most enterprises. This pressure of high targets is perhaps the most salient fact of life of the Soviet manager. Bulganin presented some dramatic evidence of this in his criticism of the high rate of underfulfillment of plans. In 1951, 31 per cent of all enterprises failed to fulfill their annual production plans; in 1952, 39 per cent; in 1953, 40 per cent; and in 1954, 36 per cent. Thus a third of all managers can regularly be expected to underfulfill their plans.

One consequence of this close margin of operation is suggested by another observation made by Bulganin. "The executives of many enterprises change much too often. In the coal industry, for example, about 40 per cent of the heads and chief engineers of the mines and some 50 per cent of the sector managers change every year." When a Soviet manager leaves his job, it is not of his own volition.

The picture which emerges is that of a system in which managers work in a rather precarious position. The difference between the successful and the lagging enterprise is not primarily that the former has an easier time of it, but that its managers are more resourceful in overcoming difficulties. Take the Cheliabinsk Tractor Plant, a great and modern establishment which fulfills its plan month after month. Here at least, one might guess, is a smoothly functioning operation. Yet when the Soviet press gives us a glimpse of its day-to-day life, we find another picture. Although the plant fulfilled its plan for the first half of 1955, it had to engage regularly in storming in order to do so. Workers are pressured by management into working on their days off and those who refuse are declared to be "absentees." One woman worker was dismissed for refusing to work on Sundays and was reinstated only after the intervention of the trade union. In September, we read, things began to look bad once more toward the end of the month; the director therefore switched the day off from Sunday, September 25, to Saturday, October 1. "It was possible," declares the reporter of the incident, "with the help of this extra day, to make do, and to make do quite well."[6] The monthly plan was fulfilled once more and the plant is still numbered among the successful.

With this slim margin of safety, any untoward accident can plunge the enterprise into underfulfillment. The breakdown of a crucial piece of equipment, the rejection of a large lot of production, can throw the enterprise off its production schedule. Even if the manager could meet his target as far as his own efforts are concerned, there is the additional source of trouble referred to by Bulganin, namely that the supplier may fall behind his schedule and thus fail to deliver urgently needed materials on time. Indeed, the unreliability of the system of interenterprise supply is perhaps the second most important fact of life in Soviet industry. The economic milieu is therefore such that the manager must often expect to fall behind his production schedule in the course of some month or other.

Given the likelihood of a lag behind the production schedule in some months, what causes the recourse to storming? One might imagine that the lost output would be considered just so much water under the dam: the manager might resume his production schedule when the machine was repaired or the materials arrived, and the month's bonus would be written off as lost. That this does not happen is due to the very special role of the accounting period, the end of the month. Ordinarily, an accounting period is a rather arbitrary date selected for the convenience of planning or for taking stock of performance. Ideally, it should be quite neutral with respect to decision-making; that is, managers should make the same decisions when the accounting date is known as they would make if they did not know on what date the books would be closed. Least of all should the accounting date itself be treated as a datum in the decision-making process.

5. Joseph S. Berliner, Informal Organization of the Soviet Firm, *Quarterly Journal of Economics*, 66 (Aug. 1952), 353–55.

6. *Current Digest of the Soviet Press*, 7 (Nov. 9, 1955), 9.

But this is precisely what happens in the Soviet enterprise, and it is this which explains the practice of storming.

This tendency for an arbitrary accounting date to become a factor in decision-making is not unique for Soviet business administration; the effect of tax law on the financial policies of American business leaps to mind. Because of the crucial role of time periods in planning, it is perhaps more serious in the Soviet economy. A vivid illustration of its unfortunate consequences was provided a few years ago by N. S. Khrushchev, in a report on agriculture.[7] For many years it had been the practice to take the livestock census on January 1. It would seem that January 1 is a rather harmless date; presumably it was selected by an innocent planner with the primary objective of facilitating planning schedules. However, the collective farms have targets of livestock holdings which they are required to meet, as well as targets of meat deliveries to the state. Ordinarily the peasants would bring their stock for slaughter in the early fall, when they are fattest from the summer grazing. But in order to meet their livestock targets on January 1, they kept their stock through the cold early winter months so that they could be counted in the census. The consequence was a disastrous loss of weight; and when they finally brought their stock for slaughter after the census date, they had to slaughter many more head of stock than planned in order to fulfill the quota of meat deliveries in kilograms of beef on the hoof. This had been going on for a number of years before it came to the attention of Khrushchev. The census date has since been moved back to October 1, and the simple shift of dates has probably solved this curious problem.

Thus an arbitrary accounting date had become a factor in the decision-making process, with the most uneconomic consequences. This is precisely what happens in the case of storming. Because of the crucial importance of the end of the month for the fortunes of the manager, any lag in the production schedule is followed by an acceleration in the rate of production in order that the planned output be attained on that vital date. The greater the lag in the early part of the month, the greater the speed-up toward the end of the month. Given this special role of the accounting period, storming is to be expected as long as lags in production are a normal occurrence.

If storming were confined to the months in which lags occurred, its prevalence would be much more limited than it is. It would be much less troublesome to the Soviets and much less interesting to us. For the remarkable thing is that at the end of the month of storming the manager is not presented with a *tabula rasa*, so that in the following month, if no lag occurred, he might hope to avoid storming. The very act of storming creates conditions which make a lag in the following month inevitable. Of the many reasons why this occurs, we can present only the most important.

A proper schedule of prophylactic maintenance and repair of equipment requires that a certain number of machines be out of operation at all times. But a machine taken down for repair is a machine which is not producing, and thus there is a constant pressure on the maintenance personnel to postpone their work until the pressure is off. "In the third ten-day period of January," we read in the newspaper of the machinery industry, "machine 'TM-132' was supposed to have been overhauled, but in the shop they decided to wait; 'the production program has to be fulfilled,' they said. Soon, however, the machine broke down completely."[8] And a correspondent of the newspaper of the iron and steel industry observes that "storming leads to the fact that at the end of the month the equipment is not stopped for maintenance. All stoppages for maintenance are postponed until the beginning of the next month."[9] The consequence is that the first part of the month following a period of storming is devoted to catching up on the most vital delayed maintenance work and to repairing the damage caused by overwork. Hence the enterprise falls once more behind its current production schedule.

In the discussion of bonuses it was pointed out that the difference between 99 per cent of the plan fulfillment and 100 per cent may be worth as much as double his salary for the plant manager. This sharp discontinuity in earning power is not exactly calculated to bring out the noblest of qualities in a man. When so much hangs upon that one per cent, it is quite understandable that the manager will stretch a point in order to achieve it. The common-

7. *Pravda*, Sept. 15, 1953, p. 2.

8. *Mashinostroenie*, Feb. 9, 1939, p. 2.

9. *Chernaia Metallurgiia*, March 4, 1941, p. 3.

set practice is the "borrowing" of output from the next month and reporting it as having been produced in the current month. The Molotov Weaving and Finishing Mill, for example, was considerably short of its monthly target on August 31. "What was most important," states the reporter of the incident, "there was no chance for a bonus." The manager called in his accountants, "giving them strict orders to include the output of the first two days of September in the August plan, and, of course, to draw up appropriate 'records' for this purpose."[10] Since the borrowed output must be "repaid," the early period of the following month is devoted to producing output which had been reported as completed in the preceding month. Hence the enterprise falls behind its current schedule once more. "It is like a tight shirt which comes out in front when you pull it down in back," remarked a former Soviet managerial official interviewed by the writer.

The available descriptions of the storming process indicate that a great deal of energy is expended, while the men work long overtime hours and the managerial officials work "round the clock." It is to be expected that when the deadline is over, there will be a letdown—if not in hours, at least in energy expended.[11]

Factors such as these impart a dynamic movement to the output of the Soviet firm, a movement which has all the formal properties of a "business cycle." Consider an enterprise which has managed to achieve an even rate of output. Any disturbance to its schedule will now generate a periodic movement in its rate of output, not only in the month in which the disturbance occurs but in a number of successive months. The oscillations will dampen down if the enterprise has succeeded in tucking away a "safety factor"; that is, if in any month the output plan is small enough that it can be fulfilled with enough time and resources left over to make up for the output deficit of the preceding month. The oscillations will become wider if the initial disturbance is reinforced in succeeding months so that the enterprise falls further and further behind its schedule. This usually ends, as the Russians say, in a great *skandal*. The manager is fired and a new hopeful takes over.

Here, then, is a nice problem for the administrator. Three integral elements of the system of industrial organization are involved; a powerful incentive to produce, a successful technique of maintaining high targets, and a system of planning and accounting. Each in its way is a useful device for what it is designed to accomplish. Yet in combination they give rise to this unfortunate and unintended practice of storming. It is interesting to speculate on changes that might succeed in eliminating the practice. Let us at the outset limit the admissible changes to simple measures which would not require far-reaching alterations in the basic features of the system of industrial organization, such as the planning and incentive systems.

In the three party reports quoted earlier, the only real administrative measure recommended was one put forth by Malenkov in the 1941 report. Certain commissariats,[12] he indicated, had introduced a system requiring every director to report daily to the commissar on the quantity of output produced the preceding day. "These reports oblige the commissar to find the causes of the failure to fulfill the daily targets immediately, and to take immediate measures for correcting the indicated deficiencies." Where the system had been introduced, stated Malenkov, there had been a significant evening-out of the rate of production.

Whatever hopes Malenkov may have had that this measure would provide the panacea must have been short-lived, for little was heard of it thereafter. At least one reason for the failure began to emerge shortly afterward. As a measure of self-defense, managers began to resort to the practice of "prolonging the work day." In an iron and steel plant, we read, "by order of Comrade Matevosian, the chief engineer, it was decided to prolong the acceptance of finished products from the rolling mill on March 15 until 1:30 A.M. of March 16. On

10. *Current Digest of the Soviet Press*, 4 (Jan. 3, 1953), 16.

11. To this may perhaps be added the survivals of peasant resistance to the harsh and demanding discipline of industrial factory life. There is a very suggestive passage in Marx's *Capital* describing the early capitalists' troubles in disciplining their recently urbanized labor force to the factory regime: "Work toward the end of the week being generally much increased in duration in consequence of the habit of the men of idling on Monday and occasionally during a part or whole of Tuesday also. . . . They lose two or three days, and then work all night to make it up" (Karl Marx, *Capital* [Modern Library], p. 523 n.).

12. In the prewar period, ministers were known as "peoples' commissars."

March 11 Comrade Matevosian authorized the inclusion in the output of the current day, of the output of the quality steel shops which had actually been completed by 6:00 A.M. of the following day."[13] In other words, the period of the storming cycle was reduced from the month to the day, but the same elements of periodicity continued to prevail. Any measure to eliminate storming must reckon with the boundless ingenuity of Soviet managers.

There were undoubtedly other reasons for the failure of Malenkov's measure. A system of daily reporting must have greatly increased the work load on the normally overlarge number of book-keepers and clerks in the plant administration. The system also required a more formalized set of daily plan targets, a further burden on the planning apparatus in the commissariat and in its hundreds of enterprises. And finally, when the lag in production was due to causes outside the enterprise's own control, such as the failure of materials shipments to arrive on time, the commissariat officials could not be expected to straighten matters out in a single day.

Would it help to lengthen the accounting period, perhaps to a three-month or six-month period instead of a one-month period?[14] This measure comes very close to violating the restriction we have set upon the range of admissible solutions, for it may well require far-reaching changes in the methods of plant administration. The system of bonus payments would have to be shifted to a longer time period. If the bonus for fulfillment of the six-month plan is to be equal to six times the bonus previously available for the monthly plan, the stakes on that last few per cent of plan fulfillment would be so high as to constitute an intolerable strain on the honesty of mortal men. Moreover, the whole system of planning and reporting is geared to a monthly basis, and if the bonus system were not similarly geared there would undoubtedly be an increase in the incidence of underfulfillment of monthly plans. For however harshly storming is indicted, the state is really rather ambivalent about it. Because of the planned interdependence of customers and suppliers, underfulfillment by one enterprise often sends a wave of underfulfillment pulsing through a number of other plants. It is therefore vitally important that each manager exert the greatest effort to fulfill his monthly plan. One suspects that the state would rather have storming-plus-fulfillment than underfulfillment-without-storming. It is true that this problem of the close interdependence of enterprises could be met by an increase in inventories and pipeline stocks, but here too is a measure which would alter the basic principles upon which Soviet industry has functioned in the past.

It is doubtful that an admissible solution could be found by the manipulation of the accounting period. It is true that this approach worked in the case of the livestock census date, but there it was merely a matter of tying the accounting period to a certain natural phenomenon which was not one of the variables of the problem but a datum.

Could a solution be found by focusing on another facet of the problem, the incentive system rather than the accounting period? When really serious problems have arisen, the Soviets have often appealed to what they clearly recognize as a major motivating factor, the bonus. Thus in recent years the award of bonuses has been made contingent upon fulfillment of a cost-reduction target and upon the production of the proper quantities of individual items of production (the assortment plan). Judging from the continued complaints about the neglect of costs and product-assortment, this method has not proved outstandingly successful, probably because the state's prime interest in production remains overriding. If the award of bonuses were made to depend on the fulfillment of too many unrealistic side conditions, fewer bonuses would actually be earned, and there is a danger that this potent incentive would be vitiated. If the state introduced and enforced a requirement that no bonus be paid if the plan were fulfilled by storming, most managers would have to write off the bonus as a paper promise.

An alternative solution along these lines would be to offer to the manager who eliminates storming a supplementary bonus which would be independent of the bonus for plan fulfillment. This too is an approach which has been used in the past to motivate managers to put more effort into increasing the production of spare parts and the production of a side line of consumer goods out of scraps and waste. The trouble is that too many supplementary bonuses

13. *Chernaia Metallurgiia*, March 22, 1941, p. 2.

14. The author is indebted to Professor Raymond T. Bye of the Wharton School of Finance and Commerce, University of Pennsylvania, for this suggestion.

tend to deflect managerial attention in the direction of the largest bonus. The commissariat of the Iron and Steel Industry, for example, once introduced a system in which managers could earn a bonus of 50 per cent of the value of fuel saved and 15 per cent of the value of materials saved.[15] The system may well have turned a good deal of effort away from materials to fuel. And when there are possibilities of substitution (perhaps by producing more consumer goods at the expense of spare parts), quite unintended decisions may be made. Thus a supplementary bonus for elimination of storming, which would be large enough to make a difference, might raise new problems in other spheres of managerial activity. In any case, the bonus must not be larger than the bonus for production plan fulfillment, and therefore it would not be likely to eliminate the causes of storming.

We cannot continue here to explore the full range of possible solutions. But enough has been said to demonstrate that storming is so deeply ingrained in the structure of the system that no simple measures can eliminate it. The argument may be concluded by considering that there is no lack of solutions if we are willing to admit fundamental changes in the system of industrial administration. Suppose, for example, that production plans were reduced well below their present high level, perhaps by eliminating the "ratchet" principle of planning. If there were enough slack in production plans, ordinary lags in production schedules could be easily made up without recourse to storming. Plans would be more often fulfilled, and there would be no need for the postponement of maintenance and the "borrowing" of output. If plans were more often fulfilled, enterprises would less often be thrown off schedule by the delayed delivery of materials from suppliers. A general reduction of plan targets would thus eliminate two of the three components of the storming mechanism: the high probability of lags behind schedule and the dynamic transmission of storming from one period to the next.

15. *Industriia*, Jan. 22, 1940, p. 3.

It is doubtful that the Soviets will accept this gratuitous suggestion and, it must be admitted, possibly with good reason. The combination of high targets and high rewards is a most effective mechanism for eliciting a high level of effort from their managers. Lower targets might very well lead to a relaxation of effort and output, which is contrary to the objectives of the state. Storming is a price which the state probably considers well worth paying for the benefits of the present system. For the administrator, it remains an embarrassing defect which his art is powerless to eliminate. "What we need if we are to solve this," said Bulganin, "is not exorcisms but elimination of the causes which breed lack of rhythm." But it is doubtful that we shall hear anything but exorcisms unless broader changes in the administrative system are admitted.

JAMES C. ABEGGLEN

# Productivity in the Japanese Factory

Thus far efforts to promote industrialization in non-Western societies have been devoted largely to problems of assistance and change in the areas of finance and technology. The results of these efforts have drawn attention to the importance of social organization and of patterns of social interaction to the process of economic change, and emphasize the need for a further understanding of the interaction between technology and human relations for effective economic development.

Japan's extraordinary history of industrialization remains a unique record of effective social change, compelling the attention of those concerned with problems of industrialization and economic development in non-Western societies. Japan strode from hard-held Asian insularity to a central role in world industry, world trade, and world power relations in a single, explosive burst of energy and remains the singular case of non-Western industrialization. The outlines of the story are familiar; its implications for present attempts effectively to bring about development in other countries are evident.

Yet there are gaps in available knowledge of the process as it took place in Japan, areas in which evidence on critical issues in Japan's transition is inadequate or contradictory. What particular changes were central to the transition; what elements of the total structure changed; what drives and needs made it possible for Japan to utilize the knowledge and skills of the West where other nations could or did not; and what kinds of people were the leaders, the men who turned away from traditional modes and directed the changes? It is in the answers to these questions that helpful insights might be found for present work in other societies.

The general view of Japan's economic transition is that the changes in Japanese society were revolutionary and entire. Far from being confined to those more superficial matters of habit, dress, and taste that peoples customarily find rather easy to adjust, they are held to have cut deep into the very roots of the nation's social system. Levy states, for example, that:

> The changes were revolutionary as far as the social structure of the society was concerned, and industrialization of a marked degree, far beyond anyone's expectations in the West, was achieved in a very short time. It is perhaps doubtful that any society ever carried out such marked changes so quickly and with so little violence. Land tenure, education, production and consumption systems, political systems—virtually everything—either changed or had its position in the total structure changed radically.[1]

What impressed observers of the transition in

Reprinted from *The Japanese Factory*, pp. 122–45, by permission of the author and The Macmillan Company. 

1. Marion J. Levy, Jr., "Contrasting Factors in the Modernization of China and Japan," in *Economic Growth: Brazil, India, Japan*, ed. by Simon Kuznets, Wilbert E. Moore, and Joseph J. Spengler (Durham: Duke University Press, 1955), pp. 532–33.

Japan was more than the extensive effects and the great speed of change. Germany too had moved toward a thorough industrialization very rapidly not long before Japan's singular adventure was undertaken. Germany, however, is of the West, the very birthplace of those attitudes and actions held to be an essential part of the process, as, for example, the Protestant world view. Japan's transition began from what was in most respects a greatly different historical and social setting. It then seemed that, in order to accomplish an effective and lasting transition, Japan would need to change rapidly in respects other than technology. As early as 1915, in characteristic turn of phrase, Thorstein Veblen stated the general implications of this picture of revolutionary technological change for social relationships and for attitudes and motives of the Japanese.

> It should, then, confidently be presumed that, as Japan has with great facility and effect taken over the occidental state of the industrial arts, so should its population be due, presently and expeditiously, to fall in with the peculiar habits of thought that make the faults and qualities of the western culture—the spiritual outlook and the principles of conduct and ethical values that have been induced by the exacting discipline of this same state of the industrial arts among the technologically more advanced and mature of the western peoples.[2]

In the interval since Veblen's presumption, the view of a close and even necessary connection between certain kinds of social systems and industrialization has been much strengthened. A series of polarities have been put forth to indicate the directions of social change, change in attitudes and social interaction, upon which change to an industrial society is held to depend. Each describes an element of a general shift in the basis of social interaction assumed necessary to the change from a preindustrial to an industrial society. The view that the outcome of industrialization would be parallel for the social system of Japan and that of the West is set forth in Lockwood's careful study of Japanese economic development:

> In the traditional East, as formerly in the West, the Industrial Revolution requires a revolution in social and political arrangements no less than in production technology. Steam and steel, joint-stock finance, and laboratory science can transform the economic life of any backward area. Yet they are only tools at best. Their successful application necessitates a whole pattern of pervasive, interlocking changes in traditional societies. They can only be put to work within a new social setting which entails a radical break with the past, led by new elements in the society who will reject the sanctity of old ways and understand the social prerequisites of the new technology.[3]

These propositions argue that economic development, in Japan and elsewhere, is dependent on a series of changes quite outside the area of finance and technology, changes in at least two broad sectors of the society. First, an issue susceptible of historical examination, the process will require a group of leaders from outside the strata that produced preindustrial leadership. Second, effective economic development will be accompanied by profound changes in the social structure, changes eventuating in patterns of interaction quite like those evolved in the West through the Industrial Revolution.

On the first of these issues, that of the leadership of Japan's industrialization, opinions differ. Central roles in the leadership of politics and industry during Japan's transition have been assigned those lesser nobility who under the feudal regime suffered a loss of economic status and who held but little power or influence before the transition period.[4] Again, the merchants of Japan, enjoying great wealth but deprived by feudal law of commensurate social status, have been seen as central figures in the changes.[5] A recent study of the early period of change assigns an important role to the peasants.[6] Still another view has lately been offered:

> The ease with which the transition was accomplished owes much not only to vigorous and imaginative leadership, but also to the fact that the political revolution represented merely a re-distribution of power within the governing class rather than an

2. Thorstein Veblen, "The Opportunity of Japan," in *Essays in Our Changing Order*, ed. by Leon Ardzrooni (New York: The Viking Press, 1943), p. 254.

3. William W. Lockwood, *The Economic Development of Japan, Growth and Structural Change*, 1868–1938 (Princeton: Princeton University Press, 1954), p. 499.

4. George B. Sansom, *The Western World and Japan, A Study in the Interaction of European and Asiatic Cultures* (New York: Alfred A. Knopf, 1950).

5. Levy, *op. cit.*

6. Thomas C. Smith, *Political Change and Industrial Development in Japan: Government Enterprise*, 1868–80 (Stanford: Stanford University Press, 1955).

upheaval destructive of the old society. Consequently Japan carried into the new era traditional sentiments and loyalties which permitted her to undergo immense material changes without the loss of social cohesion. Even high officials of the Shogunate did not usually feel themselves precluded, on the overthrow of the old order, from serving under the new Imperial regime, which was thus able to recruit many able bureaucrats trained in the business of government.[7]

There is then an unresolved question concerning the kinds of people who led the Japanese move to industrialization, their social origins, and whether in fact the change in leadership through this period was revolutionary in nature. The proposition that these new elements of leadership represented a break with the past might better be restated to indicate the underlying continuity that accompanied alterations in elite groups. It would be of considerable interest in terms of understanding Japan's experience, and of some importance to the better understanding of the process of change in other nations, to have available a thorough analysis of this leadership group in Japan.

Of more fundamental importance than the question of leadership of the transition is that concerning the degree of continuity or discontinuity in social structure and systems of social interaction from the preindustrial society to industrialization. The assumption is that industrial development on the Western model requires a social setting radically different in nature from preindustrial relationships, a system fundamentally akin to that which developed in the West. The problem is no less complex than it is important. It would be presumptuous, with the limited knowledge of Japan's social system now available, to state the answer for the Japanese case to the general proposition. Still the results of this study of the large Japanese factory bear on this issue.

It might be assumed that, more than any other institution, the large manufacturing plant would represent in its social organization the extreme accommodation of Japanese systems of organization to the demands of industrial technology. Differences in organization, retaining similarities to earlier forms, might persist in rural social groupings and not be directly relevant to this question of the connections between social change and economic change. However, such lags in adaptation would presumably be minimized in the large factory.

In the foregoing chapters a general examination of several areas of the organization of the large Japanese factory has been undertaken. The areas dealt with and the detail of the study are hardly exhaustive; it may still be possible on their review broadly to make out differences between the usual American factory organization and that common in the large factories of Japan, and to make some general statement of the nature of the differences. Leaving aside exceptions and details, some general features of the Japanese organization might be summarized.

1. Membership in the Japanese productive group is a permanent and irrevocable membership. Workers at all levels of the factory customarily work in but one company. They spend their entire career in that single firm which is entered immediately on completing their education. The firm will continue to provide the worker's income at whatever disadvantage to itself, and the worker will continue in the company's employ despite possible advantage in moving to another firm.

2. Recruitment into the productive group is based on personal qualities without reference to a particular work task or set of skills. Selection is based primarily on the individual's education, character, and general background. Inadequacy or incompetence shown subsequent to selection are not a basis for dismissal from the group.

3. Status in the group is a continuation and extension of status held in the society at the time of entrance to the group. The broad dichotomy of employees into *koin* and *shokuin* limits the movement of an individual in the factory system largely to the general category that his education entitled him to enter on recruitment.

4. Reward in the productive group is only partly in the form of money, and is based on broad social criteria rather than on production criteria. The recompense of workers is made up of such items as housing, food, and personal services, with the actual cash pay of the worker forming only part of the total. Pay is based primarily on age, education, length of service, and family size, with job rank or competence only a small part of the criteria for determining work reward.

7. G. C. Allen, and Audrey G. Donnithorne, *Western Enterprise in Far Eastern Development* (New York: The Macmillan Company, 1954), p. 188.

5. The formal organization of the factory is elaborated in a wide range and considerable number of formal positions. Formal rank and title in the hierarchy are well defined, but authority and responsibility of ranks are not. Partly in consequence, the decision-making function is exercised by groups of persons, but responsibility for the decisions is not assigned to individuals.

6. The penetration of the company into the non-business activities of the worker and the responsibility taken by the company for the worker are extensive. Management is involved in such diverse and intimate matters as the worker's personal finances, the education of his children, religious activities, and the training of the worker's wife. The company is responsible for the continued well-being of the worker and his family, and this responsibility is carried out both in formal personnel procedures and in the informal relations between the worker and supervisor.

If a single conclusion were to be drawn from this study it would be that the development of industrial Japan has taken place with much less change from the kinds of social organization and social relations of preindustrial or nonindustrial Japan than would be expected from the Western model of the growth of an industrial society. The rise and development of the industrial West is generally attributed in some considerable part to the development of an impersonalized and rationalized view of the world and of relations with others. Emphasis on individuality, the view of the workplace as a purely economic grouping clearly differentiated in goals and relationships from other areas of social interaction, the subordination of other values and interests of the economic goal in business activity, the use of money to discharge obligations for services in the business world—all these and related trends are seen as critical to the successful development of large-scale industry. In sociological theory some of these tendencies have been set forth in polarities to indicate the nature of the differences. Thus, for example, "status" and "contract" have been contrasted as indicating the difference and direction of development with industrialization from a close, intimate personal group to the more rationalized and impersonalized relations of modern business. A more recent dichotomization is the differentiation of "particularism" and "universalism," or the move from a value emphasis on particular relationships and symbols, with stress on loyalty and intragroup harmony, to an emphasis on rationalized means-end relations, with stress on efficiency and performance.

These kinds of polarities are not altogether useful in discussing the Japanese case. Although it is possible to point to elements in the organization of the Japanese factory that fit the industrial and modern end of these polarities, a very considerable part of the organizational system remains more like the preindustrial pole. It does not seem warranted to hold that Japan is now at some mid-point in development. Such an argument is inconsistent with the view that contractual, universalistic relations are necessary to successful industrialization. Nor is it sufficient to say that since Japan's industrialization is relatively recent these divergencies from the pattern as seen and set forth in the West will in time mend themselves and fit harmoniously into one of these several categories without conflict or with few conflicting elements. In point of fact, as this report has attempted to indicate, the Japanese system is on the whole self-consistent. The recruitment methods and the incentive system fit together with the rules governing employment to make a unified whole. Change in one, as, for example, in employment rules, would drastically affect and require changes in other elements of the organization.

From this examination of the Japanese factory, the factory organization seems a consistent and logical outgrowth of the kinds of relations existing in Japan prior to its industrialization. The changes that took place in Japan during the last three decades of the nineteenth century are often termed a "revolution." That they represented in many respects drastic departures from the preceding period is clear enough. The manner of the "revolution," however, seems still open to question. At repeated points in the study of the factory, parallels to an essentially feudal system of organization may be seen—not, to be sure, a replication of the feudal loyalties, commitments, rewards, and methods of leadership but a rephrasing of them in the setting of modern industry.

It may well be that the kinds of experiences undergone by the West antecedent to the development of modern industry are indeed essential to an independent and *de novo* development of industry.

The Japanese case suggests that these experiences and the organizational system used in the West are not necessary to the introduction of industry into another social system. From the observations of this study it would appear that, although the technology of modern industry was introduced into Japan, the factory organization at the same time developed consistent with the historical customs and attitudes of the Japanese and with the social system as it existed prior to the introduction of modern industry. Thus, looking beyond the modern equipment and the formal organization, the systems of relationships are more nearly similar to those which seem to have characterized an earlier Japan and which now characterize the nonindustrial areas of Japan than they are similar to the factory organization of the West.

Differences in the role of the individual in the Western and Japanese factory—the ways in which he is motivated, the extent to which responsibility and authority are assigned individuals, the kinds of rewards offered, and the behaviors that are rewarded—have a close relation to differences between the two cultural backgrounds. Japan's industry was superimposed in a matter of some few decades on a society that was profoundly and had for some centuries been feudal. The loyalty of the worker to the industrial organization, the paternal methods of motivating and rewarding the worker, the close involvement of the company in all manner of what seem to Western eyes to be personal and private affairs of the worker—all have parallels with Japan's preindustrial social organization.

This parallel does not underestimate the enormous changes that have taken place in Japan through the period of her industrialization. Japan has changed mightily; and changes continue. If the study of industrialization in Japan is to be relevant to the study of the developing economies of other Asian nations, however, the nature of the changes which have taken place must be clearly understood. What the results of this study of the social organization of the large Japanese factory suggest is that changes have taken place selectively—a point well remarked in other contexts—and, more important, that these changes have been such as to leave unchanged the underlying basis of social relationships. Rather than penetrating to the roots of the social system, the changes have been built up from the kind of social relationships pre-existing in Japan.

A compact statement of the general nature of social relations in Japan has been provided by Stoetzel. He states: "In point of fact, as Ruth Benedict rightly guessed, the whole social structure of Japan is dictated by a concept of hierarchy deriving from the kinship of the clan."[8] Stoetzel then summarizes his conclusions:

> To understand the Japanese social structure, three ideas must be brought into play, not separately, but together: (a) the idea of kinship, by blood, marriage, adoption, or service; (b) the idea of hierarchy, always conceived more or less on the *oyako* (father-son) model; (c) the idea of sharing in the protection offered by the tutelary deities, by a common cult or at least by a common burying ground. These three ideas are connected with each other, particularly the first two: wherever there is kinship there is a hierarchical relationship, and the opposite as we have seen is also true; as for the common cult, it is the symbol of the family bond [9]

Throughout this discussion of the large factory, parallels have been noted between the factory system and the clan or kinship organization. In terms of formal organization some of these have included both the manner of recruitment into the system and the kinds of reciprocal obligations thereby incurred by company and worker. Further, the formal system of motivation and reward has functional parallels to that of a kinship grouping.

In the informal organization as well the recurring relationship is modeled in the factory on the *oyako* relation, with hierarchical roles defined in terms of this pattern. This pattern is not, as pointed out earlier, the formal *oyabun-kobun* structure, but is, rather, an informal father-son type of system.

Indeed, so pervasive are the parallels to a kinship-type organization in the large Japanese factory that it is not necessary for the observer to argue their presence from indirect evidences. For example, in a 1952 speech to his managerial employees, the president of a large steel company said, "Not only is there the fact that our life's work is our employment in our company, but I feel that as people in this situation we have two occasions that can be

8. Jean Stoetzel, *Without the Chrysanthemum and the Sword: A Study of the Attitudes of Youth in Postwar Japan*, UNESCO publication (New York: Columbia University Press, 1955), p. 56.

9. *Ibid.*, p. 57.

called a 'birth.' The first is when we are born into the world as mewling infants. The second is when we all receive our commissions of adoption into the company. This is an event that has the same importance as our crying birth." Here are both a direct statement of the kinship basis of company organization and an indication of the way in which the common bond is symbolized, by treating the company, its history, and present organization as an extended family with common values, common ancestors, and common beliefs. It is for this reason, for example, that elaborate histories and geneologies of the large firms are written and that common religious shrines and ceremonies may be found.

It might be added here parenthetically and as a further evidence of the nature of these underlying relationships that the *zaibatsu* groupings in Japan are seriously misunderstood when seen as cartels or monopolies on the Western model. These are in a very real sense clans, the furthest extension of kinship-type relations in the economic and industrial sector. To treat these, by the passing of antimonopoly laws, as fundamentally economic and financial groupings was grotesque and doomed to failure from the first. It might be pertinent here to quote Lockwood again: "Too often in the case of Japan there is a tendency to apply easy labels, derived from Western experience. They may only obscure the complexities of the facts."[10] This statement does not say that the factory organization is "caused" by Japanese family organization but that both family organization and factory organization are components of a common social structure; and as such the system of relationships within each grouping has a common structural base.

It would seem from this study, then, that the very success of the Japanese experience with industrialization may well have been a function of the fact that, far from undergoing a total revolution in social structure or social relationships, the hard core of Japan's system of social relationships remained intact, allowing an orderly transition to industrialization continuous with her earlier social forms. It would in fact be remarkable if social change of this magnitude and success could occur in any other way. Discontinuity will not lead to effective adaptation; rather, it will result in chaos. The exceptional durability of Japan's social system, often remarked upon and demonstrated anew in her response to total defeat in the Second World War, is not the result of a mystic ability of the Japanese to adapt but, rather, the consequence of the fact that through change a basis for social continuity has remained intact. It is of some interest to note in this connection that the same wondrous ability to selectively take on new elements in a society is now being attributed to Indian society. But selective adaptation should not be remarkable; it would be much more remarkable if any people were able in one fell swoop to put off their past, their training, and habits of mind and don successfully and permanently totally new social paraphernalia. Efforts to change the economy of other nations in the direction of industrialization might better then be concerned with an identification of basic elements of the preindustrial social system and with the introduction of new technologies and financial systems in the context of the older relationships, than with making these nations over in the image derived from Western outcomes.

A partial explanation, therefore, of Japan's rapid industrialization might well be argued to lie in the amount and more especially in the kind of continuity throughout the transition rather than in an emphasis on change. In this connection one might note that there is reason to believe that the pressure of the family system in Japan toward social rigidity and inflexibility may be commonly overstated. Although an analysis of the family system is outside the limits of this study, in terms of the thesis of social continuity and its effects on industrial change, it should be emphasized that in two particulars at least there has been within the historical structure of the Japanese family a potentiality for flexibility and change.

The first of these is the practice of adoption, by which not only more distant relatives but also able and promising employees and servants have long been able to assume important roles in higher-status families and in family businesses. This practice, not far removed from the notion of employment as seen in the large factory, not only has made for continual social mobility and flexibility even under feudal regulations but also may well have provided a paradigm for methods of industrial recruitment.

The role of the younger son in Japan is also of some interest in this regard. Under rules of primo-

10. Lockwood, *op. cit.*, p. 200.

geniture in a country lacking sufficient land there are provided the conditions for the establishment of an urban work force. Further, there has been a tradition of continuity, despite such mobility by younger sons, through the establishment of "branch families" tied to the "main family" by bonds of obligation and duty. The main family, in, for example, a rural village, under industrialization also provided a buffer against economic hardship and depression—an advantage still in a country where social security measures are meager.

These and other elements of the Japanese family structure, aspects of family organization conducive to adaptation and change, may well have aided the transition to industrialization by making possible adjustment within the older family system rather than, as is sometimes suggested, industrialization and urbanization shattering the older family pattern. Finally, and most important from the point of view of factory organization, the principle of family loyalty and cohesion, when successfully symbolized and incorporated into military, industrial, and financial organizations, may have become an important source of energy and motivation for the transition to industrialization. It must again be emphasized that such structural elements as these would hold change within limits, order the great transition, and prevent the kind of social discontinuity which would be destructive of a society.

Turning now from such suggestions as this study of the large Japanese factory might provide for an understanding of Japan's past, we raise the question of possible future developments in the organization of Japanese industry. There is a perhaps inherent tendency in describing an ongoing social organization to emphasize the integration and harmony of the several elements of the system at the expense of an analysis of stress or of present and future changes in the system. Yet in reviewing the Japanese factory the system appears to be stable in terms of the relationships between people in the organization. The organization is internally consistent and acceptable to its members so long as the membership is drawn from backgrounds in which the forms of relationships on which the factory is based are retained.

In terms of the people in the factory, two groups in particular seem to have some difficulty in adapting themselves to this kind of organization. Young Japanese who are urban reared, born in the large cities of laboring and white-collar fathers, educated in urban schools beyond the legally prescribed minimum of middle-school education, and steeped in the impersonality of modern cities do not fit well into these factory relationships. Here is a central problem of the large Japanese factory. Workers born into traditional extended and close-knit families in the farm villages of Japan, for example, have, in the words of the factory managers, "stable natures." Products of small family groups of the large cities, unfamiliar with the elaborate systems of obligations and duties spun by kinship and friendship ties in the stable villages, do not respond to the appeals and rationale of this factory system. Women, too, who by virtue of family training or education have been schooled in a newer pattern of relationships and role expectations and who have come to expect an occupational role different from that traditionally assigned Japanese women, protest their position in the factory.

Changes in the factory organization may proceed from two causes. The first is prior changes in the organization of and relationships in primary groups in the society. The second is the pressure of changes in technology and production methods that would lead to organizational change. The demands of technology and output have been discussed in the preceding chapter on productivity. The pressure for change is great, for example, to increase the flexibility of the work force to lead to greater adaptability to economic changes. The need for change has led, on occasion, to change in a limited sphere, as, for example, when a financial crisis and a subsequent "rationalization" movement led to the discharge of employees from a number of large factories. As in the case described in an earlier chapter, however, it appears likely that makeshift and temporary adaptations which do not alter the general rules of employment and organization will be made. Real changes in factory organization will come about only when the point of view and the training of individuals in the system alter significantly. Thus the Japanese family system, under the pressure of urbanization, changes in religious thought and training, and under the constant impact of mass communication, may change the ways in which youths are trained and developed, thus changing the attitudes and expectations, motivation systems, and interaction patterns of youth. Although changes in primary group structures have not yet been carried to the point where the factory organization is in conflict with any major portion of the society's patterns of interaction, such a process of change, in large part the result of the growth of large industry, may in time alter the basis of factory organization.

It is easy here, as in looking at Japanese history, to mistake the nature of changes in cities and during the postwar period. The general formulas for the effects of urbanization have been developed out of Western experience. The almost total lack of close study of the nature of social interaction in the cities of Asia makes a prediction of the direction and kind of change induced by urbanization in Asia most hazardous. Further, it is far from clear at present as to how effective and lasting postwar experiments and adjustments may be in the Japanese case. It would be a daring observer indeed who would predict the outcome of the next two or three decades of Japanese events.

In summing up the results of this study, there appear to be two broad elements of difference between Japan and the West in relation to the nature of the social organization of the factory. First, the factory, or company, is relatively undifferentiated from other types of groups in the society. In terms of the commitment of members to the group, the nature of their recruitment and subsequent careers, and the extent of involvement of members with each other as part of the group, the Japanese factory grouping parallels other social groupings. Although the factory may be defined as an economic organization with its goals narrowly defined and relationships narrowly based on productivity and profit, the Japanese factory is not so defined. The Western view of life segments, each serving a special end with differentiated relationships in each—the family, the club or association, the workplace—makes possible a clear differentiation of activities and organization in each group. In Japan, the factory recruits involve and maintain their membership on a basis similar to that of the domestic and social groups of the society. Where the economic ends of the factory conflict with this broader definition of the group, as in the case of the incompetent employee who will not be discharged, the economic ends take a secondary position to the maintenance of group integrity.

This lack of differentiation between the large factory organization and other social groupings is not only an internal one. Status in the broader community, as reflected primarily in educational attainment, is the critical variable governing recruitment and is the dominating factor in rank and career progress in the factory. Moreover, the employee shares responsibility with the company for his family, his children, and his general well-being. The broader social activities are not set apart from his membership in the factory or company.

Closely related to this latter aspect of the lack of differentiation is the difference between the American and the Japanese organization in the extent to which there is an individualization or impersonalization of relationships in the factory. It is perhaps this lack of individualization that most sets off the day-to-day functioning of the Japanese production unit from its American counterpart. The apparatus of modern production in the West depends heavily on the assignment of individual responsibility, on individual incentive programs, on the job evaluation of the individual employee, and on a system of rewards in which individual competence and energy will be recompensed. In all of these respects the difference from Japan is marked. Individual responsibility is avoided, incentive systems have little relationship to individual output but, rather, depend on group success, and the motivating of energies appears to depend on the individual's loyalty and identification with the group and with his superior.

In short, it may be concluded from this study that, although the preindustrial experience of the West may indeed have been the necessary cause of the development of industrialization, the introduction of industry into a society like that of Japan, which has not shared these earlier experiences and has a markedly different social system, makes necessary the fitting of the industrial mechanism to the earlier social system. What must also be noted is the considerable industrial success that is possible under these circumstances. It may be true that the Western style of organization maximizes productivity, but substantial industrial progress can be made within quite a different style of organization. Rationalization and impersonalization are not, the

Japanese experience seems to argue, necessary to the adoption from the West of an industrial economy.

That the amalgam of a preindustrial system of organization and Western technology has created problems for Japanese industry is very clear, and some of the problems have been stressed in this report. It does not follow from the fact that problems exist that their solution lies in the direction of greater change toward the Western business model. This might be the case in some areas, as, for example, in terms of problems of sales and distribution where Western methods need not disrupt upon their introduction the ongoing organizational system. When other Western elements are introduced, however, whether by Western or Japanese advisers, the outcomes will often not be so harmless. Such introductions of new and Western techniques and approaches must be considered with some caution by American experts and consultants.

More relevant perhaps to present concerns of the United States are the possible implications of the Japanese experience in the problem of aiding the development of other non-Western nations. It would seem from the Japanese example that a considerable degree of tolerance—even at the cost of seeming waste—needs to be allowed local custom and methods in establishing industry in those countries with systems of interpersonal relations markedly different from those of the West. A lasting and effective transition to industrialization may be accomplished only when the changes are continuous with the preindustrial social system and are based on and grow out of the patterns of social interaction basic to the society.

# Index

# Index